INVESTMENT MANAGEMENT

INVESTMENT MANAGEMENT

FRANK J. FABOZZI, CFA

Editor
Journal of Portfolio Management

with contributions from
T. Daniel Coggin
Bruce Collins
Russell Fogler
John Ritchie, Jr.

Prentice Hall,
Englewood Cliffs, New Jersey 07632

Library of Congress Cataloging–in–Publication Data

Fabozzi, Frank J.
    Investment management/Frank J. Fabozzi.
       p.   cm.
    Includes bibliographical references and index.
    ISBN 0-13-074972-9
    1. Investments.   2. Investment analysis. I. Title.
HG4521.F26 1994   94–37833
332.6—dc20   CIP

Acquisitions Editor: Leah Jewell
Production Editor: The Total Book
Managing Editor: Frances Russello
In-House Liaison: Penelope Linskey
Development Editor: Michael Buchman
Editor-in-Chief, Development: Stephen Deitmer
Interior/Cover Designer: Joseph A. Piliero
Design Director: Linda Fiordilino
Copy Editor: Judy Duguid
Proofreader: Martha Cameron
Buyer: Patrice Fraccio
Editorial Assistant: Eileen De Guzman
Cover Art: The Stock Market

©1995 by Prentice Hall, Inc.
A Simon & Schuster Company
Englewood Cliffs, New Jersey 07632

Printed in the United States of America
10 9 8 7 6 5 4 3 2 1

ISBN 0-13-074972-9

Prentice-Hall International (UK) Limited, *London*
Prentice-Hall of Australia Pty. Limited, *Sydney*
Prentice-Hall Canada Inc., *Toronto*
Prentice-Hall Hispanoamericana, S.A., *Mexico*
Prentice-Hall of India Private Limited, *New Delhi*
Prentice-Hall of Japan, Inc., *Tokyo*
Simon & Schuster Asia Pte. Ltd., *Singapore*
Editora Prentice-Hall do Brasil, Ltda., *Rio de Janeiro*

To

the

Memory

of

My

Mother,

Josephine

Fabozzi

ABOUT THE AUTHOR

Frank J. Fabozzi is the editor of the *Journal of Portfolio Management*. In 1993 and 1994, he was an Adjunct Professor of Finance at Yale University's School of Management. From 1986 to 1992, he was a full-time professor of finance at MIT's Sloan School of Management. He has authored numerous books, including *Capital Markets: Institutions and Instruments* with Franco Modigliani and *Financial Markets and Institutions* with Franco Modigliani and Michael Ferri. He is on the board of directors of the BlackRock complex of funds and the Guardian family of funds. He is a Chartered Financial Analyst and holds a doctorate in economics (1972) from the Graduate Center of the City University of New York. In 1994 he was awarded an honorary doctorate of Humane Letters from Nova Southeastern University.

CONTENTS IN BRIEF

SECTION VI: ASSET ALLOCATION AND PERFORMANCE EVALUATION

APPENDIXES

CONTENTS

SECTION V

FIXED-INCOME ANALYSIS AND PORTFOLIO MANAGEMENT

SECTION VI

ASSET ALLOCATION AND PERFORMANCE EVALUATION

APPENDIXES

PREFACE

The job of planning, implementing, and overseeing the funds of an individual investor or an institution is referred to as investment management. The purpose of this book is to describe the process of investment management.

Many excellent investment management books are available. In deciding whether another book on the same topic merited publication, I drew upon both my experience in the training of portfolio managers at various seminars I offer throughout the world and my experience as an advisor and board member of several institutions. Here is how I thought an investment management book should differ from those available in the market.

First, I felt that the focus of an investment management book should be on the management of funds of institutional investors (depository institutions, insurance companies, investment companies, pension funds, and endowment funds and foundations), not on those of individual investors. While many of the principles are equally applicable to the investments of individual investors, there are nuances that are unique to the management of institutional funds.

Second, it has always escaped me why a book would discuss investment strategies and leave to the end a discussion of the various institutional investors and their investment objectives. Managers of the funds of institutions manage those funds to meet certain investment objectives. For many, those objectives are dictated by the nature of their liabilities. It is within the context of the asset/liability problem faced by managers of institutional funds that investment vehicles and investment strategies make any sense. Therefore, a thorough treatment of the investment objectives of institutional investors and the constraints imposed on the manager of the funds of these institutions should be clearly presented to students so that they can fully appreciate investment strategies.

Third, there should be greater emphasis on fixed-income analysis and strategies. This reflects my bias that many students who enter the business of managing funds will be employed by institutions that concentrate on fixed-income products. Historically, common stock portfolio management has been emphasized in books, leaving the student who ventures into the fixed-income portfolio management arena to "learn on the job." It has astonished me, as well as employers of college graduates majoring in finance, as to the lack of training that students receive in the area of fixed-income portfolio management.

Fourth, the use of derivative instruments—options, futures, and swaps—should be emphasized. The approach should be how these instruments can be used to effectively control a portfolio's risk and how they may be used to reduce the cost of implementing investment strategies.

Finally, an investment management book should tie together theory and practice. Investing in a theoretical world is simple; investing in a world where there are client-imposed or regulatory constraints and in which there are transactions costs means that theory must be adapted to real-world conditions.

These views are incorporated into this book and reflect what I believe to be the primary differences that distinguish this book from the others available. Other salient features of this book include an in-depth treatment of:

- The role of analysts and the various approaches used to forecast corporate earnings (Chapter 12)
- Transactions costs beyond that of simple brokerage fees and the way these costs can be measured (Chapter 13)
- The approaches used and complications that arise in constructing an equity-indexed (Chapter 14) and fixed-income-indexed (Chapter 24) portfolio
- The way to implement a hedging strategy for common stock portfolios (Chapter 16) and fixed-income portfolios (Chapter 26)
- The wide range of asset allocation strategies (Chapter 28)
- Performance measurement reporting under the new standards established by the Association for Investment Management and Research (Chapter 29)
- Techniques for evaluating investment performance beyond those of the basic measures emphasized in most books (Chapter 30)

No book is perfect, however. One of the principal drawbacks of this book is that it only covers two investment vehicles: common stock and fixed-income securities. There are other investment outlets such as real estate, timberland, commodities, and artwork that have been gaining greater acceptance in the investment community. There are two reasons why such investment vehicles are not covered in this book. First, page limitations preclude in-depth coverage of these investment vehicles. Second, for most institutional investors, common stock and fixed-income securities are the major portion of the assets they hold. Fortunately, the principles described in this book are applicable to the valuation of alternative investment vehicles. The portfolio theory concepts discussed in Section II provide a framework for assessing whether an investment vehicle would be appropriate for a particular investor.

Typically investment management books devote a separate chapter to non-U.S. common stocks. I have not elected to do so. Instead, a discussion of non-U.S. securities (both common stock and fixed-income securities), as well as non-U.S. derivative instruments, is integrated throughout the book. In fact, the discussion of derivative instruments makes clear how they can be used to gain exposure to non-U.S. securities.

On balance, I hope that the approach presented in this book provides a better alternative for teaching investment management.

ACKNOWLEDGMENTS

I am indebted to many individuals for providing me with various forms of assistance in this project.

As indicated on the title page of this book, written contributions were made by several individuals. T. Daniel Coggin of the Virginia Retirement System provided the chapter on forecasting earnings (Chapter 12) and coauthored several chapters with me (Chapters 4, 5, and 15).

Bruce Collins of Western Connecticut State University, previously the director of equity derivatives at a major Wall Street firm, coauthored with me the chapter on equity indexing (Chapter 14) and the section on transactions costs in Chapter 13.

Appendixes B, C, and D were coauthored with John Ritchie, Jr., of Temple University. In these three appendixes that deal with the analysis of financial statements, we draw on illustrations from a publication entitled *The Quality of Earnings* written by Thornton ("Ted") O'Glove. I came across Ted's work in the late 1970s and was impressed with his ability to rip apart corporate financial statements so as to identify corporations that were playing games with their earnings.

Russell Fogler of Aronson and Fogler coauthored with me a section in Chapter 15.

The writings in some of the chapters draw from my writings with Robert Arnott of First Quadrant Corp., Mark Pitts of White Oak Capital Management Corp., Gifford Fong of Gifford Fong Associates, and Sylvan Feldstein of Merrill Lynch. Parts of Section V are drawn from my book *Introduction to Fixed Income Portfolio Management*, published by Frank J. Fabozzi Associates.

K. C. Ma of Investment Research Company provided the return data used in several illustrations and end-of-chapter questions.

The person who most influenced the shaping of this book was the development editor, Michael Buchman. He made numerous suggestions about not only how to clarify the discussion of certain topics, but also how to reorganize the book to improve the flow of information.

Prentice Hall sought the advice of the following reviewers:

W. Scott Bauman (Northern Illinois University)
Alyce Campbell (University of Oregon)
Richard DeMong (University of Virginia)
Simon Hakim (Temple University)
Christopher Ma (Investment Research Company)
Kyle Mattson (Rochester Institute of Technology)
Joseph Ogden (SUNY Buffalo)
Shafiqur Rahman (Portland State University)
Mitchell Ratner (Rider College)
Kishore Tandon (Baruch College, CUNY)
Joseph Vu (DePaul University)
Avner Wolf (Baruch College, CUNY)
Tom Zwirlein (University of Colorado)

Each reviewer provided guidance for improving chapters and suggested ways to reorganize the book.

Others who have read portions of the manuscript and provided feedback include David Canuel (Aeltus Investment Management), Ravi Dattatreya (Sumitomo Bank Capital Markets), Michael Ferri (George Mason University),

Gary L. Gastineau (S. G. Warburg), Frank Jones (Guardian Life Insurance Company of America), Andrew Kalotay (Fordham University), Ed Murphy (Merchants Mutual Insurance Company), Frank Ramirez (Alex. Brown & Sons), Chuck Ramsey (Alex. Brown & Sons), Scott Richard (Miller, Anderson & Sherrerd), M. Song Jo (Alex. Brown & Sons), Richard Wilson (Fitch Investors Service), Uzi Yaari (Rutgers University), David Yuen (Alex. Brown & Sons), and Yu Zhu (Merrill Lynch).

In the end-of-chapter questions and chapter boxes, I used excerpts from *Institutional Investor* and several weekly publications of Institutional Investor Inc., *Wall Street Letter*, *Bank Letter*, *BondWeek*, *Corporate Financing Week*, *Derivatives Week*, *Money Management Letter*, and *Portfolio Letter*, along with various publications of the Association for Investment Management Research. I am grateful to Tom Lamont of *Institutional Investor* and Katherine Sherrerd of the Association for Investment Management and Research for permission to use these excerpts.

Frank J. Fabozzi
Buckingham, PA

INVESTMENT MANAGEMENT

CHAPTER 1
INTRODUCTION

LEARNING OBJECTIVES
After reading this chapter you will be able to:

- describe the steps involved in the investment management process.
- explain the difference between retail and institutional investors.
- list the factors to consider in setting investment policy.
- explain what is meant by the asset allocation decision.
- distinguish among general portfolio strategies.
- define what is meant by an efficient portfolio.
- discuss the process of evaluating portfolio performance.
- describe the structure of the money management business.

Investment management is the process of managing money. Two other terms commonly used to describe this process are **portfolio management** and **money management**. The individual who manages a portfolio of investments is referred to as an **investment manager**, **money manager**, or **portfolio manager**. (A **portfolio** is a collection of investments.) We will use these terms interchangeably throughout this book.

In industry jargon, an investment manager "runs money." The purpose of this book is to describe the process of investment management—that is, how investment managers run money. This process requires an understanding of the various investment vehicles, the way these investment vehicles are valued, and the various strategies that can be used to select the investment vehicles that should be included in a portfolio in order to accomplish investment objectives.

Investors can be classified as either retail investors or institutional investors. **Retail investors** are individuals. **Institutional investors** include insurance companies, depository institutions (i.e., banks, savings and loan associations, and credit unions), pension funds, investment companies, and endowment funds. Financial markets in the United States have shifted from being dominated by retail investors to being dominated by institutional investors, a phenomenon referred to as the **institutionalization** of financial markets. The same thing is occurring in other industrialized countries.

Our primary focus in this book is on the management of institutional investors' portfolios. The basic principles of investment management, however, are applicable to individual investors, as well.

This chapter provides an overview of the investment management process, a useful starting point for our journey, since it allows us to see the key steps involved in managing a portfolio and therefore the significance of the topics that we describe in later chapters. A description of the investment management industry follows, and the chapter concludes with a description of the chapters ahead.

THE INVESTMENT MANAGEMENT PROCESS

Regardless of the institutional investor, the investment management process involves the following five steps:

1. setting investment objectives
2. establishing investment policy
3. selecting a portfolio strategy
4. selecting the assets
5. measuring and evaluating performance

As shown by Figure 1-1, this is a cyclical process where performance evaluation may result in changes to the objectives, policies, strategies, and composition of a portfolio.

FIGURE 1-1

The investment management process.

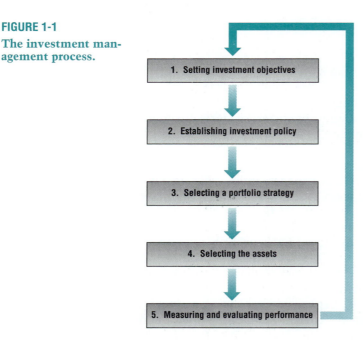

1. Setting investment objectives

2. Establishing investment policy

3. Selecting a portfolio strategy

4. Selecting the assets

5. Measuring and evaluating performance

Setting Investment Objectives

The first step in the investment management process, setting investment objectives, depends on the institution. For example, a pension fund that is obligated to pay specified amounts to beneficiaries in the future would have the objective of generating sufficient funds from its investment portfolio so as to satisfy its pension obligations. As another example, life insurance companies sell a variety of products, most of which guarantee a dollar payment at some time in the future or a stream of dollar payments over time. Therefore, the investment objective of the life insurance company would be to satisfy the obligations stipulated in the policy and to generate a profit. As a third example, in the case of institutions such as banks and savings and loan associations, funds are acquired through the issuance of certificates of deposits. These funds are then invested in loans and marketable securities. The objective would be to earn a return on invested funds that is higher than the cost of those funds.

Establishing Investment Policy

The second step in the investment management process is establishing policy guidelines to satisfy the investment objectives. Setting policy begins with the **asset allocation decision**. That is, the investor must decide how the institution's funds should be distributed among the major classes of assets in which it may invest. The major **asset classes** typically include stocks, bonds, real estate, and foreign securities.

Client and regulatory constraints must be considered in establishing an investment policy. For example, a client may wish to maintain a certain level of diversification and safety, and may limit the percentage of funds that may be invested in certain asset classes or in any particular issuer. An example of a regulatory constraint is a restriction on the asset class in which a regulated financial institution may invest. Tax and financial reporting implications must also be considered when adopting investment policies. For example, tax-exempt institutions might find tax-free investments unappealing, since these institutions are already exempt from taxes and the yields of tax-free investments are generally low. Financial reporting requirements affect the ways in which many institutional investors establish investment policies. Unfortunately, financial reporting considerations sometimes cause institutions to establish investment policies that, in the long run, may not be in the best economic interest of the institution.

Selecting a Portfolio Strategy

Selecting a portfolio strategy that is consistent with the objectives and investment policy guidelines of the client or institution is the third step in the investment management process. Portfolio strategies can be classified as either active or passive. An **active portfolio strategy** uses available information and forecasting techniques to seek a better performance than a portfolio that is simply diversified broadly. Essential to all active strategies are expectations about the factors that could influence the performance of an asset class. For example, with active common stock strategies this may include forecasts of futures earnings, dividends, or price-earnings ratios. With bond portfolios that are actively managed, expectations may involve forecasts of future interest rates. Active portfolio strategies involving foreign securities may require forecasts of future exchange rates.

A **passive portfolio strategy** involves minimal expectational input, and instead relies on diversification to match the performance of some market index.[1] In effect, a passive strategy assumes that the marketplace will reflect all available information in the price paid for securities. Between these extremes of active and passive strategies, new strategies have sprung up that have elements of both. For example, the core of a portfolio may be passively managed with the balance actively managed.

In the bond area, several strategies classified as structured portfolio strategies have been commonly used. A **structured portfolio strategy** is one in which a portfolio is designed to achieve the performance of some predetermined liabilities that must be paid out. These strategies are frequently used when trying to match the funds received from the portfolio of investment to the future liabilities that must be paid.

Given the choice among active, structured, or passive management, which should be selected? The answer depends on (1) the client's or money manager's view of how "price-efficient" the market is and (2) the nature of the client's liabilities. By **marketplace price efficiency** we mean how difficult it would be to earn a greater return than passive management would, after adjusting for the risk associated with a strategy and the transactions costs associated with implementing a strategy.

Selecting the Assets

Once a portfolio strategy is selected, the next step is to select the specific assets to be included in the portfolio. This requires an evaluation of individual securities. In an active strategy, this means trying to identify mispriced securities.

It is in this phase that the investment manager attempts to construct an **efficient portfolio**. An efficient portfolio is one that provides the greatest *expected* return for a given level of risk, or equivalently, the lowest risk for a given *expected* return. The specific meaning of return and risk cannot be provided at this time. As we develop our understanding of investment management throughout this book, we will be able to quantify what we mean by these terms.

Measuring and Evaluating Performance

The measurement and evaluation of investment performance is the last step in the investment management process. Actually, it is misleading to say that it is the last step since the investment process is an ongoing process. This step involves measuring the performance of the portfolio and then evaluating that performance relative to some benchmark. A **benchmark** is simply the performance of a predetermined set of securities, obtained for comparison purposes. The benchmark may be a popular index such as the Standard &

---

[1]A market index is a summary statistic that reflects the performance of a collection of assets.

Poor's 500 for stock portfolios or one of the bond indexes published by the major securities firms. Recently, institutional investors have worked with consultants to develop customized benchmarks.

Although a portfolio manager may have performed better than a benchmark portfolio, this does not necessarily mean that the portfolio satisfied the client's needs. For example, suppose that a financial institution established as its objective the maximization of portfolio return and allocated 75% of the fund to stocks and the balance to bonds. Suppose further that the portfolio manager responsible for the stock portfolio earned a return over a one-year horizon that is 3% higher than the established benchmark portfolio. Assuming that the risk of the portfolio was similar to that of the benchmark portfolio, it would appear that the portfolio manager outperformed the benchmark portfolio. However, suppose that in spite of this performance, the financial institution cannot meet its liabilities. Then the failure was in establishing the investment objectives and setting policy, not the portfolio manager's performance.

STRUCTURE OF THE MONEY MANAGEMENT BUSINESS

For whom does an investment manager "run money"? An investment manager runs money either for the organization that he or she is employed by or for a client of that organization. Many institutions hire investment management firms to handle portions of their funds. The managers of such a firm try to meet the investment objectives set by the client, and their performance often determines the amount of money that they manage for that client in the future. Figure 1-2 depicts institutional investors and the investment managers available to them. Organizations that require the management of funds are financial institutions such as insurance companies, depository institutions (i.e., commercial banks, savings and loan associations, credit unions), and investment companies.

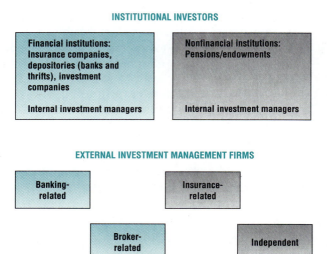

FIGURE 1-2

Institutional investors may use any combination of internal and external investment managers to shape and implement their portfolios.

BOX 1

MIAMI FIRE & POLICE HUNT FOR STOCKS & BONDS

The $575 million City of Miami Fire-fighters' & Police Officers' Retirement Trust is performing an asset allocation study and searching for a small-cap value manager and a domestic bond manager. It will also review proposals from a stock index manager, according to Elena Rodriguez, administrator.

Miami is conducting the asset allocation study as a periodic review of its investment policies, Rodriguez said, adding that consultant William Cottle at the Berkeley office of Dorn, Helliesen & Cottle is conducting the searches and study. Cottle is expected to have a short-list of candidates for the trust board's Nov. 17 meeting, during which firms will make presentations and money managers will be selected for the ventures, she said.

Allocations will be determined after reviewing the asset study and selected money management firms. Rodriguez declined to speculate how much will be allocated or how the accounts will be funded, but said no firms will be dismissed. The trust has not concluded that it will add an index stock manager, but

will include presentations from firms as part of its review of the investment style.

The trust is seeking the additional money managers to diversify its investments, Rodriguez said, adding it's happy with existing performance. For example, incumbent small-cap manager Cadence Capital Management of Boston has performed so well that its growth allocation has been increased twice. Rodriguez declined to provide the amount of assets allocated to the trust's money managers.

The trust's other managers have balanced accounts. They are Alliance Capital Management of New York, Barrow, Hanley, Mewhinney and Strauss of Dallas, Kemper Financial Services of Chicago and Sun Bank Capital Management of New Orleans. The asset allocation changes as balanced managers change their positions in response to market conditions, she said, but the firms have a target of 60% equities and 40% bonds. Comerica Trust Co. of Florida in Fort Lauderdale serves as custodian.

Adding a small-cap value manager is intended to diversify the trust's small-cap growth assets, Rodriguez explained. Since the additional equities would upset the trust's target asset mix, the trust will add a bond manager, she said. If the index equity fund is entered, the allocation for the venture will be set so that it, along with the small-cap account, will maintain the equity and bond mix, she said. The domestic bond manager will invest in both public and private instruments.

Author's Note: The types of managers that Miami Fire & Police are looking for (small-cap value manager, domestic bond manager, stock index manager) will be covered in later chapters in the book. A "balanced account" has a mixture of both stocks and bonds.

Source: Thomas Leswing, *Money Management Letter* (Oct. 25, 1993), pp. 1, 18.

Question for Box 1

1. What is an asset allocation study, and why is it essential to the investment management process?

Non-financial institutions that require the services of investment managers are pension funds and endowment funds (i.e., the funds of universities and foundations). Today, the greatest need is the management of pension assets. Organizations that have established a pension plan are referred to as **pension sponsors**. Two examples of private pension sponsors that are corporations are Allied-Signal Corporation and IBM, with total assets as of 1991 of $6.4 billion and $23.2 billion, respectively.[2] Three examples of public pension sponsors are the state of California, with total assets of $61.2 billion; the city of New York, with total assets of $39.8 billion; and the Dallas Police and Fire Department, with total pension assets of $615 million.[3] Examples of non-corporate private pension sponsors are those for TIAA-CREF, the largest pension fund in the United States (the pension plan for most college faculty and staff), and some teamsters pension funds. Box 1 describes one institutional investor's search for external money managers.

---

[2]"The Largest Corporate Plans," *Institutional Investor* (January 1992), p. 105.
[3]"The Public Pension Funds," *Institutional Investor* (January 1992), p. 133.

An organization that needs to have money managed can manage those funds internally (i.e., with its in-house money manager), engage the services of one or more outside money management firms, or use a combination of internal and external money managers. For example, Allied-Signal has 35 external money managers but also manages money internally. The Dallas Police and Fire pension system uses only outside money managers.

Who are these outside money management firms? Money management firms can be classified into four types: bank-related, insurance-related, brokerage-firm-related, and independent organizations. The first includes subsidiaries and departments of a bank. Most banks have established trust departments to manage funds of individual investors and pension sponsors. Almost all large banks have one or more money management subsidiaries. For example, as of December 31, 1992, Bankers Trust managed $158.8 billion for clients, and Norwest Bank of Minneapolis had $23.8 billion that it managed for clients, with $5.9 billion managed by three subsidiaries, Norwest Investments, Peregrine Capital Management, and United Capital Management. Insurance companies also have subsidiaries. For example, in 1992 Prudential Insurance Company of America had $174.2 billion that it managed for clients and had six subsidiaries for this purpose: Global Advisors, Jennison Associates, PDI Strategies, Prudential Fixed Income Advisors, Prudential Real Estate Investors, and PruLiquidity. Brokerage firms (i.e., securities firms) also have money management arms. For example, Merrill Lynch's subsidiary is Merrill Lynch Asset Management with $137.8 billion under management, Bear Stearns' subsidiary, Bear Stearns Asset Management, has $5.7 billion under management, and Goldman Sachs's subsidiary is Goldman Sachs Asset Management with $35.7 billion under management.

Independent money management firms are those not related to banks, insurance companies, or brokerage firms. Examples include Fidelity Investments with $203.8 billion under management as of December 31, 1992; AIM Capital Management with $20.40 billion under management; and Sanford C. Bernstein & Co. with $18.6 billion under management.

Table 1-1 lists the 10 largest institutions in the United States as of 1992. The amount under management reported in the table includes the sum of the funds of the institution and the amount managed for clients. Table 1-2 shows the top 15 managers of other people's money as of 1992.

ORGANIZATION OF THE BOOK

Now that you understand the investment management process and the structure of the money management business, let's look at the chapters that follow. The book is divided into six sections. Section I, which includes this chapter, Chapter 2, and Chapter 3, provides background information. Chapter 2 gives an overview of financial markets and the major asset classes. It presents the historical performance of the three major asset classes (common stock, bonds, and short-term securities). Chapter 3 explains secondary markets for common stock and bonds and the mechanics of trading these securities.

The three chapters in Section II set forth modern portfolio theory and capital market theory. These two theories have led to various theories about how the equilibrium price of a financial asset is determined. These theories

TABLE 1-1

TOP 10 INSTITUTIONAL INVESTORS BASED ON ALL ASSETS UNDER MANAGEMENT (THEIR OWN AND CLIENTS') AS OF 1992

Rank		Total Assets (Millions)
1	American Express Co.	$273,438
2	Prudential Insurance Co.	228,510
3	Fidelity Investments	203,758
4	Bankers Trust Co.	158,793
5	J. P. Morgan & Co.	154,084
6	Equitable Companies	151,085
7	Metropolitan Life	144,065
8	Citicorp Global Asset Mgmt	143,773
9	Merrill Lynch & Co.	140,825
10	State Street Bank & Trust Co.	137,366

This table ranks the 10 top institutions according to all assets under management—their own as well as their clients'. It includes real estate and securities investments but not commercial and personal loans.

Source: "America's Top Money Managers," *Institutional Investor* (August 1993), p. 106.

TABLE 1-2

TOP 15 INSTITUTIONAL INVESTORS BASED ON THE AMOUNT OF CLIENT ASSETS UNDER MANAGEMENT AS OF DECEMBER 1992

Rank		Total Assets (Millions)
1	Fidelity Investments	$203,758
2	American Express	192,707
3	Prudential Insurance Co.	174,217
4	Bankers Trust Co.	158,793
5	Equitable Companies	143,391
6	Merrill Lynch & Co.	140,292
7	State Street Bank & Trust Co.	129,411
8	J. P. Morgan & Co.	118,800
9	Wells Fargo Nikko Inv. Adv.	118,253
10	TIAA-CREF	111,004
11	Capital Group	109,939
12	Metropolitan Life	103,884
13	Mellon Bank Corp.	92,917
14	Franklin/Templeton Group	90,043
15	Sears Roebuck Group	80,041

This table ranks the 15 top institutions according to assets under management for clients.

Source: Adapted from "America's Top Money Managers," *Institutional Investor* (August 1993), pp. 109, 112.

have revolutionized the world of money management, contributing important methods for quantifying investment risk and return. As further confirmation of the importance of these theories, in 1990 the Alfred Nobel Memorial Prize in Economic Sciences was awarded to two of the pioneers of these theories.

As explained in this chapter, both the investment objective and the strategy selected by a money manager depend on the institution for which the money is being managed. In Section III, we review the major institutional investors. Our focus is not on how to manage an institution, but rather on how to manage the institution's investment portfolio. The factors that affect the selection of an investment policy and strategy are described in Chapter 7. These factors include the characteristics of the liabilities, liquidity and portfolio regulatory constraints, and accounting and tax considerations. Chapters 8 through 11 describe the major institutional players.

In the next two sections we discuss common stock (or equity) portfolio management (Section IV) and bond (or fixed-income) portfolio management (Section V). There are seven chapters in Section IV. Forecasting earnings is the subject of Chapter 12. Chapter 13 reviews the evidence on the pricing efficiency of the common stock market. This evidence is important because, as we noted earlier, it affects whether a client will request a money manager to pursue an active or a passive management style. In the same chapter, transactions costs are discussed in-depth. In Chapter 14, one particular form of passive management called indexing is explained. Chapter 15 reviews the major common stock investment styles and the wide range of active common stock strategies. Chapters 16 and 17 cover stock index futures and discuss options on common stock and stock indexes. The focus is on how these contracts can be used to control the risk of a portfolio and to implement portfolio strategies in a cost-effective manner. Chapter 18 explains the models for the pricing of options.

The nine chapters in Section V deal with fixed-income portfolio management. Chapter 19 provides an overview of the characteristics of fixed-income securities. The analytical tools to manage a bond portfolio are explained in Chapters 20 and 21. There is not just one interest rate in an economy. The factors affecting bond yields are explained in Chapter 22. Chapter 23 describes how bonds with embedded options and convertible bonds should be evaluated. Active bond portfolio strategies and bond indexing are the subject of Chapter 24, and structured portfolio strategies are the subject of Chapter 25. As in common stock portfolio management, futures and options can be used to control the risk of a portfolio. The various interest rate futures and options contracts available to money managers and the way they can be used to control a bond portfolio's risk are the subject of Chapter 26. The arsenal of contracts for asset/liability management available to institutional investors was augmented in the 1980s with the introduction of customized interest rate agreements: interest rate swaps, caps, and floors. These agreements are covered in Chapter 27. In recent years, customized agreements with similar features that can be used by common stock portfolio managers have been introduced. These are also explained in Chapter 27.

The last section of the book, Section VI, which consists of three chapters, is devoted to two topics. Chapter 28 covers the asset allocation decision, the mathematical models used to make the asset allocation decision, and the way an asset allocation decision can be effectively implemented. Chapter 29 describes how to measure the performance of a money manager, and, finally, Chapter 30 explains the various methodologies for evaluating the performance of a money manager.

There are four appendixes. Appendix A provides a review of the fundamental concepts of probability and statistics used in the book. Appendixes B, C, and D cover various topics for fundamental security analysis. Appendix B provides a review of the income statement and the balance sheet. The analysis of earnings is the subject of Appendix C, and the analysis of debt and cash flow is the subject of Appendix D.

■ KEY TERMS

active portfolio strategy
asset allocation decision
asset classes
benchmark
efficient portfolio
institutional investors
institutionalization

investment management
investment manager
marketplace price efficiency
money management
money manager
passive portfolio strategy
pension sponsors

portfolio
portfolio management
portfolio manager
retail investors
structured portfolio strategy

■ QUESTIONS

1. What is the difference between a retail investor and an institutional investor?

2. What is meant by the institutionalization of financial markets?

3. At a social function you were introduced to a money manager who shared his philosophy of money management with you. He said, "I don't care who my client is. Money management is money management. I would follow the same strategy and buy the same securities if I were managing the funds for a bank as I would for a retired individual." Comment on this philosophy.

4. What is meant by an active portfolio strategy?

5. What will determine whether an active or passive portfolio strategy will be pursued?

6. What is a structured portfolio strategy?

7. Explain how it can be possible for a portfolio manager to outperform a benchmark but still fail to meet the investment objective of a client.

8. What is meant by an efficient portfolio?

9. The following excerpt is from an article entitled "Shooting for Target, Louisiana Sheriffs Hire Four," in *Money Market Letter* (July 19, 1993): "The $340 million Sheriff's Pension & Relief Fund in Monroe, La., has hired its first external managers as it moves to meet its asset allocation goals. . . ."

   a. What is meant by external managers?
   b. What is meant by asset allocation goals?

10. The following excerpt is from an article entitled "Benchmarks Abounding," in *Institutional Investor* (September 1993):

    What benchmark do you use to measure your managers' performance? Once upon a time, that was a simple question with a simple response. Today, though, the task of coming up with an answer may require the services of a troop of consultants for there has been a proliferation of yardsticks in the measurement marketplace. (p. 193)

    a. What is meant by a benchmark?
    b. What role does a benchmark serve in the investment management process?

CHAPTER 2
OVERVIEW OF FINANCIAL MARKETS AND INVESTMENTS

LEARNING OBJECTIVES

After reading this chapter you will be able to:

- distinguish between financial assets and real assets.
- distinguish between a debt claim and an equity claim.
- characterize the major classes of financial instruments.
- classify financial markets.
- identify the economic functions of financial markets.
- distinguish between the capital market and money market.
- describe the globalization and institutionalization of financial markets.
- list the different sectors of the U.S. bond market.
- explain the different types of common stock and debt traded in the global market.
- distinguish the cash or spot markets from the derivative markets.
- explain the role of derivative instruments in portfolio management.
- describe the relative historical performance of stocks and bonds and the way historical performance is measured.

As discussed in Chapter 1, investors may choose among a wide range of financial instruments within several asset classes. These include common stock, bonds, real estate, precious metals, and works of art, to name a few. The specific investments within an asset class share a similar characteristic with respect to the potential reward and risk that an investor would incur. For example, the common stock of General Motors Corporation and that of ITT Corporation offer similar risks and rewards. Likewise, bonds issued by these corporations would share many characteristics.

In fact, the two major asset classes in which institutional investors allocate funds are common stock and bonds. At one time, U.S. institutional investors restricted their allocation of funds to these two asset classes because of either restrictions imposed by clients or regulations. In recent years, institutional investors have expanded their choices. Today, they are more willing to invest in residential and commercial real estate, farmlands, timberlands, works of art, and gold coins, for example. Moreover, U.S. institutional investors at one time typically restricted their allocation to the common stock and bonds of U.S. entities. Today, investors take a more global perspective and look at not only the U.S. financial market but also non-U.S. financial markets when allocating funds.

In this chapter we provide an overview of the two major asset classes in the U.S. and in other major non-U.S. markets. Sections IV and V of this book provide more information about these markets and a description of the instruments and their potential reward and risk. We also summarize the empirical evidence with respect to the relative reward and risk from investing in common stock and bonds.

FINANCIAL ASSETS

We begin with a few basic definitions. An **asset** is, broadly speaking, any possession that has value in an exchange. Assets can be classified as tangible or intangible. A **tangible asset** is one whose value depends on particular physical properties. Examples are buildings, land, or machinery. Tangible assets may be classified further into **reproducible assets** such as machinery or **nonreproducible assets** such as land, a mine, or a work of art.

An **intangible asset**, by contrast, represents legal claims to some future benefit. Its value bears no relation to the form, physical or otherwise, in which the claims are recorded. Financial assets, also called financial instruments or securities, are intangible assets. For these instruments, the typical future benefit is a claim to future cash. This book deals with investments in financial assets.

Issuers and Investors

The entity that has agreed to make future cash payments is called the **issuer** of the financial asset. The owner of the financial asset is referred to as the **investor**. Here are just three examples of financial assets:

- A bond issued by the U.S. Department of the Treasury
- A corporate bond issued by General Electric Corporation
- Common stock issued by Digital Equipment Corporation

In the case of government or corporate bonds, the government or corporation (the issuer) agrees to pay the investor (or holder) of the bond periodic interest payments until the bond matures, and then at the maturity date repay the amount borrowed. The common stock of Digital Equipment Corporation entitles the investor to receive dividends distributed by the company. The investor in this case also has a claim to a pro rata share of the net asset value of the company in case of liquidation of the company.

A particular financial asset is sometimes referred to as an **issue**. For example, rather than refer to the General Electric Corporation bond, an investor may refer to the General Electric Corporation issue.

Debt versus Equity Claims

The claim that the holder of a financial asset has may be either a fixed dollar amount or a varying, or residual, amount. In the former case, the financial asset is referred to as a **debt instrument**. The bond issued by the U.S. Department of the Treasury and the bond issued by General Electric Corporation cited above are examples of debt instruments requiring fixed dollar payments.

A **residual claim** or **equity claim** obligates the issuer of the financial asset to pay the holder an amount based on earnings, if any, after holders of debt instruments have been paid. Common stock is an example of an equity claim. A partnership share in a business is another example.

Some securities fall into both categories. Preferred stock, for example, is an equity claim that entitles the investor to receive a fixed dollar amount. This payment is contingent, however, due only after payments to debt instrument holders are made. Another instrument with both fixed and residual characteristics is the convertible bond, which allows the investor to convert debt into equity under certain circumstances. Both debt and preferred stock that pays a fixed dollar amount are called **fixed-income instruments**.

FINANCIAL MARKETS

A **financial market** provides a mechanism for creating and exchanging financial assets. Financial assets can be bought and sold privately, of course, but in most developed economies financial markets provide the opportunity to trade financial assets in some type of organized institutional structure.

Classification of Financial Markets

There are many ways to classify financial markets. One way is by the type of financial claim (see Figure 2-1). The claims traded in a financial market may be for either a fixed dollar amount or a residual amount. As explained earlier, the former financial assets are referred to as debt instruments, and the financial market in which such instruments are traded is referred to as the **debt market**. The latter financial assets are called equity instruments, and the financial market where such instruments are traded is referred to as the **equity market**, or the **stock market**. Preferred stock is an equity claim

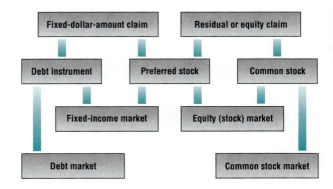

FIGURE 2-1

Classification of financial markets by type of claim.

that entitles the investor to receive a fixed dollar amount. Generally, debt instruments and preferred stock are classified as part of the **fixed-income market**. The sector of the stock market that does not include preferred stock is called the **common stock market**.

Another way to classify financial markets is by the maturity of the claims. For example, there is a financial market for short-term debt instruments, called the **money market**, and one for longer-maturity financial assets, called the **capital market**. The traditional cutoff between short term and long term is one year. That is, a financial asset with a maturity of one year or less is considered short term and therefore part of the money market. A financial asset with a maturity of more than one year is part of the capital market. Thus, the debt market can be divided into those debt instruments that are part of the money market and those that are part of the capital market, depending on the number of years to maturity. Since equity instruments are generally perpetual (i.e., they have no maturity date), they are classified as part of the capital market. This is depicted in Figure 2-2.

A third way to classify financial markets is based on whether the financial claims are newly issued or not. When an issuer sells a new financial asset to the public, it is said to "issue" the financial asset. The market for newly issued financial assets is called the **primary market**. After a certain period of time, the financial asset is bought and sold (i.e., exchanged or traded) among investors. The market where this activity takes place is referred to as the **secondary market**.

Functions of Financial Markets

Financial markets provide three important economic functions. First, markets determine the prices of the assets traded through the interactions of buyers and sellers. This is called the **price discovery process**. Second, financial markets provide a mechanism for an investor to sell a financial asset. Because of this feature, it is said that a financial market offers **liquidity**, the ability to convert an asset into cash. This is an attractive feature when circumstances either force or motivate an investor to sell. Without secondary markets, the owner of a debt would be forced to hold the debt instrument until it matures. The owner of an equity would have to wait until the company was either voluntarily or involuntarily sold (or liquidated).

The third economic function of a financial market is that it reduces the cost of transacting. Two costs are associated with transacting: search costs

FIGURE 2-2

Classification of financial markets by maturity of claim.

national market. It can be broken down into two parts: the domestic market and the foreign market. A country's **domestic market** is where issuers domiciled in the country issue securities and where those securities are subsequently traded.

A country's **foreign market** is one in which the securities of issuers not domiciled in the country are sold and traded. Foreign securities are regulated by authorities in the country in which the securities are issued. For example, securities issued by non-U.S. corporations in the United States must comply with the regulations set forth in U.S. securities law. A non-Japanese corporation that seeks to offer securities in Japan must comply with Japanese securities law and regulations imposed by the Japanese Ministry of Finance. Nicknames have been used to describe the various foreign markets. For example, the foreign market in the United States is called the **Yankee market**. In Japan the foreign market is nicknamed the *Samurai market*, in the United Kingdom the *Bulldog market*, in the Netherlands the *Rembrandt market*, and in Spain the *Matador market*.

The **external market**, also called the **international market**, includes securities with the following distinguishing features: (1) At issuance they are offered simultaneously to investors in a number of countries, and (2) they are issued outside the jurisdiction of any single country. The external market is commonly referred to as the **offshore market**, or more popularly, the **Euromarket** (even though this market is not limited to Europe, it began there).[1]

WORLD COMMON STOCK MARKETS

Table 2-1 provides a comparative analysis of the size, measured in U.S. dollars, of the common stock markets of the world. The stock markets of the United States and Japan are the largest in the world. Since the markets are measured in U.S. dollars, their relative size varies as the value of the currency of Japan, the yen, changes against the dollar; U.S. share increases when the yen depreciates and decreases when the yen appreciates. The third largest market, but trailing considerably behind those in the United States and Japan, is the U.K. market.

Euroequity issues are those securities that are initially sold to investors simultaneously in several national markets by an international syndicate. An increasing number of U.S. firms had equity offerings which included a Euroequity tranche. A **tranche** refers to one of several securities offered at the same time.

When a corporation issues equity outside its domestic market and the equity issue is subsequently traded in the foreign market, it is typically in the form of an **International Depositary Receipt (IDR)**. IDRs are issued by banks as evidence of ownership of the underlying stock of a foreign corporation that the bank holds in trust. Each IDR may represent ownership of one or more shares of common stock of a corporation. The advantage of the IDR structure is that the corporation does not have to comply with all the regulatory issu-

---

[1]The classification we use is by no means universally accepted. Some market observers and compilers of statistical data on market activity refer to the external market as consisting of the foreign market and the Euromarket.

TABLE 2-1
ESTIMATED TOTAL MARKET VALUE OF NATIONAL STOCK MARKETS INCLUDED IN MORGAN STANLEY CAPITAL INTERNATIONAL INDEXES AS OF DECEMBER 31, 1992 (IN BILLIONS OF U.S. DOLLARS)

Area and Country		Estimated Market Value
United States		$4,022.8
Canada		$ 219.7
Europe, by country:		$2,353.1
Austria	$ 22.5	
Belgium	63.3	
Denmark	32.2	
Finland	11.9	
France	333.0	
Germany	325.7	
Italy	124.4	
Netherlands	129.8	
Norway	18.0	
Spain	95.1	
Sweden	87.2	
Switzerland	195.2	
United Kingdom	914.9	
Asia and the Far East, by country:		$2,717.1
Australia	133.2	
Hong Kong	161.9	
Japan	2,331.5	
New Zealand	15.8	
Singapore/Malaysia	74.7	
South African gold mines		$ 7.4
Worldwide		$9,320.1

Source: *Morgan Stanley Capital International Perspective*, Quarterly Issue 1 (1993), p. 5. (Adapted by the author.)

ing requirements of the foreign country where the stock is to be traded. The U.S. version of the IDR is the **American Depositary Receipt (ADR)**.

WORLD BOND MARKETS

A **bond** is an instrument in which the issuer (debtor/borrower) promises to repay to the lender/investor the amount borrowed plus interest over some specified period of time. A typical bond issued in the United States specifies (1) a fixed date at which the amount borrowed (principal) is due and (2) the contractual amount of interest that would be paid every six months. The date on which the principal is required to be repaid is called the **maturity date**. Assuming that the issuer does not default or redeem the issue prior to the maturity date, an investor holding this bond until the maturity date would be assured of a known cash flow.

TABLE 2-2		
COMPOSITION OF THE U.S. BOND MARKET AS OF **DECEMBER 31, 1990 (DOLLARS IN BILLIONS)**		
U.S. Treasury securities		$2,210	(25.4%)
U.S. agencies securities		309	(3.6%)
(excluding agency mortgage-backed securities)			
Corporate bonds		1,506	(17.3%)
Domestic	1,387		
Yankee	119		
Municipal securities		852	(9.8%)
Mortgages—nonsecuritized		2,783	(32.0%)
(1–4 multifamily, farm commercial)			
Mortgage-backed securities		1,029	(11.9%)
Total U.S. bond market*		$8,599	

*Excludes asset-backed securities.

Source: This table is prepared from data supplied by Salomon Brothers Inc.

Sectors of the U.S. Bond Market

The U.S. bond market is the largest bond market in the world. The size of the U.S. bond market and its composition as of December 31, 1990, are summarized in Table 2-2.

U.S. Treasury Securities   Securities issued by the U.S. Department of the Treasury are referred to as **Treasury securities**, or simply **Treasuries**. These securities are backed by the full faith and credit of the United States government. Consequently, market participants view them as having no credit risk. Interest rates on Treasury securities are the key interest rates throughout the U.S. economy, as well as in international capital markets.

The U.S. Treasury issues three types of securities—bills, notes, and bonds. At issuance, **Treasury bills** have a maturity of 1 year or less, **Treasury notes** more than 2 years but less than 10 years to maturity, and **Treasury bonds** 10 years or more to maturity.

The Department of the Treasury is the largest single issuer of debt in the world, with Treasury securities accounting for $2.2 trillion (represented by over 180 different Treasury note and bond issues and 30 Treasury bill issues). The large volume of total debt and the large size of any single issue have contributed to making the Treasury market the most active and hence the most liquid market in the world.

Federal Agency Securities   Federally related institutions, like the Farmers Housing Administration, the Tennessee Valley Authority, and the Government National Mortgage Association, are arms of the federal government. Government-sponsored enterprises are privately owned, publicly chartered entities. Examples include the Federal Home Loan Mortgage Corporation (Freddie Mac) and the Federal National Mortgage Association (Fannie Mae). Debt securities issued by federally related institutions and government-sponsored enterprises constitute the federal agency securities market.

While there are exceptions, the debt of federally related institutions is guaranteed by the U.S. government. While government-sponsored enterprises issue their own securities, in general federally related institutions obtain all or part of their financing by borrowing from the Federal Financing Bank. As can be seen from Table 2-2, the federal government agencies market is the smallest of the sectors reported in the table.[2]

Corporate Bonds   As the name indicates, **corporate bonds** are debt obligations issued by corporations. The corporate bond sector includes bonds issued by U.S. corporations and bonds issued by non-U.S. entities in the United States. The latter market sector is called the *Yankee bond market*.

Corporate bonds are classified by the type of issuer. The four general classifications used by bond information services are (1) utilities, (2) transportations, (3) industrials, and (4) banks and finance companies. Finer breakdowns are often made to create more homogeneous groupings. For example, utilities are subdivided into electric power companies, gas distribution companies, water companies, and communication companies. Transportations are further divided into airlines, railroads, and trucking companies. Industrials are the catchall class, including all kinds of manufacturing, merchandising, and service companies.

Municipal Securities   The municipal market is the sector where state and local governments raise funds. Typically bonds issued in this sector are exempt from federal income taxes, and consequently this sector is referred to as the **tax-exempt sector**.

There are basically two different types of municipal bond security structures: general obligation bonds and revenue bonds. A **general obligation bond** is a debt instrument that is secured by the issuer's unlimited taxing power. A **revenue bond** is issued for either project or enterprise financings where the issuer pledges to the bondholders the revenues generated by the operating projects financed. Hospital revenue bonds and sewer revenue bonds are two examples of revenue bonds.

Mortgage and Mortgage-Backed Securities   Of the $8.6 trillion long-term debt market, the largest component by far is the mortgage market. A **mortgage** is a loan secured by the collateral of some specified real estate property which obliges the borrower to make a predetermined series of payments. **Mortgage-backed securities** are securities that are backed by a pool of mortgage loans. Mortgage loans that are pooled together and used as collateral (i.e., backing) for a security are said to be **securitized**.

Asset-Backed Securities   **Asset-backed securities** are securities backed by assets that are not mortgage loans. While the two most common types of asset-backed securities are those backed by automobile loans and credit card re-

---

[2]As explained in Chapter 19, a majority of the securities backed by a pool of mortgages are guaranteed by a government-sponsored enterprise of the U.S. government. These securities are classified as part of the mortgage-backed securities market rather than as U.S. government agency securities.

ceivables, there are securities backed by boat loans, recreational vehicle loans, computer leases, bank loans, accounts receivables, and Small Business Administration (SBA) loans.

Eurobond Market

A **Eurobond** is one that is (1) underwritten by an international syndicate, (2) offered at issuance simultaneously to investors in a number of countries, and (3) issued outside the jurisdiction of any single country. The Eurobond market is divided into different sectors based on the currency in which the issue is denominated. For example, when Eurobonds are denominated in U.S. dollars, they are referred to as **Eurodollar bonds**. Eurobonds denominated in Japanese yen are referred to as **Euroyen bonds**.

Non-U.S. Government Bond Markets

Prior to the 1980s, U.S. bond investors invested exclusively in U.S. domestic bonds. Among the reasons for their lack of participation in the non-U.S. bond markets were lack of familiarity with the operations of these markets, lack of familiarity with interest rate movements in these markets, concern about the liquidity of these markets, and unfamiliarity with the risks of lending to foreign governments or corporations.

In recent years, however, U.S. investors have become increasingly aware of non-U.S. interest rate movements and their relationship with U.S. interest rates. In addition, foreign countries have "liberalized" their bond markets, making them more liquid and more accessible to international investors. In many cases, withholding taxes have been eliminated or reduced. Futures and options markets have been developed on government bonds in several major countries, permitting the more effective implementation of investment strategies. And, in general, there is an increased awareness of the non-U.S. bond markets as potential sources of return enhancement and/or risk reduction. As a result, U.S. bond managers, mainly institutional investors, have increasingly adopted a global approach and invested in bonds from several countries.

Many global investors utilize only the foreign government bond markets, rather than the non-government bond markets, because of the low credit risk, the liquidity, and the simplicity of the government markets. While non-government markets ("semi-government," local government, corporate, and mortgage bond markets) provide higher yields, they also have greater credit risks, and foreign investors may not be ready to accept alien credit risks and less liquidity.

Table 2-3 shows the nine largest non-U.S. government bond markets. The Japanese government bond market is the second largest bond market in the world, followed by the German government bond market.

MONEY MARKET

Money market instruments are debt instruments that have a maturity of one year or less. The instruments traded in the money market include Treasury bills, commercial paper, bankers acceptances, short-term federal agency securities, short-term municipal obligations, certificates of deposit, repurchase agreements, and federal funds.

TABLE 2-3		
SIZE OF THE NINE LARGEST NON-U.S. GOVERNMENT BOND MARKETS AS OF JUNE 1, 1990 (IN BILLIONS OF U.S. DOLLARS)		
Country	Principal Amount	Market Value
Japan	$472.1	$460.4
Germany	213.7	201.6
United Kingdom	167.1	155.6
France	153.1	155.2
Canada	101.8	101.6
Netherlands	100.1	97.2
Denmark	33.3	34.0
Australia	21.8	21.1
Switzerland	7.1	6.6
Total (non-U.S.)	$1,270.1	$1,233.3

Our focus in this book will not be on money market instruments. However, money managers must be acquainted with these instruments because they provide an outlet for the temporary investing of funds. Thus, all money managers will use this market. Below we briefly describe Treasury bills, commercial paper, bankers acceptances, certificates of deposits, repurchase agreements, and federal funds.

As noted earlier, Treasury securities are securities issued by the U.S. Treasury. Treasury bills are one type of Treasury security, those that at the time of issuance have a maturity of one year or less. Specifically, Treasury bills are issued with a maturity of three months, six months, and one year. The current practice of the Treasury is to issue Treasury bills each month via an auction process.

Commercial paper is a name for short-term unsecured promissory notes issued by a corporation. The maturity of commercial paper is typically less than 270 days; the most common maturity range is 30 to 50 days or less.

A **bankers acceptance** is a vehicle created to facilitate commercial trade transactions, particularly international transactions. These vehicles are called bankers acceptances because a bank accepts the responsibility to repay a loan to the holder of the vehicle in case the debtor fails to perform.

A **certificate of deposit (CD)** is a certificate issued by a bank or thrift that indicates a specified sum of money has been deposited at the issuing depository institution. A CD bears a maturity date and a specified interest rate, and can be issued in any denomination. CDs issued by banks are insured by the Federal Deposit Insurance Corporation but only for amounts up to $100,000.

A **repurchase agreement** is the sale of a security with a commitment by the seller to buy the security back from the purchaser at a specified price at a designated future date. Basically, a repurchase agreement, popularly referred to as a *repo*, is a collateralized short-term loan, where the collateral is a security. The collateral in a repo may be a Treasury security, money market instrument, federal agency security, or mortgage-backed security.

The transaction is referred to as a repurchase agreement because it calls for the sale of the security and its repurchase at a future date. Both the sale price and the purchase price are specified in the agreement. The difference between the purchase (repurchase) price and the sale price is the dollar interest cost of the loan. If the agreement is for the loan of funds for one day, it is called an **overnight repo**; if the term of the agreement is for more than one day, it is called **term repo**.

As we explain in Chapter 11, depository institutions (commercial banks and thrifts) are required to maintain reserves. These reserves are deposits at their district Federal Reserve Bank, which are called **federal funds**. No interest is earned on federal funds. Consequently, a depository institution that maintains federal funds in excess of the amount required incurs an opportunity cost—the loss of interest income that could be earned on the excess reserves. At the same time, there are depository institutions whose federal funds are less than the amount required. One way that banks with less than the required reserves can bring reserves to the required level is to enter into a repo with a non-bank customer. An alternative is for the bank to borrow federal funds from a bank that has excess reserves. The market in which federal funds are bought (borrowed) by banks that need these funds and sold (lent) by banks that have excess federal funds is called the federal funds market. The equilibrium interest rate, which is determined by the supply and demand for federal funds, is the federal funds rate.

The rate determined in this market is the major factor that influences the rate paid on all the other money market instruments described above. The federal funds rate and the repo rate are tied together because both are a means for a bank to borrow. The federal funds rate is higher because the lending of federal funds is done on an unsecured basis; this differs from the repo, in which the lender has a security as collateral.

FUTURES AND OPTIONS MARKETS

The markets we have discussed thus far involve the immediate delivery of a security or instrument. Thus, they are called **cash markets** or **spot markets**. Other markets operate with contracts that specify transactions to be completed at some future date. The contract holder has either the obligation or the choice to buy or sell a financial asset at a specified future time. The price of any such contract derives its value from the price of the underlying financial asset. Consequently, these contracts are called **derivative instruments**, and the markets for these contracts are called the **derivative markets**.

The two basic types of derivative instruments are options contracts and futures contracts. An **options contract** gives the owner of the contract the right, but not the obligation, to buy (or sell) a financial asset at a specified price from (or to) another party. The buyer of the contract must pay the seller a fee, which is called the **option price**.

A **futures contract** is an agreement whereby two parties agree to transact with respect to some financial asset at a predetermined price at a specified future date. One party agrees to buy the financial asset; the other agrees to sell the financial asset. Both parties are obligated to perform, and neither party charges a fee.

Transactions using derivative instruments are not limited to financial assets. There are derivative instruments involving commodities and precious metals. Our focus in this book, however, is on derivative instruments where the underlying asset is a financial asset or some financial benchmark such as a stock index or an interest rate. We will explore how derivative markets can be used by money managers to quickly and efficiently control certain risks associated with a portfolio of financial assets.

OTHER MARKETS

While our focus in this book is on stocks and bonds, there are other markets in which an institutional investor, if permitted, may invest. The structure of the investment typically may take one of two forms: a partnership/fund or a direct investment. In the case of a partnership, there is a general partner and a limited partner. The general partner is responsible for managing the investment. An institutional investor such as a pension plan would participate as a limited partner. Below we summarize these alternative investments.

Many institutional investors invest indirectly in the real estate market through their ownership of either mortgage loans or mortgage-backed securities. The other form of participation in the real estate market is the ownership of real estate. Two particular types of real estate that institutional investors have begun to find greater interest in as an equity investment are timberlands and farmlands.

An investment in a start-up business that is perceived to have excellent growth prospects but does not have access to capital markets is referred to as **venture capital**. According to one industry source, Venture Economics of Needham, Massachusetts, there are 600 firms in the United States that manage venture capital funds with a total of $31 billion under management. As of 1990, according to Venture Economics, public and private pension funds were the major sources of capital commitments to venture funds, supplying more than half. While once a U.S. phenomenon, venture capital is now global. In Asia (including Australia and New Zealand), according to the *Asian Capital Journal*, there are 335 firms that manage venture capital funds with $19.5 billion under management.

A popular transaction used in the 1980s for taking a public corporation private is a **leveraged buy-out (LBO).** The means for financing the acquisition is through the use of debt funds: bank loans and bonds. Because of the large amount of debt relative to equity in the new corporation, the bonds are typically rated below investment grade, popularly referred to as *junk* or *high-yield* bonds. Investors can participate in an LBO through either the purchase of the debt (i.e., purchasing the bonds or participating in the bank loan) or the purchase of equity through an LBO fund that specializes in such investments. Investors may also participate in the commodities market, in particular the market for precious metals such as gold and silver. Participation in the commodities markets can be either through the ownership of the physical commodity or in the futures markets.

HISTORICAL PERFORMANCE OF STOCKS AND BONDS

There have been several studies of the historical performance of the major asset classes or sectors addressed in this book: common stocks and bonds. By historical performance, we mean the observed reward and risk from investing in an asset class. Before we discuss these studies, we provide a preliminary discussion of how reward and risk are measured.

Measuring Reward and Risk

The reward from investing is measured by the return realized over some period of time, typically one year. We discuss the nuances of measuring the return of a portfolio in Chapter 29. For purposes of our discussion here, it is sufficient to say that the return is equal to the change in the value of a portfolio over the time period divided by the initial value of the portfolio. That is,

$$\text{Return} = \frac{\genfrac{}{}{0pt}{}{\text{portfolio value at}}{\text{end of period}} - \genfrac{}{}{0pt}{}{\text{portfolio value at}}{\text{beginning of period}}}{\text{portfolio value at beginning of period}}$$

The portfolio value at the end of the period reflects the change in the market value of the assets in the portfolio plus any cash distributions during the period. The cash distributions include dividend payments received and interest income.

For example, suppose that in January 1, 19X1, the value of a portfolio is $400 million and on December 31, 19X1, the value of that portfolio is $450 million. The return is then

$$\text{Return} = \frac{\$450 \text{ million} - \$400 \text{ million}}{\$400 \text{ million}} = 0.125 = 12.5\%$$

In our illustration we have calculated the return for one year. Suppose instead that we wanted to calculate the average annual return over a five-year period. There are two ways to do this. The first is by simply calculating the annual return for each of the five years and then dividing by five. An average annual return calculated in this way is called the **arithmetic mean return**. The general formula for calculating the arithmetic mean return is

$$\text{Arithmetic mean return} = \frac{\text{return}_1 + \text{return}_2 + \ldots + \text{return}_N}{N}$$

where return_i = annual return for year i
         N = number of years

The second way to calculate an average annual return is by calculating a geometric average of the annual returns. The resulting return, which is called a **geometric mean return**, is calculated as follows:

$$\text{Geometric mean return} = [(1 + \text{return}_1)(1 + \text{return}_2) \ldots (1 + \text{return}_N)]^{1/N} - 1$$

The geometric mean return can be interpreted as follows: It is the return that will make the amount at the beginning of the period grow to the amount at the end of the period. We'll have more to say in Chapter 29 about the advantages of using the geometric mean return over the arithmetic mean return

TABLE 2-4			
U.S. FINANCIAL MARKETS: 1926–1992			
Summary Statistics of Annual Returns (Reward) and Standard Deviation (Risk)			
Sector	**Arithmetic Mean**	**Geometric Mean**	**Standard Deviation**
Common stocks*	12.4%	10.3%	20.6%
Small-company stocks	17.6	12.2	35.0
Long-term corporate bonds	5.8	5.5	8.5
Long-term Treasury bonds	5.2	4.8	8.6
Intermediate-term Treasury bonds	5.3	5.5	5.6
Treasury bills	3.6	3.7	3.3
Inflation	3.2	3.1	4.7

*As measured by the Standard & Poor's 500.

Source: *Stocks, Bonds, Bills, and Inflation 1993 Yearbook*™, Ibbotson Associates, Chicago (annually updates work by Roger G. Ibbotson and Rex A. Sinquefield). Used with permission. All rights reserved.

when looking at performance. In terms of the historical performance studies that we review below, the relative performance of asset classes is the same using either return measure.

The other element in looking at historical performance is risk. There are many dimensions to risk, and we will examine these throughout this book. In terms of historical performance, risk is generally measured as the variability of the return from period to period. That is, it is measured by how much the return varies from its average return. There are several ways that this variation can be measured. The most common way is the standard deviation of the annual returns. The calculation of the standard deviation is discussed in Appendix A.

Empirical Studies

The most extensive study and the one followed closely by most institutional investors is the one provided by Ibbotson Associates. The study is updated annually.[3] Table 2-4 shows the performance for the period 1926 to 1992 for sectors of the stock and bond markets in the United States. Two sectors of the stock market are reported: common stocks as represented by the Standard & Poor's 500 (a market index that we describe in Chapter 3) and small-company stocks. Three sectors of the bond market are reported: long-term corporate bonds, long-term Treasury bonds, and intermediate-term Treasury bonds. Also reported is the performance of Treasury bills. In addition to these market sectors, there is information on the rate of inflation as measured by the consumer price index.

A look at the average returns clearly shows that stocks have outperformed debt instruments. In fact, within the stock market, small-company stocks have performed better than the stocks in the S&P 500. Within the

---

[3]The data reported in this chapter are from Roger G. Ibbotson and Rex A. Sinquefield, *Stocks, Bonds, Bills, and Inflation 1993 Yearbook* (Chicago: Ibbotson Associates, Inc., 1993).

TABLE 2-5			
COMPARING JAPANESE AND U.S. FINANCIAL MARKETS: 1973–1987			
Summary Statistics of Annual Returns (Reward) and Standard Deviation (Risk)			
Sector in Japan	**Arithmetic Mean**	**Geometric Mean**	**Standard Deviation**
Large-capitalization stocks[a]	13.29%	12.07%	16.31%
Small-capitalization stocks[b]	16.74	14.07	26.72
Long-term corporate bonds[c]	8.90	8.76	5.56
Long-term government bonds	8.88	8.70	6.15
Short-term instruments[d]	7.26	7.24	2.74
Inflation	6.08	5.92	5.94
Sector in United States			
Large-capitalization stocks[e]	11.42%	9.86%	17.94%
Small-capitalization stocks[f]	19.24	16.18	25.68
Long-term corporate bonds	9.37	8.57	13.76
Long-term government bonds	8.88	8.53	13.30
Short-term instruments[g]	8.20	8.17	2.64
Inflation	6.96	6.90	3.57

[a]As measured by the Tokyo Stock Exchange I Index.

[b]As measured by the Tokyo Stock Exchange II Index.

[c]As measured by the long-term bonds of nine electric companies.

[d]As measured by the rate on bond repurchase agreements (called the *Gensaki rate*).

[e]As measured by the Standard & Poor's 500.

[f]As measured by the New York Stock Exchange Small Quintile.

[g]As measured by the rate on U.S. Treasury bills.

Source: Table 1 of Yasushi Hamao, "Japanese Stocks, Bonds, Bills, and Inflation: 1973–87," *Journal of Portfolio Management* (Winter 1989), p. 24.

bond market, corporate bonds have outperformed Treasury bonds.[4] Treasury bills had the worst performance. All sectors, however, realized a return that was on average greater than that of inflation.

Table 2-4 also shows the standard deviation for each asset class. As can be seen from the table, the lower the average return, the lower the risk as measured by the standard deviation. For example, the two common stock sectors had a higher average return than the three bond sectors, but a much greater standard deviation. The lowest standard deviation of all assets investigated was for Treasury bills.

This finding that the average return for an asset class is positively related to its risk is a very powerful finding. The implication is that, on average, investors have been rewarded for taking on additional risk.

The same finding has been observed in the financial markets of other countries. While we cannot review every country where there is empirical evidence, let's look at two non-U.S. financial markets. Tables 2-5 and 2-6 show

---

[4]A more detailed analysis of the return on corporate bonds found that the lower the credit quality of a corporate bond, the higher the average return. We discuss the credit quality of corporate bonds in later chapters. See Rayner Cheung, Joseph C. Bencivenga, and Frank J. Fabozzi, "Original Issue High-Yield Bonds: Historical Returns and Default Experience, 1977–1989," *Journal of Fixed Income* (September 1992), pp. 58–76.

TABLE 2-6
COMPARING CANADIAN AND U.S. FINANCIAL MARKETS: 1950–1986
Summary Statistics of Annual Returns (Reward) and Standard Deviation (Risk)

Sector in Canada	Arithmetic Mean	Geometric Mean	Standard Deviation
All stocks	11.49%	12.92%	17.87%
Long-term industrial bonds	6.22	6.63	9.82
Long-term Canada bonds	5.35	5.78	10.27
Treasury bills	5.84	5.92	4.20
Inflation	4.71	4.77	3.81
Sector in United States			
All stocks	12.79%	14.20%	17.89%
Corporate bonds	5.75	6.38	12.27
Treasury bonds	5.14	5.74	12.01
Treasury bills	5.72	5.85	5.32
Inflation	4.75	5.01	5.02

Source: James E. Hatch and Robert W. White, *Canadian Stocks, Bonds, Bills, and Inflation* (Charlottesville, VA: Institute of Chartered Financial Analysts, 1988).

the results for the Japanese and Canadian financial markets, respectively. While there are exceptions, the results reported in these tables suggest the same pattern of return and risk as in the United States. The tables also show the corresponding risk and return for the U.S. financial market for the same time period.

■ SUMMARY

An asset is any possession that has value in an exchange. A financial asset represents a legal claim to some future benefit. The typical future benefit is a claim to future cash. A financial market is a market where financial assets are exchanged.

There are many ways to classify financial markets: by types of financial claim (debt instrument versus equity claim), by the maturity of claims (money market versus capital market), and by whether the security is newly issued or seasoned (primary market versus secondary market).

Globalization means the integration of financial markets throughout the world into an international financial market. From the perspective of a given country, financial markets can be classified as either internal (also called national market) or external (also called international market, Euromarket, or offshore market). The internal market can be divided into two sec-

tors: the domestic market and the foreign market. The former is one where issuers domiciled in the country issue securities and where those securities are traded; the foreign market of a country is one in which the securities of issuers not domiciled in the country are sold and traded.

Common stock represents an ownership interest in a corporation. The stock markets of the United States and Japan are the largest in the world, followed by the U.K. market. Euroequity issues are those issued simultaneously in several national markets by an international syndicate. When a corporation issues equity outside its domestic market and the equity issue is subsequently traded in the foreign market, the equity is typically in the form of an International Depositary Receipt (IDR), the United States version being the American Depositary Receipt (ADR).

A bond is an instrument in which the issuer (debtor/borrower) promises to repay to the lender/investor the amount borrowed plus interest over some specified period of time. The U.S. bond market is the largest bond market in the world, consisting of the U.S. Treasury securities market, the federal agency securities market, the corporate bond market, the municipal securities (or tax-exempt) market, the mortgage and mortgage-backed securities market, and the asset-backed securities market.

A Eurobond is one that is (1) underwritten by an international syndicate, (2) offered at issuance simultaneously to investors in a number of countries, and (3) issued outside the jurisdiction of any single country. The Eurobond market is divided into different sectors based on the currency in which the issue is denominated. U.S. investors who invest in the national bond market of another country typically restrict their investment to the government bond market because of the low credit risk, the liquidity, and the simplicity of the securities. The Japanese government bond market is the second largest bond market in the world, followed by the German government bond market.

Money market instruments are debt instruments that have a maturity of one year or less. The instruments traded in the money market include Treasury bills, commercial paper, bankers acceptances, short-term federal agency securities, short-term municipal obligations, certificates of deposit, repurchase agreements, and federal funds.

There are two basic types of derivative instruments: options contracts and futures contracts. An options contract gives the owner of the contract the right, but not the obligation, to buy (or sell) a financial asset at a specified price from (or to) another party. A futures contract is an agreement between two parties to transact with respect to some financial asset at a predetermined price at a specified future date, one party agreeing to buy the financial asset, the other agreeing to sell the financial asset. Derivative markets can be used by money managers to quickly and efficiently control the price risk associated with a portfolio of financial assets. The market for many futures contracts has several advantages over the corresponding cash (spot) market for the financial asset.

Alternative investments to common stock and bonds include real estate (including farmland and timberland), venture capital, leveraged buy-out funds, and commodities.

There have been several studies of the historical performance of common stocks and bonds in the United States and other countries. The average return must be supplemented with information about how much variation there is in the year-to-year return which gauges the risk associated with realizing the average return. These studies suggest that the average return is positively related to the risk associated with realizing that average return.

■ **KEY TERMS**

American Depositary Receipt
    (ADR)
arithmetic mean return
asset
asset-backed securities
bankers acceptance
bond
capital market
cash markets
certificate of deposit (CD)
commercial paper
common stock market
corporate bonds
debt instrument
debt market

derivative instruments
derivative markets
domestic market
emerging markets
equity claim
equity market
Eurobond
Eurodollar bonds
Euroequity issues
Euromarket
Euroyen bonds
external market
federal funds
financial market
fixed-income instruments

fixed-income market
foreign market
futures contract
general obligation bond
geometric mean return
information costs
institutional investors
institutionalization
intangible asset
internal market
International Depositary Receipt
    (IDR)
international market
investor
issue

issuer	overnight repo	stock market
leveraged buy-out (LBO)	price discovery process	tangible asset
liquidity	primary market	tax-exempt sector
maturity date	repurchase agreement	term repo
money market	reproducible assets	tranche
mortgage	residual claim	Treasuries
mortgage-backed securities	retail investors	Treasury bills
national market	revenue bond	Treasury bonds
non-reproducible assets	search costs	Treasury notes
offshore market	secondary market	Treasury securities
option price	securitized	venture capital
options contract	spot markets	Yankee market

■ QUESTIONS

1. What is the difference between the claim of a debt holder of Ford Motor Corporation and the claim of a common stock holder of Ford Motor Corporation?

2. In September 1990 a study by the U.S. Congress, Office of Technology Assessment, entitled "Electronic Bulls & Bears: U.S. Securities Markets and Information Technology," included this statement:

   Securities markets have five basic functions in a capitalistic economy:

   1. they make it possible for corporations and governmental units to raise capital;
   2. they help to allocate capital toward productive uses;
   3. they provide an opportunity for people to increase their savings by investing in them;
   4. they reveal investors' judgments about the potential earning capacity of corporations, thus giving guidance to corporate managers; and
   5. they generate employment and income.

   For each of the functions cited above, explain how financial markets (or securities markets, in the parlance of this congressional study) perform each function.

3. In January 1992, the Korea Development Bank issued $500 million of 10-year bonds in the United States.
   a. From the perspective of the U.S. financial market, indicate whether this issue is classified as being issued in the domestic market, the foreign market, or the offshore market.

   b. From the perspective of the Korean financial market, indicate whether this issue is classified as being issued in the domestic market, the foreign market, or the offshore market.

4. In January 1992, Atlantic Richfield Corporation, a U.S.-based corporation, issued $250 million of bonds with a maturity of 30 years. From the perspective of the U.S. financial market, indicate whether this issue is classified as being issued in the domestic market, the foreign market, or the offshore market.

5. a. What is meant by the "institutionalization" of capital markets?
   b. What are the implications of the institutionalization of capital markets?

6. a. What is a Eurobond?
   b. What do you think a Eurodeutschemark bond is?

7. Indicate whether each of the following instruments trades in the money market or the capital market:
   a. General Motors Acceptance Corporation issues commercial paper.
   b. The U.S. Treasury issues a 30-year security.
   c. IBM issues common stock.
   d. Citicorp issues a 90-day certificate of deposit.

8. a. What is an International Depositary Receipt?
   b. What is the U.S. version of the International Depositary Receipt?

9. What is a Euroequity issue?

10. a. What is meant by an emerging market?
    b. What has limited the participation of institutional investors in emerging markets?

11. What is meant by the spot or cash market?

12. a. What are the two basic types of derivative instruments?
    b. "Derivative markets are nothing more than legalized gambling casinos and serve no economic function." Comment on this statement.

13. "I don't know why any rational investor would ever invest in debt instruments, particularly Treasury bills. The evidence is clear that the average return on stocks is considerably higher than that on bonds." Do you agree with this statement?

14. Consider the performance of the following portfolio:
    January 1, 19X1: $100 million December 31, 19X1: $115 million
    January 1, 19X2: $115 million December 31, 19X2: $125 million

    Assume that over this period of time, there were no cash withdrawals from the portfolio.
    a. What is the annual return for 19X1?
    b. What is the annual return for 19X2?
    c. What is the arithmetic mean return for the two years?
    d. What is the geometric mean return for the two years?
    e. Show that if $100 million is invested at the geometric mean return for two years (compounded annually), the portfolio will grow to $125 million.

15. Consider the performance of the following portfolio:
    January 1, 19X1: $100 million December 31, 19X1: $50 million
    January 1, 19X2: $ 50 million December 31, 19X2: $100 million

    Assume that over this period of time, there were no cash withdrawals from the portfolio.
    a. Without doing any calculations, what is the return on this portfolio over the two-year period?
    b. What is the annual return for 19X1?
    c. What is the annual return for 19X2?
    d. What is the arithmetic mean return for the two years?
    e. Does your answer to d make sense given your answer to a?
    f. What is the geometric mean return for the two years?
    g. Does the answer to f make sense given your answer to a?
    h. Given your answers to e and g, explain why you would prefer to use the geometric mean return rather than the arithmetic mean return.

16. A study by Daniel Wydler, "Swiss Stocks, Bonds, and Inflation, 1926–1987," published in the Winter 1989 issue of the *Journal of Portfolio Management*, found the following for Swiss stocks and bonds:

Asset	Geometric Mean	Arithmetic Mean	Standard Deviation	Highest 1-Year Return	Lowest 1-Year Return
Stocks	7.1%	8.9%	20.3%	61.4% (1985)	−33.1% (1974)
Bonds	4.4%	4.5%	3.3%	16.6% (1975)	−2.1% (1979)

Comment on the historical return and risk pattern.

CHAPTER 3
SECONDARY MARKETS AND TRADING MECHANICS

LEARNING OBJECTIVES

After reading this chapter you will be able to:

- describe the various market trading systems or locations for stocks.

- explain the trading mechanisms such as the types of orders, short selling, and margin transactions.

- differentiate between brokers and dealers, and describe the role of a dealer as a market maker and the costs associated with market making.

- explain the key structural difference between a stock exchange and an over-the-counter market.

- describe trading arrangements such as block trades and program trades, which accommodate institutional traders.

- define what the upstairs market is and its role in institutional trading.

- explain the role played by stock market indexes and how those indexes are constructed.

- identify the various indexes of U.S. and non-U.S. stock markets.

- describe the correlation of world equity markets.

Now that we have an overview of the financial markets and instruments, we will focus on the mechanisms for trading stocks and bonds and the structure of markets where they trade. It is in the secondary market for common stock that investors' opinions about the economic prospects of a company are expressed through the trades they execute. These trades result in a market price for the common stock. This market price can be viewed as the market's consensus of the value of a company's common stock. In addition, we will describe the various indexes used to gauge the performance of the stock market and take a look at stock markets outside the United States.

The secondary market for common stock has undergone significant changes since the 1960s, primarily reflecting three interacting factors: (1) the institutionalization of the stock market as a result of a shift away from traditional small investors to large institutional investors, (2) changes in government regulation of the market, and (3) innovation, largely because of advances in computer technology. The institutionalization of the market for common stock has had important implications for the design of trading systems because the demands made by institutional investors are different from those made by traditional small investors. In this chapter we will also describe special trading arrangements for institutional investors.

MARKET TRADING SYSTEMS, OR LOCATIONS

In the United States, secondary trading of common stock and bonds occurs in a number of market trading systems called *locations*: major national stock exchanges, regional stock exchanges, and the over-the-counter (OTC) market. In addition to these trading locations, independently operated electronic trading systems are available for trading common stock. While some trading of bonds takes place on exchanges, the activity of bond trading is minor compared with trading in the over-the-counter market.

Market trading systems rely on brokers and dealers. A **broker** is an entity that acts as the agent of an investor who wishes to execute orders; no position is taken by the broker in the security that is the subject of the trade. In contrast, a **dealer** is an entity that stands ready and willing to buy a security for its own account (i.e., add to its inventory of the security) or sell from its own account (i.e., reduce its inventory of the security). At a given time, dealers advertise their willingness to buy a security at a price (its **bid price**) that is less than what they are willing to sell the same security for (its **ask price** or **offer price**).

Stock Exchanges

Stock exchanges are formal organizations, approved and regulated by the Securities and Exchange Commission (SEC), that are made up of members that use the facilities to exchange certain common stocks. Stocks that are traded on an exchange are said to be **listed stocks**. The *first market* refers to the trading of listed stocks executed on the floor of the exchange. To be listed, a company must apply and satisfy requirements established by the exchange where listing is sought. Since August 1976, the listing of a common stock on more than one exchange has been permitted.

To have the right to trade securities on the floor of the exchange, firms or individuals must buy a "seat" on the exchange; that is, they must become a member of the exchange. (The cost of a seat is market-determined.) A member firm may trade for its own account or on behalf of a customer. In the latter case it is acting as a broker.

Each stock is traded at a specific location on the trading floor called a *post*. On an exchange, the market-maker role for a listed stock is performed by a **specialist**. A member firm may be designated as a specialist for the common stock of more than one company, but only one specialist can be designated for the common stock of each given company. In contrast, there can be multiple market makers in the OTC market, as we will discuss.

The two major national stock exchanges are the New York Stock Exchange (NYSE), popularly referred to as the "Big Board," and the American Stock Exchange (ASE or AMEX). The NYSE is the largest exchange in the United States. As of June 1991 about 2,300 companies were listed, with a total common stock market value of approximately $3.2 trillion. The AMEX is the second largest exchange, with 1,063 issues as of the end of 1990 and a total market value of $102 billion.

There are five regional stock exchanges: Midwest, Pacific, Philadelphia, Boston, and Cincinnati. On these exchanges two kinds of stocks are listed: (1) stocks of companies that could not qualify for listing (or do not wish to list) on one of the major national exchanges and (2) stocks that are also listed on one of the major national exchanges. The latter are called *dually listed stocks*. The benefit of dual listing for a local brokerage firm that purchases a membership on a regional exchange is that the firm can trade these stocks without having to purchase a considerably more expensive membership on the major national stock exchange. A local brokerage firm, of course, could use the services of a member of a major national stock exchange to execute an order if it were willing to give up part of its commission.

There is also the Arizona Stock Exchange in Phoenix, Arizona, which commenced trading in March 1992 and is the only after-hours electronic marketplace where anonymous participants trade stocks via personal computers.

The regional stock exchanges themselves compete with the NYSE and the AMEX for the execution of smaller trades such as those for 5,000 shares or less. Major national brokerage firms have in recent years routed such orders to regional exchanges because of the lower cost they charge for executing orders.

At one time, stock exchanges fixed minimum commissions on transactions, according to the value and volume of shares involved. The fixed-commission structure did not allow the commission rate to decline as the number of shares in the order increased, thereby ignoring the economies of scale in executing transactions. For example, brokers incurred lower total costs in executing an order of 10,000 shares of one stock for one investor than in executing 100 orders for the same stock from 100 investors. The institutional investors who had come to dominate trading activity offered larger order size, yet did not reap the benefits of the economies of scale in order execution that brokers did. Pressure from institutional investors led the SEC in April 1971 to permit negotiated commissions for that portion of trades with a market value in excess of $500,000. By May 1975, fixed minimum commissions on stocks traded on an exchange were eliminated. Commissions are now fully negotiable between investors and their brokers.

Over-the-Counter Market

The over-the-counter market is a market where listed stocks, unlisted stocks, and bonds are traded by multiple market makers. As noted earlier, bonds are traded primarily in the OTC market. Market makers in the OTC market are linked together by means of electronic display systems and telephones.

The *second market* refers to the execution of unlisted stock trades in the over-the-counter market. The *third market* refers to the trading of listed stocks in the OTC market. The third market grew as institutional investors used it in the early 1960s to avoid fixed minimum commissions, then required by the NYSE and AMEX. Dealers in this market are not members of an exchange, and therefore were not required to charge those fixed minimum commissions.

TABLE 3-1	
TRADING LOCATIONS	
A Trade Is Said To Take Place in This Location . . .	**When . . .**
First market	Listed stocks are traded on their listing exchange
Second market	Unlisted stocks are traded OTC
Third market	Stocks that are listed on an exchange are traded OTC
Fourth market	Stocks are traded directly between principals

The National Association of Securities Dealers (NASD), a private organization, represents and regulates the dealers in the OTC market under the supervision of the SEC. The National Association of Securities Dealers Automatic Quotation (NASDAQ) system is an electronic quotation system that provides price quotations to market participants for the more actively traded common stock issues in the OTC market. About 4,000 common stock issues are included in the NASDAQ system.

Independent Electronic Trading Systems

It is not always necessary for two transactors to use the services of a broker or a dealer to execute a transaction. The direct trading of stocks between two transactors without the use of a broker is called the *fourth market*. This market grew for the same reasons as the third market: the excessively high minimum commissions established by the exchanges.

The growth of the fourth market was initially limited by the availability of information on other institutions that wanted to trade. Today, computerized systems have been developed that allow institutional investors to cross trades (i.e., match buyers and sellers). The two major systems that handle large institution-to-institution trades are INSTINET and POSIT. The latter started in late 1980 and currently has 80 institutional money managers. POSIT, which stands for Portfolio System for Institutional Investors, is a trading system developed by BARRA and Jefferies & Co. POSIT is more than a simple order-matching system; it matches the purchase and sale of portfolios in such a way so as to optimize the liquidity of the system.[1] (See Table 3-1 for a brief review of the four markets.)

TYPES OF ORDERS

An investor must provide certain information to the broker about the transaction. The parameters that the investor must provide are the specific security, the number of shares in the case of common stock and the quantity in

---

[1] A description of the algorithm used to maximize the liquidity of POSIT is described in "An Inside Look at the POSIT Matching Algorithm," *POSITNEWS* (Summer/Fall 1990), p. 2.

the case of bonds, and the type of order. Below we describe the various types of orders that an investor can place.

Market Orders

When an investor wants to buy or sell a share of common stock, the price and conditions under which the order is to be executed must be communicated to a broker. The simplest type of order is the **market order**, an order executed at the best price available in the market. The best price is assured by requiring that when more than one buy order or sell order reaches the market at the same time, the order with the best price is given priority. Thus, buyers offering a higher price are given priority over those offering a lower price; sellers asking a lower price are given priority over those asking a higher price.

In the case of common stock traded on an exchange, another priority rule is needed to handle the receipt of more than one order at the same price. Most often, the priority in executing such orders is based on the time of arrival of the order—the first orders in are the first orders executed—although there may be a rule that gives higher priority to certain types of market participants over others who are seeking to transact at the same price. For example, an exchange may classify orders as either "public orders" or orders of those member firms dealing for their own account (both nonspecialists and specialists). Exchange rules require that public orders be given priority over orders of member firms dealing for their own account.

Limit Orders

The danger of a market order is that an adverse move may take place between the time the investor places the order and the time the order is executed. For example, suppose Mr. Ciola wants to buy the stock of Walt Disney Corporation at $42, but not at $44. If he places a market order when the stock is trading at $42, Mr. Ciola faces the risk that the price will rise before his order is carried out, and he will have to pay an unacceptable price. Similarly, suppose Ms. Davis owns Ford Motors and wants to sell the stock at its current price of $65, but not at $63. If Ms. Davis places a market order to sell Ford at the same time Ford announces a major recall of one of its cars, the stock would be sold at the best available price, but the price might be unacceptable.

To avoid the danger of adverse unexpected price changes, an investor can place a **limit order** that designates a price threshold for the execution of the trade. The limit order is a conditional order: It is executed only if the limit price or a better price can be obtained. A **buy limit order** indicates that the security may be purchased only at the designated price or lower. A **sell limit order** indicates that the security may be sold at the designated price or higher. For example, Mr. Ciola, who wants to purchase Disney but will not want to pay more than $42, can place a buy limit order at $42. Ms. Davis, who wants to sell Ford Motor but does not want to sell it at a price less than $65, will place a sell limit order for $65.

The danger of a limit order is that there is no guarantee that it will be executed at all. The designated price may simply not be obtainable. A limit order that is not executable at the time it reaches the market is recorded in a **limit order book** that is maintained by the specialist. The orders recorded in this book are treated equally with other orders in terms of the priority described earlier.

Stop Orders

Another type of conditional order is the **stop order**, which specifies that the order is not to be executed until the market moves to a designated price, at which time it becomes a market order. A **stop order to buy** specifies that the order is not to be executed until the market rises to a designated price (i.e., trades at or above, or is bid at or above, the designated price). A **stop order to sell** specifies that the order is not to be executed until the market price falls below a designated price (i.e., trades at or below, or is offered at or below, the designated price). Once the designated price in the stop order is reached, the order becomes a market order.

A stop order is useful when an investor cannot watch the market constantly. Profits can be preserved or losses minimized on a security position by allowing market movements to trigger a trade. In a sell stop order the designated price is less than the current market price of the security. In contrast, in a sell limit order, the designated price is greater than the current market price of the security. In a buy stop order the designated price is greater than the current market price of the security. However, in a buy limit order the designated price is less than the current market price of the security. This is depicted in Figure 3-1.

For example, suppose Mr. Ciola is uncertain about buying the Disney stock at its current price of $42 but wants to be sure that if the price moves up he does not pay more than $45. If he places a stop order to buy at $45, the order becomes a market order when the price reaches $45. In the case of the sale of Ford by Ms. Davis, suppose she wants to assure that she will not sell at less than $60 a share. She can place a stop order to sell at $60.

Two dangers are associated with stop orders. Security prices sometimes exhibit abrupt price changes, so the direction of a change in a security's price may be quite temporary, resulting in the premature trading of a security. Also, once the designated price is reached, the stop order becomes a market order and is subject to the uncertainty of the execution price noted earlier for market orders.

Stop-Limit Orders

A **stop-limit order**, a hybrid of a stop order and a limit order, is a stop order that designates a price limit. In contrast to the stop order, which becomes a market order if the stop is reached, the stop-limit order becomes a

FIGURE 3-1

Comparison of limit orders and stop orders.

limit order if the stop is reached. The order can be used to cushion the market impact of a stop order. The investor may limit the possible execution price after the activation of the stop. As with a limit order, the limit price may never be reached after the order is activated, which therefore defeats one purpose of the stop order—to protect a profit or limit a loss.

Market-If-Touched Orders

An investor may also enter a **market-if-touched order**. This order becomes a market order if a designated price is reached. However, a market-if-touched order to buy becomes a market order if the market *falls* to a given price, while a stop order to buy becomes a market order if the market rises to a given price. Similarly, a market-if-touched order to sell becomes a market order if the market rises to a specified price, while the stop order to sell becomes a market order if the market falls to a given price. We can think of the stop order as an order designed to get out of an existing position at an acceptable price (without specifying the exact price), and the market-if-touched order as an order designed to get into a position at an acceptable price (also without specifying the exact price).

Time-Specific Orders

Orders may be placed to buy or sell at the open or close of trading for the day. An opening order indicates a trade to be executed only in the opening range for the day, and a closing order indicates a trade is to be executed only within the closing range for the day.

An investor may enter orders that contain order cancellation provisions. A **fill-or-kill order** must be executed as soon as it reaches the trading floor, or it is immediately canceled. Orders may designate the time period for which the order is effective—a day, week, or month, or perhaps by a given time within the day. An **open order**, or **good-till-canceled order**, is good until the order is specifically canceled.

Size-Related Orders

For common stock, orders are also classified by their size. A **round lot** is typically 100 shares of a stock. An **odd lot** is defined as less than a round lot. For example, an order of 75 shares of Digital Equipment Corporation (DEC) is an odd-lot order. An order of 350 shares of DEC includes an odd-lot portion of 50 shares. A **block trade** is defined on the NYSE as an order of 10,000 shares of a given stock or a total market value of $200,000 or more.

Both the major national stock exchanges and the regional stock exchanges have systems for routing orders of a specified size that are submitted by brokers via computer directly to the specialists' posts where the order can be executed. On the NYSE, this system is called the *SuperDOT* (Super Designated Order Turnaround) system. The AMEX's Post Execution Reporting system allows orders of up to 2,000 shares to be routed directly to specialists. The regional stock exchanges also have computerized systems for routing small orders to specialists. The Small Order Execution system of the NASDAQ routes and executes orders of up to 1,000 shares of a given stock.

SHORT SELLING

An investor who expects that the price of a security will increase can benefit from buying the security. However, suppose that an investor expects that the price of a security will decline. How can the investor benefit from that event? By **selling short** the investor (working through a broker) borrows the security, sells it, repurchases it at a later time, and then returns it to the party who initially loaned the security. If the price has fallen, the short seller profits. When the security is returned, the investor is said to have "covered the short position."

Profiting and Losing from a Short Sale

Let's make this more concrete with an illustration. Suppose Ms. Stokes believes that Wilson Pharmaceuticals common stock is overpriced at $20 per share and wants to be in a position to benefit if her assessment is correct. Ms. Stokes calls her broker, Mr. Yats, indicating that she wants to sell 100 shares of Wilson Pharmaceuticals. Mr. Yats will do two things: (1) sell 100 shares of Wilson Pharmaceuticals on behalf of Ms. Stokes and (2) arrange to borrow 100 shares of that stock. Suppose that Mr. Yats is able to sell the stock for $20 per share and arrange to borrow the stock from Mr. Jordan. The shares borrowed from Mr. Jordan will be delivered to the buyer of the 100 shares. The proceeds from the sale (ignoring commissions) will be $2,000. However, the proceeds will not be given to Ms. Stokes because she has not given her broker the 100 shares.

Now, let's suppose one week later the price of Wilson Pharmaceuticals stock declines to $15 per share. Ms. Stokes may instruct her broker to *buy* 100 shares of Wilson Pharmaceuticals. The cost of buying the shares (once again ignoring commissions) is $1,500. The shares purchased are then delivered to Mr. Jordan, who loaned the original 100 shares to Ms. Stokes. At this point, Ms. Stokes has sold 100 shares and bought 100 shares. So she no longer has any obligation to her broker or Mr. Jordan—she has covered her short position. She is entitled to the funds in her account that were generated by the selling and buying activity. She sold the stock for $2,000 and bought it for $1,500. Thus, she realizes a profit of $500 before commissions and fees. The broker's commission and a fee charged by the lender of the stock are then subtracted from the $500. Furthermore, if any dividends were paid by Wilson Pharmaceuticals while the stock was borrowed, Ms. Stokes must return them to Mr. Jordan who still owned the stock at the time.

If instead of falling, suppose the price of Wilson Pharmaceuticals stock rises. Ms. Stokes will realize a loss when she is forced to cover her short position. For example, if the price rises to $27, Ms. Stokes will lose $700, to which must be added commissions and the cost of borrowing the stock.

Restrictions on Short Sales

Exchange-imposed restrictions specify when a short sale may be executed; they are intended to prevent investors from destabilizing the price of a stock when the market price is falling. These restrictions are the so-called **tick-test rules**. A short sale can be made only when either (1) the sale price of the particular stock is higher than the last trade price (referred to as an

up-tick trade) or (2) in cases where there is no change in the last trade price of the particular stock, the previous trade price is higher than the trade price that preceded it (referred to as a **zero up-tick**). For example, if Ms. Stokes wanted to "short" Wilson Pharmaceuticals at a price of $20 and if the two previous trade prices were $20 1/8 and then $20, she could not do so at that time because of the up-tick trade rule. If, however, the previous trade prices were $19 7/8, $19 7/8, and then $20, she could short the stock at $20 because of the up-tick trade rule. Suppose that the sequence of the last three trades is $19 7/8, $20, and $20. Ms. Stokes could short the stock at $20 because of the zero up-tick rule.

The ability of investors to sell short is an important mechanism in financial markets. In the absence of an effective short-selling mechanism, stock prices will tend to be biased toward the view of more optimistic investors.

MARGIN TRANSACTIONS

Investors can borrow cash to buy securities and use the securities themselves as collateral. For example, suppose Mr. Boxer has $10,000 to invest and is considering buying Wilson Pharmaceuticals, which is currently selling for $20 per share. With his $10,000, Mr. Boxer can buy 500 shares. Suppose his broker can arrange for him to borrow an additional $10,000 so that Mr. Boxer can buy an additional 500 shares. Thus, with a $10,000 investment, he can purchase a total of 1,000 shares. The 1,000 shares will be used as collateral for the $10,000 borrowed, and Mr. Boxer will have to pay interest on the amount borrowed.

A transaction in which an investor borrows to buy additional shares using the shares themselves as collateral is called **buying on margin**. By borrowing funds, an investor creates financial leverage. Note that Mr. Boxer, for a $10,000 investment, realizes the consequences associated with a price change of 1,000 shares rather than 500 shares. He will benefit if the price rises but be worse off if the price falls (compared with not borrowing funds).

To illustrate, let's look at what happens if the price subsequently changes. If the price of Wilson Pharmaceuticals rises to $29 per share, ignoring commissions and the cost of borrowing, Mr. Boxer will realize a profit of $9 per share on 1,000 shares, or $9,000. Had Mr. Boxer not borrowed $10,000 to buy the additional 500 shares, his profit would have been only $4,500. Now, suppose instead that the price of Wilson Pharmaceuticals stock declines to $13 per share. Then by borrowing so that he could buy 500 additional shares, he lost $7,000 ($7 per share on 1,000 shares) instead of just $3,500 ($7 on 500 shares). Table 3-2 summarizes the effect of buying on margin.

Call Money Rate
The funds borrowed to buy the additional stock are provided by the broker, and the broker gets the money from a bank. The interest rate that banks charge brokers for these transactions is known as the **call money rate** (also called the **broker loan rate**). The broker charges the investor the call money rate plus a service charge.

			Change in Position	
	Initial Investment	Shares Owned at $20/Share	At $29/Share (Gain $9/Share)	At $13/Share (Lose $7/Share)
Cash purchase	$10,000	500	+$4,500	−$3,500
Buying on 50% margin	$10,000	1000	+$9,000	−$7,000

TABLE 3-2

BUYING ON MARGIN

Margin Requirements

The broker is not free to lend as much as it wishes to the investor to buy securities. The Securities and Exchange Act of 1934 prohibits brokers from lending more than a specified percentage of the market value of the securities. The **initial margin requirement** is the proportion of the total market value of the securities that the investor must pay for in cash. The 1934 act gives the Board of Governors of the Federal Reserve the responsibility to set initial margin requirements, which it does under Regulations T and U. The initial margin requirement varies for stocks and bonds and is currently 50%, though it has been below 40%. The Fed also establishes a **maintenance margin requirement**. This is the minimum amount of equity needed in the investor's margin account as compared with the total market value. If the investor's margin account falls below the minimum maintenance margin, the investor is required to put up additional cash. The investor receives a **margin call** from the broker specifying the additional cash to be put into the investor's margin account. If the investor fails to put up the additional cash, the securities are sold.

As we will explain in Chapter 15, investors who take positions in the futures market are also required to satisfy initial and maintenance margin requirements. Margin requirements for the purchase of securities are different in concept from those in futures markets. In a margin transaction involving securities, the initial margin requirement is equivalent to a down payment; the balance is borrowed funds for which interest is paid (the call rate plus a service charge). In the futures market, the initial margin requirement is effectively "good-faith" money, indicating that the investor will satisfy the obligation of the futures contract. No money is borrowed by the investor.

THE ROLE OF DEALERS AS MARKET MAKERS IN SECONDARY MARKETS

Because of the imbalance of buy and sell orders that may reach the market at a given time, the price of a security may change abruptly from one transaction to the next, in the absence of any intervention. For example, suppose that the market price for ABC stock is $50 as determined by several recent trades, but a flow of buy orders without an accompanying supply of sell orders arrives in the market. This temporary imbalance could be sufficient to push the price of ABC stock to, say, $55. The cost of having to pay a price higher than $50 can be viewed as the price of "immediacy." By immediacy it is meant that buyers and sellers want to trade immediately rather than waiting for the arrival of sufficient orders on the other side of the trade so that the price is closer to the price of the last known transaction.

In the absence of any intervention, this temporary imbalance would have a destabilizing effect on a security's price. A flurry of unbalanced buy orders, for instance, could drive a security's price up. Rising prices could then trigger an avalanche of subsequent buying, based on the perception of rising value in the security. Of course, the market would soon correct unsubstantiated prices, resulting in a steep decline.

Dealers help stabilize the market by acting as a buffer between the buy and sell sides of the market. Dealers can be properly viewed as the suppliers of immediacy (i.e., the ability to trade promptly) to the market.[2] The bid-ask spread can, in turn, be viewed as the price charged by dealers for supplying immediacy together with short-run price stability (i.e., continuity or smoothness) in the presence of short-term order imbalances. There are two other roles that dealers play: providing better price information to market participants and, in certain market structures, providing the services of an auctioneer in bringing order and fairness to a market.[3]

The price stabilization role follows from what may happen to the price of a particular transaction in the absence of any intervention during a temporary imbalance of orders. By taking the opposite side of a trade when there are no other orders, the dealer prevents the price from materially diverging from the price at which a recent trade was consummated.

Not only are investors concerned with immediacy, but they also want to trade at prices that are reasonable, given prevailing conditions in the market. While dealers do not know with certainty the true price of a stock, they do have a privileged position in some market structures, with respect not just to market orders but also to limit orders. The latter is particularly true in market structures where one or more dealers are entitled to keep the book of limit orders. Their privileged position allows them to be in a better position to affect the quality of price information that they signal to market participants through their bids and offers.

Finally, the dealer acts as an auctioneer in some market structures, thereby providing order and fairness in the operations of the market. For example, the dealer-specialist performs this function both by organizing trading to make sure that the exchange rules for the priority of trading are followed and by keeping a limit book. The role of the dealer as market maker is summarized in Table 3-3.

Dealer Costs

A dealer's bid-ask spread is affected by its cost of doing business and by the risks it bears. One of the most important costs involves order processing costs. The costs of equipment necessary to do business and the administrative and operations staff are examples. The lower these costs, the narrower

---

[2]See George Stigler, "Public Regulation of Securities Markets," *Journal of Business* (April 1964), pp. 117–134; and Harold Demsetz, "The Cost of Transacting," *Quarterly Journal of Economics* (October 1968), pp. 35–36.

[3]For a more detailed discussion of these roles, see Robert A. Schwartz, *Equity Markets: Structure, Trading and Performance* (New York: Harper & Row, 1988), pp. 389–397.

TABLE 3-3	
THE MARKET MAKER'S ROLE	
Role	**Benefit to Market**
Sell from an inventory of securities	Immediacy, continuity, and smoothness of trading
Keep limit order book	
Process many orders	Fairness (maintain priority rules), order, better price information
Auction	

the bid-ask spread. With the reduced cost of computing and with better-trained personnel, these costs have declined since the 1960s.

Dealers also have to be compensated for bearing risk. A dealer's position may involve carrying inventory of a security (a long position) or selling a security that is not in inventory (a short position). Three types of risks are associated with maintaining a long or short position in a given security. First, there is the uncertainty about the future price of the security. A dealer that has a net long position in the security is concerned that the price will decline in the future; a dealer that is in a net short position is concerned that the price will rise.

The second type of risk has to do with the expected time it will take the dealer to unwind a position and its uncertainty. And this, in turn, depends primarily on the prevailing rate at which buy and sell orders reach the dealer (i.e., the frequency of transactions).[4] The greater the frequency of transactions, the less time a dealer will expect that it has to maintain a position. For example, if a dealer has an inventory of a particular security that is infrequently traded, then the dealer expects that it will have to hold that security in inventory for a longer time period than if the stock is frequently traded. As a result, the dealer's risk that the security's price will decline when it is held in inventory is greater for a security that is infrequently traded.

Finally, while a dealer may have access to better information about order flows (that is, buy and sell orders) than the general public, there are some trades where the dealer takes the risk of trading with someone who has better information.[5] This results in the better-informed trader obtaining a better price at the expense of the dealer. Consequently, in establishing the bid-ask spread for a trade, a dealer will assess whether the trader might have better information. Some trades that we will discuss later can be viewed as "informationless trades." This means that the dealer knows or believes that a trade is being requested to accomplish an investment objective that is not motivated by the potential future price movement of the security.

Role of Dealers in Exchanges and the OTC Market

There is an important structural difference between exchanges and the OTC market. On an exchange there is only one market maker or dealer per stock, the specialist. This type of market structure is referred to as an *auction*

---

[4]This is referred to as the *thickness* of the market.

[5]Walter Bagehot, "The Only Game in Town," *Financial Analysts Journal* (March–April 1971), pp. 12–14, 22.

market. Since there is only one specialist for a given stock, there is no competition from other market makers on the exchange. Does this mean that the specialist has a monopolistic position? Not necessarily, because specialists do face competition from several sources. The existence of public limit orders affects the bid-ask spread. There are brokers in the crowd who have public orders that compete with specialists.

In the case of multiple-listed stocks there is competition from specialists on other exchanges where the stock is listed. For stocks that are exempt from Rule 390 (restricting member firms to execute trades on the exchange), there is competition from dealers in the OTC market (discussed below). Finally, as we discuss later in this chapter, when a block trade is involved, specialists compete with the "upstairs market."

In the OTC market, in contrast, there may be more than one dealer for a stock. For this reason, this market is referred to as a *dealer market*. For example, at the time of this writing, there are more than 50 dealers for MCI Corporation. The number of dealers depends on the volume of trading in a stock. If a stock is not actively traded, there may be no need for more than one or two dealers. As trading activity in a stock increases, there are no barriers preventing more entities from becoming a dealer in that stock, other than satisfaction of capital requirements. Competition from more dealers—or the threat of new dealers—forces bid-ask spreads to more competitive levels. Moreover, the capital-raising ability of more than one dealer is believed to be more beneficial to markets than that of a single specialist in performing the role of a market maker.

The greater competition and greater potential capital arguments have been put forth by those citing the advantages of the OTC market. The exchanges, however, argue that the commitment of the dealers to provide a market in the OTC market is not the same obligation as that of the specialist on the exchange. On the NYSE, for example, Rule 104 sets forth the specialist's obligation to maintain fair and orderly markets. Failure to fulfill this obligation results in a loss of specialist status.

To what extent do specialists perform the function of stabilizing markets? That is, to what extent do public orders require the specialist itself to take the other side of a deal? Information provided by the NYSE indicates that, in 1988, 77% of all shares traded were public orders meeting public orders, and therefore not requiring dealers to take direct positions. Only 9% of shares traded involved specialist activity. The balance of trading, 14%, was by nonspecialist member firms dealing for their own accounts.[6] The 9% participation by specialists, however, may understate the importance of the role played by the specialist because the activity may have occurred under difficult market conditions.

The National Market System

In the 1960s and early 1970s, U.S. secondary markets for stocks became increasingly fragmented. By a fragmented market we mean one in which some orders for a given stock are handled differently from others, for instance, a stock that can be bought on several exchanges as well as in the over-

---

[6]James E. Shapiro, "The NYSE Trading System: Background and Issues," a paper presented at the NYSE Academic Seminar on May 5, 1989.

the-counter market. An order to buy IBM stock, for example, could be executed on one of the exchanges where IBM is listed (i.e., using the specialist system) or in the third market using the multiple-dealer system. Thus, the treatment of the order differed, depending upon where it is ultimately executed.

The concern of public policy makers was that investors were not receiving the best execution. That is, transactions were not necessarily being executed by a broker on behalf of a customer at the most favorable price available. Another concern with the increased fragmentation of the secondary market for stocks was a growing number of completed transactions in listed stocks that were not reported to the public. This occurred because transactions in the third market and on the regional exchanges were not immediately disclosed on the major national exchange ticker tapes where the stock was listed.

As a result of these concerns, Congress enacted the Securities Act of 1975 which directed the SEC to "facilitate the establishment of a national market system for securities. . . ." The SEC, in its efforts to implement a national market system, targeted the following six elements:

1. a system for public reporting of completed transactions on a consolidated basis (consolidated tape),
2. a composite system for the collection and display of bid and asked quotations (composite quotation system),
3. systems for transmitting orders to buy and sell securities and reports of completed transactions from one market to another (market linkage systems),
4. elimination of restrictions on the ability of exchange members to effect over-the-counter transactions in listed securities (off-board trading rules),
5. nationwide protection of limit price orders, against inferior execution in another market, and
6. rules defining the securities that are qualified to be traded in the NMS.[7]

The general issue that the SEC faced was how to design the national market system. Should it be structured as an electronic linkage of existing exchange floors? Or should it be an electronic trading system that was not tied to any existing exchange?

Several pilot programs were created after the passage of the 1975 act. The Intermarket Trading System (ITS), whose operations began in April 1978, was implemented for listed stocks. It was developed as an electronic system that displays the quotes posted on all the exchanges where a stock is listed, as well as in the OTC market, and provides for intermarket executions. A display system on trades on listed stocks in different market centers is provided by the Consolidated Quotation System.

While there has been a movement to a national market system for stocks, no such movement has occurred in the bond market, despite the fact that trading activity is concentrated in the over-the-counter market and that daily trading volume of U.S. Treasury securities alone exceeds $100 billion. Thus, over-the-counter bond trades are not reported. Nor is there a display of bid and ask quotations for bonds that provides reliable price quotes at which the general public can transact.

---

[7]N. S. Posner, "Restructuring the Stock Markets: A Critical Look at the SEC's National Market System," *New York University Law Review* (November–December 1981), p. 916.

BOX 3

THE EXCHANGE SYSTEM AND INSTITUTIONAL TRADING SYSTEMS

On December 7, 1987, the Institute of Chartered Financial Analysts sponsored a conference entitled "Trading Strategies and Execution Costs." The following passage is from a speech by Wayne Wagner, a partner and chief investment officer of Plexus Group.

The NYSE is not the only operating market; there are ancillary markets that provide trading facilities beyond what is available on the Exchange floor. This suggests that some needs are not well served by the process as it occurs on the Exchange. Examples of how the NYSE is augmented by other trading fa-

cilities include the supporting specialists (particularly on the regional exchange); the upstairs brokers who are willing to commit their own capital to finance a trade and provide the bridge liquidity between a natural buyer and a natural seller; direct trading markets—the third market, the fourth market, and crossing networks; and the informal floor accommodations. All of these structures are intended to accommodate trading. Without these facilities, the NYSE as it exists today probably could not exist, because it would not be sufficient to perform the task that institutional investors have asked it to perform.

Source: Wayne H. Wagner, "The Taxonomy of Trading Strategies," in Katrina F. Sherrerd (ed.), *Trading Strategies and Execution Costs* (Charlottesville, VA: The Institute of Chartered Financial Analysts, 1988).

Questions for Box 3

1. What is meant by the upstairs brokers?
2. What is meant by the third market?
3. What is meant by the fourth market?
4. What is meant by crossing networks?
5. What reasons would you give in support of Mr. Wagner's statement in the last sentence of the quote?

COMMON STOCK TRADING ARRANGEMENTS FOR INSTITUTIONAL INVESTORS

As we noted earlier in this chapter, the increase in institutional trading has required the accommodation of the trading practices of institutional investors. (See Box 3.) Evidence of institutionalization of the stock market can be seen in the ownership distribution of stocks and the share of trading by individuals (referred to as *retail* trading) and institutions (pension funds, insurance companies, investment companies, bank trusts, and endowments). In 1949, institutional ownership of stocks listed on the New York Stock Exchange was 13%; in recent years, it has been almost 50%. Moreover, more than 80% of the volume of trading on the NYSE is done by institutional investors.[8] This, of course, does not mean that ownership of stocks by individuals has diminished. Instead, institutions trade on behalf of individuals, who hold stock through mutual funds, pension funds, and so forth.

The institutionalization of the stock market has resulted in the evolution of special arrangements for the execution of certain types of orders commonly sought by institutional investors: (1) **block trades**, meaning orders requiring the execution of a trade for a large number of shares of a given stock, and (2) **program trades**, meaning orders requiring the execution of trades in a large number of different stocks at as near the same time as possible. An example of a block trade would be a mutual fund that seeks to buy 15,000 shares of IBM stock. An example of a program trade is a pension fund that seeks to buy shares of 200 "names" (by names we mean companies) at the end of a trading day.

The arrangement that has evolved to accommodate these two types of institutional trades is a network of trading desks for the major brokerage firms

---

[8]Securities Industry Association, *Trends* (Mar. 16, 1989).

and institutional investors that communicate with each other by means of electronic display systems and telephones. This network is referred to as the **upstairs market**. Participants in the upstairs market play a key role, not only in providing liquidity to the market so that such institutional trades can be executed, but also through taking part in activities that help to integrate the fragmented stock market.

Block Trades

Block trades are defined as trades of 10,000 shares or more of a given stock, or trades of shares with a market value of $200,000 or more. In 1961, there were about nine block trades per day, which accounted for about 3% of trading volume; in recent years, by contrast, there have been about 3,000 block trades per day, accounting for almost half the trading volume.[9]

As executing large numbers of block orders places strains on the specialist system, procedures have been developed to handle them. An institutional customer contacts its salesperson at a brokerage firm, indicating that it wishes to place a block order. The salesperson then gives the order to the brokerage firm's block execution department. (Notice that the salesperson does not submit the order to be executed to the exchange where the stock might be traded or, in the case of an unlisted stock, try to execute the order on the NASDAQ system.) The sales traders in the block execution department then contact other institutions in the hope of finding one or more institutions that would be willing to take the other side of the order. That is, they use the upstairs market in their search to fill the block trade order. If this can be accomplished, the execution of the order is complete.

If, on the other hand, the sales traders cannot find enough institutions to take the entire block (e.g., if the block trade order is for 40,000 shares of IBM, but only 25,000 can be exchanged, or "crossed," with other institutions), then the balance of the block trade order is given to the firm's market maker. The market maker must then make a decision about how to handle the balance of the block trade order. There are two choices: (1) The brokerage firm can take a position in the stock, in which case it is committing its own capital, or (2) the unfilled order can be executed by using the services of competing market makers.

Program Trades

Program trades involve the buying and/or selling of a large number of names *simultaneously*. Such trades are also called **basket trades**, because effectively a "basket" of stocks is being traded. An institutional investor may want to use a program trade for a variety of reasons, for example, deploying new cash into the stock market, implementing a decision to move funds between the bond market and the stock market, rebalancing the composition of a stock portfolio because of a change in investment strategy, or liquidating a stock portfolio built by a money manager whose services a plan sponsor has terminated. There are other reasons that an institutional investor may need to execute a program trade that will become apparent when we discuss certain investment strategies in Chapters 13 and 15.

---

[9]U.S. Congress, Office of Technology Assessment, *Electronic Bulls & Bears: U.S. Securities Markets & Information Technology*, OTA-CIT-469 (Washington, DC: U.S. Government Printing Office, September 1990), p. 8.

There are several commission arrangements available to an institution for a program trade. Each has numerous variants. One consideration in selecting an arrangement (besides commission costs) is the risk of failing to realize the best execution price. Another is the risk that the brokerage firms to be solicited about executing the trade will use their knowledge of the trade to benefit from the anticipated price movement that might result (i.e., they will "frontrun" the transaction).

Agency Basis   A program trade accomplished on an **agency basis** involves the selection of a brokerage firm solely on the basis of commission bids (cents per share) submitted by various brokerage firms. The brokerage firm selected uses its best efforts as an agent of the institution to obtain the best price. The disadvantage of an agency basis arrangement for a program trade is that, while commissions may be the lowest, the execution price may not be the best because of market impact costs (discussed in Chapter 13) and the potential frontrunning by the brokerage firms that were solicited to submit a commission bid.

Agency Incentive Arrangements   In an **agency incentive arrangement**, a benchmark portfolio value is established for the portfolio that is the subject of the program trade. The price for each name in the program trade is determined as either the price at the end of the previous day or the average price of the previous day. If the brokerage firm can execute the trade on the next trading day such that a better-than-benchmark portfolio value results (i.e., a higher value in the case of a program trade involving selling, or a lower value in the case of a program trade involving buying), then the brokerage firm receives a specified commission plus some predetermined additional compensation.

What if the brokerage firm does not achieve the benchmark portfolio value? Here is where the variants come into play. One arrangement may call for the brokerage firm to receive only an agreed-upon commission. Other arrangements may involve sharing the risk of not realizing the benchmark portfolio value with the brokerage firm. That is, if the brokerage firm falls short of the benchmark portfolio value, it must absorb a portion of the shortfall. In these risk-sharing arrangements, the brokerage firm is risking its own capital. The greater the risk-sharing the brokerage firm must accept, the higher the commission it will charge.

One problem that remains is the possibility of frontrunning. If brokerage firms know that an institution will execute a program trade with the prices that were determined the previous day, they may take advantage of this knowledge. To minimize the possibility of frontrunning, other types of program trade arrangements have been used. They call for a brokerage firm to receive only enough information about key portfolio parameters to allow several brokerage firms to bid on the entire portfolio, without knowing specific names or quantities. The winning bidder is then selected and given the details of the portfolio. This increases the risk to the brokerage firm of successfully executing the program trade, but the brokerage firm can use the derivative products in Chapter 15 to protect itself if the characteristics of the portfolio in the program trade are similar to those of the general market.

Brokerage firms can execute the trade in the upstairs market or send orders electronically to exchange floors or the NASDAQ system through automated order routing systems such as the NYSE SuperDOT System.

STOCK MARKET INDEXES

Market indexes have come to perform a variety of functions, from serving as benchmarks for evaluating the performance of professional money managers to answering the question "How did the market do today?" Thus, market indexes (or averages) have become a part of everyday life. Here we will discuss the various stock market indexes. We will postpone our discussion of bond indexes until Chapter 22.

The most commonly quoted stock market indicator is the Dow Jones Industrial Average. Other stock market indexes cited in the financial press are the Standard & Poor's 500 Composite, the New York Stock Exchange Composite Index, the American Stock Exchange Market Value Index, the NASDAQ Composite Index, and the Value Line Composite Index. However, there are a myriad of other stock market indexes such as the Wilshire stock indexes and the Russell stock indexes, which are followed primarily by institutional money managers.

In general, market indexes rise and fall in unison. Table 3-4 shows the correlation between the commonly cited market indexes. There are, however, important differences in the magnitude of these moves. To understand the reasons for these differences, it is necessary to understand how indexes are constructed. Three factors differentiate stock market indexes: the universe of stocks represented by the indicator, the relative weights assigned to the stocks, and the method of averaging used.

A stock market indicator can include all publicly traded stocks or a sample of publicly traded stocks. However, no stock market indicator currently available is based on all publicly traded stocks. Breadth of coverage is different for each market indicator.

The stocks included in a stock market indicator must be combined in certain proportions to construct the index or average. Each stock, therefore,

TABLE 3-4							
U.S. STOCK INDEX CORRELATIONS BASED ON MONTHLY PRICE CHANGES: JUNE 1988 TO APRIL 1993							
	S&P 500	**Dow**	**NASDAQ**	**AMEX**	**Wilshire 5000**	**Value Line**	**Russell 2000**	**NYSE**
S&P 500	1.00							
Dow	0.96	1.00						
NASDAQ	0.84	0.80	1.00					
AMEX	0.85	0.83	0.90	1.00				
Wilshire 5000	0.99	0.95	0.91	0.90	1.00			
Value Line	0.89	0.87	0.96	0.95	0.94	1.00		
Russell 2000	0.80	0.79	0.97	0.93	0.88	0.97	1.00	
NYSE	1.00	0.96	0.86	0.87	0.99	0.91	0.83	1.00

Source: Merrill Lynch Quantitative Analysis Group.

must be assigned some relative weight. One of three approaches is used to assign relative weights to the stock market indexes: (1) weighting by the market value of the company (i.e., market capitalization, which is the price of the stock times the number of shares outstanding), (2) weighting by the price of one unit of the company's stock, and (3) weighting each company equally regardless of its market value or price.

Given the stocks that will be used to create the sample and the relative weighting to be assigned to each stock, it is then necessary to average the individual components. Two methods of averaging are possible: arithmetic and geometric. All properly constructed stock market indexes are constructed using arithmetic averaging.[10]

Stock market indexes can be classified into three groups: (1) those produced by trading systems based on all stocks traded in that system, (2) those produced by organizations that subjectively select the stocks to be included in the index, and (3) those for which stock selection is based on an objective measure, such as the market capitalization of the company. In the first group we have the New York Stock Exchange Composite Index and the American Stock Exchange Market Value Index, which reflect the market value of all stocks traded on the respective stock exchange. The NASDAQ Composite Index also falls into this category.

The three most popular stock market indexes that fall into the second group are the Dow Jones Industrial Average (DJIA), the Standard & Poor's (S&P) 500, and the Value Line Composite Average (VLCA). The DJIA is constructed from 30 of the largest blue-chip industrial companies traded on the NYSE. The companies included in the average are those selected by Dow Jones & Company, publisher of the *Wall Street Journal*. The composition of the average changes over time as companies are dropped because a merger or bankruptcy has occurred, because a company's trading activity is low, or because a company not in the average becomes very prominent. When a company is replaced by another company, the average is readjusted in such a way as to provide comparability with earlier values.

The S&P 500 represents selected samples of stocks chosen from the two major national stock exchanges and the over-the-counter market. The stocks in the index at any given time are determined by a committee of Standard & Poor's Corporation, which may occasionally add or delete individual or entire industry groups. The aim of the committee is to capture overall stock market conditions representing a very broad range of economic indicators. The VLCA, produced by Arnold Bernhard & Co., covers a broad range of widely held and actively traded NYSE, AMEX, and OTC issues selected by Value Line.

In the third group we have the Wilshire Indexes produced by Wilshire Associates (Santa Monica, California) and Russell Indexes produced by the Frank Russell Company (Tacoma, Washington), a consultant to pension funds and other institutional investors. The criterion for inclusion in each of these indexes is solely market capitalization. The most comprehensive is the Wilshire 5000, which actually includes almost 6,000 companies. (At the out-

---

[10]Prior to 1988, the Value Line Composite Index was constructed using geometric averaging. Value Line still gives the geometric average for this index in its reports.

set it included 5,000 stocks.) The Wilshire 4500 includes all the stocks in the Wilshire 5000 except for those in the S&P 500. Thus, the Wilshire 4500 includes companies with smaller market capitalizations than the Wilshire 5000. The motivation for creating a stock market indicator that reflects a sector of the stock market with smaller market capitalization will be evident when we discuss market anomalies in Chapter 15.[11] The Russell 3000 encompasses the 3,000 largest companies ranked by market capitalization, while the Russell 1000 includes the largest 1,000 market capitalization companies. The Russell 2000 includes the bottom two-thirds of the companies in the Russell 3000, so it too represents a small capitalization market index.

With the exception of the DJIA and VLCA, the preeminent stock market indexes are market-value-weighted. The DJIA is a price-weighted index, with the index adjusted for stock splits and stock dividends. The VLCA is an equally weighted index.

NON-U.S. COMMON STOCK MARKETS

In this section, we will look at the non-U.S. national stock markets. In our discussion of the U.S. stock market we explained that it was once dominated by retail investors but is now dominated by institutional investors. This change has occurred in other industrialized countries as well. A key characteristic of institutional investors is that they have been more willing than retail investors to transfer funds across national borders to improve portfolio diversification and/or exploit perceived mispricing of securities in foreign countries.

Table 2-1 of Chapter 2 provides a comparative analysis of the size, measured in U.S. dollars, of the equity markets of the world. The stock markets of the United States and Japan are the largest in the world. As the markets are measured in U.S. dollars, the relative size of the U.S. and Japanese market varies as the value of the yen changes against the dollar; U.S. share increases when the yen depreciates and decreases when the yen appreciates. The third largest market, but trailing considerably behind the U.S. and Japan, is the U.K. market.

Estimated **round-trip transactions costs** as a percentage of the amount invested are higher in stock markets outside the United States, as can be seen in Table 3-5. These costs include commissions, market impact costs (discussed in Chapter 15), and taxes. Deregulation in many countries, however, is reducing the gap between transactions costs in stock markets outside the United States.

Stocks of some firms are listed for trading on stock exchanges in other countries as well as on the exchange in their own country. Some stocks of very large firms are listed on stock exchanges in several countries. The readiness of an exchange to list and trade the shares of a foreign company varies among countries and exchanges.

---

[11]For a comparison of the various small-market capitalization indexes, see Bruce M. Collins and Frank J. Fabozzi, "Considerations in Selecting a Small Capitalization Benchmark," *Financial Analysts Journal* (January–February 1990), pp. 40–46.

TABLE 3-5					
ESTIMATED ROUND-TRIP TRANSACTIONS COSTS FOR COMMON STOCKS AS A PERCENTAGE OF AMOUNT INVESTED*					
	U.S.	**Japan**	**U.K.**	**France**	**Germany**
Commissions	0.20%	0.30%	0.10%	0.20%	0.20%
Market impact cost[†]	0.57	1.00	0.90	0.80	0.60
Taxes	0.00	0.30	0.50	0.00	0.00
Total	0.77%	1.60%	1.50%	1.00%	0.80%
Avg. stock price in U.S. dollars[‡]	45	6.77	6.17	97.18	271

*Assumes a $25 million cap weighted indexed portfolio executed as agent; does not include settlement and custody fees.

[†]Trader estimate.

[‡]Local index: S&P 500, Nikkei 225, FT-SE 100, CAC-40, DAX.

Source: *Structured International Investment*, Goldman Sachs & Co., June 1992, p. 22.

International Stock Market Indexes

Many indexes of stock prices chart and measure the performance of foreign stock markets. In every country where stock trading takes place, there is at least one index that measures general share price movements. If a country has more than one stock exchange, each exchange usually has its own index. Also, news organizations and financial advisory services create indexes.

In Japan, there are two major indexes. The Tokyo Stock Exchange produces the Tokyo Stock Price Index, or TOPIX. This is a composite index based on all the shares in the Tokyo market's First Section, a designation reserved for the established and large companies whose shares are the most actively traded and widely held. A financial information firm, Nihon Keizai Shimbun, Inc., calculates and publishes the Nikkei 225 Stock Average. This average is based on 225 of the largest companies in the First Section.

The United Kingdom's London Stock Exchange is covered by several widely followed indexes. The Financial Times Industrial Ordinary Index is based on the prices of shares of 30 leading companies and is known as the *FT30*. A broader index is the Financial Times-Stock Exchange 100, commonly referred to as the *FTSE 100* (and pronounced "Footsie 100"). This index is based on the shares of the largest 100 U.K. firms, whose market value makes up a majority of the market value of all U.K. equities.[12] Indexes for different sectors and a composite index across sectors are produced by the *Financial Times* and the Institute for Actuaries. These "FT-A" indexes are very broadly based, with the composite including over 700 stocks.

The primary German stock index is the DAX, which stands for the Deutscher Aktienindex, and it is produced by the Frankfurt Stock Exchange. (The German name for this exchange is the Frankfurter Wertpapierbörse. Some financial services regularly refer to the exchange by its initials, FWB.) The DAX is based on the 30 most actively traded shares listed on the Frankfurt exchange. The FAZ Index is another popular German index. Compiled by the *Frankfurter Allgemeine Zeitung*, which is a daily newspaper, the FAZ Index is computed from the share prices of the 100 largest companies listed

---

[12]Carolyn Moses, "U.K. Equity Market," in Jess Lederman and Keith K. H. Park (eds.), *The Global Equity Markets* (Chicago: Probus Publishing Company, 1991), p. 105.

TABLE 3-6 ANNUALIZED U.S. DOLLAR RETURNS AND VOLATILITY (STANDARD DEVIATION) IN SOME MAJOR EQUITY MARKETS (1982–1992)		
Country	**Mean Return**	**Standard Deviation**
France	23.45%	24.30%
Japan	19.31%	29.62%
Germany	18.89%	23.93%
U.K.	19.12%	20.34%
U.S.	17.93%	16.25%
Switzerland	18.10%	21.77%
Canada	10.22%	20.05%
Australia	15.10%	27.00%

Source: Gary Gastineau, Gordon Holterman, and Scott Beighley, "Equity Investment across Borders: Cutting the Costs," SBC Research, Swiss Bank Corporation Banking Inc., January 1993, p. 23.

on the Frankfurt exchange. In France, a national association of stockbrokers and the Paris Bourse produce an index based on the shares of 40 large and prominent firms traded on the exchange. The index is known as the CAC 40 Index, with CAC standing for Cotation Assistée en Continu, which is the name of the Bourse's electronic trading system. Given the increasing economic integration of Europe, the CAC 40, like the FT-SE 100 and possibly the DAX, may well be a reliable indicator of the overall performance of European stocks and markets. Other widely followed national stock indexes include the Hang Seng Index produced by the Stock Exchange of Hong Kong, the TSE 300 Composite of the Toronto Stock Exchange, and the Swiss Performance Index, or SPI, which indexes almost 400 firms and is published by the stock exchanges in that country.

To meet the increased interest in global equity investing, financial institutions have crafted several respected international equity indexes. The international equity index followed the most by U.S. pension funds is the Morgan Stanley Capital International Europe, Australia, Far East Index, or EAFE Index. This index covers more than 2,000 companies in 21 countries. Relatively new international equity indexes include The Financial Times World Index (a joint product of the Institute of Actuaries in the United Kingdom, Goldman Sachs & Co., and Wood MacKenzie & Co.), the Salomon Brothers-Russell Global Equity Index (a joint product of Salomon Brothers, Inc., and Frank Russell, Inc.), and the Global Index (a joint product of First Boston Corporation and London-based *Euromoney*).

Motivation for Global Investing

Table 3-6 shows the annualized U.S. dollar returns and volatility (as measured by the standard deviation) for eight major equity markets from 1982 to 1992. Numerous studies have documented the potential portfolio diversification benefits associated with global investing.[13] In particular, those studies

---

[13]For a review of these studies, see Chapter 2 in Bruno Solnik, *International Investments* (Reading, MA: Addison-Wesley Publishing Co., 1991).

have shown that the inclusion of securities from other countries can increase a portfolio's expected return without increasing its risk, as measured by variability in returns. Similarly, including securities from other countries might reduce the portfolio's risk with no fall in its expected return.

The cause of these benefits from diversification is that international capital markets are less than perfectly correlated (see Table 3-7). As explained in Chapter 4, a correlation coefficient theoretically can vary from 1 to −1, and reflects the degree to which two events vary with respect to one another. (In fact, few stocks are negatively correlated, since economic factors tend to affect companies in the same direction.) A perfectly correlated pair of markets (correlation coefficient = 1) would rise and fall in unison and according to a constant ratio. Investing in both markets would be superfluous, since the expected results would be identical, and the transactions costs would be greater. The closer the correlation coefficient is to zero, the more independent are the two events (in this case, changes in market prices). This degree of independence is not really surprising: The different countries in which the markets are located do not tend to have the same experiences in such important areas as taxation, monetary management, banking policies, political stability and goals, population growth, and so on. Because the largest influences on stock prices are domestic or local events and policies, the prices of groups of stock from different areas tend to move up or down at somewhat different times and to somewhat different extents. As explained in Chapter 4, this pattern of dissimilar security price changes allows investors to diversify a certain amount of risk and creates the benefits of international or global investing.

Table 3-7 provides evidence regarding the degree of dissimilarity in the movement of stock prices of the eight major equity markets whose dollar returns and volatility are reported in Table 3-6. Table 3-7 presents correlation coefficients for annual returns (in U.S. dollars), which measure the overall or general level of share prices on the exchanges in those countries, for the period from 1982 to 1992.

The table reveals some interesting points. These markets are quite different from one another, and the correlations of their returns tend to be substantially less than unity. The highest coefficient is 0.81, for the United States

TABLE 3-7							
ANNUAL INTERMARKET RETURN CORRELATIONS BETWEEN COUNTRY EQUITY MARKETS (1982–1992)							
	U.S.	**France**	**U.K.**	**Japan**	**Germany**	**Switzerland**	**Canada**	**Australia**
U.S.	1.00	0.57	0.63	0.44	0.41	0.58	0.81	0.51
France		1.00	0.56	0.53	0.65	0.64	0.39	0.34
U.K.			1.00	0.51	0.38	0.45	0.52	0.53
Japan				1.00	0.30	0.30	0.30	0.30
Germany					1.00	0.75	0.27	0.22
Switzerland						1.00	0.43	0.35
Canada							1.00	0.56
Australia								1.00

Source: Gary Gastineau, Gordon Holterman, and Scott Beighley, "Equity Investment across Borders: Cutting the Costs," SBC Research, Swiss Bank Corporation Banking Inc., January 1993, p. 24.

and Canada, and many values are below 0.50. So investors can diversify by spreading their portfolio across these various markets. It is interesting that all the correlations are positive and well above zero, a value that implies complete independence of action. The positive values mean that the world's stock prices are, like their economies, somewhat integrated. Thus, the benefit of international diversification has limits. In other words, the markets of the world are members of a somewhat loosely connected system of economies, and allocating funds among the various economies provides some, but not complete, reduction of variability in returns on securities.

■ SUMMARY

Secondary trading of U.S. common stock and bonds occurs in one or more of the following market trading systems or locations: two major national stock exchanges (the NYSE and AMEX), five regional stock exchanges, and the OTC market (NASDAQ system). Independent electronic trading systems such as INSTINET and POSIT permit institution-to-institution trading without the use of a broker. The secondary market is dominated by institutional investors. While some bonds are traded on an exchange, most trading of bonds occurs in the OTC market.

Dealers provide four functions in markets: (1) opportunity for investors to trade immediately rather than waiting for the arrival of sufficient orders on the other side of the trade (i.e., immediacy), (2) maintenance of short-run price stability (i.e., continuity), (3) better price information to market participants, and (4) in certain market structures, the services of an auctioneer in bringing order and fairness to a market. An important structural difference between exchanges and the OTC market is that on exchanges there is only one market maker or dealer per stock, the specialist, while there is no restriction on the number of dealers in the OTC market.

To accommodate the trading needs of institutional investors, who tend to place orders of larger sizes and with a large number of names, special arrangements have evolved. Block trades are trades of 10,000 shares or more of a given stock or trades with a market value of $200,000 or more. Program trades, or basket trades, involve the buying and/or selling of a large number of names simultaneously. The institutional

arrangement that has evolved to accommodate these needs is the upstairs market, which is a network of trading desks of the major brokerage firms and institutional investors that communicate with each other by means of electronic display systems and telephones.

Stock market indexes are barometers of the performance of the stock market and serve as benchmarks for evaluating the performance of professional money managers. Stock market indexes can be classified into three groups: (1) those produced by stock exchanges and that include all stocks traded on the exchange, such as the New York Stock Exchange Composite Index, the American Stock Exchange Market Value Index, and the NASDAQ Composite Index; (2) those in which a committee subjectively selects the stocks to be included in the index, such as the Dow Jones Industrial Average, the Standard & Poor's 500, and the Value Line Composite Average; and (3) those in which the stocks selected are based solely on market capitalization, such as the Wilshire Indexes (Wilshire 5000 and Wilshire 4500) and the Russell Indexes (Russell 3000, Russell 2000, and Russell 1000).

Effective transactions costs (commissions and taxes) are lower for trades in stock markets in the United States than in any other stock market of the world; however, the gap has been closing as a result of deregulation in many countries. The prices of stocks in markets around the world do not move together in an exact way, because the economic systems in which those markets are located have dissimilar environments in terms of taxation, industrial growth, political stability, monetary policy, and so on. Low levels of comovement of stock prices offer investors a benefit from diversifying their holdings across the markets of countries. By investing in the shares from other countries, an investor can reduce the portfolio's risk with no fall in expected return, or equivalently, raise the

portfolio's expected return with no increase in risk. This benefit of international diversification has led many investors to allocate funds to foreign markets and shares of foreign firms.

■ KEY TERMS

agency basis
agency incentive arrangement
ask price
basket trades
bid price
block trade
broker
broker loan rate
buy limit order
buying on margin
call money rate
dealer
fill-or-kill order
good-till-canceled order

initial margin requirement
limit order
limit order book
listed stocks
maintenance margin requirement
margin call
market-if-touched order
market order
odd lot
offer price
open order
program trades
round lot
round-trip transactions costs

sell limit order
selling short
specialist
stock exchanges
stop-limit order
stop order
stop order to buy
stop order to sell
tick-test rules
upstairs market
up-tick trade
zero up-tick

■ QUESTIONS

1. The following quote is taken from Wayne H. Wagner, "The Taxonomy of Trading Strategies," in Katrina F. Sherrerd (ed.), *Trading Strategies and Execution Costs* (Charlottesville, VA: The Institute of Chartered Financial Analysts, 1988).

   When a trader decides how to bring an order to the market, he or she must deal with some very important issues; to me, the most important is: What kind of trade is this? It could be either an active or a passive trade. The type of trade will dictate whether *speed* of execution is more or less important than *cost* of execution. In other words, do I want immediate trading (a market order); or am I willing to forgo the immediate trade for the possibility of trading less expensively if I am willing to "give" on the timing of the trade (a limit order)?

   a. What is meant by a market order, and why would one be placed when a trader wants immediate trading?
   b. What is meant by a limit order, and why may it be less expensive than a market order?

2. What are the risks associated with a limit order?

3. Suppose that Mr. Mancuso has purchased the stock of Harley Davis for $45 and that he sets a maximum loss that he will accept on this stock of $6. What type of order can Mr. Mancuso place?

4. a. What does it mean to "short a stock"?
   b. What are the restrictions on shorting a stock?

5. This quotation is from an interview with William Donaldson, chairman of the New York Stock Exchange, that appeared in the *New York Times* of January 30, 1990:

   There's a need to understand the advantages of an auction market versus a dealer market. The auction market allows a buyer and a seller to get together and agree on a price and the dealer is not involved at all. That's opposed to a dealer market where the house is on both sides of the trade and the dealer makes the spread rather than having the spread shared by the buyer and the seller. . . .

   One of the things we're coming to the forefront on now is the whole idea of what makes a good market. I think the best market is where you have the maximum number of people coming together in a single location and bidding against each other. . . . That is far superior to what we are getting now, which is a fractionalization of the market. Traders on machines, trades in the closet, trades in many areas where buyers and sellers don't have the opportunity to meet.

Discuss Donaldson's opinion. In your answer be sure to address the pros and cons of the different trading locations and practices addressed in the chapter.

6. What is an informationless trade, and who would execute such a trade?

7. **a.** What is a program trade?
   b. What are the various types of commission arrangements for executing a program trade and the advantages and disadvantages of each?

8. What is the difference between a market-value-weighted index and an equally weighted index?

9. **a.** What is the most popular market index followed by institutional investors?
   b. "The stocks selected for the S&P 500 are the largest 500 companies in the United States." Indicate whether you agree or disagree with this statement.
   c. Explain how the companies in the Russell Indexes and the Wilshire Index are determined.

10. **a.** In general, the correlations between stock indexes in two countries are positively correlated. Why does this occur?
    b. Are the correlations between stock indexes in two countries perfectly positively correlated (i.e., do they have a correlation close to 1)?

11. **a.** What does the term "First Section" mean on the Tokyo Stock Exchange?
    b. What are the key differences between the two major Japanese stock market indexes, the TOPIX and the Nikkei 225?

12. Often, a news report will survey the day's trading in Europe with a statement like this: "The Footsie 100 rose 1.5% today, while the DAX dropped 0.25% and the CAC 40 finished unchanged." What are the formal names of the indexes that the reporter is citing, and to which country do they apply?

CHAPTER 4
PORTFOLIO THEORY*

LEARNING OBJECTIVES

After reading this chapter you will be able to:

- explain what is meant by an efficient portfolio.
- calculate the expected return and risk of a single asset and a portfolio of assets.
- explain why the expected return of a portfolio of assets is a weighted average of the expected return of the assets included in the portfolio.
- explain the importance of the correlation and covariance of two assets in measuring a portfolio's risk.
- differentiate between naive diversification and Markowitz diversification.

- list the assumptions underlying portfolio theory.
- describe what is meant by a Markowitz efficient frontier.
- explain what is meant by an optimal portfolio.
- describe how an optimal portfolio is selected from all the portfolios available on the Markowitz efficient frontier.
- explain the important contribution made by Markowitz portfolio theory.

In this chapter and the next two, we set forth theories that are the underpinnings for the management of portfolios: portfolio theory and capital market theory. Portfolio theory deals with the selection of portfolios that maximize expected returns consistent with individually acceptable levels of risk. Using quantitative models and historical data, portfolio theory defines "expected portfolio returns" and "acceptable levels of portfolio risk," and shows how to construct an optimal portfolio.

Capital market theory deals with the effects of investor decisions on security prices. More specifically, it shows the relationship that should exist between security returns and risk if investors constructed portfolios as indicated by portfolio theory. Together, portfolio and capital market theories provide a framework to specify and measure investment risk and to develop relationships between expected security return and risk (and hence between risk and required return on an investment). Moreover, as will be explained in Chapter 28, these theories also provide a framework for measuring the performance of managed portfolios such as mutual funds and pension funds.

*This chapter is coauthored with Dr. T. Daniel Coggin of the Virginia Retirement System.

Portfolio theory and capital market theory were once the province of academics, with money managers largely unaware of or unwilling to become interested in the subject. However, as more business school graduates trained in these theories entered the profession of money management, the situation changed. Now, money managers are receptive to these theories and often contribute new ideas themselves.

These theories have revolutionized the world of money management, by allowing managers to quantify the investment risk and expected return of a portfolio. Moreover, these theories tell us that the focus of portfolio management should be the risk of the entire portfolio, not the risk of the individual assets. That is, it is possible to combine risky assets and produce a portfolio whose expected return reflects its components, but with considerably lower risk.

Prior to portfolio theory, practitioners would often speak of risk and return, but the failure to quantify these important measures made the goal of constructing an optimal portfolio highly subjective and provided no insight about the return investors should expect. Moreover, portfolio managers would focus on the risks of individual assets without understanding how combining them into a portfolio can affect the portfolio's risk.

We will see several applications of portfolio theory and capital market theory throughout this book. In October 1990, as further confirmation of the importance of these theories, the Alfred Nobel Memorial Prize in Economic Science was awarded to Professor Harry Markowitz,[1] the developer of portfolio theory, and Professor William Sharpe, one of the developers of capital market theory.[2] Our focus in this chapter is on portfolio theory.

SOME BASIC CONCEPTS

The theories developed in this chapter draw on concepts from two fields: financial economic theory and probability and statistical theory. Appendix A at the end of this book provides a review of some of the basic concepts of probability and statistics that we use in this chapter. In this section we will describe several concepts from financial economic theory that will be used. Many of the concepts have a more technical or rigorous definition. Our goal here is to keep the explanation simple enough for the reader to appreciate the importance and applicability of these concepts to the development of the two theories.

Efficient Portfolios and an Optimal Portfolio

In constructing a portfolio, investors seek to maximize the expected return from their investment given some level of risk they are willing to accept.[3] Portfolios that satisfy this requirement are called **efficient portfolios**. The concepts of expected return and risk will be defined more specifically as we proceed in the development of portfolio theory.

---

[1]Harry M. Markowitz, "Portfolio Selection," *Journal of Finance* (March 1952), pp. 77–91, and *Portfolio Selection*, Cowles Foundation Monograph 16 (New York: John Wiley & Sons, 1959).

[2]William F. Sharpe, *Portfolio: Theory and Capital Markets* (New York: McGraw-Hill, 1970).

[3]Alternatively stated, investors seek to minimize the risk that they are exposed to given some target expected return.

To construct an efficient portfolio, it is necessary to make some assumption about how investors behave in making investment decisions. A reasonable assumption is that investors are **risk averse**. A risk-averse investor is one who when faced with two investments with the same expected return but two different risks will prefer the one with the lower risk.

Given a choice of efficient portfolios from which an investor can select, an **optimal portfolio** is the one that is most preferred.

Utility Function and Indifference Curves

In economic theory, there are many situations where entities (i.e., individuals and firms) face a trade-off between two choices. The "theory of choice" describes the decision-making process with the help of a concept called the utility function. A **utility function** is a mathematical expression that assigns a value to all possible choices. The higher the value, the greater the utility. Simply put, in portfolio theory the utility function expresses the preferences of economic entities with respect to perceived risk and expected return.

A utility function can be expressed in graphical form by an **indifference curve**. Figure 4-1 shows indifference curves labeled u_1, u_2, and u_3. The horizontal axis measures risk, and the vertical axis measures expected return. Each curve represents a set of portfolios with different combinations of risk and return. All the points on a given indifference curve indicate combinations of risk and expected return that will give the same level of utility to a given investor. For example, on utility curve u_1, there are two points u and u', with u having a higher expected return than u', but also having a higher risk. An investor has an equal preference for (or is indifferent to) any point on the curve, because the curve reflects the investor's level of risk aversion. The slope of an indifference curve reflects the fact that investors require a higher expected return in order to accept higher risk.

For the three indifference curves shown in Figure 4-1, the utility the investor receives is greater the further the indifference curve is from the horizontal axis, because that curve represents a higher level of return at every level of risk. Thus, for the three indifference curves shown in the figure, u_3 has the highest utility and u_1 the lowest.

FIGURE 4-1
Indifference curves.

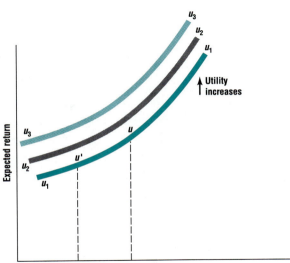

Risky Assets versus Risk-Free Assets

A **risky asset** is one for which the return that will be realized in the future is uncertain. For example, suppose an investor purchases the stock of General Motors today and plans to hold the stock for one year. At the time the investor purchases the stock, he or she does not know what return will be realized. The return will depend on the price of General Motors stock one year from now and the dividends that the company pays during the year. Thus, General Motors stock, and indeed the stock of all companies, is a risky asset. Even securities issued by the U.S. government are risky assets. For example, an investor who purchases a U.S. government bond that matures in 30 years does not know the return that will be realized if this bond is to be held for only one year. This is because a change in interest rates will affect the price of the bond one year from now and therefore the return from investing in that bond for one year.

There are assets, however, for which the return that will be realized in the future is known with certainty today. Such assets are referred to as **risk-free** or **riskless assets**. The risk-free asset is commonly defined as short-term obligations of the U.S. government. For example, if an investor buys a U.S. government security that matures in one year and plans to hold that security for one year, then there is no uncertainty about the return that will be realized. The investor knows that in one year, the maturity date of the security, the government will pay a specific amount to retire the debt. Notice how this situation differs for the U.S. government security that matures in 30 years. While the 1-year and the 30-year securities are obligations of the U.S. government, the former matures in 1 year so that there is no uncertainty about the return that will be realized. In contrast, while the investor knows what the government will pay at the end of 30 years for the 30-year bond, he or she does not know what the price of the bond will be 1 year from now.

MEASURING A PORTFOLIO'S EXPECTED RETURN

Investors are most often faced with choices among risky assets. Here we will look at how to measure the expected return of a risky asset and the expected return of a portfolio of risky assets.

Measuring Single-Period Portfolio Return

The *actual* return on a portfolio of assets over some specific time period is straightforward to calculate, as shown below:

$$R_p = w_1R_1 + w_2R_2 + \ldots + w_GR_G \tag{4-1}$$

where R_p = rate of return on the portfolio over the period
R_g = rate of return on asset g over the period
w_g = weight of asset g in the portfolio (i.e., asset g as a proportion of the market value of the total portfolio)
G = number of assets in the portfolio

In shorthand notation, Equation (4-1) can be expressed as follows:

$$R_p = \sum_{g=1}^{G} w_gR_g \tag{4-2}$$

Equation (4-2) states that the return on a portfolio of G assets (R_p) is equal to the sum of the individual asset weights in the portfolio times its return, for each asset g. The portfolio return R_p is sometimes called the **holding period return**, or the **ex post return**.

For example, consider the following portfolio consisting of three assets:

Asset	Market Value	Rate of Return
1	$ 6 million	12%
2	8 million	10%
3	11 million	5%

The portfolio's total market value is $25 million. Therefore,

$R_1 = 12\%$ and $w_1 = \$6 \text{ million}/\$25 \text{ million} = 0.24, \text{ or } 24\%$
$R_2 = 10\%$ and $w_2 = \$8 \text{ million}/\$25 \text{ million} = 0.32, \text{ or } 32\%$
$R_3 = 5\%$ and $w_3 = \$11 \text{ million}/\$25 \text{ million} = 0.44, \text{ or } 44\%$

Notice that the sum of the weights is equal to 1. Substituting into Equation (4-1), we get

$R_p = 0.24(12\%) + 0.32(10\%) + 0.44(5\%) = 8.28\%$

The Expected Return of a Portfolio of Risky Assets

Equation (4-1) shows how to calculate the actual return of a portfolio over some specific time period. In portfolio management, the investor also wants to know the expected (or anticipated) return from a portfolio of risky assets. The expected portfolio return is the weighted average of the expected return of each asset in the portfolio. The weight assigned to the expected return of each asset is the percentage of the market value of the asset to the total market value of the portfolio. That is,

$$E(R_p) = w_1 E(R_1) + w_2 E(R_2) + \ldots + w_G E(R_G) \tag{4-3}$$

The $E(\ )$ signifies expectations, and $E(R_p)$ is sometimes called the **ex ante return**, or the expected portfolio return over some specific time period.

The expected return on a risky asset is calculated as follows. First, a probability distribution for the possible rates of return that can be realized must be specified. A probability distribution is a function that associates the probability of occurrence to a possible outcome for a random variable. Given the probability distribution, the *expected value of a random variable* is simply the weighted average of the possible outcomes, where the weight is the probability associated with the possible outcome. Rather than use the term "expected value of the return of an asset," we simply use the term **expected return**. Mathematically, the expected return of asset i is expressed as

$$E(R_i) = p_1 r_1 + p_2 r_2 + \ldots + p_N r_N \tag{4-4}$$

where r_n = the nth possible rate of return for asset i
p_n = the probability of attaining the rate of return n for asset i
N = the number of possible outcomes for the rate of return

Assume that an individual is considering an investment, stock XYZ, which has a probability distribution for the rate of return for some time period as given in Table 4-1. In practice, the probability distribution is based on historical returns, as we will explain later in this chapter.

TABLE 4-1	
PROBABILITY DISTRIBUTION FOR THE RATE OF RETURN FOR STOCK XYZ	

n	Rate of Return	Probability of Occurrence
1	15%	0.50
2	10	0.30
3	5	0.13
4	0	0.05
5	−5	0.02
Total		1.00

Substituting into Equation (4-4), we get

$$E(R_{XYZ}) = 0.50(15\%) + 0.30(10\%) + 0.13(5\%) + 0.05(0\%) + 0.02(-5\%)$$
$$= 11\%$$

Thus, 11% is the expected value or mean of the probability distribution for the rate of return on stock XYZ.

MEASURING PORTFOLIO RISK

The dictionary defines *risk* as "hazard, peril, exposure to loss or injury." With respect to investment, investors have used a variety of definitions to describe risk. Professor Harry Markowitz changed how the investment community thought about risk by quantifying the concept of risk. He defined risk in terms of a well-known statistical measure known as the *variance*. Specifically, Markowitz quantified risk as the variance about an asset's expected return.

Variance as a Measure of Risk

The variance of a random variable is a measure of the dispersion of the possible outcomes around the expected value. In the case of an asset's return, the variance is a measure of the dispersion of the possible outcomes for the rate of return around the expected return.

The equation for the variance of the expected return for asset i, denoted $\text{var}(R_i)$, is

$$\text{var}(R_i) = p_1[r_1 - E(R_i)]^2 + p_2[r_2 - E(R_i)]^2 + \ldots + p_N[r_N - E(R_i)]^2$$

or

$$\text{var}(R_i) = \sum_{n=1}^{N} p_n[r_n - E(R_i)]^2 \tag{4-5}$$

Using the probability distribution of the return for stock XYZ, we can illustrate the calculation of the variance:

$$\text{var}(R_{XYZ}) = 0.50(15\% - 11\%)^2 + 0.30(10\% - 11\%)^2 + 0.13(5\% - 11\%)^2$$
$$+ 0.05(0\% - 11\%)^2 + 0.02(-5\% - 11\%)^2 = 24\%$$

The variance associated with a distribution of returns measures the tightness with which the distribution is clustered around the mean or expected return. Markowitz argued that this tightness or variance is equivalent to the uncertainty or riskiness of the investment. If an asset is riskless, it has an expected return dispersion of zero.

Standard Deviation   Since the variance is squared units, it is common to see the variance converted to the standard deviation or square root of the variance:

$$\text{SD}(R_i) = \sqrt{\text{var}(R_i)}$$

For stock XYZ, then, the standard deviation is

$$\text{SD}(R_{\text{XYZ}}) = \sqrt{24\%} = 4.9\%$$

The two are conceptually equivalent; that is, the larger the variance or standard deviation, the greater the investment risk.

Criticism of Variance as a Measure of Risk   There are two criticisms of the use of the variance as a measure of risk. The first criticism is that since the variance measures the dispersion of an asset's return around its expected value, it considers the possibility of returns above the expected return and below the expected return. Investors, however, do not view possible returns above the expected return as an unfavorable outcome. In fact, such outcomes are quite favorable. Because of this, some researchers have argued that measures of risk should not consider the possible returns above the expected return.

Markowitz recognized this limitation and, in fact, suggested a measure of downside risk—the risk of realizing an outcome below the expected return—called the *semi-variance*. The semi-variance is similar to the variance except that in the calculation no consideration is given to returns above the expected return. However, because of the computational problems with using the semi-variance and the limited resources available to him at the time, he compromised and used the variance in developing portfolio theory.

Today, various measures of downside risk are currently being used by practitioners.[4] However, regardless of the measure used, the basic principles of portfolio theory developed by Markowitz and set forth in this chapter are applicable. That is, the choice of the measure of risk may affect the calculation but doesn't invalidate the theory. In fact, in Chapter 28 we will extend the theory to consider the probability of realizing a return below some predetermined value.

The second criticism is that the variance is only one measure of how the returns vary around the expected return. When a probability distribution is not symmetrical around its expected return, then a statistical measure of the skewness of a distribution should be used in addition to the variance. Markowitz did not consider any such measure in developing portfolio theory. The variance can be justified based on empirical evidence which suggests that the historical distribution of the returns on stocks is approximately symmet-

---

[4]See Vijay S. Bawa and E. B. Lindenberg, "Mean-Lower Partial Moments and Asset Prices," *Journal of Financial Economics* (June 1977), pp. 189–200; Peter C. Fishburn, "Mean-Risk Analysis with Risk Associated with Below-Target Variance," *American Economic Review* (March 1977), pp. 230–245; R. S. Clarkson, "The Measurement of Investment Risk," paper presented to the Faculty of Actuaries (British) on February 20, 1989; and Frank A. Sortino and Robert Van Der Meer, "Downside Risk," *Journal of Portfolio Management* (Summer 1991), pp. 27–31.

rical.[5] Because expected return and variance are the only two parameters that investors are assumed to consider in making investment decisions, the Markowitz formulation of portfolio theory is often referred to as a *two-parameter model.*

Measuring the Portfolio Risk of a Two-Asset Portfolio

Equation (4-5) gives the variance for an individual asset's return. The variance of a portfolio consisting of two assets is a little more difficult to calculate. It depends not only on the variance of the two assets, but also upon how closely one asset tracks the other asset. The formula is

$$\text{var}(R_p) = w_i^2 \, \text{var}(R_i) + w_j^2 \, \text{var}(R_j) + 2w_i w_j \, \text{cov}(R_i, R_j) \tag{4-6}$$

where

$\text{cov}(R_i, R_j)$ = covariance between the return for assets i and j

In words, Equation (4-6) states that the variance of the portfolio return is the sum of the weighted variances of the two assets plus the weighted covariance between the two assets.

Covariance The covariance is a new term in this discussion and has a precise mathematical translation. However, its practical meaning is the degree to which the returns on two assets vary or change together. The covariance is not expressed in a particular unit, such as dollars or percent. A positive covariance means the returns on two assets tend to move or change in the same direction, while a negative covariance means the returns move in opposite directions. The covariance between any two assets i and j is computed using the following formula:

$$\text{cov}(R_i, R_j) = p_1[r_{i1} - E(R_i)] \, [r_{j1} - E(R_j)] + p_2[r_{i2} - E(R_i)] \, [r_{j2} - E(R_j)] \tag{4-7}$$
$$+ \ldots + p_N[r_{iN} - E(R_i)] \, [r_{jN} - E(R_j)]$$

where r_{in} = the nth possible rate of return for asset i
 r_{jn} = the nth possible rate of return for asset j
 p_n = the probability of attaining the rate of return n for assets i and j
 N = the number of possible outcomes for the rate of return

To illustrate the calculation of the covariance between two assets, we use the two stocks in Table 4-2. The first is stock XYZ that we used earlier to illustrate the calculation of the expected return and the standard deviation. The other hypothetical stock is stock ABC. Using the data in Table 4-2 in Equation (4-7), we calculate the covariance between stock XYZ and stock ABC as follows:

$$\text{cov}(R_{\text{XYZ}}, R_{\text{ABC}}) = 0.50(15\% - 11\%) \, (8\% - 8\%) +$$
$$0.30(10\% - 11\%) \, (11\% - 8\%) + 0.13(5\% - 11\%) \, (6\% - 8\%) +$$
$$0.05 \, (0\% - 11\%) \, (0 - 8\%) + 0.02(-5\% - 11\%) \, (-4\% - 8\%) = 8.9$$

Relationship between Covariance and Correlation The covariance is analogous to the correlation between the expected returns for two assets. Specifically, the

---

[5]See Chapters 1 and 2 in Eugene Fama, *Foundations of Finance* (New York: Basic Books, 1976).

TABLE 4-2			
PROBABILITY DISTRIBUTION FOR THE RATE OF RETURN FOR STOCKS XYZ AND ABC			
n	**Rate of Return for Stock XYZ**	**Rate of Return for Stock ABC**	**Probability of Occurrence**
1	15	8%	0.50
2	10	11	0.30
3	5	6	0.13
4	0	0	0.05
5	−5	−4	0.02
Total			1.00
Expected return	11%	8%	
Variance	24%	9%	
Standard deviation	4.9%	3%	

correlation between the returns for assets i and j is defined as the covariance of the two assets divided by the product of their standard deviations:

$$\text{cor}(R_i, R_j) = \frac{\text{cov}(R_i, R_j)}{\text{SD}(R_i)\, \text{SD}(R_j)} \tag{4-8}$$

The correlation and the covariance are conceptually equivalent terms. Dividing the covariance by the product of the standard deviations simply (but importantly) makes the correlation a number that is *comparable* across different assets. The correlation between the returns for stock XYZ and stock ABC is

$$\text{cor}(R_{\text{XYZ}}, R_{\text{ABC}}) = \frac{8.9}{(4.9)(3)} = 0.60$$

The correlation coefficient can have values ranging from $+1.0$, denoting perfect comovement in the same direction, to -1.0, denoting perfect comovement in opposite directions.

Calculations Using Historical Returns In our illustrations so far, the inputs we need in portfolio theory—the expected value, standard deviation, covariance, and correlation—were calculated from the probability distributions for the two stocks. As such, they are truly "expected values," since they were derived probabilistically. In practice, the estimation of these statistical measures is typically obtained from *historical* observations on the rate of returns.

Table 4-3 shows historical returns for five time periods for two hypothetical stocks, A and B. Three cases are shown. The mean, variance, standard deviation, covariance, and correlation are shown for each case, obtained by using the formulas in Appendix A.

Case I illustrates perfect positive correlation or comovement: Both A and B move up together in respectively equal increments. Case II illustrates near-zero correlation; i.e., both stocks move in a largely independent fashion. Case III illustrates perfect negative correlation: As stock A goes up, stock B goes down proportionately. In reality, few examples exactly fit these three cases. Most common stocks have a small but positive correlation of returns with each other over time. However, the three illustrations do demonstrate the basic concept of the correlation or covariance of asset returns.

		\multicolumn{5}{c}{**TABLE 4-3**}			
\multicolumn{10}{c}{**SUMMARY STATISTICS BASED ON HISTORICALLY OBSERVED RATES OF RETURN**}									
		\multicolumn{5}{c}{*Observed Return for Period*}			
Case	**Stock**	**1**	**2**	**3**	**4**	**5**	**Mean**	**Variance**	**Standard Deviation**
I	A	2%	4%	6%	8%	10%	6%	10%	3.2%
	B	4	8	12	16	20	12	40	6.3
	\multicolumn{4}{l}{Covariance = 20.2}			\multicolumn{3}{l}{Correlation ≅ +1.0}		
II	A	12	8	20	4	16	12	40	6.3
	B	8	0	4	6	2	4	10	3.2
	\multicolumn{4}{l}{Covariance = 0.0}			\multicolumn{3}{l}{Correlation = 0.0}		
III	A	2	4	6	8	10	6	10	3.2
	B	20	16	12	8	4	12	40	6.3
	\multicolumn{4}{l}{Covariance = −20.2}			\multicolumn{3}{l}{Correlation = −1.0}		

Implications   Since the variance of a portfolio depends on the covariances of its constituent securities, a portfolio's risk can be low despite the fact that the risk of individual assets making up the portfolio can be quite high. This principle has important implications not only for managing portfolios, as we shall see below, but also for challenging legal standards to judge the conduct of a professional money manager. The implications of portfolio theory as set forth by Markowitz contradicts the prevailing legal view, as explained in Box 4.

BOX 4

PORTFOLIO THEORY AND THE PRUDENT-MAN RULE

Implicit in Graham and Dodd's original theory (*Security Analysis*, 1934)* was the idea that a stock has an intrinsic value. If an investor purchased an asset or stock at a price below its intrinsic value, the asset over time would move up to its intrinsic value without risk. Graham and Dodd recognized that people hold different expectations of the future, but they had little to say about diversification. The basic idea was that, if every stock bought was below its intrinsic value, the overall portfolio would be a good one and would make money as the values of the component stocks rose to their intrinsic values.

The legal profession translated this intellectual idea into the Prudent Man rule for investing personal trusts. According to this rule, a trust manager must invest in each asset on its own merit. If each asset is safe, then the total portfolio will be safe. For example, futures cannot be used under the Prudent Man rule because they are inherently risky—even though investment managers now know that when futures are combined with other assets, they can reduce portfolio risk.

Markowitz in 1959 then developed mathematics for the efficient set. . . . This concept of looking at the entire portfolio changed the way investors think about investing.

Markowitz focused on the portfolio as a whole, not explicitly on the individual assets in the portfolio, which was clearly at odds with the Prudent Man rule for personal trusts. In fact, under the Employee Retirement Income Security Act passed in the mid-1970s, investing in derivatives to reduce the risk of a portfolio was, for the most part, legally imprudent.

*In Chapter 14 we will discuss the approach of one of the authors of this book, Benjamin Graham.

Source: Marshall E. Blume, "The Capital Asset Pricing Model and the CAPM Literature," in Diana R. Harrington and Robert A. Korajczyk (eds.), *The CAPM Controversy: Policy and Strategy Implications for Investment Management* (Charlottesville, VA: Association for Investment Management and Research, 1993), p. 5. (The first sentence was modified by Frank Fabozzi.)

Question for Box 4

1. Why is the prudent-man rule for investing a personal trust in conflict with the way to construct a portfolio as suggested by Markowitz portfolio theory?

Measuring the Risk of a Portfolio with More Than Two Assets

Thus far we have given the portfolio risk for a portfolio consisting of two assets. The extension to three assets—i, j, and k—is as follows:

$$\text{var}(R_p) = w_i^2\,\text{var}(R_i) + w_j^2\,\text{var}(R_j) + w_k^2\,\text{var}(R_k) + \tag{4-9}$$
$$2w_iw_j\,\text{cov}(R_i,R_j) + 2w_iw_k\,\text{cov}(R_i,R_k) + 2w_jw_k\,\text{cov}(R_j,R_k)$$

In words, Equation (4-9) states that the variance of the portfolio return is the sum of the weighted variances of the individual assets plus the sum of the weighted covariances of the assets. Hence, the variance of the portfolio expected return is the weighted sum of the individual variances of the assets in the portfolio plus the weighted sum of the degree to which the assets vary together.

In general, for a portfolio with G assets, the portfolio variance is

$$\text{var}(R_p) = \sum_{g=1}^{G} w_g^2\,\text{var}(R_g) + \sum_{g=1}^{G}\sum_{h=1}^{G} w_g w_h\,\text{cov}(R_g,R_h) \tag{4-10}$$
$$\text{for } h \neq g$$

USING HISTORICAL DATA TO ESTIMATE INPUTS

As we noted earlier, the inputs required for portfolio theory are estimated from historical observations on the rate of returns. The formulas for calculating the historical mean rate of return and variance of an asset and the historical covariance for the rate of return between two assets are shown in Appendix A. Given the calculated variance and covariances, the historical correlation can be calculated using Equation (4-8). The assumption is that the calculated values from historical observations are reasonable values for the inputs in the future. Portfolio managers will modify the input values if their analysis suggests that the future performance of a particular stock or stocks will differ from historical performance.

Historical returns are calculated from either monthly data or weekly data. Regardless of the time interval used to calculate a historical return, the following formula is used:

Historical return =

$$\frac{\text{beginning-period price} - \text{ending-period price} + \text{cash dividend}}{\text{beginning-period price}}$$

For example, let's look at how to calculate the historical return for IBM for the month of November 1993. The required information is given below:

Beginning period price (beginning of 11/93) = \$46.000
Ending period price (end of 11/93) = \$53.875
Cash dividend paid in November = \$0.25

Historical return for IBM for November 1993 =

$$\frac{\$53.875 - \$46.000 + \$0.25}{\$46.000} = 0.17663 = 17.663\%$$

Table 4-4 gives data on 60 monthly returns for two actual stocks, IBM and Walgreen, for the time period January 1989 to December 1993. Table 4-5 shows the mean, standard deviation, correlation, and covariance for these two stocks. The calculations are shown in Appendix A to the book. As can be

		TABLE 4-4			
		HISTORICAL DATA ON MONTHLY RETURNS FOR IBM AND WALGREEN FROM JANUARY 1989 TO DECEMBER 1993			
Month	IBM	Walgreen	Month	IBM	Walgreen
1989			1992		
January	7.179	27.273	January	1.124	−0.658
February	−6.144	−8.649	February	−1.128	−3.629
March	−10.185	1.429	March	−3.885	−1.034
April	4.467	8.451	April	8.683	−6.620
May	−2.776	8.556	May	1.333	−0.358
June	2.052	1.802	June	7.851	1.880
July	2.793	16.817	July	−3.193	5.904
August	2.900	−4.962	August	−7.298	7.331
September	−6.724	−0.533	September	−6.782	−0.326
October	−8.238	−7.237	October	−17.183	5.229
November	−1.411	3.353	November	3.865	10.000
December	−3.585	5.056	December	−26.190	−1.133
1990			1993		
January	4.781	−11.499	January	2.233	−8.596
February	6.550	−1.329	February	6.631	−1.818
March	2.166	4.618	March	−6.437	3.526
April	2.709	−1.176	April	−4.423	−5.882
May	11.202	11.786	May	9.594	12.895
June	−2.083	6.148	June	−6.398	−5.556
July	−5.106	0.758	July	−9.873	−6.811
August	−7.547	−8.352	August	3.371	3.721
September	4.417	−1.368	September	−8.197	−3.859
October	−0.940	5.276	October	9.524	13.712
November	8.977	6.818	November	17.663	−3.718
December	−0.550	1.985	December	4.872	0.307
1991					
January	12.168	9.733			
February	2.533	11.275			
March	−11.553	7.600			
April	−9.550	−2.602			
May	4.209	−0.412			
June	−8.481	2.308			
July	4.247	2.632			
August	−3.126	1.070			
September	6.968	−6.909			
October	−5.187	4.297			
November	−4.621	−2.607			
December	−3.784	17.375			

TABLE 4-5		
MEAN, VARIANCE, STANDARD DEVIATION, CORRELATION, AND COVARIANCE FOR IBM AND WALGREEN (JANUARY 1989 TO DECEMBER 1993)		
Parameter	**IBM**	**Walgreen**
Mean	−0.61%	2.05%
Variance	58.595%	53.369%
Standard deviation	7.655%	7.305%
Correlation between IBM and Walgreen: 0.21		
Covariance between IBM and Walgreen: 11.707		

seen, there is a positive correlation, but not a perfect one, between the return on the stock of IBM and Walgreen.

PORTFOLIO DIVERSIFICATION

Often, one hears investors talking about diversifying their portfolio. By this an investor means constructing a portfolio in such a way as to reduce portfolio risk without sacrificing return. This is certainly a goal that investors should seek. However, the question is how does one do this in practice.

Some investors would say that a portfolio can be diversified by including assets across all asset classes. For example, one investor might argue that a portfolio should be diversified by investing in stocks, bonds, and real estate. While that might be reasonable, two questions must be addressed in order to construct a diversified portfolio. First, how much should be invested in each asset class? Should 40% of the portfolio be in stocks, 50% in bonds, and 10% in real estate, or is some other allocation more appropriate? Second, given the allocation, which specific stocks, bonds, and real estate should the investor select?

Some investors who focus only on one asset class such as common stock argue that such portfolios should also be diversified. By this they mean that an investor should not place all funds in the stock of one corporation, but rather should include stocks of many corporations. Here, too, several questions must be answered in order to construct a diversified portfolio. First, which corporations should be represented in the portfolio? Second, how much of the portfolio should be allocated to the stocks of each corporation?

Prior to the development of portfolio theory, while investors often talked about diversification in these general terms, they never provided the analytical tools by which to answer the questions posed above. A major contribution of portfolio theory is that using the concepts discussed above, a quantitative measure of the diversification of a portfolio is possible, and it is this measure that can be used to achieve the maximum diversification benefits.

Naive Diversification

A strategy of **naive diversification** is achieved when an investor simply invests in a number of different stocks or asset types and hopes that the variance of the expected return on the portfolio is lowered. For example, a well-known rule of common stock investing holds that portfolios should be diversified across several different industries. Naive diversification is closely related to a practice Alexander and Francis[6] have termed "financial interior decorating." According to this approach, an investment counselor seeks to design portfolios to match the "financial personality" of the investor. As Alexander and Francis note, the assumption of the financial interior decorator is that certain types of investors have certain investment return requirements that can be fulfilled by artfully designing a portfolio to suit them.

For example, widows often have high current income needs; thus they should invest in so-called low-risk/high-dividend assets (such as bonds or electric utility stocks). Little or no attention is paid to the degree of correlation between the returns on the assets within these categories. Concentrating one's investments in any one asset category is an invitation to the greater risk implied by the usually high covariance of asset returns within such categories. They usually go up together, but they also tend to come down together. There is a better way to approach the diversification problem.

Markowitz Diversification

The Markowitz diversification strategy is primarily concerned with the degree of covariance between asset returns in a portfolio. Indeed a key contribution of Markowitz diversification is the formulation of an asset's risk in terms of a portfolio of assets, rather than in isolation. **Markowitz diversification** seeks to combine assets in a portfolio with returns that are less than perfectly positively correlated, in an effort to lower portfolio risk (variance) without sacrificing return. It is the concern for maintaining return, while lowering risk through an analysis of the covariance between asset returns, that separates Markowitz diversification from the naive approach and makes it more effective.

Markowitz diversification and the importance of asset correlations can be illustrated with a simple two-asset portfolio example. To do this, we will first show the general relationship between the expected risk of a two-asset portfolio and the correlation of returns of the component assets. Then we will look at the effects on portfolio risk of combining assets with different correlations.

Portfolio Risk and Correlation   In our two-asset portfolio, assume that common stock C and common stock D are available with expected returns and standard deviations as shown:

	E(R)	SD(R)
Stock C	10%	30%
Stock D	25%	60%

If an equal 50% weighting is assigned to both stocks C and D, the expected portfolio return can be calculated as

$$E(R_p) = 0.50(10\%) + 0.50(25\%) = 17.5\%$$

The variance of the return on the two-stock portfolio from Equation (4-6) is:

$$\text{var}(R_p) = w_C^2 \, \text{var}(R_C) + w_D^2 \, \text{var}(R_D) + 2w_C w_D \, \text{cov}(R_C, R_D)$$

[6]Gordon J. Alexander and Jack C. Francis, *Portfolio Analysis*, 3rd ed. (Englewood Cliffs, NJ: Prentice-Hall, 1986).

$$= (0.5)^2(30\%)^2 + (0.5)^2(60\%)^2 + 2(0.5)(0.5)\text{cov}(R_C,R_D)$$

From Equation (4-8),

$$\text{cor}(R_C,R_D) = \frac{\text{cov}(R_C,R_D)}{\text{SD}(R_C)\ \text{SD}(R_D)}$$

so

$$\text{cov}(R_C,R_D) = \text{SD}(R_C)\ \text{SD}(R_D)\ \text{cor}(R_C,R_D)$$

Since $\text{SD}(R_C) = 30\%$ and $\text{SD}(R_D) = 60\%$, then

$$\text{cov}(R_C,R_D) = (30\%)(60\%)\ \text{cor}(R_C,R_D)$$

Substituting into the expression for $\text{var}(R_p)$, we get

$$\text{var}(R_p) = (0.5)^2(30\%)^2 + (0.5)^2(60\%)^2 + 2(0.5)(0.5)(30\%)(60\%)\ \text{cor}(R_C,R_D)$$

Taking the square root of the variance gives

$$\text{SD}(R_p) = \sqrt{(0.5)^2(30\%)^2 + (0.5)^2(60\%)^2 + 2(0.5)(0.5)(30\%)(60\%)\ \text{cor}(R_C,R_D)}$$
$$= \sqrt{0.1125 + (0.09)\ \text{cor}(R_C,R_D)} \tag{4-11}$$

The Effect of the Correlation of Asset Returns on Portfolio Risk   How would the risk change for our two-asset portfolio with different correlations between the returns of the component stocks? Let's consider the following three cases for $\text{cor}(R_C,R_D)$: $+1.0$, 0, and -1.0. Substituting into Equation (4-11) for these three cases of $\text{cor}(R_C,R_D)$, we get

cor(R_C,R_D)	E(R_p)	SD(R_p)
+1.0	17.5%	45.0%
0.0	17.5	35.0
−1.0	17.5	15.0

As the correlation between the expected returns on stocks C and D decreases from $+1.0$ to 0.0 to -1.0, the standard deviation of the expected portfolio return also decreases from 45% to 15%. However, the expected portfolio return remains 17.5% for each case.

This example clearly illustrates the effect of Markowitz diversification. The phenomenon is sometimes called the **magic of diversification**. The principle of Markowitz diversification states that as the correlation (covariance) between the returns for assets that are combined in a portfolio decreases, so does the variance (hence the standard deviation) of the return for that portfolio. The magic is thus due to the degree of correlation between the expected asset returns. The good news is that investors can maintain expected portfolio return and lower portfolio risk by combining assets with lower (and preferably negative) correlations. However, the bad news is that very few assets have small to negative correlations with other assets! The problem, then, becomes one of searching among large numbers of assets in an effort to discover the portfolio with the minimum risk at a given level of expected return or, equivalently, the highest expected return at a given level of risk. The stage is now set for a discussion of Markowitz efficient portfolios and their construction.

CHOOSING A PORTFOLIO OF RISKY ASSETS

Diversification in the manner suggested by Professor Markowitz leads to the construction of portfolios that have the highest expected return at a given level of risk. Such portfolios are called **Markowitz efficient portfolios**. In order to construct Markowitz efficient portfolios, the theory makes some basic assumptions about asset selection behavior.

First, it assumes that the only two parameters that affect an investor's decision are the expected return and the variance. That is, investors make decisions using the two-parameter model formulated by Markowitz. Second, it assumes that investors are risk averse (i.e., when faced with two investments with the same expected return but two different risks, investors will prefer the one with the lower risk). Third, it assumes that all investors seek to achieve the highest expected return at a given level of risk. Fourth, it assumes that all investors have the same expectations regarding expected return, variance, and covariances for all risky assets. This assumption is referred to as the *homogeneous expectations assumption*. Finally, it assumes that all investors have a common one-period investment horizon.

Constructing Markowitz Efficient Portfolios

The technique of constructing Markowitz efficient portfolios from large groups of stocks requires a massive number of calculations. In a portfolio of G securities, there are $(G^2 - G)/2$ unique covariances to calculate. Hence, for a portfolio of just 50 securities, there are 1,224 covariances that must be calculated. For 100 securities, there are 4,950. Furthermore, in order to solve for the portfolio that minimizes risk for each level of return, a mathematical technique called *quadratic programming* (and a computer) must be used.[7] A discussion of this technique is beyond the scope of this chapter. However, it is possible to illustrate the general idea of the construction of Markowitz efficient portfolios by referring again to the simple two-asset portfolio consisting of stocks C and D.

Recall that for two assets, common stocks C and D, $E(R_C) = 10\%$, $SD(R_C) = 30\%$, $E(R_D) = 25\%$, and $SD(R_D) = 60\%$. We now further assume that $cor(R_C,R_D) = -0.5$. The expected portfolio return and standard deviation are calculated for five different proportions of C and D in the portfolio in Table 4-6. Given these available combinations of stocks C and D, it is now possible to introduce the notion of a feasible portfolio and a Markowitz efficient portfolio.

---

[7]Alternative methods that require less computer time can be used by investors who want a useful approximation to the Markowitz efficient frontier. The basic idea behind these alternative methods is that an estimated relationship between the return on a stock and some common stock market index or indexes can be used in lieu of the variance and covariance of returns. One of the approaches suggested by Sharpe uses one common stock index, and the approach is referred to as the *single-index market model*. [See William F. Sharpe, "A Simplified Model for Portfolio Analysis," *Management Science* (January 1963), pp. 277–293.] Multiple indexes have been suggested in Kalman J. Cohen and Jerry A. Pogue, "An Empirical Evaluation of Some Alternative Portfolio Selection Models," *Journal of Business* (April 1967), pp. 166–193.

TABLE 4-6
PORTFOLIO EXPECTED RETURNS AND STANDARD DEVIATIONS FOR VARYING PROPORTIONS OF STOCKS C AND D

Data for stock C: $E(R_C) = 10\%$ $SD(R_C) = 30\%$
Data for stock D: $E(R_D) = 25\%$ $SD(R_C) = 60\%$
Correlation between stock C and stock D = −0.5

Portfolio	Proportion of Stock C (w_C)	Proportion of Stock D (w_D)	$E(R_p)$	$SD(R_p)$
1	100%	0%	10.0%	30.0%
2	75	25	13.8	3.9
3	50	50	17.5	6.8
4	25	75	21.2	17.4
5	0	100	25.0	60.0

Feasible and Efficient Portfolios

A **feasible portfolio** is a portfolio that an investor can construct given the assets available. The collection of all feasible portfolios is called the **feasible set of portfolios**. With only two assets, the feasible set of portfolios is graphed as a curve that represents those combinations of risk and expected return that are attainable by constructing portfolios from the available combinations of the two assets. In Figure 4-2, the feasible set of portfolios is defined by the combinations of stocks C and D producing the $E(R_p)$ and $SD(R_p)$ given in Table 4-6, and is represented by the curve 1–5. If combinations of more than two assets were being considered, the feasible set is no longer the curved line. It would be approximated by the shaded area in Figure 4-3.

In contrast to a feasible portfolio, a Markowitz efficient portfolio is one that gives the highest expected return of all feasible portfolios with the same risk. A Markowitz efficient portfolio is also said to be a **mean-variance efficient portfolio**. Thus, for each level of risk there is a Markowitz efficient portfolio. The collection of all efficient portfolios is called the **Markowitz efficient set of portfolios**.

This can be seen graphically in Figure 4-2. Combinations of stocks C and D lie on the curve section 2–5 in the figure. These Markowitz efficient combinations of stocks C and D offer the highest expected return at a given level

FIGURE 4-2

Feasible and efficient sets of portfolios for stocks C and D.

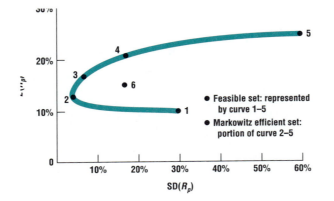

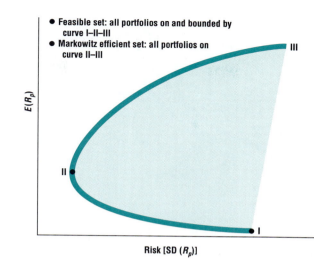

- Feasible set: all portfolios on and bounded by curve I–II–III
- Markowitz efficient set: all portfolios on curve II–III

$E(R_p)$

Risk [SD (R_p)]

FIGURE 4-3

Feasible and efficient sets of portfolios when there are more than two assets.

of risk. Notice that portfolio 1 [with $E(R_p) = 10\%$ and $SD(R_p) = 30\%$] is not included in the Markowitz efficient set, since there are three portfolios in the Markowitz efficient set (portfolios 2, 3, and 4) that have higher expected returns and lower risk levels. Portfolios to the left of section 2-3-4-5 are not attainable from combinations of stocks C and D and are, therefore, not candidates for the Markowitz efficient set. Portfolios to the right of section 2-3-4-5 are not included in the Markowitz efficient set, since there exists some other portfolio that would provide a higher expected return at the same level of risk or, alternatively, a lower level of risk at the same expected return. To see this, consider portfolio 6 in Figure 4-2. Portfolios 4 and 6 have the same level of risk, but portfolio 4 has a higher expected return. Likewise, portfolios 2 and 6 have the same expected returns, but portfolio 2 has a lower level of risk. Thus, portfolios 4 and 2 are said to dominate portfolio 6.

Figure 4-3 also shows the Markowitz efficient set. All the portfolios on the Markowitz efficient set dominate the portfolios in the shaded area.

The Markowitz efficient set of portfolios is sometimes called the **Markowitz efficient frontier**, because graphically all the Markowitz efficient portfolios lie on the boundary of the set of feasible portfolios that have the maximum return for a given level of risk. Any portfolios above the Markowitz efficient frontier cannot be achieved. Any below the Markowitz efficient frontier are dominated by portfolios on the Markowitz efficient frontier.

Choosing a Portfolio in the Markowitz Efficient Set

Now that we have constructed the Markowitz efficient set of portfolios, the next step is to determine the optimal portfolio.

An investor will want to hold one of the portfolios on the Markowitz efficient frontier. Notice that the portfolios on the Markowitz efficient frontier represent trade-offs in terms of risk and return. Moving from left to right on the Markowitz efficient frontier, the expected risk increases, but so does the expected return. The question is, which is the best portfolio to hold? The best portfolio to hold of all those on the Markowitz efficient frontier is the optimal portfolio.

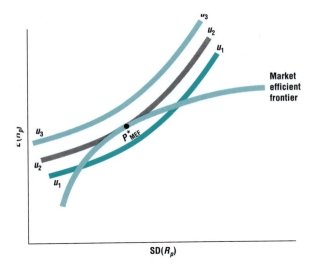

FIGURE 4-4

Selection of the optimal portfolio.

u_1, u_2, u_3 = indifference curves with $u_1 < u_2 < u_3$

P^*_{MEF} = optimal portfolio on Markowitz efficient frontier

Intuitively, the optimal portfolio should depend on the investor's preference or utility as to the trade-off between risk and return. As explained at the beginning of this chapter, this preference can be expressed in terms of a utility function.

In Figure 4-4, three indifference curves and the efficient frontier are drawn on the same diagram. In our application, the indifference curve indicates the combinations of risk and expected return that give the same level of utility. Moreover, the farther from the horizontal axis the indifference curve, the higher the utility.

From Figure 4-4, it is possible to determine the optimal portfolio for the investor with the indifference curves shown. Remember that the investor wants to get to the highest indifference curve achievable given the Markowitz efficient frontier. Given that requirement, the optimal portfolio is represented by the point where an indifference curve is tangent to the Markowitz efficient frontier. In Figure 4-4, that is the portfolio P^*_{MEF}. For example, suppose that P^*_{MEF} corresponds to portfolio 4 in Figure 4-2. From Table 4-6 we see that this portfolio is a combination of 25% of stock C and 75% of stock D, with $E(R_p)$ = 21.2% and SD(R_p) = 17.4%.

Consequently, for the investor's preferences for risk and return as determined by the shape of the indifference curves, and his or her expectations for returns and covariance of stocks C and D, portfolio 4 maximizes the utility. If this investor had a different preference for expected risk and return, there would have been a different optimal portfolio. For example, Figure 4-5 shows the same efficient frontier but three other indifference curves. In this case, the optimal portfolio is P^*_{MEF}, which has a lower expected return and risk than P^*_{MEF} in Figure 4-4.

At this point in our discussion, a natural question is how to estimate an investor's utility function so that the indifference curves can be determined. Unfortunately, there is little guidance about how to construct one. In general, economists have not been successful in measuring utility functions.

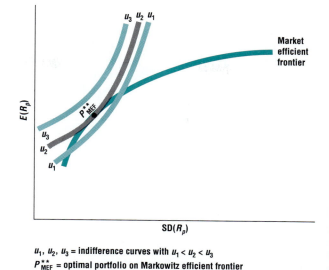

FIGURE 4-5

Selection of the optimal portfolio with different indifference curves.

u_1, u_2, u_3 = indifference curves with $u_1 < u_2 < u_3$

P^{**}_{MEF} = optimal portfolio on Markowitz efficient frontier

The inability to measure utility functions does not mean that the theory is flawed. What it does mean is that once an investor constructs the Markowitz efficient frontier, the investor will subjectively determine which Markowitz efficient portfolio is appropriate given his or her tolerance to risk.

■ SUMMARY

In this chapter we have introduced portfolio theory. Developed by Professor Harry Markowitz, this theory explains how investors should construct efficient portfolios and select the best or optimal portfolio from among all efficient portfolios. The theory differs from previous approaches to portfolio selection in that Professor Markowitz demonstrated how the key parameters should be measured. These parameters include the risk and the expected return for an individual asset and a portfolio of assets. Moreover, the concept of diversifying a portfolio, the goal of which is to reduce a portfolio's risk without sacrificing expected return, can be cast in terms of these key parameters plus the covariance or correlation between assets. All these parameters are estimated from historical data and draw from concepts in probability and statistical theory.

A portfolio's expected return is simply a weighted average of the expected return of each asset in the portfolio. The weight assigned to each asset is the market value of the asset in the portfolio relative to the total market value of the portfolio. The risk of an asset is measured by the variance or standard deviation of its return. Unlike the portfolio's expected return, a portfolio's risk is not a simple weighting of the standard deviation of the individual assets in the portfolio. Rather, the portfolio risk is affected by the covariance or correlation between the assets in the portfolio. The lower the correlation, the smaller the portfolio risk.

Markowitz has set forth the theory for the construction of an efficient portfolio, which has come to be called a Markowitz efficient portfolio, a portfolio that has the highest expected return of all feasible portfolios with the same level of risk. The collection of all Markowitz efficient portfolios is called the Markowitz efficient set of portfolios or the Markowitz efficient frontier.

The optimal portfolio is the one that maximizes an investor's preferences with respect to return and risk. An investor's preference is described by a utility function which can be represented graphically by a set of indifference curves. The utility function shows how much an investor is willing to trade off between expected return and risk. The optimal portfolio is the one where an indifference curve is tangent to the Markowitz efficient frontier.

■ KEY TERMS

efficient portfolios	indifference curve	mean-variance efficient portfolio
ex ante return	magic of diversification	naive diversification
ex post return	Markowitz diversification	optimal portfolio
expected return	Markowitz efficient frontier	risk averse
feasible portfolio	Markowitz efficient portfolios	risk-free or riskless assets
feasible set of portfolios	Markowitz efficient set of	risky asset
holding period return	portfolios	utility function

■ QUESTIONS

1. Suppose a portfolio includes four assets. The market value for each asset and the realized rate of return over some holding period are given below:

Asset	Market Value	Rate of Return
1	$15 million	11%
2	45 million	15%
3	30 million	−6%
4	10 million	1%

   Calculate the single-period rate of return for this portfolio.

2. Suppose the probability distribution for the one-period return of some asset is as follows:

Return	Probability
0.20	0.10
0.15	0.20
0.10	0.30
0.03	0.25
−0.06	0.15

   a. What is this asset's expected one-period return?

   b. What is this asset's variance and standard deviation for the one-period return?

3. What statistical measures are used in calculating the risk of an asset or a portfolio?

4. "A portfolio's expected return and variance of return are simply the weighted average of the individual asset's expected returns and variances." Do you agree with this statement?

5. Professor Harry Markowitz, corecipient of the 1990 Nobel Prize in Economics, wrote the following: "A portfolio with sixty different railway securities, for example, would not be as well diversified as the same size portfolio with some railroad, some public utility, mining, various sort of manufacturing, etc." Why is this true?

6. Two portfolio managers are discussing modern portfolio theory. Manager A states that the objective of Markowitz portfolio analysis is to construct a portfolio that maximizes expected return for a given level of risk. Manager B disagrees. He believes that the objective is to construct a portfolio that minimizes risk for a given level of return. Which portfolio manager is correct?

7. Contrast the prudent-man rule for judging individual assets with the method suggested by portfolio theory.

8. Calculate the historical rate of return for the months of January and February for the Minniefield Corporation:

Price on January 1:	$20	Cash dividends in January =	$0
Price on February 1:	$21	Cash dividends in February =	$2
Price on March 1:	$24		

9. Explain what is meant by a risk-averse investor.

10. **a.** What is meant by a Markowitz efficient frontier?

   b. Explain why all feasible portfolios are not on the Markowitz efficient frontier.

11. What is meant by an optimal portfolio, and how is it related to an efficient portfolio?

12. **a.** How does an investor select the optimal portfolio?

   b. Explain the role of an investor's preference in selecting an optimal portfolio.

13. Explain the critical role of the correlation between assets in determining the potential benefits from diversification.

14. "The maximum diversification benefits will be achieved if asset returns are perfectly correlated." Explain whether you agree or disagree with this statement.

15. Investment advisors who argue for investing in a portfolio consisting of both stocks and bonds point to the fact that the correlation of returns between these two asset classes is less than 1 and therefore there will be benefits to diversifying.

   a. What does the correlation of the returns between two asset classes measure?

   b. In what sense would a correlation of return of less than 1 between stocks and bonds suggest that there are potential diversification benefits.

16. The following excerpt is from Warren Bailey and Rene M. Stulz, "Benefits of International Diversification: The Case of Pacific Basin Stock Markets," *Journal of Portfolio Management* (Summer 1990): "Recent international diversification literature uses monthly data from foreign stock markets to make the point that American investors should hold foreign stock to reduce the variance of a portfolio of domestic stocks without reducing its expected return" (p. 57).

   a. Why would you expect that the justification of diversifying into foreign stock markets would depend on empirical evidence regarding the ability to "reduce the variance of a portfolio of domestic stocks without reducing its expected return"?

   b. Typically in research papers that seek to demonstrate the benefits of international diversification by investing in a foreign stock market, two efficient frontiers are compared. One is an efficient frontier constructed using only domestic stocks; the other is an efficient frontier constructed using both domestic and foreign stocks. If there are benefits to diversifying into foreign stocks, should the efficient frontier constructed using both domestic and foreign stocks lie above or below the efficient frontier constructed using only domestic stocks? Explain your answer.

17. The following excerpt is from John E. Hunter and T. Daniel Coggin, "An Analysis of the Diversification from International Equity Investment," *Journal of Portfolio Management* (Fall 1990):

   The extent to which investment risk can be diversified depends upon the degree to which national markets were completely dominated by a single world market factor (i.e., if all cross-national correlations were 1.00, then international diversification would have no benefit). If all national markets were completely independent (that is, if all cross-national correlations were zero), then international diversification over an infinite number of countries would completely eliminate the effect of variation in national markets. (p. 33)

   a. Why are the "cross-national correlations" critical in justifying the benefits from international diversification?

   b. Why do Hunter and Coggin argue that there would be no benefit from international diversification if these correlations are all 1.00?

18. Indicate why you agree or disagree with the following statement: "Because it is difficult to determine an investor's utility function, Markowitz portfolio theory cannot be employed in practice to construct a Markowitz efficient portfolio."

CHAPTER 5

CAPITAL MARKET THEORY AND THE
CAPITAL ASSET PRICING MODEL*

LEARNING OBJECTIVES
After reading this chapter you will be able to:

- describe the capital market line and explain the role of a risk-free asset in its construction.

- illustrate why the capital market line dominates the Markowitz efficient frontier.

- describe the security market line.

- differentiate between systematic and unsystematic risk.

- describe the capital asset pricing model, the relevant measure of risk in this model, and the limitations of the model.

- describe the market model.

- describe beta, and explain how the beta of stock and a portfolio are estimated from historical data.

- differentiate between the historical beta and fundamental beta of a stock.

- explain the empirical tests of the capital asset pricing model and the difficulties of testing this model.

Having introduced the principles of portfolio theory, we will now describe capital market theory and the implications of both that theory and portfolio theory for the pricing of financial assets. In this chapter, we focus on one well-known asset pricing model called the **capital asset pricing model (CAPM)**. In the next chapter we discuss other asset pricing models. Credit for the development of the CAPM is generally assigned to a number of individuals, including William Sharpe,[1] John Lintner,[2] Jack Treynor,[3] and Jan Mossin[4].

*This chapter is coauthored with Dr. T. Daniel Coggin of the Virginia Retirement System.

[1]William F. Sharpe, "Capital Asset Prices," *Journal of Finance* (September 1964), pp. 425–442.

[2]John Lintner, "The Valuation of Risk Assets and the Selection of Risky Investments in Stock Portfolio and Capital Budgets," *Review of Economics and Statistics* (February 1965), pp. 13–37.

[3]Jack L. Treynor, "Toward a Theory of Market Value of Risky Assets," unpublished paper, Arthur D. Little, Cambridge, MA, 1961.

[4]Jan Mossin, "Equilibrium in a Capital Asset Market," *Econometrica* (October 1966), pp. 768–783.

The asset pricing models we describe in this chapter and the next are equilibrium models. That is, given assumptions about the behavior and expectations of investors, and assumptions about capital markets, these models predict the theoretical equilibrium price of an asset. We will discuss other asset pricing models in Chapter 15.

CAPM ASSUMPTIONS

Just like the model for the selection of Markowitz efficient portfolios given in the previous chapter, capital market theory and the CAPM are abstractions of the real world and, as such, are based upon some simplifying assumptions. These assumptions simplify matters a great deal, and some of them may even seem unrealistic. However, these assumptions make the CAPM more tractable from a mathematical standpoint. The CAPM assumes (1) that investors rely on two factors in making their decisions: expected return and variance; (2) that investors are rational and risk averse and subscribe to Markowitz methods of portfolio diversification; (3) that investors all invest for the same period of time; (4) that they share all expectations about assets; (5) that there is a risk-free investment, and that investors can borrow and lend any amount at the risk-free rate; and (6) that capital markets are completely competitive and frictionless.

Two-Parameter Model

In Markowitz portfolio theory, it is assumed that investors make investment decisions based on two parameters, the expected return and the variance of returns. That is why the theory is sometimes referred to as a two-parameter model. As we noted in Chapter 4, while Markowitz used the variance of returns as a measure of risk, Markowitz himself discussed an alternative measure of risk such as the semi-variance. Other measures of downside risk have been suggested by other researchers. In any case, the model is still a two-parameter model since it would involve expected return and a single measure of risk.

Investors Are Apostles of Markowitz: Rational and Risk Averse

The two-parameter assumption tells us what investors use as inputs in making their investment decisions. Specifically, it is assumed that in order to accept greater risk, investors must be compensated by the opportunity of realizing a higher return. We referred to such investors as risk averse. This is an oversimplified definition. Actually, a more rigorous definition of risk aversion is described by a mathematical specification of an investor's utility function. However, this complexity need not be of concern here. What is important is that if an investor faces a choice between two portfolios with the same expected return, he or she will select the portfolio with the lower risk. Certainly, this is a reasonable assumption.

The CAPM also assumes that the risk-averse investor will ascribe to Markowitz's methodology of reducing portfolio risk by combining assets with counterbalancing covariances or correlations.

One-Period Investment Horizon

The CAPM assumes all investors to make investment decisions over some single-period investment horizon. How long that period is (i.e., six months, one year, two years, etc.) is not specified. In reality, the investment decision process is more complex than that, with many investors having more than one investment horizon. Nonetheless, the assumption of a one-period investment horizon is necessary to simplify the mathematics of the theory.

Homogeneous Expectations

To obtain the Markowitz efficient frontier which we will use in developing the CAPM, it was assumed that investors have the same expectations with respect to the inputs that are used to derive the efficient portfolios: asset returns, variances, and covariances. This is called the **homogeneous expectations assumption**.

Existence of a Risk-Free Asset and Unlimited Borrowing and Lending at the Risk-Free Rate

Markowitz efficient portfolios were created for portfolios consisting of risky assets. No consideration was given to how to create efficient portfolios when a risk-free asset is available. In the CAPM, it is assumed not only that there is a risk-free asset but that an investor can borrow funds at the interest paid on a risk-free rate.

Capital Market Is Perfectly Competitive and Frictionless

The previous assumptions dealt with the behavior of investors in making investment decisions. It is also necessary to make assumptions about the characteristics of the capital market in which investors transact. There are two assumptions in this regard.

First, it is assumed that the capital market is perfectly competitive. In general, this means the number of buyers and sellers is sufficiently large, and all investors are small enough relative to the market so that no individual investor can influence an asset's price. Consequently, all investors are price takers, and the market price is determined where there is equality of supply and demand.

The second assumption is that there are no transactions costs or impediments that interfere with the supply of and demand for an asset. Economists refer to these various costs and impediments as *frictions*. The costs associated with frictions generally result in buyers paying more than in the absence of frictions and/or sellers receiving less. In the case of financial markets, frictions would include commissions charged by brokers and bid-ask spreads charged by dealers. They also include taxes and government-imposed transfer fees.

CAPITAL MARKET THEORY

In the previous chapter, we distinguished between a risky asset and a risk-free asset. We described how to create Markowitz efficient portfolios from risky assets. We did not consider the possibility of constructing Markowitz efficient portfolios in the presence of a risk-free asset, that is, an asset where the return is known with certainty.

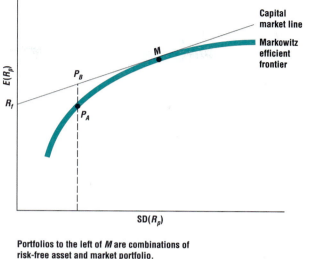

Portfolios to the left of *M* are combinations of
risk-free asset and market portfolio.

Portfolios to the right of *M* are leveraged portfolios
(borrowing at a risk-free rate to buy a market portfolio)

FIGURE 5-1

**The capital market
line.**

In the absence of a risk-free rate, portfolio theory tells us that Markowitz
efficient portfolios can be constructed based on expected return and variance
and that the optimal portfolio is the one that is tangent to the investor's indifference curve. Once a risk-free asset is introduced and assuming that investors can borrow and lend at the risk-free rate (assumption 5, above), the
conclusion of Markowitz portfolio theory can be qualified as illustrated in
Figure 5-1. Every combination of the risk-free asset and the Markowitz efficient portfolio M is shown on the **capital market line (CML)**. The line is
drawn from the vertical axis at the risk-free rate tangent to the Markowitz efficient frontier. The point of tangency is denoted by M. All the portfolios on
the capital market line are feasible for the investor to construct. Portfolios to
the left of M represent combinations of risky assets and the risk-free asset.
Portfolios to the right of M include purchases of risky assets made with funds
borrowed at the risk-free rate. Such a portfolio is called a **leveraged portfolio**
since it involves the use of borrowed funds.

Now compare a portfolio on the capital market line to the portfolio on
the Markowitz efficient frontier with the same risk. For example, compare
portfolio P_A, which is on the Markowitz efficient frontier, with portfolio P_B,
which is on the capital market line and therefore some combination of the
risk-free asset and the Markowitz efficient portfolio M. Notice that for the
same risk the expected return is greater for P_B than for P_A. A risk-averse investor will prefer P_B to P_A. That is, P_B will dominate P_A. In fact, this is true
for all but one portfolio on the line: portfolio M, which is on the Markowitz
efficient frontier.

Recognizing this, we must modify the conclusion from portfolio theory
that an investor will select a portfolio on the Markowitz efficient frontier, the
particular portfolio depending on the investor's risk preference. With the in-

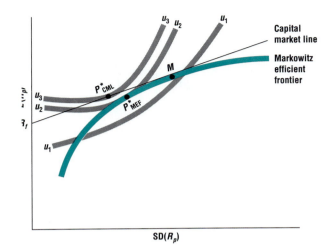

u_1, u_2, u_3 = indifference curves with $u_1 < u_2 < u_3$

M = Market portfolio

R_f = risk-free rate

P^*_{CML} = optimal portfolio on capital market line

P^*_{MEF} = optimal portfolio on Markowitz efficient frontier

FIGURE 5-2

Optimal portfolio and the capital market line.

troduction of the risk-free asset, we can now say that an investor will select a portfolio on the line, representing a combination of borrowing or lending at the risk-free rate and purchases of the Markowitz efficient portfolio M.

The particular efficient portfolio that the investor will select on the line will depend on the investor's risk preference. This can be seen in Figure 5-2, which is the same as Figure 5-1 but has the investor's indifference curves included. The investor will select the portfolio on the line that is tangent to the highest indifference curve, u_3. In the absence of a risk-free asset, it would not be possible to construct the portfolio needed to get to the indifference curve indicated by u_3. Instead, the investor could only get to u_2, which is the indifference curve that is tangent to the Markowitz efficient frontier.

It was Sharpe, Lintner, Treynor, and Mossin who demonstrated that the opportunity to borrow or lend at the risk-free rate implies a capital market where risk-averse investors will prefer to hold portfolios consisting of combinations of the risk-free asset and some portfolio M on the Markowitz efficient frontier. Sharpe called the line from the risk-free rate to portfolio M on the efficient frontier the *capital market line*, and this is the name that has been adopted in the industry.

One more key question remains: How does an investor construct portfolio M? Eugene Fama answered this question by demonstrating that M must consist of all assets available to investors, and each asset must be held in proportion to its market value relative to the total market value of all assets.[5] So, for example, if the total market value of some asset is $200 million and the total market value of all assets is $X, then the percentage of the portfolio that

---

[5]Eugene F. Fama, "Efficient Capital Markets: A Review of Theory and Empirical Work," *Journal of Finance* (May 1970), pp. 383–417.

should be allocated to that asset is $200 million divided by $X. Because portfolio M consists of all assets, it is referred to as the **market portfolio**.

Now we can restate how a risk-averse investor who makes investment decisions as suggested by Markowitz and who can borrow and lend at the risk-free rate should construct efficient portfolios. This should be done by combining an investment in the risk-free asset and the market portfolio. The theoretical result that all investors will hold a combination of the risk-free asset and the market portfolio is known as the **two-fund separation theorem**[6]—one fund consists of the risk-free asset and the other is the market portfolio. Of course, leveraged portfolios hold a negative position with respect to the risk-free asset, but they still make use of this resource. While all investors will select a portfolio on the capital market line, the optimal portfolio for a specific investor is the one that will maximize that investor's utility function.

Deriving the Formula for the Capital Market Line

Figure 5-1 shows us graphically the capital market line. But we can derive a formula for the capital market line algebraically, as well. This formula will be key in our goal of showing how a risky asset should be priced.

To derive the formula for the capital market line, we combine the two-fund separation theorem with the assumption of homogeneous expectations (assumption 4, above). Suppose an investor creates a two-fund portfolio: a portfolio consisting of w_F placed in the risk-free asset and w_M in the market portfolio, where w represents the corresponding percentage (weight) of the portfolio allocated to each asset. Thus,

$$w_F + w_M = 1 \quad \text{or} \quad w_F = 1 - w_M$$

What is the expected return and the risk of this portfolio?

As we explained in the previous chapter, the expected return is equal to the weighted average of the two assets. Therefore, for our two-fund portfolio, the expected portfolio return $E(R_p)$ is equal to

$$E(R_p) = w_F R_F + w_M E(R_M)$$

Since we know that $w_F = 1 - w_M$, we can rewrite $E(R_p)$ as follows:

$$E(R_p) = (1 - w_M)R_F + w_M E(R_M)$$

This can be simplified as follows:

$$E(R_p) = R_F + w_M[E(R_M) - R_F] \tag{5-1}$$

Now that we know the expected return of our hypothetical portfolio, we turn to the portfolio's risk as measured by the variance of the portfolio. We know from Equation (4-6) of the previous chapter how to calculate the variance of a two-asset portfolio. We repeat Equation (4-6) below:

$$\text{var}(R_p) = w_i^2 \, \text{var}(R_i) + w_j^2 \, \text{var}(R_j) + 2w_i w_j \, \text{cov}(R_i, R_j)$$

where

$\text{cov}(R_i, R_j)$ = covariance between the return for assets i and j.

[6]James Tobin, "Liquidity Preference as Behavior towards Risks," *Review of Economic Studies* (February 1958), pp. 65–86.

We can use this equation for our two-fund portfolio. Asset i in this case is the risk-free asset and asset j is the market portfolio. Then,

$$\text{var}(R_p) = w_F^2 \, \text{var}(R_F) + w_M^2 \, \text{var}(R_M) + 2w_F w_M \, \text{cov}(R_F, R_M)$$

We know that the variance of the risk-free asset, $\text{var}(R_F)$, is equal to zero. This is because there is no possible variation in the return since the future return is known. The covariance between the risk-free asset and the market portfolio, $\text{cov}(R_F, R_M)$, is zero. This is because the risk-free asset has no variability and therefore does not move at all with the return on the market portfolio which is a risky asset. Substituting these two values into the formula for the portfolio's variance, we get

$$\text{var}(R_p) = w_M{}^2 \, \text{var}(R_M)$$

In other words, the variance of the entire portfolio is represented by the weighted variance of the market portion. We can solve for the weight of the market portion by substituting standard deviations for variances.

Since the standard deviation is the square root of the variance, we can write

$$\text{SD}(R_p) = w_M \, \text{SD}(R_M)$$

and therefore

$$w_M = \frac{\text{SD}(R_p)}{\text{SD}(R_M)}$$

Now let's return to Equation (5-1) and substitute for w_M the result we just derived:

$$E(R_p) = R_F + \frac{\text{SD}(R_p)}{\text{SD}(R_M)} \, [E(R_M) - R_F]$$

Rearranging, we get

$$E(R_p) = R_F + \frac{[E(R_M) - R_F]}{\text{SD}(R_M)} \, \text{SD}(R_p) \tag{5-2}$$

Under the three assumptions stated earlier, Equation (5-2) is a straight line representing the efficient set for all risk-averse investors, which we said is the capital market line.

Interpreting the CML Formula

As we mentioned, both the capital market theory and the derivation of the Markowitz efficient frontier assume that all investors have the same expectations for the inputs into the model. With homogeneous expectations, $\text{SD}(R_M)$ and $\text{SD}(R_p)$ are the market's consensus for the expected return distributions for the market portfolio and portfolio p. The slope of the CML is

$$\frac{[E(R_M) - R_F]}{\text{SD}(R_M)}$$

Let's examine the economic meaning of the slope. The numerator is the expected return of the market beyond the risk-free return. It is a measure of the **risk premium**, or the reward for holding the risky market portfolio rather than the risk-free asset. The denominator is the risk of the market portfolio. Thus, the slope measures the reward per unit of market risk. Since the CML represents the return offered to compensate for a perceived level of risk, each point on the line is a balanced market condition, or equilibrium. The slope of the line determines the additional return needed to compensate for a unit change in risk. That is why the slope of the CML is also referred to as the **equilibrium market price of risk**.

The CML says that the expected return on a portfolio is equal to the risk-free rate plus a risk premium equal to the price of risk (as measured by the difference between the expected return on the market and the risk-free rate) times the quantity of market risk for the portfolio (as measured by the standard deviation of the portfolio). That is,

$$E(R_p) = R_F + \text{market price of risk} \times \text{quantity of market risk}$$

Deriving the CML Graphically

We derived the CML on the basis of several assumptions and simple economic principles. We can derive the same result using the graph shown in Figure 5-1. The vertical axis gives the portfolio's expected return and the horizontal axis the portfolio's standard deviation. Shown in the figure is the Markowitz efficient frontier. As we noted earlier, prior to the introduction of the risk-free asset, all that we could say is that an investor would choose one point on the Markowitz efficient frontier and that point will depend on the investor's utility. With the introduction of a risk-free asset, the investor constructs a portfolio by blending the risk-free asset and the market portfolio.

Point M in Figure 5-1 indicates a portfolio in which the investor is fully invested in the market portfolio. R_F on the vertical axis indicates a portfolio in which all the funds are fully invested in the risk-free asset. The line on which portfolio R_F and portfolio M lie is the capital market line. Each point on the line represents a portfolio consisting of different combinations of the risk-free asset and the market portfolio.

Now let's see how we get the equation for the CML from Figure 5-1. The intercept of the line (i.e., where the line intersects the vertical axis) is R_F. The slope can be determined from two points on the line. Consider the two points R_F with coordinates $(R_F, 0)$ and M with coordinates $[SD(R_M), E(R_M)]$. The slope of any line is equal to

$$\frac{\text{Difference measured on the vertical axis between two points}}{\text{Difference measured on the horizontal axis between two points}}$$

The slope of the CML is then

$$\frac{E(R_M) - R_F}{SD(R_M) - 0} = \frac{E(R_M) - R_F}{SD(R_M)}$$

The equation for the CML is then equal to

$$\text{intercept} + \text{slope } R_p$$

Substituting for the intercept and the slope the values we derived from Figure 5-1, we would get the same result as Equation (5-2).

CAPITAL ASSET PRICING MODEL

Up to this point, we know how a risk-averse investor who makes decisions based on two parameters (expected return and variance) should construct an efficient portfolio: using a combination of the market portfolio and the risk-free rate. Based on this result, we can derive a model that shows how a risky asset should be priced. In the process of doing so, we can fine-tune our thinking about the risk associated with an asset. Specifically, we can show that the appropriate risk that investors should be compensated for accepting is not the variance of an asset's return but some other quantity. In order to do this, let's take a closer look at the risk.

Systematic and Unsystematic Risk

In the development of portfolio theory, Professor Markowitz defined the variance of the rate of return as the appropriate measure of risk. However, this risk measure can be divided into two general types of risk: systematic risk and unsystematic risk.

Professor William Sharpe defined **systematic risk** as the portion of an asset's variability that can be attributed to a common factor.[7] It is also sometimes called **undiversifiable risk** or **market risk**. Systematic risk is the minimum level of risk that can be obtained for a portfolio by means of diversification across a large number of randomly chosen assets. As such, systematic risk is that which results from general market and economic conditions that cannot be diversified away.

Sharpe defined the portion of an asset's variability that can be diversified away as **unsystematic risk**. It is also sometimes called **diversifiable risk**, **unique risk, residual risk**, or **company-specific risk**. This is the risk that is unique to a company, such as a strike, the outcome of unfavorable litigation, or a natural catastrophe. As examples of this type of risk, one need only recall the case of product tampering involving Tylenol capsules (manufactured by Johnson & Johnson, Inc.) in October 1982 or the chemical accident at the Union Carbide plant in Bhopal, India, in December 1984. Both of these unforecastable and hence unexpected tragedies had negative impacts on the stock prices of the two companies involved.

How diversification reduces unsystematic risk for portfolios can be illustrated with a graph. Figure 5-3 shows that at a portfolio size of about 20 randomly selected assets (in this case, common stocks), the level of unsystematic risk is almost completely diversified away.[8] Essentially, all that is left is systematic, or market, risk.

Therefore the total risk of an asset can be measured by its variance. However, the total risk can be divided into its systematic and unsystematic risk components. Next we will show how this can be done so as to be able to quantify both components.

Market Model

The CAPM posits that there is only one factor that affects the return on a security, the market. The relationship, sometimes called the **market model** (or the **single-index model**), can be expressed as follows:

$$R_{it} = \alpha_i + \beta_i R_{Mt} + \epsilon_{it} \tag{5-3}$$

where R_{it} = return on asset i over the period t

R_{Mt} = return on the market portfolio over the period t

---

[7]William F. Sharpe, "A Simplified Model for Portfolio Analysis," *Management Science* (January 1963), pp. 277–293.

[8]Empirical evidence for Figure 5-3 is provided in Wayne H. Wagner and Sheila Lau, "The Effect of Diversification on Risks," *Financial Analysts Journal* (November–December 1971), p. 50.

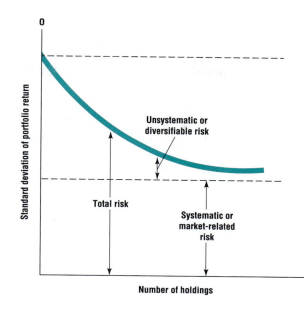

FIGURE 5-3

Systematic and unsystematic portfolio risk.

α_i = a term that represents the nonmarket component of the return on asset i

β_i = a term that relates the change in asset i's return to the change in the market portfolio

ϵ_{it} = a random error term that reflects the unique risk associated with investing in an asset

The market model says that the return on a security depends on the return on the market portfolio and the extent of the responsiveness as measured by beta (β_i). In addition, the return will also depend on conditions that are unique to the firm as measured by ϵ_{it}.

Graphical Depiction of the Market Model   Graphically, the market model can be depicted as a line fitted to a plot of asset returns against returns on the market portfolio. This is shown for a hypothetical asset in Figure 5-4. Each point represents the return of the asset and of the market portfolio during a single period of time (usually a week or month). The term β, or **beta**, is the slope of the market model for the asset, and measures the degree to which the historical returns on the asset change systematically with changes in the market portfolio's return. Hence, beta is referred to as an index of that systematic risk due to general market conditions that cannot be diversified away. For example, if a stock has a beta of 1.5, it means that, on average, on the basis of historical data, that stock had a return equal to 1.5 times that of the market portfolio's return. The beta for the market portfolio is, of course, 1.0.

The term α in the market model, popularly referred to as **alpha**, is the intercept point on the vertical axis. It is equal to the average value over time of the unsystematic returns for the stock. For most stocks, alpha tends to be small and unstable.

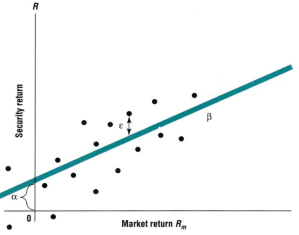

FIGURE 5-4

Graphical depiction of the market model.

Beta (β), the market sensitivity index, is the slope of the line.
Alpha (α), the average of the residual returns, is the intercept of the line on the security return axis.
Epsilon (ε), the residual returns, are the perpendicular distances of the points from the line.

Decomposing Total Risk Using the Market Model Recall from our earlier discussion, the total risk of an asset can be decomposed into market or systematic risk and unique or unsystematic risk. We can use Equation (5-3) to quantify these two risks.

To see how, let's look at the total risk of the return of asset i as measured by the variance of its return. This is done by determining the variance of Equation (5-3). We show without proof that the variance would be

$$\text{var}(R_i) = \beta_i^2 \, \text{var}(R_M) + \text{var}(\epsilon_i) \tag{5-4}$$

Equation (5-4) says that the total risk as measured by $\text{var}(R_i)$ is equal to the sum of:

(1) The market or systematic risk as measured by $\beta_i^2 \, \text{var}(R_M)$
and

(2) The unique risk as measured by $\text{var}(\epsilon_i)$

Later we explain how the market model is estimated by applying statistical techniques to historical data on returns. Table 5-1 gives estimates of beta using historical data plus systematic and unsystematic risk for 30 stocks estimated from 60 months of return data prior to July 31, 1992. For the values reported in Table 5-1, the Standard & Poor's 500 (which is a broad market index) was used as a surrogate for the return on the market portfolio.

Another product of the statistical technique used to estimate beta is the percentage of systematic risk to total risk. In statistical terms, it is measured by the **coefficient of determination** from the regression, which indicates the percentage of the variation in the return of the asset explained by the market portfolio return. The value of the coefficient ranges from 0 to 1. For example, a coefficient of determination of 0.3 for an asset means that 30% of the varia-

TABLE 5-1			
MARKET MODEL STATISTICS FOR 30 STOCKS (JULY 31, 1992)			
Stocks	Beta	Systematic Risk	Unsystematic Risk
Allied Signal	1.00	0.42	0.58
Alcoa	1.08	0.42	0.58
American Express	1.22	0.44	0.56
American Telephone	0.80	0.37	0.63
Bethlehem Steel	1.44	0.36	0.64
Boeing	1.15	0.49	0.51
Caterpillar	0.96	0.28	0.72
Chevron	0.70	0.30	0.70
Coca-Cola	0.95	0.53	0.47
Disney	1.26	0.59	0.41
DuPont	1.13	0.60	0.40
Eastman Kodak	0.76	0.37	0.63
Exxon	0.58	0.42	0.58
General Electric	1.18	0.72	0.28
General Motors	1.00	0.37	0.63
Goodyear	1.10	0.24	0.76
IBM	0.73	0.30	0.70
International Paper	1.19	0.54	0.46
McDonald's	0.96	0.51	0.49
Merck	0.84	0.49	0.51
Minnesota Mining	0.91	0.58	0.42
J.P. Morgan	1.15	0.48	0.52
Philip Morris	1.00	0.51	0.49
Procter & Gamble	0.87	0.47	0.53
Sears	1.15	0.58	0.42
Texaco	0.61	0.25	0.75
Union Carbide	0.93	0.18	0.82
United Technologies	1.38	0.74	0.26
Westinghouse	1.15	0.47	0.53
Woolworth	1.27	0.46	0.54

Note: Values estimated from 60 months of returns prior to 7/31/92.

Source: Merrill Lynch Security Evaluation Service

tion in the return of that asset is explained by the return of the market portfolio. Unsystematic or unique risk is then the amount not explained by the market portfolio's return. That is, it is 1 minus the coefficient of determination.

Studies have shown that for the average New York Stock Exchange (NYSE) common stock, systematic risk is about 30% of return variance, while unsystematic risk is about 70%. In contrast, the coefficient of determination for a well-diversified portfolio of stocks will typically exceed 90%, indicating that unsystematic risk is less than 10% of total portfolio return variance. This supports the point made in Figure 5-3 that with a well-diversified portfolio, most of the portfolio risk is systematic risk.

The Security Market Line

The capital market line represents an equilibrium condition in which the expected return on a *portfolio* of assets is a linear function of the expected return on the market portfolio. A directly analogous relationship holds for *individual security* expected returns:

$$E(R_i) = R_F + \frac{[E(R_M) - R_F]}{SD(R_M)} SD(R_i) \tag{5-5}$$

Formula (5-5) simply uses risk and return variables for an individual security in place of the portfolio values in the formula for the CML (5-2). This version of the risk-return relationship for individual securities is called the **security market line (SML)**. As in the case of the CML, the expected return for an asset is equal to the risk-free rate plus the product of the market price of risk and the quantity of risk in the security.

Another more common version of the SML relationship uses the beta of a security. To see how this relationship is developed, look back at Equation (5-4). In a well-diversified portfolio (i.e., Markowitz diversified), the unique risk is eliminated. Consequently, Equation (5-4) can be rewritten as

$$var(R_i) = \beta_i^2 \, var(R_M)$$

and the standard deviation as

$$SD(R_i) = \beta_i \, SD(R_M)$$

Therefore,

$$\beta_i = \frac{SD(R_i)}{SD(R_M)}$$

If β_i is substituted into Equation (5-5), we have the beta version of the SML or capital asset pricing model, as shown in Equation (5-6):

$$E(R_i) = R_F + \beta_i[E(R_M) - R_F] \tag{5-6}$$

This equation states that, given the assumptions of the CAPM, the expected (or required) return on an individual asset is a positive linear function of its index of systematic risk as measured by beta. The higher the beta, the higher the expected return. Notice that it is only an asset's beta that determines its expected return.

Let's look at the prediction of the CAPM for several values of beta. The beta of a risk-free asset is zero, because the variability of the return for a risk-free asset is zero and therefore it does not covary with the market portfolio. So if we want to know the expected return for a risk-free asset, we would substitute zero for β_i in Equation (5-6):

$$E(R_i) = R_F + 0[E(R_M) - R_F] = R_F$$

Thus, the return on a risk-free asset is simply the risk-free return. Of course, this is what we expect.

The beta of the market portfolio is 1. If asset i has the same beta as the market portfolio, then substituting 1 into Equation (5-6) gives

$$E(R_i) = R_F + 1[E(R_M) - R_F] = E(R_M)$$

In this case, the expected return for the asset is the same as the expected return for the market portfolio. If an asset has a beta greater than the market portfolio (i.e., greater than 1), then the expected return will be higher than for the market portfolio. The reverse is true if an asset has a beta less than the market portfolio. A graph of the SML is presented in Figure 5-5.

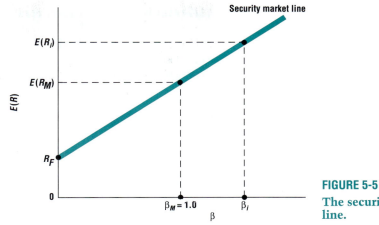

FIGURE 5-5

The security market line.

The SML and Market Risk   In equilibrium, the expected return of individual securities will lie on the SML and *not* on the CML. This is true because of the high degree of unsystematic risk that remains in individual securities that can be diversified out of portfolios of securities.

It follows that the only risk that investors will pay a premium to avoid is market risk. Hence, two assets with the same amount of systematic risk will have the same expected return. In equilibrium, only efficient portfolios will lie on both the CML and the SML. This underscores the fact that the systematic risk measure, beta, is most correctly considered as an *index* of the contribution of an individual security to the systematic risk of a well-diversified portfolio of securities.

The SML and Covariance   There is one more version of the SML that is worthwhile to discuss. In estimating beta for an asset using the statistical technique described in Appendix A, it turns out that the estimate is as follows:

$$\beta_i = \frac{\text{cov}(R_i, R_M)}{\text{var}(R_M)} \tag{5-7}$$

Substituting Equation (5-7) for β_i in the beta version of the SML given by Equation (5-6) results in another version of the SML:

$$E(R_i) = R_F + \frac{\text{cov}(R_i, R_m)}{\text{var}(R_m)}\,[E(R_M) - R_F] \tag{5-8}$$

This version of the SML emphasizes that it is not the variance or standard deviation of an asset that affects its return. It is the *covariance* of the asset's return with the market's return that affects its return. An asset that has a positive covariance will have a higher expected return than the risk-free asset; an asset with a negative covariance will have a lower expected return than the risk-free asset. The reason has to do with the benefits of diversification we discussed in the previous chapter. If the covariance is positive, this increases the risk of an asset in a portfolio and therefore investors will only purchase that asset if they expect to earn a return higher than the risk-free asset. If an asset has a negative covariance, recall from the previous chapter that this will reduce the portfolio risk and investors would be willing to accept a return less than the risk-free asset.

SML, CML, and the Market Model It is important to point out the difference between the market model and the CML and SML. The CML and the SML represent an *ex ante*, or predictive, model for expected returns. The market model is an *ex post*, or descriptive, model used to describe historical data. Hence, the market model makes no prediction of what expected returns should be.

Estimating Beta

As previously discussed, beta is an index of systematic risk for an individual asset or a portfolio of assets. It measures the sensitivity of asset returns to the return on the market portfolio. Hence, betas for individual assets or portfolios can be directly compared with betas for other assets or portfolios. The theoretical (ex ante) beta from the CAPM has been defined as essentially a measure of the expected covariance of an asset with the market portfolio, in the context of a well-diversified portfolio of assets. Now we turn to the complicated task of estimating the historical (ex post) beta for an individual stock.

Estimating Historical Beta For individual assets, the historical (or ex post) beta is estimated using a times series of the returns on the asset and returns of the market portfolio. The statistical technique used is regression analysis, which estimates the relationship between two variables. In our case, the two variables are the return on the asset whose beta we seek to estimate and the return on the market portfolio. In estimating beta, the proxy for the market portfolio is some stock market index. The stock market index typically used is the Standard & Poor's 500.

Historical beta is then estimated using the market model as follows

$$r_{it} = \alpha_i + \beta_i\, r_{Mt} + \epsilon_{it} \tag{5-9}$$

where r_{it} = return on asset i over the period t
r_{Mt} = return on the market portfolio over the period t
α_i = a term that represents the nonmarket component of the return on asset i
β_i = a term that relates the change in asset i's return to the change in the market portfolio
ϵ_{it} = a zero mean random error term

Equation (5-9) is popularly referred to as the **characteristic line** of a security.

In Appendix A, we show how to calculate the beta for IBM and Walgreen using the 60-month returns from January 1989 to December 1993 given in Table 4-4 of the previous chapter. The proxy used for the market portfolio is the S&P 500. The monthly returns for the S&P 500 for the same period are given in Appendix A. The regression results are summarized below:

Company	Alpha	Beta	Coefficient of Determination
IBM	−1.08	0.57	0.15
Walgreen	0.68	1.11	0.38

There are tests that are used to determine if the estimated values for alpha and beta are statistically significant. A discussion of these tests is beyond the scope of this chapter. We'll just report the results of these tests. The alpha for IBM and Walgreen is not significantly different from zero. This supports what we said earlier, that alpha is typically small. The beta for both companies is statistically significant, which means that there is a relationship between the return on each stock and the return on the S&P 500. The coefficient of determination indicates the strength of the relationship.

While we explained how to estimate the historical beta for a stock, the historical beta for a portfolio can also be determined. For a portfolio of G assets (β_p), the historical beta is simply a weighted average of the observed historical betas for the individual assets (β_i) in the portfolio, where the weight is the percentage of the market asset of the individual asset relative to the total market value of the portfolio. That is,

$$\beta_p = \sum_{i=1}^{G} w_i \beta_i$$

So, for example, the historical beta for a portfolio consisting of 30% of IBM (w_1) and 70% of Walgreen (w_2) is as shown below:

$$0.30\ (0.57) + 0.70\ (1.11) = 0.95$$

Beta Stability The most serious problem for the estimation of common stock betas is the fact that they are not stable; that is, beta coefficients change over time. There are at least two sources of beta instability. The first is statistical estimation error, having to do with such things as the length of the time interval over which returns are measured (e.g., daily, monthly, or quarterly). For example, monthly returns can be calculated for the past five years; thus, there would be 60 return observations for both the market index and the stock. Or weekly returns can be calculated for the past year. Nothing in the theory indicates whether weekly, monthly, or even daily returns should be used. Nor does theory indicate any specific number of observations, except that statistical methodology requires that more observations will give a more reliable measure of beta.[9]

Research has shown that stock returns vary in the speed at which they react to new information, with large-capitalization stocks reacting more quickly. Hence, there can be an interval bias in beta estimation relating to the time interval over which betas are estimated. While betas estimated for individual stocks are characteristically unstable, betas estimated for portfolios of stocks tend to be relatively more stable over ti me.

Another source of apparent beta instability has to do with the use of beta as a single index of systematic risk. As evidenced in the discussion on multi-index models in Chapter 15, common stocks have been shown to have multiple sources of systematic risk. Hence, any single risk measure that attempts to aggregate all sources of systematic risk can appear to be unstable when it encompasses one or more of the macroeconomic or microeconomic sources of systematic risk that are changing. For example, assume oil prices were a macroeconomic source of systematic risk. When the level of oil price expectations changes, all other factors remaining constant, stocks that are more sensitive to oil price expectations would react, while other stocks with the same single-index beta would not. If beta were used as the systematic risk measure, those stocks that reacted to changes in oil price expectations would

---

[9]This assumes that the economic determinants that affect the beta of a stock do not change over the measurement period.

appear to be unstable when they were actually reacting to but one of the systematic risk factors included in the traditional single-index beta. In this example, the stocks that did not react to changes in oil price expectations would appear stable. Thus, if betas are to be useful in a predictive sense, they must be updated frequently.

Adjustments to Historical Beta   Marshall Blume found that portfolio betas tend to regress toward 1.0 over time.[10] The economic logic is that the underlying riskiness of a firm tends to move toward the riskiness of the average firm. His research indicates that the following adjustment may produce a more accurate forecast beta for stock i:

$$\beta_{2i} = a + b\,\beta_{1i}$$

where β_{2i} and β_{1i} are historical betas for periods seven years apart, with β_{1i} being the earlier estimate. The parameters a and b are estimated by regression analysis and used to calculate the following:

$$\beta_{3i} = a + b\,\beta_{2i}$$

where β_{3i} is the *forecast* beta for stock i.

Two commercial vendors of beta estimates, Merrill Lynch and Value Line, currently use this method to estimate forecast betas.

Vasicek has proposed a different adjustment procedure based upon the sampling error (uncertainty) for each common stock beta estimate.[11] While Vasicek's adjustment slightly outperforms Blume's in terms of forecast accuracy, both methods outperform the unadjusted historical beta.

Some investment organizations allow investment analysts to adjust historical betas subjectively based upon their outlook for the individual firms in question. Several other researchers have suggested modifications to the beta estimation procedure that are applicable to stocks that are infrequently traded. Recent work has shown that, on average, the predictive ability of beta is inversely related to the length of the investment horizon and directly related to portfolio size, adjustments notwithstanding.

Fundamental Beta   A great deal of attention has recently been given to the development of a beta that takes explicit account of the fundamental characteristics of the firm, as well as its covariance with the market portfolio. A number of researchers have dealt with this topic. However, the best-known example of a fundamental beta was developed by Barr Rosenberg and some colleagues when he taught at the University of California at Berkeley.[12]

The basic idea of the fundamental beta is that, in addition to the single measure of the historical covariance of an asset with the market, other sources of systematic risk are related to the fundamental characteristics of the firm. Rosenberg and his later associates at BARRA (a consulting firm) made some changes to the variables in his original equation. A recent version includes 58 variables categorized into 13 groups, or *risk indices*, as Rosenberg

[10]Marshall E. Blume, "On the Assessment of Risk," *Journal of Finance* (March 1971), pp. 1–10.

[11]Oldrich A. Vasicek, "A Note on Using Cross-Sectional Information in Bayesian Estimation of Security Betas," *Journal of Finance* (December 1973), pp. 1233–1239.

[12]Barr Rosenberg and James Guy, "Prediction of Systematic Risk from Investment Fundamentals, Part I and II," *Financial Analysts Journal* (May–June 1976 and July–Aug 1976).

calls them. These include variability in markets, success, size, trading activity, growth, earnings-price ratio, book-price ratio, earnings variation, financial leverage, foreign income, labor intensity, yield, and low capitalization. The details of the most recent estimation of Rosenberg's fundamental beta system are proprietary. However, Rosenberg does claim that his system produces a better estimate of future beta than historical beta alone. Several firms offer such estimates on a commercial basis.

TESTS OF THE CAPM

The number of articles found under the general heading "tests of the CAPM" is impressive. One bibliographic compilation lists almost 1,000 papers on the topic. Consequently, only the basic results are given here. (See Box 5.)

Methodology

In general, a methodology referred to as **two-pass regression** is used to test the CAPM. The first pass involves the estimation of beta for each security by means of the time-series regression described by Equation (5-9). The betas from the first-pass regression are then used to form portfolios of securities ranked by portfolio beta. The portfolio returns, the return on the risk-free asset, and the portfolio betas are then used to estimate the second-pass, cross-sectional regression:

$$R_p - R_F = b_0 + b_1 \beta_p + e_p \tag{5-10}$$

where the parameters to be estimated are b_0 and b_1, and e_p is the error term for the regression. The return data are frequently aggregated into five-year periods for this regression.

Equation (5-10) is the empirical analogue of the equation for the CAPM. To see this, the CAPM can be rewritten as follows by subtracting R_F from both sides of Equation (5-6):

$$E(R_p) - R_F = \beta_p[E(R_M) - R_F] \tag{5-11}$$

Equation (5-11) is the CAPM in "risk-premium form" because the value on the left-hand side of the equation is the portfolio's expected return over the risk-free rate. By adding an error term to Equation (5-11) and a constant term, b_0, Equation (5-11) becomes

$$E(R_p) - R_F = b_0 + \beta_p[E(R_M) - R_F] + e_p \tag{5-12}$$

The actual process of testing the CAPM using the two-pass regression methodology involves the consideration of some econometric problems (e.g., measurement error, correlated error terms, and beta instability) that are beyond the scope of the chapter.[13]

Assuming that the capital market can be described as one in which there is no opportunity for investors to use information from previous periods to

---

[13]The interested reader should consult Merton H. Miller and Myron S. Scholes, "Rates of Return in Relation to Risk," in Michael C. Jensen (ed.), *Studies in the Theory of Capital Markets* (New York: Praeger, 1972); Eugene F. Fama, *Foundations of Finance* (New York: Basic Books, 1976); Richard Roll, "Performance Evaluation and Benchmark Errors II," *Journal of Portfolio Management* (Winter 1981), pp. 17–22; and Richard Roll, "A Critique of the Asset Pricing Theory's Tests," *Journal of Financial Economics* (March 1977), pp. 129–176, for a discussion of these issues.

BOX 5

IS THIS THE NIGHT OF THE LIVING BETA?

In July 1980 *Institutional Investor* asked the controversial—albeit esoteric—question, "Is beta dead?" The answer: Not yet, though it certainly was under attack at the time. Nonetheless, the influence of beta—a measure of a stock's price volatility relative to the market's—would mushroom in the 1980s as it became accepted in finance classes and boardrooms as financial orthodoxy.

So here it is 1992, and beta is reportedly on its deathbed once again. This time the most devastating blow has been struck by the University of Chicago's Eugene Fama and Kenneth French, whose recent study argues that long-term equity returns depend not on beta but on far more mundane factors, such as a company's size or its book-to-market ratio.*

In fact, Fama and French conclude that the commonly accepted relationship between beta and return doesn't exist at all. Says Fama, whose earlier work provided part of beta's empirical underpinning: "People have found that the [correlation between higher betas

and higher returns] is much flatter than expected by CAPM. We've found it to be *completely* flat."

The tangled tale of beta begins with Harry Markowitz. In his 1952 doctoral dissertation at the University of Chicago, Markowitz showed that the covariance among stocks in a portfolio (the correlation of returns) can be used to achieve maximum return for the degree of risk being taken on. Markowitz used a technique called mean-variance analysis to construct an "efficient" portfolio—one that provides the highest return for a given level of risk.

Markowitz's work paved the way for the development of the capital asset pricing model in the mid-1960s by Stanford University's William Sharpe and others. CAPM was designed to predict the expected return for an individual stock or portfolio by adding risk-free return, usually the rate on short-term Treasuries, to risk-adjusted market return. The latter is calculated by multiplying the average market return by the beta for that stock or portfolio.

Beta measures systematic—that is, market—risk. (Theorists assume that unsystematic risk, which results from factors unique to a particular company, can be eliminated through portfolio diversification.) If a stock's price is more volatile than the overall market, it will have a beta greater than 1; if it's less volatile, the beta will be less than 1. According to CAPM, a high-beta stock has a greater expected return than a low-beta stock. . . .

Almost from their birth, beta and CAPM have been intensely debated. "I was saying fifteen years ago that you shouldn't necessarily expect to find any relation between beta and expected return," says Richard Roll, a finance professor at the University of California at Los Angeles. "CAPM requires the true market index to be Markowitz-efficient [that is, to have minimum variance for its expected return]; then it follows mathematically. The trouble is that no truly Markowitz-efficient market index has ever been used to test CAPM." The true market index, adds Roll, "should

---

earn abnormal returns, several testable hypotheses for the empirical analogue of the CAPM can be listed.

1. The relationship between beta and return should be linear.
2. The intercept term b_0 should not differ significantly from zero. This can be seen by comparing Equations (5-11) and (5-12).:
3. The coefficient for beta, b_1, should equal the risk premium $(R_M - R_F)$. Once again, this can be seen by comparing Equations (5-11) and (5-12).
4. Beta should be the only factor that is priced by the market. That is, other factors such as the variance or standard deviation of the returns, and variables that we will discuss in later chapters such as the price-earnings ratio, dividend yield, and firm size, should not add any significant explanatory power to the equation.
5. Over long periods of time, the rate of return on the market portfolio should be greater than the return on the risk-free asset. This is because the market portfolio has more risk than the risk-free asset. Hence, risk-averse investors would price it so as to generate a greater return.

Results

The general results of the empirical tests of the CAPM are as follows:

1. The relationship between beta and return appears to be linear; hence the functional form of Equation (5-11) seems to be correct.

BOX 5

IS THIS THE NIGHT OF THE LIVING BETA (Continued)

include all the assets in the world," which would be all but impossible.

Although the Fama-French study crunched data that includes all nonfinancial shares traded on the New York Stock Exchange, the American Stock Exchange and Nasdaq between 1963 and 1990, it still failed to achieve a Markowitz-efficient market index, according to Roll. His conclusion: The paper proves nothing.

Case closed? Hardly. Fischer Black, co-inventor (with Myron Scholes) of the option pricing theory and a partner at Goldman, Sachs & Co., disagrees with Roll. To Black, people have focused so much effort on finding holes in CAPM that they have begun "data mining." "If you dig long enough," he explains, "you'll find almost any results you want." Adds Black: "There's no evidence that beta is not a good measure of risk. The only question is whether it is a good indicator of expected return."

In fact, Black argues, Fama-French's conclusions have been in the literature for years. Black himself published a study in 1972 with Scholes and then-University of Rochester professor Michael Jensen in which they showed that the actual return of stocks was flatter than expected under CAPM.

Still, the conventional wisdom about beta lives on. "We've kind of always known that beta was not an adequate measure of risk [vis-à-vis return]," says Fama, "but we've simply never faced it." Stanford's Sharpe, who calls the work of Fama and French "a neatly done study," admits that "if you reject the idea that beta is relevant for return, then you would reject CAPM too." However, he adds, "I wouldn't. I don't like going into the world without some theory."

Despite all this theoretical jousting, most finance professors will continue to teach beta and CAPM. "It's taught because it's the simplest form of a theory that gives a relation between risk and return—not because it's correct," says Roll. "Everybody agrees that there's a relation between risk and return; they disagree about how to incorporate it into a model. Teaching starts with CAPM and goes on to a multifactor model for measuring risk, such as the arbitrage pricing theory." APT, which calculates expected return by incorporating several dimensions of systematic risk, including inflation and interest rates, was developed in 1976 by Yale University economist Stephen Ross and quickly championed by Roll.† . . .

* These other factors are described in Chapter 14.

† This theory is the subject of the next chapter.

Source: Adapted from Michael Peltz, "Is This the Night of the Living Beta?" *Institutional Investor* (June 1992), pp. 42–43.

Questions for Box 5

1. What is the relationship between expected return and beta predicted by the CAPM?
2. Explain why "According to CAPM, a high-beta stock has a greater expected return than a low-beta stock."
3. Why might beta not be an adequate measure of risk?

2. The estimated intercept term b_0, is significantly different from zero and consequently different from what is hypothesized for this value.

3. The estimated coefficient for beta, b_1, is less than $R_M - R_F$. The combination of results 2 and 3 suggests that low beta stocks have higher returns than the CAPM predicts and high beta stocks have lower returns than the CAPM predicts.

4. Beta is not the only factor priced by the market. Several studies have discovered other factors that explain stock returns. These include a price-earnings factor,[14] a dividend factor,[15] a firm-size factor,[16] and both a firm-size factor and a book-market factor.[17]

5. Over long periods of time (usually 20 to 30 years), the return on the market portfolio is greater than the risk-free rate.

---

[14]See Sanjoy Basu,"Investment Performance of Common Stocks in Relation to Their Price-Earnings Ratios," *Journal of Finance* (June 1977), pp. 663–682, and "The Relationship between Earnings' Yield, Market Value and Return for NYSE Common Stocks," *Journal of Financial Economics* (June 1983), pp. 129–156.

[15]Robert Litzenberger and Krishna Ramaswamy, "The Effect of Personal Taxes and Dividends on Capital Asset Prices," *Journal of Financial Economics* (June 1979), pp. 163–195.

[16]Rolf Banz, "The Relationship between Return and Market Value of Common Stocks," *Journal of Financial Economics* (March 1981), pp. 3–18.

[17]Eugene Fama and Kenneth French, "The Cross-Section of Expected Returns," *Journal of Finance* (June 1992), pp. 427–465.

A Critique of Tests of the CAPM

One of the most controversial papers written on the CAPM is Richard Roll's "A Critique of the Asset Pricing Theory's Tests."[18] We will discuss the major points of Roll's argument here.

Following Roll's argument, the CAPM is a general equilibrium model based upon the existence of a market portfolio that is defined as the value-weighted portfolio of all investment assets. Furthermore, the market portfolio is defined to be ex ante mean-variance efficient. This means that the market portfolio lies on the ex ante Markowitz efficient frontier for all investors. Roll demonstrates that the only true test of the CAPM is whether the market portfolio is in fact ex ante mean-variance efficient. However, the *true* market portfolio is, in fact, ex ante mean-variance efficient since it includes all investment assets (e.g., stocks, bonds, real estate, art objects, and human capital).

The consequences of this "non-observability" of the true market portfolio are:

1. Tests of the CAPM are extremely sensitive to which market proxy is used, even though returns on most market proxies (e.g., the S&P 500 and the NYSE index) are highly correlated.
2. A researcher cannot unambiguously discern whether the CAPM failed a test because the true market portfolio was ex ante mean-variance inefficient or because the market proxy was inefficient. Alternatively, the researcher cannot unambiguously discern whether a test supported the CAPM because the true market portfolio was ex ante mean-variance efficient or because the market proxy was efficient.
3. The effectiveness of variables such as dividend yield in explaining risk-adjusted asset returns is evidence that the market proxies used to test the CAPM are not ex ante mean-variance efficient.

Hence, Roll submits that the CAPM is not testable until the exact composition of the true market portfolio is known, and the only valid test of the CAPM is to observe whether the ex ante true market portfolio is mean-variance efficient. As a result of his findings, Roll states that he does not believe there ever will be an unambiguous test of the CAPM. He does not say that the CAPM is invalid. Rather, Roll says that there is likely to be no unambiguous way to test the CAPM and its implications due to the non-observability of the true market portfolio and its characteristics.

Does this mean that the CAPM is useless to the financial practitioner? The answer is no, it does not. What it means is that the implications of the CAPM should be viewed with caution.

THEORETICAL ISSUES

At the outset of this chapter, we described the assumptions underlying the CAPM. Theorists have relaxed some of these assumptions either to derive modified versions of the CAPM or to reach conclusions about the validity of the model. In the next chapter, we will discuss two extensions of the CAPM,

---

[18]Roll, "A Critique of the Asset Pricing Theory's Tests," op. cit.

as well as an alternative theory of asset pricing. Here we will just point out the conclusions of two important theoretical works on what happens if the assumptions are relaxed.

First, consider the homogeneous expectations assumption (i.e., all investors have identical expectations for asset returns, variances, and covariances). The basic problem created by allowing heterogeneous expectations is that expected asset returns, variances, and covariances become complex weighted averages of individual expectations. John Lintner has examined the consequences of allowing heterogeneous expectations and has concluded that the general form of the original CAPM would still hold.[19] However, there would exist a market portfolio that is *not* necessarily efficient. The existence of heterogeneous expectations makes the CML and the SML fuzzy. The more investor expectations differ, the more uncertain predictions concerning expected asset returns become.

Stephen Ross investigated the question of the existence of a risk-free asset.[20] He found that in the absence of a risk-free asset, the pure CAPM is invalid. He also found that if there are restrictions on short selling, the CAPM is invalid. As we will discuss, one of the extensions of the CAPM described in the next chapter makes an assumption about short selling.

■ SUMMARY

This chapter explains the implications of portfolio theory, a theory that deals with the construction of Markowitz efficient portfolios by rational risk-averse investors. Once a risk-free asset is introduced, the new efficient frontier is the capital market line which represents a combination of a risk-free asset and the market portfolio.

The capital asset pricing model is an economic theory that describes the relationship between risk and expected return, or, equivalently, it is a model for the pricing of risky securities. The CAPM asserts that the only risk that is priced by rational investors is systematic risk, because that risk cannot be eliminated by diversification. Essentially, the CAPM says that the expected return of a security or a portfolio is equal to the rate on a risk-free security plus a risk premium. The risk premium in the CAPM is the product of the quantity of risk times the market price of risk.

The beta of a security or portfolio is an index of the systematic risk of the asset and is measured statistically. Historical beta is calculated from a time series of observations on both the asset's return and the market portfolio's return. This assumed relationship is called the characteristic line and is not an equilibrium model for predicting expected return, but rather a description of historical data. Another way to estimate beta is the fundamental beta approach. The basic idea of the fundamental beta is that other sources of systematic risk are related to the fundamental characteristics of the firm in addition to the single measure of the historical covariance of an asset with the market.

There have been numerous empirical tests of the CAPM, and in general, these have failed to fully support the theory. Richard Roll has criticized these studies because of the difficulty of identifying the true market portfolio. Furthermore, Roll asserts that such tests are not likely to appear soon, if at all.

---

[19]John Lintner, "The Aggregation of Investor's Diverse Judgements in Purely Competitive Security Markets," *Journal of Financial and Quantitative Analysis* (December 1969), pp. 347–400.
[20]Stephen S. Ross, "The Capital Asset Pricing Model (CAPM), Short Sales Restrictions and Related Issues," *Journal of Finance* (March 1977), pp. 177–184.

■ KEY TERMS

alpha
beta
capital asset pricing model
   (CAPM)
capital market line (CML)
characteristic line
coefficient of determination
company-specific risk
diversifiable risk

equilibrium market price of risk
homogeneous expectations
   assumption
leveraged portfolio
market model
market portfolio
market risk
residual risk
risk premium

security market line (SML)
single-index model
systematic risk
two-fund separation theorem
two-pass regression
undiversifiable risk
unique risk
unsystematic risk

■ QUESTIONS

1. **a.** Explain how the capital market line is constructed on a graph.
   b. Explain why the capital market line assumes that there is a risk-free asset and that investors can borrow or lend at the risk-free rate.
   c. Using a graph, demonstrate why the capital market line dominates the Markowitz efficient frontier.

2. How should an investor construct an efficient portfolio in the presence of a risk-free asset?

3. Would all investors invest in the same efficient portfolio? If not, what will determine the efficient portfolio that an investor will select?

4. **a.** What is meant by a two-fund separation?
   b. What do the two funds consist of?

5. Indicate why you agree or disagree with the following statement: "As a percentage of the total risk, the unsystematic risk of a diversified portfolio is greater than that of an individual asset."

6. Why is systematic risk also called market risk?

7. How many securities does it typically take to eliminate most unsystematic risk from a portfolio?

8. Indicate why you agree or disagree with the following statement: "An investor should be compensated for accepting unsystematic risk."

9. In the January 25, 1991, issue of *The Value Line Investment Survey*, you note the following:

Company	Beta
IBM	0.95
Bally Manufacturing	1.40
Cigna Corp.	1.00
British Telecom	0.60

   a. How do you interpret these betas?
   b. Is it reasonable to assume that the expected return on British Telecom is less than that on IBM shares?

   c. "Given that Cigna Corporation has a beta of 1.00, one can mimic the performance of the stock market as a whole by buying only these shares." Do you agree with this statement?
   d. Suppose you picked up *The Value Line Investment Survey* from 10 years ago. Would you expect the beta values for these companies to be the same as given above? Why or why not?

10. **a.** What is the market model, and how is it estimated?
    b. What input into the CAPM is estimated from the market model?

11. Assume the following:

    Expected market return = 15%
    Risk-free rate = 7%

    If a security's beta is 1.3, what is its expected return according to the CAPM?

12. What are the causes of the instability of beta?

13. What is meant by a fundamental beta?

14. Following is an excerpt from an article, "Risk and Reward," in *The Economist* of October 20, 1990:

    [I]s the CAPM supported by the facts? That is controversial, to put it mildly. It is a tribute to Mr. Sharpe [cowinner of the 1990 Nobel Prize in Economics] that his work, which dates from the early 1960s, is still argued over so heatedly. Attention has lately turned away from beta to more complicated ways of carving up risk. But the significance of CAPM for financial economics would be hard to exaggerate.

    a. What are the general conclusions of studies that have empirically investigated the CAPM?
    b. Summarize Roll's argument on the problems inherent in empirically verifying the CAPM.

CHAPTER 6
OTHER ASSET PRICING MODELS

LEARNING OBJECTIVES
After reading this chapter you will be able to:

- describe Black's version of the zero-beta CAPM.

- discuss the critical assumptions underlying the zero-beta CAPM and the implications for the model.

- explain the motivation behind the development of Merton's multifactor CAPM.

- describe the multifactor CAPM and the difficulties in applying it.

- define what is meant by arbitrage.

- illustrate the fundamental principles underlying the arbitrage pricing theory model.

- explain the empirical difficulties in testing the arbitrage pricing theory model and the difficulty in applying this model.

- identify the factors that researchers have found appear to affect the return on securities.

- explain the difficulty of empirically distinguishing between the multifactor CAPM and the APT model.

- discuss some fundamental investment principles concerning risk and return that are valid regardless of the asset pricing model used.

In the previous chapter we described the seminal economic theory regarding the equilibrium price of a financial asset, the capital asset pricing model (CAPM). We pointed out that several underlying assumptions of the CAPM oversimplify the real world and therefore are unrealistic. However, in developing an economic theory, it is quite common that financial economists begin with a simple set of assumptions. Then three things happen in the evolution of a theory. First, researchers will empirically test the model for its validity. Second, theorists will relax the assumptions to determine whether the conclusion of the theory is still valid or to what extent the conclusion must be modified. Third, an alternative model is offered.

In discussing the CAPM, we provided a brief review of the empirical evidence. A fair conclusion is that the empirical evidence does not support the theory. However, the validity of the empirical tests has been questioned by Richard Roll, and it appears that it will be extremely unlikely that the CAPM is testable.

In this chapter we will discuss extensions of the CAPM derived by modifying its assumptions: Black's zero-beta version of the CAPM and Merton's multifactor CAPM. We will also discuss one alternative asset pricing model, called the arbitrage pricing model. It is important to understand that as assumptions are relaxed, the derivation of a pricing model becomes much more complicated, relying on more advanced financial theories and higher-level mathematics. Yet, to understand these models, it is unnecessary to delve into the nuances of financial theory or higher mathematics. Instead of presenting rigorous mathematical proof, then, we approach these theories in a way that is conceptually useful to the investment practitioner.

BLACK'S ZERO-BETA VERSION OF THE CAPM MODEL

As we discussed in Chapter 5, in a world without a risk-free asset, an investor will select some portfolio on the Markowitz efficient frontier. When a risk-free asset is assumed, the capital market line (CML) can be generated. The CML dominates the Markowitz efficient frontier. From the CML, the CAPM is derived.

Not only is the existence of a risk-free asset important in developing the CAPM, but there are two related assumptions. First, it is assumed that investors can borrow or lend at the risk-free rate. The risk-free asset is one in which there is no uncertainty about the return that will be realized over some investment horizon. To realize that return, it is assumed the borrower will not default on its obligation. In the United States the short-term obligations of the federal government are viewed as default-free and therefore risk-free assets. As we will explain in Chapter 20, there is not just one interest rate in an economy but a structure of interest rates. The U.S. government pays the lowest interest rate, and individual borrowers pay a higher rate. The greater the perceived risk that the borrower will default, the higher the interest rate. Thus, while the U.S. government may be able to borrow at the risk-free rate, an individual investor must pay a higher rate. Consequently, this assumption does not reflect the situation facing investors in the real world.

The second related assumption is that investors can borrow and lend at the same risk-free rate. In real-world markets, investors typically lend and borrow money at different rates, the former being less than the latter. Again, the assumption does not reflect the economic situation facing investors in real-world capital markets.

Fischer Black examined the results for the original CAPM, when there is no risk-free asset in which the investor can borrow and lend.[1] He demonstrated that neither the existence of a risk-free asset nor the requirement that investors can borrow and lend at the risk-free rate is necessary for the theory to hold. However, without the risk-free asset a different form of the CAPM will result.

Black's argument is as follows. The beta of a risk-free asset is zero. That is, since there is no variability of the return on a risk-free asset, it cannot co-

---

[1]Fischer Black, "Capital Market Equilibrium with Restricted Borrowing," *Journal of Business* (July 1972), pp. 444–455.

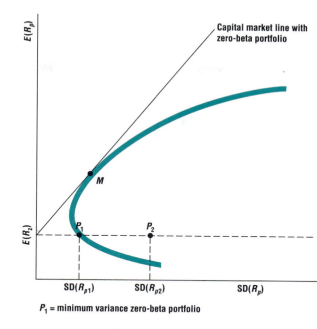

FIGURE 6-1

The capital market line with no risk-free asset but zero-beta portfolios.

P_1 = minimum variance zero-beta portfolio

vary with the market. Suppose that a portfolio can be created such that it is uncorrelated with the market. This portfolio would have a beta of zero. We shall refer to any portfolio with a beta of zero as a **zero-beta portfolio**. The assumptions necessary to create such a portfolio will be discussed later. For now, let's assume that such portfolios can be created.

Figure 6-1 shows the situation graphically. This figure includes the Markowitz efficient frontier. A tangent is drawn from the expected return axis (i.e., the vertical axis) starting at the expected return for the zero-beta portfolio to the Markowitz efficient frontier. This line will dominate the Markowitz efficient frontier and can be viewed as the capital market line when there is no risk-free asset.

Black demonstrated that if zero-beta portfolios can be constructed, then the CAPM would be modified as follows:

$$E(R_p) = E(R_Z) + \beta_p[E(R_M) - E(R_Z)] \tag{6-1}$$

where $E(R_Z)$ is the expected return on the zero-beta portfolio and $[E(R_M) - E(R_Z)]$ is the risk premium.

This version of the CAPM is the same as Equation (5-6) in Chapter 5 except that the expected return for the zero-beta portfolio is substituted for the risk-free rate. Black's zero-beta version of the CAPM is called the **two-factor model**. Empirical tests of the two-factor model suggest that it does a better job in explaining historical returns than the pure CAPM.[2]

Selecting the Zero-Beta Portfolio

Assuming that many zero-beta portfolios can be created, which zero-beta portfolio should be selected? The situation is depicted in Figure 6-1. Two

[2]Fischer Black, Michael C. Jensen, and Myron Scholes, "The Capital Asset Pricing Model," in M. C. Jensen (ed.), *Studies in the Theory of Capital Markets* (New York: Praeger, 1972).

zero-beta portfolios, P_1 and P_2, are shown. Neither portfolio is on the Markowitz efficient frontier, but both are feasible portfolios. (Recall from Chapter 4 that the feasible set includes all the portfolios that are achievable and that have the maximum expected return for a given risk. Note that P_1 is an achievable portfolio but not an efficient one.)

Given the choice of the zero-beta portfolios P_1 and P_2, which one will the investor select? Since both have the same expected return, we said that an investor will select the one with the minimum risk. That is P_1. In general, of all the possible zero-beta portfolios, an investor will select the one with the minimum risk. The portfolio is called the **minimum-variance zero-beta portfolio**.

Assumptions Needed to Construct Zero-Beta Portfolios

A natural question, of course, is how does an investor obtain a portfolio that has a zero beta? The basic principle is that by means of short selling, a zero-beta portfolio can be created from a combination of securities. As explained in Chapter 3, short selling involves selling an asset that is not owned in order to benefit from an anticipated decline in the asset's price. Since the asset has been presold at a price today, a decline in the asset's price means that an investor can buy the asset in the future at a lower price.

The reason why short selling is a necessary assumption is that since assets such as stocks are positively correlated—as we noted in the previous chapter—the only way to get a portfolio that is uncorrelated with the market portfolio is to create a portfolio in which stocks are owned and stocks are shorted. Thus, when the price of stocks increases, there will be a gain on the stocks owned in the portfolio, giving a positive return; however, there will be a loss on the stocks that have been shorted and therefore a negative return. The zero-beta portfolio is created such that this combination of stocks owned and stocks shorted will have a beta of zero.

Unfortunately, not all investors are permitted to sell short. Many institutional investors are prohibited or constrained from selling short.

Thus, the two-factor version of the CAPM avoids relying on the myth of "borrowing and lending at a risk-free rate." It still cannot reflect the real world for all investors, however, because it does require unrestricted short selling, which is not available to everyone.

MERTON'S MULTIFACTOR CAPM

In Markowitz portfolio theory and in the CAPM, it is assumed that the only risk that an investor is concerned with is the uncertainty about the future price of a security. Investors, however, usually are concerned with other risks that will affect their ability to consume goods and services in the future. Three examples would be the risks associated with future labor income, the future relative prices of consumer goods, and future investment opportunities. Consequently, using the variance of expected returns as the sole measure of risk is inappropriate.

Recognizing these other risks that investors face, Robert Merton has extended the CAPM based on consumers deriving their optimal lifetime consumption when they face these *extra-market* sources of risk.[3] These extra-market sources of risk are also referred to as *factors*, hence the model derived by Merton is called a **multifactor CAPM** and is given below:

$$E(R_p) = R_F + \beta_{p,M}[E(R_M) - R_F] + \tag{6-2}$$
$$\{\beta_{p,F1}\,[E(R_{F1}) - R_F] + \beta_{p,F2}[E(R_{F2}) - R_F] + \ldots + \beta_{p,FK}[E(R_{FK}) - R_F]\}$$

where R_F = the risk-free return
$F1, F2, \ldots, FK$ = factors or extra-market sources of risk, 1 to K
K = number of factors or extra-market sources of risk
$\beta_{p,M}$ = the sensitivity of the portfolio to the market
$\beta_{p,FK}$ = the sensitivity of the portfolio to the kth factor
$E(R_{FK})$ = the expected return of factor k

The total extra-market sources of risk are equal to

$$\beta_{p,F1}[E(R_{F1}) - R_F] + \beta_{p,F2}[E(R_{F2}) - R_F] + \ldots + \beta_{p,FK}[E(R_{FK}) - R_F] \tag{6-3}$$

This expression says that investors want to be compensated for the risk associated with each source of extra-market risk, in addition to market risk. Note that if there are no extra-market sources of risk, then Equation (6-2) reduces to the expected return for the portfolio as predicted by the CAPM:

$$E(R_p) = R_F + \beta_p[E(R_M) - R_F]$$

In the case of the CAPM, investors hedge the uncertainty associated with future security prices by diversification. This is done by holding the market portfolio, which can be thought of as a mutual fund that invests in all securities based on their relative capitalizations. In the multifactor CAPM, in addition to investing in the market portfolio, investors will also allocate funds to something equivalent to a mutual fund which hedges a particular extra-market risk (see Figure 6-2). While not all investors are concerned with the same sources of extra-market risk, those that are concerned with a specific extra-market risk will basically hedge them in the same way.

We have just described the multifactor model for a portfolio. How can this model be used to obtain the expected return for an individual security? Since individual securities are nothing more than portfolios consisting of only one security, Equation (6-2) must hold for each security i. That is,

$$E(R_i) = R_F + \beta_{i,M}[E(R_M) - R_F] + \beta_{i,F1}[E(R_{F1}) - R_F] + \tag{6-4}$$
$$\beta_{i,F2}[E(R_{F2}) - R_F] + \ldots + \beta_{i,FK}[E(R_{FK}) - R_F]$$

The multifactor CAPM is an attractive model because it recognizes non-market risks. The pricing of an asset by the marketplace, then, must reflect risk premiums to compensate for these extra-market risks. Unfortunately, it may be difficult to identify all the extra-market risks and to value each of these risks empirically. Furthermore, when these risks are taken together, the multifactor CAPM begins to resemble the arbitrage pricing theory model described next.

---

[3]Robert C. Merton, "An Intertemporal Capital Asset Pricing Model," *Econometrica* (September 1973), pp. 867–888. A less technical version is published in "A Reexamination of the CAPM," in Irwin Friend and James Bicksler (eds.), *Risk and Return in Finance* (Cambridge, MA: Ballinger Publishing, 1976). Other papers on multifactor CAPMs are John C. Cox, Jonathan E. Ingersoll, and Stephen A. Ross, "An Intertemporal Asset Pricing Model with Rational Expectations," *Econometrica* (1985), pp. 363–384, and Douglas Breeden, "An Intertemporal Asset Pricing Model with Stochastic Consumption and Investment Opportunities," *Journal of Financial Economics* (1979), pp. 265–296.

FIGURE 6-2
A Merton multifactor portfolio.

ARBITRAGE PRICING THEORY MODEL

Professor Stephen Ross has been a longtime critic of the CAPM, questioning the validity of its assumptions.[4] In 1976, he developed an alternative model based purely on arbitrage arguments, and hence called the **arbitrage pricing theory (APT)** model.[5] Since the model relies on arbitrage arguments, we will digress at this point to define what is meant by arbitrage.

Arbitrage

In its simple form, **arbitrage** is the simultaneous buying and selling of a security at two different prices in two different markets. The arbitrageur profits without risk by buying cheap in one market and simultaneously selling at the higher price in the other market. Investors don't hold their breath waiting for such situations to occur, because they are rare. In fact, a single arbitrageur with unlimited ability to sell short could correct a mispricing condition by financing purchases in the underpriced market with proceeds of short sales in the overpriced market. This means that riskless arbitrage opportunities are short-lived.

Less obvious arbitrage opportunities exist in situations where a package of securities can produce a payoff (expected return) identical to another security that is priced differently. This arbitrage relies on a fundamental principle of finance called the **law of one price**. This law states that a given security must have the same price regardless of the means by which one goes about creating that security. The law of one price implies that if the payoff of a security can be synthetically created by a package of other securities, the price of the package and the price of the security whose payoff it replicates must be equal.

When a situation is discovered whereby the price of the package of securities differs from that of a security with the same payoff, rational investors will trade these securities in such a way as to restore price equilibrium. This market mechanism is assumed by the arbitrage pricing theory, and is founded on the fact that an arbitrage transaction does not expose the investor to any adverse movement in the market price of the securities in the transaction.[6]

---

[4]Stephen A. Ross, "The Capital Asset Pricing Model (CAPM), Short Sales Restrictions and Related Issues," *Journal of Finance* (March 1977), pp. 177–184.

[5]Stephen A. Ross, "The Arbitrage Theory of Capital Asset Pricing," *Journal of Economic Theory* (December 1976), pp. 343–362, and "Return, Risk and Arbitrage," in Friend and Bicksler, op. cit. Since the publication by Ross, there have been several studies that have refined the theory. See, for example, Gur Huberman, "A Simple Approach to Arbitrage Pricing Theory," *Journal of Economic Theory* (October 1982), pp. 183–191, and Jonathan E. Ingersoll, "Some Results in the Theory of Arbitrage Pricing," *Journal of Finance* (September 1984), pp. 1021–1039.

[6]The arbitrage process that we have described above is sometimes called *riskless arbitrage*. It would seem unnecessary to qualify the term "arbitrage" by using the adjective "riskless." However, the term is sometimes carelessly used in the investment industry to mean transactions where there is some risk of an unfavorable outcome.

TABLE 6-1			
PRICES AND POSSIBLE PAYOFFS OF THREE SECURITIES			
Security	**Price**	**Payoff in State 1**	**Payoff in State 2**
A	$70	$50	$100
B	60	30	120
C	80	38	112

For example, let us consider how we can produce an arbitrage opportunity involving the three securities A, B, and C described in Table 6-1. These securities can be purchased today at the prices shown, and can each yield only one of two payoffs a year from now. The different payoffs depend on some extra-market risk (say, inflation), and we will refer to the two payoffs as occurring in state 1 and state 2.

While it is not obvious from the data in Table 6-1, we can construct a portfolio of securities A and B that will have the identical return as security C in either state 1 or state 2. Let W_A and W_B be the proportion of security A and B, respectively, in the portfolio. Then the payoff (i.e., the terminal value of the portfolio) under the two states can be expressed mathematically as follows:

If state 1 occurs: $\$50\ W_A + \$30\ W_B$
If state 2 occurs: $\$100\ W_A + \$120\ W_B$

We create a portfolio consisting of A and B that will reproduce the payoff of C regardless of the state that occurs one year from now, as shown in Table 6-2. The cost of that portfolio will be different from the cost of security C, if the three securities are mispriced in relation to one another.

Here is how: For either condition (state 1 and state 2) we set the expected return of the portfolio equal to the expected return for security C. We can solve the two equations algebraically, obtaining a value of 0.4 for W_A and 0.6 for W_B. Thus, a portfolio consisting of 0.4 of security A and 0.6 of security B

TABLE 6-2	
CONSTRUCTING AN ARBITRAGE OPPORTUNITY FROM A COMBINATION OF MISPRICED SECURITIES	
Outcome of Portfolio A + B	**Outcome of Security C**
State 1: $\$50\ W_A + \$30\ W_B$	= $38
State 2: $\$100\ W_A + \$120\ W_B$	= $112
Solving the two equations simultaneously yields:	
$W_A = 0.4$ $W_B = 0.6$	
Unit Cost	
Portfolio A + B	**Security C**
$(0.4)(70) + (0.6)(60)$	
= 64	80

TABLE 6-3			
ARBITRAGE OUTCOMES			
Security	**Investment**	**State 1**	**State 2**
A	$ 400,000	$285,715	$ 571,429
B	600,000	300,000	1,200,000
C	−1,000,000	−475,000	−1,400,000
Total	0	110,715	371,429

will have the same payoff as security C. How much will it cost us to construct this portfolio? As the prices of A and B are $70 and $60, respectively, the cost is

0.40 ($70) + 0.60 ($60) = $64

Note that the price of C is $80. Thus, for only $64 an investor can obtain the same payoff as C. This is an arbitrage opportunity that can be exploited by buying A and B in the proportions given above and shorting (selling) C. Table 6-3 shows the two outcomes for states 1 and 2 for an arbitrage involving $1 million in the portfolio consisting of A and B and shorting $1 million of C. Note that the total investment is zero. In either state 1 or 2, we profit without risk. The APT assumes that such an opportunity would be quickly eliminated by the marketplace.

Assumptions of the Arbitrage Pricing Theory

The arbitrage pricing theory model postulates that a security's expected return is influenced by a variety of factors, as opposed to just the single market index of the CAPM. Specifically, look back at Equation (5-3) in Chapter 5, which states that the return on a security is dependent on its market sensitivity index and an unsystematic return. The APT in contrast states that the return on a security is linearly related to H "factors." The APT does not specify what these factors are, but it is assumed that the relationship between security returns and the factors is linear.

For now, to illustrate the APT model, let's assume a simple world with a portfolio consisting of three securities and with two factors; otherwise more complicated mathematical notation must be introduced.[7] The following notation will be used:

$\tilde{R}_i$ = the random rate of return on security i (i = 1, 2, 3)

$E(R_i)$ = the expected return on security i (i = 1, 2, 3)

$\tilde{F}_h$ = the hth factor that is common to the returns of all three assets (h = 1, 2)

$\beta_{i,h}$ = the sensitivity of the ith security to the hth factor

$\tilde{e}_i$ = the unsystematic return for security i (i = 1, 2, 3)

The APT model asserts that the random rate of return on security i is given by the following relationship:

$$\tilde{R}_i = E(R_i) + \beta_{i,1}\tilde{F}_1 + \beta_{i,2}F_2 + \tilde{e}_i \tag{6-5}$$

---

[7]Not that some readers won't find the notation described below complicated enough.

Derivation of the APT Model

For equilibrium to exist among these three assets, the following arbitrage condition must be satisfied: Using no additional funds (wealth) and without increasing risk, it should not be possible, on average, to create a portfolio to increase return. In essence, this condition states that there is no "money machine" available in the market.

To see how this principle works, let

V_i = the *change* in the dollar amount invested in the ith security as a percentage of the investor's wealth

For example, suppose that the market value of the investor's portfolio is initially $100,000, comprised as follows: (1) $20,000 in security 1, (2) $30,000 in security 2, and (3) $50,000 in security 3. Suppose an investor changes the initial portfolio as follows: (1) $35,000 in security 1, (2) $25,000 in security 2, and (3) $40,000 in security 3. Then the V_i's would be as follows:

$$V_1 = \frac{\$35,000 - \$20,000}{\$100,000} = 0.15$$

$$V_2 = \frac{\$25,000 - \$30,000}{\$100,000} = -0.05$$

$$V_3 = \frac{\$40,000 - \$50,000}{\$100,000} = -0.10$$

Note that the sum of the V_i's is equal to zero since no additional funds were invested. That is, rebalancing the portfolio does not change the market value of the initial portfolio. Rebalancing does do two things. First, it changes the future return of the portfolio. Second, it changes the total risk of the portfolio, both the systematic risk associated with the two factors and the unsystematic risk. Let's consider the first consequence.

Mathematically, the *change* in the portfolio's future return ($\Delta \tilde{R}_p$) can be shown to be as follows:

$$\begin{aligned}\Delta \tilde{R}_p = &[V_1 E(R_1) + V_2 E(R_2) + V_3 E(R_3)] \\ &+ [V_1 \beta_{1,1} + V_2 \beta_{2,1} + V_3 \beta_{3,1}]\tilde{F}_1 \\ &+ [V_1 \beta_{1,2} + V_2 \beta_{2,2} + V_3 \beta_{3,2}]\tilde{F}_2 + [V_1 \tilde{e}_1 + V_2 \tilde{e}_2 + V_3 \tilde{e}_3]\end{aligned} \qquad (6\text{-}6)$$

Equation (6-6) indicates that the change in the portfolio return will have a component that depends on systematic risk as well as unsystematic risk. While in our example we have assumed only three securities, when there are a large number of securities, the unsystematic risk can be eliminated by diversification, as explained in Chapter 4. Thus, Equation (6-6) would reduce to

$$\begin{aligned}\Delta \tilde{R}_p = &[V_1 E(R_1) + V_2 E(R_2) + V_3 E(R_3)] + \\ &[V_1 \beta_{1,1} + V_2 \beta_{2,1} + V_3 \beta_{3,1}]\tilde{F}_1 + [V_1 \beta_{1,2} + V_2 \beta_{2,2} + V_3 \beta_{3,2}]\tilde{F}_2\end{aligned} \qquad (6\text{-}7)$$

Now let's look at the systematic risk with respect to each factor. The *change* in the portfolio risk with respect to factor 1 is just the betas of each security multiplied by their respective V_i's. Consequently, the change in the portfolio's sensitivity to systematic risk from factor 1 is

$$V_1 \beta_{1,1} + V_2 \beta_{2,1} + V_3 \beta_{3,1} \qquad (6\text{-}8)$$

For factor 2, it is

$$V_1 \beta_{1,2} + V_2 \beta_{2,2} + V_3 \beta_{3,2} \qquad (6\text{-}9)$$

One of the conditions that is imposed for no arbitrage is that the change in systematic risk with respect to each factor will be zero. That is, Equations (6-8) and (6-9) should satisfy the following:

$$V_1\beta_{1,1} + V_2\beta_{2,1} + V_3\beta_{3,1} = 0 \qquad (6\text{-}10)$$
$$V_1\beta_{1,2} + V_2\beta_{2,2} + V_3\beta_{3,2} = 0 \qquad (6\text{-}11)$$

If Equations (6-10) and (6-11) are satisfied, then Equation (6-7) reduces to

$$\Delta E(R_p) = V_1 E(R_1) + V_2 E(R_2) + V_3 E(R_3) \qquad (6\text{-}12)$$

Now let's put all the conditions for no arbitrage together in terms of the equations above. As stated earlier, using no additional funds (wealth) and without increasing risk, it should not be possible, on average, to create a portfolio to increase return. By no additional funds (wealth), this means the following condition: $V_1 + V_2 + V_3 = 0$.

The condition that there be no change in the portfolio's sensitivity to each systematic risk is set forth in Equations (6-10) and (6-11).

Finally, the expected additional portfolio return from reshuffling the portfolio must be zero. This can be expressed by setting Equation (6-12) equal to zero:

$$V_1 E(R_1) + V_2 E(R_2) + V_3 E(R_3) = 0$$

Taken together, these equations, as well as the condition that there be a sufficiently large number of securities so that unsystematic risk can be eliminated, describe mathematically the conditions for equilibrium pricing. These conditions can be solved mathematically, since the number of securities is greater than the number of factors, to determine the equilibrium value for the portfolio as well as the equilibrium value for each of the three securities. Ross has shown that the following risk and return relationship will result for each security i:

$$E(R_i) = R_F + \beta_{i,F1}[E(R_{F1}) - R_F] + \beta_{i,F2}[E(R_{F2}) - R_F] \qquad (6\text{-}13)$$

where $\beta_{i,Fj}$ = the sensitivity of security i to the jth factor

$E(R_{Fj}) - R_F$ = the excess return of the jth systematic factor over the risk-free rate, and can be thought of as the price (or risk premium) for the jth systematic risk

Equation (6-13) can be generalized to the case where there are H factors as follows:

$$E(R_i) = R_F + \beta_{i,F1}[E(R_{F1}) - R_F] + \beta_{i,F2}[E(R_{F2}) - R_F] \qquad (6\text{-}14)$$
$$+ \ldots + \beta_{i,FH}[E(R_{FH}) - R_F]$$

Equation (6-14) is the APT model. It states that investors want to be compensated for all the factors that *systematically* affect the return of a security. The compensation is the sum of the products of each factor's systematic risk ($\beta_{i,Fh}$) and the risk premium assigned to it by the financial market [$E(R_{Fh}) - R_F$]. As in the case of the other risk and return models described, an investor is not compensated for accepting unsystematic risk.

Comparison of the APT Model and CAPM

Examining the equations, we can see that the CAPM (Equation 5-6 of Chapter 5) and the multifactor CAPM are actually special cases of the APT model (Equation 6-14):

$$E(R_i) = R_F + \beta_i[E(R_M) - R_F] \tag{5-6}$$

$$E(R_i) = R_F + \beta_{i,M}[E(R_M) - R_F] + \beta_{i,F1}[E(R_{F1}) - R_F] + \tag{6-4}$$
$$\beta_{i,F2}[E(R_{F2}) - R_F] + \ldots + \beta_{i,FK}[E(R_{FK}) - R_F]$$

$$E(R_i) = R_F + \beta_{i,F1}[E(R_{F1}) - R_F] + \beta_{i,F2}[E(R_{F2}) - R_F] \tag{6-14}$$
$$+ \ldots + \beta_{i,FH}[E(R_{FH}) - R_F]$$

If the only factor in Equation (6-14) is market risk, the APT model reduces to Equation (5-6).

Now contrast Equation (6-14) with the multifactor CAPM given by Equation (6-4). They look similar. Both say that investors are compensated for accepting all systematic risk and no unsystematic risk. The multifactor CAPM states that one of these systematic risks is market risk, while the APT model does not specify the systematic risks.

Advantages of APT

Supporters of the APT model argue that it has several major advantages over the CAPM or multifactor CAPM.

First, it makes less restrictive assumptions about investor preferences toward risk and return. As explained in Chapter 5, the CAPM theory assumes investors trade off between risk and return solely on the basis of the expected returns and standard deviations of prospective investments. The APT, on the other hand, simply requires that some rather unobtrusive bounds be placed on potential investor utility functions.

Second, no assumptions are made about the distribution of security returns. Finally, since the APT does not rely on the identification of the true market portfolio, the theory is potentially testable.

Tests of the APT

The APT is a relatively new theory, and hence the financial literature continues to test its validity.[8] The research to date seems to indicate that the APT is a promising alternative to the single-factor CAPM in explaining asset returns. This research indicates that the APT may explain a significantly greater amount of the variance in common stock returns than the CAPM. However, there are some unresolved questions concerning the practical application of the APT.

There remains the question of how many factors explain security returns. (See Box 6.) One study by Nai-fu Chen, Richard Roll, and Stephen Ross suggests the following four plausible economic factors[9]:

1. Unanticipated changes in industrial production
2. Unanticipated changes in the spread between the yield on low-grade and high-grade bonds

---

[8]For a discussion of the issue of the number of factors in the APT, see Phoebus J. Dhrymes, "The Empirical Relevance of Arbitrage Pricing Models," *Journal of Portfolio Management* (Summer 1984), pp. 35-44; Stephen A. Ross, "Reply to Dhrymes: APT Is Empirically Relevant," *Journal of Portfolio Management* (Fall 1984), pp. 54–56; T. Daniel Coggin and John E. Hunter, "A Meta-Analysis of Pricing 'Risk' Factors in APT," *Journal of Portfolio Management* (Fall 1987), pp. 35–38; and Delores A. Conway and Marc R. Reinganum, "Stable Factors in Security Returns," *Journal of Business & Economic Statistics* (January 1988), pp. 1–15.

[9]Nai-fu Chen, Richard Roll, and Stephen A. Ross, "Economic Forces and the Stock Market," *Journal of Business* (July 1986), pp. 383–403.

BOX 6

THE SYSTEMATIC SOURCES OF RISK: DETAILS

The following is an excerpt from a publication by Roll & Ross Asset Management (APT: Balancing Risk and Return).

At the core of APT is the recognition that systematic factors affect the long-term average returns of financial assets.

APT does not deny the myriad factors that influence the daily price variability of individual stocks and bonds, but it focuses on the major forces that move aggregates of assets in large portfolios. The major, pervasive forces are:

- *The business cycle:* Changes in real output are measured by percentage changes in the index of industrial production.
- *Interest rates:* Changes in investors' expectations about future interest rates are measured by changes in long-term government bond yields.
- *Investor confidence:* The single most important factor, in recent years, is measured by changes in the yield spread between high- and low-grade bonds, which narrows as investor confidence increases, and vice versa.
- *Short-term inflation:* Month-to-month jumps in commodity prices, such as gold or oil, are measured by changes in the consumer price index.
- *Inflationary expectations:* Changes in expectations of inflation are measured by changes in the short-term risk-free nominal interest rate.

APT determines the extent to which any security price responds to each of these factors, using straightforward but sophisticated econometric techniques. The variables above make intuitive sense, and it also makes sense that they are indeed pervasive and "systematic." Every asset's value changes when one of these variables undergoes an unanticipated change.

It is possible, of course, to think of many other potential systematic factors, but Roll & Ross's research has found that many of them influence returns only through their impact on the factors listed above. For example,

- *Money supply:* An unpredicted change in the money supply is captured by interest rates and inflationary expectations.
- *Political risk:* Political risk—e.g., effects of wars and elections—is reflected in interest rates and investor confidence.
- *Exchange rates:* Foreign exchange rates might also be expected to have a substantial systematic effect on equity markets. Yet even here Roll & Ross analysts have found that their influence is subsumed by inflation and interest rate risk factors and that adding the foreign exchange rate as an explicit additional factor produces no larger equity returns.
- *Energy prices:* Similarly, though energy prices have a substantial influ-

ence on many companies, its influence can apparently be diversified away. Some companies are greatly benefitted by a decrease in oil prices (east coast manufacturing companies), and some are harmed (oil companies.) The overall structure of the market allows this factor to be rendered insignificant in well-managed portfolios; i.e., it is diversifiable.

APT breaks the inflation factor into two parts because different securities respond quite differently to the two types of inflation. For example, commercial real estate is a very good hedge against long-term inflation, but not against changes in commodity prices. When oil prices rise, higher fuel costs reduce profits from fixed-payment leaseholds. But when the longer-term rate of inflation rises, the value of the property also increases in anticipation of future (nominal) capital gains.

- *Roll & Ross does NOT make macroeconomic forecasts:* We position the portfolio to have high long-run average returns. We do not, for example, predict what will happen to inflation. We do predict the long-term average return and risk of inflation exposure.
- *The five systematic factors are NOT immutable:* Every month, Roll & Ross assesses the absolute and relative importance of each factor and searches for others that may have become important. Although these

---

3. Unanticipated changes in interest rates and the shape of the yield curve[10]
4. Unanticipated changes in inflation

Eric Sorensen and his colleagues at Salomon Brothers have built a model similar to the general APT formulation, which posits seven macroeconomic factors systematically affecting common stock returns: long-run economic growth, short-run business cycle risk, long-term bond yield changes, short-term Treasury bill changes, inflation shocks, dollar changes versus trading partner currencies, and residual market beta.[11]

---

[10]The yield curve is discussed in Chapter 20.

BOX 6

THE SYSTEMATIC SOURCES OF RISK: DETAILS (*Continued*)

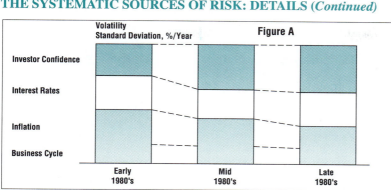

Figure A

there are five sources of systematic risk, our research indicates that this is currently the right approach for maximizing portfolio return/risk performance.

Questions for Box 6

1. What does it mean that the variables are "pervasive and 'systematic' "?
2. Explain why in the APT model it is necessary to search for factors.
3. Explain why you agree or disagree with the following statement: "According to the APT, the contribution of each factor to total volatility is constant over time."
4. In managing money according to the APT, why is the objective to predict the long-term average return and risk to a factor and not to predict the future value for the factor?

same five factors have been influential for the past forty years, the inflation factors were relatively more important in the mid-1970's than they are today. During the mid-1970's, they induced more volatility in exposed portfolios and they offered higher long-term returns as compensation. Since the October 1987 stock market crash, the investor confidence risk factor has been more important as a source of volatility and as a generator of higher long-term returns.

Figure A shows the relative contribution of the macroeconomic sources of risk to the total volatility of the S&P 500 over the past decade. For clarity, the two inflation factors are lumped together. Notice that while total volatility has changed significantly over time, the contribution of each factor has varied as well.

In Figure B, we show a recent history of the most important element of the

APT method, the return/risk ratios of the macroeconomic factors. Again, the two inflation factors are combined. The essence of APT portfolio selection is to overweight sources of risk that have high rewards relative to their contribution to short-term volatility.

Roll & Ross is actively engaged in ongoing research on the risk factors. While nothing in theory dictates that

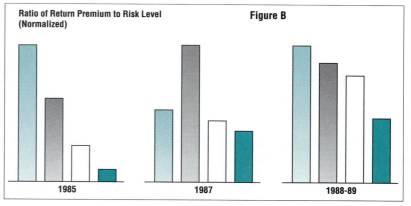

Figure B

Thus, researchers continue to search for the factors that systematically explain returns. This research is carried out not only by researchers but also by practitioners.

SOME PRINCIPLES TO TAKE AWAY

In this chapter and the last two, we have covered the heart of what is popularly called *modern portfolio theory* and *capital asset pricing theory*. We have emphasized the assumptions and their critical role in the development of

[11]Eric H. Sorensen, Joseph J. Mezrich, and Chee Thum, "The Salomon Brothers U.S. Stock Risk Attribute Model," Salomon Brothers, New York, October 1989.

these theories and explained the empirical findings. While you may understand the topics covered, you may still be uncomfortable about where we have progressed in investment management, given the lack of theoretical and empirical support for the CAPM or the difficulty of identifying the factors in the multifactor CAPM and APT model. You're not alone. A good number of practitioners and academics feel uncomfortable with these models, particularly the CAPM.

Nevertheless, what is comforting is that there are several general principles of investing and evaluating the performance of money managers that are derived from these theories that very few would question. All these principles are used in later chapters.

1. Investing has two dimensions, risk and return. Therefore, focusing only on the actual return that a money manager has achieved without looking at the risk that had to be accepted to achieve that return is inappropriate.
2. It is also inappropriate to look at the risk of an individual asset when deciding whether it should be included in a portfolio. What is important is how the inclusion of an asset into a portfolio will affect the risk of the portfolio.
3. Whether investors consider one risk or a thousand risks, risk can be divided into two general categories: systematic risks that cannot be eliminated by diversification and unsystematic risk that can be diversified away.
4. Investors should only be compensated for accepting systematic risks. Thus, it is critical in formulating an investment strategy to identify the systematic risks.

■ SUMMARY

In this chapter, two extensions of the CAPM are presented, the zero-beta CAPM, or two-factor model, developed by Black and the multifactor CAPM developed by Merton. We also explained the arbitrage pricing theory, an alternative asset pricing model to the CAPM.

Black tackles the assumption that there is a risk-free asset in which investors can borrow and lend. While he finds that the CAPM is still valid, it requires modification. The revised formulation of the CAPM requires that investors be able to create zero-beta portfolios, which are portfolios that are uncorrelated with the market portfolio. The model he derives, called the two-factor model, is the same as the pure CAPM with the exception that the expected return for the zero-beta portfolio is substituted for the risk-free rate. In selecting the zero-beta portfolio, the investor should select the one with the minimum risk. The assumption necessary to construct zero-beta portfolios is that investors are

not restricted with respect to short-selling, an assumption that does agree with the constraints imposed on many institutional investors.

The CAPM assumes that investors are concerned with only one source of risk: the risk having to do with the future price of a security. However, there are other risks, such as the capacity of investors to consume goods and services in the future. The multifactor CAPM assumes that investors face such extra-market sources of risk called factors. The expected return in the multifactor CAPM is the market risk (as in the case of the basic CAPM) plus a package of risk premiums. Each risk premium is the product of the beta of the security or portfolio with respect to the particular factor times the difference between the expected return for the factor less the risk-free rate.

The arbitrage pricing theory is developed purely from arbitrage arguments. It postulates that the expected return on a security or a portfolio is influenced by several factors. Proponents of the APT model cite its less restrictive assumptions as a feature that makes it more appealing than the CAPM or multifactor CAPM. Moreover, testing the APT model does not require identification of the "true" market portfolio. It does, however, require empirical determination of the factors because they are not specified by the theory. Consequently, the APT model replaces the problem of identifying the market portfolio in the CAPM with the problem of choosing and measuring the underlying factors. Attempts at identifying the factors empirically have not been conclusive.

Despite the fact that the theories presented are controversial or difficult to implement in practice, there are several principles of investing that are not controversial and can be used in developing investment strategies.

■ KEY TERMS

arbitrage
arbitrage pricing theory (APT)
law of one price

minimum-variance zero-beta
     portfolio
multifactor CAPM

two-factor model
zero-beta portfolio

■ QUESTIONS

1. Why is the CAPM's assumption that investors can borrow and lend at the risk-free rate questionable?

2. Comment on the following statement: "Since the CAPM depends on the existence of a risk-free asset, the CAPM cannot be supported."

3. a. What is meant by a zero-beta portfolio?
   b. If more than one zero-beta portfolio can be created, which one should an investor select?
   c. What assumption is required to create a zero-beta portfolio, and how reasonable is the assumption?

4. What was the motivation for the development of the multifactor CAPM?

5. What is meant by the extra-market sources of risk in the multifactor CAPM?

6. If there are no extra-market sources of risk, explain why the multifactor CAPM reduces to the pure CAPM.

7. What is meant by the law of one price, and what does it imply about a package of securities and a given security that have the same payoff?

8. Consider the following three securities X, Y, and Z that can be purchased today, and for which one year from now there are only two possible outcomes (state 1 and state 2):

Security	Price	Payoff in State 1	Payoff in State 2
X	$35	$25	$50
Y	30	15	60
Z	40	19	66

a. Letting W_X and W_Y be the quantity of security X and Y, respectively, in the portfolio, express the payoff (i.e., the terminal value of the portfolio) under the two states.

b. Create a portfolio consisting of X and Y that will reproduce the payoff of Z regardless of the state that occurs one year from now.

c. How much will it cost to create the portfolio found in b?

d. Given your answer to b and c, is there an arbitrage opportunity? If so, explain why it is an arbitrage opportunity.

9. What are the fundamental principles underlying the APT model?

10. What are the advantages of the APT model relative to the CAPM?

11. What are the difficulties in practice of applying the arbitrage pricing theory model?

12. Does Roll's criticism also apply to the arbitrage pricing theory model?

13. "In the CAPM investors should be compensated for accepting systematic risk; for the APT model, investors are rewarded for accepting both systematic risk and unsystematic risk." Do you agree with this statement?

14. What factors have researchers found affect security returns?

15. Comment on the following statement: "Since Markowitz portfolio theory requires so many assumptions, the notion that investors should be

concerned with the risk of the overall portfolio rather than the risk of individual securities is misleading."

16. Explain why it is difficult to empirically distinguish between the multifactor CAPM and the APT model?

17. Indicate why you agree or disagree with the following statement: "There is considerable controversy concerning the theories about how assets are priced. Therefore, the distinction between systematic risk and unsystematic risk is meaningless."

18. Indicate why you agree or disagree with the following statement: "The theories of the pricing of capital assets are highly questionable. Basically, there is only one type of risk and investors should seek to avoid it when they purchase individual securities."

CHAPTER 7
GENERAL PRINCIPLES OF ASSET/LIABILITY MANAGEMENT

LEARNING OBJECTIVES
After reading this chapter you will be able to:

- explain the various types of risk faced by investors: price risk, default risk, inflation risk, exchange rate risk, reinvestment risk, call risk, and liquidity risk.

- describe the types of liabilities that an institution may face.

- explain the two important dimensions of a liability: the amount and timing of the payment.

- explain why the same factors that affect the risk of financial assets also affect liabilities.

- describe what the goals of asset/liability management are.

- differentiate among an institution's accounting surplus, regulatory surplus, and economic surplus.

- explain how assets are handled for accounting purposes.

- use the duration of assets and liabilities to calculate the sensitivity of the economic surplus of an institution when interest rates change.

- explain the investment management objective of those money managers not facing liabilities.

In our discussion of the investment management process in Chapter 1, we explained that an investor must set objectives. For an institutional investor, objectives are influenced by the nature of the institution's liabilities. While investors are exposed to the same types of risks when they invest in financial assets, the nature of liabilities varies from institution to institution, and is therefore the key factor in a portfolio manager's selection of the asset classes to include in a portfolio.

In this chapter, we provide an overview of the various types of risks associated with investing in financial assets and a general categorization of the nature of liabilities. Armed with an understanding of the risks faced when investing in financial assets and the nature of liabilities that institutions face, we describe the basic principles underlying the management of assets relative to liabilities, popularly referred to as **asset/liability management**. In the four chapters to follow, we will describe the various institutional investors and the types of liabilities they face.

TABLE 7-1	
CLASSIFYING RISKS	
Risk	**Example**
Price risk	An asset's value drops when the investor is forced to sell.
Default risk	The issuer of an asset cannot meet its obligations.
Inflation risk	The rate of inflation erodes the value of an asset.
Exchange rate risk	The rate of exchange erodes the value of a foreign-denominated asset.
Reinvestment risk	The cash flow received must be reinvested in a similar vehicle that offers a lower return.
Call risk	The issuer of an asset exercises its right to pay off the amount borrowed.
Liquidity risk	An asset cannot easily be sold at a fair price.

RISKS ASSOCIATED WITH INVESTING IN FINANCIAL ASSETS

An investor is exposed to one or more risks when investing in financial assets. Here we will outline these risks and in later chapters explain how some of them can be quantified (see Table 7-1). In later chapters, we will introduce additional risks that are unique to a particular instrument or portfolio strategy.

Price Risk

To accomplish a certain investment objective, a portfolio manager may have to sell a security. For example, suppose a financial institution has a portfolio of securities with a market value of $10 million and must satisfy a liability obligation of $10 million two years from now. This financial institution faces the risk that two years from now, when $10 million must be withdrawn from the portfolio to satisfy this liability, the market value of the portfolio may be less than $10 million. This risk arises from the fact that the future market value of the securities in the portfolio is not known with certainty.

In general, investors are exposed to the risk that the value of a security (or a portfolio) will decline in the future. This risk is referred to as **price risk**.

As explained in Chapter 5, the general movement of the stock market as a whole is the primary factor contributing to the price risk of common stock. For bonds, changes in interest rates are the primary factor contributing to price risk, since, as explained in Chapter 21, when interest rates rise, the price of a bond declines.

Price risk is the major risk faced by an investor. We showed how price risk can be measured for individual common stocks and stock portfolios in Chapter 6, and we will show how this is done for individual bonds and bond portfolios in Chapter 21. However, in order to understand the asset/liability problem discussed in this chapter, it is necessary to introduce one of these measures here: **duration**, a common gauge of the price sensitivity of an asset or portfolio to a change in interest rates.

More specifically, duration measures the *approximate* percentage change in the price of an asset or the market value of a portfolio if interest rates change by 100 basis points.[1] So, for example, the price of a bond with a dura-

---

[1]A basis point is defined as 0.0001, or 0.01%. Therefore, 100 basis points is equal to 1 percentage point.

tion of 4 will change by approximately 4% if interest rates change by 100 basis points. The direction of the change in price is opposite the change in interest rates. An increase in interest rates of 100 basis points means that the price will decline by approximately 4%. For a 50-basis-point change in interest rates, the price of a bond with a duration of 4 will change by approximately 2%. All financial assets have a duration since they all respond to changes in interest rates. For example, if the duration of a stock is 0.5, this means that the percentage change in the price of the stock will be approximately 0.5% if interest rates change by 100 basis points.

The way duration is estimated for a bond and a bond portfolio and the limitations of this measure are explained more thoroughly in Chapter 21.

Default Risk

Default risk, also referred to as **credit risk**, is the risk that the issuer of a bond may be unable to make timely principal and interest payments on the issue. Typically, default risk is gauged by ratings assigned by commercial rating companies such as Moody's Investor Service, Standard & Poor's Corporation, Duff & Phelps Credit Rating Company, and Fitch Investors Service.

Default risk is a result of two types of risk: business risk and financial risk. **Business risk** is the risk that the cash flow of an issuer will be impaired because of adverse economic conditions, making it difficult to meet its operating expenses (e.g., payments to workers and suppliers). For example, a hotel chain with a large number of resort properties will see a reduction of its cash flow during severe economic times. **Financial risk** is the risk that the cash flow of an issuer will not be adequate to meet its financial obligations. These obligations include the repayment of debt and interest payments.

Inflation Risk

Suppose an investor purchases a debt instrument with a maturity of one year, a maturity value of $1,000, and a coupon (interest) rate of 7%. The cash flow of this bond one year from now is $1,070. Suppose further that the rate of inflation over the one year that the debt instrument is held is 5%. Then the purchasing power of the cash flow one year from now is $1,070 divided by 1 plus the rate of inflation. In our case, it is $1,070/(1.05), which is equal to $1,019. Therefore, in nominal dollars (i.e., dollars unadjusted for inflation), the return realized is 7%, but in real dollars (i.e., dollars adjusted for inflation), the return is 1.9%.

Inflation risk or **purchasing-power risk** is the risk that changes in the real return the investor will realize after adjusting for inflation will be negative. In our previous example, this would occur if the rate of inflation were greater than 7%.

Exchange Rate Risk

A U.S. investor who acquires a security whose payments are made in a foreign currency does not know what the cash flow will be in U.S. dollars. The cash flow in U.S. dollars is dependent on the exchange rate at the time the payments are received. For example, suppose an investor purchases a bond whose payments are in Japanese yen. If the yen depreciates relative to the U.S. dollar, then fewer dollars will be received. The risk of an investment's value changing because of currency exchange rates is referred to as **exchange rate risk** or **currency risk**. Should the yen appreciate relative to the U.S. dollar, the investor will benefit by receiving more dollars.

Reinvestment Risk

Reinvestment risk is the risk that proceeds received in the future will have to be reinvested at a lower potential interest rate. For example, suppose that a financial institution expects to receive $10 million from bonds maturing in four months. Suppose further that the financial institution plans to reinvest the $10 million in other bonds. The risk that this financial institution faces is that interest rates four months from now will decline, thereby forcing it to reinvest at a lower interest rate.

It should be noted that for bond portfolios, price risk and reinvestment risk are opposite each other. For example, price risk is the risk that interest rates will rise, thereby reducing the value of a bond portfolio. In contrast, reinvestment risk is the risk that interest rates will fall, resulting in any cash flow that is received being reinvested at a lower interest rate. A strategy based on these two offsetting risks is called *immunization*, and is explained in Chapter 25.

There is also reinvestment risk for stock portfolios. This arises because an investor that expects to receive proceeds in the future faces the risk that the value of the stocks will rise, and as a result, the investor will have to pay a higher price.

Call Risk

Many bonds contain a provision that allows the issuer to retire, or "call," all or part of the issue before the maturity date. The issuer usually retains this right in order to have the flexibility to refinance the bond in the future if the market interest rate drops below the coupon rate.

From the investor's perspective, there are two disadvantages to the call provision. First, the payments that will be made to the holder of a callable bond are not known with certainty. Second, because the issuer will call the bonds when interest rates have dropped, the investor is exposed to reinvestment risk; i.e., the investor will have to reinvest the proceeds when the bond is called at a lower interest rate. The combination of cash flow uncertainty and reinvestment risk introduced by a call provision is referred to as **call risk**. It is so pervasive in bond portfolio management that many market participants consider it second only to price risk in importance.

Liquidity Risk

Liquidity or *marketability* of a financial asset refers to the ease with which it can be sold at or near its value. This is an important and widely used notion, although there is at present no uniformly accepted definition of liquidity. A useful way to think of liquidity and illiquidity, proposed by Professor James Tobin, is in terms of how much sellers stand to lose if they wish to sell immediately as compared with engaging in a costly and time-consuming search.[2]

[2]James Tobin, "Properties of Assets," undated manuscript, Yale University, New Haven, CT.

The best example of a quite illiquid asset is a large and unusual house, or a work of art by a lesser artist. To sell such an asset, one must search for one of a very few suitable buyers. Less suitable buyers may be located more promptly but will have to be enticed to invest in the illiquid financial asset by an appropriate discount. **Liquidity risk**, then, arises from the difficulty of selling an asset. It can be thought of as the difference between the "true value" of the asset and the likely price, less commissions.

For many other financial assets, liquidity is determined by contractual arrangements. Ordinary bank deposits, for example, are perfectly liquid because the bank has a contractual obligation to convert them at par on demand. In the case of financial assets that are traded in the market, the primary measure of liquidity is the size of the spread between the bid price and the ask price quoted by an entity, plus commissions. The greater this spread and the commissions, the greater the liquidity risk.

NATURE OF LIABILITIES

The nature of an institutional investor's liabilities will dictate the investment strategy it will request its money manager to pursue. Depository institutions, for example, seek to generate income by the spread between the return they earn on their assets and the cost of their funds. Consequently, banking is referred to as *spread banking*. Life insurance companies are in the spread business. Pension funds are not in the spread business, in that they themselves do not raise funds in the market. Certain types of pension funds that we will describe in Chapter 9 seek to cover the cost of pension obligations at a minimum cost that is borne by the sponsor of the pension plan. Most investment companies face no explicit costs for the funds they acquire and must satisfy no specific liability obligations.

Classification of Liabilities

A **liability** is a cash outlay that must be made at a specific time to satisfy the contractual terms of an issued obligation. An institutional investor is concerned with both the amount and timing of liabilities, because its assets must produce the cash to meet any payments it has promised to make in a timely way. In fact, liabilities are classified according to the degree of certainty of their amount and timing, as shown in Table 7-2. This table assumes that the holder of the obligation will not cancel it prior to any actual or projected payout date.

TABLE 7-2		
CLASSIFICATION OF LIABILITIES OF INSTITUTIONAL INVESTORS		
Liability Type	**Amount of Cash Outlay**	**Timing of Cash Outlay**
Type I	Known	Known
Type II	Known	Uncertain
Type III	Uncertain	Known
Type IV	Uncertain	Uncertain

The description of cash outlays as either known or uncertain is undoubtedly broad. When we refer to a cash outlay as being uncertain, we do not mean that it cannot be predicted. There are some liabilities where the "law of large numbers" makes it easier to predict the timing and/or amount of cash outlays. This work is typically done by actuaries, but even actuaries have difficulty predicting natural catastrophes such as floods and earthquakes.

Below we illustrate each type of risk category. The important thing to note is that just like assets, there are risks associated with liabilities. Some of these risks are affected by the same factors that affect asset risks.

Type-I Liabilities   A Type-I liability is one for which both the amount and timing of the liabilities are known with certainty. An example would be a liability for which an institution knows that it must pay $50,000 six months from now. Banks and thrifts know the amount that they are committed to pay (principal plus interest) on the maturity date of a fixed-rate deposit, assuming that the depositor does not withdraw funds prior to the maturity date.

Type-I liabilities, however, are not limited to depository institutions. A major product sold by life insurance companies is a *guaranteed investment contract*, popularly referred to as a GIC (see Chapter 8). The obligation of the life insurance company under this contract is that, for a sum of money (called a *premium*), it will guarantee an interest rate up to some specified maturity date. For example, suppose a life insurance company, for a premium of $10 million, issues a five-year GIC agreeing to pay 10% compounded annually. The life insurance company knows that it must pay $16.11 million to the GIC policyholder in five years.[3]

Type-II Liabilities   A Type-II liability is one for which the amount of cash outlay is known, but the timing of the cash outlay is uncertain. The most obvious example of a Type-II liability is a life insurance policy. There are many types of life insurance policies, but the most basic type provides that, for an annual premium, a life insurance company agrees to make a specified dollar payment to policy beneficiaries upon the death of the insured. Naturally, the timing of the insured's death is uncertain.

Type-III Liabilities   A Type-III liability is one for which the timing of the cash outlay is known, but the amount is uncertain. A two-year floating-rate CD for which the interest rate is reset quarterly based on a market interest rate is an example. Not surprisingly, there are also floating-rate GICs; these also fall into the Type-III liabilities category.

Type-IV Liabilities   A Type-IV liability is one for which there is uncertainty about both the amount and the timing of the cash outlay. Numerous insurance products and pension obligations are in this category. Probably the most obvious examples are automobile and home insurance policies issued by property and casualty insurance companies. When, and if, a payment will have to be made to the policyholder is uncertain. Whenever damage is done to an insured asset, the amount of the payment that must be made is uncertain.

---

[3]This amount is determined as follows: $10,000,000 \times (1.10)^5$.

The liabilities of pension plans can also be Type-IV liabilities. In defined benefit plans, retirement benefits depend on the participant's income for a specified number of years before retirement and the total number of years the participant worked. This will affect the amount of the cash outlay. The timing of the cash outlay depends on when the employee elects to retire and whether the employee remains with the sponsoring plan until retirement. Moreover, both the amount and the timing will depend on how the employee elects to have payments made—over only the employee's life or over those of the employee and spouse.

Liquidity Concerns

Because of uncertainty about the timing and/or the amount of the cash outlays, an institution must be prepared to have sufficient cash to satisfy its obligations. Also keep in mind that the entity that holds the obligation against the institution may have the right to change the nature of the obligation, perhaps incurring some penalty. For example, in the case of a CD, the depositor may request the withdrawal of funds prior to the maturity date. Typically, the deposit-accepting institution will grant this request but assess an early withdrawal penalty. In the case of certain types of investment companies, shareholders have the right to redeem their shares at any time. These rights add to the uncertainty of the liability from the point of view of the financial institution.

Similarly, some life insurance products have a cash-surrender value. This means that, at specified dates, the policyholder can exchange the policy for a lump-sum payment. Typically, the lump-sum payment will penalize the policyholder for turning in the policy. Also, some life insurance products have a loan value, which means that the policyholder has the right to borrow against the cash value of the policy. Both factors increase the uncertainty of the insurance company's liabilities.

In addition to uncertainty about the timing and amount of the cash outlays, and the potential for the depositor or policyholder to withdraw cash early or borrow against a policy, an institution has to be concerned with possible reductions in cash inflows. In the case of a depository institution, this means the inability to obtain deposits. For insurance companies, it means reduced premiums because of the cancellation of policies. For certain types of investment companies, it means not being able to find new buyers for shares.

OVERVIEW OF ASSET/LIABILITY MANAGEMENT

The two goals of a financial institution are (1) to earn an adequate return on funds invested and (2) to maintain a comfortable surplus of assets beyond liabilities. The task of managing the funds of a financial institution to accomplish these goals is referred to as asset/liability management or **surplus management**. This task involves a trade-off between controlling the risk of a decline in the surplus and taking on acceptable risks in order to earn an adequate return on the funds invested. (See Box 7.) With respect to the risks, the manager must consider the risks of both the assets and the liabilities, as mentioned earlier.

BOX 7

ASSET/LIABILITY MANAGEMENT

On September 13, 1985, the Institute of Chartered Financial Analysts sponsored a conference entitled "Asset/Liability Management." The following passage is from a speech by Alfred Weinberger, a vice president in the Bond Portfolio Analysis Group of Salomon Brothers Inc:

The challenges of managing financial institutions have become formidable in recent years. While there always has been some appreciation of the link between assets and liabilities, the importance of the asset/liability management process has been dramatically heightened by the rapid changes in the broader financial environment and marketplace. The capital bases supporting financial institutions and the old rules of thumb for managing them did not envi-

sion the kinds of potential risks that have been developing in this environment of rapid change. Clearly, something had to be done. Attention focused on the subject of asset/liability management as one response to this situation. Today, asset/liability management is not just an economic exercise, it is a mainstream activity of concern to all participants, portfolio managers, and liability managers.

Asset/liability management is the prudent assessment of trade-offs. The emphasis from the asset/liability perspective is on risk control, but it is important not to lose sight of the other axis, that of profit or return enhancement. Thus, we have the fundamental trade-off of risk versus return. This relatively clear statement abstracts from a lot of difficult issues and subsidiary

trade-offs that professional asset/liability managers must tackle. Two critical questions are (1) how to define risk and return; and (2) how to discern and manage risk and return within a set of explicit and implicit corporate aims and yardsticks.

Source: Alfred Weinberger, "Strategies for Effective Asset/Liability Management," in Darwin M. Bayston and Cathryn E. Kittell (eds.), *Asset/Liability Management* (Charlottesville, VA: The Institute of Chartered Financial Analysts, 1986), p. 26.

Questions for Box 7

1. What are the different types of risk that should be considered in asset/liability management?
2. What do you think Mr. Weinberger means by "manage risk and return within a set of explicit and implicit corporate aims and yardsticks"?

Institutions may calculate three types of surpluses: economic, accounting, and regulatory. The method of valuing assets and liabilities greatly affects the apparent health of a financial institution.

Economic Surplus

The **economic surplus** of any entity is the difference between the market value of all its assets and the market value of its liabilities. That is,

Economic surplus = market value of assets − market value of liabilities

While the concept of a market value of assets may not seem unusual, one might ask, What is the market value of liabilities? This value is simply the present value of the liabilities, where the liabilities are discounted at an appropriate interest rate. A rise in interest rates will therefore decrease the present value or market value of the liabilities; a decrease in interest rates will increase the present value or market value of liabilities. Thus, the economic surplus can be expressed as

Economic surplus = market value of assets − present value of liabilities

For example, consider an institution that has a portfolio of only bonds and liabilities. Let's look at what happens to the economic surplus if interest rates rise. This will cause the bonds to decline in value; but it will also cause the liabilities to decline in value. Since both the assets and liabilities decline, the economic surplus can either increase, decrease, or remain unchanged. The net effect depends on the relative interest rate sensitivity of the assets compared with the liabilities. As we stated earlier, duration is a measure of the responsiveness of an asset to changes in interest rates. Thus, a duration can be calculated for a portfolio of assets. What we can do for assets, we can do for liabilities. We can also define the duration of liabilities as their responsiveness to a change in interest rates.

If the duration of the assets is greater than the duration of the liabilities, the economic surplus will increase if interest rates fall. For example, suppose that the current market value of a portfolio of assets is equal to $100 million and the present value of liabilities is $90 million. Then the economic surplus is $10 million. Suppose that the duration of the assets is 5 and the duration of the liabilities is 3. Consider the following two scenarios:

Scenario 1:   Interest rates decline by 100 basis points. Because the duration of the assets is 5, the market value of the assets will increase by approximately 5%, or $5 million (5% × $100 million), to $105 million. The liabilities will also increase. Since the duration of the liabilities is assumed to be 3, the present value of the liabilities will increase by $2.7 million (3% × $90 million) to $92.7 million. Thus, the surplus increased from $10 million to $12.3 million ($105 million − $92.7 million).

Scenario 2:   Interest rates rise by 100 basis points. Because the duration of the assets is 5, the market value of the assets will decrease by approximately 5% to $95 million. The liabilities will also decrease. Since the duration of the liabilities is 3, the present value of the liabilities will decrease by $2.7 million to $87.3 million. The surplus is then reduced to $7.7 million from $10 million.

Since the net effect on the surplus depends on the duration or interest rate sensitivity of the assets and liabilities, it is imperative that portfolio managers be able to measure this sensitivity for all assets and liabilities.

A variety of strategies have been used by institutional investors to either maximize economic surplus or hedge economic surplus against any adverse change in market conditions. The principles of modern portfolio theory have been used to construct an optimal portfolio of assets to maximize return without any recognition given to liabilities. In Chapter 28 we explain how modern portfolio theory can be extended to provide a framework for creating a portfolio to optimize economic surplus of an institution.

Accounting Surplus

Institutional investors must prepare periodic financial statements. These financial statements must be prepared in accordance with *generally accepted accounting principles (GAAP)*. Thus, the assets and liabilities reported are based on GAAP accounting. The accounting treatment for assets is governed by a relatively new accounting requirement, Statement of Financial Accounting Standards No. 115, more popularly referred to as FASB 115.[4] However, it does not deal with the accounting treatment for liabilities.

---

[4]FASB 115 was issued in May 1993 and became effective with fiscal years beginning after December 15, 1993.

GAAP for Assets   With respect to the financial reporting of assets, there are two possible methods for reporting: (1) amortized cost or historical cost or (2) market value. Despite the fact that the real cash flow is the same regardless of the accounting treatment, there can be substantial differences in the financial statements using these two methods.

In the amortized cost method, the value reported on the balance sheet reflects an adjustment to the acquisition cost for debt securities purchased at a discount or premium from their maturity value. This method is sometimes referred to as *book value accounting*. In the market value accounting method, the balance-sheet-reported value of an asset is its market value. When an asset is reported in the financial statements of an institution at its market value, it is said to be *marked to market*.

FASB 115 specifies which method must be followed for assets. Specifically, the accounting treatment required for a security depends on how the security is classified. There are three classifications of investment accounts: (1) held to maturity, (2) available for sale, and (3) held for trading. The definition of each account is set forth in FASB 115, and we summarize each below.

The *held-to-maturity account* includes assets that the institution plans to hold until they mature. Obviously, the assets classified in this account cannot be common stock because they have no maturity. For all assets in the held-to-maturity account, the amortized cost method must be used.

An asset is classified as in the *available-for-sale account* if the institution does not have the ability to hold the asset to maturity or intends to sell it. An asset acquired for the purpose of earning a short-term trading profit from market movements is classified in the *held-for-trading account*. For all assets in the available-for-sale and trading accounts, market value accounting is used. Thus, these two accounts more accurately reflect the economic value of the assets held by the institution.

Table 7-3 summarizes the accounting treatment of assets as set forth by FASB 115.

GAAP and Unrealized Gains and Losses   When financial statements are prepared, the change in the value of assets must be accounted for. An *unrealized gain or loss* occurs when the asset's value has changed but the gain or loss is not realized since the asset is not sold. For example, if an asset has a market value of $100 at the beginning of an accounting period and is held in the portfolio at the end of the accounting period with a market value of $110, the unrealized gain is $10.

TABLE 7-3			
SUMMARY OF KEY PROVISIONS OF FASB 115			
Account Classification	**Accounting Method for Assets**	**Will Affect Surplus**	**Will Affect Reported Earnings**
Held to maturity	Amortized cost	No	No
Available for sale	Market value	Yes	No
Held for trading	Market value	Yes	Yes

Any realized gain or loss affects the accounting surplus. Specifically, an unrealized gain increases the accounting surplus and an unrealized loss reduces it. The unrealized gain or loss may or may not affect the reported earnings.

Under FASB 115, the accounting treatment for any unrealized gain or loss depends on the account in which the asset is classified. Specifically, any unrealized gain or loss is ignored for assets in the held-to-maturity account. Thus, for assets in this account there is no affect on reported earnings or the accounting surplus. For the other two accounts, any unrealized gain or loss affects the accounting surplus as described above. However, there is a difference in how reported earnings are affected. For assets classified in the available-for-sale account, unrealized gains or losses are not included in reported earnings; in contrast, for assets classified in the held for trading account, any gains or losses are included in reported earnings. These provisions are summarized in Table 7-3.

Regulatory Surplus

Institutional investors that are regulated at the state or federal levels must provide to regulators financial reports based on regulatory accounting principles (RAP). RAP accounting for a regulated institution need not use the same rules as set forth by FASB 115 (i.e., GAAP accounting). Liabilities may or may not be reported at their present value, depending on the type of institution and the type of liability. The surplus as measured using RAP accounting is called **regulatory surplus**, and, as in the case of accounting surplus, may be materially different from economic surplus.

Dangers of Ignoring the Market Value of Assets and Liabilities

FASB 115 is a vast improvement over the previous financial reporting requirements for assets. Basically, FASB 115 has moved the accounting for assets closer to their economic value. It should be noted that the failure to require certain institutions to mark assets to market has hidden their poor financial condition. The best example of this is the savings and loan associations (S&Ls). Most readers are familiar with the financial problems these institutions have had to face. One of the reasons the S&L problems were allowed to fester was the failure of regulators to require that assets of these institutions be marked to market. With the assets of these institutions being long term in maturity, and the liabilities short term, the assets are more interest rate sensitive than the liabilities. Consequently, a rise in interest rates means that the surplus will decrease. If interest rates rise enough over a sustained period of time, the market value of assets will be less than the market value of liabilities, resulting in a negative value for the surplus. (This is called a *deficit*.) This is in fact what occurred with the S&Ls.

BENCHMARKS FOR NON-LIABILITY-DRIVEN ENTITIES

Thus far, our discussion has focused on institutional investors that face liabilities. However, not all financial institutions face liabilities. Investment companies, the topic of Chapter 11, are an example. Also, while an institution such as a pension plan may face liabilities, it may engage external money managers and set for those managers an objective that is unrelated to the pension fund's liabilities. For such money managers who do not face liabilities, the objective is to outperform some client-designated benchmark. The benchmark may be one of the stock indexes discussed in Chapter 3 or one of the bond indexes described in Chapter 24. In general, the performance of the money manager will be measured as follows:

Return on the portfolio − return on the benchmark

Active money management involves creating a portfolio that will earn a return (after adjusting for risk) greater than the benchmark. In contrast, a strategy of indexing is one in which a money manager creates a portfolio that only seeks to match the return on the benchmark.

Given our discussion of asset/liability management and the management of funds in the absence of liabilities, we can see that the investment strategy of one financial institution may be inappropriate for another. As with investment strategies, a security or asset class that may be attractive for one institutional investor may be inappropriate for the portfolio of another.

■ **SUMMARY**

An investor may be exposed to one or more risks when investing. Price risk is the risk that the price of the security will decline. This is the major risk faced by investors. This risk can be quantified. One such measure is duration, which measures the interest rate sensitivity of an asset. Default risk, also called credit risk, refers to the risk that the issuer of a bond may be unable to make timely principal and interest payments on the issue. Inflation risk or purchasing-power risk arises because of the variations in the purchasing power of the cash flows from a security due to inflation. For a security whose cash flows are not denominated in U.S. dollars, exchange rate risk or currency risk is the risk that the currency will depreciate relative to the U.S. dollar. Reinvestment risk is the risk that proceeds received in the future will have to be reinvested at a lower interest rate. An investor who buys a callable bond is exposed both to the risk that the cash flow is uncertain and to reinvestment risk; these risks are called call risk. Liquidity risk is the risk that the investor will receive less than the financial asset's true value because of a large bid-ask spread and commissions.

The nature of their liabilities, as well as regulatory considerations, determines the investment strategy pursued by all institutional investors. By nature, liabilities vary with respect to the amount and timing of their payment. The liabilities will generally fall into one of the four types shown in Table 7-2. Liabilities are affected by many of the risks that affect assets: interest rate risk, exchange rate risk, and inflation risk.

Surplus management is a more appropriate description of the activity of asset/liability management of an institution. The economic surplus of any entity is the difference between the market value of all its assets and the present value of its liabilities. Institutional investors will pursue a strategy to either maximize economic surplus or hedge economic surplus against any adverse change in market conditions. In addition to economic surplus, there is accounting surplus and regulatory surplus. The former is based on GAAP accounting, specifically, FASB 115, and the latter on RAP accounting. To the extent that these two surplus measures may not reflect the true financial condition of an institution, future financial problems may arise.

In contrast to the managers of financial institutions who face liabilities, there are managers who are free to make investment decisions without regard to liability constraints. Even though there is no liability, such managers are typically evaluated against some client-designated benchmark.

■ KEY TERMS

asset/liability management	duration	liquidity risk
business risk	economic surplus	price risk
call risk	exchange rate risk	purchasing-power risk
credit risk	financial risk	regulatory surplus
currency risk	inflation risk	surplus management
default risk	liability	

■ QUESTIONS

1. **a.** What is meant by price risk?
   b. Why may price risk and liquidity risk be unimportant to a portfolio manager who invests in a three-year bond and plans to hold that bond to the maturity date?

2. Explain why an investor in a bond that pays a fixed interest rate faces inflation risk?

3. **a.** Suppose that an investor wishes to invest $X for five years. Suppose also that the investor can purchase for $X a financial asset today which promises to pay $Y (where $Y is greater than $X) five years from now. No additional payments are made to the investor over the five-year period. Does this investor face reinvestment risk?
   b. A zero-coupon bond is one an investor purchases at some price and for which the investor receives a specified amount at the maturity date. These bonds were first issued in the early 1980s when interest rates in the United States were at an all-time high. Why do you think zero-coupon bonds were introduced at that time?

4. What risks does a U.S. investor face if he or she purchases a French corporation's bond whose cash flows are denominated in French francs?

5. For a portfolio of bonds, to what extent do price risk and reinvestment risk offset each other when interest rates change?

6. What are the two dimensions of a liability?

7. Why is it not always simple to estimate the liability of an institution?

8. A bank issues an obligation to depositors in which it agrees to pay 8% guaranteed for one year. With the funds it obtains, the bank can invest in a wide range of financial assets. What risk is involved if the bank is allowed to invest the funds in common stock?

9. Why do factors that affect the risk of a financial asset also affect liabilities?

10. Why is asset/liability management best described as surplus management?

11. **a.** What is meant by the economic surplus of an institution?
    b. What is meant by the accounting surplus of an institution?
    c. What is meant by the regulatory surplus of an institution?
    d. Which surplus best reflects the economic well-being of an institution?
    e. Under what circumstances are all three surplus measures the same?

12. Suppose that the present value of the liabilities of some financial institution is $600 million and the surplus $800 million. The duration of the liabilities is equal to 5. Suppose further that the portfolio of this financial institution includes only bonds and the duration for the portfolio is 6.
    a. What is the market value of the portfolio of bonds?
    b. What does a duration of 6 mean for the portfolio of assets?
    c. What does a duration of 5 mean for the portfolio of assets?
    d. Suppose that interest rates increase by 50 basis points. What will be the approximate new value for the surplus?
    e. Suppose that interest rates decrease by 50 basis points. What will be the approximate new value for the surplus?

13. **a.** Why is the interest rate sensitivity of an institution's assets and liabilities important?
    b. In 1986, Martin Leibowitz of Salomon Brothers Inc wrote a paper entitled "Total Portfolio Duration: A New Perspective on Asset Allocation." What do you think a total portfolio duration means?

14. If an institution has liabilities that are interest rate sensitive and invests in a portfolio of common stocks, can you determine what will happen

to the institution's economic surplus if interest rates change?

15. The following quotes are taken from Phillip D. Parker (associate general counsel of the SEC), "Market Value Accounting—An Idea Whose Time Has Come?" in Elliot P. Williams (ed.), *Managing Asset/Liability Portfolios* (Charlottesville, VA: Association for Investment Management and Research, 1991), published prior to the passage of FASB 115.
    a. "A review of the S&L crisis dramatically illustrates the danger of using accounting measures that do not reflect economic realities." Comment on this statement.
    b. "The use of market value accounting would eliminate any incentive to sell or retain investment securities for reasons of accounting treatment rather than business utility." Explain why this statement is correct. (Note that in historical accounting a loss is only recognized when a security is sold.)

16. Indicate why you agree or disagree with the following statements.
    a. "Under FASB 115 all assets must be marked to market."
    b. "The greater the price volatility of assets classified in the held-to-maturity account, the greater the volatility of the accounting surplus and reported earnings."

17. Explain the investment objectives of a manager who does not face liabilities.

CHAPTER 8
INSURANCE COMPANIES

LEARNING OBJECTIVES

After reading this chapter you will be able to:

- distinguish between a life insurance company and a property and casualty insurance company.

- explain the regulation of insurance companies.

- discuss the regulation of insurance companies' investments and the limitations imposed by regulators.

- explain what is meant by revenue, profit, regulatory surplus, adjusted regulatory capital, and risk-based capital requirements.

- distinguish between the nature of the liabilities of life insurance companies and those of property and casualty insurance companies.

- describe the risk characteristics of the types of policies sold by life insurance companies.

- explain the interest rate sensitivity of life insurance policies.

- explain the relationship between the management of a life insurance investment portfolio and the type of insurance policy issued.

- discuss the complexities associated with managing a portfolio for a property and casualty insurance company.

- explain the types of assets in which life insurance companies and property and casualty insurance companies invest.

In this chapter and the three to follow, we take a closer look at the major institutional investors. For each institution, we examine the nature of its liabilities and the strategies it may use to accomplish its investment objectives. We also look at regulations that influence investment decisions.

Our focus in this chapter is on insurance companies. Insurance companies are financial intermediaries that, for a price, will make a payment if a certain event occurs. They function as risk bearers. There are two types of insurance companies: life insurance companies (*life companies*) and property and casualty insurance companies (*P&C companies*). The principal event that the former insures against is death.[1] Upon the death of a policyholder, a life company agrees to make either a lump-sum payment or a series of payments

---

[1] Life insurance companies also sell health insurance policies.

to the beneficiary of the policy. Life insurance protection is not the only financial product sold by these companies; a major portion of the business of life companies deals with providing retirement benefits. In contrast, P&C companies insure against a wide variety of occurrences. Two examples are automobile and home insurance.

The key distinction between life and P&C companies lies in the difficulty of projecting whether a policyholder will be paid off and, if so, how much the payment will be. While this is no simple task for either type of insurance company, from an actuarial perspective it is easier for a life company. The amount and timing of claims on P&C companies are more difficult to predict because of the randomness of natural catastrophes and the unpredictability of court awards in liability cases. This uncertainty about the timing and amount of cash outlays to satisfy claims affects the investment strategies used by the managers of the P&C companies' funds.

While we have distinguished the two types of insurance companies here by the nature of their liabilities, most large insurance companies do sell both life insurance and property and casualty insurance policies. Usually a parent company has a life company subsidiary and a P&C company subsidiary.

FUNDAMENTAL CHARACTERISTICS OF THE INSURANCE INDUSTRY

We begin with the fundamental characteristics of the insurance industry that are shared by life companies and P&C companies. (See Box 8.)

The Insurance Policy and Premiums

An *insurance policy* is a legally binding contract for which the policyholder (or owner) pays *premiums* in exchange for the insurance company's promise to pay specified sums contingent on future events. The company is said to *underwrite* the owner's risk, and acts as a buffer against the uncertainties of life. The process of underwriting can include a careful evaluation of the applicant's circumstances.

When the policy is accepted by an insurance company, it becomes an asset for the owner and a liability for the insurance company. Premiums can be paid in a single payment or, more commonly, in a regular series of payments. If the owner fails to pay premiums, the policy is said to *lapse*, or *terminate*. Unless both parties renew the contract, the company loses the future stream of premiums, and the owner loses the protection the policy had promised.

Surplus and Reserves

The surplus of an insurance company is the difference between its assets and its liabilities. Since the accounting treatment of both assets and liabilities is established by state statutes covering an insurance company, surplus is commonly referred to as **statutory surplus**.

In determining the statutory surplus of an insurance company, the value of the assets and the liabilities must be determined. Later in this chapter, we will discuss how assets of life companies and property and casualty compa-

BOX 8

TO OUR POLICYHOLDERS

As Chief Executive Officer, one of my most important responsibilities is to monitor how well we are serving our policyowners. Do our products and services meet their expectations . . . and our own high performance standards?

I'm pleased to present this report because our financials best demonstrate how well we are doing. When you look at the results, you will see a growing, dynamic company which is perhaps the most financially secure company in the industry. And that's not just our opinion.

During 1992, independent rating services again conferred their highest rating on The Guardian Life Insurance Company and The Guardian Insurance & Annuity Company (GIAC):

Moody's	Aaa
Standard & Poor's	AAA
A.M. Best	A++

There are only seven companies that received top ratings in the most recent evaluations from Moody's and Standard & Poor's. Guardian Life and GIAC are two of them!

This past year was an outstanding sales year for The Guardian. Despite a still sluggish economy, record sales were set in each of our marketing areas. Here are a few highlights:

- Individual life insurance sales were $153.4 million, an increase of 28.6%.
- Individual disability income sales were $16.5 million, a 20% increase.
- Group life insurance sales were $38.8 million, a 6.2% increase.
- Group health insurance sales were $544.8 million, a 2.4% increase.
- Equity sales were $732.2 million, a 46.5% increase.

In 1992, our total individual and group life insurance in force reached $103.4 billion, a 14.5% increase over 1992.

Of course, these significant increases in sales are only a part of the overall story. How well we manage our day-to-day investments and operations are also important components of our financial strength and our ability to meet tomorrow's commitments. Let's review these aspects of our business which have enhanced our profitability and contributed to our surplus growth . . . and to our dividend distributions.

The way to maintain a profitable company is through careful expense control, sound underwriting, and quality investments. At The Guardian, we work hard at all three and have earned a reputation for a high level of profitability. Moody's Investors Service has stated: "Guardian has been very profitable—a consequence of its strong insurance operations and its sound investment strategies."

Our investment philosophy is to balance the safety of our policyowners' principal with our objective to achieve good investment returns. I'm pleased to report that in 1992 our net investment income for the parent Company was $534 million.

Surplus—our net worth—is the most important single number you will find in this report. It is the cornerstone of our financial strength. Surplus which reached $798.6 million in 1992 has grown by an average of 17.1% over the last five years.

Surplus is significant because it indicates soundness and the Company's ability to pay benefits in the years ahead. It protects the Company from unforeseen economic events. It means that the Company can afford to develop competitive products . . . and invest in its future by modernizing and improving operations.

Capital to assets is also one of the best ways to compare insurance companies. Capital, as defined by Moody's, equals surplus plus AVR* plus 50% of dividend reserve liability. In 1992, The Guardian's capital to asset ratio was 15.7%. When you compare us to other companies, you'll find that Guardian Life's surplus ratio is one of the highest in the industry. Additionally, your Company has no debt. *We don't owe a dime to anyone.* There are very few companies, in any business, that can say that.

Our efficient performance enables us to pay dividends on our permanent life policies. Policy dividends represent a share of the Company's profits, and mean a lower cost of insurance for you. We're proud of our dividend history which is discussed later in this report.

An important goal of The Guardian is to deliver the best possible products to the consumer . . . products designed to fill critical future needs. We do this through five specialized product areas, which enables us to provide the very best in products and services. You will find a commentary about these product areas on the following pages.

The Guardian does more than sell insurance. We recognize that today's marketplace demands a variety of investment vehicles. So we have been very active in the development and marketing of equity products. In 1992, more than half of our equity business came from the sale of variable annuities.

In discussing The Guardian's strengths, I cannot overlook our impressive career agent field force. Each of our agents is a trained professional with the knowledge to uncover clients' needs and suggest the best way to fill them.

˙Asset valuation reserve.

Source: Letter in the *1992 Annual Report of the Guardian* from Arthur V. Ferrara, CLU, chairman of the board and chief executive officer.

Questions for Box 8

1. Why is the rating received by Guardian Life important?
2. Why does the way to maintain a profitable life insurance company involve sound underwriting and quality investments?
3. Explain what Mr. Ferrara means when he writes: "Surplus is significant because it indicates soundness and the Company's ability to pay benefits in the years ahead."

nies are determined. As for liabilities, the complication in determining their value arises because the insurance company has committed to make payments at some time in the future and those payments are contingent on certain events occurring. To properly reflect these contingent liabilities in its financial statement, an insurance company must establish an account called a **reserve**. A reserve is not cash that is set aside by the insurance company. It is simply an accounting entry. While there are different types of reserve accounts (such as the "dividend reserve liability" mentioned in Box 8) that must be established by an insurance company, for our purposes here it is unnecessary to discuss them.

Statutory surplus is important because regulators view this as the ultimate amount that can be drawn upon to pay policyholders. The growth of this surplus for an insurance company will determine how much future business it can underwrite. Until recently, the ability of an insurance company to take on the risks associated with underwriting policies has been measured by the ratio of the annual earned premium (discussed below) to statutory surplus. Usually, this ratio is kept at between two to one and three to one. Consequently, $2 to $3 in annual premiums can be supported for each $1 available in statutory surplus.

Determination of Profits

An insurance company's revenue for a fiscal year is generated from two sources. The first is the premiums earned during the fiscal year. Not all of the premiums received are earned for that fiscal year. For example, suppose on November 1 Ms. Johnson writes a check to the All Right Insurance Company for $1,200 to cover her annual automobile insurance premium for the next 12 months. Suppose also that the insurance company's fiscal year ends on December 31. Then on December 31, the insurance company has only earned two months of the premium, or $200 ($2 \times \$1,200/12$). Thus, while Ms. Johnson paid and All Right Insurance Company received $1,200, the insurance company's earned premium is only $200. The second source of revenue is the investment income earned from invested assets.

From the revenue, costs are deducted to determine the profit. There are two general categories of costs. The first category is made up of additions to reserves. The second consists of the costs associated with selling insurance policies. If there is a profit, any portion of the profit not distributed to the owners as dividends is added to the statutory surplus. If there is a loss, the statutory surplus is decreased by the amount of the loss.

The overall profit or loss can be divided into two parts: investment income and underwriting income. **Investment income** is basically the revenue from the insurance company's portfolio of invested assets. **Underwriting income** is the difference between the premiums earned and the costs of settling claims.

Government Guarantees

Unlike the liabilities of depository institutions, insurance policies are not guaranteed by any federal entity. However, most states have statutory "guarantee associations" that provide some protection to, at least, state residents.[2] Consequently, the premiums charged by insurance companies on policies (i.e., the pricing terms) are directly related to their financial ratings. Most market participants rely on a rating system from A. M. Best, Moody's Investors Service, or Standard & Poor's Corporation.

Regulations Affecting Investment Decisions

The investments of insurance companies are also regulated primarily at the state level. Each state establishes its own regulations to ensure the safety and soundness of insurance companies doing business in that state. Model laws and regulations are developed by the National Association of Insurance Commissioners (NAIC), a voluntary association of state insurance commissioners. An adoption of a model law or regulation by the NAIC is not binding on a state, but states often use these models when writing their laws and regulations.

To insure compliance with its regulations, life insurance companies licensed to do business in a state are required to file an annual statement and supporting documents with the state's insurance department. The annual statement, referred to as the **convention statement**, shows among other things the assets, liabilities, and surplus of the reporting company. The surplus is closely watched by regulators and rating agencies because it is one of the determinants of the amount of business that an insurance company can underwrite. The convention statement must be prepared in accordance with certain accounting principles that are the same for all states.

There are three principal areas that the NAIC has addressed that affect investment decisions and strategies of insurance companies: (1) risk-based capital requirements, (2) the way assets are valued for regulatory reporting purposes, and (3) guidelines for investments. We will discuss the first two areas later in the chapter. We focus here on risk-based capital requirements.

Regulators monitor the financial well-being of insurance companies. At one time, the measure of the financial well-being related the capital of the company to its size, where size was defined as premiums earned. Capital has a well-defined meaning in the insurance industry. It is the statutory surplus plus specific statutory-defined adjustments and is referred to as *adjusted regulatory capital*. The adjustments are technical in nature and need not concern us. (See the discussion in Box 8.)

In 1993, the NAIC introduced a new approach to determining whether an insurance company had adequate adjusted regulatory capital. Rather than using asset size, the NAIC bases the capital needs of an insurance company on the nature of the risks to which it is exposed.[3] Based on these risks, the required amount of adjusted regulatory capital, referred to as the *risk-based*

---

[2] The New York State Guarantee Fund, for example, had $500 million available in 1993 for companies in liquidation.

[3] For a life insurance company, the risks are categorized as follows by the NAIC: asset risk, insurance risk, interest rate risk, and business risk. For a property and casualty insurance company, the risks are defined as asset risk, credit risk, loss/loss adjustment expense risk, and written premium risk.

TABLE 8-1

CAPITAL FACTORS FOR SELECTED ASSET CLASSES FOR LIFE COMPANIES FOR DETERMINING RISK-BASED CAPITAL REQUIREMENTS

Asset Class	Capital Factor
U.S. government securities	0.0%
Corporates, municipals, agencies, MBS, CMOs, & ABS* rated:	
NAIC (A-AAA)	0.3%
Corporates & municipals rated:	
NAIC 2 (BBB)	1.0%
NAIC 3 (BB)	2.0%
NAIC 4 (B)	4.5%
NAIC 5 (CCC)	10.0%
NAIC 6 (Default)	30.0%
Common stocks	15.0%
Mortgage & collateral loans	5.0%
Real estate	10.0%

*MBS = mortgage-backed securities, CMOs = collateralized mortgage obligations, ABS = asset-backed securities.

capital requirement, is determined. A formula is specified by the NAIC that involves weighting each asset and liability on the balance sheet by specified percentages (i.e., risk weights) to determine the risk-based capital requirement for an insurance company.

Of the risk factors considered in determining risk-based capital requirements, the one that has a direct bearing on decisions made by the manager of an insurance company's portfolio is the asset risk. More specifically, the risk-based capital requirements consider only credit risk associated with investing in an asset. To see how the risk-based capital requirement is determined just for asset risk, Table 8-1 shows various asset classes and the weight or capital factor for each. There are six asset categories for corporate and municipal bonds. The categories differ by the credit rating as shown in parentheses. In Chapter 18, we will discuss credit ratings. For now it is sufficient to note that as one moves down the table for these six asset classes, the credit risk increases. The capital factors are higher the greater the credit risk of an asset class. Therefore, the higher the portion of the portfolio invested in asset classes with a greater credit risk, the greater the risk-based capital requirement due to asset risk.

Table 8-2 gives the asset composition for two hypothetical life companies, A and B, and shows how the risk-based capital requirement due to asset risk is determined for each. Notice that while the two life companies have the same asset value, $1 billion, the risk-based capital requirements due to asset risk are $30.9 million greater for life company B than A ($72.55 million versus $41.65). This is because B allocates the greater proportion of its funds to lower-rated corporate and municipal bonds, common stock, and real estate, compared with A.

TABLE 8-2

CALCULATION OF RISK-BASED CAPITAL REQUIREMENTS FOR ASSET RISK FOR TWO HYPOTHETICAL LIFE COMPANIES

Life company: A
Assets in millions
Total assets: $1 billion

Asset Class	Capital Factor	Dollar Allocation	Capital Factor × Dollar Allocation
U.S. government securities	0.0%	$200	$ 0
Corporates, municipals, agencies, MBS, CMOs, & ABS rated:			
NAIC (A-AAA)	0.3%	300	0.90
Corporates & municipals rated:			
NAIC 2 (BBB)	1.0%	100	1.00
NAIC 3 (BB)	2.0%	50	1.00
NAIC 4 (B)	4.5%	0	0
NAIC 5 (CCC)	10.0%	0	0
NAIC 6 (Default)	30.0%	0	0
Common stocks	15.0%	150	22.50
Mortgage & collateral loans	5.0%	75	3.75
Real estate	10.0%	125	12.50
Risk-based capital requirement for asset risk			$41.65

Life company B
Assets in millions
Total assets: $1 billion

Asset Class	Capital Factor	Dollar Allocation	Capital Factor × Dollar Allocation
U.S. government securities	0.0%	$ 80	$ 0
Corporates, municipals, agencies, MBS, CMOs, & ABS rated:			
NAIC (A-AAA)	0.3%	100	0.30
Corporates & municipals rated:			
NAIC 2 (BBB)	1.0%	100	1.00
NAIC 3 (BB)	2.0%	150	3.00
NAIC 4 (B)	4.5%	50	2.25
NAIC 5 (CCC)	10.0%	50	5.00
NAIC 6 (Default)	30.0%	30	9.00
Common stocks	15.0%	220	33.00
Mortgage & collateral loans	5.0%	60	3.00
Real estate	10.0%	160	16.00
Risk-based capital requirement for asset risk			$72.55

The capital factors will affect the decision of a portfolio manager in two ways. First, insurance companies with low statutory surplus will have to limit their exposure to assets with high credit risk. Second, the decision to allocate funds to particular asset classes will depend not only on the potential yield from investing in an asset class but on the risk-based capital requirement.

LIFE INSURANCE COMPANIES

As of 1991, the total assets of U.S. life companies was $1.52 trillion.[4] The nature of the life insurance business has changed dramatically since the 1970s, due to high and variable inflation rates and increased domestic and global competitive pressures resulting from financial deregulation throughout the world. Moreover, consumer sophistication has increased, forcing life companies to offer more competitive products.

Life companies compete with other life companies in providing insurance protection. In addition, as explained below, many of the products sold by life companies have an investment feature. Because of this feature, life companies also compete both with other financial institutions that provide investment instruments and with direct market investments in securities.

Nature of the Liabilities

The liabilities of the insurance company are the insurance policies that they have underwritten. Below we will describe the various products. Before describing these policies, let's look at the liability risk that insurance companies face. As we explained in the previous chapter, there are risks in the liabilities of an institution as well as in the portfolio of assets. For a life company in particular, many of the products are interest rate sensitive. The interest rate offered on an investment-type insurance policy is called the **crediting rate**. If the crediting rate of a policy is not competitive with market interest rates or rates offered by other life companies, an owner may allow the policy to lapse or, if permissible, may begin to borrow against the policy. In either case, this will result in an outflow of cash from the life insurance company.

Term Insurance Policy Risks   **Term life insurance** is a contract that provides a death benefit but no cash buildup; it has no investment component. Further, the premium charged by the insurance company remains constant only for a specified term of years. Most policies are automatically renewable at the end of each term, but at a higher rate. When an insurance company issues this type of contract, it knows the amount of the liability it may have to pay, but it does not know the date. However, using actuarial data, the timing of the liability can be reasonably estimated for a pool of insured individuals. The premium that the insurance company charges is usually such that, no matter what happens to interest rates, the life company will have sufficient funds to meet the obligation when policyholders die.

Whole Life Policy Risks   **Whole life insurance** is a policy with two features: (1) It pays off a stated amount upon the death of the insured, and (2) it accumulates a cash value that the policyholder can borrow against. The first feature is an insurance protection feature—the same feature that term insurance provides. The second is an investment feature because the policy accumulates

---

[4]*Best's Insurance Reports—Life/Health*, 1992, p. vi. Assets are defined as "admitted assets," which means all assets approved by state insurance departments as existing property in the ownership of the company.

value and at every point in time has a **cash-surrender value**, an amount the insurance company will pay if the policyholder ends the policy. The policyholder has the option to borrow against the policy, and the amount that can be borrowed is called the **loan value**. The interest rate at which the funds can be borrowed is specified in the policy.

The liability risk associated with the investment feature of a whole life policy is that the insurance company may not be able to earn a return on its investments greater than its policies' crediting rate. This would result in a decline in the life insurance company's surplus. Offering a lower crediting rate on a whole life policy than competitors may reduce the risk that the crediting rate will not be earned, but increases the likelihood that the owner will borrow against the policy or allow it to lapse.

Universal Life Policy Risks **Universal life** is a whole life product created in response to the problem just cited for a whole life policy. The policyholder pays a premium for insurance protection, and for a separate fee he or she can invest in a vehicle that pays a competitive interest rate rather than the below-market crediting rates offered on a whole life policy. For a policyholder, the advantage of this investment alternative relative to the direct purchase of a security is that under the current tax code, the interest rate earned is tax-deferred. The risk that the insurer faces is that the return earned is not competitive with those of other insurance companies, resulting in policy lapses.

Variable Life Policy Risks A **variable life** policy is a whole life policy that provides a death benefit that depends on the market value of the insured's portfolio at the time of death. Typically the company invests premiums in common stocks, and hence variable life policies are referred to as **equity-linked policies**. While the death benefits are variable, there is a guaranteed minimum death benefit that the insurer agrees to pay regardless of the market value of the portfolio. The insurer's risk is that the return earned will be less than that of its competitors, resulting in policy lapses. In addition, the insurer faces the risk that the return earned over the insured's life is less than the guaranteed minimum death benefit specified in the policy.

Annuity Policy Risks An **annuity** is a regular periodic payment made by the insurance company to a policyholder for a specified period of time. There are two types of annuity policies. One is a life contingent policy, and the other a non-life contingent policy. To understand the first type of policy, consider a person who retires with a given amount of resources to be spread evenly over her remaining life. Clearly, she faces a problem because the length of her life is unknown. The life company, relying on the fact that the average length of life of a group can be estimated rather accurately, can offer the person a fixed annuity for the rest of her life, thus relieving her of the risk of outliving her resources. Annuities are one of the oldest types of insurance contracts.

At present most annuity policies are non-life contingency policies, and they are used primarily in connection with a pension plan. In a **single-premium deferred annuity**, the sponsor of a pension plan pays a single premium to the life insurance company, which in turn agrees to make lifelong payments to the employee (the policyholder) when that employee retires. Most policies give the policyholder the right to take the benefits in a lump sum rather than a payout over time.

Other types of non-life contingent annuity policies can also be purchased from a life insurance company. One example is the annuity policy a state might purchase to pay off a lottery winner. Most state lotteries do not offer the winnings in a lump-sum payment. That means that a winner of, say, a $3 million lottery does not receive $3 million today. Instead, there is a payout of a fixed amount over some specified period of time. The state can purchase an annuity policy from a life insurance company to make payments to the lottery winner.

A second example of a non-life contingent annuity policy is one purchased by a property and casualty insurance company to settle a legal case by making an annuity payment to someone. For example, suppose an individual is hit by an automobile and, as a result, is unable to work for the rest of his life. The individual will sue the P&C company for future lost earnings and medical care. To settle the suit, the insurance company may agree to make specified payments over time to the individual. This is called a **structured settlement**. The company will purchase a policy from a life company to make the agreed-upon payments.

Regardless of the type of annuity, the insurer faces the risk that the portfolio of assets supporting the contract will realize a return that is less than the implicit rate that the insurer has agreed to pay.

Risks Associated with Guaranteed Investment Contracts

A **guaranteed investment contract (GIC)** is a pure investment product. In a GIC, a life company agrees, for a single premium, to pay the principal amount and a predetermined annual crediting rate over the life of the investment, all of which is paid at the maturity date. For example, a $10 million five-year GIC with a predetermined crediting rate of 10% means that, at the end of five years, the life company will pay the policyholder $16,105,100 [determined as follows: $10,000,000 (1.10)^5 = $16,105,000]. What the life company is guaranteeing is the crediting rate, not the principal. The return of the principal depends on the ability of the life company to satisfy the obligation, just as in any corporate debt obligation. The risk that the insurer faces is that the rate earned on the portfolio of supporting assets is less than the rate guaranteed. The maturity of a GIC can vary from 1 year to 20 years. The interest rate guaranteed depends on market conditions and the rating of the life company. The interest rate will be a rate higher than the yield offered on U.S. Treasury securities of the same maturity. These policies typically are purchased by pension plan sponsors as an investment.

The popularity of GICs arises from their favorable financial accounting treatment. Specifically, the owner of a GIC, such as a pension plan sponsor, shows the value of a GIC in the portfolio at its purchase price, not at its current market value (i.e., it is not marked to market). Thus, a rise in interest rates, which would lower the value of any fixed-rate asset held by a pension fund, will not reduce the value of a GIC for financial reporting purposes. This preferential financial accounting treatment is being challenged by regulators who seek to require that they be marked to market, thereby forcing GICs to compete with other market instruments based purely on investment characteristics, not favorable financial accounting requirements.

The GIC that we described above is called a **bullet contract** because it is purchased with a single ("one-shot") premium; it is the most common type. The other types of GIC policies are the window contract, the floating-rate contract, and the participating contract.

In a **window contract**, instead of accepting a lump-sum payment, the life insurance company agrees to accept deposits over some future designated time period (the "window"), usually between 3 and 12 months. All deposits made are guaranteed the same crediting rate. This type of contract is used by a pension sponsor that will make periodic contributions on behalf of employees and wishes to lock in a crediting rate. The liability risk that the life insurance company faces is that if market interest rates decline below the crediting rate on the window contract, the insurance company must invest any new deposits at a lower interest rate than it has agreed to pay. Of course, if interest rates rise above the contract rate, the life insurance company will be able to invest the new deposits at a higher rate, thereby increasing its spread income. Nevertheless, to protect against a decline in interest rates, the crediting rate offered on window contracts will be below that offered on bullet contracts with the same maturity.

A **floating-rate contract** is a GIC where the crediting rate is tied to some variable ("floating") interest rate benchmark, such as a specific-maturity Treasury yield. The crediting rate will be a rate higher than the benchmark. How much higher will depend on market conditions and the rating of the life company—the lower the rating, the greater the rate.

In a **participating GIC**, the policyholder is not guaranteed a crediting rate. Instead, the policyholder's return is based on the actual experience of the portfolio managed by the life company. The assets backing the participating GIC are segregated from the other assets of the life company.

A GIC is a liability of the issuing life company, while it is an asset for a pension plan. There are money managers who specialize in managing (on behalf of pension sponsors) portfolios of GICs issued by different life companies. The issuing life company faces the problem of earning a return on the supporting assets for the GIC policy that is greater than the crediting rate by a sufficient amount to compensate for the risk associated with guaranteeing the rate.

It should be emphasized that a GIC is nothing more than the debt obligation of the life company issuing the contract. The word *guarantee* does not mean that there is a guarantor other than the life company. Effectively, a GIC is a zero-coupon bond issued by a life company, and, as such, exposes the investor to the same credit risk. This credit risk has been highlighted by the default of several major issuers of GICs in recent years. The two most publicized were the prominent GIC issuers Mutual Benefit, a New Jersey–based insurer, and Executive Life, a California-based insurer, both of which were seized by regulators in 1991.

Investments

The distribution of assets of U.S. life companies in 1991 is summarized in Table 8-3. In 1991, bonds plus mortgages constituted some 70% of total life insurance assets. In fact, life companies are the largest buyers of corporate bonds.

TABLE 8-3		
DISTRIBUTION OF ASSETS OF U.S. LIFE COMPANIES, 1991		
Asset	**Amount (000,000)**	**Percent**
Government securities	$225,805	14.9
Corporate securities		
Bonds	542,596	35.7
Common stock	56,940	3.7
Preferred stock	10,071	0.7
Total corporate securities	609,607	40.1
Mortgages	256,077	16.8
Real estate	34,949	2.3
Policy loans	61,723	4.1
Cash	5,856	0.4
Short-term investments	40,512	2.7
All others	286,001	18.7
Total admitted assets	$1,520,530	100.0

Source: A. M. Best Company, *Best's Insurance Reports—Life/Health*, 1992, p. vi.

A life company's decision to allocate most of its funds to long-term debt obligations is a result of the nature of its liabilities. As most contracts written by life companies are based on some contractually fixed interest rate that will be paid to a policyholder after an extended number of years, long-term debt obligations are a natural investment vehicle for an insurance company to use to hedge its commitments (match maturities)—or more precisely, match the duration of its liabilities.

Regulations Affecting Investment Decisions

As we noted earlier, regulations affect investment decisions and strategies of insurance companies in three ways: (1) by specifying risk-based capital requirements, (2) by stipulating how assets are valued for regulatory reporting purposes, (3) and by issuing guidelines for investments. We've already discussed risk-based capital requirements. Now we turn our attention to asset valuation and investment guidelines.

How Assets are Valued for Regulatory Reporting Purposes   In Chapter 7, we explained GAAP accounting for the financial reporting of assets as specified by FASB 115. Publicly traded life insurance companies must use GAAP accounting to report their assets. However, insurance companies must also follow regulatory accounting principles (RAP). RAP accounting requires an insurance company that buys equity or non-investment-grade bonds to report any decline in their value in the periodic financial statement. That is, market value accounting is used for these assets. An investment-grade bond, by contrast, is carried at amortized cost. Amortized cost means the cost of acquiring the asset adjusted annually for any amortization of a premium or accretion of a discount paid. Thus, if the market value of an investment-grade bond declines since the time it was acquired, the reduction in value is not recognized. In other words, historical cost accounting is used for these assets. Consequently, if $10 million is invested in a U.S. Treasury security whose market value declines to $7 million because interest rates have increased, the securities continue to be reported at $10 million (plus any accretion of a discount paid or minus any amortization of a premium paid).

RAP accounting has two important implications. First, it encourages life companies to allocate only a small portion of their funds to stock and lower quality-rated bonds because a decline in the market value of those assets below cost will reduce the life company's reported surplus. Second, it may discourage managers of life insurance companies from trying to take advantage of perceived or real opportunities in the bond market.

For example, suppose an insurance company that has invested $10 million in a U.S. Treasury security recognizes that it can improve its asset/liability position if it swaps out of these U.S. Treasury securities and into a different U.S. Treasury issue. It would be discouraged to do so if the market value of the U.S. Treasury securities it owns is less than $10 million, because once these securities are sold in order to purchase the new Treasury issue, a loss must be recognized. This would result in a reduction in the life company's surplus. It also encourages the sale of securities that have appreciated in value in order to recognize a capital gain even if the sale did not make economic sense. In 1992, the rules of the game changed. Under the current valuation system, any loss or gain is not recognized immediately but is realized gradually over the maturity of the security.

Guidelines for Investments   Restrictions are imposed by states on the acceptable investments that an insurance company may invest in and the amount that may be allocated to a particular asset class. A state will typically restrict the percentage of funds allocated to common stock investments to the lesser of 10% of assets (in some states 20%) or 100% of surplus. It will also restrict investments in bonds and preferred stock to those of a certain quality rating. A "basket provision" usually permits investments of about 5% of assets in any type of vehicle that is not explicitly prohibited by law. At the time of this writing, the NAIC is working on a model law for specific investments.

Managing the Economic Surplus

As explained in the previous chapter, the economic surplus is the difference between the market value of the assets and the present value of the liabilities. For insurance companies, not all the assets are marked to market, and liabilities are not marked to market. Thus, the surplus reported by a life company is not the economic surplus but an accounting and statutory surplus. Nevertheless, the manager of the assets of a life insurance portfolio should seek to maximize the economic surplus within accounting and regulatory constraints by various policy classes.

The investment strategies that can be used vary by the type of policy class. For example, in the case of an annuity, an investment strategy known as a *dedicated portfolio strategy* can be used to generate a cash flow that will satisfy all future obligations specified in the policy, regardless of how interest rates change in the future. For a GIC policy, an *immunization strategy* can be used to achieve the target amount that must be paid at the maturity regardless of how interest rates change. The dedicated portfolio strategy and the immunization strategy are also referred to as *structured portfolio strategies* because they involve structuring the portfolio to satisfy the liabilities. We will explain both of these strategies in Chapter 23.

There are other strategies that a portfolio manager can employ to manage the assets supporting an annuity or GIC policy. These effectively involve *betting* on interest rate movements. These bets expose the life company to the risk that the return realized will be less than the crediting rate, resulting in a decline in surplus.

Strategies for managing the supporting assets for a variable life policy are quite different. The funds are invested in a common stock portfolio. In Section IV of this book, we will describe a wide variety of common stock strategies the portfolio manager can follow.

PROPERTY AND CASUALTY INSURANCE COMPANIES

Property and casualty insurance companies provide a broad range of insurance protection against:

1. Loss, damage, or destruction of property
2. Loss or impairment of income-producing ability
3. Claims for damages by third parties because of alleged negligence
4. Loss resulting from injury or death due to occupational accidents

Property and casualty insurance products can be classified as either *personal lines* or *commercial lines*. Personal lines include automobile insurance and homeowner insurance. Commercial lines include product liability insurance, commercial property insurance, and professional malpractice insurance.

State insurance commissions regulate the premiums that may be charged for insurance coverage. Competitive pressures, however, have made the need for price regulation less important. In instances where states have imposed premiums that insurers feel are uneconomic, companies have withdrawn from offering insurance.

The amount of the liability coverage is specified in the policy. The premium is invested until the insured makes a claim on all or part of the amount of the policy and that claim is validated. For some lines of business, the P&C company will know immediately that it has incurred a liability from a policy it has underwritten; however, how much the claim is and when it will have to be paid may not be known at that time.

To illustrate this, suppose that in 1991 an automobile policy is written that provides $1 million liability coverage for Bob Smith. The policy covers him against claims by other parties resulting from an automobile accident. Let's suppose that in 1993, as a result of Bob Smith's negligence, he gets into an automobile accident that results in the permanent disability of Karen Lee, a pedestrian. The P&C company recognizes that it has a liability, but how much will it have to pay Karen Lee? It may be several years before the injured party and the company settle the matter, and a trial may be necessary to determine the monetary damages that the P&C company must pay. Money managers for P&Cs need to consider the value of claims in litigation as they formulate their investment strategies.

P&Cs also have lines of business in which a claim is not evident until several years after the policy period. For example, suppose that for the years 1987 through 1990 a P&C company wrote a product liability policy for a toy manufacturing company. It may not be until 1993 that it is discovered that one of the products manufactured by the toy company was defective, causing serious injury to children.

Nature of the Liabilities

The liabilities of P&C companies have a shorter term than those of life companies and vary with the type of policy. As noted earlier, the exact timing and amount of any liability are unknown. However, the maximum amount of the liability cannot exceed the amount of the coverage specified in the policy.

Unlike many life insurance products, P&C liabilities are not interest rate sensitive, but some are inflation sensitive. There are unique types of liability risks faced by P&C companies, the two most notable being *geographic risk* and *regulatory pricing risk*. **Geographic risk** arises when an insurer has policies within certain geographic areas. If a catastrophe such as a hurricane or an earthquake occurs in that geographic area, the liability exposure increases. **Regulatory pricing risk** arises when regulators restrict the premium rates that can be charged.

Investments

The distribution of the assets held by P&C companies at the end of 1991 is shown in Table 8-4. Because of the nature of their liabilities, P&C companies invest more heavily in equities and less so in bonds than life insurance firms do.

TABLE 8-4		
DISTRIBUTION OF ASSETS OF U.S. PROPERTY AND CASUALTY INSURANCE COMPANIES: 1991		
Asset	**Amount ($ Billions)**	**Percent of Total**
Cash & equivalents	$ 37.5	6.5
Equities	106.8	18.6
U.S. Treasury securities	96.2	16.8
Federal agency securities	31.0	5.4
Municipal bonds	140.8	24.6
Corporate & foreign bonds	102.0	17.8
Mortgages	7.7	1.3
Other	51.9	9.1
Total	$572.8	100.0

Note: These figures are from the group that the source calls "Other [Than Life] Insurance Companies."

Source: Board of Governors of the Federal Reserve System, *Flow of Funds Accounts, Financial Assets and Liabilities*, First Quarter, 1992.

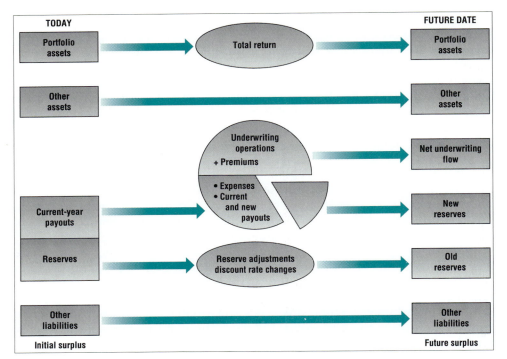

FIGURE 8-1

The dynamics of a property and casualty company.

Adapted from Alfred Weinberger and Vincent Kaminski, "Asset Allocation for Property/Casualty Insurance Companies: A Going-Concern Approach," Salomon Brothers Inc (July 1992).

Regulation of Investments

While life companies are constrained as to eligible assets, P&C companies have greater leeway for investing. For example, a P&C company might be required to invest a minimum amount in eligible bonds and mortgages. As long as this minimum is satisfied, however, a P&C company is free to allocate its investments any way it pleases among eligible assets in the other asset classes.

As in the case with life companies, equities and non-investment-grade bonds are reported at market value and investment-grade bonds at historical cost. With the exception of workers' compensation, most liabilities are carried at undiscounted cost, not their present value.

Managing Economic Surplus

Figure 8-1 shows graphically how the economic surplus of a P&C changes over time. Note that the top half of the figure shows the performance of the portfolio's assets; the lower half shows the liabilities.

In recent years, P&C companies have constructed their portfolios to have shorter maturities so as to better match the short-term and highly uncertain nature of their liabilities. The dilemma faced by P&C companies is that in an interest rate environment in which short-term interest rates decline dramatically relative to longer-term interest rates (such as in 1991 through 1993), their portfolio return will decline. Because of regulatory and competitive pricing pressures, they cannot offset that decline in investment income with an increase in underwriting income. This, in the opinion of the author, makes P&C companies the most difficult of all financial institutions to manage.

There is no one simple portfolio strategy for protecting the economic surplus. Strategies such as investing in long-term bonds, stocks, or low-quality bonds increase the risk of the economic surplus declining. In practice, the more sophisticated P&C companies perform a good deal of statistical analysis, such as simulation analysis, on both the portfolio of assets and the liabilities to determine the combination of assets that the management of the P&C company will include in its portfolio.

■ SUMMARY

Life companies and P&C companies are financial intermediaries that function as risk bearers. Insurance companies are regulated at the state level. Each state establishes its own regulations with respect to the types of securities that are eligible for investment and the way the value of those securities must be shown for regulatory reporting purposes.

The statutory surplus of an insurance company is the difference between its assets and liabilities. The accounting treatment for assets and liabilities is prescribed by state statutes. Liabilities include reserves for potential claims. Revenue is generated from two sources: premiums earned and investment income. Recently, risk-based capital requirements have been imposed on insurance companies.

While the principal event that life companies insure against is death, a major portion of their business is providing lifetime benefits in the form of retirement policies. A policy may provide only life protection or only an investment feature. Some policies provide both. The various policies include term, whole life, universal life, variable life, annuities, and guaranteed investment contracts. Insurers face various risks when they write insurance policies. Because of the nature of their liabilities, most investments made by life companies are in debt obligations. The investment strategies that can be used vary by the type of policy.

P&C companies insure against a wide variety of occurrences. They are afforded greater latitude than life companies in their investment choices. The liability for P&C companies is shorter term than for life companies and varies with the type of policy, while the exact timing and amount of any liability are unknown. P&C liabilities are not interest rate sensitive. Consequently, P&Cs tend to invest more heavily in equities and less so in bonds than life insurance firms do. The management of a P&C company is difficult when short-term interest rates decline dramatically relative to longer-term interest rates, causing its portfolio return to decline. However, regulatory and competitive pricing pressures prevent P&Cs from offsetting the decline in investment income with an increase from underwriting income. There is no one simple portfolio strategy for protecting their economic surplus.

■ KEY TERMS

annuity	guaranteed investment contract	statutory surplus
bullet GIC contract	(GIC)	structured settlement
cash-surrender value	investment income	term life insurance
convention statement	loan value	underwriting income
crediting rate	participating GIC	universal life
equity-linked policies	regulatory pricing risk	variable life
floating-rate contract	reserve	whole life insurance
geographic risk	single-premium deferred annuity	window GIC contract

■ **QUESTIONS**

1. Why are the investment strategies employed by a life insurance company different from those of a property and casualty insurance company?

2. a. How is the revenue of an insurance company determined?
   b. How is the profit of an insurance company determined?

3. What is the role of the National Association of Insurance Commissioners?

4. The risk-based capital requirements are based on the various risks faced by an insurance company. For life companies, one of these risks is referred to as asset risk. What does asset risk mean?

5. Calculate the risk-based capital requirements for asset risk for the Southwest Quality Life company (all assets are in millions of dollars):

CAPITAL FACTORS FOR SELECTED ASSETS FOR SOUTHWEST QUALITY LIFE

Asset Class	Capital Factor	Dollar Allocation
U.S. government securities	0.0%	$600
Corporates, municipals, agencies, MBS, CMOs, & ABS rated:		
NAIC (A-AAA)	0.3%	400
Corporates & municipals rated:		
NAIC 2 (BBB)	1.0%	200
NAIC 3 (BB)	2.0%	300
NAIC 4 (B)	4.5%	50
NAIC 5 (CCC)	10.0%	90
NAIC 6 (Default)	30.0%	20
Common stocks	15.0%	250
Mortgage & collateral loans	5.0%	125
Real estate	10.0%	325

6. In the chapter, only asset risk was discussed because it influences the investment decisions made by the portfolio manager of an insurance company. Another risk for life companies for which there are risk-based capital requirements is called interest rate risk. According to the NAIC, this is the risk of policyholders "lapsing."
   a. What is meant by a policy lapsing?
   b. How is the lapsing of a life insurance policy related to interest rates?

7. The chief investment officer of Guardian Life, Dr. Frank J. Jones, wrote in the 1992 annual report: "The Guardian's significant surplus allows us to invest more heavily in equities." Why does a significant surplus allow for this allocation of funds to equities?

8. The following quotation is from a recent survey in *The Economist* on the American insurance industry:

   Life insurers, like bankers, learnt the hard way about inflation and interest rates a decade ago. Insurance was a fairly straightforward business in the old days. As late as 1979, more than 80% of new premiums were for "whole life" policies with fixed premiums, benefits and surrender values; almost all the rest was "term" insurance which pays out only on death. . . .

   That comfortable world had begun to change even before inflation went into double-digits in the late 1970s. Customers realized that the cash values piling up in their insurance companies did not compare favorably with returns on other instruments. Issuers had to offer policies like universal life and variable life and permutations of the two. These gave customers market-related returns, often above a guaranteed minimum, and more flexibility.

   a. What is meant by whole life, universal life, and variable life insurance policies?
   b. In general, what have been the consequences of life companies having to offer market-related returns?

9. Why are the liabilities of a property and casualty insurance company more difficult to predict than those of a life company?

10. What does crediting rate mean on a life insurance policy?

11. a. What is a guaranteed investment contract?
    b. What does the "guaranteed" mean? Does a government entity guarantee the contract?
    c. Why does the interest rate offered on a GIC depend on the rating on the life company?
    d. What is the difference between a bullet GIC and a window GIC?

12. What risk does a life company face when it issues a GIC in which it has guaranteed a fixed interest rate over the life of the contract?

13. a. What is a single-premium deferred annuity?
    b. How might strategies differ for managing a portfolio of assets supporting a single-premium deferred annuity as opposed to one supporting a variable life insurance policy?

14. What is meant by a dedicated portfolio strategy?

15. Discuss the following excerpt from *Best's Review* of June 30, 1990:

When medical waste washed up on the beaches of New Jersey and New York in several separate incidents in 1988, the public was disgusted and scared. Many oceanfront resort operators and workers who depend on the allure of the beach for their livelihood were nearly ruined. But the financial losses from that lost summer of 1988 pale in comparison with the economic havoc that improperly handled medical waste can wreak on America's health care providers. . . . To date, no medical facility has been sued for injuries or damages caused by the disposal of medical waste, but given today's consciousness of this issue and the trend in environmental legislation, such litigation is inevitable. Clearly, this eventuality represents both an emerging liability coverage issue and a thorny challenge for the commercial insurance industry.

Your answer should address these issues:

a. The type of insurance company that would underwrite coverage for medical waste
b. Some of the problems that such companies have in estimating their liabilities to policyholders
c. The likelihood that insurance companies will be eager to start underwriting insurance for medical waste

16. a. Why is the interest rate risk of a P&C company's liability minimal?
b. What is meant by a P&C company's geographic risk?

CHAPTER 9
PENSION FUNDS AND ENDOWMENT FUNDS

LEARNING OBJECTIVES

After reading this chapter you will be able to:

- describe the features of the different types of pension plans.
- explain who bears the investment risk—the pension sponsor or the employee—for the different types of pension plans.
- list the types of assets in which pension plans invest.
- discuss the principal provisions of the Employee Retirement Income Security Act of 1974.
- explain the implications of Statement of Financial Accounting Standard No. 87 and the Omnibus Budget Reconciliation Act of 1987 for the management of pension funds.
- explain what is meant by overfunded and underfunded pension plans.
- explain what endowment funds do.
- describe the goals of managing money for endowment funds.

A **pension plan** is a fund that is established for the payment of retirement benefits. The entities that establish pension plans—called the *plan sponsors*—are private business entities acting for their employees, state and local entities acting on behalf of their employees, unions operating on behalf of their members, and individuals representing themselves.

In the old days, pension fund sponsors inhabited a quiet, comfortable world in which they turned over everything to the local bank trust officer and took a two-hour lunch. That has all changed. Today, plan sponsors are legally responsible for the investment of millions, often billions, of dollars. Often the plan sponsor is also responsible for the in-house management of assets invested in a wide range of instruments, while, at the same time, finding, hiring, and overseeing a collection of diverse outside managers whose contributions must be molded into a coherent whole.

In this chapter, we discuss pension funds and the investment considerations in managing their assets. While most of the chapter is devoted to pen-

TABLE 9-1		
TYPES OF PENSION PLANS		
Type	**Sponsor**	**Employee**
Defined contribution	Contributes to plan	Chooses investment vehicles; bears risk of investment performance
Defined benefit	Guarantees specified payout to employees; establishes funding; bears all risk	
Hybrid example: Floor-offset plan	Sets floor for payout; contributes; manages fund	Contributes when investment performance would provide payouts below the floor

sion funds, we also describe endowments. These institutional investors include colleges, private schools, museums, hospitals, and foundations.

PENSION FUNDS

Pension funds are financed by contributions by the employer and/or the employee. The total assets of U.S. pension funds have grown rapidly since World War II. They almost tripled in the 1980s. By 1989, pension fund total assets were about $2.47 trillion. The top 20 pension funds as measured by assets as of September 30, 1989, account for more than 25% of all pension assets. The assets of corporate-sponsored pension plans in 1990 were about $1.1 trillion, while those of government-sponsored pension plans totaled about $0.7 trillion.[1]

Types of Pension Plans

There are two basic and widely used types of pension plans: *defined contribution* plans and *defined benefit plans*. A new idea, a hybrid often called a "designer pension," combines features of both these types. Table 9-1 summarizes the characteristics of these plans.

Defined Contribution Plans   In a **defined contribution plan**, the plan sponsor is responsible only for making specified contributions into the plan on behalf of qualifying participants. The amount contributed is typically either a percentage of the employee's salary or a percentage of profits. The plan sponsor does not guarantee any certain amount at retirement. The payments that will be made to qualifying participants upon retirement will depend on the growth of the plan assets; that is, payment is determined by the investment perfor-

---

[1]*1990 Money Market Directory*. According to a study on pension funds by Columbia University Law School, the three largest corporate-sponsored pension funds as of September 30, 1989, are AT&T ($42.7 billion), General Motors ($40.9 billion), and IBM ($25.8 billion). The two largest government-sponsored pension funds are California Public Employees ($54.0 billion) and New York State/Local Employees ($44.2 billion). The largest public pension fund by far is TIAA/CREF, with total assets as of September 31, 1989, of $81 billion.

mance of the assets in which the pension fund are invested. Therefore, in a defined contribution plan the employee bears all the investment risk.

The plan sponsor gives the participants various investment options from which they may choose. Defined contribution pension plans come in several legal forms: money purchase pension plans, 401(k) plans, and employee stock ownership plans (ESOPs).

By far, the fastest-growing sector of the defined contribution plan is the 401(k). To the plan sponsor, this kind of plan offers fewer costs and administrative problems: The employer makes a specified contribution to a specific plan or program, and the employee chooses how it is invested.[2] To the employee, the plan offers some control over how the pension money is managed. In fact, plan sponsors frequently offer participants the opportunity to invest in one of a family of mutual funds (discussed in the next chapter). In public institutions such as state governments as well as private firms, over half of all defined contribution plans use mutual funds, and the percentage of private corporations following that path is even higher. Employees in the public and corporate sectors have responded favorably, and almost half of all assets in pensions are now invested in mutual funds, with the bulk of the money being placed in funds emphasizing equities and growth.[3] Recent regulations from the U.S. Department of Labor require firms to offer their employees a set of distinctive choices, and this development has further encouraged pension plans to opt for the mutual fund approach, because families of mutual funds can readily provide investment vehicles with different investment objectives.[4]

Defined Benefit Plan   In a **defined benefit plan**, the plan sponsor agrees to make specified dollar payments to qualifying employees at retirement (and some payments to beneficiaries in case of death before retirement). The retirement payments are determined by a formula that usually takes into account the length of service of the employee and the earnings of the employee. The pension obligations are effectively the debt obligation of the plan sponsor, which assumes the risk of having insufficient funds in the plan to satisfy the contractual payments that must be made to retired employees. Thus, unlike a defined contribution plan, in a defined benefit plan, all the investment risks are borne by the plan sponsor.

A plan sponsor establishing a defined benefit plan can use the payments made into the fund to purchase an annuity policy from a life insurance company. Defined benefit plans that are guaranteed by life insurance products are called **insured plans**[5]; those that are not are called **non-insured plans**. An insured plan is not necessarily safer than an uninsured plan, as the former depends on the ability of the life insurance company to make the contractual payments.

Whether a private pension plan is insured or non-insured, the **Pension Benefit Guaranty Corporation (PBGC),** a federal agency established in 1974 by the Employment Retirement Income Security Act (see below), insures the

---

[2]"Calling It Quits," *Institutional Investor* (February 1991), p. 125.

[3]"Taking a Fancy to Mutual Funds," *Institutional Investor* (May 1992), p. 119.

[4]"The Communication Cloud over 401(k)s," *Institutional Investor* (September 1991), p. 189.

[5]Life insurance companies also manage pension funds without guaranteeing a specified payout. In this case they are acting only as money manager, and the funds they manage are not insured plans.

vested benefits of participants. Benefits become vested when an employee reaches a certain age and completes enough years of service so that he or she meets the minimum requirements for receiving benefits upon retirement. The payment of benefits is not contingent upon a participant's continuation with the employer or union.

Hybrid Pension Plans   A recent survey by *Institutional Investor* revealed that a new phenomenon in pension planning, hybrid plans, has attracted support.[6] As noted earlier, these "designer pensions" combine features of both basic types of pensions. They first appeared in 1985 and have been adopted by 8% of companies and public employers in the United States. The appeal of these hybrids is that they overcome flaws in the basic types of plans: The defined contribution plan causes the employee to bear all the investment risk, while the defined benefit plan is expensive and hard to implement when few workers work for only one company over many years.

While hybrids come in many forms, a good example is the *floor-offset plan*. In this plan, the employer contributes a certain amount each year to a fund, as in a defined contribution approach. The employer guarantees a certain minimum level of cash benefits, depending on an employee's years of service, as in a defined benefit plan. The employer manages the pension fund and informs the employee periodically of the value of his or her account. If the managed fund does not generate sufficient growth to achieve the preset level of benefits, the employee is obliged to add the amount of the deficit. In such a plan the employer and participating employees share the risk of providing retirement benefits.

Investments

The aggregate asset mix, at the end of 1991, of the 1,000 top pension plans is summarized in Table 9-2. As can be seen, for defined benefit plans, slightly more than 80% is allocated between equities and fixed-income securities. In the allocation of assets for defined contribution plans, a large proportion of assets are placed in guaranteed investment contracts (GICs), which we discussed in Chapter 8. Qualified pension funds are exempt from federal income taxes. Thus, fund assets can accumulate tax-free. Consequently, pension funds do not invest very much in assets that have the advantage of being largely or completely tax-exempt.

There are no restrictions at the federal level on investing in non-U.S. investments. The sponsors of a fund, however, are free to restrict the allocation of the fund's assets to domestic investments. For example, the state of Oklahoma bans foreign investments for its public pension funds. It is not uncommon for union-sponsored pension funds to prohibit non-U.S. investments in their portfolios. A survey of pension fund sponsors conducted by *Institutional Investor* in 1991 found that more than half of the respondents invested in foreign securities of some type. Of those respondents that invested abroad, 96% invested in foreign stocks and 34% in foreign bonds.[7]

As can be seen from Table 9-2, the "Other" asset category is a small portion of the asset mix of pension plans. A survey by Goldman Sachs found that

TABLE 9-2	
AGGREGATE ASSET MIX FOR TOP 1,000 PENSION FUNDS IN 1991	
Asset	**Percent**
Top Defined Benefit Plans	
Equity	45.7
Fixed income	35.8
Cash equivalents	6.2
Real estate equity	3.9
Mortgages	1.0
GIC/BIC	2.3
Annuities	0.3
Other	4.8
Top Defined Contribution Plans	
Company stock	23.9
Other stock	17.6
Fixed income	11.5
Cash equivalents	7.7
GIC/BIC	33.8
Annuities	0.5
Other	5.8

Source: As reported in *Pensions & Investments*, January 20, 1992, p. 30.

---

[6]"Why Designer Pensions Are in Fashion," *Institutional Investor* (June 1992), pp. 123-131.
[7]"Pensionforum: Over There," *Institutional Investor* (February 1991), p. 70.

BOX 9

INVESTMENT POLICY ADOPTED BY A PENSION PLAN

Drafting an investment policy requires more than a cookie-cutter approach. Given the differences that exist among plan sponsors in terms of their organizations, legal restrictions, objectives, and risk tolerances, these basic components require customization to match a plan's particular characteristics and needs. This box describes the investment policy adopted by the Minnesota State Board of Investment for its largest pension plan, the $7 billion Basic Retirement Funds (BRF).

Fund's Mission

The BRF's mission statement reflects the board pension goals pursued by the Minnesota State Board of Investment in the management of this fund. Specifically, the BRF's primary mission calls for the investment of employer/employee contributions to secure sufficient funds to finance promised benefits to participating public employees upon their retirement. Secondarily, the BRF's investments should generate additional funds that permit either the reduction of contributions or the enhancement of benefits.

Risk Tolerance

The Board views its tolerance for risk in managing the BRF's assets to be rela-tively high. Given the BRF's adequate funding and its middle-aged participant demographics, the Board takes a long-term view in establishing the BRF's risk-return posture. As a consequence, the Board has adopted an aggressive, high expected return investment program consistent with the BRF's mission statement. The Board is willing to accept volatile short-term investment results with the expectation that the volatility will be more than compensated by superior long-term performance.

Investment Objectives

Based on its mission statement and risk tolerance, the Board has established the following investment objectives for the BRF:

1. To generate a total annualized rate of return 3–5% greater than the rate of inflation over a rolling 10-year period.

2. To exceed a composite of asset class target returns, weighted in accordance with the policy asset mix, over a rolling five-year period.

The investment objectives indicate the Board's high risk tolerance and long-term investment horizon with respect to managing the BRF. These ob-jectives provide direction in developing the BRF's policy asset mix and investment management structure. They also provide the basis for evaluating the performance of the BRF's investment program.

Policy Asset Mix

To achieve the investment objective of a 3–5% real rate of return necessitates that the BRF maintain a significant exposure to equity assets. The current BRF policy asset mix set by the Board is shown below:

Equities	
Domestic Common Stocks	60.0%
Real Estate	10.0
Venture Capital	2.5
Resource Funds	2.5
Total Equities	75.0%
Fixed Income	
Domestic Bonds	24.0%
Cash Equivalents	1.0
Total Fixed Income	25.0%

In conjunction with setting the BRF policy asset mix, the Board has selected appropriate targets, where available, for the asset classes that make up the BRF total portfolio.

---

from 1987 to 1991, investments other than stocks and bonds increased from $20 billion to $65 billion, an increase of more than 300%.[8] The 10 principal alternative asset classes included in the survey were venture capital, LBO funds, private debt placements, real estate mortgages, high-yield bonds, oil and gas exploration funds, turnaround funds, timberland, farmland, and commodities. The typical pension fund was found to invest in venture capital plus only one or two of the other alternative asset classes. In contrast to U.S. pension funds, the Goldman Sachs survey found that Japanese and European pension funds typically invested far more in these alternative asset classes, particularly private debt placements.

Box 9 shows the investment policy adopted by the Minnesota State Board of Investment for one of its pension plans. In addition to providing a concrete

---

[8]Thomas J. Healey and Fiachra T. O. Driscoll, "Are Alternative Investments Right for Your Pension Funds?" unpublished paper, undated.

BOX 9

Continued

Asset Class	Asset Class Target
Domestic Common Stocks	Wilshire 5000
Real Estate	Wilshire Real Estate Index
Domestic Bonds	Salomon Brothers Broad Bond Index
Cash Equivalents	90-Day Treasury Bills
Venture Capital	None selected
Resource Funds	None selected

These asset class targets represent the broad market investment opportunities available to the Board. In addition, the Board can readily access information on these indices when conducting performance evaluation.

At this time the Board has not identified appropriate asset class targets for the venture capital and resource funds. For performance evaluation purposes, the actual performance of the BRF's venture capital and resource fund investments serve as the benchmarks for those asset classes.

Investment Management Structure

The BRF investment objective of exceeding the performance of a composite of the asset class target requires that the BRF investment management structure include active management. The Board has established that a minimum of 50%

of the BRF common stock and bond investments be passively managed. The Board restricts active management to a range of 10–50% of the BRF's common stock and bond investments. The exact allocation to active mangement varies over time depending on the Board's confidence in the BRF's active managers.

While they have not been listed here due to lack of space, the Board also assigns policy allocations to each of the BRF investment managers. The Board bases its allocations on its perceptions of a manager's investment skills and the extent to which the manager's investment style serves to diversify the BRF's investments within an asset class.

Performance Evaluation

The Board conducts performance evaluation for the BRF at the total fund, asset class, and individual manager levels. At the total fund level, the Board analyzes results relative to the BRF real rate of return and composite indices objectives. Further, the Board breaks down investment results into the effects of policy decisions and the impact of deviations from policy allocations.

On the asset class and individual manager levels, the Board assigns benchmark portfolios to all BRF invest-

ment managers. These benchmarks are a vital element in the evaluation of individual and aggregate manager performance within each asset class. The Board uses these benchmarks not only to review the value added by the managers individually and in aggregate, but also to examine the extent of manager structure biases relative to the asset class targets.

Prepared by Michael J. Menssen, Investment Analyst, Minnesota State Board of Investment. (First paragraph modified by Frank Fabozzi.)

Source: Frank J. Fabozzi (ed.), *Pension Fund Investment Management* (Chicago: Probus Publishing, 1990), appendix to Chap. 2.

Questions for Box 9

1. In setting its investment policy, does the Minnesota State Board of Investment have to be concerned with FASB 87 and OBRA '87? If not, why not?
2. In describing its investment objective, what is meant by the "Board's long-term investment horizon," and why would a private pension fund not have the same long-term investment horizon?
3. What types of strategies are pursued by the money managers engaged by the Minnesota State Board?

example of the investment management process described in Chapter 1, this box gives you a flavor of the asset classes in which the Minnesota State Board has decided to invest.

ERISA and Other Federal Regulation

Because pension plans are so important for U.S. workers, Congress passed comprehensive legislation in 1974 to regulate corporate pension plans. The legislation, the Employee Retirement Income Security Act of 1974 (ERISA), is fairly technical in its details. For our purposes, it is necessary only to understand the major provisions of ERISA.

First, ERISA established minimum funding standards for the minimum contributions that a plan sponsor must make to the pension plan to satisfy the actuarially projected benefit payments. Prior to enactment of ERISA, many corporate plan sponsors followed a "pay-as-you-go" funding policy. That is, when an employee retired, the corporate plan sponsor took the necessary retirement benefits out of current operations. Under ERISA, such a practice is no longer allowed.

Second, ERISA established fiduciary standards for pension fund trustees, managers, or advisors. Specifically, all parties responsible for the management of a pension fund are guided by the judgment of a mythical "prudent man" in seeking to determine which investments are proper.[9] Because a trustee takes care of other people's money, it is necessary to make sure that the trustee takes the role seriously. In fulfillment of responsibilities, a trustee must use the care of a reasonably prudent person to acquire and use the information that is pertinent to making an investment decision.

Third, minimum vesting standards were established by ERISA. For example, after five years of employment a plan participant is entitled to 25% of accrued pension benefits. The percentage increases to 100% after 10 years. Finally, ERISA created the PBGC to insure vested benefits. The insurance program is funded from annual premiums that must be paid by pension plans.

Responsibility for administering ERISA is delegated to the Department of Labor and the Internal Revenue Service. To ensure that a pension plan is in compliance with ERISA, periodic reporting and disclosure statements must be filed with the Department of Labor and the Internal Revenue Service.

It is important to recognize that ERISA does not require that a corporation establish a pension plan. If a corporation does establish one, however, it must comply with the regulations set forth in ERISA.

In addition to ERISA, another key piece of federal legislation affects defined benefit plans, the Omnibus Budget Reconciliation Act of 1987 (OBRA). Its purpose will be explained after we discuss the financial accounting requirements for corporate defined benefit plans.

Financial Reporting Requirements for Corporate Defined Benefit Plans

While the selection of assets to include in a pension fund is dictated by the actuarially projected pension obligations, another extremely important consideration is the financial reporting requirements. Corporations report to shareholders on the basis of generally accepted accounting principles (GAAP). The reporting requirement for corporate pension obligations for defined benefit plans is promulgated by Financial Accounting Standard Board (FASB) No. 87.

Some Basics   Before explaining FASB 87, we discuss a few basic definitions used in the pension fund industry.

The *surplus* of a pension plan is the difference between the plan's assets and the plan's liabilities. The assets are measured in terms of market value; just how the liabilities are measured will be explained when we discuss FASB 87. A pension plan that has a positive surplus (i.e., assets exceed liabilities) is said to be an **overfunded pension plan**. A pension plan that has a negative surplus (i.e., liabilities exceed assets) is said to have a deficit or be an **underfunded pension plan**.

The ratio of the plan's assets to its liabilities is called the **funding ratio**. A plan that is overfunded will have a funding ratio greater than 100%; the funding ratio for a plan that is underfunded is less than 100%. If the surplus is

---

[9]The prudent-man rule developed as part of trust law.

TABLE 9-3		
FUNDING RATIOS		
Assets > liabilities	overfunded	Funding ratio > 100%
Assets < liabilities	underfunded	Funding ratio < 100%
Assets = liabilities		Funding ratio = 100%

zero (i.e., assets are equal to liabilities), the funding ratio is 100%. The funding ratio is determined at a given point in time. As assets and liabilities change over time, the funding ratio changes. These relationships are summarized in Table 9-3.

FASB 87   Prior to FASB 87, pension plan assets were reported at market value, while pension liabilities effectively were not marked to market. This was because accountants were required to determine the present value of pension plan liabilities, but they had sufficient flexibility in selecting an interest rate to discount the liabilities. The interest rate selected was supposed to reflect the return that the pension sponsor could earn over time. Typically, however, accountants arbitrarily selected interest rates that gave little recognition to prevailing market rates. Consequently, pension sponsors focused on the assets of the pension plans with no recognition of the effect of market interest rate fluctuations on the liabilities.

For example, consider ABC pension fund with $300 million in assets all invested in bonds, and with liabilities that, according to the actuary and accountant, had a present value of $285 million. The surplus of ABC pension fund would be $15 million. Suppose that interest rates decline by 100 basis points. As explained in Chapter 7, the market value of the bonds would increase by an amount that depends on the price sensitivity of the bonds to interest rate changes or, equivalently, its duration. Suppose that the duration for the bond portfolio is 7. This means that a 100-basis-point change in interest rates will change the portfolio's market value by roughly 7%. Thus, the market value of the portfolio will increase by $21 million if interest rates decline by 100 basis points, and the new market value will be $321 million. On the liability side, suppose that the accountant did not adjust the present value of the liabilities to reflect that the present value is higher as a result of a decline in interest rates. Thus, the surplus of the ABC pension plan increases from $15 million prior to the decline in interest rates to $36 million ($321 million − $285 million).

The accounting rules promulgated by FASB 87 changed this practice by requiring that both the liabilities and the assets of pension funds be marked to market. More specifically, the accountant under FASB 87 must use a market interest rate in determining the present value of liabilities.

Now let's look again at ABC pension plan's liabilities if interest rates decline by 100 basis points. Assume that the liabilities have a duration of 14. This means that a 100-basis-point decline in interest rates will increase the liabilities by 14%, or $40 million (0.14 × $285 million), to $325 million. Since it is assumed that the portfolio of bonds has a duration of 7, its market value increases to $321 million. ABC pension plan's surplus therefore declines from $15 million to −$4 million. That is, the plan went from being overfunded to being underfunded.

Prior to FASB 87, any underfunding was simply reported in the footnotes to the financial statements. Under the rules of FASB 87, if a plan is underfunded, the shortfall must be reported in the balance sheet as a liability. So, in our illustration, ABC corporation has to report a liability of $4 million. Had there been a surplus, it would *not* be reported in the balance sheet as an asset. Moreover, if ABC corporation, the plan sponsor for ABC pension plan, also had several subsidiaries with their own pension plans, ABC corporation could not aggregate the surpluses of each plan and offset any deficits with surpluses. For example, suppose that ABC corporation's one other pension plan had a surplus of $70 million after interest rates declined. The $70 million surplus could not be used to offset the $4 million deficit.

In addition to the effect on the balance sheet, FASB 87 also requires an adjustment to the reported earnings of a corporation if the change in the pension plan's surplus is large. If the surplus increases by more than 10% of either plan assets or liabilities, then this is treated as a reduction in pension expenses for the period and therefore increases earnings; if, on the other hand, the surplus decreases by more than 10% of either plan assets or liabilities, then this is treated as an increase in pension expenses and thereby reduces earnings. Thus, the *volatility* of the plan's surplus will have an effect on reported earnings.

Measuring Plan Liabilities   Two types of plan liabilities are defined in FASB 87. The **accumulated benefit obligation (ABO)** is an approximate measure of the liability of the plan in the event of a termination at the date the calculation is performed. The **projected benefit obligation (PBO)** is a measure of the plan's liability at the calculation date, assuming that the plan is ongoing and will not terminate in the foreseeable future.

The rate suggested in FASB 87 for discounting the obligations is the **settlement rate**. This is the rate at which the pension benefits could be effectively settled if the pension plan wished to terminate its pension obligation. As a guideline for the settlement rate, FASB 87 suggests looking at rates on investment-grade fixed-income securities or rates implicit in annuity contracts.

OBRA '87   As explained earlier, OBRA '87 is federal legislation that deals with defined pension plans. The act reinforces the interpretation of liabilities as stipulated in FASB 87. Specifically, it sets forth three things. First, if a plan is underfunded, the plan sponsor must accelerate contributions to the fund. Second, if a plan is underfunded, the insurance premiums that it must pay to the PBGC will be significantly increased. Finally, if the funding ratio (with liabilities measured on the basis of the ABO) exceeds 150%, the sponsor must stop making contributions to the plan.

Implications of FASB 87 and OBRA '87 for Pension Fund Management   Because of FASB 87 and OBRA '87, the corporate pension sponsor must look at managing the surplus, not just assets. With the huge liabilities of pension plans, changes in interest rates can adversely affect the surplus. In our illustration, ABC pension plan's liabilities are more sensitive to interest rate changes (a duration of 14) than the portfolio of bonds it owns (a duration of 7). This has an adverse effect when interest rates decline. If interest rates increase, the market value of the bonds and the present value of the liabilities would both decrease but the surplus would increase for ABC's pension plan. For example, suppose that interest rates increase by 100 basis points. The market value of the bond portfolio will decline by 7% from $300 million to $279 million. However, the liabilities will decline by 14% from $285 million to $245 million. The surplus thus increases from $15 million to $34 million ($279 million − $245 million).

Thus, FASB 87 not only forces corporate sponsors of defined benefit plans to manage their surplus, but sets the key factor that pension plans should look at: the interest rate sensitivity of assets and liabilities. In our illustration, we assumed that ABC pension plan's only assets are bonds. In practice, pension plans own bonds, stocks, real estate, and other asset classes (see Table 9-2). While the market value of bonds is sensitive to interest rate changes, so are stocks and real estate. Although our discussion of bond portfolio management in Section V of this book explains how to measure this sensitivity for bonds, we should note that more emphasis in the investment community is being placed on the interest rate duration of other asset classes such as stocks and real estate so that a plan sponsor can assess the sensitivity of the entire portfolio to interest rate changes.

The volatility of the surplus is also critical and must be controlled. Under FASB 87, the volatility of the surplus will affect reported earnings. This can cause greater earnings volatility for a corporate pension sponsor. Consequently, while the liabilities of a corporate pension fund tend to be long term in nature, the funds cannot be managed as if the investment horizon is solely long term. Rather, because of FASB 87, the funds are managed so as to give recognition to the long-term nature of the liabilities and the implications of the short-term volatility of the surplus. The risk tolerance that a pension sponsor will accept in setting its investment policy indicates the degree to which it will invest in potentially higher return asset classes at the risk of short-term volatility of surplus.

Unlike corporate pension funds, public pension funds do not have to comply with FASB 87. Consequently, short-term volatility of surplus is not a constraint in establishing investment policy, and the funds can be managed assuming a long-term investment horizon. In fact, historically, many public pension funds pursued conservative investment policies, in some cases prohibiting the purchase of common stock. Today, some public pension funds have become more aggressive than corporate pension funds in their allocation of funds to riskier asset classes because their view is that they are long-term investors.

Managers of Pension Funds

A plan sponsor can do one of the following with the pension assets under its control: (1) manage all the pension assets itself (i.e., use in-house management), (2) distribute the pension assets to one or more money management firms to manage (i.e., use external money managers), or (3) combine alternatives (1) and (2). Table 9-4 lists the external money managers for two corporations, Allied Signal and IBM. In addition, both pension funds have a portion of their funds managed internally. Table 9-5 lists the external money managers for two municipal pension sponsors, the New York City Retirement System and the Dallas Police & Fire Pension System. While the former plan manages a portion internally, the latter uses only external money managers.

TABLE 9-4

EXTERNAL MONEY MANAGERS FOR TWO CORPORATE PENSION PLAN SPONSORS

Allied Signal

Pension assets:
  $6.4 billion

Money managers:
  Aetna Life
  Arnhold & S. Bleichroeder Cap.
  Arnhold & S. Bleichroeder Int'l.
  Bankers Trust
  Batterymarch Fin. Mgmt.
  BMI Cap.
  Chesapeake Cap. Mgmt.
  Copley Real Estate Adv.
  Delaware Inv. Adv.
  Hancock Venture Ptnrs.
  W. R. Huff Asset Mgmt.
  John Hancock Fin. Services
  KR Cap. Adv.
  John A. Levin
  Lincoln Cap. Mgmt.
  Lord Abbett
  MIG Realty Adv.
  Montgomery Asset Mgmt.
  Morgan Grenfell Inv. Mgmt.
  Northern Trust
  Numeric Inv.
  Property Cap. Assocs.
  Prudential Asset Mgmt.
  Prudential Real Estate
  RE Adv.
  RREEF
  S Squared Technology
  Donald Smith
  State Street Bank & Trust
  Towneley Cap. Mgmt.
  Travelers Cos.
  Trust Co. of the West
  Weiss, Peck & Greer
  Westport Asset Mgmt.
  Wilshire Asset Mgmt.

IBM Corp.

Pensions assets:
  $23.137 billion

Money managers:
  Acadian Asset Mgmt.
  Aldrich, Eastman & Waltch
  Alliance Cap. Mgmt.
  American Exploration
  BEA Assocs.
  Butler Cap.
  Cabot Ptnrs.
  Capital Guardian Trust
  Chancellor Cap. Mgmt.
  Columbus Circle Inv.
  Delaware Inv. Adv.
  Dillon Read/Saratoga Ptnrs.
  Dimensional Fund Adv.
  Dreyfus Mgmt.
  DSI Int'l. Mgmt.
  Equitable Real Estate
  Fidelity Inv.
  Fischer Francis Trees & Watts
  Forstmann Little
  Freeman Spogli
  Grubb & Ellis Realty Adv.
  HD Int'l.
  Hoisington Inv. Mgmt.
  Independence Inv. Assocs.
  John Hancock Fin. Svcs.
  Lincoln Cap. Mgmt.
  Matuschka & Co.
  Miller, Anderson & Sherrerd
  Morgan Grenfell Inv. Svcs.
  J. P. Morgan Inv. Mgmt.
  NCM Cap. Mgmt.
  Nomura Cap. Mgmt.
  Oechsle Int'l. Adv.
  Olympus Adv. Ptnrs.
  Pacific Inv. Mgmt.
  Resource Inv. Mgmt.
  Rowe Price-Fleming Int'l.
  State Street Bank & Trust
  Triumph Cap.
  Warburg Pincus
  Wellington Mgmt.
  Wells Fargo Realty Adv.
  WorldInvest
  Yarmouth Group

Source: "The Largest Corporate Plans," *Institutional Investor* (January 1992), pp. 105 ff.

TABLE 9-5

**EXTERNAL MONEY MANAGERS FOR TWO
MUNICIPAL PENSION PLAN SPONSORS**

New York City Retirement System	Dallas Police & Fire Pension System

Pension assets:
  $39.759 billion
	Pension assets:
	  $615 million

Money managers:
  Alliance Cap. Mgmt.
  Bank of Ireland Asset Mgmt.
  Bankers Trust
  BEA Assocs.
  Bear Stearns Asset Mgmt.
  Capital Guardian Trust
  Clay Finlay
  Clemente Cap.
  Fidelity Inv.
  Fiduciary Trust Int'l.
  Fischer Francis Trees & Watts
  General Electric Inv.
  Investment Advisers
  Kennedy Assoc.
  Lazard Freres Asset Mgmt.
  WR Lazard
  Lehman Ark Mgmt.
  Lincoln Cap. Mgmt.
  Mellon Bond Assocs.
  Miller, Anderson & Sherrerd
  Oppenheimer Cap.
  Pacific Inv. Mgmt.
  T. Rowe Price Assocs.
  Putnam Cos.
  RCM Cap. Mgmt.
  Schroder Cap. Mgmt. Int'l.
  Scudder, Stevens & Clark
  J&W Seligman
  Smith Barney Cap. Mgmt.
  State Street Bank & Trust
  Weiss, Peck & Greer
  Wells Fargo Nikko
	Money managers:
	  Aetna Life
	  ANB Inv. Mgmt. Trust
	  CB Commercial Realty
	  Copley Real Estate Adv.
	  FS Realty Ptnrs.
	  Global Fixed Income Adv.
	  W. R. Huff Asset Mgmt.
	  JMB Inst. Realty
	  Lazard Freres Asset Mgmt.
	  Lehndorff & Babson
	  J. P. Morgan Inv. Mgmt.
	  Oak Assocs.
	  Patterson Cap.
	  Travelers Cos.
	  Trust Co. of Texas
	  Wells Fargo Nikko

Source: "The Largest Public Pension Funds," *Institutional Investor* (January 1992), pp. 133 ff.

In the case of a contributory pension plan, the plan sponsor typically allows participants to select how to allocate their contributions among funds managed by a fund group.

We already discussed in Chapter 8 how insurance companies have been involved in the pension business through their issuance of GICs and annuities. Insurance companies also have subsidiaries that manage pension funds. Aetna Life Insurance, for example, managed $48.7 billion in pension assets as of 1991, with 36% being defined contributions for 1,000 plan sponsors.[10] The trust departments of commercial banks manage funds, as do independent money management firms (i.e., firms not affiliated with an insurance com-

---

[10]"The 1992 Defined Contribution Directory," *Institutional Investor* (June 1992), p. 179.

pany or bank). For example, the trust department of Norwest Bank of Minnesota manages about $8.1 billion, of which 30% is defined contributions for 1,300 plan sponsors, while the Harris Trust and Savings Bank manages $11.6 billion of assets, of which 30% is defined contributions for 245 plan sponsors.[11] Fidelity Institutional Retirement Services, an independent money management firm that is a subsidiary of Fidelity Investments, manages $27.5 billion of defined contribution funds for 2,500 pension sponsors.[12] To give a flavor of the types of money managers sought by pension sponsors, we have listed below a few searches for managers completed in 1992[13]:

- The Los Angeles City Employees' Retirement System sought a money manager to invest internationally. The sponsors hired Scudder, Stevens & Clark.
- The U.S. Army NAF Retirement Plan wanted a money manager to invest internationally on an indexed basis and a money manager to invest in stocks of small-capitalization U.S. firms. The plan sponsor hired Wells Fargo Nikko for the former and the firm of Strong/Corneliuson Capital Management for the latter.
- Illinois Teachers' Retirement System wanted to increase its exposure to international bonds. The plan sponsor hired Smith Barney Capital Management and Julius Bear Investment Management for this purpose, giving each $60 million to manage.
- Avon Products wanted a manager for its GIC portfolio and hired Bankers Trust.
- Knight-Ridder sought more diversification of its stock investments and sought money managers specializing in small-capitalization companies, medium-size-capitalization companies, and large-capitalization companies. To accomplish this, Knight-Ridder hired four money managers specializing in these areas—Aronson & Fogler, Cadence Capital Management, Southeastern Asset Management, and SunBank Capital Management—allocating a total of $82 million to them.
- Dow Corning Corporation wanted to add equity options to its defined contribution plan. The plan sponsor hired J. P. Morgan Investment Management to manage its equity options and Wells Fargo Nikko Investment Advisors to manage its S&P 500 index option.[14]
- The District Council of Carpenters in Rhode Island sought to diversify its assets by hiring a money manager to invest in both stock and bonds (referred to as a "balanced fund"). This plan sponsor hired Bear Stearns Asset Management to manage $10–$15 million of its $60 million of pension assets.

Managers of pension fund money obtain their income from a fee charged to manage the assets. The annual fee can range from 0.75% of assets under management to as little as 0.01% of assets under management. One study found that in 1991 the average effective fees charged by external money managers for managing public pension funds was 0.31% (31 basis points) and for

---

[11]Ibid.

[12]Ibid.

[13]This information was obtained from several issues of *Money Management Letter*.

[14]We will discuss equity options and index options in Chapter 16.

managing corporate pension funds 0.41% (41 basis points).[15] The fees are lower than advisory fees for investment companies (discussed in the next chapter), in which small investors tend to invest small accounts, because of the economies of scale associated with managing large amounts of money for pension funds. Some plan sponsors have been entering into management fee contracts based on performance rather than a fixed percentage of assets under management.[16] One study found that 14% of the funds surveyed had entered into performance-based fee contracts with pension sponsors in 1991.[17]

Pension Advisors

Money managers are responsible for handling the funds allocated to them by the plan sponsor. The plan sponsor is responsible for other critical decisions in the investment management process that we explained in Chapter 1. These decisions are made in light of the consideration we discussed earlier concerning FASB 87 and OBRA '87. To assist plan sponsors in making various decisions in the investment management process, external pension fund advisors or consultants are engaged. Advisors may assist a plan sponsor in the following ways:

- Developing plan investment policy and asset allocation among the major asset classes
- Doing actuarial advising (liability modeling and forecasting)
- Designing benchmarks that the fund's money managers will be measured against
- Measuring and monitoring the performance of the fund's money managers
- Measuring trading costs and analysis of those costs
- Constructing indexed funds when a pension plan elects to manage indexed funds internally
- Searching for and recommending money managers to pension plans
- Providing specialized research

The importance of these functions will become apparent as we discuss investment management strategies in later chapters. Frank Russell Associates, SEI, BARRA, Wilshire, Callan, and Rogers, Casey are a few examples of the better-known consultants to pension funds.

ENDOWMENT FUNDS

Another group of investors that have funds to invest in financial markets are **endowment funds**. These institutions include colleges, private schools, museums, hospitals, and foundations. The investment income generated from the funds invested are used for the operation of the institution. In the case of a college, the investment income is used to meet current operating expenses and capital expenditures (i.e., the construction of new buildings and sports facilities). Many of the organizations that have endowment funds also have a pension plan for their employees. For example, the University of Kentucky

[15]"Manager Fees Head South, Greenwich Says," *Money Management Letter* (Mar. 30, 1992), p. 1.
[16]See Arjun Divecha and Nick Mencher, "Manager Fees from the Performance Viewpoint," Chap. 9 in Frank J. Fabozzi, *Pension Fund Investment Management* (Chicago: Probus Publishing, 1990).
[17]"Manager Fees Head South, Greenwich Says," op. cit., p. 23.

TABLE 9-6		
ASSETS AND GIFTS OF SELECTED LARGE ENDOWMENT FUNDS, 1990		
Name of Fund	**Assets (Billions)**	**Gifts (Millions)**
The Ford Foundation	$5.46	$227
J. Paul Getty Trust	4.82	227
Lilly Endowment, Inc.	3.54	108
W. K. Kellogg Foundation	3.51	122
J. D. and C. T. MacArthur Foundation	3.08	116
The Pew Charitable Trusts	3.08	155
The Robert Wood Johnson Foundation	2.92	112
The Rockefeller Foundation	1.97	85
The Andrew W. Mellon Foundation	1.62	75
The Kresge Foundation	1.22	75

Source: The Foundation Directory 1992 (New York: The Foundation Center, 1992), p. viii.

has a retirement system for its employees and an endowment fund of $93 million.

Most of the large endowments in the United States are independent of any firm or governmental group. Some endowments are company-sponsored or linked to certain communities. Still others are termed "operating foundations" because they award most of their gifts to their own units rather than to organizations outside the foundations. Table 9-6 lists the 10 largest endowment funds, by assets, in the United States as of 1990. All these trusts or foundations are independent, except for the Getty Trust, which is an operating foundation.[18]

As with pension funds, qualified endowment funds are exempt from taxation. The board of trustees of the endowment fund, just like the plan sponsor for a pension fund, specify the investment objectives and the acceptable investment alternatives. The endowment funds can be managed either in-house or by external money management firms. The same organizations that manage money for pension funds manage funds for endowments.

Here are a few examples of hirings by endowment funds in 1992:

- Pomona College in Claremont, California, hired its first international equity manager, The Common Fund, to manage $20 million of its endowment funds.
- The Memorial Sloan Kettering Cancer Center in New York hired two equity money managers. Hayez Sarofim was given $45 million to manage, and Spears, Benzak, Salomon & Farrell $53 million to manage.

---

[18]*The Foundation Directory 1992* (New York: The Foundation Center, 1992), p. vi.

- The Rockefeller Foundation wanted to increase its allocation to international equities. To accomplish this, it hired three money managers: Mercator Asset Management, Arnhold and S. Bleichroeder International, and Acadian Asset Management.

Typically, the managers of endowment funds invest in long-term assets and have the primary goal of safeguarding the principal of the fund. For this reason, endowments tend to favor those equities that offer a steady dividend and comparatively little price volatility. Also, endowment funds often invest in government bonds and corporate bonds of high quality. A second goal, and an important one, is to generate a stream of earnings that allow the endowment to perform its functions of supporting certain operations or institutions.

■ SUMMARY

A pension plan is a fund that is established by private employers, governments, or unions for the payment of retirement benefits. Qualified pension funds are exempt from federal income taxes, as are employer contributions. The two types of pension funds are defined contribution plans and defined benefit plans. In the former plan the sponsor is responsible only for making specified contributions into the plan on behalf of qualifying employees, but does not guarantee any specific amount at retirement. A defined benefit plan sponsor agrees to make specified payments to qualifying employees at retirement. Recently, some hybrid plans blending features of both basic types of plans have appeared.

There is federal regulation of pension funds, as embodied in the Employee Retirement Income Security Act of 1974. ERISA sets minimum standards for employer contributions, establishes rules of prudent management, and requires vesting in a specified period of time. Also, ERISA provides for insurance of vested benefits.

Financial accounting for corporate defined benefit plans is set forth in FASB 87. Prior to this accounting standard, pension sponsors focused entirely on the performance of the assets because the present value of liabilities was effectively not marked to market. FASB 87 requires marking liabilities to market and has shifted the attention of plan sponsors from a focus on only assets to that of the fund's surplus. OBRA reinforces the importance of liabilities. The key in the management of the surplus is the interest rate sensitivity of both assets and liabilities and control of the volatility of the surplus.

Pension funds are managed either by the plan sponsor or by management firms hired by the sponsor. There are advisors to provide assistance in the several phases in the investment management process.

Endowment funds include colleges, private schools, museums, hospitals, and foundations. The primary goal of managers of these funds is to safeguard the principal of the fund. As with pension funds, external money managers are engaged.

■ KEY TERMS

accumulated benefit obligation (ABO)	funding ratio	ration (PBGC)
defined benefit plan	insured plans	pension plan
defined contribution plan	non-insured plans	projected benefit obligation (PBO)
endowment funds	overfunded pension plan	settlement rate
	Pension Benefit Guaranty Corpo-	underfunded pension plan

■ **QUESTIONS**

1. a. Who are plan sponsors?
   b. What is the difference between a defined contribution plan and a defined benefit plan?

2. What is a 401(k) plan?

3. What is meant by an insured pension plan?

4. What is the function of the Pension Benefit Guaranty Corporation?

5. "Since a defined contribution plan creates liabilities for the plan sponsors, the funds must be managed to assure that the liabilities will be satisfied." Comment on this statement.

6. Why are pension funds not interested in tax-advantaged investments?

7. Are U.S. pension funds free to invest in foreign securities?

8. a. What is the major legislation regulating pension funds?
   b. Does this major legislation require that a corporation establish a pension fund?

9. On April 30, 1987, the Institute for Chartered Financial Analysts (now the Association for Investment Management and Research) sponsored a seminar titled "The Impact of FAS 87 on Investment Analysis and Portfolio Management" and subsequently published the proceedings in a book with the same title edited by Richard Brownlee and Katrina Sherrerd. The following excerpt is from an overview of the seminar:

   The management of defined benefit pension plans is a two-edged process. As fiduciaries, companies have an obligation to their active and retired employees to fund their pension plans so that participants receive the benefits to which they are entitled. On the other hand, companies also have an obligation to their shareholders to make prudent resource allocation decisions. This suggests that management has an obligation to monitor the funding status of pension plans and, in those instances where overfunding has occurred, to look for appropriate ways to capitalize on excess pension assets. Needless to say, there is considerable controversy surrounding the issues of who owns the excess pension assets and how any such excess should be determined.

   a. What is meant by the funding ratio?
   b. What is meant by a pension fund being overfunded?
   c. How does FAS 87 define whether a fund is overfunded?

10. The following excerpt is from Robert D. Arnott and Peter L. Bernstein, "Defining and Managing Pension Fund Risk," Chap. 3 in Frank J. Fabozzi (ed.), *Pension Fund Investment Management* (Chicago: Probus Publishing, 1990). The discussion refers to FASB 87 and OBRA '87:

    These two sets of rulings may have a profound effect in shortening the investment horizon of the corporate pension sponsor. For the pension fund that slides from marginal funding into underfunded territory, many ills are visited upon the corporation: . . . The stipulation that contributions must cease for well-funded plans will also have a potentially serious effect. Without contributions, the well-funded pension plans will gradually be forced down to ABO funding ratios which will result in some vulnerability to the adverse consequences detailed above. The net result may be a gradual but long-term shift in the direction of more conservative pension management policies in order to prevent the pension plan from adversely affecting corporate management or earnings. If this shift to conservatism takes place, it would be at the cost of reducing long-term rates of return for pension management and increasing the long-term cost of pension plans. (p. 40)

    a. What do the authors mean when they say "slides from marginal funding into underfunded territory"?
    b. What are the "ills" that are visited on a corporate pension sponsor whose plan slides from marginal funding to underfunding?
    c. What is meant by the ABO funding ratio?
    d. The authors argue that FASB 87 and OBRA '87 may cause a shortening of the investment horizon of corporate pension sponsors and more conservative policies. Why do you think this may be true?

11. The Moray Corporation, a manufacturing firm, has a defined benefit pension plan for its employees. Information about the characteristics of Moray Corporation's pension fund is given below:

Market value of assets	$400 million
Present value of liabilities	$350 million
Duration of assets	3
Duration of liabilities	12

    a. What is the surplus of this pension fund?
    b. What is the funding ratio of this pension fund?
    c. Is this pension overfunded or underfunded?
    d. If interest rates decrease by 100 basis points, what will happen to the surplus and funding ratio?

e. Is the pension fund overfunded or underfunded after a 100-basis-point decrease in interest rates?

f. The manager of the pension assets of Moray Corporation has told the board of directors that the fund is conservatively managed because the duration of its assets is low. That is, the assets are not sensitive to changes in interest rates. Do you agree with the manager's view?

12. In Martin L. Leibowitz, "Setting the Stage," in Eliot P. Williams (ed.), *Managing Asset/Liability Portfolios* (Charlottesville, VA: Association for Investment Management and Research), the following statements appeared on page 9:

a. "Surplus return is defined in this case as the change in surplus divided by the initial value of the APO liability." In this sentence Leibowitz is referring to the surplus return for a pension plan. Why do you think a pension sponsor would be interested in a "surplus return"?

b. "Pension fund sponsors who wish to achieve stability in the plan's surplus can do so with a bond portfolio that matches the liability in present value, duration, and volatility characteristics. Such an immunized portfolio will preserve the surplus within some reasonable range of interest rate changes..." Why would the plan's surplus be stable if Leibowitz's suggestion is followed?

c. Continuing with the previous excerpt, Leibowitz states: "Most sponsors, however, do not require this degree of safety. Typically, a plan sponsor with a 140 percent funding ratio might be willing to sustain some surplus risk, provided that the portfolio has substantial upside potential..." What do you think Leibowitz means by surplus risk, and why would a plan sponsor with a funding ratio of 140% surplus be in a better position to accept this risk compared with a plan sponsor with a funding ratio of 90%?

13. a. What are endowment funds?
    b. What is the objective of an endowment fund?

14. How does the investment objective of an endowment fund differ from that of a defined benefit pension fund?

CHAPTER 10
INVESTMENT COMPANIES

LEARNING OBJECTIVES

After reading this chapter you will be able to:

- differentiate among the types of investment companies: mutual funds, closed-end investment companies, and unit trusts.

- explain how the share prices of mutual funds and closed-end funds are determined.

- describe the structure of funds and the costs they incur.

- describe the range of investment objectives and policies adopted by funds.

- differentiate the various costs associated with managing an investment company.

- explain why institutional money managers typically do not invest in investment companies.

- describe the characteristics of a "regulated investment company."

- explain how investment companies are regulated with regard to taxes, management, diversification of assets, fees, and advertising.

- describe the characteristics of a family or complex of funds.

Investment companies sell shares to the public and invest the proceeds in a diversified portfolio of securities. Each share that they sell represents a proportionate interest in a portfolio of securities. The securities purchased could be restricted to specific types of assets such as common stock, government bonds, corporate bonds, or money market instruments. The investment strategies followed by investment companies range from high-risk active portfolio strategies to low-risk passive portfolio strategies.

An individual will find that there are several advantages of buying shares of investment companies rather than buying investments directly in the market. First, for a given amount of funds, an investor can obtain broader portfolio diversification. For example, an investor with $1,000 can acquire a diversified portfolio of common stocks and bonds by buying shares of an investment company.

Second, an investor obtains the services of professional money managers at a cost that is less than if an investor hired a money manager directly. Moreover, many money management firms would not take on a client with less than $100,000 to invest, and some firms require a minimum of $1 million. In contrast, an investor can effectively acquire the services of a professional money manager with the purchase of one share of an investment company.

Third, investment companies offer a more convenient outlet for investing. A purchase or sale of a share of an investment company represents a purchase or sale of a portion of an entire portfolio. An investor who wanted to buy or sell a proportionate amount of each security in his or her portfolio not only would have to devote time to undertake the transaction, but also would incur significant transactions costs. In contrast, the purchase or sale of a share in an investment company can be done quite easily through a broker or via a phone call to an 800 number established by the investment company. Moreover, the bookkeeping for all transactions is done by the investment company.

In this chapter, we will discuss the structure of an investment company, the expenses associated with managing one, the pertinent federal regulations, and the wide range of investment objectives and policies that an investment company may pursue. We will not focus on the selection of an investment company, because most institutional investors do not invest in them. For the individual investor, the techniques that we describe in Chapter 30 for evaluating performance can be employed to evaluate the performance of the manager of an investment company, as well.

TYPES OF INVESTMENT COMPANIES

There are three types of investment companies: open-end funds, closed-end funds, and unit trusts.

Open-End Funds

An **open-end fund**, more popularly referred to as a **mutual fund**, continually stands ready to sell new shares to the public and to redeem its outstanding shares on demand at a price equal to an appropriate share of the value of its portfolio, which is computed daily at the close of the market.

A mutual fund's share price is based on its **net asset value (NAV) per share**, which is found by subtracting from the market value of the portfolio the mutual fund's liabilities and then dividing by the number of mutual fund shares outstanding. That is:

$$\text{Net asset value per share} = \frac{\text{market value of portfolio} - \text{liabilities}}{\text{number of fund shares outstanding}}$$

For example, suppose that a mutual fund with 10 million shares outstanding has a portfolio with a market value of $215 million and liabilities of $15 million. The net asset value per share is $20, as shown below:

$$\$20 = \frac{\$215,000,000 - \$15,000,000}{10,000,000}$$

Mutual fund shares are offered directly from the mutual fund company or through a broker on its behalf. Shares are quoted on a bid-offer basis. The **offer price** is the price at which the mutual fund will sell the shares. It is equal to the net asset value per share plus any sales commission that the mutual fund may charge. The sales commission is referred to as a "load." A **load**

TABLE 10-1		
BID AND OFFER PRICES FOR SELECTED FUNDS		
Fund	**NAV**	**Offer Price**
Vanguard Hi-Yield Corporate	7.55	NL*
Safeco Equity	10.01	NL*
Templeton Growth	15.70	16.60
Putnam Tax Exempt	9.11	9.56

*NL = no load.

fund is one that tends to impose large commissions, typically ranging from 8.5% on small amounts invested down to 1% on amounts of $500,000 or over. A mutual fund that does not impose a sales commission is called a **no-load fund**. No-load mutual funds compete directly with load funds and appeal to investors who object to paying a commission (particularly because there is no empirical evidence that suggests that load funds have outperformed no-load funds after accounting for the load charge). The relative attraction of no-load funds has forced many mutual funds to convert to no-load status. (Some funds have adopted a so-called low-load strategy, that is, charging a relatively small load of around 3% to 3.5%.) For no-load funds, the offer price is the same as the net asset value per share.

The distinction between a no-load fund and a load fund is easy to spot in the price quotations that appear in the financial sections of newspapers. Also, the quotations indicate the size of the load, if there is one. Table 10-1 shows some quoted bid and offer prices from 1992.

In the table, the Hi-Yield Corporate Fund of the Vanguard Group and the Equity Fund of the Safeco Group are no-load funds. Their initial per share price to the investor equals the per share value of the fund's assets. The per share offer prices of the other two funds exceed their funds' per share net asset values. Thus, the third and fourth funds are load funds. For the Templeton Growth Fund, the load is ($16.60 − 15.70)/$15.70, or 5.7%. For the Putnam Tax Exempt Fund, the load is slightly above 5%.

Even though a fund does not charge a commission for share purchases, it may still charge investors a fee to sell (redeem) shares. Such a fund, referred to as a **back-end load fund**, may charge a commission of 4% to 6%. Some back-end load funds impose a full commission if the shares are redeemed within a designated time period after purchase, such as one year, reducing the commission the longer the investor holds the shares. The formal name for the back-end load is the **contingent deferred sales charge**, or CDSC.

There are mutual funds that do not charge an upfront or a back-end commission but instead take out up to 1.25% of average daily fund assets each year to cover the costs of selling and marketing shares. The SEC's Rule 12b-1, which was passed in 1980, allows mutual funds to use such an arrangement for covering selling and marketing costs; such funds are referred to as **12b-1 funds**.

In 1986, the SEC permitted funds to offer both types of load funds. For example, Alliance Mortgage Securities has two share classes, Class A and Class B. The former has a 3% front-end load; the latter has a back-end sales charge whose fee depends on the length of time the shares are held. Investors who

TABLE 10-2		
DISTRIBUTION OF ASSETS OF OPEN-END STOCK AND BOND FUNDS IN 1981 AND 1991		
	1981 **(in $ billions)**	**1991** **(in $ billions)**
Cash & equivalents	5.3	60.3
Corporate bonds	7.5	84.6
Preferred stock	0.4	8.0
Common stock	36.7	328.1
Municipal bonds	3.0	147.7
U.S. government bonds	2.2	170.1
Other	0.2	8.3
Total	55.2	807.1

Source: *Mutual Fund Fact Book* (Washington, DC: Investment Company Institute, 1992), p. 93.

may need to sell their shares in the short term might prefer the front-loaded Class A, while those intending to hold shares for a long period might prefer end-loaded Class B.

The number of mutual funds increased fourfold in the 1980s and early 1990s, from 250 in 1980 to more than 3,900 in 1992.[1] The amount controlled by both open-end and closed-end funds increased from $240 billion in 1982 to more than $1.5 trillion in 1992. In terms of assets under management, the funds rank behind commercial banks and nearly equal to insurance companies, but are ahead of thrifts and credit unions.[2] One reason for the growth of the assets invested in mutual funds is the use of mutual funds as an investment choice for defined contribution pension plans.

Table 10-2 shows the distribution of the assets of open-end funds across major categories of assets for 1981 and 1991 and reveals the dynamic growth of all aspects of this major institutional investor.

Closed-End Funds

In contrast to mutual funds, closed-end funds sell shares like any other corporation and usually do not redeem their shares. Shares of closed-end funds sell on either an organized exchange, such as the New York Stock Exchange, or in the over-the-counter market. Newspapers often list quotations of the prices of these shares under the heading "Publicly Traded Funds." Investors who wish to purchase closed-end funds must pay a brokerage commission at the time of purchase and again at the time of sale.

The price of a share in a closed-end fund is determined by supply and demand, so the price can fall below or rise above the net asset value per share. Shares selling below NAV are said to be "trading at a discount," while shares with prices above NAV are "trading at a premium." Though the divergence of price from NAV is often puzzling, in some cases the premium or discount is easy to understand. One fund's share price may be below the NAV because the fund has large tax liabilities on capital gains that have swelled the NAV,

---

[1] This is the number of mutual funds followed by a leading service, Lipper Analytical Services.
[2] *Mutual Fund Fact Book* (Washington, DC: Investment Company Institute, 1992), p. 25.

and investors are pricing the future after-tax distributions of the fund. Another fund's shares may trade at a premium to the NAV because the fund offers relatively cheap access to, and professional management of, stocks in another country where information is not readily available to small investors. In recent years, the Spain Fund and the Korea Fund have been prominent examples of this situation.[3]

An interesting feature of closed-end funds is that the initial investors bear the cost of underwriting the issuance of the funds' shares.[4] The proceeds that the managers of the fund have to work with equal the total paid by initial buyers of the shares minus all costs of issuance. These costs, which average around 7.5% of the total amount paid for the issue, normally include selling fees or commissions paid to the retail brokerage firms that distribute the shares to the public. The high commissions are strong incentives for retail brokers to recommend these shares to their customers who are retail (i.e., individual) investors.

Historically, closed-end funds have been far less popular than open-end funds in the United States. One estimate has it that the number of dollars in open-end funds is 12 times greater than the number in closed-end funds.[5] However, in recent years, closed-end funds have shown increasing appeal to individual investors, primarily because of their emphasis on international investment portfolios. From 1986 to 1991, the number of closed-end funds rose from 69 to 290, and their assets grew from $12 billion to $73 billion.[6]

Another reason for the popularity of closed-end funds is the introduction of a fund that has a fixed termination or maturity date. Such a fund is called a **term trust**. The first term trust, the Blackstone Target Term Trust, was a closed-end fund sponsored by Blackstone Financial Management (now called BlackRock Financial Management) in November 1988. Prior to this time, neither mutual funds nor closed-end funds had a fixed termination or maturity date. The fund invested in a portfolio of bonds, but specified a termination date for the fund. The objective of the fund was to return to shareholders the initial offering price, $10, plus a rate competitive with a Treasury security with the same maturity as the termination date of the trust. Effectively, term trusts are "synthetic bonds" whose performance over the term of the trust depends on the capability of the financial advisor. The implication for the management of such a fund is that there is a well-defined investment goal: to return to the shareholders the dollar amount specified at the offering date. Thus, the financial advisor manages the fund's portfolio using strategies that recognize a future liability, rather than using the strategies pursued by financial advisors of other mutual funds that need not be concerned with a future liability.

---

[3]The so-called country funds were popular in the late 1980s and made up a substantial portion of the closed-end funds issued at that time.

[4]Kathleen Weiss, "The Post-Offering Price Performance of Closed-End Funds," *Financial Management* (Autumn 1989), pp. 57–67.

[5]Peter Donovan, "Closed-End Funds in the United States of America," in Stefano Preda (ed.), *Funds and Portfolio Management Institutions: An International Survey* (Amsterdam: North-Holland, 1991), p. 232.

[6]Securities and Exchange Commission, *Protecting Investors: A Half-Century of Investment Company Regulation* (New York: Commerce Clearing House, Inc., 1992), p. 432.

Unit Trust

A **unit trust** is similar to a closed-end fund in that it issues a fixed number of ownership shares, called *unit certificates.* They are sold and redeemed only by the issuing company, like open-end funds, however. Unit trusts typically invest in bonds and differ in several ways from both mutual funds and closed-end funds that specialize in investing in bonds. First, there is no active trading of the bonds in the portfolio of the unit trust. Once the unit trust is assembled by the sponsor (usually a brokerage firm or bond underwriter) and turned over to a trustee, the trustee holds all the bonds until they are redeemed by the issuer. Usually the only time the trustee can sell an issue in the portfolio is if there is a dramatic decline in the issuer's credit quality. This means that the cost of operating the trust will be considerably less than costs incurred by either a mutual fund or a closed-end fund. Second, unit trusts have a fixed termination date, while mutual funds and closed-end funds (with the exception of term trusts) do not. Third, unlike the mutual fund and closed-end fund investor, the unit trust investor knows that the portfolio consists of a specific collection of bonds and has no concern that the trustee will alter the portfolio.

All unit trusts charge a sales commission. The initial sales charge for a unit trust is 3.5% to 5.5%. There is often a commission of 3% to sell units, but trusts sponsored by some organizations do not charge a commission when the units are sold. Since there is no active management of unit trusts, our focus in the balance of this chapter is on open-end (mutual) funds and closed-end funds. We shall refer to both as simply "funds."

STRUCTURE AND EXPENSES OF A FUND

A fund is structured with a board of directors, a financial advisor responsible for managing the portfolio, and a distributing and selling organization. Funds enter into contracts with a financial advisor to manage the fund, typically a company that specializes in the management of funds. The advisor can be a subsidiary of a brokerage firm, an insurance company, an investment management firm, or a bank.

Annual Fund Operating Expenses

The financial advisor to the fund charges a **management fee,** also called an *investment advisory fee.* This fee, which is one of the largest costs of administering a fund, is usually equal to 0.5% to 1.5% of the fund's average assets, but the fee per dollar of assets managed may be determined on a sliding scale that declines as the dollar amount of the fund increases. The management fee should reflect the difficulty of managing the particular fund.

Funds incur other costs in addition to the management fee. These include the expenses for maintaining shareholder records, providing shareholders with financial statements, and employing custodial and accounting services. These expenses are referred to as *other expenses* in the industry. The management fee and other expenses are referred to as **annual fund operating expenses**. Also included as part of annual fund operating expenses for 12b-1 funds are the expenses for covering selling and marketing costs.

TABLE 10-3

ANNUAL OPERATING EXPENSES FOR SELECTED FUNDS

Fidelity Magellan Fund

Management fees	0.78%
12b-1 fees	None
Other expenses	0.28%
Total fund operating expenses	1.06%

The Guardian Asset Allocation Fund

Management fees	0.65%
12b-1 fees	0.25%
Other expenses	0.76%
Total portfolio fund operating expenses	1.66%

Dreyfus New Jersey Intermediate Municipal Bond Fund

Management fees	0.60%
Other expenses	0.83%
Total fund operating expenses	1.43%

The annual fund operating expenses must be specified in the prospectus.[7] The management fee is known. How much the other expenses and the 12b-1 fees will be are not known. However, an estimate is provided in the prospectus based on the fund's historical expenses.

Table 10-3 provides excerpts from the prospectus of three funds regarding annual fund operating expenses (as a percentage of average net assets).

Average Costs of Fund Ownership

In addition to the annual fund operating expenses that the investor in a fund incurs, there is also any sales or redemption load with buying and selling shares. The load is not an annual fee but is incurred at the time the shares are purchased and/or sold. Thus, the effective annual load depends on how long the shares are held by an investor. The longer the holding period, the lower the effective annual load.

The total fees incurred by investing in a fund are then the annual fund operating expenses and the load. In mid-1992, *Money* magazine examined the prospectuses of 29 large funds to determine the average annual costs of owning a share in one of these funds. In calculating the effective annual load, *Money* magazine assumed that the shares were held for three years.

The study found that the average annual cost of owning a fund is 2.2%. The cost ranged from 0.4% to 3.5%. For 21 of the 29 funds, the cost ranged between 2% and 3%. For six of the funds, the cost was about 1%.

Portfolio Transactions

What are not included in the annual operating fund expenses are the transactions costs associated with buying and selling securities to implement the fund's portfolio strategy. We will discuss transactions costs in Chapter 13.

To give the investor some idea of portfolio trading activity, the fund re-

---

[7]A prospectus is a document approved by the Securities and Exchange Commission that describes the security offered.

ports the **portfolio turnover rate** on an annualized basis. This rate is calculated by dividing the lesser of purchases and sales by the average of portfolio assets.

The portfolio turnover rate varies from fund to fund because it depends on the investment strategy pursued by the fund. Active portfolio strategies generally require frequent buying and selling of securities and will therefore have a higher portfolio turnover rate. Passive portfolio strategies typically require less frequent portfolio transactions and therefore will have a low portfolio turnover.

For example, in the Fidelity Magellen Fund, a fund which pursues an active equity portfolio strategy, the portfolio turnover rate was 132% for the 1993 fiscal year. In contrast, for the Fidelity Market Index Fund, a fund which employs a passive equity portfolio strategy, the portfolio turnover rate was 3% for the 1993 fiscal year.

USE OF FUNDS BY MONEY MANAGERS

The managers of an investment company are paid a fee for managing the fund. Thus, a money manager hired by a client, for example, a pension plan sponsor, is unlikely to invest in the shares of an investment company because this would mean that the client would be paying two management fees. That is, a client would be paying a money manager a management fee, and, in turn, that money manager would be paying a management fee by investing in the shares of an investment company, as well as any commissions that may be incurred in buying those shares. The client could just as easily buy shares in an investment company without using a money manager as an intermediary.

Moreover, most institutions invest in sufficient amount so that they can engage the same money management firm that runs money for an investment company. For example, the largest investment company in the United States is Fidelity Investments. If IBM's pension fund wants to engage the services of the money managers of Fidelity Investments, it can hire Fidelity Investment directly rather than buying shares in one of the investment companies sponsored by Fidelity. In fact, as can been from Table 9-4 of Chapter 9, Fidelity is one of IBM's external money managers. The advantage of doing so is that the fees are considerably lower than those incurred when investing in an investment company.

Smaller institutional investors who want to invest via a pool of funds will do so by investing in so-called institutional funds or trusts. The advantages of investing in this vehicle are the lower management fees and, frequently, no-load provisions. These are typically open-end funds. Foreign institutions have used institutional trusts to invest in the U.S. capital markets. Such trusts are established in a tax haven so that foreign investors will not be taxed in the United States.

FUND OBJECTIVES AND POLICIES

When a fund is offered, a prospectus must be provided to the prospective investor. Every prospectus for a fund must include a statement about the *investment objectives* that the manager of the fund seeks to accomplish and the *policies* that the manager will follow to meet the investment objectives.

The investment objectives can only be changed by vote of a majority of the outstanding shares of the fund. The statement about policies indicates in broad terms the type of strategy that the fund manager will pursue and the asset classes in which the fund manager may invest.

Box 10 shows the statement of investment objective and policies for the Fidelity Magellan Fund, an open-end investment company. The investment objective is stated to be capital appreciation. To accomplish this objective, the fund invests in common stock and securities convertible into common stock of both domestic and foreign corporations. The portfolio strategy is described in general terms. Also note that the fund manager is permitted to use options and futures contracts.

Figure 10-1 presents excerpts of the investment objective and policies for five mutual funds. The strategies pursued are described in later chapters in this book.

Specialization of Equity Funds

There are funds that invest exclusively in equities, and others in bonds. Even within an asset class, there are funds with different objectives. In the case of funds that invest exclusively in equities, for example, the investment objective of one fund may be to emphasize stable income, another capital gains or growth, and still another a combination of income and growth. (See the investment objective and policies for Fidelity Magellan Fund in Box 10 and the excerpt for Fidelity Equity-Income II Fund in Figure 10-1.)

Some funds limit investments to specific industries so that the fund manager can presumably specialize and achieve better selection and timing. A few funds offer participation in potentially glamorous new research companies by investing in fields such as electronics, oceanography, and telecommunications. There are funds that restrict their investment to small firms, and some that invest in foreign stocks. For investors who wish to achieve maximum diversification, the latest development in the mutual fund area is "indexed funds" that hold a portfolio mimicking the composition of a broad index such as the S&P 500.

Specialization of Bond Funds

Funds that specialize in bond investments also have a wide menu of investment objectives. Government bond funds invest only in U.S. government bonds. There are corporate bond funds, which can have very different investment objectives. (See the investment objective and policies excerpt in Figure 10-1.)

Some funds invest only in high-quality corporate bonds, while others invest primarily in low-quality (junk) corporate bonds. There are funds that invest exclusively in convertible securities, mortgage-backed securities, or municipal bonds. Some funds specialize in municipal bond issuers within a given state so that investors can take advantage of the exemption of interest income from state and local taxes. (See the investment objective and policies given for the Dreyfus New Jersey Intermediate Municipal Bond Fund in Figure 10-1.)

Money Market Funds

Money market mutual funds invest in money market instruments. There are three types of money market funds: (1) general money market funds, which invest in taxable money market instruments such as Treasury bills,

BOX 10

FIDELITY MAGELLAN FUND'S INVESTMENT OBJECTIVE AND POLICIES

Investment Objective and Policies

Magellan Fund seeks capital appreciation by investing primarily in common stock and securities convertible into common stock. There is no assurance that the fund will achieve its investment objective.

Fidelity Management & Research Company (FMR), the fund's manager, seeks capital appreciation by investing primarily in common stock and securities convertible into common stock; up to 20% of the fund's assets may also be invested in debt securities of all types and qualities issued by foreign and domestic issuers if FMR believes that doing so will result in capital appreciation. No emphasis is placed on dividend income except when FMR believes that this income will have a favorable influence on the market value of the security. Because the fund has no limitation on the quality of debt securities in which it may invest, the debt securities in its portfolio may be of poor quality and may present the risk of default or may be in default.

FMR looks to the following areas for potential capital appreciation:

- domestic corporations operating primarily or entirely in the United States
- domestic corporations which have significant activities and interests outside of the United States
- foreign companies—principally large, well-known companies, but also smaller, less well-known companies which FMR believes possess unusual values, although they may involve greater risk.

There is no limitation on the amount of the fund's assets that may be invested in foreign securities or in any one country or currency except that no more than 40% of the fund's assets may be invested in companies operating exclusively in one foreign country.

The fund may invest up to 20% of its assets in lower-quality, high-yielding securities (commonly referred to as "junk bonds"). FMR can also make substantial temporary investments in investment grade–debt securities for defensive purposes when it believes that market conditions warrant.

The fund may purchase restricted securities, warrants, and interests in real estate investment trusts. The fund may also engage in repurchase agreement transactions. See the Appendix for more information.

Foreign Investments Foreign securities and securities denominated in or indexed to foreign currencies may be affected by the strength of foreign currencies relative to the U.S. dollar, or by political or economic developments in foreign countries. Foreign companies may not be subject to accounting standards or governmental supervision, comparable to U.S. companies, and there may be less public information about their operations. In addition, foreign markets may be less liquid or more volatile than U.S. markets, and may offer less protection to investors such as the fund. FMR considers these factors in making investments for the fund.

The fund may enter into currency forward contracts (agreements to exchange one currency for another at a future date) to manage currency risks and to facilitate transactions in foreign securities. Currency forward contracts will be used primarily to protect the fund from adverse exchange rate changes, but involve a risk of loss if FMR fails to predict foreign values correctly.

Options and Futures Contracts

When the fund is not fully invested in stocks, strategies such as buying calls, writing puts, and buying futures can be used to increase its exposure to stock price changes. When the fund wishes to hedge against stock market fluctuations, strategies such as buying puts, writing calls, and selling futures can be used to reduce market exposure. Since most stock index futures and options are based on broad stock market indexes, their performance tends to track the performance of common stocks generally—which may or may not correspond to the types of securities in which the fund invests. FMR expects that the underlying value of futures and options held by the fund will be less than 15% of its assets under normal conditions.

Options and futures can be volatile investments. If FMR applies a hedge at an inappropriate time or judges market conditions incorrectly, options and futures strategies may lower the fund's return. The fund could also experience losses if the prices of its options or futures positions were poorly correlated with its other investments, or if it could not close out its positions because of an illiquid secondary market. The fund's policies regarding futures and options are not fundamental and may be changed at any time without shareholder notification.

Source: Fidelity Magellan Fund's Prospectus.

Questions for Box 10

1. What is meant by a fund's investment objective and policies?
2. Why do you think there is a restriction that "no more than 40% of the fund's assets may be invested in companies operating exclusively in one foreign country"?

FIDELITY SPARTAN MARKET INDEX FUND

The investment objective of the Spartan Market Index Fund is to seek investment results that correspond to the total return (i.e., the combination of capital changes and income) of common stocks publicly traded in the United States, as represented by the Standard & Poor's 500 Composite Stock Price Index (the "S&P" 500 or "Index"), while keeping transaction costs and other expenses low. The Fund is not managed according to traditional methods of "active" investment management, which involve the buying and selling of securities based upon economic, financial, and market analyses and investment judgment. Instead, the Fund, utilizing a "passive" or "indexing" investment approach, attempts to duplicate the performance of the S&P 500. There is no assurance that the Fund will achieve its investment objective.

FIDELITY EQUITY-INCOME II FUND

The Fund's objective is to seek reasonable income by investing primarily in income-producing equity securities. In choosing these securities, the Fund will also consider the potential for capital appreciation. The Fund looks for a yield that exceeds the composite yield on securities composing the Standard & Poor's 500 Composite Stock Price Index (S&P 500). There is no assurance that the Fund will achieve its investment objective.

THE GUARDIAN INVESTMENT QUALITY BOND FUND

The primary investment objective of the Bond Fund is to secure a high level of current income and capital appreciation without undue risk to principal. The Bond Fund seeks its objective by normally investing at least 80% of the value of its assets in (1) corporate bonds and other debt obligations rated in one of the four highest rating categories established by Moody's Investors Service, Inc. ("Moody's") or Standard & Poor's Corporation ("S&P") (commonly referred to as "investment grade" bonds) and (2) U.S. government securities and obligations of U.S. government agencies and instrumentalities.

THE GUARDIAN ASSET ALLOCATION FUND

The primary investment objective of the Asset Allocation Fund is to achieve long-term total investment return consistent with moderate risk. The Asset Allocation Fund seeks its objective by investing in equities of the type permitted for the Park Avenue Fund, fixed-income securities of the type permitted for the Bond Fund and money market securities of the type permitted for the Cash Fund. GISC actively manages the allocation of assets among equity, fixed-income and money markets based upon an asset allocation strategy which uses theoretical models for investments in the equity, fixed-income and money market sectors. The theoretical models assist GISC in determining a mix of portfolio investments based on relevant economic and market trends.

DREYFUS NEW JERSEY INTERMEDIATE MUNICIPAL BOND FUND

The Fund's goal is to provide you with as high a level of current income exempt from Federal and New Jersey income taxes as is consistent with the preservation of capital. To accomplish this goal, the Fund will invest primarily in debt securities of the State of New Jersey, its political subdivisions, authorities and corporations, the interest from which is, in the opinion of bond counsel to the issuer, exempt from Federal and New Jersey income taxes (collectively, "New Jersey Municipal Obligations"). To the extent that acceptable New Jersey Municipal Obligations are at any time unavailable for investment by the Fund, the Fund will invest temporarily in other debt securities the interest from which is, in the opinion of bond counsel to the issuer, exempt from Federal, but not New Jersey, income tax. The dollar-weighted average maturity of the Fund's portfolio will range between three and ten years. The Fund's investment objective cannot be changed without approval by the majority (as defined by the Investment Company Act of 1940) of the Fund's outstanding voting shares. There can be no assurance that the Fund's investment objective will be achieved.

TABLE 10-4	
DISTRIBUTION OF NET ASSETS AMONG ALL OPEN-END FUNDS ACCORDING TO INVESTMENT OBJECTIVES, 1991	
Objective	Percent of All Funds' Net Assets
Aggressive growth	4.7%
Growth	7.8
Growth and income	9.6
Precious metals	2.2
International	1.4
Global—equity	1.3
Income—equity	2.2
Option/income	0.1
Flexible portfolio	0.7
Balanced	1.5
Income—mixed	1.9
Income—bond	2.0
U.S. government income	7.2
Ginnie Mae	2.7
Global bond	2.0
Corporate bond	1.1
High-yield bond	1.9
Municipal bond	6.6
State municipal bond	4.9
Money market—tax exempt	6.7
Money market—taxable	33.4

Source: *Mutual Fund Fact Book* (Washington, DC: Investment Company Institute, 1992), pp. 92, 112, 114.

short-term U.S. government agency issues, commercial paper, and negotiable certificates of deposit; (2) U.S. government short-term funds, which invest only in Treasury bills or U.S. government agency securities; and (3) short-term municipal funds.

Balanced Funds

A **balanced fund** is one that invests in both stocks and bonds. While there are often limits on how much a fund manager may allocate to an asset class, there is room to modify the asset mix to take advantage of what the fund manager expects will be the better-performing asset class.

The Investment Company Institute, the national association for open-end or mutual funds, recognizes all the investment objectives listed above as well as some others. Table 10-4 provides the institute's complete list and the public interest in each type of fund, as indicated by each type's percentage of total assets in all open-end funds.

Fund Families

A **fund family**, "family of funds," "group of funds," or "complex of funds" is a set of funds with different investment objectives offered by one management company. In many cases, investors may move their assets from one fund to another within the family, at little or no cost, and with only a phone call to a toll-free number. The same policies regarding load and other costs may apply to all members of the family, but it is possible for a management company to have different fee structures for different funds under its control.

REGULATION

All investment companies are regulated at the federal level according to the *Investment Company Act of 1940* and subsequent amendments to that legislation. The securities that investment companies issue must be registered with the SEC. Moreover, investment companies must provide periodic financial reports and disclose the investment policies they will follow to achieve their investment objectives to investors. The act prohibits changes in the nature of an investment company's investment objectives without the approval of shareholders. A major goal of the law was to prevent self-dealing and other examples of conflict of interest, such as the imposition of unreasonably high fees.

However, the most important feature of the Investment Company Act of 1940 has to do with what the law permits. The law frees any company that qualifies as a "regulated investment company" from taxation on its gains, from either income or capital appreciation. To qualify as such a company, the fund must distribute to its shareholders 90% of its income each fiscal year. Further, the fund must follow certain rules about the diversification and liquidity of its investments and about short-term trading and gains.

In the past, the SEC set a limit of 8.5% on a fund's load but allowed the fund to charge certain expenses under the 12b-1 rule. Recently, the SEC has amended the rule to set, for most cases effective on July 1 of 1993, a maximum of 8.5% on the total of all fees, inclusive of front-end and back-end loads as well as expenses for advertising, etc.

THE FINANCIAL ADVISOR

As we noted earlier, a fund's financial advisor (or money manager) can be a subsidiary of a brokerage firm, an insurance company, a bank, or an investment management firm. These advisors do not manage just one fund, but a family of funds. The mutual fund industry is highly concentrated, with the 10 largest mutual fund groups managing close to 50% of the market share.

The largest fund group is managed by Fidelity Investments, which was mentioned above. The second largest fund group manager is Merrill Lynch, a brokerage firm. The next three largest fund group managers are the Vanguard Group, Franklin Resources, and Dreyfus, all of which are investment management firms. These five fund groups control more than 32% of mutual fund assets.[8]

The fees realized from advising investment companies and selling their shares have attracted the interest of insurance companies and banks. For example, in 1991 Kemper Financial Services, the mutual fund operations division of the Kemper Corporation, an insurance company, generated 60% of the net income of the insurance company.[9]

---

[8]Julie Rohrer, "The Mutual Fund Battle Turns Ugly," *Institutional Investor* (September 1992), p. 41.

[9]Ibid., p. 40.

MANAGING AN INVESTMENT COMPANY

Now that we know the fundamentals about an investment company, the final topic we address in this chapter is how to manage the portfolio of an investment company.

The first thing that should be obvious is that there is no universal portfolio strategy that is followed by all fund managers. This is because each fund has its own investment objective and policies. Thus, the manager of one fund may follow one of the active common stock strategies described in Chapter 14, while the manager of another might follow one of the passive bond strategies described in Chapter 23.

The fund manager must always be sure to comply with the provisions set forth in the prospectus. Box 10, for example, indicates that the Fidelity Magellan Fund "may invest up to 20% of its assets in lower-quality, high-yielding securities." The restrictions are few for this fund. However, there are other funds with many more restrictions imposed. Consequently, internal monitoring of the fund's portfolio to assure compliance with the conditions specified by the prospectus is required.

For a given investment objective and policies, there will be a difference between the management of an open-end and closed-end fund with respect to liquidity requirements. Recall that shareholders of an open-end fund can redeem their shares at any time. Investors in closed-end funds cannot. Consequently, the manager of an open-end fund must be prepared to liquidate a portion of the portfolio to satisfy net redemptions (i.e., the difference between the shares redeemed and the new shares sold). This is not a concern to the manager of closed-end fund.

All fund managers seek to minimize the costs of operating a fund. However, high annual fund operating expenses and transactions costs are not the sign of a poorly managed fund. Some funds incur high costs because of the nature of the strategies they employ. The bottom line is how the fund performed relative to similar funds with the same investment objective and policies. The performance of a fund is measured by its annual total return after considering all fund operating expenses and the costs of portfolio transactions.

■ SUMMARY

Investment companies sell shares to the public and invest the proceeds in a diversified portfolio of securities, with each share representing a proportionate interest in the underlying portfolio of securities. There are three types of investment companies: open-end or mutual funds, closed-end funds, and unit trusts.

A fund is structured with a board of directors, a financial advisor responsible for managing the portfolio, and a distributing and selling organization. Annual fund operating expenses include the management fee and other expenses. For 12b-1 funds, the costs of distribution and marketing are also included in the annual fund operating expenses. In addition, portfolio trans-

actions costs are associated with managing a fund. These costs are not included in the annual fund operating expenses, but they are reflected in a fund's performance.

A wide range of funds with many different investment objectives and policies are available. Securities law requires that a fund clearly set forth its investment objective and policies in its prospectus.

Investment companies are extensively regulated, with most of that regulation occurring at the federal level through the Investment Company Act of 1940. The key feature of the legislation in this area allows the funds to be exempt from taxation on their gains if 90% of the gains are distributed to investors within the fund's fiscal year. There are also regulations that apply to many aspects of the funds' administration, including sales fees, asset management, degree of diversification, distributions, and advertising.

Institutional money managers are unlikely to invest in the shares of investment companies since doing so simply adds another layer of management fees. An institutional client that seeks the services of a money manager can contract for those services directly rather than buying shares in an investment company for which the money manager is the financial advisor.

A fund family refers to a choice of numerous funds with different investment objectives, which many management companies offer investors. That is, an investment advisory company actually manages dozens of different funds which span the large spectrum of investment objectives.

■ KEY TERMS

annual fund operating expenses
back-end load fund
balanced fund
contingent deferred sales charge
fund family
load fund

management fee
mutual fund
net asset value (NAV) per share
no-load fund
offer price

open-end fund
portfolio turnover rate
term trust
12b-1 funds
unit trust

■ QUESTIONS

1. An investment company with 2 million shares outstanding has total assets of $40 million and total liabilities of $2 million.
   a. What is the net asset value per share?
   b. Suppose the investment company is a no-load fund. How much would an investor have to pay to purchase one share?
   c. Suppose the investment company charged a sales commission or load of 5%. What would an investor have to pay to buy a share?

2. Suppose the investment company in the previous question is a closed-end investment company. Can you determine how much an investor would have to pay to purchase one share? If so, how? If not, why not?

3. What is a back-end load fund?

4. What is a 12b-1 fund?

5. Why does a unit trust not require active portfolio management?

6. "The manager of a fund can change the investment objective at the beginning of each fiscal year." Comment.

7. Comment on the following statement: "The management fee paid to a fund manager should be the same regardless of the fund's investment objective and policies."

8. In comparing the prospectuses of two funds, Fund A and Fund B, you note that the annual fund operating expenses as a percentage of the net assets are twice as large for Fund A as for Fund B. What does this tell you about the efficiency of the fund's manager in operating the fund?

9. In *Bogle on Mutual Funds* (Burr Ridge, IL: Irwin Professional Publishing, 1994), John C. Bogle, chairman of the Vanguard Group of Investment Companies, in his discussion of mutual fund costs wrote: "There is one large *invisible* cost, often ignored because of its invisibility. It is the cost the fund incurs in executing portfolio transactions."
   a. Why is this cost an "invisible cost"?
   b. What figure reported by a fund gives some indication of the amount of trading activity?

10. a. What is a money market fund?
    b. Explain three types of money market funds.

11. a. What types of regulatory requirements does a "regulated investment company" have to meet?
    b. What is the key advantage to a company of gaining this status?

12. You have just been engaged by General Motors to manage $50 million of its pension fund. Would you consider investing this money in the shares of one or more investment companies?

13. Indicate why you agree or disagree with the following statement: "The manager of a closed-end fund has greater liquidity concerns than the manager of an open-end fund."

CHAPTER 11
DEPOSITORY INSTITUTIONS

LEARNING OBJECTIVES
After reading this chapter you will be able to:

- explain how a depository institution generates income.

- describe what is meant by interest rate risk for a depository institution.

- explain why a depository institution must be concerned with liquidity.

- list the funding sources for a commercial bank.

- list the types of services provided by commercial banks.

- discuss the risk-based capital guidelines based on credit risk.

- discuss the proposed risk-based capital guidelines based on interest rate risk.

Depository institutions are financial intermediaries that accept deposits. They include commercial banks (or simply banks), savings and loan associations (S&Ls), savings banks, and credit unions. It is common to refer to the depository institutions other than banks as "thrifts." Depository institutions are highly regulated and supervised because of the important role that they play in the financial system. Checking accounts are still the principal means people and business entities use for making payments. Government monetary policy is implemented through various activities with banks. Because of their important role, depository institutions are afforded special privileges such as access to federal deposit insurance and access to a government entity in order to acquire funds for liquidity or emergency needs.

Deposits represent the liabilities (debt) of the deposit-accepting institution. With the funds raised through deposits and other funding sources, depository institutions make direct loans to various entities (i.e., individuals, businesses, and governments) and invest in securities. Their income is derived from the interest income from their portfolio of loans, income from their portfolio of securities, and fee income.

In this chapter we will look at the asset/liability problem of depository institutions. Our focus will be on the nature of the liabilities and considerations in managing the portfolio of securities, not the loan portfolio. After discussing the asset/liability problem, we provide an overview of the two largest types of depository institutions: banks and savings and loan associations.

THE ASSET/LIABILITY PROBLEM OF DEPOSITORY INSTITUTIONS

The asset/liability problem that depository institutions face is quite simple to explain—although not necessarily easy to solve. A depository institution seeks to earn a positive spread between the assets it invests in (loans and securities) and the cost of its funds (deposits and other sources). This difference between income and cost is referred to as **spread income** or **margin income**. The spread income should allow the institution to meet operating expenses and earn a fair profit on its capital.

In generating spread income a depository institution faces several risks. These include credit risk, regulatory risk, and interest rate (or funding) risk. Regulatory risk is the risk that regulators will change the rules so as to adversely impact the earnings of the institution. Interest rate risk is described below.

Interest Rate Risk

Simply put, **interest rate risk** is the risk that a depository institution's spread income will suffer because of changes in interest rates. This kind of risk can be explained best by an illustration. Suppose that a depository institution raises $100 million by issuing a deposit account that has a maturity of one year and by agreeing to pay an interest rate of 7%. Ignoring for the time being the fact that the depository institution cannot invest the entire $100 million because of reserve requirements, which we discuss later in this chapter, suppose that $100 million is invested in a U.S. Treasury security that matures in 15 years paying an interest rate of 9%. Because the funds are invested in a U.S. Treasury security, there is no credit risk.

It seems at first that the depository institution has locked in a spread of 2% (9% minus 7%). This spread can be counted on only for the first year, though, because the spread in future years will depend on the interest rate this depository institution will have to pay depositors in order to raise $100 million after the one-year time deposit matures. If interest rates decline, the spread will increase because the depository institution has locked in the 9% rate. If interest rates rise, however, the spread income will decline. In fact, if this depository institution must pay more than 9% to depositors for the next 14 years, the spread will be negative. That is, it will cost the depository institution more to finance the purchase of the Treasury security than it will earn on the funds invested in the security.

In our example, the depository institution has "borrowed short" (borrowed for one year) and "lent long" (invested for 15 years). This investment policy will benefit from a decline in interest rates, but suffer if interest rates rise. Suppose the institution could have borrowed funds for 15 years at 7% and invested in a U.S. Treasury security maturing in one year earning 9%—

TABLE 11-1		
EFFECT OF CHANGES IN INTEREST RATES ON SPREAD INCOME FOR TWO DEPOSITORY INVESTMENT STRATEGIES		
Strategy	If Rates Rise. . .	If Rates Fall. . .
Borrow short/lend long	Decreases	Increases
Borrow long/lend short	Increases	Decreases

borrowing long (15 years) and lending short (one year). A rise in interest rates will benefit the depository institution because it can then reinvest the proceeds from the maturing one-year government security in a new one-year government security offering a higher interest rate. In this case a decline in interest rates will reduce the spread. If interest rates fall below 7%, there will be a negative spread.

All depository institutions face this interest rate risk, or funding, problem, which is summarized in Table 11-1. Managers of a depository institution who have particular expectations about the future direction of interest rates will seek to benefit from these expectations. Those who expect interest rates to rise may pursue a policy to borrow funds for the long term and lend funds for the short term. If interest rates are expected to drop, managers may elect to borrow short and lend long.

The problem of pursuing a strategy of positioning a depository institution based on interest rate expectations is that considerable adverse financial consequences will result if those expectations are not realized. The evidence on interest rate forecasting suggests that it is a risky business. It is doubtful that there are managers of depository institutions who have the ability to forecast interest rate moves so consistently that the institution can benefit with any regularity. The goal of management should be to lock in a spread as best as possible, not to wager on interest rate movements.

Some interest rate risk, however, is inherent in any balance sheet of a depository institution. Managers must be willing to accept some risk, but they can take various measures to address the interest rate sensitivity of the institution's liabilities and its assets. A depository institution should have an asset/liability committee that is responsible for monitoring the exposure to interest rate risk. (See Box 11.) There are several asset/liability strategies for controlling interest rate risk. While a discussion of these strategies is presented in later chapters, we can point out here that the development of particular financial instruments reflects the asset/liability problem that depository institutions seek to solve.

Because of the potential adverse impact of interest rate changes on the financial well-being of a depository institution, several approaches have been suggested for measuring interest rate risk. Regulators have also proposed policies for depository institutions for measuring and reporting interest rate risk. These measures focus on the sensitivity of a depository institution's income (more specifically, net interest income) and surplus to interest rate changes. One way to measure the sensitivity to interest rate changes of the surplus is to look at the duration of the assets and the duration of the liabilities. Since

BOX 11

INTEREST RATE RISK MODELS FOR BANKS AND THRIFTS

During the last decade, most notably during the early 1980s, there has been an increasing emphasis on the measurement and management of interest-rate risk at depository institutions as volatile interest rates have caused wide swings in earnings and the value of institutions' portfolios. Many institutions have acquired models to measure their interest-rate risk or hired consultants to analyze their exposure. Interest-rate risk models have evolved from the simple maturity gap model to sophisticated measurement systems requiring detailed input data and knowledge of complex financial modeling techniques. Bank and thrift regulators have developed policies and examination guidelines outlining the responsibilities of managers and boards of directors in the area of interest-rate risk management. Bank and thrift regulators have recently developed, and will soon implement, frameworks to incorporate an interest-rate risk component into the risk-based capital requirement of the institutions they regulate. . . .

Interest-rate risk (IRR) at depository institutions is typically defined as the sensitivity of the institution's earnings and net portfolio value* to changes in interest rates. The interest-rate sensitivity of an institution's portfolio depends on the characteristics of the financial instruments that comprise the portfolio. Because deposit liabilities typically reprice faster than mortgage assets,† most thrift institutions are exposed to rising interest rates; that is, their net portfolio value and earnings decline when interest rates rise and increase when interest rates fall. Because banks typically hold shorter-term and adjustable-rate loans, they are more likely to have smaller exposures to rising rates or even be exposed to falling rates. However, many banks have increased their holdings of mortgage loans and securities in recent years and are increasingly likely to be exposed to rising interest rates.

The interest-rate sensitivity of a finan-cial instrument depends on many factors including maturity, repricing characteristics, and the presence of embedded options such as loan prepayment options, interest-rate caps on adjustable-rate loans, and deposit withdrawal options that affect the timing of the cash flows.‡

Net interest income (NII) and net portfolio value (NPV) are the two most common targets of IRR management in the banking and thrift industries. NPV is a measure of the economic value of a portfolio of financial instruments, and is equal to the estimated market value of assets, less the estimated market value of liabilities, plus or minus the estimated market value of off-balance sheet instruments.

Both the NII and NPV measures require reliable information on the amount and timing of the cash flows generated by all financial instruments in the portfolio. Because this information is frequently not known, certain assumptions must be made to perform the analysis. Depending on the type of analysis, these assumptions may include (1) how changing interest rates will affect mortgage prepayment rates and deposit withdrawal rates,§ (2) how management will administer interest rates that are under its control (such as rates on retail deposits) when the general level of interest rates changes, and (3) in NII simulation models, how management will reinvest interest and principal cash flows during the period of analysis.

Two types of models are commonly used by savings associations to estimate the interest-rate sensitivity of net interest income: maturity gap models and NII simulation models. Likewise, there are two types of models commonly used to estimate the sensitivity of net portfolio value: duration gap models and NPV simulation models.

Maturity gap and simple duration gap models are similar in that they implicitly make strict assumptions about the way interest rates and cash flows behave. For example, they assume that cash flows do not change in response to interest rate changes so that mortgage prepayment rates do not increase even when rates at which mortgages may be financed fall, and deposit withdrawal rates do not increase when market CD rates rise. Furthermore, maturity gap and duration gap models assume that when interest rates change, they all do so by the same amount, when in fact, rates on various assets and liabilities may change by differing amounts as a result of a shift in the term structure of interest rates.

NII and NPV simulation models, on the other hand, permit these assumptions to vary, but necessarily rely more heavily on the analyst to make choices about certain behavioral relationships incorporated into the model. Even though they rely more heavily on parameters set by analysts, NII and NPV simulation models can be much more accurate than their less sophisticated counterparts if appropriate assumptions are used. . . .

*Net portfolio value is the difference between the value of the assets and the present value of the liabilities. We have used the term "surplus" in the chapter.

†Mortgage assets are discussed in Chapters 21, 22, and 23.

‡How these factors affect the interest rate sensitivity is described in Section V of the book.

§Prepayments are defined in Chapter 21.

Elizabeth Mays, Ph.D., Senior Financial, Office of Thrift Supervision, Department of the Treasury.

Source: Elizabeth Mays, "Interest-Rate Risk Models Used in the Banking and Thrift Industries," Chap. 32 in Frank J. Fabozzi and T. Dessa Fabozzi (eds.), *The Handbook of Fixed Income Securities* (Burr Ridge, IL: Business One Irwin, 1994), pp. 695–696.

Questions for Box 11

1. Why is the measurement of interest rate sensitivity of a depository institution important?

2. Why are assumptions necessary in order to estimate the interest rate sensitivity of a depository institution?

the assets of a depository typically are longer term than the liabilities and therefore have a greater duration, a rise in interest rates will adversely affect the surplus: The assets will decline by more than the liabilities.

Liquidity Concerns

Depository institutions are constrained in their investment options by the level of call risk inherent in their deposits. Passbook depositors can demand their funds at any time, and holders of certificates of deposit can ask for funds prematurely, if they are willing to pay a penalty. For this reason, a portion of a depository institution's portfolio must include investments that are relatively liquid.

Regulations require that banks maintain primary reserves (discussed later in this chapter) to meet demand for withdrawals by depositors. Depository institutions keep a certain level of uninvested cash on hand, of course, but they must raise funds quickly if withdrawals greatly exceed deposits. This funding problem can be addressed in four ways. The first is to borrow at the discount window of the Federal Reserve Banks in the case of a bank and at the Federal Home Loan Banks in the case of a savings and loan association. The second alternative is to use marketable securities owned as collateral for raising funds in the repurchase agreement market. This market was reviewed in Chapter 2.

The third alternative is to sell securities that it owns. This alternative requires that the depository institution invest a portion of its funds in securities that both are liquid and have little price risk. Price risk refers to the prospect that the selling price of the security will be less than its purchase price, resulting in a loss. For example, while a 30-year U.S. Treasury security is a highly liquid security, its interest rate sensitivity or duration can be quite high. A price decline of, say, 25% would not be uncommon in a volatile interest rate environment. A 30-year Treasury bond is therefore highly liquid, but it exposes the depository institution to substantial price risk.

Holding short-term securities is the fourth alternative. In general, as we explain in Chapter 21, short-term securities entail little price risk. It is therefore short-term, or money market, debt obligations that a depository institution will hold as an investment to satisfy withdrawals, as well as to satisfy customer loan demand. It does this chiefly by lending federal funds, an investment vehicle that we discussed in Chapter 2. The term to maturity of the securities it holds affects the amount that depository institutions can borrow from some federal agencies because only short-term securities are acceptable collateral.

A disadvantage of holding securities with short maturities is that they offer a lower yield than securities with longer maturities in most interest rate environments.[1] The percentage of a depository institution's assets held for the purpose of satisfying liquidity needs will depend both on the institution's ability to raise funds from the other sources and on its management's risk preference for liquidity (safety) versus yield.

Depository institutions hold liquid assets not only for operational purposes, but also because of the regulatory requirements that we discuss below.

---

[1]In particular, it depends on the shape of the yield curve, the subject of Chapter 22.

COMMERCIAL BANKS

In 1990, there were about 13,500 commercial banks in the United States. A commercial bank can be chartered either by the state (state-chartered banks) or by the federal government (national banks).

Commercial banks provide numerous services in our financial system. The services can be broadly classified as follows: (1) individual banking, (2) institutional banking, and (3) global banking.

Individual banking encompasses consumer lending, residential mortgage lending, consumer installment loans, credit card financing, automobile and boat financing, brokerage services, student loans, and individual-oriented financial investment services such as personal trust and investment services. Interest and fee income are generated from mortgage lending and credit card financing. Fee income is also generated from brokerage services and financial investment services.

Loans to non-financial corporations, financial corporations (such as life insurance companies), and government entities (state and local governments in the United States and foreign governments) fall into the category of institutional banking. Loans and leasing generate interest income, and other services that banks offer institutional customers generate fee income. These services include management of the assets of private and public pension funds, fiduciary and custodial services, and cash management services such as account maintenance, check clearing, and electronic transfers.

Global banking covers a broad range of activities involving corporate financing and capital market and foreign exchange products and services. Most global banking activities generate fee income rather than interest income.

Bank Funding

In describing the nature of the banking business, we have focused so far on how banks generate income. Now let's take a look at how banks raise funds. There are three sources of funds for banks: (1) deposits, (2) non-deposit borrowing, and (3) common stock and retained earnings. Banks are highly leveraged financial institutions, which means that most of their funds come from borrowing—the first two sources we refer to. Included in non-deposit borrowing are borrowing from the Federal Reserve through the discount window facility, borrowing reserves in the federal funds market, and borrowing by the issuance of instruments in the money and bond markets.

Deposits   There are several types of deposit accounts. **Demand deposits** (checking accounts) pay no interest and can be withdrawn upon demand. Deposit accounts offered by savings and loan associations that look very similar to demand deposits and that do pay interest include the so-called **negotiable order of withdrawal (NOW) accounts**. **Savings deposits** pay interest, typically below-market interest rates, do not have a specific maturity, and usually can be withdrawn upon demand.

Time deposits, also called **certificates of deposit**, have a fixed maturity date and pay either a fixed or floating interest rate. A **money market demand account** is one that pays interest based on short-term interest rates.

Reserve Requirements and Borrowing in the Federal Funds Market   A bank cannot invest $1 for every $1 it obtains in deposit. All banks must maintain a specified percentage of their deposits in a non-interest-bearing account at one of the 12 Federal Reserve Banks. These specified percentages are called **reserve ratios**, and the dollar amounts based on them that are required to be kept on deposit at a Federal Reserve Bank are called **required reserves**. The reserve ratios are established by the Federal Reserve Board (the "Fed").

If actual reserves exceed required reserves, the difference is referred to as **excess reserves**. Because reserves are placed in non-interest-bearing accounts, an opportunity cost is associated with excess reserves. At the same time, penalties are imposed on banks that do not satisfy the reserve requirements. Thus, banks have an incentive to manage their reserves so as to satisfy reserve requirements as precisely as possible. Banks temporarily short of their required reserves can borrow reserves from banks that have excess reserves. The market where banks can borrow or lend reserves is the **federal funds market**. The interest rate charged to borrow funds in this market is the **federal funds rate**.

Borrowing at the Fed Discount Window   The Federal Reserve Bank is the banker's bank—or, to put it another way, the bank of last resort. Banks temporarily short of funds can borrow from the Fed at its discount window. Collateral is necessary to borrow, but not just any collateral will do. The Fed establishes (and periodically changes) the type of collateral that is eligible. The interest rate that the Fed charges to borrow funds at the discount window is called the **discount rate**. Bank borrowing at the Fed to meet required reserves is quite limited in amount, despite the fact that the discount rate generally is set below the cost of other sources of short-term funding available to a bank. This is because the Fed views borrowing at the discount window as a privilege to be used to meet short-term liquidity needs, and not a device to increase earnings.

Other Non-Deposit Borrowing   Bank borrowing in the federal funds market and at the discount window of the Fed is short term. Other non-deposit borrowing can be short term in the form of issuing obligations in the money market, or intermediate to long term in the form of issuing securities in the bond market. Banks that raise most of their funds from the domestic and international money markets, relying less on depositors for funds, are called **money center banks**.

Regulation

Because of the special role that commercial banks play in the financial system, banks are regulated and supervised by several federal and state government entities. At the federal level, supervision is undertaken by the Federal Reserve Board, the Office of the Comptroller of the Currency, and the Federal Deposit Insurance Corporation.

Here we will review some of the major regulations that affect the portfolio investment activities of commercial banks.

Beyond legislation, regulators have placed restrictions of their own on the types of securities that a bank can take a position in for its own investment portfolio. For example, while we pointed out earlier in this chapter that adjustable-rate mortgages are attractive investments, given the asset/liability problem of depository institutions, permission to invest in such mortgages had to be granted. The most recent example is the Comptroller of the Currency's restrictions on investing in certain mortgage-backed securities.

TABLE 11-2

RISK-BASED CAPITAL REQUIREMENT WEIGHT CATEGORIES FOR SAMPLE ASSETS FOR BANKS

Risk Weight	Example of Assets
0%	U.S. Treasury securities
	Mortgage-backed securities issued by the Government National Mortgage Association
20	Municipal general obligation bonds
	Mortgage-backed securities issued by the Federal Home Loan Mortgage Corporation or the Federal National Mortgage Association
50	Municipal revenue bonds
	Residential mortgages
100	Commercial loans and commercial mortgages
	LDC loans
	Corporate bonds
	Municipal IDA bonds

Risk-Based Capital Requirements   In Chapter 8, we described the risk-based capital requirements for insurance companies. In January 1989, the Federal Reserve issued risk-based capital requirements for banks. The requirements are based on a framework adopted in July 1988 by the Basle Committee on Banking Regulations and Supervisory Practices, which consists of the central banks and supervisory authorities of the G-10 countries (Belgium, Canada, France, Germany, Italy, Japan, Netherlands, Sweden, Switzerland, United Kingdom, and United States).

As with the risk-based capital requirements for insurance companies, the risk-based capital requirements for banks attempt to recognize credit risk by segmenting and weighting requirements. The risk-based capital requirements establish a credit risk weight for all assets. The weight depends on the credit risk associated with each asset. There are four credit risk classifications for banks in the United States: 0%, 20%, 50%, and 100%. Table 11-2 includes a few examples of assets that fall into each credit risk classification.

The credit risk weight is multiplied by the book value of the asset to determine the amount of core and supplementary capital that the bank will need to support that asset. For example, Table 11-3 shows sample book values of the assets of a bank and the appropriate risk-weighting calculations. The risk-weighted assets for this bank would be $420 million.[2]

An implication of the risk-based capital requirements is that when the manager of the securities portfolio considers alternative investments, the potential yield will be compared relative to the capital requirement. For example, consider an investment in a U.S. Treasury security and a corporate bond, both with a maturity of 10 years. Suppose that the yield on the Treasury security is 7% and the yield on the corporate bond is 9%. While the yield on

---

[2]The rules for determining the amount of capital required for a bank resulting from off-balance sheet items is beyond the scope of this chapter.

TABLE 11-3			
SAMPLE RISK WEIGHTING OF BANK ASSETS			
Asset	**Book Value Weight (Millions)**	**Risk**	**Product (Millions)**
U.S. Treasury securities	$400	0%	$ 0
Municipal general obligation bonds	100	20	20
Residential mortgages	200	50	100
Commercial loans	300	100	300
Risk-weighted assets			$420

the corporate bond is 200 basis points greater, the risk-based capital required would be 100%; whereas for the Treasury security there is no risk-based capital required. Thus, for each $100 invested in the Treasury security, $7 is earned that requires no risk-based capital to generate; in contrast, for each $100 invested in the corporate bond, $9 is earned that requires the generation of $100 in risk-based capital. This will make the corporate bond less attractive as an investment alternative than the Treasury security.

Proposed Interest Rate Risk Capital Requirements The risk-based capital guidelines discussed above focus on the credit risk associated with the portfolio of assets. No consideration is given to interest rate risk. The Federal Depository Insurance Corporation Improvement Act, which was passed by Congress in December 1991, required regulators of depository institutions to incorporate interest rate risk into the capital requirements no later than June 1993. The approach proposed by bank regulators is based on measuring interest rate sensitivity of the surplus based on duration.

The assets, liabilities, and off-balance sheet instruments would be partitioned into six maturity groups, or "buckets": 0 to 3 months, 3 months to 1 year, 1 to 3 years, 3 to 7 years, 7 to 15 years, and more than 15 years. For each bucket, the duration of the assets and the liabilities would be computed. The proposal by bank regulators is that a normal level of interest rate risk exposure is one in which the duration of the surplus for a given bucket is less than 1; that is, a 100-basis-point change in interest rates will change the surplus for that bucket by less than 1%. If the duration of the surplus is greater than 1, the bank must hold additional capital of an amount equal to the excess.

SAVINGS AND LOAN ASSOCIATIONS

S&Ls represent a fairly old institution. The basic motivation behind the creation of S&Ls was provision of funds for financing the purchase of a home. The collateral for the loans would be the home being financed.

Like banks, S&Ls may be chartered under either state or federal statutes. At the federal level, the primary regulator of S&Ls is, at present, the Director of the Office of Thrift Supervision (DOTS). Prior to the creation of DOTS, the primary regulator was the Federal Home Loan Bank Board (FHLBB). While the FHLBB still exists, its responsibilities have been limited to the credit-facilitating function, that is, making loans (advances) to S&Ls. Like banks, S&Ls are now subject to reserve requirements on deposits established by the Fed.

Assets

Traditionally, the only assets in which S&Ls were allowed to invest have been mortgages, mortgage-backed securities, and government securities. Mortgage loans include fixed-rate mortgages and adjustable-rate mortgages. While most mortgage loans are for the purchase of homes, S&Ls do make construction loans.

The Garn–St. Germain Act of 1982 expanded the types of assets in which S&Ls could invest. The acceptable list of investments now includes consumer loans (loans for home improvement, automobiles, education, mobile homes, and credit cards), non-consumer loans (commercial, corporate, business, and agricultural loans), and municipal securities.

S&Ls invest in short-term assets for operational (liquidity) and regulatory purposes. All S&Ls with federal deposit insurance must satisfy minimum liquidity requirements. These requirements are specified by the Federal Home Loan Bank Board. Acceptable assets include cash, short-term government agency and corporate securities, certificates of deposit of commercial banks,[3] other money market assets, and federal funds. In the case of federal funds, the S&L is lending excess reserves to another depository institution that is short of funds.

Funding

With the deregulation of interest rates, banks and S&Ls now compete head-to-head for deposits. Deregulation also expanded the types of accounts that may be offered by S&Ls—NOW accounts and money market deposit accounts (MMDAs). Beginning with the 1980s, S&Ls have been more active in raising funds in the money market than they had been. For example, they have been able to use the repurchase agreement market to raise funds. They can borrow in the federal funds market, and they have access to the Fed's discount window. S&Ls can also borrow from the Federal Home Loan Banks. These borrowings, called *advances*, can be short term or long term in maturity, and the interest rate can be fixed or floating.

Capital Requirements

The risk-based capital guidelines for S&Ls are similar to those for banks. As with commercial banks, interest rate risk must be incorporated into the capital requirements. Regulators of S&Ls, however, have taken a different approach to the measurement of interest rate risk. Rather than using a duration measure, regulators have proposed a simulation approach to assess the sensitivity of the surplus to interest rate changes.

■ SUMMARY

Depository institutions (commercial banks, savings and loan associations, savings banks, and credit unions) accept various types of deposits. With the funds raised through deposits and other funding sources, they make loans to various entities and invest in securities. A depository institution seeks to earn a positive spread between the assets it invests in and the cost of its funds. In generating spread income, a depository institution faces credit risk and interest rate

---

[3]The S&L is an investor when it holds the CD of a bank, but the CD represents the liability of the issuing bank.

(or funding) risk. In the case of a depository institution, interest rate risk is the risk that an interest rate change will adversely affect spread income.

Capital requirements are imposed on depository institutions. The risk-based capital guidelines base capital requirements on the credit risk associated with assets. These guidelines ignore the interest rate risk associated with assets and liabilities. Recent federal legislation requires that regulators adopt guidelines that will incorporate interest rate risk into capital requirements. For banks, regulators have proposed using duration as a measure of interest rate risk; for savings and loan associations, a simulation approach has been proposed.

■ KEY TERMS

certificates of deposit
demand deposits
discount rate
excess reserves
federal funds market
federal funds rate

interest rate risk
margin income
money center banks
money market demand account
negotiable order of withdrawal (NOW) accounts

required reserves
reserve ratios
savings deposits
spread income
time deposits

■ QUESTIONS

1. You and a friend are discussing the savings and loan crisis. She states that "the whole mess started in the early 80s. When short-term rates skyrocketed, S&Ls got killed—their spread income went from positive to negative. They were borrowing short and lending long."
   a. What does she mean by "borrowing short and lending long"?
   b. Are higher or lower interest rates beneficial to an institution that borrows short and lends long?

2. Why do you think a debt instrument whose interest rate is changed periodically based on some market interest rate would be more suitable for a depository institution than a long-term debt instrument with a fixed interest rate?

3. Why is a depository institution concerned with the liquidity of its assets?

4. If a depository institution needs funds quickly, what alternatives are available to the institution?

5. What are the types of services provided by commercial banks?

6. When the manager of a bank's portfolio of securities is considering alternative investments, she will also be concerned with the risk weight assigned to the security. Why?

7. Indicate why you agree or disagree with the following statement: "The risk-based capital requirements for commercial banks attempt to gauge the interest rate risk associated with a bank's balance sheet."

8. The manager of the securities portfolio of a commercial bank is considering the purchase of a 10-year corporate bond and a 10-year Treasury security. The yield on the former is 150 basis points higher than the yield on the latter. In addition to credit risk, what other factor will be important in the manager's decision about which alternative to invest in?

9. Why is it important to have a measure of interest rate risk for a depository institution?

10. How can the interest rate risk of a depository institution be measured?

11. In a publication by the ICFA Continuing Education, *Managing Asset/Liability Portfolios*, the following appeared in the article "Setting the Stage" by Martin L. Leibowitz: "The importance of surplus measurement differs for each type of financial intermediary. . . . [and] can range from being all-encompassing (as in spread banking) to almost insignificant for some highly funded corporate and public pension funds." Explain why surplus management is more important for banks than for highly funded pension funds.

CHAPTER 12
FORECASTING EARNINGS*

LEARNING OBJECTIVES
After reading this chapter you will be able to:

- distinguish between a buy-side and sell-side analyst.
- explain where company-level earnings per share are reported.
- describe how analysts forecast earnings per share and how their forecasts compare to statistical projections.
- identify the sources of error in analysts' forecasts of earnings per share.
- explain the relationship between analysts' forecasts of earnings per share and stock returns.
- describe how analysts forecast stock returns.
- explain how analysts are evaluated.
- define the role of analysts in the capital market.

In Section III we looked at the investment objectives and policies of several institutional investors and the asset/liability problem that they faced. The focus of Section IV is on the management of common stock portfolios. To begin the process, we will look at the forecasts of earnings by financial analysts. A major assumption of all investment analysis is that company earnings are strongly related to the returns to shareholders. Simply put, why else would an investor invest in a company unless he or she thought that investment was going to earn a return?

As might be expected, gathering information on companies is a time-consuming task. Since most individuals are too busy to research companies themselves, they rely on professional financial analysts to perform that task. Hence, one of the most important functions of financial analysts is to *process information* for investors in the stock market. Among the most important pieces of information supplied by analysts are forecasts of company-level earnings and earnings growth. As mentioned above, earnings and returns are closely related. Hence, professional analysts are also typically required to forecast not only earnings, but also returns for the stock they follow.

*This chapter is contributed by Dr. T. Daniel Coggin.

In this chapter we selectively review the vast amount of empirical literature that addresses how well financial analysts forecast earnings and returns, and determine whether there are individual differences in analysts' forecast ability. We then discuss how analysts are evaluated. Finally we bring all this together with a discussion of the role of the analyst in the capital market.

ANALYSTS

There are several thousand **financial analysts**—also called *securities analysts* and *investment analysts*—who analyze financial statements, interview corporate executives, and attend trade shows. Analysts develop contacts with corporate managers, and use their input together with required reports as their main sources of information. The product of all these activities is a written report recommending either purchasing, selling, or holding various stocks.

Financial analysts can be divided into two groups: "buy-side" and "sell-side" analysts. A **buy-side analyst** is employed by a non-brokerage firm, typically one of the larger money management firms that purchase securities, such as Sanford Bernstein or Fidelity Investments—hence the term *buy side*. These analysts pass along their recommendations to the portfolio managers of their organization.

A **sell-side analyst**, also popularly referred to as a *Wall Street* analyst, works for brokerage firms such as Merrill Lynch, Smith Barney, or Alex. Brown & Sons. The recommendations of sell-side analysts are passed on to the brokerage firm's customers. There may be as many as 50 analysts at a major brokerage firm, with each analyst assigned to specialized tasks. On the other hand, a small, regional brokerage firm is likely to employ only three or four analysts. Rather than specialize, these analysts are typically generalists.[1]

WHERE EARNINGS FORECASTS ARE REPORTED

There are several places one can find forecasts of company-level earnings. At the most basic level, company management regularly issues forecasts of earnings. These are called *management forecasts* and are typically provided by the investor relations officer of the company. They can be found in the business section of your local newspaper and in national financial newspapers such as *The Wall Street Journal*, *Barron's*, and *Investor's Business Daily*. At another level, sell-side analysts regularly issue company reports that include forecasts of earnings and dividends for the current year and for the next one or two years. Box 12 is an example of a report on Loral Corporation by an analyst at Kidder Peabody, a sell-side (brokerage) firm. In addition, almost every public and college library has a copy of the *Value Line Investment Survey*, which also publishes company reports that include earnings and dividends forecasts. (Figure 12-4 on page 203 is a sample page for Loral Corporation.)

Finally, at least two commercial services compile and present summary statistics on the earnings estimates of sell-side analysts for a large sample of

---

[1] In Appendix C we describe the potential conflicts between sell-side analysts and the corporation whose common stock they recommend.

BOX 12

KIDDER, PEABODY EQUITY RESEARCH

December 16, 1992   Company Comment

**Loral Corporation
(NYSE-LOR)
Stock Rating: Buy
Raising EPS Estimates Again
Addressing Several Investor
Concerns**

52-Week Range	Recent Price	Fiscal Yr-End
47–31	46	Mar.

Earnings per Share

1992	1993E	1994E	1995E
$3.85	$4.45	$5.40	$5.90

P/E Ratio		Dividend Rate	Current Yield
1994E	1995E		
8.5	7.8	$1.00	2.2%

Investment Recommendation
We are raising our F94 and F95 EPS estimates by $0.15 each, to reflect the balance sheet recapitalization announced last week. In addition to boosting EPS, the restructured balance sheet significantly deepens LOR's pockets for acquisition purposes. We have raised LOR's price target to $56 (see our December 1 report) and are reiterating our Buy rating.

This past weekend's *NY Times* business section (December 13) contained an article on Loral that was fairly objective, in our opinion, and generally favorable in tone (the December issue of the

Institutional Investor also has an upbeat interview with the CEO, Bernard Schwartz). However, a couple of quoted Wall Street analysts continued their salvo of disparaging remarks, which we observe are, in substance, contradictory in logic and/or indicative of continued incognizance of the themes propelling the defense stocks.

**Technology—Defense Electronics
Michael Lauer (212) 510-3778**

Question for Box 12

1. Why do financial analysts focus on a company's earnings per share?

---

companies and offer them to subscribers for a fee: I/B/E/S Inc. (New York) and Zacks Investment Research, Inc. (Chicago). (Figure 12-5 on page 206 is a sample page that includes Loral Corporation.)

ANALYST EARNINGS FORECASTS

When analysts forecast earnings, they typically use some sort of quantitative model to aid them. It would be impossible here to list all the possible quantitative techniques (including balance sheet and income statement approaches) employed by analysts to develop earnings forecasts. Rather, the focus here is on several well-known extrapolative statistical models that are commonly used and that are often compared with the actual forecasts of analysts.

Extrapolative Statistical Models

The three most commonly used **extrapolative statistical models** are the *simple linear trend model,* the *simple exponential model,* and the *simple autoregressive model.* An extrapolative model applies a formula to historical data and projects results for a future period. By choosing a model that best fits the data, an analyst, in effect, says that the past pattern of earnings will predict the future. All the models described below are estimated using regression analysis. Each describes a different pattern of earnings per share (EPS). The more historical earnings factors still apply, the more accurate the extrapolation is likely to be.

The **simple linear trend model** asserts that earnings have a base level and grow at a *constant amount* each period. Mathematically this model is expressed as follows:

$$\text{EPS}_t = a + b \text{ time}$$

The base level of earnings in this model is a, and the constant amount by which earnings grow each period is b. In this model, b would be expressed in dollars per period.

The graph of this relationship would be a straight line with the origin at a. Figure 12-1 illustrates the simple linear model. The table accompanying the figure presents six years of data for the earnings per share of Loral Corporation, from the beginning of 1988 to the end of 1993, with the data plotted on the graph. The figure also shows the estimated simple linear model fitted to the data for Loral Corporation, as well as the 1994 forecast of earnings per share using the estimated model.

In the **simple exponential model** it is assumed that earnings grow at a *constant rate* each period. Mathematically this model is typically expressed in logarithmic format as follows:

$$\ln(\text{EPS}_t) = a + b \text{ time}$$

In this model, ln is the natural logarithm and b is the estimated percentage growth rate per period. Figure 12-2 provides data for earnings per share of American Power Conversion Corp. from 1988 to 1993 and shows the data plotted on a graph. The estimated simple exponential model fitted to the data for American Power Conversion Corp. is shown in the figure, along with the forecast for 1994 based on the estimated model.

The **simple autoregressive model** is expressed as follows:

$$\text{EPS}_t = a + c \text{ EPS}_{t-1}$$

The special case of c equal to 1 implies that there is no information in the past history of earnings up to and including time t that can be used to predict earnings at time $t + 1$; hence earnings follow a "random walk."

Figure 12-3 provides data for earnings per share of Walgreen Company from 1988 to 1993, with the data plotted on a graph. The estimated simple autoregressive model fitted to the data for Walgreen Company is also graphed, as is the 1994 forecast based on the model.

FIGURE 12-1   Simple linear model for Loral Corp.

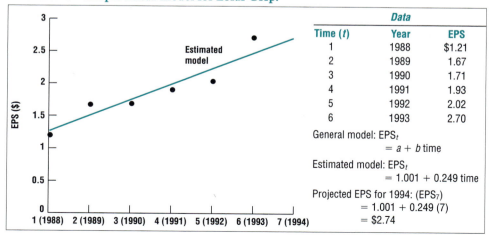

Time (t)	Year	EPS
1	1988	$1.21
2	1989	1.67
3	1990	1.71
4	1991	1.93
5	1992	2.02
6	1993	2.70

General model: $\text{EPS}_t = a + b \text{ time}$

Estimated model: $\text{EPS}_t = 1.001 + 0.249 \text{ time}$

Projected EPS for 1994: $(\text{EPS}_7) = 1.001 + 0.249\,(7) = \$2.74$

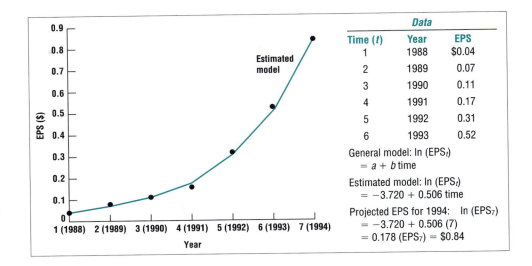

FIGURE 12-2 Simple exponential model for American Power Conversion Corp.

How does an analyst decide which of the three models (or any more complex model) to use. The selection of the model is largely based on how well the estimated model fits the data.

Now that we have defined some simple but commonly used statistical models, we can look at how well they perform in comparison with the actual forecasts by analysts.

Analyst Forecasts versus Statistical Models

A classic book by Paul Meehl compared the predictive ability of trained psychologists with statistical models of personality and behavior.[2] Meehl's fascinating study found that the statistical models did a better job of classify-

FIGURE 12-3 Simple autoregressive model for Walgreen Corp.

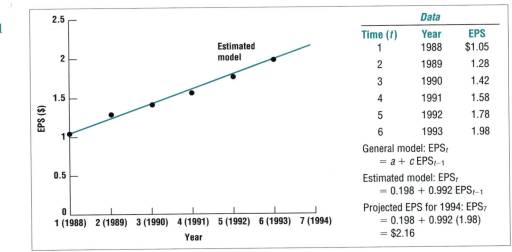

[2]Paul E. Meehl, *Clinical versus Statistical Prediction* (Minneapolis: University of Minnesota Press, 1954).

ing subjects than the psychologists. Forty years and hundreds of studies later, his basic finding has been supported in a number of areas of human judgment. That is, well-formulated statistical models tend to outperform the judgment of trained professionals. This is largely attributed to the fact that human judgment introduces biases and other imperfections in information processing that well-formulated statistical models do not.[3]

A number of studies have looked at the time-series properties of annual earnings. While some rather complicated statistical issues are involved, the general finding is that (both at the firm level and most clearly at the aggregate level) the random walk statistical model provides a reasonably accurate *description* of the time series of annual earnings.[4] However, when it comes to *predicting* annual (and quarterly) earnings, the analyst emerges as the winner in comparison with a number of statistical models (including the random walk model).[5] On the other hand, the analyst generally fails to outperform company management forecasts.[6]

Brown, Hagerman, Griffin, and Zmijewski looked at the determinants of analyst superiority relative to univariate time-series models (such as the simple autoregressive model discussed above). Their study suggests that analyst superiority is related to at least two factors.[7] One, analysts can better utilize *existing* information relative to simple univariate time-series models (a *contemporaneous* advantage). Two, analysts can use information that occurs *after* the cutoff date for the time-series date but *before* the date of the analyst forecast (a *timing* advantage). Another study by Brown, Richardson, and Schwager found that financial analyst superiority is positively related to firm size, meaning that the larger the company, the more advantage analysts have over time-series models.[8]

While the weight of the current evidence tends to favor analysts over simple statistical time-series models in predicting earnings, several studies

---

[3]For evidence that financial analysts "overreact" (exhibit excessive optimism or pessimism) in forecasting earnings, see Werner F. M. DeBondt and Richard H. Thaler, "Do Security Analysts Overreact?" *American Economic Review* (May 1990), pp. 52–57.

[4]For a more detailed discussion, see George Foster, *Financial Statement Analysis*, 2nd ed. (Englewood Cliffs, NJ: Prentice-Hall, 1986), appendix 7.C.

[5]See, for example, Lawrence D. Brown and Michael S. Rozeff, "The Superiority of Analyst Forecasts as Measures of Expectations: Evidence from Earnings," *Journal of Finance* (March 1978), pp. 1–16; T. Daniel Coggin and John E. Hunter, "Analysts' EPS Forecasts Nearer Actual Than Statistical Models," *Journal of Business Forecasting* (Winter 1982–1983), pp. 20–23; Michael S. Rozeff, "Predicting Long-Term Earnings Growth: Comparisons of Expected Return Models, Submartingales and Value Line Analysts," *Journal of Forecasting* (October–December 1983), pp. 425–435; and Patricia C. O'Brien, "Analysts' Forecasts as Earnings Expectations," *Journal of Accounting and Economics* (January 1988), pp. 53–83.

[6]See John S. Armstrong, "Relative Accuracy of Judgmental and Extrapolative Methods in Forecasting Annual Earnings," *Journal of Forecasting* (October–December 1983), pp. 437–447; and John Hassell and Robert Jennings, "Relative Forecast Accuracy and the Timing of Earnings Forecast Announcements," *Accounting Review* (January 1986), pp. 58–75.

[7]Lawrence D. Brown, Robert L. Hagerman, Paul A. Griffin, and Mark E. Zmijewski, "Security Analyst Superiority Relative to Univariate Time-Series Models in Forecasting Quarterly Earnings," *Journal of Accounting and Economics* (1987), pp. 61–87.

[8]Lawrence D. Brown, Gordon D. Richardson, and Steven J. Schwager, "An Information Interpretation of Financial Analyst Superiority in Forecasting Earnings," *Journal of Accounting Research* (Spring 1987), pp. 49–67.

suggest that individual analysts are largely *undifferentiated* in their ability to predict EPS.[9]

This finding (discussed in more detail in the next section) suggests that the consensus forecast is generally superior to the forecasts of individual analysts. The **consensus forecast** is the mean of the analysts' forecasts for a company. It should be noted that some recent studies suggest that there are benefits from *combining* statistical time-series and analyst forecasts.[10] Other studies have shown that more complex statistical models that include additional variables affecting earnings growth (such as leading economic indicators) can challenge the superiority of analysts in predicting earnings.[11]

Analyst Error in Forecasting Earnings

Having established that analysts generally do a better job of forecasting earnings than relatively simple extrapolative statistical models, it now seems appropriate to examine the general characteristics of the *errors* made by analysts. Two studies are relevant to this question, one by Elton, Gruber, and Gultekin and the other by Coggin and Hunter.

Elton, Gruber, and Gultekin　Elton, Gruber, and Gultekin studied this issue using data for the period 1976–1978.[12] One advantage of their study compared with many previous studies in this area is that they used the I/B/E/S data base of analyst EPS forecasts. (For an example, see Figure 12-4.) Earlier studies typically used very small samples of analysts or the *Value Line* analyst group.

Elton, Gruber, and Gultekin found that (1) analyst errors in forecasting annual EPS (revised monthly) declined monotonically; (2) analysts were reasonably accurate in forecasting aggregate-level EPS for the entire economy; (3) analysts were better at forecasting industry-level EPS than company-level EPS; (4) analysts had a tendency to overestimate EPS growth for companies they believed would do well and underestimate EPS growth for companies they believed would do poorly; (5) analysts had more difficulty forecasting EPS for some companies relative to others (specifically, if analysts had large errors for a company in one year, they tended to have large errors the next year); (6) analyst divergence of opinion about EPS growth for a company tended to be at its greatest during the first four months of the year; and (7) an-

---

[9] R. Malcolm Richards, "Analysts' Performance and the Accuracy of Corporate Earnings Forecasts," *Journal of Business* (July 1976), pp. 350–357; O'Brien, op. cit.; and T. Daniel Coggin and John E. Hunter, "Analyst Forecasts of EPS and EPS Growth: Decomposition of Error, Relative Accuracy and Relation to Return," Working Paper No. 89-1, Virginia Retirement System, Richmond, VA (1989).

[10] See Robert Conroy and Robert Harris, "Consensus Forecasts of Corporate Earnings: Analysts' Forecasts and Time Series Methods," *Management Science* (June 1987), pp. 725–738; Lawrence D. Brown, Robert L. Hagerman, Paul A. Griffin, and Mark E. Zmijewski, "An Evaluation of Alternative Proxies for the Market's Assessment of Unexpected Earnings," *Journal of Accounting and Economics* (1987), pp. 159–193; and John D. Guerard, Jr., "Combining Time-Series Model Forecasts and Analysts' Forecasts for Superior Forecasts of Annual Earnings," *Financial Analysts Journal* (January–February 1989), pp. 69–71.

[11] See Peter D. Chant, "On the Predictability of Corporate Earnings per Share Behavior," *Journal of Finance* (March 1980), pp. 13–21; and John E. Hunter and T. Daniel Coggin, "Analyst Judgement: The Efficient Market Hypothesis versus a Psychological Theory of Human Judgement," *Organizational Behavior and Human Decision Processes* (December 1988), pp. 284–302.

[12] Edwin J. Elton, Martin J. Gruber, and Mustafa Gultekin, "Professional Expectations: Accuracy and Diagnosis of Errors," *Journal of Financial and Quantitative Analysis* (December 1984), pp. 351–363.

LORAL CORP. NYSE-LOR

| RECENT PRICE | 46 | P/E RATIO | 10.0 | (Trailing: 11.6 / Median: 14.0) | RELATIVE P/E RATIO | 0.63 | DIV'D YLD | 2.2% | VALUE LINE | 566 |

TIMELINESS 1 (Relative Price Performance Next 12 Mos.) Highest

SAFETY 2 (Scale: 1 Highest to 5 Lowest) Above Average

BETA .80 (1.00 = Market)

1995-97 PROJECTIONS

	Price	Gain	Ann'l Total Return
High	85	(+85%)	18%
Low	55	(+20%)	7%

Insider Decisions

	M	A	M	J	J	A	S	O	N
to Buy	0	0	0	0	0	0	0	0	0
Options	0	1	0	0	0	1	1	0	0
to Sell	0	2	1	0	0	1	0	0	0

Institutional Decisions

	1Q'92	2Q'92	3Q'92
to Buy	61	51	61
to Sell	68	65	47
Hld's(000)	22591	21986	22927

Target Price Range 1995 1996 1997

6.5 x "Cash Flow" p sh

2-for-1 split

Relative Price Strength

Shaded areas indicate recessions

Options: CBOE

Percent shares traded 15.0 10.0 5.0

1976	1977	1978	1979	1980	1981	1982	1983	1984	1985	1986	1987	1988	1989	1990	1991	1992	1993	© VALUE LINE PUB., INC.	95-97
8.31	10.10	10.62	9.28	10.50	12.45	13.60	18.11	21.51	28.02	28.73	56.90	46.52	49.77	81.98	90.37	82.50	87.20	Sales per sh A	109.00
.77	.94	1.07	.94	1.27	1.52	1.75	2.09	2.57	3.47	3.67	5.83	4.96	6.36	7.34	7.85	8.00	9.35	"Cash Flow" per sh	11.90
.59	.71	.82	.92	1.00	1.15	1.29	1.45	1.79	2.21	2.35	3.01	2.41	3.34	3.41	3.85	4.40	5.15	Earnings per sh B	6.50
.08	.16	.21	.27	.32	.36	.39	.43	.47	.51	.58	.63	.70	.78	.84	.92	.98	1.04	Div'ds Decl'd per sh C	1.28
.24	.40	.39	.46	.84	1.57	1.42	1.01	1.28	1.95	1.42	2.01	1.59	2.39	3.59	2.56	2.30	2.45	Cap'l Spending per sh	3.85
2.20	2.78	3.47	6.58	6.71	7.96	8.50	9.74	11.14	13.06	15.11	17.31	20.30	22.83	25.90	31.28	31.60	35.85	Book Value per sh D	51.30
11.67	11.90	12.32	16.52	20.24	20.44	20.67	23.10	23.36	23.69	24.02	25.32	25.51	25.60	25.94	31.89	38.80	39.00	Common Shs Outst'g E	39.00
6.0	6.6	9.3	11.1	17.5	14.4	14.9	17.6	14.6	15.7	17.9	12.7	14.7	9.8	9.3	9.6	Bold figures are Value Line estimates		Avg Ann'l P/E Ratio	11.0
.77	.86	1.27	1.61	2.32	1.75	1.64	1.49	1.36	1.27	1.21	.85	1.22	.74	.69	.61			Relative P/E Ratio	.85
2.1%	3.5%	2.8%	2.6%	1.8%	2.2%	2.0%	1.7%	1.8%	1.5%	1.4%	1.6%	2.0%	2.4%	2.6%	2.4%			Avg Ann'l Div'd Yield	2.0%

CAPITAL STRUCTURE as of 9/30/92

Total Debt $839.9 mill. Due in 5 Yrs $176.2 mill.
LT Debt $788.6 mill. LT Interest $65.0 mill.
Incl. $99.7 mill. 7¼% sub. debs. ('10) conv. into 22.6 com. shs. at $44.25. Callable at declining premium. Incl. $1.0 mill. capitalized leases. Incl. $166.7 mill. non-recourse debt of subsidiary. (Total interest coverage: 7.1x) (38% of Cap'l)

Leases, Uncapitalized Annual rentals $38.0 mill.
Pension Liability None
Pfd Stock None

Common Stock 38,701,951 shs. (62% of Cap'l) as of 10/30/92

						281.1	418.3	502.3	663.8	690.0	1440.8	1187.0	1274.3	2126.8	2881.8	3200	3400	Sales ($mill) A	4250
						17.2%	17.0%	16.8%	18.5%	19.7%	17.6%	16.8%	18.7%	14.8%	14.6%	15.0%	16.0%	Operating Margin	16.5%
						9.3	14.4	18.0	29.3	30.8	73.2	66.2	78.7	100.1	128.6	150	160	Depreciation ($mill)	200
						26.8	33.9	42.1	53.0	57.5	74.3	60.3	84.1	90.4	121.8	160	205	Net Profit ($mill)	265
						42.4%	43.0%	41.0%	41.9%	41.8%	39.0%	36.4%	37.0%	37.0%	37.0%	37.0%	37.0%	Income Tax Rate	37.0%
						9.5%	8.1%	8.4%	8.0%	8.3%	5.2%	5.1%	6.6%	4.2%	4.2%	5.0%	6.0%	Net Profit Margin	6.0%
						101.4	108.4	108.7	149.9	245.6	305.4	462.8	312.6	457.7	596.2	700	805	Working Cap'l ($mill)	1075
						27.0	32.3	32.4	132.4	667.2	583.6	423.2	419.1	783.7	561.7	850	850	Long-Term Debt ($mill)	450
						175.8	225.0	260.1	309.4	362.9	438.3	517.9	584.5	672.0	997.3	1225	1395	Net Worth ($mill)	2000
						13.9%	13.8%	14.9%	13.0%	6.2%	10.3%	8.5%	10.4%	8.2%	9.8%	9.0%	10.5%	% Earned Total Cap'l	11.5%
						15.3%	15.1%	16.2%	17.1%	15.8%	17.0%	11.6%	14.4%	13.4%	12.2%	13.0%	15.0%	% Earned Net Worth	13.0%
						10.7%	10.7%	12.0%	13.2%	12.0%	13.4%	8.2%	11.0%	10.2%	9.4%	10.0%	12.0%	% Retained to Comm Eq	11.0%
						30%	29%	26%	23%	24%	21%	30%	24%	24%	23%	24%	20%	% All Div'ds to Net Prof	19%

CURRENT POSITION ($MILL)

	1990	1991	9/30/92
Cash Assets	75.1	191.1	179.7
Receivables	715.6	673.7	809.3
Inventory (FIFO) G	365.1	320.8	359.1
Other	21.7	18.8	22.0
Current Assets	1177.5	1204.4	1370.1
Accts Payable	195.6	131.0	122.2
Debt Due	37.6	15.7	51.3
Other	486.6	461.5	536.9
Current Liab.	719.8	608.2	710.4

ANNUAL RATES

of change (per sh)	Past 10 Yrs.	Past 5 Yrs.	Est'd '89-'91 to '95-'97
Sales	21.5%	23.0%	6.5%
"Cash Flow"	19.0%	17.5%	9.0%
Earnings	13.0%	13.0%	11.0%
Dividends	10.5%	10.0%	7.0%
Book Value	14.5%	15.5%	11.5%

QUARTERLY SALES ($ mill.) A

Fiscal Year Begins	Jun.30	Sep.30	Dec.31	Mar.31	Full Fiscal Year
1989	232.7	295.7	301.2	444.7	1274.3
1990	318.0	357.1	669.5	782.2	2126.8
1991	677.0	700.0	711.0	793.8	2881.8
1992	681.3	738.9	850.9	929.8	3200
1993	775	800	875	950	3400

EARNINGS PER SHARE A B

Fiscal Year Begins	Jun.30	Sep.30	Dec.31	Mar.31	Full Fiscal Year
1989	.66	.79	.89	1.00	3.34
1990	.69	.80	.79	1.13	3.41
1991	.80	.90	.91	1.22	H 3.85
1992	.83	1.02	1.15	1.40	4.40
1993	1.05	1.20	1.30	1.60	5.15

QUARTERLY DIVIDENDS PAID C

Cal-endar	Mar.31	Jun.30	Sep.30	Dec.31	Full Year
1989	.18	.18	.20	.20	.76
1990	.20	.20	.22	.22	.84
1991	.22	.22	.24	.24	.92
1992	.24	.24	.25	.25	.98
1993					

BUSINESS: Loral Corporation manufactures a variety of defense electronics systems and weather and commercial satellites. Applications include electronic combat; antisub. warfare; training and simulation; command, control, commun., and intelligence; surveillance; and space. Acq. Goodyear Aerospace, 3/87; Fairchild Weston, 6/89; Electro-Optic div. of Honeywell, 12/89; 51% stake in Ford Aerospace, 10/90; LTV Missiles, 8/92. Sold Aircraft Braking and Fabrics units, 3/89. Abt. 75% of sls. to U.S. gov't., 20% to foreign gov'ts. Co.-sponsored R&D: abt. 4% of sls. Fiscal '91 depr. rate: 9.0%. Est. plant age: 4 yrs. Has 22,200 empls., 4,500 stkhldrs. Insdrs. control 8.0% of stock. Chrmn: B. Schwartz. Inc.: NY. Addr.: 600 Third Ave., NY, NY 10016. Tel.: 212-697-1105.

Loral is successfully diversifying its program base. Many defense contractors concentrate only on a limited number of programs for the bulk of their profits, and that can prove painful when a program is cancelled. However, Loral has taken a different approach by spreading its program base over a number of areas. These diverse programs range from simulation training systems to all types of command, control, and communications systems. In addition, it focuses on upgrading existing weapons systems rather than expensive development programs, which Congress appears to want to eliminate from future defense budgets.

Loral is achieving favorable earnings comparisons despite looming defense cuts. The company posted record earnings for the first half of fiscal '92 (year ends March 31st), and we believe the second half and the next fiscal year will be even better. For one thing, the acquisition of LTV's missile subsidiary (presently called Vought Systems) last August should add about 10¢ to share earnings per quarter. In addition, Loral has called its 7¼% convertible debentures, which we believe will

be converted by the bondholders into 2.25 million shares of common stock. The company is expected to offset these additional shares through already authorized share buy backs, and this should help boost fully diluted share earnings by about 15¢ a year. Loral is taking the necessary steps to maximize its earnings capabilities. And at this time, we believe its growth prospects are superior to that of its peers in the industry.

More acquisitions are likely in view of Loral's strong financial position. We believe the company will continue to be a major player in the consolidation of the defense industry based upon its stable balance sheet and healthy cash flow. Even though this strategy of growing through external means is risky, Loral has so far been successful. Also, these shares are ranked to outperform the broader market averages over the coming 6-12 months. The stock price has increased by about 20% since our last report, which has partially discounted our projected earnings growth. As a result, appreciation potential out to '95-'97 appears a bit subpar.

Paul A. Roukis January 8, 1993

(A) Fiscal yr. ends March 31st of following calendar year. (B) Primary eqs. to 1989, fully dil. thereafter. Excludes nonrecurring gain: '89, 26¢; excludes gains from disc. ops: '88, $1.09. Factual material is obtained from sources believed to be reliable, but the publisher is not responsible for any errors or omissions contained herein. '89, 3¢. Next eqs. report due mid-Jan. (C) Next div. mtg. late Jan. Goes ex-div. mid-Feb. Dividend payment dates: about 15th of March, June, Sept., Dec. (D) Incl. intangibles. In '91: $285.9 mill., $8.95/sh. (E) In millions, adjusted for stock splits. (F) Fully diluted 3-5 years hence. (G) FIFO and Average Cost. (H) Earnings don't add due to rounding.

Company's Financial Strength	B++
Stock's Price Stability	85
Price Growth Persistence	35
Earnings Predictability	90

FIGURE 12-4 *Value Line Investment Survey* summary page on Loral Corp.

alyst divergence of opinion about EPS growth for a company was positively related to the magnitude of the EPS growth forecast error for that company. That is, the larger the EPS growth forecast error, the larger the spread of the forecasts among analysts.

Coggin and Hunter   A study by Coggin and Hunter examined the errors made by analysts in forecasting year-ahead EPS and five-year EPS growth.[13] Their study used both the I/B/E/S data base and the ICARUS data base (maintained by Zacks Investment Research). For both the one-year and the five-year forecast data, they found relatively small differences among analysts' earnings forecasts for a given company. They suggested at least four reasons for the relatively low level of diversity among individual analysts' forecasts.

First, there could be significant communication among analysts with respect to EPS forecasts. Coggin and Hunter noted that their experience in dealing with Wall Street and regional financial analysts led them to believe that there is minimal *direct* communication of EPS forecasts among analysts. However, analysts do read many of the same industry reports and journals containing short- and long-term forecasts of industry activity. This form of *indirect* communication could standardize the assumptions analysts make and thus reduce the level of idiosyncrasy in individual company forecasts.

Second, Coggin and Hunter noted that analysts often talk with company management concerning the outlook for a company. This is another source of "common information" available to analysts that could serve to further reduce the level of idiosyncratic error.[14] The third reason is that many analysts use similar financial models in deriving their forecasts. The relative uniformity of generally accepted techniques of financial analysis could help lower idiosyncratic error. Finally, they noted that their sample of companies was somewhat skewed toward larger, more well-known companies. It is possible that analysts tend to be in greater agreement concerning the future prospects for these firms.

The All-America Research Team   A recent study by Stickel profiles the performance of the *Institutional Investor* All-America Research Team in forecasting earnings.[15] The *Institutional Investor* All-America Research Team includes the top sell-side analysts selected from an annual mail survey of buy-side investment managers conducted by *Institutional Investor* magazine. The selection criteria for this list include such things as timeliness and accuracy of forecasts, accessibility, and clarity of research reports. Stickel's study suggests that the All-America analysts are more accurate and more frequent in forecasting earnings than other sell-side analysts. Stickel also found that

---

[13] Coggin and Hunter, "Analyst Forecasts of EPS and EPS Growth: Decomposition of Error, Relative Accuracy and Relation to Return," op. cit. See also Patricia C. O'Brien, "Forecast Accuracy of Individual Analysts in Nine Industries," *Journal of Accounting Research* (1990), pp. 286–304, for additional evidence of lack of diversity in analysts' earnings forecasts.

[14] A discussion of the techniques of financial analysis is provided in Appendixes B and C. Common factors considered by analysts in valuing a company are discussed in Chapter 14, where we discuss the valuation process.

[15] Scott E. Stickel, "Reputation and Performance among Security Analysts," *Journal of Finance* (December 1992), pp. 1811–1836.

the earnings forecasts of All-America analysts have a greater impact on stock prices than do those of other analysts. This leads us to a more complete discussion of the general topic of the relationship between analyst earnings forecasts and stock returns.

ANALYST EPS FORECASTS AND STOCK RETURNS

The major reason analysts are asked to perform fundamental analysis and forecast earnings per share is because there is an implied link between EPS forecasts and stock returns. Indeed, it is a fundamental tenet of financial theory that expectations for earnings for a company be related to return to stockholders. And indeed they are.

In one of the earliest studies of this relationship, Neiderhoffer and Regan verified that stock prices were strongly dependent on earnings changes—in terms of both absolute change and change relative to analysts' estimates.[16] Later studies used larger samples of analysts' expectational data to further refine our understanding of this relationship.[17] These studies showed that *current* expectations for earnings (as represented by the mean of the analysts' current forecasts) are incorporated into *current* stock prices. Furthermore, they showed that *revisions* in the consensus (i.e., mean) forecast for year-ahead earnings are *predictive* of future stock returns.

Specifically, these studies presented five key findings. First, as mentioned above, any information contained in the current consensus forecast by itself is largely reflected in the current stock price. Hence, a policy of buying stocks solely on the basis of large consensus growth estimates is generally unrewarded. Second, excess returns are available to those who can predict those stocks for which analysts will *underestimate* earnings, and even larger excess returns are possible if one can predict which stocks will experience the largest positive earnings estimate *revisions*. The phrase **excess returns** (or **abnormal returns**) here refers to returns in excess of those required by the capital asset pricing model, as explained in Chapter 5.

Third, Coggin and Hunter found that positive consensus errors were associated with higher returns for the forecast period, while negative consensus errors were associated with lower returns for the forecast period.[18] A positive consensus error refers to the case in which the consensus (mean) estimate is less than the actual earnings; a negative consensus error refers to the case in which the consensus estimate is greater than the actual earnings. These er-

---

[16] Victor Neiderhoffer and Patrick J. Regan, "Earnings Changes, Analysts' Forecasts and Stock Prices," *Financial Analysts Journal* (May–June 1972), pp. 65–71.

[17] See, for example, Edwin J. Elton, Martin J. Gruber, and Mustafa Gultekin, "Expectations and Share Prices," *Management Science* (September 1981), pp. 975–987; Eugene H. Hawkins, Stanley H. Chamberlain, and Wayne E. Daniel, "Earnings Expectations and Security Prices," *Financial Analysts Journal* (September–October 1984), pp. 24–38; and Eugene A. Imhoff and Gerald J. Lobo, "Information Content of Analysts' Composite Forecast Revisions," *Journal of Accounting Research* (Autumn 1984), pp. 541–554.

[18] Coggin and Hunter, "Analyst Forecasts of EPS and EPS Growth: Decomposition of Error, Relative Accuracy and Relation to Return," op. cit. See also Donna R. Philbrick and William E. Ricks, "Using Value Line and IBES Analyst Forecasts in Accounting Research," *Journal of Accounting Research* (Autumn 1991), pp. 397–417.

Company	Fiscal Year	EPS	5 Year Growth Rate	Stability	Year	Mean	1 Mo. Percent Chg.	Median	1 Mo. Percent Chg.	High	Low	Coefi of Variation	Total	Up	Down	P/E	Relative Price
LITCHFIELD FINL	12/91	0.58	NA	NA	92	0.73	0.0	0.73	0.0	0.73	0.73	0.2	2	0	0	15.1	1.18
					93	0.90	0.0	0.90	0.0	0.90	0.90	0.1	2	0	1	12.2	
LITTLEFUSE INC	12/91	1.18	NA	NA	92	0.04	-93.9	0.04	-94.3	0.05	0.04	11.8	4	0	0	NM	NA
					93	0.59	6.8	0.60	9.1	0.60	0.55	4.3	4	0	0	32.3	
LITTLE SWITZ INC	5/92	0.80	NA	NA	93	0.97	0.0	0.95	0.0	1.00	0.95	3.0	3	1	1	15.0	1.23
					94	1.17	0.0	1.20	0.0	1.20	1.10	4.9	3	1	1	12.4	
LITTON INDS	7/92	4.22	-6.2	25.9	93	4.59	0.0	4.55	0.0	5.02	4.30	3.4	17	1	0	9.9	0.92
					94	5.18	0.0	5.10	0.0	5.67	4.80	4.7	9	0	0	8.8	
LIVE ENTERTAINMT	12/91	-1.74	NA	NA	92	0.10	0.0	0.10	0.0	0.10	0.10		1	0	0	17.5	1.45
					93	0.25	0.0	0.25	0.0	0.25	0.25		1	0	0	7.0	
LIVING CTRS AMER	9/92	1.15	NA	NA	93	1.37	-0.4	1.37	-0.4	1.40	1.35	1.5	5	0	0	15.1	1.52
					94	1.55	NA	1.55	NA	1.55	1.55		1	0	0	13.4	
LIZ CLAIBORN	12/91	2.65	21.5	7.3	92	2.63	-0.4	2.61	-1.1	2.70	2.60	1.2	18	1	5	15.3	1.11
					93	2.87	-0.8	2.95	-0.8	3.10	2.85	2.4	18	1	4	13.5	
LOCKHEED CP	12/91	4.87	-5.5	83.1	92	5.49	0.8	5.50	0.0	5.60	5.40	1.3	19	1	1	10.2	1.17
					93	6.03	0.8	6.00	0.8	6.60	5.50	3.8	8	0	1	9.3	
LOCTITE CP	12/91	1.98	31.5	4.1	92	2.19	-0.1	2.22	0.0	2.25	1.96	4.4	8	0	2	19.2	1.01
					93	2.49	-0.5	2.50	0.0	2.55	2.40	1.8	6	0	0	16.9	
LOEWS CP	12/91	10.83	5.0	8.7	92	10.30	-1.8	10.52	-2.5	11.40	8.75	9.3	6	0	1	11.1	0.93
					93	12.07	-1.1	12.55	-0.4	12.90	10.80	7.6	5	0	0	9.4	
LOGICON INC	3/92	1.74	15.6	14.4	93	1.94	-0.5	1.95	0.0	2.00	1.90	2.2	4	0	1	10.4	1.18
					94	2.12	-0.6	2.12	-1.2	2.25	2.00	4.9	1	0	0	9.5	
LOJACK CP	2/92	-0.37	NA	NA	93	-0.22	0.0	-0.22	0.0	-0.22	-0.22		1	0	0	NM	2.00
					94	0.72	-21.8	0.72	-21.6	0.80	0.65	14.6	2	1	0	10.0	
LOMAS FINL CP	6/92	-3.49	-35.5	53.6	93	0.92	NA	0.92	NA	1.00	0.85	11.5	4	0	1	7.8	0.86
LONDON INTL GRP	3/92	1.45	NA	NA	93	1.32	-2.0	1.29	-0.4	1.48	1.20	9.3	3	1	0	15.2	NA
					94	1.55	-0.2	1.58	0.0	1.60	1.48	4.1	5	0	1	12.9	
LONE STAR STEAKH	12/92	0.34	NA	NA	93	0.87	0.2	0.90	0.0	0.91	0.80	5.3	2	1	0	41.3	2.10
					94	1.32	6.0	1.32	6.0	1.40	1.25	8.0	2	0	1	27.2	
LONE STAR TECH	12/91	0.31	NA	NA	92	0.44	0.0	0.44	0.0	0.45	0.44	1.6	2	0	0	8.3	1.19
					93	0.55	0.0	0.55	0.0	0.60	0.50	12.9	2	1	0	6.7	
LONG ISL LTG	12/91	2.15	3.6	29.2	92	2.11	0.0	2.10	0.0	2.30	2.05	2.7	21	0	0	11.9	1.00
					93	2.22	0.0	2.20	0.0	2.40	2.15	2.7	21	1	0	11.3	
LONGHORN STEAKS	12/91	0.47	NA	NA	92	0.61	0.0	0.61	0.0	0.61	0.61	0.2	2	0	0	36.5	1.42
					93	0.92	0.0	0.92	0.0	0.95	0.90	3.8	2	0	0	24.1	
LONGS DRG STRS	1/92	2.71	1.2	6.0	93	2.54	-0.2	2.55	0.0	2.60	2.45	1.8	7	1	1	14.8	1.00
					94	2.84	0.5	2.80	0.0	3.00	2.70	4.4	7	1	1	13.2	
LONGVIEW FIBRE	10/92	0.63	-26.7	20.6	93	1.12	-2.8	1.15	0.0	1.30	0.90	10.5	9	1	1	16.0	1.07
					94	1.50	0.3	1.50	2.2	1.75	1.25	23.6	2	1	2	12.0	
LONRHO LTD	9/91	0.25	NA	NA	92	0.02	NA	0.02	NA	0.03	0.01	70.7	2	0	0	55.4	0.67
					93	0.05	-63.6	0.05	-63.6	0.08	0.03	84.3	2	0	0	20.2	
LORAL CP	3/92	3.98	10.4	6.1	93	4.49	-38.9	4.50	-38.9	4.63	4.30	2.0	17	0	0	11.1	1.35
					94	4.95	0.1	4.89	0.0	5.56	4.58	4.9	15	1	3	10.1	
LOTUS DEV	12/91	1.51	-15.8	51.2	92	1.29	0.8	1.30	0.0	1.45	1.20	4.5	33	4	3	15.7	1.06
					93	1.55	0.1	1.55	0.0	1.80	1.30	8.9	33	3	3	13.1	
LVMH	12/91	9.73	24.4	5.9	92	8.59	-0.4	8.58	-2.4	8.85	8.34	3.0	3	1	1	13.4	0.81
					93	9.57	0.3	9.76	0.8	9.83	9.12	4.1	1	1	1	12.1	
LA LAND & EXPL	12/91	0.74	16.8	52.0	92	0.70	-0.4	0.70	0.0	0.90	0.50	11.8	24	1	3	46.4	0.85
					93	1.15	-1.5	1.18	-1.3	1.59	0.70	17.7	26	1	1	28.3	
LA PACIFIC CORP	12/91	1.03	-13.2	35.3	92	3.26	1.1	3.30	1.2	3.45	3.00	3.7	21	6	1	19.8	1.44
					93	4.30	2.5	4.25	3.4	5.40	3.50	11.5	21	6	0	15.1	

FIGURE 12-5   Page from I/B/E/S *Monthly Summary Data Book* including Loral Corp.

rors are commonly called positive or negative **earnings surprises** because they are different from the analysts' forecasts and hence are a "surprise." Specifically, Coggin and Hunter found that by the end of the fiscal year the market had already begun to adjust the return on a stock to the fact that actual earnings for the year were either less than or in excess of expectations. This finding extends previous research that used a statistical model to generate expected earnings,[19] and it supports results reported in Brown, Foster, and Noreen.[20]

Fourth, Coggin and Hunter also found that the variance of the analysts' five-year growth estimates was *negatively* correlated with the return for forecast periods of one through five years. This finding does not support the use of the variance of analysts' five-year growth estimates as a measure of systematic (market-related) investment risk advocated by Malkiel[21] and others. That is, financial theory states that a systematic risk measure should be positively, not negatively, related to return.

Finally, studies have shown that revisions in the consensus estimate for earnings tend to have *momentum*; that is, an increase in the consensus forecast in one month is often followed by another increase in the next month. Excess returns on such stocks have been measured to last for holding periods of from 2 to 12 months. It has been argued by some that this finding is inconsistent with the existence of an efficient market.[22] The stock market does not "instantaneously" react to changes in the consensus forecast, and it allows excess returns to a strategy that takes advantage of that fact. This topic will be briefly discussed later in this chapter.

In summary, as several stock market observers have commented, the noted British economist John Maynard Keynes appears to have been correct when he compared professional investing to participating in a contest to pick which 6 contestants out of 100 in a photo beauty contest will be chosen by the rest of the judges. In Keynes's words, ". . . each competitor has to pick, not those whose faces which he himself finds prettiest, but those which he thinks likeliest to catch the fancy of other competitors, all of whom are looking at the contest from the same point of view."[23]

ANALYST RETURN FORECASTS

As indicated earlier, a key responsibility of investment analysts is forecasting stock returns. In most cases, the analyst forecasts company-level returns directly. However, in some cases, the analyst provides input (i.e., forecasts of earnings, dividends, and growth rates) to a valuation model (such as a divi-

---

[19] See, for example, Ray Ball and Philip Brown, "An Empirical Evaluation of Accounting Income Numbers," *Journal of Accounting Research* (Autumn 1968), pp. 159–178; and George Foster, Chris Olsen, and Terry Shevlin, "Earnings Releases, Anomalies and the Behavior of Security Returns," *Accounting Review* (October 1984), pp. 574–603.

[20] Philip Brown, George Foster, and E. Noreen, *Security Analyst Multi-Year Forecasts and the Capital Market* (Sarasota, FL: American Accounting Association, 1985).

[21] Burton G. Malkiel, "Risk and Return: A New Look," Working Paper No. 700, National Bureau of Economic Research, Cambridge, MA (1981).

[22] See, for example, Dan Givoly and Josef Lakonishok, "Financial Analysts' Forecasts of Earnings: Their Value to Investors," *Journal of Banking and Finance* (September 1980), pp. 221–233.

[23] John M. Keynes, *The General Theory of Employment, Interest and Money* (New York: Harcourt, Brace & Company, 1936), p. 156.

dend discount model discussed in Chapter 15), which, in turn, forecasts returns. In either case, the analyst is central to the process of generating expected returns. These forecasts are usually in the form of "buy," "hold," and "sell" recommendations. The portfolio manager then uses these recommendations, in conjunction with other quantitative and non-quantitative aspects of evaluating a company, to construct stock portfolios for clients.

The Valuation Process

In a survey of 1,000 members of the Financial Analysts Federation, Chugh and Meador examined the process by which financial analysts evaluate common stocks.[24] They found that analysts consistently emphasize the long term over the short term. Key variables for the long term were expected change in EPS, expected return on equity (ROE), and industry outlook. Key variables for the short term were industry outlook, expected change in EPS, and general economic conditions. Other important factors mentioned by the analysts were quality and depth of management, market dominance, and "strategic credibility" (ability to achieve stated goals). According to their survey, expected growth in earnings and ROE appeared to be the most significant aspects of the valuation process. The primary sources of information for the analysts were presentations by top management, annual reports, and Form 10-K reports.

The Quality of Return Forecasts

Each quarter Zacks Investment Research tracks the performance of stocks recommended by analysts at 16 major brokerage houses and reports the results in *The Wall Street Journal*. Table 12-1 presents a summary of the results as of December 31, 1993. For one year ended December 31, 1993, the lists of stock recommended by 12 of the 16 brokerage houses outperformed the S&P 500 stock index. For five years ended December 31, 1993, all 10 who reported results outperformed the S&P 500. These returns are based on monthly rebalancing of the lists of stock and assume no transactions costs.

A number of other studies have examined the value of analysts' forecasts of stock returns. The majority of these studies have also focused on the forecasts of sell-side analysts. While there is some disagreement in this area,[25] the general finding is that there is economically valuable information in analysts' buy/sell recommendations. Specifically, recent studies by U.S., Canadian, and U.K. analysts have shown that excess returns are available to investors who

---

[24] Lal C. Chugh and Joseph W. Meador, "The Stock Valuation Process: The Analysts' View," *Financial Analysts Journal* (November–December 1984), pp. 41–48. This study expanded and updated an earlier study by Ralph A. Bing, "Survey of Practitioners' Stock Evaluation Methods," *Financial Analysts Journal* (May–June 1971), pp. 55–60.

[25] See, for example, R. E. Diefenbach, "How Good Is Institutional Brokerage Research," *Financial Analysts Journal* (January–February 1972), pp. 54–60; Clinton M. Bidwell III, "How Good Is Institutional Brokerage Research?" *Journal of Portfolio Management* (Winter 1977), pp. 26–31; and Lawrence Shepard, "How Good Is Investment Advice for Individuals," *Journal of Portfolio Management* (Winter 1977), pp. 32–36.

TABLE 12-1			
BROKERAGE HOUSES' STOCK-PICKING PROWESS IN PERIODS ENDING DECEMBER 31, 1993			
Firm	**Latest Quarter**	**One Year**	**Five Years**
PaineWebber	7.1%	39.1%	177.5%
Raymond James	11.3	34.2	413.9
Kemper	4.9	34.1	NA
Kidder Peabody	4.2	31.2	137.8
Smith Barney	6.1	28.4	150.2
Merrill Lynch	3.1	25.7	149.4
Salomon Brothers	4.7	21.1	NA
Morgan Stanley	5.0	17.8	NA
Prudential	6.0	14.7	141.2
CS First Boston	−0.1	12.2	NA
Goldman Sachs	7.3	11.4	123.1
A. G. Edwards	3.4	10.4	143.5
Bear Stearns	4.8	10.0	NA
Lehman Brothers	3.2	9.9	122.4
Dean Witter	1.2	9.0	153.7
Edward D. Jones	6.0	4.0	NA
S&P 500 INDEX	2.3	10.1	97.2

Source: The Wall Street Journal, Feb. 1, 1994, and Zacks Investment Research, Inc.

follow the published recommendations of analysts employed by brokerage houses.[26]

Put in the current jargon, these studies show that analysts' stock recommendations have a "positive IC." **Information coefficient (IC)** is an investment term defined as the correlation between predicted and actual stock returns. An IC of 1.0 indicates a perfect linear relationship between predicted and actual returns, while an IC of 0.0 indicates no linear relationship. Some researchers have argued that analysts are "worth their keep" if and only if it can be shown that they can forecast earnings and returns. The evidence to date supports the hypotheses that they can (1) outperform simple statistical models in forecasting earnings and (2) provide economically valuable information in forecasting returns.

---

[26] Peter L. Davies and Michael Canes, "Stock Prices and the Publication of Second-Hand Information," *Journal of Business* (January 1978), pp. 43–56; Kenneth Stanley, Wilbur G. Lewellen, and Gary G. Schlarbaum, "Further Evidence on the Value of Professional Investment Research," *Journal of Financial Research* (Spring 1981), pp. 1–9; James H. Bjerring, Josef Lakonishok, and Theo Vermaelen, "Stock Prices and Financial Analysts Recommendations," *Journal of Finance* (March 1983), pp. 187–204; Elroy E. Dimson and Paul Marsh, "An Analysis of Brokers' and Analysts' Unpublished Forecasts of UK Stock Returns," *Journal of Finance* (December 1984), pp. 1257–1292; and Edwin J. Elton, Martin J. Gruber, and Seth Grossman, "Discrete Expectational Data and Portfolio Performance," *Journal of Finance* (July 1986), pp. 699–714.

EVALUATING ANALYSTS' JOB PERFORMANCE

Having now established the fact that analysts are indeed a valuable component of the investment process, it seems logical to discuss how they themselves are evaluated. A mail survey of buy-side and sell-side analysts by Coggin indicated that analysts are typically evaluated on their ability to forecast earnings and returns and to communicate investment ideas and information.

A number of investment organizations have established quantitative rating systems to evaluate their analysts.[27] Several articles have been written on the topic of evaluating financial analysts.[28] These articles have focused overwhelmingly on the ability of analysts to forecast return, while other "relatively minor" issues such as the ability to communicate investment information received little or no attention. The most common elements of an analyst rating system are accuracy of stock performance forecasts, accuracy of estimate information (e.g., earnings, dividends, and growth rates), and ability to communicate investment information to portfolio managers.[29] It would then seem that ability to forecast stock return is a key (if not the key) element of an analyst's job description.

Three studies are relevant to this issue. Coggin and Hunter examined a fundamental question: Are there individual differences in analysts' abilities to forecast stock returns?[30] They analyzed the ICs both for analysts at a regional trust company over a period and for a larger sample of buy-side analysts nationwide. Coggin and Hunter showed that all apparent differences in analysts' ICs were attributable to *sampling error*. Hence, in their data, there were no real individual differences in analysts' abilities to forecast return. Dimson and Marsh replicated the Coggin and Hunter analysis on a sample of British brokers and analysts and got the same basic result.[31] Elton, Gruber, and Grossman found no evidence of one U.S. brokerage firm being consistently better than another in recommending stocks for the period investigated.[32]

It was previously noted that research suggests minimal differences in analysts' abilities to forecast earnings. We now have evidence suggesting that there are no differences in analysts' abilities to forecast returns. Thus the combined evidence suggests that rating schemes which base an individual analyst's salary and bonus on differential ability to forecast earnings and returns amount to holding a *lottery* for that award!

---

[27] The mail survey by Coggin indicated that 71% had done so.

[28] See William S. Gray, "Measuring the Analyst's Performance," *Financial Analysts Journal* (March–April 1966), pp. 56–63; Amir Barnea and Dennis E. Logue, "Evaluating the Forecasts of a Security Analyst," *Financial Management* (Summer 1973), pp. 38–45; Fred Mastrapasqua and Steven Bolten, "A Note on Financial Analyst Evaluation," *Journal of Finance* (June 1973), pp. 707–712; and Benjamin C. Korschot, "Quantitative Evaluation of Investment Research Analysts," *Financial Analysts Journal* (July-August 1978). pp. 41–46.

[29] This was found in the mail survey by Coggin.

[30] T. Daniel Coggin and John E. Hunter, "Problems in Measuring the Quality of Investment Information: The Perils of the Information Coefficient," *Financial Analysts Journal* (May–June 1983), pp. 25–33.

[31] Dimson and Marsh, "An Analysis of Brokers' and Analysts' Unpublished Forecasts of UK Stock Returns," op. cit.

[32] Elton, Gruber, and Grossman, "Discrete Expectational Data and Portfolio Performance," op. cit.

It is important to emphasize that the existing evidence does *not* suggest that analysts can't forecast returns. Indeed, there is previously cited evidence that they *can*. The mean analyst IC is not zero; rather, it is about 0.10, which is large enough to have predictive value. The point here is that the existing data suggest there are no real between-analyst differences in the ability to forecast returns.

It may seem confusing to say, on the one hand, that analysts as a group have investment information (mean IC equal to about 0.10) and then to say, on the other hand, that there are apparently no differences between analysts in predicting earnings and returns. However, the existing research does indeed suggest that analysts as a group are useful in predicting earnings and returns, but that they are not sufficiently differentiated individually to distinguish among them on this dimension.

In an effort to accommodate this finding, a regional trust company designed an analyst evaluation system that rates the analysts as a group on the return prediction dimension. At this firm, the analysts supply estimates of earnings, dividends, and growth rates to a three-phase dividend discount model (described in Chapter 15), which then calculates expected returns for a reference list of stocks. The IC is measured for the entire reference list of stocks followed by the group of analysts. If that IC is significantly positive, the analysts (as a group) are rated favorably on that dimension. Other specific criteria are then rated on an analyst-by-analyst basis, such as the ability to communicate investment information and analyses in both verbal and written form.

The preceding discussion has indicated that analysts' inputs are important to the investment decision-making process. When we add together all the investment groups and individuals in the country, we have what is called the *capital market*. The analyst is a key participant in this market.

THE ANALYST AND THE CAPITAL MARKET

At the beginning of this chapter, we noted that analysts are important information processors for investors in the stock market. In this section, we will explore this topic in more detail and shed some more light on how analysts provide this important function to the capital market.

The Analyst as Information Processor

As O'Brien has noted, accounting and finance researchers (and practitioners) are increasingly relying on analysts' forecasts as proxies for the "unobservable market expectation" for future earnings.[33] The empirical evidence that financial analysts are, in general, superior to univariate time-series models in forecasting earnings and the increasing availability of analyst forecast data (from sources like I/B/E/S and Zacks Investment Research cited above) have fostered this tendency. It is now well established that the information content of analysts' forecasts for earnings and returns is relevant to the theory and practice of accounting and finance.

In a totally efficient capital market, analysts' forecasts for earnings and returns would not matter. Every market participant (both analysts and in-

---

[33] O'Brien, "Analysts' Forecasts as Earnings Expectations," op. cit.

vestors) would have exactly the same information at exactly the same time; hence, no one would have an "informational advantage" over anyone else. However, there is mounting evidence that the stock market is not totally efficient. While the weight of the evidence suggests that analysts are generally undifferentiated in their ability to predict earnings and returns, those predictions can be profitably employed by investors in the stock market.

This chapter has cited evidence that the ability to forecast *changes* in the consensus analyst earnings forecast for a company yields excess returns in the stock market. Some studies have examined the *timing* and *speed* at which analysts' forecast information is disseminated to stock market investors.[34] This is an important area of research that will likely yield insights into just how that information is translated into excess returns. Evidence was also discussed that supports the hypothesis that analysts' buy/sell recommendations can be used to earn excess returns in the stock market. Other research has shown that one particular valuation model discussed in Chapter 15, the dividend discount model, is an economically valuable tool in predicting actual stock returns.[35]

Quantitative Methods

Recent studies have shown that a majority of investment management firms do not use quantitative methods to value common stocks. The use of quantitative methods in investment management involves extensive use of computer models, statistical analysis, and data screening utilities. Quantitative methods allow analysts to systematically and unemotionally process larger amounts of information and data than are normally possible without them; and the number of quantitative money managers is growing over time. Nonetheless, some 30 years after the "quantitative revolution" of the late 1960s, most money managers continue to rely on conventional (i.e., nonquantitative) methods of investment management. In the case of stocks, this generally means that financial analysts perform fundamental security analysis and make recommendations to portfolio managers about which stocks to buy and sell. A relatively large subjective component is then applied to the final investment decision. No doubt, this process has been successful (and will continue to be successful) for some investment management firms.

A survey reported in the November 10, 1986, issue of *Pensions & Investment Age* indicated that only 8% of respondents use quantitative methods to manage stocks, and a survey conducted by Arthur D. Little, Inc., in March 1987 reported that only 30% of respondents made intensive use of quantitative methods in their overall money management effort. This small minority of quantitative managers spans a continuum from using analysts to provide input to quantitative models to using no analysts at all, relying instead on computers and artificial intelligence to process information and select and trade stocks.

---

[34] See Chapter 4 and Appendixes A.1 and A.2 in Brown, Foster, and Noreen, *Security Analyst Multi-Year Forecasts and the Capital Market*; and O'Brien, "Analysts' Forecasts as Earnings Expectations," op. cit.

[35] See, for example, Eric H. Sorensen and David A. Williamson, "Some Evidence of the Value of Dividend Discount Models," *Financial Analysts Journal* (November–December 1985), pp. 60–69, and Chapter 15 of this book.

The fact remains that analysts provide a valuable information processing service to the majority of *active* stock market investors. There is another form of stock market investing we will discuss in Chapter 13 called *passive* investing, which includes the growing index fund business. Passive investment management assumes that securities are efficiently priced and does *not* involve the use of analysts' estimates in an effort to beat the market. Currently, however, the vast majority of money invested in the stock market is actively managed. As long as active stock market investing remains popular, analysts will be a vital component of the investment process.

■ SUMMARY

Analysts play an active role in the equity investment process. The major finding to date is that analysts do a better job than simple extrapolative models. Stock prices are strongly related to analysts' earnings forecasts—not so much to the current forecast, but to *changes* in the current forecast.

The general finding about the role of the analyst in the equity valuation process is that there is useful information in analysts' forecasts of stock returns. With regard to evaluating the job performance of analysts, while there is useful information in analysts' forecasts, there is not a great deal of difference in the individual analyst's ability to forecast company-level earnings and returns. A possible exception to this finding is the earnings forecast ability of the *Institutional Investor* All-America Team. Finally, the analyst plays important roles as an information processor for the capital market and as a key element in the process of active stock market investing.

■ KEY TERMS

abnormal returns	excess returns	sell-side analyst
buy-side analyst	extrapolative statistical models	simple autoregressive model
consensus forecast	financial analysts	simple exponential model
earnings surprises	information coefficient (IC)	simple linear trend model

■ QUESTIONS

1. Mr. Rogers is an analyst for a money management firm, and Ms. Lenox is an analyst for a West Coast brokerage firm. Which is a buy-side analyst, and which is a sell-side analyst.

2. Discuss where one can find earnings forecasts reported.

3. When comparing earnings forecasts developed using simple extrapolative statistical models with earnings forecasts developed by analysts, which kind of forecast does a better job and why?

4. Discuss the relationship between analysts' EPS forecasts and stock returns.
   a. What is an information coefficient?
   b. Is there useful information in analysts' forecasts of earnings and returns?
   c. Has research to date found significant differences in the ability of individual analysts to forecast earnings and returns?

   d. Discuss what this means for the task of evaluating analysts' job performance.

5. a. Why might it be that analysts are relatively undifferentiated in their abilities to forecast earnings for a company?
   b. What about the *Institutional Investor* All-America Team?

6. Discuss the relationship between positive and negative earnings surprises and stock returns.

7. Discuss factors used by analysts in evaluating common stocks.

8. Discuss the relationship between quantitative and nonquantitative investment management.

9. Explain why analysts will be important to the investment process as long as active investment management remains popular.

CHAPTER 13
STOCK MARKET EFFICIENCY AND TRANSACTIONS COSTS

LEARNING OBJECTIVES
After reading this chapter you will be able to:

- explain what is meant by the pricing efficiency of a market and the different forms of pricing efficiency: weak, semistrong, and strong.

- describe what is meant by the operational efficiency of a market.

- explain how abnormal returns are calculated in tests of the pricing efficiency of the market.

- characterize the empirical evidence on pricing efficiency.

- explain the implications of pricing efficiency for the selection of a common stock strategy.

- define the different components of transactions costs.

- describe what execution and opportunity costs are and how they can be measured.

- characterize the trade-off between execution cost and opportunity cost.

In this chapter and the next two chapters, we will explain the various strategies pursued by money managers of common stock portfolios. Basically, these strategies can be classified into one of two types: active and passive. The selection of a strategy depends on two factors: (1) the risk tolerance of the client and (2) the client's expectation of the efficiency of the market. A client who believes the market is efficient tends to favor a passive strategy; one who believes the market is inefficient will lean in the direction of an active strategy.

Because of the importance of transactions costs in both the selection of a strategy and the success of a strategy, we provide a detailed discussion of these costs and their measurement.

Active and passive strategies are described in the next two chapters. In this chapter, we review the evidence of the efficiency of the stock market. The findings are pretty dramatic: The stock market is reasonably efficient, so most stock pickers don't beat the market, but lots of people keep trying. Without this constant effort, though, the stock market would not be efficient. This leaves tough questions and temptations both for clients in selecting money managers and for financial entities managing funds. Should clients pursue an active strategy, thereby betting they can hire all-stars who can beat the pack this year? Is such a strategy worth the risk that the money manager hired will significantly underperform the market? Or should they require their money manager to pursue a passive strategy, the most popular form of this strategy being indexing? With a passive strategy, the client accepts the performance of the stock market.

MARKET EFFICIENCY

The term "efficient capital market" has been used in several contexts to describe the operating characteristics of a capital market. There is a distinction between an *operationally efficient* (or *internally efficient*) market and a *pricing-efficient* (or *externally efficient*) capital market.[1]

In an **operationally efficient market**, investors can obtain transaction services that reflect the true costs associated with furnishing those services. In the equity markets, for example, since the elimination of fixed minimum commissions in May 1975, the commission structure has moved closer to the competitive level dictated by the intrinsic cost of providing brokerage services. As for the dealer spread, the movement toward a national market system should tighten those spreads.

Pricing efficiency refers to a market where prices at all times fully reflect all available information that is relevant to the valuation of securities. When a market is price-efficient, strategies pursued to outperform a broad-based stock market index will not consistently produce superior returns after adjusting for (1) risk and (2) transactions costs.

PRICING EFFICIENCY OF THE STOCK MARKET AND PORTFOLIO IMPLICATIONS

There have been numerous studies of the pricing efficiency of the stock market. While it is not our intent in this chapter to provide a comprehensive review of these studies, we can summarize their basic findings and the implications for investment strategies.[2]

Definitions of Pricing Efficiency

In his seminal review article on pricing efficiency, Eugene Fama points out that in order to test whether the stock market is price-efficient, two definitions are necessary. First, it is necessary to define what it means for prices to "fully reflect" information. Second, the "relevant" set of information that is assumed to be "fully reflected" in prices must be defined.[3]

---

[1]Richard R. West, "Two Kinds of Market Efficiency," *Financial Analysts Journal* (November–December 1975), pp. 30–34.

[2]For a detailed review of these studies, see Chapters 3 to 5 in Diana R. Harrington, Frank J. Fabozzi, and H. Russell Fogler, *The New Stock Market* (Chicago: Probus Publishing, 1990).

[3]Eugene F. Fama, "Efficient Capital Markets: A Review of Theory and Empirical Work," *Journal of Finance* (May 1970), pp. 383–417.

TABLE 13-1	
FORMS OF MARKET EFFICIENCY	
Form	**Information Reflected in Prices**
Weak	Historical data
Semistrong	Historical data plus other public information
Strong	Historical data, public information, and private information

Fama, as well as others, defines "fully reflect" in terms of the expected return from holding a stock. The expected return over some holding period is equal to expected dividends plus the expected price change all divided by the initial price. The price formation process defined by Fama and others is that the expected return one period from now is a stochastic (i.e., random) variable that already takes into account the "relevant" information set.[4]

In defining the "relevant" information set that prices should reflect, Fama classified the pricing efficiency of the stock market into three forms: (1) weak form, (2) semistrong form, and (3) strong form. The distinction among these forms lies in the relevant information that is hypothesized to be impounded in the price of the security, as shown in Table 13-1. **Weak efficiency** means that the price of the security reflects the past price and trading history of the security. **Semistrong efficiency** means that the price of the security fully reflects all public information (which, of course, includes but is not limited to historical price and trading patterns). **Strong efficiency** exists in a market where the price of a security reflects all information, whether or not it is publicly available.

Formulating Empirical Tests

Tests of pricing efficiency investigate whether it is possible to generate abnormal returns. As explained in the previous chapter, an *abnormal return* (or excess return) is defined as the difference between the actual return and the expected return from an investment strategy. The expected return used in empirical tests is one predicted from a pricing model such as the capital asset pricing model or from a return-generating model such as the market model, both of which were discussed in Chapters 5 and 6. Consequently, expected return considers the risk associated with the investment. More specifically, it considers systematic risk as proxied by beta. Calculation of the actual return takes transactions costs from commissions and fees into account. Other transactions costs discussed later in this chapter are typically not considered in these studies.

To summarize, the abnormal return is calculated as follows:

Abnormal return = actual return (net of transactions costs) − expected return (from some pricing model or return-generating model)

If a strategy can be shown to consistently outperform the market, then the market is not price-efficient. To show price inefficiency, an abnormal return first must be shown to be statistically significant. If it is, it is not suffi-

---

[4]If it is assumed that investors will not invest in a stock unless its expected return is greater than zero, then the price formation process is called a *submartingale process*.

cient to conclude that the investment strategy that produced the positive abnormal return can outperform the market in the future. The reason is that the empirical test depends critically on the expected return calculated from an assumed pricing model. However, this model may be misspecified for two reasons. First, it may fail to consider the appropriate measure of risk (for example, if the arbitrage pricing model is the appropriate equilibrium pricing model). Second, the market risk parameter beta may not be estimated properly. In either instance, the results are questionable.

Tests of Weak-Form Pricing Efficiency

Tests of the weak form of pricing efficiency explore whether one or more of the following can be used to project future prices in such a way as to produce positive abnormal returns:

1. Mechanical rules such as the pattern of price movements and trading volume
2. Overreaction, that is, indications of overreaction by investors

Mechanical Rules   Mechanical rules are those in which no consideration is given to any factor other than the specified technical indicators. Mechanical rules are followed by market participants commonly referred to as **technical analysts** or **chartists**. The strategies they pursue are described in the next chapter. The overlying principle of these strategies is to detect changes in the supply of and demand for a stock and capitalize on the expected changes. The technical strategies investigated and their basic findings are presented briefly below and are summarized in Table 13-2.

Simple filter rules   The simplest of these technical strategies is to buy and sell on the basis of a predetermined movement in the price of a stock; the rule is basically that if the stock increases by a certain percentage, the stock is purchased and held until the price declines by a certain percentage, at which time the stock is sold. The percentage by which the price must change is called the **filter**. The original study of the profitability of simple filter rules was performed by Alexander in 1961.[5] Adjustments for methodological deficiencies of the Alexander study by Fama and Blume in 1966 found that price changes do show persistent trends; however, the trends were too small to exploit after considering transactions costs and other factors that must be taken into account in assessing the strategy.[6] Two more recent studies by Sweeney, however, suggest that a short-term technical trading strategy based on past price movements can produce statistically significant risk-adjusted returns after adjusting for the types of transactions costs faced by floor traders and professional money managers.[7]

---

[5]Sidney S. Alexander, "Price Movements in Speculative Markets: Trends or Random Walks," *Industrial Management Review* (May 1961), pp. 7–26.

[6]Eugene F. Fama and Marshall Blume, "Filter Rules and Stock-Market Trading," *Journal of Business* (October 1966), pp. 226–241.

[7]Richard J. Sweeney, "Some New Filter Rule Tests: Methods and Results," *Journal of Financial and Quantitative Analysis* (September 1988), pp. 285–300, and "Evidence on Short-Term Trading Strategies," *Journal of Portfolio Management* (Fall 1990), pp. 20–26.

Moving averages   Some technical analysts make their decision to buy or sell a stock based on the movement of a stock over an extended period of time (for example, 200 days). An average of the price over the time period is computed, and a rule is specified that if the price is greater than some percentage of the average, the stock should be purchased; if the price is less than some percentage of the average, the stock should be sold. The simplest way to calculate the average is to calculate a **simple moving average**. Assuming that the time period selected by the technical analyst is 200 days, then the average price over the 200 days is determined. A more complex moving average can be calculated by giving greater weight to more recent prices. The two studies that investigated strategies based on moving averages found that they produce lower returns than those of a simple buy-and-hold strategy.[8]

Relative strength   The **relative strength** of a stock is measured by the ratio of the stock price to some price index. The ratio indicates the relative movement of the stock to the index. The price index can be the index of the price of stocks in a given industry or a broad-based index of all stocks. If the ratio rises, it is presumed that the stock is in an uptrend relative to the index; if the ratio falls, it is presumed that the stock is in a downtrend relative to the index. Similarly, a relative strength measure can be calculated for an industry group relative to a broad-based index. Relative strength is also referred to as **price momentum** or **price persistence**.

Robert Levy was the first to study whether relative strength can be used to identify stocks or groups of stocks that will provide superior performance.[9] His findings suggested that a strategy based on relative strength will outperform a buy-and-hold strategy. However, Jensen noted several methodological flaws in Levy's study.[10] In a later study, Jensen and Bennington found that Levy's findings were related to the post-World War II period and therefore might not be appropriate for other time periods.[11] Subsequent studies corrected for the methodological flaws noted by Jensen and covered different time periods. Arnott, for example, after adjusting for a stock's beta, found that, contrary to conventional wisdom, a stock that has been strong in the past will tend to be weak in the future.[12] Brush examined the predictive power of eight widely used relative strength approaches combined with simple to complex rules for identifying price momentum.[13] He found that there were many similarities and some differences in the models studied. Most importantly, he found that relative strength models can be used to predict which stocks would achieve superior performance after adjusting for transac-

[8]Paul H. Cootner, "Stock Prices: Random vs. Systematic Risk," *Industrial Management Review* (Spring 1962), pp. 24–45; and F. E. James, Jr., "Monthly Moving Averages—An Effective Investment Tool?" *Journal of Financial and Quantitative Analysis* (September 1968), pp. 315–326.

[9]Robert Levy, "Conceptual Foundations of Technical Analysis," *Financial Analysts Journal* (July–August 1966), pp. 83–89.

[10]Michael C. Jensen, "Random Walks: A Comment," *Financial Analysts Journal* (November–December 1967), pp. 77–85.

[11]Michael C. Jensen and George Bennington, "Random Walks and Technical Theories: Some Additional Evidence," *Journal of Finance* (May 1970), pp. 469–482.

[12]Robert Arnott, "Relative Strength Revisited," *Journal of Portfolio Management* (Spring 1979), pp. 19–23.

[13]John S. Brush, "Eight Relative Strength Models Compared," *Journal of Portfolio Management* (Fall 1986), pp. 21–28.

TABLE 13-2

SUMMARY OF RESEARCH FINDINGS ON MECHANICAL RULES

Mechanical Rule	General Findings
Simple filter rules	Most studies found no superior performance. One recent study found superior performance.
Moving averages	Not superior to a buy-and-hold strategy.
Relative strength	Earlier studies after adjusting for methodological flaws found superior returns not possible. Recent study found superior returns after adjusting for transactions costs but not for risk.
Price and trading relationship	Mixed findings but in instances where superior performance observed appears to be a response to earnings announcements.
Multirule system	A trading system based on cumulative volume, relative strength, and moving average outperformed market after adjustments for transactions costs, trade timing, and risk.

tions costs, but not for risk. Brush found that the superior returns were only available by accepting risk in terms of volatility.

Price and trading relationship   One popular Wall Street adage is that "It takes volume to make price move." This suggests a **price-volume relationship** as a signal for detecting the price movement of a stock used in some technical analyses. The argument put forth by technical analysts is that a rise in both trading volume and price signals investor interest in the stock, and this interest should be sustained. In contrast, a rise in price accompanied by a decline in trading volume signals a subsequent decline in the price of the stock. Several studies have empirically investigated these assertions about the relationship between price and trading volume.[14] The findings vary. Ying, for example, finds that volume does tend to lead price changes (by about four days), but the relationship was not sufficiently strong to be profitably exploited.[15] To isolate the effect of the arrival of news on the price-volume relationship, Smirlock and Starks partitioned their sample into days when earnings were announced and those when no earnings were announced.[16] They find that on those trading days with an earnings announcement, up-tick (i.e., price increases) volume was higher. This suggests that price and volume increases may be a response to information. In contrast, for trading days in which there was no earnings announcement, no evidence was found to support the contention that there is a positive relationship between price change and volume.

Multirule System   The studies cited above focused on a mechanical rule based on just one technical trading rule. In a study by Pruitt and White, all

---

[14]A summary of these studies for both the stock market and the futures market is provided in Jonathan Karpoff, "The Relation between Price Changes and Trading Volume," *Journal of Financial and Quantitative Analysis* (March 1987), pp. 109–126. A theory of the price-volume relationship is provided in Thomas Epps, "Security Price Changes and Transaction Volumes: Theory and Evidence," *American Economic Review* (September 1975), pp. 586–597.

[15]Charles Ying, "Stock Market Prices and Volume of Sales," *Econometrica* (July 1976), pp. 676–685.

[16]Michael Smirlock and Laura Starks, "A Further Examination of the Stock Price Change and Transaction Volume," *Journal of Financial Research* (Fall 1985), pp. 217–225.

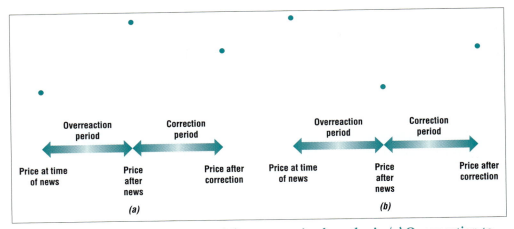

FIGURE 13-1   **Graphical depiction of the overreaction hypothesis. (*a*) Overreaction to positive news. (*b*) Overreaction to negative news.**

the technical trading rules described above (filter rules, moving averages, relative strength, and price-volume movement) are incorporated into one technical trading model, a **multirule system**.[17] Over the period 1976–1985, their model, which they call the CRISMA (cumulative volume, relative strength, moving average) Trading System, outperformed the market after adjustments for transactions costs, trade timing, and risk.

Overreaction   To benefit from favorable news or to reduce the adverse effect of unfavorable news, investors must react quickly to new information. Cognitive psychologists have shed some light on how people react to extreme events. In general, people tend to overreact to extreme events. People tend to react more strongly to recent information; and they tend to heavily discount older information.

The question is, do investors follow the same pattern? That is, do investors overreact to extreme events? The **overreaction hypothesis** suggests that when investors react to unanticipated news that will benefit a company's stock, the price rise will be greater than it should be given that information, resulting in a subsequent decline in the price of the stock. In contrast, the overreaction to unanticipated news that is expected to adversely affect the economic well-being of a company will force the price down too much, followed by a subsequent correction that will increase the price. This is depicted in Figure 13-1.

If, in fact, the market does overreact, investors may be able to exploit this to realize positive abnormal returns if they can (1) identify an extreme event and (2) determine when the effect of the overreaction has been impounded in the market price and is ready to reverse. Investors who are capable of doing this will pursue the following strategies. When positive news is identified, investors will buy the stock and sell it before the correction to the overreaction. In the case of negative news, investors will short the stock and then buy it back to cover the short position before the correction to the overreaction.

---

[17] Stephen W. Pruitt and Richard E. White, "Who Says Technical Analysis Can't Beat the Market?" *Journal of Portfolio Management* (Spring 1988), pp. 55–58.

As originally formulated by DeBondt and Thaler, the overreaction hypothesis can be described by two propositions.[18] First, the extreme movement of a stock price will be followed by a movement in the stock price in the opposite direction. This is called the *directional effect*. Second, the more extreme the initial price change (i.e., the greater the overreaction), the more extreme the offsetting reaction (i.e., the greater the price correction). This is called the *magnitude effect*. However, the directional effect and the magnitude effect may simply mean that investors overweight short-term sources of information.[19] To rectify this, Brown and Harlow added a third proposition, called the *intensity effect*, which states that the shorter the duration of the initial price change, the more extreme the subsequent response will be.[20]

Several empirical studies support the directional effect and the magnitude effect.[21] Brown and Harlow tested for all three effects (directional, magnitude, and intensity) and found that for intermediate and long-term responses to *positive* events, there is only mild evidence that market pricing is inefficient; however, evidence on short-term trading responses to *negative* events is strongly consistent with all three effects. Thus, they conclude that "the tendency for the stock market to correct is best regarded as an asymmetric, short-run phenomenon." It is asymmetric because investors appear to overreact to negative, not positive, extreme events.

Conclusions on the Weak Form of Market Efficiency   The foregoing review of the studies of the weak form of market efficiency did not cover all the technical strategies that have been investigated nor the statistical complexities and nuances of the tests. A conclusion reached by Harrington, Fabozzi, and Fogler is that:

> Technical analysis is back—after falling out of favor and taking a battering at the hands of efficient-market advocates. Profits do seem possible, albeit small, through using purely historical data. . . . [T]echnical trading rules, and investors' overreaction seem to hold potential for profit, but the profit is vulnerable to transaction costs. . . .
>
> Should you rely on technical trading rules? Not without careful thought and continued vigilance. Every investor must sort the real from the imagined. Where there is controversy, investors must do their homework (examine whether adequate commissions were considered, whether the risk adjustment was adequate, and so on).[22]

---

[18]Werner DeBondt and Richard Thaler, "Does the Market Overreact?" *Journal of Finance* (July 1985), pp. 793–805.

[19]Peter L. Bernstein, "Does the Market Overreact? Discussion," *Journal of Finance* (July 1985), pp. 806–808.

[20]Keith C. Brown and W. V. Harlow, "Market Overreaction: Magnitude and Intensity," *Journal of Portfolio Management* (Winter 1988), p. 7.

[21]DeBondt and Thaler, op. cit.; Werner DeBondt and Richard Thaler, "Further Evidence on Investor Overreaction and Stock Market Seasonality," *Journal of Finance* (July 1987), pp. 557–581; John Howe, "Evidence of Stock Market Overreaction," *Financial Analysts Journal* (July–August 1986), pp. 74–77, and Brown and Harlow, op. cit., pp. 6–13.

[22]Harrington, Fabozzi, and Fogler, op. cit., pp. 125–126.

TABLE 13-3	
MARKET ANOMALIES: POCKETS OF INEFFICIENCY	
Small-firm effect	Small-capitalization firms have outperformed the market as a whole
Low price-earnings-ratio effect	Stocks with a low P/E ratio have outperformed those with a high P/E ratio
Neglected-firm effect	Firms followed by fewer analysts outperformed those followed by many
Calendar effect	Stocks perform better at certain times: January effect, month-of-the-year effect, day-of-the-week effect, holiday effect

Tests of Semistrong-Form Pricing Efficiency

Evidence on semistrong pricing efficiency is mixed. There are studies suggesting that investors who select stocks on the basis of fundamental security analysis (i.e., analyzing financial statements, the quality of management, and the economic environment of a company) will not outperform the market. The reason is simply that there are many analysts undertaking basically the same sort of analysis, with the same publicly available data, so that the price of the stock reflects all the relevant factors that determine value.

While some studies question the usefulness of fundamental security analysis, a good number of other studies suggest that there are pockets of pricing inefficiency in the stock market. That is, there are some investment strategies that have historically produced statistically significant positive abnormal returns. These market anomalies are referred to as the *small-firm effect*, the *low-price-earnings-ratio effect*, the *neglected-firm effect*, and various *calendar effects,* and are summarized in Table 13-3.

The **small-firm effect** emerges in several studies that have shown that portfolios of small firms (in terms of total market capitalization) have outperformed the stock market (consisting of both large and small firms).[23] Because of these findings, there has been increased interest in stock market indicators that monitor small-capitalization firms.

The **low price-earnings-ratio effect** is based on studies showing that portfolios consisting of stocks with a low price-earnings ratio have outperformed portfolios consisting of stocks with a high price-earnings ratio.[24] However, another study finds that, after adjusting for transactions costs necessary to rebalance a portfolio as prices and earnings change over time, the superior performance of portfolios of low-price-earnings-ratio stocks no longer holds.[25] An explanation for the presumably superior performance is that stocks trade at low price-earnings ratios because they are temporarily out of favor with

---

[23]Marc R. Reinganum, "Misspecification of Capital Asset Pricing: Empirical Anomalies Based on Earnings Yields and Market Values," *Journal of Financial Economics* (March 1981), pp. 19–46; and Rolf W. Banz, "The Relationship between Return and Market Value of Stocks," *Journal of Financial Economics* (March 1981), pp. 103–126.

[24]Sanjoy Basu, "Investment Performance of Common Stocks in Relation to Their Price-Earnings Ratios: A Test of the Efficient Market Hypothesis," *Journal of Finance* (June 1977), pp. 663–682.

[25]Haim Levy and Zvi Lerman, "Testing P/E Ratio Filters with Stochastic Dominance," *Journal of Portfolio Management* (Winter 1985), pp. 31–40.

market participants. As fads do change, companies not currently in vogue will rebound at some indeterminate time in the future.[26]

Not all firms receive the same degree of attention from security analysts, and one school of thought is that firms that are neglected by security analysts will outperform firms that are the subject of considerable attention. One study has found that an investment strategy based on changes in the level of attention devoted by security analysts to different stocks may lead to positive abnormal returns.[27] This market anomaly is referred to as the **neglected-firm effect**.

While some empirical work focuses on selected firms according to some criterion such as market capitalization, price-earnings ratio, or degree of analysts' attention, the **calendar effect** looks at the best time to implement strategies. Examples of anomalies are the January effect, month-of-the-year effect, day-of-the-week effect, and holiday effect. It seems from the empirical evidence that there are times when the implementation of a strategy will, on average, provide a superior performance relative to other calendar time periods.

One of the difficulties with all these pricing-efficiency studies is that the factors that are believed to give rise to market anomalies are interrelated. For example, small firms may be those that are not given much attention by security analysts and that trade at a low price-earnings ratio. Current research has attempted to disentangle these effects.[28]

Aside from the various effects reviewed above, some researchers[29] claim that the pricing of equities is not rational because the variability of stock prices, particularly that of broad indexes, is too large to be consistent with rational prices. Other researchers have called attention to periods of irrational overvaluation or undervaluation of the market as a whole. In particular, Modigliani and Cohn provide some evidence that the stock market was undervalued during the 1970s because of the markets' inability to value equity correctly in the presence of significant inflation.[30]

Testing of Strong-Form Pricing Efficiency

Empirical tests of strong-form pricing efficiency fall into two groups: (1) studies of the performance of professional money managers and (2) studies of the activities of "insiders" (individuals who are either company directors, major officers, or major stockholders).

Studying the performance of professional money managers to test the strong form of pricing efficiency has been based on the belief that profes-

---

[26]David Dreman, *Contrarian Investment Strategy: The Psychology of Stock Market Success* (New York: Random House, 1979).

[27]Avner Arbel and Paul Strebel, "Pay Attention to Neglected Firms," *Journal of Portfolio Management* (Winter 1983), pp. 37–42.

[28]See Bruce I. Jacobs and Kenneth N. Levy, "Stock Market Complexity and Investment Opportunity," in Frank J. Fabozzi (ed.), *Managing Institutional Assets* (New York: Harper & Row Publishers, 1990), pp. 119–142.

[29]Robert J. Shiller, "Do Stock Prices Move Too Much to Be Justified by Subsequent Changes in Dividends?" *American Economic Review*, 71 (1981), pp. 421–435, and "The Probability of Gross Violations of a Present Value Variance Inequality," *Journal of Political Economy*, 96 (1988), pp. 1089–1092.

[30]Franco Modigliani and Richard A. Cohn, "Inflation, Rational Valuation and the Market," *Financial Analysts Journal* (March–April 1979), pp. 24–44.

sional managers have access to better information than the general public. Whether this is true is moot, because the empirical evidence suggests professional managers have not been able to outperform the market consistently. In contrast, evidence based on the activities of insiders has generally revealed that insiders consistently outperform the stock market.[31] Consequently, strong-form pricing efficiency—where the relevant information set includes non-public information—is not supported with respect to insider trading activity.

Implications for Investing in Common Stock

Common stock investment strategies can be classified into active strategies and passive strategies. Active strategies are those that attempt to outperform the market by one or more of the following: timing the selection of transactions, such as in the case of technical analysis; identifying undervalued or overvalued stocks using fundamental security analysis; or selecting stocks according to one of the market anomalies. Obviously, the decision to pursue an active strategy must be based on the belief that there is some type of gain from such costly efforts; for there to be a gain, pricing inefficiencies must exist. The particular strategy chosen depends on why the investor believes this is the case.

If investors believe that the market is efficient with respect to pricing stocks, then they should accept the implication that attempts to outperform the market cannot be successful systematically, except by luck. This does not mean that investors should shun the stock market, but rather that they should pursue a passive strategy, which is one that does not attempt to outperform the market. Is there an optimal investment strategy for someone who holds this belief in the pricing efficiency of the stock market? Indeed there is. Its theoretical basis is modern portfolio theory and capital market theory that we discussed in Chapters 4, 5, and 6. According to modern portfolio theory, the "market" portfolio offers the highest level of return per unit of risk in a market that is price-efficient. A portfolio of financial assets with characteristics similar to those of a portfolio consisting of the entire market (i.e., the market portfolio) will capture the pricing efficiency of the market.

But how can such a passive strategy be implemented? More specifically, what is meant by a "market portfolio," and how should that portfolio be constructed? In theory, the market portfolio consists of all financial assets, not just common stock. The reason is that investors compare all investment opportunities, not just stock, when committing their capital. Thus, the principles of investing we accept are based on capital market theory, not stock market theory. When the theory has been followed by those investing in the stock market, the market portfolio has been defined as consisting of a large universe of common stocks. How much of each common stock should be purchased when constructing the market portfolio? The theory states that the chosen portfolio should be an appropriate fraction of the market portfolio; hence the weighting of each stock in the market portfolio should be based on its relative market capitalization. Thus, if the aggregate market capitalization of all stocks included in the market portfolio is T and the market capitaliza-

---

[31]Researchers obtain information about the activities of insiders from reports they are required to file with the SEC. These reports are available to the public six weeks after filing.

tion of one of these stocks is A, then the fraction of this stock that should be held in the market portfolio is A/T.

The passive strategy that we have just described is called **indexing.** This strategy is the subject of Chapter 14. Because pension fund sponsors increasingly believe that money managers have been unable to outperform the stock market, the amount of funds managed using an indexing strategy has increased since the 1980s. However, index funds are still a relatively small fraction of institutional stock investments.

TRANSACTIONS COSTS[32]

Money managers are evaluated against various benchmarks, and that evaluation must take related costs into account. In an investment era where 100 basis points can make a difference, the careful analysis and management of transactions costs can yield tremendous dividends. In order to effectively manage transactions costs, money managers need to understand the different components of these costs and the various ways they can be measured. (See Box 13.)

Investment costs include research costs and transactions costs. Research costs include the cost of analysts, computers, and programmers to develop valuation models and the costs to purchase data and maintain data bases. Transactions costs consist of *commissions*, *fees*, *execution costs*, and *opportunity costs*, which can be grouped as either fixed or variable components.

Fixed Transactions Costs

The fixed components of transactions costs are easily measurable and are represented by commissions charged by brokers, taxes, and fees. The fixed components are relatively small. **Commissions** are the monies paid to brokers to execute trades. Since May 1975, commissions have been fully negotiable. According to a survey by Greenwich Associates, average commissions in cents per share have declined from $0.136 in 1977 to $0.087 in 1989.[33] Included in the category of **fees** are custodial fees and transfer fees. **Custodial fees** are the fees charged by an institution that holds securities in safekeeping for an investor. A **transfer fee** is a fee paid by the investor to transfer ownership of a stock.

Variable Transactions Costs

While commissions and fees are easily measurable, variable transactions costs—execution costs and opportunity costs—are not. **Execution costs** represent the difference between the execution price of a security and the price that would have existed in the absence of a trade. Since these two conditions cannot exist simultaneously, true transactions costs are inherently not observable. Nevertheless, there are ways to measure costs that provide useful information for the money manager. No single measure tells the whole story, and it is necessary to provide a set of measurement benchmarks that capture

---

[32]The discussion in this section draws from Bruce M. Collins and Frank J. Fabozzi, "A Methodology for Measuring Transactions Costs," *Financial Analysts Journal* (March–April 1991), pp. 27–36.

[33]"Getting Down to Business," Greenwich Associates, Greenwich, CT, 1990.

BOX 13

MONITORING TRADING COSTS

This excerpt is from a speech given by Greta E. Marshall, former Investment Manager for the California Public Employees; Retirement System, at a conference held in New York City on December 3, 1987.

My interest in trading costs began on May Day, 1975, when negotiated commissions first arrived. It had been a slow day at Deere & Co. I decided to see what commission rate external managers were able to get from the brokers. Looking through the trades, I saw a commission on an over-the-counter stock. I asked the external manager on this account why they were paying commissions on over-the-counter stocks. He told me that they were doing it through their own brokerage house to protect our identity. I replied that I did not care whether anybody knew that Deere & Co. was buying this stock; I would prefer not to pay commissions on over-the-counter trades that could go direct. Soon there was a subpoena from the SEC, which was investigating this practice. We got the subpoena because we were the only plan sponsor in the country who had ever questioned the practice of charging commissions on over-the-counter trades, which was not illegal if the broker was not the market maker in that particular stock.

The second anecdote is amusing for a different reason. It was another slow day at Deere & Co., and I was watching the INSTINET machine to see how we were trading. The market was gradually going down. I saw one stock trade down that I knew we were planning to buy. I thought that was nice; we would get it at a lower price. Our orders to the broker at that point were last sale or better— lower on the buy and higher on the sell. All of a sudden I saw 100 shares go up an eighth, and then I saw 12,700 shares last sale. That was exactly what we were buying, and so it got my attention.

I called the broker at this point, who said that they could not possibly have done anything like that. I furnished the documentation to the broker. The broker looked at all the trades they had done for our account and discovered that this had happened on 68 of the 86 trades they had done for us. The broker said that another office was handling the trades. The other office was doing what I call front running. They were buying up shares, running 100 shares through up an eighth, and then executing our trade at last sale. At that time, we were paying a commission of $0.0275 per share; but clearly up an eight meant that we were paying more like $0.14 per share.

The broker offered to do trades for us at no commission until we were paid back what they had overcharged us— which turned out to be only about $50,000. That would have meant a lot of trades with that particular broker, however, and I was not interested in continuing to trade with them, so I asked for a check. That was my first mistake. I took the check and asked our accountants how I should account for the $50,000 because it did not come in through normal channels. They said to account for it as miscellaneous income. But then our outside auditors got involved. They said that I had to back out all the trades and run them through at the right price. I refused. I would have required that of the broker because I was mad at him, but I could not do it to the custodian. Also, I did not want to do it because of the potential for errors getting into the system. I ended up before the vice president because the auditor insisted on writing this up in a management report. The auditors wanted a procedure in place that would track every trade to see whether this was happening to us on other trades. They decided, however, that it was more important for me not to forget to catch activity like this, so they removed it from the auditor's report, and I was back in business again.

When I started at CALPERS, I wanted to know what was going on in the trading area, and what kind of executions we were getting. Because it was a large fund, I did not know whether executions should be worse or better than what we had been getting at Deere & Co. Without telling our brokers, we started monitoring their trades. The first results showed that we had about equal amounts of what we defined as very good and very bad trades. These were the outliers. Outliers were identified by the admittedly crude methodology of comparing prices to closing prices on the previous day and on the next day; if we bought below the prior day's close and the next day's close, then that was a good buy; if we sold above the prior day's close and the next day's close, then it was a good sell. During the first period we had equal amounts of good and bad trades. There was no consistency among the brokers with good trades: These trades were spread over all the brokers with whom we did business. One broker had 50 percent of the bad trades, however. I mentioned to the brokers that we were investigating this, and that no one was looking especially good. I also had a conversation with the broker that 50 percent of the bad trades. In the second period, the ratio of good trades to bad trades was 10:1.

I maintain that it is possible to get good execution, but you have to watch the brokers. They have to know that you are monitoring what they are doing.

Source: Greta E. Marshall, "Execution Costs: The Plan Sponsor's View," in Katrina F. Sherrerd (ed.), *Trading Strategies and Execution Costs*, published by the Institute of Chartered Financial Analysts in 1988, p. 32.

Question for Box 13

1. Discuss three approaches that can be used to measure the market impact of trades.

the entire transactions process. Further complicating the measurement problem is the need to separate the impact of other investors and the structure of the market mechanism.

Execution costs can be further divided into *market* or *price impact* and *market timing* considerations. **Market impact costs** are the result of the bid-ask spread and a dealer's price concession. The price concession arises because of the risk the dealer takes that the investor's trade is possibly motivated by information that the investor has but the dealer does not. (Such trades are referred to as *information-motivated trades*.) **Market timing costs** are those that arise from price movement of the stock during the time of the transaction which is attributed to other activity in the stock.

Opportunity costs are defined as the difference in the performance of an actual investment and a desired investment adjusted for fixed costs and execution costs. The performance differential is a consequence of not being able to implement all desired trades.

The components of transactions costs are summarized below:

Transactions costs = fixed costs + variable costs

Fixed costs = commissions + fees + taxes

Variable costs = execution costs + opportunity costs

Execution costs = market impact costs + market timing costs

Opportunity costs = desired returns − actual returns − execution costs − fixed costs

Execution Costs   Execution costs arise out of the demand for immediate execution through both the demand for liquidity and the trading activity on the trade date. Execution costs may vary according to the investment style and the trading demands of the investor.

There is a distinction between information-motivated trades and informationless trades.[34] **Information-motivated trades** occur when an investor believes he or she possesses pertinent information not currently reflected in the stock's price. This style of trading tends to increase market impact because it emphasizes the speed of execution. It can involve the sale of one stock in favor of another. **Informationless trades** are the result of either a reallocation of wealth or an implementation of an investment strategy that only utilizes existing information.

An example of informationless trades is a pension fund's decision to invest cash in the stock market. Two other examples of informationless trades include portfolio rebalances and the investment of new money. Thus, in the case of informationless trades, the demand for liquidity alone should not lead the market maker to demand significant price concessions associated with new information. If the market maker believes a desired trade is driven by information, however, he or she will increase the bid-ask spread to provide some protection.

The problem with measuring execution costs is that the true measure, which is the difference between the price of the stock in the absence of a

---

[34]See L. J. Cuneo and W. H. Wagner, "Reducing the Cost of Stock Trading," *Financial Analyst Journal* (November–December 1975), pp. 835–843, for a further exposition of the distinction between these two classes of trades and the implications for reducing costs.

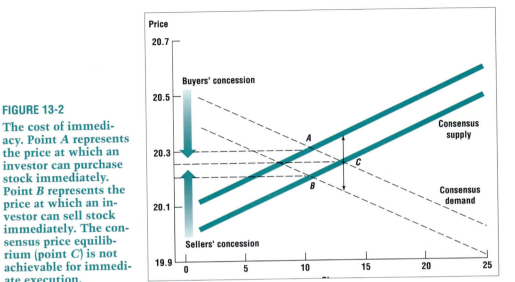

FIGURE 13-2

The cost of immediacy. Point *A* represents the price at which an investor can purchase stock immediately. Point *B* represents the price at which an investor can sell stock immediately. The consensus price equilibrium (point *C*) is not achievable for immediate execution.

money manager's trade and the execution price, is not observable. Furthermore, the execution prices are dependent on supply and demand conditions at the margin. Thus, the execution price may be influenced by competitive traders who demand immediate execution or by other investors with similar motives for trading. This means that the execution price realized by an investor is the consequence of the structure of the market mechanism, the demand for liquidity by the marginal investor, and the competitive forces of investors with similar motivations for trading.

This process is represented in Figure 13-2, where the consensus price equilibrium (point *C*) is not achievable for immediate execution.[35] The price concession necessary for immediate execution is represented by the shift in the demand and supply curves by investors who are willing to buy or sell stock immediately. In the figure, point *A* represents the price at which an investor can purchase stock immediately; it is the intersection of the supply curve of investors who are prepared to sell stock immediately and the consensus demand curve. Conversely, point *B* represents the price at which an investor can sell stock immediately.

The illustration is a static representation of the execution process. In actual markets there is a set of curves representing various levels of liquidity and price concessions. For more liquid securities the size of the shift in the demand and supply curves is smaller. Moreover, the supply and demand process for any security is a dynamic one, suggesting that as the demand for immediate execution falls, the supply and demand curves will collapse on the equilibrium price. For example, the demand for immediate execution is low for investors with low opportunity costs.

---

[35]This type of figure first appeared in H. Demsetz, "The Cost of Transacting," *Quarterly Journal of Economics* (February 1968), pp. 57–60.

Opportunity Costs   The cost of not transacting represents an opportunity cost.[36] Opportunity costs may arise when a desired trade fails to be executed. This component of costs represents the difference in performance between a money manager's desired investment and his or her actual investment after adjusting for execution costs and commissions. Opportunity costs have been characterized as the hidden cost of trading, and it has been suggested that the shortfall in the performance of many actively managed portfolios is the consequence of failing to execute all desired trades.[37]

The measurement of opportunity costs is subject to the same problems as the measurement of execution costs. The true measure of opportunity cost is derived from knowing what the performance of a stock would have been if all desired trades were executed across an investment horizon at the desired time. Since these are the desired trades that a money manager could not execute, they are inherently not observable. Nevertheless, by monitoring the performance of the desired investment as if all trades were executed, a money manager can estimate opportunity costs.

Trade-Offs

The broadest definition of investment costs is the performance difference between expected and actual outcomes. The performance expectations of a strategy can be represented by an investment benchmark which reflects the desired investment. Investment costs are revealed when there is a significant performance difference between the benchmark and the actual investment over a measurement period. The performance differential is then attributable to the cost of trading the strategy, which we refer to as execution costs, or the inability to implement the desired strategy as represented by the benchmark, which we refer to as opportunity cost. The performance shortfall, therefore, is a combination of commissions, execution costs, and opportunity costs.

All three sources of costs have to be considered in any cost management program. The reduction of one cost may be at the expense of another. For example, the dramatic decline in commission rates has altered the risk/reward characteristics for the upstairs market makers which we described in Chapter 3. The consequence may be an increase in bid-ask spreads and execution costs, or in opportunity costs because of increased search costs associated with finding the other side of the trade. A reduction in execution costs can be achieved by reducing market impact. One way to reduce execution costs is to delay trading until the price is right; however, this process may lead to missed investment opportunities.

The trade-off between execution costs and opportunity costs is illustrated in Figure 13-3. The vertical axis represents unit costs, where the units could

---

[36]See André F. Perold, "The Implementation Shortfall: Paper versus Reality," *Journal of Portfolio Management* (April 1988), pp. 4–9, for an excellent discussion of opportunity costs, presented within the context of costs defined as the implementation shortfall of an investment strategy.

[37]See L. J. Treynor, "What Does It Take to Win the Trading Game?" *Financial Analyst Journal* (January–February 1981), pp. 55–60, and Perold, op. cit., for a discussion of the consequences of high opportunity costs.

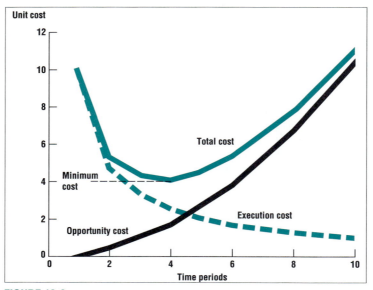

FIGURE 13-3

Cost trade-offs: execution versus opportunity costs.

be cents per share, basis points, or dollars. The horizontal axis represents time periods, which could be minutes, hours, days, etc. The downward-sloping line represents execution costs. As the line indicates, execution costs are positively related to the immediacy of execution. That means that execution costs go down as immediacy decreases, that is, as time increases. The upward-sloping line represents opportunity costs. Opportunity costs are positively related to the delay in execution. The parabola represents total costs and suggests that total costs can be minimized by appropriately trading off execution costs and opportunity costs.

Although the figure represents the general shape of execution and opportunity cost functions, the actual shapes of the curves differ across management styles. Table 13-4 is a sample of approaches to investment management and related cost structures. For example, in later chapters we will see several active investment strategies or investment styles. Value managers and growth managers have longer investment horizons, lower demand for immediate execution, and a flatter opportunity cost curve than managers that employ an earnings surprise model. Consequently, value or growth-oriented managers need not pay a high immediacy cost. As a general rule, if the slope of a money manager's opportunity cost curve is less than the slope of his or her execution cost curve, it is better to wait to find a natural transactor on the other side of the trade. Investment strategies that meet this description can be used to offset the cost of liquidity.

Measuring Transactions Costs

The measurement of transactions costs is critical for money managers in formulating investment strategies and for clients in assessing the performance of money managers. There are three dimensions to measuring transactions costs: commissions for a particular stock or trading style, determination

TABLE 13-4				
MANAGEMENT STYLE VERSUS COSTS				
Management Style	Trading Motivation	Liquidity Demands	Execution Cost	Opportunity Cost
Value	Value	Low	Low	Low
Growth	Value	Low	Low	Low
Earnings surprise	Information	High	High	High
Index fund				
Large cap*	Passive	Variable	Variable	High
Small cap	Passive	High	High	High

*The costs associated with some investment strategies that utilize futures can be low despite high opportunity costs.

of a benchmark for execution costs and opportunity costs, and separation of the influence of the trade from other factors.

Commission rates, taxes, and fees are readily observable and fixed for a transaction. The commission rates for stocks are 6 to 12 basis points. Nonetheless, this component of costs is negotiated on a pretrade basis and is known and measurable.

The measurement of other components of transactions costs, particularly the market impact component, has no unique solution. Market impact arises when a trade induces a temporary price movement. This is the result of either immediate liquidity demands or the actions of a market maker who perceives that an investor's trade contains useful information. There are alternative approaches to measuring execution costs that capture useful information about the transaction process. In general, the cost of transacting is the difference between the execution price and a fair market benchmark. That is,

Costs = execution price − fair market price

The fair price of the security is the price that would have prevailed had a money manager's trade not taken place. However, since that price is not observable, the fair price must be estimated or inferred. There are several working definitions of a fair price benchmark among practitioners. The choice of a benchmark may involve choosing either a price that represents the fair value of a stock in the absence of the money manager from the market or a price that represents the consequence of the money manager's presence in the market. We present three different approaches to measuring market impact, which we refer to as *pretrade measures, posttrade measures,* and *across-day* or *average measures.*

Pretrade benchmarks are prices occurring before or at the decision to trade, while **posttrade benchmarks** are prices occurring after the decision to trade. **Average (across-day) measures** use the average or representative price of a large number of trades. Essentially, all three approaches are attempts to measure the fair value of a stock at a point in time. Transactions costs emerge when the execution price deviates from the fair price. To the extent that any price represents an unbiased estimate of a fair price, the concept is valid. It does, however, assume that markets are efficient.

Pretrade Benchmarks   Pretrade measures use a price that existed prior to the trade as a benchmark.[38] This price may be the previous night's close or the price at which the stock last traded. The premise behind pretrade benchmarks is that the only way of knowing the impact of a money manager's trade on the price of the stock is by comparing it with conditions prior to his or her arrival in the marketplace. One way to accomplish this is by comparing the execution price with the price at which the stock last traded. Alternatively, when a time lag to last sale exists, the midpoint of the bid-ask can be used. In either case, the argument follows that market conditions before the time of execution represent the reference point for evaluating any price movement induced by a money manager's entrance into the marketplace. A positive difference between the execution price and the benchmark is regarded as a cost.

Critics of pretrade benchmarks argue that using prior prices as a benchmark violates a fundamental requirement for a good measure of execution costs: the requirement that the benchmark be independent of the trading decision. In other words, the trader should not be able to game the trade. Gaming in this context refers to structuring a trade in such a way that it satisfies or accommodates a particular cost measure. That is, gaming is rigging the apparent costs *by the person accountable for these costs* so that the manager can show low costs by rigging the measurement criteria—and the client is none the wiser. A simple example of gaming is to execute easy trades and not difficult trades.

Posttrade Benchmarks   A second approach to measuring market impact costs is using posttrade benchmarks.[39] The premise underlying the use of a posttrade benchmark is that it avoids the problem of gaming because it is independent of the trading decision. One requirement, however, is a benchmark that lies outside the influence of the trade. Thus, the measurement interval is another parameter to consider. As is the case with pretrade benchmarks, there are several choices for posttrade benchmarks. These include the next trade immediately after a trade, the closing price on the trade date, or any price subsequent to the time of execution. A price reversal is indicative of positive execution costs. A price reversal is also indicative of liquidity-driven trades versus information-motivated trades where the price does not reverse.

Average Measures   Another approach to establishing a fair price benchmark is to establish a representative price for the trade date. Two such measures

[38]See Perold, op. cit., and Gary Beebower, "Evaluating Transaction Costs," Chap. 11 in Wayne H. Wagner (ed.), *The Complete Guide to Securities Transactions* (New York: John Wiley & Sons, 1989), for a discussion of pretrade measures.

[39] For a discussion of posttrade measures of market impact, see Beebower, op. cit., and G. Beebower and W. Priest, "The Tricks of the Trade," *Journal of Portfolio Management* (Winter 1980), pp. 36–42.

TABLE 13-5			
COST MEASUREMENT TECHNIQUES			
Method	**Benchmarks**	**Advantages**	**Disadvantages**
Pretrade	Last sale Previous close	Captures current market: 1/2 bid-ask spread	May affect trading decision
Posttrade	Next sale Trade date close N-day close	Avoids gaming	Neglects pretrade information that is based on market effects
Intraday	Avg. high/low Weighted average	Measures daily market timing	Subject to gaming
Factor-adjusted	Market Industry	Captures residual effects	Difficult to measure

are the average of the high and low and the trade-weighted average price.[40] The weakness of both measures as benchmarks for measuring execution costs is that they are subject to gaming. For example, the trade-weighted average price is gamed by spreading a trade out across the trading day — periodically transacting. A major proportion of the desired trade might be transacted around the opening, closing, and large-block trades. The trader participates but does not originate a trade. The trading style is reactive and not proactive. Thus, the use of this benchmark is essentially a promise by the trader to be mediocre and may not produce the best results. These averages are better indicators of the market timing portion of costs rather than execution costs. However, proponents argue that average cost benchmarks are better measures than market impact benchmarks because the former are more representative of an equilibrium price.[41]

Other Factors   Other factors have been used to adjust costs. The movement of prices can be induced by general market movements.[42] For example, suppose several money managers would like to increase their exposure to the stock market. Suppose further that they all enter orders to buy certain stocks at the same time. As a result of these orders, the price may move between the time the order is entered and the time it is executed. Consequently, the cost of execution should be adjusted for changes in the market or other factors as-

---

[40]See S. Berkowitz and D. E. Logue, "Study of the Investment Performance of ERISA Plans," U.S. Dept. of Labor, July 1986, and S. Berkowitz, D. E. Logue, and E. A. Noser, "The Total Cost of Transactions on the N.Y.S.E.," *Journal of Finance*, 43 (March 1988), pp. 97–112, for a discussion of these measures.

[41]Peter Bernstein, consulting editor of the *Journal of Portfolio Management*, argues that the only reliable benchmarks are "representative price" benchmarks, which are essentially some form of average price, because they are more likely to represent an equilibrium price. Alternative benchmarks might incorporate market impact from competitive trades other than the one being evaluated.

[42]See Kathleen A. Condon, "Measuring Equity Transactions Costs," *Financial Analyst Journal* (September 1981), pp. 57–60, for a specification of this type of adjustment. See Stephen Bodurtha and T. Quinn, "Does Patient Trading Really Pay?" *Financial Analyst Journal* (April–May 1990), pp. 35–42, for an example of how to implement an adjustment for market changes.

sumed to affect prices. The premise underlying this approach is to specify an unbiased estimate of a fair price in the money manager's absence from the market. The measure captures the residual effects of a money manager's trade on the movement in price by adjusting the benchmark. A positive residual is indicative of a cost. The expression below is an example of a cost estimator using this approach.

$$\text{Cost} = \text{execution price} - \text{benchmark} - \text{market factor adjustment}$$

Table 13-5 summarizes the different approaches to measuring execution costs along with advantages and disadvantages.

■ SUMMARY

A market is price-efficient if at all times prices fully reflect all available information that is relevant to the valuation of securities. In such a market, strategies pursued to outperform a broad-based stock market index will not consistently produce superior returns after adjusting for risk and transactions costs. Superior performance is measured in terms of abnormal returns, which is the difference between expected returns and actual returns. There are three forms of pricing efficiency according to what is hypothesized to be the relevant information set: (1) weak form, (2) semistrong form, and (3) strong form.

While the majority of studies accept the weak form, some recent empirical evidence concerning multirule technical trading strategies and identification of market overreaction makes the total acceptance of weak-form efficiency premature. The evidence on the semistrong form is mixed, as pockets of inefficiency have been observed. These market anomalies include the small-firm effect, the low-price-earnings-ratio effect, the neglected-firm effect, and various calendar effects. Empirical tests of strong-form pricing efficiency reveal two sets of results: (1) Studies of the performance of professional money managers suggest that they have not out-performed the market, and (2) analysis of the activity of insiders generally finds that they consistently outperform the market.

Active strategies are pursued by investors who believe that markets are mispriced sufficiently to be able to capitalize on strategies that are designed to exploit the perceived inefficiency. The optimal strategy to pursue when the stock market is perceived to be price-efficient is indexing, because it allows the investor to capture the efficiency of the market.

In recent years, greater emphasis has been placed on the measurement and analysis of transactions costs. There are four general components to transactions costs: commissions, fees, execution costs, and opportunity costs. Execution costs represent the difference between the execution price of a stock and the price that would have existed in the absence of the trade, and arise out of the demand for immediate execution through both the demand for liquidity and the trading activity on the trade date. Opportunity costs arise when a desired trade fails to be executed. While commissions are fixed and measurable over a measurement period, there is no unique method to measure execution costs or opportunity costs.

■ KEY TERMS

average (across-day) measures
calendar effect
chartists
commissions
custodial fees
execution costs
fees

filter
indexing
information-motivated trades
informationless trades
low price-earnings-ratio effect
market impact costs
market timing costs

multirule system
neglected-firm effect
operationally efficient market
opportunity costs
overreaction hypothesis
posttrade benchmarks
pretrade benchmarks

price momentum
price persistence
price-volume relationship
pricing efficiency

relative strength
semistrong efficiency
simple moving average
small-firm effect

strong efficiency
technical analysts
transfer fees
weak efficiency

■ QUESTIONS

1. You overheard two investors, Mr. Stevens and Ms. Rose, talking about the efficiency of the stock market. Mr. Stevens said, "The stock market is highly efficient. I can execute trades at a very low cost." Ms. Rose stated, "I don't think that the market is efficient at all since there are investors who can outperform the market." Are Mr. Stevens and Ms. Rose referring to the same concept when they refer to the efficiency of the stock market?

2. This quotation is from an interview with William Donaldson, chairman of the New York Stock Exchange, that appeared in *The New York Times* of January 30, 1990:

   Sure it's possible to beat the market. . . . By investing for the long term with an individual selection of stocks, it's quite possible to beat the market.

   My concern is that by simply buying an index, investors are not channeling their capital into the best investments, and that has long-term negative implications for the cost of capital in this country. The risk of indexing and treating all companies the same is to give in to a very mediocre goal.

   a. What is meant by "beat the market"?
   b. What can you infer about Donaldson's views on pricing efficiency from his comment?
   c. Assuming Donaldson is correct, why do you think so few professional stock pickers have been able to beat the market?

3. The November 1985 prospectus of the Merrill Lynch Phoenix Fund, Inc., a mutual fund, stated the following investment objective:

   . . . based upon the belief that the pricing mechanism of the securities markets lacks perfect efficiency so that prices of securities of troubled issuers are often depressed to a greater extent than warranted by the condition of the issuer and that, while investment in such securities involves a high degree of risk, such investments offer the opportunity for significant capital gains.

   a. What does this strategy assume about the pricing efficiency of the stock market?
   b. Explain how this fund seems to capitalize on this theory.

4. In every issue of *The Wall Street Journal*, information appears on the performance (measured in terms of total return) for mutual funds with the same stated objective. The top 15 performers and the bottom 10 performers are shown. This information is called the "Mutual Fund Scorecard." In the Monday, February 4, 1991, issue, the following ranking was reported for several of the top performers based on the 12-month period ending January 31, 1991, for mutual funds with capital appreciation as their objective:

Fund	12-Month Total Return
Seligman Capital	20.77%
M-S Mainstay: Cap. Appre.	20.11%
Janus Twenty Fund	20.09%
Piper Jaffray: Sector	19.64%
ABT Inv: Emerging Growth	19.13%

   a. On the basis of the figures reported above, can you determine if these mutual funds beat the market?
   b. Should the total return figures reported above be used to provide a relative performance ranking?

5. What are some of the market anomalies that challenge the view that the market is price-efficient in the semistrong form?

6. "All the empirical evidence suggests that the market is efficient in regard to the weak form." Do you agree with this statement?

7. a. Explain why an abnormal return is used rather than an actual return in studies of the efficiency of the stock market.
   b. Describe how an abnormal return is calculated.
   c. What is the underlying assumption in using an abnormal return to determine if the market is price-efficient?

8. The following statements are taken from Greta E. Marshall's article "Execution Costs: The Plan Sponsor's View," which appears in *Trading Strategies and Execution Costs*, published by The

Institute of Chartered Financial Analysts in 1988. (The publication is the product of a conference held in New York City on December 3, 1987):

a. "There are three components of trading costs. First there are direct costs which may be measured—commissions. Second, there are indirect—or market impact—costs. Finally, there are the undefined costs of not trading." What are market impact costs, and what do you think the "undefined costs of not trading" represent?

b. "Market impact, unlike broker commissions, is difficult to identify and measure." Why is market impact cost difficult to measure?

9. a. What is meant by an information-motivated trade?

b. Give an example of an information-motivated trade.

10. a. What is meant by an informationless trade?

b. Give an example of an informationless trade.

11. Explain the difficulties of measuring execution costs.

12. What are the various approaches to measuring market impact cost?

13. Explain the difficulties of measuring opportunity costs.

14. What is the trade-off among the various types of transactions costs?

CHAPTER 14
EQUITY INDEXING*

LEARNING OBJECTIVES

After reading this chapter you will be able to:

- explain the two types of passive strategies: buy-and-hold and indexing.
- describe what is meant by equity indexing and a replicating portfolio.
- explain the theoretical underpinning for the use of equity indexing.
- cite the motivation for equity indexing in the United States and foreign stock markets.
- define what is meant by tracking error.

- explain why tracking error occurs.
- describe the methodologies that can be used to construct a replicating index.
- explain the considerations and describe the methodologies used in constructing an equity-indexed portfolio.
- explain the link between equity indexing and active management strategies.

In the previous chapter we reviewed the empirical evidence on the pricing efficiency of the stock market. Investors who believe that the market is efficient should pursue a passive investment strategy. There are two types of passive strategies. The first is a **buy-and-hold strategy**. This strategy is quite simple: Buy a portfolio of stocks based on some criterion and hold those stocks over some investment horizon. There is no active buying and selling of stocks once the portfolio is created.

The second approach, and the most commonly followed one, is index fund management, popularly referred to as simply **indexing**. With this approach, the money manager does not attempt to identify undervalued or overvalued stock issues based on fundamental security analysis. Nor does the money manager attempt to forecast general movements in the stock market and then structure the portfolio so as to take advantage of those movements. Instead, an indexing strategy involves designing a portfolio to track the total return performance of an index of stocks.

---

*This chapter is coauthored with Dr. Bruce Collins.

Various estimates of the amount of index funds invested in the stock market are reported in the financial press. One widely recognized authority, Robert Kirby, estimates that of the $1.25 trillion to $1.5 trillion of the total institutional investment in the stock market in 1992, about 25% to 30% was indexed.[1] Of the amount indexed, he estimates that about 85% or more was indexed to the S&P 500. As of December 1988, about 55% of the defined benefit assets of the 200 largest pension funds were indexed, with 36% of all index fund investments internally managed.[2] (See also Box 14.) There are currently several mutual funds with the investment objective to create an indexed portfolio to match some benchmark, the most common being the S&P 500.

While indexing may be a passive form of investing, there are still many issues that the money manager must address. In this chapter, we explain how an indexed portfolio is constructed and maintained.

MOTIVATION FOR EQUITY INDEXING

Both theoretical and empirical reasons underlie the increased use of common stock indexing. If a market is sufficiently price-efficient so that superior risk-adjusted return cannot be consistently earned after adjusting for transactions costs, then the appropriate strategy to pursue is a passive strategy. While both buy-and-hold and indexing are passive strategies, there is theoretical justification for indexing. The theoretical underpinning for this strategy is capital market theory, which we described in Chapter 5. According to this theory, in an efficient market the "market portfolio" offers the highest level of return per unit of risk because it captures the efficiency of the market. The theoretical market portfolio is a capitalization-weighted portfolio of all risky assets. As a proxy for the theoretical market portfolio, an index that is representative of the market should be used. With a buy-and-hold strategy, the selected stock may not capture the efficiency of the market.

This, then, is the question: Is the market efficient? As we discussed in Chapter 13, while there is evidence of pockets of pricing inefficiency, there is ample evidence that it is difficult to consistently outperform the stock market on a risk-adjusted basis after accounting for transactions costs. Moreover, a pension sponsor must pay a management fee to an external money manager. From the sponsor's perspective, even if a money manager can outperform the market after adjusting for risk and transactions costs, the amount by which it outperforms may not be greater than the management fee. So, for example, if on a risk-adjusted basis and after transactions costs, the money manager outperforms the index by 20 basis points, but the management fee is greater than 20 basis points, the manager has not added any value. Empirical studies of the performance of mutual funds (which take into consideration management fees) and money managers of pension funds indicate that professional money managers have underperformed popular indexes.

---

[1]Robert G. Kirby, "The Key Word Is 'Passive,'" *Journal of Investing* (Spring 1993), p. 21.
[2]*Pension and Investment Age* (Jan. 23, 1989), p. 14.

BOX 14

STANDING BEHIND INDEX FUNDS

Over the past decade, indexing pension assets has caught on as a low-cost way to guarantee market returns. And its use is still spreading. Nearly half of all the funds in this month's Pensionforum report that they use a domestic equity index fund. This compares with 38 percent who were indexing equity assets in 1988, the last time we ran a forum on this topic. The use of international equity index funds has also risen, to 19 percent of pension plans from 8 percent three years ago. The percentage of funds indexing domestic bonds, however, has remained steady, inching up only one point, to 16 percent.

A quarter of the respondents indicate that two years from now they expect their indexed assets to represent a higher percentage of total assets than they do now, while only some 8 percent forecast a reduction.

The trouble is, the market doesn't always rise. Sometimes it turns ugly, and the index follows suit. Yet, as the survey reveals, very few funds were scared away from indexing by last year's bear market. Only 3 percent of them reversed gears, taking assets out of index funds and putting them into the hands of active managers.

Even if there were to be a sustained bear market, the vast majority of pension funds would stick with their indexing strategies, Only 16 percent of respondents who use indexing say that in the event of a prolonged down market, they would unwind some of their indexed assets and move them into active management.

About a third of the funds that use indexing have indexed more than 20 percent of their total assets. Nearly 40 percent use this investing style for more than 25 percent of equity assets, and almost as many have indexed more than 25 percent of bonds assets. Roughly a fifth of the respondents who have indexed some equity assets have stashed part of them in enhanced funds that aim to outperform the basic index.

Source: "Pensionforum: Standing behind Index Funds," *Institutional Investor* (July 1991), p. 127.

Questions for Box 14

1. What is the difference between indexed funds and actively managed funds?
2. What is the goal of enhanced funds?

Do you currently have a portion of your assets in

A domestic equity index fund?

| Yes | 45.8% |
| No | 54.2 |

An international equity index fund?

| Yes | 19.2% |
| No | 80.8 |

An domestic bond index fund?

| Yes | 16.1% |
| No | 83.9 |

An international bond index fund?

| Yes | 1.0% |
| No | 99.0 |

Because of rounding, some responses do not total 100 percent.

If a portion of your fund is indexed, what percentage of total pension assets is indexed in either equities or fixed income?

1 to 10 percent	39.2%
11 to 20 percent	28.9
21 to 30 percent	15.7
31 to 40 percent	8.4
41 to 50 percent	3.0
More than 50 percent	4.8

If a portion of your fund is indexed, what percentage of its equity assets is currently indexed?

1 to 10 percent	23.4%
11 to 25 percent	36.7
26 to 50 percent	24.1
51 to 75 percent	12.0
More than 75 percent	3.8

If a portion of your fund is indexed, what percentage of its bond assets is currently indexed?

1 to 10 percent	40.0%
11 to 25 percent	21.5
26 to 50 percent	23.1
51 to 75 percent	3.1
More than 75 percent	12.3

If you have indexed some equity assets–domestic or international–are any of those assets in a so-called enhanced or index-plus fund, which aims to outperform its underlying index?

| Yes | 21.3% |
| No | 78.8 |

If you have indexed some bond assets–domestic or international–are any of those assets in an enhanced or indexed fund?

| Yes | 18.9% |
| No | 81.1 |

If you have indexed assets, have you de-indexed any of your assets and moved them to active managers since the stock market peaked in mid-1990?

| Yes | 3.1% |
| No | 96.9 |

In a sustained bear market, would you be likely to de-index some of your assets and move them to active managers?

| Yes | 16.0% |
| No | 84.0 |

Whether or not you currently have indexed assets, where do you expect your indexed assets–equity and fixed income–to stand two years from now, relative to today's level, in terms of percentage of total assets?

Higher	25.3%
About the same	67.0
Lower	7.6

TABLE 14-1

ANNUAL COST COMPARISON OF INDEXING VERSUS ACTIVE MANAGEMENT FOR A $40 MILLION NON-U.S. EQUITY PORTFOLIO

Management fee assumption:

Indexing: 20 basis points

Active management: 50 basis points

Cost	Indexing	Active	Index Savings
Management fees	$ 80,000	$200,000	$120,000
Brokerage commissions	4,000	78,000	73,000
Transfer taxes	5,000	90,000	85,000
Bid-offer spread	14,000	270,000	256,000
Total	$103,000	$638,000	$535,000
Impact on return	0.26%	1.60%	1.34%

Note: Annual turnover assumption is 4% for indexed portfolios and 75% for active portfolios.

Source: Larry L. Martin, "The Evolution of Passive versus Active Equity Management," *Journal of Investing* (Spring 1993), p. 18.

If these findings are accepted, then the costs associated with active equity portfolio management may not purchase an enhanced return on a portfolio. These costs, which we described in the previous section, consist of the research costs associated with uncovering mispriced stocks, the transactions costs of buying and selling stocks to take advantage of mispricing, and the transactions costs incurred in trying to time the market. Consequently, a passive approach to equity portfolio management may be more appropriate for the typical sponsor of a pension fund.

Due to the transactions costs of managing an indexed portfolio, however, indexing has also fallen short of matching the benchmark. In the case of a mutual fund, other operating expenses are associated with managing the fund. For example, the Vanguard Index 500 Fund, a mutual fund whose goal is to match the S&P 500, has an extremely low expense ratio. Due to transactions and administrative costs, during a 10-year period this mutual fund underperformed the S&P 500 by 5%.[3]

The arguments relating to low transactions costs and reduced management fee in favor of indexing in the U.S. common stock market have also been put forth by proponents of indexing in non-U.S. stock markets. This is illustrated in Table 14-1, which shows the estimates of Larry Martin, senior vice president and chief investment officer of State Street Global Advisors, of the annual cost of indexing versus active management.

Even though the preponderance of empirical evidence on the pricing efficiency of non-U.S. markets is lacking, there is evidence that active managers do not consistently outperform indexes in the non-U.S. stock markets in which they invest.[4] This can be seen in Table 14-2, which shows the stock-picking performance of managers in seven non-U.S. equity markets for two

[3]Kirby, "The Key Word Is 'Passive,'" op. cit., p. 22.

TABLE 14-2					
PERFORMANCE BASED ON STOCK PICKING IN SEVEN NON-U.S. EQUITY MARKETS					
	1984–1987			*1988–1991*	
	Median	**Index**	**Difference**	**Median**	**Index**	**Difference**
Japan	35.3%	47.8%	−12.5%	−0.5%	−1.0%	0.5%
U.K.	23.5	28.5	−5.0	10.3	13.9	−3.6
Germany	25.0	22.8	2.2	13.6	15.0	−1.4
Switzerland	26.1	22.1	4.0	9.3	10.3	−1.0
Netherlands	26.8	28.1	−1.3	16.4	15.8	0.6
Singapore	−4.7	−4.1	−0.6	23.7	20.3	3.4
Hong Kong	29.2	35.1	−5.9	22.8	22.6	0.2

Note: Returns are in U.S. dollars for the MSCI National Indexes and the InterSec Median of Active Managers.

Source: InterSec. As published in Larry L. Martin, "The Evolution of Passive versus Active Equity Management," *Journal of Investing* (Spring 1993), p. 19.

periods, 1984–1987 and 1988–1991. For the first period, the median manager underperformed an appropriately selected benchmark for a country in five of the seven non-U.S. equity markets. In the second period, the median manager underperformed in three of the seven non-U.S. equity markets. However, there was no consistency of performance over the two periods. In six of the seven countries, if the managers did well in a country in the first period, they did poorly in the second period.

SELECTING THE BENCHMARK

The first step in index fund management is the selection of the index or benchmark. In Chapter 3 we described the various stock market indexes in the United States. There are broad-based indexes and special indexes, or subindexes. A **pure index fund** is a portfolio that is managed so as to perfectly replicate the performance of the market portfolio. The market portfolio in reality is not known with certainty. Nonetheless, the S&P 500 has served as the consensus representative of the market portfolio. Recently, the Wilshire indexes and the Russell indexes have served as benchmarks for some index funds.

The major problem with the use of the S&P 500 as the benchmark is that the stocks are arbitrarily selected by a committee of the Standard & Poor's Corporation. This committee's selection criterion has nothing to do with the growth and earnings potential of a company. Nor is a selection based on whether an issue is undervalued. Thus, money managers who have a quarrel with indexing do not argue that an active strategy is better than a passive strategy, but rather that the selection of the S&P 500, or any broad-based index, is simply an arbitrary benchmark.

---

[4]See the data reported in Larry L. Martin, "The Evolution of Passive versus Active Equity Management," *Journal of Investing* (Spring 1993), pp. 17–20.

CONSIDERATIONS FOR CONSTRUCTING A REPLICATING PORTFOLIO

Once a money manager has decided to pursue an indexing strategy and has selected a benchmark, the next step is to construct a portfolio that will track the index. We refer to the portfolio constructed to match an index or benchmark as the **replicating portfolio**. The objective in constructing the replicating portfolio is to minimize the difference in performance between it and the benchmark.

Tracking Error

The difference between the performance of the benchmark and the replicating portfolio is referred to as **tracking error**. The performance of a portfolio is measured by its total return (dividends plus change in the market value of the portfolio). Thus tracking error is measured as follows:

Tracking error = total return on replicating portfolio
− total return on benchmark

Tracking error can be positive or negative. A positive tracking error means that the replicating portfolio underperformed the benchmark. A negative tracking error means that the replicating portfolio outperformed the benchmark. In indexing, the strategy is to have a tracking error of zero.

For example, suppose that two money managers pursued an indexing strategy in 1993 and that the index these two managers sought to replicate was the S&P 500. In 1993, the return on the S&P 500 was 9.99%. Further suppose that the actual return for one of the managers in 1993 was 10.08%. Then this manager's tracking error was 9 basis points. If the actual return for the other manager in 1993 was 9.89%, then this manager's tracking error was −10 basis points.

Transactions Costs and Tracking Error

Transactions costs may be particularly high for some of the smaller capitalized issues in the benchmark. In formulating an indexing strategy, the money manager seeks to minimize the costs incurred when trading in some of the smaller-capitalized issues while retaining the replicating portfolio's ability to track the index.

Designing the optimal replicating portfolio may involve holding all the stock issues in the benchmark or a subset of those issues. The number of stock issues in the replicating portfolio affects transactions costs, but holding fewer stock issues than contained in the benchmark generates tracking error. The trade-off between the number of issues in the replicating portfolio and tracking error is shown in Figure 14-1. The returns from a portfolio of 250 stocks, for example, will mistrack the S&P 500 by about 0.6%. Assuming that the probability distribution of the tracking error is normally distributed, this means that a 68% probability exists that the returns from the portfolio will fall within 0.6% of the returns from the S&P 500 on an annualized basis. The trade-off between tracking error and number of issues held must also be considered in terms of transactions costs, which increase with the number of issues traded.

It is next to impossible for a portfolio's returns to exactly match the return on the benchmark. Even if a replicating portfolio is designed to exactly

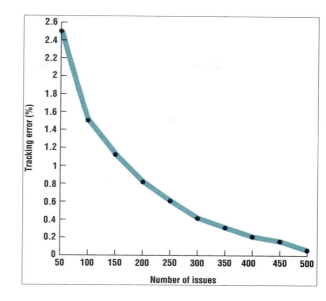

FIGURE 14-1

Trade-off between tracking error and the number of issues held for the S&P 500.

replicate a benchmark by buying all the stock issues, tracking error will result.[5] There are several reasons for this.

First, because odd-lot purchases are cumbersome, replicating portfolios usually comprise round lots, and as such the number of shares of each stock in the portfolio is rounded off to the nearest hundred from the exact number of shares indicated by the computer programs that have been developed to build the optimal replicating portfolio. This rounding may affect the ability of smaller replicating portfolios (less than $25 million) to accurately track the index. Table 14-3 shows the number of round-lot stock issues that can be included in the replicating portfolio for various dollar-sized baskets. The resulting tracking error from rounding can be derived from Figure 14-1 and Table 14-4. As can be seen, a $10 million replicating portfolio will reduce tracking error to an insignificant level. Even at this level, eight stock issues fall below the minimum round-lot threshold.

Second, and more importantly, the maintenance of a replicating portfolio is a dynamic process. Since, as explained in Chapter 3, most indexes are capitalization-weighted, the relative weights of individual issues are constantly changing. In addition, the stocks that compose the index often change. Thus, the cost of continually adjusting the portfolio, as well as timing differences, hinders an indexer's ability to accurately track a benchmark. The former problem is eliminated by holding all stocks in the benchmark. The portfolio is then self-replicating, which simply means the weights are self-adjusting. If, however, the replicating portfolio contains fewer stocks than the benchmark, the weights are not self-adjusting and may require periodic rebalancing.

Benchmark Construction and the Replicating Portfolio

The method used to construct a replicating portfolio is to formulate a procedure to determine the weight of each issue. There are three basic ways

---

[5]Through the use of relatively inexpensive forms of financing, institutional investors have access to derivative instruments (the subject of Chapters 16 and 17) that can achieve zero tracking error.

TABLE 14-3
NUMBER OF ISSUES THAT CAN BE PURCHASED PER $1 MILLION INVESTED IN THE S&P 500 WHEN THERE IS A ROUND-LOT CONSTRAINT

Amount Invested (in $ Million)	Number of Issues
$ 2	317
5	459
10	492
20	499
50	500

Based on July 28, 1988, prices. The number of stocks may change as prices increase or decrease significantly.

to look at weighting: (1) capitalization or market value, (2) price, and (3) equal dollar weighting. The market value weighting for a single stock in an index is determined by the proportion of its value to the total market value of all stocks in the index. The typical price-weighting scheme assumes equal shares invested in each stock, and the price serves as the weight. Equal dollar weighting requires investing the same dollar amount in each stock. With capitalization weighting, the largest companies naturally have the greatest influence over the index value. Consequently, underweighting or overweighting in a large-capitalization stock can lead to substantial tracking error. Also, these stocks tend to be the most liquid. Price weighting endows the highest-price stock with the greatest influence on the index value. Equal dollar weighting does the opposite. In this case, the lowest-priced stocks have the greatest potential to move the index for a given change in stock price, such as 1/8. It is important to understand these properties when constructing a replicating portfolio.

TABLE 14-4
DIFFERENCE BETWEEN WEIGHTING SCHEMES ($1 MILLION SIZE FOR REPLICATING PORTFOLIO)

Company	Price*	Total Shares (Millions)	S&P 500 Weight (%)	Cap Weight (%)	Cap Shares	Price Weight	Price Shares	Equal Dollar Weight	Equal Dollar Shares
AXP	28.625	485.445	0.4275	5.60	1,956	8.56	2,990	20	6,838
GE	105.250	852.935	2.7060	36.18	3,438	31.46	2,990	20	1,898
3M	103.250	215.791	0.6846	8.97	870	30.87	2,990	20	1,898
Merck	32.125	1,282.316	1.2500	16.60	5,167	9.60	2,990	20	6,178
Exxon	65.250	1,241.618	2.4200	32.65	5,004	19.51	2,990	20	3,083
Total	334.500		7.4881	100.00	16,435	100.00	14,950	100	19,895

Total capitalization of five stocks: $248,157.6686 million

*Prices are composite closing prices as of March 11, 1994.

Determination of weights for each issue:

Capitalization weight = capitalization of issue/total capitalization of S&P 500

Price weight = price of issue/total of all prices

Equal weight = 1/number of issues

There are two methods of constructing a replicating portfolio: arithmetic and geometric. As indicated in Chapter 3, the currently used stock market indexes use arithmetic averaging. Consequently, we focus only on arithmetic averaging. An arithmetic index is simply the weighted average of all stocks that make up the index where the weights are determined by one of the weighting schemes mentioned; that is:

$$\text{Index} = \text{constant} \times \sum_{i=1}^{N} (\text{weight}_i \times \text{price}_i)$$

where N is the number of stock issues in the index and the constant represents an arbitrary number used to initialize the value of the index.

Table 14-4 illustrates the distinction among the three weighting schemes by presenting a hypothetical index using the three alternative weighting schemes. (The footnote to the table indicates how the weights are determined for each issue for the three weighting schemes.) GE and Exxon will have the greatest influence on the index value of a capitalization-weighted index because they have the largest market value, while GE and 3M have the greatest influence on the price-weighted index. Notice that the share amounts are the same for a price-weighted index, while the weights are the same for the equal-dollar-weighted index. The performance of one index versus another depends on the relative performance of the individual stocks that compose the index. The price-weighted index will outperform the capitalization-weighted index should Merck and 3M outperform the other stocks. The reason is simply a matter of weightings. Furthermore, the same outcome would occur should Exxon and GE underperform the other stocks. The key, therefore, to understanding relative index performance is to understand the relative weights of the stocks.

Indexes based on arithmetic averages can be easily replicated regardless of the weighting scheme. Over time, however, if there are no changes in the composition of the index, as the price of a stock changes, the weights adjust automatically for consistency with the share amounts. This is only true for an arithmetic index where the share amounts do not change. Consequently, no rebalancing is necessary. However, this is not true for equally weighted indexes because share amounts must change to maintain equal dollar amounts for each stock.

The implication for the management of the replicating portfolio is that holding all the issues in the index reduces the need for rebalancing. But even if the entire index is held, rebalancing may be necessary because changes in the weighting may occur for any of the following reasons:

- Some issues may cease to exist due to merger activity.
- A company may be added to or deleted from the index should it meet or fail to meet capitalization or liquidity requirements for inclusion in an index or listing on an exchange.
- A company may split its stock or issue a stock dividend.
- New stock may be issued.
- Current stock may be repurchased.

Should any of these events occur, the constant term in the index valuation expression may require adjustment to avoid a discontinuous jump in the index value.

METHODS OF CONSTRUCTING A REPRESENTATIVE REPLICATING PORTFOLIO

As we discussed, one way to replicate an index is by purchasing all stock issues in the index in proportion to their weightings. Constructing a replicating portfolio with fewer stock issues than the index involves one of three methods.

Capitalization Method

Using the **capitalization method,** the manager purchases a number of the largest-capitalized names in the index stock issues and equally distributes the residual stock weighting across the index. For example, if the top 200 highest-capitalization stock issues are selected for the replicating portfolio and these issues account for 85% of the total capitalization of the index, the remaining 15% is evenly proportioned among the other stock issues.

Stratified Method

The second method for replicating an index is the **stratified method**. The first step in using this method is to define a factor by which the stocks that make up an index can be categorized. A typical factor is industry sector. Other factors might include risk characteristics such as beta or capitalization levels. The use of two characteristics would add a second dimension to the stratification. In the case of industry sectors, each company in the index is assigned to an industry. This means that the companies in the index have been stratified by industry. The objective of this method is then to reduce residual risk by diversifying across industry sectors in the same proportion as the benchmark. Stock issues within each stratum, or in this case industry sector, can then be selected randomly or by some other method such as capitalization ranking, valuation, or optimization.

Quadratic Optimization Method

The final method uses a quadratic optimization procedure to generate an efficient set of portfolios, and hence is called the **quadratic optimization method**. This is the same procedure that we described in Chapter 4 to generate the Markowitz efficient set. The efficient set includes minimum-variance portfolios for different levels of expected returns. The investor can select a portfolio among the set that satisfies the money manager's risk tolerance.

TRANSACTIONS COSTS

The costs of initiating and maintaining an S&P 500 index fund involve commissions, market impact costs, and rebalancing costs. Representative costs for a $50 million S&P 500 index fund are as given in Table 14-5.

Passive strategies, such as index fund investments, usually incur less turnover than active strategies when the benchmark is dominated by large-capitalization issues. Small-capitalization stock index funds incur larger transactions costs because the stocks tend to be lower priced and less liquid. Historically, the average cost for small-capitalization portfolios is 25 basis points in commissions, 75 to 125 basis points in market impact, and, due to higher turnover, 10 basis points in annual rebalancing costs.

TABLE 14-5		
TYPICAL S&P 500 INDEX FUND TRANSACTIONS COSTS		
	Basis Points	**Cents per Share**
Commissions	5–7	2–3
Market impact costs	20	9
Rebalancing costs	7	3

THE LINK WITH ACTIVE EQUITY STRATEGIES

Index fund management can be extended into active management by designing well-diversified portfolios that take advantage of superior estimates of expected returns and control market risk. Such a strategy is referred to as **enhanced indexing.** Two methods are intended to improve risk-adjusted portfolio return. The first involves creating a "tilted" portfolio, while the second utilizes the futures market.

The **tilted portfolio** can be constructed to emphasize a particular industry sector or performance factor such as fundamental measures like earnings momentum, dividend yield, and price-earnings ratio. Or it can be constructed to emphasize economic factors such as interest rates and inflation. The portfolio can be designed to maintain a strong relationship with a benchmark by minimizing the variance of the tracking error.

The second method involves the use of stock index futures. The introduction of index-derivative products has provided managers with the tools that, when used correctly, can enhance the returns to an index fund. As explained in Chapter 16, the replacement of stocks with undervalued futures contracts can add value to an indexed portfolio's annualized return without incurring any significant additional risk.

■ SUMMARY

Indexing is one form of passive equity management. This approach is supported by the findings that the stock market appears to be sufficiently price-efficient that it is difficult to consistently outperform the market after adjusting for risk and transactions costs. Moreover, pension sponsors have found that external money managers have not consistently outperformed their benchmark after taking management fees into consideration. Index fund management involves creating a portfolio to replicate an index.

The index is selected by the client, the most popular index being the S&P 500. Once an index is selected, the money manager must decide how to construct the replicating portfolio so as to minimize tracking error. In doing so the money manager must consider the trade-off between the number of stock issues in the index to include in the replicating portfolio and the transactions costs.

Constructing a replicating portfolio with fewer stock issues than are included in the index involves one of three methods: the capitalization method, stratified method, or quadratic optimization method.

Some managers utilize active strategies within an index fund management framework in an attempt to enhance returns but still control market risk. The two most popular methods are creating a tilted portfolio and utilizing the stock index futures market.

■ **KEY TERMS**

buy-and-hold strategy
capitalization method
enhanced indexing
indexing

pure index fund
quadratic optimization method
replicating portfolio

stratified method
tilted portfolio
tracking error

■ **QUESTIONS**

1. What are the two approaches to passively managing a portfolio?

2. What is the objective of equity indexing?

3. What are the theoretical arguments supporting equity indexing?

4. According to capital market theory, in a price-efficient market what does the optimal portfolio consist of?

5. The indexing approach to managing an equity portfolio is referred to as a passive strategy. However, there are several decisions that the manager must make in constructing an indexed portfolio. What are these decisions?

6. What is meant by tracking error?

7. Suppose that a manager pursued an indexing strategy last year and that the index the manager sought to replicate is the S&P 500. If the return on the S&P 500 was 7.26% and the return realized by the manager was 7.15%, how much was the tracking error?

8. Why is it difficult for a portfolio's returns to exactly match the return on the benchmark even if a replicating portfolio is designed to exactly replicate a benchmark by buying all the stock issues?

9. "If a money manager is doing a good job of equity indexing, tracking error should be positive." State why you agree or disagree with this statement.

10. "Because markets are highly efficient, all insurance companies should pursue an equity indexing strategy." State why you agree or disagree with this statement.

11. A pension sponsor who is your client just read an article by Robert G. Kirby on indexing ["The Key Word Is 'Passive,'" *Journal of Investing* (Spring 1993), p. 22]. Your client has several questions about statements made in the article.

    a. ". . . my real quarrel is with the word 'index.' An index, whether the S&P 500 or the Wilshire 1000, is more or less, a broad-based, mindless aggregation of common stocks set up on a capitalization-weighted basis. When you substitute the word 'passive' for the word 'index,' you take a giant step toward an investment approach that I can believe in." Your client thought that all passive strategies are indexing strategies and does not understand why the index is a "mindless aggregation of common stocks." Respond.

    b. "The better-than-average returns that come from an index fund are not the product of a superior common stock portfolio; they are the product of very low transaction and management costs." Your client thought that index funds provided better returns relative to active strategies because poor-performing stocks were excluded from the index. Respond.

    c. "I am sure that some efficient market theory academic would argue with me all night on this point, but common sense overwhelmingly suggests that an intelligent passive portfolio will produce a better result than a mindless passive portfolio." Your client does not understand how this intelligent passive portfolio is to be set up and thinks that this approach must incorporate an active approach to investment management. Respond.

12. Why does index fund management involve less portfolio turnover than an actively managed portfolio?

13. What is the stratified method for constructing a portfolio to replicate the index?

14. Why is the maintenance of a replicating portfolio a dynamic process?

15. Why is it important to understand how the index the manager seeks to replicate is constructed?

16. "Indexing is costly to implement because an equal dollar amount of all stock issues in the index must be purchased." Comment on this statement.

17. What is meant by a tilted portfolio?

CHAPTER 15
ACTIVE EQUITY MANAGEMENT*

LEARNING OBJECTIVES
After reading this chapter you will be able to:

- distinguish between active equity management and passive equity management.

- distinguish between the top-down and bottom-up styles of investment management.

- discuss the different subcategories of investment style: value managers, growth managers, group rotation managers, technicians, market timers, and hedgers.

- explain the dividend discount model and its variants—the constant-growth model and the three-phase dividend model.

- explain how to apply the dividend discount model and the underlying assumptions of the model.

- describe what multifactor models are.

- explain the various multifactor models used by practitioners.

- describe how a portfolio manager can change exposure to factors.

- describe the Benjamin Graham low-P/E model, the relative strength model, and homogeneous group/group rotation models.

- discuss the potential problems in the design and implementation of strategies.

In Chapter 13, we reviewed the evidence about the pricing efficiency of the common stock market. A client who believes the market is efficient tends to favor a passive strategy, with indexing being the most common form of passive strategy. By contrast, active equity management begins with the notion, explicitly stated or implied, that the stock market is not totally efficient. Put another way, active equity management assumes that all historical and current information is not "fully and correctly" reflected in the current price of every stock. Hence, there exist stocks that are *undervalued*, *fairly valued*, and *overvalued*. The task of the active equity manager is to decide which stocks are which and invest accordingly.

*This chapter is coauthored with Dr. T. Daniel Coggin and Dr. H. Russell Fogler.

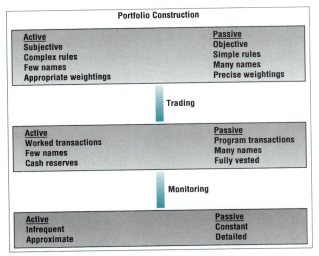

FIGURE 15-1   Active equity management versus passive equity management.

Source: Jeffery L. Skelton, "Investment Opportunities with Indexing," in Katrina F. Sherrerd (ed.), *Equity Markets and Valuation Methods* (Charlottesville, VA: The Institute of Chartered Financial Analysts 1988).

A useful way of thinking about active versus passive management is in terms of the following three activities performed by the manager: (1) portfolio construction (deciding on the stocks to buy and sell), (2) trading of securities, and (3) portfolio monitoring.[1] Figure 15-1 summarizes the differences in the three activities for active management and passive management. Generally, active managers devote the majority of their time to portfolio construction. In contrast, with passive strategies such as indexing, managers devote less time to this activity.

This chapter focuses on the active management of common stock portfolios. We begin with a brief discussion of the primary active investment styles. In our description of the various strategies pursued by active equity managers, we will introduce several models used by practitioners. The underlying theory behind two of these models, the capital asset pricing model and the multifactor model, was described in Chapters 5 and 6, respectively. Here we will see how theory is put into practice.

ACTIVE EQUITY INVESTMENT STYLES

The primary styles of active equity management are *top-down* and *bottom-up*. Even though there are few pure examples of these two styles, they serve as a useful point of reference. A manager who uses a **top-down equity management style** begins with an assessment of the overall economic environment and a forecast of its near-term outlook and makes a general asset allo-

---

[1]Jeffery L. Skelton, "Investment Opportunities with Indexing," in Katrina F. Sherrerd (ed.), *Equity Markets and Valuation Methods* (Charlottesville, VA: The Institute of Chartered Financial Analysts, 1988).

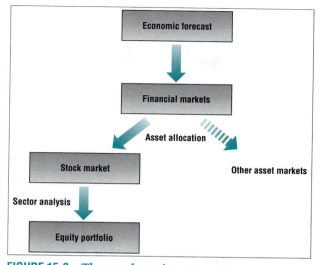

FIGURE 15-2   **The top-down investment process.**

cation decision regarding the relative attractiveness of the various sectors of the financial markets (e.g., stocks, bonds, real estate, and cash equivalents).[2] The top-down manager then analyzes the stock market in an attempt to identify economic sectors and industries that stand to gain or lose from the manager's economic forecast. After identifying attractive and unattractive sectors and industries, the top-down manager finally selects a portfolio of individual stocks. Figure 15-2 presents this process as a diagram.

A manager who uses a **bottom-up equity management style** de-emphasizes the significance of economic and market cycles and focuses instead on the analysis of individual stocks. Using financial analysts and/or computer screening techniques, the bottom-up manager seeks out stocks that have certain characteristics that are deemed attractive (e.g., low price-earnings ratios, small capitalization, low analyst coverage). A variety of management styles can be subsumed under the general bottom-up management category. Notable active equity managers who fit this basic style include Dean LeBaron (Batterymarch Financial Management), Peter Lynch (formerly of Fidelity Magellan Fund), and Warren Buffett (Berkshire Hathaway, Inc.).

In addition to the strategies discussed below, managers recognize the need to carefully monitor and control transactions costs. We discussed these costs in Chapter 13.

SUBCATEGORIES OF ACTIVE EQUITY MANAGEMENT

Having defined the two major styles of active equity management, we next discuss some of the major subcategories.

---

[2]The asset allocation decision-making process is described in Chapter 28.

Value Managers

The **value manager** seeks to buy stocks that are at a discount to their "fair value" and sell them at or in excess of that value. Value managers can fall into either the top-down or the bottom-up category. Value managers use dividend discount models (discussed later), price-earnings (P/E) ratios, earnings surprise, and other similarly motivated constructs. Value managers are sometimes called **contrarians** because they see value where many other market participants do not. In terms of portfolio characteristics, value managers have relatively low betas, low price-book and P/E ratios, and high dividend yields.

Growth Managers

The **growth manager** seeks to buy stocks that are typically selling at relatively high P/E ratios due to high earnings growth, with the expectation of continued high (or higher) earnings growth. Growth managers can be classified as either top-down or bottom-up. Growth managers are often divided into large-capitalization and small-capitalization subgroups. The portfolios of growth managers are characterized by relatively high betas, price-book and P/E ratios, high returns on equity and growth rates, and relatively low dividend yields.

Group Rotation Managers

The **group rotation manager** is in a subcategory of the top-down management style. While there are few pure group rotation managers, many investment firms use group rotation to some degree. The basic idea behind this technique is that the economy goes through reasonably well-defined phases of the business cycle. Some general names for these phases are recession, recovery, expansion, and credit crunch. The group rotator believes he can discern the current phase of the economy and forecast into which phase it will evolve. He can then select those economic sectors and industries that are about to benefit. For example, if the economy were perceived to be on the verge of moving from recession to recovery, the group rotator would begin to purchase stocks in the appropriate sectors (e.g., credit cyclicals, consumer cyclicals, technology, and transportation) and specific industries (e.g., building materials, savings and loans, autos, electronics, and trucking) that are sensitive to a pickup in the economy. Thus the portfolio of the group rotation manager is characterized by concentrations in a small number of "economically timely" industries.

Technicians

Perhaps the boldest assault on the notion of an efficient market comes from the technicians. As explained in Chapter 13, **technicians** (sometimes called *technical analysts* or *chartists*) discern market cycles (not economic cycles) and pick stocks solely on the basis of historical price movements as they relate to the projected price movements. By reading a chart of the price action of a stock (or a group of stocks) and artfully discerning patterns, the technician hopes to be able to predict the future path of the price action.

Even though numerous academic studies have shown technical analysis to be of little or no value in predicting common stock returns, it still survives as a technique that deserves mention in any survey of contemporary active equity management styles. There are still some pure technical analysts around, and many investment management firms have a "token" technician on staff.

Market Timers

The **market timer** is typically in a subcategory of the top-down investment style and comes in many varieties. The basic assumption of the market timer is that she can forecast when the stock market will go up (or continue to go up) and when it will go down (or continue to go down). In this sense, the market timer is a not-too-distant relative of the technical analyst. The portfolio of the market timer is not always fully invested in common stocks. Rather, she moves in and out of the stock market as her economic, analytical, and technical work dictates. While academic studies of market-timing ability suggest that it rarely exists, many investment managers still feel compelled to attempt market timing in varying degrees. Market timing is viewed by some as an essential ingredient to the solution of the asset allocation problem discussed in Chapter 28.

Hedgers

The **hedger** seeks to buy common stocks, but also to place well-defined limits on his investment risk. One popular hedging technique that will be described in Chapter 16 involves simultaneously purchasing a stock and a put option on that stock. The put option sets a floor on the amount of loss that can be sustained (if the stock price goes down), while the potential profit (if the stock price goes up) is diminished only by the original cost of the put. This is an example of a relatively simple "hedge." Much more complicated hedge strategies are followed by some practitioners.

One particular type of hedger that is currently growing in popularity is the **hedge fund** manager. The hedge fund can take many forms. One application is the "long-short" portfolio in which a valuation model is used to select attractive stocks to purchase, or "go long," and unattractive stocks to sell, or "go short." The idea here is to benefit from both stocks which go up and stocks which go down. Of course, the key assumption is that the valuation model is a good predictor of each.

A small group of managers have expanded the long-short stock model to include other assets. These managers often include domestic and foreign stocks and bonds, currencies, and commodities. Hedge fund managers typically charge relatively high fees. A standard agreement is that the manager will take 20% of the profits above a prespecified base-level 20% investment return. That is, no fees are paid until a 20% return is obtained. A few of these managers have impressive track records, while others have one or two good years followed by several relatively bad years. The SEC permits only very high net worth individuals and institutions to invest in hedge funds.

EQUITY VALUATION MODELS

Having discussed some of the various styles of active management, we turn now to a discussion of some of the actual models of equity valuation used by active equity managers. The purpose of these models is to identify whether a

BOX 15

APPROACHING EARNINGS FROM BOTH ENDS

On March 31, 1991, the Association of Investment Management Research sponsored a conference entitled *Improving the Investment Decision Process—Better Use of Economic Inputs in Security Analysis and Portfolio Management*. The following passage is from a speech by Elaine Garzarelli, Director of Quantitative Strategies at Lehman Brothers:

I use both a bottom-up and a top-down approach for determining S&P 500 earnings. My bottom-up process uses 60 econometric models for S&P industry groups, including the steel, automobile, home appliance, retailing, and banking industries. Each model has 14 equations and includes economic inputs for the factors that are important for the industry. I run the models once a month to estimate earnings for each industry, and then I add these estimates to get the S&P earnings.

My top-down model is a least-squares model that looks at aggregate price-cost ratios for the nonfarm economy. The inputs include GDP projections through the end of the coming year, the capitalization rate, earnings from the rest of the world, the dollar exchange rate, and profits in the national income accounts. The model has about an 88 percent coefficient of determination on a year-to-year change basis.

My bottom-up and top-down numbers rarely match, so I spend two weeks every month going through every industry and adjusting the numbers until the bottom-up result is within about 0.5 percent of the top-down result. This is a good methodology; it requires a lot of structure and you must keep your emotions out, which is why it works.

Earnings alone are not enough to predict stock prices. You need an equation to predict the price-earnings ratio (P/E). The P/E for the S&P 500 is a function of three figures: the three-month Treasury bill rate, the 30-year Treasury bond yield, and the rate of inflation. Based on data going back to 1954, the regression analysis has an r^2 of about 85 percent. I never predict interest rates; I just use what is available today.

The Treasury bill rate is at 4 percent, the Treasury bond yield is at 8 percent, the rate of inflation is at 3 percent, so the fair P/E for the market today should be 15.8 times earnings. My earnings number for 1992 is 27 and 30 for 1993. With the S&P 500 at the 406 or 407 level, it is at 13.5 times earnings, and it should be at 15.8. The fair value for the S&P 500 on 1993 earnings is about 471, which is about 3,670 on the Dow.

Source: Elaine Garzarelli, "Selecting Equity Securities," in H. Kent Baker (ed.), *Improving the Investment Decision Process—Better Use of Economic Inputs in Security Analysis and Portfolio Management* (Charlottesville, VA: Association of Investment Management Research, 1991), p. 46.

Questions for Box 15

1. Explain why the model described in the first paragraph of the excerpt is a bottom-up approach.
2. Explain why the model described in the second paragraph of the excerpt is a top-down approach.
3. Why is a model needed to predict the price-earnings ratio?

stock is mispriced. (See Box 15.) Stocks that are undervalued should be purchased; stocks that are overpriced should be shorted—assuming that the manager is given authority by the client to short stocks.

Dividend Discount Model

The fundamental model for valuing the common stock of a company is the **dividend discount model (DDM)**. The basis for the DDM is simply the application of present value analysis, which asserts that the price of an asset is the present value of the expected cash flows. In the case of common stock, the cash flows are the expected dividend payouts and the expected sale price of the stock at some future date. The sale price is also called the *terminal price*.

The dividend discount model can be expressed mathematically as follows:

$$P = \frac{D_1}{(1+r_1)} + \frac{D_2}{(1+r_2)^2} + \cdots + \frac{D_N}{(1+r_N)^N} + \frac{P_N}{(1+r_N)^N} \tag{15-1}$$

where P = the fair value or theoretical value of the common stock

D_t = the expected dividend for year t

P_N = the expected sale price (or terminal price) in the horizon year N

N = the number of years in the horizon

r_t = the appropriate discount or capitalization rate for year t

The DDM represents a bottom-up investment management style. In theory, the DDM is unbiased and thus rationally reflects the consensus of market participants for the value of a stock. However, proponents of the DDM argue that market "inefficiencies" such as superior information and market psychology do exist and can be translated by the DDM to reveal overvaluation and undervaluation.

The DDM can be used in combination with fundamental security analysis (described in Appendixes B and C and in Chapter 13) in trying to obtain a fair value for the stock. To illustrate, we will use an actual company, the American Broadcasting Corporation, ABC. (We've used examples of a hypothetical "ABC" company in other places in this book, but in this case we are talking about a real company.) ABC was acquired in 1986 by Capital Cities Communications for $121 per share. The date of the analysis is December 31, 1984, so in referring to years, the first year is 1985, the second year is 1986, etc. While this illustration deals with a case a decade ago, we feel it still represents the key points in applying the DDM and the inherent dangers of applying the model blindly.

In many applications the discount rate is assumed to be the same for each year, so that each cash flow is discounted at the same rate of r. For example, if ABC's 1984 dividend of $1.60 per share were projected to grow annually at 10% for the next five years, with the following dividends:

$D_1 = \$1.60\,(1.10) = \$1.76$

$D_2 = \$1.60\,(1.10)^2 = \$1.94$

$D_3 = \$1.60\,(1.10)^3 = \$2.13$

$D_4 = \$1.60\,(1.10)^4 = \$2.34$

$D_5 = \$1.60\,(1.10)^5 = \$2.57$

the DDM for January 1985 would have looked like this:

$$P_{\text{Jan.85}} = \frac{1.76}{1+r} + \frac{1.94}{(1+r)^2} + \frac{2.13}{(1+r)^3} + \frac{2.34}{(1+r)^4} + \frac{2.57}{(1+r)^5} + \frac{P_5}{(1+r)^5}$$

As the above equation illustrates, three forecasts are needed to calculate the fair value or price of ABC common stock:

1. The expected terminal price (P_5)
2. The dividends up to year 5 (D_1 to D_5)
3. The discount rate (r)

Thus the relevant question is, How accurately can these inputs be forecast?

The terminal price is the most difficult of the three forecasts. According to theory, P_N is the present value of all future dividends after N; that is, D_{N+1}, $D_{N+2}, \ldots, D_{\text{infinity}}$. Also, the future discount rate (r) must be forecast. In practice, forecasts are made of either dividends (D_N) or earnings (E_N) first, and then the price P_N is estimated by assigning an "appropriate" requirement for yield, price-earnings ratio, or capitalization rate. While the present value of the expected terminal price $P_N/(1 + r)^N$ becomes very small if N is very large, in our simple illustration we use a time horizon of five years. In practice, managers might project returns using several terminal prices with associated probabilities, thus incorporating the investor's uncertainty.

The forecasting of dividends is somewhat easier. Usually, past history is available, management can be queried, and flow of funds can be projected for a given scenario. In our example, ABC had been paying a $1.60 dividend a year for the past five years, so it was reasonable to expect an increase in dividends, assuming that the cash was available. A growth rate of 10% is assumed in our example.

Forecasting r is more complex than forecasting dividends, although not nearly as difficult as forecasting the terminal price (which requires a forecast of future discount rates as well). First, an investor must determine if a single rate is to be used or whether a different rate should be used for each year. If multiple rates are to be used, an explicit interest rate forecast must be developed. One procedure is to examine the current yield curve for bonds and then to calculate the implied forward discount rate (discussed in Chapter 21). Finally, given two stocks with identical dividend forecasts, if one stock is riskier, then that stock should have a lower valuation; thus r must be adjusted upward for company risk.

With the above caveats in mind and accepting the dividend forecast for ABC, the next step is to forecast a terminal price five years from now (P_5). Two valuation methods have been used by practitioners for this task.

Constant-Growth Model If future dividends are assumed to grow at an assumed rate (g) and a single discount rate is used, then the dividend discount model given by Equation (15-1) becomes

$$P = \frac{D_0(1 + g)}{1 + r} + \frac{D_0(1 + g)^2}{(1+r)^2} + \cdots + \frac{D_0(1 + g)^N}{(1 + r)^N} + \frac{P_N}{(1 + r)^N} \tag{15-2}$$

and it can be shown that if N is assumed to approach infinity, Equation (15-2) is equal to

$$P = \frac{D_0}{r - g} \tag{15-3}$$

where D_0 is the current dividend. Equation (15-3) is called the **constant-growth model** or the **Gordon-Shapiro model**.[3]

Let us suppose that for ABC r is equal to 13% and the dividend growth rate g is 10%; since D_5 is $2.57, we can then estimate the terminal price in year 5 as

$$P_5 = \frac{D_5}{r - g} = \frac{2.57}{0.13 - 0.10} = 85.67$$

Price-Earnings Model A simpler version of the same idea is the price-earnings model. If a company retains or holds back a percentage of its earnings, it can be shown that Equation (15-2) becomes

---

[3]Myron Gordon and E. Shapiro, "Capital Equipment Analysis: The Required Rate of Profit," *Management Science* (October 1956), pp. 102–110. The model was first developed in John B. Williams, *The Theory of Investment Value* (Cambridge, MA: Harvard University Press, 1938).

$$P = \frac{(1-b)E}{r-g} \tag{15-4}$$

where b is the percentage of present earnings (E) held back or retained, popularly referred to as the **retention rate** or **plowback rate**. Thus,

$$\frac{P}{E} = \frac{1-b}{r-g}$$

For example, in 1984 ABC paid out $1.60 from earnings of $6.39, or about 25%, and therefore retained about 75%. The price-earnings ratio in year 5 is therefore estimated as

$$\frac{P_5}{E_5} = \frac{1-0.75}{0.13-0.10} = 8.33$$

The expected terminal price in year 5 would then be the product of the estimated earnings in year 5 and the estimated price-earnings ratio. For ABC, 1984 earnings were $6.39. If 1984 earnings are assumed to grow at 10% per year (versus 4.28% for 1980 through 1984), then E_5 would equal $10.29 and the forecasted price (P_5) would be $85.72, found by multiplying $10.29 by 8.33. Furthermore, if we assume that 13% is a fair rate of return for this investment, the theoretical value of ABC's common stock according to Equation (15-2) would be

$$\begin{aligned}
P_{\text{Jan.85}} &= \frac{1.76}{1.13} + \frac{1.94}{(1.13)^2} + \frac{2.13}{(1.13)^3} + \frac{2.34}{(1.13)^4} + \frac{2.57}{(1.13)^5} + \frac{85.67}{(1.13)^5} \\
&= \frac{1.76}{1.13} + \frac{1.94}{1.28} + \frac{2.13}{1.44} + \frac{2.34}{1.63} + \frac{2.57}{1.84} + \frac{85.67}{1.84} = 53.88
\end{aligned}$$

The market price of ABC at the time of the analysis was $64. Our analysis suggests that the value of ABC's stock is only $53.88. Thus, an investor using the results of this analysis would not have bought ABC for his or her portfolio in December 1984 since the DDM indicates that the stock is overvalued.

Estimating the Expected Return   An alternative use of the DDM is to calculate the expected return from buying the stock now and holding it for five years, with the implicit assumption that the stock can be sold at the forecasted price. Thus, assuming we could have bought ABC at $64 a share in December 1984 and assuming from the constant-growth model above that the price five years from December 1984 equals $85.67, the equation to be solved to obtain the expected return is simply the internal rate of return:

$$64 = \frac{1.76}{1+r} + \frac{1.94}{(1+r)^2} + \frac{2.13}{(1+4)^3} + \frac{2.34}{(1+r)^4} + \frac{2.57}{(1+r)^5} + \frac{85.67}{(1+r)^5}$$

The solution is that r is equal to 8.98%. Since the investor required a 13% return, this approach also implies that ABC is an unattractive investment.

Adding Fundamental Security Analysis   It may be worthwhile to take another look at ABC from a different perspective. Specifically, as explained in Appendixes C and D, security analysts look at the capital structure of the company (i.e., the relative amount of debt and equity) in performing fundamental security analysis. ABC had been changing its financial complexion. Its long-term debt of $220.3 million in 1980 had been reduced to $140.5 million in 1984.

This reduction, about $16 million a year, occurred while the equity base grew from $870.1 million to $1,352.3 million. Moreover, this reduction made a lot of sense. The early 1980s were years of very high interest rates, and ABC earned less on new investments than the rate of interest on new debt, thus effecting negative leverage.

If we assume that ABC simply stopped reducing its debt by approximately $16 million a year and paid dividends instead, its current dividend would rise from $1.60 to $2.15 in 1985 and grow at 10%. Using our previous techniques, we would get these estimates:

Dividends to 1989 at 10% growth:

$D_1 = \$2.15;$ $D_2 = \$2.37;$ $D_3 = \$2.60;$ $D_4 = \$2.86;$ $D_5 = \$3.15$

Earnings per share 1989 at 10% growth: $10.29

The projected sale price in 1989 (i.e., the terminal price) based on the constant-growth model given by Equation (15-3) is

$$P_5 = \frac{3.15}{0.13 - 0.10} = 105.00$$

The projected sale price in 1989 based on the price-earnings model given by Equation (15-4) is

$$\frac{P_5}{E_5} = \frac{1 - b}{0.13 - 0.10}$$

Based on the assumptions above, the forecasted dividend in year 5 is $3.15 and the forecasted earnings in year 5 is $10.29. Thus, the amount retained is $7.14, and the retention rate b is equal to 0.6939 ($7.14/$10.29) and

$$\frac{P_5}{E_5} = \frac{1 - 0.6939}{0.13 - 0.10} = 10.20$$

The projected terminal price at year 5 is then $104.96 (10.20 times $10.29).

With the above estimates, the present value equation can be used to estimate either a fair price in December 1984 or the expected return at a price of $64 per share. For example, using $105 for P_5, we can determine the fair value as

$$P_{\text{Jan.85}} = \frac{2.15}{1.13} + \frac{2.37}{(1.13)^2} + \frac{2.60}{(1.13)^3} + \frac{2.86}{(1.13)^4} + \frac{3.15}{(1.13)^5} + \frac{105.00}{(1.13)^5}$$

$$= \frac{2.15}{1.13} + \frac{2.37}{1.28} + \frac{2.60}{1.44} + \frac{2.86}{1.63} + \frac{3.15}{1.84} + \frac{105.00}{1.84}$$

$$= \$66.01$$

Using the current stock price of $64, we find expected return by solving for r in the following equation:

$$64 = \frac{2.15}{1 + r} + \frac{2.37}{(1 + r)^2} + \frac{2.60}{(1 + r)^3} + \frac{2.86}{(1 + r)^4} + \frac{3.15}{(1 + r)^5} + \frac{105.00}{(1 + r)^5}$$

The solution is that r, the expected return, is 13.74%.

Thus, after more detailed analysis, ABC would have been expected to earn a 0.74% return after risk adjustment. This return, of course, assumes that no transactions costs are incurred to purchase ABC. Thus the market value of ABC in December 1984 appears fair at first glance.

Sensitivity Analysis   Further analysis is warranted, though. How sensitive is the foregoing valuation to the assumptions used in applying the DDM? For example, what if a different P_5 had been estimated? What if ABC becomes a takeover candidate? How would this development affect our assessment of its relative attractiveness?

The impact of different expected terminal prices can be handled easily by recomputing the present values and expected returns under new assumptions. For example, if P_5 were assumed to equal $115.41, then the theoretical price is $71.76 and the expected return is 15.73%. The analysis of the impact of the the fair price based on different assumptions for the inputs is called *sensitivity analysis*.

Issues such as what price might be paid in a merger are more difficult to deal with. In general, the above theoretical prices and expected returns would need adjustment for potential synergies.

Probabilistic DDM   One approach to dealing with these uncertainties is to assign probabilities to the various outcomes. These probabilities, of necessity, are subjective—the result of experience, research, and even intuition. For example, assume that the probability distribution in Table 15-1 reflects an investor's assessment of the probable distribution of the terminal price. This analysis would have suggested ABC as a buy in December 1984. The expected value or mean of the price of the distribution is $67.23, with a standard deviation of $7.91. But the probability of results above the December price of $64 is 80% versus a 20% probability for results below the current price.

The subsequent takeover battle and buyout of ABC by Capital Cities Communications at $121 per share reflected projected synergies well above the implicit estimates in the above analysis. It would be erroneous to infer that through the quantitative analysis described above, one could have anticipated the takeover and the resultant extraordinary return. An unfavorable event as significant as the takeover could have occurred and caused ABC's return to be sharply negative. As explained in Chapter 4, over time and with diversified portfolios, unpredictable events should cancel each other out so that the fruits of careful quantitative analysis and sound judgment are manifested. The ABC example indicates that there was no one conclusive course of action

TABLE 15-1

INVESTOR'S SUBJECTIVE PROBABILITY DISTRIBUTION OF ABC'S TERMINAL PRICE

Terminal Price	Probability
$55	0.10
60	0.10
65	0.30
70	0.30
75	0.10
80	0.10

that the investor should have followed. Rather, it should be clear that there are several ways of using the DDM to value a stock, and some of these ways might have suggested a buy for ABC.

The function of security analysis and valuation may be to "skew" the distribution in the investor's favor, realizing that incredible upside potential can seldom be foreseen but downside risks can be reduced.

Three-Phase DDM   While we have used the constant-growth DDM in our illustrations, the assumption of constant growth is unrealistic and can even be misleading. The version of the DDM most commonly used by practitioners is the **three-phase DDM**. This model assumes that all companies go through three phases, analogous to the concept of the product life cycle. In the **growth phase**, a company experiences rapid earnings growth as it produces new products and expands market share. In the **transition phase**, the company's earnings begin to mature and decelerate to the rate of growth of the economy as a whole. At this point, the company is in the **maturity phase**, in which earnings continue to grow at the rate of the general economy. Figure 15-3 depicts this pattern.

Different companies are assumed to be at different phases in the three-phase model. An emerging growth company would have a longer growth phase than a more mature company. Some companies are considered to have higher initial growth rates and hence longer growth and transition phases. Other companies may be considered to have lower current growth rates and hence shorter growth and transition phases.

In the typical investment organization, analysts supply the projected earnings, dividends, growth rates for earnings, and dividend and payout ratios using the fundamental security analysis framework described in Appendixes B, C, and D. The growth rate at maturity for the entire economy is applied to all companies. As a generalization, approximately 25% of the expected return from a company (projected by the DDM) comes from the growth phase, 25% from the transition phase, and 50% from the maturity phase. However, a company with high growth and low dividend payouts shifts the relative contribution toward the maturity phase, while a company with low growth and a high payout shifts the relative contribution toward the growth and transition phases.

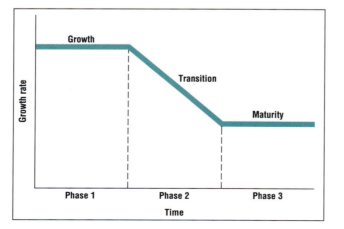

FIGURE 15-3

The generalized three-phase dividend discount model.

TABLE 15-2		
ACTUAL COMPOUND TOTAL RETURNS BY THREE-PHASE DDM QUINTILE RANK FOR 250 STOCKS: 1973–1986		
	Actual Return	**Annual Rate**
Quintile 1	819.2%	17.2%
Quintile 2	584.5	14.7
Quintile 3	361.0	11.5
Quintile 4	194.9	8.0
Quintile 5	99.8	5.1
Total sample (equal-weighted)	348.6	11.3
S&P 500 (equal-weighted)	586.8	14.8
S&P 500 (market-weighted)	287.6	10.2

Note: The quintile returns are equal-weighted and based on annual rebalancing. Quintile 1 contains the stocks with the highest expected returns from the DDM, and quintile 5 contains the stocks with the lowest expected returns.

Applying the DDM to the Stock Selection Process   In applying the DDM, the most common procedure is to estimate the expected return rather than the fair price. Expected returns are usually ranked high to low and then separated into five equal-sized groupings.[4] Quintile 1 contains stocks with the highest expected return, which are, all other things being equal, the most attractive for purchase. Quintile 5 contains stocks with the lowest expected return, which are the least attractive and hence the strongest candidates for sale.[5]

Table 15-2 shows the results of a study of the three-phase DDM, using a sample of 250 large- to medium-capitalization stocks over the 14-year period, 1973–1986. This DDM used the current market price and a forecasted dividend stream and solved for the expected return.[6]

The entries in Table 15-2 are actual total returns (assuming no transactions costs) that would have resulted from buying the stocks ranked by expected return quintiles once a month, holding the stocks for the entire month, and rebalancing at the beginning of the next month. Each expected re-

---

[4]See Russell J. Fuller, "Programming the Three-Phase Dividend Discount Model," *Journal of Portfolio Management* (Summer 1979), pp. 28-32, and Richard W. Taylor, "Portfolio Management with a Hand-Held Calculator," *Journal of Portfolio Management* (Summer 1984), pp. 27–31.

[5]The notion of systematic risk in the sense described by the capital asset pricing model (see Chapter 5) is not explicitly included in the DDM calculation. Nonetheless, some practitioners [see, e.g., William L. Fouse, "Risk and Liquidity," *Financial Analysts Journal* (May–June 1976)] have suggested that further quintile ranking of expected returns by beta is useful. However, assuming that 250 or more stocks broadly diversified across industries are to be ranked, the mean beta for each expected return quintile is typically about 1.0. In the data presented in this chapter, there is no systematic tendency for higher expected return quintiles to have mean betas that are significantly different from those for lower expected return quintiles as calculated by the DDM.

[6]See Richard W. Taylor, "Make Life Easy: Bond Analysis and DDM on the PC," *Journal of Portfolio Management* (Fall 1985), pp. 54–57, for a handy computer program for the PC that will solve for the expected return or the price in the three-phase DDM.

turn quintile contained 50 stocks. The results presented in Table 15-2 are striking and illustrate the potential utility of the DDM as a stock valuation tool. A number of current investment managers use the DDM (in varying degrees) as an input to the equity valuation decision.

DDM Assumptions   Whenever DDMs are used, the following three implicit assumptions should be recognized.

Assumption 1: There is attribute bias   **Attribute bias** means that stocks preferred by the DDM tend to be biased toward certain equity attributes. Examples of equity attributes are low price-earnings ratios, high dividend yield, high book value ratio, or a particular industry sector. To test for such biases, Jacobs and Levy conducted a study.[7] They analyzed over 1,000 stocks on a quarterly basis for five years (mid-1982 to mid-1987) and estimated the expected return for each stock using a DDM. Given the expected return, they then used multiple regression analysis to estimate the relationship between 25 equity attributes and 38 industry categories and the expected return. What Jacobs and Levy found is that expected returns from a DDM are related to equity attributes such as low price-earnings ratio, book-value-to-price ratio, dividend yield, beta, and firm size. Thus, while the DDM assumes no attribute bias, this is not supported by empirical research.[8]

Assumption 2: Investor and model time horizons are equal   The DDM assumes that the investor's horizon matches the time used in the model. In practice, this is often not true. Users of DDMs typically hold stocks for much shorter time periods than those implied by the model.

Assumption 3: $(r - g)$ is estimated accurately   When applying quantitative methods, one should always ask, Which variables can affect the analysis most dramatically? In the dividend discount model, the denominator of $(r - g)$ is the answer. For instance, in our ABC example assume three estimates of r: 12%, 13%, and 14%. Using our previous dividend forecast, we would calculate the terminal prices as $128.50, $85.67, and $64.25. Thus, inaccuracy of 200 basis points in estimating either r or g leads to terminal price forecasts that are 100% different. This is extremely critical, as both r and g are difficult to estimate.

The Benjamin Graham Low-P/E Model
The legendary Benjamin Graham proposed a classic investment model in 1949 for the "defensive investor"—one without the time, expertise, or temperament for aggressive investment. The model was updated in each subse-

---

[7]Bruce I. Jacobs and Kenneth N. Levy, "On the Value of Value," *Financial Analysts Journal* (July–August 1988), pp. 47–62.

[8]Another study that has suggested such attribute bias is Richard Michaud, "A Scenario-Dependent Dividend Discount Model: Bridging the Gap between Top-Down Investment Information and Bottom-Up Forecasts," *Financial Analysts Journal* (November–December 1985), pp. 49–59.

quent edition of his book, *The Intelligent Investor*.[9] Some of the basic investment criteria outlined in the 1973 edition are representative of the approach:

1. A company must have paid a dividend in each of the last 20 years.
2. Minimum size of a company is $100 million in annual sales for an industrial company and $50 million for a public utility.
3. Positive earnings must have been achieved in each of the last 10 years.
4. Current price should not be more than 1 1/2 times the latest book value.
5. Market price should not exceed 15 times the average earnings for the past three years.

Graham considered the P/E ratio as a measure of the price paid for value received. He viewed high P/Es with skepticism and as representing a large premium for difficult-to-forecast future earnings growth. Hence, lower-P/E, higher-quality companies were viewed favorably as having less potential for earnings disappointments and the resulting downward revision in price.

A study by Oppenheimer and Schlarbaum reveals that over the period 1956–1975 significant risk-adjusted excess returns were obtained by following Graham's strategy, even after allowing for transactions costs.[10] While originally intended for the defensive investor, numerous variations of Graham's low-P/E approach are currently followed by a number of professional investment advisors.[11]

The Relative Strength Model

The notion of relative strength was made popular by the doctoral dissertation of Robert Levy written in 1966 and his article in *Financial Analysts Journal* in 1967.[12] As we explained in Chapter 13, relative strength models come in several varieties, but the basic idea is that stocks that have had better-than-average price performance in the recent past will continue (for some time in the future) to have above-average price performance. These models generally calculate percentage change in stock price over some recent period, rank-order the percentages from high to low, and purchase the stocks with the largest percentage increases.

While not a pure version of the relative strength model, the well-known Value Line timeliness ranking system includes a relative strength component in its calculation.[13] The record of the Value Line timeliness rank is impres-

---

[9]This model is fully described in Benjamin Graham, *The Intelligent Investor*, 4th rev. ed. (New York: Harper & Row, 1973), Chap. 14.

[10]Henry R. Oppenheimer and Gary G. Schlarbaum, "Investing with Ben Graham: An *Ex Ante* Test of the Efficient Market Hypothesis," *Journal of Financial and Quantitative Analysis* (September 1981), pp. 341–360.

[11]For a thorough presentation of the low-P/E investment strategy, see David Dreman, *The New Contrarian Investment Strategy* (New York: Random House, 1982).

[12]Robert A. Levy, "Random Walks: Reality or Myth," *Financial Analysts Journal* (November–December 1967), pp. 129–132. See also the comment by Michael C. Jensen in the same issue and the reply by Levy in the January–February 1968 issue.

[13]See Arnold Bernhard, *Value Line Methods of Evaluating Common Stocks* (New York: Arnold Bernhard & Co., 1979), Part 4, for a complete description of the Value Line timeliness rank.

sive. Assuming no transactions costs, the stocks ranked in the top group (Value Line group 1) had a total return of 26,815% over the period April 16, 1965, to December 30, 1992 (allowing for changes in rank during the year), and a total return of 5,059% (if ranks are changed only once a year). A study by Copeland and Mayers documents the existence of significant abnormal performance (based on the market model) for Value Line predictions over the period 1965–1978, before transactions costs.[14] A recent article by John Brush demonstrates the predictive ability of eight *pure* relative strength models of varying complexity over the period 1969–1984.[15]

Homogeneous Group/Group Rotation Models

The homogeneous group model of James Farrell uses **cluster analysis**, a statistical technique which identifies clusters of stocks whose returns are highly correlated within each cluster and relatively uncorrelated between clusters.[16] Using this technique, Farrell determined that there are at least four clusters of stocks in the market: growth, cyclical, stable, and energy.

Managers who use the group rotation approach can apply cluster analysis to define homogeneous groups of stocks whose returns strongly covary. As Farrell shows, a substantial reward awaits the manager who can select valid clusters and then correctly forecast those the market will favor. Specifically, in a study spanning the period 1970–1977, Farrell found that the net advantage to perfect group rotation over a buy-and-hold S&P 500 portfolio was 289%. While it is highly unlikely that any manager was able to forecast exactly which groups would be in favor during this (or any other) period, it is clearly demonstrated that reasonable accuracy can produce attractive returns.

A study by Coggin[17] and another by Sorensen and Burke[18] use the notion of relative strength to show that a group rotation strategy of buying industry groups with superior relative price performance results in superior returns. The Coggin study shows evidence of persistence of superior returns for subsequent periods of one year, while the Sorensen and Burke study demonstrates superior returns for periods of at least two quarters.

Multifactor Models

The idea that common stock prices can be described by an econometric model with a small number of well-chosen explanatory variables dates back at least to the 1930s. In many cases, these variables are simply financial data or the regression coefficients attached to them, but because of an early allusion to variables that were generated by a statistical procedure called factor

[14]Thomas E. Copeland and David Mayers, "The Value Line Enigma (1965–1978)," *Journal of Financial Economics* (November 1982), pp. 289–321.

[15]John S. Brush, "Eight Relative Strength Models Compared," *Journal of Portfolio Management* (Fall 1986), pp. 21–28.

[16]See James L. Farrell, Jr., "Homogeneous Stock Groupings: Implications for Portfolio Management," *Financial Analysts Journal* (May–June 1975), pp. 50–62, and *Guide to Portfolio Management* (New York: McGraw-Hill, 1983), Chap. 8.

[17]T. Daniel Coggin, "On the Persistence of S&P 500 Industry Group Returns, 1975–1985," unpublished study, 1986.

[18]Eric H. Sorensen and Terry Burke, "Portfolio Returns from Active Industry Group Rotation," *Financial Analysts Journal* (September–October 1986), pp. 43–50.

analysis, such variables are currently labeled *factors*. Some practitioners refer to them as *attributes* or *indexes*.

The simplest idea was that one factor (beta) was sufficient. But just as most practitioners scoff at such a simplistic notion, quantitative analysts also indicate that more sophisticated models add insights. Certainly, it seems plausible to create models such as

$$r_i = B_{i,0} + B_{i,1}(\text{BETA}) + B_{i,2}(\text{SIZE}) + B_{i,3}(\text{P/E}) + e_i$$

which merely states that stock i's return (r_i) is a function of its beta (BETA), capitalization (SIZE), price-earnings ratio (P/E), and sensitivities to each variable $(B_{i,j})$, as well as other unmeasured effects that are assumed to act as independent errors (e_i). By using the statistical technique of multiple regression analysis, it is easy to estimate the average sensitivity coefficients (i.e., the Bs) for a group of stocks.

How many factors are there? A practical answer is, there are several. A rigorous scientific answer is, we do not know. Most studies suggest at least three to five systematic factors, although some practitioners use more factors in their models. It should be understood that certain factors are important only some of the time, and even then they may be of only minor importance. If the risk of such factors can be diversified away, these transient factors might affect returns periodically. However, no risk premium would attach to them, because risk premiums are only related to nondiversifiable risk. Despite the fact that we do not know the exact number of factors, factor models can be very valuable for understanding portfolio returns. This type of research activity is sometimes referred to as top-down. As this term suggests, factor models are concerned with identifying systematic factors that affect security returns. This approach requires the investor to estimate the factor exposures in order to identify companies that will be most affected by these factors.

Below we describe two examples of multifactor models of equity valuation in current use. Then we illustrate how a portfolio manager can alter a portfolio to factor exposures.

Factor Models in Use One multifactor model used by institutional investors has been developed by the consulting firm BARRA of Berkeley, California. The BARRA model contains 13 common factors (called *risk indexes* in their terminology): (1) variability, (2) success, (3) size, (4) trading activity, (5) growth, (6) earnings/price, (7) book/price, (8) earnings variation, (9) financial leverage, (10) foreign income, (11) labor intensity, (12) yield, and (13) low capitalization. In addition, 55 industry designators are provided, as well as measurements for beta and shifts in beta. This model has a wide following among institutional investors because it is consistently estimated and is comprehensive. Since a large number of institutional investors are using BARRA analyses, we will describe both the model and the variables in more detail in the appendix of this chapter. In Chapter 30 we illustrate how a factor model can also be used to evaluate the performance of a money manager.

Another multifactor model has been developed by Chen, Roll, and Ross.[19] Their model is consistent with the arbitrage pricing theory (APT) developed

---

[19]This model is described and tested in Nai-Fu Chen, Richard Roll, and Stephen A. Ross, "Economic Forces and the Stock Market," *Journal of Business* (July 1986), pp. 382–403.

TABLE 15-3		
FACTOR SENSITIVITIES OF AN EQUALLY WEIGHTED PORTFOLIO		
	Portfolio	**S&P**
Expected return (DDM forecast)	12.57%	13.10%
Yield	3.09%	4.28%
P/E ratio	12.86	11.14
Growth	9.60%	8.30%
Factor price sensitivities		
Real GNP	26.53	21.48
Short-term interest rates	−2.77	−2.76
Inflation	−10.09	−8.37
Oil prices	.64	1.20
Defense spending	−1.26	−1.20

Source: Michelle Clayman et al., *Stockfacts* (New York: Salomon Brothers, 1985).

by Stephen Ross and expanded by several others, as explained in Chapter 6. Richard Roll and Stephen Ross have a money management firm, Roll & Ross Asset Management Corp. (Culver City, California), which uses a proprietary version of this model. This model is important because it serves as the prototype for almost all subsequent APT-based, multifactor investment models. The basic model proposed by Chen, Roll, and Ross asserts that asset prices depend upon their exposure to the "state variables" which describe the economy. Their testing revealed four economic variables that are significant in explaining monthly stock returns over the period 1958–1984: the monthly growth rate in industrial production, unanticipated inflation (defined as the monthly first difference in the logarithm of the CPI minus a variable representing the expected inflation rate), unanticipated change in the term structure of interest rates (defined as the spread between long- and short-term bond returns), and unanticipated change in the risk premium (defined as the spread between low- and high-grade bond returns).

Building a Portfolio with Factor Bets Now let's look at how to use a multifactor model to alter the risk exposure, or, equivalently, make factor bets. To do this, we use the data in Table 15-3 for two equally weighted portfolios: a money manager's portfolio and the S&P 500. The factor sensitivities in the table indicate relative return sensitivity to changes in each economic factor.[20] For example, the real GNP sensitivity indicates that a change of 1% in real GNP would cause a 26.53% change in our portfolio's price versus a change of 21.48% in the price of the S&P index. These factor sensitivities were estimated by simulating alternative economic scenarios and measuring the resulting return changes as forecast by a dividend discount model.

Several portfolio characteristics are immediately evident. For example, the portfolio has a lower expected return than the S&P 500 (12.57% versus

---

[20]This illustration is abstracted from Michelle Clayman et al., *Stockfacts* (New York: Salomon Brothers, 1985), pp. 35–40.

13.10%). It has slightly more GNP sensitivity, slightly lower oil sensitivity, and slightly higher defense sensitivity.

After examining the portfolio, suppose that the portfolio manager decides upon the following objectives:

- Raise the expected return without increasing exposure to the GNP.
- Reduce the oil sensitivity.
- Raise the defense sensitivity.
- Turn over not more than 20% of the portfolio.

At this portfolio construction phase, both specific security returns (bottom-up analysis) and economic factor bets (top-down economic analysis) must be combined.

Table 15-4 contains four sections. The first section identifies the oil-sensitive stocks, the second section contains GNP-sensitive stocks with low expected return, the third section shows defense-sensitive stocks, and the last section has companies with high expected returns.

Suppose the portfolio manager wanted the expected return for the portfolio to be equal to the expected return for the S&P 500 of 13.10% (see Table 15-3). The following transactions would have created this expected return: (1) sell Rowan Companies, Halliburton, Advanced Micro Devices, Intel, and Motorola and (2) buy General Dynamics, Sundstrand, NED Bancorp, Kimberly-Clark, and Warner-Lambert. Although not shown here, the restructured portfolio would have an energy sensitivity that is zero and a GNP price sensitivity that is reduced slightly. The portfolio's defense sensitivity would be higher. This means that if there were no changes in economic expectations, the portfolio could be expected to perform in line with the S&P 500. If, however, expectations for defense spending were to rise or expectations for GNP and oil prices were to fall, then the portfolio would be likely to perform better than the S&P 500.

As the portfolio was actively tracked from the end of the third quarter 1984 to the end of the first quarter 1985, the original portfolio had a total return of 9.5%, while the restructured portfolio was up to 15.2% (the corresponding return for the S&P 500 was 11%). In this case, the alteration of the portfolio's economic sensitivities along with the identification of "cheap" stocks from the DDM added 470 basis points in incremental return.

Market Anomaly Models

If the stock market were totally efficient, then there would be no systematic gain from investing in stocks with certain easily identifiable characteristics, such as low P/E, small capitalization, and low analyst coverage. However, numerous academic studies have shown that such market anomalies do in fact exist. A summary article by Donald Keim discusses five sources of anomalous return in the stock market: high-dividend stocks, small-capitalization stocks, low-P/E stocks, abnormally high returns for the month of January, and abnormally high returns for stocks rated "1" in the Value Line timeliness rank.[21] As explained in Chapter 13, other studies have noted abnormally low returns for stocks on Monday, as compared with the rest of the week.

---

[21]Donald B. Keim, "The CAPM and Equity Return Regularities," *Financial Analysts Journal* (May–June 1986), pp. 19–34.

TABLE 15-4

FOUR SCREENS FOR PORTFOLIO ADJUSTMENTS

Screen	Factor Sensitivity	Expected Return
1. High oil sensitivities		
Rowan Cos	0.54	
Texaco	0.50	
Halliburton	0.30	
Texas Instruments	0.15	
Nalco Chemical	0.05	
2. High GNP sensitivities (low expected returns)		
Rexnord	1.42	12.73
Advanced Micro Devices	1.25	12.36
Intel	1.25	11.69
Motorola	1.25	12.93
LTV	1.12	0.00
Abbott Laboratories	1.10	13.11
Halliburton	1.04	12.70
Hewlett-Packard	1.04	12.70
New York Times Co—Class A	1.03	12.03
3. High defense sensitivities		
General Dynamics	0.36	14.83
Boeing	0.28	13.57
Lockheed	0.24	14.34
Advanced Micro Devices	0.02	12.36
Intel	0.02	11.69
Texas Instruments	0.01	11.82
Sundstrand	0.01	13.72
4. High expected returns		
Boeing		13.57
Citicorp		16.77
Clorox		13.83
General Dynamics		14.83
General Signal		13.92
International Business Machines		13.74
ITT		14.65
Kimberly-Clark		13.96
Lockheed		14.34
Ned Bancorp		16.12
J. C. Penney		13.89
Security Pacific		15.66
Sundstrand		13.72
United Technologies		14.58
Warner-Lambert		13.51

Source: Michelle Clayman et al., *Stockfacts* (New York: Salomon Brothers, 1985).

The low-P/E strategy and the Value Line timeliness rank were mentioned earlier. There is a growing interest in active investment strategies that attempt to capture excess returns available to other stock market anomalies as well. Dimensional Fund Advisors, Inc. (Santa Monica, California) now has available small-capitalization stock funds that invest in the United States, Japan, and the United Kingdom. Several money managers now use "extent of coverage by Wall Street analysts" (sometimes called the *neglect effect*) as one of their investment criteria. (We mentioned the neglected-firm effect in Chapter 13.) The strategy in this case is to buy attractive stocks which are underfollowed by Wall Street and hence have (potentially) undiscovered value. Time will tell whether or not these anomalies persist as more market participants become aware of them—also, whether large institutional investors could profit after the market impact cost of transacting is subject to question. For now at least, their existence presents appealing investment opportunities.

The CAPM

No discussion of models of equity valuation would be complete without including the CAPM, which we described in Chapter 5. While its promise has not been fully realized, and the APT (arbitrage pricing theory) looms on the horizon as its successor, some money managers still employ its basic insights.

Those who use the CAPM for active equity management employ its prediction that, in equilibrium, the expected return on a stock is an exact linear function of the risk-free rate, the beta for the stock (i.e., its expected covariance with the market portfolio), and the expected return on the market portfolio. This linear relationship is called the *security market line*.

In theory, a stock whose expected return from a valuation model (such as the DDM) equals the expected return from the CAPM is said to be *in equilibrium*. If the expected return from the DDM were greater than the expected return from the CAPM, then the market would adjust the price of the stock upward and hence lower its expected return. If the expected return from the DDM were less than the expected return from the CAPM, then the market would adjust the price of the stock downward and hence raise its expected return. Figure 15-4 presents this relationship in the form of a graph.

The 45-degree dotted line in Figure 15-4 represents the equilibrium condition where the expected return for a stock as predicted from the DDM is equal to the expected return from the CAPM [i.e., where $E(R_{DDM})=E(R_{CAPM})$]. Following this logic, stocks X, Y, and Z are undervalued; stocks A, B, and C are fairly valued,; and stocks R, S, and T are overvalued. Hence, all other things being equal, the CAPM manager would buy stocks X, Y, and Z; hold stocks A, B, and C; and sell stocks R, S, and T. A variation of this basic approach has been implemented by a number of professional investment advisors.

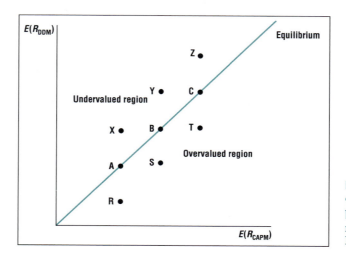

FIGURE 15-4

The relationship between the expected return based on the DDM and the CAPM.

TABLE 15-5

HISTORICAL PERFORMANCE OF SEVEN POPULAR MODELS OF EQUITY VALUATION

Model	*Annualized Total Return Relative to S&P 500*	
	30 June 1968– 30 June 1987	**30 June 1986– 30 June 1987**
Dividend discount model	+7.0%	−6.8%
Low P/E	+4.7	−8.6
Price momentum	+7.6	−5.0
Historical EPS growth	+4.7	−12.0
Low earnings uncertainty	+1.3	−6.4
Low analyst coverage	+7.0	−1.0
Small capitalization	+9.3	−1.7

Note: Returns are defined as annualized total return percentage for the top 20% of stocks ranked by each model in excess of (+) or less than (−) the return on the S&P 500 stock index.

Source: Goldman Sachs.

How the Valuation Models Have Performed

Several studies have examined the performance of the various models described above. A study by Robert C. Jones of Goldman Sachs sheds some light on this question.[22] Table 15-5 shows the record of seven historically popular equity valuation models over the 19 years prior to June 30, 1987, and over the 12 months ending June 30, 1987. As revealed in Table 15-5, none of the seven models continued in its historical track record in the year ended June 30, 1987, and none of the seven outperformed the S&P 500 stock index for this period.

According to Jones, this never happened before in the 19-year history of his backtests. The stocks that did outperform the S&P index over the 12-month period were overvalued, large-capitalization, low-earnings-growth, high-P/E, low-dividend, high-analyst-coverage stocks. These stocks as a group fit no single investment style currently in use! When these results were reported in *The Wall Street Journal*, none of the commentators interviewed in the article could explain this phenomenon. However, they did agree that the market was unlikely to continue to ignore the "value" for long—undervalued stocks must eventually come back into favor. And, indeed, the value investment style came roaring back in 1991 and 1992.

Other studies suggest that simple multifactor models can outperform other models. Jacobs and Levy have compared the contribution of a simple factor model with a traditional dividend discount model.[23] They found that less than one-half of 1% of the quarterly average actual returns is explained by the DDM. In contrast, about 43% of the average actual returns is ex-

---

[22]Robert Jones, *Stock Selection* (New York: Goldman Sachs & Co., December 1987).

[23]Jacobs and Levy, "On the Value of Value," op. cit.

TABLE 15-6

PERFORMANCE OF PORTFOLIOS BASED ON ONE FACTOR VERSUS TWO FACTORS

Portfolio	Period 1 Return	Period 2 Return	Two-Period Return
Factor 1 portfolio	+100%	−50%	0%
Factor 2 portfolio	−50%	+100%	0%
Equal-weighted portfolio	+25%	+25%	+56.25%

plained by a factor model which includes the DDM and other factors. Thus, in their study the factor model outperformed the DDM hands down.

Another study by Robert C. Jones of Goldman Sachs examined the net return of the top-quartile stocks over the bottom-quartile stock returns for 12 factors, along with the returns for two factor models: an equal-weighted (EW) multifactor model and a combination of the multifactor model plus a dividend discount model. The results for the multifactor model were the highest for various time periods from the 1970s through 1988. The DDM can be either a stand-alone model (as some practitioners use it) or one of several inputs to a multifactor model (as some other practitioners use it and as shown above).

This winning performance for the multifactor model comes from both stock rebalancing and factor diversification. We can state the following generalization: Over a long time horizon, if the correlation between two factors with equal long-run returns is not +1.0 or −1.0, and if rebalancing is used and transactions costs are zero, multifactor models will outperform single-factor models. The multifactor model is always poised to take advantage of the undervalued factor. To illustrate this, consider two portfolios, each based on only one factor. The return for each portfolio for each of two periods and the two-period return are shown in Table 15-6, as is the return for a portfolio consisting of an equal weighting of both portfolios. As can be seen from the table, the equal-weighted portfolio will outperform the two portfolios that are constructed using only one factor. Although this two-period example uses exaggerated returns, the message is clear: Rebalancing a multifactor portfolio by using a low or negative correlation between the factors results in gains. Of course, if everyone were rebalancing using the same multifactor models, prices would quickly reflect this.

The final question is whether the returns to the factors will persist. In their research, Levy and Jacobs included 25 factors and 38 industry variables in their model.[24] They found consistent returns for a number of factor strategies (low P/E, small size, high sales/price, trends in earnings estimates, earnings surprises, relative strength, and residual reversals). Indeed, to the extent that these strategies represent either future earnings risk or uncertainty because of recent changes, one might expect continued higher returns for this risk.

[24]Jacobs and Levy, "On the Value of Value," op. cit.

CONSIDERATIONS IN DEVELOPING AND SELECTING QUANTITATIVE STRATEGIES

Robert Hagin of Miller, Anderson & Sherrerd defines quantitative strategies as "engineered investment strategies."[25] According to Hagin, these strategies have at least three characteristics. First, the strategy should be based on a sound theory. That is, there should be not only a reason why the strategy worked in the past, but, more importantly, a reason why it should be expected to work in the future. Second, the strategy should be put in quantified terms. Finally, a determination should be made of how the strategy would have performed in the past. This last characteristic is critical and is the reason why investment strategies are backtested.

A portfolio manager encounters many potential problems in the design, testing, and implementation of engineered investment strategies. These include:[26]

1. *Insufficient rationale*. There is insufficient rationale for why a strategy worked in the past and why it is anticipated that it will work in the future.

2. *Blind assumptions*. Some strategies are based on blind assumptions that certain factors are always "good" or always "bad."

3. *Data mining*. Data mining occurs when so many strategies are tested that, by the laws of chance, one works. This is related to the problem of insufficient rationale and blind assumptions. Data mining is suspected when an investment researcher uncovers statistical relationships that are not related to any investment theory or substantive model and may well be just a result of the type of data or statistical model used or pure chance.

4. *Quality of data*. In searching for engineered investment strategies, managers use computer-based historical data. These data bases often suffer from problems of inaccuracy, omissions, and survivor bias. Survivor bias occurs when the companies that disappeared are eliminated from the data base. As a result, any testing of a potential strategy that includes only surviving companies would be biased in favor of "survivors."

5. *Look-ahead bias*. This bias involves testing an investment strategy using data that would not have been available at the time the strategy was implemented. For example, suppose that a manager is testing a strategy involving the price-earnings ratio and performs the following test: If the price-earnings ratio is greater than a specified value on December 31, then sell the stock on January 1; if it is less than the specified value, then buy the stock on January 1. The look-ahead bias here is that the price-earnings ratio based on actual earnings for the year ending December 31 cannot be calculated on December 31 because actual earnings for the year ending December 31 are reported in the first quarter (or later) of the following year. Thus, in conducting this backtest, the manager would be using data

---

[25]Robert L. Hagin, "Engineered Investment Strategies: Problems and Solutions," in Katrina F. Sherrerd (ed.), *Equity Markets and Valuation Methods* (Charlottesville, VA: The Institute of Chartered Financial Analysts, 1988), p. 16.

[26]Hagin, "Engineered Investment Strategies," op. cit., pp. 17–19.

on December 31 that were not available on that date. To have a valid backtest of this investment strategy, the manager would have to design the test so as to use earnings data that would have been available on December 31 (e.g., an analyst's *estimate* of earnings as of December 31).

6. *Multiple factors.* As demonstrated by Jacobs and Levy,[27] many of the observed market anomalies are highly correlated. Adding highly correlated factors to a model neither enhances return nor lowers risk. Factors that by themselves seem not to be important may be important when combined with other factors. A manager must be able to untangle these relationships.

7. *Statistical assumptions and techniques.* A product of a test of a strategy using historical data is predicted investment returns or excess returns. These returns are then subjected to statistical tests to determine if they are statistically different from zero (i.e., they did not result merely by chance). Statistical tests require that assumptions be made about the probability distribution for the return of stocks. For example, it is common to assume that returns are normally distributed. Yet empirical evidence does not support this assumption. Therefore, in this case, the manager must assess the extent to which the test of a strategy is affected by the underlying assumption about the probability distribution of returns.

8. *Linear models.* In the valuation models presented in this chapter and Chapter 6, it is assumed that there is a linear relationship between a factor and the expected return. Empirical evidence does seem to suggest that factors conform to a linear model. For example, Richard Grinold of BARRA tested 12 of the 13 factors in the BARRA model that we noted above and found that 83% conformed to linear models, which suggests that 17% are best described by a nonlinear relationship. Thus, a manager may test a linear factor model and find it not to be statistically significant; yet a more complex nonlinear model in fact may produce a highly significant correlation between return and the factors.

9. *Market impact.* As explained in Chapter 13, in implementing a strategy, one of the transactions costs faced is market impact cost. This must be recognized in conducting tests of strategies. Predicted excess returns can be wiped out by market impact.

10. *"Reference" or "normal" portfolios.* In designing a test of the historical performance of a strategy, performance should be measured against a suitable benchmark, called the *reference* or *normal* portfolio. We will turn to the issue of selecting an appropriate benchmark in Chapter 30.

■ SUMMARY

Active equity management begins with the notion that stock prices are sufficiently mispriced that excess returns after adjusting for risk and transactions costs can be realized by identifying mispriced stocks and exploiting the mispricing. The two basic investment styles of active equity management are the bottom-up approach and the top-down approach. In turn, investment styles can be further categorized as value managers, growth managers, group rotation managers, technicians, market timers, and hedgers.

---

[27]Bruce Jacobs and Kenneth Levy, "Disentangling Equity Return Regularities: New Insights and Investment Opportunities," *Financial Analysts Journal* (May–June 1988), pp. 18–43.

The various equity valuation models employed by practitioners are the three-phase dividend discount model, the Benjamin Graham low-P/E model, the relative strength model, the homogeneous group/group rotation models, the multifactor model, and the market anomalies model. Whereas some of these models, such as the DDM, allow a manager to construct portfolios from a bottom-up perspective, multifactor models provide the technology to construct portfolios from the top down. If a manager is skillful at anticipating the direction of factors, it is possible to identify companies that will benefit by their exposure to various factors. These approaches are not mutually exclusive. Rather, many of these models can be used in combination with each other and especially in combination with sound judgment.

APPENDIX: THE BARRA MULTIFACTOR MODEL

The BARRA E2 model estimates factors for 13 risk indexes and 55 industry groups. For 12 of these risk indexes and the 55 industry groups, the model is estimated for BARRA's HICAP universe (1,000 of the largest-capitalization companies plus selected slightly smaller companies to fill underrepresented industry groups) using statistical techniques. The universe has varied from 1,170 to 1,300 companies.

Each risk index is built from a number of underlying fundamental data items that capture an element of the risk BARRA is trying to measure. Combining them produces a multifaceted measure of risk that best characterizes the single concept that is being measured. The individual data items are called *descriptors*, and the combined descriptors make up the 13 risk indexes.

1. *Variability in Markets* (VIM) This risk index is a predictor of the market volatility of a stock based on its behavior and the behavior of its options in the capital markets. It uses measures such as cumulative trading range and daily stock price standard deviation to identify stocks with highly variable stock prices.

2. *Success* (SCS) The success index identifies stocks that have been successful recently in terms of both earnings and stock prices. The success of the company is measured over both the past year and the past five years in two ways: first, as measured by earnings growth (five-year growth in earnings, growth in earnings in the latest year, and present growth in earnings implied by the I/B/E/S data); and second, as measured by price behavior in the market over the past five years and the past year (historical alpha and relative strength). In addition, frequency of dividend cuts is used as a negative indication.

3. *Size* (SIZ) The size index is based on the value of total assets and the total market capitalization for a company.

4. *Trading Activity* (TRA) The trading activity index captures various descriptors of the activity of the shares traded in the market. Most important are the share-turnover variables. Also incorporated are the ratio of trading volume to price variability, the logarithm of price, and the number of analysts following the stock, as reported in the I/B/E/S data base. The stocks with more rapid share turnover, lower price, and signs of greater trading activity are generally the higher-risk stocks. This index can be thought of as an indicator of institutional popularity.

5. *Growth* (GRO) The growth index estimates earnings growth for the next five years using regression techniques on historical data. It includes descriptors of payout, asset growth, historical growth in earnings, the level of earnings to price, and variability in capital structure.

6. *Earnings-Price Ratio* (EPR) The earnings-price risk index is a combination of measures of past, current, and estimated future earnings.

7. *Book-Price Ratio* (BPR) This index is simply the book value of common equity divided by the market capitalization.

8. *Earnings Variation* (EVR) This index is a measure of the company's historical earnings variability. In addition to a five-year variance of earnings descriptor, it includes both a component capturing the relative variability of earnings forecasts taken from the I/B/E/S

data base and a measure of the industry concentration of the firm's activities.

9. *Financial Leverage* (FLV) The financial leverage index is based on the debt-assets ratio, leverage at book value, and probability of fixedcharges not being covered.

10. *Foreign Income* (FOR) This index reflects the fraction of operating income earned outside the United States.

11. *Labor Intensity* (LBI) The labor intensity index measures the importance of labor, relative to capital, in the operations of the firm. It is based on descriptors of labor expense relative to assets, of fixed plant and equipment relative to equity, and of the ratio of depreciated plant value to total plant cost. A higher value on the index indicates a larger ratio of labor expense to capital costs.

12. *Yield* (YLD) This index is a predictor of dividend yield for the coming year.

13 *LOCAP* The LOCAP characteristic singles out those companies that are not in the HICAP universe. It permits an adjustment to the average returns of those companies, relative to the predicted values from the factors estimated within the HICAP universe. The LOCAP factor in any month is roughly the difference between the average returns of non-HICAP companies and the average value predicted by the factor exposures of those companies. The factor is, in a sense, an extension of the size factor, allowing the smaller-company returns to deviate from an exact linear relationship with the size index.

■ **KEY TERMS**

attribute bias
bottom-up equity management
  style
cluster analysis
constant-growth model
contrarians
dividend discount model (DDM)
Gordon-Shapiro model

group rotation manager
growth manager
growth phase
hedge fund
hedger
market timer
maturity phase
plowback rate

retention rate
technician
three-phase DDM
top-down equity management
  style
transition phase
value manager

■ **QUESTIONS**

1. *Morningstar* is a publication that evaluates mutual funds. For each mutual fund discussed in the publication, there is a box labeled "Style" that looks as follows:

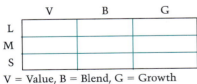

V = Value, B = Blend, G = Growth
L = Large, M = Medium, S = Small

For each mutual fund, the box that best represents the style of the manager of the mutual fund is shaded.

a. What is meant by a money manager's style?

b. What do you think *Morningstar* means by Value, Blend, and Growth?

c. What do you think *Morningstar* means by Large, Medium, and Small?

2. In its write-up of the Guardian Park Avenue Fund, *Morningstar* described the investment approach of the fund manager, Chuck Albers, as a quantitative stock picking in which the "model combines three kinds of factors: valuation, price and earnings momentum, and technical analysis. Based on the model's real-world performance, Albers continually fine-tunes the weightings given to each of these factors. Albers looks at the stocks rated in the top 10% by the model and checks their fundamentals before buying."

a. Describe each of the three factors that are considered in Mr. Albers's model: valuation, price and earnings momentum, and technical analysis.

b. What do you think it means that Mr. Albers "checks their fundamentals before buying"?

3. a. What is meant by the top-down equity management style?

b. What is meant by the bottom-up equity management style?

4. A study of the 10-year returns of more than 650 managers that was conducted by Plan Sponsor Network, and reported in the July 1991 issue of *Institutional Investor*, found the following returns through the first quarter of 1991:

Equity Style	1 Year	5 Years	10 Years
Growth	19.42%	13.77%	16.43%
Small-cap growth	24.21	13.92	16.81
Value	11.39	12.10	16.73
Large cap	14.36	13.02	16.62
Small cap	15.56	12.44	16.73
Contrarian	9.39	11.34	16.52
Income	10.10	12.10	16.81

The results are net of commission but do not reflect management fees. In the study, the 650 managers were grouped according to their own professed styles. Based on the evidence reported above, does it appear that the equity style makes a difference?

5. Suppose an investor applies the constant-growth version of the dividend discount model to estimate the price of the Peoria Corporation. The current dividend per share is $3.

a. Assuming the current dividend will grow at a constant rate of 10% per year and the discount rate is 12%, what is the estimated value of a share of Peoria Corporation?

b. Suppose the market price of a share of Peoria Corporation is $12. What spread between the discount rate and the growth rate is consistent with the current dividend, the observed market price, and the constant growth version of the dividend discount model?

c. What are the limitations of the constant-growth dividend discount model?

6. a. What are the assumptions underlying the three-phase dividend discount model?

b. Rather than estimate the price in a three-phase dividend discount model, the expected return can be calculated. Explain how this is done.

c. On the basis of the estimated expected return from the three-phase dividend discount model,

how does an investor determine whether the stock is fairly priced?

d. Explain how the capital asset pricing model can be used in answering item c.

7. What is meant by attribute bias in using the dividend discount model?

8. The following is an excerpt from an article by H. Russell Fogler ("Common Stock Management in the 1990s") published in the Winter 1990 issue of the *Journal of Portfolio Management*:

> To begin, one might ask: "Is security analysis relevant anymore?" Before you judge this question ludicrous, be aware that Jacobs and Levy have compared the contribution of a simple factor model to a traditional dividend discount model (DDM)—the factor model outperformed the DDM hands down!
>
> Answering this question is easy by referring to the factor model equation:
>
> $$R_i = B_{i,1}f_1 + B_{i,2}f_2 + \ldots + B_{i,k}f_k + e_k$$
>
> where R_i is the return on stock i;
>
> f_i is the return attributable to factor k (e.g., P/E, low capitalization, etc.);
>
> $B_{i,k}$ is the sensitivity of stock i's return to the return of the kth factor, and
>
> e_i is the unexplained portion.
>
> Suppose that three factors, beta, P/E, and size, were sufficient to explain 90% of a portfolio's return—then, for a three-factor model, the other 10% would be in the error term, e_i. Clearly, whether it is less or more than 10% will depend on the model, but any such return is relevant, just as is any security analysis behind it.
>
> Although it sounds facetious, a modern definition of security analysis is discovering stocks with positive error terms. Any investor can construct a portfolio with a specified beta, P/E, and size (or any other commonly used factors)—one needs only a personal computer and some software. Real security analysis requires analyzing a company's fundamentals (à la Graham and Dodd), as well as projecting its future prospects (à la John Burr Williams and DDMs). Merely screening for a low P/E or low P/B, or plugging in an I/B/E/S earnings forecast, doesn't qualify as security analysis (for example, factor models such as BARRA Associates' already utilize I/B/E/S forecasts, relative strength measures, and other generally available data base items.). . .

By this definition, security analysis is idiosyncratic. In other words, real security analysis doesn't follow the herd. For example, if the error term is viewed as

$e_i = f(x_1, x_2, \ldots, x_n)$

then x_i are i variables that knowledgeable security analysts utilize. To ensure profits these variables can be known to only a few. If the variables are widely known, they can be replicated—then they become a factor.

a. What is a factor model?

b. According to Fogler, a factor model would be needed to be able to identify mispriced securities. Why?

c. Explain what Fogler means that "If the variables are widely known, they can be replicated—then they become a factor."

d. Explain whether you agree or disagree with Fogler's definition of modern security analysis.

9. In "Common Stock Management in the 1990s" published in the Winter 1990 issue of the *Journal of Portfolio Management*, H. Russell Fogler makes the following statement: "Active added value comes from one of three sources: timing short-term factor trends, market timing, or security analysis." Explain each of these sources of added value.

10. In "A Modern Theory of Security Analysis," published in the Spring 1993 issue of the *Journal of Portfolio Management*, H. Russell Fogler makes the following statement:

The message to all security analysts is straightforward. Although trading in our capital markets has changed (e.g., institutional domination, synthetic securities, reduced alphas, and faster analysis and execution via computers), Ben Graham's fundamental principle remains. The issue isn't traditional versus quantitative security analysts. Rather, modern security analysts must provide idiosyncratic value that can't be supplied by a computer.

a. What is "Ben Graham's fundamental principle" that Fogler refers to in the excerpt?

b. What does Fogler mean when he says "modern security analysts must provide idiosyncratic value that can't be supplied by a computer"?

11. In "Investment Opportunities with Indexing" [appearing in Katrina F. Sherrerd (ed.), *Equity Markets and Valuation Methods*, (Charlottesville, VA: The Institute of Chartered Financial Analysts, 1988)], Jeffrey L. Skelton argues

that "active and passive management styles may be compared along three dimensions: portfolio construction, trading and monitoring." He included Figure 15-1 to illustrate the differences.

a. Skelton states that "the typical active manager expends the majority of its resources on portfolio construction—the process of deciding which stocks to buy or sell. . . . By contrast, portfolio construction for passive managers is very simple." Explain why this statement is true.

b. Skelton states that "trading techniques in both styles of management are an expression of the need to accommodate the results of portfolio construction." He goes on to say: "The challenge to active managers is to execute an extraordinarily large number of transactions quickly, precisely, and at minimum cost. Most passive trading is in the form of packages or programs, in which hundreds or thousands of stocks are traded at one moment in time." Explain why the foregoing is true.

c. Discussing the monitoring of a portfolio, Skelton states: "Perhaps because an active portfolio has subjective weightings for securities and is difficult to control, the monitoring of its structure is infrequent and imprecise. For exactly the opposite reasons, monitoring of the structure of indexed portfolios must be constant and as complete as possible." Explain why this statement is true.

12. a. The following is from Robert L. Hagin, "Engineered Investment Strategies: Problems and Solutions," in Katrina F. Sherrerd (ed.), *Equity Markets and Valuation Methods* (Charlottesville, VA: The Institute of Chartered Financial Analysts, 1988):

I was at a conference recently where a participant reported he had discovered the exact mix of factors that would have provided the highest returns over a sample period. The strategy was then "tested" on the same sample period. As you might guess, it worked pretty well. Then came an even bigger leap of faith: The researcher introduced an investment management product into the marketplace that uses this exact mix of factors—making the rather heroic assumption that the same factors and the same weights would remain stationary in the future. Of course, they would not. (This problem can be corrected by using a hold-out sample—by specifying a model using data from one period and testing the model using data from another period.)

Financial researchers should never forget two important facts: the world is not perfect and there is very little historical information. If a researcher conducts 1,000 experiments on purely random variables, with 99 percent level of confidence, on average 10 should appear to satisfy the objective function.

Hagin gives a list of potential problems in engineered investment strategies. What problem (or bias) is the above an example of?

b. The following is also taken from the article by Hagin:

What is worse, everyone scrutinizes the same data. If purely accidental relationships are there—and statisticians know they should be—they will be discovered. Thus, the publication of several papers on the same anomaly merely serves to confirm that the anomaly was there in the past, not that it will necessarily be there in the future!

In my opinion, good financial research starts with a rationale for why an investment strategy should work. . . .

Explain why you agree or disagree with the above statement.

CHAPTER 16
USING STOCK INDEX FUTURES IN INVESTMENT MANAGEMENT

LEARNING OBJECTIVES
After reading this chapter you will be able to:

- explain what a futures contract is.
- describe the mark-to-market and margin requirements of a futures contract.
- describe the basic features of U.S. stock index futures contracts.
- determine the theoretical price of a futures contract.
- explain how the futures and cash market are tied together by the cost of carry.
- explain why stock index futures prices may diverge from their theoretical price.
- describe what basis means.
- explain how money managers can use stock index futures to hedge and describe the risks associated with hedging.
- describe how index fund managers can use stock index futures to create an indexed portfolio.
- explain what a stock replacement strategy is and how it can be used by an index fund manager to enhance the return on an index fund.

Thus far in this section of the book, our attention has been on the implementation of investment strategies by buying or selling individual securities. For many types of strategies in the stock market, there may be a more efficient way to implement an investment strategy: buying or selling stock index futures contracts. With the advent of stock index futures, as well as stock index options described in the next chapter, it is now possible for managers to alter the market exposure sensitivity of a stock portfolio or implement a strategy economically and quickly, thereby reducing transactions costs.

Our purpose in this chapter is to explain stock index futures contracts and how they can be used by investment managers. The effective use of stock index futures requires an understanding of how they are priced. Thus, we will also look at how the fair price of a stock index futures contract is determined.

As we discussed in Chapter 2, the value of a futures contract is derived from the value of the underlying asset. Thus, futures contracts are commonly called *derivative instruments*. In the next chapter we will discuss another derivative instrument, an option contract.

FUTURES CONTRACTS

As discussed in Chapter 2, a **futures contract** is a firm legal agreement between a buyer and a seller in which:

1. The buyer agrees to take delivery of something at a specified price at the end of a designated period of time.
2. The seller agrees to make delivery of something at a specified price at the end of a designated period of time.

Of course, no one buys or sells anything when entering into a futures contract. Rather, those who enter into a contract agree to buy or sell a specific amount of a specific item at a specified future date. When we speak of the "buyer" or the "seller" of a contract, we are simply adopting the jargon of the futures market which refers to parties of the contract in terms of the future obligation they are committing themselves to.

Let's look closely at the key elements of this contract. The price at which the parties agree to transact in the future is called the **futures price**. The designated date at which the parties must transact is called the **settlement date** or **delivery date**. The "something" that the parties agree to exchange is called **the underlying**.

To illustrate, suppose a futures contract is traded on an exchange where the underlying to be bought or sold is asset XYZ, and the settlement is three months from now. Assume further that Bob buys this futures contract, and Sally sells this futures contract, and the price at which they agree to transact in the future is $100. Then $100 is the futures price. At the settlement date, Sally will deliver asset XYZ to Bob. Bob will give Sally $100, the futures price.

When an investor takes a position in the market by buying a futures contract (or agreeing to buy at the future date), the investor is said to be in a **long position** or to be **long futures**. If, instead, the investor's opening position is the sale of a futures contract (which means the contractual obligation to sell something in the future), the investor is said to be in a **short position** or **short futures**.

The buyer of a futures contract will realize a profit if the futures price increases; the seller of a futures contract will realize a profit if the futures price decreases. For example, suppose one month after Bob and Sally take their positions in the futures contract, the futures price of asset XYZ increases to $120. Bob, the buyer of the futures contract, could then sell the futures contract and realize a profit of $20. Effectively, at the settlement date he has agreed to buy asset XYZ for $100 and agreed to sell asset XYZ for $120. Sally, the seller of the futures contract, will realize a loss of $20.

If the futures price falls to $40 and Sally buys back the contract at $40, she realizes a profit of $60 because she agreed to sell asset XYZ for $100 and now can buy it for $40. Bob would realize a loss of $60. Thus, if the futures price decreases, the buyer of the futures contract realizes a loss while the seller of the futures contract realizes a profit.

Liquidating a Position

Most financial futures contracts have settlement dates in the months of March, June, September, or December. This means that at a predetermined time in the contract settlement month the contract stops trading, and a price is determined by the exchange for settlement of the contract. For example, on January 4, 199X, suppose Bob buys and Sally sells a futures contract that settles on the third Friday of March of 199X. Then on that date, Bob and Sally must perform—Bob agreeing to buy asset XYZ at $100 and Sally agreeing to sell asset XYZ at $100. The exchange will determine a settlement price for the futures contract for that specific date. For example, if the exchange determines a settlement price of $130, then Bob has agreed to buy asset XYZ for $100 but can settle the position for $130, thereby realizing a profit of $30. Sally would realize a loss of $30.

Instead of Bob or Sally entering into a futures contract on January 4, 199X, that settles in March, they could have selected a settlement in June, September, or December. The contract with the closest settlement date is called the **nearby futures contract**. The **next futures contract** is the one that settles just after the nearby contract. The contract farthest away in time from settlement is called the **most distant futures contract**.

A party to a futures contract has two choices regarding the liquidation of the position. First, the position can be liquidated prior to the settlement date. For this purpose, the party must take an offsetting position in the same contract. For the buyer of a futures contract, this means selling the same number of identical futures contracts; for the seller of a futures contract, this means buying the same number of identical futures contracts. An identical contract means the contract for the same underlying and the same settlement date. So, for example, if Bob buys one futures contract for asset XYZ with settlement in March 199X on January 4, 199X, and wants to liquidate a position on February 14, 199X, he can sell one futures contract for asset XYZ with settlement in March 199X. Similarly, if Sally sells one futures contract for asset XYZ with settlement in March 199X on January 4, 199X, and wants to liquidate a position on February 22, 199X, she can buy one futures contract for asset XYZ with settlement in March 199X. A futures contract on asset XYZ that settles in June 199X is not the same contract as a futures contract on asset XYZ that settles in March 199X.

The alternative is to wait until the settlement date. At that time the party purchasing a futures contract accepts delivery of the underlying; the party that sells a futures contract liquidates the position by delivering the underlying at the agreed-upon price. For the futures contracts that we shall describe later, stock index futures contracts, settlement is made in cash only. Such contracts are referred to as **cash settlement contracts**.

A useful statistic for measuring the liquidity of a contract is the number of contracts that have been entered into but not yet liquidated. This figure is called the contract's **open interest**. An open interest figure is reported by an exchange for every futures contracts traded on the exchange.

The Role of the Clearinghouse

Associated with every futures exchange is a clearinghouse, which performs several functions. One of these functions is to guarantee that the two parties to the transaction will perform. Because of the clearinghouse, the two parties need not worry about the financial strength and integrity of the other party taking the opposite side of the contract. After initial execution of an order, the relationship between the two parties ends. The clearinghouse interposes itself as the buyer for every sale and the seller for every purchase. Thus the two parties are then free to liquidate their positions without involving the other party in the original contract, and without worry that the other party may default.

Margin Requirements

When a position is first taken in a futures contract, the investor must deposit a minimum dollar amount per contract as specified by the exchange. This amount, called **initial margin**, is required as a deposit for the contract. Individual brokerage firms are free to set margin requirements above the minimum established by the exchange. The initial margin may be in the form of an interest-bearing security such as a Treasury bill. The initial margin is placed in an account, and the amount in this account is referred to as the **investor's equity**. As the price of the futures contract fluctuates each trading day, the value of the investor's equity in the position changes.

At the end of each trading day, the exchange determines the "settlement price" for the futures contract. The settlement price is different from the closing price, which many people know from the stock market and which is the price of the security in the final trade of the day (whenever that trade occurred during the day). By contrast, the **settlement price** is that value which the exchange considers to be representative of trading at the end of the day. The representative price may in fact be the price of the day's last trade. But if there is a flurry of trading at the end of the day, a committee of the exchange, called the **pit committee**, looks at all trades in the last few minutes and identifies a median or average price among those trades. The exchange uses the settlement price to **mark to market** the investor's position, so that any gain or loss from the position is quickly reflected in the investor's equity account.

A **maintenance margin** is the minimum level (specified by the exchange) by which an investor's equity position may fall as a result of unfavorable price movements before the investor is required to deposit additional margin. The maintenance margin requirement is a dollar amount that is less than the initial margin requirement. It sets the floor that the investor's equity account can fall to before the investor is required to furnish additional margin. The additional margin deposited, called **variation margin**, is an amount necessary to bring the equity in the account back to its initial margin level. Unlike initial margin, variation margin must be in cash, not interest-bearing instruments. Any excess margin in the account may be withdrawn by the investor. If a party to a futures contract who is required to deposit variation margin fails to do so within 24 hours, the futures position is liquidated by the clearinghouse.[1]

---

[1]Although there are initial and maintenance margin requirements for buying securities on margin, the concept of margin differs for securities and futures. When securities are acquired on margin, the difference between the price of the security and the initial margin is borrowed from the broker. The security purchased serves as collateral for the loan, and the investor pays interest. For futures contracts, the initial margin, in effect, serves as "good-faith" money, an indication that the investor will satisfy the obligation of the contract. Normally no money is borrowed by the investor.

To illustrate the mark-to-market procedure, let's assume the following margin requirements for asset XYZ:

Initial margin $7 per contract

Maintenance margin $4 per contract

Suppose that Bob buys 500 contracts at a futures price of $100 and Sally sells the same number of contracts at the same futures price. The initial margin for both Bob and Sally is $3,500, which is determined by multiplying the initial margin of $7 by the number of contracts, 500. Bob and Sally must put up $3,500 in cash or Treasury bills or other acceptable collateral. At this time, $3,500 is the equity in the account. The maintenance margin for the two positions is $2,000 (the maintenance margin per contract of $4 multiplied by 500 contracts). That means the equity in the account may not fall below $2,000. If it does, the party whose equity falls below the maintenance margin must put up additional margin, which is the variation margin.

Regarding the variation margin, note two things: First, the variation margin must be cash. Second, the amount of variation margin required is the amount to bring the equity up to the initial margin, not the maintenance margin.

Now to illustrate the mark-to-market procedure we will assume the following settlement prices at the end of four consecutive trading days after the transaction was entered into:

Trading Day	Settlement Price
1	$ 99
2	97
3	98
4	95

First consider Bob's position. At the end of trading day 1, Bob realizes a loss of $1 per contract, or $500 for the 500 contracts he bought. Bob's initial equity of $3,500 is reduced by $500 to $3,000. No action is taken by the clearinghouse since Bob's equity is still above the maintenance margin of $2,000. At the end of the second day, Bob realizes a further loss as the price of the futures contract declines $2 to $97, resulting in an additional reduction in his equity position by $1,000. Bob's equity is then $2,000. Despite the loss, no action is taken by the clearinghouse, since the equity is not less than the $2,000 maintenance margin requirement. At the end of trading day 3, Bob realizes a profit from the previous trading day of $1 per contract, or $500. Bob's equity increases to $2,500. The drop in price from 98 to 95 at the end of trading day 4 results in a loss for the 500 contracts of $1,500 and a reduction of Bob's equity to $1,000. Since Bob's equity is now below the $2,000 maintenance margin, Bob is required to put up additional margin of $2,500 (variation margin) to bring the equity up to the initial margin of $3,500. If Bob cannot put up the variation margin, his position will be liquidated. That is, his contracts will be sold by the clearinghouse.

Now let's look at Sally's position. Since Sally sold the futures contract, she benefits if the price of the futures contract declines. As a result, her equity increases at the end of the first two trading days. In fact, at the end of trading day 1, she realizes a profit of $500, which increases her equity to $4,000. She is entitled to remove the $500 profit and utilize these funds elsewhere. Suppose she does, and as a result, her equity remains at $3,500 at the end of trading day 1. At the end of trading day 2, she realizes an additional profit of $1,000 that she can withdraw. At the end of trading day 3, she realizes a loss of $500 since the price increased from $97 to $98. This results in a reduction of her equity to $3,000. Finally, on trading day 4, she realizes a profit of $1,500, making her equity $4,500. She can withdraw $1,000.

Leveraging Aspect of Futures

When taking a position in a futures contract, a party need not put up the entire amount of the investment. Instead, the exchange requires that only the initial margin be invested. To see the crucial consequences of this fact, suppose Bob has $100 and wants to invest in asset XYZ because he believes its price will appreciate. If asset XYZ is selling for $100, he can buy one unit of the asset in the cash market, the market where goods are delivered upon purchase. His payoff will then be based on the price action of one unit of asset XYZ.

Suppose that the exchange where the futures contract for asset XYZ is traded requires an initial margin of only 5%, which in this case would be $5. Then Bob can purchase 20 contracts with his $100 investment. (This example ignores the fact that Bob may need funds for variation margin.) His payoff will then depend on the price action of 20 units of asset XYZ. Thus he can leverage the use of his funds. (The degree of leverage equals 1/margin rate. In this case, the degree of leverage equals 1/0.05, or 20.) While the degree of leverage available in the futures market varies from contract to contract, as the initial margin requirement varies, the leverage attainable is considerably greater than in the cash market.

At first, the leverage available in the futures market may suggest that the market benefits only those who want to speculate on price movements. This is not true. As we shall see, futures markets can be used to reduce price risk. Without the leverage possible in futures transactions, the cost of reducing price risk using futures would be too high for many market participants.

The Role of Futures Contracts in Investment Management

Without financial futures, money managers would have only one trading location to alter portfolio positions when they get new information that is expected to influence the value of assets they manage—the *cash market*, also called the *spot market*. If adverse economic news is received, money managers can reduce their price risk exposure to that asset by selling the asset. The opposite is true if the new information is expected to impact the value of that asset favorably: A money manager would increase price risk exposure to that asset, buying additional quantities of that asset. There are, of course, transactions costs associated with altering exposure to an asset—explicit costs (commissions) and hidden or execution costs (bid-ask spreads and market impact costs), which we discussed in Chapter 13.

The futures market is an alternative market that money managers can use to alter their risk exposure to an asset when new information is acquired. But which market—cash or futures—should the money manager employ to alter a position quickly on the receipt of new information? The answer is simple: the one that more efficiently achieves the investment objective of the money manager. The factors to consider are liquidity, transactions costs, speed of execution, and leverage potential.

It is easier and less costly to alter a portfolio position using stock index futures than using the cash market. A comparison of transactions costs indicates that they are substantially lower in the stock index futures market, both in the United States and in other countries, as will be seen later in this chapter. The speed at which orders can be executed also gives the advantage to the stock index futures market. It has been estimated that to sell a block of stock at a reasonable price would take about two to three minutes, while a futures transaction can be accomplished in 30 seconds or less.[2] The advantage is also on the side of the stock index futures market when it comes to the amount of money that must be put up in a transaction (i.e., leverage). As we explained earlier, margin requirements for transactions in the stock market are considerably higher than in the stock index futures market.

STOCK INDEX FUTURES CONTRACTS

Now that we have a general understanding of futures contracts, we can turn to the specific type of futures contract used by managers of stock portfolios: stock index futures. We described the more popular stock indexes in Chapter 3, such as the Standard & Poor's 500 and the New York Stock Exchange Index. A stock index futures contract is a futures contract in which the underlying is a specific stock index. An investor who buys a stock index futures contract agrees to buy the stock index, and the seller of a stock index futures contract agrees to sell the stock index. In principle, this investor is no different from an investor who buys or sells a futures contract in which the underlying is asset XYZ. The only difference is in the features of the contract that must be established so that it is clear how much of the particular stock index is being bought or sold (which we describe later).

The first stock index futures contracts were introduced in 1982. Table 16-1 lists the countries with stock index futures as of January 1993 and indicates those approved for trading by U.S. investors. Table 16-2 shows the currently traded major stock index futures contracts in the United States. The most actively traded contract is the S&P 500 futures contract. There are no futures contracts on individual stocks.

Basic Features of Stock Index Futures

The dollar value of a stock index futures contract is the product of the futures price and the **futures contract multiple**. The multiple is indicated in Table 16-2. The dollar value of a stock index futures contract is then

Dollar value of a stock index futures contract = futures price × multiple

For all contracts except the Major Market Index, the multiple is $500. For the Major Market index it is $250. To illustrate, if the futures price for the S&P 500 is 400, the dollar value of the stock index futures contract is

400 × $500 = $200,000

If an investor buys an S&P 500 futures contract at 400 and sells it at 420, the investor realizes a profit of 20 times $500, or $10,000. If the futures contract is sold instead for 350, the investor will realize a loss of 50 times $500, or $25,000.

---

[2]Thomas Byrne, "Program Trading—A Trader's Perspective," *Commodities Law Letter*, VI, Nos. 9 and 10, p. 9.

TABLE 16-1

COUNTRIES WITH STOCK INDEX FUTURES

Country	Approved for Use by U.S. Investors
Australia	Yes
Canada	Yes
Denmark	No
France	Yes
Germany	No
Hong Kong	No
Japan	Yes
Netherlands	No
New Zealand	No
Spain	No
Sweden	No
Switzerland	No
United Kingdom	Yes
United States	Yes

TABLE 16-2

SUMMARY OF MAJOR STOCK INDEX FUTURES CONTRACTS TRADED IN THE UNITED STATES (AS OF JUNE 1991)

Contract	Exchange	Multiple	Initial Margin Speculator	Hedger	Last Trading Day in Delivery Month
S&P 500 Index	CBOE	$500	$22,000	$9,000	Thurs. prior to third Friday
NYSE Index	NYSE	500	9,000	4,000	Thurs. prior to third Friday
Major Market Index	AMEX	250	21,000	7,500	Third Friday
Value Line Maxi Index	KCBT	500	7,000	5,000	Third Friday

Features common to all contracts:

1. The contract value is the futures price × the multiple.
2. All contracts settle in cash.
3. The expiration day is the Saturday after the third Friday of the expiration month.

Stock index futures contracts are cash settlement contracts. This means that at the settlement date, cash will be exchanged to settle the contract. For example, if an investor buys an S&P 500 futures contract at 400 and the futures settlement price is 420, settlement would be as follows. The investor has agreed to buy the S&P 500 for 400 times $500, or $200,000. The S&P 500 value at the settlement date is 420 times $500, or $210,000. The seller of this futures contract must pay the investor $10,000 ($210,000 − $200,000). Had the futures price at the settlement date been 330 instead of 420, the dollar value of the S&P 500 futures contract would be $165,000 (330 × $500). In this case, the investor must pay the seller of the contract $35,000 ($200,000 − $165,000).

The minimum price fluctuation, or *tick,* for all stock index futures contracts is 0.05. The dollar value of a tick is found by multiplying 0.05 by the contract's multiple. For stock index futures contracts with a multiple of $500, the dollar value of a tick is $25 (0.05 × $500).

The margin requirements (initial, maintenance, and variation) for futures contracts are revised periodically. As shown in Table 16-2, traders are classified as speculators or hedgers.[3] The initial and maintenance requirements for the S&P 500 futures contract are $22,000 and $9,000, respectively, per contract. If the futures price for the contract is 400, the dollar value of the contract is $200,000. The initial margin is therefore about 11% of the contract value, and the maintenance margin is 4%. For a speculator who purchases stock on margin, however, the initial margin requirement is 50% of the stock position, and the maintenance margin requirement is 25%. Margin requirements for traders classified as hedgers are lower. For the S&P 500 futures contract, the initial margin requirement is $8,000 instead of $22,000. The maintenance margin is the same ($8,000).

Round-Trip Transactions Costs

Table 16-3 shows the estimated round-trip transactions costs (commissions, market impact cost, and taxes) as a percentage of the amount invested for five countries. As can be seen, transactions costs are less for stock index futures than in the cash market. The largest cost differential is in the United States.

TABLE 16-3					
ESTIMATED ROUND-TRIP TRANSACTIONS COSTS AS A PERCENTAGE OF AMOUNT INVESTED FOR STOCKS AND STOCK INDEX FUTURES*					
			Country‡		
Stocks	U.S.	Japan	U.K.	France	Germany
Commissions	0.20%	0.30%	0.10%	0.20%	0.20%
Market impact cost†	0.57	1.00	0.90	0.80	0.60
Taxes	0.00	0.30	0.50	0.00	0.00
Total	0.77%	1.60%	1.50%	1.00%	0.80%
			Country‡		
Futures§	U.S.	Japan	U.K.	France	Germany
Commissions	0.01%	0.11%	0.03%	0.03%	0.03%
Market impact cost†	0.10	0.30	0.40	0.40	0.30
Taxes	0.00	0.00	0.00	0.00	0.00
Total	0.11%	0.41%	0.43%	0.43%	0.33%

*Assumes a $25 million portfolio; does not include settlement and custody fees.

†Trader estimate.

‡Local index: S&P 500, Nikkei 225, FT-SE 100, CAC-40, DAX.

§All contracts are quarterly except for the CAC-40.

Source: Structured International Investment, Goldman Sachs & Co., June 1992, p. 22.

[3]As explained later in this chapter, investors commonly use stock index futures to hedge a position. The clearinghouse requires less margin for investors who are using contracts for this purpose.

Like the commissions on common stock transactions, the commissions on stock index futures trades are fully negotiable. The commissions charged on stock index futures contracts are based on a round trip (i.e., they cover buying and selling the contract). For individual investors, the commissions range from $40 to $100 per contract at a full-service brokerage firm. For institutional investors, the typical commission per contract is less than $15. The cost of transacting is typically less than 0.1% (0.001) of the contract value. A round-trip commission for a portfolio consisting of the underlying stocks would be roughly 1% of the value of the stocks.

PRICING OF FUTURES CONTRACTS

To understand what determines the futures price, consider once again the futures contract where the underlying is asset XYZ. The following assumptions will be made:

1. Asset XYZ is selling for $100 in the cash market.
2. Asset XYZ pays the holder (with certainty) $12 per year in four quarterly payments of $3, and the next quarterly payment is exactly three months from now.
3. The futures contract requires delivery three months from now.
4. The current three-month interest rate at which funds can be loaned or borrowed is 8% per year.

What should the price of this futures contract be? We will explore this question with two examples of mispriced futures contracts, followed by an example of a futures contract in equilibrium with the spot market.

Suppose the price of the futures contract is $107. Consider this strategy:

Sell the futures contract at $107.
Purchase asset XYZ in the cash market for $100.
Borrow $100 for three months at 8% per year.

The borrowed funds are used to purchase asset XYZ, resulting in no initial cash outlay for this strategy. At the end of three months, $3 will be received from holding asset XYZ. Three months from now, asset XYZ must be delivered to settle the futures contract, and the loan must be repaid. This strategy produces an outcome as follows:

1. *From the settlement of the futures contract:*

Proceeds from the sale of asset XYZ to settle the futures contract	107
Dividend received from investing in asset XYZ for 3 months	3
Total proceeds	110

2. *From the loan:*

Repayment of the principal of the loan	100
Interest on the loan (2% for 3 months)	2
Total outlay	102

3. *Profit* 8

Notice that this strategy will guarantee a profit of $8. Moreover, this profit is generated with no investment outlay, as we pointed out above. The profit will be realized regardless of what the futures price at the settlement date is. In financial terms, the profit arises from a riskless arbitrage between the price of XYZ in the cash or spot market and the price of XYZ in the futures market. Obviously, in a well-functioning market, arbitrageurs who could realize this riskless gain for a zero investment would sell the futures contract and buy asset XYZ, forcing the futures price down and bidding up asset XYZ's price so as to eliminate this profit.

Suppose instead that the futures price is $92, and not $107. Let's consider the following strategy:

Buy the futures contract at $92.
Sell (short) asset XYZ for $100.
Invest (lend) $100 for three months at 8% per year.[4]

Once again, there is no initial cash outlay for the strategy: The cost of a long position in a futures contract is zero, and there is no cost to selling the asset short and lending the money. Three months from now, asset XYZ must be purchased to settle the long position in the futures contract. Asset XYZ accepted for delivery will then be used to cover the short position (i.e., to cover the short sale of asset XYZ in the cash market). Shorting asset XYZ requires the short seller to pay the lender of asset XYZ the proceeds that the lender would have earned for the quarter. Therefore, the strategy requires a payment of $3 to the lender of asset XYZ. The outcome in three months would be as follows:

1. *From the settlement of the futures contract:*

Price paid for the purchase of asset XYZ to settle the futures contract	92
Proceeds to the lender of asset XYZ in order to borrow the asset	3
Total outlay	95

2. *From the loan:*

Principal from the maturing of the loan	100
Interest earned from the 3-month loan ($2 for 3 months)	2
Total proceeds	102

3. *Profit*   7

The $7 profit from this strategy is also the result of a riskless arbitrage. This strategy requires no initial cash outlay, but will generate a profit regardless of what the price of asset XYZ is at the settlement date. Clearly, this opportunity would lead arbitrageurs to buy futures and short asset XYZ, and the effect of these two actions would be to raise the futures price and lower the cash price until the profit disappeared.

At what futures price would the arbitraging stop? Asked another way, is there a futures price that would prevent the opportunity for the riskless arbitrage profit? Yes, there is. There will be no arbitrage profit if the futures price is $99. Let's look at what would happen if the two previous strategies are followed, assuming a futures price of $99.

Consider the first strategy, which had these elements:

---

[4]Technically, a short seller may not be entitled to the full use of the proceeds resulting from the sale. We will discuss this later in this section.

Sell the futures contract at $99.
Purchase asset XYZ for $100.
Borrow $100 for three months at 8% per year.

In three months the outcome will be as follows:

1. *From the settlement of the futures contract:*

Proceeds from the sale of asset XYZ to settle the futures contract	99
Payment received from investing in asset XYZ for 3 months	3
Total proceeds	102

2. *From the loan:*

Repayment of the principal of the loan	100
Interest ($2 for 3 months)	2
Total outlay	102
3. *Profit*	0

Therefore, if the futures price is $99, the arbitrage profit has disappeared.
Next, consider a strategy consisting of these actions:

Buy the futures contract at $99.
Sell (short) asset XYZ for $100.
Invest (lend) $100 for 3 months at 8% per year.

The outcome in three months would be as follows:

1. *From the settlement of the futures contract:*

Price paid for the purchase of asset XYZ to settle the futures contract	99
Proceeds to the lender of asset XYZ in order to borrow asset XYZ	3
Total outlay	102

2. *From the loan*

Proceeds received from the maturing of the investment	100
Interest earned from the 3-month loan investment ($2 for 3 months)	2
Total proceeds	102
3. *Profit*	0

If the futures price is $99, neither strategy would result in an arbitrage profit.
Hence, a futures price of $99 is the equilibrium price because any higher or
lower futures price will permit riskless arbitrage profits.

Theoretical Futures Price Based on Arbitrage Model

According to the arbitrage arguments we have just presented, we see that
the equilibrium futures price can be determined on the basis of the following
information:

1. The price of the asset in the cash market
2. The cash yield earned on the asset until the settlement date
3. The "financing cost," which is the interest rate for borrowing and lending
   until the settlement date

To develop a theory of futures pricing, we will use the following notation:

r = financing cost (%)
y = cash yield (%)
P = cash market price ($)
F = futures price ($)

Now, consider this strategy:

Sell (or take a short position in) the futures contract at F.
Purchase asset XYZ for P.
Borrow P, at a rate of r, until the settlement date.

The outcome at the settlement date would be:

1. *From the settlement of the futures contract:*

Proceeds from the sale of asset XYZ to settle the futures contract	F
Payment received from investing in asset XYZ for 3 months	yP
Total proceeds	$F + yP$

2. *From the loan:*

Repayment of the principal of the loan	P
Interest on the loan	rP
Total outlay	$P + rP$

The profit will equal total proceeds − total outlay

$$\text{Profit} = (F + yP) - (P + rP)$$

The equilibrium futures price is the price that ensures that the profit from this arbitrage strategy is zero. Thus, equilibrium requires that

$$0 = (F + yP) - (P + rP)$$

Solving for the theoretical futures price gives this equation:

$$F = P + P(r - y)$$

In other words, the equilibrium futures price is simply a function of the cash price, the financing cost, and the cash yield on the asset.

Alternatively, let us consider the second strategy which was illustrated in our example above and which looks like this:

Buy the futures contract at F.
Sell (short) asset XYZ for P.
Invest (lend) P at r until the settlement date.

The outcome at the settlement date would be:

1. *From the settlement of the futures contract:*

Price paid for the purchase of asset XYZ to settle the futures contract	F
Payment to the lender of asset XYZ in order to borrow the asset	yP
Total outlay	$F + yP$

2. *From the loan:*

Proceeds received from the maturing of the loan investment	P
Interest earned	rP
Total proceeds	$P + rP$

The profit will equal total proceeds − total outlay

Profit = $(P + rP) − (F + yP)$

Setting the profit equal to zero so that there will be no arbitrage profit and solving for the futures price, we obtain the same equation for the futures price as derived earlier:

$$F = P + P(r − y)$$

It is instructive to apply this equation to our previous example to determine the theoretical futures price. In that example, the key variables have these values:

$r = 0.02$

$y = 0.03$

$P = \$100$

Then, the theoretical futures price is

$F = \$100 − \$100(0.03 − 0.02)$

$\quad = \$100 − \$1 = \$99$

This agrees with the equilibrium futures price we proposed earlier. We refer to the equilibrium futures price as the **theoretical futures price** or the **fair price**.

The theoretical futures price may be at a premium to the cash market price (higher than the cash market price) or at a discount from the cash market price (lower than the cash market price), depending on $(r − y)$. The term $r − y$, which reflects the difference between the cost of financing and the asset's cash yield, is called the **net financing cost**. The net financing cost is more commonly called the **cost of carry** or, simply, **carry**. **Positive carry** means that the yield earned is greater than the financing cost; **negative carry** means that the financing cost exceeds the yield earned. Table 16-4 summarizes the effect of carry on the difference between the futures price and the cash market price.

Basis   The **basis** of a futures contract is defined as the difference between the cash price and the futures price observed in the market. That is,

Basis = cash price − futures price

For example, if the cash price of asset XYZ is 100 and the futures price is 102, the basis is −2 $(100 − 102)$.

If a futures contract is properly priced, the theoretical basis should be equal to the cost of carry. For example, suppose the cost of carry for the futures contract in which the underlying is asset XYZ is 2%. This means

---

TABLE 16-4

**THE EFFECT OF NET FINANCING COST ("CARRY")
ON FUTURES PRICING**

Carry	Futures Price
Positive $(y > r)$	Will sell at a discount to cash price $(F < P)$
Negative $(y < r)$	Wili sell at a premium to cash price $(F > P)$
Zero $(r = y)$	Will be equal to the cash price $(F = P)$

that the financing rate is greater than the cash yield. Therefore, carry is negative and the futures price should exceed the cash price by 2%. In our example, the futures price exceeds the cash price for asset XYZ by 2, which is 2% of $100.

To the extent that the actual basis in the market differs from the theoretical basis, arbitrage opportunities exist.

Price Convergence at the Delivery Date   At the delivery date, which is when the futures contract settles, the futures price must equal the cash market price, because a futures contract with no time left until delivery is equivalent to a cash market transaction. Thus, as the delivery date approaches, the futures price will converge to the cash market price. This fact is evident from the equation for the theoretical futures price. As the delivery date approaches, the financing cost approaches zero, and the yield that can be earned by holding the investment approaches zero. Hence the cost of carry approaches zero, and the futures price will approach the cash market price. Therefore, at the delivery date the basis will be zero.

Theoretical Price of a Stock Index Futures Contract

Since dividends are paid on stocks in the index, in the case of stock index futures contracts, the cash yield is simply the dividend yield on the stocks in the index. The cost of carry is then the difference between the annual financing rate and the annualized dividend yield adjusted for the number of days to settlement of the futures contract. More specifically, in the case of stock index futures, the cost of carry is calculated as follows:

Cost of carry = (annual financing rate − annualized dividend yield) × (days to settlement/365)

For example, suppose that the annual financing rate is 6.5%, the annualized dividend yield is 2%, and the number of days to settlement is 60. Then the cost of carry is equal to

$$(0.065 - 0.02) \times (60/365) = 0.007397$$

If the cash index's value is 410, then the theoretical futures price would be

$$410 + 410 (0.007397) = 413.03$$

If the actual futures price is 413.03, then the basis would be −3.03, the difference between the cash index value of 410 and the futures price of 413.03.

To derive the theoretical futures price using the arbitrage argument, we made several assumptions. When the assumptions are violated, the actual futures price will diverge from the theoretical futures price. That is, the difference between the two prices will differ from the value as indicated by the cost of carry. Or expressed in terms of basis, the difference will not be equal to the theoretical basis. Below we will examine the assumptions underlying the arbitrage pricing model and identify practical reasons why the actual price of a stock index futures contract tends to deviate from its theoretical price.

Interim Cash Flows   Our theoretical pricing model assumes that no interim cash flows arise because of changes in futures prices and the need for variation margin. In addition, the model implicitly assumes that any dividend payments are paid at the delivery date rather than at some time between initiating the cash position and the settlement date of the futures contract. However, we know that interim cash flows of either type can and do occur in practice.

In the case of stock index futures, incorporating interim dividend payments into the pricing model is necessary because a cash position in a set of 100 or 500 stocks (the number of stocks underlying an index) generates cash flows in the form of dividends from the stocks. Fortunately, incorporating these interim payments is not difficult. The only problem is that the value that the interim dividend payments will accrue to by the settlement date will depend on the interest rate at which they can be reinvested. The lower the dividend, and the closer the dividend payments to the settlement date of the futures contract, the less important the reinvestment income is in determining the futures price.

Differences between Lending and Borrowing Rates   In deriving the theoretical futures price, we assumed that the investor's borrowing rate and lending rate are equal. Typically, however, the borrowing rate is greater than the lending rate. The impact of this inequality is important and easy to identify. We will begin by adopting these symbols for the two rates:

r_B = borrowing rate

r_L = lending rate

Now, consider this familiar strategy:

Sell the futures contract at F.
Purchase the asset for P.
Borrow P until the settlement date at r_B.

Clearly, the futures price that would produce no arbitrage profit is

$$F = P + P(r_B - y)$$

Recall that the second arbitrage strategy was this:

Buy the futures contract at F.
Sell (short) the asset for P.
Invest (lend) P at r_L until the settlement date.

The futures price that would prevent a riskless profit is

$$F = P + P(r_L - y)$$

These two equations together provide boundaries between which the futures price will be in equilibrium. Figure 16-1 illustrates this. The first equation establishes the upper boundary, and the second equation the lower boundary. For example, assume that the borrowing rate is 8% per year, or 2% for three months, while the lending rate is 6% per year, or 1.5% for three months. According to the first equation, the upper boundary is

$$F \text{ (upper boundary)} = \$100 + \$100 (0.02 - 0.03) = \$99$$

The lower boundary according to the second equation is

$$F \text{ (lower boundary)} = \$100 + \$100 (0.015 - 0.03) = \$98.50$$

Thus, equilibrium arises if the futures price takes on any value between the two boundaries. In other words, equilibrium requires that $\$98.50 < F < \$99$.

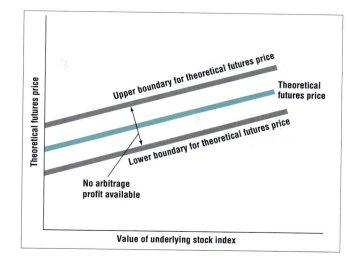

FIGURE 16-1
Boundaries for theoretical futures prices.

Uncertainty about the Dividend Yield   When the futures pricing model is applied to stock index futures, the cash yield represents the dividends that would be paid on the stocks in the index and is referred to as the **dividend yield**. Determining the cost of carry for stock index futures requires knowledge of both the financing cost and the dividend yield on the stocks included in the index. The development of the theoretical futures price assumes that (1) the dividends are known with certainty and (2) the timing of receipt of dividends from each stock in the index is known with certainty. Because neither condition is met in practice, the actual futures price may diverge from the theoretical futures price.

Transactions Costs   In deriving the theoretical futures price, we ignored the transactions costs of the elements in the arbitrage strategies. In actuality, the costs of entering into and closing the cash position as well as round-trip transactions costs for the futures contract do affect the futures price. It is easy to show, as we did above for borrowing and lending rates, that transactions costs widen the boundaries for the futures price. The details need not concern us here.

Short Selling   In the strategy involving short selling of asset XYZ when the futures price is below its theoretical value, we explicitly assumed that the proceeds from the short sale are received and reinvested. In practice, for individual investors, the proceeds are not received, and, in fact, the individual investor is required to put up margin (securities margin and not futures margin) to short-sell. For institutional investors, the asset may be borrowed, but there is a cost to borrowing. This cost of borrowing can be incorporated into the model by reducing the yield on the asset.

For strategies applied to stock index futures, a short sale of the stocks in the index means that all the stocks that constitute the index must be sold simultaneously. The stock exchange rule for the short selling of stock, which was explained in Chapter 3, may prevent an investor from implementing the arbitrage strategy.[5] If the arbitrage requires selling the stocks in the index simultaneously, and the last transaction for some of the stocks is not an uptick, the stocks cannot be shorted simultaneously. Thus, an institutional rule may in effect keep arbitrageurs from bringing the actual futures price in line with the theoretical futures price.

The Deliverable Is a Basket of Securities   In our pricing illustration, we assumed that the underlying is an asset, asset XYZ. For a stock index futures contract, however, the underlying is an index that comprises more than one stock. The problem in arbitraging such a futures contract is that it is too expensive to buy or sell every stock included in the index. Instead, a portfolio containing a smaller number of assets may be constructed to "track" the index (which means having price movements that are very similar to changes in the index). Nonetheless, arbitrage based on this tracking portfolio is no longer risk-free because of the risk that the portfolio will not track the index exactly. Clearly, then, the actual price of futures based on baskets of assets may diverge from the theoretical price because of the transactions costs and uncertainty about the outcome of the arbitrage.

Several studies have examined the pricing efficiency of the stock index futures. These studies have found that after adjusting the theoretical pricing model for various factors discussed above and for taxes, the actual prices do not differ significantly from theoretical prices.[6]

APPLICATIONS

Now that we know what stock index futures are and how they are priced, we can look at how they can be used by institutional investors. Prior to the development of stock index futures, an investor who wanted to speculate on the future course of stock prices had to buy or short individual stocks. Now, the stock index can be bought or sold in the futures market. But making speculation easier for investors is not the main function of stock index futures contracts. The other strategies discussed below show how institutional investors can effectively use stock index futures to meet investment objectives. Box 16 reports the use of stock index futures and other derivatives (described in later chapters) by pension funds.

Controlling the Risk of a Stock Portfolio

A money manager who wishes to alter exposure to the market can do so by revising the portfolio's beta. This can be done by rebalancing the portfolio with stocks that will produce the target beta, but there are transactions costs associated with rebalancing a portfolio. Because of the leverage inherent in futures contracts, money managers can use stock index futures to achieve a target beta at a considerably lower cost. Buying stock index futures will increase a portfolio's beta; and selling will reduce it.

---

[5]The short-selling rule for stocks specifies that a short sale can be made only at a price that is higher than the previous trade (referred to as an up-tick) or at a price that is equal to the previous trade (referred to as a zero-tick) but higher than the last trade at a different price.

[6]For a discussion of these studies, see Frank J. Fabozzi and Franco Modigliani, *Capital Markets* (Englewood Cliffs, NJ: Prentice-Hall, 1992), pp. 307–309.

BOX 16

FUNDS SEE DERIVATIVES AS MORE OF AN OPTION

Pension funds are increasingly crossing over into a dimension that's once removed from their familiar investing world. In other words, they're using derivatives.

More than a third of plan officers in this month's Pensionforum report that they use them. And among those who haven't ventured into the derivatives zone, almost one fourth say they are considering it.

Nearly one quarter of those using derivatives have only a vague idea about how much of their fund's assets are invested in the instruments at any moment, since they give their managers discretion to buy and sell them at will. But another quarter say they have between $11 million and $50 million in derivatives, and about 30 percent indicate they've invested more than that in them.

A tally not shown here indicates that corporate plans tend to own greater amounts of derivatives than do public funds. Less than 12 percent of the funds surveyed place some or all of their derivatives investments into a separate asset class.

Plan officers are divided as to what should be their primary goals in using derivatives. Almost 37 percent claim to be interested equally in both hedging and enhancing returns. About 28 percent say they're in derivatives for hedging purposes first. And 27 percent say their top priority is enhancing returns. Respondents say the uses of their futures contracts range from tactical asset allocation (37 percent) to hedging active managers' portfolios (29 percent) to adding to returns through arbitrage (27 percent).

Does your pension fund invest in derivatives?

Yes	35.6%
No	64.4

If so, how much does your fund have invested in derivatives at any one time, on average?

Less than $11 million	20.7%
$11 million to $50 million	24.8
$51 million to $100 million	12.4
$101 million to $500 million	15.7
$501 million to $1 billion	1.7
More than $1 billion	0.8
Don't know, since amount invested in derivatives is left to the discretion of the fund's managers	24.0

What is your fund's primary goal in its derivatives investing?

Hedging returns	28.3%
Enhancing returns	26.7
Both hedging and enhancing returns, equally	36.7
Lowering transaction costs	4.2
Other	4.2

If you use derivatives, have you used any of the following strategies?

Equity swaps	14.8%
Equitizing or securitizing cash	29.6
Market-neutral investing	15.7
Protective equity notes	5.6
Collars	12.0
Transporting alphas	2.8
None of the above	49.1

If you are using futures contracts, in which of the following contexts are you employing them?

As an occasional hedge against fund's index fund holdings	15.2%
As an occasional hedge against active managers' portfolios	28.6
As a hedge against equity holdings that have to be liquidated in a manager transition	19.0
As a hedge against equity holdings that have to be liquidated in changing overall asset mix	16.2
To maintain equity exposure during manager transitions	21.9
As a quick and low-cost way of adjusting equity exposure in expectation of big market moves (tactical asset allocation)	37.1
To add to returns through arbitrage	26.7
Other	15.2

Do you use derivatives to create synthetic indexes?

Yes	15.4%
No	84.6

Do you treat some or all of your derivatives investments as a separate asset class?

Yes	11.5%
No	88.5

If you are not using derivatives, are you considering doing so?

Yes	24.2%
No	75.8

If your fund is not using derivatives and is not considering their use, why not?

Legal and/or accounting reasons	12.9%
Senior management is opposed	35.4
Don't understand these vehicles and their usefulness	22.4
Barred from using derivatives	23.1
Other	26.5

Source: "Pensionforum: Funds See Derivatives as More of an Option," *Institutional Investor* (November 1993), p.147.

Questions for Box 16

1. How can stock index futures be used for hedging?
2. How can stock index futures be used for enhancing returns?
3. How can stock index futures be used to synthetically create a stock index?

Hedging against Adverse Stock Price Movements

The major economic function of futures markets is to transfer price risk from hedgers to speculators. **Hedging** is the employment of futures contracts as a substitute for a transaction to be made in the cash market. If the cash and futures markets move together, any loss realized by the hedger on one position (whether cash or futures) will be offset by a profit on the other position. When the profit and loss are equal, the hedge is called a **perfect hedge.**

Short Hedge and Long Hedge   A **short hedge** is used by a hedger to protect against a decline in the future cash price of the underlying. To execute a short hedge, the hedger sells a futures contract. Consequently, a short hedge is also referred to as a **sell hedge**. By establishing a short hedge, the hedger has fixed the future cash price and transferred the price risk of ownership to the buyer of the contract.

As an example of a money manager who would use a short hedge, consider a pension fund manager who knows that the beneficiaries of the fund must be paid a total of $3 million four months from now. This will necessitate liquidating a portion of the fund's common stock portfolio. If the value of the shares that she intends to liquidate in order to satisfy the payments to be made decline in value four months from now, a larger portion of the portfolio will have to be liquidated. The easiest way to handle this situation is for the money manager to sell the needed amount of stocks and invest the proceeds in a Treasury bill that matures in four months. However, suppose that for some reason the money manager is constrained from making the sale today. The pension fund manager can use a short hedge to lock in the value of the stocks that will be liquidated.

A **long hedge** is undertaken to protect against rising prices of future intended purchases. In a long hedge, the hedger buys a futures contract, so this hedge is also referred to as a **buy hedge**. As an example, consider once again a pension fund manager. This time suppose that the manager expects a substantial contribution from the plan sponsor four months from now and that the contributions will be invested in common stock of various companies. The pension fund manager expects the market price of the stocks in which he will invest the contributions to be higher in four months and therefore takes the risk that he will have to pay a higher price for the stocks. The manager can use a long hedge to effectively lock in a future price for these stocks now.

Return on a Hedged Position   Hedging is a special case of controlling a stock portfolio's exposure to adverse price changes. In a hedge, the objective is to alter a current or anticipated stock portfolio position so that its beta is zero. A portfolio with a beta of zero should generate a risk-free interest rate. This is consistent with the capital asset pricing model discussed in Chapter 5. Thus, in a perfect hedge, the return will be equal to the risk-free interest rate. More specifically, it will be the risk-free interest rate corresponding to a maturity equal to the number of days until settlement of the futures contract.

Therefore, say, a portfolio that is identical to the S&P 500 (i.e., an S&P 500 index fund) is fully hedged by selling an S&P 500 futures contract with 60 days to settlement which is priced at its theoretical value. The return on this hedged position will be the 60-day risk-free return.

Notice what has been done. If a manager wanted to temporarily eliminate all exposure to the S&P 500, she could sell all the stocks and, with the funds received, invest in a Treasury bill. By using futures contract, the manager can eliminate exposure to the S&P 500 by hedging, and the hedged position will earn the same return as that on a Treasury bill. The manager thereby saves on the transactions costs associated with selling a stock portfolio. Moreover, when the manager wants to get back into the stock market, rather than having to incur the transactions costs associated with buying stocks, she simply removes the hedge by buying an identical number of stock index futures contracts.

Cross Hedging   In practice, hedging is not a simple exercise. When hedging with stock index futures, a perfect hedge can only be obtained if the return on the portfolio being hedged is identical to the return on the futures contract.

The effectiveness of a hedged stock portfolio is determined by:

1. The relationship between the cash portfolio and the index underlying the futures contract
2. The relationship between the cash price and futures price when a hedge is placed and when it is lifted (liquidated)

Recall that the difference between the cash price and the futures price is the basis. It is only at the settlement that the basis is known with certainty. As explained earlier, at the settlement date the basis is zero. If a hedge is lifted at the settlement date, the basis is therefore known. However, if the hedge is lifted at any other time, the basis is not known in advance. The uncertainty about the basis at the time a hedge is to be lifted is called **basis risk**. Consequently, *hedging involves the substitution of basis risk for price risk*.

A stock index futures contract has a stock index as its underlying. Since the portfolio that a money manager seeks to hedge will typically have different characteristics from the underlying stock index, there will be a difference in return pattern of the portfolio being hedged and the futures contract. This practice—hedging with a futures contract that is different from the underlying being hedged—is called **cross hedging**. In the commodity futures markets this occurs, for example, when a farmer who grows okra hedges that crop by using corn futures contracts since there are no exchange-traded contracts in which okra is the underlying. In the stock market, a money manager who wishes to hedge a stock portfolio must choose the stock index, or combination of stock indexes, that best (but imperfectly) tracks the portfolio.

Consequently, cross hedging adds another dimension to basis risk, because the portfolio does not track the return on the stock index perfectly. Mispricing of a stock index futures contract is a major portion of basis risk and is largely random. Mispricing is measured as the divergence between the actual futures price and the theoretical futures price as a percentage of the actual futures price. That is, mispricing can be specified as follows:

$$\text{Mispricing} = \frac{\text{actual futures price} - \text{theoretical futures price}}{\text{actual futures price}}$$

The foregoing points about hedging will be made clearer in the illustrations below.

Hedge Ratio   To implement a hedging strategy, it is necessary to determine not only which stock index futures contract to use, but also how many of the contracts to take a position in (i.e., how many to sell in a short hedge and buy in a long hedge). The number of contracts depends on the relative return volatility of the portfolio to be hedged and the return volatility of the futures contract. The **hedge ratio** is the ratio of volatility of the portfolio to be hedged and the return volatility of the futures contract.

It is tempting to use the portfolio's beta as a hedge ratio because it is an indicator of the sensitivity of a portfolio's return to the stock index return. It appears, then, to be an ideal way to adjust for the sensitivity of the return of the portfolio to be hedged. However, applying beta relative to a stock index as a sensitivity adjustment to a stock index futures contract assumes that the index and the futures contract have the same volatility. If futures always sold at their fair price, this would be a reasonable assumption. However, mispricing is an extra element of volatility in a stock index futures contract. One study found that mispricing adds 20% to the volatility of a stock index futures contract.[7] Since the futures contract is more volatile than the underlying index, using a portfolio beta as a sensitivity adjustment would result in a portfolio being overhedged.

The most accurate sensitivity adjustment would be the beta of a portfolio relative to the futures contract. It can be shown that the beta of a portfolio relative to a futures contract is equivalent to the product of the portfolio relative to the underlying index and the beta of the index relative to the futures contract.[8] The beta in each case is estimated using regression analysis in which the data are historical returns for the portfolio to be hedged, the stock index, and the stock index futures contract. The regression estimated is

$$r_P = a_P + B_{PI}r_I + e_P$$

where r_P = the return on the portfolio to be hedged
r_I = the return on the stock index
B_{PI} = the beta of the portfolio relative to the stock index
a_P = the intercept of the relationship
e_P = the error term

and

$$r_I = a_I + B_{IF}r_F + e_I$$

where r_F = the return on the stock index futures contract
B_{IF} = the beta of the stock index relative to the stock index futures contract
a_I = the intercept of the relationship
e_I = the error term

Given B_{PI} and B_{IF}, the minimum risk hedge ratio can then be expressed as

Hedge ratio = $B_{PI} \times B_{IF}$

The coefficient of determination of the regression will indicate how good the estimated relationship is and thereby allow the money manager to assess the likelihood of success of the proposed hedge.

The number of contracts needed can be calculated using the following three steps after B_{PI} and B_{IF} are estimated:

Step 1. Determine the *equivalent market index units* of the market by divid-

[7]Ed Peters, "Hedged Equity Portfolios: Components of Risk and Return," *Advances in Futures and Options Research*, 1B, 1987, pp. 75–92.

[8]Peters, "Hedged Equity Portfolios," ibid.

ing the market value of the portfolio to be hedged by the current index price of the futures contract:

Equivalent market index units

$$= \frac{\text{market value of the portfolio to be hedged}}{\text{current index value of the futures contract}}$$

Step 2. Multiply the equivalent market index units by the hedge ratio to obtain the *beta-adjusted equivalent market index units*:

Beta-adjusted equivalent market index units
= hedge ratio × equivalent market index units

or

Beta-adjusted equivalent market index units
= $B_{PI} \times B_{IF} \times$ equivalent market index units

Step 3. Divide the beta-adjusted equivalent units by the multiple specified by the stock index futures contract:

$$\text{Number of contracts} = \frac{\text{beta-adjusted equivalent market index units}}{\text{multiple of the contract}}$$

Illustrations   We will use two examples to illustrate the implementation of a hedge and the risks associated with hedging.[9]

In our first illustration, consider a portfolio manager on July 1, 1986, who is managing a $1 million portfolio that is identical to the S&P 500. The manager wants to hedge against a possible market decline. More specifically, the manager wants to hedge the portfolio until August 31, 1986. To hedge against an adverse market move during the period July 1, 1986, to August 31, 1986, the portfolio manager decides to enter into a short hedge by selling the S&P 500 futures contracts that settled in September 1986. On July 1, 1986, the September 1986 futures contract was selling for 253.95.

Since the portfolio to be hedged is identical to the S&P 500, the beta of the portfolio relative to the index (B_{PI}) is, of course, 1. The beta relative to the futures contract (B_{IF}) was estimated to be 0.745. Therefore, the number of contracts needed to hedge the $1 million portfolio is computed as follows:

Step 1
$$\text{Equivalent market index units} = \frac{\$1,000,000}{253.95} = \$3,937.78$$

Step 2
Beta-adjusted equivalent market index units = 1 × 0.745 × $3,937.78
= $2,933.648

Step 3. The multiple for the S&P 500 contract is 500. Therefore,

$$\text{Number of contracts to be sold} = \frac{\$2,933.648}{\$500} = 5.87$$

This number will be rounded up to six contracts. This means that the futures position was equal to $761,850 (6 × 500 × 253.95). On August 31, 1986, the hedge was removed. The portfolio that mirrored the S&P 500 had lost $67,965.40. At the time the hedge was lifted, the September 1986 S&P 500

[9]These two examples are taken from Frank J. Fabozzi and Edgar E. Peters, "Hedging with Stock Index Futures," Chap. 13 in Frank J. Fabozzi and Gregory M. Kipnis (eds.), *The Handbook of Stock Index Futures and Options* (Homewood, IL: Richard D. Irwin, 1989).

contract was selling at 233.15. Since the contract was sold on July 1, 1986, for 253.95 and bought back on August 31, 1986, for 233.15, there was a gain of 20.8 index units per contract. For the six contracts, the gain was $62,400 (20.8 × 500 × 6). This results in a trivial loss of $5,565.40 ($62,400 gain on the futures position and $67,965.40 loss on the portfolio). The total transactions costs for the futures position would have been less than $120. Remember, had the money manager not hedged the position, the loss would have been $67,965.40.

Let's analyze this hedge to see not only why it was successful but also why it was not a perfect hedge. As explained earlier, in hedging, basis risk is substituted for price risk. Consider the basis risk in this hedge. At the time the hedge was placed, the cash index was at 252.04 and the futures contract was selling at 253.95. The basis was equal to −1.91 index units (the cash index of 252.04 minus the futures price of 253.95). At the same time, it was calculated that, based on the cost of carry, the theoretical basis was −1.26 index units. That is, the fair value for this futures contract at the time the hedge was placed should have been 253.3. Thus, the futures contract was mispriced by 0.65 index unit.

When the hedge was removed at the close of August 31, 1986, the cash index stood at 234.91 and the futures contract at 233.15. Thus, the basis changed from −1.91 index units at the time the hedge was initiated to +1.76 index units (234.91 − 233.15) when the hedge was lifted. The basis had changed by 3.67 index units (1.91 + 1.76) alone, or $1,835 per contract (3.67 times the multiple of $500). This means that the basis alone returned $11,010 for the six contracts ($1,835 × 6). The index dropped 17.13 index units for a gain of $8,565 per contract, or $51,390. Thus, the futures position returned $11,010 due to the change in the basis risk and $51,390 due to the change in the index. Combined, this comes out to be the $62,400 gain in the futures position.

In this illustration, the two-beta hedge ratio minimized the effects of the basis, which swung 3.67 index units. If B_{PI} had been used rather than the two-beta hedge ratio, the number of contracts for hedging would have been calculated to be eight rather than six. This would have resulted in a 1.5% gain in the position. While it is preferable to have a gain rather than a loss, the purpose of hedging is to neutralize the price exposure of a portfolio. While in this case using B_{PI} to obtain the hedge ratio worked out better, this will not always be the case, and its use will subject the hedger to greater basis risk than a two-beta hedge ratio.

In our illustration, we examined basis risk. Since we were hedging a portfolio that was constructed to replicate the S&P 500 index using the S&P 500 futures contract, there was no cross-hedging risk. However, most portfolios are not matched to the S&P 500. Consequently, cross-hedging risk results because the estimated beta for the price behavior of the portfolio may not behave as predicted by B_{PI}. To illustrate this situation, suppose that a money manager owned all the stocks in the Dow Jones Industrial Average on July 1, 1986. The market value of the portfolio held was $1 million. Also assume that the portfolio manager wanted to hedge the position against a decline in stock prices from July 1, 1986, to August 31, 1986, using the September 1986 S&P 500 futures contract. Since the S&P 500 futures September contract is used here to hedge a portfolio of Dow Jones Industrials to August 31, 1986, this is a cross hedge.

Information about the S&P 500 cash index and futures contract when the hedge was placed on July 1, 1986, and when it was removed on August 31, 1986, was given in the previous illustration. The beta of the index relative to the futures contract (B_{IF}) was 0.745. The Dow Jones Index in a regression analysis was shown to have a beta relative to the S&P 500 of 1.05 (with a coefficient of determination of 93%). We follow the three steps enumerated above to obtain the number of contracts to sell:

Step 1

$$\text{Equivalent market index units} = \frac{\$1,000,000}{253.95} = \$3,937.78$$

Step 2

$$\text{Beta-adjusted equivalent market index units} = 1.05 \times 0.745 \times \$3,937.78$$
$$= \$3,080.328$$

Step 3. The multiple for the S&P 500 contract is 500. Therefore,

$$\text{Number of contracts to be sold} = \frac{\$3,080.328}{\$500} = 6.16$$

Again, this would be rounded to six contracts. During the period of the hedge, the Dow Jones index actually lost $73,500. This meant a loss of 7.35% on the portfolio consisting of the Dow Jones stocks. Since the same number of S&P 500 futures contracts were sold as in the previous illustration, the gain from the futures position was the same as in that illustration, $62,400. This means that the hedged position resulted in a loss of $11,100, or equivalently, a return of −1.11%.

We already analyzed why this was not a perfect hedge. In the previous illustration, we explained how changes in the basis affected the outcome. Let's look at how the relationship between the Dow Jones and the S&P 500 index affected the outcome. As stated in the previous illustration, the S&P 500 over this same period declined in value by 6.8%. With the beta of the portfolio relative to the S&P 500 index (1.05), the expected decline in the value of the portfolio based on the movement in the S&P 500 was 7.14% (1.05 × 6.8%). Had this actually occurred, the Dow Jones portfolio would have lost only $71,400 rather than $73,500, and the net loss from the hedge would have been only $9,000, or −0.99%. Thus there is a difference of a $2,100 loss due to the Dow Jones performing differently than predicted by beta.

Constructing an Indexed Portfolio

As we explained in Chapter 14, an increasing number of institutional equity funds are indexed to some broad-based stock market index. There are management fees and transactions costs associated with creating a portfolio to replicate a stock index that has been targeted to be matched. The higher these costs, the greater the divergence between the performance of the indexed portfolio and the target index. Moreover, because a fund manager creating an indexed portfolio will not purchase all the stocks that make up the index, the indexed portfolio is exposed to tracking error risk. Instead of using the cash market to construct an indexed portfolio, the manager can use stock index futures. In fact, *Pension and Investments* reports that of the 60 or so largest pension funds that are indexed, about one third use stock index futures in managing the fund.

Let's illustrate how and under what circumstances stock index funds can be used to create an indexed portfolio. If stock index futures are priced according to their theoretical value, a portfolio consisting of a long position in stock index futures and Treasury bills will produce the same portfolio return as that of the underlying cash index. To see this, suppose that an index fund manager wishes to index a $9 million portfolio using the S&P 500 as the target index. Also assume the following:

1. The S&P 500 is currently 300.
2. The S&P 500 futures index with six months to settlement is currently selling for 303.
3. The expected dividend yield for the S&P 500 for the next six months is 2%.
4. Six-month Treasury bills are currently yielding 3%.

The theoretical futures price is 303.[10]

Consider two strategies that the index fund manager may choose to pursue:

Strategy 1. Purchase $9 million of stocks in such a way as to replicate the performance of the S&P 500.
Strategy 2. Buy 60 S&P 500 futures contracts with settlement six months from now at 303, and invest $9 million in six-month Treasury bills.[11]

How will the two strategies perform under various scenarios for the S&P 500 value when the contract settles six months from now? Let's investigate three scenarios: The S&P 500 increases to 330, remains at 300, and declines to 270. At settlement, the futures price converges to the value of the index. Table 16-5 shows the value of the portfolio for both strategies for each of the three scenarios. As can be seen, for a given scenario, the performance of the two strategies is identical.

This result should not be surprising because a futures contract can be replicated by buying the instrument underlying the futures contract with borrowed funds. In the case of indexing, we are replicating the underlying instrument by buying the futures contract and investing in Treasury bills. Therefore, if stock index futures contracts are properly priced, index fund managers can use stock index futures to create an index fund.

Several points should be noted. First, in strategy 1 the ability of the portfolio to replicate the S&P 500 depends on how well the portfolio is constructed to track the index. On the other hand, assuming that the expected dividends are realized and that the futures contract is fairly priced, the futures/Treasury bill portfolio (strategy 2) will mirror the performance of the S&P 500 exactly. Thus, tracking error is reduced. Second, the cost of transact-

---

[10]The theoretical futures price is found using the formula presented earlier:

Cash market price + cash market price (financing cost − dividend yield)

The financing cost is 3%, and the dividend yield is 2%. Therefore, 300 + 300 (0.03 − 0.02) = 303.

[11]There are two points to note here. First, this illustration ignores margin requirements. The Treasury bills can be used for initial margin. Second, 60 contracts are selected in this strategy because with the current market index at 300 and a multiple of $500, the cash value of 60 contracts is $9 million.

TABLE 16-5

COMPARISON OF PORTFOLIO VALUE FROM PURCHASING STOCKS TO REPLICATE AN INDEX AND A FUTURES/TREASURY BILL STRATEGY WHEN THE FUTURES CONTRACT IS FAIRLY PRICED

Assumptions:

1. Amount to be invested = $9 million
2. Current value of S&P 500 = 300
3. Current value of S&P futures contract = 303
4. Expected dividend yield = 2%
5. Yield on Treasury bills = 3%
6. Number of S&P 500 contracts to be purchased = 60

Strategy 1: Direct Purchase of Stocks

	Index Value at Settlement*		
	330	300	270
Change in index value	10%	0%	−10%
Market value of portfolio that mirrors the index	$ 9,900,000	$9,000,000	$ 8,10,000
Dividends			
0.02 × $9,000,000	$ 180,000	$ 180,000	$ 180,000
Value of portfolio	$10,080,000	$9,180,000	$8,280,000
Dollar return	$ 1,080,000	$ 180,000	$ (720,000)

Strategy 2: Futures/T-Bill Portfolio

	Index Value at Settlement*		
	330	300	270
Gain for 60 contracts			
60 × $500 × gain per contract	$ 810,000	$ (90,000)	$ (999,000)
Value of Treasury bills			
$9,000,000 × 1.03	$ 9,270,000	$9,270,000	$9,270,000
Value of portfolio	$10,080,000	$9,180,000	$8,280,000
Dollar return	$ 1,080,000	$ 180,000	$ (720,000)

* Because of convergence of cash and futures price, the S&P 500 cash index and stock index futures price will be the same.

---

ing is less for strategy 2. For example, if the cost of one S&P 500 futures is $15, then the transactions costs for strategy 2 would be only $900 for a $9 million fund. This would be considerably less than the transactions costs associated with the acquisition and maintenance of a broadly diversified stock portfolio designed to replicate the S&P 500. In addition, for a large fund that wishes to index, the market impact cost is lessened by using stock index futures rather than using the cash market to create an index. The third point is that custodial costs are obviously less for an index fund created using stock index futures. The fourth point is that the performance of the synthetically created index fund will depend on variation margin. Finally, in the analysis of the performance of each strategy, the dollar value of the portfolio at the end of the six-month period is the amount in the absence of taxes. For strategy 1, no taxes will be paid if the securities are not sold, though taxes will be paid on dividends. For strategy 2, taxes must be paid on the interest from the Treasury bills and on any gain from the liquidation of the futures contract.

Enhanced Indexing

In synthetically creating an index fund, we assumed that the futures contract was fairly priced. Suppose instead that the stock index futures price is less than the theoretical futures price (i.e., the futures contracts are cheap). If that situation occurs, the index fund manager can enhance the indexed portfolio's return by buying the futures and buying Treasury bills. That is, the return on the futures/Treasury bill portfolio will be greater than that on the underlying index when the position is held to the settlement date.

To see this, suppose that in our previous illustration the current futures price is 301 instead of 300, so that the futures contract is cheap (undervalued). The futures position for the three scenarios in Table 16-5 would be $60,000 greater (2 index units × $500 × 60 contracts). Therefore, the value of the portfolio and the dollar return for all three scenarios will be greater by $60,000 by buying the futures contract and Treasury bills rather than buying the stocks directly.

Alternatively, if the futures contract is expensive based on its theoretical price, an index fund manager who owns stock index futures and Treasury bills will swap that portfolio for the stocks in the index. An index fund manager who swaps between the futures/Treasury bills portfolio and a stock portfolio based on the value of the futures contract relative to the cash market index is attempting to enhance the portfolio's return. This strategy, referred to as a **stock replacement strategy,** is one of several strategies used to attempt to enhance the return of an indexed portfolio.[12]

Transactions costs can be reduced measurably by using a return enhancement strategy. Whenever the difference between the actual basis and the theoretical basis exceeds the market impact of a transaction, the aggressive manager should consider replacing stocks with futures or vice versa.

Once the strategy has been put into effect, several subsequent scenarios may unfold. For example, consider an index manager who has a portfolio of stock index futures and Treasury bills. First, should the futures contract become sufficiently rich relative to stocks, the futures position is sold and the stocks repurchased. Program trading is used to execute the buy orders. Second, should the futures contract remain at fair value, the position is held until expiration, when the futures settle at the cash index value and stocks are repurchased at the market at close using a program trade.

Should an index manager own a portfolio of stocks and the futures contract becomes cheap relative to stocks, then the manager will sell the stocks and buy the stock index futures contracts. A program trade will be used to execute the sale of the stocks.

Creating Portfolio Insurance

In the next chapter we will explain how put options on a stock index can be used to protect the value of a stock portfolio. Alternatively, an institutional investor can create a put option synthetically by using either (1) stock index futures or (2) stocks and a riskless asset. Allocation of the portfolio's funds to stock index futures or between stocks and a riskless asset is adjusted as market conditions change. A strategy that seeks to ensure the value of a

---

[12]For a further discussion of this strategy, see Bruce M. Collins, "Index Fund Investment Management," Chap. 10 in Frank J. Fabozzi (ed.), *Portfolio and Investment Management* (Chicago: Probus Publishing, 1989).

portfolio using a synthetic put option strategy is called **dynamic hedging**, or **portfolio insurance**.

Given that put options on stock indexes are available to portfolio managers, why should they bother with dynamic hedging? We give these reasons in Chapter 17. They will be better understood after we explain options.

■ SUMMARY

This chapter has explained the basic features of stock index futures. A buyer (seller) of a futures contract realizes a profit if the futures price increases (decreases). The buyer (seller) of a futures contract realizes a loss if the futures price decreases (increases). Because only initial margin is required when an investor takes a futures position, futures markets provide investors with substantial leverage for the money invested.

Investors can use the futures market or the cash market to react to economic news that is expected to change the value of an asset. Futures markets are the market of choice for altering asset positions because of the lower transactions costs involved and the greater speed with which orders can be executed.

With the use of arbitrage arguments, the theoretical price of a futures contract can be shown to be equal to the cash market price plus the cost of carry. The cost of carry is the net financing cost, that is, the difference between the financing rate and the cash yield on the underlying asset. Developing the theoretical futures price with arbitrage arguments requires certain assumptions. When these assumptions are violated for a specific futures contract, the theoretical futures price must be modified.

Money managers can use stock index futures contracts in a variety of ways. Managers can use them to alter the risk exposure of a stock by quickly and inexpensively changing a portfolio's beta. In hedging a portfolio, the key factor is the basis, which is the difference between the cash price and the futures price. The basis should equal the cost of carry. Basis risk is the risk that the basis might change between the time a hedge is placed and the time it is lifted. Hedging eliminates price risk but exposes hedged positions to basis risk. Cross hedging occurs when the underlying of the futures contract is different from the financial instrument or portfolio to be hedged, and most hedging of stock portfolios involves cross hedging. The risk associated with cross hedging is that the financial instrument or portfolio to be hedged will have price changes that are different from those of the instrument underlying the futures contract and, therefore, different from those of the contract itself. If this occurs, the futures contract is said to have failed to track the hedged instrument in an exact way.

When the futures contract is priced fairly relative to the cash index, the futures contract can be used to synthetically create an indexed portfolio by buying futures and investing in Treasury bills. When futures contracts are mispriced, a money manager can enhance the return of an indexed portfolio. This strategy is called a stock replacement strategy. Finally, stock index futures can be used to establish a minimum value for a portfolio, a strategy referred to as portfolio insurance or dynamic hedging.

■ KEY TERMS

basis
basis risk
buy hedge
carry
cash settlement contracts
cost of carry
cross hedging
delivery date
dividend yield

dynamic hedging
fair price
futures contract
futures contract multiple
futures price
hedge ratio
hedging
initial margin
investor's equity

long futures
long hedge
long position
maintenance margin
mark to market
most distant futures contract
nearby futures contract
negative carry
net financing cost

next futures contract

open interest

perfect hedge

pit committee

portfolio insurance

positive carry

sell hedge

settlement date

settlement price

short futures

short hedge

short position

stock replacement strategy

theoretical futures price

the underlying

variation margin

■ QUESTIONS

1. **a.** What is a cash settlement futures contract?
   b. What two contracts in the United States are cash settlement futures contracts?

2. Explain the functions of a clearinghouse associated with a futures exchange.

3. What is the dollar value of the S&P 500 futures contract if the futures price is 343?

4. You notice that the S&P 500 index is 380. The dividend yield for the stocks composing the index is 4%. The interest rate for 12 months is 12%. The S&P 500 futures contract for settlement in 12 months' time is currently selling at 412.
   a. Is there an arbitrage opportunity? If so, how would you take advantage of it?
   b. What considerations would you want to address before executing this trade?

5. On April 1, 1992, you bought a stock index futures contract for 200 and were required to put up an initial margin of $10,000. The value of the contract was 200 times the $500 multiple, or $100,000. On the next three days, the contract's settlement price was at these levels: day 1, 205; day 2, 197; day 3, 190.
   a. Calculate the value of your margin account on each day.
   b. If the maintenance margin for the contract is $7,000, how much variation margin did the exchange require you to put up at the end of the third day?
   c. If you had failed to put up that much, what would the exchange have done?

6. How do margin requirements in the futures market differ from margin requirements in the cash market?

7. Suppose that a money manager wishes to hedge a $20 million stock portfolio against a decline in market value and has selected the S&P 500 futures contract as the hedging vehicle. Assume the following:

   Cash price of S&P 500 index = 335

   S&P 500 futures price = 340

   Beta of S&P 500 relative to S&P 500 futures contract (B_{IF}) = 0.80

   Beta of portfolio to be hedged to S&P 500 (B_{PI}) = 1.1

   The futures contract settles in 90 days, and the portfolio manager intends to hedge the portfolio for two months.
   a. What is the basis at the time the hedge is placed?
   b. What is the hedge ratio?
   c. What is the risk associated with the hedge?

8. "By using futures to hedge, a portfolio manager substitutes basis risk for price risk." Explain why this statement is true.

9. In the August 18, 1989, issue of *The Wall Street Journal* there appeared an article entitled "Program Trading Spreads from Just Wall Street Firms." Following are two quotations from that article.

   The first quotation states: "Brokerage firms in the business, which tiptoed back into program trading after the post-crash furor died down, argue that such strategies as stock-index arbitrage—rapid trading between stock index futures and stocks to capture fleeting price differences—link two related markets and thus benefit both."

   The second quotation in the article is from a senior vice president at Twenty-First Securities Corp.: "Program trading is a product that is here, links markets, and it is not going to disappear. It is a function of the computerization of Wall Street."

   Do you agree with these statements?

10. On April 28, 1992, a portfolio manager who wanted to hedge a position was considering both the June and December contracts on the S&P 500. Open interest for the S&P 500 June 1992 futures contract was 129,623. Open interest for the December 1992 contract was 1,244. What is open interest, and why would the portfolio manager want to know the open interest figures for the June and December contracts?

11. Suppose you bought five Nikkei 225 contracts (with multiples of $5 each) on the Chicago Board

of Trade when the futures price was 17,400. Suppose the price went to 18,200 over the next month. How many dollars did you earn on this investment?

12. The following excerpt appeared in "Prudential Reduces FT-SE Futures Exposure in Favour of CAC-40," in the December 7, 1992, issue of *Derivatives Week*:

    Prudential Portfolio Managers in London, which manages over £10 billion in pension fund assets, recently used futures to reduce an overweight position in U.K. equities while increasing its exposure to French equities, according to Martin Bookes, assistant director. Last June, Prudential used LIFFE-traded FT-SE futures to overweight U.K. equities by 2–3% compared to benchmark indices which have a 60% exposure.

    a. Explain how this money manager was able to increase its exposure to French equities using futures.
    b. Explain how this money manager was able to decrease its exposure to U.K. equities using futures.

13. Shortly after stock index futures began trading, it was reported that Westinghouse Electric Corporation's pension fund bought 400 stock index contracts between July 29 and August 11, 1982. ["Stock Futures Used in Rally," *Pension & Investment Age* (Oct. 25, 1982), pp. 1, 52.] The reason cited by a company source for purchasing these contracts, which were worth over $20 million, was that the company was not "ready to buy individual stocks in such a short period of time." A company source stated that stock index futures gave the pension fund "a quick way of putting money into the market," and one "much cheaper" than if the fund had purchased stock in the cash market.
    a. Was the hedging strategy used by Westinghouse a long hedge or short hedge?
    b. Elaborate on the reasons Westinghouse decided to use stock index futures rather than the cash market.

14. The following excerpt is from the article "Salomon Downplays Japan Stock Index Arbitrage" that appeared in the June 22, 1992, issue of *Derivatives Week*:

    Salomon Brothers Asia is deemphasizing Japanese equity index arbitrage, according to a spokesman for the firm. The increasing efficiency of the Tokyo market made index arbi-

trage less attractive, he explained. "It's a brokerage's work to find a market's inefficiency and earn profit, but [stock index arbitrage offers] less now," the Salomon spokesman said. The past two years, during which foreign firms dominated the business, were unusual, he added (p. 2).

    a. What is stock index arbitrage?
    b. On the basis of the comments in the excerpt, explain why the experience with stock index arbitrage in Japan is the same as in the United States.

15. a. The following excerpt is from an article entitled "Spanish Equity Futures Trade at Massive Discount," which appeared in the August 10, 1992, issue of *Derivative Week*:

    A spectacular arbitrage window opened up in Spanish IBEX equity futures when the contract traded down to a 80 point discount to the theoretical value of the underlying stocks, according to Spanish traders.
        Jose-Luis Perez, a futures and options trader at Banco Santander, said that the futures were trading at around 50–60 points under theoretical value. "If I had stock, I would sell it all," he said.

    Explain why Mr. Perez would pursue the strategy he suggested.

    b. Jose Martin, a trader at Banco Bilbao Vizcaya, in the same article stated: "Without the proper credit facilities and without being able to trade stock baskets, arbitrage is very difficult for Spaniards." Why are credit facilities and the ability to trade stock baskets important in implementing stock index arbitrage?

16. The following excerpt, published in the September 7, 1992, issue of *Derivatives Week*, is taken from an article entitled "Trafalgar Reproduces EAFE with Futures": "Ontario-based Trafalgar Capital Management has been using equity index futures from five different countries to replicate the performance of the EAFE index, according to Vidis Vaicunas, v.p.-investment systems and trading at the firm. The EAFE index tracks the performance of 18 different equity markets in Europe, Australia and the Far East."
    a. What is the advantage of using this approach over buying individual shares in each country?
    b. What are the risks associated with this approach?

CHAPTER 17
USING EQUITY OPTIONS IN INVESTMENT MANAGEMENT

LEARNING OBJECTIVES
After reading this chapter you will be able to:

- explain what an option contract is and the basic features of options.
- describe the differences between a futures contract and an option contract.
- differentiate between a stock option and a stock warrant.
- describe the risk/return characteristics of an option.
- explain the basic components of the option price and the factors that affect the option price.
- explain how equity options can change the risk/return profile of a stock portfolio.
- explain the different stock option strategies that institutional investors use.
- comment on the empirical evidence as to whether there is a stock option strategy that consistently beats other strategies.

In the previous chapter we showed how stock index futures contracts can be used by a money manager to accomplish certain investment objectives. In this chapter we introduce a second derivative contract, an option contract. Our focus will be on two types of options: one option in which the underlying is the common stock of a corporation and another option in which the underlying is a common stock index. We refer to the former option as a **stock option** and to the latter as a **stock index option**. Collectively, these two types of options are called **equity options**, since the underlying is the common stock of one or more corporations.

The purpose of this chapter is to explain the risk/return characteristics and basic strategies of equity options. We will then see how equity options can be used by managers to accomplish investment objectives. A critical aspect in using equity options is their pricing. This is a complicated topic, and we devote the next chapter to it.

There are also options on stock index futures; however, these options are not as widely used as options on stock indexes. Options on futures contracts are the contracts of choice in the interest rate options market. We will postpone our discussion of options on futures until Chapter 26.

Warrants

A **warrant** is a contract that gives the holder of the warrant the right but not the obligation to buy or to sell a designated number of shares of a stock or a stock index at a specified price before a set date. Consequently, a warrant is nothing more than an option.

At one time, the only type of common stock warrants were those issued by a corporation with common stock outstanding. These warrants allow the purchase of common stock and are therefore call-type options. They were typically bundled with the offering of some security of an issuer. For example, a corporation could issue bonds or preferred stock with attached warrants. The security to which the warrant is attached is called the **host security**. Usually warrants may be detached from the host security and then traded separately on either an exchange or in the over-the-counter market.

There are several differences between the exchange-traded call options on common stocks and the warrants we have just described. First, at the time of issuance, the length of time over which the investor in an exchange-traded call option may exercise is much shorter than that for a warrant. There are some warrants, for example, that have no expiration date; these are called **perpetual warrants**. Second, and most important, the issuer of a warrant is the company itself. Consequently, when a warrant is exercised, the number of shares of stock outstanding will increase accordingly. This will result in a dilution of the issuer's earnings.

More recently, there has been an explosion in warrants on stock indexes. These warrants are called **index warrants**. As with a stock index option, the buyer of an index warrant can purchase the underlying stock index. Index warrants are issued by either a corporate or sovereign entity as part of a security offering. They are guaranteed by an option clearing corporation.

THE OPTION PRICE

The option price is a reflection of the option's **intrinsic value** and any additional amount over its intrinsic value. The premium over intrinsic value is often referred to as the time value or **time premium**. While the former term is more common, we will use the term *time premium* to avoid confusion with the time value of money.

Determination of the theoretical or fair value of an option is much more complicated than for a futures contract. For this reason, we have devoted the next chapter to this topic. Here we focus only on the two basic components of an option and the factors that affect the price of an option.

Intrinsic Value

The intrinsic value of an option is its economic value if it is exercised immediately. If no positive economic value would result from exercising the option immediately, then the intrinsic value is zero.

For a call option, the intrinsic value is positive if the current stock price is greater than the strike price. The intrinsic value is then the difference between the two prices. If the strike price of a call option is greater than or equal to the current stock price, the intrinsic value is zero. For example, if the strike price for a call option is $100 and the current stock price is $105, the intrinsic value is $5. That is, an option buyer exercising the option and simultaneously selling the underlying stock would realize $105 from the sale of the stock, which would be covered by acquiring the stock from the option writer for $100, thereby netting a $5 gain.

When an option has intrinsic value, it is said to be *in the money*. When the strike price of a call option exceeds the current stock price, the call option is said to be *out of the money*; it has no intrinsic value. An option for which the strike price is equal to the current stock price is said to be *at the money*. Both at-the-money and out-of-the-money options have an intrinsic value of zero because they are not profitable to exercise. Our call option with a strike price of $100 would be (1) in the money when the current stock price is greater than $100, (2) out of the money when the current stock price is less than $100, and (3) at the money when the current stock price is equal to $100.

For a put option, the intrinsic value is equal to the amount by which the current stock price is below the strike price. For example, if the strike price of a put option is $100 and the current stock price is $92, the intrinsic value is $8. The buyer of the put option who exercises the put option and simultaneously sells the underlying stock will net $8 by exercising since the stock will be sold to the writer for $100 and purchased in the market for $92. The intrinsic value is zero if the strike price is less than or equal to the current market price.

For our put option with a strike price of $100, the option would be (1) in the money when the stock price is less than $100, (2) out of the money when the stock price exceeds $100, and (3) at the money when the stock price is equal to $100.

We can summarize the relations above in Table 17-3.

TABLE 17-3		
INTRINSIC VALUE OF OPTIONS		
If Stock Price > *Strike Price*		
	Call option	**Put Option**
Intrinsic value	Stock price − strike price	Zero
Jargon	In the money	Out of the money
If Stock Price < *Strike Price*		
	Call option	**Put Option**
Intrinsic value	Zero	Strike price − stock price
Jargon	Out of the money	In the money
If Stock price = *Strike Price*		
	Call option	**Put Option**
Intrinsic value	Zero	Zero
Jargon	At the money	At the money

Time Premium

The time premium of an option is the amount by which the option price exceeds its intrinsic value. The option buyer hopes that, at some time prior to expiration, changes in the market price of the underlying stock will increase the value of the rights conveyed by the option. For this prospect, the option buyer is willing to pay a premium above the intrinsic value. For example, if the price of a call option with a strike price of $100 is $9 when the current stock price is $105, the time premium of this option is $4 ($9 minus its intrinsic value of $5). Had the current stock price been $90 instead of $105, then the time premium of this option would be the entire $9 because the option has no intrinsic value. Other factors equal, the time premium of an option will increase with the amount of time remaining to expiration, since the opportunity for a favorable change in the price is greater.

There are two ways in which an option buyer may realize the value of a position taken in the option: The first is to exercise the option, and the second is to sell the call option. In the first example above, since the exercise of an option will realize a gain of only $5 and will cause the immediate loss of any time premium ($4 in our first example), it is preferable to sell the call. In general, if an option buyer wishes to realize the value of a position, selling will be more economically beneficial than exercising. However, there are circumstances under which it is preferable to exercise prior to the expiration date, depending on whether the total proceeds at the expiration date would be greater by holding the option or by exercising it and reinvesting any cash proceeds received until the expiration date.

Factors That Influence the Option Price

Six factors influence the option price:

1. Current price of the underlying stock
2. Strike price
3. Time to expiration of the option
4. Expected price volatility of the underlying stock over the life of the option
5. Short-term risk-free interest rate over the life of the option
6. Anticipated dividends on the underlying stock over the life of the option

The impact of each of these factors depends on whether (1) the option is a call or a put and (2) the option is an American option or a European option. A summary of the effect of each factor on put and call option prices is presented in Table 17-4. In the case of a warrant, an additional factor results from the fact that the exercise of a warrant dilutes earnings.

Current Price of the Underlying Stock   The option price will change as the price of the underlying stock changes. For a call option, as the price of the underlying stock increases (holding all other factors constant), the option price increases, because the intrinsic value increases. The opposite holds for a put option: As the price of the underlying stock increases, the price of a put option decreases.

TABLE 17-4		
SUMMARY OF FACTORS THAT AFFECT THE PRICE OF AN AMERICAN OPTION		
	Effect of an Increase of Factor on:	
Factor	**Call Price**	**Put Price**
Current price of underlying stock	Increase	Decrease
Strike price	Decrease	Increase
Time to expiration of option	Increase	Increase
Expected price volatility	Increase	Increase
Short-term interest rate	Increase	Decrease
Anticipated cash dividends	Decrease	Increase

Strike Price   The strike price is fixed for the life of the option. All other factors being equal, the lower the strike price, the higher the price of a call option. For example, if the stock price is trading at $110, the intrinsic value for a call option with a strike price of $100 will be $10 while the intrinsic value for a call option with a strike price of $105 will only be $5. For put options, the higher the strike price, the higher the option price.

Time to Expiration of the Option   An option is a "wasting asset." That is, after the expiration date passes, the option has no value. Holding all other factors equal, the longer the time to expiration of the option, the greater the option price. The reason for this is that as the time to expiration decreases, less time remains for the underlying stock's price to rise (for a call buyer) or to fall (for a put buyer)—that is, to compensate the option buyer for any time premium paid—and, therefore, the probability of a favorable price movement decreases. Consequently, for American options, as the time remaining until expiration decreases, the option price approaches its intrinsic value.

Expected Price Volatility of the Underlying Stock over the Life of the Option   All other factors being equal, the greater the expected volatility (as measured by the standard deviation or variance) of the price of the underlying stock, the more an investor would be willing to pay for the option, and the more an option writer would demand it. This is because the greater the volatility, the greater the probability that the price of the underlying stock will move in favor of the option buyer at some time before expiration.

Notice that it is the standard deviation or variance, not the systematic risk as measured by beta, that is relevant in the pricing of options.

Short-Term Risk-Free Interest Rate over the Life of the Option   Buying the underlying stock ties up one's money. Buying an option on the same quantity of the underlying stock makes the difference between the stock price and the option price available for investment at the risk-free rate. Consequently, holding all other factors constant, the higher the short-term risk-free interest rate, the greater the cost of buying the underlying stock and carrying it to the expiration date of the call option. Hence, the higher the short-term risk-free interest rate, the more attractive the call option will be relative to the direct purchase of the underlying stock. As a result, the higher the short-term risk-free interest rate, the greater the price of a call option.

Anticipated Dividends on the Underlying Stock over the Life of the Option   Cash dividends on the underlying stock tend to decrease the price of a call option because they make it more attractive to hold the underlying stock than to hold the option. For put options, cash dividends on the underlying stock tend to increase their price.

RISK AND RETURN CHARACTERISTICS OF OPTIONS

Here we illustrate the risk and return characteristics of the four basic option positions—buying a call option (long a call option), selling a call option (short a call option), buying a put option (long a put option), and selling a put option (short a put option). We will use stock options in our example. The illustrations assume that each option position is held to the expiration date and not exercised early. Also, to simplify the illustrations, we assume that each option is for 1 share of stock rather than 100 shares and we ignore transactions costs.

Buying Call Options

Assume that there is a call option on stock XYZ that expires in one month and has a strike price of $100. The option price is $3. Suppose that the current price of stock XYZ is $100. The profit and loss will depend on the price of stock XYZ at the expiration date. Table 17-5 and Figure 17-1 show the profit and loss potential for buying a call option. The buyer of a call option benefits if the price rises above the strike price. If the price of stock XYZ is equal to $103, the buyer of a call option breaks even. The maximum loss is the option price, and there is substantial upside potential if the stock price rises above $103.

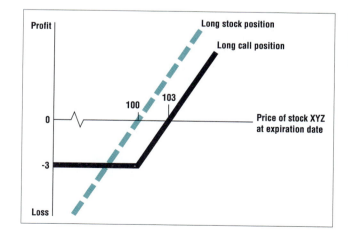

FIGURE 17-1

Profit/loss profile of a long call position and a long stock position.

TABLE 17-5

PROFIT/LOSS PROFILE OF A LONG CALL OPTION AND A LONG STOCK POSITION

Assumptions:

Price of stock XYZ = $100
Option price = $3
Strike price = $100
Time to expiration = 1 month

Price of Stock XYZ at Expiration Date	*Profit/Loss for:* Long Call[*]	Long Stock XYZ[†]
$150	$47	$50
140	37	40
130	27	30
120	17	20
115	12	15
114	11	14
113	10	13
112	9	12
111	8	11
110	7	10
109	6	9
108	5	8
107	4	7
106	3	6
105	2	5
104	1	4
103	0	3
102	−1	2
101	−2	1
100	−3	0
99	−3	−1
98	−3	−2
97	−3	−3
96	−3	−4
95	−3	−5
94	−3	−6
93	−3	−7
92	−3	−8
91	−3	−9
90	−3	−10
89	−3	−11
88	−3	−12
87	−3	−13
86	−3	−14
85	−3	−15
80	−3	−20
70	−3	−30
60	−3	−40

[*]Price at expiration − $100 − $3
Maximum loss = − $3

[†]Price at expiration − $100

It is worthwhile to compare the profit and loss profile of the call option buyer with that of an investor taking a long position in one share of stock XYZ. The payoff from the position depends on stock XYZ's price at the expiration date. Table 17-5 and Figure 17-1 provide this comparison. This comparison clearly demonstrates the way in which an option can change the risk/return profile for investors. An investor who takes a long position in stock XYZ realizes a profit of $1 for every $1 increase in stock XYZ's price. As stock XYZ's price falls, however, the investor loses, dollar for dollar. If the price drops by more than $3, the long position in stock XYZ results in a loss of more than $3. The long call position, in contrast, limits the loss to only the option price of $3 but retains the upside potential, which will be $3 less than for the long position in stock XYZ.

Which alternative is better, buying the call option or buying the stock? The answer depends on what the investor is attempting to achieve. This will become clearer as we explain various strategies using either option positions or cash market positions.

We can also use this hypothetical call option to demonstrate the speculative appeal of options. Suppose an investor has strong expectations that stock XYZ's price will rise in one month. At an option price of $3, the speculator can purchase 33.33 call options for each $100 invested. If stock XYZ's price rises, the investor realizes the price appreciation associated with 33.33 units of stock XYZ. With the same $100, however, the investor can purchase only one unit of stock XYZ selling at $100, thereby realizing the appreciation associated with one unit if stock XYZ's price increases. Now, suppose that in one month the price of stock XYZ rises to $120. The long call position will result in a profit of $566.50 [($20 × 33.33) − $100], or a return of 566.5% on the $100 investment in the call option. The long position in stock XYZ results in a profit of $20, only a 20% return on $100.

This greater leverage attracts investors to options when they wish to speculate on price movements. There are drawbacks to this leverage, however. Suppose that stock XYZ's price is unchanged at $100 at the expiration date. The long call position results in this case in a loss of the entire investment of $100, while the long position in stock XYZ produces neither a gain nor a loss.

Writing Call Options

To illustrate the option seller's, or writer's, position, we use the same call option we used to illustrate buying a call option. The profit and loss profile of the short call position (that is, the position of the call option writer) is the mirror image of the profit and loss profile of the long call position (the position of the call option buyer). That is, the profit of the short call position for any given price for stock XYZ at the expiration date is the same as the loss of the long call position.[1] Consequently, the maximum profit the short call position can produce is the option price. The maximum loss is not limited because it is the highest price reached by stock XYZ on or before the expiration date, less the option price; this price can be indefinitely high. This can be

---

[1] For this reason, the combined position of the long and the short call option positions is referred to as a *zero-sum game*.

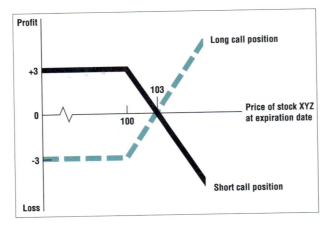

FIGURE 17-2

Profit/loss profile for a short call position and a long call position.

seen in Figure 17-2, which shows the profit/loss profile for a short call position, as well as the profit/loss profile for a long call position.

Buying Put Options

To illustrate a long put option position, we assume a hypothetical put option on one share of stock XYZ with one month to maturity and a strike price of $100. Assume that the put option is selling for $2 and the current price of stock XYZ is $100. The profit or loss for this position at the expiration date depends on the market price of stock XYZ. The buyer of a put option benefits if the price falls.

The profit/loss profile of a long put position is shown in Table 17-6 and Figure 17-3. As with all long option positions, the loss is limited to the option price. The profit potential, however, is substantial: The theoretical maximum profit is generated if stock XYZ's price falls to zero. Contrast this profit potential with that of the buyer of a call option. The theoretical maximum profit for a call buyer cannot be determined beforehand because it depends on the highest price that can be reached by stock XYZ before or at the option expiration date.

FIGURE 17-3

Profit/loss profile for a long put position and a short stock position.

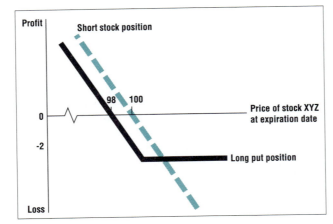

TABLE 17-6

PROFIT/LOSS PROFILE OF A LONG PUT OPTION AND A SHORT STOCK POSITION

Assumptions:

Price of Stock XYZ = $100

Option price = $2

Strike price = $100

Time to expiration = 1 month

Price of Stock XYZ at Expiration Date	Profit/Loss for:	
	Long Put*	Short Stock XYZ†
$150	−$2	−$50
140	−2	−40
130	−2	−30
120	−2	−20
115	−2	−15
110	−2	−10
105	−2	−5
100	−2	0
99	−1	1
98	0	2
97	1	3
96	2	4
95	3	5
94	4	6
93	5	7
92	6	8
91	7	9
90	8	10
89	9	11
88	10	12
87	11	13
86	12	14
85	13	15
84	14	16
83	15	17
82	16	18
81	17	19
80	18	20
75	23	25
70	28	30
65	33	35
60	38	40

*$100 − price at expiration −$2
  Maximum loss = −$2

†$100 − price at expiration

To see how an option alters the risk/return profile for an investor, we again compare it with a position in stock XYZ. The long put position is compared with a short position in stock XYZ because such a position would also realize a profit if the price of the stock falls. A comparison of the two positions is shown in Table 17-5 and Figure 17-3. While the investor taking a short stock position faces all the downside risk as well as the upside potential, an investor taking the long put position faces limited downside risk (equal to the option price) while still maintaining upside potential reduced by an amount equal to the option price.

Writing Put Options

The profit and loss profile for a short put option is the mirror image of the long put option. The maximum profit to be realized from this position is the option price. The theoretical maximum loss can be substantial should the price of the underlying fall; if the price were to fall all the way to zero, the loss would be as large as the strike price less the option price. Figure 17-4 graphically depicts this profit and loss profile for both a short put position and a long put position.

Summary of Profit/Loss from Option Positions

To summarize, buying calls or selling puts allows the investor to gain if the price of the underlying stock rises. Buying calls gives the investor unlimited upside potential but limits the loss to the option price. Selling puts limits the profit to the option price but provides no protection if the stock price falls, with the maximum loss occurring if the stock price falls to zero.

Buying puts and selling calls allows the investor to gain if the price of the underlying stock falls. Buying puts gives the investor upside potential, with the maximum profit realized if the stock price declines to zero. However, the loss is limited to the option price. Selling calls limits the profit to the option price but provides no protection if the stock price rises, with the maximum loss being theoretically unlimited.

Considering the Time Value of Money and Dividends

Our illustrations of the four option positions do not address the time value of money. Specifically, the buyer of an option must pay the seller the option price at the time the option is purchased. Thus, the buyer must finance the purchase price of the option or, assuming the option's purchase price does not have to be borrowed, the buyer loses the income that can be earned by investing the amount of the option price until the option is sold or exercised. In contrast, assuming the seller does not have to use the option

FIGURE 17-4

Profit/loss profile for a short put position and a long put position.

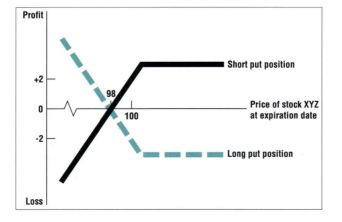

price as margin for the short position or can use an interest-earning asset as security, the seller has the opportunity to earn income from the proceeds of the option sale.

The time value of money changes the profit/loss profile of the option positions we have discussed. The break-even price for the buyer and the seller of an option will not be the same as in our illustrations. The break-even price for the underlying stock at the expiration date is higher for the buyer of the option; for the seller, it is lower.

Our comparisons of the option position with positions in the underlying stock also ignore the time value of money. We have not considered the fact that the underlying stock may pay dividends. The buyer of a call option is not entitled to any dividends paid by the corporation. The buyer of the underlying stock, however, would receive any interim cash flows and would have the opportunity to reinvest them. A complete comparison of the long call option position and the long position in the underlying stock must take into account the additional dollars gained from reinvesting any dividends. Moreover, any effect on the price of the underlying stock as a result of the distribution of cash must also be considered. This occurs, for example, when as a result of a dividend payment, the stock declines in price. For simplicity's sake, however, we continue to ignore the time value of money and dividends in the discussions in this chapter.

OPTION STRATEGIES

Now let's look at the various strategies using options. While there are several ways to categorize the wide range of option strategies employed by participants in the options market, a useful classification is as follows: (1) naked strategies, (2) hedge strategies, (3) combination strategies, and (4) spread strategies. Naked option strategies use one of the four option positions exclusively, while the other strategies combine option positions with other positions to balance risks and rewards differently.

Naked Strategies

Naked strategies include the exclusive use of any of the four option positions described above: long call strategy (buying call options), short call strategy (selling or writing call options), long put strategy (buying put options), and short put strategy (selling or writing put options). By themselves, these positions are called *naked* strategies because they do not involve an offsetting or risk-reducing position in another option or the underlying common stock.

The resulting profit or loss from each strategy depends on the price of the underlying stock at the expiration date (on the assumption that the option is not exercised or sold early). The most that the option buyer can lose with each strategy is the option price. At the same time, the option buyer preserves the benefits of a favorable price movement of the underlying stock (a price increase for a call option and a price decline for a put option) reduced by the option price. In contrast, the maximum profit that the option writer can realize is the option price, while remaining exposed to all the risks associated with an unfavorable price movement.

The long call strategy (buying call options) is the most straightforward option strategy for taking advantage of an anticipated increase in the stock price, while at the same time limiting the maximum loss to the option price. The speculative appeal of call options is that they provide an investor with the opportunity to capture the price action of more shares of common stock for a given number of dollars available for investment. An investor who believes that the price of some common stock will decrease or change very little can, if the expectation is correct, realize income by writing (selling) a call option (i.e., following a short call strategy). The profit and loss of the option writer is the mirror image of the option buyer's.

Following a long put strategy (buying put options) is the most straightforward option strategy for benefiting from an expected decrease in the price of some common stock, while avoiding the unfavorable consequences should the price rise. The short put strategy (selling put options) is employed if the investor expects the price of a stock to increase or stay the same. The maximum profit from this strategy is the option price. If the price of the stock declines to zero at or before the expiration date, the investor will experience the maximum loss for the short put strategy.

To summarize, long calls and short puts allow the investor to gain if the price of the underlying stock rises. Short calls and long puts allow the investor to gain if the price of the underlying stock falls. The strategy that an investor would want to use depends on the market view the investor has. Table 17-7 summarizes the naked option strategies to use based on market view.

Covered (Hedge) Strategies

In contrast to naked option strategies, **covered** or **hedge option strategies** involve a position in an option as well as a position in the underlying stock. The aim is for one position to help offset any unfavorable price movement in the other. The two most popular covered or hedge strategies are (1) the covered call writing strategy and (2) the protective put buying strategy.

Covered Call Writing Strategy   A **covered call writing strategy** involves writing a call option on stocks that the investor owns in his portfolio. That is, the investor takes a short position in a call option on stock in which he or she has a long position. If the price of the stock declines, there will be a loss on the long stock position. However, the income generated from the sale of the call option will either (1) fully offset, (2) partially offset, or (3) more than offset the loss in the long stock position so as to generate a profit.

To illustrate, suppose that a money manager holds 100 shares of XYZ Corporation and that the current price of a share is $100. The total value of

TABLE 17-7

NAKED STRATEGIES AND MARKET VIEW

Market View	Strategy
Very bullish	Buy call options
Slightly bullish	Write put options
Slightly bearish	Write call options
Very bearish	Buy put options

the portfolio is $10,000. Also suppose that a call option on 100 shares of XYZ with a $100 strike price that expires in three months can be sold for $700. (The option is at the money when it is purchased because the strike price is equal to the current price of the stock.) If the money manager has decided to hold the 100 shares and write one call option (each call option is for 100 shares of the underlying stock), the profit or loss for this strategy will depend on the price of XYZ stock at the expiration date. One of the following outcomes will occur:

1. If the price of XYZ stock is greater than $100, the call option buyer will exercise the option and pay the option writer $100 per share. The 100 shares in the portfolio are exchanged for $10,000. The value of the portfolio at the expiration date is then $10,700 ($10,000 received from the option buyer exercising the option plus $700 received from writing the call option). In fact, more than $10,700 will be in the portfolio if the $700 is invested when it is received. At a minimum, though, the profit from this strategy if the price of XYZ stock is greater than $100 is $700, the option price. If the price of XYZ stock rises above $107, however, there will also be an opportunity loss equal to the excess of the value of the stock over $10,700.

2. If the price of XYZ stock is equal to $100 at the expiration date, the call option buyer will not exercise the option. The value of the portfolio will still be at least $10,700: 100 shares of XYZ with a market value of $100 per share and the proceeds of $700 received from writing the call option.

3. If the price of XYZ stock is less than $100 but greater than $93, there will be a profit, but it will be less than $700. For example, suppose that the price of the stock is $96. The long stock position will have a value of $9,600, while the short call position generated $700. The portfolio value is therefore $10,300, resulting in a profit of $300.

4. At a price of $93, the long stock position will have a value of $9,300 and the short call position generated $700, resulting in no profit or loss, as the portfolio value is $10,000.

5. Should the price of XYZ stock be less than $93 at expiration, the portfolio will realize a loss. For example, suppose that the price of the stock at expiration is $88. The portfolio value will be $9,500: The long stock position will be worth $8,800, and the short call position will have produced $700. Hence, there is a loss of $500. The worst case is if the price of XYZ stock declines to zero. This would result in a portfolio value of $700 and a loss of $9,300.

The profit and loss profile for this covered call writing strategy is graphically portrayed in Figure 17-5. There are two important points to note in this illustration. First, this strategy has allowed the investor to reduce the downside risk for the portfolio. In this example, for the at-the-money call option, the risk is reduced by an amount equal to the option price. In exchange for this reduction of downside risk, the investor has agreed to cap the potential profit. For the at-the-money option used in our illustration, the maximum profit is the option price.

The second point can be seen by comparing Figure 17-4 with Figure 17-5. Notice that the shape of the two profit and loss profiles is the same. That is, the covered call writing strategy has the same profit and loss profile as a naked

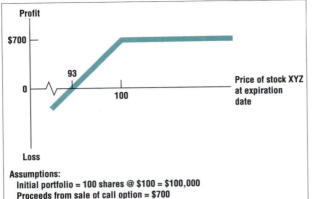

FIGURE 17-5

Profit/loss profile for a covered call writing position.

short put strategy. Indeed, in our example, the covered call writing strategy has the same profit and loss outcome as writing a put on 100 shares of XYZ stock with a strike price of $100 and three months to expiration (provided the price of the call and put options is the same). This is not an accident. As we explain in the next chapter, portfolios with equivalent payoffs can be constructed with different positions in options and the underlying stock.

While we have focused on stock options, stock index options would be used to write call options on a diversified portfolio.

Protective Put Buying Strategy　An investor may want to protect the value of a stock held in the portfolio against the risk of a decline in market value. One way of doing this with options is to buy a put option on that stock. (See Box 17.) By doing so, the investor is guaranteed the strike price of the put option less the cost of the option. Should the stock price rise rather than decline, the investor is able to participate in the price increase, with the profit reduced by

---

BOX 17

FIDELITY GUARDS AGAINST TRADITIONAL AUTUMN

Fidelity Investments has hedged one of its fund's long positions in U.S. stocks with put options to guard against aftershocks from the European currency crisis and the traditional fall in the U.S. stock market in the fourth quarter, according to Bob Beckwitt, portfolio manager. The put options are also providing insurance against the 2% fall in the S&P 500 index which occurred since the Presidential conventions, another traditional market response when there is an expectation that the incumbent President will lose the election, he continued. Beckwitt manages $4 billion of Fidelity's assets under management and

the put options were purchased for the Fidelity Asset Manager Fund.

Fidelity bought the over-the-counter put options on the S&P 500 between mid-August and mid-September. They expire at the end of November, have a strike of 420 and a premium cost of 2–3%. The options covered a notional amount of $300 million. Fidelity used the over-the-counter market as it was more liquid than the exchanges, he said. The puts were in-the-money on October 22, with the S&P 500 at a level of 415.

This excerpt was taken from an article in the October 26, 1992, issue of *Derivative Week*, "Fidelity Guards against Traditional Autumn Drop in S&P 500."

Questions for Box 17

1. Explain the put option strategy used by Mr. Beckwitt to hedge the Fidelity Asset Manager Fund.

2. Mr. Beckwitt used over-the-counter options. How does an over-the-counter option differ from an exchange-traded option? Who is the counterparty to each agreement?

3. Why do you think the over-the-counter market in this case was more liquid than the exchange?

4. Explain why the puts were in the money on October 22.

the cost of the option. This strategy is called a **protective put buying strategy**; it involves a long put position (buying a put option) and a long position in the underlying stock that is held in the portfolio.

To illustrate, suppose that a money manager has 100 shares of XYZ stock in a portfolio and that the current market value of the stock is $100 per share (a portfolio value of $10,000). Assume further that a two-month put option selling for $500 can be purchased on 100 shares of XYZ stock with a strike price of $100. Two months from now at the expiration date, the profit or loss can be summarized as follows:

1. If the price of XYZ stock is greater than $105, the investor will realize a profit from this strategy. For example, if the price is $112, the long stock position will have a value of $11,200. The cost of purchasing the put option was $500, so the value of the portfolio is $10,700, for a profit of $700.
2. If the price of XYZ stock is equal to $105, no profit or loss will be realized from this strategy.
3. There will be a loss if the price of XYZ stock is less than $105, but at least $100. For example, a price of $102 will result in a loss of $300: a gain in the long stock position of $200, but a loss of $500 to acquire the long put position.
4. In none of the previous outcomes will the investor exercise the put option, but if the price of XYZ stock is below $100 per share, the option will be exercised. At any price below $100 per share, the investor will be assured of receiving $100 per share for the 100 shares of stock. In this case, the value of the portfolio will be $10,000 minus the cost of the option ($500), resulting in a loss of $500.

The graphical presentation of the profit and loss profile for this protective put buying strategy is shown in Figure 17-6. By implementing this strategy, the money manager has effectively assured a price of $95 per share. The money manager has maintained all the upside potential, reduced only by the cost of the put option.

An important consideration in a protective put buying strategy is the strike price. The higher the strike price, the higher the minimum price being established for the price of the underlying stock. However, this does not come without a cost: The higher the strike price, the higher the put option's price.

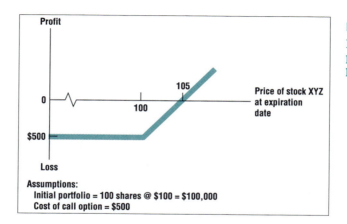

FIGURE 17-6

Profit/loss profile for a protective put buying position.

Now consider an institutional investor that holds a portfolio consisting of a large number of stock issues. To protect against an adverse price movement, the institutional investor would have to buy a put option on every stock issue in the portfolio, which would be quite costly. But by taking an appropriate position in a suitable stock index option, an institutional investor with a diversified portfolio can protect against adverse price movements.[2]

For example, suppose that an institutional investor holding a diversified portfolio of common stock which is highly correlated with the S&P 100 is concerned that the stock market will decline in value over the next three months. Suppose that a three-month put option on the S&P 100 is available. If an institutional investor purchases this put option (i.e., follows a protective buying put strategy) rather than liquidating the portfolio, adverse movements in the value of the portfolio due to a decline in the stock market will be offset (in whole or in part) by the gain in the put option, because the put option buyer gains when the price of the underlying stock index declines.

Combination Strategy

In a **combination strategy**, a put and a call on the same underlying stock with the same strike price and expiration are either both bought or both sold. When the same position is taken in the same number of puts as calls, the strategy is called a **straddle**, the most popular type of combination. An example of a straddle would be the purchase of one put and one call on XYZ stock with a strike price of $100 and an expiration date of one month. Since a long position is taken in both options, this strategy is called a **long straddle**. If one put and one call are sold, the position is called a **short straddle**.

Unlike a long naked option position, which benefits only if the underlying's price moves in the anticipated direction, a long straddle benefits if there is a large enough price movement in either direction so that the gain on one of the options will be greater than the cost of establishing the position. For example, suppose that both the put option and the call option on stock XYZ have a strike price of $100, an expiration of one month, and a price of $2. Also assume that the current price of stock XYZ is $100 (i.e., the options are at the money). The cost of establishing a long straddle would be $4. For the investor to benefit, the price of stock XYZ must either increase by more than $4 (i.e., to a price greater than $104) or decrease by more than $4 (i.e., to a price less than $96). Rather than betting on the direction of the price movement, the investor who pursues a long straddle strategy is betting on future price volatility. It is the volatility of the price of the underlying, not its direction, that will affect the outcome of this strategy. A portfolio manager who expects price volatility to increase before the expiration of the option, but is uncertain about the direction of the price change, can employ a long straddle strategy to enhance returns if her expectations are realized.

For a short straddle strategy, the investor realizes fee income if the price does not move enough to wipe out the fee received for both the put and call. For a short straddle position in the options on stock XYZ, this means that the price does not rise above $104 or fall below $96. Once again, this is a play on

---

[2]The appropriate number of stock index options to buy depends on the beta of the portfolio with respect to the underlying stock. The procedure for calculating the appropriate position in a stock index option is beyond the scope of this chapter.

future price volatility, not its direction. A portfolio manager who expects that the price of stock XYZ will remain flat (i.e., there will be little price volatility) can generate fee income and thereby enhance return if her expectations are realized.

Spread Strategy

A **spread strategy** involves a position in one or more options so that the cost of buying an option is funded entirely or in part by selling another option on the same underlying. There are many types of spread strategies. These include bull spreads, bear spreads, vertical spreads, horizontal spreads, diagonal spreads, and butterfly spreads. Here we look at just the bull spread.

In a **bull spread**, an investor buys an out-of-the-money put option on the underlying and finances this purchase by selling an out-of-the-money call option on the same underlying. For example, suppose that the current price of stock XYZ is $100 and that the following two options that expire in one month are available: (1) a call option with a strike price of $105 and an option price of $3 and (2) a put option with a strike price of $95 and an option price of $3. Both options are out of the money. The purchase of the put option for $3 would be financed by the sale of the call option for $3.

Let's look at the payoff of this bull spread strategy at the expiration date. If the price of stock XYZ is between $95 and $105, neither option will be exercised. If the stock price rises above $105, the call option will be exercised, and as a result, the investor will sell the stock for the strike price, $105. Thus, the investor realizes a gain of $5, but forgoes the opportunity to benefit from a stock price higher than $105. On the other hand, if the price falls below $95, the investor exercises the put option and thereby sells the stock for the strike price of $95. The maximum loss is $5. Effectively, this strategy is similar to a long position in stock XYZ except that the price of stock XYZ at expiration is forced to be between the two strike prices. The strategy thereby allows the investor to set a maximum price and a minimum price, and the cost of establishing the position is zero.

Is There a Superior Options Strategy?

The development of the options market brought with it a number of myths about strategies that were alleged to generate consistently superior returns over purchasing stocks. For example, both the popular literature and advertising by the options industry have recommended that individual and institutional investors follow a covered call strategy that could be expected to generate "extra return" from the income received by selling (writing) a call option on stocks held in their portfolios. The proliferation of such popular literature and misleading advertisements led Fischer Black to write: "For every fact about options, there is a fantasy—a reason given for trading or not trading in options that doesn't make sense when examined carefully."[3]

Is there indeed an options strategy that has consistently outperformed a simple strategy of buying common stocks? Numerous empirical studies have

---

[3]Fischer Black, "Fact and Fantasy in the Use of Options," *Financial Analysts Journal* (July-August 1975), pp. 36–41, 61–72.

examined this issue. These studies have focused on strategies with stock options rather than strategies with stock index options.[4]

While all the studies have shortcomings due to the complexity of testing various strategies, the majority—particularly those conducted in more recent years after the equity options market fully developed—indicate that there is no one superior option strategy. The empirical evidence suggests that option strategies have investment characteristics that are consistent with the familiar trade-off between risk and return: The higher the expected return, the more the expected risk as measured by return volatility. The relative risk characteristics of the strategies are consistent with those that are expected from the risk/return characteristics of the portfolio. This view is best summarized by the authors of one study:

> The specific levels of the returns generated, however, are strongly dependent on the actual experience of the underlying stocks during the simulation period. To avoid the creation of new myths about option strategies, the reader is warned not to infer from our findings that any one of the strategies is superior to the others for all investors. Indeed, if options and their underlying stocks are correctly priced, then there is no single best strategy for all investors.[5]

The last sentence is particularly noteworthy. In a market that prices options fairly, there should be no options strategy that is superior. In the next chapter we will turn to the question of whether equity options are indeed fairly priced.

■ SUMMARY

An option grants its buyer the right either to buy (in the case of a call option) or to sell (in the case of a put option) the underlying asset to the seller (writer) of the option at a stated price called the strike (exercise) price by a stated date called the expiration date. The price that the option buyer pays to the writer of the option is called the option price or option premium.

The buyer of an option cannot realize a loss greater than the option price, and has all the upside potential. By contrast, the maximum gain the writer (seller) of an option can realize is the option price; the writer is exposed to all the downside risk.

The option price consists of two components: the intrinsic value and the time premium. The intrinsic value is the economic value of the option if it is exercised immediately. (If exercising immediately yields no positive economic value, then the intrinsic value is zero.) The time premium is the amount by which the option price exceeds the intrinsic value. There are other factors that can influence the option price: current price of the underlying stock, the strike price, the time to expiration of the option, expected price volatility of the underlying stock over the life of the option, the short-term risk-free interest rate over the life of the option, and anticipated dividends on the underlying stock over the life of the option.

Equity options include options on common stock and options on stock indexes. The underlying stock market index may be a broad-based index or a narrow-based index. The dollar value of a contract is determined by the product of the cash index value and the contract's multiple. Unlike options on individual common

---

[4]For a detailed discussion of these studies, see Chapters 6 and 7 of Diana R. Harrington, Frank J. Fabozzi, and H. Russell Fogler, *The New Stock Market* (Chicago: Probus Publishing, 1990).

[5]Robert C. Merton, Myron S. Scholes, and Matthew L. Gladstein, "The Return and Risk of Alternative Call Option Portfolio Investment Strategies," *Journal of Business*, 51, No. 2 (1978), pp. 183–243.

stock, stock index products are cash settlement contracts.

Stock options permit investors to mold the shape of the return distribution to meet investment objectives better. Among the strategies that institutional investors use to control portfolio risk are basic naked strategies, covered call writing, protective put buying, combination strategies, and spread strategies. The empirical evidence suggests that no options strategy dominates any other.

■ KEY TERMS

American option
bull spread
call option
combination strategy
counterparty risk
covered call writing strategy
covered strategies
equity options
European option
exercise price
expiration date
hedge option strategies

host security
index warrants
intrinsic value
long straddle
naked strategies
option
option premium
option price
option seller
option writer
options contract multiple
perpetual warrants

protective put buying strategy
put option
short straddle
spread strategy
stock index option
stock option
straddle
strike index
strike price
time premium
warrant

■ QUESTIONS

1. **a.** What is the difference between a put option and a call option?
    b. What is the difference between an American option and a European option?
    c. Why do stock index options involve cash settlement rather than delivery of the underlying stocks?

2. Explain how this statement can be true: "A long call position offers potentially unlimited gains if the underlying stock's price rises, but a fixed, maximum loss if the underlying stock's price drops to zero."

3. **a.** Suppose a call option on a stock has a strike price of $70 and a cost of $2, and suppose you buy the call. Identify the profit at the expiration date for each of these values of the underlying stock: $25, $70, $100, $400.
    b. Suppose you had sold the call option in a. What would your profit be at expiration for each of those stock prices?

4. Explain why you agree or disagree with this statement: "Buying a put is just like short-selling the underlying stock. You gain the same thing from either position if the underlying stock's price falls. If the price goes up, you have the same loss."

5. Suppose that you buy an index call option for 5.50 with a strike price of 200 and at expiration you exercise it. Suppose, too, that at the time you exercise the call option, the index has a value of 240.
    a. If the index option has a multiple of $100, how much money does the writer of this option pay you?
    b. What profit do you realize from buying this call option?

6. "There's no real difference between options and futures. Both are hedging tools, and both are derivative products. It's just that with options you have to pay an option premium, while futures require no upfront payment except for `good-faith' margin. I can't understand why anyone would use options." Do you agree with this statement?

7. **a.** "If a put option is in the money, a call option on the same underlying and strike price will also be in the money." Explain why you agree or disagree with this statement.
    b. Suppose the current price of a stock is $46. A call option on that stock with a strike price of $50 is selling for $9. What is the intrinsic value and time premium of this call option?

c. Suppose the current price of a stock is $84. A put option on that stock with a strike price of $95 is selling for $13. What is the intrinsic value and time premium of this put option?

d. What is the time premium of an out-of-the money option?

e. What is the time premium of an option at the expiration date?

8. "The option price depends on the volatility of the underlying stock. Since capital market theory asserts that the appropriate measure of volatility is a stock's beta, then the option price should depend on the stock's beta." Explain why you agree or disagree with this statement.

9. What is the difference between a stock option and a stock warrant?

10. The following excerpt is from an article entitled "Scudder Writes Covered Calls on S&P 500" that appeared in the July 13, 1992, issue of *Derivatives Week*:

> Scudder, Stevens & Clark writes covered calls on the S&P 500 Index to enhance the return of some of its equity portfolios, according to Harry Hitch, principal at Scudder. Hitch, who advises Scudder's equity portfolio managers on derivatives use, said that the S&P 500 has been in a trading range since the beginning of the year, making it a good candidate for covered call writing. Half of the index is made up of growth stocks, a group that Scudder sees as overbought, whereas the other half is probably increasing in price. The combination of one half appreciating with the other half depreciating creates the range, rather than a decided one-way movement.
>
> The goal is to write calls at the top of the trading range, take the premium and wait for the options to expire worthless. . . . Typically, Scudder takes 1,000 contract positions, worth around $42 million. (p. 7)

Explain the risks and rewards of the strategy discussed in this excerpt.

11. You are meeting with a pension plan sponsor who has asked you for advice on several investment policy guidelines that it has formulated for its money managers. One of the guidelines involves the use of options for hedging: "Protective put buying and covered call writing strategies are recognized by the investment community as means for hedging a stock position. The former will not be permitted by any of our fund managers because it involves a cost that may not be recouped

if the put option is not exercised. We will permit covered call writing because there is no cost generated to protect the portfolio." What advice would you give the plan sponsor concerning this investment policy guideline?

12. Suppose an investor wants to follow a protective put buying strategy for a stock she owns that has a market price of $60. She is told that three 180-day put options are available on that stock with strike prices of $56, $58, and $60.

a. Which put option will give her the greatest price protection?

b. Which put option will be the most expensive?

c. Which put option should be selected?

13. What is the difference between a naked strategy and a combination strategy?

14. What naked strategy or strategies would an investor pursue if she thought that a stock's price was going to rise?

15. The quote following is from the June 22, 1992, issue of *Derivatives Week*:

> Aetna Investment Management, the London-based fund management arm of U.S. insurer Aetna Life & Casualty, expects to start using derivatives within weeks in more than £200 million of U.K. equity holdings, according to Tom Chellew, director. The firm has not used derivatives before in its total of £700 million under management in the U.K.
>
> Aetna is talking to trustees over the next two weeks and expects to get approval to start dealing thereafter, he said. Initially, it will only use derivatives in its more than £200 million of U.K. holdings in its £250 million of unit trusts under management.
>
> Chellew said initial strategies are likely to include writing covered calls and writing puts on stock Aetna doesn't mind buying. The firm will likely be interested in both U.K. index and individual stock options.
>
> Subsequently, Aetna expects to expand use into other holdings—specifically, equity and later possibly fixed income—and into pension and life insurance money under management, he said. Aetna will use derivatives to enhance yields and for risk reduction, and will trade futures for asset allocation .(p. 4)

a. What does Mr. Chellew mean by writing puts on "stock Aetna doesn't mind buying"?

b. How can futures be used to "enhance yields and for risk reduction"? (How futures can be used for asset allocation is the subject of Chapter 28.)

16. The following is from an article entitled "Analytic Uses Options to Protect Tenneco Position" that appeared in the November 16, 1992, issue of *Derivatives Week*:

> Analytic Investment Management in Irvine, Ca., last Monday sold 70 Nov. 40 puts and bought 70 Feb. 35 puts on Tenneco for its Analytic Optioned Equity Fund—a derivatives-driven mutual fund, according to Chuck Dobson, the fund's executive v.p. By selling and buying an equal number of exchange-traded puts, the firm maintained a fully-hedged position while using profits on its options to counterbalance paper losses on the 7,000 Tenneco shares it owns for a net gain of 1 7/8 per option, Dobson said.
>
> Though Dobson could not give the price at which the stock was bought, he noted that since Tenneco was trading around $35 last Monday, the 7,000 shares were worth roughly $245,000, or about 0.27% of the total $91 million portfolio. Dobson explained that the firm takes a non-directional approach to picking stock, relying instead on the stock's volatility, option premium and dividends.
>
> Dobson explained that the fund, which contains 130–140 mostly high capitalization stocks, is governed by four basic derivatives-linked strategies: 1) buy a stock and sell a call on the stock; 2) buy a stock and a put on the stock; 3) sell a put and place the exercise price in a cash reserve fund; and 4) buy a call and place the exercise price in a money market fund. (p. 7)

a. Explain the option strategy cited in the first paragraph of this excerpt. Be sure to explain what Mr. Dobson meant by the "firm maintained a fully-hedged position."

b. What does Mr. Dobson mean in the second approach when he says the "firm takes a non-directional approach to picking stock, relying instead on the stock's volatility."

c. Explain the first two strategies listed in the third paragraph.

17. Two option-type products that were issued in the market are "Primes" and "Scores." Primes and Scores separate the cash flow components of certain stocks into two components: dividend income and capital appreciation. Specifically, a Prime entitles the holder of the security to receive (1) the dividends of the underlying stock and (2) the market value of the stock at a specified future date up to a preset amount, called the *termination value*. The term *Prime* stands for "prescribed right to income." A Score entitles the instrument holder to all the appreciation above the termination value. Usually, the termination value is 20% to 25% above the current stock price. The term *Score* stands for "special claim on residual income." There were 25 trusts issued, and all matured some time in 1992.

Primes and Scores on individual stocks are not issued originally as securities. Instead, a trust is created in which the stock of a specific company is placed. The trust then issues a Prime and a Score for each share of stock placed in the trust. The trust has a maturity of five years, with its size restricted to no more than 5% of the total number of shares of the outstanding stock of the company. At the end of five years, the trust is terminated, and the Prime and Score holders receive the agreed-upon amount. Before the termination date, the Prime and Score created are traded separately on the American Stock Exchange. At any time during a trading day, a combination of one unit of a Prime and one unit of a Score may be redeemed from the trust for one share of the underlying stock. There is no charge for the redemption.

While probably no new Primes and Scores will be created in the future because of adverse tax circumstances, it is still interesting to examine these instruments in order to understand that there are instruments that have option features even though they are not labeled options.

a. Explain why the Score has the payoff profile of a call option.

b. Explain why the Prime has the payoff profile of a covered call option.

c. In an efficient market, a package of a Prime and a Score should sell for the same price as the underlying stock after adjusting for transactions costs. However, in a study on the pricing of Primes and Scores, two researchers found that the Primes and Scores were mispriced relative to the underlying stock [Robert A. Jarrow and Maureen O'Hara, "Primes and Scores: An Essay on Market Imperfections," *Journal of Finance* (December 1989), pp. 1263–1287]. More specifically, they found that a package of Primes and Scores often exceed the price of the underlying stock by a considerable amount. They explain the discrepancy as arising from market imperfections with respect to short selling and transactions costs. Explain why these two factors could cause the discrepancy.

18. Comment on the following statement: "Investors should pay closer attention to the options markets since option strategies offer risk and reward opportunities that are clearly superior to investing directly in common stock."

CHAPTER 18
EQUITY OPTION PRICING MODELS

LEARNING OBJECTIVES
After reading this chapter you will be able to:

- explain the relationship between the price of a put and a call option.

- calculate the theoretical price of a stock option using the Black-Scholes option pricing model.

- describe how the Black-Scholes option pricing has been modified.

- calculate the theoretical price of a stock option using the binomial option pricing model.

- describe the findings regarding the pricing efficiency of the equity options market.

- describe how the option price changes when factors affecting the value of an option change, and identify measures of how the price of an option changes when the factors affecting its value change: delta, gamma, theta, and kappa.

- explain how price volatility of a stock can be estimated: implied volatility and standard deviation based on historical data.

- describe what is meant by an option replication strategy, and explain how an option replicating portfolio is created, why it must be rebalanced, and what must be reconsidered in rebalancing.

- explain what one option replicating strategy called portfolio insurance is and why it might be employed by an institutional investor.

- describe the risks associated with portfolio insurance.

- explain the advantages and disadvantage of using stock index futures in rebalancing a replicating portfolio.

In the previous chapter, we discussed the basic characteristics of stock and stock index options, strategies employing equity options, and the factors that influence the price of an equity option. In this chapter, we focus on how to determine the fair value or theoretical price of an equity option. The model for doing so is more complicated than the model for determining the fair value of a futures contract that we described in Chapter 17. We then look at the pricing efficiency of the equity options market.

The performance of a stock index option position can be replicated using stock index futures. Such strategies are called *option replication strategies*, the most popular being portfolio insurance. At the end of this chapter, we dis-

337

cuss option replication strategies, the motivation for institutional investors using such strategies, and the associated risks.

PUT-CALL PARITY RELATIONSHIP

There is a relationship between the price of a call option and the price of a put option on the same underlying instrument with the same strike prices and the same expiration dates. To see this relationship, commonly referred to as the **put-call parity relationship**, let's use an example.

In our illustrations in the previous chapter, we used a put and call option on the same underlying stock (stock XYZ), with one month to expiration and with a strike price of $100. The price of the underlying stock was assumed to be $100. The call price and put price were assumed to be $3 and $2, respectively. Consider this strategy:

Buy stock XYZ at a price of $100.
Sell a call option at a price of $3.
Buy a put option at a price of $2.

This strategy involves:

Long stock XYZ.
Short the call option.
Long the put option.

Table 18-1 shows the profit and loss profile at the expiration date for this strategy for selected stock prices. For the long stock position, there is no profit. That is because at a price above $100, stock XYZ will be called from the investor at a price of $100, and at a price below $100, stock XYZ will be

TABLE 18-1
PROFIT/LOSS PROFILE FOR A STRATEGY INVOLVING A LONG POSITION IN STOCK XYZ, SHORT CALL OPTION POSITION, AND LONG PUT OPTION POSITION

Assumptions:

Price of stock XYZ = $100

Call option price = $3

Put option price = $2

Strike price = $100

Time to expiration = 1 month

Price of Stock XYZ at Expiration Date	Profit from Stock XYZ*	Price Received for Call	Price Paid for Put	Overall Profit
$150	0	3	−2	1
130	0	3	−2	1
120	0	3	−2	1
110	0	3	−2	1
100	0	3	−2	1
90	0	3	−2	1
80	0	3	−2	1
70	0	3	−2	1
60	0	3	−2	1

*There is no profit, because at a price above $100, stock XYZ will be called from the investor at a price of $100, and at a price below $100, stock XYZ will be put by the investor at a price of $100.

put by the investor at a price of $100. No matter what stock XYZ's price is at the expiration date, this strategy will produce a profit of $1 without anybody making any net investment. Ignoring (1) the cost of financing the long position in stock XYZ and the long put position and (2) the return from investing the proceeds from the sale of the call, this situation cannot exist in an efficient market. By implementing the strategy to capture the $1 profit, the actions of market participants will have one or more of the following consequences which tend to eliminate the $1 profit: (1) the price of stock XYZ will increase, (2) the call option price will drop, and/or (3) the put option price will rise.

Assuming stock XYZ's price does not change, the call price and the put price will tend toward equality. However, this is true only when we ignore the time value of money (financing cost, opportunity cost, cash payments, and reinvestment income). Also, our illustration does not consider the possibility of early exercise of the option. Thus, we have been considering a put-call parity relationship applicable for only European options.

It can be shown that the put-call parity relationship for an option where the underlying stock makes cash dividends is

Put option price − call option price = present value of strike price
+ present value of dividends − price of underlying stock   (18-1)

This relationship is actually the put-call parity relationship for European options; it is approximately true for American options. If this relationship does not hold, arbitrage opportunities exist. That is, portfolios consisting of long and short positions in the stock and related options that provide an extra return with (practical) certainty will exist.

OPTION PRICING MODELS

In Chapter 17, we illustrated that the theoretical price of a futures contract can be determined on the basis of arbitrage arguments. Theoretical boundary conditions for the price of an option also can be derived using arbitrage arguments. For example, it can be shown that the minimum price for an American call option is its intrinsic value; that is,

Call option price $\geq$ max [0, (price of stock − strike price)]   (18-2)

This expression says that the call option price will be greater than or equal to either the difference between the price of the underlying stock and the strike price (intrinsic value) or zero, whichever is higher.

The boundary conditions can be "tightened" by using arbitrage arguments coupled with certain assumptions about the cash distribution of the stock.[1] The extreme case is an option pricing model that uses a set of assumptions to derive a single theoretical price, rather than a range. As we shall see below, deriving a theoretical option price is much more complicated than deriving a theoretical futures price because the option price depends on the expected price volatility of the underlying stock over the life of the option.

Several models have been developed to determine the theoretical value of an option. The most popular one was developed by Fischer Black and Myron

---

[1]See John C. Cox and Mark Rubinstein, *Option Markets* (Englewood Cliffs, NJ: Prentice-Hall, 1985), Chap. 4.

HOW WE CAME UP WITH THE OPTION FORMULA

First, we concentrated on the fact that the option formula was going to depend on the underlying stock's volatility—not on its expected return. That meant that we could solve the problem using any expected return for the stock.

We decided to try assuming that the stock's expected return was equal to the interest rate. (We were assuming a constant interest rate, so short-term and long-term rates were equal.) In other words, we assumed that the stock's beta was zero; all of its risk could be diversified away.

As we also assumed that the stock's volatility was constant (when expressed in percentage terms) it was easy to figure the likelihood of each possible value of an investment in the stock at the time the option expired. We knew that the stock's terminal value (including reinvested dividends) would have to fit a lognormal distribution.

Other writers on options had made the same sort of assumption about the underlying stock, but they had not assumed an expected return equal to the interest rate. They had, however, assumed a constant expected return, which means a lognormal distribution for the terminal value of a stock that pays no dividends.

If you know the distribution for the stock's terminal value, you can cut it off at the option's exercise price and have the distribution for the option's terminal value. The expected value of that cutoff distribution gives you the expected terminal value of the option.

An article by Case Sprenkle presented a formula for the expected terminal value of an option with these same assumptions, except that Sprenkle allowed the stock to have any constant expected return. By putting the interest rate for the expected stock return into his formula, we got the expected terminal value of the option under our assumptions.

But we didn't want the expected terminal value of the option. We wanted the present value of the option: the value at some time before maturity. So we had to find some way to discount the option's expected terminal value to the present.

Rather suddenly, it came to us. We were looking for a formula relating the option value to the stock price. If the stock had an expected return equal to the interest rate, so would the option. After all, if all the stock's risk could be diversified away, so could all the option's risk. If the beta of the stock were

zero, the beta of the option would have to be zero too.

If the option always had an expected return equal to the interest rate, then the discount rate that would take us from the option's expected future value to its present value would always be the interest rate. The discount rate would not depend on time or on the stock price, as it would if the stock had an expected return other than the interest rate.

So we discounted the expected terminal value of the option at the constant interest rate to get the present value of the option. Then we took Sprenkle's formula, put in the interest rate for the expected return on the stock, and put in the interest rate again for the discount rate for the option. We had our option formula.

Source: Fischer Black, "How We Came Up with the Option Formula," *Journal of Portfolio Management* (Winter 1989), p. 6.

Questions for Box 18

1. Why does the option price depend on the underlying stock's volatility and not on the expected return of the underlying stock?
2. What interest rate is Black referring to?

Scholes in 1973 for valuing European call options.[2] (In Box 18, Fischer Black explains how he and Myron Scholes came up with the formula for the option pricing model.) Several modifications to their model have followed since then. Another pricing model that overcomes some of the drawbacks of the Black-Scholes option pricing model is the binomial option pricing model.

Basically, the idea behind the arbitrage argument in deriving these option pricing models is that if the payoff from owning a call option can be replicated by (1) purchasing the stock underlying the call option and (2) borrowing funds, then the price of the option will be (at most) the cost of creating the replicating strategy.

Black-Scholes Option Pricing Model

Arbitrage conditions provide boundaries for option prices; but to identify investment opportunities and construct portfolios to satisfy their investment

---

[2] Fischer Black and Myron Scholes, "The Pricing of Corporate Liabilities," *Journal of Political Economy* (May-June 1973), pp. 637–659.

objectives, investors want an exact price for an option. By imposing certain assumptions (to be discussed later) and using arbitrage arguments, the **Black-Scholes option pricing model** computes the fair (or theoretical) price of a European call option on a non-dividend-paying stock with the following formula:

$$C = SN(d_1) - Xe^{-rt} N(d_2)$$ (18-3)

where $d_1 = \dfrac{\ln(S/X) + (r + 0.5s^2t)}{s\sqrt{t}}$ (18-4)

$d_2 = d_1 - s\sqrt{t}$ (18-5)

ln = natural logarithm
C = call option price
S = current stock price
X = strike price
r = short-term risk-free interest rate
e = 2.718 (natural antilog of 1)
t = time remaining to the expiration date (measured as a fraction of a year)
s = standard deviation of the stock price
$N(.)$ = the cumulative probability density. The value for $N(.)$ is obtained from a normal distribution function that is tabulated in most statistics textbooks

Notice that five of the factors that we said in the previous chapter influence the price of an option are included in the formula. However, the sixth factor, anticipated cash dividends, is not included because the model is for a non-dividend-paying stock. In the Black-Scholes model, the direction of the influence of each of these factors is the same as stated in the previous chapter. Four of the factors—strike (exercise) price, stock price, time to expiration, and risk-free interest rate—are easily observed. The standard deviation of the stock price must be estimated.

The option price derived from the Black-Scholes option pricing model is "fair" in the sense that if any other price existed, it would be possible to earn riskless arbitrage profits by taking an offsetting position in the underlying stock. That is, if the price of the call option in the market is higher than that derived from the Black-Scholes option pricing model, an investor could sell the call option and buy a certain number of shares in the underlying stock. If the reverse is true, that is, the market price of the call option is less than the "fair" price derived from the model, the investor could buy the call option and sell short a certain number of shares in the underlying stock. This process of hedging by taking a position in the underlying stock allows the investor to lock in the riskless arbitrage profit. The number of shares necessary to hedge the position changes as the factors that affect the option price change, so the hedged position must be changed constantly.

Computing a Call Option Price   To illustrate the Black-Scholes option pricing formula, assume the following values:

Strike price = $45
Time remaining to expiration = 183 days
Current stock price = $47
Expected price volatility = standard deviation = 25

Risk-free rate = 10%

In terms of the values in the formula:

$S = 47$

$X = 45$

$t = 0.5$ (183 *days*/365, *rounded*)

$s = 0.25$

$r = 0.10$

Substituting these values into Equations (18-4) and (18-5), we get

$$d_1 = \frac{\ln(47/45) + [0.10 + 0.5 (0.25)^2] \, 0.5}{0.25\sqrt{0.5}} = 0.6172$$

$$d_2 = 0.6172 - 0.25 \sqrt{0.5} = 0.4404$$

From a normal distribution table:

$$N(0.6172) = 0.7315 \quad \text{and} \quad N(0.4404) = 0.6702$$

Then

$$C = 47 \, (0.7315) - 45 \, (e^{-(0.10)(0.5)}) \, (0.6702) = \$5.69$$

Let's look at what happens to the theoretical option price if the expected price volatility is 40% rather than 25%. Then

$$d_1 = \frac{\ln(47/45) + [0.10 + 0.5 (0.40)^2] \, 0.5}{0.40\sqrt{0.5}} = 0.4719$$

$$d_2 = 0.4719 - 0.40 \sqrt{0.5} = 0.1891$$

From a normal distribution table:

$$N(0.4719) = 0.6815 \quad \text{and} \quad N(0.1891) = 0.5750$$

Then

$$C = 47 \, (0.6815) - 45 \, (e^{-(0.10)(0.5)} \, (0.5750) = \$7.42$$

Notice that the higher the assumed expected price volatility of the underlying stock price, the higher the price of a call option.

Table 18-2 shows the option value as calculated from the Black-Scholes option pricing model for different assumptions concerning (1) the standard deviation, (2) the risk-free rate, and (3) the time remaining to expiration. Notice that the option price varies directly with three variables: volatility, the risk-free rate, and the time remaining to expiration. That is, (1) the lower (higher) the volatility, the lower (higher) the option price; (2) the lower (higher) the risk-free rate, the lower (higher) the option price; and (3) the shorter (longer) the time remaining to expiration, the lower (higher) the option price. All of this agrees with what we stated in the previous chapter (see Table 17-4) about the effect of a change in one of the factors on the price of a call option.

Computing a Put Option Price We have focused our attention on call options. How do we value put options? Recall that the put-call parity relationship as given by Equation (18-1) gives the relationship among the price of the common stock, the call option price, and the put option price. If we can calculate the fair value of a call option, the fair value of a put with the same strike price and expiration on the same stock can be calculated from the put-call parity relationship.

TABLE 18-2
COMPARISON OF BLACK-SCHOLES CALL OPTION PRICE VARYING ONE FACTOR AT A TIME

Base Case
Call option:
  Strike price = $45
  Time remaining to expiration = 183 days
  Current stock price = $47
  Expected price volatility = standard deviation = 25%
  Risk-free rate = 10%

Holding All Factors Constant except Expected Price Volatility

Expected Price Volatility	Call Option Price
15%	4.69
20	5.17
25 (base case)	5.69
30	6.26
35	6.84
40	7.42

Holding All Factors Constant except the Risk-Free Rate

Risk-Free Interest Rate	Call Option Price
7%	5.27
8	5.41
9	5.50
10 (base case)	5.69
11	5.84
12	5.99
13	6.13

Holding All Factors Constant except Time Remaining to Expiration

Time Remaining to Expiration	Call Option Price
30 days	2.85
60	3.52
91	4.15
183 (base case)	5.69
273	6.99

Assumptions Underlying the Black-Scholes Model and Extensions

The Black-Scholes model is based on several restrictive assumptions. These assumptions were necessary to develop the hedge to realize riskless arbitrage profits if the market price of the call option deviates from the value obtained from the model. First, we will look at these assumptions and mention some extensions of the model that make pricing more realistic. We will later examine these extensions of the basic model.

The Option Is a European Option   The Black-Scholes model assumes that the call option is a European call option. Because the Black-Scholes model is on a non-dividend-paying stock, early exercise of an option will not be economic because by selling rather than exercising the call option, the option holder can recoup the option's time premium. The binomial option pricing model which we describe next, can easily handle American call options.[3]

---

[3]John C. Cox, Stephen A. Ross, and Mark Rubinstein, "Option Pricing: A Simplified Approach," *Journal of Financial Economics* (September 1979), pp. 229–263.

Variance of the Stock Price   The Black-Scholes model assumes that the variance of the stock price is (1) constant over the life of the option and (2) known with certainty. If (1) does not hold, an option pricing model can be developed that allows the variance to change. The violation of (2), however, is more serious. As the Black-Scholes model depends on the riskless hedge argument and, in turn, the variance must be known to construct the proper hedge, if the variance is not known, the hedge will not be riskless.

Stochastic Process Generating Stock Prices   To derive an option pricing model, an assumption is needed about the way stock prices move. The Black-Scholes model is based on the assumption that stock prices are generated by one kind of stochastic (random) process called a **diffusion process**. In a diffusion process, the stock price can take on any positive value, but when it moves from one price to another, it must take on all values in between. That is, the stock price does not jump from one stock price to another, skipping over interim prices. An alternative assumption is that stock prices follow a jump process; that is, prices are not continuous and smooth but do jump from one price across intervening values to the next. Merton[4] and Cox and Ross[5] have developed option-pricing models assuming a jump process.

Risk-Free Interest Rate   In deriving the Black-Scholes model, two assumptions were made about the risk-free interest rate. First, it was assumed that the interest rates for borrowing and lending were the same. Second, it was assumed that the interest rate was constant and known over the life of the option. The first assumption is unlikely to hold, because borrowing rates are higher than lending rates. The effect on the Black-Scholes model is that the option price will be between the call price derived from the model using the two interest rates. The model can handle the second assumption by replacing the risk-free rate over the life of the option by the geometric average of the period returns expected over the life of the option.[6]

Dividends   The original Black-Scholes model is for a non-dividend-paying stock. In the case of a dividend-paying stock, it may be advantageous for the holder of the call option to exercise the option early. To understand why, suppose that a stock pays a dividend such that if the call option is exercised, dividends would be received prior to the option's expiration date. If the dividends plus the accrued interest earned from investing the dividends from the time they are received until the expiration date are greater than the time premium of the option, then it would be optimal to exercise the option.[7] In the case where dividends are not known with certainty, it will not be possible to develop a model using the riskless arbitrage argument.

---

[4]Robert Merton, "The Theory of Rational Option Pricing," *Bell Journal of Economics and Management Science*, 4 (Spring 1973), pp. 141–183.

[5]John C. Cox and Stephen A. Ross, "The Valuation of Options for Alternative Stochastic Processes," *Journal of Financial Economics*, 3 (March 1976), pp. 145–166.

[6]Returns on short-term Treasury bills cannot be known with certainty over the long term; only the expected return is known, and there is a variance around it. The effects of variable interest rates are considered in Merton, "The Theory of Rational Option Pricing," op. cit.

[7]Recall from the previous chapter that the time premium is the excess of the option price over its intrinsic value.

In the case of known dividends, a shortcut to adjust the Black-Scholes model is to reduce the stock price by the present value of the dividends. Black has suggested an approximation technique to value a call option for a dividend-paying stock.[8] A more accurate model for pricing call options in the case of known dividends has been developed by Roll,[9] Geske,[10] and Whaley.[11]

Taxes and Transactions Costs   The Black-Scholes model ignores taxes and transactions costs. The model can be modified to account for taxes, but the problem is that there is not just one tax rate. Transactions costs include both commissions and the bid-ask spreads for the stock and the option, as well as other costs associated with trading options.

Binomial Option Pricing Model

To overcome some of the limitations of the Black-Scholes option pricing model, the binomial option pricing model was developed. To derive a one-period binomial option pricing model for a call option, we begin by constructing a portfolio consisting of (1) a long position in a certain amount of the stock and (2) a short call position in this underlying stock. The amount of the underlying stock purchased is such that the position will be hedged against any change in the price of the stock at the expiration date of the option. That is, the portfolio consisting of the long position in the stock and the short position in the call option is riskless and will produce a return that equals the risk-free interest rate. A portfolio constructed in this way is called a **hedged portfolio**.

We can show how this process works with an extended illustration. Let us first assume that there is a stock that has a current market price of $80 and that only two possible future states can occur one year from now. (Because the model assumes that there are only two possible outcomes, it is called a *binomial* model.) Each state is associated with one of only two possible values for the stock, and they can be summarized in this way:

State	Price
1	$100
2	70

We assume further that there is a call option on this stock with a strike price of $80 (the same as the current market price) that expires in one year. Let us suppose an investor forms a hedged portfolio by acquiring 2/3 of a unit of the stock and selling one call option. The 2/3 of a unit of the stock is the so-called **hedge ratio**, the amount of the stock purchased per call sold (how

[8]See Fischer Black, "Fact and Fantasy in the Use of Options," *Financial Analysts Journal* (July-August 1975), pp. 36–41, 61–72. The approach requires that the investor at the time of purchase of the call option and for every subsequent period specify the exact date the option will be exercised.

[9]Richard Roll, "An Analytic Formula for Unprotected American Call Options on Stocks with Known Dividends," *Journal of Financial Economics* (November 1977), pp. 251–258.

[10]Robert Geske, "A Note on an Analytical Formula for Unprotected American Call Options on Stocks with Known Dividends," *Journal of Financial Economics* (December 1979), pp. 375–380, and Robert Geske, "Comment on Whaley's Note," *Journal of Financial Economics* (June 1981), pp. 213–215.

[11]Robert Whaley, "On the Valuation of American Call Options on Stocks with Known Dividends," *Journal of Financial Economics* (June 1981), pp. 207–211.

we derive the hedge ratio will be explained later). Let us consider the outcomes for this hedged portfolio corresponding to the two possible outcomes for the stock.

If the price of the stock one year from now is $100, the buyer of the call option will exercise it. This means that the investor will have to deliver one unit of the stock in exchange for the strike price, 80. As the investor has only a 2/3 unit of the stock, she has to buy 1/3 at a cost of 33 1/3 (the market price of 100 times 1/3). Consequently, the outcome will equal the strike price of 80 received, minus the 33 1/3 cost to acquire the 1/3 unit of the stock to deliver, plus whatever price the investor initially sold the call option for. That is, the outcome will be

$$80 - 33\ 1/3 + \text{call option price} = 46\ 2/3 + \text{call option price}$$

If, instead, the price of the stock one year from now is $70, the buyer of the call option will not exercise it. Consequently, the investor will own 2/3 of a unit of the stock. At the price of 70, the value of 2/3 of a unit is 46 2/3. The outcome in this case is the value of the stock plus whatever price the investor received when she initially sold the call option. That is, the outcome will be

$$46\ 2/3 + \text{call option price}$$

It is apparent that, given the possible stock prices, the portfolio consisting of a short position in the call option and 2/3 of a unit of the stock will generate an outcome that hedges changes in the price of the stock; hence, the hedged portfolio is riskless. Furthermore, this holds regardless of the price of the call, which affects only the magnitude of the outcome.

Deriving the Hedge Ratio   To show how the hedge ratio can be calculated, we will use the following notation:

S = current stock price

u = 1 plus the percentage change in the stock's price if the price goes up in the next period

d = 1 plus the percentage change in the stock's price if the price goes down in the next period

r = a risk-free one-period interest rate (the risk-free rate until the expiration date)

C = current price of a call option

C_u = intrinsic value of the call option if the stock price goes up

C_d = intrinsic value of the call option if the stock price goes down

E = strike price of the call option

H = hedge ratio, that is, the amount of the stock purchased per call sold

In our illustration,

u = 1.250 ($100/$80)

d = 0.875 ($70/$80)

H = 2/3

Further, state 1 in our illustration means that the stock's price goes up, and state 2 means that the stock's price goes down.

The investment made in the hedged portfolio is equal to the cost of buying H amount of the stock minus the price received from selling the call option. Therefore, because

Amount invested in the stock = HS

then

Cost of the hedged portfolio = $HS - C$

The payoff of the hedged portfolio at the end of one period is equal to the value of the H amount of the stock purchased minus the call option price. The payoffs of the hedged portfolio for the two possible states are defined in this way:

State 1, if the stock's price goes up: $uHS - C_u$
State 2, if the stock's price goes down: $dHS - C_d$

In our illustration, we have these payoffs:

If the stock's price goes up: 1.250 H $80 − C_u or $100 H − C_u
If the stock's price falls: 0.875 H $80 − C_d or $70 H − C_d

If the hedge is riskless, the payoffs must be the same. Thus,

$$uHS - C_u = dHS - C_d \qquad (18\text{-}6)$$

Solving Equation (18-6) for the hedge ratio H, we have

$$H = \frac{C_u - C_d}{(u - d)S} \qquad (18\text{-}7)$$

To determine the value of the hedge ratio H, we must know C_u and C_d. These two values are equal to the difference between the price of the stock and the strike price in the two possible states. Of course, the minimum value of the call option, in any state, is zero. Mathematically, the differences can be expressed as follows:

If the stock's price goes up: $C_u = max\,[0, (uS - E)]$
If the stock's price goes down: $C_d = max\,[0, (dS - E)]$

As the strike price in our illustration is $80, uS is $100, and dS is $70, then,

If the stock's price goes up: $C_u = max\,[0, (\$100 - \$80)] = \$20$
If the stock's price goes down: $C_d = max\,[0, (\$70 - \$80)] = \$0$

To continue with our illustration, we substitute the values of u, d, S, C_u and C_d into Equation (18-7) to obtain the hedge ratio's value:

$$H = \frac{\$20 - \$0}{(1.25 - 0.875)\,\$80} = 2/3$$

This value for H agrees with the amount of the stock purchased when we introduced this illustration.

Now we can derive a formula for the call option price. Figure 18-1 diagrams the situation. The top left half of the figure shows the price of the stock for the current period and at the expiration date. The lower left-hand portion of the figure does the same thing using the notation above. The upper right-hand side of the figure gives the current price of the call option and the

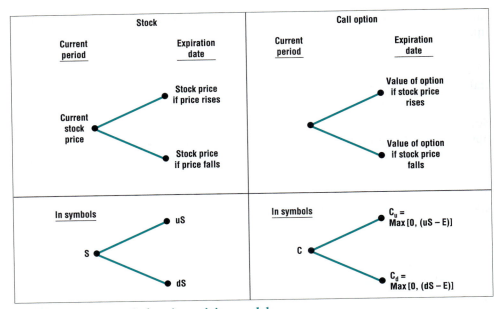

FIGURE 18-1   One-period option-pricing model.

value of the call option at the expiration date; the lower right-hand side does the same thing using our notation. Figure 18-2 uses the values in our illustration to construct the outcomes for the stock and the call option.

    Deriving the Price of a Call Option   To derive the price of a call option, we can rely on the basic principle that the hedged portfolio, being riskless, must have a return equal to the risk-free rate of interest. Given that the amount invested in the hedged portfolio is $HS - C$, the amount that should be generated one period from now is

$$(1 + r)(HS - C) \tag{18-8}$$

We also know what the payoff will be for the hedged portfolio if the stock's price goes up or down. Because the payoff of the hedged portfolio will be the

FIGURE 18-2   One-period option-pricing model illustration.

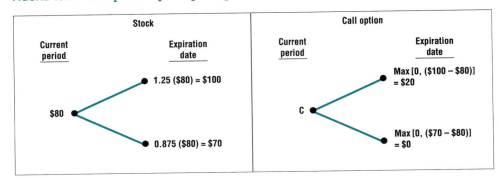

same whether the stock's price rises or falls, we can use the payoff if it goes up, which is

$$uHS - C_u$$

The payoff of the hedged portfolio given above should be the same as the initial cost of the portfolio given by Equation (18-8). Equating the two, we have

$$(1 + r)(HS - C) = uHS - C_u \tag{18-9}$$

Substituting Equation (18-7) for H in Equation (18-9) and solving for the call option price C, we find

$$C = \left(\frac{1 + r - d}{u - d}\right)\left(\frac{C_u}{1 + r}\right) + \left(\frac{u - 1 - r}{u - d}\right)\left(\frac{C_d}{1 + r}\right) \tag{18-10}$$

Applying Equation (18-10) to our illustration
where $u = 1.250$
$$d = 0.875$$
$$r = 0.10$$
$$C_u = \$20$$
$$C_d = \$0$$

we get

$$C = \left(\frac{1 + 0.10 - 0.875}{1.25 - 0.875}\right)\left(\frac{\$20}{1 + 0.10}\right) + \left(\frac{1.25 - 1 - 0.10}{1.25 - 0.875}\right)\left(\frac{\$0}{1 + 0.10}\right)$$
$$= \$10.90$$

Equation (18-10) is the formula for the one-period binomial option pricing model. We would have derived the same formula if we had used the payoff for a decline in the price of the underlying stock. This derivation is left as an exercise for the reader.

The approach we presented for pricing options may seem oversimplified, given that we assume only two possible future states for the price of the underlying stock. In fact, we can extend the procedure by making the periods smaller and smaller, and in that way calculate a fair value for an option. It is important to note that extended and comprehensive versions of the binomial pricing model are in wide use throughout the world of finance. Moreover, the other popular option pricing model, the Black-Scholes model mentioned earlier, is in reality the mathematical equivalent of the binomial approach as the intervals become very small. Therefore, the approach we have described in detail here provides the conceptual framework for much of the analysis of option prices that today's financial market participants regularly perform.

Extension to a Two-Period Model By dividing the time to expiration into two periods, we can represent price changes within the time period to maturity and add more realism to our model. The extension to two intermediate periods requires that we introduce more notation. To help understand the notation, look at Figure 18-3. The left panel of the figure shows, for the stock, the initial price, the price one period from now if the price goes up or goes down, and the price at the expiration date (two periods from now) if the price in the previous period goes up or goes down. The right panel of Figure 18-3 shows the value of the call option at the expiration date and the value one period prior to the expiration date.

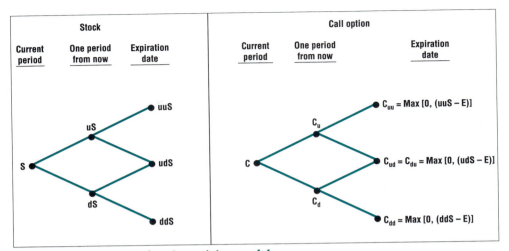

FIGURE 18-3   Two-period option-pricing model.

The new notation has to do with the value of the call option at the expiration date. We now use two subscripts. Specifically, C_{uu} is the call value if the stock's price went up in both periods, C_{dd} is the call value if the stock's price went down in both periods, and C_{ud} (which is equal to C_{du}) is the call value if the stock's price went down in one period and up in one period.

We solve for the call option price C by starting at the expiration date to determine the value of C_u and C_d. This can be done by using Equation (18-10) because that equation gives the price of a one-period call option. Specifically,

$$C_u = \left(\frac{1 + r - d}{u - d}\right)\frac{C_{uu}}{1 + r} + \left(\frac{u - 1 - r}{u - d}\right)\frac{C_{ud}}{1 + r} \tag{18-11}$$

and

$$C_d = \left(\frac{1 + r - d}{u - d}\right)\frac{C_{du}}{1 + r} + \left(\frac{u - 1 - r}{u - d}\right)\frac{C_{dd}}{1 + r} \tag{18-12}$$

Once C_u and C_d are known, we can solve for C using Equation (18-10).

To make this more concrete, let's use numbers. We will assume that the stock's price can go up by 11.8% per period or down by 6.46% per period. That is,

$u = 1.118$ and $d = 0.9354$

Then, as shown in the top left panel of Figure 18-4, the stock can have three possible prices at the end of two periods:

Price goes up both periods: $uuS = (1.118)(1.118)\,\$80 = \$100$
Price goes down both periods: $ddS = (0.9354)(0.9354)\,\$80 = \$70$
Price goes up one period and down the other: $udS = (1.118)(0.9354)\,\$80 = duS = (0.9354)(1.118)\,\$80 = \$83.66$

Notice that the first two prices are the same as in the one-period illustration. By breaking the length of time until expiration to two periods rather than one, and adjusting the change in the stock price accordingly, we now

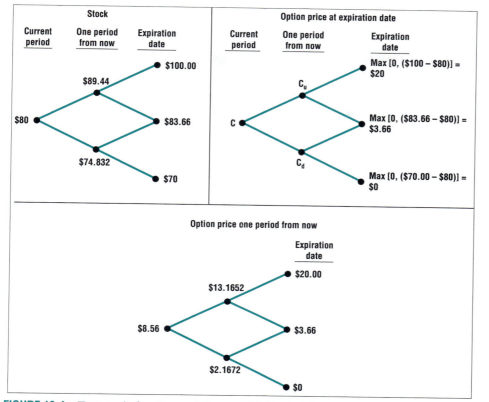

FIGURE 18-4 Two-period option-pricing model illustration.

have three possible outcomes. If we break down the length of time to expiration into more periods, the number of possible outcomes that the stock price may take on at the expiration date will increase. Consequently, what seemed like an unrealistic assumption about two possible outcomes for each period becomes more realistic with respect to the number of possible outcomes that the stock price may take at the expiration date.

Now we can use the values in the top right panel of Figure 18-4 to calculate C. In our example we assumed a risk-free interest rate of 10%. When we divide our holding period in two, the riskless interest rate for one period is now 4.88% because when compounded this rate will produce an interest rate of 10% from now to the expiration date (two periods from now). First, consider the calculation of C_u using Equation (18-11). From Figure 18-4 we see that

$$C_{uu} = \$20 \quad \text{and} \quad C_{ud} = \$3.66$$

Therefore,

$$C_u = \left(\frac{1 + 0.0488 - 0.9354}{1.118 - 0.9354}\right) \frac{\$20}{1 + 0.0488}$$

$$+ \left(\frac{1.118 - 1 - 0.0488}{1.118 - 0.9354}\right) \frac{\$3.66}{1 + 0.0488} = \$13.1652$$

From Figure 18-4,

$$C_{dd} = \$0 \qquad \text{and} \qquad C_{du} = \$3.66$$

Therefore,

$$C_d = \left(\frac{1 + 0.0488 - 0.9354}{1.118 - 0.9354}\right)\frac{\$3.66}{1 + 0.0488}$$

$$+ \left(\frac{1.118 - 1 - 0.0488}{1.118 - 0.9354}\right)\frac{\$0}{1 + 0.0488} = \$2.1672$$

We have inserted the values for C_u and C_d in the bottom panel of Figure 18-4 and can now calculate C by using Equation (18-11) as follows:

$$C = \left(\frac{1 + 0.0488 - 0.9354}{1.118 - 0.9354}\right)\frac{\$13.1652}{1 + 0.0488}$$

$$+ \left(\frac{1.118 - 1 - 0.0488}{1.118 - 0.9354}\right)\frac{\$2.1672}{1 + 0.0488} = \$8.58$$

Dividends can be incorporated into the binomial pricing model by using the dividend amount at each point for the value of the stock. So if the dividend one period from now is expected to be \$1, then S_u and S_d in the left panel of Figure 18-3 would be $S_u + \$1$ and $S_d + \$1$, respectively. In Figure 18-4, this means that in the top left panel, the value for the stock one period from now would be \$90.44 and \$75.832, instead of \$89.44 and \$74.832.

SENSITIVITY OF THE OPTION PRICE TO A CHANGE IN FACTORS

In employing options in investment strategies, a money manager would like to know how sensitive the price of an option is to a change in any one of the factors that affect its price. Here we look at the sensitivity of a call option's price to changes in the price of the underlying stock, the time to expiration, and expected price volatility.[12]

The Call Option Price and the Price of the Underlying Stock

In developing an option-pricing model, we have seen the importance of understanding the relationship between the option price and the price of the underlying stock. Moreover, a money manager employing options to control the price risk of a portfolio wants to know how the option position will change as the price of the underlying stock changes.

Figure 18-5 shows the theoretical price of a call option based on the price of the underlying stock. The horizontal axis is the price of the underlying stock at any point in time. The vertical axis is the call option price. The shape of the curve representing the theoretical price of a call option, given the price of the underlying stock, would be the same regardless of the actual option pricing model used. In particular, the relationship between the price of the underlying stock and the theoretical call option price is convex.

---

[12]For a detailed explanation of the role of these measures in option strategies, see Chapter 4 in Richard M. Bookstaber, *Option Pricing and Investment Strategies* (Chicago: Probus Publishing, 1991).

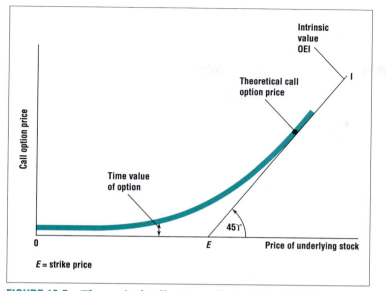

Time value of option

45°

0

E

Price of underlying stock

Call option price

Intrinsic value OEI

Theoretical call option price

I

E = strike price

FIGURE 18-5   Theoretical call price and price of underlying stock.

The line from the origin to the strike price on the horizontal axis in Figure 18-5 is the intrinsic value of the call option when the price of the underlying stock is less than the strike price, since the intrinsic value is zero. The 45-degree line extending from the horizontal axis is the intrinsic value of the call option once the price of the underlying stock exceeds the strike price. The reason is that the intrinsic value of the call option will increase by the same dollar amount as the increase in the price of the underlying stock. For example, if the strike price is $100 and the price of the underlying stock increases from $100 to $101, the intrinsic value will increase by $1. If the price of the stock increases from $101 to $110, the intrinsic value of the option will increase from $1 to $10. Thus, the slope of the line representing the intrinsic value after the strike price is reached is 1.

Since the theoretical call option price is shown by the convex line, the difference between the theoretical call option price and the intrinsic value at any given price for the underlying stock is the time value of the option.

Figure 18-6 shows the theoretical call option price, but with a tangent line drawn at the price of p^*. The tangent line in the figure can be used to estimate what the new option price will be (and therefore what the change in the option price will be) if the price of the underlying stock changes. Because of the convexity of the relationship between the option price and the price of the underlying stock, the tangent line closely approximates the new option price for a small change in the price of the underlying stock. For large changes, however, the tangent line does not provide as good an approximation of the new option price.

The slope of the tangent line shows how the theoretical call option price will change for small changes in the price of the underlying stock. The slope

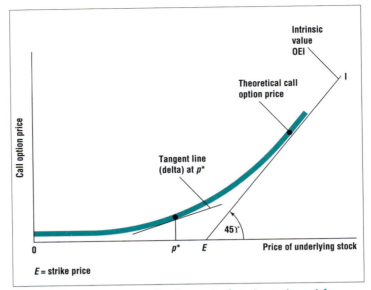

FIGURE 18-6 **Estimating the theoretical option price with a tangent line.**

of the tangent line is what we referred to earlier as the hedge ratio. It is more popularly referred to as the **delta** of the option. Specifically,

$$\text{Delta} = \frac{\text{change in price of call option}}{\text{change in price of underlying stock}}$$

For example, a delta of 0.4 means that a $1 change in the price of the underlying stock will change the price of the call option by approximately $0.40.

Figure 18-7 shows the curve of the theoretical call option price with three tangent lines drawn. The steeper the slope of the tangent line, the greater the delta. When an option is deep out of the money (that is, the price of the underlying stock is substantially below the strike price), the tangent line is nearly flat (see line 1 in Figure 18-7). This means that delta is close to zero. To understand why, consider a call option with a strike price of $100 and two months to expiration. If the price of the underlying stock is $20, its price would not increase by much, if anything, should the price of the underlying stock increase by $1, from $20 to $21.

For a call option that is deep in the money, the delta will be close to 1. That is, the call option price will increase almost dollar for dollar with an increase in the price of the underlying stock. In terms of the graph in Figure 18-7, the slope of the tangent line approaches the slope of the intrinsic value line after the strike price. As we stated earlier, the slope of that line is 1.

Thus, the delta for a call option varies from zero (for call options deep out of the money) to 1 (for call options deep in the money). The delta for a call option at the money is approximately 0.5.

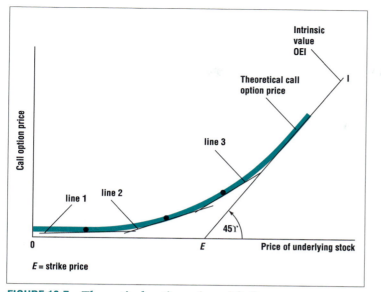

FIGURE 18-7   Theoretical option price with three tangents.

The curvature of the convex relationship can also be approximated. This is the rate of change of delta as the price of the underlying stock changes. The measure is commonly referred to as **gamma** and is defined as follows:

$$\text{Gamma} = \frac{\text{change in delta}}{\text{change in price of underlying stock}}$$

The Call Option Price and Time to Expiration

All other factors constant, the longer the time to expiration, the greater the option price. Since each day the option moves closer to the expiration date, the time to expiration decreases. The **theta** of an option measures the change in the option price as the time to expiration decreases, or equivalently, it is a measure of **time decay**. Theta is measured as follows:

$$\text{Theta} = \frac{\text{change in price of option}}{\text{decrease in time to expiration}}$$

Assuming that the price of the underlying stock does not change (which means that the intrinsic value of the option does not change), theta measures how quickly the time premium of the option changes as the option moves toward expiration.

Buyers of options prefer a low theta so that the option price does not decline quickly as it moves toward the expiration date. An option writer benefits from an option that has a high theta.

The Call Option Price and Expected Price Volatility

All other factors constant, a change in the expected price volatility will change the option price. The **kappa** of an option measures the dollar price change in the price of the option for a 1% change in the expected price volatility. That is,

$$\text{Kappa} = \frac{\text{change in option price}}{1\% \text{ change in expected price volatility}}$$

ESTIMATING EXPECTED PRICE VOLATILITY

The only factor whose value is not known in an option-pricing model is expected price volatility. Market participants estimate expected price volatility in one of two ways: (1) by calculating the implied volatility from current option prices or (2) by calculating the standard deviation using historical daily price changes for the stock.

Implied Volatility

An option pricing model relates a given volatility estimate to a unique price for the option. Similarly, if the option price is known, the same option pricing model can be used to determine the corresponding volatility. This is known as **implied volatility**.

In addition to its use as input in an option-pricing model to determine the value of another option, implied volatility has other applications in strategies employing options. The most straightforward application is a comparison of implied volatility with the estimate of volatility using historical price data that we describe next. If an investor believes that the estimated volatility using historical data is a better estimate than implied volatility, then the two volatility estimates can be compared to assess whether an option is cheap or expensive. More specifically, if the estimate of volatility using historical data is higher than implied volatility, then the option is cheap; if it is less than implied volatility, then the option is expensive.

In addition to identifying options that may be rich or expensive, implied volatility can be used to compare options on the same underlying stock and time to expiration but with different strike prices. For example, suppose that the implied volatility for a call option with a strike price of 90 is 8% when a call option with a strike of 100 has an implied volatility of 12%. Then on a relative basis, the call option with a strike of 90 is cheaper than the call option with a strike of 100. Put and call options on the same stock and with the same time to expiration can also be compared using implied volatility.

Calculating Standard Deviation from Historical Data

The second method used to estimate expected price volatility is the calculation of the standard deviation of historical daily price changes. Market practice with respect to the number of days that should be used to calculate the daily standard deviation varies. The number of days can be as few as 10 days or as many as 100 days.

Since market participants are interested in annualized volatility, the daily standard deviation must be annualized as follows:

Daily standard deviation $\times \sqrt{\text{number of days in a year}}$

Market practice varies with respect to the number of days in the year that should be used in the annualizing formula above. Typically, either 250 days,

260 days, or 365 days is used. The first two are used because they represent the number of actual trading days for certain options.

Thus, in calculating an annual standard deviation, the money manager must decide on:

1. The number of daily observations to use to calculate the daily standard deviation
2. The number of days in the year to use to annualize the daily standard deviation

As a result of these two choices, the volatility estimate based on historical daily price changes can vary significantly.

PRICING EFFICIENCY OF THE EQUITY OPTIONS MARKETS

A market is said to be efficient if investors cannot earn abnormal returns after accounting for risk and transactions costs. In Chapter 13 we mentioned the problems associated with testing for the pricing efficiency of the stock market. Here we focus on tests of the pricing efficiency of the market for equity options.

A problem encountered by researchers in this area is that tests require information on the price of two instruments at the exact same time—the stock price and the option price. When prices are available on both assets at the same time, the data are said to be **synchronous data**. In empirical tests, prices used may be non-synchronous because of data availability limitations. That is, the stock price used in a study may be the closing price for the day, while the option price may be the price at the beginning of the same trading day. An empirical study that finds abnormal trading profits using non-synchronous data does not necessarily indicate that the options market is inefficient.

Beyond the problem of non-synchronous data, there is the problem of determining the fair price of an option to be used in the empirical tests. Thus, researchers must rely on some option-pricing model, which makes the findings only as good as the option-pricing model employed. Table 18-3 summarizes the general findings.

Evidence for Stock Options

Tests of market efficiency fall into two categories. The first category is tests using no option-pricing model. Instead, violations of boundary conditions or violations of put-call parity are examined to determine if abnormal trading profits are possible after transactions costs. The studies on stock options have found that while there may be opportunities for abnormal trading profits before transactions costs, these opportunities disappear after considering transactions costs.[13]

Tests in the second category employ various option-pricing models to assess whether mispriced options can be identified and exploited. The earlier

---

[13]See Mihtu Bhattacharya, "Transactions Data Tests of Efficiency of the Chicago Board Options Exchange," *Journal of Financial Economics*, 12 (August 1983), pp. 161–165; Robert C. Klemkosky and Bruce G. Resnick, "Put-Call Parity and Market Efficiency," *Journal of Finance* (December 1979), pp. 1141–1155, and Robert C. Klemkosky and Bruce G. Resnick, "An Ex Ante Analysis of Put-Call Parity," *Journal of Financial Economics*, 8 (1980), pp. 363–378.

<table>
<tr><td colspan="3" align="center">**TABLE 18-3**</td></tr>
<tr><td colspan="3" align="center">**TESTS OF EQUITY OPTION PRICE EFFICIENCY**</td></tr>
<tr><td>**Test Category**</td><td>**Findings of Abnormal Profit Opportunities?**</td><td>**Comment**</td></tr>
<tr><td>*For Stock Options*</td><td></td><td></td></tr>
<tr><td>Seeking violations of boundary or parity conditions</td><td>Not after transactions costs</td><td></td></tr>
<tr><td>Comparing theoretical and actual prices</td><td>Not after transactions costs</td><td>Transactions costs differ among participants</td></tr>
<tr><td>*For Stock Index Options*</td><td></td><td></td></tr>
<tr><td>Seeking lower boundary violations</td><td>Yes</td><td>Possibly explained by non-synchronous information used in the study</td></tr>
<tr><td>Seeking violations of the put-call parity relationship</td><td>Yes, and more so for European than American options</td><td>Arbitrage problems: 1. Expense of creating a cash market replicating portfolio 2. Estimating stock index dividends</td></tr>
</table>

studies in the 1970s reported mixed results concerning market efficiency.[14] Criticisms of these studies were that the researchers failed to take transactions costs into consideration. In the options market, transactions costs include (1) floor trading and clearing costs, (2) any state transfer tax that might be imposed, (3) SEC transactions fees, (4) margin requirements, (5) net capital charges, and (6) bid-ask spreads. The magnitude of these costs needs to be considered in empirical studies that investigate market efficiency. These costs vary for market makers, arbitrageurs, and individuals in the options markets, so the market may be efficient for one type of market participant but not another. Studies that took one or more of these costs into account found that the abnormally high returns reported in earlier studies were eliminated.[15]

Thus, in the stock options market, the hypothesis that the options market is efficient is supported.

Evidence for Stock Index Options

Empirical tests of the pricing of index options are subject to the same problems as empirical tests of the pricing of stock options. Moreover, there is the added problem of estimating the amount and timing of dividends for the stocks in the index. One study tested for violations of the lower boundary

---

[14]See, for example, Fischer Black and Myron Scholes, "The Valuation of Option Contracts and a Test of Market Efficiency," *Journal of Finance* (May 1972), pp. 399–417; Dan Galai, "Tests of Market Efficiency and the Chicago Board Options Exchange," *Journal of Business*, 50 (1970), pp. 167–197; Dan Galai, "Empirical Tests of Boundary Conditions for CBOE Options," *Journal of Financial Economics*, 6 (1978), pp. 187–211; Robert Trippi, "A Test of Option Market Efficiency Using a Random-Walk Valuation Model," *Journal of Economics and Business*, 29 (1977), pp. 93–98; Donald Chiras and Steven Manaster, "The Information Content of Option Prices and a Test of Market Efficiency," *Journal of Financial Economics* 6 (1978), pp. 213–234.

[15]See Susan M. Phillips and Clifford W. Smith, "Trading Costs for Listed Options: Implications for Market Efficiency," *Journal of Financial Economics*, 8 (1980), pp. 179–201; and Edward C. Blomeyer and Robert C. Klemkosky, "Tests of Market Efficiency for American Call Options," in Menachem Brenner (ed.), *Option Pricing* (Lexington, MA: Heath, 1983), pp. 101–121.

(that is, instances where the ask price of the call was below the difference between the value of the cash index and the strike price).[16] Using an extensive data base that eliminated many of the data problems discussed above, the researchers found many instances of violations. Moreover, there were occasions when the size of the violation became so large that even "upstairs traders" would have been capable of taking advantage of these violations. The authors of the study suggested that the reason for the violations was that despite the detailed data used, there was still a non-synchronous data problem during periods when prices were changing rapidly.

Two studies tested for violations of the put-call parity relationship.[17] Both of these studies found a significant number of violations.[18] The results of one of these studies suggest that if stock index options are treated as European options, significant profit opportunities are possible. The violations suggest that the S&P 100 index call options were underpriced (which means that the puts were overpriced). The reverse is true for another exchange-traded stock index option. Even if the options are considered American options, these results suggest that there were profit opportunities.

Why do we observe these violations in the stock index options market? The reason is more than likely attributable to the difficulty of arbitraging between the index options market and the cash market. Two problems in arbitraging are (1) the difficulty and expense of creating a portfolio to replicate the performance of the cash market index and (2) the difficulty of estimating dividends for the stocks in the index.

OPTION REPLICATION STRATEGIES

From our discussion of option pricing, we can see that the same payoff can be created by taking a leveraged position in the underlying stock and adjusting the position as market prices change. The advantage of an option is that it may be a more transactionally efficient vehicle for creating a desired payoff.

Nevertheless, there are still instances in which a money manager may benefit from replicating an option position using the cash instrument. Here are just two examples. Options do not exist on all financial products, and therefore a money manager seeking the risk/reward payoff of an option must create it synthetically. For instance, suppose a money manager has a portfolio of stocks in a foreign country that does not have an equity index options market. If the money manager wants to protect against a decline in the value of the portfolio, it may be possible to synthetically create the payoff of a put option on the equity index.

The second case in which a money manager would consider replicating an option rather than buying one is when she believes that the option price is too high. For example, suppose that a money manager wants to insure a minimum value for a stock portfolio. The money manager could buy an exchange-traded put option. The cost of insuring the minimum value of the portfolio is

---

[16]Jeremy Evnine and Andrew Rudd, "Index Options: The Early Evidence," *Journal of Finance* (July 1985), pp. 743–756.

[17]Evnine and Rudd, "Index Options: The Early Evidence," op. cit.; and; Don M. Chance, "Parity Tests of Index Options," *Advances in Futures and Options Research*, 2 (1987), pp. 47–64.

[18]Evnine and Rudd, "Index Options: The Early Evidence," op. cit.

the cost of the put option. Since the option price is known upfront, the cost of the insurance is known. The cost will depend on expected price volatility. Thus, by buying a put option to insure a minimum value for a portfolio, the money manager knows the cost of that insurance, and the cost is determined by the market's expectation of future price volatility.

Suppose, however, that a money manager believes that the market's expectation of future price volatility is too high. This means that the cost of insuring the portfolio by buying a put option would be too expensive. Given that an option can be replicated by creating a leveraged portfolio in the underlying stock, the money manager can synthetically create a put option. This particular type of option replication strategy is popularly referred to as creating **portfolio insurance**.

What will be the cost of insuring the portfolio? The answer is that it depends on the actual price volatility of the market over the planned investment horizon. This is because, as we explain below, the strategy involves rebalancing the portfolio. The actual transactions costs depend on the actual market price volatility. The greater the actual volatility, the more rebalancing necessary and therefore the greater the transactions costs. If the money manager expects future price volatility to be less than the market's expectation for future price volatility, then there could be a cost savings by synthetically creating a put option rather than buying one. Whether the money manager does realize the cost savings depends on the actual price volatility. Thus, when a money manager buys a put option, the manager knows the cost of the insurance upfront. In contrast, a money manager who synthetically creates a put option does not know beforehand the cost of the insurance. The actual price volatility will determine the cost.

Creating a Portfolio to Replicate an Option

The basic principles of creating a portfolio to replicate a target option can be illustrated for a one-stock portfolio. In our illustration we will create a portfolio to replicate a target put option; that is, we will create an insured portfolio. To do this, consider the non-dividend-paying stock used in the illustration of the binomial option pricing model. The assumptions are as follows:

1. The current market price of the stock is $80.
2. Based on the money manager's expectation, the following two possible future states are expected to occur one year from now:

State	Price	
1	$100	(up market)
2	70	(down market)

Since these two states indicate how the money manager feels the stock price can move, it is effectively her volatility assumption.
3. The risk-free interest rate is 10% per year.

Finally, assume that the money manager wants to insure that one year from now the market value of the portfolio is not less than its current market price of $80. This is equivalent to saying that the money manager wants a minimum return over the one year of 0%.

Let's consider what happens if the money manager creates a portfolio consisting of the stock and a one-year zero-coupon risk-free security. We will use a one-year Treasury bill as the risk-free security. Since a Treasury bill is a zero-coupon instrument, the price of the one-year Treasury security with a maturity value of $100 selling to yield 10% would be $90.91 ($100 divided by 1.10). The market value of the portfolio would then be equal to

$$w_s(\text{price of stock}) + w_f(\text{price of Treasury})$$

where w_s is equal to the market value of the stock relative to the market value of the portfolio, and w_f is the market value of the Treasury security relative to the market value of the portfolio.

One year from now the money manager knows the market value of the portfolio will depend on which of the two states for the price of the stock occurs. The value of the Treasury security will not depend on the state that occurs for the stock price. The value of the Treasury security will be $100, its maturity value.

Now remember that the money manager's objective is to have the same payoff as a put option on the stock, ignoring the cost of acquiring the put option. If an up market occurs, the money manager wants the market value of the portfolio to be $100, the same as the payoff if a put option were purchased. That is,

$$w_s\$100 + w_f\$100 = \$100 \tag{18-13}$$

If a down market occurs, the money manager wants the minimum value for the portfolio to be equal to $80, just as if a put option with a strike price of $80 were purchased. That is,

$$w_s\$70 + w_f\$100 = \$80 \tag{18-14}$$

Equations (18-13) and (18-14) represent two equations with two unknowns. Solving these two equations simultaneously for w_s and w_f gives 2/3 for w_s and 1/3 for w_f. Let's verify that with these weights the insured portfolio produces the same portfolio value one year from now as a put option (ignoring the cost of the option). If the stock's price increases to $100, then from Equation (18-14):

$$(2/3)\$100 + (1/3)\$100 = \$100$$

If the stock's price declines to $70, then from Equation (18-14):

$$(2/3)\$70 + (1/3)\$100 = \$80$$

To create this insured portfolio which includes 2/3 of the stock and 1/3 of the Treasury security, the following must be invested at current market prices:

$$(2/3)\$80 + (1/3)\$90.91 = \$83.64$$

Since an uninsured portfolio would cost $80 (the current price of the stock), this means that the cost of the insurance is $3.64.

With an $80 investment and an $83.64 total cost of an insured portfolio, the money manager would buy 95.65% ($80/$83.64) of an insured portfolio.

Portfolio Rebalancing

Remember that the objective of an option replication strategy is to reproduce the payoff of an option at all times. In our illustration above, the money manager established an initial portfolio to replicate the put option. Also, it was assumed that the stock's price will change only once. In practice, the price of the underlying stock changes daily. The option replication strategy requires that the payoff or performance of the replicating portfolio be the same as the payoff of the actual option. This requires that the replicating portfolio be rebalanced periodically.

To understand why, suppose that a money manager wants to replicate a call option. Suppose that the delta of the call option is 0.4. This means that if the price of the stock changes by $1, the price of the option will change by approximately $0.40. In establishing the amount of the initial replicating portfolio, 40% of the underlying stock will be purchased. (This is effectively what we did in our earlier illustration even though we did not specifically introduce the delta into our analysis.) Consequently, if a money manager is seeking to replicate a call option on 100,000 shares of the stock, the initial replicating portfolio will include 40,000 shares of the stock. If the stock price increases by $1, the call option would increase by $40,000 given a delta of 0.4, and the replicating portfolio with 40,000 shares of stock would also increase by $40,000.

Over time, as the price of the underlying stock changes, the delta of the call option changes. (We discussed this earlier in the chapter using Figure 18-7.) Suppose that the price of the stock rises by $10 so its delta increases to, say, 0.70. Thus, a further change in the price of the stock by $1 will change the value of a call option on 100,000 shares by approximately $70,000. However, the replicating portfolio only has 40,000 shares of the stock, so a $1 increase in the price of the stock will increase the portfolio value by only $40,000. Thus, the performance of the replicating portfolio does not match the performance of the call option. To prevent this from happening, the number of shares of the stock in the replicating portfolio must be adjusted to reflect the changing delta.

An option-replicating strategy is illustrated in Figures 18-6 and 18-7. At a given point in time, these two figures show the curve representing the theoretical option value for different prices of the underlying stock. The option-replicating strategy seeks to reproduce that curve representing the theoretical option value. The first approximation of the curve is the tangent line, which we stated is the delta, or hedge ratio. However, as explained earlier, delta does not do a good job of approximating the price change for a large change in the price. To correct for this, the gamma of the option should be employed. Finally, the curve representing the theoretical option value changes as the option moves closer to the expiration date. Thus, replicating the option performance requires not only allowing for changes in the stock's price but also allowing for time decay, as measured by the option's theta.

Consequently, while we focused on the delta in discussing how the stock position must be rebalanced, a more careful analysis requires consideration of the gamma and theta of the option. In fact, the other factors that affect the option price such as the short-term interest rate and expected price volatility also change and must be considered. How this is done in practice is beyond the scope of this book.[19] Because an option replication strategy involves rebalancing, it is often referred to as **dynamic hedging**.

---

[19]The interested reader is referred to Chapter 6 in Bookstaber, *Option Pricing and Investment Strategies*, op. cit.

Risks Associated with Option Replication Strategies

Several risks are associated with trying to replicate an option. First, there is the risk that the option-pricing model used to estimate the performance of the target option to be replicated is incorrect. As a result, the delta, gamma, and theta that are used in the replicating portfolio and rebalancing portfolio will be incorrect, and the replicating portfolio will not match the performance of the target option.

Second, the actual cost of the synthetic option may be more than the target option. As noted earlier, it is not possible to know with certainty what the cost of the synthetic option will be. It depends on the actual volatility of the stock's price, which, in turn, affects the transactions costs associated with rebalancing the portfolio. In practice, estimates of this cost are made using simulation analysis. In contrast, the cost of the purchase of the target option is known with certainty.

Finally, a critical assumption in an option replication strategy is that prices change smoothly over time and do not jump (i.e., price changes follow a diffusion process and not a jump process). If there are time periods where prices do jump, as in the October 1987 stock market crash, then it will be difficult to properly adjust the replicating portfolio, and accordingly, there will be no assurance the portfolio insurance strategy will turn out as expected.

Use of Futures in an Option Replication Strategy

In our illustration, we looked at an option replication strategy for one stock. In practice, money managers employ an option replication strategy for a broad-based portfolio of stocks. Buying and selling a large number of stocks in order to rebalance the portfolio can be costly. Instead, stock index futures contracts are typically used to rebalance a portfolio.

The advantages of using stock index futures rather than the actual stocks were explained in Chapter 17, one of these advantages being the considerably lower transactions costs. The disadvantage of using stock index futures is that they might be mispriced relative to their fair value (too cheap when the futures are sold and too expensive when they are purchased).

Consequently, when the futures are fairly priced or mispriced in favor of the money manager (i.e., expensive when futures are being sold and cheap when they are being purchased), futures rather than the actual stocks will be used in the strategy. If futures are mispriced to the money manager's disadvantage by an amount more than the additional transactions costs associated with buying or selling the actual stock, the money manager can rebalance using the actual stock.

Portfolio Insurance and Black Monday

Portfolio insurance is one type of option replication strategy that seeks to match a put option. The rebalancing requirements for a portfolio insurance strategy involve buying stocks or futures when the market is rising and selling when the market is falling. The concern with this strategy as expressed by the SEC Division of Market Regulation and other critics is that it may have a "cascade" effect when stock prices decline.

To understand this argument, consider what would happen if stock prices decline and portfolio insurance is employed using stocks and a risk-free security. The strategy requires that stocks be sold. But if many institutional investors are following a portfolio insurance strategy, this will mean a substantial number of stocks will be sold, causing further decline in stock prices. In turn, more stocks must be sold, leading to more decline in stock prices.

The same would happen if stock index futures are used to implement a portfolio insurance strategy. Their sales in the futures market would depress futures prices. What would arbitrageurs do? They would take offsetting positions in futures (by buying futures) and in stocks (by selling stocks). This action, it is argued, would lower cash prices further and cause portfolio insurers to sell futures, resulting in a spiraling effect.

Proponents of portfolio insurance argue that the cascade effect is unlikely. At some point, value-oriented investors would step in when stocks are priced below their value based on economic fundamentals. However, Grossman (in a paper published several months before Black Monday) presented theoretical arguments that suggest that the imbalance of buyers and sellers of portfolio insurance could change stock market volatility. Specifically, if the demand for portfolio insurance exceeds the amount that market participants are willing to supply (that is, the amount of put options that market participants are willing to sell), volatility will increase; it would decrease if supply exceeded demand.[20]

Critics of portfolio insurance have argued that this strategy was responsible for the stock market crash of October 19, 1987 (Black Monday). It is interesting to note that in the morning of that day, several options exchanges did begin trading in long-term index options that were designed to satisfy the needs of the portfolio insurance market.[21] A supply of long-term put index options—that is, actual exchange-traded put options—it is argued, could have satisfied the demand from portfolio insurers. Two things probably prevented that from happening. First, the new exchange-traded contracts did not have sufficient time to develop so that market participants could be comfortable with using them. Second, even if market participants did want to use these new contracts, position limits imposed on investors by the exchange may have prevented them from doing so. In discussing Black Monday, SEC Commissioner Joseph A. Grundfest in an article published in mid-1989 wrote:

> Had all investors involved in portfolio insurance found it possible, and desirable, to satisfy their demand for "insurance" by buying puts instead of relying on dynamic hedges, the market would have had more information about the intensity of investor concern about a downside move. Under those circumstances, there's reason to believe that prices might not have fallen as low on the downside had the market simply been better informed of investors' own concerns. Thus, to the extent position limits on index options forced investors away from the options market and into secret dynamic hedging strategies, the government's position limit restrictions may have unwittingly exacerbated the market's decline.[22]

Thus, the culprit might not be dynamic hedging/portfolio insurance but, instead, (1) the inability to develop a long-term exchange-traded index options

---

[20]Sanford J. Grossman, "An Analysis of the Implications for Stock and Futures Price Volatility of Program Trading and Dynamic Hedging Strategies," presented at the Conference on the Impact of Stock Index Futures Trading at the Center for the Study of Futures Markets, Columbia University, June 8, 1987. The paper was subsequently published in the July 1988 issue of the *Journal of Business.* A less technical version of this paper is "Insurance Seen and Unseen: The Impact of Markets," *Journal of Portfolio Management* (Summer 1988), pp. 5–8.

[21]Gary L. Gastineau, *Eliminating Option Position Limits: A Key Structural Reform* (New York: Salomon Brothers Inc, Aug. 30, 1988), p. 3.

[22]Joseph A. Grundfest, "Perestroika on Wall Street: The Future of Securities Trading," *Financial Executive* (May-June 1989), p. 25.

market and (2) government imposition of a regulatory feature—position limits—that impeded the use of the exchange-traded market. Whether or not one is willing to accept this hypothesis, it should be understood that it is entirely untested and has therefore no empirical underpinning.

■ SUMMARY

In this chapter we turned our attention to the pricing of options and the pricing efficiency of the options market. There is a relationship between the price of a put option and the price of a call option, called the put-call parity relationship. Several models have been developed to determine the fair value of an option: the Black-Scholes option pricing model, extensions of the Black-Scholes model, and the binomial option pricing model. The arbitrage argument employed in deriving these option-pricing models is that the payoff from owning an option can be replicated by a position in the underlying asset and by borrowing funds to create the leverage associated with an option. The cost of the option is then (at most) the cost of creating the portfolio to replicate the option.

The price of an option depends on six factors. The sensitivity of the option price to changes in these factors can be estimated. We discussed several of these measures: The delta and the gamma of an option measure the sensitivity of the option price to a change in the price of the underlying stock; the theta of an option measures the time decay of an option; and the kappa of an option measures the sensitivity of an option's price to a change in expected price volatility.

The unknown in an option-pricing model is expected price volatility. There are two ways to estimate expected price volatility: implied volatility and the standard deviation of daily price changes from historical data. Implied volatility has several applications in addition to its use in an option-pricing model. In estimating the standard deviation based on observed daily price changes, a decision must be made

about how many daily observations should be used and how the daily standard deviation should be annualized. As a result of these two choices, there could be a significant difference in the estimated price volatility using historical data.

The empirical evidence on the pricing efficiency of the options market suggests that, after considering transactions costs, the market appears to be price-efficient.

There are instances in which a money manager may want to replicate the performance of an option position. This occurs when either no option is available on the underlying asset or where the money manager believes that the option is too expensive. The technology for replicating an option follows from the basic principles of how to determine the fair value of an option. The strategy requires a rebalancing of the replicating portfolio as the factors that affect the value of an option change. Rebalancing results in transactions costs, and such costs are the costs of replicating the target option.

Several risks are associated with creating a synthetic option: The option-pricing model will be misestimated, transactions costs will be higher than the outright purchase of an option, and a jump in stock prices may prevent the successful implementation of the rebalancing required. When an option-replicating strategy is employed for a portfolio of stocks, stock index futures rather than stocks are used to rebalance the portfolio. While critics of one type of option replicating strategy, portfolio insurance, have argued that followers of this strategy caused the stock market crash of October 1987, there is no empirical evidence to support this.

■ KEY TERMS

Black-Scholes option pricing model
delta
diffusion process
dynamic hedging

gamma
hedge ratio
hedged portfolio
implied volatility
kappa

portfolio insurance
put-call parity relationship
synchronous data
theta
time decay

■ QUESTIONS

1. What is the relationship between the price of a put and a call with the same underlying stock, strike price, and expiration date.

2. **a.** Assuming the values below for a European call option, calculate the theoretical option price using the Black-Scholes model:

    Strike price = $100

    Current stock price = $100

    Dividend = $0

    Risk-free rate = 8%

    Expected price volatility = 20%

    Time to expiration = 91 days

   b. What are the intrinsic value and the time premium for this call option?

3. For the call option in the previous question, what would be the theoretical option price, intrinsic value, and time premium if:

    a. The current stock price is $55 instead of $100?

    b. The current stock price is $150 instead of $100?

4. **a.** Calculate the option value for a two-period European call option with the following terms:

    Current price of underlying asset = $100

    Strike price = $10

    One-period risk-free rate = 5%

    The stock price can either go up or go down by 10% at the end of one period.

   b. Recalculate the value for the option when the stock price can move either up or down by 50% at the end of one period. Compare your answer with the calculated value in part a. Why is the answer different from what you might have expected?

5. **a.** Explain why it would not be economic for the buyer of an American call option on a non-dividend-paying stock to exercise the option prior to the expiration date.

    b. Is this true for an American call option on a dividend-paying stock? Under what circumstances (if any) would early exercise be economic?

    c. Would it be economic for the buyer of an American put option to exercise the option early? (*Hint*: Think about what happens if the

price of the stock falls to zero before the expiration date.)

6. Two portfolio managers have estimated the standard deviation of the price change of IBM stock using daily data. Why might the two estimates be markedly different?

7. **a.** What is meant by implied volatility?

    b. How can implied volatility be used to compare options on the same stock but with different strike prices?

8. **a.** What does the delta of an option measure?

    b. Why would you expect that the delta of a deep out-of-the-money call option would be close to zero?

    c. Why is the delta of an option not constant over the life of the option?

    d. What is meant by the gamma of an option?

9. **a.** What does the theta of an option measure?

    b. A seller of a call option would prefer an option with a low theta. Do you agree with this statement?

10. Give two reasons why a money manager would prefer to synthetically create a put option.

11. Suppose that a money manager has a portfolio of one stock with a market value of $100. Also assume the following: (1) The stock price one year from now can be either $110 or $90, (2) a one-year Treasury bill with a maturity value of $100 has a market price of $95.24, and (3) the money manager wants to create an insured portfolio with a minimum value one year from now of $100.

    a. Express in equation form the market value of the portfolio, one year from now, that the money manager seeks if the market price increases.

    b. Express in equation form the market value of the portfolio, one year from now, that the money manager seeks if the market price decreases.

    c. Indicate how much of the stock and the Treasury bill should be purchased to create the initial insured portfolio.

    d. Show that these amounts will produce the target outcome for the insured portfolio if the stock price rises or if it falls one year from now.

e. What is the cost of the portfolio insurance?

f. How much of the insured portfolio should the money manager buy?

12. In an article titled "The Mechanics of Portfolio Insurance," [*Journal of Portfolio Management* (Spring 1988)], Thomas J. O'Brien wrote in summary:

This article has presented a line of analysis designed to clarify the mysteries of the basic portfolio insurance concept. A simplified abstraction of reality shows that portfolio insurance works. With an understanding of the mechanics and cost concepts presented here, the analyst may proceed to consider aspects of real-world application.

There are many periods and possible horizon states in actual practice, rather than the four used in the examples here. Therefore, the Black-Scholes model is the starting point for calculating deltas and expected insurance costs in the real world. Advanced applications would try to make use of extensions to the Black-Scholes model to factor in the impact of certain real-world issues. . . .

In the simple, abstract environment assumed here, dynamic portfolio insurance has been shown to work. No guarantee can be made that dynamic replication will be effective against a catastrophe that occurs during a time when the market is closed, or against a "market meltdown" during trade hours. Indeed, the macro-effect of dynamic insurance on the market is still in question. [The words of this concluding paragraph were written prior to October 19, 1987!] (p.47)

a. What is meant by portfolio insurance?

b. What is the basic underlying principle with respect to creating an insured portfolio?

c. Why does the author indicate that deltas have to be calculated?

d. The author states that extensions of the Black-Scholes model should be used to calculate the deltas. Explain at least two extensions of the Black-Scholes model.

e. What does it mean that there is no guarantee that portfolio insurance will work if there is a market meltdown during trading hours?

13. In an article by Joanne Hill, Anshuman Jain, and Robert Wood, Jr., entitled "Insurance: Volatility Risk and Futures Mispricing" (which appeared in the Winter 1988 issue of the *Journal of Portfolio Management*), the authors state:

Almost all "dynamic" portfolio protection strategies are implemented with futures trades motivated by the pattern of changing prices in the protected asset or portfolio over the investment horizon. The realized costs of the programs therefore are affected by futures mispricing and the pattern of realized price volatility over the period the program is in effect. (p. 23)

a. What do you think the authors mean by "dynamic" portfolio protection strategies?

b. What do the authors mean when they say that the futures trades are motivated by the "pattern of changing prices in the protected asset or portfolio over the investment horizon"?

c. Why do money managers use futures rather than the underlying asset to implement the required trades?

d. Why are the realized costs of the program affected by (1) "futures mispricing" and (2) "the pattern of realized price volatility over the period the program is in effect"?

14. A money manager that you are advising read an article by Yu Zhu and Robert Kavee, "Performances of Portfolio Insurance Strategies," in the Spring 1988 issue of the *Journal of Portfolio Management*. He tells you that the authors used elaborate simulations of synthetic put options and found that they do reduce downside risk and retain some upside gains. Nevertheless, the authors found the strategies are costly and do not guarantee a floor.

a. Your client is confused about why it was necessary for the authors to simulate the strategy in order to determine the cost of the synthetic put option. He thought that the cost of the insurance is known upfront. Explain why the simulations are necessary.

b. Your client also did not understand what was meant by the strategy being costly. Explain what this means.

c. Finally, it was unclear to your client that the strategy does not guarantee a floor. He thought that the purpose of an insurance program is to set a floor or minimum value for the portfolio. Explain why a floor is not guaranteed.

CHAPTER 19
FIXED-INCOME SECURITIES

LEARNING OBJECTIVES
After reading this chapter you will be able to:

- distinguish between the different types of fixed-income securities.
- explain the fundamental features of bonds.
- describe the different types of securities issued by the Treasury.
- show how zero-coupon Treasury securities are created.
- describe provisions for paying off a corporate bond issue prior to the maturity date.
- identify the different credit ratings for a corporate bond issue.
- distinguish between the two types of municipal bonds: general obligation bonds and revenue bonds

- identify types of securities issued in the Eurobond market.
- describe the characteristics of preferred stock.
- explain the cash flow characteristics of a mortgage loan and the meaning of prepayment risk.
- describe the three types of mortgage-backed securities: mortgage pass-through securities, collateralized mortgage obligations, and stripped mortgage-backed securities.
- describe the different types of asset-backed securities.

Our focus in Section IV was on managing a common stock portfolio. Now we turn our attention to investing in the other major asset class, fixed-income securities. In this chapter we will provide an overview of these securities. We will look at their basic features and then delve into the various types of fixed-income securities: Treasury securities, corporate bonds, municipal securities, preferred stock, mortgage-backed securities, and asset-backed securities. Our goal is to provide a general description of these securities and the features that allow issuers or investors to alter their cash flows. In later chapters we will explain the pricing and performance characteristics of fixed-income securities, which involves these cash–flow–related features. The most complicated of all fixed-income securities are mortgage-backed securities, and our purpose of introducing these securities is simply to provide an introduction to this complex, yet large and growing, sector of the fixed-income securities market.

We cover the pricing, yield calculations, and price volatility characteristics in the next two chapters. In Chapter 22 we discuss the reasons that interest rates are not equal for all fixed-income securities and the factors that affect the interest rate that must be offered on a particular security. The principles of valuing fixed-income securities covered in Chapters 20 and 22 are extended to the valuation of complicated bond structures and convertible securities in Chapter 23. Bond portfolio strategies are explained in Chapters 24 and 25, and the use of derivative instruments for managing bond portfolios is presented in Chapters 26 and 27.

BOND FUNDAMENTALS

A fixed-income security is one in which the issuer (borrower) has agreed to make income payments that are fixed by contract. For example, every six months for the next 10 years an issuer can agree to pay $50. Another example is a security in which the issuer agrees to make an income payment based on the interest rate paid on six-month certificates of deposit. In this example, the dollar amount of the income will fluctuate every six months depending on the interest rate on six-month certificates of deposit. However, this security is a fixed-income security because the contractual amount is fixed. The investor can realize no more than this amount, and assuming the issuer is capable of satisfying its obligation, the investor will receive no less than this amount.

Fixed-income securities can be divided into two categories: debt obligations and equity. With a debt obligation, the borrower makes interest payments. Failure to make the contractual interest payments means that the borrower is in default. In general, in the remainder of this book we will refer to securities that represent debt obligations as *bonds*. In contrast to debt obligations, preferred stock is an equity instrument in which the securityholders have agreed to a fixed-income payment called *dividends*. Below we describe the basic features of bonds. We postpone a discussion of preferred stock to later in this chapter.

A key feature of any bond is its **term to maturity,** which is the date on which the debt will cease to exist and the borrower will have completely paid off the amount borrowed. In practice, the words *maturity* and *term* are used interchangeably to refer to the number of years remaining in the life of a bond. Technically, however, maturity denotes the date the debt will be paid off completely, and term or term to maturity denotes the number of years until that date.

The amount that the issuer agrees to pay at the maturity date is called the **par value**, **maturity value**, or **face value**. A bond's **coupon** is the periodic interest payment made to the bondholders during the life of the bond. As Table 19-1 shows, bonds can be classified by coupon type.

In referring to a bond, the coupon cited is in fact the **coupon rate,** or rate of interest, that, when multiplied by the par value, indicates the dollar value of the coupon payment. Typically, but not universally, for bonds issued in the United States half of the coupon payment is made in semiannual installments.

There are bonds in which no periodic coupon interest rate is paid over the life of the contract. Instead, both the principal and the interest are paid at the

TABLE 19-1

CLASSIFICATION OF BONDS BY COUPON TYPE

| Bond Type | Interest Payments | |
	Timing	Rate
Fixed coupon	Periodic (e.g., every 6 months)	Unchanging (e.g., 5.5%)
Floating coupon	Periodic	Variable, expressed as a benchmark ± a spread (e.g., LIBOR + 30 basis points)
Zero coupon	At maturity	Usually fixed

maturity date. Such bonds are called **zero-coupon bonds**. The investor in a zero-coupon bond realizes interest as the difference between the maturity value and the purchase price.

A floating-rate security is one in which the coupon rate is reset periodically. The new coupon rate for the period is contractually determined to be some reference rate adjusted for a spread. The spread can be either added to or subtracted from the value of the reference rate, and is expressed in *basis points* (hundredths of a percent). Two examples of the coupon reset formula for a floating-rate security are

Reference rate + 100 basis points
Reference rate − 50 basis points

U.S. TREASURY SECURITIES

There are two categories of U.S. Treasury securities—discount and coupon securities. Current Treasury practice is to issue all securities with maturities of one year or less (Treasury bills) as discount securities. All securities with maturities of two years or longer are issued as coupon securities. As we said in Chapter 2, at issuance Treasury notes have a maturity between 2 and 10 years, and Treasury bonds have a maturity at issuance greater than 10 years. Although Treasury notes are not callable, many outstanding Treasury bond issues are callable within five years of maturity. Treasury bonds issued since February 1985 are not callable.

Interest income from Treasury securities is subject to federal income taxes but is exempt from state and local income taxes.

Treasury securities typically are issued on an auction basis according to regular cycles for securities of specific maturities. Three-month and six-month Treasury bills are auctioned every Monday. The 1-year (52-week bill) Treasury bills are auctioned in the third week of every month. The Treasury regularly issues coupon securities with maturities of 2, 3, 5, 10, and 30 years. Each month, 2- and 5-year notes are auctioned. At the beginning of the second month of each calendar quarter (February, May, August, and November), the Treasury conducts its regular refunding operations. At this time, it auctions 3-year, 10-year, and 30-year Treasury securities.

The secondary market for Treasury securities is an over-the-counter market where a group of U.S. government securities dealers provide continuous bids and offers on specific outstanding Treasuries. This secondary market is the most liquid financial market in the world.

In the secondary market, the most recently auctioned Treasury issues for each maturity are referred to as *on-the-run* or *current-coupon* issues. They are also referred to as the **benchmark issues** or **bellwether issues**. Issues auctioned prior to the current coupon issues typically are referred to as *off-the-run* issues; they are not as liquid as on-the-run issues. That is, the bid-ask spread is larger for off-the-run issues relative to on-the-run issues because they are not as liquid.

Quotation Convention for Treasury Bills

The convention for quoting bids and offers is different for Treasury bills and Treasury coupon securities. Unlike bonds that pay coupon interest, Treasury bills are quoted not in terms of price but rather in terms of yield. More specifically the convention is to quote Treasury bills on a **bank discount basis**. The yield on a bank discount basis is computed as follows:

$$Y_d = \frac{D}{F} \times \frac{360}{t}$$

where Y_d = annualized yield on a bank discount basis (expressed as a decimal)

D = dollar discount, which is equal to the difference between the face value and the price

F = face value

t = number of days remaining to maturity

As an example, a Treasury bill that has 100 days to maturity and a face value of $100,000 and is selling for $97,569 would be quoted at 8.75% on a bank discount basis:

$$D = \$100,000 - \$97,569$$
$$= \$2,431$$

Therefore:

$$Y_d = \frac{\$2,431}{\$100,000} \times \frac{360}{100}$$
$$= 8.75\%$$

The quoted yield on a bank discount basis is not a meaningful measure of the return from holding a Treasury bill for two reasons. First, the measure is based on a face value investment rather than on the actual dollar amount invested. Second, the yield is annualized according to a 360-day rather than 365-day year, making it difficult to compare Treasury-bill yields with yields from Treasury notes and bonds, which pay interest on a 365-day basis. The use of 360 days for a year is a money-market convention for some money-market instruments. Despite its shortcomings as a measure of return, this is the method dealers have adopted to quote Treasury bills.

Price Quotation Convention for Treasury Coupon Securities

Treasury coupon securities are quoted differently from Treasury bills. They trade on a dollar price basis in price units of 1/32 of 1% of par (par is taken to be $100). For example, a quote of 92-14 refers to a price of 92 and 14/32. On the basis of $100,000 par value, a change in price of 1% equates to $1,000, and 1/32 equates to $31.25. A plus sign following the number of 32nds means that a 64th is added to the price. For example, 92-14+ refers to a price of 92 and 29/64 or 92.453125% of par value.

Stripped Treasury Securities

In the next chapter, we will explain why investors may find it beneficial to invest in zero-coupon securities that are backed by the U.S. government. Unfortunately, the U.S. Treasury does not issue zero-coupon notes or bonds. In August 1982, however, both Merrill Lynch and Salomon Brothers created synthetic zero-coupon Treasury receipts. Merrill Lynch marketed its Treasury receipts as Treasury Income Growth Receipts (TIGRs), Salomon Brothers marketed its as Certificates of Accrual on Treasury Securities (CATS). The procedure was to purchase Treasury bonds and deposit them in a bank custody account. The firms then issued receipts representing an ownership interest in each coupon payment on the underlying Treasury bond in the account and a receipt on the underlying Treasury bond's maturity value. This process of separating each coupon payment, as well as the principal, to sell securities against them is referred to as *coupon stripping*. Although the receipts created from the coupon stripping process are not issued by the U.S. Treasury, the underlying bond deposited in the bank custody account is a debt obligation of the U.S. Treasury, so the cash flow from the underlying security is certain.

To illustrate the process, suppose $100 million of a Treasury bond with a 20-year maturity and a coupon rate of 10% is purchased to create zero-coupon Treasury securities. The cash flow from this Treasury bond is 40 semiannual payments of $5 million each ($100 million times 0.10 divided by 2) and the repayment of principal (corpus) of $100 million 20 years from now. This Treasury bond is deposited in a bank custody account. Receipts are then issued, each with a different single payment claim on the bank custody account. As there are 41 different payments to be made by the Treasury, a receipt representing a single payment claim on each payment is issued, which is effectively a zero-coupon bond. The amount of the maturity value for a receipt on a particular payment, whether coupon or corpus, depends on the amount of the payment to be made by the Treasury on the underlying Treasury bond. In our example, 40 coupon receipts each have a maturity value of $5 million, and one receipt, the corpus, has a maturity value of $100 million. The maturity dates for the receipts coincide with the corresponding payment dates by the Treasury.

Other investment banking firms followed suit by creating their own receipts. They all are referred to as *trademark* zero-coupon Treasury securities because they are associated with a particular firm. Receipts of one firm were rarely traded by competing dealers, so the secondary market was not liquid for any one trademark. To broaden the market and improve liquidity of these receipts, a group of primary dealers in the government market agreed to issue generic receipts that would not be directly associated with any of the participating dealers. These generic receipts are referred to as *Treasury receipts* (TRs). Rather than representing a share of the trust as the trademarks do, TRs represent ownership of a Treasury security. In February 1985 the U.S. Treasury announced its Separate Trading of Registered Interest and Principal of Securities (STRIPS) program to facilitate the stripping of Treasury securities.

The zero-coupon Treasury securities created under the STRIPS program are direct obligations of the U.S. government. Creation of the STRIPS program ended the origination of trademarks and generic receipts.

FEDERAL AGENCY SECURITIES

The federal agency securities market can be divided into two sectors—the **government-sponsored enterprises securities market** and the **federally related institutions securities market**. Government-sponsored enterprises are privately owned, publicly chartered entities. They were created by Congress to reduce the cost of capital for certain borrowing sectors of the economy deemed to be important enough to warrant assistance. The entities in these privileged sectors include farmers, homeowners, and students. Government-sponsored enterprises issue securities directly in the marketplace.

Federally Related Institutions Securities

Federally related entities are arms of the federal government that typically do not issue securities directly in the marketplace. These include the Export-Import Bank of the United States, the Commodity Credit Corporation, the Farmers Housing Administration, the General Services Administration, the Government National Mortgage Association, the Maritime Administration, the Private Export Funding Corporation, the Rural Electrification Administration, the Rural Telephone Bank, the Small Business Administration, and the Washington Metropolitan Area Transit Authority. The Tennessee Valley Authority is a federally related institution that now issues its own securities. All federally related institutions are exempt from SEC registration. With the exception of securities of the Private Export Funding Corporation and the Tennessee Valley Authority, the securities are backed by the full faith and credit of the United States government.

Government-Sponsored Enterprise Securities

There are eight government-sponsored enterprises. The Federal Farm Credit Bank System is responsible for the credit market in the agricultural sector of the economy. The Farm Credit Financial Assistance Corporation was created in 1987 to address problems in the existing Farm Credit System. Three government-sponsored enterprises—Federal Home Loan Bank, Federal Home Loan Mortgage Corporation, and Federal National Mortgage Association—are responsible for providing credit to the mortgage and housing sectors. The Student Loan Marketing Association provides funds to support higher education. The Financing Corporation was created in 1987 to recapitalize the Federal Savings and Loan Insurance Corporation. Because of continuing difficulties in the savings and loan association industry, the Resolution Trust Corporation was created in 1989 to liquidate or bail out insolvent institutions.

With the exception of the securities issued by the Farm Credit Financial Assistance Corporation, government-sponsored enterprise securities are not backed by the full faith and credit of the U.S. government, as is the case with Treasury securities. Consequently, an investor who purchases a security issued by a government-sponsored enterprise is exposed to credit risk.

The price quotation convention for securities issued by government-sponsored enterprises is the same as that for Treasury coupon securities.

Some issues of government-sponsored enterprises trade with almost the same liquidity as Treasury securities. Other issues that are only supported by a few dealers trade much like off-the-run corporate bonds.

CORPORATE BONDS

The promises of a corporate bond issuer and the rights of investors are set forth in great detail in a contract called a **bond indenture**. The essential features of a corporate bond are relatively simple, however. The corporate issuer promises to pay a specified percentage of par value on designated dates (known as the *coupon payments*) and to repay par or principal value of the bond at maturity. Failure to pay either the principal or interest when due constitutes legal default, and court proceedings can be instituted to enforce the contract. Bondholders, as creditors, have a prior legal claim over common and preferred stockholders on both income and assets of the corporation for the principal and interest due them.

There are really two secondary corporate bond markets: the exchange market (New York Stock Exchange and American Stock Exchange) and the over-the-counter (OTC) market. Almost all trading volume takes place in the OTC market, which is the market used by institutional investors and professional money managers.

In a typical corporate bond, options are embedded in the issue. An **embedded option** is part of the structure of a bond, as opposed to a *bare option*, which trades separately from any underlying security. As we describe the features of a corporate bond issue, these embedded options should be recognized since their presence, as we shall see in Chapter 23, affects the value of a bond.

Most corporate bonds are **term bonds**; that is, they run for a term of years and then become due and payable. Term bonds are often referred to as *bullet-maturity*, or simply *bullet*, bonds. The term may be long or short. As with Treasuries, obligations due less than 10 years from the date of issue are called **notes**; however, we do not make the distinction in this chapter. Term bonds may be retired by payment at final maturity or retired prior to maturity if provided for in the indenture. Some corporate bond issues are so arranged that specified principal amounts become due on specified dates. Such issues are called **serial bonds**.

A **medium-term note** is another corporate debt instrument. The unique characteristic of medium-term notes is that they are continuously offered to investors over a period of time by an agent of the issuer. Investors can select from the following maturity bands: 9 months to 1 year, more than 1 year to 18 months, more than 18 months to 2 years, etc., up to 30 years.

Security for Bonds

Either real property or personal property may be pledged to offer security beyond that of the general credit standing of the issuer. With a **mortgage bond**, the issuer has granted the bondholders a lien against the pledged assets. A lien is a legal right to sell mortgaged property to satisfy unpaid obligations to bondholders. In practice, foreclosure and sale of mortgaged property are unusual. If a default occurs, there is usually a financial reorganization of the issuer in which provision is made for settlement of the debt to bondholders. The mortgage lien is important, though, because it gives the mortgage bond-

TABLE 19-2
CLAIM PRIORITY OF CORPORATE BONDHOLDERS

Corporate Bonds	Pledged Property	Priority of Claim
Secured		
Mortgage bonds	Fixed assets or real property	First against pledged property; then as general claimant against issuer
Collateral trust bonds	Securities	First against pledged property; then as general claimant against issuer
Unsecured		
Debenture bonds	None	As general claimant
Subordinate debenture bonds	None	As claimant after debenture bondholders

holders a very strong bargaining position relative to other creditors in determining the terms of a reorganization.

Some companies do not own fixed assets or other real property and so have nothing on which they can give a mortgage lien to secure bondholders. Instead, they own securities of other companies; they are holding companies and the other companies are subsidiaries. To satisfy the desire of bondholders for security, the issuer grants investors a lien on stocks, notes, bonds, or whatever other kind of financial asset it owns. These assets are termed *collateral* (or personal property), and bonds secured by such assets are called **collateral trust bonds**.

Debenture bonds are not secured by a specific pledge of property, but that does not mean that holders have no claim on property of issuers or on their earnings. Debenture bondholders have the claim of general creditors on all assets of the issuer not pledged specifically to secure other debt. And they even have a claim on pledged assets to the extent that these assets have value greater than necessary to satisfy secured creditors. **Subordinated debenture bonds** are issues that rank after secured debt, after debenture bonds, and often after some general creditors in the claim on assets and earnings.

Table 19-2 provides a summary of claim priority of corporate bondholders.

It is important to recognize that while a superior legal status will strengthen a bondholder's chance of recovery in case of default, it will not absolutely prevent bondholders from suffering financial loss when the issuer's ability to generate cash flow adequate to pay its obligations is seriously eroded. Claims against a weak lender are oftentimes satisfied for less than face value.

Provisions for Paying Off Bonds

Most corporate issues have a **call provision** whereby the issuer has an option to buy back all or part of the issue prior to maturity. Some issues specify that the issuer must retire a predetermined amount of the issue periodically. Various types of call provisions found in corporate bonds are discussed below.[1]

---

[1]For a more detailed explanation of call provisions in corporate bonds, see Richard S. Wilson and Frank J. Fabozzi, *The New Corporate Bond Market* (Chicago: Probus Publishing, 1990).

Call and Refund Provisions An important question in negotiating the terms of a new bond issue is whether the issuer shall have the right to redeem the *entire amount* of bonds outstanding on a date before maturity. Issuers generally want this right because they recognize that at some time in the future the general level of interest rates may fall sufficiently below the issue's coupon rate, so redeeming the issue and replacing it with another issue with a lower coupon rate would be attractive. For the reasons discussed in Chapter 23, this right is a disadvantage to the bondholder. Thus, a call option is an embedded option granted to the issuer.

The usual practice is a provision that denies the issuer the right to redeem bonds during the first 5 to 10 years following the date of issue with proceeds received from issuing lower-cost debt obligations ranking equal to or superior to the debt to be redeemed. This type of redemption is called **refunding**. While most long-term issues have these refunding restrictions, they may be immediately callable, in whole or in part, if the source of funds comes from other than lower-interest cost money. Cash flow from operations, proceeds from a common stock sale, or funds from the sale of property are examples of such sources.

Investors often confuse refunding protection with call protection. Call protection is much more absolute in that bonds cannot be redeemed *for any reason*. Refunding restrictions only provide protection against the one type of redemption mentioned above. Failure to recognize this difference has resulted in unnecessary losses for some investors. When less than the entire issue is called, the procedure for calling the issue is specified in the indenture. The specific bonds to be called are selected either randomly or on a pro rata basis.

As a rule, corporate bonds are callable at a premium above par. Generally, the amount of the premium declines as the bond approaches maturity and often reaches par after a number of years have passed since issuance.

Sinking-Fund Provision Corporate bond indentures may require the issuer to retire a specified portion of an issue each year. This is referred to as a **sinking fund** requirement. This kind of provision for repayment of corporate debt may be designed to liquidate all of a bond issue by the maturity date, or it may be arranged to pay only a part of the total by the end of the term. If only a part is paid, the remainder is called a **balloon maturity**. The purpose of the sinking fund provision is to reduce credit risk.

Generally, the issuer may satisfy the sinking fund requirement by either (1) making a cash payment of the face amount of the bonds to be retired to the corporate trustee who then calls the bonds for redemption using a lottery or (2) delivering to the trustee bonds with a total face value equal to the amount that must be retired from bonds purchased in the open market. Usually, the sinking fund call price is the par value if the bonds were originally sold at par.

Many corporate bond indentures include a provision that grants the issuer the right (i.e., option) to *accelerate* the repayment of the principal. This is another embedded option granted to the issuer since the issuer can take advantage of this provision if interest rates decline below the coupon rate. While the acceleration provision is supposedly included in an indenture to reduce the credit risk of an issuer by allowing the issuer to retire more of the principal prior to the maturity date, it effectively is a call option granted to the issuer.

Other Features

Other features can be included in a bond issue. These features are described below.

Convertible and Exchangeable Bonds The conversion provision in a corporate bond issue grants the bondholder the right to convert the bond to a predetermined number of shares of common stock of the issuer. Exchangeable bonds grant the bondholder the right to exchange the bonds for the common stock of a firm *other* than the issuer of the bond. We will discuss convertible and exchangeable bonds in more detail in Chapter 23.

Issues of Debt with Warrants When a bond is issued, warrants may be attached as part of the offer. A warrant grants the holder the right to purchase a designated security at a specified price. The warrant may permit the holder to purchase the common stock of the issuer of the debt or the common stock of a firm other than the issuer's. Or the warrant may grant the holder the right to purchase a debt obligation of the issuer.

Generally, warrants can be detached from the bond and sold separately. The warrant can generally be exercised by using cash or by exchanging the debt at par that was part of the unit offering. In the case of convertible and exchangeable bonds, only the bond may be used to exercise the investor's option to convert the bond into stock.

The warrant may permit the bondholder to buy common stock of the issuer, as does a convertible bond. However, the embedded call option in the convertible bond cannot be sold separately from the bond, while a warrant can be. Thus, the holder of a bond and a warrant is in a long position in the corporate bond of the issuer and a long position in a call option on the common stock of the issuer. The same is true of a unit of debt with warrants to buy common stock of a firm other than the issuer. The holder of a bond and a warrant in this case is in a long position in the corporate bond of the issuer and a long position in a call option on the common stock of some other firm.

Putable Bonds A putable bond grants the bondholder the right to sell the issue back to the issuer at par value on designated dates. The advantage to the bondholder is that if interest rates rise after the issue date, thereby reducing the value of the bond, the bondholder can put the bond to the issuer for par. Thus, a putable corporate bond is a package composed of a non-putable corporate bond plus a long put option on the corporate bond. This will insure that the bond will stay close to par somewhat like instruments earning a short-term floating rate (see below), except that the former, but not the latter, also provide protection against deterioration in credit rating.

Floating-Rate Securities The coupon interest on floating-rate securities is reset periodically based on some reference interest rate. For example, the coupon rate may be reset every six months at a rate equal to a spread of 100 basis points over the six-month Treasury bill rate. Floating-rate securities are attractive to some institutional investors because the securities allow investors to buy an asset with an income stream that more closely matches the floating nature of some of their liabilities.

Special Features in High-Yield Bonds   As explained later in this section, bonds with a quality rating below triple B are called **high-yield bonds**, or more commonly, **junk bonds**. There are complex bond structures in the junk bond area, particularly for bonds issued for leveraged buyout (LBO) financing and recapitalizations producing higher debt. In an LBO or recapitalization, the heavy interest payment places severe cash flow constraints on the firm. To reduce this burden, firms involved in LBOs and recapitalizations have issued deferred coupon structures that permit the issuer to avoid using cash to make interest payments for a period of three to seven years. There are three types of deferred-coupon structures: (1) deferred-interest bonds, (2) step-up bonds, and (3) payment-in-kind bonds.

Deferred-interest bonds are the most common type of deferred-coupon structure. These bonds sell at a deep discount and do not pay interest for an initial period, typically from three to seven years. **Step-up bonds** do pay coupon interest. However, the coupon rate is low for an initial period and then increases ("steps up") to a higher coupon rate thereafter. Finally, **payment-in-kind (PIK) bonds** give the issuer an option to pay cash at a coupon payment date or give the bondholder a similar bond (i.e., a bond with the same coupon rate and a par value equal to the amount of the coupon payment that would have been paid). The period within which the issuer can make this choice varies from 5 to 10 years.

Credit Ratings

Professional money managers use various techniques to analyze information on companies and bond issues in order to estimate the ability of the issuer to live up to its future contractual obligations. This activity is known as **credit analysis**.

Some large institutional investors and most investment banking firms have their own credit analysis departments. Few individual investors and institutional bond investors do their own analysis, though. Instead, they rely primarily on commercial rating companies that perform credit analysis and issue their conclusions in the form of ratings. The four commercial rating companies are (1) Duff and Phelps Credit Rating Co. (D&P), (2) Fitch Investors Service, (3) Moody's Investors Service, and (4) Standard & Poor's Corporation. The rating systems use similar symbols, as shown in Table 19-3.

The two most widely used systems of bond ratings are Moody's and Standard & Poor's. In both systems the term *high grade* means low credit risk, or conversely, high probability of future payments. The highest-grade bonds are designated by Moody's by the letters Aaa and by Standard & Poor's by AAA. The next highest grade is Aa or AA; for the third grade both rating agencies use A. The next three grades are Baa or BBB, Ba or BB, and B, respectively. There are also C grades. Standard & Poor's uses plus or minus signs to provide a narrower credit quality breakdown within each class, and Moody's uses 1, 2, or 3 for the same purpose. Bonds rated triple A (AAA or Aaa) are said to be prime; double A (AA or Aa) are of high quality; single A issues are called upper medium grade, and triple B are medium grade. Lower-rated bonds are said to have speculative elements or be distinctly speculative.

Bond issues that are assigned a rating in the top four categories are referred to as **investment-grade bonds**. Issues that carry a rating below the top

TABLE 19-3

SUMMARY OF CORPORATE BOND RATING SYSTEMS AND SYMBOLS

Moody's	S&P	Fitch	D&P	Brief Definition
Investment Grade: High Creditworthiness				
Aaa	AAA	AAA	AAA	Gilt edge, prime, maximum safety
Aa1	AA+	AA+	AA+	
Aa2	AA	AA	AA	Very high grade, high quality
Aa3	AA−	AA−	AA−	
A1	A+	A+	A+	
A2	A	A	A	Upper medium grade
A3	A−	A−	A−	
Baa1	BBB+	BBB+	BBB+	
Baa2	BBB	BBB	BBB	Lower medium grade
Baa3	BBB−	BBB−	BBB−	
Non-investment Grade: Distinctly Speculative—Low Creditworthiness				
Ba1	BB+	BB+	BB+	
Ba2	BB	BB	BB	Low grade, speculative
Ba3	BB−	BB−	BB−	
B1	B+	B+		
B2	B	B	B	Highly speculative
B3	B−	B−		
Non-investment Grade: Predominantly Speculative—Substantial Risk or in Default				
	CCC+			
Caa	CCC	CCC	CCC	Substantial risk, in poor standing
	CCC−			
Ca	CC	CC		May be in default, extremely speculative
C	C	C		Even more speculative than those above
	CI			CI=Income bonds—no interest is being paid
		DDD		Default
		DD	DD	
	D	D		

four categories are referred to as *non-investment-grade bonds*, or more popularly as *high-yield bonds* or *junk bonds*. Thus, the corporate bond market can be divided into two sectors: the investment grade and non-investment-grade markets.

Occasionally the ability of an issuer to make interest and principal payments changes seriously and unexpectedly because of (1) a natural or industrial accident or some regulatory change or (2) a takeover or corporate restructuring. These risks are referred to generically as **event risk** and will result in a downgrading of the issuer by the rating agencies.

Box 19 provides a summary of the changing United States corporate bond market.

BOX 19

THE CHANGING U.S. CORPORATE BOND MARKET

The corporate bond market has changed substantially in size and structure over the past 20 years. While the investment-grade corporate market has grown 468%, or 9.1% per annum since 1973, the size of the overall bond market has increased by 1,666%, or 15.4% annually. This growth has been driven by an increased rate of Treasury borrowing as well as the emergence of a huge market in mortgage-backed securities. Today, investment-grade corporates compose 17% of the overall bond market; the addition of high-yield bonds would increase this to 21%.

In 1973 the corporate market was dominated by highly rated, long-maturity callable utility issues. By 1992 each of these characteristics had changed significantly. Utilities declined from 63% of the corporate market to 26% over the 20-year period while industrials grew from 24% to 36%, financials from 13% to 24%, and Yankees from 0% to 14%.

The average credit rating of corporate bonds has also declined significantly. AAA- and AA-rated issues composed 58% of the market in 1973 (see figure). Twenty years later the market has evolved into an A and BBB orientation, with these two rating categories composing over 71% of the market. Incorporating high-yield bonds raises the percentage of bonds rated A or below to nearly 80%.

Increased financial and industrial issuance has altered the average maturity and callability of the corporate market. Today 60% of outstanding issues mature in less than 10 years, and fully 25% have a maturity of less than five years.

Finally, noncallable bonds have become much more prevalent. As recently as 1980 nearly 100% of all corporate bonds outstanding were callable prior to maturity. By December 1992 64% of all outstanding issues were noncallable, and about 90% of ongoing issuance was in call-free securities.

Source: Adapted from Appendix One in Thomas L. Bennett, Stephen F. Esser, and Christian G. Roth, *Corporate Credit Risk and Reward,* published in 1993 by Miller Anderson & Sherrerd, an investment management firm in West Conshohocken, PA.

Questions for Box 19

1. What is meant by investment-grade corporates?
2. What is meant by high-yield bonds?
3. What is a callable bond?

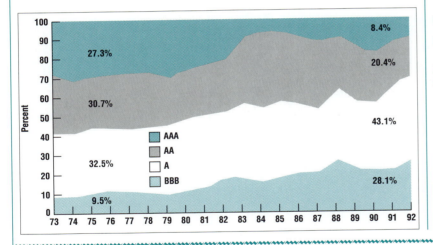

MUNICIPAL SECURITIES

Municipal securities are issued by state and local governments and by the governments' creations, such as "authorities" and special districts. There are municipal zero-coupon bonds, floating-rate bonds, and putable bonds. There are both tax-exempt and taxable municipal bonds. Interest on tax-exempt municipal bonds is exempt from federal income taxation. The large majority of municipal bonds outstanding are tax-exempt. Interest may or may not be taxable at the state and local level.

Municipal bonds are issued with one of two debt retirement structures or a combination of both. Either a bond has a serial maturity structure or a term maturity structure. A serial maturity structure requires a portion of the debt obligation to be retired each year. A term maturity structure provides for the debt obligation to be repaid on a final date. Usually term bonds have maturities ranging from 20 to 40 years and retirement schedules (sinking fund provisions) that begin 5 to 10 years before the final term maturity. Municipal bonds may be called prior to the stated maturity date, either according to a mandatory sinking fund or at the option of the issuer.

An **official statement** describing the issue and the issuer is prepared for new offerings. The same commercial rating companies that rate corporate bonds also rate municipal bonds.

Municipal bonds are traded in the over-the-counter market supported by municipal bond dealers across the country. Markets are maintained on smaller issuers (referred to as *local credits*) by regional brokerage firms, by local banks, and by some of the larger Wall Street firms. Larger issuers (referred to as *general names*) are supported by the larger brokerage firms and banks, many of which have investment banking relationships with these issuers. There are brokers who serve as intermediaries in the sale of large blocks of municipal bonds among dealers and large institutional investors. In addition to these brokers and the daily offerings sent out over The Bond Buyer's "munifacts" teletype system, many dealers advertise their municipal bond offering for the retail market in what is known as *The Blue List*. This is a 100-plus-page booklet published every weekday by the Standard & Poor's Corporation that gives municipal securities offerings and prices.

There are basically two different types of municipal bond security structures: general obligation bonds and revenue bonds. There are also securities that share characteristics of both general obligation and revenue bonds.

General Obligation Bonds

As explained in Chapter 2, general obligation bonds are debt instruments issued by states, counties, special districts, cities, towns, and school districts. Usually, a general obligation bond is secured by the issuer's unlimited taxing power. However, not all general obligation bonds are secured that way. Some are backed by taxes that are limited as to revenue sources. Such bonds are known as **limited-tax general obligation bonds**. For smaller governmental entities such as school districts and towns, the only available unlimited taxing power is on property. For larger general obligation bond issuers such as states and big cities, tax revenue sources are more diverse, and may include corporate and individual income taxes, sales taxes, and property taxes. The security pledges for these larger issuers, such as states, are sometimes referred to as being **full faith and credit obligations**.

Additionally, certain general obligation bonds are secured not only by the issuer's general taxing powers to create revenues accumulated in a general fund, but also by certain identified fees, grants, and special charges, which provide additional revenues from outside the general fund. Such bonds are known as double-barreled in security because of the dual nature of the revenue sources.

Revenue Bonds

The second basic type of security structure is found in a revenue bond. Such bonds are issued for either project or enterprise financings where the bond issuers pledge to the bondholders the revenues generated by the operating projects financed. A feasibility study is performed before the endeavor is undertaken to determine whether it will be self-supporting.

The revenue of the enterprise is pledged to service the debt of the issue. The details of how revenue received by the enterprise will be disbursed are set forth in the trust indenture. Typically, the flow of funds for a revenue bond is as follows. First, all revenues from the enterprise are placed into a **revenue fund**. It is from the revenue fund that disbursements for expenses are made to the following funds: *operation and maintenance fund, sinking fund, debt service reserve fund, renewal and replacement fund, reserve maintenance fund*, and *surplus fund*.

Cash needed to operate the enterprise is deposited from the revenue fund to the operation and maintenance fund. Operations of the enterprise have priority over the servicing of the issue's debt. This is the typical structure of a revenue bond. The pledge of revenue to the bondholders is a net revenue pledge, *net* meaning after operation expenses. Cash required to service the debt is deposited in the sinking fund, and disbursements are then made to bondholders as specified in the bond indenture. Any remaining cash is then distributed to the reserve funds. The purpose of the debt service reserve fund is to accumulate cash to cover any shortfall of future revenue to service the issue's debt. The specific amount that must be deposited is stated in the trust indenture. The function of the renewal and replacement fund is to accumulate cash for regularly scheduled major repairs and equipment replacement. The function of the reserve maintenance fund is to accumulate cash for extraordinary maintenance or replacement costs that might arise. Finally, if any cash remains after disbursement for operations, debt servicing, and reserves, it is deposited in the surplus fund. The issuer can use the cash in this fund in any way it deems appropriate.

Various restrictive covenants are included in the trust indenture for a revenue bond to protect the bondholders. A rate, or user-charge, covenant dictates how charges will be set on the product or service sold by the enterprise. The covenant could specify that the minimum charges be set so as to satisfy both expenses and debt servicing, or it could specify a higher rate to provide for a certain amount of reserves. An additional bond covenant indicates whether additional bonds with the same lien may be issued. If additional bonds with the same lien may be issued, conditions that must be satisfied are specified. Other covenants would specify whether the facility may not be sold, how much insurance must be maintained, what requirements for record keeping and for auditing the enterprise's financial statements by an independent accounting firm are necessary, and what requirements for maintaining the facilities in good order must be met.

Examples of revenue bonds include airport revenue bonds, college and university revenue bonds, hospital revenue bonds, resource recovery revenue bonds, seaport revenue bonds, sports complex and convention center revenue bonds, student loan revenue bonds, toll road and gas tax revenue bonds, and water revenue bonds.

Hybrid Bond Securities

Some municipal bonds that have the basic characteristics of general obligation bonds and revenue bonds have more issue-specific structures as well. Two important examples are insured bonds and refunded bonds.

Insured bonds are backed by insurance policies written by commercial insurance companies, as well as by the credit of the municipal issuer. Municipal bond insurance is a contractual commitment by an insurance company to pay the bondholder any bond principal and/or coupon interest that is due on a stated date but that has not been paid by the bond issuer. Once issued, this municipal bond insurance usually extends for the term of the bond issue, and it cannot be canceled by the insurance company.

Refunded bonds (also called **prefunded bonds**) are bonds that originally may have been issued as general obligation or revenue bonds but that are now secured by an "escrow fund" consisting entirely of direct U.S. government obligations that are sufficient for paying the bondholders.

EUROBONDS

As described in Chapter 2, a bond is classified as a Eurobond if (1) it is underwritten by an international syndicate, (2) at issuance it is offered simultaneously to investors in a number of countries, and (3) it is issued outside the jurisdiction of any single country. When Eurobonds are denominated in U.S. dollars, they are referred to as *Eurodollar bonds*. Eurobonds denominated in Japanese yen are referred to as *Euroyen bonds*.

Although Eurobonds are typically registered on a national stock exchange, the most common being the Luxembourg, London, and Zurich exchange, the bulk of all trading is in the over-the-counter market. Listing on a stock exchange is done purely to circumvent restrictions imposed on some institutional investors that are prohibited from purchasing securities not listed on an exchange. Some of the stronger issuers privately place issues with international institutional investors.

The Eurobond market has been characterized by new and innovative bond structures to accommodate the particular needs of issuers and investors. There are, of course, the "plain vanilla," fixed-rate coupon bonds, referred to as **Euro straights**. Because they are issued on an unsecured basis, they are usually issued by high-quality entities.

Coupon payments are made annually, rather than semiannually, because of the higher cost of distributing interest to geographically dispersed bondholders. There are also zero-coupon bond issues, deferred-coupon issues, and step-up issues, all of which were described earlier.

There are issues that pay coupon interest in one currency but pay the principal in a different currency. Such issues are called **dual-currency issues**. A **convertible Eurobond** is one that can be converted into another asset. Bonds with attached warrants represent a large part of the Eurobond market. A warrant grants the owner of that option the right to enter into another financial transaction with the issuer. Most warrants are detachable from the host bond; that is, the bondholder may detach the warrant from the bond and sell it.

There are a wide variety of floating-rate Eurobond notes. In the Eurobond market, almost all floating-rate notes are denominated in U.S. dollars, with non-U.S. banks being the major issuers. The coupon rate on a Eurodollar floating-rate note is some stated margin over the London interbank offered rate (LIBOR).

PREFERRED STOCK

Preferred stock is a class of stock, not a debt instrument, but it shares characteristics of both common stock and debt. Like the holder of common stock, the holder of preferred stock is entitled to dividends. Unlike those on common stock, however, dividends are a specified percentage of par or face value. The percentage is called the **dividend rate**; it need not be fixed, but may float over the life of the issue.

Failure to make preferred stock dividend payments cannot force the issuer into bankruptcy. Should the issuer not make the preferred stock dividend payment, usually made quarterly, one of two things can happen, depending on the terms of the issue. In one case, the dividend payment can accrue until it is fully paid. Preferred stock with this feature is called **cumulative preferred stock**. In the other case, the securityholder must forgo the payment. Such preferred stock is said to be **non-cumulative preferred stock**. Failure to make dividend payments may result in imposition of certain restrictions on management. For example, if dividend payments are in arrears, holders of preferred stock might be granted voting rights.

Unlike debt, dividend payments made to holders of preferred stock are treated as a distribution of earnings. This means that the dividend payments are not tax-deductible to the corporation under the current tax code (whereas interest payments are tax-deductible). While this raises the after-tax cost of funds if a corporation issues preferred stock rather than borrowing, there is a factor that reduces the cost differential: A provision in the tax code exempts 70% of qualified dividends from federal income taxation if the recipient is a qualified corporation. For example, if corporation A owns the preferred stock of corporation B, for each $100 of dividends received by A, only $30 will be taxed at A's marginal tax rate. The purpose of this provision is to mitigate the effect of double taxation of corporate earnings. There are two implications of this tax treatment of preferred stock dividends. First, the major buyers of preferred stock are corporations seeking tax-advantaged investments. Second, the cost of preferred stock issuance is lower than it would be in the absence of the tax provision because buyers are willing to accept a lower dividend rate in exchange for the tax benefits.

Preferred stock has some important similarities with debt, particularly in the case of cumulative preferred stock: (1) The returns to holders of preferred stock promised by the issuer are fixed, and (2) holders of preferred stock have priority over holders of common stock with respect to dividend payments and distribution of assets in the case of bankruptcy. (The position of non-cumulative preferred stock is considerably weaker.) It is because of this second feature that preferred stock is called a *senior* security. On a balance sheet, preferred stock is classified as equity.

Almost all preferred stock has a sinking fund provision, and some preferred stock is convertible into common stock. Preferred stock may be issued without a maturity date. This is called *perpetual preferred stock*.

The same four commercial companies that assign ratings to corporate bond issues also rate preferred stock issues.

MORTGAGES AND MORTGAGE-BACKED SECURITIES

The mortgage market is the largest sector of the fixed-income market. This market includes the market for individual mortgage loans (both residential mortgages and commercial mortgages) and **mortgage-backed securities (MBS)**. Mortgage-backed securities are securities that are backed by pools (i.e., collections) of mortgage loans. While any type of mortgage loans, residential or commercial, can be used as collateral for a mortgage-backed security, most are backed by residential mortgages.

Mortgage-backed securities include the following securities: (1) mortgage pass-through securities, (2) collateralized mortgage obligations, and (3) stripped mortgage-backed securities. In the world of fixed-income securities, the growth of the U.S. mortgage-backed securities markets holds all records.

Mortgages

As discussed in Chapter 2, a mortgage is a loan secured by the collateral of some specified real estate property which obliges the borrower to make a predetermined series of payments. The mortgage gives the lender (**mortgagee**) the right, if the borrower (the **mortgagor**) defaults (i.e., fails to make the contracted payments), to *foreclose* on the loan and seize the property in order to ensure that the debt is paid off. The interest rate on the mortgage loan is called the **mortgage rate**. Our focus in this section is on residential mortgage loans.

When the lender makes the loan based on the credit of the borrower and on the collateral for the mortgage, the mortgage is said to be a **conventional mortgage**. The lender also may take out mortgage insurance to guarantee the fulfillment of the borrower's obligations. Some borrowers can qualify for mortgage insurance guaranteed by one of three U.S. government agencies: the Federal Housing Administration (FHA), the Veterans Administration (VA), and the Farmers Home Administration. There are also private mortgage insurers. The cost of mortgage insurance is paid to the guarantor by the mortgage originator, but it is passed along to the borrower in the form of higher mortgage payments.

Cash Flow Characteristics of a Mortgage Loan

A borrower can select from many types of mortgage loans. In this section, our purpose is to understand the basic cash flow characteristics of a mortgage loan. To illustrate these characteristics we will use the most common mortgage design: the level-payment, fixed-rate mortgage.[2]

The basic idea behind the design of the level-payment, fixed-rate mortgage, or simply level-payment mortgage, is that the borrower pays interest

---

[2] Other types of mortgage designs include adjustable-rate mortgages, graduated-payment mortgages, growing-equity mortgages, balloon/reset mortgages, and tiered-payment mortgages. These mortgage designs are discussed in Chapters 6 and 7 in Frank J. Fabozzi and Franco Modigliani, *Mortgage and Mortgage-Backed Securities Markets* (Boston: Harvard Business School Press, 1992).

and repays principal in equal installments over an agreed-upon period of time, called the *maturity* or *term of the mortgage*. Thus at the end of the term, the loan has been fully amortized.

For a level-payment mortgage, each monthly mortgage payment is due on the first of each month and consists of:

1. Interest of 1/12th of the fixed annual mortgage rate times the amount of the outstanding mortgage balance at the beginning of the previous month
2. A repayment of a portion of the outstanding mortgage balance (principal)

The difference between the monthly mortgage payment and the portion of the payment that represents interest equals the amount that is applied to reduce the outstanding mortgage balance. The monthly mortgage payment is designed so that after the last scheduled monthly payment of the loan is made, the amount of the outstanding mortgage balance is zero (i.e., the mortgage is fully repaid).

To illustrate a level-payment, fixed-rate mortgage, consider a 30-year (360-month), $100,000 mortgage with an 8.125% mortgage rate. The monthly mortgage payment would be $742.50. Table 19-4 shows for selected months how each monthly mortgage payment is divided between interest and repayment of principal. At the beginning of month 1, the mortgage balance is $100,000, the amount of the original loan. The mortgage payment for month 1 includes interest on the $100,000 borrowed for the month. Since the mortgage rate is 8.125%, the monthly interest rate is 0.0067708 (0.08125 divided by 12). Interest for month 1 is therefore $677.08 ($100,000 times 0.0067708). The $65.41 difference between the monthly mortgage payment of $742.50 and the interest of $677.08 is the portion of the monthly mortgage payment which represents repayment of principal. This $65.41 in month 1 reduces the mortgage balance.

The mortgage balance at the end of month 1 (beginning of month 2) is then $99,934.59 ($100,000 minus $65.41). The interest for the second monthly mortgage payment is $676.64, the monthly interest rate (0.0067708) times the mortgage balance at the beginning of month 2 ($99,934.59). The difference between the $742.50 monthly mortgage payment and the $676.64 interest is $65.86, representing the amount of the mortgage balance paid off with that monthly mortgage payment. Notice that the last monthly mortgage payment is sufficient to pay off the remaining mortgage balance. When a loan repayment schedule is structured in this way, so that the payments made by the borrower will completely pay off the interest and principal, the loan is said to be **self-amortizing**. Table 19-4 is then referred to as an **amortization schedule**.

As Table 19-4 clearly shows, *the portion of the monthly mortgage payment applied to interest declines each month and the portion applied to reducing the mortgage balance increases.* The reason for this is that as the mortgage balance is reduced with each monthly mortgage payment, the interest on the mortgage balance declines. Since the monthly mortgage payment is fixed, an increasingly larger portion of the monthly payment is applied to reduce the principal in each subsequent month.

Mortgage Cash Flow with Servicing Fee   Unlike the other fixed-income instruments, every mortgage loan must be serviced. Servicing of a mortgage loan involves collecting monthly payments and forwarding proceeds to owners of

TABLE 19-4

AMORTIZATION SCHEDULE FOR A LEVEL-PAYMENT, FIXED-RATE MORTGAGE

Mortgage loan: $100,000   Mortgage rate: 8.125%

Monthly payment: $742.50   Term of loan: 30 years (360 months)

Month	Beginning Mortgage Balance	Monthly Payment	Monthly Interest	Scheduled Principal Repayment	Ending Mortgage Balance
1	100,000.00	742.50	677.08	65.41	99,934.59
2	99,934.59	742.50	676.64	65.86	99,868.73
3	99,868.73	742.50	676.19	66.30	99,802.43
4	99,802.43	742.50	675.75	66.75	99,735.68
25	98,301.53	742.50	665.58	76.91	98,224.62
26	98,224.62	742.50	665.06	77.43	98,147.19
27	98,147.19	742.50	664.54	77.96	98,069.23
74	93,849.98	742.50	635.44	107.05	93,742.93
75	93,742.93	742.50	634.72	107.78	93,635.15
76	93,635.15	742.50	633.99	108.51	93,526.64
141	84,811.77	742.50	574.25	168.25	84,643.52
142	84,643.52	742.50	573.11	169.39	84,474.13
143	84,474.13	742.50	571.96	170.54	84,303.59
184	76,446.29	742.50	517.61	224.89	76,221.40
185	76,221.40	742.50	516.08	226.41	75,994.99
186	75,994.99	742.50	514.55	227.95	75,767.04
233	63,430.19	742.50	429.48	313.02	63,117.17
234	63,117.17	742.50	427.36	315.14	62,802.03
235	62,802.03	742.50	425.22	317.28	62,484.75
289	42,200.92	742.50	285.74	456.76	41,744.15
290	41,744.15	742.50	282.64	459.85	41,284.30
291	41,284.30	742.50	279.53	462.97	40,821.33
321	25,941.42	742.50	175.65	566.85	25,374.57
322	25,374.57	742.50	171.81	570.69	24,803.88
323	24,803.88	742.50	167.94	574.55	24,229.32
358	2,197.66	742.50	14.88	727.62	1,470.05
359	1,470.05	742.50	9.95	732.54	737.50
360	737.50	742.50	4.99	737.50	0.00

the loan, sending payment notices to mortgagors, reminding mortgagors when payments are overdue, maintaining records of principal balances, administering an escrow balance for real estate taxes and insurance purposes, initiating foreclosure proceedings if necessary, and furnishing tax information to mortgagors when applicable.

An investor who acquires a mortgage may service the mortgage or sell the right to service the mortgage. In the first case, the investor's cash flow is the entire cash flow from the mortgage. In the second case, it is the cash flow net of the servicing fee. The monthly cash flow from a mortgage loan, regardless of the mortgage design, can therefore be divided into three parts: (1) the servicing fee, (2) the interest payment net of the servicing fee, and (3) the scheduled principal repayment.

Prepayments and Cash Flow Uncertainty We assumed that the homeowner would not pay off any portion of the mortgage balance prior to the scheduled due date. But most times homeowners do pay off all or part of their mortgage balance before the maturity date. Payments made in excess of the scheduled principal repayments are called **prepayments**.

Prepayments occur for one of several reasons. First, homeowners prepay the entire mortgage when they sell their home. The sale of a home may be due to (1) a change of employment that necessitates moving, (2) the purchase of a more expensive home ("trading up"), or (3) a divorce in which the settlement requires sale of the marital residence. Second, as we explained earlier in this chapter, the borrower has the right to pay off all or part of the mortgage balance at any time. The borrower may be moved to pay off the loan as market rates fall below the mortgage rate on the loan. Third, in the case of homeowners who cannot meet their mortgage obligations, the property is repossessed and sold. The proceeds from the sale are used to pay off the mortgage in the case of a conventional mortgage. For an insured mortgage, the insurer will pay off the mortgage balance. Finally, if property is destroyed by fire or another insured catastrophe occurs, the insurance proceeds are used to pay off the mortgage.

The effect of prepayments is that the cash flow from a mortgage is not known with certainty—by this we mean that the amount and the timing of the cash flow is uncertain. For example, the investor in a $100,000, 8.125% 30-year government-insured mortgage knows that as long as the loan is outstanding, interest will be received and the principal will be repaid at the scheduled date each month. At the end of the 30 years, the investor would receive $100,000 in principal payments. What the investor does not know—the uncertainty—is for how long the loan will be outstanding and therefore the timing of the principal payments. This is true for all mortgage loans.

Mortgage Pass-Through Securities

A **mortgage pass-through security**, or simply a *pass-through*, is created when one or more mortgage holders form a collection (pool) of mortgages and sell shares or participation certificates in the pool. As we discussed in Chapter 2, mortgage loans that are included in a pool to create a pass-through are said to be securitized. The process of creating a pass-through is referred to as **securitization**.

We will illustrate the creation of a pass-through using Figures 19-1 and 19-2 and the motivation for its creation. Figure 19-1 shows 10 mortgage loans and the cash flows from these loans. For simplicity, we will assume that the amount of each loan is $100,000 so that the aggregate value of all 10 loans is $1 million. The cash flows are monthly and consist of three components: (1) interest, (2) scheduled principal repayment, and (3) prepayments (that is, payments in excess of the regularly scheduled principal repayment).

An investor who owns one of the mortgage loans shown in Figure 19-1 faces prepayment risk. For an individual loan, it may be difficult to predict prepayments. If an individual investor purchased all 10 loans, then the investor may be able to better predict prepayments. In fact, if there were 500 mortgage loans in Figure 19-1 rather than 10, the investor may be able to use historical prepayment experience to improve his or her predictions about prepayments.

Suppose, instead, that some entity purchases all 10 loans in Figure 19-1 and pools them. The 10 loans can be used as collateral for the issuance of a pass-through, with the cash flow from that security reflecting the cash flow

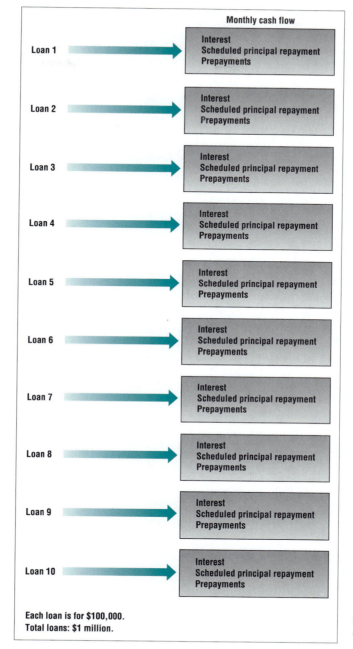

FIGURE 19-1
Ten mortgage loans.

from the 10 loans, as depicted in Figure 19-2. Suppose that 40 units of this pass-through are issued. Thus, each unit is initially worth $25,000 ($1 million divided by 40). Each unit would be entitled to 2.5% (1/40) of the cash flow.

Payments are made to securityholders each month. The monthly cash flow for a pass-through is less than the monthly cash flow of the underlying mortgages by an amount equal to servicing and other fees. The other fees are

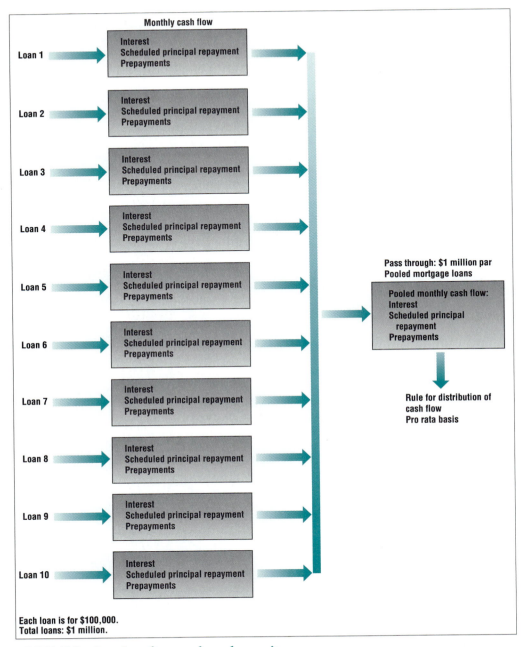

FIGURE 19-2   Creation of a pass-through security.

those charged by the issuer or guarantor of the pass-through for guaranteeing the issue.[3] The coupon rate on a pass-through, called the **pass-through coupon rate**, is less than the mortgage rate on the underlying pool of mortgage loans by an amount equal to the servicing and guaranteeing fees.

[3]Actually, the servicer pays the guarantee fee to the issuer or guarantor.

Because of prepayments, the cash flow of a pass-through is not known with certainty. Estimating the cash flow from a pass-through requires making an assumption about future prepayments. The rate at which prepayments are assumed to be made is called the **prepayment speed** or, simply, **speed**. The major dealers in pass-throughs and a number of independent vendors have developed statistical models that estimate prepayment speed.

Types of Pass-Throughs   There are three major types of pass-throughs guaranteed by the following organizations: Government National Mortgage Association ("Ginnie Mae"), Federal Home Loan Mortgage Corporation ("Freddie Mac"), and Federal National Mortgage Association ("Fannie Mae"). These are called **agency pass-throughs**. Ginnie Mae is a federally related institution. Freddie Mac and Fannie Mae are government-sponsored enterprises. Because Ginnie Mae is a federally related institution, its pass-throughs are guaranteed by the full faith and credit of the U.S. government. For this reason, Ginnie Mae pass-throughs are viewed as free of default risk, just like Treasury securities. Because Freddie Mac and Fannie Mae are government-sponsored enterprises, their guarantee is not a guarantee by the U.S. government. Non-agency pass-throughs are called **conventional pass-throughs** or **private-label pass-throughs** and are a small but growing sector of the pass-through market.

An agency can provide one of two types of guarantee. One type of guarantee is the timely payment of both interest and principal, meaning the interest and principal will be paid when due, even if any of the mortgagors fail to make their monthly mortgage payments. Pass-throughs with this type of guarantee are referred to as **fully modified pass-throughs**. All three agencies issue fully modified pass-throughs. The second type guarantees both interest and principal payments; however, it only guarantees the timely payment of interest. The scheduled principal is passed through as it is collected, with a guarantee that the scheduled payment will be made no later than a specified time after it is due. Pass-throughs with this type of guarantee are called **modified pass-throughs**. Only Freddie Mac has issued such pass-throughs in the past.

Collateralized Mortgage Obligations

A **collateralized mortgage obligation (CMO)** is a security backed by a pool of pass-throughs. CMOs are structured so that there are several classes of bondholders with varying maturities. The different bond classes are also called *tranches*. The principal payments from the underlying pool of pass-through securities are used to retire the bonds on a priority basis as specified in the prospectus.

The CMO was created as a better vehicle for managing the asset/liability needs of institutional investors. From an asset/liability perspective, pass-throughs are an unattractive investment for many institutional investors because of prepayment risk. This risk is reduced by a CMO that redirects cash flows from a pool of pass-through securities to the different bond classes.

To illustrate a simple CMO structure, consider the 10 mortgage loans in Figure 19-1. Suppose that instead of distributing the monthly cash flow on a pro rata basis as in the case of a pass-through, the principal (both scheduled payments and prepayments) is distributed on some prioritized basis. How this is done is illustrated in Figure 19-3.

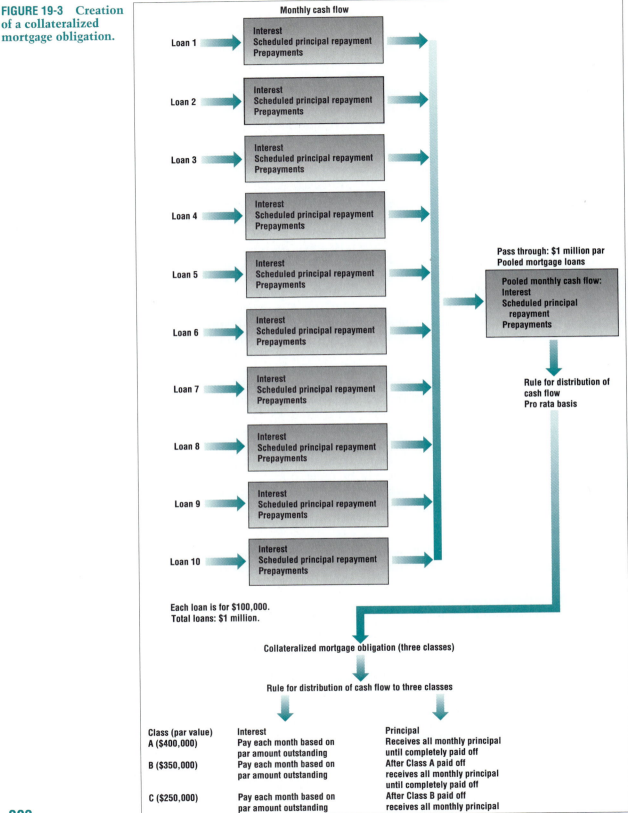

FIGURE 19-3 Creation of a collateralized mortgage obligation.

Monthly cash flow

Loan 1 → Interest / Scheduled principal repayment / Prepayments

Loan 2 → Interest / Scheduled principal repayment / Prepayments

Loan 3 → Interest / Scheduled principal repayment / Prepayments

Loan 4 → Interest / Scheduled principal repayment / Prepayments

Loan 5 → Interest / Scheduled principal repayment / Prepayments

Loan 6 → Interest / Scheduled principal repayment / Prepayments

Loan 7 → Interest / Scheduled principal repayment / Prepayments

Loan 8 → Interest / Scheduled principal repayment / Prepayments

Loan 9 → Interest / Scheduled principal repayment / Prepayments

Loan 10 → Interest / Scheduled principal repayment / Prepayments

Pass through: $1 million par
Pooled mortgage loans

Pooled monthly cash flow:
Interest
Scheduled principal repayment
Prepayments

Rule for distribution of cash flow
Pro rata basis

Each loan is for $100,000.
Total loans: $1 million.

Collateralized mortgage obligation (three classes)

Rule for distribution of cash flow to three classes

Class (par value)	Interest	Principal
A ($400,000)	Pay each month based on par amount outstanding	Receives all monthly principal until completely paid off
B ($350,000)	Pay each month based on par amount outstanding	After Class A paid off receives all monthly principal until completely paid off
C ($250,000)	Pay each month based on par amount outstanding	After Class B paid off receives all monthly principal

Figure 19-3 shows the cash flow of our original 10 mortgage loans and the pass-through. Also shown are three classes of bonds or tranches, the par value of each class, and a set of rules indicating how the principal from the pass-through is to be distributed to each. Note the following. The sum of the par value of the three classes is equal to $1 million. While not shown in the figure, for each of the three classes there will be units representing a proportionate interest in a class. For example, suppose that for Class A, which has a par value of $400,000, 50 units of Class A are issued. Each unit would receive a proportionate share (2%) of what is received by Class A.

The rule for the distribution of principal shown in Figure 19-3 is that Class A will receive all principal (both scheduled payments and prepayments) until that class receives its entire par value of $400,000. Then, Class B receives all principal payments until it receives its par value of $350,000. After Class B is completely paid off, Class C receives principal payments. The rule for the distribution of cash flow in Figure 19-3 indicates that each of the three classes will receive interest based on the amount of par value outstanding.

Let's look at what has been accomplished. The total prepayment risk for the CMO is the same as the total prepayment risk for the 10 mortgage loans. However, the prepayment risk has been redistributed among the three classes of the CMO. Class A absorbs prepayments first, then Class B, and then Class C. The result of this is that Class A will effectively be a shorter-term security than the other two classes; Class C will have the longest maturity. Institutional investors will be attracted to the different classes, given the nature of their liability structure and the effective maturity of the CMO class. Moreover, the uncertainty about the maturity of each class of the CMO is far less than the uncertainty about the maturity of the pass-through. Thus, by redirecting the cash flow from the underlying mortgage pool, classes of bonds have been created that are more attractive to institutional investors to satisfy asset/liability objectives than a pass-through.

The CMO we depicted in Figure 19-3 has a simple set of rules for prioritizing the distribution of principal. Today, much more complicated CMO structures exist.[4] The purpose is to provide certain CMO classes with less uncertainty about prepayment risk. However, this can occur only if the reduction in prepayment risk for such classes is absorbed by other classes in the CMO structure.

Stripped Mortgage-Backed Securities

A pass-through divides the cash flow from the underlying pool of mortgages on a pro rata basis to the securityholders. Stripped mortgage-backed securities, introduced by Fannie Mae in 1986, are created by altering the distribution of principal and interest from a pro rata distribution to an *unequal* distribution. Consider once again the 10 mortgage loans in Figure 19-1. In the CMO there was a set of rules for prioritizing the distribution of the principal payments among the various classes. In a stripped mortgage-backed security, the principal and interest are divided between two classes unequally. For example, one class may be entitled to receive all of the principal and the other class all of the interest. This is depicted in Figure 19-4.

---

[4]For an explanation of these bond classes, see Frank J. Fabozzi, Chuck Ramsey, and Frank Ramirez, *Collateralized Mortgage Obligations: Structures and Analysis* (Buckingham, PA: Frank J. Fabozzi Associates, 1994).

FIGURE 19-4 Creation of a stripped mortgage-backed security.

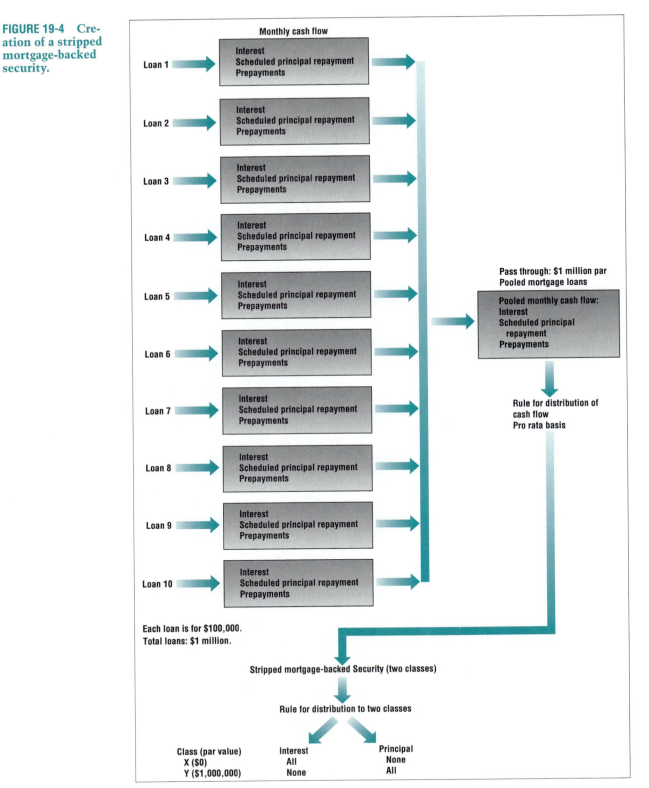

The most popular type of stripped MBS is one in which all of the interest is allocated to one class (the *interest-only*, or IO, class) and all of the principal to the other class (the *principal-only*, or PO, class). The IO class receives no principal payments. What may be confusing is why such securities are created. It is sufficient to say that the risk/return characteristics of these instruments make them attractive for the purposes of hedging a portfolio of pass-throughs and mortgage loans. They should not be used as stand-alone investment vehicles.

ASSET-BACKED SECURITIES

Asset-backed securities are securities collateralized by assets that are not mortgage loans. In structuring an asset-backed security, issuers have drawn from the structures used in the mortgage-backed securities market. Asset-backed securities have been structured as pass-throughs and as structures with multiple bond classes just like a CMO. Credit enhancement can be provided externally by mechanisms such as a letter of credit or recourse to the issuer, or it can be provided internally by creating senior and subordination interests in the cash flow or by using collateral whose par value is greater than the par value owed to the holders of the security. This is referred to as *overcollateralizing* the structure.

The two most common types of asset-backed securities are those backed by automobile loans and credit card receivables. Because of credit enhancements, all these issues have received ratings of at least double A. Cash flow for automobile-loan-backed securities is either monthly or quarterly. Stated final maturities range from three to five years, but have average lives of one to three years. The uncertainty about the cash flow is due to prepayments. For securities backed by automobile loans, prepayments result from (1) sales and trade-ins requiring full payoff of the loan, (2) repossession and subsequent sale of the automobile, (3) loss or destruction of the vehicle, (4) payoff of the loan with cash to save interest cost, and (5) refinancing of the loan at a lower interest cost.

While refinancings may be a major reason for prepayments of mortgage loans, they are of minor importance for automobile loans. Moreover, the interest rates for the automobile loans underlying several issues are substantially below market rates if they are offered by manufacturers as part of a sales promotion. There is good historical information on the other causes of prepayments. Therefore, the cash flow of securities backed by automobile loans does not have a great deal of uncertainty despite prepayments.

Credit-card-backed issues represent participation in a fixed pool of credit card accounts. Unlike mortgage-backed securities and automobile-loan-backed issues, credit-card-backed issues are backed by revolving loans. The principal repayment from the loan is not distributed to the securityholder. Instead, it is retained by a trustee and reinvested in additional credit card receivables.

While automobile-loan-backed issues and credit-card-backed issues are the two largest sectors of the asset-backed securities market, there are securities backed by boat loans, recreational vehicle loans, computer leases, senior bank loans, accounts receivables, and Small Business Administration loans.

■ SUMMARY

In this chapter we provided an overview of the instruments traded in the fixed-income market and their basic features (term to maturity, par value, and coupon rate). The U.S. Treasury issues three types of securities: bills, notes, and bonds. Zero-coupon Treasury securities include trademarks, Treasury receipts, and STRIPS. Creation of the first two types of zero-coupon Treasury securities has ceased; STRIPS now dominate the market.

Government-sponsored enterprises securities and federally related institution securities constitute the federal agency securities market. The former are privately owned, publicly chartered entities created to reduce the cost of borrowing for certain sectors of the economy. Federally related institutions are arms of the federal government whose debt is guaranteed by the U.S. government.

Corporate bonds are debt obligating a corporation to pay periodic interest with full repayment of principal at maturity. Special corporate bond features include convertible and exchangeable bonds, units of debt with warrants, putable bonds, zero-coupon bonds, and floating-rate securities.

Municipal securities are issued by state and local governments and their authorities, with the coupon interest on most issues being exempt from federal income taxes. The two basic security structures are general obligation bonds and revenue bonds.

The Eurobond market is divided into different sectors based on the currency in which the issue is denominated. Eurobonds can be denominated in any currency, the most popular issues being U.S. dollar-denominated, called Eurodollar bonds.

Preferred stock as a class of stock shares characteristics of both common stock and debt. A distinctive feature of preferred stock is the favorable tax treatment of the dividends for qualified corporations.

A mortgage is a loan secured by the collateral of some specified real estate property which obliges the borrower to make a predetermined series of payments. The monthly cash flow from a mortgage loan, regardless of the mortgage design, can be broken down into three parts: (1) the servicing fee, (2) the interest payment, and (3) the scheduled principal repayment. Uncertainty is associated with investing in a mortgage because the rate of prepayments is uncertain.

Mortgage-backed securities are securities backed by a pool of mortgage loans. While any type of mortgage loan, residential or commercial, can be used as collateral for a mortgage-backed security, most are backed by residential mortgages. A mortgage pass-through security is created when mortgage holders form a collection (pool) of mortgages and sell shares or participation certificates in the pool. Estimating the cash flow from a pass-through requires forecasting prepayments. Because of prepayment risk, pass-throughs are an unattractive investment for many institutional investors from an asset/liability perspective.

To address the prepayment risks associated with investing in mortgage pass-through securities, collateralized mortgage obligations were created. CMOs redirect cash flows from a pool of pass-throughs to different bond classes based on a set of rules for distribution of interest and principal. A stripped MBS is created by altering the distribution of principal and interest of the underlying pass-through security in unequal portions to two classes of bonds.

Asset-backed securities are backed by loans other than mortgage loans. The two most common types of asset-backed securities are those backed by automobile loans and those backed by credit card receivables. Issuers have used pass-through structures and a multiple class structure similar to a CMO. Credit enhancements are also used.

■ KEY TERMS

agency pass-throughs	bank discount basis	bond indenture
amortization schedule	bellwether issues	call provision
balloon maturity	benchmark issues	collateral trust bonds

collateralized mortgage obligation (CMO)
conventional mortgage
conventional pass-throughs
convertible Eurobond
corpus
coupon
coupon rate
credit analysis
cumulative preferred stock
debenture bonds
deferred-interest bonds
dividend rate
dual-currency issues
embedded option
event risk
Euro straights
face value
federally related institutions securities market
full faith and credit obligations

fully modified pass-throughs
government-sponsored enterprises securities market
high-yield bonds
insured bonds
investment-grade bonds
junk bonds
limited-tax general obligation bonds
maturity value
medium-term note
modified pass-throughs
mortgage-backed securities (MBS)
mortgage bond
mortgage pass-through security
mortgage rate
mortgagee
mortgagor
non-cumulative preferred stock
notes
official statement

par value
pass-through coupon rate
payment-in-kind (PIK) bonds
preferred stock
prepayment speed
prepayments
prerefunded bonds
private-label pass-throughs
refunded bonds
refunding
revenue fund
securitization
self-amortizing
serial bonds
sinking fund
speed
step-up bonds
subordinated debenture bonds
term bonds
term to maturity
zero-coupon bonds

■ QUESTIONS

1. Indicate whether you agree or disagree with the following statements:
   a. "All fixed-income securities are debt obligations."
   b. "In order to qualify as a fixed-income security, the coupon interest rate must be a fixed interest rate for the life of the security."

2. For a 10-year bond that pays interest semiannually, the coupon rate is 8% and the par value is $1,000. How much will the investor receive every six months for the next 10 years?

3. Explain how an investor realizes interest when he purchases a zero-coupon bond?

4. a. What is the difference between a Treasury bill and coupon Treasury security?
   b. What is an on-the-run and an off-the-run Treasury issue?

5. a. Suppose that the price of a Treasury bill with 90 days to maturity and a $1 million face value is $980,000. What is the yield on a bank discount basis?
   b. Determine the dollar price for the following Treasury coupon securities:

	Price Quoted	Par
i.	95-4	$ 100,000
ii.	87-16	1,000,000
iii.	102-10	10,000,000
iv.	116-30	10,000
v.	102-4+	100,000

6. a. Explain how a stripped Treasury security can be created from $3 billion of a 7% coupon, 30-year Treasury bond.
   b. When stripped Treasury securities were first created, callable 30-year Treasury bonds were being issued by the Treasury. Such issues could be called by the Treasury five years before the maturity date. Why would the presence of a call feature make it difficult to strip a Treasury security?

7. a. What is the difference between a government-sponsored enterprise and a federally related institution?
   b. Are government-sponsored enterprise securities backed by the full faith and credit of the U.S. government?

8. What are the two major companies that assign credit ratings?

9. What is event risk?

10. What is the difference between a non-callable bond and a non-refundable bond?

11. a. What is the difference between a convertible bond and an exchangeable bond?
    b. What is a payment-in-kind bond?

12. A Merrill Lynch note structure called a Liquid Yield Option Note (LYON) has the following characteristics:

It is a zero-coupon instrument.
It is convertible into the common stock of the issuer.
It is putable.
It is callable.
It is a subordinated note.

a. Describe all the embedded options granted to the corporation that issues a LYON.

b. Describe all the embedded options granted to the investor that purchases a LYON.

c. What is meant by a subordinated note?

13. a. What is the difference between a general obligation bond and a revenue bond?

b. Which type of bond would an investor analyze using an approach similar to that for analyzing a corporate bond?

14. "An insured municipal bond is safer than an uninsured municipal bond." Do you agree with this statement?

15. What is a refunded bond?

16. What is a dual-currency bond?

17. Why are corporate treasurers the main buyers of preferred stock?

18. Why is the interest rate on a mortgage loan not necessarily the same as the interest rate that the investor receives?

19. a. What are the three components of the cash flow of a mortgage loan?

b. Why is the cash flow of a mortgage unknown?

c. In what sense has the investor in a mortgage granted the borrower (homeowner) a call option?

20. a. What is a mortgage pass-through security?

b. Describe the cash flow characteristics of a mortgage pass-through security.

c. Which type of agency pass-through carries the full faith and credit of the U.S. government?

21. a. What is meant by a fully modified pass-through?

b. What is meant by a modified pass-through?

22. Why is it necessary to forecast prepayments for a pass-through security?

23. How does a collateralized mortgage obligation alter the cash flow from mortgages so as to shift the prepayment risk across various classes of bondholders?

24. "By creating a CMO, an issuer eliminates the prepayment risk associated with the underlying mortgages." Do you agree with this statement?

25. a. What is a principal-only security?

b. What is an interest-only security?

26. Suppose that 8% coupon pass-throughs are stripped into two classes. Class X-1 receives 75% of the principal and 10% of the interest. Class X-2 receives 25% of the principal and 90% of the interest.

a. What is the effective coupon rate on Class X-1?

b. What is the effective coupon rate on Class X-2?

27. a. Is the prepayment risk of an automobile-loan-backed security as great as for a mortgage pass-through security?

b. In a credit-card-backed security is the principal repaid periodically to the investor?

CHAPTER 20
BOND PRICING

LEARNING OBJECTIVES

After reading this chapter you will be able to:

- calculate the price of a bond.
- explain why the price of a bond changes in the direction opposite to the change in required yield.
- explain why the price of a bond changes.
- calculate the yield to maturity and yield to call of a bond.
- describe and evaluate the sources of a bond's return.

- explain the limitations of conventional yield measures.
- calculate two portfolio yield measures and explain the limitations of these measures.
- calculate the total return for a bond.
- explain why the total return is superior to conventional yield measures.
- use scenario analysis to assess the potential return performance of a bond.

In the previous chapter we discussed the fundamental characteristics of bonds and the wide range of bonds available in the market. In this chapter and the one to follow, we explain the fundamental analytical tools necessary to understand how to analyze bonds and assess their potential performance.

In this chapter, we explain how to determine the price of a bond and explain the relationship between price and yield. Then we discuss various yield measures and their meaning for evaluating the potential performance over some investment horizon. In particular, we explain the various conventions for measuring the yield of a bond and then demonstrate why conventional yield measures fail to identify the potential return from investing in a bond over some investment horizon. A better measure for assessing the potential return from investing in a bond is the total return. We will see how to calculate the potential total return from investing in a bond over some investment horizon. In the next chapter, we explain the price volatility characteristics of a bond and describe measures to quantify price volatility.

PRICING OF BONDS

The price of any financial instrument is equal to the present value of the expected cash flows from the financial instrument. Therefore to determine the price requires:

1. An estimate of the expected cash flows
2. An estimate of the appropriate required yield

The expected cash flows for some financial instruments are simple to compute; for others, the task is more difficult. The **required yield** reflects the yield for financial instruments with *comparable risk*, or so-called alternative (or substitute) investments.

The first step in determining the price of a bond is to determine its cash flow. The cash flow for a bond that the issuer cannot retire prior to its stated maturity date (that is, a *non-callable bond*[1]) consists of:

1. Periodic coupon interest payments to the maturity date
2. The par value at maturity (also known as maturity value)

Our illustrations of bond pricing use three assumptions to simplify the analysis:

1. The coupon payments are made every six months. (For most U.S. bond issues, coupon interest is in fact paid semiannually.)
2. The next coupon payment for the bond is received exactly six months from now.
3. The coupon interest is fixed for the term of the bond.

Consequently, the cash flows for a non-callable bond consists of an annuity of a fixed coupon interest payment paid semiannually and the par, or maturity, value. For example, a 20-year bond with a 10% coupon rate and a par, or maturity, value of $1,000 has the following cash flows from coupon interest:

Annual coupon interest = $1,000 × 0.10 = $100
Semiannual coupon interest = $100/2 = $50

Therefore there are 40 semiannual cash flows of $50, and there is a $1,000 cash flow 40 six-month periods from now.

Notice the treatment of the par value. It is not treated as if it is received 20 years from now. Instead, it is treated on a basis consistent with the coupon payments, which are semiannual.

The required yield is determined by investigating the yields offered on comparable bonds in the market. In this case, comparable investments would be non-callable bonds of the same credit quality and the same maturity. The required yield typically is expressed as an annual interest rate. When the cash flows occur semiannually, the market convention is to use one-half the annual interest rate as the periodic interest rate with which to discount the cash flows.

Given the cash flows of a bond and the required yield, we have all the information needed to price a bond. As the price of a bond is the present value of the cash flows, it is determined by adding these two present values:

1. The present value of the semiannual coupon payments

---

[1]In Chapter 21 we discuss the pricing of callable bonds.

2. The present value of the par, or maturity, value at the maturity date

   In general, the price of a bond can be computed using the following formula:

$$P = \frac{C}{(1+r)^1} + \frac{C}{(1+r)^2} + \frac{C}{(1+r)^3} + \ldots + \frac{C}{(1+r)^n} + \frac{M}{(1+r)^n}$$

or

$$P = \sum_{t=1}^{n} \frac{C}{(1+r)^t} + \frac{M}{(1+r)^n} \tag{20-1}$$

where P = price (in $)

n = number of periods (number of years × 2)

C = *semiannual* coupon payment (in $)

r = periodic interest rate (required annual yield ÷ 2)

M = maturity value

t = time period when the payment is to be received

Because the semiannual coupon payments are equivalent to an ordinary annuity, the present value of the coupon payments can be determined from the following formula:

$$\text{Present value of coupon payments} = C \left[\frac{1 - \dfrac{1}{(1+r)^n}}{r} \right] \tag{20-2}$$

To illustrate how to compute the price of a bond, consider a 20-year 10% coupon bond with a par value of $1,000. Let's suppose that the required yield on this bond is 11%. The cash flows for this bond are as follows:

1. 40 semiannual coupon payments of $50
2. $1,000 to be received 40 six-month periods from now

The semiannual or periodic interest rate (or periodic required yield) is 5.5% (11% divided by 2).

The present value of the 40 semiannual coupon payments of $50 discounted at 5.5% is $802.31, calculated as

$$C = \$50 \qquad n = 40 \qquad r = 0.055$$

$$\text{Present value of coupon payments} = 50 \left[\frac{1 - \dfrac{1}{(1.055)^{40}}}{0.055} \right]$$

$$= 50 \left(\frac{1 - 0.117463}{0.055} \right) = \$802.31$$

The present value of the par, or maturity, value of $1,000 received 40 *six-month periods from now*, discounted at 5.5%, is $117.46, as follows:

$$\frac{\$1,000}{(1.055)^{40}} = \frac{\$1,000}{8.51332} = \$117.46$$

The price of the bond is then equal to the sum of the two present values:

Present value of coupon payments   = $802.31

+ Present value of par (maturity value) = <u>117.46</u>

Price   = $919.77

Suppose that instead of an 11% required yield, the required yield is 6.8%. The price of the bond would then be $1,347.04, demonstrated as follows:

The present value of the coupon payments using a periodic interest rate of 3.4% (6.8%/2) is

$$\text{Present value of coupon payments} = 50 \left[\frac{1 - \dfrac{1}{(1.034)^{40}}}{0.034} \right] = \$1,084.51$$

The present value of the par, or maturity, value of $1,000 received 40 *six-month periods from now* discounted at 3.4% is

$$\frac{\$1,000}{(1.034)^{40}} = \$262.53$$

The price of the bond is then

Present value of coupon payments	=	$1,084.51
+ Present value of par (maturity value)	=	262.53
Price	=	$1,347.04

If the required yield is equal to the coupon rate of 10%, it can be demonstrated that the price of the bond would be its par value, $1,000.

Zero-coupon bonds do not make any periodic coupon payments. Instead, the investor realizes interest as the difference between the maturity value and the purchase price. The price of a zero-coupon bond is calculated by substituting zero for C in Equation (20-1):

$$P = \frac{M}{(1 + r)^n} \tag{20-3}$$

Equation (20-3) states that the price of a zero-coupon bond is simply the present value of the maturity value. In the present value computation, however, the number of periods used for discounting is not the number of years to maturity of the bond, but rather double the number of years. The discount rate is one-half the required annual yield.

Price/Yield Relationship

A fundamental property of a bond is that its price changes in the opposite direction from the change in the required yield. The reason is that the price of the bond is the present value of the cash flows. As the required yield increases, the present value of the cash flows decreases; hence the price decreases. The opposite is true when the required yield decreases: The present value of the cash flows increases, and therefore the price of the bond increases. This can be seen by examining the price for the 20-year, 10% bond when the required yield is 11%, 10%, and 6.8%. Table 20-1 shows the price of the 20-year, 10% coupon bond for various required yields.

If we graph the price/required yield relationship for any non-callable bond, we will find that it has the bowed shape shown in Figure 20-1. This shape is referred to as **convex**. The convexity of the price/yield relationship has important implications for the investment properties of a bond, as we explain later in this chapter.

TABLE 20-1			
PRICE/YIELD RELATIONSHIP FOR A 20-YEAR, 10% COUPON BOND			
Yield	Price	Yield	Price
0.045	$1,720.32	0.110	919.77
0.050	1,627.57	0.115	883.50
0.055	1,541.76	0.120	849.54
0.060	1,462.30	0.125	817.70
0.065	1,388.65	0.130	787.82
0.070	1,320.33	0.135	759.75
0.075	1,256.89	0.140	733.37
0.080	1,197.93	0.145	708.53
0.085	1,143.08	0.150	685.14
0.090	1,092.01	0.155	663.08
0.095	1,044.41	0.160	642.26
0.100	1,000.00	0.165	622.59
0.105	958.53		

Relationship between Coupon Rate, Required Yield, and Price

As yields in the marketplace change, the only variable that can change to compensate an investor in an existing bond is the price of that bond. When the coupon rate is equal to the required yield, the price of the bond will be equal to its par value, as we demonstrated for the 20-year, 10% coupon bond.

When yields in the marketplace rise above the coupon rate at a given point in time, the price of the bond adjusts so that the investor can realize some additional interest. This is accomplished by the price falling below its par value. The capital appreciation realized by holding the bond to maturity represents a form of interest to the investor to compensate for a coupon rate

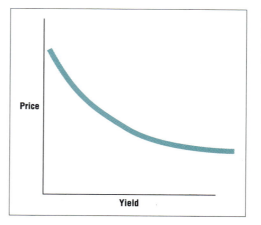

FIGURE 20-1

Shape of the price/yield relationship.

that is lower than the required yield. When a bond sells below its par value, it is said to be selling at a **discount**. In our earlier calculation of bond price we saw that when the required yield is greater than the coupon rate, the price of the bond is always lower than the par value ($1,000).

When the required yield in the market is below the coupon rate, the bond must sell above its par value. This is because investors who would have the opportunity to purchase the bond at par would be getting a coupon rate in excess of what the market requires. As a result, investors would bid up the price of the bond because its yield is so attractive. The price would eventually be bid up to a level where the bond offers the required yield in the market. A bond whose price is above its par value is said to be selling at a **premium**.

The relationship between coupon rate, required yield, and price can be summarized as follows:

Coupon rate < required yield → price < par (discount bond)
Coupon rate = required yield → price = par
Coupon rate > required yield → price > par (premium bond)

Relationship between Bond Price and Time If Interest Rates Are Unchanged

If the required yield does not change between the time the bond is purchased and the maturity date, what will happen to the price of the bond? For a bond selling at par value, the coupon rate is equal to the required yield. As the bond moves closer to maturity, the bond will continue to sell at par value. The price of a bond will not remain constant for a bond selling at a premium or a discount, however. A discount bond's price increases as it approaches maturity, assuming the required yield does not change. For a premium bond, the opposite occurs. For both bonds, the price will equal par value at the maturity date.

Reasons for the Change in the Price of a Bond

The price of a bond will change for one or more of the following three reasons:

1. There is a change in the required yield owing to changes in the credit quality of the issuer. That is, the required yield changes, because the market now compares the bond yield with yields from a different set of bonds with the same credit risk.
2. There is a change in the price of the bond selling at a premium or a discount, without any change in the required yield, simply because the bond is moving toward maturity.
3. There is a change in the required yield owing to a change in the yield on comparable bonds. That is, market interest rates change.

Complications

The framework for pricing a bond discussed in this chapter assumes that:

1. The next coupon payment is exactly six months away.
2. The cash flows are known.
3. One rate is used to discount all cash flows.

Let's look at the implications for the pricing of a bond if each assumption is not true.

Next Coupon Payment Due in Less Than Six Months   When an investor purchases a bond whose next coupon payment is due in less than six months, the accepted method for computing the price of the bond is as follows:

$$P = \sum_{t=1}^{n} \frac{C}{(1 + r)^v (1 + r)^{t-1}} + \frac{M}{(1 + r)^v (1 + r)^{n-1}} \tag{20-4}$$

where

$$v = \frac{\text{days between settlement and next coupon}}{\text{days in six-month period}}$$

Note that when v is 1 (that is, when the next coupon payment is six months away), Equation (20-4) reduces to Equation (20-1).

The Cash Flows May Not Be Known   For non-callable bonds, assuming that the issuer does not default, the cash flows are known. For most bonds, however, the cash flows are not known with certainty. This is because an issuer may call a bond before the stated maturity date. With callable bonds, the cash flows will, in fact, depend on the level of current interest rates relative to the coupon rate. For example, the issuer will typically call a bond when interest rates drop far enough below the coupon rate so that it is economic to retire the bond issue prior to maturity and issue new bonds at a lower coupon rate.[2] Consequently, the cash flows of bonds that may be called prior to maturity are dependent on current interest rates in the marketplace.

Different Discount Rates Apply to Each Cash Flow   Our pricing analysis has assumed that it is appropriate to discount each cash flow using the same discount rate. As explained in Chapter 22, a bond can be viewed as a package of zero-coupon bonds, in which case a unique discount rate should be used to determine the present value of each cash flow.

Price Quotes

We have assumed in our illustrations that the maturity, or par, value of a bond is $1,000. A bond may have a maturity, or par, value greater or less than $1,000. Consequently, when quoting bond prices, traders quote the price as a percentage of par value. A bond selling at par is quoted as 100, meaning 100% of its par value. A bond selling at a discount will be selling for less than 100; a bond selling at a premium will be selling for more than 100.

The procedure for converting a price quote to a dollar price is as follows:

(Price per $100 of par value/100) × par value

For example, if a bond is quoted at 96 1/2 and has a par value of $100,000, then the dollar price is

(96.5/100) × $100,000 = $96,500

---

[2]Mortgage-backed securities are another example; the borrower has the right to prepay all or part of the obligation prior to maturity.

If a bond is quoted at 103 19/32 and has a par value of $1 million, then the dollar price is

$$(103.59375/100) \times \$1,000,000 = \$1,035,937.50$$

Accrued Interest

When an investor purchases a bond between coupon payments, the investor must compensate the seller of the bond for the coupon interest earned from the time of the last coupon payment to the settlement date of the bond. This amount is called **accrued interest**. (The exceptions are bonds that are in default. Such bonds are said to be quoted at a **flat price**, that is, without accrued interest.)

In order to calculate accrued interest, the number of days between the last coupon and the settlement date of the bond must be determined. There are different conventions in bond markets within the U.S. and in other countries for determining the number of days. These conventions are called *day-count conventions*, and they are described in Box 20.

CONVENTIONAL YIELD MEASURES

Related to the price of a bond is its yield. The price of a bond is calculated from the cash flows and the required yield. The yield of a bond is calculated from the cash flows and the market price. In this section we discuss various yield measures and their meaning for evaluating the relative attractiveness of a bond.

There are three bond yield measures commonly quoted by dealers and used by portfolio managers: (1) current yield, (2) yield to maturity, and (3) yield to call.

Current Yield

Current yield relates the annual coupon interest to the market price. The formula for the current yield is

$$\text{Current yield} = \frac{\text{annual dollar coupon interest}}{\text{price}}$$

For example, the current yield for a 15-year, 7% coupon bond with a par value of $1,000 selling for $769.40 is 9.10%, as shown:

$$\text{Current yield} = \frac{\$70}{\$769.40} = 0.091\% = 9.1\%$$

The current yield calculation takes into account only the coupon interest and no other source of return that will affect an investor's yield. No consideration is given to the capital gain that the investor will realize when a bond is purchased at a discount and held to maturity; nor is there any recognition of the capital loss that the investor will realize if a bond purchased at a premium is held to maturity. The time value of money is also ignored.

Yield to Maturity

The **yield to maturity** is the interest rate that will make the present value of a bond's remaining cash flows (if held to maturity) equal to the price (plus accrued interest, if any). Mathematically, the yield to maturity, y, for a bond

> ## BOX 20
>
> ### ACCRUED INTEREST AND DAYCOUNT CONVENTIONS
>
> Accrued interest is calculated as follows:
>
> AI = (DAYS × Coupon)/AY
>
> where   AI = accrued interest
>   DAYS = number of days between the two days
>   AY = number of days in a year
>   Coupon = annual coupon rate (%)
>
> There are various ways to calculate the number of days between two dates (DAYS) and the number of days in a year (AY). In our discussion, we will let "D1/M1/Y1" denote the previous coupon date and "D2/M2/Y2" denote the value date.
>
> *Number of days between two days (DAYS)*: One of the following three daycount conventions may be used:
>
> 1. *ACT*
>   Actual number of days between two dates
> 2. *30*
>   Calculate number of days between the two dates assuming 30-day months using the following calculations: The number of days between the dates D1/M1/Y1 and D2/M2/Y2 is:
>
>   - if D1 is 31, change to 30
>   - if D2 is 31 and D1 is 30 or 31, change D2 to 30, otherwise, leave at 31.
>   - Then, the number of days between the two dates is:
>
>   ((Y2 − Y1) × 360) + ((M2 − M1) × 30) + (D2 − D1)
>
>   - Thus, there are 29 days between May 1 and May 30, and 30 days between May 1 and May 31.
>
> 3. *30E*
>   Calculate the number of days between the two dates assuming 30-day months using the following calculation: The number of days between dates D1/M1/Y1 and D2/M2/Y2 is given by:
>
>   - if D1 is 31, change to 30
>   - if D2 is 31, change to 30
>   - Then the number of days between the two dates is:
>
>   ((Y2 − Y1) × 360) + ((M2 − M1) × 30) + (D2 − D1)
>
>   - Thus, there are 29 days between May 1 and May 30, and 30 days between May 1 and May 31.
>   - The 30E method is used in the Euromarkets and some continental European domestic markets.
>
> *Number of days in a year (AY)*: One of the following three daycount conventions may be used:
>
> 1. *365*
>   Assume a year of 365 days.
> 2. *ACT*
>   AY is the number of days in the current coupon period multiplied by the number of coupon payments per year. For a semi-annual coupon, the number of days in a coupon period can range from 181 to 184 days so AY can range from 362 to 368 days.
> 3. *360*
>   Assume a year of 360 days.
>
> *Daycount conventions in practice*: Of the nine possible combinations of DAYS and AY, only the following five are used in practice:
>
> 1. ACT/365 (U.K., Japan)
> 2. ACT/360
> 3. 30/360 (U.S. Federal Agencies; U.S. Corporates)
> 4. 30E/360 (Eurobonds; Germany; Holland)
> 5. ACT/ACT (U.S. Treasuries; France; Australia)
>
> *Source*: Frank Jones and Frank J. Fabozzi, *The International Government Bond Markets* (Chicago: Probus Publishing, 1992), pp. 16–18.
>
> ### Questions for Box 20
>
> 1. What is accrued interest?
> 2. Why is the number of days between the settlement dates and the date of the last coupon payment important?
> 3. Do all bond markets throughout the world assume that there are 365 days in a year for the purpose of calculating accrued interest?

that pays interest semiannually and that has no accrued interest is found by solving the following equation:

$$P = \frac{C}{(1+y)^1} + \frac{C}{(1+y)^2} + \frac{C}{(1+y)^3} + \ldots + \frac{C}{(1+y)^n} + \frac{M}{(1+y)^n}$$

This expression can be rewritten in shorthand notation as

$$P = \sum_{t=1}^{n} \frac{C}{(1+y)^t} + \frac{M}{(1+y)^n} \qquad (20\text{-}5)$$

Since the cash flows are every six months, the yield to maturity y found by solving Equation (20-5) is a semiannual yield to maturity. This yield can be annualized by either (1) doubling the semiannual yield or (2) compounding the yield. The market convention is to annualize the semiannual yield by simply doubling its value. The yield to maturity computed on the basis of this market convention is called the **bond-equivalent yield**. It is also referred to as a yield on a **bond-equivalent basis**.

The computation of the yield to maturity requires a trial-and-error (iterative) procedure. To illustrate the computation, consider the bond that we used to compute the current yield. The cash flow for this bond is (1) 30 coupon payments of $35 every six months and (2) $1,000 to be paid 30 six-month periods from now. To get y in Equation (20-5), different interest rates must be tried until the present value of the cash flows is equal to the price of $769.42. The present value of the cash flows of the bond for several periodic interest rates is shown in Table 20-2.

When a 5% semiannual interest rate is used, the present value of the cash flows is $769.42. Therefore y is 5%, and is the semiannual yield to maturity. As noted before, the convention in the market is to double the semiannual yield to obtain an annualized yield. Thus the yield on a bond-equivalent basis for our hypothetical bond is 10%.

It is much easier to compute the yield to maturity for a zero-coupon bond. To find the yield to maturity, we substitute zero for the coupon in Equation (20-5) and solve for y:

$$y = \left(\frac{M}{P}\right)^{1/n} - 1 \qquad (20\text{-}6)$$

For example, for a 10-year zero-coupon bond with a maturity value of $1,000, selling for $439.18:

$$y = \left(\frac{\$1,000}{\$439.18}\right)^{1/20} - 1 = 0.042 = 4.2\%$$

Note that the number of periods is equal to 20 semiannual periods, which is double the number of years. The number of years is not used because we want a yield value that may be compared with alternative coupon bonds. To get the bond-equivalent annual yield, we must double y, which gives us 8.4%.

			TABLE 20-2	
		ITERATIVE PROCEDURE FOR CALCULATING THE YIELD TO MATURITY		
Annual Interest Rate ($2y$)	**Semiannual Rate (y)**	**Present Value of 30 Payments of $35**	**Present Value of $1,000 30 Periods from Now**	**Present Value of Cash Flows**
9.00	4.50	570.11	267.00	837.11
9.50	4.75	553.71	248.53	802.24
10.00	5.00	538.04	231.38	769.42*
10.50	5.25	532.04	215.45	738.49
11.00	5.50	508.68	200.64	709.32

*Market price.

TABLE 20-3
RELATIONSHIP BETWEEN COUPON RATE, CURRENT YIELD, YIELD TO MATURITY, AND BOND PRICE

Bond Selling At	Relationship
Par	Coupon rate = current yield = yield to maturity
Discount	Coupon rate < current yield < yield to maturity
Premium	Coupon rate > current yield > yield to maturity

The yield-to-maturity calculation takes into account not only the current coupon income but also any capital gain or loss the investor will realize by holding the bond to maturity. In addition, the yield to maturity considers the timing of the cash flows.

The relationship among the coupon rate, current yield, yield to maturity, and bond price is shown in Table 20-3.

Yield to Call

Call dates are specified times before maturity when the issuer of a bond may retire part of the bond for a specified **call price**. Both call dates and prices are set at time of issuance, and, as discussed in Chapter 19, allow the issuer to retire the issue prior to maturity should market interest rates fall below the coupon rate. For a bond that may be called prior to the stated maturity date, another yield measure is commonly quoted—the **yield to call**. The cash flows for computing the yield to call are those that will result if the issue is called on its first call date. In effect, the yield to call is calculated like the yield to maturity, only using the first call date and price in place of the maturity date and price. The yield to call is the interest rate that will make the present value of the cash flows equal to the price of the bond if the bond is held to the first call date.

Mathematically, the yield to call can be expressed as follows:

$$P = \frac{C}{(1 + y_c)^1} + \frac{C}{(1 + y_c)^2} + \frac{C}{(1 + y_c)^3} + \cdots + \frac{C}{(1 + y_c)^{n^*}} + \frac{M^*}{(1 + y_c)^{n^*}}$$

$$P = \sum_{t=1}^{n^*} \frac{C}{(1 + y_c)^t} + \frac{M^*}{(1 + y_c)^{n^*}} \tag{20-7}$$

where M^* = call price (in \$)
  n^* = number of periods until first call date
  y_c = yield to call

For a bond that pays coupon interest semiannually, doubling y_c gives the yield to call on a bond-equivalent basis.

To illustrate the computation, consider an 18-year, 11% coupon bond with a maturity value of \$1,000 selling for \$1,168.97. Suppose that the first call date is 13 years from now and that the call price is \$1,055. The cash flows for this bond if it is called in 13 years are (1) 26 coupon payments of \$55 every six months and (2) \$1,055 due in 26 six-month periods from now.

The value for y_c in Equation (20-7) is the one that will make the present value of the cash flows to the call date equal to the bond's price of \$1,168.97.

In this case that periodic interest rate is 4.5%. Therefore the yield to call on a bond-equivalent basis is 9%.

Investors typically compute both the yield to call and the yield to maturity for a callable bond selling at a premium. They then select the lower of the two as a measure of return. The lowest yield based on every possible call date and the yield to maturity is referred to as the **yield to worst**.

Potential Sources of a Bond's Dollar Return

An investor who purchases a bond can expect to receive a dollar return from one or more of these sources:

1. The periodic coupon interest payments made by the issuer
2. Income from reinvestment of the periodic interest payments (the interest-on-interest component)
3. Any capital gain (or capital loss–negative dollar return) when the bond matures, is called, or is sold

Any measure of a bond's potential yield should take into consideration each of these three potential sources of return. The current yield considers only the coupon interest payments. No consideration is given to any capital gain (or loss) or to interest-on-interest. The yield to maturity takes into account coupon interest and any capital gain (or loss). It also considers the interest-on-interest component; implicit in the yield-to-maturity computation, however, is the assumption that the coupon payments can be reinvested at the computed yield to maturity. The yield to maturity, therefore, is a **promised yield**; that is, it will be realized only if (1) the bond is held to maturity and (2) the coupon interest payments are reinvested at the yield to maturity. If either (1) or (2) fails to occur, the actual yield realized by an investor can be greater than or less than the yield to maturity.

The yield to call also takes into account all three potential sources of return. In this case, the assumption is that the coupon payments can be reinvested at the yield to call. Therefore the yield-to-call measure suffers from the same drawback inherent in the implicit assumption of the reinvestment rate for the coupon interest payments. Also, it assumes that the bond will be held until the first call date, at which time the bond will be called.

Determining the Interest-on-Interest Dollar Return   The interest-on-interest component can represent a substantial portion of a bond's potential return. Letting r denote the semiannual reinvestment rate, we can find the interest-on-interest plus the total coupon payments from the following formula[3]:

$$\text{Coupon interest} + \text{interest-on-interest} = C\left[\frac{(1 + r)^n - 1}{r}\right] \qquad (20\text{-}8)$$

The total dollar amount of coupon interest is found by multiplying the semiannual coupon interest by the number of periods:

$$\text{Total coupon interest} = nC$$

The interest-on-interest component is then the difference between the coupon interest plus interest-on-interest and the total dollar coupon interest, as expressed in Equation (20-9):

---

[3]This is the formula for the future value of an annuity.

$$\text{Interest-on-interest} = C\left[\frac{(1 + r)^n - 1}{r}\right] - nC \tag{20-9}$$

The yield-to-maturity measure assumes that the reinvestment rate is the yield to maturity. For example, let's consider the 15-year, 7% bond that we have used to illustrate how to compute current yield and yield to maturity. The yield to maturity for this bond is 10%. Assuming an annual reinvestment rate of 10% or a semiannual reinvestment rate of 5%, the interest-on-interest plus total coupon payments using Equation (20-8) is

$$\text{Coupon interest} + \text{interest-on-interest} = \$35\left[\frac{(1.05)^{30} - 1}{0.05}\right]$$
$$= \$2{,}325.36$$

Using Equation (20-9), we calculate the interest-on-interest component as

$$\text{Coupon interest} = 30\,(\$35) = \$1{,}050.00$$
$$\text{Interest-on-interest} = \$2{,}325.36 - \$1{,}050 = \$1{,}275.36$$

Yield to Maturity and Reinvestment Risk   Let's look at the potential total dollar return from holding this bond to maturity. As mentioned earlier, the total dollar return comes from three sources. In our example:

1. Total coupon interest of $1,050 (coupon interest of $35 every six months for 15 years)
2. Interest-on-interest of $1,275.36 earned from reinvesting the semiannual coupon interest payments at 5% every six months
3. A capital gain of $230.60 ($1,000 par value minus $769.40 purchase price)

The potential total dollar return if the coupons can be reinvested at the yield to maturity of 10% is then $2,555.96.

Notice that if an investor places the money that would have been used to purchase this bond, $769.40, in a savings account earning 5% semiannually for 15 years, the future value of the savings account would be

$$\$769.40\,(1.05)30 = \$3{,}325.30$$

For the initial investment of $769.40, the total dollar return is $2,555.96.

So an investor who invests $769.40 for 15 years at 10% per year (5% semiannually) expects to receive at the end of 15 years the initial investment of $769.40 plus $2,555.96. This is precisely what we found by breaking down the dollar return on the bond, assuming a reinvestment rate equal to the yield to maturity of 10%. Thus it can be seen that for the bond to yield 10%, the investor must generate $1,275.36 by reinvesting the coupon payments. This means that to generate a yield to maturity of 10%, approximately half ($1,275.36/$2,555.96) of this bond's total dollar return must come from the reinvestment of the coupon payments.

The investor will realize the yield to maturity at the time of purchase only if the bond is held to maturity and the coupon payments can be reinvested at the yield to maturity. The risk that the investor faces is that future reinvestment rates will be less than the yield to maturity at the time the bond is purchased. This risk, as we indicated in Chapter 7, is called *reinvestment risk*.

Two characteristics of a bond determine the importance of the interest-on-interest component and therefore the degree of reinvestment risk: maturity and coupon. For a given yield to maturity and a given coupon rate, the longer the maturity, the more dependent the bond's total dollar return is on the interest-on-interest component in order to realize the yield to maturity at the time of purchase. In other words, the longer the maturity, the greater the reinvestment risk. The implication is that the yield-to-maturity measure for long-term coupon bonds tells little about the potential yield that an investor may realize if the bond is held to maturity. For long-term bonds, the interest-on-interest component may be as high as 80% of the bond's potential total dollar return.

Turning to the coupon rate, for a given maturity and a given yield to maturity, the higher the coupon rate, the more dependent the bond's total dollar return will be on the reinvestment of the coupon payments in order to produce the yield to maturity anticipated at the time of purchase. This means that when maturity and yield to maturity are held constant, premium bonds are more dependent on the interest-on-interest component than are bonds selling at par. Discount bonds are less dependent on the interest-on-interest component than are bonds selling at par. For zero-coupon bonds, none of the bond's total dollar return is dependent on the interest-on-interest component. So a zero-coupon bond has no reinvestment risk if held to maturity. Thus the yield earned on a zero-coupon bond held to maturity is equal to the promised yield to maturity.

PORTFOLIO YIELD MEASURES

Two conventions have been adopted by practitioners to calculate a portfolio yield: (1) weighted-average portfolio yield and (2) internal rate of return. We describe each below.

Weighted-Average Portfolio Yield

Probably the most common—and most flawed—method for calculating a portfolio yield is the **weighted-average portfolio yield**. It is found by calculating the weighted average of the yield of all the bonds in the portfolio. The yield is weighted by the proportion of the portfolio that a security makes up. In general, if we let

w_i = the market value of bond i relative to the total market value of the portfolio

y_i = the yield on bond i

K = the number of bonds in the portfolio

then the weighted-average portfolio yield is

$$w_1y_1 + w_2y_2 + w_3y_3 + \ldots + w_Ky_K$$

For example, consider the three-bond portfolio in Table 20-4. In this illustration, the total market value of the portfolio is $57,259,000, K is equal to 3, and

$w_1 = $ 9,209,000/57,259,000 = 0.161 $y_1 = 0.090$
$w_2 = $ 20,000,000/57,259,000 = 0.349 $y_2 = 0.105$
$w_3 = $ 28,050,000/57,259,000 = 0.490 $y_3 = 0.085$

TABLE 20-4					
THREE-BOND PORTFOLIO					
Bond	Coupon Rate	Maturity	Par Value	Market Value	Yield to Maturity
B1	7.0%	5 years	$10,000,000	$ 9,209,000	9.0%
B2	10.5	7	20,000,000	20,000,000	10.5
B3	6.0	3	30,000,000	28,050,000	8.5
Total			$60,000,000	$57,259,000	

The weighted-average portfolio yield is then

$$0.161 (0.090) + 0.349 (0.105) + 0.490 (0.085) = 0.0928 = 9.28\%$$

While it is the most commonly used measure of portfolio yield, the average yield measure provides little insight into the potential yield of a portfolio. To see this, consider a portfolio consisting of only two bonds: a six-month bond offering a yield to maturity of 11% and a 30-year bond offering a yield to maturity of 8%. Suppose that 99% of the portfolio is invested in the six-month bond and 1% in the 30-year bond. The weighted-average yield for this portfolio would be 10.97%. But what does this yield mean? How can it be used within any asset/liability framework? The portfolio is basically a six-month portfolio even though it has a 30-year bond. Would a manager of a depository institution feel confident offering a two-year CD with a yield of 9%? This would suggest a spread of 197 basis points above the yield on the portfolio, based on the weighted-average portfolio yield. This would be an imprudent policy since the yield on this portfolio over the next two years will depend on interest rates six months from now.

Portfolio Internal Rate of Return

Another measure used to calculate a portfolio yield is the **portfolio internal rate of return**. It is computed by first determining the cash flows for all the bonds in the portfolio and then finding the interest rate that will make the present value of the cash flows equal to the market value of the portfolio.

To illustrate how to calculate a portfolio's internal rate of return, we will use the three-bond portfolio in Table 20-4. To simplify the illustration, it is assumed that the coupon payment date is the same for each bond. The cash flow for each bond and the portfolio's cash flows are shown in Table 20-5. The portfolio's internal rate of return is the interest rate that will make the present value of the portfolio's cash flows (the last column in Table 20-5) equal to the portfolio's market value of $57,259,000. The interest rate is 4.77%. Doubling this rate to 9.54% gives the portfolio's internal rate of return on a bond-equivalent basis.

The portfolio internal rate of return, while superior to the weighted-average portfolio yield, suffers from the same problems as yield measures in general that we discussed earlier: It assumes that the cash flows can be reinvested at the calculated yield. In the case of a portfolio internal rate of return, it assumes that the cash flows can be reinvested at the calculated internal rate of return. Moreover, it assumes that the portfolio is held till the maturity of the longest-maturity bond in the portfolio. For example, if in our illustra-

		TABLE 20-5		
		CASH FLOW OF THREE-BOND PORTFOLIO		
Period Cash Flow Received	**Bond B1**	**Bond B2**	**Bond B3**	**Portfolio**
1	$350,000	$1,050,000	$900,000	$2,300,000
2	350,000	1,050,000	900,000	2,300,000
3	350,000	1,050,000	900,000	2,300,000
4	350,000	1,050,000	900,000	2,300,000
5	350,000	1,050,000	900,000	2,300,000
6	350,000	1,050,000	30,900,000	32,300,000
7	350,000	1,050,000	-	1,400,000
8	350,000	1,050,000	-	1,400,000
9	350,000	1,050,000	-	1,400,000
10	10,350,000	1,050,000	-	11,400,000
11	-	1,050,000	-	1,050,000
12	-	1,050,000	-	1,050,000
13	-	1,050,000	-	1,050,000
14	-	21,050,000	-	21,050,000

tion one of the bonds had a maturity of 30 years, it is assumed that the portfolio is held for 30 years and all interim cash flows (coupon interest and maturing principal) are reinvested.

TOTAL RETURN

At the time of purchase an investor is promised a yield, as measured by the yield to maturity, if both of the following conditions are satisfied: (1) The bond is held to maturity, and (2) all coupon interest payments are reinvested at the yield to maturity.

We focused on the second assumption, and we showed that the interest-on-interest component for a bond may constitute a substantial portion of the bond's total dollar return. Therefore reinvesting the coupon interest payments at a rate of interest less than the yield to maturity will produce a lower yield than the yield to maturity.

Rather than assume that the coupon interest payments are reinvested at the yield to maturity, an investor can make an explicit assumption about the reinvestment rate based on money manager's expectations. The **total return** is a measure of yield that incorporates an explicit assumption about the reinvestment rate.

Let's take a careful look at the first assumption—that a bond will be held to maturity. Suppose, for example, that an investor who has a five-year investment horizon is considering the four bonds shown in Table 20-6. Assuming that all four bonds are of the same credit quality, which one is most attractive to this investor? An investor who selects bond C because it offers the highest yield to maturity is failing to recognize that the investment horizon calls for selling the bond after five years, at a price that depends on the yield

TABLE 20-6			
FOUR ALTERNATIVE INVESTMENTS			
Bond	**Coupon**	**Maturity**	**Yield to Maturity**
A	5%	3 years	9.0%
B	6%	20 years	8.6%
C	11%	15 years	9.2%
D	8%	5 years	8.0%

required in the market for 10-year, 11% coupon bonds at the time. Hence there could be a capital gain or capital loss that will make the return higher or lower than the yield to maturity promised now. Moreover, the higher coupon on bond C relative to the other three bonds means that more of this bond's return will be dependent on the reinvestment of coupon interest payments.

Bond A offers the second highest yield to maturity but matures before the investment horizon is reached. On the surface, it seems to be particularly attractive because it eliminates the problem of realizing a possible capital loss when the bond must be sold prior to the maturity date. Moreover, the reinvestment risk seems to be less than for the other three bonds because the coupon rate is lowest. However, the investor would not be eliminating the reinvestment risk because after three years the proceeds received at maturity must be reinvested for two more years. The yield that the investor will realize depends on interest rates after three years on two-year bonds when the proceeds must be rolled over.

The yield to maturity doesn't seem to be helping us to identify the best bond. How, then, do we find out which is the best bond? The answer depends on the investor's expectations. Specifically, it depends on the interest rate at which the coupon interest payments can be reinvested until the end of the investor's planned investment horizon. Also, for bonds with a maturity longer than the investment horizon, it depends on the investor's expectations about required yields in the market at the end of the planned investment horizon. Consequently, any of these bonds can be the best alternative, depending on some reinvestment rate and some future required yield at the end of the planned investment horizon. The total return measure takes these expectations into account and will determine the best investment for the investor depending on money manager's expectations.

Computing the Total Return for a Bond

The idea underlying total return is simple. The objective is first to compute the total future dollars that will result from investing in a bond assuming a particular reinvestment rate. The total return is then computed as the interest rate that will make the initial investment in the bond grow to the computed total future dollars.

The procedure for computing the total return for a bond held over some investment horizon can be summarized as follows.

Step 1. Compute the total coupon payments plus the interest-on-interest based on the assumed reinvestment rate using Equation (20-8). The reinvestment rate in this case is one-half the annual interest rate that the investor assumes can be earned on the reinvestment of coupon interest payments.

Step 2. Determine the projected sale price at the end of the planned investment horizon. The projected sale price will depend on the projected required yield at the end of the planned investment horizon. The projected sale price will be equal to the present value of the remaining cash flows of the bond discounted at the projected required yield.

Step 3. Sum the values computed in steps 1 and 2. The sum is the total future dollars that will be received from the investment, given the assumed reinvestment rate and the projected required yield at the end of the investment horizon.

Step 4. Obtain the semiannual total return using the formula:

$$\left(\frac{\text{Total future dollars}}{\text{Purchase price of bond}} \right)^{1/h} - 1 \tag{20-10}$$

where h is the number of six-month periods in the investment horizon.

Step 5. The semiannual total return found in step 4 must be annualized. There are two alternatives. The first is simply to double the semiannual total return found in step 4. The resulting interest rate is the total return on a bond-equivalent yield basis. The second is to calculate the annual return by compounding the semiannual total return. This is done as follows:

$$(1 + \text{semiannual total return})^2 - 1 \tag{20-11}$$

A total return calculated using Equation (20-11) is called a total return on an *effective rate basis.*

Determination of how to annualize the semiannual total return depends on the situation at hand. The first approach is just a market convention. If an investor is comparing the total return with the return either on other bonds or on a bond index (discussed in Chapter 23) in which yields are calculated on a bond-equivalent basis, then this approach is appropriate. However, if the portfolio objective is to satisfy liabilities that the institution is obligated to pay and those liabilities are based on semiannual compounding, then the second approach is appropriate.

To illustrate computation of the total return, suppose that an investor with a 3-year investment horizon is considering purchasing a 20-year, 8% coupon bond for $828.40. The yield to maturity for this bond is 10%. The investor expects to be able to reinvest the coupon interest payments at an annual interest rate of 6% and at the end of the planned investment horizon the then-17-year bond will be selling to offer a yield to maturity of 7%. The total return for this bond is found as follows.

Step 1. Compute the total coupon payments plus the interest-on-interest, assuming an annual reinvestment rate of 6%, or 3% every six months. The coupon payments are $40 every six months for three years or six periods (the planned investment horizon). Applying Equation (20-8), we get the total coupon interest plus interest-on-interest, which is $258.74.

Step 2. Determining the projected sale price at the end of three years, assuming that the required yield to maturity for 17-year bonds is 7%, is accomplished by calculating the present value of 34 coupon payments of $40 plus the present value of the maturity value of $1,000, discounted at 3.5%. The projected sale price is $1,098.51.

Step 3. Adding the amounts in steps 1 and 2 gives total future dollars of $1,357.25.

Step 4. To obtain the semiannual total return, compute the following:

$$\left(\frac{\$1,3725}{\$828.40}\right)^{1/6} - 1 = 0.0858, \text{ or } 8.58\%$$

Step 5: Doubling 8.58% gives a total return on a bond-equivalent basis of 17.16%. Using Equation (20-11), we get the total return on an effective rate basis:

$$(1.0858)^2 - 1 = 17.90\%$$

Applications of Total Return (Horizon Analysis)

The total return measure allows a portfolio manager to project the performance of a bond on the basis of the planned investment horizon and expectations concerning reinvestment rates and future market yields. This permits the portfolio manager to evaluate which of several potential bonds considered for acquisition will perform the best over the planned investment horizon. As we have emphasized, this cannot be done using the yield to maturity.

Using total return to assess performance over some investment horizon is called **horizon analysis**. When a total return is calculated over an investment horizon, it is referred to as a **horizon return**. In this book we use the terms *horizon return* and *total return* interchangeably.

An often-cited objection to the total return measure is that it requires the portfolio manager to formulate assumptions about reinvestment rates and future yields, as well as to think in terms of an investment horizon. Unfortunately, some portfolio managers find comfort in measures such as the yield to maturity and yield to call simply because they do not require incorporating any particular expectations. The horizon analysis framework, however, enables the portfolio manager to analyze the performance of a bond under different interest rate scenarios for reinvestment rates and future market yields. This procedure is referred to as **scenario analysis**. Only by investigating multiple scenarios can the portfolio manager see how sensitive the bond's performance will be to each scenario.

To illustrate scenario analysis, consider a portfolio manager who is deciding on whether to purchase a 20-year, 9% non-callable bond selling at $109.896 per $100 of par value. The yield to maturity for this bond is 8%. Assume also that the portfolio manager's investment horizon is three years and that the portfolio manager believes the reinvestment rate can vary from 3% to 6.5% and the projected yield at the end of the investment horizon can vary from 5% to 12%. The first panel in Table 20-7 shows different projected yields at the end of the three-year investment horizon, and the second panel gives the corresponding price for the bond at the end of the investment horizon. (This is step 2 in the total return calculation discussed earlier.) For example, consider the 10% projected yield at the end of the investment horizon. The price of a 17-year non-callable bond with a coupon rate of 9% would be 91.9035. The third panel of Table 20-7 shows the total future dollars at the end of three years under various scenarios for the reinvestment rate and the projected yield at the end of the investment horizon. (This is step 3

TABLE 20-7

SCENARIO ANALYSIS

Bond A: 9% coupon, 20-year non-callable bond

Price: $109.896

Yield to maturity: 8.00%

Investment horizon: 3 years

Projected Yield at End of Investment Horizon

5.00%	6.00%	7.00%	8.00%	9.00%	10.00%	11.00%	12.00%

Projected Sale Price at End of Investment Horizon

145.448	131.698	119.701	109.206	100.000	91.9035	84.763	78.4478

Total Future Dollars

Reinv. Rate	5.00%	6.00%	7.00%	8.00%	9.00%	10.00%	11.00%	12.00%
3.0%	173.481	159.731	147.734	137.239	128.033	119.937	112.796	106.481
3.5%	173.657	159.907	147.910	137.415	128.209	120.113	112.972	106.657
4.0%	173.834	160.084	148.087	137.592	128.387	120.290	113.150	106.834
4.5%	174.013	160.263	148.266	137.771	128.565	120.469	113.328	107.013
5.0%	174.192	160.443	148.445	137.950	128.745	120.648	113.508	107.193
5.5%	174.373	160.623	148.626	138.131	128.926	120.829	113.689	107.374
6.0%	174.555	160.806	148.809	138.313	129.108	121.011	113.871	107.556
6.5%	174.739	160.989	148.992	138.497	129.291	121.195	114.054	107.739

Total Return (Effective Rate)

Reinv. Rate	5.00%	6.00%	7.00%	8.00%	9.00%	10.00%	11.00%	12.00%
3.0%	16.44	13.28	10.37	7.69	5.22	2.96	0.87	−1.05
3.5%	16.48	13.32	10.41	7.73	5.27	3.01	0.92	−0.99
4.0%	16.52	13.36	10.45	7.78	5.32	3.06	0.98	−0.94
4.5%	16.56	13.40	10.50	7.83	5.37	3.11	1.03	−0.88
5.0%	16.60	13.44	10.54	7.87	5.42	3.16	1.08	−0.83
5.5%	16.64	13.49	10.59	7.92	5.47	3.21	1.14	−0.77
6.0%	16.68	13.53	10.63	7.97	5.52	3.26	1.19	−0.72
6.5%	16.72	13.57	10.68	8.02	5.57	3.32	1.25	−0.66

1. Price of a 9%, 17-year non-callable bond selling to yield the assumed projected yield at the end of the investment horizon.

2. Projected sale price at the end of the investment horizon plus coupon interest plus interest-on-interest at the assumed reinvestment rate.

3. Semiannual total return calculated as follows:

$$\left(\frac{\text{total future dollars}}{\$109.896} \right)^{1/6} - 1$$

Total return (effective rate) = $(1 + \text{semiannual total return})^2 - 1$

in the total return calculation discussed above.) For example, with a reinvestment rate of 4% and a projected yield at the end of the investment horizon of 10%, the total future dollars would be 120.290. The bottom panel shows the total return on an effective rate basis for each scenario.

Table 20-7 is useful for a portfolio manager in assessing the potential outcome of a bond (or a portfolio) over the investment horizon. For example, a portfolio manager knows that the maximum and minimum total return for the scenarios shown in the table will be 16.72% and −1.05%, respectively, and the scenarios under which each will be realized.

Another way to use scenario analysis is in assessing the likelihood that an investment objective will not be realized. For example, suppose that a life insurance company has issued a three-year guaranteed investment contract in which it has guaranteed an effective annual interest rate of 7.02%. Suppose that the premiums are invested in the bond analyzed in Table 20-7 and that the portfolio manager's investment objective is a minimum return of 7.02% plus a spread of 100 basis points. The spread represents the profit that the life insurance company seeks to earn. Thus, the minimum return is 8.02%. From Table 20-7 the portfolio manager can see that if the yield at the end of the investment horizon is 8% or greater and the reinvestment rate over the three-year investment horizon is less than 6.5%, a total return on an effective rate basis will be less than the investment objective of a minimum return of 8.02%.

Total Return and Bond Price Volatility

Earlier we explained the three sources of return from investing in a bond. The importance of each source of return from holding a bond over some investment horizon depends on the characteristics of the bond (coupon and maturity) and the length of the investment horizon. For long investment horizons, a coupon bond's reinvestment income will be a major component of the total return. For short investment horizons, reinvestment income is not an important source of return. However, for short investment horizons, the potential price change is of major importance. This can be seen from the first two panels of Table 20-7. The price at the beginning of the investment horizon is 109.896. The projected price at the end of the investment horizon can vary from 145.448 to 78.4478 if the projected yield at the investment horizon is between 5% and 12%.

Because of the importance of the price volatility of a bond on its total return over some investment horizon, it is critical to understand the characteristics of a bond that affect its price volatility and to know how to quantify potential price volatility. This is the subject of the next chapter.

■ SUMMARY

The price of a bond is the present value of the bond's cash flows, the discount rate being equal to the yield offered on comparable bonds. For an option-free bond, the cash flows are the coupon payments and the maturity value. For a zero-coupon bond, there are no coupon payments. The price is equal to the present value of the maturity value. The higher (lower) the required yield, the lower (higher) the price of a bond. Therefore a bond's price changes in the opposite direction from the change in the required yield. When the coupon rate is equal to the required yield, the bond will sell at its par value. When

the coupon rate is less (greater) than the required yield, the bond will sell for less (more) than its par value and is said to be selling at a discount (premium).

The conventional yield measures commonly used by bond market participants are the current yield, yield to maturity, and yield to call. We reviewed the three potential sources of dollar return from investing in a bond—coupon interest, interest-on-interest, and capital gain (or loss)—and showed that none of the three conventional yield measures deals satisfactorily with all these sources. The current yield measure fails to consider both interest-on-interest and capital gain (or loss). The yield to maturity considers all three sources, but it is deficient in assuming that all coupon interest can be reinvested at the yield to maturity. The risk that the coupon payments will be reinvested at a rate less than the yield to maturity is called reinvestment risk. The yield to call has the same shortcoming; it assumes that the coupon interest can be reinvested at the yield to call.

There are two measures of a portfolio yield: weighted-average yield to maturity and portfolio

internal rate of return. Both these measures are deficient in that they offer little insight to the potential return from holding a portfolio over some investment horizon.

The total return measure is more meaningful than either yield to maturity or yield to call for assessing the relative attractiveness of a bond given the portfolio manager's expectations and planned investment horizon. Scenario analysis can be used to assess the performance of a bond under various sets of assumptions and the conditions under which an investment objective may not be satisfied.

■ KEY TERMS

accrued interest
bond-equivalent basis
bond-equivalent yield
call date
call price
convex
discount

flat price
horizon analysis
horizon return
portfolio internal rate of return
premium
promised yield
required yield

scenario analysis
total return
weighted-average portfolio yield
yield to call
yield to maturity
yield to worst

■ QUESTIONS

1. Calculate for each of the bonds below the price per $1,000 of par value assuming semiannual coupon payments.

Bond	Coupon Rate	Years to Maturity	Required Yield
A	8%	9	7%
B	9	20	9
C	6	15	10
D	0	14	8

2. Consider a bond selling at par ($100) with a coupon rate of 6% and 10 years to maturity.
   a. What is the price of this bond if the required yield is 15%?
   b. What is the price of this bond if the required yield increases from 15% to 16%, and by what percentage did the price of this bond change?
   c. What is the price of this bond if the required yield is 5%?
   d. What is the price of this bond if the required yield increases from 5% to 6%, and by what percentage did the price of this bond change?
   e. From your answers to parts b and d, what can you say about the relative price volatility of a

bond in high compared with low interest rate environments?

3. Suppose you purchased a debt obligation three years ago at its par value of $100,000. The market price of this debt obligation today is $90,000. What are some of the reasons why the price of this debt obligation could have declined since you purchased it three years ago?

4. Suppose you are reviewing a price sheet for bonds and see the following prices (per $100 par value) reported. You observe what seems to be several errors. Without calculating the price of each bond, indicate which bonds seem to be reported incorrectly, and explain why.

Bond	Price	Coupon Rate	Required Yield
U	90	6%	9%
V	96	9	8
W	110	8	6
X	105	0	5
Y	107	7	9
Z	100	6	6

5. What is the maximum price of a bond?

6. What is meant by the accrued interest of a bond?

7. **a.** What is meant by the yield to maturity of a bond?

   b. What is meant by the yield to maturity calculated on a bond-equivalent basis?

8. **a.** Show the cash flows for the four bonds below, each of which has a par value of $1,000 and pays interest semiannually:

Bond	Coupon Rate	Years to Maturity	Price
W	7%	5	$884.20
X	8	7	948.90
Y	9	4	967.70
Z	0	10	456.39

   b. Calculate the yield to maturity for the four bonds.

9. A portfolio manager is considering buying two bonds. Bond A matures in three years and has a coupon rate of 10% payable semiannually. Bond B, of the same credit quality, matures in 10 years and has a coupon rate of 12% payable semiannually. Both bonds are priced at par.

   a. Suppose the portfolio manager plans to hold the bond for three years. Which would be the best bond for the portfolio manager to purchase?

   b. Suppose the portfolio manager plans to hold the bond for six years instead of three years. In this case, which would be the best bond for the portfolio manager to purchase?

   c. Suppose that the portfolio manager is managing the assets of a life insurance company that has issued a five-year guaranteed investment contract (GIC). The interest rate that the life insurance company has agreed to pay is 9% on a semiannual basis. Which of the two bonds should the portfolio manager purchase to assure that the GIC payments will be satisfied and that a profit will be generated for the life insurance company?

10. Demonstrate that the yield to call for an 11% coupon bond, callable in six years at a call price of $1,055 and selling for $1,233.64, is 7.1%.

11. An investor is considering the purchase of a 20-year, 7% coupon bond selling for $816 and with a par value of $1,000. The yield to maturity for this bond is 9%.

    a. What would be the total future dollars if this investor invested $816 for 20 years earning 9% compounded semiannually?

    b. What are the total coupon payments over the life of this bond?

   c. What would be the total future dollars from the coupon payments and the repayment of principal at the end of 20 years?

   d. In order for the bond to produce the same total future dollars as in part a, how much must the interest-on-interest be?

   e. Calculate the interest-on-interest from the bond assuming that the semiannual coupon payments can be reinvested at 4.5% every six months and demonstrate that the resulting amount is the same as in part d.

12. **a.** Consider a three-bond portfolio as follows:

Bond	Coupon Rate	Maturity	Par Value	Market Value	Yield to Maturity
A	5%	5 years	$ 2,000,000	$ 1,756,000	8%
B	7%	2 years	$ 5,000,000	$ 5,000,000	7%
C	3%	1 years	$12,000,000	$11,655,600	6%
			Total market value $18,412,200		

   Calculate the weighted-average yield of the portfolio.

   b. Do you think that the weighted-average yield of the portfolio is a meaningful measure of the potential return of a portfolio?

   c. Demonstrate that the cash flows of the portfolio are as shown below. To simplify, assume that the coupon payment date is the same for each bond.

Period Cash Flow Received	Portfolio
1	$ 405,000
2	12,405,000
3	225,000
4	5,225,000
5	50,000
6	50,000
7	50,000
8	50,000
9	50,000
10	2,050,000

   d. Show that the internal rate of return for this portfolio is 6.88% on a bond-equivalent basis.

   e. What are the drawbacks of the internal return measure?

13. What is the total return for a 20-year zero-coupon bond selling to offer a yield to maturity of 8%?

14. Explain why the total return from holding a bond to maturity will fall between the yield to maturity and reinvestment rates.

15. For a long-term, high-coupon bond, do you think that the total return from holding a bond to ma-

turity will be closer to the yield to maturity or to the reinvestment rate?

16. Suppose that an investor with a five-year investment horizon is considering purchasing a seven-year, 9% coupon bond selling at par. The investor expects that the coupon payments can be reinvested at an annual interest rate of 9.4% and that at the end of the investment horizon two-year bonds will be selling to offer a yield to maturity of 11.2%. What is the total return for this bond?

CHAPTER 21
BOND PRICE VOLATILITY

LEARNING OBJECTIVES
After reading this chapter you will be able to:

- explain the factors that affect the price volatility of a bond when yields change.

- describe the price volatility properties of an option-free bond.

- calculate the price value of a basis point.

- calculate and explain what is meant by Macaulay duration, modified duration, and dollar duration.

- explain why duration is a measure of the price sensitivity of a bond to yield changes.

- discuss the limitations of using duration as a measure of price volatility.

- explain how price change estimated by duration can be adjusted for the bond's convexity.

As we explained in the previous chapter, a fundamental property of a bond is that its price will change in the opposite direction from the change in the required yield for the bond. This property follows from the fact that the price of a bond is equal to the present value of its expected cash flows. While all bonds change in price when the required yield changes, they do not change by the same percentage. For example, when the required yield increases by 100 basis points for two bonds, the price of one might fall by 15%, while that of the other might fall by only 1%. To effectively implement bond portfolio strategies, it is necessary to understand why bonds react differently to yield changes. In addition, it is necessary to quantify how a bond's price might react to yield changes. Ideally, a portfolio manager would like a measure that indicates the relationship between changes in required yields and changes in a bond's price. That is, a manager would want to know how a bond's price is expected to change if yields change by, say, 100 basis points.

In this chapter, we discuss the characteristics of a bond's price that affect its price volatility. We present two measures that are used to quantify a bond's price volatility. One of these measures, duration, is a measure of the approximate percentage change in a bond's price if yield changes by 100 basis points. Duration, however, provides only an approximation of how the price will change. Duration can be supplemented with another measure that we will discuss, convexity. Together duration and convexity do an effective job of estimating how a bond's price will change when yields change. In later chapters, we will use these two measures in bond portfolio management strategies and demonstrate the limitations of the measures.

PRICE VOLATILITY PROPERTIES OF OPTION-FREE BONDS

The inverse relationship between bond price and yield for an option-free bond is illustrated in Table 21-1 for six hypothetical bonds. The bond prices are shown assuming a par value of $100. When the price/yield relationship for any option-free bond is graphed, it exhibits the convex shape shown in Figure 20-1 of Chapter 20 (page 403). The price/yield relationship is for a given point in time. We know from the properties of a bond described in the previous chapter that over time the price of a bond changes as its maturity changes.

Table 21-2 shows for the six hypothetical bonds in Table 21-1 the percentage change in the bond's price for various changes in the required yield, assuming that the initial yield for all six bonds is 9%. For example, consider the 9%, 25-year bond. If the bond is selling to yield 9%, its price would be 100 (see Table 21-1). If the required yield declines to 8%, the price of that bond would be 110.741 (see Table 21-1). Thus, a decline in yield from 9% to 8% would increase the price by 10.74% [(110.741 − 100)/100]. This is the value shown in Table 21-2.

An examination of Table 21-2 reveals several properties concerning the price volatility of an option-free bond.

Property 1. For very small changes in the required yield, the percentage price change for a given bond is roughly the same, whether the required yield increases or decreases.

Property 2. For large changes in the required yield, the percentage price change is not the same for an increase in the required yield as it is for a decrease in the required yield.

Property 3. For a large change in basis points, the percentage price increase is greater than the percentage price decrease. The implication of this property is that if an investor owns a bond, the price appreciation that will be realized if the required yield decreases is greater than the capital loss that will be realized if the required yield rises by the same number of basis points.

An explanation for these three properties of bond price volatility lies in the convex shape of the price/yield relationship. We will investigate this in more detail later in the chapter.

FACTORS THAT AFFECT A BOND'S PRICE VOLATILITY

Two features of an option-free bond determine its price volatility: coupon and term to maturity. In addition, the yield level at which a bond trades affects its price volatility. This is demonstrated below.

TABLE 21-1
PRICE/YIELD RELATIONSHIP FOR SIX HYPOTHETICAL OPTION-FREE BONDS

| Required Yield | *Price at Required Yield* | | | | | |
| | *Coupon/Maturity in Years* | | | | | |
	9%/5	9%/25	6%/5	6%/25	0%/5	0%/25
6.00%	112.7953	138.5946	100.0000	100.0000	74.4094	22.8107
7.00	108.3166	123.4556	95.8417	88.2722	70.8919	17.9053
8.00	104.0554	110.7410	91.8891	78.5178	67.5564	14.0713
8.50	102.0027	105.1482	89.9864	74.2587	65.9537	12.4795
8.90	100.3966	100.9961	88.4983	71.1105	64.7017	11.3391
8.99	100.0395	100.0988	88.1676	70.4318	64.4236	11.0975
9.00	100.0000	100.0000	88.1309	70.3570	64.3928	11.0170
9.01	99.9604	99.9013	88.0943	70.2824	64.3620	11.0445
9.10	99.6053	99.0199	87.7654	69.6164	64.0855	10.8093
9.50	98.0459	95.2339	86.3214	66.7773	62.8723	9.8242
10.00	96.1391	90.8720	84.5565	63.4881	61.3913	8.7204
11.00	92.4624	83.0685	81.1559	57.6712	58.5431	6.8767
12.00	88.9599	76.3572	77.9197	52.7144	55.8395	5.4288

TABLE 21-2
INSTANTANEOUS PERCENTAGE PRICE CHANGE FOR SIX HYPOTHETICAL BONDS

Six Hypothetical Bonds, Priced Initially to Yield 9%

9% coupon,	5 years to maturity,	Price = 100.0000
9% coupon,	25 years to maturity,	Price = 100.0000
6% coupon,	5 years to maturity,	Price = 88.1309
6% coupon,	25 years to maturity,	Price = 70.3570
0% coupon,	5 years to maturity,	Price = 64.3928
0% coupon,	25 years to maturity,	Price = 11.0710

| Required Yield Changes to | Change in Basis Points | *Percentage Price Change, Coupon/Maturity in Years* | | | | | |
		9%/5	9%/25	6%/5	6%/25	0%/5	0%/25
6.00%	−300	12.80%	38.59%	13.47%	42.13%	15.56%	106.04%
7.00	−200	8.32	23.46	8.75	25.46	10.09	61.73
8.00	−100	4.06	10.74	4.26	11.60	4.91	27.10
8.50	−50	2.00	5.15	2.11	5.55	2.42	12.72
8.90	−10	0.40	1.00	0.42	1.07	0.48	2.42
8.99	−1	0.04	0.10	0.04	0.11	0.05	0.24
9.01	1	−0.04	−0.10	−0.04	−0.11	−0.05	−0.24
9.10	10	−0.39	−0.98	−0.41	−1.05	−0.48	−2.36
9.50	50	−1.95	−4.75	−2.05	−5.09	−2.36	−11.26
10.00	100	−3.86	−9.13	−4.06	−9.76	−4.66	−21.23
11.00	200	−7.54	−16.93	−7.91	−18.03	−9.08	−37.89
12.00	300	−11.04	−23.64	−11.59	−25.08	−13.28	−50.96

The Effect of the Coupon Rate

Consider the three 25-year bonds in Table 21-2. For a given change in yield, the zero-coupon bond has the largest price volatility, and the largest coupon bond (the 9% coupon bond) has the smallest price volatility. This is also true for the three 5-year bonds. *In general, for a given term to maturity and initial yield, the lower the coupon rate, the greater the price volatility of a bond.*

The Effect of Maturity

Consider the two 9% coupon bonds in Table 21-2. For a given change in yield, the 25-year bond has the largest price volatility, and the shortest-maturity bond (the 5-year bond) has the smallest price volatility. This is also true for the two 6% coupon bonds and the two zero-coupon bonds in Table 21-2. *In general, for a given coupon rate and initial yield, the longer the maturity, the greater the price volatility of a bond.*

Effects of Yield to Maturity on Price Volatility

The price volatility of a bond is also affected by the level of interest rates in the economy. Specifically, the higher the level of yields, the lower the price volatility. To illustrate this, let's compare the 9%, 25-year bond trading at two yield levels: 7% and 13%. If the yield increases from 7% to 8%, the bond's price declines by 10.3%; but if the yield increases from 13% to 14%, the bond's price declines by 6.75%.

This is also demonstrated in Figure 21-1. The figure shows the price change at two different yield levels. Notice at the lower yield level the price changes are significant when the yield changes. At the higher yield level the price changes are much less for the same change in yield. This means that for a given change in yields, price volatility is greater when yield levels in the market are low, and price volatility is lower when yield levels are high.

FIGURE 21-1

Comparison of price change at a low- and high-yield level.

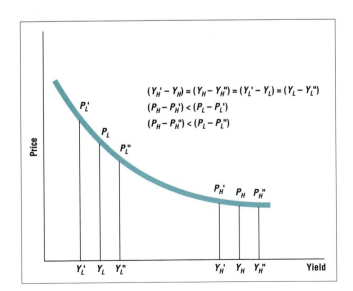

$$(Y_H' - Y_H) = (Y_H - Y_H'') = (Y_L' - Y_L) = (Y_L - Y_L'')$$
$$(P_H - P_H') < (P_L - P_L')$$
$$(P_H - P_H'') < (P_L - P_L'')$$

MEASURES OF PRICE VOLATILITY

We now know that the coupon rate, maturity, and yield level at which a bond trades all affect its price volatility. To control the price volatility of a bond portfolio, it is essential to have a measure that quantifies a bond's potential price volatility. The most popular measures used are the price value of a basis point and duration.

Price Value of a Basis Point

The **price value of a basis point (PVBP)**, also referred to as the **dollar value of an 01**, measures the change in the price of the bond if the required yield changes by one basis point. Note that this measure of price volatility indicates dollar price volatility as opposed to percentage price volatility (price change as a percentage of the initial price). Typically, the price value of a basis point is expressed as the absolute value of the change in price. Owing to property 1 of the price/yield relationship, price volatility is the same for an increase or a decrease of one basis point in required yield.

We can illustrate how to calculate the price value of a basis point by using the six bonds in Table 21-1. For each bond, the initial price, the price after increasing the yield by one basis point (from 9% to 9.01%), and the price value of a basis point (the difference between the two prices) are shown in Table 21-3.

Because this measure of price volatility is in terms of dollar price change, dividing the price value of a basis point by the initial price gives the percentage price change for a one-basis-point change in yield. We will see how to use this measure in Chapter 26 when we demonstrate how to hedge a position in a bond.

Duration

The second measure of price volatility is duration. This measure is derived using calculus. The basic principle is based on a well-known principle in calculus: The change in the value of a mathematical function can be estimated by taking the first derivative of that mathematical function. Turning

TABLE 21-3			
PRICE VALUE OF A BASIS POINT			
Bond	**Initial Price (9% Yield)**	**Price at 9.01%**	**Price Value of a Basis Point***
5 years, 9% coupon	100.0000	99.9604	0.0396
25 years, 9% coupon	100.0000	99.9013	0.0987
5 years, 6% coupon	88.1309	88.0945	0.0364
25 years, 6% coupon	70.3570	70.2824	0.0746
5 years, zero coupon	64.3928	64.3620	0.0308
25 years, zero coupon	11.0710	11.0445	0.0265

*Absolute value per $100 of par value.

to the bond price, Equation (20-1) of Chapter 20 indicates that the price of a bond can be expressed as a mathematical function of the required yield. The equation is repeated below:

$$P = \sum_{t=1}^{n} \frac{C}{(1+r)^t} + \frac{M}{(1+r)^n} \tag{21-1}$$

where P = price (in $)
       n = number of periods (number of years × 2)
       C = *semiannual* coupon payment (in $)
       r = periodic interest rate (required annual yield ÷ 2)
       M = maturity value
       t = time period when the payment is to be received

Thus, if we seek to estimate how the bond's price changes if the required yield changes, the first derivative of Equation (21.1) should be calculated. The approximation of the price change would be good for small changes in yield. Dividing by the initial price gives the approximate percentage price change.

If the first derivative of Equation (21-1) is calculated and then divided by the initial price, the following equation would result:

Approximate percentage price change

$$= -\frac{1}{(1+y)}\left[\frac{1C}{(1+y)^1} + \frac{2C}{(1+y)^2} + \cdots + \frac{nC}{(1+y)^n} + \frac{nM}{(1+y)^n}\right]\frac{1}{P} \tag{21-2}$$

The term in brackets is the weighted-average term to maturity of the cash flows from the bond, where the weights are the present value of the cash flow divided by the price (or here multiplied by the reciprocal of the price). It is commonly referred to as **Macaulay duration.**[1] That is,

$$\text{Macaulay duration} = \left[\frac{1C}{(1+y)^1} + \frac{2C}{(1+y)^2} + \cdots + \frac{nC}{(1+y)^n} + \frac{nM}{(1+y)^n}\right]\frac{1}{P}$$

Investors commonly refer to the ratio of Macaulay duration to $(1 + y)$ as **modified duration**; that is,

$$\text{Modified duration} = \frac{\text{Macaulay duration}}{(1+y)}$$

Substituting modified duration into Equation (21-2) gives

Approximate percentage price change = − modified duration   (21-3)

Equation (21-3) states that modified duration is related to the approximate percentage change in price for a given change in yield. This is what we stated in earlier chapters. Because for all option-free bonds modified duration is positive, Equation (21-3) states that there is an inverse relationship between modified duration and the approximate percentage change in price for

[1]In 1938, Frederick Macaulay coined this term and used this measure rather than maturity as a proxy for the average length of time that a bond investment is outstanding. See Frederick Macaulay, *Some Theoretical Problems Suggested by the Movement of Interest Rates, Bond Yields, and Stock Prices in the U.S. Since 1856* (New York: National Bureau of Economic Research, 1938).

TABLE 21-4

CALCULATION OF MACAULAY DURATION AND MODIFIED DURATION FOR A 6%, 5-YEAR BOND SELLING TO YIELD 9%*

Coupon rate = *6%*   *Term (years)* = *5*   *Initial yield* = *9%*   *Price* = *88.1309*

Period(*t*)	Cash Flow[†]	PV of $1 at 0.045[‡]	PV of CF	*t* × PVCF
1	$3.00	0.956938	2.870814	2.87081
2	3.00	0.915729	2.747190	5.49437
3	3.00	0.876296	2.628890	7.88666
4	3.00	0.838561	2.515684	10.06273
5	3.00	0.802451	2.407353	12.03676
6	3.00	0.767895	2.303687	13.82212
7	3.00	0.734828	2.204485	15.43139
8	3.00	0.703185	2.109555	16.87644
9	3.00	0.672904	2.018713	18.16841
10	103.00	0.643927	66.324551	663.24551
Total			88.130922	765.89522

$$\text{Macaulay duration (in half years)} = \frac{765.89522}{88.130928} = 8.69$$

$$\text{Macaulay duration (in years)} = \frac{8.69}{2} = 4.35$$

$$\text{Modified duration (in years)} = \frac{4.35}{1.0450} = 4.16$$

*PV = present value. CF = cash flow

†Cash flow per $100 of par value.

‡4.5% is one-half the bond's yield to maturity

a given yield change. This is to be expected from the fundamental principle that bond prices move in the opposite direction of interest rates.

Table 21-4 shows the computation of the Macaulay duration and modified duration for a 6%, five-year bond selling to yield 9%. The durations are shown for half years because the cash flows of the bond occur every six months. To adjust the durations to an annual figure, the durations must be divided by 2, as shown at the bottom of Table 21-4. In general, if the cash flows occur m times per year, the durations are adjusted by dividing by m. Macaulay duration and modified duration in years for the six hypothetical bonds are shown in Table 21-5.

Properties of Duration   As can be seen from the durations computed for the six hypothetical bonds, the modified duration and Macaulay duration of a coupon bond are less than the maturity. It should be obvious from the formula that the Macaulay duration of a zero-coupon bond is equal to its maturity; a zero-coupon bond's modified duration, however, is less than its maturity. Also, the lower the coupon, generally the greater the modified and Macaulay duration of the bond.[2]

---

[2]This property does not hold for long-maturity deep-discount bonds.

TABLE 21-5		
DURATIONS FOR SIX HYPOTHETICAL BONDS		
Bond	**Macaulay Duration (in Years)**	**Modified Duration (in Years)**
9%/5 years	4.13	3.96
9%/25 years	10.33	9.88
6%/ 5 years	4.35	4.16
6%/25 years	11.10	10.62
0%/ 5 years	5.00	4.78
0%/25 years	25.00	23.92

There is a consistency between the properties of bond price volatility we discussed earlier and the properties of modified duration. We showed earlier that when all other factors are constant, the longer the maturity, the greater the price volatility. A property of modified duration is that when all other factors are constant, the longer the maturity, the greater the modified duration. We also showed that the lower the coupon rate, all other factors being constant, the greater the bond price volatility. As we have just seen, generally the lower the coupon rate, the greater the modified duration. Thus, the greater the modified duration, the greater the price volatility. (See Box 21.)

Finally, as we noted earlier, another factor that will influence the price volatility is the yield to maturity. All other factors being constant, the higher the yield level, the lower the price volatility. The same property holds for modified duration. For example, the modified duration of a 25-year, 9% coupon bond trading at a yield of 7% is 11.21, but at a yield of 14% it is 7.66.

Approximating the Percentage Price Change   If we multiply equation (21-3) by the change in the required yield, we have the following relationship:

Approximate percentage price change
= −modified duration × yield change (in decimal)   (21-4)

Equation (21-4) can be used to approximate the percentage price change for a given change in required yield. To illustrate the relationship, consider the 6%, 25-year bond selling at 70.3570 to yield 9% shown in Table 21-1. The modified duration for this bond is 10.62. If yields increase instantaneously from 9% to 9.10%, a yield change of +0.0010 (10 basis points), the approximate percentage change in price using Equation (21-4) is

$$-10.62 \, (+0.0010) = -0.0106 = -1.06\%$$

Notice from Table 21-2 that the actual percentage change in price is −1.05%. Similarly, if yields decrease instantaneously from 9% to 8.90% (a 10-basis-point decrease), the approximate percentage change in price using Equation (21-4) would be +1.06%. According to Table 20-2, the actual percentage price change would be +1.07%. This example illustrates that for small changes in the required yield, modified duration gives a good approximation of the percentage change in price.

<table>
<tr><td colspan="3" align="center">BOX 21</td></tr>
<tr><td colspan="3" align="center">DENVER INVESTMENT TO MAKE $800 MILLION TREASURY MOVE</td></tr>
</table>

Denver Investment Advisors will swap $800 million of long zero-coupon Treasuries for intermediate Treasuries when long bond yields hit bottom at 7.40-7 1/2% before the end of the first quarter, said John Cormey, portfolio manager. The move would shorten the duration of its $2.5 billion fixed-income	portfolio from 5 1/2-5.6 years to neutral to its indexes, such as the Lehman Brothers Government/Corporate Bond Index, at 5.17 years last week, Cormey said. *Source:* "Denver Investment to Make $800 Million Treasury Move," *BondWeek* (Dec. 9, 1991), p. 1	**Question for Box 21** **1.** Why would the swap of long-term zero-coupon Treasuries for intermediate Treasuries shorten the duration?

Instead of a small change in required yield, let's assume that yields increase by 200 basis points, from 9% to 11% (a yield change of +0.02). The approximate percentage change in price using Equation (21-4) is

$$-10.62\,(+0.02) = -0.2124 = -21.24\%$$

As can be seen from Table 20-2, the actual percentage change in price is only −18.03%. Moreover, if the required yield decreased by 200 basis points, from 9% to 7%, the approximate percentage change in price based on duration would be +21.24, compared with an actual percentage change in price of +25.46%. Modified duration provides not only a flawed approximation but also a symmetric percentage price change, which, as we pointed out earlier in this chapter, is not a property of the price/yield relationship for bonds when there are large changes in yield.

We can use Equation (21-4) to provide an interpretation of modified duration. Suppose that the yield on any bond changes by 100 basis points. Then, substituting 100 basis points (0.01) into Equation (21-4) and ignoring the minus sign, the following is obtained:

Modified duration × (0.01) = modified duration %

Thus, *modified duration can be interpreted as the approximate percentage change in price for a 100-basis-point change in yield.* For example, a bond with a modified duration of 6 means that its price will change by approximately 6% for a 100-basis-point change in yield. A bond with a modified duration of 8 means that its price will change by approximately 8% for a 100-basis-point change in yield and 4% for a 50-basis-point change in yield.

Approximating the Dollar Price Change   Modified duration is a proxy for the percentage change in price. Investors also like to know the dollar price volatility of a bond. The dollar price change for a given change in yield can be approximated as follows:

Approximate dollar price change

= −modified duration × initial price × yield change (in decimal)   (21-5)

The product of modified duration and the initial price is called **dollar duration**. That is,

Dollar duration = modified duration × initial price   (21-6)

For small changes in the required yield, Equation (21-6) does a good job in estimating the change in price. For example, consider the 6%, 25-year bond selling at 70.3570 to yield 9% with a modified duration of 10.62. For a 1-basis-point (0.0001) increase in the required yield, the estimated price change per $100 of face value is

$$-(10.62)(70.3570)(0.0001) = -\$0.0747$$

From Table 21-1, we see that the actual price is 70.2824. The actual price change would therefore be 0.0746 (70.284 − 70.3570). Notice that the dollar duration for a one-basis-point change is the same as the price value of a basis point.

Now let's see what happens when there is a large change in the required yield for the same bond. If the required yield increases from 9% to 11% (or 200 basis points), the approximate dollar price change per $100 par value is

$$-(10.62)(70.3570)(0.02) = -\$14.94$$

From Table 21-1, we see that if the required yield is 11% the actual price for this bond is 57.6712. Thus the actual price decline is 12.6858 (57.6712 − 70.3570). The estimated dollar price change is more than the actual price change. The reverse is true for a decrease in the required yield. This result is consistent with what we illustrated earlier. When there are large movements in the required yield, neither dollar duration nor modified duration is adequate to approximate the price reaction. Duration will overestimate the price change when the required yield rises, thereby underestimating the new price. When the required yield falls, duration will underestimate the price change and thereby underestimate the new price.

Concerns with Using Duration   Care must be exercised in using duration as a measure of the price sensitivity of a bond to changes in interest rates. First, as we demonstrate, duration is only an approximation of price sensitivity and does not do a good job for large changes in yield. Second, in the derivation of the relationship between modified duration and bond price volatility, we start with the price equation (21-1). This price equation assumes that all cash flows for the bond are discounted at the same discount rate. The appropriateness of this assumption is examined in the next chapter, where we analyze the yield curve. Essentially, the duration assumes that the yield curve is flat and all shifts are parallel. In Chapter 24, we show the limitations of applying duration to a bond portfolio when this assumption does not hold, and the yield curve does not shift in a parallel fashion.

Our final concern is misapplication of duration to bonds with embedded options. The principles we have illustrated apply only to option-free bonds. When changes in yields result in a change in the expected cash flows for a bond, which is the case for bonds with embedded options, the duration measure is appropriate only in certain circumstances. We discuss the price volatility of bonds with embedded options in Chapter 23.

Convexity

Duration is only a first approximation of the percentage change in the price of a bond. The duration measure can be supplemented with an additional measure to capture the curvature or convexity of a bond. Here we tie

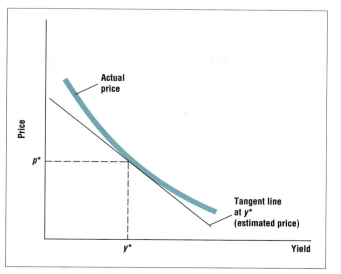

FIGURE 21-2

Line tangent to the price/yield relationship.

together the convex price/yield relationship for a bond and several of the properties of bond price volatility discussed earlier.

In Figure 21-2, a tangent line is drawn to the price/yield relationship at yield y^*. The tangent shows the rate of change of price with respect to a change in interest rates at that point (yield level). The slope of the tangent line is closely related to dollar duration. Consequently, for a given starting price, the tangent (which tells the rate of absolute price changes) is closely related to the duration of the bond (which tells about the rate of percentage price changes). The steeper the tangent line, the greater the duration; the flatter the tangent line, the lower the duration. Thus, for a given starting price, the tangent line and the duration can be used interchangeably and can be thought of as one and the same method of estimating the rate of price change.

Notice what happens to duration (steepness of the tangent line) as yield changes: As yield increases (decreases), duration decreases (increases). This property holds for all option-free bonds, as we noted earlier.

If we draw a vertical line from any yield (on the horizontal axis), as in Figure 21-3, the distance between the horizontal axis and the tangent line represents the price approximated by using duration starting with the initial yield y^*. The approximation will always understate the actual price. This agrees with what we demonstrated earlier about the relationship between duration (and the tangent line) and the approximate price change. For small changes in yield (points y_2 and y_3 in Figure 21-3), the tangent line and duration do a good job in estimating the actual price. However, the farther away from the initial yield y^* (points y_1 and y_4 in Figure 21-3), the worse the approximation. It should be apparent that the accuracy of the approximation depends on the convexity of the price/yield relationship for the bond.

Adjusting Duration for Convexity   Duration (modified or dollar) attempts to estimate a convex relationship with a straight line (the tangent line). It can be

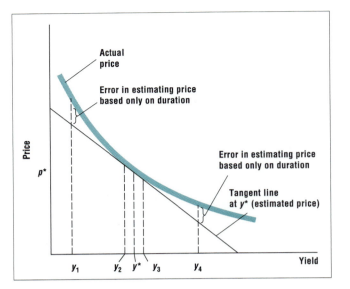

FIGURE 21-3

Price approximation using duration.

shown that an adjustment to the percentage change estimated using duration is equal to

Convexity adjustment = 0.5 (convexity) (yield change in basis points)^2 (21-7)

$$\text{Convexity} = \frac{\dfrac{1(2)C}{(1 + y)^1} + \dfrac{2(3)C}{(1 + y)^2} + \ldots + \dfrac{n(n + 1)C}{(1 + y)^n} + \dfrac{n(n + 1)M}{(1 + y)^n}}{(1 + y)^2 P}$$ (21-8)

Table 21-6 shows the calculation of convexity for the 6%, five-year bond selling to yield 9%. The convexity is in terms of periods per year squared. To annualize the convexity, the convexity calculated from Equation (21-8) is divided by 4, the square of the number of periods (2^2).

To illustrate the adjustment, consider the 6%, 25-year bond selling to yield 9%. The modified duration for this bond is 10.62, and the convexity is 182.92. If the required yield increases by 200 basis points, from 9% to 11%, the approximate percentage change in the price of the bond is

    Percentage change in price due to duration from Equation (21-2)
    = −modified duration × yield change (in decimal)
    −(10.62) (0.02) = −0.2124 = −21.24%

Convexity adjustment from Equation (21-7) is

    0.5 (182.92) (−0.02)^2 = 0.0366 = 3.66%

The estimated percentage price change due to duration after adjusting for convexity is

    −21.24% + 3.66% = −17.58%

From Table 21-2 we see that the actual change is −18.03%. Using duration and convexity measures together gives a better approximation of the actual price change for a large movement in the required yield. Suppose, instead, that the required yield *decreases* by 200 basis points. Then the approximate percentage change in the price of the bond using duration would be 21.24%.

TABLE 21-6

CALCULATION OF CONVEXITY FOR A 6%, 5-YEAR BOND SELLING TO YIELD 9%*

Coupon rate = 6%

Initial yield = 9%

Term (years) = 5

Price = 88.1309

Period(t)	Cash Flow†	PV of $1 at 0.045	PV of CF	$t(t + 1)$ PVCF
1	$ 3.00	0.956938	2.870814	5.7416
2	3.00	0.915729	2.747190	16.4831
3	3.00	0.876296	2.628890	31.5467
4	3.00	0.838561	2.515684	50.3137
5	3.00	0.802451	2.407353	72.2206
6	3.00	0.767895	2.303687	96.7549
7	3.00	0.734828	2.204485	123.4512
8	3.00	0.703185	2.109555	151.8880
9	3.00	0.672904	2.018713	181.6842
10	103.00	0.643927	66.324551	7,295.7006
Total			88.130922	8,025.7850

$$\text{Convexity (half years)} = \frac{8,025.7850}{(1.045)^2(88.130923)} = 83.39245$$

$$\text{Convexity (years)} = \frac{83.39245}{4} = 20.8481$$

*PV = present value. CF = cash flow.

†Cash flow per $100 of par value.

The convexity adjustment would be 3.66%. Therefore, the estimated percentage price change would be 24.9% (21.24% + 3.66%). From Table 21-2 we see that the actual change is +25.46%. Once again, using both duration and convexity provides a good approximation of the actual price change for a large movement in the required yield.

Positive Convexity   All option-free bonds have the following convexity property: As the required yield increases (decreases), the convexity of a bond decreases (increases). This property is referred to as **positive convexity**. An implication of positive convexity is that the duration of an option-free bond moves in the expected direction as market yields change. That is, if market yields rise, the price of a bond will fall. The price decline is slowed down by a decline in the duration of the bond as market yields rise. In contrast, should market yields fall, duration increases so that percentage price change accelerates. With an option-free bond, both these changes in duration occur.

This is portrayed graphically in Figure 21-4. The slope of the tangent line in the figure gets flatter as the required yield increases. A flatter tangent line means a smaller duration as the required yield rises. In contrast, the tangent line gets steeper as the required yield decreases, implying that the duration gets larger. This property will hold for all option-free bonds. Also, from this graphical presentation we can see that the convexity is actually measuring the rate of change of the dollar duration as market yields change.

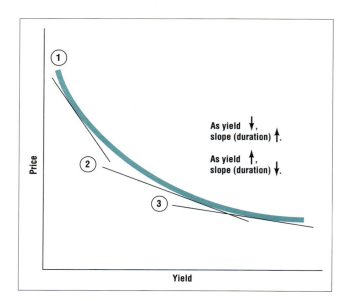

FIGURE 21-4

Change in duration as the required yield changes.

The Value of Convexity   Up to this point, we have focused on how taking convexity into account can improve the approximation of a bond's price change for a given yield change. The convexity of a bond, however, has another important investment implication, which is illustrated in Figure 21-5. The figure shows two bonds, A and B. The two bonds have the same duration and are offering the same yield; they have different convexities, however. Bond B is more convex (bowed) than bond A.

What is the implication of the greater convexity for B? Whether the market yield rises or falls, B will have a higher price. That is, if the required yield

FIGURE 21-5

Comparison of convexity of two bonds.

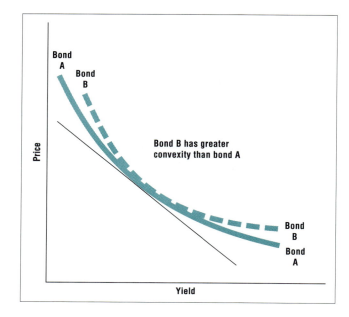

rises, the capital loss on bond B will be less than it will be on bond A. A fall in the required yield will generate greater price appreciation for B than for A.

Generally, the market will take the greater convexity of B compared with A into account in pricing the two bonds. That is, the market will price convexity. Consequently, while there may be times when a situation such as that depicted in Figure 21-5 will exist, generally the market will require investors to "pay up" (accept a lower yield) for the greater convexity offered by bond B.

The question is, how much should the market want investors to pay up for convexity? Look again at Figure 21-5. Notice that if investors expect that market yields will change by very little—that is, they expect low interest rate volatility—the advantage of owning bond B over bond A is insignificant because both bonds will offer approximately the same price for small changes in yields. In this case, investors should not be willing to pay much for convexity. In fact, if the market is pricing convexity high, which means that A will be offering a higher yield than B, investors with expectations of low interest rate volatility would probably be willing to "sell convexity"—that is, to sell B if they own it and buy A. In contrast, if investors expect substantial interest rate volatility, bond B would probably sell at a much lower yield than A.

■ SUMMARY

The price/yield relationship for all option-free bonds is convex. There are three properties of the price volatility of an option-free bond: (1) For small changes in yield, the percentage price change is symmetric; (2) for large changes in yield, the percentage price change is asymmetric; and (3) for large changes in yield, the price appreciation is greater than the price depreciation for a given change in yield.

The price volatility of an option-free bond is affected by two characteristics of a bond—maturity and coupon—and the yield level at which a bond trades. For a given maturity and yield, the lower the coupon rate, the greater the price volatility. For a given coupon rate and yield, the lower the coupon rate, the greater the price volatility. For a given coupon rate and maturity, the price volatility is greater the lower yield.

There are two measures of bond price volatility: price value of a basis point and duration. We focused on the various duration measures—Macaulay duration, modified duration, and dollar duration—showing the relationship between bond price volatility and each of these measures. Modified duration is the approximate percentage change in price for a 100-basis-point change in yield. The dollar duration is the approximate dollar price change.

Duration does a good job of estimating a bond's percentage price change for a small change in yield. However, it does not do as good a job for a large change in yield. The percentage price change due to convexity can be used to supplement the approximate price change using duration. Together, the duration and convexity measures provide an excellent approximation of the price change when yields change.

■ KEY TERMS

dollar duration
dollar value of an 01

Macaulay duration
modified duration

positive convexity
price value of a basis point (PVBP)

■ QUESTIONS

1. The price value of a basis point will be the same whether the yield is increased or decreased by one basis point. The yield value of 100 basis points (i.e., the change in price for a 100-basis-point change in interest rates), however, will not be the same if the yield is increased or decreased by 100 basis points. Why?

2. Calculate the requested measures for bonds A and B (assume each bond pays interest semiannually):

	Bond A	Bond B
Coupon	8%	9%
Yield to maturity	8%	8%
Maturity (in years)	2	5
Par	100.00	100.00
Price	100.000	104.055

   a. Price value of a basis point
   b. Macaulay duration
   c. Modified duration
   d. Convexity

3. For bonds A and B in question 2:
   a. Calculate the actual price of the bonds for a 100-basis-point increase in interest rates.
   b. Using duration, estimate the price of the bonds for a 100-basis-point increase in interest rates.
   c. Using duration and the adjustment for convexity, estimate the price of the bonds for a 100-basis point increase in interest rates.
   d. Comment on the accuracy of your results in parts b and c, and state why one approximation is closer to the actual price than the other.
   e. Without working through calculations, indicate whether the duration of the two bonds would be higher or lower if the yield to maturity is 10% rather than 8%.

4. From the information below, can you tell which of the following three bonds will have the greatest price volatility, assuming each is trading to offer the same yield to maturity?

Bond	Coupon Rate	Maturity
X	8%	9 years
Y	10	11 years
Z	11	12 years

5. State why you would agree or disagree with the following statement: "As the duration of a zero-coupon bond is equal to its maturity, the responsiveness of a zero-coupon bond to yield changes is the same regardless of the level of interest rates."

6. State why you would agree or disagree with the following statement: "When interest rates are low, there will be little difference between the Macaulay duration and modified duration measures."

7. State why you would agree or disagree with the following statement: "If two bonds have the same dollar duration, yield, and price, their dollar price sensitivity will be the same for a given change in interest rates."

8. State why you would agree or disagree with the following statement: "For a one-basis-point change in yield, the price value of a basis-point is equal to the dollar duration."

9. The November 26, 1990, issue of *BondWeek* includes an article entitled "Van Kampen Merritt Shortens." The article begins as follows: "Peter Hegel, first v.p. at Van Kampen Merritt Investment Advisory, is shortening his $3 billion portfolio from 110% of his normal duration of 6 1/2 years to 103–105% because he thinks that in the short run the bond rally is near an end." Explain Hegel's strategy and his use of the duration measure in this context.

10. Consider two Treasury securities:

Bond	Price	Modified Duration
A	100	6
B	80	7

Which bond will have the greater dollar price volatility for a 25-basis-point change in interest rates?

11. What are the limitations of using duration as a measure of a bond's price sensitivity to interest rate changes?

CHAPTER 22
FACTORS AFFECTING BOND YIELDS

LEARNING OBJECTIVES
After reading this chapter you should be able to:

- explain why the yield on a Treasury security is the base interest rate.

- enumerate the factors that affect the yield spread between two bonds.

- describe what a yield curve is.

- explain what a spot rate and a spot rate curve mean.

- calculate the theoretical spot rates from the Treasury yield curve.

- explain what the term structure of interest rates is.

- explain why the price of a Treasury bond should be based on spot rates.

- explain what is meant by a forward rate and be able to calculate a forward rate.

- describe how long-term rates are related to the current short-term rate and short-term forward rates.

- explain the different theories about the determinants of the shape of the term structure: pure expectations theory, the liquidity theory, the preferred habitat theory, and the market segmentation theory.

In Chapter 19, we described a variety of bonds. There is not just one yield offered on all bonds. For example, the yield offered on bonds issued by General Motors that mature in 10 years will not be the same as the yield offered on U.S. Treasury securities that mature in 30 years. The yield offered on a particular bond depends on a myriad of factors having to do with the type of issuer, the characteristics of the bond issue, and the state of the economy.

In this chapter we will look at the factors that affect the yield offered in the bond market. We begin with the minimum interest rate that an investor wants from investing in a bond, the yield on U.S. Treasury securities. Then we describe why the yield on a non-U.S. Treasury security will differ from that of a U.S. Treasury security. Finally, we focus on one particular factor that affects the yield offered on a security: maturity. The pattern of interest rates on securities of the same issuer but with different maturities is called the *term structure of interest rates*. The importance of analyzing the term structure of interest rates for U.S. Treasury securities will be explained.

TABLE 22-1	
YIELDS FOR ON-THE-RUN TREASURIES ON AUGUST 27, 1992	
Maturity	**Yield**
3 months	3.22%
6 months	3.33
1 year	3.47
2 years	4.22
3 years	4.74
5 years	5.65
7 years	6.18
10 years	6.63
20 years	7.02
30 years	7.42

Source: Weekly Market Update, Goldman Sachs & Co., Fixed Income Research (Aug. 28, 1992), p. A-1.

THE BASE INTEREST RATE

The securities issued by the United States Department of the Treasury are backed by the full faith and credit of the United States government. Consequently, market participants throughout the world view them as having no credit risk. As such, interest rates on Treasury securities are the key interest rates in the U.S. economy, as well as in international capital markets. The large size of any single issue has contributed to making the Treasury market the most active and hence the most liquid market in the world.

The minimum interest rate that investors want is referred to as the **benchmark interest rate** or **base interest rate** that investors will demand for investing in a non-Treasury security. This rate is the yield to maturity (hereafter referred to as simply *yield*) offered on a comparable-maturity Treasury security that was most recently issued (on the run). So, for example, if an investor wanted to purchase a 10-year bond on August 27, 1992, the minimum yield the investor would seek is 6.63%, the yield on the most recently issued 10-year Treasury (see Table 22-1).

RISK PREMIUM

Market participants talk of interest rates on non-Treasury securities as "trading at a spread" to a particular on-the-run Treasury security. For example, if the yield on a 10-year non-Treasury security is 9% and the yield on a 10-year Treasury security is 8%, the spread is 100 basis points. This spread, called a **risk premium**, reflects the additional risks the investor faces by acquiring a security that is not issued by the U.S. government. Thus we can express the interest rate offered on a non-Treasury security as

base interest rate + spread

or equivalently,

base interest rate + risk premium

The factors that affect the spread include (1) the type of issuer, (2) the issuer's perceived creditworthiness, (3) the term or maturity of the instrument, (4) provisions that grant either the issuer or the investor the option to do something, (5) the taxability of the interest received by investors, and (6) the expected liquidity of the security. (See Box 22.)

Types of Issuers

The bond market is classified by the type of issuer, including the U.S. government, U.S. government agencies, municipal governments, corporations (domestic and foreign), and foreign governments. These classifications are referred to as **market sectors**. Different sectors are generally perceived to represent different risks and rewards. Some market sectors are further subdivided into categories intended to reflect common economic characteristics. For example, within the corporate market sector, issuers are classified as follows: (1) utilities, (2) transportations, (3) industrials, and (4) banks and finance companies. Excluding the Treasury market sector, the other market sectors have a wide range of issuers, each with different abilities to satisfy their con-

---

BOX 22

POPULAR EXPLANATIONS OF SPREAD PATTERNS

The simplest and most naive theory of yield spreads relies upon temporary imbalances between the supply of and demand for a particular class of bond and government bonds. Take A-rated industrial corporate bonds as an example. The supply–demand imbalance theory holds that, as the supply of 'A' industrials increases relative to governments, the relative yield premium demanded by investors increases. Similarly, as the supply of governments increases relative to 'A' industrials, the yield spread narrows.

To believe the supply–demand theory, we must assume that, independent of cash flow uncertainty, bonds are not fungible, investors do not adequately assess risk–reward trade-offs in the short run, or that there is an embedded short-term illiquidity in the market. In an investment world dominated by computers, telecommunications, and tremendous amounts of arbitrage capital, an assumption that investors are slow to respond to profit opportunity seems unbelievable. The illiquidity argument is equally unbelievable, when we observe that the average *daily* volume of trading on government bonds with longer maturities through both dealers and the futures exchange is $30 billion.

The supply–demand theory assumes that Treasury securities and inter-market securities approximate perfect substitutes. They are, in fact, imperfect substitutes because of differences in the certainty of the timing and size of cash flows. The certainty of those cash flows is affected by the differences in liquidity, credit, tax, and optionable attributes of various forms of inter-market bonds in contrast to similar duration Treasury securities. The pricing of these attributes is largely a function of macroeconomic volatility and is independent of a simple fungible microeconomic supply–demand framework. It is the pricing of these variable attributes at given levels of volatility that, in fact, determines the equilibrium level of inter-market yield spreads. The quantification of these attributes along the volatility spectrum creates fungibility among bonds, allowing them to be good substitutes for one another.

The quality spread theory links the changing of inter-market spreads (primarily corporate and municipal bond spreads) with the economic cycle. This is the most often cited explanatory theory. This theory holds that spreads are reduced during economic recoveries and widen during periods of recession. In fact, some point to these changes in spreads as leading indicators of recession or recovery.

The quality spread theory is appealing intuitively. An important determinant in the ability of a company to meet its debt obligations is cash flow generation. There is little doubt that cash flow increases during recoveries and diminishes during recessions. Therefore, the ability to service the debt is enhanced during economic recoveries and diminished during economic recessions. The perceived quality improvement causes spreads to narrow and the perceived credit depreciation causes spreads to widen.

The empirical support for these yield spread relations is also strong. No doubt the stage of the economic cycle influences inter-market spreads. The influence may, however, be more directly linked to the more important general side effects of declining rates accompanying recessions and increasing rates accompanying recoveries. Nevertheless, much of the volatility in spreads remains unexplained.

Source: Chris P. Dialynas, "Bond Yield Spreads Revisited," *Journal of Portfolio Management* (Winter 1988), pp. 57–58.

Questions for Box 22

1. Why are the cash flows of a bond "affected by the differences in liquidity, credit, tax, and optionable attributes of various forms of inter-market bonds in contrast to similar duration Treasury securities"?
2. Why does the pricing of optionable attributes determine the "equilibrium level of inter-market yields spreads"?
3. How does the stage of the economic cycle affect yield spreads?

---

tractual obligations. Therefore, a key feature of a debt obligation is the nature of the issuer.

The spread between the interest rate offered in two sectors of the bond market for bonds with the same maturity is referred to as an **intermarket sector spread**. For instance, the intermarket sector spread between securities issued by government-sponsored enterprises and those issued by domestic corporations would reflect the consensus of risk between those two sectors. The spread between two issues within a market sector is called an **intramarket sector spread**. For example, for the week of August 27, 1992, the yield on 5-

year industrial corporate bonds and 5-year utility corporate bonds with the same credit rating was 5.85% and 5.79%, respectively.[1] Therefore, the intra-market sector spread was 6 basis points.

Perceived Creditworthiness of the Issuer

Default risk or credit risk refers to the risk that the issuer of a bond may be unable to make timely principal or interest payments. Most market participants rely primarily on commercial rating companies to assess the default risk of an issuer. We discussed these rating companies in Chapter 19.

The spread between Treasury securities and non-Treasury securities that are identical in all respects except for quality is referred to as a **quality spread** or **credit spread**. For example, for the week of August 27, 1992, the yield on single-A-rated 10-year industrial bonds was 7.28%, and the corresponding yield for the 10-year on-the-run Treasury was 6.53%.[2] Therefore, the quality spread was 75 basis points.

Inclusion of Options

It is not uncommon for a bond issue to include a provision that gives the bondholder and/or the issuer an option to take some action against the other party. Such embedded options were discussed in Chapter 19.

The most common type of option in a bond issue is the call provision that grants the issuer the right to retire the debt, fully or partially, before the scheduled maturity date. The inclusion of a call feature benefits issuers by allowing them to replace an old bond issue with a lower interest cost issue, should interest rates in the market decline. Effectively, a call provision allows the issuer to alter the maturity of a bond. A call provision is detrimental to the bondholder because the bondholder must reinvest the proceeds received at a lower interest rate.

The presence of an embedded option has an effect on the spread of an issue relative to a Treasury security and the spread relative to otherwise comparable issues that do not have an embedded option. In general, market participants will require a larger spread to a comparable Treasury security for an issue with an embedded option that is favorable to the issuer (e.g., a call option) than for an issue without such an option. In contrast, market participants will require a smaller spread to a comparable Treasury security for an issue with an embedded option that is favorable to the investor (e.g., a put option or conversion option). In fact, for a bond with an option that is favorable to an investor, the interest rate on an issue may be less than that on a comparable Treasury security!

Taxability of Interest

Unless exempted under the federal income tax code, interest income is taxable at the federal level. In addition to federal income taxes, there may be state and local taxes on interest income.

---

[1]These yields were estimated from *Cross-Sector Weekly*, Lehman Brothers, Fixed Income Research (Sept. 8, 1992), p. 2.

[2]*Cross-Sector Weekly*, op. cit., p. 2.

TABLE 22-2		
YIELD ON HIGH-GRADE, TAX-EXEMPT SECURITIES ON AUGUST 27, 1992		
Maturity	Yield	Yield as a Percent of Treasury Yield
1 year	3.05%	87.8%
3 years	4.10	86.5
5 years	4.60	81.4
10 years	5.40	81.4
30 years	6.15	82.9

Source: *Weekly Market Update*, Goldman Sachs & Co., Fixed Income Research (Aug. 28, 1992), p. A-5.

The federal tax code specifically exempts from taxation at the federal level any interest income earned from qualified municipal bond issues. Because of the tax-exempt feature of municipal bonds, the yield on municipal bonds is less than that on Treasuries with the same maturity. Table 22-2 shows this relationship on August 27, 1992, for high-grade, tax-exempt securities. The difference in yield between tax-exempt securities and Treasury securities is typically measured not in basis points but in percentage terms. More specifically, it is measured as the percentage of the yield on a tax-exempt security relative to a comparable Treasury security. This is reported in Table 22-2.

The yield on a taxable bond issue after federal income taxes are paid is called *after-tax yield*.

$$\text{After-tax yield} = \text{pretax yield} \times (1 - \text{marginal tax rate})$$

Of course, the marginal tax rate varies among investors. For example, suppose a taxable bond issue offers a yield of 9% and is acquired by an investor facing a marginal tax rate of 31%. The after-tax yield would then be

$$\text{After-tax yield} = 0.09 \times (1 - 0.31) = 0.0621 = 6.21\%$$

Alternatively, we can determine the yield that must be offered on a taxable bond issue to give the same after-tax yield as a tax-exempt issue. This yield is called the **equivalent taxable yield** and is determined as follows:

$$\text{Equivalent taxable yield} = \frac{\text{tax-exempt yield}}{(1 - \text{marginal tax rate})}$$

For example, consider an investor facing a 31% marginal tax rate who purchases a tax-exempt issue with a yield of 6.21%. The equivalent taxable yield is then

$$\text{Equivalent taxable yield} = \frac{0.0621}{(1 - 0.31)} = 0.09 = 9\%$$

Notice that the higher the marginal tax rate, the higher the equivalent taxable yield. For example, in our previous example, if the marginal tax rate is 36% rather than 31%, the equivalent taxable yield would be 9.7% rather than 9%, as shown below:

$$\text{Equivalent taxable yield} = \frac{0.0621}{(1 - 0.36)} = 0.097 = 9.7\%$$

State and local governments may tax interest income on bond issues that are exempt from federal income taxes. Some municipalities exempt interest income from all municipal issues from taxation; others do not. Some states exempt interest income from bonds issued by municipalities within the state but tax the interest income from bonds issued by municipalities outside the state. The implication is that two municipal securities of the same quality rating and the same maturity may trade at some spread because of the relative demand for bonds of municipalities in different states. For example, in a high income tax state such as New York, the demand for bonds of municipalities will drive down their yield relative to municipalities in a low income tax state such as Florida.

Municipalities are not permitted to tax the interest income from securities issued by the U.S. Treasury. Thus, part of the spread between Treasury securities and taxable non-Treasury securities of the same maturity reflects the value of the exemption from state and local taxes.

Expected Liquidity of an Issue

Bonds trade with different degrees of liquidity. The greater the expected liquidity, the lower the yield that investors would require. As noted earlier, Treasury securities are the most liquid securities in the world. The lower yield offered on Treasury securities relative to non-Treasury securities reflects the difference in liquidity. Even within the Treasury market, on-the-run issues have greater liquidity than off-the-run issues.

Term to Maturity

As we explained in Chapter 20, the price of a bond will fluctuate over its life as yields in the market change. The time remaining on a bond's life is referred to its **term to maturity**, or simply *maturity*. As demonstrated in Chapter 21, the volatility of a bond's price is dependent on its term to maturity. More specifically, with all other factors constant, the longer the term to maturity of a bond, the greater the price volatility resulting from a change in market yields. Generally, bonds are classified into three "maturity sectors": bonds with a term to maturity of between 1 and 5 years are considered *short term*; bonds with a term to maturity between 5 and 12 years are viewed as *intermediate term*, and *long-term* bonds are those with a term to maturity greater than 12 years. The spread between any two maturity sectors of the market is called a **maturity spread**. The relationship between the yields on otherwise comparable securities with different maturities is called the **term structure of interest rates**.

THE TERM STRUCTURE OF INTEREST RATES

The term structure of interest rates plays a key role in the valuation of bonds. For this reason, we devote a good deal of space to this important topic.

The Yield Curve

The graphical depiction of the relationship between the yield on bonds of the same credit quality but different maturities is known as the **yield curve**. In the past, most investors have constructed yield curves from observations of prices and yields in the Treasury market. Two reasons account for this tendency. First, Treasury securities are free of default risk, and differences in creditworthiness do not affect yields. Therefore, these instruments are directly comparable. Second, as the largest and most active bond market, the Treasury market offers the fewest problems of illiquidity or infrequent trading. That is to say, the prices of Treasuries are the most current in the market, reflecting the most recent information. Figure 22-1 shows several recent Treasury yield curves.

From a practical viewpoint, as we explained earlier in this chapter, the key function of the Treasury yield curve is to serve as a benchmark for pricing bonds and to set yields in many other sectors of the debt market—bank loans, mortgages, corporate debt, and international bonds. However, market participants are coming to realize that the traditionally constructed Treasury yield curve is an unsatisfactory measure of the relation between required yield and maturity. The key reason is that securities with the same maturity may actually carry different yields. As we will explain below, this phenomenon reflects the role and impact of differences in the bonds' coupon rates. Hence, it is necessary to develop more accurate and reliable estimates of the Treasury yield curve. In what follows, we will show the problems posed by traditional approaches to the Treasury yield curve, and we will offer an increasingly popular approach to building a yield curve. Our approach consists of identifying yields that apply to zero-coupon bonds and, therefore, eliminates the problem of coupon rate differences in the yield-maturity relationship.

Why the Yield Curve Should Not Be Used to Price a Bond

The price of a bond is the present value of its cash flow. However, in our illustrations and our discussion of the pricing of a bond in the previous chap-

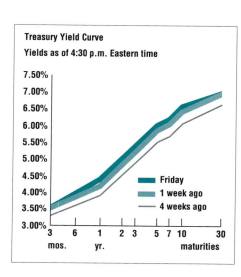

FIGURE 22-1

Recent Treasury yield curves.

(Source: Thompson Technical Data Corp's BondData Technical Service Telerate page 8005.)

ter, we assume that one interest rate should be used to discount all the bond's cash flows. The appropriate interest rate is the yield on a Treasury security, with the same maturity as the bond, plus an appropriate risk premium.

As noted above, however, there is a problem with using the Treasury yield curve to determine the appropriate yield at which to discount the cash flow of a bond. To illustrate this problem, consider the following two hypothetical five-year Treasury bonds, A and B. The difference between these two Treasury bonds is the coupon rate, which is 12% for A and 3% for B. The cash flow for these two bonds per $100 of par value for the 10 six-month periods (five years) to maturity would be:

Period	Cash Flow for A	Cash Flow for B
1–9	$ 6.00	$ 1.50
10	106.00	101.50

Because of the different cash flow patterns, it is not appropriate to use the same interest rate to discount all cash flows. Instead, each cash flow should be discounted at a unique interest rate appropriate for the time period in which the cash flow will be received. But what should be the interest rate for each period?

The correct way to think about bonds A and B is not as bonds but as packages of cash flows. More specifically, they are packages of zero-coupon instruments. Thus, the interest earned is the difference between the maturity value and the price paid. For example, bond A can be viewed as 10 zero-coupon instruments: one with a maturity value of $6 maturing 6 months from now; a second with a maturity value of $6 maturing 1 year from now; a third with a maturity value of $6 maturing 1.5 years from now, etc. The final zero-coupon instrument matures 10 six-month periods from now and has a maturity value of $106. Likewise, bond B can be viewed as ten zero-coupon instruments with maturity values of $1.50 for the first nine periods and $101.50 for the last period. Obviously, in the case of each coupon bond (A or B), the value or price of the bond is equal to the total value of its component zero-coupon instruments.

In general, any bond can be viewed as a package of zero-coupon instruments. That is, each zero-coupon instrument in the package has a maturity equal to its coupon payment date or, in the case of the principal, the maturity date. The value of the bond should equal the value of all the component zero-coupon instruments. If this does not hold, it is possible for a market participant to generate riskless profits by stripping off the coupon payments and creating stripped securities (see Chapter 19).

To determine the value of each zero-coupon instrument, it is necessary to know the yield on a zero-coupon Treasury with that same maturity. This yield is called the **spot rate**, and the graphical depiction of the relationship between the spot rate and its maturity is called the **spot rate curve**. Because there are no zero-coupon Treasury debt issues with a maturity greater than one year, it is not possible to construct such a curve solely from observations of market activity. Rather, it is necessary to derive this curve from theoretical considerations as applied to the yields of the actually traded Treasury debt securities.[3] Such a curve is called a **theoretical spot rate curve** and is the graphical depiction of the term structure of interest rate.

Constructing the Theoretical Spot Rate Curve

To explain the process of estimating the theoretical spot rate curve from observed yields on Treasury securities, we use the data for the hypothetical price, annualized yield (yield to maturity), and maturity of the 20 Treasury securities shown in Table 22-3. Each security is assumed to have a market price equal to its par value so that the yield to maturity and the coupon rate are equal.

Throughout the analysis and illustrations to come, it is important to remember that the basic principle is that the value of the Treasury coupon security should be equal to the value of the package of zero-coupon Treasury securities that duplicates the coupon bond's cash flow.

Consider the 6-month Treasury bill in Table 22-3. Since a Treasury bill is a zero-coupon instrument, its annualized yield of 5.25% is equal to the spot rate. Similarly, for the 1-year Treasury, the cited yield of 5.5% is the 1-year spot rate. Given these two spot rates, we can compute the spot rate for a theoretical 1.5-year zero-coupon Treasury. The price of a theoretical 1.5-year zero-coupon Treasury should equal the present value of three cash flows from an actual 1.5-year coupon Treasury, where the yield used for discounting is the spot rate corresponding to the cash flow. Table 22-3 shows the coupon rate for a 1.5 year Treasury as 5.75%. Using $100 as par, the cash flow for this Treasury is

0.5 year	$0.0575 \times \$100 \times 0.5$	$= \$\ \ 2.875$
1.0 year	$0.0575 \times \$100 \times 0.5$	$= \$\ \ 2.875$
1.5 years	$0.0575 \times \$100 \times 0.5 + 100$	$= \$102.875$

The present value of the cash flow is then

$$\frac{2.875}{(1 + z_1)^1} + \frac{2.875}{(1 + z_2)^2} + \frac{102.875}{(1 + z_3)^3}$$

where z_1 = one-half the annualized 6-month theoretical spot rate
z_2 = one-half the 1-year theoretical spot rate
z_3 = one-half the annual value of the 1.5-year theoretical spot rate

Since the 6-month spot rate and 1-year spot rate are 5.25% and 5.50%, respectively, we know these facts:

---

[3]In practice, the Treasury securities used to construct the theoretical spot rate curve are the on-the-run (most recently auctioned) Treasury securities of a given maturity. As we explained in Chapter 19, there are actual zero-coupon Treasury securities with a maturity greater than one year that are outstanding in the market. These securities are not issued by the U.S. Treasury but are created by certain market participants from actual coupon Treasury securities. It would seem logical that the observed yield on zero-coupon Treasury securities can be used to construct an actual spot rate curve. However, there are problems with this approach. First, the liquidity of these securities is not as great as that of the coupon Treasury market. Second, there are maturity sectors of the zero-coupon Treasury market that attract specific investors who may be willing to trade off yield in exchange for an attractive feature associated with that particular maturity sector, thereby distorting the term structure relationship.

$$z_1 = 0.02625 \quad \text{and} \quad z_2 = 0.0275$$

We can compute the present value of the 1.5-year coupon Treasury security as

$$\frac{2.875}{(1.02625)^1} + \frac{2.875}{(1.0275)^2} + \frac{102.875}{(1 + z_3)^3}$$

Since the price of the 1.5-year coupon Treasury security is $100, the following relationship must hold:

$$100 = \frac{2.875}{(1.02625)^1} + \frac{2.875}{(1.0275)^2} + \frac{102.875}{(1 + z_3)^3}$$

We can solve for the theoretical 1.5-year spot rate as follows:

$$100 = 2.801461 + 2.723166 + \frac{102.875}{(1 + z_3)^3}$$

$$94.47537 = \frac{102.875}{(1 + z_3)^3}$$

$$(1 + z_3)^3 = 1.028798$$

$$z_3 = 0.028798$$

TABLE 22-3

MATURITY AND YIELD TO MATURITY FOR 20 HYPOTHETICAL TREASURY SECURITIES

Period	Years	Yield to Maturity/ Coupon Rate
1	0.5	5.25%
2	1.0	5.50
3	1.5	5.75
4	2.0	6.00
5	2.5	6.25
6	3.0	6.50
7	3.5	6.75
8	4.0	6.80
9	4.5	7.00
10	5.0	7.10
11	5.5	7.15
12	6.0	7.20
13	6.5	7.30
14	7.0	7.35
15	7.5	7.40
16	8.0	7.50
17	8.5	7.60
18	9.0	7.60
19	9.5	7.70
20	10.0	7.80

Note: All bonds with the exception of the six-month and one-year issues are at par (100). For these issues the coupon rate is equal to the yield to maturity. The six-month and one-year issues are zero-coupon instruments, and the price is less than par.

Doubling this yield, we obtain the bond-equivalent yield of 0.0576, or 5.76%, which is the theoretical 1.5-year spot rate. That rate is the rate that the market would apply to a 1.5-year zero-coupon Treasury security if, in fact, such a security existed.

Given the theoretical 1.5-year spot rate, we can obtain the theoretical 2-year spot rate. The cash flow for the 2-year coupon Treasury in Table 22-3 is

0.5 year	$0.060 \times \$100 \times 0.5$	= $	3.00
1.0 year	$0.060 \times \$100 \times 0.5$	= $	3.00
1.5 years	$0.060 \times \$100 \times 0.5$	= $	3.00
2.0 years	$0.060 \times \$100 \times 0.5 + 100$	= $	103.00

The present value of the cash flow is then

$$\frac{3.00}{(1 + z_1)^1} + \frac{3.00}{(1 + z_2)^2} + \frac{3.00}{(1 + z_3)^3} + \frac{103.00}{(1 + z_4)^4}$$

where z_4 = one-half the 2-year theoretical spot rate. Since the 6-month spot rate, 1-year spot rate, and 1.5-year spot rate are 8.0%, 8.3%, and 8.93%, respectively, then

$$z_1 = 0.02625 \qquad z_2 = 0.0275 \qquad z_3 = 0.028798$$

Therefore, the present value of the 2-year coupon Treasury security is

$$\frac{3.00}{(1.002625)^1} + \frac{3.00}{(1.0275)^2} + \frac{3.00}{(1.028798)^3} + \frac{103.00}{(1 + z_4)^4}$$

Since the price of the 2-year coupon Treasury security is $100, the following relationship must hold:

$$100 = \frac{3.00}{(1.00265)^1} + \frac{3.00}{(1.0275)^2} + \frac{3.00}{(1.028798)^3} + \frac{103.00}{(1 + z_4)^4}$$

We can solve for the theoretical 2-year spot rate as follows:

$$100 = 2.92326 + 2.84156 + 2.75506 + \frac{103.00}{(1 + z_4)^4}$$

$$91.48011 = \frac{103.00}{(1 + z_4)^4}$$

$$(1 + z_4)^4 = 1.125927$$

$$z_4 = 0.030095$$

Doubling this yield, we obtain the theoretical 2-year spot rate bond-equivalent yield of 6.02%.

One can follow this approach sequentially to derive the theoretical 2.5-year spot rate from the calculated values of z_1, z_2, z_3, and z_4 (the 6-month, 1-year, 1.5-year, and 2-year rates) and the price and coupon of the bond with a maturity of 2.5 years. Further, one could derive theoretical spot rates for the remaining 15 half-yearly rates. The process of creating a theoretical spot rate curve in this way is called **bootstrapping**.

The spot rates using this process are shown in Table 22-4. They represent the term structure of interest rates for maturities up to 10 years, at the particular time to which the bond price quotations refer.

TABLE 22-4		
THEORETICAL SPOT RATES		
Period	**Years**	**Spot rate**
1	0.5	5.25%
2	1.0	5.50
3	1.5	5.76
4	2.0	6.02
5	2.5	6.28
6	3.0	6.55
7	3.5	6.82
8	4.0	6.87
9	4.5	7.09
10	5.0	7.20
11	5.5	7.26
12	6.0	7.31
13	6.5	7.43
14	7.0	7.48
15	7.5	7.54
16	8.0	7.67
17	8.5	7.80
18	9.0	7.79
19	9.5	7.93
20	10.0	8.07

Using the Theoretical Spot Rate Curve

We can now apply the spot rates to price a bond. In Chapter 20, we showed how to price a bond assuming that each cash flow is discounted at one discount rate. Table 22-5 shows how to properly value a Treasury bond using the theoretical spot rates. The bond in the illustration is a hypothetical 10-year Treasury security with a coupon rate of 10%.

The third column of the table shows the cash flow per $100 of par value for each of the 20 six-month periods. The fourth column shows the theoretical spot rate for each maturity as per Table 22-4. The fifth column gives the present value of $1 when discounted at the theoretical spot rate shown in the third column. The last column gives the present value of the cash flow, found by multiplying the third column by the fifth column. The theoretical price of this bond is the sum of the present values in the last column, $115.4206.

While we have stated that the price of a Treasury security should be equal to the present value of its cash flow where each cash flow is discounted at the theoretical spot rates, the question is, what forces a Treasury to be priced based on the spot rates? The answer is that arbitrage forces this. For example, the theoretical price of $115.4206 can be viewed as the value of a package of zero-coupon instruments. That is, if this 10%, 10-year Treasury security is purchased and then stripped, it will generate proceeds of $115.4206. The stripped Treasury securities created are the securities we described in Chapter 20.

Now, suppose instead that the market priced the 10%, 10-year Treasury security based on the yield to maturity of 10-year Treasury securities as indicated by the yield curve. As can be seen in Table 22-3, the yield to maturity for 10-year Treasury securities is 7.8%. If the 10%, 10-year Treasury security

| | | | | **TABLE 22-5** | | |

DETERMINING THE THEORETICAL VALUE OF A 10%, 10-YEAR TREASURY SECURITY USING THE THEORETICAL SPOT RATES

Period	Year	Cash Flow	Spot Rate	PV of $1 @Spot Rate	PV of Cash Flow
1	0.5	5	5.25%	0.974421	4.872107
2	1.0	5	5.50	0.947188	4.735942
3	1.5	5	5.76	0.918351	4.591756
4	2.0	5	6.02	0.888156	4.440782
5	2.5	5	6.28	0.856724	4.283619
6	3.0	5	6.55	0.824206	4.12103
7	3.5	5	6.82	0.790757	3.953783
8	4.0	5	6.87	0.763256	3.81628
9	4.5	5	7.09	0.730718	3.653589
10	5.0	5	7.20	0.701952	3.509758
11	5.5	5	7.26	0.675697	3.378483
12	6.0	5	7.31	0.650028	3.250138
13	6.5	5	7.43	0.622448	3.112238
14	7.0	5	7.48	0.597889	2.989446
15	7.5	5	7.54	0.573919	2.869594
16	8.0	5	7.67	0.547625	2.738125
17	8.5	5	7.80	0.521766	2.608831
18	9.0	5	7.79	0.502665	2.513325
19	9.5	5	7.93	0.477729	2.388643
20	10.0	105	8.07	0.453268	47.59317
Theoretical value					115.4206

is priced using a discount rate of 7.8%, its price would be $115.0826, a price that is less than its theoretical value. A government securities dealer who had the opportunity to buy this Treasury security for $115.0826 would buy it, strip it, and then sell the zero-coupon securities created. The total proceeds from this process, as we just noted, would be $115.4206. Thus, the dealer would realize an arbitrage profit of $0.338 per $100 of par value purchased. The actions of dealers to capture this arbitrage profit would drive up the price of this Treasury security. Only when the price reaches $115.4206—the theoretical value when the cash flows are discounted at the theoretical spot rates—will the arbitrage disappear. It is this action that forces Treasury securities to be priced based on the theoretical spot rates.

We can now modify our earlier statement about the base interest rate for a given maturity. It is not simply the yield on the on-the-run Treasury security for that maturity, but the theoretical Treasury spot rate for that maturity. It is the theoretical Treasury spot rates to which a risk premium must be added in order to value a non-Treasury security.

Forward Rates

Thus we have seen that from the yield curve we can extrapolate the theoretical spot rates. In addition, we can extrapolate the market's consensus of future interest rates. To see the importance of knowing the market's consensus for future interest rates, consider the following two investment alternatives for an investor who has a one-year investment horizon:

Alternative 1. Buy a one-year instrument.
Alternative 2. Buy a six-month instrument, and when it matures in six months, buy another six-month instrument.

With alternative 1, the investor will realize the one-year spot rate, and that rate is known with certainty. In contrast, with alternative 2, the investor will realize the six-month spot rate, but the six-month rate six months from now is unknown. Therefore, for alternative 2, the rate that will be earned over one year is not known with certainty. This is illustrated in Figure 22-2.

Suppose that this investor expected that six months from now six-month rates will be higher than they are today. The investor might then feel alternative 2 would be the better investment. However, this is not necessarily true. To understand why it is necessary to know what the market's consensus of future interest rates is and to appreciate the need to understand why, let's continue with our illustration.

The investor will be indifferent to the two alternatives if they produce the same total dollars over the one-year investment horizon. Given the one-year spot rate, there is some rate on a six-month instrument six months from now that will make the investor indifferent between the two alternatives. We will denote that rate by f.

The value of f can be readily determined given the theoretical one-year spot rate and the six-month spot rate. If an investor placed $100 in a one-year instrument (alternative 1), the total dollars generated at the end of one year is

Total dollars at end of year for alternative 1 = $100 $(1 + z_2)^2$ (22-1)

where z_2 is the one-year spot rate. (Remember we are working in six-month periods, so the subscript 2 represents two six-month periods, or one year.)

The proceeds from investing at the six-month spot rate will generate the following total dollars at the end of six months:

Total dollars at end of six month for alternative 2 = $100 $(1 + z_1)$ (22-2)

where z_1 is the six-month spot rate. If the amount in Equation (22.2) is reinvested at the six-month rate six months from now, which we denoted as f, then the total dollars at the end of one year would be

Total dollars at end of year for alternative 2 = $100 $(1 + z_1)(1 + f)$ (22-3)

The investor will be indifferent between the two alternatives if the total dollars are the same. This will occur if Equation (22-1) is equal to Equation (22-3). Setting these two equations equal, we get

$$\$100(1 + z_2)^2 = \$100\ (1 + z_1)(1 + f) \qquad (22\text{-}4)$$

FIGURE 22-2

Two alternative one-year investments.

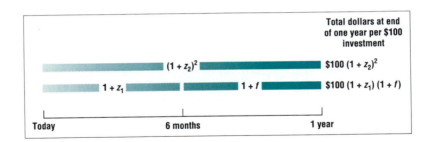

Solving Equation (22-4) for f, we get

$$f = \frac{(1 + z_2)^2}{(1 + z_1)} - 1 \qquad (22\text{-}5)$$

Doubling f gives the bond-equivalent yield for the six-month rate six months from now that we are interested in.

We can illustrate the use of Equation (22-5) with the theoretical spot rates shown in Table 22-4. From that table, we know that

Six-month spot rate = 0.0525   therefore z_1 = 0.02625
One-year spot rate   = 0.0550   therefore z_2 = 0.02750

Substituting into Equation (22-5), we have

$$f = \frac{(1.02750)^2}{1.02625} - 1$$

$$= 0.028752$$

Therefore, the annual rate for f on a bond-equivalent basis is 5.75% (2.8752% × 2).

Here is how we use this rate of 5.75%. If the six-month rate six months from now is less than 5.75%, then the total dollars at the end of one year would be higher by investing in the one-year instrument (alternative 1). If the six-month rate six months from now is greater than 5.75%, then the total dollars at the end of one year would be higher by investing in the six-month instrument and reinvesting the proceeds six months from now at the six-month rate at the time (alternative 2). Of course, if the six-month rate six months from now is 5.75%, the two alternatives give the same total dollars at the end of one year.

Now that we have the rate for f that we are interested in and we know how that rate can be used, let's return to the question we posed at the outset. From Table 22-4, the six-month spot rate is 5.25%. Suppose that the investor expects that six months from now the six-month rate will be 5.60%. That is, the investor expects that the six-month rate will be higher than its current level. Should the investor select alternative 2 because the six-month rate six months from now is expected to be higher? The answer is no. As we explained in the previous paragraph, if the rate is less than 5.75%, then alternative 1 is the better alternative. Since this investor expects a rate of 5.6%, he should select alternative 1 despite the fact that he expects the six-month rate to be higher than it is today.

This is a somewhat surprising result for some investors. The reason for this is that the market prices its expectations of future interest rates into the rates offered on investments with different maturities. This is why knowing the market's consensus of future interest rates is critical. The rate that we determined for f is the market's consensus for the six-month rate six months from now. A future interest rate calculated from either the spot rates or the yield curve is called a **forward rate**.

Relationship between Six-Month Forward Rates and Spot Rates   In general, the relationship between a t-period spot rate, the current six-month spot rate, and the six-month forward rates is as follows:

$$z_t = [(1 + z_1)(1 + f_1)(1 + f_2)(1 + f_3) \dots (1 + f_{t-1})]^{1/t} - 1 \qquad (22\text{-}6)$$

where f_t is the six-month forward rate beginning t six-month periods from now.

To illustrate how to use Equation (22-6), let's look at how the five-year (ten-year) spot rate is related to the six-month forward rates. Six-month forward rates were calculated from the spot rates given in Table 22-4. The values for f_1 through f_9 are given below:

$f_1 = 0.02875$ $f_2 = 0.03140$ $f_3 = 0.03670$ $f_4 = 0.03945$

$f_5 = 0.04320$ $f_6 = 0.03605$ $f_7 = 0.04455$ $f_8 = 0.04100$

$f_9 = 0.03885$

The six-month spot rate is 2.625% (5.25% on a bond-equivalent basis). Substituting these values into Equation (22-6), we have

$$z_{10} = [(1.02875)(1.02875)(1.03140)(1.03670)(1.03945)(1.04320)(1.03605)(1.04455)(1.04100)(1.03855)]^{1/10} - 1 = 0.072 = 7.2\%$$

Note that this value agrees with the five-year (ten-period) spot rate shown in Table 22-4.

Other Forward Rates   We can take this sort of analysis much further. It is not necessary to limit ourselves to six-month forward rates. The spot rates can be used to calculate the forward rate for any time in the future for any investment horizon. As examples, the following can be calculated:

- The two-year forward rate five years from now
- The six-year forward rate ten years from now
- The seven-year forward rate three years from now

A natural question about forward rates is how well they do at predicting future interest rates. Studies have demonstrated that forward rates do not do a good job in predicting future interest rates.[4] Then why the big deal about understanding forward rates? The reason, as we demonstrated in our illustration of how to select between two alternative investments, is that forward rates indicate how an investor's expectations must differ from the market consensus in order to make the correct decision. In our illustration, the six-month forward rate may not be realized. That is irrelevant. The fact is that the six-month forward rate indicated to the investor that if his expectation about the six-month rate six months from now is less than 5.75%, he would be better off with alternative 1.

Determinants of the Shape of the Term Structure

If we plot the term structure—the yield to maturity, or the spot rate, at successive maturities against maturity—what is it likely to look like? Figure 22-3 shows four shapes that have appeared with some frequency over time. Panel (*a*) shows an upward-sloping yield curve; that is, yield rises steadily as maturity increases. This shape is commonly referred to as a "normal," or "positive," yield curve. Panel (*b*) shows a downward-sloping, or "inverted," yield curve, where yields decline as maturity increases. Panel (*c*) shows a "humped" yield curve. Finally, panel (*d)* shows a "flat" yield curve.

Two major theories have evolved to account for these observed shapes of the yield curve: the *expectations theory* and the *market segmentation theory.*

---

[4]Eugene F. Fama, "Forward Rates as Predictors of Future Spot Rates," *Journal of Financial Economics*, 3, 4 (1976), pp. 361–377.

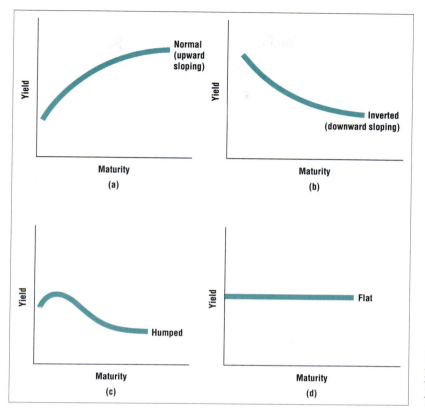

FIGURE 22-3

Four shapes that have been observed for the yield curve.

There are several forms of the expectations theory—the *pure expectations theory*, the *liquidity theory*, and the *preferred habitat theory*. The **expectations theories** share a hypothesis about the behavior of short-term forward rates and also assume that the forward rates in current long-term contracts are closely related to the market's expectations about future short-term rates. These three theories differ, however, on whether other factors also affect forward rates, and how. The pure expectations theory postulates that no systematic factors other than expected future short-term rates affect forward rates; the liquidity theory and the preferred habitat theory assert that there are other factors. Accordingly, the last two forms of the expectations theory are sometimes referred to as **biased expectations theories**. Figure 22-4 depicts the relationship among these three theories.

The Pure Expectations Theory   According to the **pure expectations theory**, the forward rates exclusively represent the expected future rates. Thus, the entire term structure at a given time reflects the market's current expectations of the family of future short-term rates. Under this view, a rising term structure, as in Panel (*a*) of Figure 22-3, must indicate that the market expects short-term rates to rise throughout the relevant future. Similarly, a flat term structure reflects an expectation that future short-term rates will be mostly constant, while a falling term structure must reflect an expectation that future short rates will decline steadily.

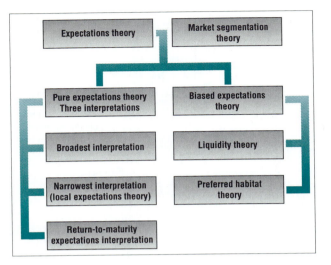

FIGURE 22-4

Term structure theories.

We can illustrate this theory by considering how an expectation of a rising short-term future rate would affect the behavior of various market participants, so as to result in a rising yield curve. Assume an initially flat term structure, and suppose that economic news subsequently leads market participants to expect interest rates to rise.

1. Those market participants interested in a long-term investment would not want to buy long-term bonds because they would expect the yield structure to rise sooner or later, resulting in a price decline for the bonds and a capital loss on the long-term bonds purchased. Instead, they would want to invest in short-term debt obligations until the rise in yield had occurred, permitting them to reinvest their funds at the higher yield.

2. Speculators expecting rising rates would anticipate a decline in the price of long-term bonds and therefore would want to sell any long-term bonds they own and possibly to short-sell some they do not now own. (Should interest rates rise as expected, the price of longer-term bonds will fall. Since the speculator will sell these bonds short and then purchase them at a lower price to cover the short sale, a profit will be earned.) Speculators will reinvest in short-term debt obligations.

3. Borrowers wishing to acquire long-term funds would be pulled toward borrowing now, in the long end of the market, by the expectation that borrowing at a later time would be more expensive.

All these responses would tend either to lower the net demand for or to increase the supply of long-maturity bonds, and all three responses would increase demand for short-term debt obligations. This would require a rise in long-term yields in relation to short-term yields; that is, these actions by investors, speculators, and borrowers would tilt the term structure upward until it is consistent with expectations of higher future interest rates. By analogous reasoning, an unexpected event leading to the expectation of lower future rates will result in the yield curve sloping down.

Unfortunately, the pure expectations theory suffers from one shortcoming, which, qualitatively, is quite serious. It neglects the risks inherent in investing in bonds and like instruments. If forward rates were perfect predictors of future interest rates, then the future prices of bonds would be known with certainty. The return over any investment period would be certain and independent both of the maturity of the instrument initially acquired and of the time at which the investor needed to liquidate his instrument. However, with uncertainty about future interest rates and hence about future prices of bonds, these instruments become risky investments in the sense that the return over some investment horizon is unknown.

Two risks cause uncertainty about the return over some investment horizon: price risk and reinvestment risk. The first is the uncertainty about the price of the bond at the end of the investment horizon. For example, an investor who plans to invest for 5 years might consider the following three investment alternatives: (1) invest in a 5-year bond and hold it for 5 years, (2) invest in a 12-year bond and sell it at the end of 5 years, (3) invest in a 30-year bond and sell it at the end of 5 years. The return that will be realized for the second and third alternatives is not known, because the price of each long-term bond at the end of 5 years is not known. In the case of the 12-year bond, the price will depend on the yield on 7-year debt securities 5 years from now; and the price of the 30-year bond will depend on the yield on 25-year bonds 5 years from now. Since forward rates implied in the current term structure for a future 12-year bond and a future 25-year bond are not perfect predictors of the actual future rates, there is uncertainty about the price for both bonds 5 years from now. Thus, there is price risk, that is, the risk that the price of the bond will be lower than currently expected at the end of the investment horizon. As explained in the previous chapter, an important feature of price risk is that it is greater the longer the maturity of the bond.

The second risk has to do with the uncertainty about the rate at which the proceeds from a bond can be reinvested until the expected maturity date, that is, reinvestment risk. For example, an investor who plans to invest for five years might consider the following three alternative investments: (1) invest in a five-year bond and hold it for five years; (2) invest in a six-month instrument, and when it matures, reinvest the proceeds in six-month instruments over the entire five-year investment horizon; and (3) invest in a two-year bond, and when it matures, reinvest the proceeds in a three-year bond. The risk in the second and third alternatives is that the return over the five-year investment horizon is unknown because rates at which the proceeds can be reinvested until maturity are unknown.

There are several interpretations of the pure expectations theory that have been put forth by economists. These interpretations are not exact equivalents, nor are they consistent with each other, in large part because they offer different treatments of the two risks we have just explained.[5]

The broadest interpretation of the pure expectations theory suggests that investors expect the return for any investment horizon to be the same, regardless of the maturity strategy selected.[6] For example, consider an investor

---

[5]These formulations are summarized by John Cox, Jonathan Ingersoll, Jr., and Stephen Ross, "A Re-examination of Traditional Hypotheses about the Term Structure of Interest Rates," *Journal of Finance* (September 1981), pp. 769–799.

[6]F. Lutz, "The Structure of Interest Rates," *Quarterly Journal of Economics* (1940–1941), pp. 36–63.

who has a five-year investment horizon. According to this theory, it makes no difference if a five-year, twelve-year, or thirty-year bond is purchased and held for five years since the investor expects the return from all three bonds to be the same over five years. A major criticism of this very broad interpretation of the theory is that, because of price risk associated with investing in bonds with a maturity greater than the investment horizon, the expected returns from these three very different bond investments should differ in significant ways.[7]

A second interpretation, referred to as the **local expectations theory**, a form of the pure expectations theory, suggests that the returns on bonds of different maturities will be the same over a short-term investment horizon. For example, if an investor has a six-month investment horizon, buying a five-year, ten-year, or twenty-year bond will produce the same six-month return. It has been demonstrated that the local expectations formulation, which is narrow in scope, is the only one of the interpretations of the pure expectations theory that can be sustained in equilibrium.[8]

The third and final interpretation of the pure expectations theory suggests that the return an investor will realize by rolling over short-term bonds to some investment horizon will be the same as holding a zero-coupon bond with a maturity that is the same as that investment horizon. (Since a zero-coupon bond has no reinvestment risk, future interest rates over the investment horizon do not affect the return.) This variant is called the **return-to-maturity expectations interpretation**. For example, let's assume that an investor has a five-year investment horizon. By buying a five-year zero-coupon bond and holding it to maturity, the investor's return is the difference between the maturity value and the price of the bond, all divided by the price of the bond. According to return-to-maturity expectations, the same return will be realized by buying a six-month instrument and rolling it over for five years. The validity of this interpretation is currently subject to considerable doubt.

The Liquidity Theory   We have explained that the drawback of the pure expectations theory is that it does not consider the risks associated with investing in bonds. There is the risk in holding a long-term bond for one period, and that risk increases with the bond's maturity because maturity and price volatility are directly related.

Given this uncertainty, and the reasonable consideration that investors typically do not like uncertainty, some economists and financial analysts have suggested a different theory. This theory states that investors will hold longer-term maturities if they are offered a long-term rate higher than the average of expected future rates by a risk premium that is positively related to the term to maturity.[9] Put differently, the forward rates should reflect both

[7]Cox, Ingersoll, and Ross, op. cit., pp. 774–775.

[8]Cox, Ingersoll, and Ross, op. cit.

[9]John R. Hicks, *Value and Capital* (London: Oxford University Press, 1946), 2nd ed., pp. 141–145.

interest rate expectations and a "liquidity" premium (really a risk premium), and the premium should be higher for longer maturities.

According to this theory, which is called the **liquidity theory of the term structure**, the implied forward rates will not be an unbiased estimate of the market's expectations of future interest rates because they embody a liquidity premium. Thus, an upward-sloping yield curve may reflect expectations that future interest rates either (1) will rise or (2) will be flat or even fall, but with a liquidity premium increasing fast enough with maturity so as to produce an upward-sloping yield curve.

The Preferred Habitat Theory

Another theory, known as the **preferred habitat theory**, also adopts the view that the term structure reflects the expectation of the future path of interest rates as well as a risk premium. However, the preferred habitat theory rejects the assertion that the risk premium must rise uniformly with maturity.[10] Proponents of the habitat theory say that the risk premium would rise uniformly with maturity only if all investors intend to liquidate their investment at the shortest possible date while all borrowers are anxious to borrow long. This assumption can be rejected since institutions have holding periods dictated by the nature of their liabilities.

The preferred habitat theory asserts that, to the extent that the demand for and supply of funds in a given maturity range do not match, some lenders and borrowers will be induced to shift to maturities showing the opposite imbalances. However, they will need to be compensated by an appropriate risk premium whose magnitude will reflect the extent of aversion to either price or reinvestment risk.

Thus, this theory proposes that the shape of the yield curve is determined by both expectations of future interest rates and a risk premium, positive or negative, to induce market participants to shift out of their preferred habitat. Clearly, according to this theory, yield curves that are upward-sloping, downward-sloping, flat, or humped are all possible.

Market Segmentation Theory

The **market segmentation theory** also recognizes that investors have preferred habitats dictated by the nature of their liabilities. This theory also proposes that the major reason for the shape of the yield curve lies in asset/liability management constraints (either regulatory or self-imposed) and/or creditors (borrowers) restricting their lending (financing) to specific maturity sectors.[11] However, the market segmentation theory differs from the preferred habitat theory in that it assumes that neither investors nor borrowers are willing to shift from one maturity sector to another to take advantage of opportunities arising from differences between expectations and forward rates. Thus, for the segmentation theory, the shape of the yield curve is determined by supply of and demand for securities within each maturity sector.

---

[10]Franco Modigliani and Richard Sutch, "Innovations in Interest Rate Policy," *American Economic Review* (May 1966), pp. 178–197.

[11]This theory was suggested in J. M. Culbertson, "The Term Structure of Interest Rates," *Quarterly Journal of Economics* (November 1957), pp. 489–504.

■ SUMMARY

In all economies, there is not just one interest rate but a structure of interest rates. The difference between the yield on any two bonds is called the yield spread. The base interest rate is the yield on a Treasury security. The yield spread between a non-Treasury security and a comparable on-the-run Treasury security is called a risk premium. The factors that affect the spread include (1) the type of issuer (e.g., agency, corporate, municipality), (2) the issuer's perceived creditworthiness as measured by the rating system of commercial rating companies, (3) the term or maturity of the instrument, (4) the embedded options in a bond issue (e.g., call, put, or conversion provisions), (5) the taxability of interest income at the federal and municipal levels, and (6) the expected liquidity of the issue.

The relationship between yield and maturity is referred to as the term structure of interest rates.

The graphical depiction of the relationship between the yield on bonds of the same credit quality but different maturities is known as the yield curve. The yield on Treasury securities is the base interest rate used in determining the yield required on non-government bonds.

There is a problem with using the Treasury yield curve to determine the one yield at which to discount all the cash payments of any bond. Each cash flow should be discounted at a unique interest rate that is applicable to the time period when the cash flow is to be received. Since any bond can be viewed as a package of zero-coupon instruments, its value should equal the value of all the component zero-coupon instruments. The rate on a zero-coupon bond is called the spot rate. The relationship between the spot rate and maturity is also called the term structure of interest rates. The theoretical spot rate curve for Treasury securities can be estimated from the Treasury yield curve using a methodology known as bootstrapping.

Under certain assumptions, the market's expectation of future interest rates can be extrapolated from the theoretical Treasury spot rate curve. The resulting forward rate is called the implied forward rate. The spot rate is related to the current six-month spot rate and the implied six-month forward rates.

Several theories have been proposed about the determination of the term structue: pure expectations theory, the biased expectations theory (the liquidity theory and preferred habitat theory), and the market segmentation theory. All the expectation theories hypothesize that the one-period forward rates represent the market's expectations of future actual rates. The pure expectations theory asserts that it is the only factor. The biased expectations theory asserts that there are other factors.

■ KEY TERMS

base interest rate
benchmark interest rate
biased expectations theories
bootstrapping
credit spread
equivalent taxable yield
expectations theories
forward rate
intermarket sector spread
intramarket sector spread

liquidity theory of the term
    structure
local expectations theory
market sectors
market segmentation theory
maturity spread
preferred habitat theory
pure expectations theory
quality spread

return-to-maturity expectations
    interpretation
risk premium
spot rate
spot rate curve
term structure of interest rates
term to maturity
theoretical spot rate curve
yield curve

■ QUESTIONS

1. In the *Weekly Market Update* of May 29, 1992, published by Goldman Sachs & Co., the following information was reported in various exhibits for the Treasury market as of the close of business Thursday, May 28, 1992:

ON-THE-RUN TREASURIES

Maturity	Yield
3 months	3.77%
6 months	3.95
1 year	4.25
2 years	5.23
3 years	5.78
5 years	6.67
7 years	7.02
10 years	7.37
20 years	7.65
30 years	7.88

KEY OFF-THE-RUN TREASURIES

Issue	Yield
Old 10-year	7.42%
Old 30-year	7.90

   a. What is the credit risk associated with a Treasury security?
   b. Why is the Treasury yield considered the base interest rate?
   c. What is meant by on-the-run Treasuries?
   d. What is meant by off-the-run Treasuries?
   e. What is the yield spread (1) between the off-the-run 10-year Treasury issue and the on-the-run 10-year Treasury issue and (2) between the off-the-run 30-year Treasury issue and the on-the-run 30-year Treasury issue?
   f. What does the yield spread between the off-the-run Treasury issue and the on-the-run Treasury issue reflect?

2. In the *Weekly Market Update* of May 29, 1992, published by Goldman Sachs & Co., the following information was reported in various exhibits for certain corporate bonds as of the close of business Thursday, May 28, 1992:

Issuer	Rating	Yield	Spread	Treasury Benchmark
General Electric Capital Co	Triple A	7.87%	50	10
Mobile Corp	Double A	7.77	40	10
Southern Bell Tel & Teleg	Triple A	8.60	72	30
Bell Tel Co Pa	Double A	8.66	78	30
AMR Corp	Triple B	9.43	155	30

   a. What does rating mean?
   b. Which of the five bonds has the greatest credit risk?

   c. What is meant by spread?
   d. What is meant by Treasury benchmark?
   e. Using the information for the Treasury market reported for May 29, 1992, in question 1, explain how each of the spreads reported above was determined.
   f. Why do each of the spreads reported above reflect a risk premium?

3. For the corporate bond issues reported in the previous question, answer the following questions:

   a. Should a triple-A-rated bond issue offer a higher or lower yield than a double-A-rated bond issue of the same maturity?
   b. What is the spread between the General Electric Capital Co. issue and the Mobile Corp. issue?
   c. Is the spread reported in part b consistent with your answer to part a?
   d. The yield spread between these two bond issues reflects more than just credit risk. What other factors would the spread reflect?
   e. The Mobile Corp. issue is not callable. However, the General Electric Capital Co. issue is callable. How does this information help you in understanding the spread between these two issues?

4. For the corporate bond issues reported in question 2, answer the following questions:

   a. What is the yield spread between the Southern Bell Telephone and Telegraph bond issue and the Bell Telephone Company (Pennsylvania) bond issue?
   b. The Southern Bell Telephone and Telegraph bond issue is not callable, but the Bell Telephone Company (Pennsylvania) bond issue is callable. What does the yield spread in part a reflect?
   c. AMR Corp. is the parent company of American Airlines and is therefore classified in the transportation industry. The issue is not callable. What is the yield spread between the AMR Corp. and Southern Bell Telephone and Telegraph bond issue, and what does this spread reflect?

5. In the *Weekly Market Update* of May 29, 1992, published by Goldman Sachs & Co., the following information was reported in an exhibit for high-grade, tax-exempt securities as of the close of business Thursday, May 28, 1992:

Maturity	Yield	Yield as a Percent of Treasury Yield
1 year	3.20%	76.5%
3 years	4.65	80.4
5 years	5.10	76.4
10 years	5.80	78.7
30 years	6.50	82.5

a. What is meant by a tax-exempt security?

b. What is meant by a high-grade issue?

c. Why is the yield on a tax-exempt security less than the yield on a Treasury security of the same maturity?

d. What does equivalent taxable yield mean?

e. Also reported in the same issue of the Goldman Sachs report is information on intramarket yield spreads. What is an intramarket yield spread?

6. a. What is an embedded option in a bond?

b. Give three examples of an embedded option that might be included in a bond issue.

c. Does an embedded option increase or decrease the risk premium relative to the base interest rate?

7. a. What is a yield curve?

b. Why is the Treasury yield curve the one most closely watched by market participants?

8. What is a spot rate?

9. Explain why it is inappropriate to use one yield to discount all the cash flows of a financial asset.

10. Explain why a financial asset can be viewed as a package of zero-coupon instruments.

11. How are spot rates related to forward rates?

12. You are a financial consultant. At various times you have heard comments on interest rates from one of your clients. How would you respond to each comment?

a. "The yield curve is upward-sloping today. This suggests that the market consensus is that interest rates are expected to increase in the future."

b. "I can't make any sense out of today's term structure. For short-term yields (up to three years) the spot rates increase with maturity; for maturities greater than three years but less than eight years, the spot rates decline with maturity; and for maturities greater than eight years the spot rates are virtually the same for each maturity. There is simply no theory that explains a term structure with this shape."

c. "When I want to determine the market's consensus of future interest rates, I calculate the forward rates."

13. You observe the yields of Treasury securities below (all yields are shown on a bond-equivalent basis):

Year	Yield to Maturity	Spot Rate
0.5	5.25%	5.25%
1.0	5.50	5.50
1.5	5.75	5.76
2.0	6.00	?
2.5	6.25	?
3.0	6.50	?
3.5	6.75	?
4.0	7.00	?
4.5	7.25	?
5.0	7.50	?
5.5	7.75	7.97
6.0	8.00	8.27
6.5	8.25	8.59
7.0	8.50	8.92
7.5	8.75	9.25
8.0	9.00	9.61
8.5	9.25	9.97
9.0	9.50	10.36
9.5	9.75	10.77
10.0	10.00	11.20

All the securities maturing from 1.5 years on are selling at par. The 0.5-year and 1-year securities are zero-coupon instruments.

a. Calculate the missing spot rates.

b. What should the price of a six-year, 6% coupon Treasury security be?

c. What is the six-month forward rate starting in the sixth year?

14. You observe the following Treasury yields (all yields are shown on a bond-equivalent basis):

Year	Yield to Maturity	Spot Rate
0.5	10.00%	10.00%
1.0	9.75	9.75
1.5	9.50	9.48
2.0	9.25	9.22
2.5	9.00	8.95
3.0	8.75	8.68
3.5	8.50	8.41
4.0	8.25	8.14
4.5	8.00	7.86
5.0	7.75	7.58
5.5	7.50	7.30
6.0	7.25	7.02
6.5	7.00	6.74
7.0	6.75	6.46
7.5	6.50	6.18
8.0	6.25	5.90
8.5	6.00	5.62
9.0	5.75	5.35
9.5	5.50	?
10.0	5.25	?

All the securities maturing from 1.5 years on are selling at par. The 0.5-year and 1-year securities are zero-coupon instruments.

a. Calculate the missing spot rates.
b. What should the price of a four-year, 5% coupon Treasury security be?

15. What actions force a Treasury's bond price to be valued in the market at the present value of the cash flows discounted at the Treasury spot rates?

16. Explain the role that forward rates play in making an investment decision?

17. "Forward rates are poor predictors of the actual future rates that are realized. Consequently, they are of little value to an investor." Explain why you agree or disagree with this statement.

18. Bart Simpson is considering two alternative investments. The first alternative is to invest in an instrument that matures in two years. The second alternative is to invest in an instrument that matures in one year and at the end of one year to reinvest the proceeds in a one-year instrument. He believes that one-year interest rates one year from now will be higher than they are today and therefore is leaning in favor of the second alternative. What would you recommend to Bart Simpson?

19. a. What is the common hypothesis about the behavior of short-term forward rates shared by the various forms of the expectations theory?
b. What are the types of risks associated with investing in bonds and how do these two risks affect the pure expectations theory.
c. Give three interpretations of the pure expectations theory.

20. a. What are the two biased expectations theories about the term structure of interest rates?
b. What are the underlying hypotheses of these two theories?

CHAPTER 23
VALUATION OF BONDS WITH EMBEDDED OPTIONS

LEARNING OBJECTIVES

After reading this chapter you will be able to:

- explain the disadvantages of a callable bond from the investor's perspective.

- describe what is meant by the yield to worst and outline the pitfalls of the traditional approach to valuing callable bonds.

- illustrate the price/yield relationship for a callable bond.

- explain what negative convexity means and when a callable bond may exhibit it.

- describe how the value of a bond with an embedded option can be decomposed and why an options approach is needed to value such bonds.

- explain the limitations of using modified duration and standard convexity as a measure of the price sensitivity of a bond with an embedded option.

- distinguish between effective duration and modified duration.

- describe the different types of convertible securities.

- describe the basic features of a convertible security.

- explain and calculate the conversion value, market conversion price, conversion premium per share, conversion premium ratio, and premium over straight value of a convertible bond.

- discuss the investment features of a convertible security.

- describe why an option-pricing approach is needed to properly value convertible securities.

In Chapters 20 and 21, we discussed pricing, return measures, and price volatility for bonds without options. We saw that the price of a bond was based on the present value of its cash flows. A bond with an embodied option is one in which either the issuer or the bondholder has the option to alter a bond's cash flows. In this chapter, we look at how to value bonds with embedded options.

Since the most common type of option embedded in a bond is a call option, our primary focus will be on callable bonds. We begin by looking at the disadvantages of the call feature from a bondholder's perspective and therefore at the reasons that potential investors want to receive compensation for the risk that the issuer might call the bond. We review the limitations of the traditional methodology used to evaluate bonds with embedded options and then provide a conceptual framework for thinking about how to value them. Because of the complexities in building models to value bonds with embedded options, we do not delve into these models. In the last section of this chapter, we look at how to value convertible bonds and the risk/return characteristics of these bonds.

CALLABLE BONDS

The holder of a callable bond has given the issuer the right to call the issue prior to the maturity date. A mortgage-backed security is also a callable security since the homeowner has the right to pay off all or part of the mortgage loan balance at any time.

As we discussed in Chapter 19, the presence of a call option results in two disadvantages to the bondholder. First, callable bonds expose bondholders to reinvestment risk, since an issuer will call a bond when the yield on bonds in the market is lower than the issue's coupon rate. For example, if the coupon rate on a callable corporate bond is 13% and prevailing market yields are 7%, the issuer will find it economical to call the 13% issue and refund it with a 7% issue. From the investor's perspective, the proceeds received will have to be reinvested at a lower interest rate.

Second, as we explain later in this chapter, the price appreciation potential for a callable bond in a declining interest rate environment is limited compared to an otherwise comparable non-callable bond. This is because the market will increasingly expect the bond to be redeemed at the call price as interest rates fall. This phenomenon for a callable bond is referred to as price compression.

Because of the disadvantages associated with callable bonds, these instruments often feature a period of call protection, an initial period when bonds may not be called. Still, given both price compression and reinvestment risk, why would any investor want to own a callable bond? If the investor receives sufficient potential compensation in the form of a higher potential yield, an investor would be willing to accept call risk.

Traditional Valuation Methodology

When a bond is callable, the practice has been to calculate a yield to call as well as a yield to maturity. The former yield calculation assumes that the issuer will call the bond at the first call date. As explained in Chapter 19, the procedure for calculating the yield to call is the same as for any yield calculation: Determine the interest rate that will make the present value of the expected cash flows equal to the price. In the case of yield to call, the expected cash flows are the coupon payments to the first call date and the call price.

According to the traditional approach, conservative investors should compute the yield to call and yield to maturity for a callable bond selling at a premium, selecting the lower of the two as a measure of potential return. The smaller of the two yield measures should be used to evaluate the relative value of bonds. More recently, the traditional approach has been extended to compute not just the yield to the first call date, but the yield to all possible call dates. Since most bonds can be called at any time after the first call date, the approach has been to compute the yield to every coupon anniversary date following the first call date. Then, all the yield to calls calculated and the yield to maturity are compared. The lowest of these yields is called the **yield to worst**, which is the yield that the traditional approach has investors believing should be used in relative value analysis.

We explained the limitations of the yield to call as a measure of the potential return of a security in Chapter 20. The yield to call does consider all three sources of potential return from owning a bond. However, as in the case of the yield to maturity, it assumes that all cash flows can be reinvested at the computed yield—in this case the yield to call—until the assumed call date. Moreover, the yield to call assumes that (1) the investor will hold the bond to the assumed call date and (2) the issuer will call the bond on that date.

Oftentimes, these underlying assumptions about the yield to call are unrealistic since they do not take into account how an investor will reinvest the proceeds if the issue is called. For example, consider two bonds, M and N. Suppose that the yield to maturity for bond M, a five-year non-callable bond, is 10%, while the yield to call for bond N is 10.5% assuming the bond will be called in three years. Which bond is better for an investor with a five-year investment horizon? It is not possible to tell for the yields cited. If the investor intends to hold the bond for five years and the issuer calls the bond after three years, the total dollars available at the end of five years will depend on the interest rate that can be earned from investing funds from the call date to the end of the investment horizon.

Price/Yield Relationship for a Callable Bond

As explained in Chapter 20, the price/yield relationship for an option-free bond is convex. Figure 23-1 shows the price/yield relationship for both a non-callable bond and the same bond if it is callable. The convex curve a–a' is the

FIGURE 23-1

Price/yield relationship for a non-callable bond and a callable bond.

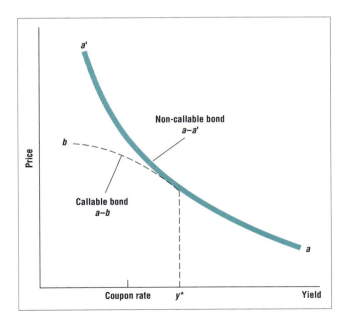

price/yield relationship for the non-callable (option-free) bond. The unusual-shaped curve denoted by a–b is the price/yield relationship for the callable bond.

The reason for the shape of the price/yield relationship for the callable bond is as follows. When the prevailing market yield for comparable bonds is higher than the coupon interest on the bond, it is unlikely that the issuer will call the bond. For example, if the coupon rate on a bond is 8% and the prevailing yield on comparable bonds is 16%, it is highly improbable that the issuer will call an 8% coupon bond so that it can issue a 16% coupon bond. Since the bond is unlikely to be called, the callable bond will have the same convex price/yield relationship as a non-callable bond when yields are greater than y^*. However, even when the coupon rate is just below the market yield, investors may not pay the same price for the callable bond had it been non-callable because there is still the chance the market yield may drop further, making it beneficial for the issuer to call the bond.

As yields in the market decline, the likelihood that yields will decline further so that the issuer will benefit from calling the bond increases. The exact yield level at which investors begin to view the issue likely to be called may not be known, but we do know that there is some level. In Figure 23-1, at yield levels below y^*, the price/yield relationship for the callable bond departs from the price/yield relationship for the non-callable bond. Consider a bond that is callable at 104. If market yield would price a comparable non-callable bond at 109, rational investors would not pay 109 for the callable bond. If they did and the bond were called, investors would receive 104 (the call price) for a bond they purchased for 109.

Notice that for a range of yields below y^*, there is price compression—that is, there is limited price appreciation as yields decline. The portion of the callable bond price/yield relationship below y^* is said to be *negatively convex*.

Negative convexity means that the price appreciation will be less than the price depreciation for a large change in yield of a given number of basis points. For a bond that is option-free and exhibits positive convexity, the price appreciation will be greater than the price depreciation for a large change in yield. The price changes resulting from bonds exhibiting positive convexity and negative convexity are shown in Table 23-1.

It is important to understand that a bond can still trade above its call price even if it is highly likely to be called. For example, consider a callable bond with a 10-year, 13% coupon rate that is callable in 1 year at a call price of 104. Suppose that the yield on 10-year bonds is 6% and that the yield on 1-year bonds is 5%. In a 6% interest rate environment for 10-year bonds, investors will expect that the issue will be called in 1 year. Thus, investors will

TABLE 23-1		
PRICE VOLATILITY IMPLICATIONS OF POSITIVE AND NEGATIVE CONVEXITY		
Change in Interest Rates	**Absolute Value of Percentage Price Change for:**	
	Positive Convexity	**Negative Convexity**
-100 basis points	X%	Less than Y%
+100 basis points	Less than X%	Y%

treat this issue as if it is a 1-year bond and price it accordingly. The price must reflect the fact that the investor will receive a 13% coupon rate for 1 year. The price of this bond would be the present value of the two cash flows, which are (1) $6.5 (per $100 of par value) of coupon interest 6 months from now and (2) $6.50 coupon interest plus the call price of $104 1 year from now. Discounting the two cash flows at the 5% prevailing market yield (2.5% every 6 months) for 1-year bonds, the price is

$$\frac{\$6.5}{(1.025)^1} + \frac{\$110.5}{(1.025)^2} = \$111.52$$

In a case such as this, an investor will be willing to pay a higher price than the call price to purchase this bond.

The Components of a Bond with an Embedded Option

To develop an analytical framework for valuing a bond with an embedded option, it is necessary to decompose a bond into its component parts. A callable bond is a bond in which the bondholder has sold the issuer an option (more specifically, a call option) that allows the issuer to repurchase the contractual cash flows of the bond from the time the bond is first callable until the maturity date.

Consider the following two bonds: (1) a callable bond with an 8% coupon, 20 years to maturity and callable in 5 years at 104 and (2) a 10-year 9% coupon bond callable immediately at par. For the first bond, the bondholder owns a 5-year non-callable bond and has sold a call option granting the issuer the right to call away from the bondholder 15 years of cash flows 5 years from now for a price of 104. The investor who owns the second bond has a 10-year non-callable bond and has sold a call option granting the issuer the right to immediately call the entire 10-year contractual cash flows, or any cash flows remaining at the time the issue is called, for 100.

Effectively, the owner of a callable bond is entering into two separate transactions. First, she buys a non-callable bond from the issuer for which she pays some price. Then, she sells the issuer a call option for which she receives the option price.

In terms of price, a callable bond is therefore equal to the price of the two components parts. That is,

Callable bond price = non-callable bond price − call option price

The reason the call option price is subtracted from the price of the non-callable bond is that when the bondholder sells a call option, she receives the option price. Graphically this can be seen in Figure 23-2. The difference between the price of the non-callable bond and the callable bond at any given yield is the price of the embedded call option.[1]

---

[1]Actually, the position is more complicated than we just described. The issuer may be entitled to call the bond at the first call date and any time thereafter, or at the first call date and any subsequent coupon anniversary. Thus the investor has effectively sold an American-type call option to the issuer, but the call price may vary with the date the call option is exercised. This is because the call schedule for a bond may have a different call price, depending on the call date. Moreover, the underlying bond for the call option is the remaining coupon payments that would have been made by the issuer had the bond not been called. For exposition purposes, it is easier to understand the principles associated with the investment characteristics of callable corporate bonds by describing the investor's position as long a non-callable bond and short a call option.

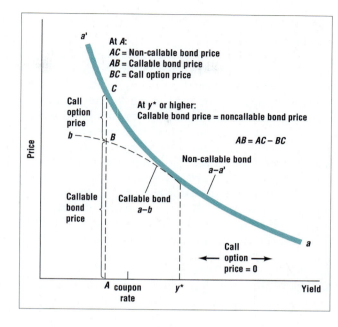

FIGURE 23-2

Decomposition of the price of a callable bond.

The same logic applies to putable bonds. In the case of a putable bond, the bondholder has the right to sell the bond to the issuer at a designated price and time. A putable bond can be broken into two separate transactions. First, the investor buys a non-putable bond. Second, the investor buys an option from the issuer that allows the investor to sell the bond to the issuer. The price of a putable bond is then

Putable bond price = non-putable bond price + put option price

Options Approach to the Valuation of Bonds with Embedded Options

The discussion in the previous section provides a useful way to conceptualize a bond with an embedded option. More specifically, in the case of a callable bond, its value is equal to the value of a comparable non-callable bond minus the value of the call option. Therefore, to value a callable bond it is necessary to determine its value if it is not callable and to subtract the value of the embedded option. In the case of a putable bond, it is necessary to value the bond if it is not putable and to add to that value the value of the put option.

The procedure for valuing a bond with an embedded option therefore requires an option-pricing model that can value the embedded option. We discussed various option-pricing models for the valuation of stock options. Here we are interested in option-pricing models that value an option on a fixed-income security. Such models are more complex than option-pricing models for stock. The reason for this is more fully explained in Chapter 26.

Nevertheless, it is critical to understand that the factors that affect options prices that we discussed in Chapter 18 are those that affect the value of an option on a bond. Consequently, the same factors will affect the value of a bond with an embedded option. For example, all other factors constant, the value of an option on a bond increases when expected interest rate volatility increases. Thus, if expected interest rate volatility increases, the value of a callable bond decreases because the value of the embedded call option increases.

The valuation procedure gives the theoretical value of a callable corporate bond.[2] An investor can then compare that value with the market price of the bond. If the theoretical value is greater than the market price, the bond is cheap; if the reverse is true, then the bond is expensive. If the theoretical value is equal to the market price, the bond is fairly priced.

The valuation procedure need not stop here, however. Instead, it can convert the divergence between the theoretical value and the market price into a yield spread measure. This step is necessary since most market participants find it more convenient to think about yield spread than about price differences.

The **option-adjusted spread** (**OAS**) was developed as a measure of the yield spread that can be used to convert dollar differences between theoretical value and market price. Thus, basically, the OAS is used to reconcile value with market price. But what is it a "spread" over? As we explained in Chapter 22, the proper procedure for valuing a bond is the spot rate curve. While we discussed the Treasury spot rate curve, it is possible to develop a theoretical spot rate curve for every issuer. The OAS is a spread over an issuer's spot rate curve. The spot rate curve itself is not a single curve, but a series of spot rate curves that allow for changes in interest rates due to interest rate volatility. The reason the resulting spread is referred to as "option-adjusted" is because in the valuation process the cash flows of the bond whose value we seek are adjusted to reflect the embedded option.

Effective Duration and Effective Convexity

Money managers also want to know the price sensitivity of a bond when interest rates change. As explained in Chapter 21, modified duration is a measure of the sensitivity of a bond's price to interest rate changes, *assuming that the expected cash flows do not change with interest rates*. Consequently, modified duration may not be an appropriate measure for bonds with embedded options because the expected cash flows change as interest rates change. For example, when interest rates fall, the expected cash flows for a callable bond may change. In the case of a putable bond, a rise in interest rates may change the expected cash flows.

While modified duration may be inappropriate as a measure of a bond's price sensitivity to interest rate changes, there is a duration measure that is more appropriate for bonds with embedded options. Since duration measures price responsiveness to changes in interest rates, the duration for a bond with an embedded option can be estimated by letting interest rates change by a small number of basis points above and below the prevailing yield and then seeing how the prices change. In general, the duration for *any* bond can be *approximated* as follows:

$$\text{Duration} = \frac{P_- - P_+}{(P_0)\,(y_+ - y_-)}$$

---

[2]For a discussion of the two valuation procedures—the binomial method and the Monte Carlo method—see Chapters 6 and 7 in Frank J. Fabozzi, *Valuation of Fixed Income Securities* (Summit, NJ: Frank J. Fabozzi Associates, 1994).

where P_- = price if yield is decreased by x basis points
  P_+ = price if yield is increased by x basis points
  P_0 = initial price (per \$100 of par value)
  y_+ = initial yield plus x basis points
  y_- = initial yield minus x basis points

Application of this formula to an option-free bond gives the modified duration because the cash flows do not change when yields change. For example, consider a 20-year, 7% coupon bond selling at \$74.26. The yield to maturity for this bond is 10%. The Macaulay duration for this bond using the formula for the Macaulay duration presented in Chapter 21 is 9.64. Therefore, modified duration is 9.18, as shown below:

$$\text{Modified duration} = \frac{9.64}{(1 + 0.10/2)} = 9.18$$

Suppose, instead, we used the formula given above to approximate duration, evaluating the price changes for a 20-basis-point change up and down. Then, with

  P_- = 75.64
  P_+ = 72.92
  P_0 = 74.26
  y_+ = 0.102
  y_- = 0.098

substituting into the formula gives

$$\frac{75.64 - 72.92}{(74.26)(0.102 - 0.098)} = 9.16$$

The approximation of 9.16 is close to the 9.18 modified duration calculated using the exact formula.

When the approximate duration formula is applied to a bond with an embedded option, the new prices at the higher and lower yield levels should reflect the expected change in the cash flows. For example, in the case of a callable bond, the new prices are based on what the cash flows are expected to be, given the issuer's right to call the bond. For mortgage-backed securities, the new prices must consider how prepayments will change as interest rates change. Duration calculated in this way is called **effective duration**.

In general, the relationships between duration, modified duration, and effective duration are as follows. Duration is a generic concept that indicates the responsiveness of a bond to a change in interest rates. Modified duration is a duration measure in which the cash flows are not assumed to change when interest rates change. In contrast, effective duration measures the responsiveness of a bond's price, taking into account that the expected cash flows will change as interest rates change due to the embedded option. The difference between modified duration and effective duration for a bond with an embedded option can be quite dramatic. For example, a callable bond could have a modified duration of 7 and an effective duration of 3. For certain highly leveraged mortgage-backed securities, the bond could have a modified duration of 7 and an effective duration of 50! The difference between modified duration and effective duration is summarized in Figure 23-3.

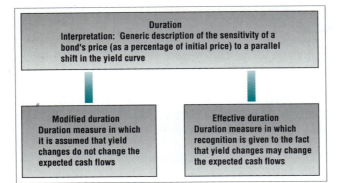

FIGURE 23-3

Modified duration versus effective duration.

Similarly, the standard convexity measure may be inappropriate for a bond with embedded options because it does not consider the effect of a change in interest rates on the bond's cash flows. The convexity of any bond can be approximated using the following formula:

$$\frac{P_+ + P_- - 2(P_0)}{(P_0)[0.5\,(y_+ - y_-)]^2}$$

When the prices used in this formula assume that the cash flows do not change when yields change, the resulting convexity is a good approximation of the standard convexity for an option-free bond. When the prices used in the formula are derived by changing the cash flows when yields change, the resulting convexity is called **effective convexity**. (See Box 23.)

CONVERTIBLE SECURITIES[3]

A **convertible security** is a security that can be converted into common stock at the option of the securityholder. These securities include **convertible bonds** and **convertible preferred stock**. As of October 31, 1992, the total market value of convertible securities issued by U.S. corporations was $85.8 billion.[4] Of this amount, $47.2 billion (55%) were convertible bonds and $38.6 (45%) were convertible preferred stock. Convertible bonds are also issued outside the United States, in national bond markets and the Eurobond market. For example, of the $47.2 billion of convertible bonds issued by U.S. corporations, about $6.7 billion were issued in the Eurobond market.

Basic Features of Convertible Securities

The conversion provision of a convertible security grants the securityholder the right to convert the security into a predetermined number of shares of common stock of the issuer. A convertible security is therefore a security with an embedded call option to buy the common stock of the issuer.

---

[3]This section draws from Chapter 9 of Fabozzi, *Valuation of Fixed Income Securities*, op. cit.

[4]Preston M. Harrington II, Bernie Moriarty, and Hareesh Paranjape, *LYONs Review* (November/December 1992 Quarterly Update), Merrill Lynch, Pierce, Fenner & Smith, Inc., p. 2. All the data reported in this chapter on the size of the market are taken from this source.

BOX 23

EXPECTED VOLATILITY AND THE VALUATION OF CALLABLE, FIXED-INCOME SECURITIES

Most U.S. fixed-income securities carry embedded call options that allow the borrower to redeem the liability before maturity. The loans underlying mortage-backed securities can, in general, be pre-paid at par at any time and about 75% of outstanding corporate bonds are callable at the issuer's descretion at some time before maturity. Until recently, participants in fixed-income markets lacked effective tools for evaluating these options. Some commonly used valuation measures assumed that interest rates would not change, that is, that interest rate volatility would be zero. Thus, mortage-backed securities were quoted on a cash flow yield basis, on the assumption that prepayments would proceed according to a fixed schedule, and callable corporates were bought and sold on the basis of their "yield to worst" (the minimum of the yield to maturity and the yield to call). The impact of changing rate levels was analyzed by viewing the security's performance for a small number of arbitrarily chosen scenarios.

Two related concepts—*effective duration and option-adjusted spread* (*OAS*)—provide a more precise measurement of the relative value and performance characteristics of securities carrying differing degrees of call protection. The effective duration of a callable corporate or mortage security gives the sensitivity of the issue's price to interest rate changes; the OAS is the basis-point spread offered by the security over U.S. Treasuries, after adjusting for the effect of its option features.

Unlike the yield to worst or the cash flow yield, the OAS explicitly accounts for the possibility that interest rates might change. Consequently, the value of a given callable security, as measured by its OAS, will vary depending on how much interest rates are likely to change. For example, consider a callable bond trading at a discount. If interest rates are not expected to vary beyond a very narrow range, then it is unlikely that the issuer will exercise the option to call the bond before maturity. Thus, at low volatility levels, the embedded call option will have little effect on the bond's value, and the OAS of the bond will be close to the standard spread over Treasuries given by the bond's yield to maturity. The effective duration of such a bond would be approximately equal to its nominal duration (the modified duration based on the cash flows to maturity). By contrast, if interest rates are expected to be highly volatile, then there is a much greater probability that the issuer will call the bond before maturity. In this case, the effective duration of the callable bond will be shorter than its nominal duration, and the OAS will be narrower than the yield to maturity spread.

Source: William M. Boyce, Webster Hughes, Peter S. A. Niculescu, and Michael Waldman, "The Implied Volatility of Fixed Income Markets," in Frank J. Fabozzi (ed.), *Advances and Innovations in the Bond and Mortgage Markets* (Chicago: Probus Publishing, 1989), pp. 17–18.

Questions for Box 23

1. What is the difference between modified duration and effective duration?
2. Why in a low interest rate volatility environment will a bond's effective duration be approximately the same as its modified duration?

An **exchangeable security** grants the securityholder the right to exchange the security for the common stock of a firm *other* than the issuer of the security. For example, some Ford Motor Credit convertible bonds are exchangeable for the common stock of the parent company, Ford Motor Company. Throughout this chapter we use the term "convertible security" to refer to both convertible and exchangeable securities.

In illustrating the calculation of the various concepts described below, we will use the General Signal Corporation (ticker symbol "GSX") 5 3/4% convertible issue due June 1, 2002. Information about the issue and the stock of this issuer is provided in Table 23-2.

Conversion Ratio The number of shares of common stock that the securityholder will receive from exercising the call option of a convertible security is called the **conversion ratio**. The conversion privilege may extend for all or only some portion of the security's life, and the stated conversion ratio may fall over time. It is always adjusted proportionately for stock splits and stock

---

TABLE 23-2

INFORMATION ABOUT GENERAL SIGNAL CORPORATION CONVERTIBLE BOND 5 3/4% DUE JUNE 1, 2002, AND COMMON STOCK

Convertible Bond

Market price (as of 10/7/93): $106.50

Issue proceeds: $100 million

Issue date: 6/1/92

Maturity date: 6/1/02

Non-call until 6/1/95

Call price schedule:

6/1/95	103.59
6/1/96	102.88
6/1/97	102.16
6/1/98	101.44
6/1/99	100.72
6/1/00	100.00
6/1/01	100.00

Coupon rate: 5 3/4%

Conversion ratio: 25.320 shares of GSX shares per $1,000 par value

Rating: A3/A-

GSX Common Stock

Stock price: $33

Dividend per share: $0.90 per year

Dividend yield (as of 10/7/93): 2.727%

Expected volatility: 17%

---

dividends. For the GSX convertible issue the conversion ratio is 25.32 shares. This means that for each $1,000 of par value of this issue the securityholder exchanges for GSX common stocks, she will receive 25.32 shares.

At the time of issuance of a convertible security, the issuer effectively grants the securityholder the right to purchase the common stock at a price equal to

$$\frac{\text{par value of convertible security}}{\text{conversion ratio}}$$

This price is referred to in the prospectus as the **stated conversion price**. Sometimes the issue price of a convertible security may not be equal to par. In such cases, the stated conversion price at issuance is usually determined by the issue price.

The conversion price for the GSX convertible issue is

$$\text{Conversion price} = \frac{\$1,000}{25.32} = \$39.49$$

Call Provisions   Almost all convertible issues are callable by the issuer. Typically there is a non-call period (i.e., a time period from the time of issuance that the convertible security may not be called). The GSX convertible issue had a non-call period of three years at the time of issuance, as indicated in Table 23-2 (issued in 6/1/92 but could not be called until 6/1/95).

Some issues have a **provisional call feature** that allows the issuer to call the issue during the non-call period if the stock reaches a certain price. For example Whirlpool Corporation issued a zero-coupon convertible bond on 5/14/91 with a non-call period of two years and a conversion ratio that translated to a stated conversion price of $52.35. This bond would be due 5/14/11 but could not be called before 5/14/93 unless the stock price reached $52.35, at which time the issuer had the right to call the issue. Another example is the Eastman Kodak zero-coupon convertible bond due 10/15/11. The issuer could not call the issue before 10/15/93 unless the common stock traded at a price of at least $70.73 for at least 20 to 30 trading days.

The call price schedule of a convertible security is specified at the time of issuance. Typically, the call price declines over time. The call price schedule for the GSX convertible issue is shown in Table 23-2.[5]

Put Provisions   A put option grants the bondholder the right to require the issuer to redeem the issue at designated dates for a predetermined price. Some convertible bonds are putable. For example, Eastman Kodak zero-coupon convertible bond due 10/15/11 is putable. The put schedule is as follows: 32.35 if put on 10/15/94; 34.57 if put on 10/15/95; 36.943 if put on 10/15/96; 51.486 if put on 10/15/01; and 71.753 if put on 10/15/06.

Put options can be classified as "hard" puts and "soft" puts. A hard put is one in which the convertible security must be redeemed by the issuer only for cash. In the case of a soft put, the issuer has the option to redeem the convertible security for cash, common stock, subordinated notes, or a combination of the three.

Traditional Analysis of a Convertible Security

Now that we are familiar with the basic features of a convertible issue, let's look at how to analyze a convertible issue. There are two approaches: the traditional approach and the option-based approach. The latter approach uses the option-pricing theory described in Chapter 18 to value a convertible bond. We postpone this approach to the end of this section. The traditional approach that we describe now makes no attempt to value the option that the securityholder has been granted.

Minimum Value of a Convertible Security   The **conversion value**, or **parity value**, of a convertible security is the value of the security if it is converted immediately.[6] That is,

Conversion value = market price of common stock × conversion ratio

---

[5]In the case of a zero-coupon convertible bond, the call price is based on an accreted value. For example, for the Whirlpool Corporation zero-coupon convertible, the call price on 5/14/93 is $28.983 and thereafter accretes daily at 7% per annum compounded semiannually. So if the issue is called on 5/14/94, the call price would be $31.047 ($28.983 times 1.035^2).

[6]Technically, the standard textbook definition of conversion value given here is theoretically incorrect because as bondholders convert, the price of the stock will decline. The theoretically correct definition for the conversion value is that it is the product of the conversion ratio and the stock price *after* conversion.

The minimum price of a convertible security is the greater of:

1. Its conversion value.

or

2. Its value as a security without the conversion option—that is, based on the convertible security's cash flows if not converted (a plain vanilla security). This value is called its **straight value** or **investment value**.

To estimate the straight value, we must determine the required yield on a non-convertible security with the same quality rating and similar investment characteristics. Given this estimated required yield, the straight value is then the present value of the security's cash flows using this yield to discount the cash flows.

If the convertible security does not sell for the greater of these two values, arbitrage profits could be realized. For example, suppose the conversion value is greater than the straight value, and the security trades at its straight value. An investor can buy the convertible security at the straight value and convert it. By doing so, the investor realizes a gain equal to the difference between the conversion value and the straight value. Suppose, instead, the straight value is greater than the conversion value, and the security trades at its conversion value. By buying the convertible at the conversion value, the investor will realize a higher yield than a comparable straight security.

For the GSX convertible issue, the conversion value on 10/7/93 per $1,000 of par value was equal to

Conversion value = $33 × 25.32 = $835.56

Therefore, the conversion value per $100 of par value was 83.556.

To simplify the analysis of the straight value of the bond, we will discount the cash flows to maturity by the yield on the 10-year on-the-run Treasury at the time of the analysis, 5.32%, plus a credit spread of 70 basis points that appeared to be appropriate at that time. The straight value using a discount rate of 6.02% for theoretical purposes only is 98.19. Actually, the straight value would be less than this because no recognition was given to the call feature. Since the minimum value of the GSX convertible issue is the greater of the conversion value and the straight value, the minimum value is 98.19.

Market Conversion Price   The price an investor effectively pays for the common stock if the convertible security is purchased in the market and then converted into the common stock is called the **market conversion price** (it is also called the **conversion parity price**). It is found as follows:

$$\text{Market conversion price} = \frac{\text{market price of convertible security}}{\text{conversion ratio}}$$

The market conversion price is a useful benchmark, because once the actual market price of the stock rises above the **market conversion price,** any further stock price increase is certain to increase the value of the convertible security by at least the same percentage. Therefore, the market conversion price can be viewed as a break-even point.

An investor who purchases a convertible security, rather than the underlying stock, pays a premium over the current market price of the stock. This premium per share is equal to the difference between the market conversion price and the current market price of the common stock. That is,

Market conversion premium per share

= market conversion price − current market price

The market conversion premium per share is usually expressed as a percentage of the current market price as follows:

Market conversion premium ratio

$$= \frac{\text{market conversion premium per share}}{\text{market price of common stock}}$$

Why would someone be willing to pay a premium to buy the stock? Recall that the minimum price of a convertible security is the greater of its conversion value or its straight value. Thus, as the common stock price declines, the price of the convertible security will not fall below its straight value. The straight value therefore acts as a floor for the convertible security's price.

Viewed in this context, the market conversion premium per share can be seen as the price of a call option. As explained in Chapter 17, the buyer of a call option limits the downside risk to the option price. In the case of a convertible security, for a premium the securityholder limits the downside risk to the straight value of the security. The difference between the buyer of a call option and the buyer of a convertible security is that the former knows precisely the dollar amount of the downside risk, while the latter knows only that the most that can be lost is the difference between the convertible security's price and the straight value. The straight value at some future date, however, is unknown; the value will change as interest rates in the economy change.

The calculation of the market conversion price, market conversion premium per share, and market conversion premium ratio for the GSX convertible issue based on market data as of 10/7/93 is shown below:

Market conversion price $= \dfrac{\$1,065}{25.32} = \$42.06$

Market conversion premium per share $= \$42.06 - \$33 = \$9.06$

Market conversion premium ratio $= \dfrac{\$9.06}{\$33} = 0.275 \qquad$ or 27.5%

Current Income of Convertible Security versus Common Stock As an offset to the market conversion premium per share, investing in the convertible security rather than buying the stock directly, means generally that the investor realizes higher current income from the coupon interest paid in the case of a convertible bond and from dividends in the case of a convertible preferred than would be received as common stock dividends paid on the number of shares equal to the conversion ratio. Analysts evaluating a convertible security typically compute the time it takes to recover the premium per share by computing the **premium payback period** (which is also known as the **break-even time**). This is computed as follows:

Premium payback period $= \dfrac{\text{market conversion premium per share}}{\text{favorable income differential per share}}$

where the favorable income differential per share is equal to the following for a convertible bond:

$$\frac{\text{coupon interest} - (\text{conversion ratio} \times \text{common stock dividend per share})}{\text{conversion ratio}}$$

And for convertible preferred stock:

$$\frac{\text{preferred dividends} - (\text{conversion ratio} \times \text{common stock dividend per share})}{\text{conversion ratio}}$$

Notice that the premium payback period does *not* take into account the time value of money.

For the GSX convertible issue, the market conversion premium per share is $9.06. The favorable income differential per share is found as follows:

Coupon interest from bond = 0.0575 × $1,000 = $57.50
Conversion ratio × dividend per share = 25.32 × $0.90 = $22.79

Therefore,

$$\text{Favorable income differential per share} = \frac{\$57.50 - \$22.79}{25.32} = \$1.37$$

and

$$\text{Premium payback period} = \frac{\$9.06}{\$1.37} = 6.6 \text{ years}$$

Without considering the time value of money, the investor would recover the market conversion premium per share in about seven years.

Downside Risk with a Convertible Security   Investors usually use the straight value as a measure of the downside risk of a convertible security, because the price of the convertible security cannot fall below this value. Thus, the straight value acts as the *current* floor for the price of the convertible bond. The downside risk is measured as a percentage of the straight value and is computed as follows:

$$\text{Premium over straight value} = \frac{\text{market price of the convertible security}}{\text{straight value}} - 1$$

The higher the premium over straight value, all other factors constant, the less attractive the convertible security.

Despite its use in practice, this measure of downside risk is flawed, because the straight value (the floor) changes as interest rates change. If interest rates rise (fall), the straight value falls (rises), making the floor fall (rise). Therefore, the downside risk changes as interest rates change.

For the GSX convertible issue, since the market price of the convertible security is 106.5 and the straight value is 98.19, the premium over straight value is

$$\text{Premium over straight value} = \frac{\$106.50}{\$98.19} - 1 = 0.085 \quad \text{or} \quad 8.5\%.$$

Upside Potential of a Convertible Security   The evaluation of the upside potential of a convertible security depends on the prospects for the underlying common stock. Thus, the techniques for analyzing common stocks discussed in earlier chapters of this book should be undertaken.

Investment Characteristics of Convertible Securities

The investment characteristics of a convertible security depend on the common stock price. If the price is low, so that the straight value is considerably higher than the conversion value, the security will trade much like a straight security. The convertible security in such instances is referred to as a **fixed-income equivalent** or a **busted convertible**.

When the price of the stock is such that the conversion value is considerably higher than the straight value, then the convertible security will trade as if it were an equity instrument; in this case it is said to be a **common stock equivalent**. In such cases, the market conversion premium per share will be small.

Between these two cases, fixed-income equivalent and equity equivalent, the convertible security trades as a **hybrid security**, having the characteristics of both a fixed-income security and a common stock instrument. These investment characteristics are summarized in Table 23-3.

An Option-Based Valuation Approach

The traditional valuation approach did not address the following questions:

1. What is a fair value for the conversion premium per share?
2. How do we handle convertible securities with call and/or put options?
3. How does a change in interest rates affect the stock price?

Consider first a non-callable/non-putable convertible security. The investor who purchases this security would be entering into two separate transactions: (1) buying a non-callable/non-putable straight security and (2) buying a call option on the stock where the number of shares that can be purchased with the call option is equal to the conversion ratio.

The question is, what is the fair value for the call option? The fair value depends on the factors discussed in Chapter 18 that affect the price of a call option. One key factor is the expected price volatility of the stock: The more the expected price volatility, the greater the value of the call option. The theoretical value of a call option can be valued using the Black-Scholes

TABLE 23-3		
INVESTMENT CHARACTERISTICS OF CONVERTIBLE SECURITIES		
Condition		*Characteristics*
Low stock price	Straight value > Conversion value	Fixed-income equivalent
Mid stock price	Straight value ≈ Conversion value	Hybrid security
High stock price	Straight value < Conversion value	Common stock equivalent

option-pricing model. As a first approximation to the value of a convertible security, the formula would be

Convertible security value
$$= \text{straight value} + \text{value of the call option on the stock}$$

The value of the call option is added to the straight value because the investor has purchased a call option on the stock.

Now let's add in a common feature of a convertible security: the issuer's right to call the security. The issuer can force conversion by calling the security. For example, suppose the call price is 103 and the conversion value is 107. If the issuer calls the security, the optimal strategy for the investor is to convert the security and receive shares worth \$107.[7] The investor, however, loses any premium over the conversion value that is reflected in the market price. Therefore, the analysis of convertible securities must take into account the value of the issuer's right to call. This depends, in turn, on (1) future interest rate volatility and (2) economic factors that determine whether it is optimal for the issuer to call the security. The Black-Scholes option-pricing model cannot handle this situation. To link interest rates and stock prices together (the third question we raise above), statistical analysis of historical movements of these two variables must be estimated and incorporated into the model.

Valuation models based on an option-pricing approach have been suggested by several researchers.[8] Many dealers of convertible bonds have developed such models, which they make available to institutional clients. One example is the model developed by Merrill Lynch Equity Capital Markets that can handle a combination of call and put features found in convertible securities, as well as changing conversion ratios and provisional call features.[9] The key input to the theoretical valuation model is expected stock price volatility, expected interest rate volatility, the interest rate on the issuer's non-convertible securities, the current common stock dividend, and the expected growth of common stock dividends. The inputs not known with certainty can be changed to test the sensitivity of the model.

Consider the GSX convertible issue. As indicated in Table 23-2, the assumed standard deviation (expected volatility) of the stock price return is 17%. The valuation model used by Merrill Lynch would have determined a theoretical value for the GSX convertible issue as of 10/7/93 to be 106.53. This value was in fact equal to the actual market price at the time, 106.5, which suggests that the issue is fairly priced.

---

[7]Actually, the conversion value would be less than \$107 because the per share value after conversion would decline.

[8]See, for example: Michael Brennan and Eduardo Schwartz, "Convertible Bonds: Valuation and Optimal Strategies for Call and Conversion," *Journal of Finance* (December 1977), pp. 1699–1715; Jonathan Ingersoll, "A Contingent-Claims Valuation of Convertible Securities," *Journal of Financial Economics* (May 1977), pp. 289–322; Michael Brennan and Eduardo Schwartz, "Analyzing Convertible Bonds," *Journal of Financial and Quantitative Analysis* (November 1980), pp. 907–929; and George Constantinides, "Warrant Exercise and Bond Conversion in Competitive Markets," *Journal of Financial Economics* (September 1984), pp. 371–398.

[9]Mihir Bhattacharya and Yu Zhu, "Valuation and Analysis of Convertible Securities," Chap. 36 in Frank J. Fabozzi and T. Dessa Fabozzi (eds.), *The Handbook of Fixed Income Securities* (Homewood, IL: Irwin Professional Publishing, 1994).

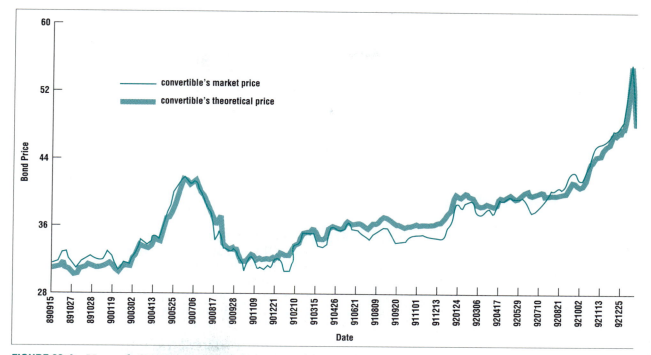

FIGURE 23-4   **Motorola LYONs: market price versus theoretical value (9/7/89–3/26/93).**

Source: Mihir Bhattacharya and Yu Zhu, "Valuation and Analysis of Convertible Securities," Chap. 6 in Frank J. Fabozzi and ˈ Dessa Fabozzi, (eds.), *The Handbook of Fixed Income Securities* (Homewood, IL: Irwin Professional Publishing, 1994).

The difference between the value of the convertible bond as determined from the valuation model and the straight value (properly adjusted for the call option granted to the issuer and any put option) is the value of the embedded call option for the stock. That is,

Value of the embedded call option for underlying stock

= theoretical value of convertible bond − straight value

For the GSX convertible issue, since the theoretical value for the issue is 106.53 and the straight value is 98.19 (recall that this was not adjusted for the issuer's call option), the approximate value of the embedded call option for the underlying stock is 8.43.

The valuation model as applied to the GSX issue indicated that the issue was fairly priced. Figure 23-4 compares the theoretical value of Motorola's Liquid Yield Option Notes (LYONs)[10] with the actual market price of the convertible issue from the issue date (9/7/89) to 3/26/93. During this period, the price of Motorola's stock increased from $28 1/16 to $65 1/4. In January 1991, the market conversion premium ratio reached a high of 44%. The figure indicates that the valuation appears to track the market price well.

---

[10]LYON is a Merrill Lynch trademark name for zero-coupon convertible bonds that are both callable and putable.

TABLE 23-4

SENSITIVITY OF MERRILL LYNCH'S VALUATION MODEL APPLIED TO WHIRLPOOL CORPORATION ZERO-COUPON BOND DUE 5/14/11

	Theoretical Value (% Change)	
	11/20/92	**11/20/93**
Base case	$33.16	$33.33
Stock volatility = 20%	32.67 (-1.0%)	33.07 (0.2%)
Stock price up 25%	39.52 (19.8%)	39.46 (19.6%)
Stock price down 25%	29.59 (-10.3%)	30.93 (-6.3%)
Interest rate down 100 basis points	33.47 (1.44%)	33.66 (1.9%)
Interest rate up 100 basis points	32.89 (-0.3%)	33.05 (0.15%)

Because the inputs into the valuation model are not known with certainty, it is important to test the sensitivity of the model. As an example, the Merrill Lynch theoretical valuation model was used to value, as of November 20, 1992, the Whirlpool Corporation zero-coupon bond due 5/14/11 (a LYON), assuming the following as a base case: a common stock price of 43 5/8, volatility for the stock price at 25.21%, a constant dividend yield, a yield to maturity of 8.10%, and a yield to put of 6.98%.[11] The theoretical value for the Whirlpool issue for this base case was $33.16.[12] The market price for this issue at the time was $33, so the issue appeared to be cheap relative to its theoretical value. Results of tests of the sensitivity of the model to the base case inputs are shown for the theoretical value as of 11/20/92 and also one year later by changing each input in Table 23-4.

The results for the stock volatility analysis indicate that if stock price volatility is 20% rather than the 25.21% assumed in the base case, the theoretical value as of 11/20/92 would be less. This is expected since the value of a call option on a stock is lower the lower the expected stock price volatility. Thus, while the Whirlpool issue would be cheap relative to its market price of $33 if stock price volatility is 25.21%, it is expensive if stock price volatility is 20%.

The Risk/Return Profile of a Convertible Security

Let's use the GSX convertible issue and the valuation model to look at the risk/return profile in investing in a convertible issue or the underlying common stock.

Suppose on 10/7/93 an investor is considering the purchase of either the common stock of GSX or the 5 3/4% convertible issue due 6/1/02. The stock can be purchased in the market for $33. By buying the convertible bond, the investor is effectively purchasing the stock for $42.06 (the market conversion price per share). Table 23-5 shows the total return for both alternatives one

---

[11]A yield to put is the interest rate that will make the present value of the cash flow to the first put date equal to the market price (plus accrued interest).

[12]Preston M. Harrington II, Bernie Moriarty, and Hareesh Paranjape, *LYONs Review* (November/December 1992 Quarterly Update), Merrill Lynch, Pierce, Fenner & Smith, Inc., p. 104.

TABLE 23-5
COMPARISON OF ONE-YEAR RETURN FOR GSX STOCK AND CONVERTIBLE ISSUE FOR ASSUMED CHANGES IN STOCK PRICE

Beginning of horizon: 10/7/93

End of horizon: 10/07/94

Price of GSX stock on 10/7/93: $33

Assumed volatility of GSX stock return: 17%

Stock Price Change (%)	GSX Stock Return (%)	Convertible's Theoretical Value	Convertible's Return (%)
-25%	-22.24%	100.47	-0.16%
-10	-7.24	102.96	2.14
0	2.76	105.27	4.27
10	12.76	108.12	6.90
25	27.76	113.74	12.08

year later, assuming that the stock price does not change, that it increases by +10%, and that it changes by +25%. The convertible's theoretical value is based on the Merrill Lynch valuation model.

If the GSX's stock price is unchanged, the stock position will underperform the convertible position despite the fact that a premium was paid to purchase the stock by acquiring the convertible issue. The reason is that even though the convertible's theoretical value decreased, the income from the coupon more than compensates for the capital loss. In the two scenarios where the price of GSX declines, the convertible position outperforms the stock position because the straight value provides a floor for the convertible. In contrast, the stock position outperforms the convertible position in the two cases where the stock rises in price because of the premium paid to acquire the stock via the convertible's acquisition.

One of the critical assumptions in this analysis is that the straight value does not change except for the passage of time. If interest rates rise, the straight value will decline. Even if interest rates do not rise, the perceived creditworthiness of the issuer may deteriorate, causing investors to demand a higher yield. The illustration clearly demonstrates that there are benefits and drawbacks of investing in convertible securities. The disadvantage is the upside potential give-up because a premium per share must be paid. An advantage is the reduction in downside risk (as determined by the straight value).

■ SUMMARY

Most bonds issued in bond markets throughout the world have at least one type of embedded option. In this chapter, we provide a framework for evaluating such bonds. Our primary focus was on callable bonds and convertible bonds.

The disadvantages of the call feature from the investor's perspective as interest rates decline are twofold. First, there is reinvestment risk. Second, the upside potential of a callable bond is limited compared with that of an otherwise non-callable bond, a feature referred to as price compression or negative convexity. The limitations of using the conventional methodology for evaluating callable bonds are explained, and the general principles of valuing convertible bonds are discussed.

Modified duration and standard convexity used to measure the interest rate sensitivity of an option-free bond may be inappropriate for a bond with an embedded option because these measures assume that cash flows do not change as interest rates change. The duration and convexity can be approximated for any bond whether it is option-free or has an embedded option. The approximation involves determining how the price of the bond changes if interest rates go up or down by a small number of basis points. If when interest rates are changed it is assumed that the cash flows do not change, then the resulting measures are modified duration and standard convexity. However, when the cash flows are allowed to change when interest rates change, the resulting measures are called effective duration and effective convexity.

Convertible and exchangeable securities can be converted into shares of common stock. A convertible security can be either a bond or a share of preferred stock. The conversion ratio is the number of common stock shares for which a convertible security may be converted. All convertible securities are callable, and some are putable. There are zero-coupon convertible bonds. A LYON is an example of a zero-coupon convertible bond that is callable and putable.

Analysis of a convertible security requires calculation of the conversion value, straight value, market conversion price, market conversion premium ratio, and premium payback period.

The downside risk of a convertible security usually is estimated by calculating the premium over straight value. The limitation of this measure is that the straight value (the floor) changes as interest rates change. Convertible security-holders are also exposed to call risk and takeover risk.

Because of the embedded options in a convertible security, an option-pricing approach can be used to determine the theoretical or fair value of a convertible security. These embedded options include the call option on the common stock that the securityholder possesses and the call option on the convertible security that the issuer has. If the issue is putable, this option must also be considered. Convertible security valuation models based on an option approach have been developed by many dealer firms and made available to their institutional clients.

■ KEY TERMS

break-even time	convertible security	option-adjusted spread (OAS)
busted convertible	effective convexity	parity value
call protection	effective duration	premium payback period
common stock equivalent	exchangeable security	price compression
conversion parity price	fixed-income equivalent	provisional call feature
conversion ratio	hybrid security	stated conversion price
conversion value	investment value	straight value
convertible bonds	market conversion price	yield to worst
convertible preferred stock	negative convexity	

■ QUESTIONS

1. **a.** What does negative convexity mean?
   b. Does a callable bond have negative or positive convexity?

2. Why is the investor of a callable bond or a mortgage-backed security exposed to reinvestment risk?

3. Suppose you are given the following information about two callable bonds that can be called immediately:

Estimated Percentage Change in Price If Interest Rates Change by:

	-100 Basis Points	+100 Basis Points
Bond ABC	+15%	−20%
Bond XYZ	+22%	−16%

You are told that both these bonds have the same maturity and that the coupon rate of one bond is 7% and the other 13%. Suppose that the yield curve for both issuers is flat at 8%. Based on this information, determine which bond is the lower-coupon bond and which is the higher-coupon bond. Explain why.

4. Given the following information, determine the theoretical value of the call option:

   Theoretical value of non-callable bond = $103
   Theoretical value of callable bond = $101

5. Explain why you agree or disagree with the following statement: "The value of a putable bond is never greater than the value of an otherwise comparable option-free bond."

6. The following excerpt is taken from an article entitled "Call Provisions Drop Off," which appeared in the January 27, 1992, issue of *BondWeek*:

   Issuance of callable long-term bonds dropped off further last year as interest rates fell, removing the incentive for many issuers to pay extra for the provision, said Street capital market officials.
   . . . The shift toward non-callable issues, which began in the late 1980s, reflects the secular trend of investors' unwilling to bear prepayment risk and possibly the cyclical trend that corporations believe that interest rates have hit all time lows. . . .(p. 2)

   a. What incentive is this article referring to in the first sentence of the excerpt?
   b. Why would issuers not be willing to pay for this incentive if they feel that interest rates will continue to decline?

7. Explain why you agree or disagree with the following statement: "An investor should be unwilling to pay more than the call price for a bond that is likely to be called."

8. The following excerpt is taken from an article entitled "Eagle Eyes High-Coupon Callable Corporates," which appeared in the January 20, 1992 issue of *BondWeek*:

   If the bond market rallies further, Eagle Asset Management may take profits, trading $8 million of seven to 10-year Treasuries for high-coupon single-A industrials that are callable in two to four years according to Joseph Blanton, senior v.p. He thinks a further rally is unlikely, however.
   . . .The corporates have a 95% chance of being called in two to four years and are treated as two-to-four year paper in calculating the duration of the portfolio, Blanton said... (p. 7)

   a. Why is modified duration an inappropriate measure for a high-coupon callable bond?
   b. What would be a better measure than modified duration?
   c. Why would the replacement of 10-year Treasuries with high-coupon callable bonds reduce the portfolio's duration?

9. Why is interest rate volatility important to take into consideration in valuing a bond with an embedded option?

10. Explain how an increase in expected interest rate volatility can decrease the value of a callable bond.

11. Suppose that a 7% coupon corporate bond is immediately callable. Also suppose that if this issuer issued new bonds, the coupon rate would be 12%. Why would the modified duration be a good approximation for the effective duration for this bond?

12. In calculating the effective duration for a mortgage-backed security, a prepayment model is needed to determine what would happen to the cash flows if interest rates change. Why?

13. In the October 26, 1992, prospectus summary of The Staples 5% convertible subordinated debentures due 1999, the offering stated: "Convertible into Common Stock at a conversion price of $45 per share..." Since the par value is $1,000, what is the conversion ratio?

14. In the November/December 1992 issue of *LYONs Review*, the following statement was made: "Because of the put option at three or five years after issuance, the price of a LYON tends to be less sensitive to interest rate changes than a 20–25 year maturity bond. This can provide significant price support in the event of a rise in interest rates or a decline in the price of the underlying stock" (p. 101). Explain why this statement is correct.

15. This excerpt is taken from an article entitled "Caywood Looks for Convertibles," which appeared in the January 13, 1992, issue of *BondWeek*: "Caywood Christian Capital Management will invest new money in its $400 million high-yield portfolio in 'busted convertibles,' double- and triple-B rated convertible bonds of companies . . . , said James Caywood, ceo. Caywood likes these convertibles as they trade at discounts and are unlikely to be called, he said" (p. 7).

   a. What is a busted convertible?
   b. What is the premium over straight value at which these bonds would trade?

c. Why does Mr. Caywood seek convertibles with higher investment-grade ratings?

d. Why is Mr. Caywood interested in call protection?

16. Explain the limitation of using premium over straight value as a measure of the downside risk of a convertible security.

17. This excerpt is from an article entitled "Bartlett Likes Convertibles," which appeared in the October 7, 1991, issue of *BondWeek*:

    Bartlett & Co. is selectively looking for opportunities in convertible bonds that are trading cheaply because the equity of the issuer has dropped in value, according to Dale Rabiner, director of fixed income at the $800 million Cincinnati-based fund. Rabiner said he looks for five-year convertibles trading at yields comparable to straight bonds of companies he believes will rebound. (p. 7)

    Discuss this strategy for investing in convertible bonds.

18. Consider the following hypothetical convertible bond:

    Par value = $1,000

    Coupon rate = 9.5%

    Market price of convertible bond = $1,000

    Conversion ratio = 37.383

    Estimated straight value of bond = $510

    Yield to maturity of straight bond = 18.7%

Assume that the price of the common stock is $23 and that the dividend per share is $0.75 per year.

a. Calculate each of the following:
   (1) Conversion value
   (2) Market conversion price
   (3) Conversion premium per share
   (4) Conversion premium ratio
   (5) Premium over straight value
   (6) Yield advantage of bond
   (7) Premium payback period

b. Suppose that the price of the common stock increases from $23 to $46.
   (1) What will be the approximate return realized from investing in the convertible bond?
   (2) What would be the return realized if $23 had been invested in the common stock?
   (3) Why would the return on investing directly in the common stock be higher than investing in the convertible bond?

c. Suppose that the price of the common stock declines from $23 to $8.
   (1) What will be the approximate return realized from investing in the convertible bond?
   (2) What would be the return realized if $23 had been invested in the common stock?
   (3) Why would the return on investing in the convertible bond be higher than the return on investing directly in the common stock?

CHAPTER 24
BOND PORTFOLIO MANAGEMENT STRATEGIES

LEARNING OBJECTIVES
After reading this chapter you will be able to:

- identify the different types of active bond portfolio strategies: interest rate expectations strategies, yield curve strategies, yield spread strategies, and individual security selection strategies.

- explain what is meant by a bullet, a barbell, and a ladder yield curve strategy.

- explain the limitations of using duration and convexity to assess the potential performance of bond portfolio strategies.

- describe why it is necessary to use the dollar duration when implementing a yield spread strategy.

- discuss the advantages and disadvantages of bond indexing.

- describe the methodologies for constructing an indexed portfolio.

- explain the difficulties associated with implementing a bond-indexing strategy.

- explain what is meant by enhanced bond indexing.

As explained in Chapter 1, selecting a bond portfolio strategy that is consistent with the objectives and policy guidelines of the client or institution is a major step in the investment management process. Bond portfolio strategies, just like stock portfolio strategies, can be classified as either active or passive. Essential to all active strategies is specification of expectations about the factors that influence the performance of an asset class. Passive strategies involve minimal expectational input.

This chapter describes active bond portfolio strategies and one type of passive strategy, indexing. Active portfolio strategies can be classified into four categories: interest rate expectations strategies, yield curve strategies, yield spread strategies, and individual security selection strategies. The passive strategy described in this chapter, bond indexing, has the same objective as equity indexing described in Chapter 14—to match the performance of some predetermined index. We will describe other passive strategies in the next chapter.

STRATEGIES

N.Y. Firm Buys Long Treasuries

Alan Kral, portfolio manager at New York-based **Trevor Stewart Burton & Jacobsen**, says he is putting new cash coming into the firm's $400 million taxable fixed-income portfolio into 30-year Treasuries. Kral is bullish on long bonds, predicting yields will fall throughout the year as inflation remains subdued.

The portfolio is currently barbelled in three- and 30-year Treasuries as he predicts the yield curve will flatten with short-term rates rising and 30-year bond yields dropping to around 6% by year end. With the **Federal Reserve** determined to keep a lid on inflation, long bond yields will come down, he predicts. Kral anticipates the yield on the 30-year **Treasury** bond will drop to 5% before the end of the decade. The portfolio holds short-term Treasuries to target duration and as a hedge against a rate backup on the long end.

The mortgage-backed position contains 7 1/2% coupon Z-bonds. These bonds accrue interest on principal until the deal pays down, he notes. He does not plan to add to the mortgage-backed position as he is bullish on Treasuries. He has no plans to buy corporates either as spreads are tight. He says he is more comfortable making an interest rate bet rather than taking credit risk at this time. The duration on the portfolio is 12

years, Kral says, adding that he does not target any index. The portfolio is currently allocated 87% to Treasuries and 13% to mortgage-backeds.

USAA Boosts Utility Stocks, Reduces Pass-Throughs

Jack Saunders, manager of **USAA Mutual Income Fund**'s $2 billion portfolio, will use new cash and cash from maturing agency mortgage pass-throughs to add approximately $100 million in utility stocks over the next two to three months. Saunders says utility stocks cheapened as the stock market corrected following the **Federal Reserve**'s recent move to tighten interest rates, and he expects the stocks' prices will rise over the next few months as the market rebounds. The move will increase the fund's allocation to stocks to 20% from 15% and reduce the allocation to pass-throughs to 65% from 70%, he notes.

Saunders believes the yield curve will flatten over the year with short rates rising about 50 basis points and long rates staying in the 6–6.34% range. While he expects the Fed will tighten again this year, he does not believe inflation will be high enough to prompt significant moves in long-term interest rates. He will hold onto the fund's long bonds, which constitute 5% of the portfolio, as he believes the long bond yield

is currently at the high end of its trading range and has room to fall. He will also hold onto investment-grade corporates, which make up 10% of the portfolio, as they offer attractive yields, he says. To buy the utility stocks, Saunders will slightly reduce the allocation to mortgage-backeds, which include **Government National Mortgage Association** and **Federal National Mortgage Association** pass-throughs with average coupons of 7% and average lives of about 12 years, he says. He will continue to maintain on overweighted position in pass-throughs, however, as he believes they will continue to offer value this year as rates climb slightly and prepayments slow.

Oregon Firm Buys Munies

As corporate spreads to Treasuries have narrowed, **Thompson/Rubinstein Investment Management** is investing $5 million from maturing short-term corporate bonds in tax-exempt 12-year municipal bonds, says **Tim Ellis**, portfolio manager. By also selling corporates that have about one year left till maturity, the portfolio can pick up approximately 100 basis points in yield and gets the added benefit of selling taxable securities for non-taxable ones, Ellis says.

The manager is selling investment-grade corporates in the insurance, industrial and utility sectors. About 70% of

---

We emphasize throughout these chapters that the total return framework should be employed to analyze the effect of a strategy. Recall from Chapter 20 that yield measures are inadequate for assessing the potential performance of an individual bond. For a bond portfolio, the meaning of a "portfolio yield" is questionable and certainly provides no insight into the return for a portfolio over some investment horizon.

ACTIVE PORTFOLIO STRATEGIES

The starting point in our discussion of active strategies is an investigation of the various sources of return from holding a fixed-income portfolio. As we explained in Chapter 20, the three sources of return are coupon income, any capital gain (or loss), and reinvestment income. Here we explore the factors

BOX 24

Continued

Thompson/Rubinstein's $100 million fixed-income portfolio is invested on behalf of property/casualty insurance companies, whose tax rates have risen, making municipal bonds attractive. These portfolios require high liquidity in order to make potential claims payments. In addition, the firm tends to buy short and intermediate paper to lower risk and stabilize income, Ellis says. Not all cash is reinvested as insurance clients dip into their portfolios to pay annual claims. The portfolio's duration is less than four years, and the move will slowly lengthen duration by one to 15 days per month.

The Portland, Ore.-based firm's portfolio is allocated 50% to Treasuries, 25% to corporates, and 15% to tax exempt municipals and 10% to cash. The firm does not buy mortgage-backeds to avoid prepayment risk.

SCI Capital Shortens

John Finnerty, portfolio manager and fixed-income strategist at **SCI Capital Management**, says he recently shortened the firm's $190 million fixed-income portfolio by putting proceeds from the sale of nine-year Treasuries into two-year Treasuries and cash. The move reduced the **Treasury** position to 89% from 95% and boosted its cash position to 6% from 0%, Finnerty says. The

move also shortened the portfolio's duration to 2 3/4 years from 3 3/4 years, he adds.

Finnerty predicts first-quarter Gross Domestic Product will grow around 4%, higher than the market expectation of 2 1/2–3%. He believes this stronger growth will cause short- and long-term rates to rise about 40 basis points over the next three months. he shortened the portfolio's duration to avoid price depreciation on the long end. Longer term, Finnerty sees economic growth slowing, causing long rates to fall to 6% by year end though short rates will stay relatively stable. After long rates rise to the 6 3/4–7% range, Finnerty will consider reversing the recent move and extending the portfolio's duration by swapping two-year Treasuries and cash for 10-year Treasuries, he says.

The remainder of the Cedar Rapids, Iowa-based firm's portfolio is allocated 5% to investment-grade corporates, which he will not sell as they offer attractive yields over Treasuries. He has no plans to buy mortgage-backeds as prepayment risk is too high, he says.

Source: *BondWeek* (Feb. 28, 1994), p. 5.

Questions for Box 24

1. For the strategy followed by Alan Kral of Trevor Stewart Burton & Ja-

cobsen, answer the following questions:
   a. What is meant by a barbell strategy?
   b. Why is the purchase of a 3- and 30-year Treasury a barbell strategy?
   c. Why does a barbell strategy benefit if the yield curve flattens?

2. For the strategy followed by Jack Saunders of USAA Mutual Income fund, why do expectations that over the year short rates will rise about 50 basis points and long rates will stay at about the same range they currently are mean a flattening of the yield curve?

3. For the strategy followed by Tim Ellis of Thompson/Rubinstein Investment Management, why does the increase in tax rates faced by the property/casualty companies on whose behalf he invests, make municipal bonds attractive?

4. For the strategy followed by John Finnerty of SCI Capital Management, answer the following questions:
   a. Why did putting proceeds from the sale of nine-year Treasuries into two-year Treasuries and cash decrease the duration of the portfolio?
   b. Why does shortening the duration avoid price depreciation in the long end if long rates are expected to increase 40 basis points?

---

that affect one or more of these sources. In general, the following factors affect a portfolio's return:

1. Changes in the level of interest rates
2. Changes in the shape of the yield curve
3. Changes in yield spreads among bond sectors
4. Changes in the yield spread (risk premium) for a particular bond

Box 24 is a page from the February 28, 1994, issue of *BondWeek*, describing various strategies that are being employed by some portfolio managers who are willing to share their strategies with readers of the publication.

Manager Expectations versus the Market Consensus

A money manager who pursues an active strategy will position a portfolio to capitalize on expectations about future interest rates. But the potential outcome (as measured by total return) must be assessed before an active strategy is implemented. The primary reason for assessing the potential outcome is that the market (collectively) has certain expectations for future interest rates and these expectations are embodied in the market price of bonds. One lesson we learned in Chapter 22 when we discussed forward rates is that the outcome of a strategy will depend on how a manager's expectation differs from that of the market. Moreover, it does not make a difference if the market's expectation is correct. What is relevant is that the price of a bond embodies those expectations. The same is true for the strategies we discuss in this chapter.

Consequently, while some managers might refer to an "optimal strategy" that should be pursued given certain expectations, that is insufficient information in making an investment decision. If the market's expectations are the same as the manager's, bond prices reflect these expectations. For this reason we emphasize below the use of the total return framework for evaluating active strategies rather than blind pursuit of a strategy based merely on general statements such as "if you expect . . . , then you should pursue . . . " strategy.

Interest Rate Expectations Strategies

A money manager who believes that he or she can accurately forecast the future level of interest rates will alter the portfolio's sensitivity to interest rate changes. As duration is a measure of interest rate sensitivity, this involves increasing a portfolio's duration if interest rates are expected to fall and reducing duration if interest rates are expected to rise. For those managers whose benchmark is a bond index, this means increasing the portfolio duration relative to the benchmark index if interest rates are expected to fall and reducing it if interest rates are expected to rise. The degree to which the duration of the managed portfolio is permitted to diverge from that of the benchmark index may be limited by the client.

A portfolio's duration may be altered by swapping (or exchanging) bonds in the portfolio for new bonds that will achieve the target portfolio duration. Such swaps are commonly referred to as **rate anticipation swaps**. Alternatively, a more efficient means for altering the duration of a bond portfolio is to use interest rate futures contracts. As we explain in Chapter 26, buying futures increases a portfolio's duration, while selling futures decreases it.

The key to this active strategy is, of course, an ability to forecast the direction of future interest rates. The academic literature, however, does not support the view that interest rates can be forecasted so that risk-adjusted excess returns can be consistently realized. It is doubtful whether betting on future interest rates will provide a consistently superior return.

While a manager may not pursue an active strategy based strictly on future interest rate movements, there can be a tendency to make an interest rate bet to cover inferior performance relative to a benchmark index. For example, suppose a manager holds himself or herself out to a client as pursuing one of the active strategies discussed later in this chapter. Suppose further that the manager is evaluated over a one-year investment horizon, and that three months before the end of the investment horizon, the manager is performing below the client-specified benchmark index. If the manager believes the account will be lost because of underperformance, there is an incentive to bet on interest rate movements. If the manager is correct, the account will be saved, although an incorrect bet will result in underperforming the benchmark index by a greater amount. In this case, the account might well be lost regardless of the level of underperformance. A client can prevent this type of gaming by a manager by imposing constraints on the degree that the portfolio's duration can vary from that of the benchmark index. Also, in the performance evaluation stage of the investment management process described in Chapter 30, decomposing the portfolio's return into the factors that generated the return will highlight the extent to which a portfolio's return is attributable to changes in the level of interest rates.

There are other active strategies that rely on forecasts of future interest rate levels. Future interest rates, for instance, affect the value of options embedded in callable bonds and the value of prepayment options embedded in mortgage-backed securities. Callable corporate and municipal bonds with coupon rates above the expected future interest rate will underperform relative to non-callable bonds or low-coupon bonds. This is because callable bonds have the negative convexity feature described in Chapter 23. For the wide range of mortgage-backed securities described in Chapter 19, the effect of interest rates on prepayments causes some to benefit from higher future interest rates and others to benefit from lower future interest rates.

Yield Curve Strategies

As we explained in Chapter 22, the yield curve for U.S. Treasury securities shows the relationship between their maturities and yields. The shape of this yield curve changes over time. **Yield curve strategies** involve positioning a portfolio to capitalize on expected changes in the shape of the Treasury yield curve. In this section we will describe the different ways in which the Treasury yield curve has shifted, the different types of yield curve strategies, the usefulness of duration as a measure of the price sensitivity of a bond or portfolio when the yield curve shifts, and the way to assess the potential outcome of yield curve strategies.

Types of Shifts in the Yield Curve and Impact on Historical Returns A shift in the yield curve refers to the relative change in the yield for each Treasury maturity. A **parallel shift in the yield curve** refers to a shift in which the change in the yield on all maturities is the same. A **non-parallel shift in the yield curve** means that the yield for each maturity does not change by the same number of basis points.

Historically, two types of non-parallel yield curve shifts have been observed: a twist in the slope of the yield curve and a change in the humpedness of the yield curve. All these shifts are graphically portrayed in Figure 24-1. A twist in the slope of the yield curve refers to a flattening or steepening of the yield curve. In practice, the slope of the yield curve is measured by the spread between some long-term Treasury yield and some short-term Treasury yield. For example, some practitioners refer to the slope as the difference between the 30-year Treasury yield and the 1-year Treasury yield. Others refer to it as the spread between the 20-year Treasury yield and the 2-year Treasury yield. Regardless of how it is defined, a **flattening of the yield curve** means that the

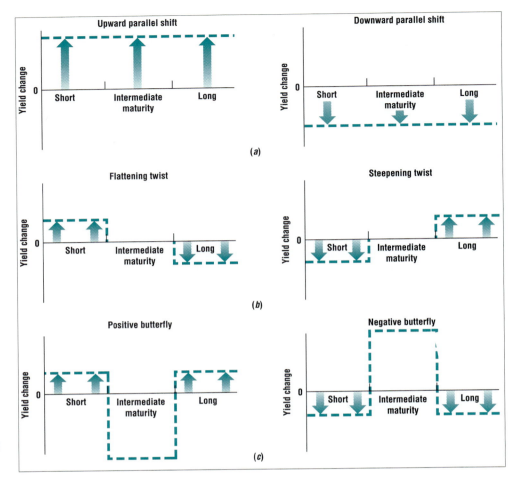

FIGURE 24-1

Types of yield curve shifts: (*a*) parallel shifts, (*b*) twists, and (*c*) butterfly shifts.

yield spread between the yield on a long-term and a short-term Treasury has decreased; a **steepening of the yield curve** means that the yield spread between a long-term and a short-term Treasury has increased. The other type of non-parallel shift, a change in the humpedness of the yield curve, is referred to as a **butterfly shift**.

Frank Jones analyzed the types of yield curve shifts that occurred between 1979 and 1990.[1] He found that the three types of yield curve shifts are not independent, with the two most common types of yield curve shifts being (1) a downward shift in the yield curve combined with a steepening of the yield curve and (2) an upward shift in the yield curve combined with a flattening of the yield curve. These two types of shifts in the yield curve are depicted in Figure 24-2. For example, his statistical analysis indicated that an upward parallel shift in the Treasury yield curve and a flattening of the yield curve have a correlation of 0.41. This suggests that an upward shift of the yield curve by 10 basis points is consistent with a 2.5-basis-point flattening of the yield curve. Moreover, he finds that an upward shift and flattening of the

[1]Frank J. Jones, "Yield Curve Strategies," *Journal of Fixed Income* (September 1991), pp. 43–41.

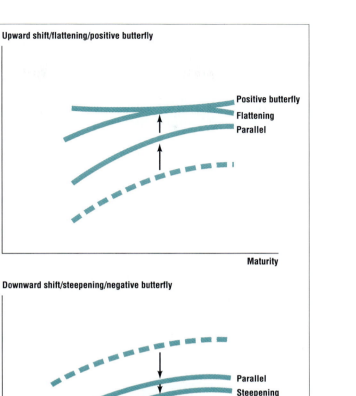

FIGURE 24-2

Combinations of yield curve shifts.

yield curve is correlated with a positive butterfly (less humpedness), while a downward shift and steepening of the yield curve is correlated with a negative butterfly (more humpedness).

Jones also provides empirical evidence of the importance of changes in the yield curve in determining returns of Treasury securities for various maturity sectors from 1979 to 1990. He finds that parallel shifts and twists in the yield curve are responsible for 91.6% of Treasury returns, while 3.4% of the returns is attributable to butterfly shifts and the balance, 5%, to unexplained factor shifts.[2] This discussion indicates that yield curve strategies require a forecast of the direction of the shift and a forecast of the type of twist.

Yield Curve Strategies   In portfolio strategies that seek to capitalize on expectations based on short-term movements in yields, the dominant source of return is the change in the price of the securities in the portfolio. This means

---

[2]These findings are consistent with those reported in Robert Litterman and Jose Scheinkman, "Common Factors Affecting Bond Returns," _Journal of Fixed Income_ (June 1991), pp. 54–61.

that the maturity of the securities in the portfolio will have an important impact on the portfolio's return. For example, a total return over a one-year investment horizon for a portfolio consisting of securities all maturing in one year will not be sensitive to changes in how the yield curve shifts one year from now. In contrast, the total return over a one-year investment horizon for a portfolio consisting of securities all maturing in 30 years will be sensitive to how the yield curve shifts because one year from now the value of the portfolio will depend on the yield offered on 29-year securities. As we know from Chapter 21, long-maturity bonds have substantial price volatility when yields change.

A portfolio consisting of equal proportions of securities maturing in one year and securities maturing in 30 years will have quite a different total return over a one-year investment horizon than the two portfolios we previously described when the yield curve shifts. The price of the one-year securities in the portfolio will not be sensitive to how the one-year yield has changed, but the price of the 30-year securities will be highly sensitive to how long-term yields have changed.

The key point is that for short-term investment horizons, the spacing of the maturity of bonds in the portfolio will have a significant impact on the total return. Consequently, yield curve strategies involve positioning a portfolio with respect to the maturities of the securities across the maturity spectrum included in the portfolio. There are three yield curve strategies: (1) bullet strategies, (2) barbell strategies, and (3) ladder strategies. Each of these strategies is depicted in Figure 24-3.

In a **bullet strategy**, the portfolio is constructed so that the maturities of the securities in the portfolio are highly concentrated at one point on the yield curve. In a **barbell strategy**, the maturities of the securities included in the portfolio are concentrated at two extreme maturities. Actually, in practice, when managers refer to a barbell strategy, it is relative to a bullet strategy. For example, a bullet strategy might be to create a portfolio with maturities concentrated around 10 years, while a corresponding barbell strategy might be a portfolio with 5-year and 20-year maturities. In a **ladder strategy**, the portfolio is constructed to have approximately equal amounts of each maturity. So, for example, a portfolio might have equal amounts of securities with one year to maturity, two years to maturity, etc.

Each of these strategies will result in a different performance when the yield curve shifts. The actual performance will depend on both the type of shift and the magnitude of the shift. Thus, no general statements can be made about the optimal yield curve strategy. The framework for analyzing a yield curve strategy will be discussed later.

Duration and Yield Curve Shifts   Before discussing how to analyze yield curve strategies, let's reconsider the concept of duration and its role in approximating the price volatility of a bond portfolio when the yield curve shifts. In Chapter 21 we explained how duration is a measure of the sensitivity of the price of a bond or the value of a bond portfolio to changes in market yields. Thus, a portfolio with a duration of 4 means that if market yields increase by 100 basis points, the portfolio will change by approximately 4%.

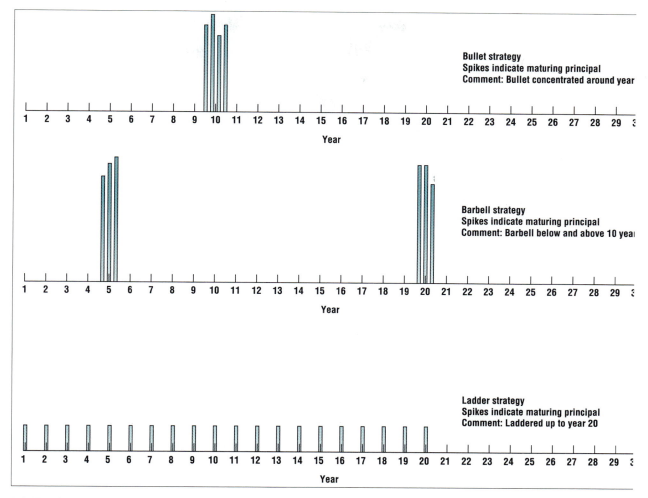

FIGURE 24-3

Yield curve strategies: bullet, barbell, and ladder.

In explaining the limitations of duration, we indicated that an assumption is made about how market yields change. Specifically, if a portfolio of bonds consists of 5-year bonds, 10-years bonds, and 20-year bonds, and the portfolio's duration is 4, what market yield is assumed to change when we say that this portfolio will change in value by 4% if yields change by 100 basis points? Is it the 5-year yield, 10-year yield, or 20-year yield? In fact, the assumption made when using duration as a measure of how the value of a portfolio will change if market yields change is that the yield on *all* maturities will change by the same number of basis points. Thus, if our three-bond portfolio has a duration of 4, the statement that the portfolio's value will change by 4% for a 100-basis-point change in yields actually should be stated as follows: The portfolio's value will change by 4% if the yields on 5-year

			TABLE 24-1			
			THREE HYPOTHETICAL TREASURY SECURITIES			
Bond	**Coupon**	**Maturity (Years)**	**Price plus Accrued Interest**	**Yield to Maturity**	**Dollar Duration**	**Dollar Convexity**
A	8.50%	5	100	8.50%	4.005	19.8164
B	9.50	20	100	9.50	8.882	124.1702
C	9.25	10	100	9.25	6.434	55.4506

bonds, 10-year bonds, and 20-year bonds all change by 100 basis points. That is, it is assumed that there is a parallel yield curve shift.

An illustration of what happens to a bond portfolio when the yield curve shift is not parallel is demonstrated below. The key point of the illustration is that two portfolios with the same duration may perform quite differently when the yield curve shifts.

Analysis of Expected Yield Curve Strategies   The proper way to analyze any portfolio strategy is to look at its potential total return. We indicated this at the outset of this chapter. If a manager wants to assess the outcome of a portfolio for any assumed shift in the Treasury yield curve, this should be done by calculating the potential total return if that shift actually occurs.

We will illustrate this by looking at the performance of two hypothetical portfolios of Treasury securities, assuming different shifts in the Treasury yield curve. The three hypothetical Treasury securities shown in Table 24-1 are considered for inclusion in our two portfolios.[3] Thus, for our illustration, the Treasury yield curve consists of these three Treasury securities: a short-term security (A, the 5-year security), an intermediate-term security (C, the 10-year security), and a long-term security (B, the 20-year security).

Consider the following two yield curve strategies: a bullet strategy and a barbell strategy. We will label the portfolios created based on these two strategies as the "bullet portfolio" and the "barbell portfolio," and they comprise the following:

Bullet portfolio: 100% bond C
Barbell portfolio: 50.2% bond A and 49.8% bond B

The bullet portfolio consists of only bond C, the 10-year bond. In our hypothetical portfolio, all the principal is received when bond C matures in 10 years. The barbell portfolio consists of almost an equal amount of the short-term and long-term securities. The principal will be received at two ends of the maturity spectrum. Specifically, relative to the bullet portfolio, which in our illustration has all its principal being returned in 10 years, for the barbell portfolio the principal is being returned at shorter (5 year) and longer (20 year) dates.

---

[3]This illustration is adapted from Ravi E. Dattatreya and Frank J. Fabozzi, *Active Total Return Management of Fixed Income Portfolios* (Chicago: Probus Publishing, 1989).

The dollar duration of the bullet portfolio per 100-basis-point change in yield is 6.43409. As we explained in Chapter 21, dollar duration is a measure of the dollar price sensitivity of a bond or a portfolio. As indicated in Table 24-1, the dollar duration for the bullet portfolio is 6.434. For the barbell portfolio, the dollar duration is just the weighted average of the dollar duration of the two bonds. Therefore,

Dollar duration of barbell portfolio = 0.502(4.005) + 0.498(8.882) = 6.434

The dollar duration of the barbell portfolio is the same as the dollar duration of the bullet portfolio. (In fact, the barbell portfolio was designed to produce this result.)

As we explained in Chapter 21, duration is just a first approximation of the change in price resulting from a change in interest rates. Convexity provides a second approximation. While we did not discuss "dollar convexity," it has a similar meaning to convexity in that it provides a second approximation to the dollar price change. For two portfolios with the same dollar duration, the greater the convexity, the better the performance of a bond or a portfolio when yields change. What is necessary to understand for this illustration is that the larger the dollar convexity, the greater the dollar price change due to a portfolio's convexity. As shown in Table 24-1, the dollar convexity of the bullet portfolio is 55.4506. The dollar convexity of the barbell portfolio is a weighted average of the dollar convexity of the two bonds. That is,

Dollar convexity of barbell portfolio = 0.502(19.8164) + 0.498(124.1702)
= 71.7846

Therefore, the dollar convexity of the barbell portfolio is greater than that of the bullet portfolio.

The "yield" for the two portfolios likewise is not the same. The yield for the bullet portfolio is simply the yield to maturity of bond C, 9.25%. The traditional yield calculation for the barbell portfolio, which is found by taking a weighted average of the yield to maturity of the two bonds included in the portfolio, is 8.998%, as shown below:

Portfolio yield for barbell portfolio = 0.502(8.50%) + 0.498(9.50%)
= 8.998%

This approach suggests that the "yield" of the bullet portfolio is 25.2 basis points greater than that of the barbell portfolio (9.25% − 8.998%). Although both portfolios have the same dollar duration, the yield of the bullet portfolio is greater than the yield of the barbell portfolio. However, the dollar convexity of the barbell portfolio is greater than that of the bullet portfolio. The difference in the two yields is sometimes referred to as the *cost of convexity* (i.e., giving up yield to get better convexity).

Now, suppose that a portfolio manager with a six-month investment horizon has a choice of investing in the bullet portfolio or the barbell portfolio. Which one should he choose? The manager knows that (1) the two portfolios have the same dollar duration, (2) the "yield" for the bullet portfolio is greater than that for the barbell portfolio, and (3) the dollar convexity of the barbell portfolio is greater than that of the bullet portfolio. Actually, this information is not adequate for making the decision. What is necessary is to assess the potential total return when the yield curve shifts.

	TABLE 24-2						
RELATIVE PERFORMANCE OF BULLET PORTFOLIO AND BARBELL PORTFOLIO OVER A SIX-MONTH INVESTMENT HORIZON*							
Yield Change	**Parallel Shift***	**Flattening†**	**Steepening‡**	**Yield Change**	**Parallel Shift***	**Flattening†**	**Steepening‡**
−5.000	−7.19%	−10.69%	−3.89%	0.250	0.24	−1.01	1.41
−4.750	−6.28	−9.61	−3.12	0.500	0.21	−0.98	1.32
−4.500	−5.44	−8.62	−2.44	0.750	0.16	−0.97	1.21
−4.250	−4.68	−7.71	−1.82	1.000	0.09	−0.98	1.09
−4.000	−4.00	−6.88	−1.27	1.250	0.01	−1.00	0.96
−3.750	−3.38	−6.13	−0.78	1.500	−0.08	−1.05	0.81
−3.500	−2.82	−5.44	−0.35	1.750	−0.19	−1.10	0.66
−3.250	−2.32	−4.82	0.03	2.000	−0.31	−1.18	0.49
−3.000	−1.88	−4.26	0.36	2.250	−0.44	−1.26	0.32
−2.750	−1.49	−3.75	0.65	2.500	−0.58	−1.36	0.14
−2.500	−1.15	−3.30	0.89	2.750	−0.73	−1.46	−0.05
−2.250	−0.85	−2.90	1.09	3.000	−0.88	−1.58	−0.24
−2.000	−0.59	−2.55	1.25	3.250	−1.05	−1.70	−0.44
−1.750	−0.38	−2.24	1.37	3.500	−1.21	−1.84	−0.64
−1.500	−0.20	−1.97	1.47	3.750	−1.39	−1.98	−0.85
−1.250	−0.05	−1.74	1.53	4.000	−1.57	−2.12	−1.06
−1.000	0.06	−1.54	1.57	4.250	−1.75	−2.27	−1.27
−0.750	0.15	−1.38	1.58	4.500	−1.93	−2.43	−1.48
−0.500	0.21	−1.24	1.57	4.750	−2.12	−2.58	−1.70
−0.250	0.24	−1.14	1.53	5.000	−2.31	−2.75	−1.92
0.000	0.25	−1.06	1.48				

*Performance is based on the difference in total return over a six-month investment horizon. Specifically:

　Bullet portfolio's total return − barbell portfolio's total return

Therefore a negative value means that the barbell portfolio outperformed the bullet portfolio.

†Change in yield for bond C. Non-parallel shift as follows (flattening of yield curve):

　Yield change bond A = yield change bond C + 25 basis points

　Yield change bond B = yield change bond C − 25 basis points

‡Change in yield for bond C. Non-parallel shifts as follows (steepening of yield curve):

　Yield change bond A = yield change bond C − 25 basis points

　Yield change bond B = yield change bond C + 25 basis points

Table 24-2 provides an analysis of the six-month total return of the two portfolios when the yield curve shifts.[4] The numbers reported in the table are the difference in the total return for the two portfolios. Specifically, the following is shown:

Difference in total return
　　　= bullet portfolio's total return − barbell portfolio's total return

Thus a positive value means that the bullet portfolio outperformed the barbell portfolio, while a negative sign means that the barbell portfolio outperformed the bullet portfolio.

Let's focus on the second column of Table 24-2, which is labeled "Parallel Shift." This is the relative total return of the two portfolios over the six-month investment horizon, assuming that the yield curve shifts in a parallel

---

[4]Note that no assumption is needed for the reinvestment rate because the three bonds shown in Table 24-1 are assumed to be trading right after a coupon payment has been made and therefore there is no accrued interest.

fashion. In this case, parallel movement of the yield curve means that the yields for the short-term bond (A), the intermediate-term bond (C), and the long-term bond (B) change by the same number of basis points, shown in the "Yield Change" column of the table.

Which portfolio is the better investment alternative if the yield curve shifts in a parallel fashion and the investment horizon is six months? The answer depends on the amount by which yields change. Notice that when yields change by less than 100 basis points, the bullet portfolio outperforms the barbell portfolio. The reverse is true if yields change by more than 100 basis points.

This illustration makes two key points. First, even if the yield curve shifts in a parallel fashion, two portfolios with the same dollar duration will not give the same performance. The reason is that the two portfolios do not have the same dollar convexity. The second point is that while, with all other things equal, it is better to have more convexity than less, the market charges for convexity in the form of a higher price or a lower yield. But the benefit of the greater convexity depends on how much yields change. As can be seen from the second column of Table 24-2, if market yields change by less than 100 basis points (up or down), the bullet portfolio, which has less convexity, will provide a better total return.

Now let's look at what happens if the yield curve does not shift in a parallel fashion. The last two columns of Table 24-2 show the relative performance of the two portfolios for a non-parallel shift of the yield curve. Specifically, the first non-parallel shift column, the "flattening" column, assumes that if the yield on bond C (the intermediate-term bond) changes by the amount shown in the first column, bond A (the short-term bond) will change by the same amount plus 25 basis points, whereas bond B (the long-term bond) will change by the same amount shown in the first column less 25 basis points. Measuring the steepness of the yield curve as the spread between the long-term yield (yield on bond B) and the short-term yield (yield on Bond A), we find the spread has decreased by 50 basis points. As we noted earlier, such a non-parallel shift means a flattening of the yield curve. As can be seen in Table 24-2, for this assumed yield curve shift, the barbell outperforms the bullet.

In the last column, the "steepening" column, the non-parallel shift assumes that for a change in bond C's yield, the yield on bond A will change by the same amount less 25 basis points, whereas that on bond B will change by the same amount plus 25 points. Thus, the spread between the long-term yield and the short-term yield has increased by 50 basis points, and therefore the yield curve has steepened. In this case, the bullet portfolio outperforms the barbell portfolio so long as the yield on bond C does not rise by more than 250 basis points or fall by more than 325 basis points.

The key point here is that looking at measures such as yield (yield to maturity or some type of portfolio yield measure), duration, or convexity tells us little about performance over some investment horizon, because performance depends on the magnitude of the change in yields and the way the yield curve shifts.

Therefore, when a manager wants to position a portfolio based on expectations of how he or she might expect the yield curve to shift, it is imperative to perform total return analysis. For example, in a steepening yield curve environment, it is often stated that a bullet portfolio would be better than a bar-bell portfolio. However, as can be seen from Table 24-2, it is not the case that a bullet portfolio would outperform a barbell portfolio. Whether the bullet portfolio outperforms the barbell depends on how much the yield curve steepens. An analysis similar to that in Table 24-2 based on total return for different degrees of steepening of the yield curve clearly demonstrates to a manager whether a particular yield curve strategy will be superior to another. The same analysis can be performed to assess the potential outcome of a lad-der strategy.

Yield Spread Strategies

As discussed in Chapter 22, the bond market is classified into sectors in several ways: by type of issuer (Treasury, agencies, corporates, and mortgage-backeds), quality or credit (risk-free Treasuries, triple A, double A, etc.), coupon (high-coupon/premium bonds, current-coupon/par bonds, and low-coupon/discount bonds), and maturity (short, intermediate, or long term). Yield spreads between maturity sectors involve changes in the yield curve, as we have discussed in the previous section.

Yield spread strategies involve positioning a portfolio to capitalize on ex-pected changes in yield spreads between sectors of the bond market. Swaps that involve exchanging one bond for another when the manager believes (1) that the prevailing yield spread between the two bonds in the market is out of line with the bonds' historical yield spread and (2) that the yield spread will realign by the end of the investment horizon are called **intermarket spread swaps**.

Yield spreads can be measured in terms of the difference between the yield on two bonds. The difference is measured in basis points. Unless other-wise stated, yield spreads are typically measured in this way. Yield spreads can also be measured on a relative basis by taking the ratio of the yield spread to the yield level. This is called a **relative yield spread**.

$$\text{Relative yield spread} = \frac{\text{yield on bond A} - \text{yield on bond B}}{\text{yield on bond B}}$$

Sometimes bonds are compared in terms of a **yield ratio**, the quotient of two bond yields:

$$\text{Yield ratio} = \frac{\text{yield on bond A}}{\text{yield on bond B}}$$

Credit Spreads Credit or quality spreads change because of expected changes in economic prospects. Credit spreads between Treasury and non-Treasury issues widen in a declining or contracting economy and narrow dur-ing economic expansion. The economic rationale is that in a declining or con-tracting economy, corporations experience a decline in revenue and reduced cash flows, making it difficult for corporate issuers to service their contrac-tual debt obligations. To induce investors to hold non-Treasury securities of lower-quality issuers, the yield spread relative to Treasury securities must widen. The converse is that during economic expansion and brisk economic activity, revenue and cash flows pick up, increasing the likelihood that corpo-rate issuers will have the capacity to service their contractual debt obliga-tions. Yield spreads between Treasury and federal agency securities will vary,

	TABLE 24-3				
	RELATIVE YIELD				
Period	**Average 10-Year Treasury Yield (%)**	**Average BBB Utility Yield (%)**	**Average Spread (%)**	**Relative Yield (%)**	**Yield Ratio**
1955–1959	3.46	4.21	75	22	1.217
1960–1964	4.03	4.79	76	19	1.189
1965–1969	5.32	6.22	95	17	1.169
1970–1974	6.82	8.75	197	28	1.283
1975–1979	8.17	10.04	191	23	1.229
1980–1984	12.30	15.18	276	23	1.234
1985–1989	8.81	10.92	209	24	1.240

Source: Chris P. Dialynas and David H. Edington, "Bond Yield Spreads—A Postmodern View," *Journal of Portfolio Management* (Fall 1992).

depending on investor expectations about the prospects that an implicit government guarantee will be honored. Yield spreads are also related to the level of interest rates. For example, in 1957, when the yield on Treasuries was 3%, the yield spread between a triple-B-rated utility bond and Treasuries was 40 basis points. This represented a relative yield spread of 13% (0.4% divided by 3%). When the yield on Treasuries exceeded 10% in 1985, however, a yield spread of 40 basis points would have meant only a relative yield spread of 4%.[5] Consequently, the yield spread measured in basis points had to be greater than 40 basis points to produce a similar relative yield. Table 24-3 suggests that the relative yield spread—as measured by the ratio of the yield spread to the level of Treasury yields—and the yield ratio—the ratio of non-Treasury and Treasury yields—tend to be relatively stable over time.

Spreads between Callable and Non-Callable Securities   Spreads attributable to differences in callable and non-callable bonds and differences in coupons of callable bonds will change as a result of expected changes in (1) the direction of the change in interest rates and (2) interest rate volatility. An expected drop in the level of interest rates will widen the yield spread between callable bonds and non-callable bonds as the prospects that the issuer will exercise the call option increase. The reverse is true: The yield spread narrows if interest rates are expected to rise. As we explain in Chapter 26, an increase in interest rate volatility increases the value of the embedded call option, and thereby increases the yield spread between callable bonds and non-callable bonds. Expectations about the direction of the change in interest rates and interest rate volatility will affect the yield spread between Treasury and mortgage pass-through securities and the yield spread between low-coupon and high-coupon pass-throughs in the same way as it affects the yield spreads for corporates.

The Importance of Dollar Duration Weighting of Yield Spread Strategies   What is critical in assessing yield spread strategies is to compare positions that have the same dollar duration. To understand why, consider two bonds, X and Y. Sup-

---

[5]Chris P. Dialynas and David H. Edington, "Bond Yield Spreads—A Postmodern View," *Journal of Portfolio Management* (Fall 1992), pp. 68–75.

pose that the price of bond X is 80 and has a modified duration of 5, while bond Y has a price of 90 and has a modified duration of 4. Since modified duration is the approximate percentage change per 100-basis-point change in yield, a 100-basis-point change in yield for bond X would change its price by about 5%. Based on a price of 80, its price will change by about $4 per $80 of market value. Thus, its dollar duration for a 100-basis-point change in yield is $4 per $80 of market value. Similarly, for bond Y, its dollar duration for a 100-basis-point change in yield per $90 of market value can be determined. In this case it is $3.6. So if bonds X and Y are being considered as alternative investments in some strategy other than one based on anticipating interest rate movements, the amount of each bond in the strategy should be such that they will both have the same dollar duration.

To illustrate this, suppose that a portfolio manager owns $10 million of par value of bond X, which has a market value of $8 million. The dollar duration of bond X per 100-basis-point change in yield for the $8 million market value is $400,000. Suppose further that this portfolio manager is considering exchanging bond X in her portfolio for bond Y. If the portfolio manager wants to have the same interest rate exposure (i.e., dollar duration) for bond Y that she currently has for bond X, she will buy a market value amount of bond Y with the same dollar duration. If the portfolio manager purchased $10 million of *par value* of bond Y and therefore $9 million of *market value* of bond Y, the dollar price change per 100-basis-point change in yield would be only $360,000. If, instead, the portfolio manager purchased $10 million of *market value* of bond Y, the dollar duration per 100-basis-point change in yield would be $400,000. Since bond Y is trading at 90, $11.11 million of par value of bond Y must be purchased to keep the dollar duration of the position from bond Y the same as for bond X.

Mathematically, this problem can be expressed as follows:

Let $\$D_X$ = dollar duration per 100-basis-point change in yield for bond X for the market value of bond X held

MD_Y = modified duration for bond Y

MV_Y = market value of bond Y needed to obtain the same dollar duration as bond X

Then, the following equation sets the dollar duration for bond X equal to the dollar duration for bond Y:

$$\$D_X = (MD_Y/100)MV_Y$$

Solving for MV_Y, we get

$$MV_Y = \$D_X/(MD_Y/100)$$

Dividing by the price per $1 of par value of bond Y gives the par value of Y that has a dollar duration approximately equivalent to that of bond X.

In our illustration, $\$D_X$ is $400,000 and MD_Y is 4. Then

$$MV_Y = \$400,000/(4/100) = \$10,000,000$$

Since the market value of bond Y is 90 per $100 of par value, the price per $1 of par value is 0.9. Dividing $10 million by 0.9 indicates that the par value of bond Y that should be purchased is $11.11 million.

Failure to adjust a portfolio repositioning based on some expected change in yield spread so as to hold the dollar duration the same means that the outcome of the portfolio will be affected by not only the expected change in the yield spread but also a change in the yield level. Thus, a manager would be making a conscious yield spread bet and possibly an undesired bet on the level of interest rates.

Individual Security Selection Strategies

There are several active strategies that money managers pursue to identify mispriced securities. The most common strategy identifies an issue as undervalued because either (1) its yield is higher than that of comparably rated issues or (2) its yield is expected to decline (and price therefore rise) because credit analysis indicates that its rating will improve.

A swap in which a money manager exchanges one bond for another bond that is similar in terms of coupon, maturity, and credit quality, but offers a higher yield, is called a **substitution swap**. This swap depends on a capital market imperfection. Such situations sometimes exist in the bond market owing to temporary market imbalances and the fragmented nature of the non-Treasury bond market. The risk the money manager faces in making a substitution swap is that the bond purchased may not be truly identical to the bond for which it is exchanged. Moreover, typically bonds will have similar but not identical maturities and coupons. This could lead to differences in the convexity of the two bonds, and any yield spread may reflect the cost of convexity.

An active strategy used in the mortgage-backed securities market is to identify individual issues of pass-throughs, CMO classes, or stripped MBSs that are mispriced, given the assumed prepayment speed to price the security. Another active strategy commonly used in the mortgage-backed securities market is to create a package of securities that will have a better return profile for a wide range of interest rate and yield curve scenarios than similar-duration securities available in the market. Because of the fragmented nature of the mortgage-backed securities market and the complexity of the structures, such opportunities are not unusual.

BOND INDEXING STRATEGY

Bond indexing means designing a portfolio so that its performance will match the performance of some bond index. In indexing, performance is measured in terms of total rate of return achieved (or simply, total return) over some investment horizon. Total return over some investment horizon incorporates all three sources of return from holding a portfolio of bonds.

As we explained in Chapter 14, indexing an equity portfolio is commonplace. On the bond side, indexing is a relatively recent phenomenon. In 1980, for example, only $40 million of assets was managed under bond indexing strategies.[6] Currently, more than $75 billion of funds under fixed-income management is indexed.[7]

---

[6]Sharmin Mossavar-Rahmani, "Understanding and Evaluating Index Fund Management," in Frank J. Fabozzi and T. Dessa Garlicki (eds.), *Advances in Bond Analysis and Portfolio Strategies* (Chicago: Probus Publishing, 1987), p. 433.

[7]Sharmin Mossavar-Rahmani, *Bond Index Funds* (Chicago: Probus Publishing, 1991), p. vii.

Advantages and Disadvantages of Bond Indexing

Several factors explain the recent popularity and phenomenal growth rate of bond indexing.[8] First, the empirical evidence suggests that historically the overall performance of active bond managers has been poor. SEI Funds Evaluation Corporation ranked the performance of active bond managers by total return and compared the relative performance with that of the Salomon Brothers Investment Grade Index. For various time periods ending in 1989, the median return of the active bond money managers was lower than the index return. In fact, in most periods investigated, more than 75% underperformed the index. The second factor explaining the popularity of bond indexing is reduced advisory management fees charged for an indexed portfolio compared with active management advisory fees. Advisory fees charged by active managers typically range from 15 to 50 basis points. The range for indexed portfolios, in contrast, is 1 to 20 basis points, with the upper range representing the fees for enhanced and customized benchmark funds, discussed later in this chapter.[9] Some pension funds have decided to do away with advisory fees and to manage some or all of their funds in-house following an indexing strategy.

Lower non-advisory fees, such as custodial fees, make up the third explanation for the popularity of indexing. Finally, sponsors have greater control over external managers when an indexing strategy is selected. For example, in an actively managed portfolio, a sponsor who specifies a restriction on the portfolio's duration still gives the manager ample leeway to pursue strategies that may significantly underperform the index selected as a benchmark. In contrast, requiring an investment advisor to match an index gives little leeway to the manager and therefore should result in performance that does not significantly diverge from a benchmark.

Critics of indexing point out that while an indexing strategy matches the performance of some index, the performance of that index does not necessarily represent optimal performance. For the five-year period ending September 1981, for example, 50% of active managers outperformed a popular index.[10] Moreover, matching an index does not mean that the manager will satisfy a client's return-requirement objective. For example, if the objective of a life insurance company or a pension fund is to have sufficient funds to satisfy a predetermined liability, indexing only reduces the likelihood that performance will not be materially worse than the index. The index's return is not necessarily related to the sponsor's liability. Finally, matching an index means that a money manager is restricted to the sectors of the bond market that are in the index, even though there may be attractive opportunities in market sectors excluded from the index. While the broad-based bond market indexes typically include agency pass-through securities, other mortgage-backed securities such as private-label pass-throughs and collateralized mortgage obligations are generally not included. Yet it is in these fairly new markets that at-

---

[8]Ibid., pp. 2–12.

[9]Mossavar-Rahmani, "Understanding and Evaluating Index Fund Management," op. cit., p. 434.

[10]As reported in Mossavar-Rahmani, "Understanding and Evaluating Index Fund Management," op. cit., pp. 436–437.

TABLE 24-4	
ADVANTAGES AND DISADVANTAGES OF BOND INDEXING	
Advantages	**Disadvantages**
No dependence on expectations and little risk of underperforming the index	Bond indexes do not reflect optimal performance
Reduced advisory and non-advisory fees	A bond index may not match the sponsor's liabilities
Greater sponsor control	Restrictions on fund management ignore opportunities

tractive returns to enhance performance may be available. Table 24-4 summarizes the advantages and disadvantages of bond indexing.

Factors to Consider in Selecting an Index

A money manager who wishes to pursue an indexing strategy must determine which bond index to replicate. There are a number of bond indexes from which to select, and several factors influence the decision. The first is the investor's risk tolerance. Selection of an index that includes corporate bonds will expose the investor to credit risk. If this risk is unacceptable, an investor should avoid an index that includes this sector.

The second factor influencing the selection of an index is the investor's objective. For example, while the total return of the various indexes tends to be highly positively correlated, the variability of total returns has been quite different. Therefore, an investor whose objective may be to minimize the variability of total returns will be biased toward one that has had, and expects to continue to have, low variability (i.e., a shorter duration relative to other indexes). Moreover, variability of total return may not be symmetric in rising and falling markets. Investors who have expectations about the future direction of interest rates will favor the index that is expected to perform better given their expectations.

Bond Indexes

The wide range of bond market indexes available can be classified as broad-based market indexes and specialized market indexes.

The three broad-based market indexes most commonly used by institutional investors are the Lehman Brothers Aggregate Index, the Salomon Brothers Broad Investment-Grade Bond Index, and the Merrill Lynch Domestic Market Index. The bond market sectors covered by these three indexes are the Treasury, agency, investment-grade corporate, mortgage-backed, and Yankee markets.

The specialized market indexes focus on only one sector of the bond market or a subsector of the bond market. Indexes on sectors of the market are published by the three investment banking firms that produce the broad-based market indexes. For example, Salomon Brothers publishes both a corporate bond index (a sector index) and a high-grade corporate bond index that includes AAA- and AA-rated corporate bonds (a subindex of the corporate bond index). Firms that do not produce one of the three broad-based market indexes may provide specialized indexes. Some examples are the Morgan Stanley Actively Traded MBS Index, the Donaldson Lufkin & Jenrette High Yield Index, the First Boston High Yield Index, the Goldman Sachs Convertible 100, and the Ryan Labs Treasury Index.

In recent years, money managers in consultation with their clients have been moving in the direction of **customized benchmarks**. A customized benchmark is a benchmark that is designed to meet a client's requirements and long-term objectives.[11] For example, in December 1986, Salomon Brothers Inc introduced its Large Pension Fund Baseline Bond Index as a standardized customized benchmark tailor-made for large pension funds "seeking to establish long-term core portfolios that more closely match the longer durations of their nominal dollar liabilities."[12]

Why have broker/dealer firms developed and aggressively marketed their bond indexes? Enhancing the firm's image is only a minor reason. The key motivation lies in the potential profit that the firm will make by executing trades to set up an indexed portfolio and rebalance it. Typically, a broker/dealer charges a money manager who wants to set up or rebalance an index a nominal amount for providing the necessary data, but expects that the bulk of the trades will be executed through its trading desks. Also, by keeping the makeup of the index proprietary, those firms attempt to lock in customers to using their index.

Indexing Methodologies

Once a money manager has decided to pursue an indexing strategy and has selected an index (broad-based bond market index, specialized market index, or customized benchmark), the next step is to construct a portfolio that will track the index. As with equity indexing (Chapter 14), any discrepancy between the performance of the indexed portfolio and the index (whether positive or negative) is referred to as tracking error. Tracking error has three sources: (1) transactions costs in constructing the indexed portfolio, (2) differences in the composition of the indexed portfolio and the index itself, and (3) discrepancies between prices used by the organization constructing the index and transactions prices paid by the indexer.

One approach in constructing the indexed portfolio is for the money manager to purchase all the issues in the index according to their weight in the benchmark index. However, substantial tracking error will result from the transactions costs (and other fees) associated with purchasing all the issues and reinvesting cash flow (maturing principal and coupon interest). A broad-based market index could include over 5,000 issues, so large transactions costs may make this approach impractical. In addition, some issues in the index may not be available at the prices used in constructing the index. Instead of purchasing all issues in the index, the money manager may purchase just a sample of issues. While this approach reduces tracking error resulting from high transactions costs, it increases tracking error resulting from the mismatch of the indexed portfolio and the index.

---

[11]For a discussion of customized benchmarks and the reasons for the growing interest in them, see Sharmin Mossavar-Rahmani, "Customized Benchmarks in Structured Management," *Journal of Portfolio Management* (Summer 1987), pp. 65–68.

[12]Martin L. Leibowitz, Thomas Klaffky, and Steven Mandel, *Introducing the Salomon Brothers Large Pension Fund Baseline Bond Index* (New York: Salomon Brothers Inc, December 1986), p. 1.

Generally speaking, the fewer the number of issues used to replicate the index, the smaller the tracking error due to transactions costs but the greater the tracking error risk due to the mismatch of the characteristics of the indexed portfolio and the index. In contrast, the more issues purchased to replicate the index, the greater the tracking error due to transactions costs and the smaller the tracking error risk due to the mismatch of the indexed portfolio and the index. Obviously, then, there is a trade-off between tracking error and the number of issues used to construct the indexed portfolio.

There are three methodologies for designing a portfolio to replicate an index: (1) the stratified sampling, or cell, approach, (2) the optimization approach, and (3) the variance minimization approach. For each of these approaches, the initial question that the indexer must ask is, what are the factors that affect a bond index's performance? Each approach assumes that the performance of an individual bond depends on a number of systematic factors that affect the performance of all bonds and on a factor unique to the individual issue. This last risk is diversifiable risk. The objective of the three approaches is to construct an indexed portfolio that eliminates this diversifiable risk.

Stratified Sampling, or Cell, Approach Under the **stratified sampling approach to indexing**, the index is divided into cells, each cell representing a different characteristic of the index. The most common characteristics used to break down an index are (1) duration, (2) coupon, (3) maturity, (4) market sectors (Treasury, corporate, mortgage-backed), (5) credit rating, (6) call factors, and (7) sinking fund features. The last two factors are particularly important because the call and sinking fund features of an issue will impact its performance.

For example, suppose that a manager selects the following characteristics to partition a Treasury/agency/corporate bond index:

Characteristic 1: Effective duration range: (1) less than or equal to 5 and (2) greater than 5
Characteristic 2: Maturity range: (1) less than 5 years, (2) between 5 and 15 years, and (3) greater than or equal to 15 years
Characteristic 3: Market sectors: (1) Treasury, (2) agencies, and (3) corporates
Characteristic 4: Credit rating: (1) triple A, (2) double A, (3) single A, and (4) triple B.

The total number of cells would be equal to 72 (= $2 \times 3 \times 3 \times 4$).

The objective is then to select from all the issues in the index one or more issues in each cell that can be used to represent that entire cell. The total dollar amount purchased of the issues from each cell will be based on the percentage of the index's total market value that the cell represents. For example, if 40% of the market value of all the issues in the index is made up of corporate bonds, then 40% of the market value of the indexed portfolio should be composed of corporate bond issues.

The number of cells that the indexer uses will depend on the dollar amount of the portfolio to be indexed. In indexing a portfolio of less than $50 million, for example, using a large number of cells would require purchasing odd lots of issues. This increases the cost of buying the issues to represent a cell, and thus would increase the tracking error. Reducing the number of cells to overcome this problem increases tracking error risk of index mismatch because the characteristics of the indexed portfolio may differ materially from those of the index.

Optimization Approach   In the **optimization approach to indexing**, the money manager seeks to design an indexed portfolio that will match the cell breakdown just as described and satisfy other constraints, but also optimize some objective. An objective might be to maximize the portfolio yield, to maximize convexity, or to maximize expected total returns.[13] Constraints other than matching the cell breakdown might include not purchasing more than a specified amount of one issuer or group of issuers, or overweighting certain sectors for enhanced indexing (discussed later).

The computational technique used to derive the optimal solution to the indexing problem in this approach is mathematical programming. When the objective function that the indexer seeks to optimize is a linear function, linear programming (a specific form of mathematical programming) is used. If the objective function is quadratic, then the particular mathematical programming technique used is quadratic programming.

Variance Minimization Approach.   The **variance minimization approach to indexing** is by far the most complex. This approach requires using historical data to estimate the variance of the tracking error. This is done by estimating a price function for every issue in the index. The price function is estimated on the basis of two sets of factors: (1) the cash flows from the issue discounted at the theoretical spot rates and (2) other factors such as the duration or sector characteristics discussed earlier. The price function is estimated, using a large universe of issues and statistical techniques, from historical data. Once the price function for each issue is obtained, a variance equation for the tracking error can be constructed. The objective then is to minimize the variance of the tracking error in constructing the indexed portfolio. As the variance is a quadratic function (the difference between the benchmark return and the indexed portfolio's return, squared), quadratic programming is used to find the optimal indexed portfolio in terms of minimized tracking error. The biggest problem with this approach is that estimating the price function from historical data is very difficult in the Treasury market, let alone the corporate market or the new-issue market. Also, the price function may not be stable.

Although the stratified sampling (or cell) approach seems to be the easiest to use, it is extremely difficult to implement when large, diversified portfolios are taken as the benchmark. In this case, many cells are required, and the problem becomes complex. Also, because the handpicking of issues to match each cell is subjective, tracking error may result. Mathematical programming

---

[13]For a mathematical presentation of this approach as well as the variance minimization approach, see Christina Seix and Ravi Akoury, "Bond Indexation: The Optimal Quantitative Approach," *Journal of Portfolio Management* (Spring 1986), pp. 50–53. For an illustration, see Philip Galdi, "Indexing Fixed Income Portfolios," in Fabozzi and Garlicki (eds.), op. cit.

reduces the complexity of the problem when well-defined constraints are employed, allowing the indexer to analyze large quantities of data optimally.

Tracking Error and the Optimization Approach to Indexing

How well do indexed portfolios constructed using an optimization approach track benchmark indexes? Table 24-5 presents the results of a study by Salomon Brothers on the tracking error for the Salomon Brothers Broad Based Investment-Grade Bond Index and three subindexes using an optimal indexed portfolio methodology devised by Salomon Brothers. The tracking error was computed each month between January 1985 and November 1986 as the difference between the monthly return on the indexed portfolio and the monthly return on the benchmark index. A positive (negative) tracking error indicates that the monthly return on the indexed portfolio outperformed (underperformed) the monthly return on the index. Summary statistics (standard deviation, mean, high, and low) for the monthly tracking error and the cumulative tracking error over the entire two-year period are shown in Table 24-5.

The table indicates that tracking error varies according to the benchmark. The smallest tracking error results when the index benchmark comprises only government securities. This is expected, because most government securities have similar features, no credit risk, and minimal call risk if any. By far the more difficult sector to track is the corporate bond market. This is probably because of the difference between the call and sinking fund characteristics of the indexed portfolio and those of the index, as well as the smaller diversification (higher unique risk) for the indexed portfolio relative to the index. For the broad market index, the tracking performance was similar to that of the government index. This is understandable, because the government index made up 60% of the broad market index at the time of the study.

					Total Return	
Sector	Standard Deviation	Mean	High	Low	Cumulative	Annualized
Broad market	54	2	13	−6	69	34
Governments	2	2	5	−1	63	31
Corporates	17	9	40	−26	301	156
Mortgages	3	0	6	−7	6	3
Broad market (Including transactions costs)	5	0	11	−8	−12	−6

TABLE 24-5 TRACKING ERROR OF MONTHLY RETURNS IN BASIS POINTS*

*Analysis between January 1985 and November 1986.

Source: Sharmin Mossavar-Rahmani, "Understanding and Evaluating Index Fund Managment," in Frank J. Fabozzi and T. Dessa Garlicki (eds.), *Advances in Bond Analysis and Portfolio Strategies* (Chicago: Probus Publishing, 1987), Based on Salomon Brothers Broad Investment-Grade Bond Index and its components.

Logistical Problems in Implementing an Indexing Strategy[14]

An indexer faces several logistical problems in constructing an indexed portfolio. First of all, the prices for each issue used by the organization that publishes the index may not be the execution prices available to the indexer. In fact, they may be materially different from the prices offered by some dealers.

In addition, the prices used by organizations reporting the value of indexes are based on bid prices. Dealer ask prices, however, are the ones that the money manager would have to transact at when constructing or rebalancing the indexed portfolio. Thus there will be a bias between the performance of the index and the indexed portfolio that is equal to the bid-ask spread.

Furthermore, there are logistical problems unique to certain sectors in the bond market. Consider first the corporate bond market. There are typically about 3,500 issues in the corporate bond sector of a broad-based index. Because of the illiquidity of this sector of the bond market, not only may the prices used by the organization that publishes the index be unreliable, but also many of the issues may not even be available. Next, consider the mortgage-backed securities market. There are over 300,000 agency pass-through issues. The organizations that publish indexes lump all these issues into a few hundred generic issues. The indexer is then faced with the difficult task of finding pass-through securities with the same risk/return profiles of these hypothetical issues.

Finally, recall that the total return depends on the reinvestment rate available on coupon interest. If the organization publishing the index regularly overestimates the reinvestment rate, then the indexed portfolio could underperform the index by 10 to 15 basis points a year.[15]

Enhanced Indexing

So far we have discussed straight, or "plain vanilla," indexing. The objective of an **enhanced indexing** strategy is to replicate the total return performance of some predetermined index. In enhanced indexing (also called *indexing plus*), the objective is consistently to exceed the total return performance of the index by an amount sufficient to justify a higher management advisory fee and a higher level of risk of underperforming the index. The total return on the index becomes the minimum total return objective rather than the target total return. Thus enhanced indexing brings active strategies back into the portfolio management process, although enhanced indexing strategies are assumed to employ only low-risk strategies.

What are some of the strategies employed in enhanced indexing? We have discussed most of them at the beginning of this chapter. Any of the strategies employed would involve only those issues in the index. Another strategy for enhancing total return is to use securities not included in the index. For ex-

---

[14]For a more detailed discussion, see Mossavar-Rahmani, "Understanding and Evaluating Index Fund Management," op. cit., pp. 438–440.

[15]Fran Hawthorne, "The Battle of the Bond Indexes," *Institutional Investor* (April 1986), p. 122.

ample, the broad-based indexes do not include derivative mortgage-backed securities such as collateralized mortgage obligations. If money managers pursuing enhanced index strategies believe that derivative mortgage-backed securities will outperform the agency pass-through securities in the index, they can substitute the former securities for the latter. Or the money manager may be able to create synthetic agency pass-through securities by using stripped mortgage-backed securities (interest-only and principal-only securities) that would exhibit better performance in certain interest rate environments.[16]

■ SUMMARY

Active bond portfolio strategies seek to capitalize on expectations about changes in factors that will affect the price and therefore the performance of an issue over some investment horizon. The factors that affect a portfolio's return are (1) changes in the level of interest rates, (2) changes in the shape of the yield curve, (3) changes in yield spreads among bond sectors, and (4) changes in the yield spread for a particular bond. The total return framework should be used to assess how changes in these factors will affect the performance of a strategy over some investment horizon.

Indexing a portfolio means designing a portfolio so that its total return will match the performance of some predetermined index. Indexing requires selecting a bond index to be replicated and constructing a portfolio so as to minimize tracking error. The methodologies used to construct an indexed portfolio include the stratified sampling, or cell, approach, the optimization approach, and the variance minimization approach. In an enhanced indexing strategy the performance of the index becomes the minimum return objective that the portfolio manager attempts to achieve.

■ KEY TERMS

barbell strategy
bond indexing
bullet strategy
butterfly shift
customized benchmarks
enhanced indexing
flattening of the yield curve
intermarket spread swaps

ladder strategy
non-parallel shift in the yield curve
optimization approach to indexing
parallel shift in the yield curve
rate anticipation swaps
relative yield spread
steepening of the yield curve

stratified sampling approach to indexing
substitution swap
variance minimization approach to indexing
yield curve strategies
yield ratio
yield spread strategies

---

[16]For a discussion of strategies to outperform an index, see Mark L. Dunetz and James M. Mahoney, "Indexation and Optimal Strategies in Portfolio Management," in Frank J. Fabozzi (ed.), *Fixed Income Portfolio Strategies* (Chicago: Probus Publishing, 1989). For an illustration of enhanced indexing within the Treasury sector of the market, see H. Gifford Fong and Frank J. Fabozzi, "How to Enhance Bond Returns with Naive Strategies," *Journal of Portfolio Management* (Summer 1985), pp. 57–60.

■ QUESTIONS

1. What are the limitations of using duration and convexity measures in active portfolio strategies?

2. Below are two portfolios with a market value of $500 million. The bonds in both portfolios are trading at par value. The dollar duration of the two portfolios is the same.

BONDS IN PORTFOLIO I

Issue	Years to Maturity	Par Value ($ million)
A	2.0	$120
B	2.5	30
C	20.0	150
D	20.5	100

BONDS IN PORTFOLIO II

Issue	Years to Maturity	Par Value ($ million)
E	9.7	$200
F	10.0	230
G	10.2	70

   a. Which portfolio can be characterized as a bullet portfolio?

   b. Which portfolio can be characterized as a barbell portfolio?

   c. Since the two portfolios have the same dollar duration, explain whether their performance will be the same if interest rates change.

   d. If they will not perform the same, how would you go about determining which would perform best, assuming that you have a six-month investment horizon?

3. Explain why you agree or disagree with the following statements:

   a. "It is always better to have a portfolio with more convexity than less convexity."

   b. "A bullet portfolio will always outperform a barbell portfolio with the same dollar duration if the yield curve steepens."

4. What is a laddered portfolio?

5. A portfolio manager owns $5 million par value of bond ABC. The bond is trading at 70 and has a modified duration of 6. The portfolio manager is considering swapping out of bond ABC and into bond XYZ. The price of this bond is 85, and it has a modified duration of 3.5.

   a. What is the dollar duration of bond ABC per 100-basis-point change in yield?

   b. What is the dollar duration for the $5 million position of bond ABC?

   c. How much in market value of bond XYZ should be purchased so that the dollar duration of bond XYZ will be approximately the same as that of bond ABC?

   d. How much in par value of bond XYZ should be purchased so that the dollar duration of bond XYZ will be approximately the same as that of bond ABC?

6. Explain why in implementing a yield spread strategy it is necessary to keep the dollar duration constant.

7. The excerpt following is taken from an article entitled "Smith Plans to Shorten," which appeared in the January 27, 1992, issue of *BondWeek*:

   When the economy begins to rebound and interest rates start to move up, Smith Affiliated Capital will swap 30-year Treasuries for 10-year Treasuries and those with average remaining lives of nine years, according to Bob Smith, executive v.p. The New York firm doesn't expect this to occur until the end of this year or early next, however, and sees the yield on the 30-year Treasury first falling below 7%. Any new cash that comes in now will be put into 30-year Treasuries, Smith added. (p. 6)

   What type of portfolio strategy is Smith Affiliated Capital pursuing?

8. The following excerpt is taken from an article entitled "MERUS to Boost Corporates," which appeared in the January 27, 1992, issue of *BondWeek*:

   MERUS Capital Management will increase the allocation to corporates in its $790 million long investment-grade fixed-income portfolio by $39.5 million over the next six months to a year, according to George Wood, managing director. MERUS will add corporates rated single A or higher in the expectation that spreads will tighten as the economy recovers and that some credits may be upgraded. (p. 6)

   What types of active portfolio strategies is MERUS Capital Management pursuing?

9. This excerpt comes from an article entitled "Eagle Eyes High-Coupon Callable Corporates," published in the January 20, 1992, issue of *BondWeek*:

   If the bond market rallies further, Eagle Asset Management may take profits, trading $8 million of seven to 10-year Treasuries for high-coupon single-A industrials that are callable in two to four years according to Joseph Blanton, senior v.p. He thinks a further rally is unlikely, however.

Eagle has already sold seven- to 10-year Treasuries to buy $25 million of high-coupon, single-A nonbank financial credits. It made the move to cut the duration of its $160 million fixed income portfolio from 3.7 to 2.5 years, substantially lower than the 3.3-year duration of its bogey . . . because it thinks the bond rally has run its course.

. . . Blanton said he likes single-A industrials and financial with 9 1/2–10% coupons because these are selling at wide spreads of about 100–150 basis points off Treasuries. (p. 7)

What types of active portfolio strategies are being pursued by Eagle Asset Management?

10. The excerpt below is taken from an article entitled "W. R. Lazard Buys Triple Bs," which appeared in the November 18, 1991, issue of *BondWeek*:

W. R. Lazard & Co. is buying some corporate bonds rated triple B that it believes will be upgraded and some single As that the market perceives as risky but Lazard does not, according to William Schultz, v.p. The firm, which generally buys corporates rated single A or higher, is making the move to pick up yield, Schultz said. (p. 7)

What types of active portfolio strategies are being followed by W.R. Lazard & Co.?

11. In an article entitled "Signet to Add Pass-Throughs," which appeared in the October 14, 1991, issue of *BondWeek*, it was reported that Christian Goetz, assistant vice president of Signet Asset Management, "expects current coupons to outperform premium pass-throughs as the Fed lowers rates because mortgage holders will refinance premium mortgages" (p. 5). If Goetz pursues a strategy based on this, what type of active strategy is it?

12. This excerpt comes from an article entitled "Securities Counselors Eyes Cutting Duration," published in the February 17, 1992, issue of *BondWeek*: Securities Counselors of Iowa will shorten the 5.3 year duration on its $250 million fixed-income portfolio once it is convinced interest rates are moving up and the economy is improving. . . . It will shorten by holding in cash equivalents the proceeds from the sale of an undetermined amount of 10-year Treasuries and adding a small amount of high-grade electric

utility bonds that have short maturities if their spreads widen out at least 100 basis points. . . .

. . . The portfolio is currently allocated 85% Treasuries and 15% to agencies. It has not held corporate bonds since 1985, when it perceived as risky the barrage of hostile corporate takeovers . . . . (p. 5)

a. Why would Securities Counselors want to shorten duration if it believes interest rates will rise?

b. How does the purchase of cash equivalents and short-maturity high-grade utilities accomplish the goal of shortening the duration?

c. If the economy does improve, do you think that the spread on short-maturity high-grade corporate bonds will widen out?

d. What risk is Securities Counselors indicating in the last sentence of the excerpt that it is seeking to avoid by not buying corporate bonds?

13. This next excerpt is taken from an article entitled "Wood Struthers to Add High-Grade Corporates," which appeared in the February 17, 1992, issue of *BondWeek*:

Wood Struthers & Winthrop is poised to add a wide range of high-grade corporates to its $600 million fixed-income portfolio. . . . It will increase its 25% corporate allocation to about 30% after the economy shows signs of improving. . . . It will sell Treasuries and agencies of undetermined maturities to make the purchase. . . .

. . . Its duration is 4 1/2-5 years and is not expected to change significantly. . . . (p. 5)

Comment on this portfolio strategy.

14. What factors led to the use of bond indexing?

15. Is there any problem with a commercial bank using an indexing strategy to invest one-year funds on which the bank has agreed to pay a fixed rate?

16. What are the three most commonly used broad-based bond market indexes used by institutional investors?

17. Why does tracking error occur in a bond indexing strategy?

18. What is the stratified sampling, or cell, approach to indexing?

19. What are the various types of enhanced bond indexing strategies?

CHAPTER 25
LIABILITY FUNDING STRATEGIES

LEARNING OBJECTIVES

After reading this chapter you will be able to:

- explain what a liability funding strategy is.
- discuss the risks associated with mismatching portfolio assets and liabilities.
- explain what is meant by immunizing a portfolio.
- explain the basic principles of an immunization strategy and the role of duration in an immunization strategy.
- identify the risks associated with immunizing a portfolio.
- describe what is meant by a contingent immunization strategy and the key factors in implementing such a strategy.

- describe the two liability funding strategies when there are multiple liabilities: multiperiod liability immunization and cash flow matching.
- explain the advantages and disadvantages of a multiple liability immunization strategy versus a cash flow matching strategy.
- describe how liability funding strategies can be extended to cases in which the liabilities are not known with certainty.
- explain what is an active/immunization combination strategy and how the amount allocated to each active and immunized components can be determined.

A **structured portfolio strategy** is one that seeks to match the performance of a predetermined benchmark. Bond portfolio indexing, discussed in the previous chapter, is an example of such a strategy. For bond portfolio indexing, the benchmark is based on a bond index, but it may not actually satisfy the needs of the sponsoring institution. In this chapter we will discuss **liability funding strategies** which select assets so that cash flows will equal or exceed the client's obligations. The client's liabilities, then, serve as the benchmark for portfolio performance. Specifically, when the liability is a single liability, an *immunization strategy* is employed. When there are multiple liabilities, there are two strategies to choose from: *multiperiod immunization* and *cash flow matching*.

Tens of billions of dollars in pension monies went into these liability funding strategies in the early and mid-1980s when interest rates were high because of the strong incentive to reduce pension costs by locking in these rates. The insurance industry has also made widespread use of these strategies for their fixed-liability insurance products.

IMMUNIZATION OF A PORTFOLIO TO SATISFY A SINGLE LIABILITY

The individual generally credited with pioneering the **immunization strategy**, F. M. Reddington, defined immunization in 1952 as "the investment of the assets in such a way that the existing business is immune to a general change in the rate of interest."[1]

To comprehend the basic principles underlying the immunization of a portfolio against interest rate changes so as to satisfy a single liability, consider the situation faced by a life insurance company that sells a guaranteed investment contract (GIC). Under this policy, for a lump-sum payment a life insurance company guarantees that specified dollars will be paid to the policyholder at a specified future date. Or, equivalently, the life insurance company guarantees a specified rate of return on the payment. For example, suppose that a life insurance company sells a GIC that guarantees an interest rate of 6.25% every 6 months (12.5% on a bond-equivalent yield basis) for 5.5 years (eleven 6-month periods). Also suppose that the payment made by the policyholder is $8,820,262. Then the value that the life insurance company has guaranteed the policyholder 5.5 years from now is

$8,820,262(1.0625)^{11} = \$17,183,033$

When investing the $8,820,262, the target accumulated value for the portfolio manager of the life insurance company is $17,183,033 after 5.5 years, which is the same as a target yield of 12.5% on a bond-equivalent basis.[2]

Suppose the portfolio manager buys $8,820,262 par value of a bond selling at par with a 12.5% yield to maturity that matures in 5.5 years. Will the portfolio manager be assured of realizing the target yield of 12.5% or, equivalently, a target accumulated value of $17,183,033? As we explained in Chapter 20, the portfolio manager will realize a 12.5% yield only if the coupon interest payments can be reinvested at 6.25% every 6 months. That is, the accumulated value will depend on the reinvestment rate.

To demonstrate this, we will suppose that immediately after investing the $8,820,262 in the 12.5% coupon, 5.5-year-maturity bond, yields in the market change and stay at the new level for the remainder of the 5.5 years. Table 25-1 illustrates what happens at the end of 5.5 years. The first column shows the new yield level. The second column shows the total coupon interest payments (which remain constant). The third column gives the interest-on-interest over the entire 5.5 years if the coupon interest payments are reinvested at the new yield level shown in the first column. The price of the bond

---

[1]The theory of immunization was first set forth in F. M. Reddington, "Review of the Principle of Life Office Valuation," *Journal of the Institute of Actuaries* (1952), pp. 286–340.

[2]Actually, the life insurance company will not guarantee the interest rate that it expects to earn, but a lower rate. The spread between the interest rate earned and the interest rate it guarantees is the return for the risk of not achieving the target return.

TABLE 25-1

ACCUMULATED VALUE AND TOTAL RETURN AFTER 5.5 YEARS: 5.5-YEAR, 12.5% BOND SELLING TO YIELD 12.5%

Investment horizon (years)	= 5.5
Coupon rate	= 0.125
Maturity (years)	= 5.5
Yield to maturity	= 0.125
Price	= 100
Par value purchased	= $8,820,262
Purchase price	= $8,820,262
Target accumulated value	= $17,183,033

			After 5.5 years		
New Yield*	Coupon Interest	Interest-on-Interest	Price of Bond†	Accumulated Value	Total Return
0.160	$6,063,930	$3,112,167	$8,820,262	$17,996,360	0.1340
0.155	6,063,930	2,990,716	8,820,262	17,874,908	0.1326
0.145	6,063,930	2,753,177	8,820,262	17,637,369	0.1300
0.140	6,063,930	2,637,037	8,820,262	17,521,230	0.1288
0.135	6,063,930	2,522,618	8,820,262	17,406,810	0.1275
0.130	6,063,930	2,409,984	8,820,262	17,294,086	0.1262
0.125	6,063,930	2,298,840	8,820,262	17,183,033	0.1250
0.120	6,063,930	2,189,433	8,820,262	17,073,625	0.1238
0.115	6,063,930	2,081,648	8,820,262	16,965,840	0.1225
0.110	6,063,930	1,975,462	8,820,262	16,859,654	0.1213
0.105	6,063,930	1,870,852	8,820,262	16,755,044	0.1201
0.100	6,063,930	1,767,794	8,820,262	16,651,986	0.1189
0.095	6,063,930	1,666,266	8,820,262	16,550,458	0.1178
0.090	6,063,930	1,566,246	8,820,262	16,450,438	0.1166
0.085	6,063,930	1,467,712	8,820,262	16,351,904	0.1154
0.080	6,063,930	1,370,642	8,820,262	16,254,834	0.1143
0.075	6,063,930	1,275,014	8,820,262	16,159,206	0.1132
0.070	6,063,930	1,180,808	8,820,262	16,065,000	0.1120
0.065	6,063,930	1,088,003	8,820,262	15,972,195	0.1109
0.060	6,063,930	996,577	8,820,262	15,880,769	0.1098
0.055	6,063,930	906,511	8,820,262	15,790,703	0.1087
0.050	6,063,930	817,785	8,820,262	15,701,977	0.1077

*Immediate change in yield.

†Maturity value.

at the end of 5.5 years shown in the fourth column is the par value. The fifth column is the accumulated value from all three sources: coupon interest, interest-on-interest, and bond price. The total return on a bond-equivalent yield basis is shown in the last column, according to the formula[3]

$$\text{Total return} = 2\left[\left(\frac{\text{accumulated value}}{\$8,820,262}\right)^{1/11} - 1\right]$$

If yields do not change, so that the coupon payments can be reinvested at 12.5% (6.25% every 6 months), the portfolio manager will achieve the target accumulated value. If market yields rise, an accumulated value (total return) higher than the target accumulated value (target yield) will be achieved. This

---

[3] The procedure for calculating the total return is given in Chapter 20.

TABLE 25-2

ACCUMULATED VALUE AND TOTAL RETURN AFTER 5.5 YEARS: 15-YEAR, 12.5% BOND SELLING TO YIELD 12.5%

Investment horizon (years) = 5.5
Coupon rate   = 0.1250
Maturity (years)   = 15
Yield to maturity   = 0.1250
Price   = 100
Par value purchased   = $8,820,262
Purchase price   = $8,820,262
Target accumulated value = $17,183,033

New Yield*	Coupon Interest	After 5.5 years			
		Interest-on-Interest	Price of Bond	Accumulated Value	Total Return
0.160	$6,063,930	$3,112,167	$7,337,902	$16,514,000	0.1173
0.155	6,063,930	2,990,716	7,526,488	16,581,134	0.1181
0.145	6,063,930	2,753,177	7,925,481	16,742,587	0.1200
0.140	6,063,930	2,637,037	8,136,542	16,837,510	0.1211
0.135	6,063,930	2,522,618	8,355,777	16,942,325	0.1223
0.130	6,063,930	2,409,984	8,583,555	17,057,379	0.1236
0.125	6,063,930	2,298,840	8,820,262	17,183,033	0.1250
0.120	6,063,930	2,189,433	9,066,306	17,319,699	0.1265
0.115	6,063,930	2,081,648	9,322,113	17,467,691	0.1282
0.110	6,063,930	1,975,462	9,588,131	17,627,523	0.1299
0.105	6,063,930	1,870,852	9,864,831	17,799,613	0.1318
0.100	6,063,930	1,767,794	10,152,708	17,984,432	0.1338
0.095	6,063,930	1,666,266	10,452,281	18,182,477	0.1359
0.090	6,063,930	1,566,246	10,764,095	18,394,271	0.1382
0.085	6,063,930	1,467,712	11,088,723	18,620,366	0.1406
0.080	6,063,930	1,370,642	11,462,770	18,861,342	0.1431
0.075	6,063,930	1,275,014	11,778,867	19,117,812	0.1457
0.070	6,063,930	1,180,808	12,145,682	19,390,420	0.1485
0.065	6,063,930	1,088,003	12,527,914	19,679,847	0.1514
0.060	6,063,930	996,577	12,926,301	19,986,808	0.1544
0.055	6,063,930	906,511	13,341,617	20,312,058	0.1576
0.050	6,063,930	817,785	13,774,677	20,656,393	0.1609

*Immediate change in yield.

is because the coupon interest payments can be reinvested at a higher rate than the initial yield to maturity. Contrast this with what happens when the yield declines. The accumulated value (total return) will be less than the target accumulated value (target yield). *Therefore investing in a coupon bond with a yield to maturity equal to the target yield and a maturity equal to the investment horizon does not assure that the target accumulated value will be achieved.*

Suppose that instead of investing in a bond maturing in 5.5 years, the portfolio manager invests in a 15-year bond with a coupon rate of 12.5% that is selling at par to yield 12.5%. Table 25-2 presents the accumulated value and total return if the market yield changes immediately after the bond is purchased and remains at the new yield level. The fourth column of the table is the market price of a 12.5% coupon, 9.5-year bond (since 5.5 years have passed), assuming the market yields shown in the first column. If the market

TABLE 25-3

CHANGE IN INTEREST-ON-INTEREST AND PRICE DUE TO INTEREST RATE CHANGE AFTER 5.5 YEARS: 15-YEAR, 12.5% BOND SELLING TO YIELD 12.5%

New Yield	Change in Interest-on-Interest	Change in Price	Total Change in Accumulated Value
0.160	$813,327	-$1,482,360	-$669,033
0.155	692,875	-1,293,774	-601,898
0.145	454,336	-894,781	-440,445
0.140	338,197	-683,720	-345,523
0.135	223,778	-464,485	-240,707
0.130	111,054	-236,707	-125,654
0.125	0	0	0
0.120	-109,407	246,044	136,636
0.115	-217,192	501,851	284,659
0.110	-323,378	767,869	444,491
0.105	-427,989	1,044,569	616,581
0.100	-531,046	1,332,446	801,400
0.095	-632,574	1,632,019	999,445
0.090	-732,594	1,943,833	1,211,239
0.085	-831,128	2,268,461	1,437,333
0.080	-928,198	2,606,508	1,678,309
0.075	-1,023,826	2,958,605	1,934,779
0.070	-1,118,032	3,325,420	2,207,388
0.065	-1,210,838	3,707,652	2,496,814
0.060	-1,302,263	4,106,039	2,803,776
0.055	-1,392,329	4,521,355	3,129,026
0.050	-1,481,055	4,954,415	3,473,360

yield increases, the portfolio will fail to achieve the target accumulated value; the opposite will be true if the market yield decreases—the accumulated value (total return) will exceed the target accumulated value (target yield).

The reason for this result can be seen in Table 25-3, which summarizes the change in interest-on-interest and the change in price resulting from a change in the market yield. For example, if the market yield rises instantaneously by 200 basis points, from 12.5% to 14.5%, interest-on-interest will be $454,336 greater; however, the market price of the bond will decrease by $894,781. The net effect is that the accumulated value will be $440,445 less than the target accumulated value. The reverse will be true if the market yield decreases. The change in the price of the bond will more than offset the decline in the interest-on-interest, resulting in an accumulated value that exceeds the target accumulated value.

Now we can see what is happening to the accumulated value. There is a trade-off between interest rate (or price) risk and reinvestment risk. For this 15-year bond, the target accumulated value will be realized only if the market yield does not increase.

Because neither a coupon bond with the same maturity nor a bond with a longer maturity ensures realization of the target accumulated value, maybe a bond with a maturity shorter than 5.5 years will. Consider a 12.5% bond with 6 months remaining to maturity selling at par. Table 25-4 shows the accumulated value and total return over the 5.5-year investment horizon. The second column shows the accumulated value after 6 months. The third column shows the value that is accumulated after 5.5 years by reinvesting the value accumulated after 6 months at the yield shown in the first column. That is,

$$\$9,371,528\left(1 + \frac{\text{New yield}}{2}\right)^2$$

By investing in this 6-month bond, the portfolio manager incurs no interest rate risk, although there is reinvestment risk. The target accumulated

TABLE 25-4
ACCUMULATED VALUE AND TOTAL RETURN: 6-MONTH, 12.5% BOND SELLING TO YIELD 12.5%

Investment horizon (years)	= 5.5		
Coupon rate	= 0.125		
Maturity (years)	= 0.5		
Yield to maturity	= 0.125		
Price	= 100		
Par value purchased	= $8,820,262		
Purchase price	= $8,820,262		
Target accumulated value	= $17,183,033		

		After 5.5 years	
New Yield*	**After 6 Months**	**Accumulated Value**	**Total Return**
0.160	$9,371,528	$20,232,427	0.1568
0.155	9,371,528	19,768,932	0.1523
0.145	9,371,528	18,870,501	0.1432
0.140	9,371,528	18,435,215	0.1386
0.135	9,371,528	18,008,986	0.1341
0.130	9,371,528	17,591,647	0.1295
0.125	9,371,528	17,183,033	0.1250
0.120	9,371,528	16,782,980	0.1205
0.115	9,371,528	16,391,330	0.1159
0.110	9,371,528	16,007,924	0.1114
0.105	9,371,528	15,632,609	0.1068
0.100	9,371,528	15,265,232	0.1023
0.095	9,371,528	14,905,644	0.0977
0.090	9,371,528	14,553,697	0.0932
0.085	9,371,528	14,209,247	0.0886
0.080	9,371,528	13,872,151	0.0841
0.075	9,371,528	13,542,270	0.0795
0.070	9,371,528	13,219,466	0.0749
0.065	9,371,528	12,903,604	0.0704
0.060	9,371,528	12,594,550	0.0658
0.055	9,371,528	12,292,175	0.0613
0.050	9,371,528	11,996,349	0.0567

*Immediate change in yield.

value will be achieved only if the market yield remains at 12.5% or rises. Once again, the portfolio manager is not assured of achieving the target accumulated value.

If we assume there is a one-time instantaneous change in the market yield, is there a coupon bond that the portfolio manager can purchase to assure the target accumulated value whether the market yield rises or falls? The portfolio manager should look for a coupon bond so that however the market yield changes, the change in the interest-on-interest will be offset by the change in the price.

Consider, for example, an 8-year, 10.125% coupon bond selling at 88.20262 to yield 12.5%. Suppose $10,000,000 of par value of this bond is purchased for $8,820,262. Table 25-5 provides the same information for this bond as Tables 25-1 and 25-2 did for the previous bonds. Looking at the last two columns, we see that the accumulated value and the total return are never less than the target accumulated value and the target yield. Thus the

TABLE 25-5
ACCUMULATED VALUE AND TOTAL RETURN: 8-YEAR, 10.125% BOND SELLING TO YIELD 12.5%

Investment horizon (years) = 5.5
Coupon rate   = 0.10125
Maturity (years)   = 8
Yield to maturity   = 0.125
Price   = 88.20262
Par value purchased   = $10,000,000
Purchase price   = $8,820,262
Target accumulated value = $17,183,033

		After 5.5 years			
New Yield*	**Coupon Interest**	**Interest-on-Interest**	**Price of Bond**	**Accumulated Value**	**Total Return**
0.160	$5,568,750	$2,858,028	$8,827,141	$17,253,919	0.1258
0.155	5,568,750	2,746,494	8,919,852	17,235,096	0.1256
0.145	5,568,750	2,528,352	9,109,054	17,206,156	0.1253
0.140	5,568,750	2,421,697	9,205,587	17,196,034	0.1251
0.135	5,568,750	2,316,621	9,303,435	17,188,807	0.1251
0.130	5,568,750	2,213,102	9,402,621	17,184,473	0.1250
0.125	5,568,750	2,111,117	9,503,166	17,183,033	0.1250
0.120	5,568,750	2,010,644	9,605,091	17,184,485	0.1250
0.115	5,568,750	1,911,661	9,708,420	17,188,831	0.1251
0.110	5,568,750	1,814,146	9,813,175	17,196,071	0.1251
0.105	5,568,750	1,718,078	9,919,380	17,206,208	0.1253
0.100	5,568,750	1,623,436	10,027,059	17,219,245	0.1254
0.095	5,568,750	1,530,199	10,136,236	17,235,185	0.1256
0.090	5,568,750	1,438,347	10,246,936	17,254,033	0.1258
0.085	5,568,750	1,347,859	10,359,184	17,275,793	0.1260
0.080	5,568,750	1,258,715	10,473,006	17,300,472	0.1263
0.075	5,568,750	1,170,897	10,588,428	17,328,075	0.1266
0.070	5,568,750	1,084,383	10,705,477	17,358,610	0.1270
0.065	5,568,750	999,156	10,824,180	17,392,086	0.1273
0.060	5,568,750	915,197	10,944,565	17,428,511	0.1277
0.055	5,568,750	832,486	11,066,660	17,467,895	0.1282
0.050	5,568,750	751,005	11,190,494	17,510,248	0.1268

*Immediate change in yield.

TABLE 25-6				
CHANGE IN INTEREST-ON-INTEREST AND PRICE DUE TO INTEREST RATE CHANGE AFTER 5.5 YEARS: 8-YEAR, 10.125% BOND SELLING TO YIELD 12.5%				
New Yield	**Change in Interest-on-Interest**	**Change in Price**	**Total Change in Accumulated Value**
---	---	---	---
0.160	$746,911	-$676,024	$70,887
0.155	635,377	-583,314	52,063
0.145	417,235	-394,112	23,123
0.140	310,580	-297,579	13,001
0.135	205,504	-199,730	5,774
0.130	101,985	-100,544	1,441
0.125	0	0	0
0.120	-100,473	101,925	1,452
0.115	-199,456	205,254	5,798
0.110	-296,971	310,010	13,038
0.105	-393,039	416,215	23,176
0.100	-487,681	523,894	36,212
0.095	-580,918	633,071	52,153
0.090	-672,770	743,771	71,000
0.085	-763,258	856,019	92,760
0.080	-852,402	969,841	117,439
0.075	-940,221	1,085,263	145,042
0.070	-1,026,734	1,202,311	175,578
0.065	-1,111,961	1,321,014	209,053
0.060	-1,195,921	1,441,399	245,478
0.055	-1,278,632	1,563,494	284,862
0.050	-1,360,112	1,687,328	327,216

target accumulated value is assured regardless of what happens to the market yield. Table 25-6 shows why. When the market yield rises, the change in the interest-on-interest more than offsets the decline in price. When the market yield declines, the increase in price exceeds the decline in interest-on-interest.

What characteristic of this bond assures that the target accumulated value will be realized regardless of how the market yield changes? The Macaulay duration for each of the four bonds we have considered is shown in Table 25-7.

Notice that the last bond, which assures that the target accumulated value will be achieved regardless of what happens to the market yield, has a

TABLE 25-7	
MACAULAY DURATIONS OF SELECTED BONDS	
Bond	**Macaulay Duration**
---	---
5.5-year, 12.5% coupon, selling at par	4.14 years
15-year, 12.5% coupon, selling at par	7.12 years
6-month, 12.5% coupon, selling at par	0.50 year
8-year, 10.125% coupon, selling for 88.20262	5.50 years

Macaulay duration equal to the length of the investment horizon. *This is the key. To immunize a portfolio's target accumulated value (target yield) against a change in the market yield, a portfolio manager must invest in a bond (or a bond portfolio) such that:*

1. The Macaulay duration is equal to the investment horizon.
2. The initial present value of the cash flow from the bond (or bond portfolio) equals the present value of the future liability.

Rebalancing an Immunized Portfolio

Our illustrations of the principles underlying immunization assume a one-time instantaneous change in the market yield. In practice, the market yield will fluctuate over the investment horizon. As a result, the Macaulay duration of the portfolio will change as the market yield changes. In addition, the Macaulay duration will change simply because of the passage of time.

Even in the face of changing market yields, a portfolio can be immunized if it is rebalanced so that its Macaulay duration is equal to the remaining time of the investment horizon. For example, if the investment horizon is initially 5.5 years, the initial portfolio should have a Macaulay duration of 5.5 years. After 6 months the investment horizon will be 5 years, but the Macaulay duration of the portfolio will probably be different from 5 years. This is because duration depends on the remaining time to maturity and the new level of yields, and there is no reason why the change in these two values should reduce the duration by exactly 6 months. Thus the portfolio must be rebalanced so that its Macaulay duration is equal to 5. After 6 months, the portfolio must be rebalanced again so that its Macaulay duration will equal 4.5 years. And so on.

How often should the portfolio be rebalanced to adjust its Macaulay duration? On the one hand, the more frequent rebalancing increases transactions costs, thereby reducing the likelihood of achieving the target yield. On the other hand, less frequent rebalancing will result in the Macaulay duration wandering from the target Macaulay duration, which will also reduce the likelihood of achieving the target yield. Thus the portfolio manager faces a trade-off: Some transactions costs must be accepted to prevent the Macaulay duration from wandering too far from its target; but some maladjustment in the Macaulay duration must be accepted, or transactions costs will become prohibitively high.

Immunization Risk

The sufficient condition for the immunization of a single liability is that the Macaulay duration of the portfolio be equal to the length of the investment horizon. However, a portfolio will be immunized against interest rate changes only if the yield curve is flat and any changes in the yield curve are parallel changes (that is, interest rates move either up or down by the same number of basis points for all maturities). Recall from Chapter 21 that Macaulay duration is a measure of price volatility for parallel shifts in the yield curve. If there is a change in interest rates that does not correspond to this shape-preserving shift, matching the Macaulay duration to the investment horizon will not assure immunization. That is, the target yield will no longer be the minimum total return for the portfolio.

Empirical studies of the effectiveness of immunization strategies based on Macaulay duration clearly demonstrate that immunization does not work perfectly in the real world. In the first study of immunization, Fisher and Weil found that the duration-based immunization strategy would have come closer to the target yield or exceeded it more often than a strategy based on matching the maturity of the portfolio to the investment horizon (for the period 1925 through 1968), even after considering transactions costs.[4] When Ingersoll critically evaluated the Fisher-Weil study, using actual prices rather than the indexes they used, he did not find support for the claim that a duration-matching strategy outperforms a maturity strategy.[5] However, studies by Bierwag, Kaufman, Schweitzer, and Toevs;[6] Hackett;[7] Lau;[8] and Leibowitz and Weinberger[9] all support the theory that a duration-matched portfolio will outperform a maturity-matched portfolio. Yet, contrary to what immunization theory would lead us to expect, a common finding has been that when a duration-matched strategy is employed, the total return is frequently below the target yield. As for the magnitude of the divergence, Leibowitz and Weinberger found that for 5-year investment horizons from January 1958 to January 1975, the total return did not fall below the target yield by more than 25 basis points.

The divergence of the total return from the target yield arises from the fact that, contrary to assumptions of Macaulay duration, the yield curve is not always flat and often changes in a non-parallel fashion. Several researchers have relaxed these assumptions and developed different measures of duration.

Bierwag, Kaufman, Schweitzer, and Toevs, for example, empirically examine how duration strategies based on more complex duration measures assuming different yield curve shifts would perform compared with Macaulay duration. They conclude that Macaulay duration "immunized almost as well as the more complex [duration] strategies and appears to be the most cost effective."[10] Lau reaches the same conclusion—Macaulay duration is just about as effective as the more complex duration measures.

As there are many Macaulay duration-matched portfolios that can be constructed to immunize a liability, is it possible to construct one that has the lowest risk of not realizing the target yield? That is, in light of the uncertain

---

[4]Lawrence Fisher and Roman L. Weil, "Coping with the Risk of Interest Rate Fluctuations: Returns to Bondholders from Naive and Optimal Strategies," *Journal of Business* (October 1971), pp. 408–431.

[5]Jonathan E. Ingersoll, "Is Immunization Feasible? Evidence from the CRSP Data," in George G. Kaufman, G. O. Bierwag, and Alden Toevs (eds.), *Innovations in Bond Portfolio Management: Durations and Analysis and Immunization* (Greenwich, CT: JAI Press, 1983).

[6]G. O. Bierwag, George G. Kaufman, Robert Schweitzer, and Alden Toevs, "The Art of Risk Management in Bond Portfolios," *Journal of Portfolio Management* (Spring 1981), pp. 27–36.

[7]T. Hackett, "A Simulation Analysis of Immunization Strategies Applied to Bond Portfolios," unpublished doctoral dissertation, University of Oregon, 1981.

[8]Patrick W. Lau, "An Empirical Examination of Alternative Interest Rate Immunization Strategies," unpublished doctoral dissertation, University of Wisconsin at Madison, 1983.

[9]Martin L. Leibowitz and Alfred Weinberger, "Contingent Immunization—Part II: Problem Areas," *Financial Analysts Journal* (January–February 1983), pp. 35–50.

[10]Bierwag, Kaufman, Schweitzer, and Toevs, "The Art of Risk Management in Bond Portfolios," op. cit., p. 33.

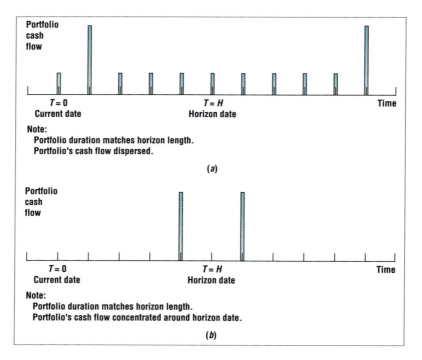

way in which the yield curve may shift, is it possible to develop a criterion for minimizing the risk that a Macaulay duration-matched portfolio will not be immunized? Fong and Vasicek[11] and Bierwag, Kaufman, and Toevs[12] explore this question. Figure 25-1 graphically illustrates how to minimize immunization risk.

The spikes in the two panels of Figure 25-1 represent actual portfolio cash flows. The taller spikes depict the actual cash flows generated by securities that have matured, and the smaller spikes represent coupon payments. Both portfolio A and portfolio B are composed of two bonds with a duration equal to the investment horizon. Portfolio A is, in effect, a barbell portfolio—one composed of short and long maturities and interim coupon payments. For portfolio B, the two bonds mature very close to the investment horizon, and the coupon payments are nominal over the investment horizon. Portfolio B is, in effect, a bullet portfolio.

We can now see why the barbell portfolio should be riskier than the bullet portfolio. Assume that both portfolios have Macaulay durations equal to the horizon length, so that each is immune to parallel changes in the yield curve. Suppose that the yield curve changes in a non-parallel way so that short-term interest rates decline while long-term interest rates increase. Both portfolios would then produce an accumulated value at the end of the investment horizon that is below the target accumulated value, because they would

[11]H. Gifford Fong and Oldrich Vasicek, "A Risk Minimizing Strategy for Multiple Liability Immunization," *Journal of Finance* (December 1984), pp. 1541–1546.

[12]G. O. Bierwag, George G. Kaufman, and Alden Toevs, "Bond Immunization and Stochastic Process Risk," working paper, Center for Capital Market Research, University of Oregon, July 1981.

experience a capital loss owing to the higher long-term interest rate and less interest-on-interest resulting from the lower reinvestment rate when the short-term interest rate declines. The accumulated value for the barbell portfolio at the end of the investment horizon, however, would miss the target accumulated value by more than the bullet portfolio.

There are two reasons for this. First, the lower reinvestment rates are experienced on the barbell portfolio for larger interim cash flows over a longer time period than on the bullet portfolio. Second, the portion of the barbell portfolio still outstanding at the end of the investment horizon is much longer than the maturity of the bullet portfolio, resulting in a greater capital loss for the barbell compared with the bullet. Thus the bullet portfolio has less risk exposure than the barbell portfolio to any changes in the interest rate structure that might occur.

What should be evident from this analysis is that immunization risk is the risk of reinvestment. The portfolio that has the least reinvestment risk will have the least immunization risk. When there is a high dispersion of cash flows around the investment horizon date, the portfolio is exposed to high reinvestment risk. When the cash flows are concentrated around the investment horizon date, as in the case of the bullet portfolio, the portfolio is subject to low reinvestment risk.

Fong and Vasicek have developed a measure of immunization risk. They have demonstrated that if the yield curve shifts in any arbitrary way, the relative change in the portfolio value will depend on the product of two terms. The first term depends solely on the characteristics of the investment portfolio. The second term is a function of interest rate movement only. The second term characterizes the nature of the change in the shape of the yield curve. Because that change will be impossible to predict a priori, it is not possible to control for it. The first term, however, can be controlled for when constructing the immunized portfolio, because it depends solely on the composition of the portfolio. This first term, then, is a measure of risk for immunized portfolios and is equal to

$$\frac{CF_1(1 - H)^2}{(1 + y)^1} + \frac{CF_2(2 - H)^2}{(1 + y)^2} + \cdots + \frac{CF_n(n - H)^2}{(1 + y)^n}$$

where CF_t = cash flow of the portfolio at time period t
       H = length (in years) of the investment horizon
       y = yield for the portfolio
       n = time to receipt of the last cash flow

The immunization risk measure agrees with our earlier graphic analysis of the relative risk associated with a barbell and a bullet portfolio. For the barbell portfolio (portfolio A in Figure 25-1), the portfolio's cash flow payments are widely dispersed in time, and the immunization risk measure would be high. The portfolio cash flow payments for the bullet portfolio (portfolio B in Figure 25-1) are close to the investment horizon, so the immunization risk measure is low.

Notice that if all the cash flows are received at the investment horizon, the immunization risk measure is zero. In such a case, the portfolio is equivalent to a pure discount security (zero-coupon security) that matures on the investment horizon date. If a portfolio can be constructed that replicates a pure discount security maturing on the investment horizon date, that portfolio will be the one with the lowest immunization risk. Typically, however, it is not possible to construct such an ideal portfolio.

The objective in constructing an immunized portfolio, then, is to match the Macaulay duration of the portfolio to the investment horizon and select the portfolio that minimizes the immunization risk. The immunization risk measure can be used to construct approximate confidence intervals for the target yield and the target accumulated value.

Zero-Coupon Bonds and Immunization

So far we have dealt with coupon bonds. An alternative approach to immunizing a portfolio against changes in the market yield is to invest in zero-coupon bonds with a maturity equal to the investment horizon. This is consistent with the basic principle of immunization, because the Macaulay duration of a zero-coupon bond is its maturity. However, in practice, the yield on zero-coupon bonds is typically lower than the yield on coupon bonds. Thus using zero-coupon bonds to fund a bullet liability requires more funds, because a lower target yield (equal to the yield on the zero-coupon bond) is being locked in.

Suppose, for example, that a portfolio manager must invest funds to satisfy a known liability of $20 million 5 years from now. If a target yield of 10% on a bond-equivalent basis (5% every 6 months) can be locked in using zero-coupon Treasury bonds, the funds necessary to satisfy the $20 million liability will be $12,278,260, the present value of $20 million using a discount rate of 10% (5% semiannually).

Suppose, instead, that by using coupon Treasury securities, a target yield of 10.3% on a bond-equivalent basis (5.15% every 6 months) is possible. Then the funds needed to satisfy the $20 million liability will be $12,104,240, the present value of $20 million discounted at 10.3% (5.15% semiannually). Thus a target yield higher by 30 basis points would reduce the cost of funding the $20 million by $174,020 ($12,278,260 − $12,104,240). But the reduced cost comes at a price—the risk that the target yield will not be achieved.

Credit Risk and the Target Yield

The target yield may not be achieved if any of the bonds in the portfolio default, or decrease in value because of credit quality deterioration. Restricting the universe of bonds that may be used in constructing an immunized portfolio to Treasury securities eliminates default risk. The target yield that can be achieved, however, will be lower than that for bonds with credit risk, so that the cost of funding a liability would be increased.

In most immunization applications, the client specifies an acceptable level of credit risk. Issues selected for the immunized portfolio are then restricted to those with that quality rating or higher. The more credit risk the client is willing to accept, the higher the achievable target yield, but the greater the risk that the immunized portfolio will fail to meet that target yield because of defaulted or downgraded issues. Once the minimum credit risk is specified and the immunized portfolio is constructed, the portfolio manager must then monitor the individual issues for possible decreases in credit quality. Should an issue be downgraded below the minimum quality rating, that issue must be sold or the acceptable level of risk changed.

Call Risk

When the universe of acceptable issues includes corporate bonds, the target yield may be jeopardized if a callable issue is included that is subsequently called. Call risk can be avoided by restricting the universe of acceptable bonds to non-callable bonds and deep-discount callable bonds. This strategy does not come without a cost. Because non-callable and deep-discount bonds offer lower yields in a low interest rate environment, restricting the universe to these securities reduces the achievable target yield and therefore increases the cost of funding a liability. Also, it may be difficult to find acceptable non-callable bonds.

An immunized portfolio that includes callable bond issues must be carefully monitored so that issues likely to be called are sold and replaced with bond issues that have a lower probability of being called.

Constructing the Immunized Portfolio

Once the universe of acceptable issues is established and any constraints are imposed, the portfolio manager has a large number of possible securities from which to construct an initial immunized portfolio and from which to select to rebalance an immunized portfolio. An objective function can be specified, and a portfolio that optimizes the objective function using mathematical programming tools can be determined. A common objective function, given the risk of immunization discussed earlier, is to minimize the immunization risk measure.[13]

Contingent Immunization

Contingent immunization is a strategy that consists of identifying both the available immunization target rate and a lower safety-net level return with which the investor would be minimally satisfied.[14] The money manager pursues an active portfolio strategy until an adverse investment experience drives the then-available potential return—the combined active return from actual past experience and immunized return from expected future experience—down to the safety-net level. When that point is reached, the money manager is obligated to immunize the portfolio completely and lock in the safety-net level return. As long as the safety net is not violated, the money manager can continue to actively manage the portfolio. Once the immunization mode is activated because the safety net is violated, the manager can no longer return to the active mode, unless, of course, the contingent immunization plan is abandoned.

---

[13]For a discussion of alternative objective functions, see H. Gifford Fong and Frank J. Fabozzi, *Fixed Income Portfolio Management* (Homewood, IL: Dow Jones-Irwin, 1985), Chap. 6; Peter E. Christensen and Frank J. Fabozzi, "Bond Immunization: An Asset Liability Optimization Strategy," Chap. 31 in Frank J. Fabozzi and Irving M. Pollack (eds.), *The Handbook of Fixed Income Securities* (Homewood, IL Dow Jones-Irwin, 1987); and Peter E. Christensen and Frank J. Fabozzi, "Dedicated Bond Portfolios," Chap. 32 in Fabozzi and Pollack (eds.), ibid.

[14]Martin L. Leibowitz, "The Uses of Contingent Immunization," *Journal of Portfolio Management* (Fall 1981), pp. 51–55.

To illustrate this strategy, suppose that a client investing $50 million is willing to accept a 10% rate of return over a 4-year planning horizon at a time when a possible immunized rate of return is 12%. The 10% return is called the **safety-net return**. The difference between the immunized return and the safety-net return is called the **safety cushion**. In our example, the safety cushion is 200 basis points (12% minus 10%).

Because the initial portfolio value is $50 million, the minimum target value at the end of 4 years, based on semiannual compounding, is $73,872,772 [= $50,000,000(1.05)^8]. The rate of return at the time is 12%, so the assets required at this time to achieve the minimum target value of $73,872,772 represent the present value of $73,872,772 discounted at 12% on a semiannual basis, which is $43,348,691 [= $73,872,772/(1.06)^8]. Therefore the safety cushion of 200 basis points translates into an initial **dollar safety margin** of $6,651,309 ($50,000,000 − $43,348,691). Had the safety net of return been 11% instead of 10%, the safety cushion would have been 100 basis points and the initial dollar safety margin $1,855,935. In other words, the smaller the safety cushion, the smaller the dollar safety margin. Table 25-8 illustrates the contingency immunization strategy by showing the portfolio's value at initial investment and for two scenarios six months later.

The money manager initially pursues an active portfolio strategy within the contingent immunization strategy. Suppose that the money manager puts all the funds into a 20-year, 12% coupon bond selling at par to yield 12%. Let's look at what happens if the market yield falls to 9% at the end of 6 months. The value of the portfolio at the end of 6 months would consist of (1) the value of the 19.5-year, 12% coupon bond at a 9% market yield and (2) 6 months' coupon interest. The price of the bond would increase from 100 to 127.34, so that the price of $50 million of these bonds would rise to $63.67 million. Coupon interest is $3 million (0.50 × 0.12 × $50 million). Thus the portfolio value at the end of 6 months is $66.67 million.

TABLE 25-8

CONTINGENCY IMMUNIZATION: TWO SCENARIOS

Initial Conditions	Initial Investment		
$50 million investment	20-year, 12% coupon bond, selling at		
Achievable immunization rate = 12%	par to yield 12%		
Safety-net return = 10%			
Planning horizon = 4 years			
Scenario/Interest Rates	**Initial Rate 12%**	**Drops to 9% in 6 Months**	**Rises to 14.26% in 6 Months**
Minimum target value to horizon	$73,872,772	$73,872,772	$73,872,772
Current portfolio value	$50,000,000	$66,670,000	$45,615,776
Present value of minimum target	$43,348,691	$54,283,888	$45,614,893
Dollar safety margin (Current value − present value of minimum target)	$ 6,651,309	$12,386,112	$ 883
Management strategy	Active	Active	Immunize

How much would be necessary to achieve the minimum target return of $73,872,772 if a portfolio can be immunized at the current interest rate of 9%? The required dollar value is found by computing the present value of the minimum target return at 9% for 3.5 years. The required dollar amount is $54,283,888 [= $73,872,772/(1.045)^7].

The portfolio value of $66.67 million is greater than the required portfolio value of $54,283,888. The money manager can therefore continue to manage the portfolio actively. The dollar safety margin is now $12,386,112 ($66,670,000 − $54,283,888). As long as the dollar safety margin is positive (that is, the portfolio value is greater than the required portfolio value to achieve the minimum target value at the prevailing interest rate), the portfolio is actively managed.

Suppose that instead of declining to 9% in six months, interest rates rose to 14.26%. The market value of the bond would decline to $42,615,776. The portfolio value would then equal $45,615,776 (the market value of the bonds plus $3 million of coupon interest). The required dollar amount to achieve the minimum target value of $73,872,772 at the current interest rate (14.26%) would be $45,614,893 [= $73,872,772/(1.0713)^7]. The required dollar amount is approximately equal to the portfolio value (that is, the dollar safety margin is almost zero). Thus the money manager would be required to immunize the portfolio in order to achieve the minimum target value (safety-net return) over the investment horizon.

The three key factors in implementing a contingent immunization strategy are (1) establishing accurate immunized initial and ongoing available target returns, (2) identifying a suitable and immunizable safety-net return; and (3) designing an effective monitoring procedure to ensure that the safety-net return is not violated.

STRUCTURING A PORTFOLIO TO SATISFY MULTIPLE LIABILITIES

Thus far we have discussed immunizing a single liability. For pension funds, multiple liabilities must be satisfied—payments to the beneficiaries of the pension fund. A stream of liabilities must also be satisfied for a life insurance company that sells an insurance policy requiring multiple payments to policyholders, such as an annuity policy. Two strategies can be used to satisfy a liability stream: (1) multiperiod immunization and (2) cash flow matching.

Multiperiod Immunization

Multiperiod immunization is a portfolio strategy in which a portfolio is created that will be capable of satisfying more than one predetermined future liability regardless if interest rates change. Even if there is a parallel shift in the yield curve, Bierwag, Kaufman, and Toevs demonstrate that matching the duration of the portfolio to the duration of the liabilities is not a sufficient condition to immunize a portfolio seeking to satisfy a liability stream.[15] Instead, it is necessary to decompose the portfolio payment stream in such a way that each liability is immunized by one of the component streams. The

---

[15]G. O. Bierwag, George G. Kaufman, and Alden Toevs, "Immunization Strategies for Funding Multiple Liabilities," *Journal of Financial and Quantitative Analysis* (March 1983), pp. 113–124.

key to understanding this approach is recognizing that the payment stream on the portfolio, not the portfolio itself, must be divided in this manner. There may be no actual bonds that would give the component payment stream.

In the special case of a parallel shift of the yield curve, Fong and Vasicek demonstrate the necessary and sufficient conditions that must be satisfied to assure the immunization of multiple liabilities.[16]

1. The portfolio's duration must equal the duration of the liabilities.
2. The distribution of durations of individual portfolio assets must have a wider range than the distribution of the liabilities.[17]
3. The present value of the cash flows from the bond portfolio must equal the present value of the liability stream.

However, these conditions will immunize only in the case of a parallel shift in the yield curve. To cope with the problem of failure to immunize because of non-parallel shifts in the yield curve, Fong and Vasicek generalize the immunization risk measure for a single liability discussed earlier in this chapter to the multiple-liability case. An optimal immunization strategy is to minimize this immunization risk measure subject to the three constraints above (duration, dispersion of assets and liabilities, and equality of present value of asset cash flows and liability stream), as well as any other constraints that a client may impose.

In a series of articles, Reitano has explored the limitations of the parallel shift assumption.[18] He has also developed models that generalize the immunization of multiple liabilities to arbitrary yield curve shifts. His research makes it clear that classical multiple-period immunization can disguise the risks associated with non-parallel yield curve shifts and that a model that protects against one type of yield curve shift may allow a great deal of exposure and vulnerability to other types of shifts.

Cash Flow Matching

An alternative to multiperiod immunization is **cash flow matching**. This approach, also referred to as **dedicating a portfolio**, can be summarized as follows. A bond is selected with a maturity that matches the last liability stream. An amount of principal plus final coupon equal to the amount of the last

---

[16]Fong and Vasicek, "A Risk Minimizing Strategy for Multiple Liability Immunization," op. cit.

[17]The reason for the second condition can be illustrated using an example. Suppose that a liability stream with 10 payments of $5 million each year is funded with a zero-coupon bond with a maturity (duration) equal to the duration of the liability stream. Suppose also that when the first $5 million payment is due, interest rates rise so that the value of the zero-coupon bond falls. Even though interest rates have increased, there is no offset to reinvestment income because the bond is a zero-coupon bond. Thus there is no assurance that the portfolio will generate sufficient cash flows to satisfy the remaining liabilities. In the case of a single liability, the second condition is automatically satisfied.

[18]Robert R. Reitano, "A Multivariate Approach to Immunization Theory," *Actuarial Research Clearing House*, 2 (1990), and "Multivariate Immunization Theory," *Transactions of the Society of Actuaries*, XLIII (1991). For a detailed illustration of the relationship between the underlying yield curve shift and immunizations, see Robert R. Reitano, "Non-Parallel Yield Curve Shifts and Immunization," *Journal of Portfolio Management* (Spring 1992), pp. 36–43.

liability stream is then invested in this bond. The remaining elements of the liability stream are then reduced by the coupon payments on this bond, and another bond is chosen for the new, reduced amount of the next-to-last liability. Going backward in time, this cash flow matching process is continued until all liabilities have been matched by the payment of the securities in the portfolio.

Figure 25-2 provides a simple illustration of this process for a five-year liability stream. Mathematical programming techniques can be employed to construct a least-cost cash flow matching portfolio from an acceptable universe of bonds. As with immunization, there are constraints imposed when constructing a cash flow–matched portfolio (see Box 25).

The differences between the cash flow matching and multiperiod immunization strategies should be understood. First, unlike the immunization approach, the cash flow matching approach has no duration requirements. Second, with immunization, rebalancing is required even if interest rates do not change. In contrast, no rebalancing is necessary for cash flow matching except to delete and replace any issue whose quality rating has declined below an acceptable level. Third, there is no risk that the liabilities will not be satisfied (barring any defaults) with a cash flow–matched portfolio. For a portfolio constructed using multiperiod immunization, there is immunization risk due to reinvestment risk.

The differences just cited may seem to favor the use of cash flow matching. However, what we have ignored is the relative cost of the two strategies. Using the cost of the initial portfolio as an evaluation measure, Gifford Fong Associates has found that cash flow–matched portfolios, using a universe of corporate bonds rated at least double A, cost from 3% to 7% more in dollar terms than multiperiod immunized portfolios. The reason cash flow matching is more expensive is that, typically, the matching of cash flows to liabilities is not perfect. This means that more funds than necessary must be set aside to match the liabilities. Optimization techniques used to design cash flow–matched portfolios assume that excess funds are reinvested at a conservative reinvestment rate. With multiperiod immunization, all reinvestment returns are assumed to be locked in at a higher target rate of return. Therefore money managers face a trade-off in deciding between the two strategies: avoidance of the risk of not satisfying the liability stream under cash flow matching versus the lower cost attainable with multiperiod immunization.

In the basic cash flow matching technique, only asset cash flows occurring prior to a liability date can be used to satisfy the liability. The technique has been extended to handle situations in which cash flows occurring both before and after the liability date can be used to meet a liability.[19] This technique, called **symmetric cash matching**, allows for the short-term borrowing of funds to satisfy a liability prior to the liability due date. The opportunity to borrow short term so that symmetric cash matching can be employed results in a reduction in the cost of funding a liability.

---

[19]T. Dessa Fabozzi, Tom Tong, and Yu Zhu, "Extensions of Dedicated Bond Portfolio Techniques," Chap. 44 in Frank J. Fabozzi (ed.), *The Handbook of Fixed Income Securities: 3rd ed.* (Homewood, IL: BusinessOne-Irwin, 1991).

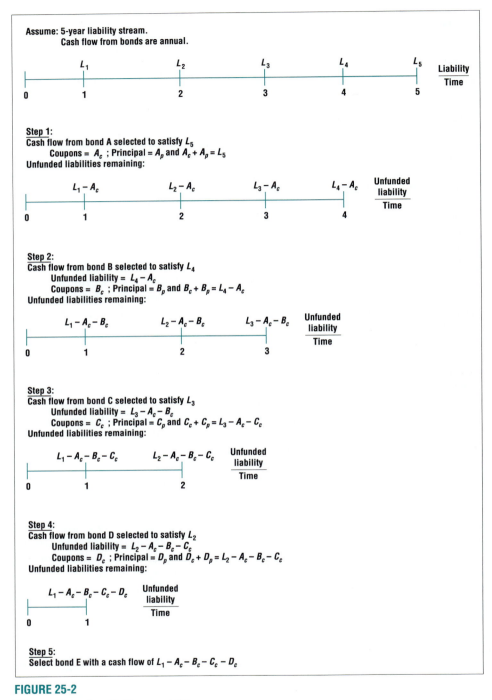

Assume: 5-year liability stream.
        Cash flow from bonds are annual.

Step 1:
Cash flow from bond A selected to satisfy L_5
     Coupons $= A_c$; Principal $= A_p$ and $A_c + A_p = L_5$
Unfunded liabilities remaining:

Step 2:
Cash flow from bond B selected to satisfy L_4
     Unfunded liability $= L_4 - A_c$
     Coupons $= B_c$; Principal $= B_p$ and $B_c + B_p = L_4 - A_c$
Unfunded liabilities remaining:

Step 3:
Cash flow from bond C selected to satisfy L_3
     Unfunded liability $= L_3 - A_c - B_c$
     Coupons $= C_c$; Principal $= C_p$ and $C_c + C_p = L_3 - A_c - C_c$
Unfunded liabilities remaining:

Step 4:
Cash flow from bond D selected to satisfy L_2
     Unfunded liability $= L_2 - A_c - B_c - C_c$
     Coupons $= D_c$; Principal $= D_p$ and $D_c + D_p = L_2 - A_c - B_c - C_c$
Unfunded liabilities remaining:

Step 5:
Select bond E with a cash flow of $L_1 - A_c - B_c - C_c - D_c$

FIGURE 25-2
Illustration of cash flow matching process.

Box 25

PORTFOLIO CONSTRAINTS IN A CASH FLOW–MATCHING STRATEGY

In practice, cash-flow-matching portfolios are subject to a variety of constraints imposed by both the logic of the problem and the degree of conservatism sought by the fund sponsor. These constraints relate to call vulnerability, quality, type of issuer, diversification across type and individual issuer, and the utilization of holdings from preexisting portfolios, among other things.

The call/prepayment vulnerability of specific bonds or mortgage-backed securities—whether for refunding, sinking fund or other purposes—is an important concern for any portfolio designed to provide a prescribed cash flow. The problem can be avoided by purchasing only noncallable securities. Such a prohibition would rule out many higher-yielding securities, however. A more practical approach is to accept fixed income securities that have coupons low enough that the prospect of

a refunding call or mortgage prepayment is either improbable or so productive in terms of windfall gain as to assure adequate reinvestment income.

Similarly, the ultimate in credit quality would be a portfolio consisting of all U.S. Treasury securities. Again, this would prove to be expensive. In most cases, corporate securities of different qualities are acceptable, provided the mixture is appropriately diversified across industries and issuers. . . .

Another important constraint relates to preexisting bond portfolios. In many cases, a fund sponsor may wish to construct cash-flow-matching portfolios using as many existing holdings as possible. This may reduce the new cash required to establish the matching portfolio, reduce transaction costs, and avoid problems associated with the recognition of realized gains or losses in the existing portfolio.

The specific structure, aberrations and peculiarities of the marketplace at a given time will have a huge impact on the optimal cash-matched portfolio. The key is to apply the most modern computer optimization techniques to the broadest possible universe of truly available bonds identified with their truly available prices.

Source: Martin L. Leibowitz, "The Dedicated Bond Portfolio in Pension Funds—Part I: Motivations and Basics," *Financial Analysts Journal* (January/February 1986), pp. 705–506.

Questions for Box 25

1. Why is "call/prepayment vulnerability of specific bonds or mortgage-backed securities . . . an important concern for any portfolio designed to provide a prescribed cash flow"?

2. Why would a cash flow portfolio constrained to include only Treasury securities "prove to be expensive"?

A popular variation of multiperiod immunization and cash flow matching to fund liabilities is one that combines the two strategies. This strategy, referred to as **combination matching** or **horizon matching**, creates a portfolio that is duration-matched with the added constraint that it be cash-matched in the first few years, usually five years. The advantage of combination matching over multiperiod immunization is that liquidity needs are provided for in the initial cash flow–matched period. Cash flow matching the initial portion of the liability stream reduces the risk associated with non-parallel shifts of the yield curve. The disadvantage of combination matching over multiperiod immunization is that the cost is slightly greater.

Within the immunization and dedicated cash flow strategies, some portfolio managers are permitted to manage the portfolio actively by entering into bond swaps to enhance portfolio performance. Obviously, only small bets can be made in order to minimize the likelihood that the liability payments will not be satisfied.

EXTENSIONS OF LIABILITY FUNDING STRATEGIES

As we explained in Chapter 7, liabilities may be uncertain with respect to both timing and amount of payment. We referred to these liabilities as Type II, III, and IV in Table 7-1 of Chapter 7. In the techniques we have discussed in this chapter, we have assumed that the timing and the amount of the cash payment of liabilities are known with certainty. That is, we assume that the liabilities are deterministic.

We assume, moreover, that the cash flows from the assets are known with certainty, although you have learned that most non-Treasury securities have embedded options that permit the borrower or the investor to alter the cash flows. Thus, the models presented in this chapter are referred to as **deterministic models**, because they assume that the liability payments and the asset cash flows are known with certainty.

Since the mid-1980s, a good number of models have been developed to handle real-world situations in which liability payments and/or asset cash flows are uncertain. Such models are called **stochastic models**.[20] Such models require that the portfolio manager incorporate an interest rate model, that is, a model that describes the probability distribution for interest rates. Optimal portfolios then are solved for using a mathematical programming technique known as *stochastic programming*.

The complexity of stochastic models, however, has limited their application in practice. Nevertheless, they are gaining in popularity as more portfolio managers become comfortable with their sophistication. There is increasing awareness that stochastic models reduce the likelihood that the liability objective will not be satisfied, and that transactions costs can be reduced through less frequent rebalancing of a portfolio derived from these models.

COMBINING ACTIVE AND IMMUNIZATION STRATEGIES

In our discussion of contingent immunization, the money manager is permitted to actively manage the portfolio until the safety net is violated. However, contingent immunization is not a combination or mixture strategy. The money manager is either in the immunization mode (by choice or because the safety net is violated) or in the active management mode. In contrast to an immunization strategy, an active/immunization combination strategy is a mixture of two strategies that are pursued by the money manager at the same time.

The immunization component of this strategy could be either a single-liability immunization or a multiple-liability immunization using the techniques discussed earlier in this chapter. In the single-liability immunization case, an assured return would be established so as to serve to stabilize the portfolio's total return. In the multiple-liability immunization case, the component to be immunized would be immunized now, with new requirements, as they become known, taken care of through reimmunization. This would be an adaptive strategy in that the immunization component would be based on an initial set of liabilities and modified over time to changes in future liabilities (e.g., for actuarial changes for the liabilities in the case of a pension fund). The active portion would continue to be free to maximize expected return, given some acceptable risk level.

---

[20]For a review of such models, see Randall S. Hiller and Christian Schaack, "A Classification of Structured Bond Portfolio Modeling Techniques," *Journal of Portfolio Management* (Fall 1990), pp. 37–48.

The following formula suggested by Gifford Fong Associates in Walnut Creek, California, can be used to determine the portion of the initial portfolio to be actively managed, with the balance immunized[21]:

Active component

$$= \frac{\text{immunization target rate} - \text{minimum return established by client}}{\text{immunization target rate} - \text{expected worse case active return}}$$

In the formula it is assumed that the immunization target return is greater than either the minimum return established by the client or the expected worse case return from the actively managed portion of the portfolio.

As an illustration, assume that the available immunization target return is 7% per year, the minimum return acceptable to the client is 5%, and the expected worse case return for the actively managed portion of the portfolio is 2%. Then the percentage in the active portion of the portfolio would be

$$\text{Active component} = \frac{0.07 - 0.05}{0.07 - 0.02} = 0.40, \text{ or } 40\%$$

Notice from the formula for determining the active component that for any given immunization target return, the smaller the minimum acceptable return to the client and the larger the expected worse case active return, the larger the percentage allocated to active management. Since the return values in the formula change over time, the money manager must monitor these values constantly, adjusting and rebalancing the allocation between the immunized and active components as appropriate. As long as the worse case scenario is not violated—that is, as long as the actual return experienced does not drop below the expected worse case active return—the minimum return for the portfolio established by the client will be achieved.

■ SUMMARY

This chapter has demonstrated liability funding strategies that involve designing a portfolio to produce sufficient funds to satisfy liabilities whether or not interest rates change. When only one future liability is to be funded, an immunization strategy can be used. An immunization strategy is designed so that as interest rates change, interest rate risk and reinvestment risk will offset each other in such a way that the minimum accumulated value (or minimum rate of return) becomes the target accumulated value (or target yield). An immunization strategy requires that a money manager create a bond portfolio with a duration equal to the investment horizon. Because immunization theory is based on parallel shifts in the yield curve, the risk is that a portfolio will not be immunized even if the duration-matching condition is satisfied. Immunization risk can be quantified so that a portfolio that minimizes this risk can be constructed.

When multiple liabilities are to be satisfied, either multiperiod immunization or cash flow matching can be used. Multiperiod immunization is a duration-matching strategy that exposes the portfolio to immunization risk. The cash flow–matching strategy does not impose any duration requirement. While the only risk that the liabilities will not be satisfied is that issues will be called or will default, the dollar cost of a cash flow–matched portfolio may be higher than that of a portfolio constructed using a multiperiod immunization strategy.

---

[21]Gifford Fong Associates, *The Costs of Cash Flow Matching*, 1981.

Liability funding strategies where the liability payments and the asset cash flows are known with certainty are deterministic models. In a stochastic model, either the liability payments or the asset cash flows, or both, are uncertain. Stochastic models require specification of a probability distribution for the process that generates interest rates.

A combination of active and immunization strategies can be pursued. Allocation of the portion of the portfolio to be actively managed is based on the immunization target rate, the minimum return acceptable to the client, and the expected worse case return from the actively managed portfolio. In a contingent immunization strategy, a money manager is either actively managing the portfolio or immunizing it. Since both strategies are not pursued at the same time, contingent immunization is not a combination or mixture strategy.

■ KEY TERMS

cash flow matching	dollar safety margin	safety cushion
combination matching	horizon matching	safety-net return
contingent immunization	immunization strategy	stochastic models
dedicating a portfolio	liability funding strategies	structured portfolio strategy
deterministic models	multiperiod immunization	symmetric cash matching

■ QUESTIONS

1. What is meant by immunizing a bond portfolio?

2. a. What is the basic underlying principle in an immunization strategy?
   b. Why may the matching of the maturity of a coupon bond to the maturity of a liability fail to immunize a portfolio?

3. Why must an immunized portfolio be rebalanced periodically?

4. What are the risks associated with a bond immunization strategy?

5. "I can immunize a portfolio by simply investing in zero-coupon Treasury bonds." Comment on this statement.

6. Why is there greater risk in a multiperiod immunization strategy than a cash flow–matching strategy?

7. a. What is a contingent immunization strategy?
   b. What is meant by the safety-net cushion in a contingent immunization strategy?
   c. Is it proper to classify a contingent immunization as a combination active/immunization strategy?

8. What is a combination matching strategy?

9. In a stochastic liability funding strategy, why is an interest rate model needed?

10. Suppose that a client has granted a money manager permission to pursue an active/immunization combination strategy. Suppose further that the minimum return expected by the client is 9% and that the money manager believes that an achievable immunized target return is 4% and the worst possible return from the actively managed portion of the portfolio is 1%. Approximately how much should be allocated to the active component of the portfolio?

11. One of your clients, a newcomer to the life insurance business, questioned you about the following excerpt from Peter E. Christensen, Frank J. Fabozzi, and Anthony LoFaso, "Dedicated Bond Portfolios," Chap. 43 in Frank J. Fabozzi (ed.), *The Handbook of Fixed Income Securities* (Homewood, IL: BusinessOne-Irwin, 1991):

For financial intermediaries such as banks and insurance companies, there is a well-recognized need for a complete funding perspective. This need is best illustrated by the significant interest-rate risk assumed by many insurance carriers in the early years of their Guaranteed Investment Contract (GIC) products. A large volume of compound interest (zero coupon) and simple interest (annual pay) GICs were issued in three-through seven-year maturities in the positively sloped yield-curve environment of the mid-1970s. Proceeds from hundreds of the GIC issues were reinvested at higher rates in the longer 10- to 30-year private placement, commercial mortgage, and public bond instruments. At the time, industry expectations were that the GIC product would be very profitable because of the large positive spread between the higher "earned" rate on the longer assets and the lower "credited" rate on the GIC contracts.

By pricing GICs on a spread basis and investing the proceeds on a mismatched basis, companies gave little consideration to the rollover risk they were assuming in volatile markets. As rates rose dramatically in the late 1970s and early 1980s, carriers were exposed to disintermediation as GIC liabilities matured and the corresponding assets had 20 years remaining to maturity and were valued at only a fraction of their original cost.

Answer the following questions posed to you by your client.

a. "It is not clear to me what risk an issuer of a GIC is facing. Since a carrier can invest the proceeds in assets offering a higher yield than they are guaranteeing to GIC policyholders, what's the problem? Isn't it just default risk which can be controlled by setting tight credit standards?"

b. "I understand that disintermediation means that when a policy matures, the funds are withdrawn from the insurance company by the policyholder. But why would a rise in interest rates cause GIC policyholders to withdraw their funds. The insurance company can simply guarantee a higher interest rate."

c. "What do the authors mean by 'pricing GICs on a spread basis and investing the proceeds on a mismatched basis' and what is this 'rollover risk' that they are referring to?"

12. CFA Global Foundation has recently hired Strategic Allocation Associates (SAA) to review and make recommendations concerning allocation of its $5 billion endowment portfolio. Global has indicated an interest in introducing a structured approach (where structured management is broadly defined as indexing, immunization, dedication, etc.) to at least a portion of the fund's fixed-income component.

After analysis of Global's current asset mix, investment objectives, international exposure, and cash flow data, SAA has recommended that the overall asset mix be: 50% equity, 5% real estate, and 45% fixed-income securities. Within the fixed-income component, SAA further recommended the following allocation:

- 50% Structured Management;

- 40% Specialty Active Management (20% Market Timing, 10% High-Yield, 10% Arbitrage); and
- 10% Nondollar/International Active Management.

Global's investment committee has asked you, as a senior partner in SAA, to address several issues.

a. Compare structured management to active management with specific focus on *each* of the following aspects:

- predictability of returns,
- level of return, and
- cash flow characteristics.

b. Explain the potential impact on the active managers' strategies and freedoms of action resulting from the introduction of a structured portfolio component.

13. Suppose that a life insurance company sells a 5-year guaranteed investment contract that guarantees an interest rate of 7.5% per year on a bond-equivalent yield basis (or, equivalently, 3.75% every six months for the next ten six-month periods). Also suppose that the payment made by the policyholder is $9,642,899. Consider the following three investments that can be made by the portfolio manager:

Bond X: Buy $9,642,899 par value of a bond selling at par with a 7.5% yield to maturity that matures in 5 years.

Bond Y: Buy $9,642,899 par value of a bond selling at par with a 7.5% yield to maturity that matures in 12 years.

Bond Z: Buy $10,000,000 par value of a 6-year, 6.75% coupon bond selling at 96.42899 to yield 7.5%.

a. Holding aside the spread that the insurance company seeks to make on the invested funds, demonstrate that the target accumulated value to meet the GIC obligation 5 years from now is $13,934,413.

b. Complete Exhibit 1 assuming that the manager invests in bond X and immediately following the purchase, yields change and stay the same for the 5-year investment horizon.

c. Based on Exhibit 1, under what circumstances will the investment in bond X fail to satisfy the target accumulated value?

d. Complete Exhibit 2 assuming that the manager invests in bond Y and immediately following the purchase, yields change and stay the same for the 5-year investment horizon.

EXHIBIT 1
ACCUMULATED VALUE AND TOTAL RETURN AFTER 5 YEARS: 5-YEAR, 7.5% BOND SELLING TO YIELD 7.5%

Investment horizon (years)	*5*
Coupon rate	*7.50%*
Maturity (years)	*5*
Yield to maturity	*7.50%*
Price	*100.00000*
Par value purchased	*$9,642,899*
Purchase price	*$9,642,899*
Target accumulated value	*$13,934,413*
* After 5 years*	

New yield	Coupon	Interest on interest	Price of bond	Accumulated value	Total return
11.00%	$3,616,087	$1,039,753	$9,642,899	$14,298,739	8.04%
10.00	3,616,087				
9.00	3,616,087				
8.00	3,616,087				
7.50	3,616,087				
7.00	3,616,087				
6.00	3,616,087				
5.00	3,616,087				
4.00	3,616,087	343,427	9,642,899	13,602,414	7.00

EXHIBIT 2
ACCUMULATED VALUE AND TOTAL RETURN AFTER 5 YEARS: 12-YEAR, 7.5% BOND SELLING TO YIELD 7.5%

Investment horizon (years)	*5*
Coupon rate	*7.5%*
Maturity (years)	*12*
Yield to maturity	*7.5%*
Price	*100.00000*
Par value purchased	*$9,642,899*
Purchase price	*$9,642,899*
Target accumulated value	*$13,934,413*
* After 5 years*	

New yield	Coupon	Interest on Interest	Price of Bond	Accumulated Value	Total Return
11.00%	$3,616,087	$1,039,753	$8,024,639	$12,680,479	5.55%
10.00%	3,616,087				
9.00	3,616,087				
8.00	3,616,087				
7.50	3,616,087				
7.00	3,616,087				
6.00	3,616,087				
5.00	3,616,087				
4.00	3,616,087	343,427	11,685,837	15,645,352	9.92

EXHIBIT 3
ACCUMULATED VALUE AND TOTAL RETURN AFTER 5 YEARS: 6-YEAR, 6.75% BOND SELLING TO YIELD 7.5%

Investment horizon (years) 5
Coupon rate   6.75%
Maturity (years)   6
Yield to maturity   7.5%
Price   96.42899
Par value purchased $10,000,000
Purchase price $9,642,899
Target accumulated value $13,934,413

After 5 years

New yield	Coupon	Interest on Interest	Price of Bond	Accumulated Value	Total Return
11.00%	$3,375,000	$970,432	$9,607,657	$13,953,089	7.53%
10.00	3,375,000				
9.00	3,375,000				
8.00	3,375,000				
7.50	3,375,000				
7.00	3,375,000				
6.00	3,375,000				
5.00	3,375,000				
4.00	3,375,000	320,531	10,266,965	13,962,495	7.54

e. Based on Exhibit 2, under what circumstances will the investment in bond Y fail to satisfy the target accumulated value?

f. Complete Exhibit 3 assuming that the manager invests in bond Z and immediately following the purchase, yields change and stay the same for the 5-year investment horizon.

g. Based on Exhibit 3, under what circumstances will the investment in bond Y fail to satisfy the target accumulated value?

h. Complete the following table for the three bonds assuming that each bond is trading to yield 7.5%:

BOND	MACAULAY DURATION
5-year 7.5% coupon, selling at par	
12-year 7.5% coupon, selling at par	
6-year 6.75% coupon, selling for 96.42899	

i. For which bond is the Macaulay duration equal to the investment horizon?

CHAPTER 26
USING INTEREST RATE FUTURES AND OPTIONS
IN INVESTMENT MANAGEMENT

LEARNING OBJECTIVES
After reading this chapter you will be able to:

- explain the differences between a futures and forward contract.

- describe the basic features of interest rate futures contracts.

- explain what the cheapest-to-deliver issue is and how it is determined.

- discuss counterparty risk in regard to forward contracts and buyers of over-the-counter options.

- describe the delivery options embedded in the Treasury bond futures contract and their impact on the futures price.

- identify how futures contracts can be used in bond portfolio management: speculation, changing duration, yield enhancement, and hedging.

- calculate the hedge ratio and the number of contracts to short when hedging with Treasury bond futures contracts.

- describe the basic features of interest rate options contracts.

- explain why over-the-counter interest rate options are used by institutional investors.

- describe futures options, their trading mechanics, and the reasons for their popularity.

- identify the limitations of applying the Black-Scholes option-pricing model to options on fixed-income securities.

- explain how futures options can be used to hedge.

In Chapters 16 and 17, we explained how stock index futures and equity options can be employed by managers to control the risk of a stock portfolio and other strategies to potentially enhance the performance of stock portfolios. The difference in the risk/return characteristics between futures and options was also explained in the two chapters.

In this chapter we focus on interest rate futures and options and the role they play in the management of a fixed-income portfolio. We need not repeat the general characteristics of these two derivative contracts here. Rather, we will explain the contract specifications of the more popular interest rate futures and options contracts employed by portfolio managers, the modifications to the pricing models for stock index futures and options necessary to price these contracts, and the unique considerations in employing them for interest rate risk control. We will introduce a new type of option—options on interest rate futures. It is this option contract that portfolio managers use in implementing option strategies rather than options on cash market fixed-income instruments.

While we limit our discussion to interest rate futures and options traded in the United States, similar contracts are traded in other major capital markets. Thus, the same strategies can be employed when managing foreign bonds.

INTEREST RATE FUTURES AND FORWARD CONTRACTS

The fundamental features of stock index futures contracts that we described in Chapter 16 apply equally to interest rate futures. Here we will add a discussion of *forward contracts*, which are sometimes used in bond portfolio management.

Forward Contracts

A **forward contract**, just like a futures contract, is an agreement for the future delivery of the underlying at a specified price at the end of a designated period of time. Futures contracts are standardized agreements as to the delivery date (or month) and quality of the deliverable, and are traded on organized exchanges. A forward contract differs in that it is usually non-standardized (that is, the terms of each contract are negotiated individually between buyer and seller), there is no clearinghouse, and secondary markets are often nonexistent or extremely thin. Unlike a futures contract, which is an exchange-traded product, a forward contract is an over-the-counter instrument.

Because there is no clearinghouse that guarantees the performance of a counterparty in a forward contract, the parties to a forward contract are exposed to *counterparty risk*, the risk that other party to the transaction will fail to perform.

Although both futures and forward contracts set forth terms of delivery, futures contracts are not intended to be settled by delivery. In fact, generally less than 2% of outstanding contracts are settled by delivery. Forward contracts, in contrast, are intended for delivery.

Futures contracts are marked to market at the end of each trading day, while forward contracts usually are not. Consequently, futures contracts are subject to interim cash flows because additional margin may be required in the case of adverse price movements or because cash may be withdrawn in the case of favorable price movements. There are no interim cash flows with forward contracts because no variation margin is required.

Finally, the parties in a forward contract are exposed to credit risk because either party may default on the obligation. Credit risk is minimal in the case of futures contracts because the clearinghouse associated with the exchange guarantees the other side of the transaction.

Other than these differences, most of what we say about futures contracts applies to forward contracts, too.

TABLE 26-1

SELECTED INTEREST RATE FUTURES CONTRACTS*

Futures Contracts	CBT 30-Year T-bonds	CBT 10-Year T-notes	CBT 5-Year T-notes	FINEX 5-Year T-notes	IMM 90-Day T-bills	IMM Eurodollars Futures
Trading unit	U.S. T-bonds with a face value of $100,000	U.S. T-notes with a face value of $100,000	U.S. T-notes with a face value of $100,000	U.S. T-notes with a face value of $100,000	U.S. T-bills with a face value of $1,000,000	$1,000,000 3-month Eurodollar time deposit
Deliverable grade	U.S. T-bonds that mature at least 15 years from the delivery date, or if callable, not callable for at least 15 years from the first day of the delivery month	U.S. T-notes that mature no less than 6 1/2 and no more than 10 years from the first day of the delivery month	Any of the four most recently auctioned five-year T-notes. Specifically, US T-notes that have an original maturity of not more than 5 1/2 years and not less than 4 1/4 years, as of the first day of the delivery month.	U.S. T-notes with original maturity of 4 1/2 to 5 1/2 years, and a maturity of 4 1/2 to 5 1/2 years at delivery	U.S. T-bills maturing 90, 91, or 92, days from the delivery date	(Actual delivery not allowed)
Price quotation	Percentage of par in minimum increments of one 32nd of a point, or $31.25 per tick	Percentage of par in minimum increments of one 32nd of a point, or $31.25 per tick	Percentage of par in minimum increments of one-half of one 32nd of a point, or $15.625	Percentage of par in minimum increments of one-half of one 32nd of a point or $15.625	Index (100 minus annualized discount rate) in minimum increments of 0.01 or one basis point, or $25.00 (*Example:* 100 − 8.00 = 92.00)	Index (100 minus annualized discount rate) in minimum increments of 0.01 or one basis point, or $25.00 (*Example:* 100 − 8.00 = 92.00)
Last trading day	The eighth to last business day of the delivery month	The eighth to last business day of the delivery month	The eighth to last business day of the delivery month	The eighth to last business day of the delivery month	Business day preceding the first day of the contract month on which a 13-week T-bill is issued and a one-year T-bill has 13 weeks remaining to maturity	Second London business day before third Wednesday of contract month
First delivery date	First business day of the delivery month	First business day of the delivery month	First business day of the the delivery month	First business day of the delivery month	First business day following the last day of trading	(Actual delivery not allowed)
Last delivery date	Last business day of the delivery month	Last business day of the delivery month	Last business day of the delivery month	Last business day of the delivery month	First business day following the last day of trading	(Actual delivery not allowed)

*Contract specifications are subject to change without notice. The settlement months for all futures contracts are March, June, September, and December.

Exchange-Traded Interest Rate Futures Contracts

Table 26-1 summarizes the currently traded interest rate futures contracts. Interest rate futures contracts can be classified by the maturity of their underlying security. Short-term interest rate futures contracts have an underlying security that matures in less than one year. The maturity of the underlying security of long-term futures exceeds one year. Examples of the former are futures contracts in which the underlying is a three-month Treasury bill and a three-month Eurodollar certificate of deposit. Examples of the latter are futures contracts in which the underlying is a coupon Treasury security, a municipal bond index, and a mortgage pass-through security. Our focus will be on futures contracts in which the underlying is a Treasury coupon security—a Treasury bond or a Treasury note. These contracts are the most widely used by money managers of bond portfolios, and we begin with the specifications of the contract.

Treasury Bond Futures   As we explained in Chapter 16, futures are contracts that are traded on any exchange. The Treasury bond futures contract is traded on the Chicago Board of Trade (CBT).

The underlying instrument for a Treasury bond futures contract is $100,000 par value of a hypothetical 20-year, 8% coupon bond. The futures price is quoted in terms of par being 100. Quotes are in 32nds of 1%. Thus a quote for a Treasury bond futures contract of 97-16 means 97 and 16/32nds, or 97.50. So if a buyer and seller agree on a futures price of 97-16, this means that the buyer agrees to accept delivery of the hypothetical underlying Treasury bond and pay 97.50% of par value and the seller agrees to accept 97.50% of par value. Since the par value is $100,000, the futures price that the buyer and seller agree on for this hypothetical Treasury bond is $97,500.

The minimum price fluctuation for the Treasury bond futures contract is a 32nd of 1%. The dollar value of a 32nd for a $100,000 par value (the par value for the underlying Treasury bond) is $31.25. Thus, the minimum price fluctuation is $31.25 for this contract.

We have been referring to the underlying as a hypothetical Treasury bond. Does this mean that the contract is a cash settlement contract as is the case with stock index futures? The answer is no. The seller of a Treasury bond futures who decides to make delivery rather than liquidate his or her position by buying back the contract prior to the settlement date must deliver some Treasury bond. But what Treasury bond? The CBT allows the seller to deliver one of several Treasury bonds that the CBT declares is acceptable for delivery. The specific bonds that the seller may deliver are published by the CBT prior to the initial trading of a futures contract with a specific settlement date. Table 26-2 shows the Treasury issues that the seller can select from to deliver to the buyer of the futures contract. The CBT makes its determination of the Treasury issues that are acceptable for delivery from all outstanding Treasury issues that meet the following criteria: An issue must have at least 15 years to maturity from the date of delivery if not callable; in the case of callable bonds, the issue must not be callable for at least 15 years from the first day of the delivery month.

The delivery process for the Treasury bond futures contract makes the contract interesting. At the settlement date, the seller of a futures contract (the short) is required to deliver the buyer (the long) $100,000 par value of

TABLE 26-2

TREASURY ISSUES ACCEPTABLE FOR DELIVERY TO SATISFY THE U.S. TREASURY BOND FUTURES CONTRACT FOR SETTLEMENT IN SEPTEMBER 1994 AND THEIR CONVERSION FACTOR

Issue		
Coupon	**Maturity**	**Conversion Factor**
7 1/4	05/15/16	0.923600
7 1/2	11/15/16	0.948600
8 3/4	05/15/17	1.077700
8 7/8	08/15/17	1.090800
9 7/8	11/15/15	1.189200
8 1/8	08/15/19	1.013200
8 7/8	02/15/92	1.092800
9 1/8	05/15/18	1.118400
8 1/2	02/15/20	1.053700
9 1/4	02/15/16	1.126500
8 3/4	05/15/20	1.081100
10 5/8	08/15/15	1.263400
8 1/8	08/15/21	1.013500
11 1/4	02/15/15	1.323000
8	11/15/21	1.000000
7 1/4	08/15/22	0.916700
7 5/8	11/15/22	0.958300
11 3/4	11/15/14	1.324200
7 1/8	02/15/23	0.902400
9	11/15/18	1.106000
6 1/4	08/15/23	0.804000
8 3/4	08/15/20	1.081100
7 7/8	02/15/21	0.986200
8 1/8	05/15/21	1.013700
10 5/8	08/15/15	1.263400
8 1/8	08/15/21	1.013500
11 1/4	02/15/15	1.323000
8	11/15/21	1.000000
7 1/4	08/15/22	0.916700
7 5/8	11/15/22	0.958300
11 3/4	11/15/14	1.324200
7 1/8	02/15/23	0.920400
9	11/15/18	1.106000

an 8%, 20-year Treasury bond. Since no such bond exists, the seller must choose from one of the acceptable deliverable Treasury bonds that the CBT has specified. Suppose the seller is entitled to deliver $100,000 of a 6%, 20-year Treasury bond to settle the futures contract. The value of this bond of course is less than the value of an 8%, 20-year bond. If the seller delivers the 6%, 20-year bond, this would be unfair to the buyer of the futures contract who contracted to receive $100,000 of an 8%, 20-year Treasury bond. Alternatively, suppose the seller delivers $100,000 of a 10%, 20-year Treasury bond. The value of a 10%, 20-year Treasury bond is greater than that of an 8%, 20-year bond, so this would be a disadvantage to the seller.

How can this problem be resolved? To make delivery equitable to both parties, the CBT has introduced **conversion factors** for determining the invoice price of each acceptable deliverable Treasury issue against the Treasury bond futures contract. The conversion factor is determined by the CBT before a contract with a specific settlement date begins trading. Table 26-2 shows for each of the acceptable Treasury issues the corresponding conversion factor.[1] The conversion factor is constant throughout the trading period of the futures contract. The short must notify the long of the actual bond that will be delivered one day before the delivery date.

The price that the buyer must pay the seller when a Treasury bond is delivered is called the **invoice price**. The invoice price is the settlement futures price plus accrued interest. However, as just noted, the seller can deliver one of several acceptable Treasury issues, and to make delivery fair to both parties, the invoice price must be adjusted based on the actual Treasury issue delivered. It is the conversion factors that are used to adjust the invoice price. The invoice price is

Invoice price = contract size × futures contract settlement price
× conversion factor + accrued interest

Suppose that the Treasury bond futures contract settles at 94-08 and that the short elects to deliver a Treasury bond issue with a conversion factor of 1.20. The futures contract settlement price of 94-08 means 94.25% of par value. As the contract size is $100,000, the invoice price the buyer pays the seller is

$100,000 × 0.9425 × 1.20 + accrued interest = $113,100 + accrued interest

In selecting the issue to be delivered, the short will select from all the deliverable issues the one that is cheapest to deliver. This issue is referred to as the **cheapest-to-deliver issue**; it plays a key role in the pricing of this futures contract. The cheapest-to-deliver issue is determined by participants in the market as follows. For each of the acceptable Treasury issues from which the seller can select, the seller calculates the return that can be earned by buying that issue and delivering it at the settlement date. Note that the seller can calculate the return since he knows the price of the Treasury issue now and the futures price that he agrees to deliver the issue. The return so calculated is called the **implied repo rate**. The cheapest-to-deliver issue is then the one issue among all acceptable Treasury issues with the highest implied repo rate since it is the issue that would give the seller of the futures contract the highest return by buying and then delivering the issue. This is depicted in Figure 26-1.

In addition to the choice of which acceptable Treasury issue to deliver—sometimes referred to as the **quality option** or **swap option**—the short position has two more options granted under CBT delivery guidelines. The short position is permitted to decide when in the delivery month delivery actually will take place. This is called the **timing option**. The other option is the right of the short position to give notice of intent to deliver up to 8:00 p.m. Chicago time after the closing of the exchange (3:15 p.m. Chicago time) on

---

[1]The conversion factor is based on the price that a deliverable bond would sell for at the beginning of the delivery month if it were to yield 8%.

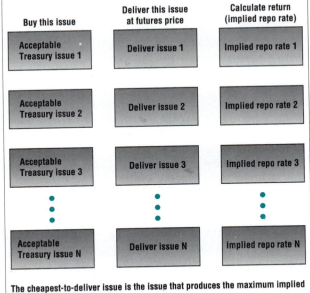

FIGURE 26-1

Determination of cheapest-to-deliver issue based on the implied repo rate.

the date when the futures settlement price has been fixed. This option is referred to as the **wild card option**. The quality option, the timing option, and the wild card option (in sum referred to as the **delivery options**) mean that the long position can never be sure of which Treasury bond will be delivered or when it will be delivered. The delivery options are summarized in Table 26-3.

Treasury Note Futures   Modeled after the Treasury bond futures contract, the underlying instrument for the Treasury note futures contract is $100,000 par value of a hypothetical 10-year, 8% Treasury note. Several acceptable Treasury issues may be delivered by the short. An issue is acceptable if the maturity is not less than 6.5 years and not greater than 10 years from the first day

TABLE 26-3	
DELIVERY OPTIONS GRANTED TO THE SHORT (SELLER) OF A CBT TREASURY BOND FUTURES CONTRACT	
Delivery Option	**Description**
Quality or swap option	Choice of which acceptable Treasury issue to deliver
Timing option	Choice of when in the delivery month to deliver
Wild card option	Choice to deliver after the closing price of the futures contract is determined

of the delivery month. The delivery options granted to the short position and the minimum price fluctuation are the same as for the Treasury bond futures contract.

Pricing of Interest Futures Contracts

In Chapter 16, we discussed the theoretical or fair value of a futures. We demonstrated that the theoretical futures price is

$$F = P + P(r - y) \qquad (26\text{-}1)$$

In other words, Equation (26-1) states that the equilibrium futures price (F) is simply a function of the cash price (P), the financing cost (r), and the cash yield on the asset (y). The difference between the financing cost and the cash yield on the asset ($r - y$) is the *cost of carry*, or simply *carry*. Positive carry means that the cash yield on the asset is greater than the financing cost; negative carry means that the financing cost exceeds the cash yield on the asset.

In our discussion of the pricing of stock index futures, we took a closer look at the reasons why the actual (observed or market) futures price might deviate from the theoretical futures price as given by Equation (26-1). Here we will review how several of the assumptions in the pricing model may be inappropriate for interest rate futures such as Treasury bond and note futures.

Deliverable Bond Is Not Known   The arbitrage arguments used to derive Equation (26-1) assumed that only one instrument is deliverable. But the futures contracts on Treasury bonds and Treasury notes are designed to allow the short the choice of delivering one of a number of deliverable issues (the quality or swap option). Because there may be more than one deliverable, market participants track the price of each deliverable bond and determine which bond is the cheapest to deliver. The futures price will then trade in relation to the cheapest-to-deliver issue.

There is the risk that while an issue may be the cheapest to deliver at the time a position in the futures contract is taken, it may not be the cheapest to deliver after that time. A change in the cheapest-to-deliver issue can dramatically alter the futures price.

What are the implications of the quality (swap) option on the futures price? Because the swap option is an option granted by the long to the short, the long will want to pay less for the futures contract than indicated by Equation (26-1). Therefore, as a result of the quality option, the theoretical futures price as given by Equation (26-1) must be adjusted as follows:

$$F = P + P(r - y) - \text{value of quality option} \qquad (26\text{-}2)$$

Market participants have employed theoretical models in attempting to estimate the fair value of the quality option. These models are beyond the scope of this chapter.

Delivery Date Is Not Known   In the pricing model based on arbitrage arguments, a known delivery date is assumed. For Treasury bond and note futures contracts, the short has a timing and wild card option, so the long does not know when the securities will be delivered. The effect of the timing and wild card options on the theoretical futures price is the same as the effect of the quality option. These delivery options should result in a theoretical futures price that is lower than the one suggested in Equation (26-1), as shown below:

$$F = P + P(r - y) - \text{value of quality option} - \text{value of timing option}$$
$$- \text{value of wild card option} \qquad (26\text{-}3)$$

or alternatively,

$$F = P + P(r - y) - \text{delivery options} \qquad (26\text{-}4)$$

Market participants attempt to value the delivery option in order to apply Equation (26-4).

Bond Portfolio Management Applications

There are various ways a money manager can use interest rate futures contracts in addition to speculating on the movement of interest rates.

Controlling the Interest Rate Risk of a Portfolio Money managers can use interest rate futures to alter the interest rate sensitivity or duration of a portfolio. Those with strong expectations about the direction of the future course of interest rates will adjust the duration of their portfolios so as to capitalize on their expectations. Specifically, a money manager who expects rates to increase will shorten duration; a money manager who expects interest rates to decrease will lengthen duration. While money managers can use cash market instruments to alter the durations of their portfolios, using futures contracts provides a quicker and less expensive means for doing so (on either a temporary or permanent basis).

Besides adjusting a portfolio for anticipated interest rate movements, money managers can use futures in strategies such as immunization (described in Chapter 25) to construct a portfolio with a longer duration than would be available with cash market securities. Suppose that in a given interest rate environment a pension fund manager must structure a portfolio to have a duration of 10 years to accomplish a particular investment objective. Bonds with such a long duration may not be available, but buying the appropriate number and kind of interest rate futures contracts can allow a pension fund manager to increase the portfolio's duration to the target level of 10. A formula to approximate the number of futures contracts necessary to adjust the portfolio duration to a new level is

$$\text{Approximate number of contracts} = \frac{(D_T - D_I)\, P_I}{D_F\, P_F} \qquad (26\text{-}5)$$

where D_T = target modified duration for the portfolio
$\ \ D_I$ = initial modified duration for the portfolio
$\ \ P_I$ = initial market value of the portfolio
$\ \ D_F$ = modified duration for the futures contract
$\ \ P_F$ = market value of the futures contract

Notice that if the money manager wishes to increase the duration, then D_T will be greater than D_I, and the formula will have a positive sign. This means that futures contracts will be purchased. The opposite is true if the objective is to shorten the portfolio duration.

Creating Synthetic Securities for Yield Enhancement A cash market security can be created synthetically by taking a position in the futures contract together with the deliverable instrument. If the yield on the synthetic security is the same as the yield on the cash market security, there will be no arbitrage opportunity. Any difference between the two yields can be exploited so as to enhance the yield on the portfolio.

To see how, consider an investor who owns a 20-year Treasury bond and sells Treasury futures that call for the delivery of that particular bond 3 months from now. While the maturity of the Treasury bond is 20 years, the investor has effectively shortened the maturity of the bond to 3 months.

Consequently, the long position in the 20-year bond and the short futures position are equivalent to a long position in a 3-month riskless security. The position is riskless because the investor is locking in the price to be received 3 months from now—the futures price. By being long the bond and short the futures, the investor has synthetically created a 3-month Treasury bill. The return the investor should expect to earn from this synthetic position should be the yield on a 3-month Treasury bill. If the yield on the synthetic 3-month Treasury bill is greater than the yield on the cash market Treasury bill, the investor can realize an enhanced yield by creating the synthetic short-term security. The fundamental relationship for creating synthetic securities is

$$RSP = CBP - FBP \qquad (26\text{-}6)$$

where   RSP = riskless short-term security position
CBP = cash bond position
FBP = bond futures position

A negative sign before a position means a short position. In terms of our previous example, CBP is the long cash bond position, the negative sign before FBP refers to the short futures position, and RSP is the riskless synthetic 3-month security or Treasury bill.

Equation (26-6) states that an investor who is long the cash market security and short the futures contract should expect to earn the rate of return on a risk-free security with the same maturity as the futures delivery date. Solving Equation (26-6) for the long bond position, we have

$$CBP = RSP + FBP \qquad (26\text{-}7)$$

Equation (26-7) states that a cash bond position equals a short-term riskless security position plus a long bond futures position. Thus, a cash market bond can be created synthetically by buying a futures contract and investing in a Treasury bill.

Solving Equation (26-7) for the bond futures position, we have

$$FBP = CBP - RSP \qquad (26\text{-}8)$$

Equation (26-8) tells us that a long position in the futures contract can be created synthetically by taking a long position in the cash market bond and shorting the short-term riskless security. But shorting the short-term riskless security is equivalent to borrowing money. Notice that it was Equation (26-8) that we used in deriving the theoretical futures price when the futures contract was underpriced in Chapter 16. Recall that when the actual futures price is greater than the theoretical futures price, the strategy to obtain an arbitrage profit is to sell the futures contract and create a synthetic long futures position by buying the asset with borrowed funds. This is precisely what Equation (26-8) states. In this case, instead of creating a synthetic cash market instrument as we did with Equations (26-6) and (26-7), we have created a synthetic futures contract. The fact that the synthetic long futures position is cheaper than the actual long futures position provides an arbitrage opportunity.

If we reverse the sign of both sides of Equation (26-8), we can see how a short futures position can be created synthetically.

In an efficient market the opportunities for yield enhancement should not exist very long. But even in the absence of yield enhancement, money managers can use synthetic securities to hedge a portfolio position that they find difficult to hedge in the cash market either because of lack of liquidity or because of other constraints.

Hedging   As we explained in Chapter 16, hedging with futures calls for taking a futures position as a temporary substitute for transactions to be made in the cash market at a later date. If cash and futures prices move together, any loss realized by the hedger from one position (whether cash or futures) will be offset by a profit on the other position. When the net profit or loss from the positions is exactly as anticipated, the hedge is referred to as a *perfect hedge.*

In practice, hedging is not that simple. The amount of net profit will not necessarily be as anticipated. Recall from Chapter 16 that the outcome of a hedge will depend on the relationship between the cash price and the futures price both when a hedge is placed and when it is lifted. The difference between the cash price and the futures price is the basis. The risk that the basis will change in an unpredictable way is called *basis risk.*

In bond portfolio management, typically the bond to be hedged is not identical to the bond underlying the futures contract. Thus the type of hedging done is cross hedging. There may be substantial basis risk in cross hedging. An unhedged position is exposed to price risk, the risk that the cash market price will move adversely. A hedged position substitutes basis risk for price risk. Box 26 describes the factors to be considered by a manager in hedging with interest rate futures, as well as with interest rate options that are described later in this chapter.

A short (or sell) hedge is used to protect against a decline in the cash price of a bond. To execute a short hedge, futures contracts are sold. A long (or buy) hedge is undertaken to protect against an increase in the cash price of a bond. In a long hedge, the hedger buys a futures contract to lock in a purchase price. A pension fund manager might use a long hedge when substantial cash contributions are expected and the manager is concerned that interest rates will fall. Also, a money manager who knows that bonds are maturing in the near future and expects that interest rates will fall can employ a long hedge to lock in a rate for the proceeds to be reinvested.

As we explained in Chapter 16, conceptually, cross hedging is somewhat more complicated than hedging deliverable securities, because it involves two relationships. In the case of interest rate futures contracts, the first relationship is between the cheapest-to-deliver issue and the futures contract. The second relationship in the case of interest rate futures contracts is the relationship between the security to be hedged and the cheapest-to-deliver issue.

The key to minimizing risk in a cross hedge is to choose the right hedge ratio. The hedge ratio depends on volatility weighting, or weighting by rela-

Box 26

RISK IDENTIFICATION AND CONTROL WHEN HEDGING WITH FUTURES AND OPTIONS

You would take several preliminary steps before setting up a futures or options hedge. The first step is to define your risk. The second is to identify your desired risk-return profile. The third is to determine which instrument, or combination of instruments, can be used to generate the desired profile.

Define Your Risk

Risk identification generally consists of analyzing your portfolio to see what types of risks are present. There are two basic risk positions—symmetric risk and asymmetric risk. With symmetric risk, the gain when interest rates rise by 10 basis points is roughly the same magnitude as the loss when rates fall by 10 basis points. Thus if you hold a long position in 30-year Treasury bonds, you face symmetric risk. If rates go down you gain by roughly the same amount as if rates go up. The amount of symmetric risk you face can be quantified—it is the price sensitivity of your portfolio to a small change in rates. It is often called the *duration* of your portfolio.

By contrast, if you hold a bond with an embedded option, (such as a mortgage security or a corporate bond with a call option,) you would face an element of asymmetric risk. Your loss if interest rates rise is greater than your gain if interest rates fall. Most corporate bonds have call features. We can think about the holder of a mortgage-backed security as long a bond and short a call option. That is, as interest rates go down, the homeowner has the right to call the mortgage and refinance his house at the new low rates. . . .

Identifying Your Desired Risk-Return Profile

After identifying the risks, the next step is to identify the desired risk-return profile. You must decide which risks reward you sufficiently for keeping them and which you wish to lay off. If you are a money manager with a long position in a 30-year Treasury security, and you expect interest rates to rise more than is reflected in the term structure of interest rates, you may want to neutralize this position by hedging. That is, you may want to turn the long bond position, in effect, into a position in a money market instrument. Conversely, if you have a long position in a 30-year Treasury security and you expect interest rates to fall, you will not want to hedge your position.

You may also want to convert a symmetric risk position into an asymmetric risk position. That is, if you hold a portfolio of 30-year Treasury bonds, the purchase of a put option will place a maximum loss on your position, while preserving your upside. The portfolio will gain if rates decline. The option can be put if rates rise. If interest rates remain steady you will lose the option premium.

In sum, if you are a portfolio manager with a long symmetric position, you have three alternatives: keep the long symmetric position, neutralize the long symmetric position or convert the long symmetric position into an asymmetric position by purchasing puts. Combinations of these alternatives are, of course, possible. Thus, if you hold a long symmetric bond position and choose to shorten but not eliminate your position, the return will be a combination of the long symmetric position and the neutralized position. . . .

Which Instrument or Instruments Should Be Used to Hedge?

Futures positions are generally used to neutralize symmetric risk. Futures are very actively traded, and it is possible to execute a very large order at one time rather than "working the order." Futures contracts exist on a number of different interest rate instruments. . . .

In contrast to futures, options are usually used to convert symmetric risk to asymmetric risk. Options can be either exchange-traded or over-the-counter and can be written on either physical bonds or bond futures. . . .

The choice of OTC options versus exchange-traded options, or options on futures versus options on bonds, depends on your need to tailor the hedge to a specific date, security, or strike price, as well as on the liquidity of the market. Exchange-traded options, if appropriate, can be less costly than OTC options, since they eliminate the dealer's bid-asked spread. Sometimes, however, exchange-traded options will not meet your needs. Expiration dates on exchange-traded options are spaced three months apart, strike prices are spaced two points apart, and the longest expiration date is only nine months out. Moreover, they are based on only a small universe of bonds. The advantage, however, is that exchange-traded options are more liquid—if you no longer need the option, you can resell it at any time. By contrast, OTC options often can only be resold to the original seller, entailing fairly large transactions costs.

Source: Laurie S. Goodman, "Hedging with Futures and Options," Chap. 17 in Frank J. Fabozzi (ed.), *Fixed Income Portfolio Strategies* (Chicago: Probus Publishing, 1989), pp. 321–324.

Questions for Box 26

1. How does a short futures contract on a Treasury bond position neutralize a long Treasury bond futures positon?

2. How does the purchase of a put option on a Treasury bond by the owner of a Treasury bond change a symmetric risk position into an asymmetric risk position?

3. Why does the choice of OTC options versus exchange-traded options, or options on futures versus options on bonds, depend on an investor's need to tailor a hedge?

tive changes in value. The purpose of a hedge is to use gains or losses from a futures position to offset any difference between the target sale price and the actual sale price of the asset. Accordingly, the hedge ratio is chosen with the intention of matching the volatility (that is, the dollar change) of the futures contract to the volatility of the asset. Consequently, the hedge ratio is given by

$$\text{Hedge ratio} = \frac{\text{volatility of bond to be hedged}}{\text{volatility of hedging instrument}} \qquad (26\text{-}9)$$

As Equation (26-9) shows, if the bond to be hedged is more volatile than the hedging instrument, more of the hedging instrument will be needed.

While it might be fairly clear why volatility is the key variable in determining the hedge ratio, "volatility" has many definitions. For hedging purposes we are concerned with volatility in absolute dollar terms. To calculate the dollar volatility of a bond, one must know the precise time that volatility is to be calculated (because volatility generally declines as a bond seasons) as well as the price or yield at which to calculate volatility (because higher yields generally reduce dollar volatility for a given yield change). The relevant point in the life of the bond for calculating volatility is the point at which the hedge will be lifted. Volatility at any other point is essentially irrelevant because the goal is to lock in a price or rate only on that particular day. Similarly, the relevant yield at which to calculate volatility initially is the target yield. Consequently, the "volatility of bond to be hedged" referred to in Equation (26-9) is the price value of a basis point for the bond on the date the hedge is expected to be delivered.[2]

An example shows why volatility weighting leads to the correct hedge ratio.[3] Suppose that on April 19, 1985, an investor owned the Southern Bell 11 3/4% bonds of 2023 and sold June 1985 Treasury bond futures to hedge a future sale of the bonds. This is an example of a cross hedge. Suppose that (1) the Treasury 7 5/8s of 2007 were the cheapest-to-deliver issue on the contract and that they were trading at 11.50%, (2) the Southern Bell bonds were at 12.40%, and (3) the Treasury bond futures were at a price of 70. To simplify, assume also that the yield spread between the two bonds remains at 0.90% (i.e., 90 basis points) and that the anticipated sale date was the last business day in June 1985.

Because the conversion factor for the deliverable 7 5/8s for the June 1985 contract was 0.9660, the target price for hedging the 7 5/8s would be 67.62 (from 70 × 0.9660), and the target yield would be 11.789% (the yield at a price of 67.62). The yield on the telephone bonds is assumed to stay at 0.90% above the yield on the 7 5/8s, so the target yield for the Southern Bell bonds would be 12.689%, with a corresponding price of 92.628. At these target levels, the price values of a basis point (PVBP) for the 7 5/8s and telephone bonds are, respectively, 0.056332 and 0.072564. As indicated earlier, all these calculations are made using a settlement date equal to the anticipated sale date, in

---

[2]The yield that is to be used on this date in order to determine the price value of a basis point is the forward rate. We discussed forward rates in Chapter 22.

[3]This example is adapted from Mark Pitts and Frank J. Fabozzi, *Interest Rate Futures and Options* (Chicago: Probus Publishing, 1989).

this case the end of June 1985. Thus, the relative price volatilities of the bonds to be hedged and the deliverable security are easily obtained from the assumed sale date and target prices.

However, to calculate the hedge ratio [Equation (26-9)] we need the volatility not of the cheapest-to-deliver issue, but of the hedging instrument, that is, of the futures contract. Fortunately, knowing the volatility of the bond to be hedged relative to the cheapest-to-deliver issue and the volatility of the cheapest-to-deliver bond relative to the futures contract, we can easily obtain the relative volatilities that define the hedge ratio:

$$\text{Hedge ratio} = \frac{\text{volatility of bond to be hedged}}{\text{volatility of CTD issue}} \times \frac{\text{volatility of CTD bond}}{\text{volatility of hedging instrument}} \quad (26\text{-}10)$$

where CTD = cheapest to deliver. The second ratio can be shown to equal the conversion factor for the CTD issue. Assuming a fixed yield spread between the bond to be hedged and the cheapest-to-deliver issue, Equation (26-10) can be rewritten as:

$$\text{Hedge ratio} = \frac{\text{PVBP of bond to be hedged}}{\text{PVBP of CTD issue}} \times \text{conversion factor for CTD issue} \quad (26\text{-}11)$$

The hedge ratio at hand is therefore approximately 1.24 [from $(0.072564/0.056332) \times 0.9660$].

Given the hedge ratio, the number of contracts that must be short is determined as follows:

$$\text{Number of contracts} = \text{hedge ratio} \times \frac{\text{par value to be hedged}}{\text{par value of contract}} \quad (26\text{-}12)$$

Since the amount to be hedged is $10 million and each Treasury bond futures contract is for $100,000, this means that the number of futures contracts that must be sold is

$$\text{Number of contracts} = \text{hedge ratio} \times \frac{\$10,000,000}{\$100,000}$$

$$= 1.24 \times 100 = 124 \text{ contracts}$$

Table 26-4 shows that, if the simplifying assumptions hold, a futures hedge using the recommended hedge ratio very nearly locks in the target price for $10 million face value of the telephone bonds.[4]

Another refinement in the hedging strategy is usually necessary for hedging non-deliverable securities. This refinement concerns the assumption about the relative yield spread between the cheapest-to-deliver bond and the bond to be hedged. In the prior discussion, we assumed that the yield spread was constant over time. Yield spreads, however, are not constant over time. They vary with the maturity of the instruments in question and the level of rates, as well as with many unpredictable and non-systematic factors.

---

[4]In practice, most of the remaining error could be eliminated by frequent adjustments to the hedge ratio to account for the fact that the price value of a basis point changes as rates move up or down.

	TABLE 26-4					
	HEDGING A NONDELIVERABLE BOND TO A DELIVERY DATE WITH FUTURES					

Instrument to be hedged: Southern Bell 11 3/4% of 4/19/23

Hedge ratio = 1.24

Price of futures contract when sold = 70

Target price for Southern Bell bonds = 92.628

Actual Sale Price of Telephone Bonds	Yield at Sale	Yield on Treas. 7 5/8*	Price of Treas. 7 5/8	Futures Price†	Gain (Loss) on 124 Contracts ($10/0.01/Contract)	Effective Sale Price‡
$7,600,000	15.468%	14.568%	54.590	56.511	$1,672,636	$9,272,636
7,800,000	15.072	14.172	56.167	58.144	1,470,144	9,270,144
8,000,000	14.696	13.769	57.741	59.773	1,268,148	9,268,148
8,200,000	14.338	13.438	59.313	61.401	1,066,276	9,266,276
8,400,000	13.996	13.096	60.887	63.030	864,280	9,264,280
8,600,000	13.671	12.771	62.451	64.649	663,524	9,263,524
8,800,000	13.359	12.459	64.018	66.271	462,396	9,262,396
9,000,000	13.061	12.161	65.580	67.888	261,888	9,261,888
9,200,000	12.776	11.876	67.134	69.497	62,372	9,262,372
9,400,000	12.503	11.603	68.683	71.100	(136,400)	9,263,600
9,600,000	12.240	11.340	70.233	72.705	(335,420)	9,264,580
9,800,000	11.988	11.088	71.773	74.299	(533,076)	9,266,924
10,000,000	11.745	10.845	73.312	75.892	(730,608)	9,269,392
10,200,000	11.512	10.612	74.839	77.473	(926,652)	9,273,348
10,400,000	11.287	10.387	76.364	79.052	(1,122,448)	9,277,552
10,600,000	11.070	10.170	77.884	80.625	(1,317,500)	9,282,500
10,800,000	10.861	9.961	79.394	82.188	(1,511,312)	9,288,688
11,000,000	10.659	9.759	80.889	83.746	(1,704,504)	9,295,496
11,200,000	10.463	9.563	82.403	85.303	(1,897,572)	9,302,428

*By assumption, the yield on the 7 5/8s of 2007 is 90 basis points lower than the yield on the Southern Bell bond.

†By convergence, the futures price equals the price of the 7 5/8s of 2007 divided by 0.9660 (the conversion factor).

‡Transactions costs and the financing of margin flows are ignored.

Regression analysis allows the hedger to capture the relationship between yield levels and yield spreads and use it to advantage. For hedging purposes, the variables are the yield on the bond to be hedged and the yield on the cheapest-to-deliver bond. The regression equation takes the form

$$\text{Yield on bond to be hedged} = a + b \times \text{yield on CTD security} + \text{error}$$
(26-13)

The regression procedure provides an estimate of b (the yield beta), which is the expected relative change in the two bonds. Our example that used constant spreads implicitly assumes that the yield beta, b in Equation (26-13) equals 1.0 and a equals 0.90 (because 0.90% is the assumed spread).

For the two issues in question, that is, the Southern Bell 11 3/4s and the Treasury 7 5/8s, the estimated yield beta was 1.05. Therefore, yields on the corporate issue are expected to move 5% more than yields on the Treasury issue. To calculate the relative volatility of the two issues correctly, this fact must be taken into account; thus, the hedge ratio derived in our earlier example is multiplied by the factor 1.05. Consequently, instead of shorting 124

Treasury bond futures contracts to hedge $10 million of telephone bonds, the investor would short 130 contracts.

The formula for the hedge ratio, Equation (26-11), is revised as follows to incorporate the impact of the yield beta:

$$\text{Hedge ratio} = \frac{\text{PVBP of bond to be hedged}}{\text{PVBP of CTD issue}}$$

$$\times \text{ conversion factor for CTD issue} \times \text{yield beta} \qquad (26\text{-}14)$$

where the yield beta is derived from the yield of the bond to be hedged regressed on the yield of the cheapest-to-deliver issue. As before, PVBP stands for the change in price for a one-basis-point change in yield.

INTEREST RATE OPTIONS

In Chapter 17, we described the basic features of options and then focused on two types of equity options: options on common stock and options on stock indexes.

Interest rate options can be written on a fixed-income security or an interest rate futures contract. The former options are called **options on physicals**. The most liquid exchange-traded option on a fixed-income security at the time of this writing is an option on Treasury bonds traded on the Chicago Board Options Exchange. For reasons to be explained later, options on interest rate futures have been far more popular than options on physicals. However, portfolio managers have made increasingly greater use of over-the-counter options on Treasury and mortgage-backed securities.

Institutional investors who want to purchase an option on a specific Treasury security or a Ginnie Mae pass-through can do so on an over-the-counter basis. There are government and mortgage-backed securities dealers who make a market in options on specific securities. Over-the-counter options, also called **dealer options**, typically are purchased by institutional investors that want to hedge the risk associated with a specific security. For example, a thrift may be interested in hedging its position in a specific mortgage pass-through security. Typically, the maturity of the option coincides with the time period over which the buyer of the option wants to hedge, so the buyer is not concerned with the option's liquidity.

Besides options on fixed-income securities, there are OTC options on the shape of the yield curve or the yield spread between two securities (such as the spread between mortgage pass-through securities and Treasuries or between double-A corporates and Treasuries). A discussion of these options is beyond the scope of this chapter.

As explained earlier with forward contracts, in the absence of a clearinghouse the parties to any over-the-counter contract are exposed to counterparty risk. In the case of a forward contract where both parties are obligated to perform, both parties face counterparty risk. In contrast, in the case of an option, once the option buyer pays the option price, the buyer has satisfied his or her obligation. It is only the seller that must perform if the option is exercised. Thus, the option buyer is exposed to counterparty risk—the risk that the option seller will fail to perform.

Exchange-Traded Futures Options

An option on a futures contract, commonly referred to as a **futures option**, gives the buyer the right to buy from or sell to the writer a designated futures contract at the strike price at any time during the life of the option. If the futures option is a call option, the buyer has the right to purchase one designated futures contract at the strike price. That is, the buyer has the right to acquire a long futures position in the designated futures contract. If the buyer exercises the call option, the writer acquires a corresponding short position in the futures contract.

A put option on a futures contract grants the buyer the right to sell one designated futures contract to the writer at the strike price. That is, the option buyer has the right to acquire a short position in the designated futures contract. If the put option is exercised, the writer acquires a corresponding long position in the designated futures contract. Table 26-5 summarizes these positions. There are futures options on all the interest rate futures contracts mentioned earlier in this chapter.

Mechanics of Trading Futures Options   As the parties to the futures option will realize a position in a futures contract when the option is exercised, the question is, what will the futures price be? That is, at what price will the long be required to pay for the instrument underlying the futures contract, and at what price will the short be required to sell the instrument underlying the futures contract?

Upon exercise, the futures price for the futures contract will be set equal to the strike price. The position of the two parties is then immediately marked to market in terms of the then-current futures price. Thus, the futures position of the two parties will be at the prevailing futures price. At the same time, the option buyer will receive from the option seller the economic benefit from exercising. In the case of a call futures option, the option writer must pay the difference between the current futures price and the strike price to the buyer of the option. In the case of a put futures option, the option writer must pay the option buyer the difference between the strike price and the current futures price.

For example, suppose an investor buys a call option on some futures contract in which the strike price is 85. Assume also that the futures price is 95

	TABLE 26-5		
	FUTURES OPTIONS		
Type	**Buyer Has the Right to . . . and Then Has**	**If Exercised, the Seller Then Has . . .**	**And the Seller Pays the Buyer...**
Call	Purchase one futures contract at the strike price	A short futures position	Current futures price − strike price
	A long futures position		
Put	Sell one futures contract at the strike price	A long futures position	Strike price − current futures price
	A short futures position		

and that the buyer exercises the call option. Upon exercise, the call buyer is given a long position in the futures contract at 85 and the call writer is assigned the corresponding short position in the futures contract at 85. The futures positions of the buyer and the writer are immediately marked to market by the exchange. Because the prevailing futures price is 95 and the strike price is 85, the long futures position (the position of the call buyer) realizes a gain of 10, while the short futures position (the position of the call writer) realizes a loss of 10. The call writer pays the exchange 10, and the call buyer receives from the exchange 10. The call buyer, who now has a long futures position at 95, can either liquidate the futures position at 95 or maintain a long futures position. If the former course of action is taken, the call buyer sells a futures contract at the prevailing futures price of 95. There is no gain or loss from liquidating the position. Overall, the call buyer realizes a gain of 10. The call buyer who elects to hold the long futures position will face the same risk and reward of holding such a position, but still realizes a gain of 10 from the exercise of the call option.

Suppose instead that the futures option is a put rather than a call, and the current futures price is 60 rather than 95. If the buyer of this put option exercises it, the buyer would have a short position in the futures contract at 85; the option writer would have a long position in the futures contract at 85. The exchange then marks the position to market at the then-current futures price of 60, resulting in a gain to the put buyer of 25 and a loss to the put writer of the same amount. The put buyer who now has a short futures position at 60 can either liquidate the short futures position by buying a futures contract at the prevailing futures price of 60 or maintain the short futures position. In either case the put buyer realizes a gain of 25 from exercising the put option.

There are no margin requirements for the buyer of a futures option once the option price has been paid in full. Because the option price is the maximum amount that the buyer can lose, regardless of how adverse the price movement of the underlying instrument, there is no need for margin.

Because the writer (seller) of an option has agreed to accept all of the risk (and none of the reward) of the position in the underlying instrument, the writer (seller) is required to deposit not only the margin required on the interest rate futures contract position if that is the underlying instrument, but also (with certain exceptions) the option price that is received for writing the option. In addition, as prices adversely affect the writer's position, the writer would be required to deposit variation margin as the position is marked to market.

Price Quotes for Futures Options   The price of a futures option is quoted in 64ths of 1% of par value. For example, a price of 24 means 24/64ths of 1% of par value. Since the par value of a Treasury bond futures contract is $100,000, an option price of 24 means

$$[(24/64)/100] \times \$100,000 = \$375$$

In general, the price of a futures option quoted at Q is equal to

$$\text{Option price} = [(Q/64)/100] \times \$100,000$$

Reasons for the Popularity of Futures Options   There are three reasons why futures options on fixed-income securities have largely supplanted options on physicals as the options vehicle of choice for institutional investors. First, unlike options on fixed-income securities, options on Treasury coupon futures do not require payments for accrued interest to be made. Consequently, when a futures option is exercised, the call buyer and the put writer need not compensate the other party for accrued interest.

Second, futures options are believed to be "cleaner" instruments because of the reduced likelihood of delivery squeezes. Market participants who must deliver an instrument are concerned that at the time of delivery the instrument to be delivered will be in short supply, resulting in a higher price to acquire the instrument. As the deliverable supply of futures contracts is more than adequate for futures options currently traded, there is no concern about a delivery squeeze.

Finally, in order to price any option, it is imperative to know at all times the price of the underlying instrument. In the bond market, current prices are not as easily available as price information on the futures contract. The reason is that, as explained in Chapter 19, bonds trade in the over-the-counter market and there is no reporting system with recent price information. Thus, an investor who wanted to purchase an option on a Treasury bond would have to call several dealer firms to obtain a price. In contrast, a futures is traded on exchanges, and as a result, price information on the most recent trade is reported.

Option-Pricing Models for Interest Rate Options

The two most popular models for the pricing of equity options are the Black-Scholes option-pricing model and the binomial option-pricing model. There are some problems in using these models to price options on a bond. To illustrate the problems with the Black-Scholes option-pricing model if applied to the pricing of interest rate options, consider a three-month European call option on a three-year zero-coupon bond.[5] The maturity value of the underlying bond is $100, and the strike price is $120. Suppose further that the current price of the bond is $75.13, the three-year risk-free rate is 10% annually, and expected price volatility is 4%. What would be the fair value for this option? Do you really need an option-pricing model to determine the value of this option?

Think about it. This zero-coupon bond will never have a price above $100 because that is the maturity value. As the strike price is $120, the option will never be exercised; its value is therefore zero. If you can get anyone to buy such an option, any price you obtain will be free money. Yet an option buyer armed with the Black-Scholes option-pricing model will input the variables we assume above and come up with a value for this option of $5.60! Why is the Black-Scholes model off by so much? The answer lies in its underlying assumptions (see Table 26-6).

---

[5]This example is given in Lawrence J. Dyer and David P. Jacob, "Guide to Fixed-Income Option Pricing Models," in Frank J. Fabozzi (ed.), *The Handbook of Fixed-Income Options* (Chicago: Probus Publishing, 1989), pp. 81–82.

TABLE 26-6

LIMITATIONS IN APPLYING THE BLACK-SCHOLES OPTION-PRICING MODEL TO PRICE INTEREST RATE OPTIONS

Assumptions	Fixed-Income Realities
1. The price of the underlying has some possibility of rising to any price.	There is a maximum price for a bond, and any higher price assumes a negative interest rate is possible.
2. Short-term rates remain constant.	Changes in short-term rates cause bond price to change.
3. Volatility (variance) of price is constant over the life of the option.	Bond price volatility decreases as the bond approaches maturity.

Three assumptions underlie the Black-Scholes model that limit its use in pricing options on interest rate instruments. First, the probability distribution for the prices assumed by the Black-Scholes option-pricing model permits some probability—no matter how small—that the price can take on any positive value. But in the case of a zero-coupon bond, the price cannot take on a value above $100. In the case of a coupon bond, we know that the price cannot exceed the sum of the coupon payments plus the maturity value. For example, for a five-year, 10% coupon bond with a maturity value of $100, the price cannot be greater than $150 (five coupon payments of $10 plus the maturity value of $100). Thus, unlike stock prices, bond prices have a maximum value. The only way that a bond's price can exceed the maximum value is if negative interest rates are permitted. This is not likely to occur, so any probability distribution for prices assumed by an option-pricing model that permits bond prices to be higher than the maximum bond value could generate nonsensical option prices. The Black-Scholes model does allow bond prices to exceed the maximum bond value (or, equivalently, allows negative interest rates). That is one of the reasons why we can get a senseless option price for the three-month European call option on the three-year zero-coupon bond.

The second assumption of the Black-Scholes option-pricing model is that the short-term interest rate is constant over the life of the option. Yet the price of an interest rate option will change as interest rates change. A change in the short-term interest rate changes the rates along the yield curve. Therefore, to assume that the short-term rate will be constant is inappropriate for interest rate options. The third assumption is that the variance of prices is constant over the life of the option. Recall from Chapter 21 that as a bond moves closer to maturity, its price volatility declines. Therefore, the assumption that price variance is constant over the life of the option is inappropriate.

While we have illustrated the problem of using the Black-Scholes model to price interest rate options, we can also show that the binomial option-pricing model based on the price distribution of the underlying bond suffers from the same problems. A way around the problem of negative interest rates is to use a binomial option-pricing model based on the distribution of interest rates rather than prices and construct the binomial tree.[6] Once a binomial interest rate tree is constructed, it can be converted into a binomial price tree by using the interest rates on the tree to determine the price of the bond. Then we follow the standard procedure for calculating the option price by working backward from the value of the call option at the expiration date.

While the binomial option-pricing model based on yields is superior to models based on prices, it still has a theoretical drawback. All option-pricing models to be theoretically valid must satisfy the put-call parity relationship explained in Chapter 18. The problem with the binomial model based on yields is that it does not satisfy this relationship. It violates the relationship in that it fails to take into consideration the yield curve, thereby allowing arbitrage opportunities.

The most elaborate models that take the yield curve into consideration and as a result do not permit arbitrage opportunities are called **yield curve option-pricing models** or **arbitrage-free option-pricing models**. These models can incorporate different volatility assumptions along the yield curve. The most popular model employed by dealer firms is the Black-Derman-Toy model.[7]

Options and Duration

The price of an interest rate option will depend on the price of the underlying instrument, which, in turn, depends on the interest rate on the underlying instrument. Thus, the price of an interest rate option depends on the interest rate of the underlying instrument. Consequently, the interest rate sensitivity or duration of an interest rate option can be determined.

The modified duration of an option can be shown to be equal to

Modified duration for an option = Modified duration of underlying instrument

$$\times \text{ delta} \times \frac{\text{price of underlying instrument}}{\text{price of option}}$$

As expected, the modified duration of an option depends on the modified duration of the underlying instrument. It also depends on the price responsiveness of the option to a change in the underlying instrument, as measured by the option's delta. We described this measure in Chapter 18. The leverage created by a position in an option comes from the last ratio in the formula. The higher the price of the underlying instrument relative to the price of the option, the greater the leverage (i.e., the more exposure to interest rates for a given dollar investment).

It is the interaction of all three factors that affects the modified duration of an option. For example, a deep out-of-the-money option offers higher lever-

---

[6]For example, in constructing the binomial tree based on interest rates, the following formula can be used:

If yield increases: If yield decreases:

$$Y_{t+1} = Y_t e^{+s} \qquad\qquad Y_{t+1} = Y_t e^{-s}$$

where Y_{t+1} = yield to maturity in time period $t + 1$
           Y_t = yield to maturity in time period t
           s = expected interest rate volatility
           e = 2.7182818

[7]Fischer Black, Emanuel Derman, and William Toy, "A One-Factor Model of Interest Rates and Its Application to Treasury Bond Options," *Financial Analysts Journal* (January–February 1990), pp. 24–32.

age than a deep in-the-money option, but the delta of the former is less than that of the latter.

Since the delta of the call option is positive, the modified duration of an interest rate call option will be positive. Thus, when interest rates decline, the value of an interest rate call option will rise. A put option, however, has a delta that is negative. Thus, modified duration is negative. Consequently, when interest rates rise, the value of a put option rises.

Hedging with Futures Options

The most common application of options is to hedge a portfolio. We explained two hedge strategies with options in Chapter 17, protective put buying and covered call writing. In this section, we demonstrate these two strategies using futures options. The exercise is worthwhile because it shows how complicated hedging with futures options is and which key parameters are involved in the process. We also compare the outcome of hedging with futures and hedging with futures options.[8]

Hedging Long-Term Bonds with Puts on Futures   Investors often want to hedge their bond positions against a possible increase in interest rates. Buying puts on futures is one of the easiest ways to purchase protection against rising rates. To illustrate this strategy, we can use the same utility bond example that we used to demonstrate how to hedge with Treasury bond futures. In that example, an investor held 11 3/4% bonds of 2023 and used futures to lock in a sale price for those bonds on a futures delivery date. Now we want to show how the hedger could have used futures options instead of futures to protect against rising rates.

In the example (summarized at the top of Table 26-7), rates were already fairly high; the hedged bonds were selling at a yield of 12.40%; the Treasury 7 5/8% of 2007 (the cheapest-to-deliver issue at the time) were at 11.50%. For simplicity, we assumed that this yield spread would remain at 90 basis points. In terms of a yield regression, this would be equivalent to a regression in which the beta equals 1.0 and the intercept term is 0.90%.

The hedger must determine the minimum price that he or she wants to establish for the hedged bonds. In our illustration it is assumed that the minimum price is 87.668. This is equivalent to saying that the hedger wants to establish a strike price for a put option on the hedged bonds of 87.668. But the hedger is not buying a put option on the utility bonds. He or she is buying a put option on a Treasury bond futures contract. Therefore, the hedger must determine the strike price for a put option on a Treasury bond futures contract that is equivalent to a strike price of 87.668 for the utility bonds.

This can be done with the help of Figure 26-2. We begin at the top left-hand box of the figure. Since the minimum price is 87.668 for the utility bonds, this means that the hedger is attempting to establish a maximum yield of 13.41%. This is found from the relationship between price and yield: Given a price of 87.668 for the utility bond, this is equivalent to a yield of 13.41%. (This gets us to the lower left-hand box in Figure 26-2.) From our assumption that the spread between the utility bonds and the cheapest-to-de-

---

[8]The illustrations in this section are taken from Chapter 10 of Mark Pitts and Frank J. Fabozzi, op. cit.

TABLE 26-7

HEDGING A NON-DELIVERABLE BOND
TO A DELIVERY DATE WITH PUTS ON FUTURES

Instrument to be hedged: 11 3/4% of 4/19/23

Hedge ratio = 1.24

Strike price for puts on futures = 66-0

Target minimum price for hedged bonds = 87.203

Future price per contract = $375

Actual Sale Price of Hedged Bonds	Futures Price*	Value of 124 Put Options†	Cost of 124 Put Options	Effective Sale Price‡
$ 7,600,000	56.511	$1,176,636	$46,500	$8,730,136
7,800,000	58.144	974,144	46,500	8,727,644
8,000,000	59.773	772,148	46,500	8,725,648
8,200,000	61.401	570,276	46,500	8,723,776
8,400,000	63.030	368,280	46,500	8,721,780
8,600,000	64.649	167,524	46,500	8,721,024
8,800,000	66.271	0	46,500	8,753,500
9,000,000	67.888	0	46,500	8,953,500
9,200,000	69.497	0	46,500	9,153,500
9,400,000	71.100	0	46,500	9,353,500
9,600,000	72.705	0	46,500	9,553,500
9,800,000	74.299	0	46,500	9,753,500
10,000,000	75.892	0	46,500	9,953,500
10,200,000	77.473	0	46,500	10,153,500
10,400,000	79.052	0	46,500	10,353,500
10,600,000	80.625	0	46,500	10,553,500
10,800,000	82.188	0	46,500	10,753,500
11,000,000	83.746	0	46,500	10,953,500
11,200,000	85.303	0	46,500	11,153,500

*These numbers are approximate because futures trade in even 32nds.

†From 124 × $1,000 × max{ (66 − futures price), 0}.

‡Does not include transaction costs or the financing of the options position.

liver issue is a constant 90 basis points, setting a maximum yield of 13.41% for the utility bond is equivalent to setting a maximum yield of 12.51% for the cheapest-to-deliver issue. (Now we are at the lower box in the middle column of Figure 26-2.) Given the yield of 12.51% for the cheapest-to-deliver issue, the minimum price can be determined (the top box in the middle column of the figure). A 12.51% yield for the Treasury 7 5/8% of 2007 (the cheapest-to-deliver issue at the time) is 63.756. The corresponding futures price is found by dividing the price of the cheapest-to-deliver issue by the conversion factor. This gets us to the box in the right-hand column of Figure 26-2. Since the conversion factor is 0.9660, the futures price is about 66 (63.7567 divided by 0.9660). This means that a strike price of 66 for a put option on a Treasury bond futures contract is roughly equivalent to a put option on the utility bonds with a strike price of 87.668.

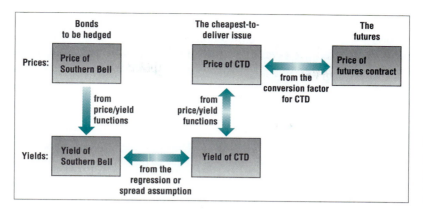

FIGURE 26-2

Calculating equivalent prices and yields for hedging with futures options.

The foregoing steps are always necessary to obtain the appropriate strike price on a put futures option. The process is not complicated. It simply involves (1) the relationship between price and yield, (2) the assumed relationship between the yield spread between the hedged bonds and the cheapest-to-deliver issue, and (3) the conversion factor for the cheapest-to-deliver issue. As with hedging employing futures, illustrated earlier in this chapter, the success of the hedging strategy will depend on (1) whether the cheapest-to-deliver issue changes and (2) what the yield spread between the hedged bonds and the cheapest-to-deliver issue is.

The hedge ratio is determined using Equation (26-12) since we will assume a constant yield spread between the security to be hedged and the cheapest-to-deliver issue. For increased accuracy, we calculate the price values of a basis point at the option expiration date (assumed to be June 28, 1985) and at the yields corresponding to the futures strike price of 66 (12.51% for the cheapest-to-deliver issue and 13.41% for the hedged bonds). The respective price values of a basis point are 0.065214 and 0.050969. This results in a hedge ratio of 1.236 for the options hedge, or 1.24 with rounding.

To create a table for the protective put hedge, we can use some of the numbers from Table 26-4. Everything will be the same except the last two columns. For the put option hedge we have to insert the value of the 124 futures put options in place of the 124 futures contracts in the next-to-last column. This is easy because the value of each option at expiration is just the strike price of the futures option (66) minus the futures price (or zero if that difference is negative), all multiplied by $1,000. The effective sale price for the hedged bonds is then just the actual market price for the hedged bonds, plus the value of the options at expiration, minus the cost of the options.

Suppose that the price of the put futures option with a strike price of 66 is 24. As we explained earlier, an option price of 24 means 24/64 of 1% of par value, or $375. With a total of 124 options, the cost of the protection would have been $46,500 (124 × $375, not including financing costs and commissions). This cost, together with the final value of the options, is combined with the actual sale price of the hedged bonds to arrive at the effective sale price for the hedged bonds. These final prices are shown in the last column of Table 26-7. This effective price is never less than 87.203. This equals the price of the hedged bonds equivalent to the futures strike price of 66 (i.e., 87.668), minus the cost of the puts (that is, $0.4650 = 1.24 \times 24/64$). This minimum effective price is something that can be calculated before the hedge is ever initiated. (As prices decline, the effective sale price actually exceeds the projected effective minimum sale price of 87.203 by a small amount. This is due only to rounding and the fact that the hedge ratio is left unaltered although the relative price values of a basis point that go into the hedge ratio calculation change as yields change.) As prices increase, however, the effective sale price of the hedged bonds increases as well; unlike the futures hedge shown in Table 26-7, the options hedge protects the investor if rates rise, but allows the investor to profit if rates fall.

Covered Call Writing with Futures Options   Unlike the protective put strategy, covered call writing is not entered into with the sole purpose of protecting a portfolio against rising rates. The covered call writer, believing that the market will not trade much higher or much lower than its present level, sells out-of-the-money calls against an existing bond portfolio. The sale of the calls brings in premium income that provides partial protection in case rates increase. The premium received does not, of course, provide the kind of protection that a long put position provides, but it does provide some additional income that can be used to offset declining prices. If, on the other hand, rates fall, portfolio appreciation is limited because the short call position constitutes a liability for the seller, and this liability increases as rates go down. Consequently, there is limited upside potential for the covered call writer. Of course, this is not so bad if prices are essentially going nowhere; the added income from the sale of options is obtained without sacrificing any gains.

To see how covered call writing with futures options works for the bond used in the protective put example, we construct a table much as we did before. With futures selling around 71-24 on the hedge initiation date, a sale of a 78 call option on futures might be appropriate. As before, it is assumed that the hedged bond will remain at a 90-basis-point spread off the cheapest-to-deliver Treasury bond, the 7 5/8% of 2007. We also assume for simplicity that the price of the 78 calls is 24/64. The number of options contracts sold will be the same, namely 124 contracts for $10 million face value of underlying bonds. Table 26-8 shows the results of the covered call writing strategy given these assumptions.

To calculate the effective sale price of the bonds in the covered call writing strategy, the premium received from the sale of calls is added to the actual sale price of the bonds, while the liability associated with the short call position is subtracted from the actual sale price. The liability associated with each call is the futures price minus the strike price of 78 (or zero if this difference is negative), all multiplied by $1,000. The middle column in the table is just this value multiplied by 124, the number of options sold.

Just as the minimum effective sale price could be calculated beforehand for the protective put strategy, the maximum effective sale price can be calculated beforehand for the covered call writing strategy. The maximum effective sale price will be the price of the hedged security corresponding to the strike price of the option sold, plus the premium received. In this case, the

---

TABLE 26-8

HEDGING A NON-DELIVERABLE BOND
TO A DELIVERY DATE WITH CALLS ON FUTURES

Instrument to be hedged: 11 3/4% of 4/19/23

Hedge ratio = 1.24

Strike price for calls on futures = 78-0

Expected maximum price for hedged bonds = 103.131

Future price per contract = $375

Actual Sale Price of Hedged Bonds	Futures Price*	Liability of 124 Call Options†	Premium from 124 Call Options	Effective Sale Price‡
$ 7,600,000	56.511	$ 0	$46,500	$ 7,646,500
7,800,000	58.144	0	46,500	7,846,500
8,000,000	59.773	0	46,500	8,046,500
8,200,000	61.401	0	46,500	8,246,500
8,400,000	63.030	0	46,500	8,446,500
8,600,000	64.649	0	46,500	8,646,500
8,800,000	66.271	0	46,500	8,846,500
9,000,000	67.888	0	46,500	9,046,500
9,200,000	69.497	0	46,500	9,246,500
9,400,000	71.100	0	46,500	9,446,500
9,600,000	72.705	0	46,500	9,646,500
9,800,000	74.299	0	46,500	9,846,500
10,000,000	75.892	0	46,500	10,046,500
10,200,000	77.473	0	46,500	10,246,500
10,400,000	79.052	130,448	46,500	10,316,052
10,600,000	80.625	325,500	46,500	10,321,000
10,800,000	82.188	519,312	46,500	10,327,188
11,000,000	83.746	712,504	46,500	10,333,996
11,200,000	85.303	905,572	46,500	10,340,928

*These numbers are approximate because futures trade in even 32nds.

†From $124 \times \$1,000 \times \max\{$ (futures price $- 78), 0\}$.

‡Does not include transactions costs or the financing of the options position.

---

strike price on the futures call option was 78. A futures price of 78 corresponds to a price of 75.348 (from 78 times the conversion factor), and a corresponding yield of 10.536% for the cheapest-to-deliver bond, the 7 5/8% of 2007. The equivalent yield for the hedged bond is 90 basis points higher, or 11.436%, for a corresponding price of 102.666. Adding on the premium received, 0.465 point, the final maximum effective sale price will be about 103.131. As Table 26-8 shows, if the hedged bond does trade at 90 basis points over the cheapest-to-deliver issue as assumed, the maximum effective sale price for the hedged bond is, in fact, slightly over 103. The discrepancies shown in the table are due to rounding and the fact that the position is not adjusted even though the relative price values of a basis point change as yields change.

Comparing Alternative Strategies In this chapter we have covered three basic hedging strategies for hedging a bond position: (1) hedging with futures, (2) hedging with out-of-the-money protective puts, and (3) covered call writing with out-of-the-money calls. Similar, but opposite, strategies exist for those whose risks are that rates will decrease. As might be expected, there is no "best" strategy. Each strategy has its advantages and its disadvantages, and we never get something for nothing. To get anything of value, something else of value must be forfeited.

To make a choice among strategies, it helps to lay the alternatives side by side. Using the futures and futures options examples from this chapter, Table 26-9 shows the final values of the portfolio for the various alternatives. (These are just the unhedged values together with the final columns from Tables 26-4, 26-7, and 26-8.) It is easy to see from Table 26-9 that if one alternative is superior to another alternative at one level of rates, it will be inferior at some other level of rates. This is even more obvious in Figure 26-3, which displays the numbers in Table 26-9 graphically. Consequently, we cannot conclude that one strategy is the best strategy. The manager who makes the strategy decision makes a choice among probability distributions, not usually among specific outcomes. Except for the perfect hedge, there is always some range of possible final values of the portfolio. Of course, exactly what that range is, and the probabilities associated with each possible outcome, is a matter of opinion.

TABLE 26-9

ALTERNATIVE HEDGING STRATEGIES

Actual Sale Price of Bonds	Effective Sale Price with Futures Hedge	Effective Sale Price with Protective Puts	Effective Sale Price with Covered Calls
$ 7,600,000	$9,272,636	$ 8,730,136	$ 7,646,500
7,800,000	9,270,144	8,727,644	7,846,500
8,000,000	9,268,148	8,725,648	8,046,500
8,200,000	9,266,276	8,723,776	8,246,500
8,400,000	9,264,280	8,721,780	8,446,500
8,600,000	9,263,524	8,721,024	8,646,500
8,800,000	9,262,396	8,753,500	8,846,500
9,000,000	9,261,888	8,953,500	9,046,500
9,200,000	9,262,372	9,153,500	9,246,500
9,400,000	9,263,600	9,353,500	9,446,500
9,600,000	9,264,580	9,553,500	9,646,500
9,800,000	9,266,924	9,753,500	9,846,500
10,000,000	9,269,392	9,953,500	10,046,500
10,200,000	9,273,348	10,153,500	10,246,500
10,400,000	9,277,552	10,353,500	10,316,052
10,600,000	9,282,500	10,553,500	10,321,000
10,800,000	9,288,688	10,753,500	10,327,188
11,000,000	9,295,496	10,953,500	10,333,996
11,200,000	9,302,428	11,153,500	10,340,928

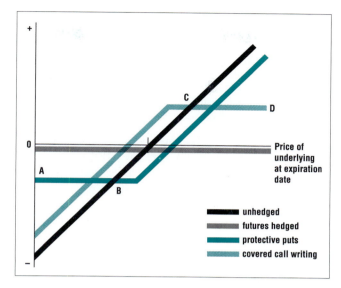

FIGURE 26-3
Alternative hedging strategies compared graphically.

■ SUMMARY

In this chapter, we described interest rate futures and options contracts. We looked closely at the Treasury bond futures contract because it is commonly used in bond portfolio management. The theoretical futures price of a Treasury bond futures contract must be adjusted for the delivery options granted to the seller.

Interest rate futures contracts can be used by money managers to speculate on the movement of interest rates, to control the interest rate risk of a portfolio, and to enhance returns when futures are mispriced. A corporate bond position can be hedged with a Treasury bond futures contract.

Interest rate options include options on fixed-income securities and options on interest rate futures contracts. The latter, more commonly called futures options, are the preferred exchange-traded vehicle for implementing investment strategies. Because of the difficulties of hedging particular bond issues or pass-through securities, many institutions find over-the-counter options more useful; these contracts can be customized to meet specific investment goals.

Counterparty risk is the risk that the other party to a derivative contract will default. Participants in the derivative market view counterparty risk as negligible for exchange-traded derivatives because of the clearinghouse that guarantees performance. In contrast, for forward contracts the two parties are exposed to counterparty risk; for over-the-counter options, the buyer of the option is exposed to counterparty risk.

The assumptions underlying the Black-Scholes option-pricing model and the binomial model based on prices limit their application to options on fixed-income instruments. The binomial option model based on yields is a better model, but it still suffers from the problem that it does not satisfy the put-call parity relationship. More sophisticated models called yield curve or arbitrage-free pricing models overcome this drawback by incorporating the yield curve into the pricing model. Strategies using interest rate options include speculating on interest rate movements and hedging. Two hedge strategies, a protective put buying strategy and a covered call writing strategy, with futures options can be implemented to hedge a corporate bond position.

■ **KEY TERMS**

arbitrage-free option-pricing
  models
cheapest-to-deliver issue
conversion factors
dealer options
delivery options

forward contract
futures option
implied repo rate
invoice price
options on physicals
quality option

swap option
timing option
wild card option
yield curve option-pricing
  models

■ **QUESTIONS**

1. Explain the differences between a futures contract and a forward contract.

2. a. What is meant by counterparty risk?
  b. Why do both the buyer and seller of a forward contract face counterparty risk?
  c. Why does the buyer and not the seller of an over-the-counter option face counterparty risk?

3. a. What does it mean if the cost of carry is positive for a Treasury bond futures contract?
  b. How do you think the cost of carry will affect the decision of the short of when in the delivery month the short will elect to deliver?

4. What are the delivery options granted to the seller of the Treasury bond futures contract?

5. How is the theoretical futures price of a Treasury bond futures contract affected by the delivery options granted to the short?

6. Suppose that the conversion factor for a particular Treasury bond that is acceptable for delivery in a Treasury bond futures contract is 0.85 and that the futures price settles at 105. Assume also that the accrued interest for this Treasury bond is 4. What is the invoice price if the seller delivers this Treasury bond at the settlement date?

7. What is the implied repo rate?

8. Explain why the implied repo rate is important in determining the cheapest-to-deliver issue.

9. A manager wishes to hedge a bond with a par value of $20 million by selling Treasury bond futures. Suppose that (1) the conversion factor for the cheapest-to-deliver issue is 0.91, (2) the price value of a basis point of the cheapest-to-deliver issue at the settlement date is 0.06895, and (3) the price value of a basis point of the bond to be hedged is 0.05954.
  a. What is the hedge ratio?
  b. How many Treasury bond futures contracts should be sold to hedge the bond?

10. Suppose that a manager wants to reduce the duration of a portfolio. Explain how this can be done using Treasury bond futures contracts.

11. The following excerpt appeared in the article "Duration," in the November 16, 1992, issue of *Derivatives Week*: "... TSA Capital Management in Los Angeles must determine duration of the futures contract it uses in order to match it with the dollar duration of the underlying, explains David Depew, principal and head of trading at the firm. Futures duration will be based on the duration of the underlying bond most likely to be delivered against the contract ..." (p. 9).
  a. Explain why it is necessary to know the dollar duration of the underlying in order to hedge.
  b. Why can the price value of basis point be used instead of the dollar duration?

12. An investor owns a call option on bond X with a strike price of 100. The coupon rate on bond X is 9% and has 10 years to maturity. The call option expires today at a time when bond X is selling to yield 8%. Should the investor exercise the call option?

13. An investor wants to protect against a rise in the market yield on a Treasury bond. Should the investor purchase a put option or a call option to obtain protection?

14. What arguments would be given by those who feel that the Black-Scholes model does not apply in pricing interest rate options?

15. Here are some excerpts from an article entitled "It's Boom Time for Bond Options as Interest-Rate Hedges Bloom," published in the November 8, 1990, issue of the *Wall Street Journal*.
  a. "The threat of a large interest-rate swing in either direction is driving people to options to hedge their portfolios of long-term Treasury bonds and medium-term Treasury notes, said Steven Northern, who manages fixed-income mutual funds for Massachusetts Financial Ser-

vices Co. in Boston." Why would a large interest rate swing in either direction encourage people to hedge?

b. "If the market moves against an option purchaser, the option expires worthless, and all the investor has lost is the relatively low purchase price, or 'premium,' of the option." Comment on the accuracy of this statement.

c. "Futures contracts also can be used to hedge portfolios, but they cost more, and there isn't any limit on the amount of losses they could produce before an investor bails out." Comment on the accuracy of this statement.

d. Mr. Northern said Massachusetts Financial has been trading actively in bond and note put options. "The concept is simple," he said. "If you're concerned about interest rates but don't want to alter the nature of what you own in a fixed-income portfolio, you can just buy puts." Why might put options be a preferable means of altering the nature of a fixed-income portfolio?

16. What is the difference between an option on a bond and an option on a bond futures contract?

17. a. "I don't understand how money managers can calculate the duration of an interest rate option. Don't they mean the amount of time remaining to the expiration date?" Respond to this question.

b. What factors affect the modified duration of an interest rate option?

c. "A deep in-the-money option always provides a higher modified duration for an option than a deep out-of-the-money option." Comment.

d. "The modified duration of all options is positive." Is this statement correct?

18. The excerpt following is from "Dutch and German Debt Warrants Offer Interest Rate Plays," which appeared in the October 12, 1992, issue of *Derivatives Week*:

Bankers Trust International launched its first warrants deal on Dutch State Loans last week, according to a bank official. A possible convergence of Dutch and German interest rates will make the call warrants attractive, said the official. Dutch interest rates are around 20–40 basis points over German rates in the 10–20 year maturities and there is a general market expectation that Dutch and European interest rates are likely to fall, he argued. . . .

The Bankers Trust deal comprises 3.5 million American-style call warrants which had an at-the-money strike of 103.81. The issue price was DFl 2.70 for DFl 100 of notional underlying.

The calls were trading last Thursday slightly out-of-the-money with the underlying in the range of 104.62–103.72, said the official. The warrants expire in April 1994.
[Note that DFl denotes the Dutch currency, guilders.]

a. Why is this an example of an over-the-counter interest rate option?

b. What role does Bankers Trust International play in this transaction?

c. When can these options be exercised?

d. Why would an investor who anticipated that Dutch interest rates would decline consider using this option to capitalize on this expectation?

e. The excerpt indicated that the option the previous Thursday was trading slightly out of the money in the range of 104.62–103.72. Is this statement correct?

19. Here is an excerpt from an article entitled "Dominguez Barry Looks at Covered Calls," which appeared in the July 20, 1992, issue of *Derivatives Week*:

SBC Dominguez Barry Funds Management in Sydney, with A$5.5 billion under management, is considering writing covered calls on its Australian bond portfolio to take advantage of very high implied volatilities, according to Carl Hanich, portfolio manager. The implied price volatility on at-the-money calls is 9.8%, as high as Hanich can ever remember. . . .

In response to rising volatility, Hanich is thinking about selling calls with a strike of 8.5%, generating premium income. "I'd be happy to lose bonds at 8.5%, given our market's at 8.87% now," he said. (p. 7)

Explain the strategy Mr. Hanich is considering.

20. a. On June 3, 1992, Danish voters rejected increased European integration. As a result, there were increased concerns that yields in many European countries would rise. The excerpt following is from the June 22, 1992, issue of *Derivatives Week*, ". . . As Guinness Blocks Italian Fallout":

In the wake of Denmark's rejection of European unity, Guinness Flight Global Asset Management [sold/bought] the Italian BTP Bond future to hedge most of its underlying Italian bond portfolio, which is in tens of millions of pounds, according to Director Philip Saunders. . . .

What did Guinness do, sell or buy the Italian BTP futures contract? Explain why.

b. The article also stated:

> The illiquidity of the cash markets on the heels of the Danish no vote made putting on a hedge using the future a more attractive alternative, Saunders noted. . . . with bid-offer spreads on Italian bonds widening to at least 200 basis points from their norm of 10 points and prices initially falling by more than those on futures. Additionally, dealing in the future meant that the hedge could be taken off subsequently without disturbing the underlying portfolio, said Saunders.

Elaborate further on the advantages of using futures contracts to hedge.

c. From the same article:

> As of last Monday, Guinness Flight was maintaining the hedge, Saunders said. The future stood at 95 and the cash was still down, so its losses in the cash market were offset by gains on the future, he said.

Isn't the whole idea behind using the futures contract to realize a profit, so that just offsetting the loss by using futures means that the hedge was ineffective?

CHAPTER 27

USING SWAPS, CAPS, AND FLOORS IN INVESTMENT MANAGEMENT

LEARNING OBJECTIVES
After reading this chapter you should be able to:

- explain what an interest rate swap is and how it can be used by institutional investors.

- describe the relationship between an interest rate swap and forward contracts.

- explain how interest rate swap terms are quoted in the market.

- describe the primary determinants of the price of an interest rate swap.

- explain what an option on an interest rate swap is and how it can be used by institutional investors.

- describe an equity swap and the various market conventions for quoting equity swap terms.

- describe how an equity swap can be used to replicate an index or enhance returns.

- explain what a rate cap and floor are and how these agreements can be used by institutional investors.

- describe the relationship between a cap and floor and options.

- explain how an interest rate collar can be created.

In previous chapters we discussed how futures and options can be used to control portfolio risk and/or enhance portfolio returns. There are other derivative contracts that can be used by money managers that have been customized by commercial banks and investment banks for their clients. The more popular contracts are interest rate swaps and interest rate agreements (caps and floors). These contracts have been used by money managers since the early 1980s to control interest rate risk. In more recent years, similar swaps have been introduced to control the risk of equity portfolios.

While there has already been widespread use of swaps, caps, and floors in the management of taxable institutions, increased use by pension funds, endowment funds, and other tax-exempt investors is expected as a result of an important Internal Revenue Service regulation in July 1992. Specifically, under Section 512 of the Internal Revenue Code, income from contracts such as swaps, caps, and floors (called *notional principal contracts*) is excluded from the Unrelated Business Income Tax. Prior to this ruling, there was concern that the income realized by tax-exempt investors using these contracts would be treated as Unrelated Business Income Tax and therefore taxed.

In this chapter we will review each of these derivative contracts—interest rate swaps, equity swaps, interest rate agreements, and equity caps and floors—and explain how they can be used by institutional investors.

INTEREST RATE SWAPS

Institutions sometimes find that their assets and liabilities are unavoidably mismatched. For instance, a bank will generally borrow short and lend long. As we discussed in Chapter 11, a rise in interest rates can create losses for the bank. Its cost of funds and therefore liability payments would increase, as depositors demanded higher rates, while its cash flow from existing assets (long-term loans) would remain the same. In contrast, an institution may borrow long and invest short by issuing long-term bonds and investing in floating-rate securities. If interest rates fall, the institution loses. Clearly, these two institutions could reduce their interest rate risk exposure by exchanging the interest elements of their positions.

In an **interest rate swap**, two parties (called **counterparties**) agree to exchange periodic interest payments. The dollar amount of the interest payments exchanged is based on some predetermined dollar principal, which is called the **notional principal amount**. The dollar amount each counterparty pays to the other is the agreed-upon periodic interest rate times the notional principal amount. The only dollars exchanged between the parties are the interest payments, not the notional principal amount. In the most common type of swap, one party agrees to pay the other party fixed interest payments at designated dates for the life of the contract. This party is referred to as the **fixed-rate payer**. The other party, who agrees to make interest rate payments that float with some reference rate, is referred to as the **floating-rate payer**. The frequency with which the interest rate that the floating-rate payer must pay is called the **reset frequency**.

The reference rates used for the floating rate in an interest rate swap are those on various money market instruments: Treasury bills, the London interbank offered rate, commercial paper, bankers acceptances, certificates of deposit, the federal funds rate, and the prime rate. The most common is the London interbank offered rate (LIBOR). LIBOR is the rate at which prime banks offer to pay on Eurodollar deposits available to other prime banks for a given maturity. Basically, it is viewed as the global cost of bank borrowing. There is not just one rate but a number of rates for different maturities—for example, a one-month LIBOR, a three-month LIBOR, and a six-month LIBOR.

To illustrate an interest rate swap, suppose that for the next five years party X agrees to pay party Y 10% per year, while party Y agrees to pay party X six-month LIBOR (the reference rate). Party X is a fixed-rate payer/floating-rate receiver, while party Y is a floating-rate payer/fixed-rate receiver. Assume that the notional principal amount is $50 million and that payments are exchanged every six months for the next five years. This means that every six months, party X (the fixed-rate payer/floating-rate receiver) will pay party Y $2.5 million (10% times $50 million divided by 2). The amount that party Y (the floating-rate payer/fixed-rate receiver) will pay party X will be six-month LIBOR times $50 million divided by 2. If six-month LIBOR is 7%, party Y will pay party X $1.75 million (7% times $50 million divided by 2). Note that we divide by 2 because one-half year's interest is being paid.

Later we will illustrate how market participants can use an interest rate swap to alter the cash flow character of assets or liabilities from a fixed-rate basis to a floating-rate basis, or vice versa.

Entering Into a Swap and Counterparty Risk

Interest rate swaps are over-the-counter instruments. This means that they are not traded on an exchange. An institutional investor wishing to enter into a swap transaction can do so through either a securities firm or a commercial bank that transacts in swaps.[1] These entities can do one of the following. First, they can arrange or broker a swap between two parties that want to enter into an interest rate swap. In this case, the securities firm or commercial bank is acting in a brokerage capacity. For example, an institutional investor who seeks a swap position can use the brokerage services of Smith Barney Shearson. This firm can set up a swap with a party that it has an arrangement with, say, AIG (an insurance company). Thus, Smith Barney Shearson arranges the swap between an institutional investor that wants a swap position and AIG, but Smith Barney Shearson is not itself a party to the swap agreement. The institutional investor looks to AIG to fulfill its obligations to make the swap payments, and AIG looks to the institutional investor to fulfill its obligations to make the swap payments.

The second way in which a securities firm or commercial bank can get an institutional investor into a swap position is by taking the other side of the swap. This means that the securities firm or the commercial bank is a dealer rather than a broker in the transaction. Acting as a dealer, the securities firm or the commercial bank must hedge its swap position in the same way that it hedges its position in other securities that it holds. Also it means that the dealer (which we refer to as a *swap dealer*) is the counterparty to the transaction. Merrill Lynch, for example, is a swap dealer. If an institutional investor entered into a swap with Merrill Lynch, the institutional investor will look to Merrill Lynch to satisfy the obligations of the swap; similarly, Merrill Lynch looks to the institutional investor to fulfill its obligations as set forth in the swap. Today, most swaps are transacted using a swap dealer.

The risks that the two parties take on when they enter into a swap is that the other party will fail to fulfill its obligations as set forth in the swap agreement. That is, each party faces default, or *counterparty risk*. In any agreement between two parties that must perform according to the terms of a contract, counterparty risk is the risk that the other party will default. With futures and exchange-traded options the counterparty risk is the risk that the clearinghouse established to guarantee performance of the contracts will default. Market participants view this risk as small. In contrast, counterparty risk in a swap can be significant.

Because of counterparty risk, not all securities firms and commercial banks can be swap dealers. Several securities firms have actually established

---

[1] Don't get confused here about the role of commercial banks. A bank can use a swap in its asset/liability management. Or a bank can transact (buy and sell) swaps to clients to generate fee income. It is in the latter sense that we discuss here the role of a commercial bank in the swap market.

subsidiaries that are separately capitalized so that they have a high credit rating, which permits them to enter into swap transactions as a dealer.

Thus, it is imperative to keep in mind that any party that enters into a swap is subject to counterparty risk.

Risk/Return Characteristics of an Interest Rate Swap

The value of an interest rate swap will fluctuate with market interest rates. To see how, let's consider our hypothetical swap. Suppose that interest rates change immediately after parties X and Y enter into the swap. First, consider what would happen if the market demanded that in any five-year swap the fixed-rate payer must pay 11% in order to receive six-month LIBOR. If party X (the fixed-rate payer) wants to sell its position to party A, then party A will benefit by having to pay only 10% (the original swap rate agreed upon) rather than 11% (the current swap rate) to receive six-month LIBOR. Party X will want compensation for this benefit. Consequently, the value of party X's position has increased. Thus, if interest rates increase, the fixed-rate payer will realize a profit and the floating-rate payer will realize a loss.

Next, consider what would happen if interest rates decline to, say, 6%. Now a five-year swap would require a new fixed-rate payer to pay 6% rather than 10% to receive six-month LIBOR. If party X wants to sell its position to party B, the latter would demand compensation to take over the position. In other words, if interest rates decline, the fixed-rate payer will realize a loss, while the floating-rate payer will realize a profit.

The risk/return profile of the two positions when interest rates change is summarized in Table 27-1.

Interpreting a Swap Position

A swap position can be interpreted in two ways: (1) a package of forward/futures contracts and (2) a package of cash flows from buying and selling cash market instruments.

Package of Forward Contracts.   Contrast the position of the counterparties in an interest rate swap summarized above to the position of the long and short interest rate futures (forward) contract discussed in the previous chapter. The long futures position gains if interest rates decline and loses if interest rates rise—this is similar to the risk/return profile for a floating-rate payer. The risk/return profile for a fixed-rate payer is similar to that of the short futures position: a gain if interest rates increase and a loss if interest rates decrease. By taking a closer look at the interest rate swap, we can understand why the risk/return relationships are similar.

Consider party X's position. Party X has agreed to pay 10% and receive six-month LIBOR. More specifically, assuming a $50 million notional principal amount, X has agreed to buy a commodity called "six-month LIBOR" for $2.5 million. This is effectively a six-month forward contract where X agrees to pay $2.5 million in exchange for delivery of six-month LIBOR. If interest rates increase to 11%, the price of that commodity (six-month LIBOR) is higher, resulting in a gain for the fixed-rate payer, who is effectively long a six-month forward contract on six-month LIBOR. The floating-rate payer is effectively short a six-month forward contract on six-month LIBOR. There is therefore an implicit forward contract corresponding to each exchange date.

TABLE 27-1		
EFFECT OF RATE CHANGES ON INTEREST RATE SWAP COUNTERPARTIES		
	Interest Rates Decrease	**Interest Rates Increase**
Floating-rate payer	Gain	Loss
Fixed-rate payer	Loss	Gain

Now we can see why there is a similarity between the risk/return relationship for an interest rate swap and a forward contract. If interest rates increase to, say, 11%, the price of that commodity (six-month LIBOR) increases to $2.75 million (11% times $50 million divided by 2). The long forward position (the fixed-rate payer) gains, and the short forward position (the floating-rate payer) loses. If interest rates decline to, say, 9%, the price of our commodity decreases to $2.25 million (9% times $50 million divided by 2). The short forward position (the floating-rate payer) gains, and the long forward position (the fixed-rate payer) loses.

Consequently, interest rate swaps can be viewed as a package of more basic interest rate control tools, such as forwards. The pricing of an interest rate swap will then depend on the price of a package of forward contracts with the same settlement dates in which the underlying for the forward contract is the same index.

While an interest rate swap may be nothing more than a package of forward contracts, it is not a redundant contract for several reasons. First, maturities for forward or futures contracts do not extend out as far as those of an interest rate swap; an interest rate swap with a term of 15 years or longer can be obtained. Second, an interest rate swap is a more transactionally efficient instrument. By this we mean that in one transaction an entity can effectively establish a payoff equivalent to a package of forward contracts. The forward contracts would each have to be negotiated separately. Third, the interest rate swap market has grown in liquidity since its establishment in 1981; interest rate swaps now provide more liquidity than forward contracts, particularly long-dated (i.e., long-term) forward contracts.

Package of Cash Market Instruments   To understand why a swap can also be interpreted as a package of cash market instruments, consider an investor who enters into the transaction below:

- Buy a $50 million par of a five-year floating-rate bond that pays six-month LIBOR every six months.
- Finance the purchase by borrowing $50 million for five years on terms requiring 10% annual interest rate paid every six months.

The cash flows for this transaction are set forth in Table 27-2. The second column of the table shows the cash flow from purchasing the five-year floating-rate bond. There is a $50 million cash outlay and then 10 cash inflows. The amount of the cash inflows is uncertain because they depend on future LIBOR. The next column shows the cash flow from borrowing $50 million on a fixed-rate basis. The last column shows the net cash flow from the entire

TABLE 27-2

CASH FLOW FOR THE PURCHASE OF A FIVE-YEAR FLOATING-RATE BOND FINANCED BY BORROWING ON A FIXED-RATE BASIS

Transaction:
Purchase for $50 million
five-year, floating-rate bond: Floating rate = LIBOR
Semiannual pay

Borrow $50 million for five years: fixed rate = 10%,
semiannual payments

Cash Flow (in Millions of Dollars) From:

Six-Month Period	Floating-Rate Bond (*)	Borrowing Cost	Net
0	$-\$50$	$+\$50.0$	$\$0$
1	$+(LIBOR_1/2) \times 50$	-2.5	$+ (LIBOR_1/2) \times 50 - 2.5$
2	$+(LIBOR_2/2) \times 50$	-2.5	$+ (LIBOR_2/2) \times 50 - 2.5$
3	$+(LIBOR_3/2) \times 50$	-2.5	$+ (LIBOR_3/2) \times 50 - 2.5$
4	$+(LIBOR_4/2) \times 50$	-2.5	$+ (LIBOR_4/2) \times 50 - 2.5$
5	$+(LIBOR_5/2) \times 50$	-2.5	$+ (LIBOR_5/2) \times 50 - 2.5$
6	$+(LIBOR_6/2) \times 50$	-2.5	$+ (LIBOR_6/2) \times 50 - 2.5$
7	$+(LIBOR_7/2) \times 50$	-2.5	$+ (LIBOR_7/2) \times 50 - 2.5$
8	$+(LIBOR_8/2) \times 50$	-2.5	$+ (LIBOR_8/2) \times 50 - 2.5$
9	$+(LIBOR_9/2) \times 50$	-2.5	$+ (LIBOR_9/2) \times 50 - 2.5$
10	$+(LIBOR_{10}/2) \times 50 + 50$	-52.5	$+ (LIBOR_{10}/2) \times 50 - 2.5$

Note: The subscript for LIBOR indicates the six-month LIBOR as per the terms of the floating-rate bond at time *t*.

transaction. As the last column indicates, there is no initial cash flow (no cash inflow or cash outlay). In all 10 six-month periods, the net position results in a cash inflow of LIBOR and a cash outlay of $2.5 million. This net position, however, is identical to the position of a fixed-rate payer/floating-rate receiver.

It can be seen from the net cash flow in Table 27-2 that a fixed-rate payer has a cash market position that is equivalent to a long position in a floating-rate bond and a short position in a fixed-rate bond—the short position being the equivalent of borrowing by issuing a fixed-rate bond.

What about the position of a floating-rate payer? It can be easily demonstrated that the position of a floating-rate payer is equivalent to purchasing a fixed-rate bond and financing that purchase at a floating rate, where the floating rate is the reference interest rate for the swap. That is, the position of a floating-rate payer is equivalent to a long position in a fixed-rate bond and a short position in a floating-rate bond.

Duration of a Swap

As with any fixed-income contract, the value of a swap will change as interest rates change. Dollar duration is a measure of the interest rate sensitivity of a fixed-income contract (see Chapter 20). From the perspective of the party who pays floating and receives fixed, the interest rate swap position can be viewed as follows:

long a fixed-rate bond + short a floating-rate bond

This means that the dollar duration of an interest rate swap from the perspective of a floating-rate payer is simply the difference between the dollar duration of the two bond positions that make up the swap. That is,

Dollar duration of a swap = dollar duration of a fixed-rate bond
− dollar duration of a floating-rate bond

Most of the dollar price sensitivity of a swap due to interest rate changes will result from the dollar duration of the fixed-rate bond because the dollar duration of the floating-rate bond will be small. The closer the swap is to the date that the coupon rate is reset, the smaller the dollar duration of a floating-rate bond.

Terminology, Conventions, and Market Quotes

Here we review some of the terminology used in the swaps market and explain how swaps are quoted. The date that the counterparties commit to the swap is called the **trade date**. The date that the swap begins accruing interest is called the **effective date**, while the date that the swap stops accruing interest is called the **maturity date**.

While our illustrations assume that the timing of the cash flows for both the fixed-rate payer and floating-rate payer will be the same, this is rarely the case in a swap. In fact, an agreement may call for the fixed-rate payer to make payments annually but for the floating-rate payer to make payments more frequently (semiannually or quarterly). Also, the way in which interest accrues on each leg of the transaction differs, because there are several day count conventions in the fixed-income markets.

The terminology used to describe the position of a party in the swap markets combines cash market jargon and futures jargon, given that a swap position can be interpreted as a position in a package of cash market instruments or a package of futures/forward positions. As we have said, the counterparty to an interest rate swap is either a fixed-rate payer or a floating-rate payer. Table 27-3 describes these positions in several ways.

The first two expressions in Table 27-3 to describe the position of a fixed-rate payer and floating-rate payer are self-explanatory. To understand why the fixed-rate payer is viewed as short the bond market and the floating-rate payer is viewed as long the bond market, consider what happens when interest rates change. Those who borrow on a fixed-rate basis will benefit if interest rates rise because they have locked in a lower interest rate. But those who have a short bond position will also benefit if interest rates rise. Thus, a fixed-rate payer can be said to be short the bond market. A floating-rate payer benefits if interest rates fall. A long position in a bond also benefits if interest rates fall, so terminology describing a floating-rate payer as long the bond market is not surprising. From our discussion of the interpretation of a swap as a package of cash market instruments and the duration of a swap, describing a swap in terms of the sensitivities of long and short cash positions follows naturally.

TABLE 27-3*

DESCRIBING THE COUNTERPARTIES TO A SWAP

Fixed-Rate payer	Floating-Rate payer
Pays fixed rate in the swap	Pays floating rate in the swap
Receives floating in the swap	Receives fixed in the swap
Is short the bond market	Is long the bond market
Has bought a swap	Has sold a swap
Is long a swap	Is short a swap
Has established the price sensitivities of a longer-term liability and a floating-rate asset	Has established the price sensitivities of a longer-term asset and a floating-rate liability

*Source: Robert F. Kopprasch, John Macfarlane, Daniel R. Ross, and Janet Showers, "The Interest Rate Swap Market: Yield Mathematics, Terminology, and Conventions," Chap. 58 in Frank J. Fabozzi and Irving M. Pollack (eds.), *The Handbook of Fixed Income Securities* (Homewood, IL: Dow Jones-Irwin, 1987).

The convention that has evolved for quoting swap levels is that a swap dealer sets the floating rate equal to the index and then quotes the fixed rate that will apply. To illustrate this convention, consider a 10-year swap offered by a dealer to market participants, shown in Table 27-4.

The offer price that the dealer would quote the fixed-rate payer would be to pay 8.85% and receive LIBOR "flat" (flat meaning with no spread to LIBOR). The bid price that the dealer would quote the floating-rate payer would be to pay LIBOR flat and receive 8.75%. The bid-offer spread is 10 basis points.

The fixed rate is some spread above the Treasury yield curve with the same term to maturity as the swap. In our illustration, suppose that the 10-year Treasury yield is 8.35%. Then the offer price that the dealer would quote to the fixed-rate payer is the 10-year Treasury rate plus 50 basis points versus receiving LIBOR flat. For the floating-rate payer, the bid price quoted would be LIBOR flat versus the 10-year Treasury rate plus 40 basis points. The dealer would quote such a swap as 40-50, meaning that the dealer is willing to enter into a swap to receive LIBOR and pay a fixed rate equal to the 10-year Treasury rate plus 40 basis points; and the dealer would be willing to enter into a swap to pay LIBOR and receive a fixed rate equal to the 10-year Trea-

---

TABLE 27-4

MEANING OF A "40-50" QUOTE FOR A 10-YEAR SWAP WHEN TREASURIES YIELD 8.35%*

	Floating-Rate Payer	Fixed-Rate Payer
Pay	Floating rate of six-month LIBOR	Fixed rate of 8.85%
Receive	Fixed rate of 8.75%	Floating rate of six-month LIBOR

*Bid-offer spread of 10 basis points.

sury rate plus 50 basis points. The difference between the fixed rate paid and received is the bid-offer spread.

Application of a Swap to Asset/Liability Management

So far we have merely described an interest rate swap and looked at its characteristics. Here we will illustrate how these swaps can be used in asset/liability management. Other types of interest rate swaps have been developed that go beyond the generic, or "plain vanilla," swap described; however, we will confine our discussion to the generic swap.[2]

An interest rate swap can be used to alter the cash flow characteristics of an institution's assets so as to provide a better match between assets and liabilities. The two institutions we use for illustration are a commercial bank and a life insurance company.

Suppose a bank has a portfolio consisting of five-year-term commercial loans with a fixed interest rate. The principal value of the portfolio is $50 million, and the interest rate on all the loans in the portfolio is 10%. The loans are interest-only loans; interest is paid semiannually, and the principal is paid at the end of five years. That is, assuming no default on the loans, the cash flow from the loan portfolio is $2.5 million every six months for the next five years and $50 million at the end of five years. To fund its loan portfolio, assume that the bank is relying on the issuance of six-month certificates of deposit. The interest rate that the bank plans to pay on its six-month CDs is six-month LIBOR plus 40 basis points.

The risk that the bank faces is that six-month LIBOR will be 9.6% or greater. To understand why, remember that the bank is earning 10% annually on its commercial loan portfolio. If six-month LIBOR is 9.6%, it will have to pay 9.6% plus 40 basis points, or 10%, to depositors for six-month funds, and so there will be no spread income. Worse, if six-month LIBOR rises above 9.6%, there will be a loss; that is, the cost of funds will exceed the interest rate earned on the loan portfolio. The bank's objective is to lock in a spread over the cost of its funds.

The other party in the interest rate swap illustration is a life insurance company that has committed itself to pay a 9% rate for the next five years on a guaranteed investment contract (GIC) it has issued. The amount of the GIC is $50 million. Suppose that the life insurance company has the opportunity to invest $50 million in what it considers an attractive five-year floating-rate instrument in a private-placement transaction. The interest rate on this instrument is six-month LIBOR plus 160 basis points. The coupon rate is set every six months. The risk that the life insurance company faces in this instance is that six-month LIBOR will fall so that the company will not earn enough to realize a spread over the 9% rate that it has guaranteed to the GIC holders. If six-month LIBOR falls to 7.4% or less, no spread income will be generated. To understand why, suppose that six-month LIBOR at the date the floating-rate instrument resets its coupon is 7.4%. Then the coupon rate for the next six months will be 9% (7.4% plus 160 basis points). Because the life

---

[2]For a discussion of these swaps and their application, see Anand Bhattacharya and Frank J. Fabozzi, "Interest Rate Swaps," Chap. 56 in Frank J. Fabozzi and T. Dessa Fabozzi (eds.), *The Handbook of Fixed Income Securities* (Burr Ridge, IL: Irwin Professional Publishing, 1994).

TABLE 27-5

AN INTEREST RATE SWAP OPPORTUNITY

	Bank	**Insurance Company**
Long-term position	Lending	Borrowing
Short-term position	Borrowing	Lending
Exposure	Spread income falls if reference rate increases	Spread income falls if reference rate decreases

insurance company has agreed to pay 9% on the GIC policy, there will be no spread income. Should six-month LIBOR fall below 7.4%, there will be a loss.

Table 27-5 summarizes the asset/liability problems of the bank and the life insurance company. We can also sum it up this way:

Bank

1. It has lent long term and borrowed short term.
2. If six-month LIBOR rises, spread income declines.

Life insurance company

1. Has effectively lent short term and borrowed long term.
2. If six-month LIBOR falls, spread income declines.

Now let's suppose the market has available a five-year interest rate swap with a notional principal amount of $50 million. The swap terms available to the bank are as follows:

1. Every six months the bank will pay 8.45% (annual rate).
2. Every six months the bank will receive LIBOR.

The swap terms available to the insurance company are as follows:

1. Every six months the life insurance company will pay LIBOR.
2. Every six months the life insurance company will receive 8.40%.

What has this interest rate contract done for the bank and the life insurance company? Table 27-6 shows what the interest rate spread will be for each participant for every six-month period for the life of the swap agreement.

As you can see from Table 27-6, regardless of what happens to six-month LIBOR, the bank locks in a spread of 115 basis points, and the life insurance company locks in a spread of 100 basis points. The interest rate swap has allowed each party to accomplish its asset/liability objective of locking in a spread.[3] It permits the two financial institutions to alter the cash flow characteristics of its assets: from fixed to floating in the case of the bank, and from floating to fixed in the case of the life insurance company. This type of transaction is referred to as an **asset swap**. Another way the bank and the life in-

---

[3]Whether the size of the spread is adequate is not an issue to us in this illustration.

TABLE 27-6	
ANALYZING THE EFFECT OF A SWAP	

$50 million notional
8.45% fixed
floater at six-month LIBOR

Bank **(Fixed-Rate Payer)**		**Insurance Company** **(Floating-Rate Payer)**	
Annual interest rate received:		Annual interest rate received:	
*From commercial loan portfolio = 10.00%		*From floating-rate instrument = 1.6% + six-month LIBOR	
From interest rate swap	= six-month LIBOR	From interest rate swap	= 8.40%
Total	= 10.00% + six-month LIBOR	Total	= 10.00% + six-month LIBOR
Annual interest rate paid:		Annual interest rate paid:	
*To CD depositors	= six-month LIBOR	*To GIC policyholders	= 9.00%
From interest rate swap	= 8.45%	On interest rate swap	= six-month LIBOR
Total	= 8.45% + six-month LIBOR	Total	= 9.00% + six-month LIBOR
Outcome:		Outcome:	
To be received	= 10.00% + six-month LIBOR	To be received	= 10.00% + six-month LIBOR
To be paid	= 8.45% + six-month LIBOR	To be paid	= 9.00% + six-month LIBOR
Spread income	= 1.15%, or 115 basis points	Spread income	= 1.0%, or 100 basis points

*Assets and liabilities predating the swap.

surance company could use the swap market would be to change the cash flow nature of their liabilities. Such a swap is called a **liability swap**.

Of course, there are other ways that two such institutions can accomplish the same objectives. The bank might refuse to make fixed-rate commercial loans. However, if borrowers can find another company willing to lend on a fixed-rate basis, the bank has lost these customers. The life insurance company might refuse to purchase a floating-rate instrument. But suppose that the terms on a private-placement instrument offered to the life insurance company were more attractive than those available on a floating-rate instrument with a comparable credit risk, and that by using the swap market the life insurance company can earn more than it could by investing directly in a five-year, fixed-rate bond. For example, suppose the life insurance company can invest in a comparable-credit-risk, five-year, fixed-rate bond with a yield of 9.8%. Assuming that it commits itself to a GIC with a 9% rate, this would result in spread income of 80 basis points—less than the 100-basis-point spread income it achieves by purchasing the floating-rate instrument and entering into the swap.

Consequently, not only can an interest rate swap be used to change the risk of a transaction by changing the cash flow characteristics of assets or liabilities, but under certain circumstances, it can also be used to enhance returns. Obviously, this depends on the existence of market imperfections.

Primary Determinants of Swap Spreads

Earlier we provided two interpretations of a swap: (1) a package of futures/forward contracts and (2) a package of cash market instruments. The swap spread is determined by the same factors that influence the spread over Treasuries on financial instruments (futures/forward contracts or cash) that produce a similar return or funding profile. As we explain below, the key determinant of the swap spread for swaps with maturities of five years or less is the cost of hedging in the Eurodollar CD futures market. For longer-maturity swaps, the key determinant of the swap spread is the credit spreads in the corporate bond market.

Given that a swap is a package of futures/forward contracts, the swap spread can be determined by looking for futures/forward contracts with the same risk/return profile. A Eurodollar CD futures contract is a swap where a fixed dollar payment (i.e., the futures price) is exchanged for three-month LIBOR. There are available Eurodollar CD futures contracts that have maturities every three months for five years. A market participant can synthesize a (synthetic) fixed-rate security or a fixed-rate funding vehicle of up to five years by taking a position in a strip of Eurodollar CD futures contracts (i.e., a position in every three-month Eurodollar CD up to the desired maturity date).

For example, consider a financial institution that has fixed-rate assets and floating-rate liabilities. Both the assets and liabilities have a maturity of three years. The interest rate on the liabilities resets every three months based on three-month LIBOR. This financial institution can hedge this mismatched asset/liability position by buying a three-year strip of Eurodollar CD futures contracts. By doing so, the financial institution is receiving LIBOR over the three-year period and paying a fixed dollar amount (i.e., the futures price). The financial institution is now hedged because the assets are fixed rate, and the strip of long Eurodollar CDs futures synthetically creates a fixed-rate funding arrangement. From the fixed dollar amount over the three years, an effective fixed interest rate that the financial institution pays can be calculated. Alternatively, the financial institution can synthetically create a fixed-rate funding arrangement by entering into a three-year swap in which it pays fixed and receives three-month LIBOR. The financial institution will use the vehicle that gives the lowest cost of hedging the mismatched position. This will drive the synthetic fixed rate in the swap market to that available by hedging in the Eurodollar CD futures market.

For swaps with maturities longer than five years, the spread is determined primarily by the credit spreads in the corporate bond market. Since a swap can be interpreted as a package of long and short positions in a fixed-rate bond and a floating-rate bond, it is the credit spreads in those two market sectors that will be the key determinant of the swap spread. Boundary conditions for swap spreads based on prices for fixed-rate and floating-rate corporate bonds can be determined.[4] Several technical factors, such as the relative supply of fixed-rate and floating-rate corporate bonds and the cost to dealers of hedging their inventory position of swaps, influence where between the boundaries the actual swap spread will be.[5]

---

[4]These boundary conditions are derived in the appendix to Ellen Evans and Gioia Parente Bales, "What Drives Interest Rate Swap Spreads?" Chap. 13 in Carl R. Beidleman (ed.), *Interest Rate Swaps* (Homewood, IL: Richard D. Irwin, 1991).

[5]For a discussion of these other factors, see Evans and Bales, ibid., pp. 293–301.

Secondary Market Swap Transactions

There are three general types of transactions in the secondary market for swaps. These include (1) a swap reversal, (2) a swap sale (or assignment), and (3) a swap buy-back (or close-out or cancellation). Table 27-7 summarizes the secondary market for swaps.

In a **swap reversal**, the party that wants out of the transaction will arrange for a swap in which (1) the maturity on the new swap is equal to the time remaining for the original swap, (2) the reference rate is the same, and (3) the notional principal amount is the same. For example, suppose party X enters into a five-year swap with a notional principal amount of $50 million in which it pays 10% and receives LIBOR, but two years later, X wants out of the swap. In a swap reversal, X would enter into a three-year interest rate swap, with a counterparty different from the original counterparty, let's say Z, in which the notional principal amount is $50 million, and X pays LIBOR and receives a fixed rate. The fixed rate that X receives from Z will depend on prevailing swap terms for floating-rate receivers at the initiation of the three-year swap.

While party X has effectively terminated the original swap in economic terms, there is a major drawback to this approach: Party X is still liable to the original counterparty Y, as well as to the new counterparty, Z. That is, party X now has two offsetting interest rate swaps on its books instead of one swap, and as a result it has increased its default risk exposure.

The **swap sale** or **swap assignment** overcomes this drawback. In this secondary market transaction, the party that wishes to close out the original swap finds another party that is willing to accept its obligations under the swap. In our illustration, this means that X finds another party, say, A, that

TABLE 27-7			
TYPES OF SECONDARY MARKET SWAP TRANSACTIONS			
	Swap Reversal	**Swap Sale**	**Swap Buy-Back**
Purpose	Counterbalance a swap until maturity	End the party's obligation	End the party's obligation
Strategy	Take the opposite side of a swap with equivalent: • maturity • reference rate • notional principal	Seek another party to accept the obligation	Sell the swap back to the original counterparty
Drawbacks	Having two swaps increases counterparty risk	Counterparty must be willing to accept the credit of the new party	Counterparty must be willing to buy

will agree to pay 10% to Y and receive LIBOR from Y for the next three years. Party A might have to be compensated to accept the position of party X, or A might have to be willing to compensate X. Who will receive compensation depends on the swap terms at the time. For example, if interest rates have risen so that to receive LIBOR for three years a fixed-rate payer would have to pay 12%, then A would have to compensate X because A has to pay only 10% to receive LIBOR. The compensation would be equal to the present value of a three-year annuity of 2% times the notional principal amount.[6] If, instead, interest rates have fallen so that to receive LIBOR for three years a fixed-rate payer would have to pay 6%, then X would have to compensate A. The compensation would be equal to the present value of a three-year annuity of 4% times the notional principal amount.

Once the transaction is completed, it is then A, not X, that is obligated to perform under the swap terms. (Of course, an intermediary could act as principal and become party A to help its client X.) In order to accomplish a swap sale, the original counterparty, Y in our example, must agree to the sale. A key factor in whether Y will agree is whether it is willing to accept the credit of A. For example, if A's credit rating is double B while X's is double A, Y would be unlikely to accept A as a counterparty.

A **swap buy-back** (or *close-out sale* or *cancellation*) involves the sale of the swap to the original counterparty. As in the case of a swap sale, one party might have to compensate the other, depending on how interest rates and credit spreads have changed since the inception of the swap. There have been proposals to create a swap clearing corporation, similar to the clearing corporations for futures and options, in which case swaps could be marked to market and credit exposure to a swap would be reduced.

Options on Swaps

The second generation of products in the interest rate swap market consists of options on interest rate swaps, which are referred to as **swaptions**. The buyer of a swaption has the right to enter into an interest rate swap agreement by some specified date in the future. The swaption agreement will specify whether the buyer of the swaption will be a fixed-rate receiver or a fixed-rate payer. The writer of the swaption becomes the counterparty to the swap if the buyer exercises.

If the buyer of the swaption has the right to enter into a swap as a fixed-rate payer, the swap is called a **call swaption**. The writer therefore becomes the fixed-rate receiver/floating-rate payer. If the buyer of the swaption has the right to enter into a swap as a floating-rate payer, the swap is called a **put swaption**. The writer of the swaption therefore becomes the floating-rate receiver/fixed-rate payer.

The strike rate of the swaption indicates the fixed rate that will be swapped versus the floating rate. The swaption will also specify the maturity date of the swap. A swaption may be European or American. Of course, as in

---

[6]It is three years because this is the time remaining for the swap. The 2% represents the difference between the prevailing rate of 12% and the fixed rate of 10% on the swap.

all options, the buyer of a swaption pays the writer a premium, although the premium can be structured into the swap terms so that no upfront fee has to be paid.

A swaption can be used to hedge a portfolio strategy that uses an interest rate swap but where the cash flows of the underlying asset or liability are uncertain. The cash flows of the asset would be uncertain if it (1) is callable, as in the case of a callable corporate bond, a mortgage loan, a pass-through security, or a loan that can be prepaid, and/or (2) exposes the investor/lender to default risk.[7]

To illustrate the use of a swaption, suppose a savings and loan association enters into a four-year swap in which it agrees to pay 9% fixed and receive LIBOR. The fixed-rate payments will come from a portfolio of mortgage pass-through securities with a coupon rate of 9%. Suppose that one year after the swap begins, mortgage rates decline to 6%, resulting in large prepayments. The prepayments received will have to be reinvested at a rate lower than 9%, but the S&L must still pay 9% under the terms of the swap. As the S&L is paying fixed and receiving floating, it would seek to use a swaption that allows it to unwind the original swap by receiving fixed and paying floating. More specifically, the S&L will enter into a swaption that will allow it to receive 9% and pay LIBOR. The purchase of a call swaption with a strike rate of 9% (and a LIBOR floating rate) would be the appropriate swaption to terminate the original swap.

EQUITY SWAPS

In recent years, the concept of swapping cash flows has been applied to the equity area (see Box 27). In an **equity swap**, the cash flows that are swapped are based on the total return on some stock market index and an interest rate (either a fixed rate or a floating rate). Moreover, the stock market index can be a non-U.S. stock market index and the payments could be non-dollar-denominated. For example, a money manager can enter into a two-year, quarterly-reset equity swap based on the German DAX market index versus the LIBOR in which the money manager receives the market index in deutsche marks and pays the floating rate in deutsche marks.

As with interest rate swaps, the notional principal amount of the contract is not exchanged by the counterparties, but both parties are exposed to counterparty risk. An important difference between an equity swap and an interest rate swap is that it is possible that one of the parties in an equity swap, specifically, the party receiving the stock market index, will realize a negative total return. This means that party must pay to the counterparty the amount of the negative total return plus the payment on the reference interest rate.

---

[7]For an explanation of how swaptions can be used to manage a portfolio of callable bonds, see Robert M. Stavis and Victor J. Haghani, "Putable Swaps: Tools for Managing Callable Assets," Chap. 20 in Frank J. Fabozzi (ed.), *The Handbook of Fixed Income Options* (Chicago: Probus Publishing, 1989).

BOX 27

SWAPS AND THE DIVISION OF LABOR

Outstanding managers will find improved opportunities for increased business from their existing accounts, because the account's allocation to an outstanding manager is no longer limited by the need for exposure to that manager's specialty. Of course, a key assumption behind this expectation is that the specialty manager's performance tracks a swappable benchmark. This assumption is valid in the vast majority of cases and it will be even more applicable as the swap market expands and matures.

An obvious corollary to business gains for successful managers will be greater difficulties for mediocre managers. A manager who was held onto an account only because the fund administrator could not find a better manager in his specialty will be at risk. The fund can now hire someone with better performance *in another market* and swap into the index return for the former manager's asset class.

Source: Gary Gastineau, *Swaps and the Division of Labor*, published by SBC Research, Swiss Bank

Corporation Investment Banking Inc., January 1993.

Question for Box 27

1. Explain why development of the interest rate swap and equity swap will have the results described in the excerpt.

As an example, Figure 27-1 shows what the cash flows would have been for the period June 30, 1990, to June 30, 1992, for a two-year, quarterly-reset equity swap based on the German DAX market index versus LIBOR with all payments denominated in deutsche marks. The top panel shows the cash flows as a percent of the notional principal for the party receiving the DAX return and paying LIBOR in deutsche marks. Notice that in two of the quarters there is a negative return on the DAX. The bottom panel shows the resulting net cash flow of the party receiving the DAX return and paying LIBOR in deutsche marks. The greatest exposure over this two-year period for the party receiving the DAX return is a net cash flow of about 20% of the notional principal.

Applications

A swap is nothing more than a package of forward contracts. The advantage of the swap is that it is more transactionally efficient for accomplishing many investment objectives.

In the case of an equity swap, two uses have been suggested. The first is to create a portfolio that replicates an index. As explained in Chapter 14, an indexed portfolio can be created by buying all or some of the stocks that compose the index. In Chapter 16, we then explained how this can be done more efficiently—in terms of cost and speed of execution—by buying stock index futures contracts and investing funds in Treasury bills. The stock index futures position must then be rolled over before the settlement date into a new futures position. Equity swaps provide a third alternative that have three advantages: (1) There are quarterly cash flows, (2) the money manager can specify the maturity of the contract so that frequent rolling of a futures position is unnecessary, and (3) there is no concern with the mispricing of the futures contract. Another distinct advantage of an equity swap is that since it is customized, a money manager can use a swap to index a non-U.S. stock market index. We saw this in our earlier illustration of swapping the DAX market index for deutsche marks LIBOR. Moreover, an equity swap can be used to

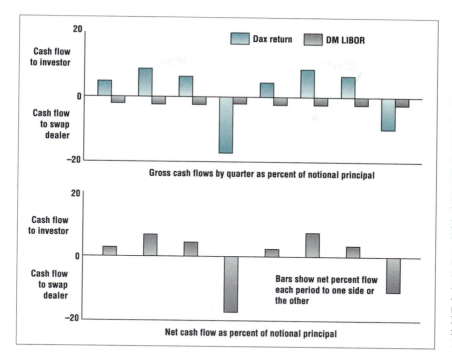

FIGURE 27-1

Cash flows for the period June 30, 1990, to June 30, 1992, for a two-year quarterly-reset equity swap based on the German DAX market index versus LIBOR with all payments in deutsche marks

Source: Gary Gastineau, Gordon Holterman, and Scott Beighley, *Equity Investment across Borders: Cutting the Costs* (SBC Research, Swiss Bank Corporation Investment Banking Inc., 1992), p. 15.

hedge the currency risk. For example, an equity swap can be structured in which the money manager receives in U.S. dollars the DAX market index total return and pays in U.S. dollars LIBOR. There are two disadvantages of using an equity swap rather than stock index futures: (1) There is counterparty risk, and (2) there is less liquidity in swaps compared with the very liquid stock index futures contract.

The second way it has been suggested that equity swaps can be used is to enhance return.[8] For example, suppose a pension plan sponsor has allocated a small portion of the portfolio to a specialty equity manager who has exhibited on a fairly consistent basis superior investment performance relative to some stock market benchmark. Diversification and other constraints may prevent more funds from being allocated to this manager. Also suppose that the plan sponsor has established an asset allocation policy, fixing the amount in three-year Treasury securities. Using an equity swap, the pension plan sponsor can enter into a swap in which the sponsor receives over the next three years a fixed coupon rate based on three-year Treasuries and agrees to pay the total return on the stock market benchmark that the specialty equity manager has outperformed. The amount allocated to this manager can be increased. Then, if the manager can outperform the benchmark, the excess return over the benchmark is retained by the pension plan sponsor. The total return for the pension plan would then be the three-year Treasury fixed coupon rate plus the excess return over the benchmark. The risk, of course, is

---

[8]Gary Gastineau, *Swaps and the Division of Labor* (SBC Research, Swiss Bank Corporation Investment Banking Inc., January 1993), p. 2.

that the specialty equity manager underperforms the index. The plan's return is then reduced by the amount of underperformance. Depending on the actual performance of the specialty equity manager, it is possible for the fund's return to be negative.

Market Conventions

In the case of interest rate swaps, the market convention for quoting swap terms is now standardized. Because the equity swap market is in its infancy, no standardization for quoting these swaps exists at the time of this writing. This makes it difficult to compare swap terms among the various dealer firms that are making markets in these swaps. For example, some dealers quote swaps in terms of the change in the stock market index without including dividends. That is, the return being received or paid just considers price changes. Other dealers quote the total return (price change and dividends) for the index. In the case of non-U.S. stock market indexes, a dealer may quote the swap in terms of the total return after deducting foreign withholding taxes.

INTEREST RATE AGREEMENTS (CAPS AND FLOORS)

An **interest rate agreement** is an agreement between two parties whereby one party, for an upfront premium, agrees to compensate the other at specific time periods if a designated interest rate, called the **reference rate**, is different from a predetermined level. When one party agrees to pay the other whenever the reference rate exceeds a predetermined level, the agreement is referred to as an **interest rate cap**, or *ceiling*. The agreement is referred to as an **interest rate floor** when one party agrees to pay the other whenever the reference rate falls below a predetermined level. The predetermined interest rate level is called the *strike rate*.

The terms of an interest rate agreement include:

1. The reference rate.
2. The strike rate that sets the ceiling or floor.
3. The length of the agreement.
4. The frequency of settlement.
5. The notional principal amount.

Suppose that C buys an interest rate cap from D with terms as follows:

1. The reference rate is six-month LIBOR.
2. The strike rate is 8%.
3. The agreement is for seven years.
4. Settlement is every six months.
5. The notional principal amount is $20 million.

Under this agreement, every six months for the next seven years, D will pay C whenever six-month LIBOR exceeds 8%. The payment will equal the dollar value of the difference between six-month LIBOR and 8% times the notional principal amount divided by 2. For example, if six months from now six-month LIBOR is 11%, then D will pay C 3% (11% minus 8%) times $20 million divided by 2, or $300,000. If six-month LIBOR is 8% or less, D does not have to pay anything to C.

In the case of an interest rate floor, assume the same terms as the interest rate cap we just illustrated. In this case, if six-month LIBOR is 11%, C receives nothing from D, but if six-month LIBOR is less than 8%, D compensates C for the difference. For example, if six-month LIBOR is 7%, D will pay C $100,000 (8% minus 7% times $20 million divided by 2).

Interest rate caps and floors can be combined to create an interest rate collar. This is done by buying an interest rate cap and selling an interest rate floor. Some commercial banks and investment banking firms now write options on interest rate agreements for customers.

Risk/Return Characteristics

In an interest rate agreement, the buyer pays an upfront fee, which represents the maximum amount that the buyer can lose and the maximum amount that the writer of the agreement can gain. The only party that is required to perform is the writer of the interest rate agreement. The buyer of an interest rate cap benefits if the underlying interest rate rises above the strike rate because the seller (writer) must compensate the buyer. The buyer of an interest rate floor benefits if the interest rate falls below the strike rate, because the seller (writer) must compensate the buyer.

To better understand interest rate caps and interest rate floors, we can look at them as, in essence, equivalent to a package of options on interest rates. Since the buyer benefits if the interest rate rises above the strike rate, an interest rate cap is similar to purchasing a package of call options on the reference rate; the seller of an interest rate cap has effectively sold a package of put options. The buyer of an interest rate floor benefits from a decline in the interest rate below the strike rate. Therefore, the buyer of an interest rate floor has effectively bought a package of put options on the reference rate from the writer of the option. An interest rate collar is equivalent to buying a package of call options and selling a package of put options. Once again, a complex contract can be seen to be a package of basic contracts, or options in the case of interest rate agreements.

Applications

To see how interest rate agreements can be used for asset/liability management, consider the problems faced by the commercial bank and the life insurance company we discussed in demonstrating the use of an interest rate swap.[9]

Recall that the bank's objective is to lock in an interest rate spread over its cost of funds. Yet because it borrows short term, its cost of funds is uncertain. The bank may be able to purchase a cap, however, so that the cap rate plus the cost of purchasing the cap is less than the rate it is earning on its fixed-rate commercial loans. If short-term rates decline, the bank does not

---

[9]For additional applications in the insurance industry, see David F. Babbel, Peter Bouyoucos, and Robert Stricker, "Capping the Interest Rate Risk in Insurance Products," Chap. 21 in Frank J. Fabozzi (ed.), *Fixed Income Portfolio Strategies* (Chicago: Probus Publishing, 1989).

benefit from the cap, but its cost of funds declines. The cap therefore allows the bank to impose a ceiling on its cost of funds while retaining the opportunity to benefit from a decline in rates. This is consistent with the view of an interest rate cap as simply a package of options.

The bank can reduce the cost of purchasing the cap by selling a floor. In this case, the bank agrees to pay the buyer of the floor if the underlying rate falls below the strike rate. The bank receives a fee for selling the floor, but it has sold off its opportunity to benefit from a decline in rates below the strike rate. By buying a cap and selling a floor, the bank has created a predetermined range for its cost of funds (i.e., a collar).

Recall the problem of the life insurance company that guarantees a 9% rate on a GIC for the next five years and is considering the purchase of an attractive floating-rate instrument in a private-placement transaction. The risk that the company faces is that interest rates will fall so that it will not earn enough to realize the 9% guaranteed rate plus a spread. The life insurance company may be able to purchase a floor to set a lower bound on its investment return, yet retain the opportunity to benefit should rates increase. To reduce the cost of purchasing the floor, the life insurance company can sell an interest rate cap. By doing so, however, it gives up the opportunity of benefiting from an increase in the six-month LIBOR above the strike rate of the interest rate cap.

EQUITY CAPS AND FLOORS

An **equity cap** is an agreement in which one party, for an upfront premium, agrees to compensate the other at specific time periods if a designated stock market benchmark is greater than a predetermined level. An **equity floor** is an agreement in which one party agrees to pay the other at specific time periods if a specific stock market benchmark is less than a predetermined level. By buying an equity floor and selling an equity cap, a money manager can create an **equity collar**.

As with equity swaps, these are relatively new derivative contracts. As with interest rate caps and floors, these contracts are nothing more than packages of options and are therefore more transactionally efficient vehicles. They can be customized for any stock market benchmark, United States or foreign. However, they are less liquid than exchange-traded options.

■ SUMMARY

An interest rate swap is an agreement specifying that the parties exchange interest payments at designated times. In a typical swap, one party will make fixed-rate payments and the other will make floating-rate payments, with payments based on the notional principal amount. Participants in financial markets use interest rate swaps to alter the cash flow characteristics of their assets or liabilities and to capitalize on perceived capital market inefficiencies. A swap position can be interpreted as either a package of forward/futures contracts or a package of cash flows from buying and selling cash market instruments.

In an equity swap, the counterparties agree to exchange the return on some stock market index for an interest rate (either a fixed or floating rate). Equity swaps can be used to create an indexed portfolio to match some U.S. or non-U.S. stock market benchmark and, under certain circumstances, enhance a portfolio's return.

An interest rate agreement allows one party, for an upfront premium, the right to receive compensation from the writer of the agreement if a designated interest rate is different from a predetermined level. An interest rate cap calls for one party to receive a payment if a designated interest rate is above the predetermined level.

An interest rate floor lets one party receive a payment if a designated interest rate is below the predetermined level. An interest rate cap can be used to establish a ceiling on the cost of funding; an interest rate floor can be used to establish a floor return. Buying a cap and selling a floor creates a collar. Similarly, an equity cap and floor can be used to establish a ceiling or floor on any stock market benchmark.

■ KEY TERMS

asset swap	floating-rate payer	reference rate
call swaption	interest rate agreement	reset frequency
counterparties	interest rate cap	swap assignment
effective date	interest rate floor	swap buy-back
equity cap	interest rate swap	swap reversal
equity collar	liability swap	swap sale
equity floor	maturity date	swaptions
equity swap	notional principal amount	trade date
fixed-rate payer	put swaption	

■ QUESTIONS

1. Why can a fixed-rate payer in an interest rate swap be viewed as short the bond market and the floating-rate payer be viewed as long the bond market?

2. Why is an interest rate swap similar to a futures (or forward) contract?

3. How can the dollar duration of an interest rate swap be calculated?

4. Suppose that a life insurance company has issued a three-year GIC with a fixed rate of 10%. Under what circumstances might it be feasible for the life insurance company to invest the funds in a floating-rate security and enter into a three-year interest rate swap in which it pays a floating rate and receives a fixed rate?

5. The following excerpt is taken from an article entitled "IRS Rule to Open Swaps to Pension Funds," which appeared in the November 18, 1991, issue of *BondWeek*:

A proposed Internal Revenue Service rule that gives tax-free status to income earned on swaps by pension funds and other tax-exempt institutions is expected to spur pension fund use of these products, say swap and pension fund professionals. . . .

. . . UBS Asset Management has received permission from most of its pension fund clients to use interest rate and currency swaps in its fixed-income portfolios and is awaiting the IRS regulation before stepping into the market, says Kenneth Choie, v.p. and head of research and product development. . . "The IRS' proposed rule is great news for pension fund managers," as the use of swaps can enhance returns and lower transaction costs, Choie says. . . .

While some pension funds are exploring the swap market, pension fund consultants underscore that the funds' entrance into the market is likely to be slow. Counterparty risk has been a more formidable obstacle than the ambiguity of the tax status of income from interest rate and currency swaps, says Paul Burik, director of research at Ennis, Knupp & Associates, a pension fund consulting firm. (pp. 1, 2)

a. What is the status of the proposed IRS regulation?

b. In the article, Choie indicates that one "possible application that UBS is considering is to switch between fixed- and floating-rate income streams without incurring the transaction costs of trading chunks of securities." Explain how an interest rate swap can be used for this application.

c. What is meant by counterparty risk?

d. How can counterparty risk be reduced?

6. What is a swaption?

7. What is the relationship between an interest rate agreement and an option on an interest rate?

8. How can an interest rate collar be created?

9. a. What are the advantages of using an equity swap relative to stock index futures when constructing an indexed portfolio?

   b. What are the disadvantages?

10. Suppose that a swap dealer offers a money manager the following terms for a one-year equity swap with a quarterly reset frequency between the Nikkei 225 and LIBOR with all cash flows denominated in Japanese yen:

    Receive: Nikkei 225 return minus 15 basis points

    Pay: LIBOR

    a. What question would you ask the dealer concerning the swap terms?

    b. Why is it possible for a quarterly payment made by the money manager to be greater than LIBOR?

    c. Explain why the money manager is exposed to foreign exchange risk.

11. In recent years, a new fixed-income security has been created in which the coupon interest rate changes periodically in the opposite direction of some reference rate. This instrument is called an *inverse floater*. It is created by taking a fixed-rate bond and splitting its cash flows so as to create a floating-rate security and the corresponding inverse floating-rate security. The combined coupon payments on the floating-rate security and inverse floating-rate security always total to the coupon payment of the fixed-rate bond from which they are created.

    As an example, suppose that an issuer sells to a trust $80 million of a bond with a 9% coupon rate. The trust then creates two securities, a floating-rate security with a par value of $64 million and the following coupon rate that is reset semiannually:

    six-month LIBOR + 0.65%

and an inverse floating-rate security with a par value of $16 million and the following coupon rate that is reset semiannually:

42.4% − 4 × six-month LIBOR

a. Suppose that six-month LIBOR is 5% at a coupon payment date. What is the coupon rate for the floater and the inverse floater?

b. Show that if six-month LIBOR is 5% at a coupon payment date, the combined coupon payments to the floater and the inverse floater total to the coupon interest paid by the fixed- rate bond from which they were created.

c. Suppose that six-month LIBOR is 12% at a coupon payment date. What would the coupon rate of the inverse floater be if no restriction is imposed?

d. Based on your answer to part c, explain why a floor for the inverse floater is always established.

e. Show that if an interest rate floor of zero percent is set for the coupon rate on the inverse floater, then a maximum coupon rate of 11.25% must be set for the floater.

f. Explain why a position in an inverse floater can be viewed as being long a fixed-rate bond and short a floater (in which the reference rate on the floater is the same reference rate as the inverse floater).

g. Given your answer to part f, explain why the position of an investor who owns an inverse floater is as follows:

   Receive a fixed rate every six months

   Pay a floating rate every six months

h. Given your answer to part g, why is an inverse floater similar to a position in an interest rate swap?

i. Participants in the inverse floater market often state that one way they can determine if an inverse floater is fairly priced is by looking at the interest rate swap market and the interest rate cap market. From part h, the motivation for looking at the swap market can be understood. Why do market participants also look at the interest rate cap market in trying to assess if an inverse floater is fairly priced?

CHAPTER 28
ASSET ALLOCATION

LEARNING OBJECTIVES

After reading this chapter you will be able to:

- discuss the different types of asset allocation decisions.
- explain what policy asset allocation is.
- explain what dynamic asset allocation is.
- explain what tactical asset allocation is.
- outline the different types of tactical asset allocation strategies.
- describe the various types of asset allocation optimization models.
- explain the importance of considering liabilities in asset allocation optimization models.
- identify the advantages of using futures contracts to implement an asset allocation decision.

In the first chapter of this book, we described the steps in the investment management process. One of the major steps is the allocation of funds among major asset classes. It may seem strange that if the asset allocation process is so important, why we postponed coverage of this topic to the end of the book. The reason is that the asset allocation decision cannot be made without an understanding of the nature of the asset/liability problems faced by institutional investors, the investment characteristics of common stocks and fixed-income securities, and the use of futures contracts. All these topics were covered earlier in this book. Now we're ready to tackle the asset allocation decision.

The term "asset allocation" means different things to different people in different contexts. Asset allocation can loosely be divided into three categories: *policy* asset allocation, *dynamic* asset allocation, and *tactical* strategies for asset allocation. We discuss each in this chapter. We also discuss the various asset allocation optimization models and ways to implement an asset allocation using futures contracts.

POLICY ASSET ALLOCATION[1]

The **policy asset allocation** decision can loosely be characterized as a long-term asset allocation decision, in which the investor seeks to assess an appropriate long-term "normal" asset mix that represents an ideal blend of controlled risk and enhanced return. The strategies that offer the greatest prospects for strong long-term rewards tend to be inherently risky strategies. The strategies that offer the greatest safety tend to offer only modest return opportunities. The balancing of these conflicting goals is what we call *policy asset allocation.*

Even within this definition of policy asset allocation, there are many considerations that the investor must address. *What* risks and *what* rewards are to be contemplated in this evaluation? For the investor with a short investment horizon and a need to preserve capital such as a depository institution, the relevant definition of risk is very different from a long-horizon investor such as a pension fund or an endowment fund. Ironically, the lowest-risk strategy for a short-horizon investor may be a high-risk strategy for a long-horizon investor.

For many investors, more than one definition of risk may have a bearing on the policy asset allocation decision. In Chapter 4, one measure of risk we presented was the risk that the actual outcome will deviate from the expected outcome. In that chapter our focus was on returns. We can use risk in a more general sense here: It is the risk of falling short of any investment target. We can refer to this risk as **shortfall risk**. For example, as explained in Chapter 9, the pension sponsor needs to be concerned with volatility of assets, volatility of liabilities, volatility of the surplus, and volatility of earning per share, as well as a handful of other factors. But risk is not just volatility. Under FASB 87, the pension accounting requirements for U.S.–based corporations described in Chapter 9, the shortfall risk is the risk that inadequacy in performance of the fund's investment portfolio will lead to an unfunded liability reported in the balance sheet.

Box 28 is a list of questions that one investment advisor uses in working with pension fund clients to select a policy asset allocation.

In assessing the policy asset allocation, there is even a host of different tools at the investor's disposal. Should the investor use optimization techniques? Should optimization techniques with a shortfall constraint be the basis for the policy asset mix decision? How does the suitable policy mix shift with different investor circumstances? All of these are questions that can and must be addressed in assessing the policy asset allocation decision. We will describe such techniques later in this chapter.

DYNAMIC ASSET ALLOCATION

Some of the more intriguing and controversial strategies to emerge in recent years are described as **dynamic asset allocation**, in which the asset mix is mechanistically shifted in response to changing market conditions. The most well-publicized variant of these dynamic strategies would be *portfolio insurance,* which we described in Chapter 17. The objective of portfolio insurance

---

[1]This section and the two to follow are adapted from Robert D. Arnott and Frank J. Fabozzi, "The Many Dimensions of the Asset Allocation Decision," Chap. 1 in Robert D. Arnott and Frank J. Fabozzi (eds.), *Active Asset Allocation* (Chicago: Probus Publishing, 1992).

BOX 28

QUESTIONS PENSION SPONSORS SHOULD ASK WHEN ESTABLISHING
A POLICY ASSET ALLOCATION

I. How much exposure to illiquid or non-traditional assets is appropriate?
  A. Real estate.
  B. Venture capital.
  C. Non-U.S. stocks, bonds, real estate.
  D. Specialty categories:
    1. Limited partnerships.
    2. Energy partnerships.
    3. Timber leases.

II. How sensitive are we to funding ratio considerations?
  A. Avoiding the "four ills." Newly underfunded plans face:
    1. A new liability on the balance sheet.
    2. An earnings reduction due to a rise in pension expense.
    3. A cash flow cost due to sharply accelerated pension contributions.

    4. A cash flow cost due to increased PBGC insurance premiums.
  B. If well funded, how do we stay there?
    1. Reduce the volatility of funding ratios?
    2. Accept funding ratio volatility in the quest for high returns, thereby sustaining the funding ratios through strong returns.
    3. What is the risk to tolerance of my "customer" (likely the pension committee of the board)? Will my customer permit a long investment horizon or not?

III. What mixture of stocks, bonds, cash, global and illiquid assets offer the best long-term rewards, without exceeding our tolerance for risk?

Source: Robert D. Arnott, "Managing the Asset Mix," Chap. 4 in Robert D. Arnott and Frank J. Fabozzi (eds.), *Active Asset Allocation* (Chicago: Probus Publishing, 1992), p. 50.

Questions for Box 28

1. What is meant by a policy asset allocation?
2. Why is a pension fund concerned with the liquidity of non-traditional assets?
3. How is shortfall risk related to the sensitivity of funding ratio considerations?

---

is to construct and then rebalance a portfolio so as to create a floor (or minimum) return but to maintain the upside potential for the portfolio. Effectively, portfolio insurance replicates the risk/return profile of a synthetically created put option.

Dynamic strategies can be used for a host of purposes which go well beyond simple portfolio insurance, for all its potential merits or demerits. In essence, these dynamic strategies enable the money manager to reshape the entire return distribution. By dynamically shifting the asset mix, investors can control both downside risk and surplus volatility, can directly build a "shortfall constraint" into their strategy, and in essence can reshape the return distribution as they see fit. Dynamic strategies are notable for their mechanistic nature and for their potential impact on policy asset allocation. They are mechanistic in the sense that any action in the capital markets triggers a prescribed reaction in the portfolio of assets.

Dynamic strategies have an interesting implication for the policy asset allocation decision. If a dynamic strategy is employed, it can represent a long-term policy asset allocation *response* to changing market conditions. Many advocates of portfolio insurance have also been advocates of a more aggressive asset allocation stance, leaning more heavily toward equities in response to the protection offered by portfolio insurance. Other investment practitioners have argued for the opposite strategy: selling portfolio insurance. Such a process would involve boosting equity exposure after a decline and lowering it after a rally, thereby ostensibly providing a "built-in" policy response to changing market conditions. Such strategies clearly provide greatly increased flexibility in investment management and greatly improved control over the nature of the portfolio, *if the dynamic strategy can be implemented at a reasonable cost*. This last issue has been the focal point of much of the controversy regarding dynamic strategies in the wake of the October 1987 market crash.

TACTICAL ASSET ALLOCATION

Once the policy asset allocation has been established, the investor can turn attention to the possibility of active departures from the normal asset mix established by policy. That is, suppose that the long-run asset mix is established as 60% equities and 40% fixed income. A departure from this mix under certain circumstances may be permitted. If a decision to deviate from this mix is based upon rigorous objective measures of value, it is often called **tactical asset allocation** (**TAA**). Tactical asset allocation is not a single, clearly defined strategy. Many variations and nuances are involved in building a tactical allocation process.

One of the problems in reviewing the concepts of asset allocation is that the same terms are often used for different concepts. The term "dynamic asset allocation" has been used to refer to the long-term policy decision and to intermediate-term efforts to strategically position the portfolio to benefit from major market moves, as well as to refer to aggressive tactical strategies. Even the words "normal asset allocation" convey a stability that is not consistent with the real world. As an investor's risk expectations and tolerance for risk change, the normal or policy asset allocation may change. It is critical in exploring asset allocation issues to know what *element* of the asset allocation decision is the subject of discussion, and to know *in what context* the words "asset allocation" are being used. Figure 28-1 shows asset allocation terminology as we use it in this chapter.

Tactical asset allocation broadly refers to active strategies that seek to enhance performance by opportunistically shifting the asset mix of a portfolio in response to the changing patterns of reward available in the capital markets. Notably, tactical asset allocation tends to refer to disciplined processes for evaluating prospective rates of return on various asset classes and establishing an asset allocation response intended to capture higher rewards. In the various implementations of tactical asset allocation, there are different investment horizons and different mechanisms for evaluating the asset allocation decision. These merit a brief review.

Tactical asset allocation can refer to either an intermediate-term or a short-term process. Some tactical processes seek to measure the relative attractiveness of the major asset classes that participate in major movements in the stock or bond markets. Other approaches are more short-term in nature, designed to capture short-term movements in the markets. The shared attributes of these tactical asset allocation processes are several.

First, they tend to be objective processes, based on analytical tools, such as regression analysis or optimization, rather than relying on subjective judgment. Second, they tend to be driven primarily by objective measures of prospective values within an asset class. Investors *know* the yield on cash, in-

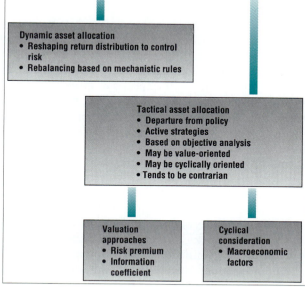

FIGURE 28-1
Asset allocation.

vestors *know* the yield to maturity on long bonds, and the earning yield on the stock market represents a reasonable and objective proxy for long-term rewards available in stocks. These objective measures of reward lead to an inherently value-oriented process.

Finally, tactical asset allocation processes tend to buy after a market decline and sell after a market rise. As such, they can be inherently contrary. By objectively measuring which asset classes are offering the greatest prospective rewards, tactical asset allocation disciplines measure which asset classes are most out of favor. In so doing, they steer investments into unloved asset classes. These assets are priced to reflect the fact that they are out of favor and the corresponding fact that investors demand a premium reward for an out-of-favor investment. Therein lies the effectiveness of tactical asset allocation disciplines.

Thus, the key distinction in shifting the mix of a portfolio using tactical asset allocation and dynamic asset allocation is as follows. Tactical asset allocation seeks to enhance return by allocating funds to asset classes that are expected based on some objective measures to outperform other asset classes. The risk posture of the portfolio may change significantly in expectation of the better return possible from the shift in funds. With dynamic asset allocation, the key is risk control. Funds are shifted in attempting to control the risk that there may be a shortfall. For both asset allocation strategies, when and how much to shift funds to the various asset classes is determined by a specified set of rules.

It has been estimated that as of early 1991, over $42 billion was under management in which tactical asset allocation strategies were pursued.[2]

Approaches to Tactical Asset Allocation

Tactical asset allocation disciplines cover a wide spectrum. Some are simple, objective comparisons of available rates of return. Others seek to enhance the timeliness of these value-driven decisions by incorporating macroeconomic measures, sentiment measures, volatility measures, and even technical measures. In essence, the users of these more elaborate approaches would argue that, just as an undervalued stock can get more undervalued, so too an undervalued asset class can grow more undervalued. The investor who buys an asset as soon as it becomes undervalued does less well than the investor who buys that same asset class shortly before it finally rebounds.

In general, tactical asset allocation models can be divided into three groups: (1) valuation approaches, (2) cyclical considerations, and (3) a combination of the first two.[3]

Valuation Approaches   In general, asset classes that are identified as expensive should be sold and those identified as cheap should be purchased. The trick is in identifying when an asset class is expensive or cheap. The valuation approach seeks to identify the relative value of an asset class.

The most common valuation approach is the **risk premium approach**, or *spread approach*. Basically, if the expected return on equities relative to bonds is above average, an above-average allocation is made to equities; however, if the expected return on equities relative to bonds is below average, a below-average allocation is made to equities. There are several approaches for determining the expected return for each asset class. For bonds, the expected return is fairly straightforward: It is the yield to maturity for long-term Treasury bonds. For cash equivalents, it is the yield on short-term Treasury bills. For equities, forecasting the expected return is much more complicated. It involves determining the equity market discount rate, or, equivalently, the cost of capital. There are a variety of techniques for doing this.

The risk premiums used to determine the relative attractiveness of an asset allocation are (1) stock/bills risk premium (expected return for equities minus expected return for Treasury bills), (2) bonds/bills risk premium (expected return for bonds minus expected return for Treasury bills), and (3) stocks/bonds risk premium (expected return for equities minus expected return for bonds).

Table 28-1, for example, shows for the years 1951 to 1989 the historical results of the stocks/bills risk premium for forecasting the returns of stocks versus bills in subsequent periods. The premium range is shown in the first column, and the number of months in which a risk premium occurred within the range is shown in the second column. For example, there were 96 months in this time period in which the risk premium was between 2% and 3.9%

---

[2]Eric J. Weigel, "The Performance of Tactical Asset Allocation," *Financial Analysts Journal* (September/October 1991), p. 63.

[3]For a detailed description of these approaches, see Charles H. DuBois, "Tactical Asset Allocation: A Review of the Current Techniques," Chap. 12 in Arnott and Fabozzi (eds.), op cit.

		Average Subsequent Excess Return			Probability of Positive Excess Return		
Premium Range	**# Mo. Obs.**	**1 mo.**	**3 mo.**	**12 mo.**	**1 mo.**	**3 mo.**	**12mo.**
> 10	10	2.5%	6.8%	26.1%	80%	80%	100%
8–9.9	64	1.9	4.8	16.7	66	78	89
6–7.9	102	0.5	2.0	6.1	57	63	63
5–5.9	64	0.7	1.6	4.8	61	70	67
4–4.9	107	0.4	1.8	2.7	60	64	62
2–3.9	96	(0.1)	(1.4)	2.8	48	42	60
< 2	25	(1.8)	(1.7)	(6.9)	32	36	40
	468	0.5	1.5	5.7	57	61	66

TABLE 28-1

STOCKS/BILLS PREMIUM* AND SUBSEQUENT PERFORMANCE OF STOCKS VERSUS BILLS, 1951–1989

*Long-term expected equity return minus 3-month T-bill yield.

Source: Charles H. DuBois, "Tactical Asset Allocation: A Review of the Current Techniques," Chap. 12 in Robert D. Arnott and Frank J. Fabozzi (eds.), *Active Asset Allocation* (Chicago: Probus Publishing, 1992), Exhibit 1, p. 244.

(i.e., 200 to 390 basis points). The next three columns show the average excess return over three time horizons: 1 month, 3 months, and 1 year. The average excess return is the difference between the actual return on equities and the Treasury bill. The last three columns report the percentage of observations within a premium range that were followed by positive excess returns for the corresponding time horizons.

Look at the first premium range, risk premiums in excess of 10%. The table indicates that in the 10 months in which this risk premium is observed, the one-year average excess return was 26.1% and this occurred in every month. Overall, the results suggest there are meaningful differences associated with the actual excess return in one month and the risk premium in prior months using these simple measures. In practice, other measures are used, such as the information coefficient that we described in Chapter 12.

Cyclical Considerations   This approach is premised on the view that cycles in stock prices and bond yields are closely tied together in very important ways because of macroeconomic factors. For example, movements in the stock market typically precede changes in economic activity. Identifying one or more components of general economic activity that have been historically observed to be a predicator or leading indicator of stock market movements is what is sought by followers of this approach. Typically, this approach can be used to construct cyclical equity indexes and cyclical bond indexes using historical data.

Empirical Evidence

As with dynamic asset allocation, there is considerable debate over whether tactical asset allocation can enhance risk-adjusted returns after transactions costs.

First is the issue of whether stock and bond market returns can be predicted. The empirical evidence suggests that stock and bond returns are predictable over long investment horizons.[4] For shorter time intervals, market returns also appear to be predictable, but at more modest levels.[5]

What has been the actual performance of those following some type of tactical asset allocation strategy? One study examines this issue by looking at the actual and simulated performance of a sample of 17 U.S. money managers who follow tactical asset allocation strategies. The time period investigated was 1980 to 1989.[6] The author of this study, Eric Weigel of Frank Russell Company, found that these money managers displayed market-timing skill over the sample period. Whether there will be opportunities in the future as more practitioners enter the market armed with the strategies that have been documented to be successful in the past remains to be seen.

ASSET ALLOCATION OPTIMIZATION MODELS[7]

In this section we describe several asset allocation models. The basic principles of these models is Markowitz portfolio theory, which we described in Chapter 4. In that chapter we explained portfolio theory in terms of individual securities. In asset allocation, rather than dealing with individual securities, the analysis is cast in terms of asset classes. As we will explain, the basic Markowitz model has been embellished in several ways to provide investors with information about the risks associated with achieving a specified return and to allow for short-term/long-term asset allocations.

All the asset allocation models described in this section are solved by a technique called **mathematical programming**. This is an operations research technique that solves problems in which an optimal value is sought subject to specified constraints. There are many types of mathematical programming models: linear programming, quadratic programming, and dynamic programming. The particular mathematical programming technique used is determined by the nature of the problem. We are not concerned here with mathematical programming techniques and how they are solved. Rather, our focus is on the asset allocation models themselves.

Basic Inputs

The basic inputs for the asset allocation models we will discuss are the expected returns, expected cash yields, risk estimates, and correlations (or covariances) for each asset class included in the analysis. The appropriate

---

[4]See the following three papers by Eugene F. Fama and Kenneth R. French: "Permanent and Transitory Components of Stock Prices," *Journal of Political Economy* (1987), pp. 246–273; "Dividend Yields and Expected Stock Returns," *Journal of Financial Economics* (1988), pp. 3–25, and "Business Conditions and Expected Returns on Stocks and Bonds," *Journal of Financial Economics* (1989), pp. 27–59.

[5]See, for example; Robert D. Arnott and James N. von Germeten, "Systematic Asset Allocation," *Financial Analysts Journal* (November/December 1983), pp. 31–38; Donald B. Keim and Robert F. Stambaugh, "Predicting Returns in the Stock and Bond Markets," *Journal of Financial Economics*, 17 (1986), pp. 357–390; William Breen, Lawrence R. Glosten, and Ravi Jagannathan, "Economic Significance of Predictable Variations in Stock Index Returns," *Journal of Finance* (December 1989), pp. 1177–1190.

[6]Weigel, op. cit.

[7]The material in this section is adapted from H. Gifford Fong and Frank J. Fabozzi, "Asset Allocation Optimization Models," Chap. 8 in Arnott and Fabozzi (eds.), op. cit.

<table>
<tr><td colspan="4">**TABLE 28-2**</td></tr>
<tr><td colspan="4">**EXPECTATIONAL INPUTS FOR TWO ASSET CLASSES**</td></tr>
<tr><td>**Asset Class**</td><td>**Expected Return**</td><td>**Variance**</td><td>**Standard Deviation**</td></tr>
<tr><td>Stocks</td><td>0.13</td><td>0.0342</td><td>0.185</td></tr>
<tr><td>Bonds</td><td>0.08</td><td>0.0036</td><td>0.060</td></tr>
<tr><td colspan="4">Correlation between stocks and bonds = 0.20</td></tr>
</table>

source for these inputs is the money manager, since he or she is most directly concerned with these factors on a day-to-day basis. Additional insights can be achieved by using historical estimates, either from a lengthy past period or from more recent experience. The objective is to use the proxy that will best represent the future horizon of interest. Typically, a money manager will use his or her own return expectation in conjunction with historical risk measures based on the variance and covariance from a historical series.

Two-Asset Class Allocation Model

To introduce the basic principles of an asset allocation optimization model, we begin with only two asset classes, stocks and bonds. Table 28-2 summarizes the expectational inputs (expected return, variance, standard deviation, and correlation of returns).

As explained in Chapter 4, when the two assets are combined to form a portfolio, the expected return for the portfolio is simply the weighted average of the expected return for the two asset classes. The weight for each asset class is equal to the dollar value of the asset class as a percent of the dollar value of the portfolio. The sum of the two weights, of course, must equal 1. Unlike the portfolio's expected return, the portfolio's variance (standard deviation) is not simply a weighted average of the variance (standard deviation) of the two asset classes. Instead, the portfolio variance depends on the correlation (covariance) between the two asset classes.

The portfolio expected return, variance, and standard deviation for different allocations of funds between the two asset classes using the input in Table 28-2 and the formulas in Chapter 4 are shown in tabular form in Table 28-3. Figure 28-2 graphically portrays the portfolio expected return and standard deviation presented in Table 28-3. With respect to Figure 28-2, the following should be noted:

1. Every point on XYZ denotes a portfolio consisting of a specific allocation of funds between stocks and bonds. Not all of the portfolios are shown in Table 28-3. We filled in the gaps when we plotted the results.
2. XYZ represents all possible portfolios consisting of these two asset classes. XYZ is therefore the feasible set.[8]
3. It would never be beneficial for an investor to allocate funds between stocks and bonds to produce a portfolio on that portion of XYZ between Y and Z (excluding portfolio Y).[9] The reason is that for every portfolio on segment

---

[8]The portfolios on XYZ include portfolios in which there is short selling of either asset class.

[9]The portfolio represented by point Y is the minimum variance that can be obtained by holding these two asset classes in any combination.

TABLE 28-3

PORTFOLIO EXPECTED RETURN, VARIANCE, AND STANDARD DEVIATION FOR DIFFERENT ALLOCATIONS OF FUNDS BETWEEN STOCKS AND BONDS

Allocation		Expected Return	Variance	Standard Deviation
W_1	W_2	$E(R_p)$	$Var(R_p)$	$Std(R_p)$
0.0	1.0	0.080	0.0036000	0.0600000
0.1	0.9	0.085	0.0036570	0.0604769
0.2	0.8	0.090	0.0043820	0.0661978
0.3	0.7	0.095	0.0057740	0.0759872
0.4	0.6	0.100	0.0078330	0.0885054
0.5	0.5	0.105	0.0105596	0.1027600
0.6	0.4	0.110	0.0139532	0.1181240
0.7	0.3	0.115	0.0180141	0.1342160
0.8	0.2	0.120	0.0227421	0.1508050
0.9	0.1	0.125	0.0281375	0.1677420
1.0	0.0	0.130	0.0342000	0.1849320

*Asset class 1 = stocks

Asset class 2 = bonds.

See Table 28-2 for the expectational inputs for these two asset classes.

YZ there is a portfolio that dominates it on the XY segment of the feasible set. That is, for a given portfolio standard deviation (risk level), an investor can realize a higher portfolio expected return. This can be seen on Figure 28-2 by examining portfolios A and A'. These portfolios have the same portfolio standard deviation; however, the expected return for portfolio A is higher than for portfolio A'. Consequently, all portfolios on XY of the feasible set dominate the portfolios on YZ of the feasible set. XY is therefore the Markowitz efficient set or efficient frontier. A portfolio on the efficient set is said to be an efficient portfolio.

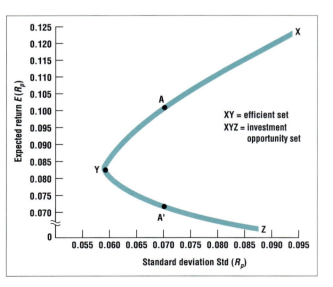

FIGURE 28-2

Feasible set and efficient set for two asset classes (stocks and bonds).

The efficient set indicates the expected trade-off between return and risk (standard deviation) faced by the investor. Just which portfolio in the efficient set the investor selects depends on the investor's preference.

To see the impact of the correlation of the two assets on the efficient set, Figure 28-3 shows the efficient set for each different assumed correlation between the returns on stocks and bonds. As can be seen, the lower the correlation of returns, the better off the investor. That is, for a given set of expected returns and standard deviations for the two asset classes, the investor will be exposed to a lower level of risk (standard deviation) for a given portfolio if the correlation of returns is lower. Notice that if the correlation is 1, the efficient set is a straight line and the portfolio standard deviation is therefore a weighted average of the standard deviations of the two asset classes.

Asset Allocation Model for More Than Two Asset Classes

The principles we have discussed for the efficient set for the two-asset class allocation model can easily be extended to the general case of N-asset classes using the formulas for a portfolio given in Chapter 4.

Graphically, the efficient set of portfolios in the N-asset class case can be portrayed in the same manner as in the two-asset class case. Figure 28-4 shows all possible portfolios for the N-asset class case. This figure is analogous to Figure 28-2. The difference is that the feasible set in the two-asset class case does not include points (portfolios) in the interior of XYZ. In the N-asset class case, interior points are also feasible portfolios. However, as in the two-asset class case, the portfolios represented by the segment XY dominate portfolios in the interior of the feasible set.

Although the efficient set for the simple two-asset class case can be easily determined, the computation of the efficient set when funds are to be allocated to more than two asset classes becomes more difficult. Fortunately, the efficient set of the N-asset class problem can be solved using a mathematical programming technique called quadratic programming. This algorithm can

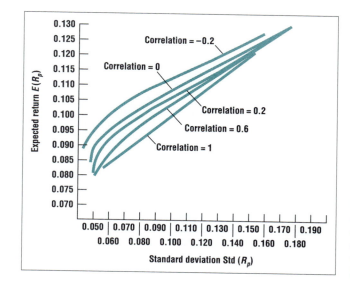

FIGURE 28-3

Comparison of efficient set for different correlations between two asset classes (stocks and bonds).

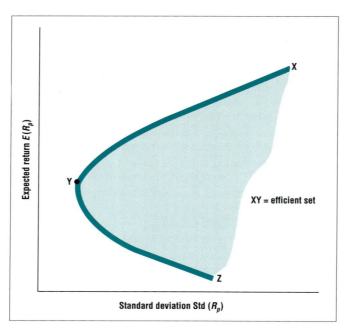

FIGURE 28-4

Feasible set and efficient set in an *N*-asset class portfolio case.

also accommodate other constraints that might be imposed, such as limitations on the concentration of funds in a given asset class.

Let us now illustrate the three-asset class allocation model. Assume that an investor wishes to allocate available investment funds among the following three asset classes: stocks, bonds, and Treasury bills. Table 28-4 presents the annual expected return, expected cash yield, variance, standard deviation, and correlations for the three asset classes for two scenarios. The expected cash yield component of the expected return is the amount of the return at-

TABLE 28-4				
EXPECTATIONAL INPUTS FOR THREE ASSET CLASSES FOR TWO SCENARIOS				
Asset Class	**Expected Return**	**Expected Cash Yield**	**Variance**	**Standard Deviation**
Scenario 1:				
Stock	0.13	0.05	0.034200	0.185
Bonds	0.08	0.08	0.003600	0.060
Treasury bills	0.06	0.06	0.000016	0.004
Scenario 2:				
Stock	0.15	0.05	0.034200	0.185
Bonds	0.08	0.08	0.003600	0.060
Treasury bills	0.05	0.05	0.000016	0.004

	Correlations for both Scenarios		
	Stocks	**Bonds**	**Treasury Bills**
Stocks	1.00	0.20	−0.15
Bonds	0.20	1.00	−0.12
Treasury bills	−0.15	−0.12	1.00

tributable to dividends in the case of stocks and to interest payments in the case of bonds. The difference between the expected return and the expected cash yield is therefore the return attributable to capital appreciation.

The efficient set can be determined using quadratic programming. The results for scenario 1, assuming a one-year horizon and no constraints, are shown in Table 28-5, while the results for scenario 2 are shown in Table 28-6. For each identified level of portfolio expected return, the corresponding standard deviation, yield component of total return, and minimum risk concentrations (weights) of each class are shown on both tables. The columns under the heading "Probability of Annual Return of Less Than" will be explained shortly.

To make sure you understand the two tables, let's interpret one of the results. For scenario 1, the minimum risk (standard deviation) that the investor will be exposed to if he or she seeks a 9% return for the 12-month period is 6.552%. No other allocation produces a 9% return with a standard deviation less than 6.552%. The asset mix associated with this efficient or optimal portfolio is 24.8% in stocks, 64.2% in bonds, and 10.9% in Treasury bills. (The total does not equal 100% because of rounding.) The annual expected return of 9% will have an expected cash yield of 7.04%. Therefore, 1.96% of the total annual expected return will be attributable to capital appreciation.

Extension of the Asset Allocation Model to Risk-of-Loss

In the portfolio risk minimization process, the variance (standard deviation) of returns was the proxy measure for portfolio risk. As a supplement, the probability of not achieving a portfolio expected return can be calculated. This type of analysis would be useful in determining the most appropriate mix from the set of optimal portfolio allocations.

TABLE 28-5									
OPTIMAL ASSET ALLOCATION FOR SCENARIO 1: SAMPLE PORTFOLIOS IN THE EFFICIENT SET (12-MONTH HORIZON)									
Annual Expected Return	Annual Standard Deviation	Annual Expected Cash Yield	*Probability of Annual Return of Less Than*				*Minimum Risk Asset Mix*		
			0.0%	5.0%	7.0%	10.0%	Stocks	Bonds	T-Bills
6.00%	0.400%	6.00%	0.9%	0.9%	99.1%	100.00%	0.0%	0.0%	100.0%
6.04	0.389	6.02	0.0	0.5	99.0	100.0	0.3	1.0	98.7
6.50	1.097	6.18	0.0	9.7	66.7	99.8	4.1	10.9	84.9
7.00	2.174	6.35	0.1	19.2	50.0	90.0	8.3	21.7	70.0
7.50	3.271	6.52	1.3	23.5	44.3	76.0	12.5	32.4	55.1
8.00	4.368	6.70	3.8	25.8	41.5	66.4	16.6	43.1	40.3
8.50	5.462	6.84	6.6	27.3	39.9	60.0	20.7	53.7	25.6
9.00	6.552	7.04	9.3	28.3	38.8	55.6	24.8	64.2	10.9
9.50	7.649	7.09	11.6	29.0	38.1	52.4	30.4	69.6	0.0
10.00	8.918	6.79	14.1	30.0	37.7	50.0	40.5	59.5	0.0
10.50	10.356	6.48	16.5	31.0	37.7	48.2	50.5	49.5	0.0
11.00	11.895	6.19	18.8	31.9	37.8	46.9	60.5	39.5	0.0
11.50	13.497	5.89	20.8	32.7	37.9	46.0	70.4	29.6	0.0
12.00	15.142	5.59	22.5	33.3	38.0	45.2	80.3	19.7	0.0
12.50	16.813	5.29	24.0	33.9	38.2	44.6	90.2	9.8	0.0
13.00	18.500	5.00	25.2	34.4	38.3	44.2	100.0	0.0	0.0

				TABLE 28-6						
			OPTIMAL ASSET ALLOCATION FOR SCENARIO 2: SAMPLE PORTFOLIOS IN THE EFFICIENT SET (12-MONTH HORIZON)							
Annual Expected Return	**Annual Standard Deviation**	**Annual Cash Yield**	*Probability of Annual Return of Less Than*				*Minimum Risk Asset Mix*			
			0.0%	**5.0%**	**7.0%**	**10.0%**	**Stocks**	**Bonds**	**T-Bills**	
5.00%	0.400%	5.00%	0.0%	50.1%	100.0%	100.0%	0.0%	0.0%	100.0%	
5.06	0.389	5.03	0.0	44.3	100.0	100.0	0.3	1.0	98.7	
5.50	0.784	5.24	0.0	27.2	96.5	100.0	2.8	7.9	89.3	
6.00	1.501	5.47	0.0	26.3	73.5	99.3	5.5	15.7	78.7	
6.50	2.248	5.70	0.2	26.3	58.3	92.6	8.3	23.5	68.2	
7.00	3.003	5.94	1.2	26.4	50.0	82.3	11.0	31.2	57.7	
7.50	3.757	6.17	2.6	26.4	45.0	73.1	13.8	38.9	47.3	
8.00	4.509	6.40	4.3	26.5	41.8	65.9	16.5	46.6	36.9	
8.50	5.258	6.63	5.9	26.5	39.5	60.4	19.2	54.2	26.6	
9.00	6.005	6.85	7.4	26.5	37.8	56.1	21.9	61.8	16.3	
9.50	6.750	7.08	8.8	26.6	36.5	52.7	24.6	69.4	6.0	
10.00	7.505	7.13	10.0	26.6	35.5	50.0	29.1	70.9	0.0	
10.50	8.374	6.91	11.5	26.9	34.9	47.8	36.4	63.6	0.0	
11.00	9.345	6.69	13.0	27.4	34.6	46.1	43.6	56.4	0.0	
11.50	10.386	6.48	14.5	28.0	34.4	44.8	50.7	49.3	0.0	
12.00	11.478	6.26	15.9	28.5	34.4	43.7	57.8	42.2	0.0	
12.50	12.605	6.05	17.3	29.0	34.4	42.9	64.9	35.1	0.0	
13.00	13.756	5.84	18.5	29.5	34.4	42.2	72.0	28.0	0.0	
13.50	14.927	5.63	19.6	29.9	34.5	41.6	79.1	29.9	0.0	
14.00	16.109	5.42	20.5	30.3	34.5	41.1	86.1	13.9	0.0	
14.50	17.302	5.21	21.4	30.6	34.6	40.7	93.0	7.0	0.0	
15.00	18.500	5.00	22.2	30.9	34.7	40.4	100.0	0.0	0.0	

We refer to this analysis as the *risk of loss*. A technical description of the analysis is beyond the scope of this chapter.[10] The columns under the heading "Probability of Annual Return Less Than" in Tables 28-5 and Tables 28-6 show the results of the risk-of-loss analysis for four annual levels. The interpretation of the results for the 9% expected return for scenario 1 (Table 28-5) is as follows: There is a 9.3% probability that the annual return will be negative, a 28.3% probability that the annual return will be less than 5%, a 38.8% probability that the annual return will be less than 7%, and a 55.6% probability that the annual return will be less than 10%.

In the context of setting investment strategy for a pension fund that has a long-term normal asset allocation policy established, the value of the probability of loss for the desired return benchmark over the long-term horizon can be used as the maximum value for the short term. For example, if the long-term policy has a 15% probability of loss for 0% return, the mix may be changed over the short run, as long as the probability of loss of the new mix has a maximum of 15%. Therefore, by taking advantage of short-term expectations to maximize return, the integrity of the long-term policy is retained.

A floor, or **base probability of loss**, is therefore established that can provide boundaries within which strategic return/risk decisions may be made. As long as the alteration of the asset allocation mix does not violate the probability of loss, increased return through strategies such as tactical asset allocation can be pursued.

---

[10] This is provided in Appendix A to Fong and Fabozzi, op.cit., pp. 156–159.

Extension of the Asset Allocation Model to Multiple Scenarios

The asset allocation model described above can be extended to multiple possible scenarios. Each assumed scenario is believed to be an assessment of the asset performance in the long run, over the investment horizon. If a probability can be assigned to each scenario, an efficient set can be constructed for the composite scenario. The procedure for computing the optimal asset allocation when there are multiple scenarios which are discrete or mutually exclusive and each scenario can be assigned a probability of occurrence is beyond the scope of this chapter.[11]

Asset Allocation Optimization Models with Liabilities Considered

Other asset allocation optimization models have been developed by Martin Leibowitz and his colleagues at Salomon Brothers Inc.[12] The models have been applied to the assets and liabilities of various financial institutions. One of the advantages of their model is that it incorporates liabilities. That is, it is the return distribution of not only the assets classes that must be considered in an optimization model, but also the liabilities.

As an example, consider a pension fund. The plan sponsor is concerned with the performance of the assets and maintenance of acceptable levels of downside risk as measured by the standard deviation. But this is not the only concern of the plan sponsor. The other concern is the performance of the fund's surplus (i.e., the difference between the market value of the assets and the present value of the liabilities) and the maintenance of acceptance levels of downside risk for the surplus. By considering the surplus as specified by FASB 87—and hence the liabilities—a better asset allocation can be achieved than in models that simply consider assets.

Leibowitz and his colleagues have developed an asset allocation model for pension funds that strikes a balance between asset performance and the maintenance of acceptable levels of its downside risk and between surplus performance and the maintenance of acceptable levels of its downside risk. This model has also been applied to the asset allocation problem faced by property and casualty insurance companies.[13] Consideration is given to statutory surplus that we explained in Chapter 8.

Another important point made by Leibowitz is that those involved in the asset allocation decision should not lump together all fixed-income securities into one asset class. Rather, within an asset/liability framework, there is a continuum of fixed-income instruments each with a different duration. Since, as we noted in Chapter 7, liabilities are often interest rate sensitive and therefore have a duration, the variety of durations of bonds is hidden by lumping them into one asset class. Asset allocation models that consider liabilities and a continuum of fixed-income instruments along the yield curve will be superior to those in which only assets are considered and in which all fixed-income securities are lumped together as one asset class.

---

[11]For a description of not only this extension but other extensions with multiple possible scenarios in which there are short-term and long-term expectations, see Fong and Fabozzi, ibid.

[12]Martin L. Leibowitz, Stanley Kogelman, and Lawrence N. Bader, "Asset Performance and Surplus Control—A Dual-Shortfall Approach," Chap. 9 in Arnott and Fabozzi (eds.), op. cit.

[13]Alfred Weinberger, *Allocation for Property/Casualty Insurance Companies: A Going Concern Approach* (Salomon Brothers Inc, New York, July 1991).

TABLE 28-7

USING FINANCIAL FUTURES INSTEAD OF ASSET PURCHASES AND SALES TO IMPLEMENT ASSET ALLOCATION

Advantages	Disadvantage
Lower transactions costs	Possible mispricing of futures
Faster execution	
Reduced market impact costs	
No disruption of money managers	

USING DERIVATIVE PRODUCTS TO IMPLEMENT AN ASSET ALLOCATION DECISION

The product of an asset allocation decision is the asset mix. This will necessitate the shifting of funds among the asset classes. Funds can be shifted in one of two ways. The most obvious is by buying or selling the amount specified in the asset mix in the cash market. The costs associated with shifting funds in this manner are the transactions costs with respect to commissions, bid-ask spreads, and market impact. Moreover, there will be a disruption of the activities of the money managers who are managing funds for each asset class. For example, a pension sponsor typically engages certain money managers for managing equity funds and different ones for managing bond funds. An asset allocation decision requiring the reallocation of funds will necessitate the withdrawal of funds from some managers and the placement of funds with others. If the shift is temporary as a result of a tactical asset allocation decision, there will be a subsequent revision of the asset allocation, further disrupting the activities of money managers.

An alternative approach is to use the futures market to change an exposure to an asset class. As we explained in Chapter 16 where we described stock index futures and Chapter 26 where we described interest rate futures, buying futures contracts increases exposure to the asset class underlying the futures contract, while selling futures contracts reduces it.

As Table 28-7 shows, the advantages of using financial futures contracts are (1) transactions costs are lower, (2) execution is faster in the futures market, (3) market impact costs are avoided or reduced as the sponsor has more time to buy and sell securities in the cash market, and (4) activities of the money managers employed by the pension sponsor are not disrupted. A strategy of using futures for asset allocation by pension sponsors to avoid disrupting the activities of money managers is sometimes referred to as an **overlay strategy**. Futures contracts involving the stock indexes and interest rates of non-U.S. markets have been particularly useful for U.S. portfolio managers investing in these markets.

The major disadvantage of using futures contracts is that the futures contract may be mispriced; more specifically, the futures contract of the asset class that is being purchased may be too expensive relative to its fair value, and/or the futures contract of the asset class that is being sold is too cheap relative to its fair value.

SUMMARY

There are several dimensions to the asset allocation decision. Policy asset allocation can loosely be characterized as a long-term asset allocation decision, in which the investor seeks to assess an appropriate long-term "normal" asset mix that represents an ideal blend of controlled risk and enhanced return. Dynamic asset allocation strategies involve shifting the asset mix mechanistically in response to changing market conditions so as to reshape the return distribution (i.e., control risk). Portfolio insurance is the most publicized strategy in this category. Tactical asset allocation broadly refers to active strategies that seek to enhance performance by opportunistically shifting the asset mix of a portfolio in response to the changing patterns of reward available in the capital markets.

Asset allocation optimization models are based on the Markowitz portfolio framework, replacing individual assets with asset classes.

The basic Markowitz model has been embellished to provide investors with information about the risks associated with achieving a specified expected return. Other models allow for multiple scenarios. The basic inputs for all these models are the expected returns, expected cash yields, risk estimates, and correlations (or covariances) for each asset class included in the analysis. Optimization models should consider not only asset distributions, but also the distribution of liabilities.

The actual implementation of an asset allocation decision can be done in either the cash market or the futures market. The advantages of using futures rather the cash market are the lower transaction costs, the speed of execution, and the avoidance of disruption of existing money managers. The disadvantage is that the futures contract may be mispriced such that it will reduce the return on the portfolio compared with transacting in the cash position.

KEY TERMS

base probability of loss
dynamic asset allocation
mathematical programming

overlay strategy
policy asset allocation
risk premium approach

shortfall risk
tactical asset allocation (TAA)

QUESTIONS

1. Why is the reference to an "asset allocation decision" ambiguous?

2. Distinguish between a policy asset allocation and a dynamic asset allocation.

3. What is meant by a shortfall?

4. In a paper entitled "Global Asset Allocation" by Robert Arnott and Roy Henriksson [Chapter 15 in Robert D. Arnott and Frank J. Fabozzi (eds.) *Active Asset Allocation* (Chicago: Probus Publishing, 1992)], the authors state: "In a Stage I asset allocation model, one assumes that objective measures of prospective relative return (or value) are positively correlated with subsequent actual relative returns. . . . In essence, a Stage I model assumes that there is an equilibrating mechanism between asset classes, whereby unusual market conditions give rise to unusual subsequent relative performance" (p. 339). What type of asset allocation are the authors referring to and why?

5. What is the controversy surrounding tactical asset allocation?

6. In "Tactical Asset Allocation: A Review of Current Techniques," Chapter 12 in *Active Asset Allocation*, Charles DuBois writes:

One of the principal historical drawbacks of TAA was the cost of transacting, particularly as asset size increased. Costs included. . . . About 15–40% of the historical value-added of the more active TAA strategies could have been lost as a consequence of the transaction costs associated with trading in the traditional stock and bond markets.

Today, however, costs have been reduced in a number of ways. The list includes lower commissions, the use of index funds, and most significantly, the availability of high volume futures markets for both stocks and bonds. Currently transaction costs of TAA implementations appear to be less than a tenth of those that existed, say, 10 years ago. Hence, a significant impediment to the viability of TAA strategies has been largely eliminated for today's TAA managers. (p. 234)

    a. Why are transaction costs important in the implementation of a TAA strategy?

    b. What are transaction costs?

    c. How does the existence of futures markets improve the likelihood that a tactical asset allocation strategy will add value?

7. What is an overlay strategy, and what is the advantage of using this strategy for pension sponsors?

8. a. In a tactical asset allocation strategy, what is meant by a valuation-oriented approach?

    b. What is meant by a risk premium, and which risk premiums are estimated by a money manager who is a tactical asset allocator?

9. a. What is meant by risk-of-loss analysis?

    b. Explain one way in which risk-of-loss analysis can be used by a pension fund sponsor.

10. What is the limitation of an asset-only asset allocation model?

11. Why is it useful in an asset allocation model not to lump all fixed-income securities into one asset class?

CHAPTER 29
MEASURING PERFORMANCE

LEARNING OBJECTIVES

After reading this chapter you will be able to:

- explain the difference between performance measurement and performance evaluation.

- describe the various methods for calculating the rate of return over some evaluation period: the arithmetic average rate of return, the time-weighted rate of return, and the dollar-weighted rate of return.

- explain the impact of client contributions and withdrawals on the calculated return.

- identify the method of calculating returns that minimizes the effect of client contributions and withdrawals.

- explain the objectives of the Association for Investment Management and Research's Performance Presentation Standards, the key requirements and mandatory disclosures to be in compliance with the standards, and some key guidelines and disclosures recommended in the standards.

In this chapter and the next, we will see how to evaluate the investment performance of a money manager. In doing so, we must distinguish between performance measurement and performance evaluation. **Performance measurement** involves the calculation of the return realized by a money manager over some time interval which we call the **evaluation period**. As we will see, several important issues must be addressed in developing a methodology for calculating a portfolio's return. Because different methodologies are available and these methodologies can lead to quite disparate results, it is difficult to compare the performances of money managers. Consequently, there is a great deal of confusion concerning the meaning of the data provided by money managers to their clients and their prospective clients. This has led to abuses by some managers in reporting performance results that are better than actual performance. To mitigate this problem the Committee for Performance Standards of the Association for Investment Management and Research has established standards both for calculating performance results and for presenting those results.

Performance evaluation is concerned with two issues: (1) determining whether the money manager added value by outperforming the established benchmark and (2) determining how the money manager achieved the calculated return. For example, as explained in Chapter 15, there are several strategies an equity money manager can employ. Did the money manager achieve the return by market timing, by buying undervalued stocks, by buying low-capitalization stocks, by overweighting specific industries, etc.? The decomposition of the performance results to explain the reasons why those results were achieved is called **performance attribution analysis**. Moreover, performance evaluation requires the determination of whether a money manager achieved superior performance (i.e., added value) by skill or by luck.

Our focus in this chapter is on performance measurement. In the next chapter we cover the more difficult topic of performance evaluation.

ALTERNATIVE RETURN MEASURES

The starting point for evaluating the performance of a money manager is measuring return. From our discussions in Chapters 2 and 4, this might seem quite simple, but several practical issues make the task complex.

Throughout our discussions we have assumed that no distributions are made from a portfolio during the holding period. Of course, in reality, distributions and withdrawals are common. The **dollar return** realized on a portfolio for any evaluation period (i.e., a year, month, or week), then, is equal to the sum of (1) the difference between the market value of the portfolio at the end of the evaluation period and the market value at the beginning of the evaluation period and (2) any distributions made from the portfolio. It is important that any capital or income distributions from the portfolio to a client or beneficiary of the portfolio be included.

The rate of return, or simply return, expresses the dollar return in terms of the amount of the market value at the beginning of the evaluation period. Thus, the return can be viewed as the amount (expressed as a fraction of the initial portfolio value) that can be withdrawn at the end of the evaluation period while maintaining the initial market value of the portfolio intact.

In equation form, the portfolio's **return** can be expressed as follows:

$$R_p = \frac{MV_1 - MV_0 + D}{MV_0} \tag{29-1}$$

where R_p = the return on the portfolio

MV_1 = the portfolio market value at the end of the evaluation period

MV_0 = the portfolio market value at the beginning of the evaluation period

D = the cash distributions from the portfolio to the client during the evaluation period

To illustrate the calculation of a return, assume the following information for an external money manager for a pension plan sponsor: The portfolio's market value at the beginning and end of the evaluation period is $25 million and $28 million, respectively, and during the evaluation period $1 million is distributed to the plan sponsor from investment income. Thus:

$$MV_1 = \$28,000,000$$
$$MV_0 = \$25,000,000$$
$$D = \$1,000,000$$

Then,

$$R_p = \frac{\$28,000,000 - \$25,000,000 + \$1,000,000}{\$25,000,000}$$

$$= 0.16 = 16\%$$

There are three assumptions in measuring return as given by Equation (29-1), summarized in Table 29-1. The first assumption is that cash inflows into the portfolio from dividends and interest that occur during the evaluation period but are not distributed are reinvested in the portfolio. For example, suppose that during the evaluation period $2 million is received from dividends. This amount is reflected in the market value of the portfolio at the end of the period.

The second assumption is that if there are distributions from the portfolio, they either occur at the end of the evaluation period or are held in the form of cash until the end of the evaluation period. In our example, $1 million is distributed to the plan sponsor. But when did that distribution actually occur? To understand why the timing of the distribution is important, consider two extreme cases: (1) the distribution is made at the end of the evaluation period, as assumed by Equation (29-1), and (2) the distribution is made at the beginning of the evaluation period. In the first case, the money manager had the use of the $1 million to invest for the entire evaluation period. By contrast, in the second case, the money manager loses the opportunity to invest the funds until the end of the evaluation period. Consequently, the timing of the distribution will affect the return, but this is not considered in Equation (29-1).

The third assumption is that there is no cash paid into the portfolio by the client. For example, suppose that sometime during the evaluation period the plan sponsor gives an additional $1.5 million to the external money manager to invest. Consequently, the market value of the portfolio at the end of the evaluation period, $28 million in our example, would reflect the contribution of $1.5 million. Equation (29-1) does not reflect that the ending market value of the portfolio is affected by the cash paid in by the sponsor. Moreover, the timing of this cash inflow will affect the calculated return.

Thus, while the return calculation for a portfolio using Equation (29-1) can be determined for an evaluation period of any length of time such as one day, one month, or five years, from a practical point of view the assumptions discussed above limit its application. The longer the evaluation period, the

TABLE 29-1

ASSUMPTIONS IN EQUATION (29-1) FOR CALCULATING PORTFOLIO RATE OF RETURN

1. Undistributed proceeds are reinvested in the portfolio during the evaluation period.
2. Distributions are made at the end of the evaluation period (or held as cash until then).
3. No new funds are invested in the portfolio during the evaluation period.

more likely the assumptions will be violated. For example, it is highly likely that there may be more than one distribution to the client and more than one contribution from the client if the evaluation period is five years. Thus, a return calculation made over a long period of time, if longer than a few months, would not be very reliable because of the assumption underlying the calculations that all cash payments and inflows are made and received at the end of the period.

Not only does the violation of the assumptions make it difficult to compare the returns of two money managers over some evaluation period, but it is also not useful for evaluating performance over different periods. For example, Equation (29-1) will not give reliable information to compare the performance of a one-month evaluation period and a three-year evaluation period. To make such a comparison, the return must be expressed per unit of time, for example, per year.

The way to handle these practical issues is to calculate the return for a short unit of time such as a month or a quarter. We call the return so calculated the **subperiod return**. To get the return for the evaluation period, the subperiod returns are then averaged. So, for example, if the evaluation period is one year and 12 monthly returns are calculated, the monthly returns are the subperiod returns, and they are averaged to get the one-year return. If a three-year return is sought and 12 quarterly returns can be calculated, quarterly returns are the subperiod returns, and they are averaged to get the three-year return. The three-year return can then be converted into an annual return by the straightforward procedure described later.

Three methodologies have been used in practice to calculate the average of the subperiod returns: (1) the arithmetic average rate of return, (2) the time-weighted rate of return (also called the *geometric rate of return*), and (3) the dollar-weighted return. Table 29-2 compares these methods side by side.

Arithmetic Average (Mean) Rate of Return

As explained in Chapter 2, the **arithmetic average (mean) rate of return** is an unweighted average of the subperiod returns. The general formula is

$$R_A = \frac{R_{P1} + R_{P2} + \ldots + R_{PN}}{N} \tag{29-2}$$

where R_A = the arithmetic average rate of return

R_{Pk} = the portfolio return for subperiod k as measured by Equation (29-1), where $k = 1, \ldots, N$

N = the number of subperiods in the evaluation period

For example, if the portfolio returns [as measured by Equation (29-1)] were -10%, 20%, and 5% in months July, August, and September, respectively, the arithmetic average monthly return is 5%, as shown below:

$$N = 3 \qquad R_{P1} = -0.10 \qquad R_{P2} = 0.20 \qquad \text{and} \qquad R_{P3} = 0.05$$

$$R_A = \frac{-0.10 + 0.20 + 0.05}{3} = 0.05 = 5\%$$

There is a major problem with using the arithmetic average rate of return. To see this problem, suppose the initial market value of a portfolio is

---

TABLE 29-2

THREE METHODS FOR AVERAGING SUBPERIOD RETURNS

Method	Interpretation	Limitations
Arithmetic average (mean) rate of return	• Average value of the withdrawals (expressed as a fraction of the initial portfolio market value) that can be made at the end of each subperiod while keeping the initial portfolio market value intact	• Overvalues total return when subperiod returns vary greatly •Assumes the maintenance of initial market value
Time-weighted (geometric) rate of return	• The compounded rate of growth of the initial portfolio market value during the evaluation period	• Assumes all proceeds are reinvested
Dollar-weighted rate of return (internal) return	• The interest rate that will make the present value of the sum of the subperiod cash flows (plus the terminal market value) equal to the initial market value of the portfolio	• Is affected by client contributions and withdrawals beyond the control of the money manager

---

$28 million and the market values at the end of the next two months are $56 million and $28 million, respectively, and assume that there are no distributions or cash inflows from the client for either month. Then using Equation (29-1) we find the subperiod return for the first month (R_{P1}) is 100% and the subperiod return for the second month (R_{P2}) is -50%. The arithmetic average rate of return using Equation (29-2) is then 25%. Not a bad return! But think about this number. The portfolio's initial market value was $28 million. Its market value at the end of two months is $28 million. The return over this two-month evaluation period is zero. Yet Equation (29-2) says it is a whopping 25%.

Thus, it is improper to interpret the arithmetic average rate of return as a measure of the average return over an evaluation period. The proper interpretation is as follows: It is the average value of the withdrawals (expressed as a fraction of the initial portfolio market value) that can be made at the end of each subperiod while keeping the initial portfolio market value intact. In our first example above in which the average monthly return is 5%, the investor must add 10% of the initial portfolio market value at the end of the first month, can withdraw 20% of the initial portfolio market value at the end of the second month, and can withdraw 5% of the initial portfolio market value at the end of the third month. In our second example, the average monthly return of 25% means that 100% of the initial portfolio market value ($28 million) can be withdrawn at the end of the first month and 50% must be added at the end of the second month.

Time-Weighted Rate of Return

The **time-weighted rate of return** measures the compounded rate of growth of the initial portfolio market value during the evaluation period, assuming that all cash distributions are reinvested in the portfolio. As discussed in Chapter 2, this return is also commonly referred to as the **geometric mean return** since it is computed by taking the geometric average of the portfolio subperiod returns calculated from Equation (29-1). The general formula is

$$R_T = [(1 + R_{P1})(1 + R_{P2})\ldots(1 + R_{PN})]^{1/N} - 1 \qquad (29\text{-}3)$$

where R_T is the time-weighted rate of return and R_{Pk} and N are as defined earlier.

For example, let us assume the portfolio returns were -10%, 20%, and 5% in July, August, and September, as in the first example above. Then the time-weighted rate of return as given by Equation (29-3) is

$$R_T = \{[1 + (-0.10)](1 + 0.20)(1 + 0.05)\}^{1/3} - 1$$
$$= [(0.90)(1.20)(1.05)]^{1/3} - 1 = 0.043$$

Since the time-weighted rate of return is 4.3% per month, one dollar invested in the portfolio at the beginning of July would have grown at a rate of 4.3% per month during the three-month evaluation period.

The time-weighted rate of return in the second example is 0%, as expected, as shown below:

$$R_T = \{(1 + 1.00)[1 + (-0.50)]\}^{1/2} - 1$$
$$= [(2.00)(0.50)]^{1/2} - 1 = 0\%$$

In general, the arithmetic and time-weighted average returns will give different values for the portfolio return over some evaluation period. This is because in computing the arithmetic average rate of return, the amount invested is assumed to be maintained (through additions or withdrawals) at its initial portfolio market value. The time-weighted return, on the other hand, is the return on a portfolio that varies in size because of the assumption that all proceeds are reinvested.

In general, the arithmetic average rate of return will exceed the time-weighted average rate of return. The exception is in the special situation where all the subperiod returns are the same, in which case the averages are identical. The magnitude of the difference between the two averages is smaller the less the variation in the subperiod returns over the evaluation period. For example, suppose that the evaluation period is four months and that the four monthly returns are as follows:

$$R_{P1} = 0.04 \qquad R_{P2} = 0.06 \qquad R_{P3} = 0.02 \qquad \text{and} \qquad R_{P4} = -0.02$$

The arithmetic average rate of return is 2.5%, and the time-weighted average rate of return is 2.46%. Not much of a difference. In our earlier example in which we calculated an average rate of return of 25% but a time-weighted average rate of return of 0%, the large discrepancy is due to the substantial variation in the two monthly returns.

Dollar-Weighted Rate of Return

The **dollar-weighted rate of return** is computed by finding the interest rate that will make the present value of the cash flows from all the subperiods in the evaluation period plus the terminal market value of the portfolio equal to the initial market value of the portfolio. The cash flow for each subperiod reflects the difference between the cash inflows due to investment income (i.e., dividends and interest) and to contributions made by the client to the portfolio and the cash outflows reflecting distributions to the client. Notice that it is not necessary to know the market value of the portfolio for each subperiod to determine the dollar-weighted rate of return.

The dollar-weighted rate of return is simply an internal rate of return calculation, and hence it is also called the **internal rate of return**. The general formula for the dollar-weighted return is

$$V_0 = \frac{C_1}{(1 + R_D)} + \frac{C_2}{(1 + R_D)^2} + \cdots + \frac{C_N + V_N}{(1 + R_D)^n} \tag{29-4}$$

where R_D = the dollar-weighted rate of return
V_0 = the initial market value of the portfolio
V_N = the terminal market value of the portfolio
C_k = the cash flow for the portfolio (cash inflows minus cash outflows) for subperiod k, where $k = 1, 2, \ldots, N$

For example, consider a portfolio with a market value of $100,000 at the beginning of July, capital withdrawals of $5,000 at the end of months July, August, and September, no cash inflows from the client in any month, and a market value at the end of September of $110,000. Then

$$V_0 = \$100,000 \quad N = 3 \quad C_1 = C_2 = C_3 = \$5,000 \quad \text{and} \quad V_3 = \$110,000$$

and R_D is the interest rate that satisfies the following equation:

$$\$100,000 = \frac{\$5,000}{(1 + R_D)} + \frac{\$5,000}{(1 + R_D)^2} + \frac{\$5,000 + \$110,000}{(1 + R_D)^3}$$

It can be verified that the interest rate that satisfies the above expression is 8.1%. This, then, is the dollar-weighted return.

The dollar-weighted rate of return and the time-weighted rate of return will produce the same result if no withdrawals or contributions occur over the evaluation period and all investment income are reinvested. The problem with the dollar-weighted rate of return is that it is affected by factors that are beyond the control of the money manager. Specifically, any contributions made by the client or withdrawals that the client requires will affect the calculated return. This makes it difficult to compare the performance of two money managers.

To see this, suppose that a pension plan sponsor engaged two money managers, A and B, giving $10 million to A to manage and $200 million to B. Suppose that (1) both money managers invest in identical portfolios (that is, the two portfolios have the same securities and are held in the same proportion), (2) for the following two months the rate of return on the two portfolios is 20% for month 1 and 50% for month 2, and (3) the amount received in investment income is in cash. Also assume that the plan sponsor does not make an additional contribution to the portfolio of either money manager. Under these assumptions, it is clear that the performance of both money managers would be identical. Suppose, however, that the plan sponsor withdraws $4 million from A at the end of month 1. This means that A could not invest the entire amount at the end of month 1 and capture the 50% increase in the portfolio value. A's net cash flow would be as follows: In month 1 the net cash flow is $-$2 million since $2 million is realized in investment income and $4 million is withdrawn by the plan sponsor. The dollar-weighted rate of return is then calculated as follows:

$$\$10 = \frac{-\$2}{(1 + R_D)} + \frac{\$12}{(1 + R_D)^2} \qquad R_D = 0\%$$

For B, the cash inflow for month 1 is $40 million ($200 million times 20%) and the portfolio value at the end of month 2 is $360 million ($240 million times 1.5). The dollar-weighted rate of return is

$$\$200 = \frac{\$40}{(1 + R_D)} + \frac{\$360}{(1 + R_D)^2} \qquad R_D = 44.5\%$$

These are quite different results for two money managers we agreed had identical performance. The withdrawal by the plan sponsor and the size of the withdrawal relative to the portfolio value had a significant effect on the calculated return, Notice also that even if the plan sponsor had withdrawn $4 million from B at the beginning of month 2, this would not have had as significant an impact. The problem would also have occurred if we assumed that the return in month 2 is -50% and that instead of A realizing a withdrawal of $4 million, the plan sponsor contributed $4 million.

Despite this limitation, the dollar-weighted rate of return does provide information. It indicates information about the growth of the fund which a client will find useful. This growth, however, is not attributable to the performance of the money manager because of contributions and withdrawals.

Annualizing Returns

The evaluation period may be less than or greater than one year. Typically, return measures are reported as an average annual return. This requires the annualization of the subperiod returns. The subperiod returns are usually calculated for a period of less than one year for the reasons described earlier. The subperiod returns are then annualized using the following formula:

$$\text{Annual return} = (1 + \text{average period return})^{\text{number of periods in year}} - 1 \qquad (29\text{-}5)$$

So, for example, suppose the evaluation period is three years and a monthly period return is calculated. Suppose further that the average monthly return is 2%. Then the annual return would be

$$\text{Annual return} = (1.02)^{12} - 1 = 26.8\%$$

Suppose instead that the period used to calculate returns is quarterly and the average quarterly return is 3%. Then the annual return is

$$\text{Annual return} = (1.03)^4 - 1 = 12.6\%$$

AIMR PERFORMANCE PRESENTATION STANDARDS

As explained above, there are subtle issues in calculating the return over the evaluation period. There are also industry concerns about how money managers should present results to clients and how money managers should dis-

---

BOX 29

THE SEC'S PHILOSOPHICAL APPROACH TO ADVERTISING PERFORMANCE RESULTS

The focus on money management performance is a relatively recent development. When the Advisers Act was adopted in 1940, money managers largely served wealthy clients who relied on them for assistance in managing private securities portfolios and other family financial affairs. These relationships tended to be long term. As the industry shifted to institutional rather than individual accounts, and as computers provided an efficient means to crunch the numbers, client demand, or advisor competition for clients—or both—brought performance advertising to the forefront of investment advisor promotional materials.

The SEC's historical approach to regulating performance advertising and all other aspects of advisor advertising has been to prevent the presentation from being misleading or deceptive. It has not required comparability of presentations. This is in contrast to investment company advertising, where, with money market fund yields and recently with comprehensive rules for all equity and debt funds, the SEC has required investment companies in their advertising of performance to compute performance in accordance with specified formulas.

The AIMR Performance Presentation Standards are directed not just at preventing fraud in advisor advertisements but also at promoting comparability. Although the SEC itself has not moved in the direction of mandating comparability, I believe it would not object to the industry establishing these Standards. In fact, AIMR should be commended for its efforts to develop standard investment performance presentation principles for advisors. The industry, clients, and regulators have known for some time that if all money managers can put their performance in the top quartile, something is wrong with the performance reporting system. The present system permits everybody to be good at something and allows the manager to pick what that something is.

Source: Mary Podesta, "Where the SEC Stands on Performance Advertising and Other Issues," in *Performance Reporting for Investment Managers: Applying the AIMR Performance Presentation Standards* (Charlottesville, VA: AIMR, 1991), pp. 20.

Question for Box 29

1. Explain how the "AIMR Performance Presentation Standards are directed not just at preventing fraud in advisor advertisements but also at promoting comparability."

---

close performance data and records to prospects from whom they are seeking to obtain funds to manage. According to Claude N. Rosenberg, Jr., chairman of the **Committee for Performance Presentation Standards (CPPS)** of the **Association for Investment Management and Research (AIMR)**:

> There is little consistency within the investment management industry in the presentation of performance data and records. There certainly has been a great deal of confusion about what should be reported to clients and prospects. The investment management industry has pretty much operated on an honor system, and although there is a great deal of honor in our industry, there are too many approaches that make this whole subject a real hornet's nest. Because there has been confusion, there has been misuse, and some of the misuse must, bluntly, be recognized as deception, and in some cases—we hope not too many—misuse has been motivated by outright dishonesty.[1]

The Securities and Exchange Commission (SEC) has established standards for advertising performance results under the antifraud provisions of the Investment Advisers Act of 1940. Box 29 explains the SEC's philosophical approach to advertising performance results. The SEC's rule for advertising the performance of investment advisors, however, is not very specific.[2]

---

[1]Claude N. Rosenberg, Jr., panel discussion, as reported in *Performance Measurement: Setting the Standards, Interpreting the Numbers* (Charlottesville, VA: The Institute for Chartered Financial Analysts, 1989), p. 15.

[2]However, there are specific rules for advertising performance that are required for investment companies (mutual funds and closed-end funds).

Accordingly, the CPPS was charged with developing standards for disclosure. The standards adopted by the AIMR went into effect in 1993 and "are a set of guiding ethical principles intended to promote full disclosure and fair representation by investment managers in reporting their investment results."[3] A secondary objective of the standards is to ensure uniformity in the presentation of results so it is easier for clients to compare the performance of money managers. It is important to emphasize that the AIMR standards deal with the presentation of the data and what must be disclosed, not with how the money manager should be evaluated.

In developing these standards, the CPPS recognized that in practice no single ideal set of performance presentation standards is applicable to all users. There are provisions in the standards to prevent certain abusive practices. Rather than mandating other practices, the standards provide guidelines and recommendations for reporting. Thus, the standards can be broken down into (1) the requirements and mandatory disclosures for compliance and (2) the practices recommended. Below we highlight some of the standards.

Requirements and Mandatory Disclosures

To be considered in compliance with the standards, the following practices and disclosures *must* be followed:

- Calculate performance on a total return basis.
- Employ accrual accounting rather than cash accounting in calculating return (except for dividends and calculations of performance for periods prior to 1993).
- Calculate return using the time-weighted rate of return methodology, with valuation on at least a quarterly basis and geometric linking of period returns. (We will discuss this further below.)
- Include all actual fee-paying, discretionary portfolios in one composite or aggregate measure. This prevents a money manager from misleading a potential client by showing only the performance of selective accounts that have performed well. The number of portfolios, the amount of assets in the composite, and the percentage of the firm's total assets the composite represents must be disclosed. The firm must also disclose the existence of any minimum size below which portfolios are excluded from a composite and the inclusion of any non-fee-paying portfolios in the composite.
- Do not link the results of simulated and model portfolios with actual portfolio performance. That is, only actual portfolio performance, not the performance that would have been realized if a certain strategy had been employed, can be reported.
- Deduct all trading costs in calculating the return.
- Disclose whether the performance results are calculated gross or net of management fees. If net results are reported, then the average weighted management fee must be disclosed.
- Disclose the tax rate assumption if the results are reported after taxes.

---

[3]*Performance Presentation Standards: 1993* (Charlottesville, VA: Association for Investment Management and Research, 1993).

- Present at least a 10-year performance record. If the firm has been in existence for less than 10 years, then the performance since inception must be reported.
- Present annual returns for all years.
- Provide a complete list and description of all the firm's composites.

Other required practices and disclosures deal with the reporting of results of accounts that have been terminated, the treatment of new portfolios added to a composite, and special requirements for international and real estate portfolios.

Table 29-3 is a sample presentation.

Recommended Guidelines and Disclosures

Some of the practices that the AIMR encourages are:

- Revalue a portfolio whenever inflows or outflows of cash and market action combine to distort performance. We'll focus on this below when we discuss the return calculation under the standards.
- Present performance gross of management fees in one-on-one presentations to clients.[4] The results should be presented before taxes.
- Treat convertible and other hybrid securities consistently across and within composites.
- Disclose external risk measures such as standard deviation of composite returns across time.
- Disclose benchmarks that parallel the risk or investment style the client is expected to track. We will discuss benchmarks in the next chapter.
- For leveraged portfolios, disclose the results on an unleveraged basis where possible.

There are specific recommended guidelines and disclosures for international portfolios.

Calculating Returns under the Standards

In our illustrations of the various ways to measure portfolio return, we used the same length of time for the subperiod (e.g., a month or a quarter). The subperiod returns were averaged, with the preferred method being geometric averaging. The AIMR standards require that the return measure minimize the effect of contributions and withdrawals so that cash flow beyond the control of the money manager is minimized. If the subperiod return is calculated daily, the impact of contributions and withdrawals will be minimized. The time-weighted return measure can then be calculated from the daily returns.

From a practical point of view, the problem is that calculating a daily return requires that the market value of the portfolio be determined at the end of each day. While this does not present a problem for a mutual fund that must calculate the net asset value of the portfolio each business day, it is a time-consuming administrative problem for other money managers.

---

[4]This is also acceptable to the SEC for one-on-one presentations with clients. If a money manager distributes the information to more than one client, the SEC requires that the returns be reported after deducting management fees.

TABLE 29-3					
SAMPLE PRESENTATIONS					
XYZ INVESTMENT FIRM PERFORMANCE RESULTS JANUARY 1, 1984–DECEMBER 31, 1993, GROWTH-PLUS-INCOME BALANCED COMPOSITE					
Year	Total Return	Benchmark Return*	Number of Portfolios	Total Assets End of Period ($Millions)	Percent of Firm Assets
1984	12.1%	9.4%	6	$ 50	80%
1985	24.2	26.4	10	85	82
1986	17.0	16.4	15	120	78
1987	(3.3)	(1.7)	14	100	80
1988	15.8	12.8	18	124	75
1989	16.0	14.1	26	165	70
1990	2.2	1.8	32	235	68
1991	22.4	24.1	38	344	65
1992	7.1	6.0	45	445	64
1993	8.5	8.0	48	520	62

Notes:

1. These results have been prepared and presented in compliance with the AIMR Performance Presentation Standards for the period 1/1/88 through 12/31/93. The full period is not in compliance. Prior to 1/1/88, not all fully discretionary portfolios were represented in appropriate composites. Composite results for the years 1984 through 1987 include the five largest institutional portfolios that were managed in accordance with the growth-plus-income strategy. These five accounts were consistently represented in the composite for the full period from 1984 through 1987.

2. Results for the full historical period are time weighted. From 1984 through 1990, results are calculated yearly, and the composites are asset weighted by beginning-of-year asset values. After January 1, 1991, composites are valued quarterly, and portfolio returns are weighted by using beginning-of-quarter market values plus weighted cash flows.

3. The benchmark: 60% S&P 500; 40% Lehman Intermediate Aggregate, Annualized Compound Composite Return = 11.9%. Annualized Compound Benchmark Return = 11.4%.

4. Standard deviation in annual composite returns equals 8.24% versus a standard deviation in the yearly benchmark returns of 8.53%.

5. The dispersion of annual returns as measured by the range between the highest and lowest performing portfolios in the composite is as follows: 1984, 3.2%; 1985, 5.4%; 1986, 3.8%; 1987, 1.2%; 1988, 4.3%; 1989, 4.5%; 1990, 2.0%; 1991, 5.7%; 1992, 2.8%; 1993, 3.1%.

6. Performance results are presented before management and custodial fees. The management fee schedule is attached.

7. No alteration of composites as presented here has occurred because of changes in personnel or other reasons at any time.

8. Settlement-date accounting is used prior to 1990.

9. A complete list of firm composites and performance results is available upon request.

*Presentation of benchmark returns is not required.

Source: *Performance Presentation Standards: 1993* (Charlottesville, VA: Association for Investment Management and Research, 1993), p. 65.

Moreover, there are asset classes in which the determination of daily prices would be difficult (e.g., certain fixed-income securities, securities in emerging markets, and real estate).

An alternative to the time-weighted rate of return has been suggested. This is the dollar-weighted rate of return, which as we noted earlier is less desirable in comparing the performance of money managers because of the effect of withdrawals and contributions beyond the control of the money manager. The advantage of this method from an operational perspective is that market values do not have to be calculated daily. The effect of withdrawals and contributions is minimized if they are small relative to the length of the subperiod. However, if the cash flow is over 10% at any time, the AIMR standards require that the portfolio be revalued on that date.[5]

Once the subperiod returns in an evaluation period are calculated, they are compounded. The AIMR standards specify that for evaluation periods of less than one year the returns should *not* be annualized. Thus, if the evaluation period is seven months and the subperiod returns calculated are monthly, the seven-month return should be reported by calculating the compounded seven-month return instead.

■ SUMMARY

Performance measurement involves the calculation of the return realized by a money manager over some evaluation period. Performance evaluation is concerned with determining whether the money manager added value by outperforming the established benchmark and how the money manager achieved the calculated return.

The rate of return expresses the dollar return in terms of the amount of the initial investment (i.e., the initial market value of the portfolio). Three methodologies have been used in practice to calculate the average of the subperiod returns: (1) the arithmetic average rate of return, (2) the time-weighted (or geometric) rate of return, and (3) the dollar-weighted return. The arithmetic average rate of return is the average value of the withdrawals (expressed as a fraction of the initial portfolio market value) that can be made at the end of each period while keeping the initial portfolio market value intact. The time-weighted rate of return measures the compounded rate of growth of the initial portfolio over the evaluation period, assuming that all cash distributions are reinvested in the portfolio. The time-weighted return is the return on a portfolio that varies in size because of the assumption that all proceeds are reinvested. In general, the arithmetic average rate of return will exceed the time-weighted average rate of return. The magnitude of the difference between the two averages is smaller the less the variation in the subperiod returns over the evaluation period.

The dollar-weighted rate of return is computed by finding the interest rate that will make the present value of the cash flows from all the subperiods in the evaluation period plus the terminal market value of the portfolio equal to the initial market value of the portfolio. The dollar-weighted rate of return is an internal rate-of-return calculation and will produce the same result as the time-weighted rate of return if (1) no withdrawals or contributions occur over the evaluation period and (2) all cash flows are reinvested. The problem with using the dollar-weighted rate of return to evaluate the performance of money managers is that it is affected

---

[5]For a further discussion of the implementation of the AIMR Standards, see Deborah H. Miller, "How to Calculate the Numbers According to the Standards," in *Performance Reporting for Investment Managers: Applying the AIMR Performance Presentation Standards* (Charlottesville, VA: AIMR, 1991).

by factors beyond the control of the money manager. Specifically, any contributions made by the client or withdrawals that the client requires will affect the calculated return, making it difficult to compare the performance of two money managers.

The AIMR has adopted standards for the presentation and disclosure of performance results.

In developing them, the CPPS of the AIMR recognized that in practice no single ideal set of performance presentation standards is applicable to all users. There are provisions in the standards to prevent certain abusive practices. Rather than mandating other practices, the standards provide guidelines and recommendations for reporting.

■ KEY TERMS

arithmetic average (mean) rate of return
Association for Investment Management and Research (AIMR)
Committee for Performance Presentation Standards (CPPS)

dollar return
dollar-weighted rate of return
evaluation period
geometric mean return
internal rate of return
performance attribution analysis

performance evaluation
performance measurement
return
subperiod return
time-weighted rate of return

■ QUESTIONS

1. What is the difference between performance measurement and performance evaluation?

2. Suppose that the monthly return for two money managers is as follows:

Month	Manager I	Manager II
1	9%	25%
2	13%	13%
3	22%	22%
4	−18%	−24%

   a. What is the arithmetic average monthly rate of return for the two managers?
   b. What is the time-weighted average monthly rate of return for the two managers?
   c. Why does the arithmetic average monthly rate of return diverge more from the time-weighted monthly rate of return for manager II than for manager I?

3. Smith & Jones is a money management firm. One of its clients gave the firm $100 million to manage. The market value for the portfolio for the four months after receiving the funds was as follows:

End of Month	Market Value (in Millions)
1	$ 50
2	$150
3	$ 75
4	$100

   a. Calculate the rate of return for each month.

   b. Smith & Jones reported to the client that over the four-month period the average monthly rate of return was 33.33%. How was that value obtained?
   c. Is the average monthly rate of return of 33.33% indicative of the performance of Smith & Jones? If not, what would be a more appropriate measure?

4. The Mercury Company is a money management firm that manages the funds of pension plan sponsors. For one of its clients it manages $200 million. The cash flow for this particular client's portfolio for the past three months was $20 million, −$8 million, and $4 million. The market value of the portfolio at the end of three months was $208 million.
   a. What is the dollar-weighted rate of return for this client's portfolio over the three-month period?
   b. Suppose that the $8 million cash outflow in the second month was a result of withdrawals by the plan sponsor and that the cash flow after adjusting for this withdrawal is therefore zero. What would the dollar-weighted rate of return then be for this client's portfolio?

5. a. If the average monthly return for a portfolio is 1.23%, what is the annualized return?
   b. If the average quarterly return for a portfolio is 1.78%, what is the annualized return?

6. The High Quality Corporation is a money management firm that was started five years ago. The firm has 20 discretionary, fee-paying accounts with an aggregate amount under management of $500 million. In preparing a report for a client that it is prospecting for funds, it has done the following:

   1. Presented the return for the past three years for five representative portfolios
   2. Calculated the arithmetic average annual return over the past three years where the return subperiod was measured each year
   3. Disclosed what the return would have been for the past ten years based on the actual performance for the past three years and simulated returns for the seven prior years using the same strategy it employed for the actual portfolio
   4. Calculated the return before transactions costs and management fees

Based on the above, explain whether High Quality Corporation is in compliance with the AIMR standards.

7. In *Performance Measurement: Setting the Standards, Interpreting the Numbers* (Charlottesville, VA: The Institute for Financial Analysts, 1989), John Sherrerd, a member of the Performance Presentation Standards Committee of the AIMR, stated:

   It is important to keep in mind that the objective of these performance statistics is to measure the capabilities of the manager, not the cash flows. It is not an attempt to measure how many dollars the client has earned over a period of time. If the performance of the manager is being measured, those results should not be influenced by whether the client is taking money out and spending it, the way most endowments might, or leaving it in, as many corporations do.

   a. Why is the dollar-weighted rate of return affected by contributions and withdrawals by the client?
   b. What rate of return methodology do the AIMR standards require?

8. In the calculation of return, the AIMR standards recommend the use of a daily return.

   a. Explain why it would be ideal to calculate daily returns.
   b. Why is it difficult to calculate daily returns?

9. In "Performance Basics: Simple in Theory, Hard to Apply—Part I," published in *Performance Measurement: Setting the Standards, Interpreting the Numbers*, Edward D. Baker III of BARRA states:

   Performance numbers are often used to form expectations for future performance, either for an investment strategy or for the evaluation of a potential manager. For this application, the arithmetic average return is superior to the geometric compound return. In fact, the arithmetic average is an unbiased forecast for next period's return. It is the preferred method for selecting an investment or manager when the next period is the relevant performance outcome. However, if we are interested in a long-term performance expectation we should, indeed, consider the geometric compound return.

   Explain why you agree or disagree with the above statement.

10. In "A Bank Trust Department's Perspective," by Mary E. McFadden, published in *Performance Reporting for Investment Managers: Applying the AIMR Performance Presentation Standards* (Charlottesville, VA: AIMR, 1991), Mary McFadden states: "Eventually, bank trust departments probably will calculate rates of return both on a daily time-weighted basis and a dollar-weighted basis for master trust accounts. Plan sponsors need to see both calculations to measure how well their overall assets are doing." Explain why, despite the drawbacks of the dollar-weighted rate of return, it is useful for plan sponsors.

11. One of the pioneers in the area of performance measurement is Professor Lawrence Fisher. In a 1968 study for the Bank Administration Institute ("Measuring Rates of Return," *Investment Performance of Pension Funds*) he wrote: "One of the vital statistics for measuring the performance of pension funds is the rate of return. Rate of return has many possible definitions, probably none of which is right for all purposes. It is hoped that at least one is useful for each purpose." Explain why you agree or disagree with this statement.

CHAPTER 30
EVALUATING PERFORMANCE

LEARNING OBJECTIVES
After reading this chapter you will be able to:

- explain why it is necessary to establish a benchmark.
- describe the different types of benchmarks: market indexes, generic-investment-style indexes, Sharpe benchmarks, and normal portfolios.
- discuss the problems with generic-investment-style indexes.
- explain how Sharpe benchmarks are created.
- describe the way normal portfolios are created and the difficulties of creating them.
- describe the single-index performance evaluation measures (Treynor Index, Sharpe Index, and Jensen Index) and their limitations.
- explain what a performance attribution model is and why it is useful in assessing the performance of a money manager.
- describe how Sharpe benchmarks are used to evaluate performance.

Money managers may pursue a great variety of active investment strategies, and in the previous chapter, we concentrated on ways of measuring performance and the AIMR performance reporting standards. But a performance measure does not answer two questions: (1) How did the manager perform after adjusting for the risk associated with the active strategy employed and (2) how did the manager achieve the reported return?

The answers to these two questions are critical in assessing how well or how poorly the manager performed relative to some benchmark. In answering the first question, we must draw upon the various measures of risk that we described in Chapters 4, 5 and 6. We can then judge whether the performance was aceptable in the face of the risk.

The answer to the second question tells us whether the manager, in fact, achieved a return by following the anticipated strategy. While a client would expect that any superior return accomplished is a result of a stated strategy, that may not always be the case. For example, suppose a manager solicits funds from a client by claiming he can achieve superior common stock performance by selecting underpriced stocks. Suppose also that this manager does generate a superior return compared with the S&P 500 Index. The client should not be satisfied with this performance until the return realized by the manager is segregated into the various components that generated the return. A client may find that the superior performance is the result of the manager's timing of the market (i.e., revising the beta in anticipation of market movements), rather than of his selecting underpriced stocks. In such an instance, the manager may have outperformed the S&P 500 (even after adjusting for risk), but not by following the strategy the manager told the client he intended to pursue.

In this chapter, we look at the state-of-the-art technology for adjusting returns for risk so as (1) to determine whether a superior return was realized and (2) to analyze the actual return of a portfolio to uncover the reasons why a return was realized. We refer to this analysis as *performance evaluation*. We begin this chapter with a discussion of the various benchmarks that can be used to evaluate the performance of a manager.

BENCHMARK PORTFOLIOS

To evaluate the performance of a money manager, a client must specify a benchmark against which the manager will be measured. In fact, as the following example will demonstrate, it is important to use a benchmark *portfolio* rather than a broad-based index like the S&P 500.

Figure 30-1 shows the cumulative excess return for the evaluation period January 1984–June 1988 of one of the external money managers engaged by the Bell Atlantic pension plan. This money manager is a growth manager. As

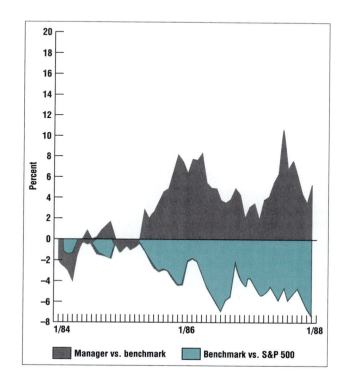

FIGURE 30-1

Cumulative excess return for a growth manager of Bell Atlantic.

Source: Edward P. Rennie and Thomas J. Cowhey, "The Successful Use of Benchmark Portfolios," in Darwin M. Bayston and H. Russell Fogler (eds.), *Improving Portfolio Performance with Quantitative Models* (Charlottesville, VA: Institute of Chartered Financial Analysts, 1989), p. 34.

can be seen, the money manager outperformed the benchmark portfolio specified by the plan sponsor; that is, the money manager added value. The benchmark portfolio, however, underperformed the S&P 500. The decision to select a growth manager was that of the plan sponsor, and that decision may not have been optimal.

Four types of benchmarks have been used in practice: (1) market indexes, (2) generic-investment-style indexes, (3) Sharpe benchmarks, and (4) normal portfolios. We discussed the various types of market indexes in Chapter 2. The other types of benchmarks are discussed below.

Generic-Investment-Style Indexes

Developed by various consulting firms, a generic-investment-style index measures the various investment styles described in Chapter 15. For example, those developed by Frank Russell Company (the Russell Style Indexes) include growth, market-oriented, and value styles.

The problem with these indexes is that it is often difficult to classify a money manager by a particular investment style. To illustrate this problem, suppose a money manager buys equal amounts of 80 stocks—the 40 highest-dividend-yield stocks in the Russell 1000 index and the 40 lowest-price-earnings stocks in the Russell 2000 index.[1] The Russell 1000 index includes the largest-capitalization stocks. So the manager could be classified as following a large-capitalization style. Conversely, the stocks selected from within this index have a high dividend yield, a characteristic of stocks selected by a value manager. Thus, the manager can be classified as having this style. Finally, since half the portfolio comprises stocks in the Russell 2000 and this index includes the smallest-capitalization stocks, this manager can be classified as following a small-capitalization style.

Sharpe Benchmarks

Because of the difficulty of classifying a money manager into any one of the generic investment styles, William Sharpe suggested that a benchmark can be constructed using multiple regression analysis from various specialized market indexes.[2] The rationale is that potential clients can buy a combination of tilted index funds to replicate a style of investing. A benchmark can be statistically created that adjusts for a manager's index-like tendencies. Such a benchmark is called a **Sharpe benchmark**.

The 10 mutually exclusive indexes suggested by Sharpe to provide asset class diversification are (1) the Russell Price-Drive Stock Index (an index of large-value stocks), (2) the Russell Earnings-Growth Stock Index (an index of large-growth stocks), (3) the Russell 2000 Small Stock Index, (4) the Salomon Brothers 90-Day Bill Index, (5) the Lehman Intermediate Government Bond Index, (6) the Lehman Long-Term Government Bond Index, (7) the Lehman

---

[1]This illustration is from H. Russell Fogler, "Normal Style Indexes—An Alternative to Manager Universes?" in *Performance Measurement: Setting the Standards, Interpreting the Numbers* (Charlottesville, VA: Association of Management and Investment Research, 1991), p. 97.

[2]William F. Sharpe, "Determining a Fund's Effective Asset Mix," *Investment Management Review* (September/October 1988), pp. 16–29.

Corporate Bond Index, (8) the Lehman Mortgage-Backed Securities Index, (9) the Salomon Brothers Non-U.S. Government Bond Index, and (10) the Financial Times Actuaries Euro-Pacific Index.

Later in this chapter we will see how to use the Sharpe benchmark to evaluate performance.

Normal Portfolios[3]

A **normal portfolio** is a customized benchmark that includes "a set of securities that contains all of the securities from which a manager normally chooses, weighted as the manager would weight them in a portfolio."[4] Thus, a normal portfolio is a specialized index. It is argued that normal portfolios are more appropriate benchmarks than market indexes because normal portfolios control for investment management style, thereby representing a passive portfolio against which a manager can be evaluated. In effect, the manager is being challenged to beat his or her average.

The construction of a normal portfolio for a particular money manager is no simple task.[5] The principle is to construct a portfolio that, given the historical portfolios held by the money manager, will reflect that manager's style in terms of assets and the weighting of those assets. The construction of a normal portfolio for a money manager requires (1) defining the stocks to be included in the normal portfolio and (2) determining how these stocks should be weighted (i.e., equally weighted or capitalization-weighted).

Defining the set of stocks to be included in the normal portfolio begins with discussions between the client and the money manager to determine the money manager's investment style. Based on these discussions, the universe of all publicly traded stocks is reduced to a subset that includes those stocks that the money manager considers eligible given his investment style. For example, suppose that the money manager's investment style is to invest in only stocks with a price-earnings ratio less than the average of all publicly traded stocks; all such stock would be included in the normal portfolio.

Given these stocks, the next question is how they should be weighted in the normal portfolio. The two choices are equal weighting and capitalization weighting of each stock. To illustrate the importance of the weighting, Figure 30-2 compares the performance of the S&P 500 stocks based on an equal weighting and a capitalization weighting of the stocks for the five years 1984 through 1988.

Various methodologies can be used to determine the weights. These methodologies typically involve a statistical analysis of the historical holdings of a money manager and the risk exposure contained in those holdings. As an example, Bell Atlantic uses a money manager's month-end portfolios over the past five years as a guide in determining weights. These historical

---

[3]The term "normal portfolio" was first introduced by the founder of BARRA, Barr Rosenberg.

[4]Jon Christopherson, "Normal Portfolios and Their Construction," in Frank J. Fabozzi (ed.), *Portfolio and Investment Management* (Chicago: Probus Publishing, 1989), p. 382.

[5]See Mark Kritzman, "How to Build a Normal Portfolio in Three Easy Steps," *Journal of Portfolio Management* (Spring 1987), pp. 21–23.

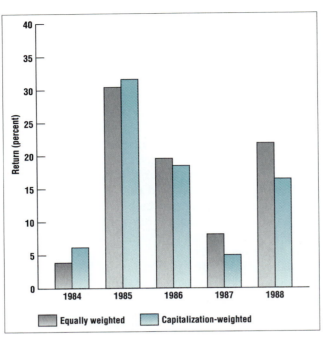

FIGURE 30-2

Comparison of S&P 500 performance assuming equal weighting and capitalization weighting: 1984–1988.

Source: Edward P. Rennie and Thomas J. Cowhey, "The Successful Use of Benchmark Portfolios," in Darwin M. Bayston and H. Russell Fogler (eds.), *Improving Portfolio Performance with Quantitative Models* (Charlottesville, VA: Institute of Chartered Financial Analysts, 1989), p. 34.

portfolios are then used to determine the average exposure of the actual portfolio to each of the factors defined by the BARRA factor model.[6] The weighting is adjusted using these average exposures.

Figure 30-3 shows the average exposure (as measured by the standard deviation) for the actual portfolio of a Bell Atlantic money manager over the period December 1984–November 1988. The figure compares this exposure to (1) the benchmark portfolio based on the methodology described above for obtaining the weights, (2) a benchmark portfolio if a capitalization weighting had been used, and (3) a benchmark portfolio if an equal weighting had been used. Notice that the difference in the method used to weight the assets in the portfolio affects the risk exposure of the benchmark that might be selected.

Plan sponsors work with pension consultants to develop normal portfolios for a money manager. The consultants use commercially available systems that have been developed for performing the needed statistical analysis and the necessary optimization program to create a portfolio exhibiting similar factor positions to replicate the "normal" position of a manager.[7] (See Box 30.) A plan sponsor must recognize that there is a cost to developing and updating the normal portfolio.

There are some who advocate that the responsibility of developing normal portfolios should be left to the manager. However, many clients are re-

---

[6]Edward P. Rennie and Thomas J. Cowhey, "The Successful Use of Benchmark Portfolios," in Darwin M. Bayston and H. Russell Fogler, (eds.), *Improving Portfolio Performance with Quantitative Models* (Charlottesville, VA: Institute of Chartered Financial Analysts, 1989), p. 34.

[7]The procedure for creating normals using the BARRA system is explained in the following two publications of the firm: *The Normalbook* (September 1988) and Arjun Divecha and Richard Grinold, *Normal Portfolios: Issues for Sponsors, Managers, and Consultants* (February 1989).

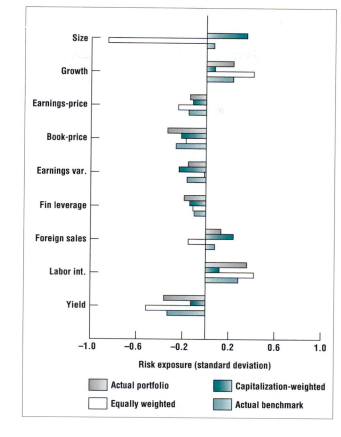

FIGURE 30-3

Comparison of investment manager risk factor analysis: 1984–1988.

Source: Edward P. Rennie and Thomas J. Cowhey, "The Successful Use of Benchmark Portfolios," in Darwin M. Bayston and H. Russell Fogler (eds.), *Improving Portfolio Performance with Quantitative Models* (Charlottesville, VA: Institute of Chartered Financial Analysts, 1989), p. 36.

luctant to let their managers control the construction of normal portfolios because they believe that the managers will produce easily beaten, or "slow rabbit," benchmarks. Bailey and Tierney demonstrate that under reasonable conditions there is no long-term benefit for the manager to construct a "slow rabbit" benchmark and explain the disadvantage of a manager pursuing such a strategy.[8] In addition, they recommend that clients should let managers control the benchmarks. Clients should, instead, focus their efforts on monitoring the quality of the benchmarks and the effectiveness of the managers' active management strategies.

While normal portfolios are theoretically ideal benchmarks, the problems and costs with their creation have engendered criticism. A study by Jon Christopherson of the consulting firm Frank Russell Company found, based on a small sample of managers, that normal portfolios may not adequately capture the manager's investment process.[9] Moreover, he finds that normal portfolios are no better or worse in explaining performance than generic-investment-style indexes.

---

[8]Jeffrey V. Bailey and David E. Tierney, "Gaming Manager Benchmarks," *Journal of Portfolio Management* (Summer 1993), pp. 37–41.

[9]Jon Christopherson, "Selecting an Appropriate Benchmark," unpublished manuscript, Frank Russell Company, 1993.

BOX 30

SELECTING AN APPROPRIATE BENCHMARK

The following excerpt is from a paper entitled "Selecting an Appropriate Benchmark," by Jon Christopherson of Frank Russell Company.

The results in this paper are troubling, however, because many plan sponsors are not experienced normal portfolio users nor do they have the luxury of an array of normal portfolios against which to evaluate each of their managers. Sponsors could demand that managers take control of the normal creation process, thereby relieving the sponsors of the burden. Unfortunately, this solution raises the danger of the manager ensuring a self-serving "slow rabbit."

Sponsors usually hire one vendor to create their normals. They rely on the vendor's professional skill to do the job well. Unfortunately, plan sponsors often cannot be entirely sure that the normals they buy are good, and there is no readily available evaluation service to answer this question. This is not a trivial management problem for sponsors and managers, because poorly built normals can lead to the sponsor being unduly harsh on a manager who trails his normal or, conversely, giving too much credit to a manager when the normal is a slow rabbit.

Questions for Box 30

1. What is a normal portfolio?
2. What it meant by a slow rabbit, and what are the dangers referred to in the above excerpt.

SINGLE-INDEX PERFORMANCE EVALUATION MEASURES

In the 1960s, several single-index measures were used to evaluate the relative performance of money managers. These measures of performance evaluation did not specify how or why a money manager may have outperformed or underperformed a benchmark. The three measures, or indexes, are the *Treynor Index*,[10] the *Sharpe Index*,[11] and the *Jensen Index*.[12] All three indexes assume that there is a linear relationship between the portfolio's return and the return on some broad-based market index.

In the early studies of investment managers, these measures were used to evaluate the performance of the managers of mutual funds. However, they are of very limited use in the evaluation of money managers today because of the development of the performance attribution models discussed later in the chapter.

Treynor Index

The **Treynor Index** is a measure of the excess return per unit of risk. The excess return is defined as the difference between the portfolio's return and the risk-free rate of return over the same evaluation period. The risk measure in the Treynor Index is the relative systematic risk as measured by the portfolio's beta, which can be estimated from the portfolio's characteristic line (see Chapter 4). Treynor argues that this is the appropriate risk measure since in a

---

[10]Jack Treynor, "How to Rate Management of Investment Funds," *Harvard Business Review* (January–February 1965), pp. 63-75.

[11]William F. Sharpe, "Mutual Fund Performance," *Journal of Business* (January 1966), pp. 119–138.

[12]Michael C. Jensen, "The Performance of Mutual Funds in the Period 1945-1964," *Journal of Finance* (May 1968), pp. 389–416.

well-diversified portfolio the unsystematic risk is close to zero. In equation form, the Treynor Index is:

$$\frac{\text{portfolio return} - \text{risk-free rate}}{\text{portfolio's beta}}$$

Sharpe Index

As with the Treynor Index, the **Sharpe Index** is a measure of the reward/risk ratio. The numerator is the same as in the Treynor Index. The risk of the portfolio is measured by the standard deviation of the portfolio. The Sharpe Index is therefore:

$$\frac{\text{portfolio return} - \text{risk-free rate}}{\text{standard deviation of portfolio}}$$

Thus the Sharpe Index is a measure of the excess return relative to the total variability of the portfolio.[13] The Sharpe and Treynor indexes will give identical rankings if the portfolios evaluated are well diversified. If they are poorly diversified, the rankings could be quite different.

Jensen Index

The **Jensen Index** uses the capital asset pricing model that we described in Chapter 5 to determine whether the money manager outperformed the market index. The empirical analogue of the CAPM is

$$E(R_p) - R_F = \beta_p\,[E(R_M) - R_F] + e$$

where $E(R_p)$ = the expected return on the portfolio
        R_F = the risk-free rate
        β_p = the beta of the portfolio
        $E(R_M)$ = expected return on the market
        e = random error term

In words:

Excess return = beta × [excess return on the market index]
                     + random error term

If the excess return produced by the manager does not exceed the excess return described by this formula, however, the manager has added nothing. After all, the historical beta of the portfolio represents an expectation of information-free performance; a random portfolio should perform this well. Jensen, then, added a factor to represent the portfolio's performance that diverges from its beta. This **alpha** is a measure of the manager's performance.

---

[13]Since the standard deviation is affected by the number of observations, there is a bias if the number of observations is small. Robert Korkie ["External vs. Internal Performance Evaluation," *Journal of Portfolio Management* (Spring 1983), pp. 36-42] has suggested that the bias introduced into the Sharpe Index can be corrected as follows:

$$\frac{\text{portfolio return} - \text{risk-free rate}}{\text{standard deviation of portfolio}} \times \frac{\text{no. of observations}}{\text{no. of observations} + 0.75}$$

Using time-series data for the return on the portfolio and the market index, we can estimate the following equation by regression analysis:

$$R_{pt} - R_{Ft} = \alpha_p + \beta_p \left[R_{Mt} - R_{Ft} \right] + e_{pt}$$

The intercept term alpha, α_p, in the above equation is the unique return realized by the money manager. That is,

Excess return = unique return + beta
$\times$ [excess return on the market index] + random error term

The Jensen measure is the alpha or unique return that is estimated from the above regression. If the alpha is not statistically different from zero, there is no unique return. A statistically significant alpha that is positive means that the money manager outperformed the market index; a negative value means that the money manager underperformed the market index.

As with the Treynor Index, the Jensen measure assumes that the portfolio is fully diversified so that the only risk remaining in the portfolio is systematic risk.

The estimated alpha is sensitive to the beta level of the portfolio. To correct for this, the alpha can be divided by the expected return for the portfolio to reflect its systematic risk.

EQUITY PERFORMANCE ATTRIBUTION MODELS

The active added value provided by a money manager of a common stock portfolio comes from pursing one or more of the active strategies discussed in Chapter 15. Recall that we discussed these strategies in terms of equity investment styles. Active managers could be classified by style as value managers, growth managers, group rotation managers, technicians, market timers, and hedgers. Also recall that we explained that the return on a portfolio depends on factors that are expected to systematically affect the return on securities.

In broad terms, the return performance of a common stock portfolio can be explained by three actions followed by a manager. The first is actively managing a portfolio to capitalize on factors that are expected to perform better than other factors. For example, if a manager believes that low-price-earnings stocks will outperform high-price-earnings stocks, the manager can tilt the portfolio in favor of low-price-earnings stocks. The second is actively managing a portfolio to take advantage of anticipated movements in the market. For example, the manager can increase the beta of a portfolio when the market is expected to increase and decrease it when the market is expected to decline. The third is actively managing the portfolio by buying stocks that are believed to be undervalued and selling (or shorting) stocks that are believed to be overvalued. The valuation methods described in Chapter 15 can be used to identify mispriced stocks.

We can categorize the sources of return of a common stock portfolio in terms of these three active management strategies. The three sources are referred to as *timing short-term factor trends, market timing,* and *security*

TABLE 30-1			
PERFORMANCE ATTRIBUTION ANALYSIS FOR THREE MONEY MANAGERS OF BELL ATLANTIC			
	Manager A	**Manager B**	**Manager C**
Actual return	19.1%	17.0%	12.6%
Benchmark portfolio	14.9	15.2	12.6
Active management return	4.2% (99)	1.8% (53)	0.0% (3)
Components of return:			
Market timing	-0.2% (40)	-0.6% (64)	-0.5% (73)
Industry exposure	0.2 (20)	-2.0 (89)	0.3 (34)
Sector emphasis	2.2 (99)	3.9 (99)	0.3 (51)
Security selection	1.9 (84)	0.6 (43)	0.1 (7)
Unreconciled return*	0.1	-0.1	-0.2

( ) denotes confidence level

* Difference between actual management return and sum of components of return.

Source: Edward P. Rennie and Thomas J. Cowhey, "The Successful Use of Benchmark Portfolios," in Darwin M. Bayston and H. Russell Fogler (eds.), *Improving Portfolio Performance with Quantitative Models* (Charlottesville, VA: Institute of Chartered Financial Analysts, 1989), p. 37.

analysis. Thus, understanding a managed portfolio's return comes down to answering these four questions:

1. What were the major sources of added value?
2. Was short-term factor timing statistically significant?
3. Was market timing statistically significant?
4. Was security selection statistically significant?

Notice that for the last three questions we must determine whether the result is statistically significant or just a result of luck. For this reason, statistical analysis must be employed.

The methodology for answering these questions is called **performance attribution analysis**. The single indexes discussed above do not help answer these questions. However, for stock portfolios, multifactor models, which we described in Chapter 6, can be used to answer the above questions.

The most popular model used by large-plan sponsors and their consultants to evaluate the performance of equity money managers is **BARRA's performance analysis (PERFAN) factor model**. BARRA is a consulting firm in Berkeley, California. We described the factors used in the BARRA factor model in the appendix to Chapter 15. A discussion of the statistical analysis employed to derive the BARRA model for performance analysis is beyond the scope of this chapter. Instead we will look at how BARRA's performance attribution model has been used by a plan sponsor.

Rennie and Cowhey report the performance of three external money managers for Bell Atlantic.[14] Table 30-1 shows the results for the three money managers since they began managing funds for Bell Atlantic. The values shown in parentheses in Table 30-1 are statistical measures that indicate the probability that the estimated value is statistically different from zero. The

---

[14]Rennie and Cowhey, op. cit., pp. 37–38.

value in parentheses is referred to as a *confidence level.* The higher the confidence level, the more likely the estimated value is different from zero and therefore performance can be attributed to skill rather than luck.

The active management return represents the difference between the actual portfolio return and the benchmark return. Manager A's active management return is 420 basis points and thus seems to have outperformed the benchmark. But was this by investment skill or luck? The confidence level of 99% suggests that it was through investment skill. The lower panel of the table shows how this was achieved. Of the four components of return, two are statistically significant—sector emphasis and security selection. The other two components—market timing and industry exposure—are not statistically significant. This means that either manager A's skills in these two areas did not significantly impact the portfolio's return or the manager did not emphasize these skills. In fact, this manager's stated investment style is to add value through sector emphasis and security selection and neutralize market timing and industry exposure. The results of the performance attribution analysis are consistent with this investment style.

An analysis of the results of manager B indicates that the manager outperformed the benchmark by 180 basis points. The confidence level, however, is 53%. In most statistical tests, this confidence level would suggest that the 180 basis points is not statistically different from zero. That is, the 180-basis-point active management return can be attributed to luck rather than skill. However, Rennie and Cowhey state that this is an acceptable level of confidence for Bell Atlantic, but that it does provide a warning to the company to carefully monitor this manager's performance for improvement or deterioration. The stated investment style of this manager is to identify undervalued securities. The component return of 60 basis points from security selection with a confidence level of only 43% suggests that this manager is not adding value in this way. This is another warning sign that this manager must be more carefully monitored.

Manager C has to be carefully monitored since this manager did not outperform the benchmark and none of the component returns are statistically significant. This manager is a candidate for termination. What is the minimum active management return that Bell Atlantic expects from its active equity managers? According to Rennie and Cowhey, it is 1% per year over a 2.5-year investment horizon with a confidence level of at least 70%. Moreover, the component analysis should corroborate what the manager states is the manager's investment style.

Before leaving this illustration, let's look at the unreconciled return, the last row in Table 30-1. This is the difference between the active management return and the four components of return. A large value for the unreconciled return can mean that the model is not sufficiently robust to capture all the factors that are affecting the portfolio's performance. For example, as pointed out by Rennie and Cowhey, the performance attribution analysis reported in Table 30-1 is based on end-of-month holdings and therefore does not capture the effects of intramonth trading and the associated transactions costs. Another reason is that the portfolio may have had debt instruments such as high-yield bonds or hybrid securities such as convertible bonds whose performance is affected by other factors, most notably, the level of interest rates and yield spreads.

FIXED-INCOME PERFORMANCE ATTRIBUTION MODELS[15]

As with equity performance attribution models, fixed-income attribution models seek to identify the active management decisions that contribute to the performance of a portfolio and give a quantitative assessment of the contribution of these decisions. In Chapter 24 we explained four active strategies in managing a fixed-income portfolio: interest rate expectations strategies, yield curve expectations strategies, yield spread strategies, and individual security selection strategies. The performance of a portfolio can be decomposed in terms of these four strategies.

The performance attribution described in this section is that of Gifford Fong Associates of Walnut Creek, California. The particular system that monitors and evaluates the performance of a fixed-income portfolio as well as the individual securities held in the portfolio is called **BONDPAR**. BONDPAR segregates the return into those elements beyond the manager's control, such as the interest rate environment and client-imposed duration policy constraints, and those that the management process contributes to, such as interest rate management, sector/quality allocations, and individual bond selection.

BONDPAR answers the following six questions: (1) How does each element of the manager's return compare with the same elements of return of the benchmark? (2) What is the cost of being in the bond market? (3) What effect do client policies have on portfolio returns? (4) Has the manager successfully anticipated interest rate changes? (5) Has the manager been successful at selecting the issuing sector and quality groups that enhance the portfolio's performance? And (6) has the manager improved returns by selecting individual bonds because of company fundamentals?

An explanation of the technology for decomposing the portfolio's return so that these questions can be answered is beyond the scope of this chapter.[16] Instead we illustrate the product of the system with a hypothetical portfolio for the period February 28, 1990–March 31, 1990, showing how it answers the six questions. Table 30-2 gives the holdings of the portfolio and the transactions during the period. Also shown for each security are the beginning and ending par amount, proceeds, accrued value, interest paid during the evaluation period, and capital gain or loss.

Table 30-3 shows the results of the performance attribution analysis for the portfolio in Table 30-2. Let's look first at the three columns in the table. The "Evaluation Period Return" column presents the return and components of return for the portfolio over the evaluation period. The "Bond Equivalent Annualized Return" column gives the annualized return and components of return for the portfolio over the evaluation period. The "Salomon B.I.G. Index" column shows the evaluation period return of a market index (benchmark).

The decomposition of the evaluation period return is shown in Sections I, II, III, and IV. Section I, "Interest Rate Effect," is the return over the evaluation period of the full Treasury index. The values in this section are interpreted as follows. The subtotal 0.09 means that the actual monthly return on

---

[15]This section is adapted from Chapter 12 in Frank J. Fabozzi and H. Gifford Fong, *Advanced Fixed Income Portfolio Management* (Chicago: Probus Publishing, 1994).

[16]An explanation of the technology is provided in Fabozzi and Fong, ibid.

TABLE 30-2

BOND PERFORMANCE ANALYSIS: INDIVIDUAL SECURITY LISTING AND TRANSACTIONS

Individual Security Listing

Cusip	Bond Description	Initial/ Last Date	Beg/End Par ($000)	Beg/End Prc (%)	Beg/End Acc ($000)	Interest Paid ($000)	Capital Gain/Loss ($000)
041033BM	ARKANSAS POWER & LIGHT CO						
1	14.125% 11/1/14 E4	2/28/90	24500.000	98.689	1124.70		
		3/31/90	20000.000	98.765	1177.08	0.00	17.99
16161OBA	CHASE MANHATTAN CORP						
2	9.750% 9/15/99 F3	2/28/90	25000.000	99.969	1103.65		
		3/31/90	30000.000	100.080	130.00	1462.50	69.05
172921CT	CITICORP MORTGAGE SECS INC						
3	9.500% 1/1/19 PS	2/28/90	76151.720	86.250	542.58		
		3/31/90	76151.720	85.031	602.87	602.87	−928.29
3024519X	FHA INSURED PROJECT MORTGAGE						
4	7.400% 2/1/21 PS	2/28/90	73071.970	84.438	405.55		
		3/31/90	73071.970	83.875	450.61	450.61	−411.40
313400KK	FEDERAL HOME LOAN MTG CORP						
5	12.250% 3/15/95 AG	2/28/90	30600.000	106.250	1718.93		
		3/31/90	30600.000	105.813	162.98	1874.25	−133.72
4581829H	INTER-AMERICAN DEVELOPMENT						
6	11.000% 12/11/92 X1	2/28/90	5600.000	103.313	131.76		
		3/31/90	5600.000	102.813	188.22	0.00	−28.00
674599AW	OCCIDENTAL PETROLEUM CORP						
7	11.750% 3/15/11 04	2/28/90	34000.000	102.875	1808.85		
		3/31/90	34000.000	102.500	177.56	1997.50	−127.50

TABLE 30-2 CONTINUED
BOND PERFORMANCE ANALYSIS: INDIVIDUAL SECURITY LISTING AND TRANSACTIONS

Individual Security Listing

Cusip	Bond Description	Initial/ Last Date	Beg/End Par ($000)	Beg/End Prc (%)	Beg/End Acc ($000)	Interest Paid ($000)	Capital Gain/Loss ($000)
912827TQ	UNITED STATES TREASURY NOTES						
8 7.375% 5/15/96 TR		2/28/90	93500.000	94.156	2000.11		
		3/31/90	93500.000	93.594	2590.62	0.00	−525.47
912827WN	UNITED STATES TREASURY NOTES						
9 9.250% 8/15/98 TR		3/13/90	92000.000	102.531	658.23		
		3/31/90	92000.000	102.969	1034.36	0.00	402.96
912827XM	UNITED STATES TREASURY NOTES						
10 9.000% 5/15/92 TR		2/28/90	85900.000	101.031	2242.42		
		3/10/90	0.000	100.750	2498.69	0.00	−241.38

The *Individual Security Listing* is an optional report that is used to review the beginning and ending holdings, price, and accrued interest for all individual securities held during the evaluation period. This report also displays the amount of interest paid for individual securities during the evaluation period.

Transactions Report

Cusip	Bond Description	Type of/ Transact	Trade Date	Settle Date	Par ($000)	Acc ($000)	Prc (%)	Cost/Proceeds ($000)
041033BM	ARKANSAS POWER & LIGHT CO							
1 14.125% 11/1/14 E4		Sale	3/5/90	3/12/90	4500.000	231.30	98.751	4675.1
161610BA	CHASE MANHATTAN CORP							
2 9.750% 9/15/99 F3		Purchase	3/6/90	3/13/90	5000.000	241.04	99.254	5203.7
912827XM	UNITED STATES TREASURY NOTES							
10 9.000% 5/15/92 TR		Termsale	3/10/90	3/12/90	85900.000	2498.69	100.750	89042.9
912827WN	UNITED STATES TREASURY NOTES							
9 9.250% 8/15/98 TR		Purchase	3/13/90	3/15/90	92000.000	658.23	102.531	94986.8

The *Transactions Report* can be used to review the total cost and proceeds of all purchase and sale transactions during the evaluation period. This report displays the type of transaction, the trade and settlement date, the par amount in ($000), the price of the transaction, and the accued interest calculated by the BONDPAR system.

TABLE 30-3

PERFORMANCE ATTRIBUTION ANALYSIS FOR A PORTFOLIO WITH BONDPAR

	Eval. Period Return %	Bond Equiv. Annualized Return %	Salomon B.I.G. Index Eval. Period Return %
I. Interest rate effect (SAL Treasury Index)			
1. Expected	0.66	7.93	0.66
2. Unexpected	−0.57	−6.87	−0.57
Subtotal	0.09	1.06	0.09
II. Policy effect			
3. Portfolio duration reqt. (4.60 years)	0.01	0.07	0.01
III. Interest rate management effect			
4. Duration	0.06	0.69	0.00
5. Convexity	−0.07	−0.84	−0.10
6. Yield curve shape change	−0.15	−1.78	0.10
Subtotal (options adjusted)	−0.16	−1.93	0.00
IV. Other management effects			
7. Sector/quality	0.18	2.15	0.10
8. Bond selectivity	0.32	3.79	0.00
9. Transactions cost	−0.03	−0.38	0.00
Subtotal	0.47	5.56	0.10
V. Total return	0.41	4.76	0.20
VI. Sources of return			
1. Capital gains	−0.44	−5.20	
2. Interest income	0.85	9.96	
Total return	0.41	4.76	

Treasuries was 9 basis points. The value of 0.66 indicates that the expected monthly return from investing in Treasury bonds over this period was 66 basis points. Where does this value come from? Recall from Chapter 22 that we demonstrated that forward rates can be calculated from the Treasury yield curve. These rates are the market's consensus of rates that can be earned. It is the forward rate that is the expected return reported in the row "Expected." The unexpected return, −57 basis points, is the difference between the actual return of 9 basis points and the expected return of 66 basis points.

The results reported in the section "Interest Rate Effect" can be interpreted as the cost of being in the bond market. That is, if any investor wanted to invest in default-free bonds (i.e., Treasury securities) and simply bought a portfolio of Treasury securities, the return would have been 9 basis points. Therefore, this component of return is considered out of the manager's control since such a return would have been realized by anyone who decided to commit funds to the bond market.

Section II shows the *policy effect*. This section provides the necessary information to analyze the duration policy constraint specified by the manager's client. BONDPAR calculates the portion of the total return due to the policy constraint and separates it from the *interest rate management effect*. This effect is shown in Section III and gives the option-adjusted default-free return for the portfolio. This component of return shows whether the manager has successfully anticipated interest rate changes. The interest rate management effect is broken into the following three subcomponents: (1) *duration effect*, which is the effect on the return due to the magnitude of the yield curve shift[17]; (2) *convexity effect*, which is the return component of managing the convexity of the portfolio; and (3) *yield curve shape change effect*, which is the return due to the change in the shape of the yield curve (i.e., the residual return component not measured by duration and convexity).

Other management effects are shown in Section IV. These are divided into three effects. The *sector/quality effect* is the return component that shows whether the manager successfully selected the sector and quality groups that performed better over the evaluation period. The *bond selectivity effect* is the return component due to the selection of individual bonds in the portfolio. *Transactions cost* refers to the hypothetical effect of the costs that transactions had on the portfolio's return.

The last two sections, V and VI, provide summary information. The *Total Return* section is the time-weighted total return for the evaluation period. This is the sum of the preceding sections, "Interest Rate Effect," "Policy Effect," "Interest Rate Management Effect," and "Other Management Effects." The "Sources of Return" section separates the return into capital gains (the change in price) and interest income.

While Table 30-3 shows the decomposition of return for the entire portfolio, the same analysis can be done for each security. This is shown in Table 30-4.

PERFORMANCE EVALUATION USING SHARPE BENCHMARKS

As explained earlier, Sharpe benchmarks are determined by regressing subperiod (e.g., monthly) returns on various market indexes. For example, a Sharpe benchmark was used for an actual common stock portfolio managed by Aronson & Fogler, a money management firm in Philadelphia. The evaluation period was for the period January 1981 through July 1988. After adjustments, the resulting Sharpe benchmark based on monthly observations was[18]

Sharpe benchmark = 0.43 × (FRC price-driven index) + 0.13
× (FCR earnings-growth index) + 0.44 × (FRC 2000 index)

where FRC is an index produced by Frank Russell Company.

---

[17]Consistent with the concept of using the Treasury index to measure the unmanaged interest rate effect, this component is measured relative to the duration of the Treasury index.

[18]See Fogler, op. cit., p. 102.

TABLE 30-4

PERFORMANCE ATTRIBUTION ANALYSIS FOR EACH SECURITY WITH BONDPAR

Init. Face Value ($000) Bond Description	Initial Date	Last Date	Market Perf.			Portfolio Management			Total Return %	Return Source	
			Market Expect.	+ Rate Change	+ Int. Rate	+ Sector /Qual.	+ Selectivity	+ Trans Cost	=	Capit. Gains	+ Inter. Income
1 041033BM 24500.0 ARKANSAS POWER & LIGHT CO 14.125% 11/1/14 E4	2/28/90	3/31/90	0.66	-0.57	0.37	0.69	0.25	-.07	1.33	0.07	1.25
2 161610BA 25000.0 CHASE MANHATTAN CORP 9.750% 9/15/99 F3	2/28/90	3/31/90	0.66	-0.57	-0.19	0.01	1.12	-.04	0.98	0.11	0.88
3 172921CT 76151.7 CITICORP MORTGAGE SECS INC 9.500% 1/1/19 PS	2/28/90	3/31/90	0.66	-0.57	-0.04	0.25	-0.70	00.00	-0.40	-1.31	0.91
4 3024519X 73072.0 FHA INSURED PROJECT MORTGAG 7.400% 2/1/21 PS	2/28/90	3/31/90	0.66	-0.57	-0.55	0.70	-0.10	00.00	0.14	-0.59	0.73
5 313400KK 30600.0 FEDERAL HOME LOAN MTG CORP 12.250% 3/15/95 AG	2/28/90	3/31/90	0.66	-0.57	-0.08	0.06	0.50	00.00	0.57	-0.39	0.96
6 4581829H 5600.0 INTER-AMERICAN DEVELOPMENT 11.000% 12/11/92 X1	2/28/90	3/31/90	0.66	-0.57	0.05	-0.03	0.37	00.00	0.48	-0.47	0.95
7 674599AW 34000.0 OCCIDENTAL PETROLEUM CORP 11.750% 3/15/11 O4	2/28/90	3/31/90	0.66	-0.57	-0.31	0.05	0.84	00.00	0.68	-0.35	1.02
8 91282TTQ 93500.0 UNITED STATES TREASURY NOTE 7.375% 5/15/96 TR	2/28/90	3/31/90	0.66	-0.57	-0.19	0.00	0.17	00.00	0.07	-0.58	0.66
9 912827WN 92000.0 UNITED STATES TREASURY NOTE 9.250% 8/15/98 TR	3/13/90	3/31/90	0.39	-0.33	-0.15	0.00	0.99	-0.06	0.82	0.42	0.40
10 912827XM 85900.0 UNITED STATES TREASURY NOTE 9.000% 5/15/96 TR	2/28/90	3/10/90	0.21	-0.18	0.13	00.00	-0.08	-0.06	0.02	-0.27	0.29

The *Individual Security Performance* report lists the return components for all individual securities held during the evaluation period.

- *Initial Face Value* indicates in ($000) the beginning holding position for the bond.
- *Bond Description* displays the security's portfolio bond number, cusip number, coupon, maturity date, and sector/quality.
- *Initial Date* and *Last Date* display the evaluation period for the security being analyzed.
- The remaining columns break down the components of return for the individual security over the evaluation period.

Notice that the sum of the three coefficients is equal to 1. The coefficient of determination for this regression was 97.6%. The intercept term for this regression was 0.365%, which represents the average excess monthly return and is a statistic similar to Jensen's alpha explained earlier.

By subtracting the style benchmark's monthly return from the manager's monthly portfolio return, we can measure performance. This difference, which we refer to as *added-value residuals*, is what the manager added over the return from three "index funds" in the appropriate proportions. For example, suppose that in some month the return realized by this manager was 1.75%. In the same month, the returns for the three indexes were as follows: 0.7% for the FRC price-driven index, 1.4% for the FRC earnings-growth index, and 2.2% for the FRC 2000 Index. The added-value residual for this month would be determined as follows. First, calculate the value of the Sharpe benchmark:

$$\text{Sharpe benchmark} = 0.43 \times (0.7\%) + 0.13 \times (1.4\%) + 0.44 \times (2.2\%)$$
$$= 1.45\%$$

The added-value residual is then

$$\text{Added-value residual} = \text{actual return} - \text{Sharpe benchmark return}$$

Since the actual return for the month is 1.75%,

$$\text{Added-value residual} = 1.75\% - 1.45\% = 0.3\%.$$

Notice that if this manager had been benchmarked against a single-investment-style index such as the FRC price-driven index, she would have outperformed the benchmark by a wide margin (1.05%). In contrast, if the FRC 2000 Index is used as the benchmark, the manager would have underperformed by 0.45%.

Figure 30-4 shows monthly added-value residuals. This is a way of visualizing the risk of a manager underperforming. The standard deviation was 0.797%, so one would expect only 15% of the months to have a return of more than 80 basis points below the average excess return (i.e., 0.365%).

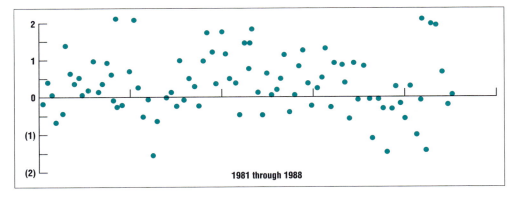

FIGURE 30-4
Monthly added value over benchmark.

■ SUMMARY

The role of performance evaluation is to determine if a money manager added value beyond what could have been achieved by a passive strategy in a benchmark portfolio. Four types of benchmarks have been used in practice: (1) market indexes, (2) generic-investment-style indexes, (3) Sharpe benchmarks, and (4) normal portfolios.

Generic-investment-style indexes have been developed by various consulting firms to measure particular investment styles. Because of the difficulty of classifying a money manager into one of the generic investment styles, Sharpe benchmarks are a useful alternative since they can be constructed using multiple regression from various specialized market indexes. A normal portfolio is a customized benchmark that includes a set of securities that contains the universe of securities that a manager normally selects from and whose securities are weighted as the manager would weight them in a portfolio. Advocates claim that normal portfolios are more appropriate benchmarks than market indexes because they control for investment management style, thereby representing a passive portfolio against which a manager can be evaluated. It is neither an easy nor costless process to construct normal portfolios.

Three single-index measures were developed in the 1960s to evaluate the relative performance of money managers: the Treynor Index, the Sharpe Index, and the Jensen Index. These measures fail to identify how or why a money manager may have outperformed or underperformed a benchmark.

In contrast to single-index measures, performance attribution models identify the sources of return. In the equity area, multifactor models are the foundation for performance attribution models, and these models can be used to determine whether active added value provided by a money manager comes from one of three sources: timing short-term factor trends, market timing, or security analysis. In the fixed-income area, returns are attributed to those elements beyond the manager's control, such as the interest rate environment and duration policy constraints imposed by a client, and those that the management process contributes to, such as interest rate management, sector/quality allocations, and individual bond selection.

Sharpe benchmarks can also be used to evaluate performance by calculating added-value residuals.

■ KEY TERMS

alpha	Jensen Index	Sharpe benchmark
BARRA's performance analysis (PERFAN) factor model	normal portfolio	Sharpe Index
	performance attribution analysis	Treynor Index
BONDPAR		

■ QUESTIONS

1. The following is an excerpt from H. Russell Fogler that appeared in "Normal Style Indexes— An Alternative to Manager Universes?" in *Performance Measurement: Setting the Standards, Interpreting the Numbers* (Charlottesville, VA: Association of Management and Investment Research, 1991):

   A desirable performance measurement system should have at least three characteristics: (1) it is easy to use and understand; (2) it accounts for average factor effects; and (3) it can accurately separate factor timing and selection ability. Style universes seem to satisfy the first criterion and partially address the second criterion; normal portfolios address the second criterion, but are weak on the first and third criteria. An alternate method, called Sharpe benchmarks, seems to satisfy both the first and second criteria while ignoring the third. (p. 97)

Explain why the above is true for generic-invest-ment-style indexes (referred to as "style uni-verses" in the quote), Sharpe benchmarks, and normal portfolios.

2. What are the difficulties of using generic-invest-ment-style indexes as a benchmark?

3. What are the difficulties of constructing a normal portfolio?

4. Indicate whether you agree or disagree with the following statement: "The three single-index measures (Treynor Index, Sharpe Index, and Jensen Index) assume that the portfolio is com-posed of a well-diversified group of stocks."

5. The following statement was made by H. Russell Fogler in "Common Stock Management in the 1990s," *Journal of Portfolio Management* (Winter 1990): "Once we appreciate the simplicity and power of multiple-factor models, single index measurement will join the archives of perfor-mance measurement history, where it belongs" (p. 34). The Treynor Index, Sharpe Index, and Jensen Index are examples of single-index mea-surements. Indicate whether you agree with the statement made by Dr. Fogler.

6. In the *AIMR Performance Presentation Stan-dards* (1993), the following statement appears: "The inclusion of attribution as summary infor-mation in presentations is encouraged. Because different methodologies for calculating attribu-tion can lead to different results, attribution analysis should be accompanied by a clear expla-nation of the methodology used" (p. 47). Explain why you agree or disagree with this statement.

7. The Izzobaf Corporation engages three external active equity money managers to manage its $300 million pension fund. The results of a per-formance attribution analysis of the three man-agers over the past four years are shown below:

	Manager X	Manager Y	Manager Z
Actual return	15.2	17.3%	21.4%
Benchmark portfolio	12.0	15.2	22.9
Active management return	3.2% (90)	2.1% (95)	−1.5% (83)
Components of Return			
Market timing	5.2% (99)	−0.4% (24)	−3.5% (88)
Industry exposure	−0.3 (10)	0.2 (39)	0.5 (24)
Sector emphasis	0.2 (20)	0.6 (89)	−0.3 (41)
Security selection	−2.0 (97)	1.5 (93)	−0.2 (10)

( ) denotes confidence level.

a. Why is it incorrect to state that manager Z outperformed the other two managers over this four-year period based on the actual re-turn?

b. Which manager appears to have done the best job in adding value?

c. The stated investment style of manager X is to select undervalued securities and neutralize market risk. Is the performance of this manager consistent with this stated investment style?

d. The component analysis supported manager Y's stated investment style. What is this man-ager's investment style?

e. Manager Z's stated investment style is to time the market and neutralize individual security selection by diversifying the portfolio with eq-uities and convertible bonds. Is the perfor-mance of this manager consistent with this stated investment style?

f. Calculate the unreconciled return for the three managers.

g. Which money manager should Izzobaf Corpo-ration consider terminating?

h. Suppose that manager Z offered Izzobaf Corpo-ration its services simply for market timing. Should these services be used?

8. The following is a statement from John H. Watts, chairman of Fischer Francis Trees & Watts, as published in *Performance Reporting for Invest-ment Managers: Applying the AIMR Perfor-mance Presentation Standards* (Charlottesville, VA: AIMR, 1991):

Results are often analyzed, for either comparison or evaluation purposes, over an arbitrary speci-fied number of years. The period we see most often used is five years. Particularly for fixed-in-come portfolios, an arbitrarily chosen period can lead to an unintended, if not perverse, conclu-sion. For example, if a five-year reporting period happens to fall within a bull market, a manager that has a long-term bond bias will look strong, and vice versa. (p. 57)

a. Why is this statement true for fixed-income portfolios if comparisons are based on actual returns?

b. How does performance attribution analysis re-duce the risk of distorting performance results for a fixed-income portfolio?

9. The following statement concerning a policy of Bell Atlantic is from Edward P. Rennie and

Thomas J. Cowhey, "The Successful Use of Benchmark Portfolios," in Darwin M. Bayston and H. Russell Fogler (eds.), *Improving Portfolio Performance with Quantitative Models* (Charlottesville, VA: Institute of Chartered Financial Analysts, 1989):

Typically, we exclude the first month's performance of a new investment manager from the analysis because of the transaction costs and the initial imbalance of the portfolio. Therefore, in our process an investment manager is not penalized because of the initial start-up costs. To the extent the first month's performance is included in the analysis, transaction costs should be assessed to the benchmark. (p. 39)

Explain the logic for the practice in the last sentence of the above quote.

10. Suppose that a plan sponsor using monthly returns has determined the following Sharpe benchmark for one of its money managers:

Sharpe benchmark = 0.785
$$\times \text{(FRC price-driven index)}$$
$$+ .055 \text{ (FRC earnings-growth index)}$$
$$+ 0.160 \text{ (FRC 2000 index)}$$

Suppose that in some month the return realized by this manager was 0.8%. In the same month, the returns for the three indexes were as follows: 0.5% for the FRC price-driven index, 2.0% for the FRC earnings-growth index, and 3% for the FRC 2000 Index.

a. What is the added-value residual for this month?
b. Did this manager outperform the benchmark?
c. Suppose that instead of using a Sharpe benchmark, the manager would have been classified using a single generic-investment-style. What would the appropriate index have been?
d. Suppose that the manager would have been classified according to the generic investment style based on your answer to part c. Would this manager have outperformed or underperformed the benchmark?
e. Does your conclusion about the performance of the manager change when the benchmark is the Sharpe benchmark and the generic-investment-style index?

APPENDIX A
STATISTICAL CONCEPTS

LEARNING OBJECTIVES
After reading this appendix you will be able to:

- explain what is meant by a random variable.
- describe what is meant by a probability distribution and a cumulative probability distribution.
- describe the fundamental properties of the normal distribution.
- calculate the variance and standard deviation.
- calculate the parameters of a simple linear regression.
- calculate and explain the meaning of the coefficient of determination.
- calculate the correlation and covariance between two random variables.

In most applications in investment management, the outcome of a decision will depend on variables that are not known with certainty at the time a decision is made. As a result, portfolio decisions rely on probability and statistical theory. Also, it is important to estimate relationships among variables. Such relationships can be estimated using regression analysis and correlation analysis. In this appendix, the fundamentals of probability and statistical theory, regression analysis, and correlation analysis are explained.

PROBABILITY THEORY

A probability measures the decision maker's degree of belief in the likelihood of a given outcome. A decision maker may formulate a probability based on empirical evidence. For example, if a money manager wants to estimate the probability that the return on the S&P 500 will increase by more than 5% in a given month, the manager can look at historical returns on the S&P 500 and base her probability on the percentage of times that a return greater than 5% occurred. In some instances, however, empirical evidence may not be available. The manager, then, draws on a variety of information and her experience to formulate a probability.

Random Variable and Probability Distribution

A **random variable** is a variable for which a probability can be assigned to each possible value that can be taken by the variable. A **probability distribution** or **probability function** is a function that describes all the values that the random variable can take on and the probability associated with each. A **cumulative probability distribution** is a function that shows the probability that the random variable will attain a value less than or equal to each value that the random variable can take on.

Let's use some notation. If we let X denote a random variable, then we use a subscript to denote specific values of the random variable. For example, X_i refers to the ith value for the random variable X. The probability of a specific value for the random variable X is typically denoted by stating the specific value [i.e., $P(X = $ specific value$)$] or by using the subscript notation [i.e., $P(X_i)$].

To illustrate the above concepts, suppose that the probability distribution of the rate of return of the common stock of the Hall Corporation over the next year is as shown in Table A-1. Nine possible outcomes are shown. Notice that the sum of the probabilities is 1.

The seventh outcome in Table A-1 represents a rate of return of 14.2%. The probability assigned to that rate of return is 10%. That is, $P(X = 14.2\%)$, or $P(X_7)$ is 10%. The probability that the total return will be less than 14.2% is the cumulative probability for the first six outcomes and is shown in the fourth column of Table A-1. The probability is 77%.

Statistical Measures of a Probability Distribution

Various measures are used to summarize the probability distribution of a random variable. The two most often used measures are the expected value and the variance (or standard deviation).

Expected Value The **expected value** of a probability distribution is the weighted average of the distribution. The weights in this case are the probabilities associated with the random variable X. The expected value of a random variable is denoted by $E(X)$ and is computed using the following expression:

$$E(X) = P_1X_1 + P_2X_2 + \ldots + P_nX_n$$

where P_i is the probability associated with the outcome X_i.

For example, the expected value for the one-year rate of return for the Hall Corporation whose probability distribution is shown in Table A-1 is found as follows:

TABLE A-1

PROBABILITY DISTRIBUTION FOR THE ONE-YEAR RATE OF RETURN OF THE HALL CORPORATION

i	Rate of Return	Probability	Cumulative Probability
1	−10.15%	0.05	0.05
2	−6.65	0.08	0.13
3	−3.02	0.10	0.23
4	0.85	0.16	0.39
5	5.00	0.22	0.61
6	9.44	0.16	0.77
7	14.20	0.10	0.87
8	19.31	0.08	0.95
9	24.79	0.05	1.00

$$E(X) = 0.05(-10.15) + 0.08(-6.65) + 0.10(-3.02) + 0.16(0.85) + 0.22(5.00)$$
$$+ 0.16(9.44) + 0.10(14.42) + 0.08(19.31) + 0.05(24.79) = 5.61\%$$

The expected value for the one-year rate of return is 5.61%.

Variance and Standard Deviation   A portfolio manager is interested not only in the expected value of a probability distribution but also in the dispersion of the random variable around the expected value. A measure of dispersion of the probability distribution is the **variance** of the distribution. The variance of a random variable X, denoted by var(X), is computed from the following formula:

$$\text{var}(X) = [X_1 - E(X)]^2 P_1 + [X_2 - E(X)]^2 P_2 + \ldots + [X_n - E(X)]^2 P_n$$

Notice that the variance is simply a weighted average of the deviations of each possible outcome from the expected value, where the weight is the probability of an outcome occurring. The greater the variance, the greater the distribution of the possible outcomes for the random variable. The reason that the deviations from the expected value are squared is to avoid outcomes above and below the expected value from canceling each other out.

The problem with using the variance as a measure of dispersion is that variance is expressed in terms of squared units of the random variable. Consequently, the square root of the variance, called the **standard deviation**, is a more meaningful measure of the degree of dispersion. Mathematically this can be expressed as follows:

$$\text{std}(X) = \sqrt{\text{var}(X)}$$

where std(X) denotes the standard deviation of the random variable X.

The variance for the one-year rate of return for the Hall Corporation whose probability distribution is given in Table A-1 is calculated as follows:

$$\text{var}(X) = (-10.15 - 5.61)^2 \, 0.05 + (-6.65 - 5.61)^2 \, 0.08 + (-3.02 - 5.61)^2$$
$$0.10 + (0.85 - 5.61)^2 \, 0.16 + (5.00 - 5.61)^2 \, 0.22 + (9.44 - 5.61)^2 \, 0.16 +$$
$$(14.42 - 5.61)^2 \, 0.10 + (19.31 - 5.61)^2 \, 0.08 + (24.79 - 5.61)^2 \, 0.05$$
$$= 78.73\%$$

The standard deviation is 8.87%, which is the square root of the variance, 78.73%.

Normal Probability Distribution

In many applications involving probability distributions, it is assumed that the underlying probability distribution is a **normal distribution**. An example of a normal distribution is shown in Figure A-1.

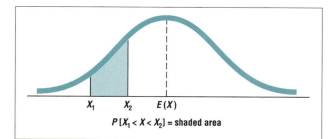

FIGURE A-1

Example of a normal distribution (or normal curve).

The area under the normal distribution or normal curve between any two points on a horizontal axis is the probability of obtaining a value between those two values. For example, the probability of realizing a value for the random variable X that is between X_1 and X_2 in Figure A-1 is shown by the shaded area. Mathematically, the probability of realizing a value for X between these two variables can be written as follows:

$P(X_1 < X < X_2)$

The entire area under the normal curve is equal to 1.

Properties of the Normal Distribution The normal distribution has the following properties:

1. The point in the middle of the normal curve is the expected value for the distribution.
2. The distribution is symmetric around the expected value. That is, half the distribution is to the left of the expected value and the other half is to the right. Thus, the probability of obtaining a value less than the expected value is 50%. The probability of obtaining a value greater than the expected value is also 50%. Mathematically, this can be expressed as follows:

    $P[X < E(X)] = 0.5$ and $P[X > E(X)] = 0.5$

3. The probability that the actual outcome will be within a range of one standard deviation above the expected value and one standard deviation below the expected value is 68.26%, rounded off to 68.3%.
4. The probability that the actual outcome will be within a range of two standard deviations above the expected value and two standard deviations below the expected value is 95.46%, rounded off to 95.5%.
5. The probability that the actual outcome will be within a range of three standard deviations above the expected value and three standard deviations below the expected value is 99.74%, rounded off to 99.7%.

Suppose that the one-year rate of return for a portfolio has an expected value of 7% and a standard deviation of 4% and that the probability distribution is a normal distribution. The probability is 68.3% that the one-year rate of return will be between 3% (the expected value of 7% minus one standard deviation of 4%) and 11% (the expected value of 7% plus one standard deviation of 4%). The probability is 95.5% that the one-year rate of return will be between −1% (the expected value minus two standard deviations) and 15% (the expected value plus two standard deviations).

Suppose that the standard deviation for the one-year rate of return in the previous illustration is 2% rather than 4%. Then the probability is 68.3% that the one-year rate of return will be between 5% and 9%; the probability is 95.5% that the one-year rate of return will be between 3% and 11%. *Notice that the smaller the standard deviation, the smaller the range of the possible outcome for a given probability.*

Using Normal Distribution Tables Tables are available that give the probability of obtaining a value between any two values of a normal probability distribution. All that must be known in order to determine the probability is the expected value and the standard deviation. However, the normal distribution table is constructed for a normal distribution that has an expected value of 0 and a standard deviation of 1. In order to use the table, therefore, it is necessary to convert the normal distribution under consideration into a distribution that has an expected value of 0 and a standard deviation of 1. This is done by standardizing the values of the distribution under consideration.

The procedure is as follows. Suppose that a normal distribution for some random variable X has an expected value $E(X)$ and a standard deviation denoted by std(X). To standardize any particular value, say X_1, the following is computed:

$$z_1 = \frac{X_1 - E(X)}{std(X)}$$

where z_1 is the **standardized value** or **normal deviate** for X_1.

Table A-2 is an abridged table that shows the area under the normal curve, which, as stated before, represents probability. This particular table shows the probability of obtaining a value greater than some specified value in standardized form in the right-hand tail of the distribution. This is the shaded area shown in the normal curve at the top of Table A-2. For instance, the table indicates that the probability of getting a value greater than one standard deviation is 15.87%.

Lognormal Distribution

The rate of return on securities calculated for short time periods such as one day, one month, or one quarter can be well approximated by a normal distribution. For returns calculated over longer time periods, empirically it has been demonstrated that such returns are better described as following a **lognormal distribution**. A distribution is said to be lognormal if the logarithm of the variable follows a normal distribution.

Calculating Variance and Standard Deviation from Historical Data

In several topics in this book, we explain the role of volatility. For example, in our discussion of Markowitz portfolio theory in Chapter 4, we need the volatility of the return on stocks as an input into the model. In our discussion of the pricing of options in Chapter 18, we explain that the volatility is an input into all option-pricing models.

As we indicate in our discussions of volatility, the variance (or standard deviation) is a proxy for volatility, since it measures the variation of a random variable around its mean or expected value. Here we will demonstrate how to calculate historical volatility.

Formula for Calculating Variance from Historical Data   Earlier, we showed how to calculate the standard deviation and variance of a random variable given a probability distribution. The variance of a random variable using historical data is calculated using the following formula:

$$\text{Variance} = \sum_{t=1}^{T} \frac{(X_t - \overline{X})^2}{T - 1} \tag{A-1}$$

and then

TABLE A-2

NORMAL DISTRIBUTION TABLE FOR S.TANDARDIZED VALUE (OR NORMAL DEVIATE) z

z	.00	.01	.02	.03	.04	.05	.06	.07	.08	.09
0.0	.5000	.4960	.4920	.4880	.4840	.4801	.4761	.4721	.4681	.4641
0.1	.4602	.4562	.4522	.4483	.4443	.4404	.4364	.4325	.4286	.4247
0.2	.4207	.4168	.4129	.4090	.4052	.4013	.3974	.3936	.3897	.3859
0.3	.3821	.3783	.3745	.3707	.3669	.3632	.3594	.3557	.3520	.3483
0.4	.3446	.3409	.3372	.3336	.3300	.3264	.3228	.3192	.3156	.3121
0.5	.3085	.3050	.3015	.2981	.2946	.2912	.2877	.2843	.2810	.2776
0.6	.2743	.2709	.2676	.2643	.2611	.2578	.2546	.2514	.2483	.2451
0.7	.2420	.2389	.2358	.2327	.2296	.2266	.2236	.2206	.2177	.2148
0.8	.2110	.2090	.2061	.2033	.2005	.1977	.1949	.1922	.1894	.1867
0.9	.1841	.1814	.1788	.1762	.1736	.1711	.1685	.1660	.1635	.1611
1.0	.1587	.1562	.1539	.1515	.1492	.1469	.1449	.1423	.1401	.1379
1.1	.1357	.1335	.1314	.1292	.1271	.1251	.1230	.1210	.1190	.1170
1.2	.1151	.1131	.1112	.1093	.1075	.1056	.1038	.1020	.1003	.0985
1.3	.0968	.0951	.0934	.0918	.0901	.0885	.0869	.0853	.0838	.0823
1.4	.0808	.0793	.0778	.0764	.0749	.0735	.0721	.0708	.0694	.0681
1.5	.0668	.0655	.0643	.0630	.0618	.0606	.0594	.0582	.0571	.0559
1.6	.0548	.0537	.0526	.0516	.0510	.0495	.0485	.0475	.0465	.0455
1.7	.0446	.0436	.0427	.0418	.0409	.0401	.0392	.0384	.0375	.0367
1.8	.0359	.0351	.0344	.0336	.0329	.0322	.0314	.0307	.0301	.0294
1.9	.0287	.0281	.0274	.0268	.0262	.0256	.0250	.0244	.0239	.0233
2.0	.0228	.0222	.0217	.0212	.0207	.0202	.0197	.0192	.0188	.0183
2.1	.0179	.0174	.0170	.0166	.0162	.0158	.0154	.0150	.0146	.0143
2.2	.0139	.0136	.0132	.0129	.0125	.0122	.0119	.0116	.0113	.0110
2.3	.0107	.0104	.0102	.0099	.0096	.0094	.0091	.0089	.0087	.0084
2.4	.0082	.0080	.0078	.0075	.0073	.0071	.0069	.0068	.0066	.0064
2.5	.0062	.0060	.0059	.0057	.0055	.0054	.0052	.0051	.0049	.0048
2.6	.0047	.0045	.0044	.0043	.0041	.0040	.0039	.0038	.0037	.0036
2.7	.0035	.0034	.0033	.0032	.0031	.0030	.0029	.0028	.0027	.0026
2.8	.0026	.0025	.0024	.0023	.0023	.0022	.0021	.0021	.0020	.0019
2.9	.0019	.0018	.0018	.0017	.0016	.0016	.0015	.0015	.0014	.0014
3.0	.0013	.0013	.0013	.0012	.0012	.0011	.0011	.0011	.0010	.0010

Standard deviation = $\sqrt{\text{variance}}$

where X_t = observation t on variable X
$\bar{X}$ = the average sample value for variable X_t
T = the number of observations in the sample

TABLE A-3							
WORSHEET FOR THE CALCULATION OF THE VARIANCE AND STANDARD DEVIATION FOR THE MONTHLY RETURN ON IBM: JANUARY 1989 TO DECEMBER 1993							
Month	**t**	**X_t**	**X_t^2**	**Month**	**t**	**X_t**	**X_t^2**
Jan. 89	1	7.1790	51.5380	Aug. 91	32	−3.1260	9.7719
Feb. 89	2	−6.1440	37.7487	Sept. 91	33	6.9680	48.5530
Mar. 89	3	−10.1850	103.7342	Oct. 91	34	−5.1870	26.9050
Apr. 89	4	4.4670	19.9541	Nov. 91	35	−4.6210	21.3536
May 89	5	−2.7760	7.7062	Dec. 91	36	−3.7840	14.3187
June 89	6	2.0520	4.2107	Jan. 92	37	1.1240	1.2634
July 89	7	2.7930	7.8008	Feb. 92	38	−2.1280	4.5284
Aug. 89	8	2.9000	8.4100	Mar. 92	39	−3.8850	15.0932
Sept. 89	9	−6.7240	45.2122	Apr. 92	40	8.6830	75.3945
Oct. 89	10	−8.2380	67.8646	May 92	41	1.3330	1.7769
Nov. 89	11	−1.4110	1.9909	June 92	42	7.8510	61.6382
Dec. 89	12	−3.5850	12.8522	July 92	43	−3.1930	10.1952
Jan. 90	13	4.7810	22.8580	Aug. 92	44	−7.2980	53.2608
Feb. 90	14	6.5500	42.9025	Sept. 92	45	−6.7820	45.9955
Mar. 90	15	2.1660	4.6916	Oct. 92	46	−17.1830	295.2555
Apr. 90	16	2.7090	7.3387	Nov. 92	47	3.8650	14.9382
May 90	17	11.2020	125.4848	Dec. 92	48	−26.1900	685.9161
June 90	18	−2.0830	4.3389	Jan. 93	49	2.2330	4.9863
July 90	19	−5.1060	26.0712	Feb. 93	50	6.6310	43.9702
Aug. 90	20	−7.5470	56.9572	Mar. 93	51	−6.4370	41.4350
Sept. 90	21	4.4170	19.5099	Apr. 93	52	−4.4230	19.5629
Oct. 90	22	−0.9400	0.8836	May 93	53	9.5940	92.0448
Nov. 90	23	8.9770	80.5865	June 93	54	−6.3980	40.9344
Dec. 90	24	−0.5500	0.3025	July 93	55	−9.8730	97.4761
Jan. 91	25	12.1680	148.0602	Aug. 93	56	3.3710	11.3636
Feb. 91	26	2.5330	6.4161	Sept. 93	57	−8.1970	67.1908
Mar. 91	27	−11.5530	133.4718	Oct. 93	58	9.5240	90.7066
Apr. 91	28	−9.5500	91.2025	Nov. 93	59	17.6630	311.9816
May 91	29	4.2090	17.7157	Dec. 93	60	4.8720	23.7364
June 91	30	−8.4810	71.9274				
July 91	31	4.2470	18.0370	Total		−36.5160	3479.3256

It can be demonstrated that Equation (A-1) is equivalent to the following:

$$\text{Variance} = \frac{\sum_{t=1}^{T} X_t^2 - \frac{1}{T}\left(\sum_{t=1}^{T} X_t\right)^2}{T - 1} \tag{A-2}$$

We will demonstrate how to use Equation (A-2) by computing the monthly variance for the return on a stock. In Chapter 4, the monthly return on IBM stock for the 60-month period beginning January 1989 and ending December 1993 is presented in Table 4-4. Table A-3 shows the worksheet. The first column shows the month, the second column the return for IBM for that month [X_t in the notation of Equation (A-2)], and the last column the square of the monthly return [X_t^2 in the notation of Equation (A-2)]. The last row shows the sum of the second and third columns. Therefore from Table A-3 we know

$$\sum_{t=1}^{60} X_t = -36.516 \qquad \sum_{t=1}^{60} X_t^2 = 3,479.326$$

Substituting these values into Equation (A-2), we obtain

$$\text{Variance} = \frac{3{,}479.326 - \dfrac{1}{60}(-36.516)^2}{60 - 1}$$

$$= 58.90$$

The standard deviation is then

$$\text{Standard deviation} = \sqrt{58.90} = 7.675\%$$

Annualizing Volatility   In option-pricing models, most market participants calculate the volatility of return or price using daily data. Market practice with respect to the number of days that should be used to calculate the daily standard deviation varies. The number of days can be as few as 10 days or as many as 100 days.

Since market participants are interested in the annual volatility, the daily standard deviation must be annualized as follows:

annual standard deviation

$$= \text{daily standard deviation} \times \sqrt{\text{number of days in a year}}$$

Market practice varies with respect to the number of days that should be used in the annualizing formula above. Typically, either 250 days, 260 days, or 365 days are used.

Thus, in calculating an annual standard deviation, the portfolio manager must decide on:

1. The number of daily observations to use
2. The number of days in the year to use to annualize the daily standard deviation

Interpreting the Annualized Standard Deviation   What does it mean if the annual standard deviation or annual volatility for a security's return is, say, 15%? It means that if the prevailing expected return is 7%, the standard deviation of the one-year return is 105 basis points (7% times 15%).

Assuming that the return is approximately normally distributed, this means that there is a 68.3% probability that the one-year return will be within one standard deviation below and above 7%. Thus, there is a 68.3% probability that the security's return will be between 5.95% and 8.05%. Similarly, from the properties of a normal distribution we know that there is a 95.5% probability that the security's return will be within a range of two standard deviations (between 4.9% and 9.10%); there is a 99.7% probability it will be within a range of three standard deviations (3.85% and 10.15%).

Notice that the larger the volatility, the larger the range of the security's possible return. This means that there is greater uncertainty about the return. For example, if the annual volatility or standard deviation is 20% rather than 15%, this translates into a return volatility of 140 basis points (20% times 7%). Assuming a normal distribution, there is a 68.3% probability that the security's return will be between 5.6% and 8.4%, a 95.5% probability that it will be between 4.2% and 9.8%, and a 99.7% probability that it will be between 2.8% and 11.2%.

REGRESSION ANALYSIS

In many applications in investment management, a relationship between two or more random variables must be estimated. **Regression analysis** is a statistical technique that can be used to estimate relationships between variables. Regression analysis will be explained with an illustration.

The Simple Linear Regression Model

Suppose that a portfolio manager wants to estimate the relationship between the monthly return on IBM stock and the S&P 500. This is, in fact, an important relationship, called the *single-index market model,* which we discussed in Chapter 5. Assume that the portfolio manager believes that the monthly relationship can be expressed as follows:

IBM monthly return $= \alpha + \beta$(S&P 500 monthly return)   (A-3)

The values α and β are called the *parameters* of the model. The objective of regression analysis is to estimate the parameters.

There are several points to note about this relationship. First there are only two variables in the relationship—the return on IBM stock and the return on the S&P 500. Because there are only two variables and the relationship is linear, this regression model is called a **simple linear regression**. Since the return on IBM is assumed to depend on the return on the S&P 500, the return on IBM is referred to as the *dependent variable.* The return on the S&P 500 is referred to as the *explanatory* or *independent variable* because it is used to explain the return on IBM. Second, it is highly unlikely that the estimated relationship for Equation (A-3) will describe the true relationship between the two returns exactly because, as explained in Chapter 6, other factors may influence the return on IBM in addition to the return on the S&P 500. Consequently, the relationship may be more accurately described by adding a random error term to Equation (A-3). That is, the relationship can be expressed as follows:

IBM monthly return $= \alpha + \beta$(S&P 500 monthly return)

$+$ random error term   (A-4)

The expression can be simplified as follows:

$$Y = \alpha + \beta X + e$$

where Y = monthly return on IBM
X = monthly return on the S&P 500
e = random error term

Estimating the Parameters of the Simple Linear Regression Model

In order to estimate the parameters of the simple linear regression model, historical information on the monthly returns of IBM and the S&P 500 is needed. The third and fourth columns in Table A-4 give the monthly returns for the S&P 500 and IBM, respectively, for 60 months beginning January 1989 and ending December 1993. Each pair of values for the two variables X and Y is referred to as an *observation.* The 60 observations shown in Table A-4 will be used to estimate Equation (A-4). The 60 observations are plotted in Figure A-2. When observations are plotted in this fashion, the resulting diagram is called a *scatter diagram.*

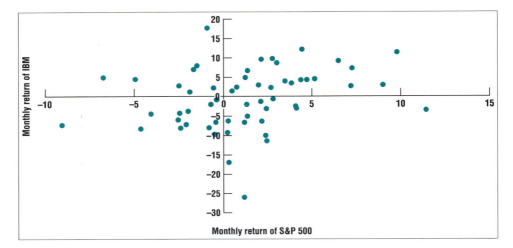

FIGURE A-2

Scatter diagram with observations for the monthly returns on IBM and the S&P 500.

One possible way of estimating the relationship between the two returns is simply to draw a line through the observations which are believed to best represent the relationship. Selecting two points on this line will determine the estimated relationship. The obvious pitfall is that there is no specified criterion for drawing the line, and hence different individuals would obtain different estimates of the relationship based on the same observations.

The regression method specifies a logical criterion for estimating the relationship. To understand this criterion, first rewrite the simple linear regression so that it shows the estimated relationship for each observation. This is done as follows[1]:

$$Y_t = \alpha + \beta X_t + e_t$$

where the subscript t denotes the observation for the tth month. For example, for the fourth observation $(t = 4)$, the above expression is

$$4.467 = \alpha + \beta(5.13) + e_4$$

For observation 18 $(t = 18)$, the expression is

$$-2.083 = \alpha + \beta(-0.60) + e_{18}$$

The values for e_4 and e_{18} are referred to as the *observed error term for the observation*. Note that the value of the observed error term for both observations will depend on the values selected for α and β. This suggests a criterion for selecting the two parameters. The parameters should be estimated in such a way that the sum of the observed error terms for all observations is as small as possible.

Although this is a good standard, it presents one problem. Some observed error terms will be positive, and others will be negative. Consequently, positive and negative observed error terms will offset each other. To overcome this problem, each error term could be squared. On the basis of that criterion, the objective would then be to select parameters so as to minimize the sum

---

[1]The notation for the variables in the single index market model in Chapter 5 is

$$X_t = r_{Mt} \quad \text{and} \quad Y_t = r_{it}$$

where r stands for return and the subscripts M and i represent the S&P 500 and stock i, respectively.

of the square of the observed error terms. This is precisely the criterion used to estimate the parameters in regression analysis. Because of this property, regression analysis is sometimes referred to as the *method of least squares.*

The formulas that can be used to estimate the parameters on the basis of this criterion are derived from differential calculus. Their use will be illustrated. If a hat (^) over the parameter denotes the estimated value and T denotes the total number of observations, then the estimated parameters for α and β are computed from the observations using the following formulas:

$$\hat{\beta} = \frac{\sum_{t=1}^{T} X_t Y_t - \frac{1}{T} \sum_{t=1}^{T} X_t \sum_{t=1}^{T} Y_t}{\sum_{t=1}^{T} X_t^2 - \frac{1}{T} \left(\sum_{t=1}^{T} X_t \right)^2} \tag{A-5}$$

and

$$\hat{\alpha} = \frac{1}{T} \sum_{t=1}^{T} Y_t - \frac{1}{T} (\hat{\beta}) \sum_{t=1}^{T} X_t \tag{A-6}$$

Although the formulas look complicated, they are easy to apply. In actual problems with a large number of observations, there are regression analysis programs that will compute the value of the parameters using the above formulas. Most electronic spreadsheets are preprogrammed to perform simple linear regression analysis.

The above formulas may be used to compute the estimated parameters on the basis of the 60 observations given in Table A-4. The worksheet for the sums needed to apply the formula is shown as Table A-4 and summarized below.

$$\sum_{t=1}^{60} X_t = 72.03 \qquad \sum_{t=1}^{60} Y_t = -36.516$$

$$\sum_{t=1}^{60} X_t Y_t = 401.8848 \qquad \sum_{t=1}^{60} X_t^2 = 909.5345$$

Substituting into Equation (A-5) yields

$$\hat{\beta} = \frac{401.8848 - \frac{1}{60}(72.01)(-36.516)}{909.5345 - \frac{1}{60}(72.01)^2}$$

$$= 0.5415$$

Substituting into Equation (A-6) yields

$$\hat{\alpha} = \frac{1}{60}(-36.516) - \frac{1}{60}(0.5415)(72.01)$$

$$= -1.2585$$

The estimated relationship between the monthly return on IBM and the S&P 500 is then

$$Y = -1.2585 + 0.5415X$$

TABLE A-4

WORKSHEET FOR THE ESTIMATION OF THE PARAMETERS OF THE SIMPLE LINEAR REGRESSION: RELATIONSHIP BETWEEN MONTHLY RETURN ON IBM AND S&P 500

X_t = monthly return on S&P 500 Y_t = monthly return on IBM

Month	t	X_t	Y_t	$X_t Y_t$	X_t^2	Y_t^2
Jan. 89	1	7.2100	7.1790	51.7606	51.9841	51.5380
Feb. 89	2	−2.5000	−6.1440	15.3600	6.2500	37.7487
Mar. 89	3	2.3600	−10.1850	−24.0366	5.5696	103.7342
Apr. 89	4	5.1300	4.4670	22.9157	26.3169	19.9541
May 89	5	4.0400	−2.7760	−11.2150	16.3216	7.7062
June 89	6	−0.5500	2.0520	−1.1286	0.3025	4.2107
July 89	7	8.9800	2.7930	25.0811	80.6404	7.8008
Aug. 89	8	1.9300	2.9000	5.5970	3.7249	8.4100
Sept. 89	9	−0.3900	−6.7240	2.6224	0.1521	45.2122
Oct. 89	10	−2.3600	−8.2380	19.4417	5.5696	67.8646
Nov. 89	11	2.0700	−1.4110	−2.9208	4.2849	1.9909
Dec. 89	12	2.3900	−3.5850	−8.5682	5.7121	12.8522
Jan. 90	13	−6.7200	4.7810	−32.1283	45.1584	22.8580
Feb. 90	14	1.2900	6.5500	8.4495	1.6641	42.9025
Mar. 90	15	2.6200	2.1660	5.6749	6.8644	4.6916
Apr. 90	16	−2.4800	2.7090	−6.7183	6.1504	7.3387
May 90	17	9.7500	11.2020	109.2195	95.0625	125.4848
June 90	18	−0.6900	−2.0830	1.4373	0.4761	4.3389
July 90	19	−0.3200	−5.1060	1.6339	0.1024	26.0712
Aug. 90	20	−9.0400	−7.5470	68.2249	81.7216	56.9572
Sept. 90	21	−4.9200	4.4170	−21.7316	24.2064	19.5099
Oct. 90	22	−0.3700	−0.9400	0.3478	0.1369	0.8836
Nov. 90	23	6.4300	8.9770	57.7221	41.3449	80.5865
Dec. 90	24	2.7500	−0.5500	−1.5125	7.5625	0.3025
Jan. 91	25	4.3600	12.1680	53.0525	19.0096	148.0602
Feb. 91	26	7.1500	2.5330	18.1110	51.1225	6.4161
Mar.91	27	2.4200	−11.5530	−27.9583	5.8564	133.4718
Apr. 91	28	0.2400	−9.5500	−2.2920	0.0576	91.2025
May 91	29	4.3200	4.2090	18.1829	18.6624	17.7157
June 91	30	−4.5800	−8.4810	38.8430	20.9764	71.9274
July 91	31	4.6600	4.2470	19.7910	21.7156	18.0370

Goodness of Fit

The portfolio manager will be interested in knowing how "good" the estimated relationship is before relying upon it for any investment strategy. Statistical tests determine in some sense how good the relationship is between the dependent variable and the explanatory variable. A measure of the "goodness of fit" of the relationship is the coefficient of determination.

The explanatory or independent variable X is being used to try to explain movements in the dependent variable Y. But what movements is it trying to explain? The variable X is trying to explain why the variable Y would deviate from its mean. It can be shown that if no explanatory variable is used to try to explain movements in Y, the method of least squares would give the mean of Y as the value estimate of Y. Thus the ability of X to explain deviations of Y from its mean is of interest. In regression analysis, when we refer to the variation in a variable we mean its deviation from its mean.

The coefficient of determination indicates the percentage of the variation of the dependent variable that is explained by the explanatory variable (i.e.,

TABLE A-4 (continued)						
WORKSHEET FOR THE ESTIMATION OF THE PARAMETERS OF THE SIMPLE LINEAR REGRESSION: RELATIONSHIP BETWEEN MONTHLY RETURN ON IBM AND S&P 500						

X_t = monthly return on S&P 500 Y_t = monthly return on IBM

Month	t	X_t	Y_t	X_tY_t	X_t^2	Y_t^2
Aug. 91	32	2.3700	−3.1260	−7.4086	5.6169	9.7719
Sept. 91	33	−1.6700	6.9680	−11.6366	2.7889	48.5530
Oct. 91	34	1.3400	−5.1870	−6.9506	1.7956	26.9050
Nov. 91	35	−4.0300	−4.6210	18.6226	16.2409	21.3536
Dec. 91	36	11.4400	−3.7840	−43.2890	130.8736	14.3187
Jan. 92	37	−1.8600	1.1240	−2.0906	3.4596	1.2634
Feb. 92	38	1.3000	−2.1280	−2.7664	1.6900	4.5284
Mar. 92	39	−1.9500	−3.8850	7.5758	3.8025	15.0932
Apr. 92	40	2.9400	8.6830	25.5280	8.6436	75.3945
May 92	41	0.4900	1.3330	0.6532	0.2401	1.7769
June 92	42	−1.4900	7.8510	−11.6980	2.2201	61.6382
July 92	43	4.0900	−3.1930	−13.0594	16.7281	10.1952
Aug. 92	44	−2.0500	−7.2980	14.9609	4.2025	53.2608
Sept. 92	45	1.1800	−6.7820	−8.0028	1.3924	45.9955
Oct. 92	46	0.3500	−17.1830	−6.0141	0.1225	295.2555
Nov. 92	47	3.4100	3.8650	13.1797	11.6281	14.9382
Dec. 92	48	1.2300	−26.1900	−32.2137	1.5129	685.9161
Jan. 93	49	0.7300	2.2330	1.6301	0.5329	4.9863
Feb. 93	50	1.3600	6.6310	9.0182	1.8496	43.9702
Mar. 93	51	2.1500	−6.4370	−13.8396	4.6225	41.4350
Apr. 93	52	−2.4200	−4.4230	10.7037	5.8564	19.5629
May 93	53	2.6800	9.5940	25.7119	7.1824	92.0448
June 93	54	0.2900	−6.3980	−1.8554	0.0841	40.9344
July 93	55	−0.4000	−9.8730	3.9492	0.1600	97.4761
Aug. 93	56	3.7900	3.3710	12.7761	14.3641	11.3636
Sept. 93	57	−0.7700	−8.1970	6.3117	0.5929	67.1908
Oct. 93	58	2.0700	9.5240	19.7147	4.2849	90.7066
Nov. 93	59	−0.9500	17.6630	−16.7799	0.9025	311.9816
Dec. 93	60	1.2100	4.8720	5.8951	1.4641	23.7364
Total		72.0100	−36.5160	401.8848	909.5345	3479.3256

explained by the regression).[2] That is,

$$\text{Coefficient of determination} = \frac{\text{variation of } Y \text{ explained by } X}{\text{variation of } Y} \qquad \text{(A-7)}$$

The coefficient of determination can take on a value between 0 and 1. If all the variation of Y is explained by X, then the coefficient of determination is 1. When none is explained by X, the coefficient of determination is 0. Hence, the closer the coefficient of determination is to 1, the stronger the relationship between the variables.

Another interpretation of the coefficient of determination is that it measures how close the observed points are to the regression line. The closer the observed points are to the regression line, the closer the coefficient of

---

[2]In statistics textbooks, the terms "total sum of squares" and "explained sum of squares" are used instead of variation in Y and variation in Y explained by X.

determination will be to 1. On the other hand, the greater the scatter of the observed points from the regression line, the closer the coefficient of determination will be to 0.

The coefficient of determination is commonly referred to as "R-squared" and denoted by R^2. Computation of the coefficient of determination is as follows.

To compute variation of Y, the following formula is used:

$$\text{Variation of } Y = \sum_{t=1}^{T} Y_t^2 - \frac{1}{T}\left(\sum_{t=1}^{T} Y_t\right)^2 \tag{A-8}$$

The variation of Y explained by X is computed using the following formula:

$$\text{Variation of } Y \text{ explained by } X = \hat{\beta}\left(\sum_{t=1}^{T} X_t Y_t - \frac{1}{T}\sum_{t=1}^{T} X_t \sum_{t=1}^{T} Y_t\right) \tag{A-9}$$

The coefficient of determination is then found by dividing the variation of Y explained by X by the variation of Y.

From the worksheet shown as Table A-4,

$$\sum_{t=1}^{60} X_t = 72.03 \qquad \sum_{t=1}^{60} Y_t = -36.516$$

$$\sum_{t=1}^{60} X_t Y_t = 401.8848 \qquad \sum_{t=1}^{60} Y_t^2 = 3{,}479.326$$

Then substituting into Equation (A-7), we get

$$\text{Variation of } Y = 3{,}479.326 - \frac{1}{60}(-36.516)^2$$

$$= 3{,}457.142362$$

and substituting into Equation (A-8), we get

$$\text{Variation of } Y \text{ explained by } X = (0.5415)[401.8848 - \frac{1}{60}(72.01)(-36.516)]$$

$$= 241.3500215$$

The coefficient of determination is therefore

$$\text{Coefficient of determination} = \frac{241.3500215}{3{,}457.142362} = 0.07$$

A coefficient of determination of 0.07 means that approximately 7% of the variation in the monthly return of IBM is explained by the monthly return of the S&P 500.

Tests can be performed to determine whether the coefficient of determination is statistically significant. Alternatively, the statistical significance of the estimated β parameter can be tested. The test involves determining whether the estimated β is statistically different from zero. If there is no relationship between the two variables, the estimated β would not be statistically different from zero. A discussion of these tests is provided in statistics textbooks.

Extension of the Simple Linear Regression Model

In many applications, a dependent variable may be best explained by more than one explanatory variable. When such a relationship is estimated, it is referred to as a **multiple regression**. The computations for obtaining the parameters of a multiple regression are difficult to compute by hand. Fortunately, there are numerous multiple regression analysis programs for computing the parameters of a multiple regression.

The interpretation of the coefficient of determination is the same in multiple regression as it is in simple linear regression. In the latter case, it is the total sum of squares explained by the explanatory variable X. In multiple regression, the coefficient of determination is the variation in Y explained by all the explanatory variables. By adding an explanatory variable to a regression model, the belief is that the new explanatory variable will significantly increase the variation in Y explained by the regression. For example, suppose that a simple linear regression is estimated and that the variation in Y is 1,000 and the variation explained by the single explanatory variable X is 600. Suppose that another explanatory variable is added to the regression model and that the inclusion of this explanatory variable increased the variation in Y explained from 600 to 750. Thus, it would increase the coefficient of determination from 60% to 75% (750/1,000). This new explanatory variable would appear to have contributed substantially to explaining the variation in Y. On the other hand, had the variation in Y explained by the regression increased from 600 to 610, the coefficient of determination would increase from 60% to only 61%. Thus it appears that the new explanatory variable did not do much to help explain the dependent variable.

CORRELATION ANALYSIS

The correlation coefficient measures the association between two variables. No cause and effect are assumed when a correlation coefficient is computed. Therefore, when a correlation coefficient between two variables is computed, there is no assumption about which one is the dependent variable and which is the explanatory variable. In regression analysis, one variable is assumed to be dependent on the other.

Calculating the Correlation

The formula for calculating the correlation between two random variables X and Y is

$$\text{cor} = \frac{T\sum_{t=1}^{T} X_t Y_t - \sum_{t=1}^{T} X_t \sum_{t=1}^{T} Y_t}{\sqrt{\left[T\sum_{t=1}^{T} X_t^2 - \left(\sum_{t=1}^{T} X_t\right)^2\right] - \left[T\sum_{t=1}^{T} Y_t^2 - \left(\sum_{t=1}^{T} Y_t\right)^2\right]}} \tag{A-10}$$

To illustrate how to use Equation (A-10), we will calculate the correlation between the monthly return on IBM (X) and that on Walgreen (Y) for the 60-month period January 1989–December 1993. The data are provided in Table A-5. The last row of the table indicates that

TABLE A-5

CALCULATION OF THE CORRELATION BETWEEN THE MONTHLY RETURN ON WALGREEN AND IBM: JANUARY 1989 AND DECEMBER 1993

X_t = monthly return on IBM Y_t = monthly return on Walgreen

Month	t	X_t	Y_t	X_t^2	Y_t^2	X_tY_t
Jan. 89	1	7.1790	27.2730	51.5380	743.8165	195.7929
Feb. 89	2	−6.1440	−8.6490	37.7487	74.8052	53.1395
Mar. 89	3	−10.1850	1.4290	103.7342	2.0420	−14.5544
Apr. 89	4	4.4670	8.4510	19.9541	71.4194	37.7506
May 89	5	−2.7760	8.5560	7.7062	73.2051	−23.7515
June 89	6	2.0520	1.8020	4.2107	3.2472	3.6977
July 89	7	2.7930	16.8170	7.8008	282.8115	46.9699
Aug. 89	8	2.9000	−4.9620	8.4100	24.6214	−14.3898
Sept. 89	9	−6.7240	−0.5330	45.2122	0.2841	3.5839
Oct. 89	10	−8.2380	−7.2370	67.8646	52.3742	59.6184
Nov. 89	11	−1.4110	3.3530	1.9909	11.2426	−4.7311
Dec. 89	12	−3.5850	5.0560	12.8522	25.5631	−18.1258
Jan. 90	13	4.7810	−11.4990	22.8580	132.2270	−54.9767
Feb. 90	14	6.5500	−1.3290	42.9025	1.7662	−8.7050
Mar. 90	15	2.1660	4.6180	4.6916	21.3259	10.0026
Apr. 90	16	2.7090	−1.1760	7.3387	1.3830	−3.1858
May 90	17	11.2020	11.7860	125.4848	138.9098	132.0268
June 90	18	−2.0830	6.1480	4.3389	37.7979	−12.8063
July 90	19	−5.1060	0.7580	26.0712	0.5746	−3.8703
Aug. 90	20	−7.5470	−8.3520	56.9572	69.7559	63.0325
Sept. 90	21	4.4170	−1.3680	19.5099	1.8714	−6.0425
Oct. 90	22	−0.9400	5.2760	0.8836	27.8362	−4.9594
Nov. 90	23	8.9770	6.8180	80.5865	46.4851	61.2052
Dec. 90	24	−0.5500	1.9850	0.3025	3.9402	−1.0918
Jan. 91	25	12.1680	9.7330	148.0602	94.7313	118.4311
Feb. 91	26	2.5330	11.2750	6.4161	127.1256	28.5596
Mar. 91	27	−11.5530	7.6000	133.4718	57.7600	−87.8028
Apr. 91	28	−9.5500	−2.6020	91.2025	6.7704	24.8491
May 91	29	4.2090	−0.4120	17.7157	0.1697	−1.7341
June 91	30	−8.4810	2.3080	71.9274	5.3269	−19.5741
July 91	31	4.2470	2.6320	18.0370	6.9274	11.1781

$$\sum_{t=1}^{60} X_t = -36.516 \qquad \sum_{t=1}^{60} Y_t = 123.288 \qquad \sum_{t=1}^{60} X_tY_t = 627.3633$$

$$\sum_{t=1}^{60} X_t^2 = 3,479.3256 \qquad \sum_{t=1}^{60} Y_t^2 = 3,402.0807$$

Substituting these values into Equation (A-10) yields

$$\text{cor} = \frac{60\,(627.3633) - (-36.516)(123.288)}{\sqrt{[60(3,479.3256) - (-36.516)^2][60(3,402.0807) - (123.288)^2]}}$$

$$= 0.21$$

Relationship between the Correlation Coefficient and Coefficient of Determination

The **coefficient of determination** turns out to be equal to the square of the correlation coefficient. Thus, the square root of the coefficient of determination is the correlation coefficient. Since the coefficient of determination can be between 0 and 1, the correlation coefficient will be between −1 and 1. The

		TABLE A-5 (continued)				
	CALCULATION OF THE CORRELATION BETWEEN THE MONTHLY RETURN ON WALGREEN AND IBM: JANUARY 1989 AND DECEMBER 1993					
X_t = monthly return on IBM		Y_t = monthly return on Walgreen				
Month	**t**	X_t	Y_t	X_t^2	Y_t^2	X_tY_t
Aug. 91	32	−3.1260	1.0700	9.7719	1.1449	−3.3448
Sept. 91	33	6.9680	−6.9090	48.5530	47.7343	−48.1419
Oct. 91	34	−5.1870	4.2970	26.9050	18.4642	−22.2885
Nov. 91	35	−4.6210	−2.6070	21.3536	6.7964	12.0469
Dec. 91	36	−3.7840	17.3750	14.3187	301.8906	−65.7470
Jan. 92	37	1.1240	−0.6580	1.2634	0.4330	−0.7396
Feb. 92	38	−2.1280	−3.6290	4.5284	13.1696	7.7225
Mar. 92	39	−3.8850	−1.0340	15.0932	1.0692	4.0171
Apr. 92	40	8.6830	−6.6200	75.3945	43.8244	−57.4815
May 92	41	1.3330	−0.3580	1.7769	0.1282	−0.4772
June 92	42	7.8510	1.8800	61.6382	3.5344	14.7599
July 92	43	−3.1930	5.9040	10.1952	34.8572	−18.8515
Aug. 92	44	−7.2980	7.3310	53.2608	53.7436	−53.5016
Sept. 92	45	−6.7820	−0.3260	45.9955	0.1063	2.2109
Oct. 92	46	−17.1830	5.2290	295.2555	27.3424	−89.8499
Nov. 92	47	3.8650	10.0000	14.9382	100.0000	38.6500
Dec. 92	48	−26.1900	−1.1330	685.9161	1.2837	29.6733
Jan. 93	49	2.2330	−8.5960	4.9863	73.8912	−19.1949
Feb. 93	50	6.6310	−1.8180	43.9702	3.3051	−12.0552
Mar. 93	51	−6.4370	3.5260	41.4350	12.4327	−22.6969
Apr. 93	52	−4.4230	−5.8820	19.5629	34.5979	26.0161
May 93	53	9.5940	12.8950	92.0448	166.2810	123.7146
June 93	54	−6.3980	−5.5560	40.9344	30.8691	35.5473
July 93	55	−9.8730	−6.8110	97.4761	46.3897	67.2450
Aug. 93	56	3.3710	3.7210	11.3636	13.8458	12.5435
Sept. 93	57	−8.1970	−3.8590	67.1908	14.8919	31.6322
Oct. 93	58	9.5240	13.7120	90.7066	188.0189	130.5931
Nov. 93	59	17.6630	−3.7180	311.9816	13.8235	−65.6710
Dec. 93	60	4.8720	0.3070	23.7364	0.0942	1.4957
Total		−36.5160	123.2880	3479.3256	3402.0807	627.3633

sign of the correlation coefficient will be the same as the sign of the slope of the regression, β. For example, earlier we calculated that the coefficient of determination between the monthly return of IBM and the S&P 500 is 0.07. The correlation coefficient is therefore 0.26.

Covariance

The covariance measures how two random variables vary together. The covariance is related to the correlation coefficient as follows:

$$\text{Covariance} = \text{std}(X)\text{std}(Y)(\text{correlation coefficient}) \qquad \text{(A-11)}$$

The covariance between IBM (X) and Walgreen (Y) for the 60-month period January 1989–December 1993 is found as follows. Earlier we calculated the standard deviation of IBM and found it to be 7.675. The standard deviation of Walgreen is 7.305. The correlation between Walgreen and IBM is 0.21. Therefore from Equation (A-11):

$$\text{Covariance} = 7.675(7.305)(0.21) = 11.77$$

■ SUMMARY

A random variable is a variable that can take on more than one possible value in the future. A probability distribution gives the probability of obtaining the values that the random variable can realize. One particular type of probability distribution is the normal distribution.

For all probability distributions an expected value and a standard deviation (variance) can be computed. The expected value is the weighted average of the distribution. The standard deviation measures the dispersion of the possible outcomes around the expected value.

Regression analysis is used to estimate the relationship between variables. A simple linear regression includes one explanatory variable and a dependent variable. A multiple regression includes more than one explanatory variable. The method of least squares is used to estimate the

parameters of the relationship, creating a line of best fit for the scatter plot of the observations.

The coefficient of determination is a measure of the goodness of fit of the linear relationship. The coefficient of determination is the ratio of the explained sum of squares to the total sum of squares and consequently varies between 0 and 1. The larger the coefficient of determination, the better the relationship. The coefficient of determination is related to the correlation coefficient.

The correlation coefficient and covariance measure the association between two random variables. The correlation coefficient can have a value between –1 and 1. The correlation coefficient is just the square root of the coefficient of determination.

■ KEY TERMS

coefficient of determination
cumulative probability
    distribution
expected value
lognormal distribution
multiple regression

normal deviate
normal distribution
probability distribution
probability function
random variable
regression analysis

simple linear regression
standard deviation
standardized value
variance

■ QUESTIONS

1. a. What is a random variable?
   b. What is probability distribution and a cumulative probability distribution?

2. a. Complete the following table which contains information about the probability distribution for the one-year rate of return of the Rice Corporation:

Outcome	Rate of Return	Probability	Cumulative Probability
1	−12.35%	0.05	0.05
2	−7.25	0.10	?
3	−4.15	0.15	?
4	−0.50	0.20	?
5	1.90	0.18	?
6	5.65	0.12	?
7	9.20	0.08	?
8	13.30	?	?
9	24.79	0.05	1.00

   b. Calculate the expected value of the one-year rate of return.
   c. Calculate the variance and the standard deviation of the one-year rate of return.

3. Suppose that the one-year rate of return for a portfolio has an expected value of 5% and a standard deviation of 2.5%, and that the probability distribution can be characterized as following a normal distribution.

   a. What is the probability that the one-year rate of return will be between 2.5% and 7.5%?
   b. What is the probability that the one-year rate of return will be between 0% and 10%?
   c. What is the probability that the one-year rate of return will be negative?
   d. What is the probability that the one-year rate of return will be greater than 15%?

4. Suppose that the standard deviation for the one-year rate of return in the previous question is 10% rather than 2.5%.

   a. What is the probability of realizing a one-year rate of return less than zero?
   b. What is the probability of realizing a one-year rate of return greater than 15%?

5. Calculate the variance and standard deviation for the monthly rate of return for the historical series beginning May 1989 and ending April 1994 for Quaker Oats, Sprint, the S&P 500, and the New York Stock Exchange Composite Index given below:

	Quaker Oats	Sprint	S&P 500	NYSE
1989				
May	5.33%	20.00%	3.51%	3.30%
June	5.57	−4.69	0.10	−0.53
July	10.04	12.50	8.84	8.16
Aug.	−8.76	9.43	1.55	1.49
Sept.	0.76	−1.66	0.15	−0.67
Oct.	−1.20	−6.46	−2.52	−2.95
Nov.	−2.02	7.41	1.65	1.63
Dec.	−4.16	−4.08	2.97	1.93
1990				
Jan.	−13.42	−13.82	−6.88	−6.92
Feb.	−7.75	11.45	0.85	0.87
March	2.11	10.27	3.26	2.06
April	4.81	−4.06	−2.69	−2.87
May	3.06	19.87	9.20	8.51
June	−4.75	−13.32	−0.00	−0.74
July	−1.31	−38.17	−0.52	−0.45
Aug.	−10.34	4.59	−9.43	−9.06
Sept.	6.84	5.91	−4.19	−5.15
Oct.	5.03	−6.05	−0.67	−1.00
Nov.	3.72	−9.90	5.99	5.95
Dec.	9.26	3.30	3.45	2.52
1991				
Jan.	−3.07	5.91	4.15	3.93
Feb.	9.27	−0.51	6.73	6.99
March	5.16	−1.02	2.98	2.29
April	−0.85	6.25	0.03	0.03
May	0.43	13.73	3.86	3.71
June	7.11	2.59	−3.96	−4.47
July	5.44	−6.78	4.49	4.36
Aug.	−1.03	−4.09	1.96	2.05
Sept.	−1.36	−2.84	−1.12	−1.55
Oct.	7.01	−8.37	1.19	1.50
Nov.	8.33	0.00	−4.39	−4.06
Dec.	10.34	3.23	11.97	10.44
1992				
Jan.	−12.85	1.05	−1.99	−1.41
Feb.	−2.87	−11.98	0.96	0.89
March	−12.14	7.69	−1.48	−2.17
April	−7.69	6.11	2.79	2.26
May	10.29	−3.66	0.10	0.25
June	1.65	−4.35	−0.96	−1.98
July	3.08	6.90	3.94	3.93
Aug.	2.14	0.54	−2.40	−2.20
Sept.	5.62	5.35	1.68	0.63
Oct.	7.78	5.13	0.21	0.48
Nov.	5.19	2.93	3.03	2.98
Dec.	−7.77	−2.37	1.71	1.16
1993				
Jan.	−1.15	5.39	0.70	0.71
Feb.	7.20	4.65	1.05	0.89
March	−2.03	9.33	2.55	2.19
April	−2.80	1.64	−2.54	−2.39
May	13.24	6.05	2.27	2.11
June	3.36	7.60	0.80	0.20
July	−14.85	2.49	−0.53	−0.24
Aug.	1.74	3.47	3.44	3.38
Sept.	2.90	−0.68	−0.31	−0.64
Oct.	5.97	−2.04	1.94	1.63
Nov.	3.17	−8.33	−1.29	−1.77
Dec.	−2.35	6.11	1.68	1.68
1994				
Jan.	−7.04	4.32	3.25	3.10
Feb.	−3.79	2.07	−3.00	−2.95
March	−0.54	−6.76	−3.90	−4.69
April	2.79	7.30	1.15	1.34

6. For the historical returns in the previous question, calculate the correlation and covariance between Quaker Oats and Sprint.

7. a. For the historical returns of Sprint in question 5, estimate the parameters of the following regression:

   $$\text{Sprint return} = \alpha + \beta(\text{S\&P 500 return})$$
   $$+ \text{ random error term}$$

   b. Calculate the coefficient of determination for the relationship and explain what it means.
   c. What is the correlation coefficient between the monthly return on Sprint and the S&P 500?

8. a. For the historical returns of Sprint in question 5, estimate the following regression:

   $$\text{Sprint return} = \alpha + \beta(\text{NYSE return})$$
   $$+ \text{ random error term}$$

   b. Calculate the coefficient of determination for the relationship and explain what it means.
   c. Compare the β and the coefficient of determination found in b with that found in question 6b.

9. Suppose that the daily standard deviation of the yield changes for a Treasury security is found to be 0.9%.

   a. How can the annual standard deviation be determined?

b. Why might two investors calculate a different annual standard deviation even if they find that the daily standard deviation is the same.

10. A bond portfolio manager wants to estimate the relationship between the yield on new single-A-rated medium-term industrial bonds and the yield on 10-year Treasuries. Assume that the portfolio manager believes that the industrial/Treasury yield relationship can be expressed as follows:

Industrial yield = $\alpha + \beta$(Treasury yield) + error term

That is,

$Y = \alpha + \beta X + e$

where Y = yield on new single-A medium-term industrial bonds
X = yield on 10-year Treasuries
e = random error term

The portfolio manager collects the following data for 45 months:

Date	t	Yield on Treasury	Industrial
11/30/88	1	9.057	9.900
12/30/88	2	9.140	10.000
1/31/89	3	8.983	9.800
2/28/89	4	9.298	10.250
3/31/89	5	9.279	10.100
4/28/89	6	9.057	9.950
5/31/89	7	8.598	9.550
6/30/89	8	8.079	9.000
7/31/89	9	7.808	8.700
8/31/89	10	8.256	9.150
9/29/89	11	8.298	9.250
10/31/89	12	7.913	9.000
11/30/89	13	7.833	8.950
12/29/89	14	7.924	9.100
1/31/90	15	8.418	9.380
2/28/90	16	8.518	9.550
3/30/90	17	8.636	9.650
4/30/90	18	9.028	10.050
5/31/90	19	8.599	9.550
6/29/90	20	8.414	9.400
7/31/90	21	8.341	9.200
8/31/90	22	8.854	9.875
9/28/90	23	8.800	10.000
10/31/90	24	8.620	9.850
11/30/90	25	8.252	9.500
12/31/90	26	8.069	9.350

Date	t	Yield on Treasury	Industrial
1/31/91	27	8.011	9.200
2/28/91	28	8.036	9.100
3/28/91	29	8.059	9.050
4/30/91	30	8.013	8.900
5/31/91	31	8.059	8.875
6/28/91	32	8.227	9.050
7/31/91	33	8.147	9.000
8/30/91	34	7.814	8.600
9/30/91	35	7.443	8.250
10/31/91	36	7.462	8.250
11/29/91	37	7.378	8.125
12/31/91	38	6.700	7.600
1/31/92	39	7.281	8.000
2/28/92	40	7.257	8.050
3/31/92	41	7.530	8.230
4/30/92	42	7.583	8.300
5/29/92	43	7.325	8.000
6/30/92	44	7.123	7.750
7/31/92	45	6.709	7.300

a. Using regression analysis, estimate the parameters of the relationship.
b. What is the goodness of fit of the estimated relationship?

11. Explain why you agree or disagree with the following statement: "The correlation coefficient indicates the degree to which one random variable depends on another."

12. A portfolio manager estimates a simple linear regression between the monthly rate of return on a stock and the S&P 500 and finds that the coefficient of determination is 0.45. The manager believes that another explanatory variable would improve the statistical relationship. Suppose that the explanatory variable is added to the regression and the coefficient of determination rises to 0.46.

a. Explain why the relationship is called a multiple linear regression.
b. Explain whether you believe that the explanatory variable that was added to the regression added much to the portfolio manager's understanding of what affects the rate of return on the stock.

APPENDIX B

REVIEW OF THE INCOME STATEMENT AND BALANCE SHEET

LEARNING OBJECTIVES
After reading this appendix you will be able to:

- describe the sources of financial information for analyzing a company.

- explain what the auditors' opinion is and the potential conflicts that arise for independent auditors.

- explain what is meant by generally accepted accounting standards.

- describe how the shareholders' letter can be used.

- explain the underlying principles in constructing the income statement.

- describe the key items in the income statement and the key focus that requires the analyst's attention.

- explain how the inventory valuation method selected by a corporation affects reported income.

- describe the key items in the balance sheet and the key focus that requires the analyst's attention.

- explain how the judgments in preparing financial statements and the choices available make the comparison among firms difficult.

In Chapter 12 we described the role of analysts in forecasting the earnings of a company. A key source of information in analyzing the earnings of a company as well as its economic well-being is provided in various financial reports the company is required to publish. Our focus in this appendix and the two that follow is on considerations in analyzing a company's financial statements.

In this appendix, we review two key elements of an annual financial report: the income statement and the balance sheet. In Appendix C, our concern is with the analysis of earnings, and in Appendix D, debt and cash flow analysis. It is assumed that the reader has taken a course in financial accounting. This is a typical prerequisite at most universities for a course in finance. Our

---

*This appendix is coauthored with Professor John C. Ritchie, Jr., of Temple University. Some material in this appendix has been taken from various issues of Thornton L. O'Glove's *Quality of Earnings Reports*. Permission to use this material is granted by Thornton L. O'Glove.

discussion in the three appendixes is not on the construction of financial statements (the terms "debits" and "credits" are never mentioned), but on important issues in analyzing these financial statements.

SOURCES OF INFORMATION FOR ANALYZING A COMPANY

There are several documents that investors can use to prepare an analysis of a company. The first are documents prepared by the company itself. These documents can be divided into two groups: (1) documents that the corporation prepares and files with the Securities and Exchange Commission (SEC) and (2) documents that the corporation prepares and distributes to shareholders. A summary of the contents of these documents is given in Table B-1. The former (the ones filed with the SEC) include the 10-K (an annual filing), the 8-Q (a quarterly filing), and the proxy statement. The documents that the corporation prepares and distributes to shareholders include the annual report and the quarterly financial report. The annual report is the principal document used by corporations to communicate with shareholders. It is not an official SEC filing; consequently, companies have significant discretion in deciding on what types of information will be reported and the way it is reported. In addition, when a corporation offers a new security to the public, the SEC requires that the corporation prepare and file a registration statement and pro-

---

TABLE B-1

SUMMARY OF DOCUMENTS THAT A CORPORATION PREPARES

1. Documents That the Corporation Must Prepare and File with the SEC

Document: Form 10-K

When must be filed: 90 days after close of corporation's fiscal year

Contents:
 Part I. Covers business, properties, legal proceedings, principal securityholders, and securityholdings of management
 Part II. Covers selected financial data, management's discussion and analysis of financial conditions and results of operations, financial statements, and supplementary data
 Part III. Covers directors and executive officers and remuneration of directors and officers
 Part IV. Provides complete, audited annual financial information
 Part V. Provides schedule of various items.

Document: Form 8-Q

When must be filed: 45 days after close of corporation's each fiscal quarter

Contents:
 Part I. Quarterly financial statements provided
 Part II. Covers legal proceedings, changes in securities, defaults upon senior securities, changes in amount outstanding of securities or indebtedness, submission of matters to a vote of securityholders, and other materially important events

Document: Proxy statement

Contents: Notifies designated classes of stockholders of matters to be voted upon at a shareholders' meeting.

2. Documents That the Corporation Prepares and Distributes to Shareholders (Not Official SEC Filings)

Document: Annual report to shareholders

Contents: Provides financial information on annual operations and often non-financial information about the business that are not reported elsewhere.

Document: Quarterly report to shareholders

Contents: Provides quarterly financial information on operations.

vide a condensed version of this statement, called a *prospectus*, to potential investors.

The reports filed with the SEC are bland and legalistic. The best place to start the analysis of a corporation would be with the annual report sent to shareholders. One of the reasons companies issue annual reports is to comply with the mandate set down in Rule 14a-3 of the Securities Exchange Act of 1934, which enumerates the specific financial information that must be revealed, but not the form in which it is to be presented. Annual reports contain some basic accounting and statistical data and commentaries. It is in the commentaries that there is a chance that management will inadvertently include information that can be helpful to the investor in going beyond the numbers reported in the accounting and statistical sections of the report.

More specifically, in every annual report is the **shareholders' letter**. In this section of the annual report one can often find discussions by management of successful and failed strategies. Also, the shareholders' letter is usually jargon-free. Occasionally an investor can come across letters that communicate problems and possibilities clearly, in such a way as to simultaneously illuminate the situation at the firm and provide guidance for the probing of the rest of the report, which necessarily must follow. In fact, this is the prime purpose of these letters. We'll see an example of this in Appendix C.

In addition to the documents listed in Table B-1 that the corporation prepares, there are publications by commercial services. Some of the more popular are the publications put out by Standard & Poor's Corporation, Moody's Investor Service, and Value Line.

THE ROLE OF THE AUDITOR

The financial statements of a company are prepared by the firm's management. Therefore, there is the potential that the accounting data may be presented in a biased and/or fraudulent manner. It is the role of the independent auditor, who is paid by the firm being audited, to review its accounting books and issue an opinion on the veracity of the financial statements. The auditor's opinion is presented in a section of the financial statements called the **auditor's report**.

Financial statements are prepared in accordance with **generally accepted accounting principles (GAAP)**. But what exactly is GAAP? Before 1964, the pronouncements of the Committee on Accounting Procedure and the Accounting Principles Board (APB) were viewed by the accounting profession as GAAP. However, those pronouncements were not backed by enforcement power, and so accountants did not necessarily comply with the recommendations of GAAP. In 1964, the Council of the American Institute of Certified Public Accountants (AICPA) incorporated Rule 203 into its rule of ethics. Rule 203 states:

> A member shall not express an opinion that financial statements are presented in conformity with generally accepted accounting principles if such statements contain any departure from an accounting principle promulgated by the body designated by the Council to establish such principles which has a material effect on the statements taken as a whole, unless the member can demonstrate that due to unusual circumstances the financial statements would otherwise have been

misleading. In such cases his report must describe the departure, the approximate effects thereof, if practicable, and the reasons why compliance with the principle would result in a misleading statement.

Since 1973, the Financial Accounting Standards Board (FASB) has been the accounting standard-setting body of the accounting profession. This means that the accounting standards issued by the FASB are GAAP. The FASB is a private entity whose board members are full time and include members of the accounting profession, representatives from private industry, and financial analysts.

One might think that an auditor who operates under these professional guidelines could certainly be relied upon. That is, if anything in the financial statements is to be accepted at face value, it would be the auditor's report. If the auditor finds items that smack of deceit, he or she can—indeed, must—say so in the opinion.

In fact, there are four categories of opinions that might be awarded:

1. A **clean opinion** means that there is an unqualified acceptance by the auditor of the financial statements.
2. A **subject to opinion** means that the auditor accepts the financial statements subject to pervasive uncertainty that cannot be adequately measured, such as information relating to the value of inventories, reserves for losses, or other matters subject to judgment.
3. An **except for opinion** means that the auditor was unable to audit certain areas of the company's operations because of restrictions imposed by management or other conditions beyond the auditor's control.
4. A **disclaimer of opinion** is a statement from the auditor disclaiming any opinion regarding the company's financial condition.

Most opinions are clean, and disclaimers are rare.

The issuance of an opinion would seem to be very scientific, precise, and legalistic. Unfortunately this is not always the case. While the accounting profession maintains that the opinions remain a good indication of the accuracy of financial statements, many shareholder suits allege that the auditors have not been doing their jobs as well as they might. For example, Baldwin-United, Penn Square Bank, and Continental Illinois all failed. They also have something else in common: All received clean opinions in the most recent report prior to collapse. And these are only the more spectacular cases.[1] That these incidents are out of the ordinary is certainly true, but that can hardly console stockholders in the failed companies who thought the clean auditor's report meant that everything was as represented.

The reason for this is not necessarily incompetence. Rather, its roots are in the unusual relationship between auditors and their clients. The client pays the bill to have an independent audit and will be displeased if the auditor discovers irregularities sufficient to prevent him or her from offering a clean opinion. Putting that in writing may mean the loss of an account in

---

[1]For additional examples, see Thornton L. O'Glove (with Robert Sobel), *Quality of Earnings* (New York: Free Press, 1987), Chap. 2.

an industry marked by intense competition, in which raids for clients and price slashing have become the rule. A full audit for a large corporation can cost from $1 million to $6 million and can open the door for other services and fees.

In April of 1985, the SEC issued a warning to registrants and independent auditors attempting to engage in "opinion shopping." The practice of **opinion shopping** involves a corporation that attempts to obtain reporting objectives by following questionable accounting principles and a pliable auditor willing to go along with the desired treatment.

The average investor probably never even looks at the auditor's statement—but he or she should consider it carefully and with discretion.

THE INCOME STATEMENT

The **income statement** shows the revenues, expenses, and income (the difference between revenue and expenses) of a corporation over some period of time. A corporation must prepare income statements for its fiscal year and interim periods (quarterly). For many years, major emphasis has been placed on the income statement—not only in the case of common stock analysis, but also in the case of bonds and preferred stock analysis. The margin of safety for fixed-income securityholders is provided by a corporation's earnings and cash flow. The value of the business reflects the amount that can be earned on the invested capital and the cash flow generated by that firm. Therefore, the analyst must determine a true earnings base of recurring earnings from which growth and volatility of earnings and dividends may be projected. All a common stockholder can receive from an investment are dividends and/or capital appreciation. Both are dependent on future earnings—and expectations by investors of future earnings and dividends.

Security analysts seek information from the income statement in order to answer the following questions:

1. What is the true recurring earnings base that serves as a starting point for generating useful projections of future performance?
2. How has the company performed over a relatively long time horizon (10 years of data often are studied to encompass a business cycle) and in the recent past? What factors underlie the revenue and cost trends exhibited?
3. Is earnings growth consistent or is the company in decline? Do the earnings patterns from year to year display significant variability? If so, what causes this variability?
4. How does the earnings growth of the company being analyzed compare with the earnings growth of the economy and the industry in which it participates? How does the company compare with competitors in terms of revenue, cost behavior, and profitability?
5. Does the company appear to have good control of costs?

The focal point of common stock analysis is on the growth and profitability of the firm. Table B-2 provides the income statement appearing in the 1991 Annual Report of The Home Depot, Inc., for its 1991 and 1990 fiscal years.

TABLE B-2		
THE HOME DEPOT, INC. INCOME STATEMENT, 1991 AND 1990 (Dollars in Thousands)		
	1991	**1990**
Net sales	$3,815,356	$2,758,535
Cost of goods sold	2,751,085	1,991,777
Gross profit	1,064,271	766,758
Operating expenses	693,657	504,363
General & administration	91,664	67,901
Pre-opening expense	13,315	9,845
Net operating profit	$265,635	$184,649
Interest expense (net)	5,807	2,634
Earnings before taxes	259,828	182,015
Income taxes	96,400	70,061
Net income	$163,428	$111,954

Matching Revenues and Expenses

The most fundamental accounting principle applied to the income statement is that which requires the matching of revenues and expenses. Revenue is recognized when it is realized, not when the cash is received. The **matching concept** requires the recognition of all costs that are associated with the generation of the revenue reported in the income statement. For this reason, corporations are required to use accrual accounting. Many subjective judgments are made by accountants in matching costs and revenues, leading to potential limitations of the figures in the income statement and possibly to misleading conclusions if not properly considered by the analyst.

Below we discuss the major items in the income statement and note the careful attention required by the analyst. The relationship between items in the income statement usually is explored by means of ratio analysis, which will be discussed separately in Appendix D.

Revenues

The revenues of a company are its net sales. Sales can be divided into cash sales and installment sales. Cash sales do not present a problem. The major concern of the analyst is installment sales. Many companies recognize the entire profit for an installment sale when the sale is made, assuming the company is reasonably certain it will be paid. Certain types of sales may, however, result in periodic installment payments which could stretch over several years (e.g., a land development company). One could then raise the question about the number of payments that would have to be received before the buyer has a sufficient stake to make continued payments relatively certain. The AICPA has issued standards governing the accounting for installment sales, but some companies may follow practices that are more conservative than the required standards while other companies follow only the minimally acceptable standards.

Expenses

Any income statements offered by firms today separate the results achieved through regular operations from those produced by non-operating and/or extraordinary activities of the company. Moreover, expenses often are classified by functions, e.g., the cost to produce and sell goods, selling expenses, administrative expenses, and other expenses. This facilitates year-by-year comparisons of key expense categories and forecasting efforts.

Expenditures for items where the benefits are expected to be received over a period longer than one year typically are **capitalized** (i.e., recorded in asset accounts) and then depreciated or amortized over the life of the asset. Where the benefit is expected to be received within a year, the cost of the item is **expensed** (i.e., directly charged to an expense account) and fully reduces reported profit of that year. Many items are not easily labeled as short or long term, and some companies may capitalize a given item (a liberal policy since it increases reported income), while other companies expense it (a conservative policy since it decreases reported income). This can lead to noncomparability of reported profits among firms.

There are numerous items that a corporation may expense in its tax return but capitalize in its published balance sheet. Many companies have followed such a procedure in regard to advertising and promotional expenses. Analysts are cynical about capitalization and deferral of expense items. When companies defer items that more properly should be currently expensed, the result is higher reported profit. The analyst must make adjustments, increasing reported expenses and decreasing reported profits for these and similar expense items that should be expensed in the current year rather than deferred to later years.

Other items that are capitalized in annual reports, but expensed in tax returns, are intangible drilling costs of oil and natural gas producers and exploration and development expenses of mining companies. These all raise a problem for the analyst attempting to place different companies on a comparable basis.

Inventory Valuation Methods and Cost of Goods Sold   At the moment that net income is increased by revenues derived from the sale of a product, it is also decreased by the costs associated with producing that product. Accountants determine the total cost of goods sold for a period by a process of deduction. The value of inventory on hand at the beginning of the period is added to that acquired during the period to determine the total cost for all goods available for sale. Those units still on hand at the end of the period obviously were not sold. Accordingly, the value of goods on hand at the end of the period is determined by means of a physical inventory and subtracted from the cost of goods available for sale to determine the cost-of-goods-sold figure used in the income statement.

Inventory, in accordance with accounting standards, should be valued "at cost or market, whichever is lower." Application of this rule, however, requires the determination of cost. If prices were constant, the determination of cost of goods sold would be simple. Prices to acquire units of inventory do change, however, and one must determine which particular units were sold to match costs and revenues. How are the units sold and those in ending inventory valued? The two most widely used methods for assigning these costs are **first-in–first-out (FIFO)** and **last-in–first-out (LIFO)**.

To illustrate the problem, assume the inventory data shown in Table B-3.

The FIFO method is based on the assumption that the first merchandise acquired is the first merchandise sold. The ending inventory, therefore, consists of the most recently acquired goods. The key to calculating the cost of goods sold is to calculate the value of the ending inventory of 200 units that was determined by physical count. The value of the ending inventory is $5,730, calculated as follows:

70 units purchased December 12	$2,450
70 units purchased September 28	1,960
60 units purchased June 13 (@ $22/unit)	1,320
Total: 200 units	$5,730

Cost of goods sold is $3,160, calculated as follows:

Beginning inventory	$1,680
Plus purchases	7,210
Cost of goods available for sale	$8,890
Less ending invenory	5,730
Cost of goods sold	$3,160

Under the LIFO method, the most recently acquired goods are assumed to be sold first, and the ending inventory consists of "old" goods acquired through the earliest purchases. For purposes of measuring income, the flow of costs may be more significant than the actual flow of goods. LIFO seems realistic in this context since costs stated in more current dollars are matched against revenues stated in relatively current dollars.

The value of the ending inventory under the LIFO method is $2,760, calculated as follows:

140 units, beginning inventory	$1,680
60 units, February 26 purchase	1,080
Total: 200 units	$2,760

TABLE B-3

INVENTORY PURCHASES AND COSTS

	Number of Units	Cost per Unit	Total Cost
Beginning inventory	140	$12	$1,680
Purchase, February 26	70	18	1,260
Purchase, June 13	70	22	1,540
Purchase, September 28	70	28	1,960
Purchase, December 12	70	35	2,450
Available for sale	420		$8,890
Units sold	220		
Units in ending inventory	200		

Cost of goods sold is $6,130, calculated as follows:

Beginning inventory	$1,680
Plus purchases	7,210
Cost of goods available for sale	$8,890
Less ending Inventory	2,760
Cost of goods sold	$6,130

Assuming that net sales for the period were $13,200, the gross profit as reported under each of the above methods is shown below:

	FIFO	LIFO
Net sales	$13,200	$13,200
Less costs of goods sold	3,160	6,130
Gross profit	$10,040	$7,070

As can be seen, the inventory valuation method can have a significant impact on the gross profit during a period of rising prices.

The specific inventory valuation method used by a corporation is indicated in the footnotes to the financial statements.

Expenditures Included in Inventory Management has a great deal of flexibility in determining which expenses will be capitalized in the inventory accounts and which expenses will be written off directly as cost of the period. For example, if the personnel department was housed in the building used for administrative staff, the expenses associated with its operation are likely to be written off directly as part of administrative expense. If the personnel department staff were housed in an operating plant, at least part of the expenses of its operation are likely to be capitalized in the inventory account. A liberal interpretation of the question of capitalizing versus expensing such costs could improve reported income for a given period. Moreover, different decisions about whether to capitalize in the inventory account or directly expense could distort comparability of reported income data between companies or through time.

Current tax laws practically allow any business firm to adopt LIFO, regardless of the actual flow of goods through the firm, and many firms have adopted the method since the 1950s. A firm that uses LIFO for financial reporting purposes must use the same system for tax purposes.

As illustrated above, during a period of rising prices the use of LIFO will result in lower reported profits, and, therefore, the firm will incur a lower income tax liability than under FIFO. This is because "old" inventory costs that do not reflect current replacement costs are matched against revenues stated in current dollars. In contrast, during periods of rising prices, FIFO inventory valuation will overstate income. It is important to understand that a significant portion of reported net income of companies using the FIFO method may be inventory profits that will melt away as inventory must be replaced in the future. Furthermore, if prices were to fall, then the firm using FIFO would report the lower profits and higher cost of goods sold.

Profits appear to be more volatile when FIFO rather than LIFO costing is used to determine ending inventory values. This occurs because FIFO accounting tends to cause inventory profits to be added to regular operating profits when prices are rising since current cost is not matched with current revenue. The opposite will occur during a recession, thus increasing volatility. Where selling prices are less flexible than new-material prices, however, profits may not be more volatile under FIFO than under LIFO.

Finally, LIFO could show illusory profits if a firm does not replenish inventory in a given year and digs into the "old"-cost LIFO reserve to meet sales at current prices. The firm will have to restock eventually at the higher current replacement cost, causing a sharp decline in future profits. This can occur, for example, when a firm faces an extended strike by employees and attempts to continue sales from existing inventory.

When inventories are not a significant asset, the analyst need not be overly concerned about differences in inventory costing systems. In many cases, however, misleading conclusions may be drawn if the analyst is not careful to adjust when different systems are used.

The footnotes to the financial statements, unfortunately, rarely facilitate an accurate adjustment, unless a company has just switched from one method to the other. When a company has changed inventory costing methods, it must report the dollar and cents impact on inventory, cost of goods sold, taxes, and profits in the financial report of that year. These data need not be repeated, however, in future annual reports.

FASB Statement No. 33 (*Financial Reporting and Changing Prices*) requires that large corporations disclose what it would cost to replace their inventories at year-end and what their cost of goods sold would be if computed using current replacement cost at the date of sale. These data can help the analyst better frame reasonable adjustments when two companies use different inventory costing systems.

For comparative purposes, either the LIFO or FIFO firm could be adjusted to the system used by the other firm. Some analysts prefer LIFO reporting on the grounds that this system reports more meaningful profit data. Therefore, it would seem best to adjust the firm using FIFO to the LIFO approach. Unfortunately, an analyst is likely to find that available information facilitates adjusting LIFO to FIFO, using current replacement cost information. When contrasting two companies using different inventory costing methods, the analyst can only subjectively adjust the data of one to the system used by the other company.[2]

Finally, it is important to recognize that the choice of an inventory costing system also affects the balance sheet. A period of sustained inflation tends to cause assets to be valued in the balance sheet at amounts substantially below their current replacement cost, especially when the LIFO costing system is used. This occurs because inventory is carried at "old" costs to acquire, which deviate more and more from current replacement costs as infla-

---

[2]Sometimes analysts assume that the gross profit margin percentages would have been the same if the companies had used the same inventory costing procedures, to facilitate an adjustment. This is not a useful technique, however, since this will wash out differing efficiencies between companies, which is what the analyst is looking for.

tion continues. Accordingly, a company using LIFO may have a low current ratio (discussed in Appendix D) relative to a company using FIFO.

Depreciation   Depreciation of production facilities would be a cost entering into the determination of cost of goods sold, but depreciation of sales office space properly would be shown as a selling expense. Depreciation may, therefore, affect the determination of several major subdivisions of the income statement.

Because the accounting charge for depreciation does not represent a corresponding outlay of cash, some investors and analysts have implied that depreciation is not a real expense by using the term "cash earnings per share" or "cash flow earnings per share" and have even substituted these terms for "net earnings per share." Strong criticism of this position by the AICPA, the New York Stock Exchange, and the Financial Analysts Federation has sharply reduced the use of these terms in brokerage houses and annual corporate reports.

Since fixed assets, particularly plant and equipment, represent such a substantial outlay, it would be impractical to write them off entirely as an expense charged against the income of the year in which they are purchased, especially since benefits from their use will be received over an extended period. Furthermore, as soon as it is purchased, a fixed asset begins to depreciate. To ignore this fact would be to experience a gradual loss of capital without any reflection on the books of account. Accountants consider the original cost of a fixed asset to be a prepaid expense that must be amortized during the service life of the asset by regular periodic charges to the depreciation expense account. After deduction of the annual charge, the remaining amount is the unamortized cost; but in no way, except by coincidence, does this amount represent the economic value of the asset at that time.

Reflecting Replacement Costs of Capital Equipment   Concern with inflation has led many to advocate a policy of substituting replacement cost for original cost as the basis for determining depreciation charges in the income statement. Corporate management has been especially vocal on this subject. The basic function of depreciation charges is to amortize the cost of a capital asset over its useful life. Management is concerned with a second function: providing the funds needed for replacement of assets after they have worn out or become technologically obsolete. Depreciation charges do not provide a company with cash. However, they are tax-deductible, and they do protect cash generated by sales operations from the burden of taxes.

When replacement costs have risen far above original cost, prudent business management must recognize this capital erosion and set aside the additional funds necessary to continue operating the business. Such funds must be provided from retained earnings, because the income tax laws do not recognize the inflation situation. Income taxes must be paid on the capital lost through inflation, which makes the problem of maintaining a company's capital doubly difficult.

Depreciation Methods   Although corporate laws and accounting principles require that corporations make some charge for depreciation, corporate management is permitted numerous alternatives in the manner in which it amortizes the cost of fixed assets over their useful life on its books and in published reports.

The straight-line method provides for the regular distribution of the original cost of fixed assets, less their estimated salvage value, over their estimated service lives. In addition to the straight-line method of depreciation, two other depreciation methods are permitted for financial reporting purposes: the declining-balance method and the sum-of-the-years-digits method. These two methods allow for a faster write-off of the asset in the earlier years of the service life and are thus referred to as *accelerated depreciation*.

For tax reporting purposes, prior to the Economic Recovery Tax Act of 1981, fixed assets could be depreciated using any of the three methods. The 1981 tax act substantially revised the method of computing depreciation by introducing the Accelerated Cost Recovery System (ACRS), a modified version of which is still used today. Under this system, taxpayers have virtually no choice in selecting a useful life for depreciable property, and salvage value is ignored. The Tax Reform Act of 1986 provided less liberal write-offs, especially of real estate, but retained the ACRS approach. The shorter depreciable lives mandated by ACRS introduce another factor that can cause taxable income to differ from reported accounting income, since different depreciation methods may be used for purposes of preparing financial statements and tax returns.

Since 1954, most corporations have reported publicly on a straight-line basis to stockholders, while taking advantage of the rapid amortization permitted for tax reporting purposes. What this means is that when reporting to shareholders, a lower depreciation expense is taken, resulting in higher reported income than if accelerated depreciation is used. In contrast to reporting to shareholders, the objective is to minimize reported income when preparing tax returns. Thus, accelerated depreciation is used, resulting in higher depreciation charges and lower reported income compared with what would be reported if straight-line depreciation is used for tax accounting purposes. This practice of reporting to shareholders using straight-line depreciation and accelerated depreciation for tax purposes and "flowing through" the lower income taxes actually paid to the financial statement prepared for shareholders is called the **flow-through method**.

Until fiscal 1968, income statements in annual reports of numerous corporations reported depreciation by using the flow-through method. However, other corporations reported depreciation by the **normalizing method**, making a charge in the income account equivalent to the tax savings and thus washing out the benefits of the tax savings as far as final net income in their financial statements to shareholders. In financial statements, the charge for deferred taxes (the difference between the taxes as reported in the income statement prepared for shareholders and the tax return) resulting from the use of the flow-through method usually is included in the total item entitled "Federal Income Taxes."

APB Opinion No. 11 stated categorically that the deferred method of tax allocation should be followed. An exception would be allowed for regulated companies such as public utilities, where particular regulatory authorities may require the use of flow-through accounting.

Those who favor the normalizing method state that the use of rapid amortization for tax purposes will result in lower taxes being paid in the earlier years of the life of the assets than under the straight-line method because of higher depreciation charges, but that in later years depreciation will be less than straight-line rates; taxes will therefore be higher than in the earlier years. Total taxes for the entire life of the assets should be the same under either the straight-line method or rapid amortization. Thus, tax savings are temporary and deferred until later years of lower depreciation charges. Those holding this viewpoint, including the AICPA and the SEC, therefore wish to eliminate any effect of tax savings on net income in the earlier years of the asset's life.

Those who have advocated the flow-through method, including numerous state public utility commissions (not the SEC), have argued that as long as a company is regularly expanding and purchasing fixed assets, the new assets will have the advantage of rapid amortization, therefore offsetting the declining depreciation on older assets. The lower taxes paid in the earlier years, therefore, are not deferred to later years, but payment will be deferred indefinitely. Thus, there will be a constantly increasing "deferred taxes" account on the balance sheet.

Although depreciation is a real expense, it does not involve an outlay of cash in the period charged; therefore, the sales revenues allocated to the depreciation charges do represent a tax-protected source of funds to the business enterprise. While the total depreciation charged over the life of the asset is not affected by the method used, the greater amounts of revenues protected in early years by the declining-balance method and sum-of-the-years-digits method have a higher present value than funds that might be protected in later years. Rapid amortization is similar to an interest-free loan from the Treasury Department. Depreciation charges often are substantial, and the estimates made have a material effect on the reported profits or losses of a given year. Profits are overstated when depreciation charges understate the actual depletion of assets during the production process. Depreciation charges can be understated by increasing the estimated life of an asset beyond the time the asset is useful economically or by overstating salvage value. For example, several American airlines extended the depreciable life of their aircraft between 1968 and 1970, thereby reducing annual depreciation expense and increasing reported earnings at a time when airline earnings generally were depressed.

Accountants cannot know in advance how long an asset will last or what its salvage value will be. The depreciation expense charged in the income statement is a rough estimate of cost and does not allow for the effects of inflation. Determining the adequacy of depreciation charges is difficult. The following tests are suggested:

1. The consistency of the rate of depreciation charged over time can be explored by studying depreciation as a percentage of gross plant assets and sales over an extended period of time.
2. Depreciation rates of a given company should be compared with those utilized by similar companies.

Amortization of Intangibles In addition to the major non-cash charges for depreciation and depletion in the income statement, the amortization of intangibles such as goodwill, patents, and trademarks represents non-cash charges in the income account. The problem of determining the time over which the values recognized for intangibles are consumed is a difficult one, and differing judgments can lead to non-comparability of reported income data by different companies.

Goodwill, and the accounting for goodwill, has become important to analysts with the tremendous merger movement that has occurred since World War II. The costs of acquisitions often have been well in excess of the book value of the assets acquired, and a balancing item of goodwill has been added in the balance sheet. The AICPA requires that the item of goodwill be amortized annually as a charge against income over a period of not more than 40 years. Since firms may write off goodwill using any time span within the 40-year period, profit comparability can be distorted.

Other Expenses Selling expenses, administrative expenses, other expenses, and taxes must be deducted from gross profit, and other income must be added, to determine net income. These expenses are not identifiable specifically with or assigned to production. Some costs may be included here because they are difficult to allocate; it is, therefore, possible that parts of these expense items should affect production costs.

The main classifications under operating expenses in the income statement are selling, general, and administrative expenses. Expenses related to storing and displaying merchandise for sale, advertising, sales salaries, and delivery costs are the main items included under selling expenses. General and administrative expenses include costs related to the operation of the general offices, costs of the accounting department, costs of the personnel office, and costs of the credit and collections departments. Certain expenses may be listed separately under operating expenses, including depreciation, depletion and amortization, maintenance and repair expenses, research and development (R&D) expenses, rental expenses, costs of exploration, and employee benefit payments (mainly pension costs), though they should have been part of the determination of cost of goods sold.

The analyst should calculate each of the listed expenses as a percentage of sales. This will highlight the changing importance of expense items, trend patterns, and the relationship of costs to sales activity. A useful comparison also can be made between the behavior of individual expense items relative to sales, both over time and with industry composite figures.

Below we describe the various operating expenses.

1. *Maintenance and repairs.* The significance of maintenance and repair costs will vary with the amount invested in plant, equipment, and productive activity. These costs typically are composed of both fixed and variable elements. While it is useful to look at their behavior in relation to sales, one should not make much of this comparison—a consistent relationship with sales is not to be expected. Also, it is useful to look at annual maintenance and repair costs in relation to total plant and equipment. Unfortunately, maintenance and repair expense is not always presented separately in the financial statements.

These costs are discretionary and can be postponed within limits. Sometimes, management may be tempted to postpone needed maintenance and repairs when revenues are falling to maintain the level of income reported to stockholders. This can lead to continued future deterioration in profits. Also, inadequate maintenance and repairs can shorten the useful lives of assets, thereby invalidating depreciation expense charges, which are related to useful life estimates. The analyst must make sure that reasonable amounts are being spent to maintain competitive facilities.

2. *Rental expenses.* A large number of corporations have chosen to lease rather than purchase assets. Lease rental costs, therefore, can become important expense items. Where a long-term lease is involved, the resulting rental expense can be characterized as a required series of payments over many years that include elements of both principal amortization and interest expense. To an important extent, the payment requirements on a long-term lease are equivalent to fixed charges incurred when debt is utilized to acquire an asset, and the fixed-charge obligation of a lease can force a company into financial difficulties just as readily as can fixed charges on funded or other debt. An analyst should determine the future minimum lease payments required, for both capital leases and operating leases, and relate the payment requirements to expected cash flow to ensure that the firm has not overcommitted itself.

3. *Pension costs.* As explained in Chapter 9, pension plans come in two basic forms: defined contribution and defined benefit plans. A defined contribution plan is one in which the firm's contribution rate is fixed. Once a company has made the required contribution, it has no liability for additional payments. The recognition of the required contribution as expense, therefore, assures proper recognition of pension costs in the income account.

A defined benefit plan, by contrast, is one in which the benefits are determined by formula and the employer contributions are treated as variable. The estimation of the size of the pension obligation is difficult and subject to great uncertainty in terms of what the company actually will be obligated to pay in the future.

Under a defined benefit plan, the employer's commitment is to fund a future benefit. The required annual contribution to the plan is not fixed, but is being redefined constantly in terms of changing wage rates, earnings rates of the fund, and other variables.

When a firm establishes a defined benefit plan, it commits itself to two undetermined costs: (1) past-service costs that arise because of contracted obligations to employees for years served before either the founding of a plan or a change in the plan and (2) current-period costs as required by the plan. APB Opinion 8 and FASB Statement No. 87 are the basic guides to accounting for pension costs.

In determining pension costs, there are various assumptions that the actuary who is responsible for calculating these costs must make. One assumption is the interest rate assumption, which represents the annual rate of return that the actuary expects the pension fund assets to earn. Another assumption is the wage assumption, which represents the annual rate at which covered wages are expected to grow. The higher the interest rate assumption and the lower the wage growth assumption, the smaller will be the reported unfunded pension liability and the lower the required company contribution. In actuality, the setting of these assumptions is more art than science, making it difficult to compare pension costs among firms and to judge the adequacy of the costs charged for funding purposes. Therefore, reported profits can be distorted in a comparative sense because of different assumptions used in determining annual charges, both over time and between companies.

4. *Other employee benefits.* Accounting requires the disclosure of the costs of past employment benefits. The costs of health and life insurance benefits are the main components of these costs, and such benefits usually continue after an employee reaches retirement and often include the spouse and children. These costs are potentially large and should receive careful consideration in terms of the liability they create and their impact on future income.

5. *Research and development costs.* Research and development (R&D) costs are difficult to properly account for because (1) the ultimate results are highly uncertain and (2) the amount of time that can go by between the initiation of a research project and the determination of its ultimate success or failure is difficult to predict. Such expenditures are often substantial and must be considered when analyzing current income and forecasting future profits. FASB Statement No. 2 concludes that, subject to certain exceptions, all R&D costs should be charged to expense in the year incurred.

The analyst should attempt to judge the success of past R&D expenditures and the likelihood of future successes when evaluating a firm. It is the future that is of importance when evaluating a common stock, and accounting for R&D expenses is not helpful in this regard. Evaluation of the potential future success generated by R&D outlays requires information on the types of research performed, the outlays by category, the technical feasibility of projects being undertaken, and the quality of the research staff; and it is useful to know the company's success-failure experience in the past.

BALANCE SHEET ANALYSIS

A **balance sheet** (also called the *statement of financial condition)* is a technical accounting term. "In this view, a balance sheet may be defined as a tabular statement or summary of balances (debt and credit) carried forward after an actual or constructive closing of books of account kept according to principles of accounting."[3] This is as far as accountants are willing to go. The investor must expect neither more nor less than this. A balance sheet does not purport to list economic or investment values, which are related more to the cash flow and earning power of a firm.

Investors must understand what balance sheets demonstrate. One examines a balance sheet to determine the company's current financial position, the amount and nature of invested capital, the sources of invested capital, the

---

[3]*Accounting Research Study No. 7* (New York: American Institute of Certified Public Accountants, 1965), p. 226.

proportionate division of corporate capitalization, and, with the income statement, the rate of return earned on total assets, on total capitalization, and on stockholders' equity.

Balance Sheet Values

The word "value" is used in accounting to describe the figure at which an asset or liability is carried in the accounts, although the amount may represent something different than "value" as the word is used ordinarily. Accounting is based predominantly on cost, and assets usually are carried at cost or some modification of cost. For example, accountants report the original cost of fixed assets on the balance sheet, less amortization of that cost over the useful life of the asset. Inventories will reflect the cost to purchase the items included, unless current market value falls below that cost. Accounting values, therefore, are not intended to represent current market value, replacement value, or liquidation value of assets.

Accounting values are book values that signify only the amount at which an item is stated in accordance with the accounting principles related to the item. The term **book value** also is used to represent the total owners' equity shown in the balance sheet; book value per share is the owners' equity divided by the number of shares of common stock outstanding. Book value per share should not be thought of as an indicator of economic worth.

Balance Sheet Information Sought by Analysts

The major types of information that the analyst seeks from the balance sheet are as follows:

1. The sources of funds that have been used to acquire the corporate assets:
   a. The long-term funds invested by creditors, preferred stockholders, and common stockholders. In the case of common stockholders, it includes earnings retained in the business (not paid out as dividends) and capital in excess of par.
   b. The short-term funds supplied by banks, commercial paper houses, factors and trade creditors, etc.
   On the basis of the above information, the investor can calculate the proportion of invested capital contributed by creditors, preferred stockholders, and common stockholders and can determine such ratios as long-term debt to stockholders' equity. It is worthwhile for the investor to calculate the market value of the corporation's securities and the ratios of each component to the total capitalization. In this calculation par value often is used for bonds and preferred stock, but market value is used for common stock: hence the term "total capitalization with common at market" (number of shares times market value).
2. The strength of the corporation's working capital position as indicated by the various working capital ratios. These ratios indicate the corporation's assumed ability to meet current liabilities, which are expected to be paid with current assets.
3. The assets of the corporation, which indicate the sources of the corporation's income and the manner in which capital was invested, as well as providing a base for assessing the adequacy of total assets and the mix of assets to support expected levels of operation.

4. Data for an analysis of the balance sheet combined with an analysis of the income statements to indicate:
   a. The amount and the rate of return on total long-term capitalization
   b. The rate of return on total assets
   c. The rate of return on the stockholders' equity
   d. A check of the retained earnings account in the balance sheet with the earnings reported over a period of years in the income statement. [Retained earnings at the beginning of the period plus earnings (less losses) for the entire period less dividends paid should give the total in the retained earnings account at the end of the period, except for charges or credits made directly to the retained earnings account that may not have been recorded in any income statement but that should have been disclosed in annual reports.]

In essence, the balance sheet when combined with income statement data offers a basis for a long-term study of earning power relative to asset mix and financial structure.

We will discuss the ratios mentioned above in much greater detail in Appendix D. Table B-4 shows the balance sheet for The Home Depot, Inc., for the fiscal years 1991 and 1990.

Assets Section of the Balance Sheet

In considering assets in the balance sheet as offsets to the liabilities and capital, the analyst must recognize what asset figures really mean. The ana-

TABLE B-4		
THE HOME DEPOT, INC. BALANCE SHEET, 1991 AND 1990 **(Dollars in Thousands)**		
	1991	**1990**
Assets		
Cash	$ 137,296	$ 135,381
Receivables (net)	49,235	38,993
Inventory	509,022	381,452
Other	17,931	10,474
Total current assets	$ 713,574	$ 566,240
Plant, property & equipment	963,619	568,690
Less accumulated depreciation	(84,889)	(54,250)
Net plant, property & equipment	$ 878,730	$ 514,440
Other assets	47,199	36,854
Total assets	$1,639,503	$1,117,534
Liabilities		
Accounts payable	$ 235,267	$ 172,876
Accrued liabilities	166,734	118,066
Other current liabilities	10,706	1,447
Total current liabilities	$ 12,707	$ 292,389
Long-term debt	530,774	302,901
Capital lease obligations	12,620	10,115
Stockholder's equity		
Retained earnings	439,770	289,177
Paid-in-capital	264,301	233,458
Other	(26,572)	(10,506)
Total stockholders' equity	$ 683,402	$ 512,129
Total liability & equity	$1,639,503	$1,117,534

lyst should not be under the illusion that these offsets to liabilities and capital represent reliable estimates of economic value, except to some extent in the case of current assets; and even in this case, book figures may be far removed from economic values, especially in regard to inventories.

Current Assets   **Current assets** of a business (also called *circulating assets* or *working assets*) represent its working capital. For accounting purposes the term "current assets" is used to designate cash and other assets or resources commonly identified as those that are expected to be realized in cash or sold or consumed during the normal operating cycle of the business. This generally encompasses the following resources: cash available for current operations and items that are the equivalent of cash, inventories, receivables, marketable securities representing the temporary investment of cash, and prepaid expenses. The ordinary operations of a business involve a circulation of capital within the current asset group. Expenditures are accumulated as inventory cost. Inventory costs, on sale of the products, are converted into trade receivables and ultimately into cash again. The average time intervening between the acquisition of materials or services entering this process and the final cash realization constitutes an **operating cycle**.

The character of a borrower's working capital has been of prime interest to grantors of credit. Bond indentures, credit agreements, and preferred stock agreements commonly contain provisions restricting corporate actions that would affect a reduction or impairment of working capital (and would impair the ability to satisfy debt requirements). Such restrictions can affect the future financing possibilities of a firm, its growth, and its dividend-paying capacity, thereby affecting the common stockholders' interest. Net working capital is represented by the excess of current assets over current liabilities and identifies the relatively liquid portion of total enterprise capital that constitutes a margin or buffer for meeting obligations within the ordinary operating cycle of the business.

Cash-equivalent items include temporary investments of currently excess cash in short-term, high-quality investment media such as Treasury bills and bankers acceptances. There is little or no chance of loss in the event that these items have to be liquidated. Sometimes cash and cash-equivalent items are segregated arbitrarily and not included in current assets. If such segregated items have been excluded from current assets and if these items are, in fact, subject to the full control of management and not required to be segregated by regulations or contract agreements, the analyst should add them back to the current assets.

Receivables, less any allowance for doubtful accounts, are included as current assets on the grounds that the firm intends to convert them to cash in the ordinary operating cycle of the business. Accordingly, receivables may be included as current assets when the payment period runs beyond a year, as with installment sales discussed below. This must be kept in mind when judging the firm's ability to pay current liabilities. The analyst must consider the nature of the receivables in terms of the characteristics of the industry and the company's business. The analyst should determine whether the receivables are proportionately larger than normal in respect to current assets for the type of business and whether the deductions for estimated doubtful accounts are reasonable in terms of industry averages and firm experience.

Schedule VIII of a firm's 10-K filing with the SEC offers useful information for evaluating the adequacy of the reserve for doubtful accounts of a firm, especially when compared with other firms operating in the same industry.

The estimate for doubtful or uncollectible accounts must be reasonable in relation to receivables in the case of installment sales, and this is true if profits on installment sales are taken into income in the period that the sales are accomplished rather than when receivables are collected. If a corporation sells (or "factors") its installment notes to banks or finance companies, it should note whether they have been sold outright or on a "recourse basis." In the latter case, the corporation has a contingent liability, which usually is not shown in the balance sheet but is included as a footnote. The analyst must consider the size of these contingent liabilities and the likelihood of the contingency materializing in the light of industry and company experience and the character of the receivables.

Inventories are classified as raw materials, work in process, and finished goods. In investigating inventory, the analyst must consider the implications of FIFO and LIFO inventory accounting as applied to analysis between companies and over a period of years for the same company if company reports do not provide actual figures indicating the effect of a change from FIFO to LIFO or vice versa. One must be careful to make appropriate adjustments when comparing two firms if one uses LIFO while the other uses FIFO. The firm using LIFO will report a lower profit and inventory than the firm using FIFO, when there are no real differences, assuming rising prices.

Non-Current Assets   One of the non-current classifications applicable to assets is that of investments. Investments owned by business enterprises include shares of stock, bonds, and other securities; mortgages and contracts receivable; life insurance policies on the lives of officers that designate the company as beneficiary; and special funds to finance plant expansion or to retire long-term debt. Temporary investments are classified as current assets. Only long-term holdings of securities are classified as investments.

A basic accounting position on the reporting of long-term investments and non-current assets is quoted below.

> Long-term investments in securities should be carried at the lower of aggregate cost or market. When market quotations are available, the aggregate quoted amounts (and information as to whether aggregate cost or market is the carrying amount) should be disclosed. Investments in affiliates should be segregated from other investments.[4]

Fixed assets consist of land, plant, and equipment reported at cost less depreciation, i.e., amortization of cost. The process of depreciation is the process of amortization of cost over the estimated life of the asset and is in no sense a process of valuation, as discussed earlier. The economic value of fixed assets is their earning power, which bears no necessary relationship to the amount at which they are carried in the books.

---

[4]Quoted from *Accounting Research Study No. 7*, ibid., pp. 259–260, and APB Opinion No. 18, except for changes made by FASB Statement No. 12 (December 1975).

Intangibles that appear in the balance sheet come from two sources: (1) intangible assets purchased outright and (2) intangible assets initially developed in the regular course of business. Such assets have no physical existence and depend on future anticipated benefits for their value. Intangibles purchased outright are intangibles (such as goodwill) that have been acquired in exchange for an issue of securities, for cash, or for other considerations. The AICPA stated in APB Opinion No. 17 that the costs of all intangible assets, including those arising from a "purchase" type of business combination, should be recorded as assets and should be amortized by systematic charges to income over estimated benefit periods, the period of amortization not to exceed 40 years.

Liabilities and Shareholders' Equity of the Balance Sheet

The balance sheet furnishes information on the amount of funds raised from creditors, both short- and long-term obligations, and from owners (including retained earnings). Investors should analyze the long-term capitalization of the corporation (long-term debt plus owners' equity), by means of ratios, to indicate both the degree of financial leverage being utilized by the corporation and the rates of return being earned on capitalization. Short-term obligations should be analyzed in terms of the current assets and cash flow factors from which payment must come.

Current Liabilities   Current liabilities designate obligations that must be paid within one year from the date of the balance sheet. The current liability classification, however, is not intended to include a contractual obligation that falls due at an early date and that is expected to be refunded, or debts to be liquidated by funds that are carried in non-current asset accounts. Liquidation of such liabilities could reasonably be expected to require the use of current assets or the creation of other current liabilities. Current liabilities are therefore related to current assets when assessing the possibility that the firm will experience liquidity problems. The ratios used in such an analysis will be given in Appendix D.

Long-Term Debt   This section consists of long-term obligations such as bonds, private-placement notes, equipment obligations, and bank loans with a maturity of more than one year. The amounts that appear on the balance sheet generally can be assumed to state accurately the amount of long-term obligations currently outstanding. Notes to financial statements will furnish additional information about the debt contracts, such as restrictive clauses against charges to retained earnings for dividends and officers' salaries. Such restrictions are important to common stockholders, since these restrictions can limit financing opportunities to support growth and dividend payments.

In the post–World War II period, leasing has become a major method of financing the use of property and equipment; annual rentals under leases run into billions of dollars. Leasing differs in technique, although often not in substance, from conventional purchase of assets. FASB Statement No. 13 contains guidelines for classifying leases, along with accounting and reporting standards for each class of lease. According to FASB Statement No. 13, leases are classified as either (1) capital leases or (2) operating leases. Operating leases are those that the lessor will reacquire to lease again. They are to be accounted for as rental expense to the lessee and as rental income to the lessor. Capital leases must be capitalized by the lessee on the balance sheet as an asset and an obligation. The treatment is as if the firm purchased the asset with borrowed funds. Consequently, each period the capitalized asset is depreciated and the obligation is amortized, giving rise to depreciation expense and interest expense.

When a corporation establishes a pension fund, it accepts two costs: (1) past-service costs that have not been funded and (2) current pension costs based on current payrolls. The problem as far as the balance sheet is concerned is that of past-service cost—the unfunded pension costs covering the period prior to the inauguration of the pension plan. These funds were not set aside previously but would have been funded if a pension plan had been in effect. The amount of these unfunded pension costs is often substantial and in the case of large corporations may amount to several billion dollars. These unfunded pension costs are a liability of the corporation. However, many pension fund agreements provide that annual payments to amortize unfunded pension costs may be skipped in years of poor earnings, sometimes for as many as three consecutive years.

The Accounting Principles Board of the AICPA stated that a major objective of Opinion No. 8 was to eliminate inappropriate fluctuation in recorded pension costs. It stated that "costs should not be limited to the amounts for which the company has a legal liability." The principles involved are that the pension cost accounting method should be applied consistently from year to year and that the amount recognized for past pension service costs should be relatively stable from year to year.[5] Opinion No. 8 does not require that certified statements disclose the amount of unfunded or otherwise-unprovided-for past or prior service costs. However, the SEC does require such disclosure.

Preferred Stock   If the corporation has preferred stock outstanding, the balance sheet will disclose the number of shares, the par or stated value per share, and the total dollar amount of the preferred stock. In the balance sheet, preferred stock is listed in the shareholders' equity section along with the common stock. Although preferred stock is essentially an equity security, it is a strictly limited equity security.

Preferred stock is senior to common stock. The amount shown in the balance sheet should represent the claim of preferred stock coming ahead of the common stock, but this is not always the manner in which it is reported. If the preferred stock has a par value or a stated value relatively close to its legal claim (for example, liquidating value) ahead of the common stock, then the balance sheet closely reflects the actual situation. However, if the stated value is only a nominal amount and is not close to the claim of the preferred stock, then the preferred stock on the balance sheet (number of shares of preferred stock times the stated value) does not reflect the true situation. If the balance sheet does not reflect the preferred stock's claim properly, the analyst

[5]Julia W. Phoenix, Jr., and William D. Bosse, "Accounting for the Cost of Pension Plans—More Information on APB No. 8," *Journal of Accountancy* (October 1967); and "Pension Reform," *Journal of Accountancy* (May 1972), p. 76.

should reconstruct the balance sheet so that it reflects the preferred claims that are senior to the common stock.

In addition, there may be dividend arrears, which, while they are not liabilities of the corporation, do represent a claim senior to the common stock. However, such arrearages usually are not shown on the balance sheet but are disclosed only as a footnote.

Common Stock and Retained Earnings   Common stock is classified as part of shareholders' equity. Because the common stock is the residual claimant to the assets and the earnings of the corporation, the shareholder's equity section of the balance sheet is divided into paid-in capital and retained earnings. The latter is earnings that have not been distributed to shareholders.

■ SUMMARY

Analysts rely on the financial information prepared by the corporation. Financial statements must be prepared in accordance with generally accepted accounting principles. While financial statements are audited by an independent accountant, there are potential conflicts that may bias the auditor's opinion about how the financial statements were prepared by management.

The shareholders' letter in the annual report occasionally communicates actual and potential problems in a jargon-free manner that can provide guidance to the investor for the probing of the rest of the annual report.

Two key financial statements that must be prepared by a corporation are the income statement and the balance sheet. In this chapter we discussed the key items in these two financial statements and how the judgments in preparing financial statements and the accounting policy choices available make comparison among firms difficult.

■ KEY TERMS

auditor's report
balance sheet
book value
capitalized
cash-equivalent items
clean opinion
current assets
disclaimer of opinion

except for opinion
expensed
first-in–first-out (FIFO)
flow-through method
generally accepted accounting
    principles (GAAP)
income statement
last-in–first-out (LIFO)

matching concept
normalizing method
operating cycle
opinion shopping
shareholders' letter
subject to opinion

■ QUESTIONS

1. What is the difference between the 10-K and an annual report?

2. Comment on the following statement: "Since the accounting rules are specified by GAAP, the management of a corporation has no discretion in reporting its income."

3. **a.** What are the four categories of opinions that an auditor can give?
   b. What is meant by opinion shopping?

4. What conflicts may arise with respect to the auditor's responsibility to fairly present the financial statements?

5. Comment on the following statement: "Since the shareholders' letter is not subject to audit, the investor should ignore it in analyzing the company."

6. What is meant by the matching concept in regard to preparing the income statement?

7. **a.** What is meant by the capitalization of an expense?
   b. What is meant by the expensing of an expense?
   c. How does management's decision to capitalize or expense a particular expenditure affect the income statement and the balance sheet?

8. What are the key assumptions in determining pension costs?

9. Discuss briefly the effect on both the balance sheet and the income statement of using the LIFO method of inventory valuation rather than the FIFO method during a period of rising prices.

10. **a.** Explain the current practice for depreciating fixed assets.
    b. Does the value reported in the balance sheet reflect the market value of the fixed asset? If not, could there be a major discrepancy between the book value and the market value?

11. What is the difference between the flow-through method and the normalizing method of accounting for fixed assets?

12. What is an intangible asset? Give three examples.

13. How must an accountant handle research and development costs?

14. How should an analyst treat research and development costs?

15. What is the difference between expenses shown in the "Cost of goods sold" section of the income statement and the "Operating expenses and other items" section.

16. What is the distinction between current liabilities and long-term debt?

17. Explain how the judgments in preparing financial statements and the choices available make the comparison among firms difficult.

APPENDIX C
ANALYSIS OF EARNINGS*

LEARNING OBJECTIVES
After reading this chapter you will be able to:

- identify the limitations of the use of earnings-per-share figures by themselves.

- discuss the potential conflicts facing sell-side analysts.

- explain how earnings per share are calculated and the difference between primary earnings per share and fully diluted earnings per share.

- describe what non-operating/non-recurring items are and what their effect is on earnings.

- explain why it is important to analyze the differences in income for financial reporting purposes and tax reporting purposes.

- explain what differential disclosure means and how caution should be exercised when an investor encounters it.

- explain how changes in discretionary expenses can affect the quality of a company's earnings.

- discuss and calculate ratios for assessing the profitability of a company.

- explain the reasons for the growth of a company's earnings per share.

- describe the importance of analyzing accounts receivable and inventories in assessing profitability.

- explain how to analyze a company's sales.

In financial circles, two measures often used to evaluate common stocks are earnings per share and the related ratio of market price to earnings per share, the price-earnings ratio. Accountants and financial analysts have criticized the undue emphasis often placed on earnings per share, especially when reviewed in isolation without taking into consideration the accounting limitations inherent in their calculation and other income statement items. Moreover, reported net income and earnings per share are not good surrogates for cash flow from operations when considering bill-paying capacity and ability to finance company growth and operations.

The three major criticisms of the use of earnings-per-share figures by themselves are (1) unless associated with an income statement review and

* This chapter is coauthored with Professor John C. Ritchie, Jr., of Temple University. Some material in this chapter has been taken from various issues of Thornton L. O'Glove's *Quality of Earnings Report*. Permission to use this material is granted by Thornton L. O'Glove.

analysis, they can lead to erroneous conclusions; (2) reported earnings per share may be non-comparable over time or between companies; and (3) they concentrate the investor's attention on a single figure without reference to the corporation as a whole, which would provide information on the sources and the nature of income and provide some basis for a reasonable projection of earnings and dividends. An analyst of financial statements should carefully review the income statement and adjust where needed to represent economic and comparable income over time and between firms. In this appendix we show how this should be done.

SELL-SIDE RECOMMENDATIONS AND CONFLICTS OF INTEREST

As we explained in Chapter 12, analysts are responsible for analyzing the earnings of companies that they cover. There are sell-side ("Wall Street") and buy-side analysts. Investment management firms that have their own analysts—buy-side analysts—rely on their analysis. Investment management firms that do not have their own analysts, as well as individual investors, rely on the recommendations of sell-side analysts—analysts employed by brokerage firms—that appear in published reports.

The question is, why is it necessary to undertake an analysis of earnings if this task is being performed by sell-side analysts? The reason is that a sell-side analyst is working for a brokerage firm, not the investor, and so potential conflicts can arise. For example, the analyst is expected to be on good terms with the management of the companies he covers, so he can scout for new business for the brokerage firm. A conflict of interest arises since a favorable report about a firm might be beneficial to the brokerage firm that employs the analyst in prospecting for the opportunity to underwrite the next issue of securities or perform some other investment banking function such as arranging a merger.

Prospecting is basically the way that analysts earn their keep, since low commission rates are typically not adequate to support the compensation of analysts.[1] This conflict probably accounts for the greater number of buy recommendations than sell recommendations in sell-side analysts' reports.

This conflict of interest is one reason why investors must be careful about blindly accepting sell-side analyst recommendations. Another reason is that analysts are typically reluctant to deviate from what other analysts are saying about a particular company. Renegades are often severely criticized and, in extreme cases, have lost their jobs.

EARNINGS PER SHARE

One figure analysts consider is **earnings per share**, which are calculated by dividing the earnings available to common stock holders (earnings after taxes less any required preferred stock dividends) by the weighted average number

---

[1]Claire Makin, "Has the Compensation Bubble Burst?" *Institutional Investor* (December 1984), p. 109.

of common shares outstanding over the year for which the calculation takes place. That is,

$$\text{Earnings per share} = \frac{\text{earnings available to common}}{\text{average number of common shares}}$$

But what if a corporation has issued securities or entered into contracts that may increase the number of outstanding shares of common stock? Such securities might include convertible securities, options, warrants, or other stock issue agreements. These instruments are referred to as *dilutive securities* because they can dilute the earnings per share since they can increase the number of shares outstanding. When there are dilutive securities that do in fact result in the dilution of earnings per share, generally accepting accounting principles (GAAP) require that the potential dilutive effects be taken into consideration.[2] A company must make two presentations of earnings per share in such instances: (1) *primary earnings per share* and (2) *fully diluted earnings per share.*

Calculating Primary and Fully Diluted Earnings per Share

An illustrative calculation can clarify the meaning of primary and fully diluted earnings per share. Assume a company has outstanding 20 million shares of common stock. Further assume there is $400 million of 5% preferred stock outstanding, of which $200 million is convertible into 10 million common shares. Also assume there is $400 million of 10% long-term debenture bonds outstanding, of which $200 million is convertible into 5 million common shares. Finally, assume this company has earnings before interest charges and income taxes of $200 million and is subject to an effective income tax rate of 34%.

Table C-1 shows what the earnings per share would be if the potential dilution of earnings per share resulting from dilutive securities is ignored. The resulting earnings per share are called the undiluted earnings per share. As can be seen from Table C-1, the undiluted earnings per share are $4.28.

Next the potential dilution of dilutive securities must be considered. GAAP requires that only dilutive securities classified as *common stock equivalents* must be considered and that the resulting earnings per share are called primary diluted earnings per share. GAAP has specific rules for classifying a dilutive security as a common stock equivalent. We will discuss the classification rules here. Let's assume that in our previous example the $200 million of convertible bonds are treated as a common stock equivalent. The accountant then calculates the earnings per share, assuming that (1) the convertible bonds are converted into common stock and (2) the interest expense that was paid to convertible bond holders is not paid. In our illustration, the number of shares used in calculating the earnings per share would be 25 million (20 million plus 5 million treating the bonds as converted) and interest expense would decline by $20 million (10% times $200 million). This is shown in Table C-1 where primary diluted earnings per share are discussed. Since the primary diluted earnings per share in our illustration are $3.95, which is less than the undiluted earnings per share ($4.28), there was a dilu-

---

[2]*Accounting Principles Bulletin No. 15.*

TABLE C-1

CALCULATION OF PRIMARY AND FULLY DILUTED EARNINGS PER SHARE
(Dollars in Millions)

Assumptions:
  Common shares outstanding: 20 million
  Preferred stock: $400 million @ 5%; $200 million convertible into 10 million
    shares
  Bonds: $400 million @ 10%; $200 milion convertible into 5 million shares and
    are treated as common stock equivalents

	Undiluted	Primary Diluted	Fully Diluted
Earnings before interest and taxes	$200.0	$200.0	$200.0
Interest expense	40.0	20.0	20.0
Earnings before taxes	160.0	180.0	180.0
Taxes at 34%	54.4	61.2	61.2
Earnings after taxes	105.6	118.8	118.8
Preferred dividend	20.0	20.0	10.0
Earnings available to common stock holders	85.6	98.8	108.8
Number of shares	20	25	35
Earnings per share	$4.28	$3.95	$3.11

Undiluted earnings per share: Dilution potential of the two dilutive securities is ignored.

Primary diluted earnings per share: Dilution potential of the $200 million of bonds that are assumed to be common stock equivalents is considered; the interest expense is reduced by $20 million ($200 million times 10%), and the number of shares increases by 5 million to 25 million. The dilution potential of the convertible preferred stock is ignored.

Fully diluted earnings per share: Dilution potential of the $200 million of bonds that are assumed to be common stock equivalents and the $200 of convertible preferred stock is considered; the interest expense is reduced by $20 million ($200 million times 10%), and preferred stock dividends are reduced by $10 million ($200 million times 5%). The number of shares of common stock increases by 15 million (5 million for the convertible bonds and 10 million for the convertible preferred stock).

---

tive effect. Because of this, in our illustration the corporation must report primary diluted earnings per share, not the undiluted earnings per share.

In addition, fully diluted earnings per share must be reported. This figure is the earnings per share after taking into account the dilutive effects of all dilutive securities. In our illustration, this means taking into account the dilutive effects of the $200 million of convertible preferred stock and the $200 million of the convertible bonds. This is shown in Table C-1 and indicates that the fully diluted earnings per share are $3.11. Consequently, this firm will report primary diluted earnings per share of $3.95 and fully diluted earnings per share of $3.11.

Analysts should use both primary diluted earnings per share and fully diluted earnings per share when evaluating the investment merits of common stock. The analyst will then determine two intrinsic values and can use them as a range of potential value.

Price-Earnings Ratio

A **price-earnings (P/E) ratio** is the current market price of the stock divided by some measure of earnings per share. Reported price-earnings ratios may use either (1) the latest available 12 months' earnings per share, (2) earnings per share projected for the next 12 months, (3) the average or midpoint of projected earnings per share for the next 5 or 6 years, or (4) the earnings-per-share expectation in a target year 3 to 6 years hence. The most commonly used denominator is the latest available 12 months' earnings per share.

P/E ratios are used commonly as indicators of relative value for various common stocks. P/E ratios can, however, give a distorted view of relative value due to different accounting techniques and definitions that may be employed by various firms or by the same firm over time. Moreover, a common stock holder is concerned with the future performance of the firm, while a P/E ratio is based on past performance. This is why estimates of future earnings are sometimes used in calculating such ratios. P/E ratios provide only a crude indication of relative investment merit, and must be used with great caution. Still, they do provide an indication of market expectations if earnings are properly adjusted when calculating the ratio. The higher the expected growth rate and the less the volatility of earnings, the higher the P/E ratio awarded to a firm.

CLOSER EXAMINATION OF EARNINGS PER SHARE[3]

In Appendix B we explained the alternative acceptable accounting principles that could be used by a firm to construct its financial statements. Below we focus on factors that the analyst should consider in assessing the quality of reported earnings.

Non-Operating and/or Non-Recurring Income

Two reference standards in the investment community, Standard & Poor's *Stock Reports* and Moody's *Handbook of Common Stocks*, indicated that the earnings per share of Pepsico increased from $2.40 in 1982 to $3.01 in 1983, an increase of 25%. Another standard source of information about earnings per share, *The Value Line Investment Survey*, indicated that the earnings were $3.24 in 1982 and $3.01 in 1983, for a decline of 7%. This is not a trivial difference. According to S&P and Moody's, the company was growing; by contrast, according to Value Line, the company was stagnating.

The reason for the difference in the earnings reported by these standard references involves the matter of non-operating and/or non-recurring income. The debate on this topic can become quite complex, but the fundamental principles involved are not difficult to comprehend. The issue in some cases can be crucial when deciding whether to invest in a company' stock. We use the difference in Pepsi's earnings to illustrate the fundamental principles involved in the debate.

In 1982 Pepsico reported an "unusual charge" relating to the write-down of overseas bottling assets. Previously these facilities had been overvalued due to the application of an improper accounting technique. The charge amounted to $79.4 million, or $0.84 per share. It would seem that such

---

[3]Much of this section is taken from the writing of Thornton O'Glove.

charges are unusual and so might be considered non-recurring. For this reason, Value Line decided to exclude the item from Pepsico's earnings and so reported the higher figure. This was not the stance taken by S&P and Moody's, which decided to include the charge and so came up with the lower figure.

At one time, any charge or earnings not resulting from the company's prime business would almost automatically be classified as non-recurring. The accounting profession reconsidered this position in the 1970s. Pepsi's accountant took the stance that companies have write-offs of assets on a regular basis, which means that write-offs are not extraordinary and so should not be reported as non-recurring. Another accounting firm might take a different view of the matter.

Most of the time the differences between operating and non-operating income are quite clear; the problem comes on close calls. One can readily agree that some charges are unusual, for instance, the expropriation of assets by a foreign government or a loss due to a natural disaster such as a fire when destroyed properties are uninsured. On a more individual level, a million dollars won in a lottery drawing could be seen as non-recurring.

Take the example of a company that sells a property on which it makes a $15 million profit. Is that non-recurring? It probably is if the firm is a small manufacturer of electronic parts moving to a new location after a couple of decades in one place. However, what about a real estate operator who engages in this kind of transaction on a regular basis? What is unusual for the electronics firm is bread and butter for a real estate operator.

Not only is the distinction difficult to make, but unlike many other items we will be discussing, there is no single place in the annual report or quarterly financial statement in which the items are isolated and analyzed in just these terms. Investors have to be prepared to ferret the information out of the shareholders' letter, the analysis and discussion section, and footnotes, as well as the profit and loss statement. Occasionally an investor can learn of developments that impact upon whole industries or individual corporations from the front pages or business sections of the daily press. Alterations in the tax laws provide one clear example of this.

Differential Disclosure

Differential disclosure refers to the possibility that what the company says in one document is markedly different from what it says in another. Or there may be more complete information on a particular topic in one than another. Here we are not referring to press releases and interviews by reporters, but rather to the annual and quarterly reports and the 10-Ks and 10-Qs.

An analyst should exercise caution when encountering any significant divergences between annual and quarterly financial statements and the reports mandated by the SEC. The reason for differential disclosure is that the annual reports and quarterly financial statements are meant to be read by stockholders, most of whom, in the opinion of management, tend to be more impressed by glossy presentations and hyped writing than statistics and footnotes. The 10-Ks and 10-Qs are official reports filed with the SEC. No chief executive officer will go to jail if, in the face of declining business and stiffer competition, he predicts a rosy future in the stockholders' letter. But he could be in trouble if the 10-K and 10-Q do not conform to SEC guidelines. Generally speaking, the narrative portion of annual reports is put together with the assistance of public relations experts, whereas the financial part of the annuals is compiled by the accounting staff of the company and reviewed by the external auditors. The 10-K is the direct responsibility of accountants and lawyers.

If this is the case, why should an investor bother reading the annual reports and quarterly financial statements at all? Why not go straight to the 10-Ks and 10-Qs if that is where one can get more accurate statements? The answer has in part been provided in Appendix B, namely that only in the stockholders' letter can one discover the ideas and rationale behind management's actions and decisions. It is there that CEOs talk about their strategies, defend past actions, and, if you are fortunate, disclose plans. Moreover, a comparative study of all these statements can indicate their credibility.

Shifting Tides at P&G. A prime example of differential disclosure can be found in Procter & Gamble's *1984 Annual Report*. For the fiscal year ended June 30, 1984, P&G earned $5.35 per share versus $5.22 in 1983, hardly an earth-shattering increase. Moreover, the company revealed that part of the improvement came from changes in its corporate tax rate, which declined to 37.6% from 44.1% in 1983 (the equivalent of $0.56 per share). Finally, the 1984 figure included an $0.18-per-share special item, compared with one of $0.10 in 1983, both resulting from swaps of stock for debt. So the company actually experienced an operating earnings decline in 1984, a fact which is noted elsewhere in the "Analysis and Discussion" section—located in the back of the report.[4]

In the letter, management explained that the "modest earnings increase . . . reflects the cost of broadening the Company's product base and augurs well for the long-term health and vitality of the business." So it would appear that P&G believed it would reap a bountiful harvest from the investment in new products somewhere down the line. All's well and good, for this is a sign of vigor and health. In some new-product areas increased marketing expenses can be an indication that better bottom-line results are in the offing. But this was not the case at the time.

Changes in family structure had something to do with it. Says an advertising executive who once worked at P&G, "There is no way the traditional housewife, who is generally a smart shopper, is going to go for something like a toothpaste pump. Today's consumer will [go for such gimmicks], however, and that's the kind of thing P&G might not see."

As a result of the breakdown of the nuclear family, the increase in two-job families, women's liberation, and related social changes, men do more of the shopping than they used to. Studies show that husbands select different brands than their wives 43% of the time. So it was that P&G's Crest toothpaste, long an industry leader, was being seriously challenged by Colgate. Tide was threatened by Wisk, and Pampers, which once had 75% of the disposable diaper market, was down to less than 33% in 1985.

---

[4]Procter & Gamble, *1984 Annual Report*, pp. 2–5; O'Glove, *Quality of Earnings Report* (Sept. 25, 1984), p. 116.

Increased advertising budgets, which in the past had enabled P&G to increase market share, were also not working well. None of these basic problems are discussed in the P&G annual report—we would not expect them to be. But in the "Analysis and Discussion" section we encounter this explanation: In addition to the aggressive investment program there was "the highly competitive climate faced by many of the Company's established brands in the U.S. consumer business"—which is another way of saying that rivals have turned in a remarkable job of "catch-up." That this would be a long-term problem could be seen in the fact that for the fiscal year ended June 30, 1985, P&G's earnings dropped for the first time in three decades.

Divergent Information from Convergent Technologies Convergent Technologies (CVGT), once one of the hottest stocks of the microcomputer age, also offers a good example of differential disclosure. For 1983 the company reported earnings of $0.40 a share compared with $0.42 in 1982. CVGT's annual report and letter were both optimistic, but the 10-K provided a somewhat different picture.

Among CVGT's more important products were multiprocessor super-minicomputers known as the NGEN workstations and the MegaFrame, upon which the company had pinned much of its hopes. The letter to stockholders in the annual report started out by noting that "1983 was a year of progress and challenge for Convergent Technologies." Now this word "challenge" should put an analyst on guard; corporate management often uses "challenge" to mean "trouble."

Although most of the rest of the letter was relatively upbeat, there were exceptions. For example, NGEN shipments were below expectations and costs were above expectations. The reason: "Slow manufacturing start up and disappointing performance by some suppliers." There were words of praise for WorkSlate, a powerful portable microcomputer that can also function as a terminal. "These machines were sent as 'high tech stocking stuffers' to initial customers ordering through the American Express Christmas catalog," with a good reception.[5]

Some of the numbers looked great, but some were not at all pleasing. Revenues rose from $96.4 million to $163.5 million, net income went from $11.9 million to $14.9 million, but CVGT earned only $0.40 per share compared with $0.42 in 1982 due to a substantial increase in the number of shares outstanding.[6] Despite this, the letter ended on a note of triumph. "Upon reflection, 1983 was a year of investment and a year of rewards. . . . We have retained our tough operating culture and entrepreneurial spirit, and will continue to set demanding goals for ourselves."[7]

The 10-K presented quite a different picture, one of the clearest examples of differential disclosure. In that document we learn that there was only one supplier for the advanced microprocessor upon which MegaFrame is based and only one for the disk drives. "To date the disk drives have been manufac-

---

[5]Convergent Technologies, *1983 Annual Report Commission*, pp. 2–3.

[6]Ibid., p. 19.

[7]Ibid., p. 3.

tured in limited quantities and the microprocessor is on allocation from its manufacturer." The report went on to claim that this had no material impact upon the business, but later in the 10-K we read that "with the increased demand for certain components in the computer system industry the Company believes that there is a greater likelihood that the Company will experience such delays." Further, "some of these new components have yet to be manufactured in volume by their suppliers. The Company's ability to manufacture these products may be adversely affected by the inability of the Company's vendors to supply high quality components in adequate quantities."[8] A similar situation existed for the company's other product, WorkSlate.

Changes in Discretionary Expenses

There are scores of examples by which earnings are increased or decreased through one-time changes in discretionary expenses, and others in which earnings remain the same but the quality can be altered. Examples of discretionary expenses are maintenance repair costs, the cost of replacement of obsolete equipment, advertising costs, and the costs of training programs. Changes in these expenditures are the result of business decisions made by management, not accounting decisions.

Either cutting a discretionary cost or postponing it to a future accounting period can favorably impact a company's earnings in the current period but have a detrimental effect on future earnings. For example, consider the case where a company in the last month of its fiscal year decides to cut advertising expenditures for the remainder of the fiscal year and in future years. The immediate effect might be to improve earnings in the current fiscal year. But future earnings will be adversely affected if the reduction in advertising reduces future sales by a greater amount.

Changes in discretionary expenses could also have the opposite effect: It could decrease earnings but result in a favorable impact on earnings in future periods. An increase in advertising and the acquisition of more efficient capital equipment are examples of positive discretionary expenses.

In summary, the financial analyst must read all the publications of a corporation and be alert to unusual charges and sources of income, changes and large differences in changes in discretionary expenses, and differences in information disclosed. By reading between the lines, the astute analyst can uncover issues that corporate managers may be asked to address.

PROFITABILITY ANALYSIS

Profitability ratios are utilized to explore the underlying causes of a change in earnings per share. They show the combined effects of liquidity and asset and debt management on the profitability of the firm. These ratios break earnings per share into their basic determinants for purposes of assessing the factors underlying the profitability of the firm. These ratios help to assess the adequacy of historical profits, and to project future profitability through better understanding of its underlying causes.

---

[8]Convergent Technologies, *1983 10-K Report to the Securities & Exchange Commission.*

Standards for a given ratio will vary according to the operating characteristics of the company being analyzed and general business conditions; such standards cannot be stated as fixed and immutable. Experience plays an important role in setting such standards.

It is assumed that the analyst has made all adjustments deemed necessary to reflect the comparable and true earning power of the corporation before calculating the ratios discussed below. It is important to stress that ratios are utilized to raise significant questions requiring further analysis, not to provide answers. Ratios must be viewed in the context of other ratios and other facts, derived from sources other than the financial statements, such as cash flow analysis, which is discussed in Appendix D.

Determinants of Earnings per Share

Profit is the ultimate measure of the success of a firm, but the analyst must relate it to total assets and common stock holders' equity to avoid being misled. For example, assume a firm with 1,000,000 common shares outstanding earned $1,000,000 after taxes. Earnings per share, assuming only that class of common stock outstanding, would be $1 per share. Now assume the company could earn an additional $500,000 after taxes by utilizing the funds raised through selling an additional 1,000,000 common shares. While total earnings would increase, this would not be advantageous to the stockholder. There are now 2,000,000 shares outstanding, and since earnings would be $1,500,000 after taxes, earnings per share would fall to $0.75 per share. Return on the total owners' investment also would fall. This suggests concentrating, at least initially, on earnings per share and their determinants rather than earnings after taxes.

The two basic determinants of earnings per share are the return on stockholders' equity and the book value per share, as shown by the equation below:

$$\text{Earnings per share} = \frac{\text{earnings available to common}}{\text{average number of common shares}}$$

$$= \frac{\text{earnings available to common}}{\text{stockholders' equity}} \times \frac{\text{stockholders' equity}}{\text{average number of common shares}}$$

The first ratio is the return on stockholders' equity:

$$\text{Return on stockholders' equity} = \frac{\text{earnings available to common}}{\text{stockholders' equity}}$$

The second ratio is **book value per share:**

$$\text{Book value per share} = \frac{\text{stockholders' equity}}{\text{average number of common shares}}$$

To illustrate the calculation of the ratios above and other ratios discussed in this appendix, we use the 1991 and 1990 balance sheet and income statement of The Home Depot, Inc., the largest participant in the home-center industry.[9] We presented these two financial statements in Appendix B. Table C-

---

[9]The source of the data on Home Depot is a research report by Christopher E. Vroom of Alex. Brown & Sons, Inc., dated September 5, 1991.

2 reproduces the income statement, and Table C-3 the balance sheet. (The last two columns in both tables will be discussed later in this appendix.) Table C-4 shows the calculation of the various financial measures discussed throughout this appendix.

Growth in Book Value per Share

As one can see from the partitioning of the earnings-per-share measure earlier, all other things being equal, a higher book-value-per-share ratio is better than a low one. How can a firm get growth in book value per share? There are three basic ways.

First, the company can retain earnings. By doing so, owners' equity increases, but there is no change in the number of common shares outstanding. This assumes that the retained earnings can be utilized as effectively as past owners' equity has been; in other words, the return on owners' equity is at least maintained.

The growth rate in earnings supported by retained earnings can be calculated by multiplying the rate of return earned on owners' equity by the retention rate of the firm (retained earnings divided by earnings after taxes). A firm that earns 10% on its owners' equity and has a **retention rate** of 40% builds a 4% growth rate for earnings per share. To illustrate, assume

Earnings per share = $1
Book value per share = $10
Retention rate = 40%

Forty cents will be retained for each dollar earned per share, increasing book value per share to $10.40. If, however, the firm continues to earn 10% on the owners' capital ($1/$10), the earnings per share will rise to $1.04, or a 4% growth rate. If the rate earned on owners' capital fell because of the added production capacity, earnings per share could fall, even with retention. For

			Common Size Analysis*	
TABLE C-2 THE HOME DEPOT, INC. INCOME STATEMENT, 1991 AND 1990 (Dollars in Thousands)				
	1991	**1990**	**1991**	**1990**
Net sales	$3,815,356	$2,758,535	100.00%	100.00%
Cost of goods sold	2,751,085	1,991,777	72.11	72.20
Gross profit	$1,064,271	$ 766,758	27.89	27.80
Operating expenses	$ 693,657	$ 504,363	18.18	18.28
General & admin.	91,664	67,901	2.40	2.46
Preopening expense	13,315	9,845	0.35	0.36
Net operating profit	$ 265,635	$ 184,649	6.96	6.69
Interest expense (net)	5,807	2,634	0.15	0.10
Earnings before taxes	$ 259,828	$ 182,015	6.81	6.60
Income taxes	96,400	70,061	2.53	5.54
Net income	$ 163,428	$ 111,954	4.28	4.06

* All items expressed as a percentage of net sales.

TABLE C-3

THE HOME DEPOT, INC.
BALANCE SHEET, 1991 AND 1990
(Dollars in Thousands)

	1991	1990	Common Size Analysis* 1991	1990
Assets				
Cash	$ 137,296	$ 135,381	8.37%	12.11%
Receivables (net)	49,325	38,933	3.01	3.48
Inventory	509,022	381,452	31.05	34.13
Other	17,931	10,474	1.09	0.94
Total current assets	$ 713,574	$ 566,240	43.52	50.67
Plant, prop., & equip.	963,619	568,690	58.78	50.89
Less accumulated dep.	(84,889)	(54,250)	(5.18)	(4.85)
Net plant, prop., & equip.	$ 878,730	$ 514,440	53.60	46.04
Other assets	47,199	36,854	2.88	3.30
Total assets	$1,639,503	$1,117,534	100.00	100.00
Liabilities				
Accounts payable	$ 235,267	$ 172,876	14.35	15.47
Accrued liabilities	166,734	118,066	10.17	10.56
Other current liability	10,706	1,447	0.65	0.13
Total current liabilities	$ 412,707	$ 292,389	25.17	26.16
Long-term debt	530,774	302,901	32.37	27.10
Capital lease obligations	12,620	10,115	0.77	0.91
Stockholder's equity				
Retained earnings	439,770	289,177	26.82	25.88
Paid-in-capital	264,301	233,458	16.12	20.89
Other	(20,669)	(10,506)	(1.26)	(0.94)
Total stockholders' equity	$ 683,402	$ 512,129	41.68	45.83
Total liabilities & equity	$1,639,503	$1,117,534	100.00	100.00

* All items expressed as a percentage of total assets.

TABLE C-4

CALCULATION OF FINANCIAL RATIOS FOR THE HOME DEPOT, INC.: 1991 AND 1990

The balance sheet and income statement are shown in Tables C-2 and C-3, respectively.
Additional information:
    Average number of shares of common stock outstanding: 1991 = 181,252,000; 1990 = 177,472,000
    Year-end 1989 accounts receivable = $17,614,000
    Year-end 1989 inventory = $294,274,000

Since there is no preferred stock in the capital structure, net income = earnings available to common

Financial Measure	1991		1990	
Earnings per share:				
$\dfrac{\text{Earnings available to common}}{\text{Average number of common shares}}$	$\dfrac{\$163,428,000}{181,252,000}$	$= \$0.90$	$\dfrac{\$111,954,000}{177,472,000}$	$= \$0.63$
Return on stockholders' equity:				
$\dfrac{\text{Earnings available to common}}{\text{Stockholders' equity}}$	$\dfrac{\$163,428,000}{\$683,402,000}$	$= 23.91\%$	$\dfrac{\$111,954,000}{\$512,129,000}$	$= 21.86\%$

			TABLE C-4			

CALCULATION OF FINANCIAL RATIOS FOR THE HOME DEPOT, INC.: 1991 AND 1990 (Continued)

Financial Measure	1991			1990		
Book value per share:						
$\dfrac{\text{Stockholders' equity}}{\text{Average number of common shares}}$	$\dfrac{\$683,402,000}{181,252,000}$	= $3.77		$\dfrac{\$512,129,000}{177,472,000}$	= $2.88	
Return on total assets:						
$\dfrac{\text{Earnings available to common}}{\text{Total assets}}$	$\dfrac{\$163,428,000}{\$1,639,503,000}$	= 9.97%		$\dfrac{\$111,954,000}{\$1,117,534,000}$	= 10.02%	
Asset/equity ratio:						
$\dfrac{\text{Total assets}}{\text{Stockholders' equity}}$	$\dfrac{\$1,639,503,000}{\$683,402,000}$	= 2.40		$\dfrac{\$1,117,534,000}{\$512,129,000}$	= 2.18	
Gross profit margin:						
$\dfrac{\text{Gross profit}}{\text{Net sales}}$	$\dfrac{\$1,064,271,000}{\$3,815,356,000}$	= 27.89%		$\dfrac{\$766,758,000}{\$2,758,535,000}$	= 27.80%	
Net operating margin:						
$\dfrac{\text{Net operating income}}{\text{Net sales}}$	$\dfrac{\$265,635,000}{\$3,815,356,000}$	= 6.96%		$\dfrac{\$184,649,000}{\$2,758,535,000}$	= 6.69%	
Before-tax profit margin:						
$\dfrac{\text{Net income before taxes}}{\text{Net sales}}$	$\dfrac{\$259,828,000}{\$3,815,356,000}$	= 6.81%		$\dfrac{\$182,015,000}{\$2,758,535,000}$	= 6.60%	
After-tax profit margin:						
$\dfrac{\text{Net income}}{\text{Net sales}}$	$\dfrac{\$163,428,000}{\$3,815,356,000}$	= 4.28%		$\dfrac{\$111,954,000}{\$2,758,535,000}$	= 4.06%	
Total asset turnover:						
$\dfrac{\text{Net sales}}{\text{Total assets}}$	$\dfrac{\$3,815,356,000}{\$1,639,503,000}$	= 2.33		$\dfrac{\$2,758,535,000}{\$1,117,534,000}$	= 2.47	
Accounts receivable turnover:						
$\dfrac{\text{Net sales}}{\text{Average accounts receivable*}}$	$\dfrac{\$3,815,356,000}{\$44,114,000}$	= 86.49		$\dfrac{\$2,758,535,000}{\$28,303,500}$	= 97.46	
Days sales in accounts receivable:						
$\dfrac{\text{360 days}}{\text{Average accounts receivable turnover}}$	$\dfrac{360}{86.49}$	= 4.2 days		$\dfrac{360}{97.46}$	= 3.7 days	
Inventory turnover:						
$\dfrac{\text{Cost of goods sold}}{\text{Average inventory†}}$	$\dfrac{\$2,751,085,000}{\$445,237,000}$	= 6.2		$\dfrac{\$1,991,777,000}{\$337,863,000}$	= 5.9	
Days to sell inventory:						
$\dfrac{\text{360 days}}{\text{Inventory turnover}}$	$\dfrac{360}{6.2}$	= 58 days		$\dfrac{360}{5.9}$	= 61 days	

* Average Accounts Receivable =   ($49,235,000 + $38,993,000)/2   ($38,993,000 + $17,614,000)/2

† Average Inventory =   ($509,022,000 + $381,452,000)/2   ($381,452,000 + $294,274,000)/2

example, if return on owners' capital fell to 8%, the earnings per share would be only 83 cents (0.08 × $10.40 = $0.832).

The second way to get growth in book value per share is to buy back company stock at a price less than book value per share. The third way is to sell stock at a price above book value per share. Mergers can result in an increase in book value per share for the surviving company since the book value of the acquired shares may be greater than the book value of the shares given in exchange. While it is true that book value per share has no necessary relationship to market value per share, investors should follow what happens to book value since it is an important determinant of earnings.

Return on Stockholders' Equity

Stockholders are the residual claimants to the profits earned after taxes less any preferred dividends (earnings available to common). The rate earned on the stockholders' invested capital (return on owners' equity) and the behavior of the basic components determining that return are the key criteria when selecting stocks. The two basic determinants of return on stockholders' equity are the return on total assets and the proportion of assets financed by owners, as opposed to creditors. This is demonstrated in the equation below:

$$\frac{\text{Earnings available to common}}{\text{Stockholders' equity}} = \frac{\text{earnings available to common}}{\text{total assets}}$$
$$\times \frac{\text{total assets}}{\text{stockholders' equity}}$$

The first ratio is the **return on total assets**:

$$\text{Return on total assets} = \frac{\text{earnings available to common}}{\text{total assets}}$$

The second ratio, the **asset/equity ratio**, indicates the amount of total assets relative to stockholders' equity:

$$\text{Asset/equity ratio} = \frac{\text{total assets}}{\text{stockholders' equity}}$$

The reciprocal of the asset/equity ratio is the percentage of the firm's assets provided by the stockholders.

Leveraged Capital Structures Most firms have a leveraged capitalization, which means that debt has been used as a source of funds. This will cause profits and the return to owners to be much more variable than if only equity capital were used to raise funds. The effects of financial leverage are compounded by the effects of operating leverage introduced by fixed operating costs. To illustrate, assume the following data for Temple Corporation:

1. The product of the firm is sold at $3 per unit.
2. Fixed costs are $180,000.
3. Variable costs are $1.50 per unit and vary in direct proportion.
4. The firm is capitalized as follows: (a) $300,000 of 10% coupon bonds and (b) $300,000 of common equity representing 3,000 shares of common stock outstanding.

5. The firm currently is selling 160,000 units.
6. The effective income tax rate applicable to the firm is 40%.

The effect of a 10% increase in units sold and a 10% decrease in units sold is illustrated in Table C-5. Earnings per share rise 80% when sales increase 10%, but fall by 80% when sales decrease by 10%.

The difference between the rate of return on total capital invested and the rate of return on the equity of common stock holders indicates the effect of financial leverage. Favorable financial leverage means that the rate of return on the total capital invested exceeds the cost of borrowed funds. When this occurs, the rate of return on the equity of common stock holders will exceed the rate earned on total invested capital.

Return on Total Assets

As explained above, return on total assets is a key determinant of the return earned on owners' equity. There are two basic determinants of the return on total assets: (1) the cents of profit generated by each dollar of sales (the margin) and (2) the dollars of sales generated on average for each dollar of assets (the turnover of assets). This is demonstrated in the equation below:

$$\text{Return on total assets} = \frac{\text{earnings available to common}}{\text{total assets}} \times \frac{\text{net sales}}{\text{total assets}}$$

TABLE C-5

TEMPLE CORPORATION—THE DETERMINATION OF EARNINGS PER SHARE FOR THE THREE LEVELS OF SALES

Units sold	144,000	160,000	176,000
Sales	$432,000	$480,000	$528,000
Less costs			
Fixed costs	$180,000	$180,000	$180,000
Variable costs	216,000	240,000	264,000
Total costs	$396,000	$420,000	$444,000
EBIT*	$ 36,000	$ 60,000	$ 84,000
Less interest expense	30,000	30,000	30,000
Taxable income	$ 6,000	$ 30,000	$ 54,000
Less taxes	2,400	12,000	21,600
Earnings after taxes	$ 3,600	$ 18,000	$ 32,400
Number of shares	3,000	3,000	3,000
Earnings per share	$ 1.20	$ 6.00	$ 10.80

Percentage increase in earnings per share for 10% rise in sales:

$$\frac{10.80 - 6}{6} = \frac{4.80}{6} = 80\%$$

Percentage decrease in earnings per share for 10% drop in sales:

$$\frac{6 - 1.2}{6} = \frac{4.80}{6} = 80\%$$

*EBIT 5 earnings before interest and taxes.

The first ratio is called the **profit margin** and the second the **total asset turnover**; that is,

$$\text{Profit margin} = \frac{\text{net earnings}}{\text{net sales}}$$

$$\text{Total asset turnover} = \frac{\text{net sales}}{\text{total assets}}$$

Return on total assets and the behavior of its components offer some of the most useful statistics for studying the operating efficiency of a firm.

Profit Margin

To aid in studying the operating efficiency of a firm, an analyst can calculate and assess each of the following margin ratios.

Gross Profit Margin **Gross profit margin** is calculated by dividing gross profit by net sales:

$$\text{Gross profit margin} = \frac{\text{gross profit}}{\text{net sales}}$$

This ratio is a useful indicator of the productive efficiency of the plant floor of a firm. It should be analyzed in terms of its trend over time and in relationship to other companies operating in the same industry. As noted in Appendix B, the method of inventory valuation used by the firm (e.g., LIFO versus FIFO) is important, and the analyst must be sure that the figures used for comparison are, in fact, comparable.

Net Operating Margin **Net operating margin** is calculated by dividing net operating income by net sales:

$$\text{Net operating margin} = \frac{\text{net operating income}}{\text{net sales}}$$

The net operating margin is the complement of the net operating expense ratio, since the two when added must always equal 100%. This ratio indicates the percentage of sales dollars not used up in the generation of sales. In other words, this is the percentage of sales dollars available to meet finance charges, pay taxes, pay dividends, and finance corporate capital needs.

Before-Tax and After-Tax Profit Margins The **before-tax profit margin** and the **after-tax profit margin** are calculated as shown below:

$$\text{Before-tax profit margin} = \frac{\text{net income before taxes}}{\text{net sales}}$$

$$\text{After-tax profit margin} = \frac{\text{net income}}{\text{net sales}}$$

The before-tax profit margin is a more useful intermediate determinant of the return on assets than the after-tax profit margin, for purposes of assessing the efficiency with which assets are used.

The percentage of sales brought down to before-tax profit may be low (as for a food retailer), but if inventory turnover and/or capital investment turnover are high, then the rate of return on assets may still be big. Conversely, the before-tax margin may be relatively high (as for a public utility), but if inventory turnover and/or capital asset turnover is low, the return on assets may be low. These ratios are components of the return on assets and must be interpreted in relation to asset turnovers. It is the return on capital committed that is important to an investor, not how that return is generated. Breaking the return on investment into its basic components, however, helps gain a better understanding of the firm's operating record and provides a better basis for forecasting.

Asset Turnover

Asset turnover is calculated by dividing the net sales by the total assets. There are numerous combinations of asset turnover and gross profit margin that will produce a given return on assets. One should compare both the turnover ratios and the gross profit margins of a company with those of competitive companies or companies in the same industry. Such an analysis, especially when buttressed by information gained in the analysis of the economy, can reveal the weaknesses as well as the potential strengths of a firm.

One must go beyond a mere calculation of these ratios and a comparison to competitors. A weak margin suggests problems in controlling expenses for a firm. Vertical and horizontal analyses can help explore these problems. **Vertical analysis** is accomplished by dividing each expense item in the income statement of a given year by net sales. One would expect expenses to rise as sales rise. However, when a particular expense item rises at a faster rate than sales, it should be explored carefully. In **horizontal analysis**, each expense item of a given year is divided by that same expense item in the base year. This allows for the exploration of changes in the relative importance of expense items over time and the behavior of expense items as sales change.

The turnover of assets may fall sharply when a firm undertakes a major expansion. The large asset investment causes this, since there has not yet been adequate time for these assets to generate the anticipated growth in sales that motivated the expansion. One must, therefore, be careful to review capital expenditures when assessing asset turnover ratios.

Leased assets treated as operating leases are not recorded on the balance sheet and are not, therefore, a part of the total assets shown on the balance sheet. Still, leased assets do result in sales. A rising or relatively high turnover ratio could, therefore, be generated by a firm that increases the use of leasing to acquire assets. This would not indicate more efficient use of asset investment.

One of the best ways analysts can predict future downward earnings is through a careful analysis of accounts receivable and inventories. Two signs can indicate problems: a larger than average accounts receivable situation and/or a bloated inventory. Either situation is a signal that the analyst should play the devil's advocate when assessing that particular company.

Accounts Receivable   The **accounts receivable turnover** can be determined by dividing the net credit sales by the average accounts receivable. That is,

$$\text{Accounts receivable turnover} = \frac{\text{annual net credit sales}}{\text{average accounts receivable}}$$

Here the average accounts receivable is equal to the average of the accounts receivable at the beginning of the year (i.e., the accounts receivable at the end of the previous fiscal year) and the accounts receivable at the end of the current fiscal year.

In practice, the net sales figure typically is used as the numerator because information is not available about the portion of sales that were on credit terms. This does tend to overstate the liquidity of receivables when cash sales are significant, as for a retailer.

The turnover may be converted into the number of days' sales outstanding in receivables by dividing the accounts receivable turnover figure into 360. That is,

$$\text{Days' sales in accounts receivable} = \frac{360 \text{ days}}{\text{accounts receivable turnover}}$$

One would expect the accounts receivable turnover to be relatively in line with the firm's terms of sale. A high accounts receivable turnover could make a relatively low current ratio (discussed in Appendix D) acceptable from a liquidity standpoint and could lead to a higher return on assets. On the other hand, a high turnover could suggest that credit terms are too tight, causing sales and profits to be restricted.

Increases in days' sales in accounts receivable can illustrate the granting of more liberal credit terms and/or difficulty in obtaining payment from customers. However, even more importantly, the analysis of sales and accounts receivable may provide a clue about whether a company is merely shifting inventory from the corporate level to its customers because of a hard-sell sales campaign or costly incentives. In such an instance, this type of sales may constitute "borrowing from the future." Within this context, it is important to note that in most instances a sale is recorded by a company when the goods are shipped to the customer. Also, there is an added cost to the company in carrying an above-average amount of accounts receivable.

Inventories **Inventory turnover** is computed by dividing the cost of goods sold by the average inventory for a year. That is,

$$\text{Inventory turnover} = \frac{\text{cost of goods sold}}{\text{average inventory}}$$

The analyst is interested in determining the physical turnover of the inventory, and needs a numerator (cost of goods sold) that is calculated on the same basis as the inventory. Price changes could distort this ratio, as an indicator of physical turnover, when the net sales figure is used as a numerator.

A low ratio suggests the possibility that investment in inventory is too high for the sales capacity of the business. This will hurt future profitability, because of both the interest costs incurred by borrowing to support the inventory investment and the storage costs. On the other hand, a high ratio relative to the industry tends to suggest that inventories are too low. Sales might be lost by a firm because of inadequate selection for its customers.

The number of days' sales outstanding in inventory can be calculated by dividing the approximate number of days in a year (360) by the inventory turnover ratio:

$$\text{Days to sell inventory} = \frac{360 \text{ days}}{\text{inventory turnover}}$$

For example, if the inventory turnover ratio were 12, the number of days' sales outstanding would be 30. This would mean that if the firm continued to sell at the same rate it has in the past, it would sell the entire inventory shown on the balance sheet in 30 days.

Why is inventory analysis so important? Obviously, higher-trending inventories in relation to sales can lead to inventory markdowns, write-offs, etc. In addition, it is important to note that an excess of inventories has repeatedly proved to be a good indicator of future slowdown in production. Within this context, it is important to analyze the components of inventories. If the finished goods segment of inventories is rising much more rapidly than raw materials and/or work in process, it is likely that the company has an abundance of finished goods and will have to slow down production. Akin to accounts receivable, bulging inventories are costly to carry.

Importance of Accounts Receivable and Inventory Analysis Accounts receivable are monies due from customers for goods shipped and/or services performed. By itself this isn't a problem: Just about every operation has accounts receivable. The difficulty comes when accounts receivable rise substantially over what they had been in the same reporting period during previous years. This can result from any of several factors. A spell of economic hard times for the country, industry, or region will often cause stretch-outs in payments. A poor collection job might be another reason. Perhaps the firm, its back against the wall and eager to make sales, has offered its customers liberal credit terms. This often happens in the auto industry during slack periods. In the retail business, this is the equivalent of end-of-season sales and the dumping of unfashionable merchandise. One dramatic instance of this occurred at RCA just prior to that company's departure from the computer business, when mainframes were being leased literally on a "two for the price of one" basis simply to move them out of inventory prior to the news being released. Whatever the cause, major increases in days' sales in accounts receivable are a danger sign.

An analysis of the relationships between sales, accounts receivable, and inventories may provide a clue about whether a company is merely shifting inventory from the warehouses to its customers due to hard-sell campaigns or costly incentives. In such an instance, these kinds of sales may constitute borrowing from the future or rectifying past errors. In this context, it is important to recall that in most instances revenues are recorded by a company when the goods are shipped to the customer. Also, there are the added money costs of carrying accounts receivable.

Now for inventories. These are stores of raw materials and finished and semifinished products. Manufacturing concerns may have very large inventories as a ratio to sales, while service companies have smaller ones. Indeed, the key distinction between the manufacturing and service sectors is just that: Companies can stockpile inventory products, but not services. For example, a stock market advisory service has an inventory of paper, back copies, postage stamps, and the like, which can be quite minor when set beside gross income. Knowing the inventory for such an operation is not very useful. On the other hand, a furniture factory can have an inventory larger than annual sales. As just noted, the specific amount of inventory is not particularly meaningful in and of itself. What matters are comparisons with the same reporting period in previous years.

Increases in raw materials inventories from reporting period to reporting period might mean that the company had decided to stock up in anticipation of a price boost, but this is not very likely, since the company has to lay out money for inventory and wants to move it as quickly as possible. Indeed, one of the reasons the Japanese carmakers are more efficient than those from Detroit is inventory management; Toyota does far better in this regard than General Motors. So an increase in raw materials inventories usually means business is speeding up, and this will be reflected in future revenues and profits.

More interesting are major changes in semifinished and finished goods. If business is sluggish due to economic conditions, or to the fact that a furniture manufacturer decided to produce colonial when customers decided they wanted Scandinavian contemporary, this figure could rise substantially. On the other hand, should the manufacturer have targeted the market correctly, retailers would be pounding on its door pleading for sofas and cabinets and the manufacturer would be drawing down its finished goods inventories.

Examples abound of how considerable increases in inventory and/or accounts receivable can forecast downward earnings and surprises. This is especially true in those industries subject to rapid changes in products and taste. Expect to find them in companies dealing with high fashion, seasonal goods, and especially high tech. No investor seriously involved with stocks in these industries can afford to ignore accounts receivable and inventories.

Profitability Analysis and Physical Data Ratios

Analysts frequently calculate physical data ratios and reduce them to a per share basis, to aid in studying profitability. These ratios are useful when calculated on the basis of specific characteristics of a given industry and used for comparing companies in that industry.

Physical Reserves   Reserves are of utmost importance to companies dependent on wasting assets for their operations (such as oil or timber companies). Reported reserves by major companies normally provide a conservative representation of such assets. The analyst should note the quality or grade of reserves as well as the quantity, with special attention to changes in grade from year to year. Changes from year to year indicate current extractive policy and possibly "high grading" (mining primarily the highest-grade ores in the deposit) in any given year.

Reserves of oil and gas, normally stated in terms of millions of barrels and billions of cubic feet, respectively, frequently are reported on a per share basis. The estimated value of reserves can be computed by multiplying the number of units in reserve by the going market price per unit. The value of reserves per share often is compared with current market price per share when looking for undervalued companies. This is not necessarily a valid indicator of value, however, since market prices for the physical resource can rise or fall sharply in the future (witness oil).

Capacity   Producers and processors of various materials normally have specific productive or fabricating capacities that may be expressed in physical terms. These data can be reduced to a per share or a per employee basis for comparison between companies. Capacity also can be related to order backlogs, in both units and dollars. Persistent excess capacity often is a symptom of decline for a firm.

Production Data   Production data in units can be related to capacity figures to assess whether or not excess capacity is present. This information should be compared with that for other firms in the industry. In companies concentrating principally on one type of product (e.g., crude oil, ingot steel, or copper), production data in units can be used to estimate selling prices, production costs, and profits per unit. Such data also help the analyst to determine the effects of changes in costs and selling prices, not the profit margins of the company.

Freight Volume and Other Specialized Ratios   Detailed information relative to volume, product composition, and geographical distribution of freight carried is valuable to the analyst in appraising the outlook for a transportation company such as a railroad, airline, trucking service, or barge line. Other examples of specialized physical ratios could be residential and commercial load for utilities, ton miles per dollar of debt for railroads, or the load factor for airlines. In the case of The Home Depot, Inc., information on the sales per average store and the sales per square foot should be analyzed.

SALES ANALYSIS

Analysts have long stressed growth in demand for a company's products as important to successful investment. However, growth in earnings power, not sales per se, is the desired objective. This makes cost behavior important. Since cost economies are rarely repeated on a yearly basis, continued growth in profits is not likely unless sales are growing.

The aim of sales analysis is to project revenues for the next three to five years as a basis for generating cost and profit expectations. When studying historical revenue data, the analyst should be concerned with the size, trend, composition, and underlying determinants of those revenue patterns.

For the purposes of developing future sales forecasts, the analyst could:

1. Calculate the compound growth rate in sales over a period of about 10 years, to insure including the effects of the business cycle
2. Calculate a standard deviation around the average of the above data to assess the stability of revenue patterns over time
3. Observe the resistance of company sales to negative economic and other factors
4. Assess the major factors underlying the sales pattern observed

Market Share Analysis and Sales Growth

Analysts typically compare the sales patterns for a given company with those of its principal competitors and appropriate aggregate data (such as

GNP data). Above-average sales growth for a company usually is predicated on expected rapid growth of the industry in which the company operates. A company may, however, accomplish above-average growth by gaining an increased share of total industry demand. Forecasting end-use demand for a company's products is therefore useful.

Many sophisticated systems of forecasting demand are based on past demand-supply relationships. Such systems rest on **input-output tables** which indicate how much each industry requires of the production of every other industry in order to produce each dollar of its own output. The various industrial subdivisions are listed both vertically and horizontally, similar to an intercity mileage chart on a road map. The individual inputs into a given industry read vertically, while the industry's dollar sales to other specific industries are read horizontally. The U.S. Department of Commerce publishes these tables on an infrequent basis in the *Survey of Current Business*.

Trends and Common Size Statements

In a **common size statement**, all items are expressed as a percentage of a base figure. Common size statements can be useful for purposes of analyzing trends and the changing relationship between financial statement items. For example, all items in each year's income statement could be presented as a percentage of net sales. This is shown for The Home Depot, Inc., in the last two columns of Table C-2. By reviewing several years of such statements, one could observe what changes in the relative importance of cost items occurred and how cost items vary as sales change. In the case of the balance sheet, all items can be expressed as a percentage of total assets, as shown in the last two columns of Table C-2.

Horizontal analysis is also a useful tool. In horizontal analysis, each item in the income statement is expressed as an index number calculated by dividing a given year's number by the number of a base year.

Calculating Growth Rates

Analysts typically calculate compound annual growth rates when studying long-term trends in sales and other variables. A compound annual growth rate is that rate that, if applied each year for a given number of years to a beginning balance, will cause the balance to grow to the ending known value. An analyst should always use a compound annual growth rate for time series, rather than a simple average growth rate. A simple average growth rate usually will overstate the growth experienced.

Regression analysis can be used to examine the relationship between variables, in either a cross-sectional or a time-series analysis. An analyst using a simple regression analysis, for example, could assess the strength of the relationship between disposable personal income and a company's sales. Moreover, the regression line developed through such an analysis could be used as a beginning framework for generating a sales forecast. Actually, in generating a sales forecast more than one independent variable might be used in the regression analysis (multiple regression).

TABLE C-6					
THE HOME DEPOT SALES MIX BY PRODUCT CATEGORY: FISCAL YEARS 1987 TO 1991					
Product Category	**1987**	**1988**	**1989**	**1990**	**1991**
Plumbing, heating & electrical supplies	29.2%	28.9%	29.0%	29.5%	28.9%
Building Materials, lumber, floor/wall covering	29.1	29.5	31.0	31.0	32.1
Hardware and tools	13.1	12.7	12.2	12.1	12.1
Seasonal and specialty items	14.4	14.8	14.6	14.5	15.2
Paint and furniture	14.2	14.1	13.2	12.9	11.7
	100.0%	100.0%	100.0%	100.0%	100.0%

Conglomerates and Sales Breakdowns

Analysts of diversified businesses face the problem of separating and understanding the impact that the individual segments of the business have on the operational results of a firm. Opportunities for growth will vary among the different product lines, and this must be taken into account when forecasting sales and profitability. Analysts require information that is broken down to represent homogeneous groupings whose characteristics are similar in terms of growth potential, variability, and risk. Table C-6 shows the breakdown of the sales mix of Home Depot by product category from fiscal years 1987 to 1991.

The degree of disclosure of product-line breakdown varies widely among companies. There are numerous difficulties, including problems of allocating overhead and interdivisional transfer pricing (i.e., prices charged by one division to another within a company), in preparing such data. Moreover, management is reluctant to divulge information that might help competitors.

FASB Statement No. 14 requires disclosure concerning information about operations in different industries, foreign operations, and major customers. Companies are required in their annual reports to offer breakdowns of significant segments in terms of revenues, operating profit, and identifiable assets. Also, the method of accounting for transfer pricing and cost allocations is to be disclosed. A segment is significant if sales, operating profit, or identifiable assets are 10% or more of the combined accounts for all of a company's industry segments.

While disclosure of information on business segments is helpful, one must recognize the many judgments necessary for preparing such data, which limit its usefulness. Cost allocations are often arbitrary, and there are no generally accepted principles governing such allocations. Information on business segments must be treated as highly qualitative, and one must not attribute undue accuracy to such data.

Industry Analysis

A firm's sales and profits typically are affected by economy-wide factors (e.g., interest rates and price-level fluctuations), by factors specific to the product line or industry areas in which the firm operates, and by factors specific to the firm itself (e.g., quality of management and locational factors). Therefore, a part of the sales and earnings of a corporation is determined by industry forces.

Some writers, notably Julius Grodinsky,[10] draw a rough parallel between industry growth and the human life cycle. They point out that when new industries are born, there often is a rush by many companies to enter the field in this period of initial and rapid growth. This is followed by a shakeout period, which only a few survive, and then by a continuing period of strong growth, although the rate of growth is slower than in the initial period. Grodinsky described these first two periods as (1) the pioneering stage and (2) the expansion stage. Finally, industries are expected to stop growing, either living a relatively stable existence for an extended period of time or dying.

Grodinsky pointed out the great risk of selecting stocks in the pioneering stage, where little information about participants may be available. There is little or no past record to guide investors or aid in preparing future projections.

Michael Porter has suggested six basic factors that should be considered in projecting the sales of a firm:

1. The threat of new entrants to the major markets served by the company
2. The threat posed by substitute products or services
3. The possible new entry of products by the company under analysis
4. The rivalry among existing firms serving the markets important to the company, and the company's present and expected position in those markets
5. The company's strategy for maintaining its leadership position in its market and its financial and other abilities to carry out these strategies
6. The position in the life-cycle analysis approach of the major product lines of the company[11]

Once again, we return to Home Depot, a company in the do-it-yourself home improvement industry. According to Christopher E. Vroom, an analyst in the Growth Retailers Group of Alex. Brown & Sons, this industry

> is a large, relatively stable and fast-growing component of residential construction accounting for over $100 billion in sales, or 24% of overall building activity (versus 16% in 1980). The industry has grown at a compound annual rate of 9% for the past ten years, driven largely by gains in the remodeling segment, which comprise roughly 70% of total sales.[12]

Vroom then goes on to highlight the favorable demographic and income shifts that "will drive sustained, strong growth in remodeling sales while the continued aging of the housing stock will likely spur growth in the repair business."

The five largest chains in the do-it-yourself industry account for only 12% of industry sales. Thus, this industry can be categorized as extremely fragmented. The five market leaders and their sales in 1986 and 1990 are shown in Table C-7.

[10]Julius Grodinsky, *Investments* (New York: Ronald Press, 1953), Part II.

[11]Michael Porter, *Competitive Strategy: Techniques for Analyzing Industries and Competitors* (New York: Free Press, 1980)

[12]Research report on The Home Depot, Inc., September 5, 1991.

TABLE C-7			
DO-IT-YOURSELF INDUSTRY LEADERS: 1986 AND 1990			
(Sales in Billions)			
Company	**1986**	**1990**	**% Change**
Lowe's Cos.	$2.5	$2.8	12.0%
Wickes Cos.	2.0	0.9	-55.0
Payless Cashways	1.5	2.2	46.7
Grossman's	1.0	0.8	-20.0
The Home Depot	1.0	3.8	280.0

Source: The Home Depot, Inc., Research report by Christopher E. Vroom of Alex. Brown & Sons, Inc., dated September 5, 1991.

■ SUMMARY

The earnings per share of a company are closely followed by participants in the stock market. Earnings per share are calculated by dividing the earnings available to common stock holders by the weighted average number of common shares outstanding over the year for which the calculation takes place. Two measures are calculated: primary diluted earnings per share and fully diluted earnings per share.

In analyzing the quality of reported earnings per share, the analyst should consider, in addition to the accounting policies, the treatment of non-operating and non-recurring items and the manipulation of discretionary expenses. When an analyst encounters differential disclosure (i.e., what the company says in one document is markedly different from what it says in another), caution should be exercised and the reasons for the differences should be investigated.

Profitability ratios are utilized to explore the underlying causes of a change in earnings per share. Profit is the ultimate measure of the success of a firm, but it must be related to total assets and owners' capital to be meaningful. The two basic determinants of earnings per share are the return on stockholders' equity and the book value per share. The two basic determinants of return on owners' equity are the return on total assets and the proportion of assets financed by owners as opposed to creditors. Return on total assets and the behavior of its components offer probably the most useful statistics for studying the operating efficiency of a firm. Two key ratios to look at in this area are those involving accounts receivable and inventories. Analysts frequently calculate physical data ratios, and reduce them to a per share basis, to aid in studying profitability.

Analysts must examine sales and cost structure to assess the future growth of earnings. Sales analysis typically involves comparing the sales patterns for a given company with those of its principal competitors and appropriate aggregate data. A firm's sales and profits typically are affected by economy-wide factors, by factors specific to the product line or industry areas in which the firm operates, and by factors specific to the firm itself.

■ KEY TERMS

accounts receivable turnover
after-tax profit margin
asset/equity ratio
asset turnover
before-tax profit margin
book value per share
common size statement

differential disclosure
earnings per share
gross profit margin
horizontal analysis
input-output tables
inventory turnover
net operating margin

price-earnings (P/E) ratio
profit margin
retention rate
return on stockholders' equity
return on total assets
total asset turnover
vertical analysis

■ QUESTIONS

1. What are the three major criticisms of the use of earnings-per-share figures by themselves?

2. A study by Zacks Investment Research found that during the 1981–1984 period 86% of brokerage house recommendations were either neutral or buys, 12% were sells, and 2% were strong sells. How would you explain the dominance of buy or neutral recommendations?

3. A glowing report on a company by a sell-side analyst includes a disclaimer saying "The information contained herein is based on sources believed to be reliable, but is neither all-inclusive nor guaranteed by our firm." It ends with these words: "We have been an underwriter, manager, or co-manager, or have previously placed securities of the company within the last three years, or were a previous underwriter of this company." What should an investor keep in mind when reviewing this report?

4. **a.** In the calculation of earnings per share, what is meant by dilutive securities?
   b. Explain why a company that has issued dilutive securities may have to calculate two earnings-per-share figures.

5. What is the difference between primary diluted earnings per share and fully diluted earnings per share?

6. The first four paragraphs from Land End's six-month shareholders' letter, dated August 28, 1989, for the reporting period ending July 31, 1989, is reproduced below:

The quarter ended July 31 showed mixed results for Lands' End. Sales continued to show good gains (up 23 percent for the quarter and 27 percent for the first six months). Earnings, however, failed to keep pace. Net income was off 54 percent in the quarter and 36 percent in the six months.

The first half of last year was exceptionally strong, and we knew we had tough comparisons; but clearly, we expected to do better than we did. However, in the context of what we are trying to accomplish and in line with our long-term goals, we are not too disappointed. In fact, I believe the course we're on is correct.

Although sales were softer than expected at the outset of the quarter. I'm encouraged by the strengthening that set in as the second quarter progressed.

Gross profit as a percent of net sales was below that of last year, but we continue to make progress on our plan to close the gap between costs and selling prices which developed early in the year.

Land End's 10-Q report for the same period contained the following commentary in reference to "Results of Operations":

Net sales in the second quarter of fiscal 1990 were $104.2 million, an increase of 23.2 percent from $84.6 million in the second quarter of fiscal 1989. Management attributes the sales increase to an increase in the number of catalogs mailed, the creative presentation of products offered, continued development and merchandising of new products and improved order fulfillment. Management believes the overall rate of response to the company's catalog mailings was lower in the second quarter of fiscal 1990 than in the second quarter of fiscal 1989, in part because the company benefitted from improved mailing list segmentation techniques in the prior year to reduce its mailings to less productive names on its list due to a relatively weaker inventory position.

Gross profit increased 16.9 percent to $24.9 million in the second quarter as a result of the increase in net sales. As a percentage of net sales, gross profit was 41.2 percent in fiscal 1990 compared to 43.4 percent in fiscal 1989. The percentage decrease resulted primarily from product cost increases principally incurred in the latter part of fiscal 1989, that were not entirely passed through to customers in the form of higher selling prices during the second quarter of fiscal 1990.

Selling, general and administrative expenses totaled $39.4 million in the second quarter of fiscal 1990, an increase of 34.0 percent from $29.4 million in the second quarter of last year. The increase was due primarily to higher variable operating expenses and catalog advertising associated with the increased sales volume. Selling, general and administrative expenses as a percentage of net sales increased from 34.8 percent in the second quarter of fiscal 1989 to 37.8 percent in the second quarter of fiscal 1990, due principally to the overall weaker response to catalog mailings and additional prospecting for new customers.

a. What is meant by differential disclosure?
b. Explain why the above is an example of differential disclosure.

7. For the year ended December 31, 1988, National Education Corp. (NEC) earned $1.57 per share compared with a loss of $0.03 a share in the year 1987. NEC's revenues in 1988 totaled $457.5 million, 15% higher than in 1987.

   In 1987, NEC wrote down $34 million of assets. Explain why this "big bath" writedown contributed to the increase in earnings per share from 1987 to 1988.

8. In NEC's 1988 annual report the following appears under the section "Summary of Significant Accounting Policies Associated with Revenues and Costs":

Training Contract Revenues consist primarily of rental contract, custom contract and industrial contract revenues. Rental contract revenues under ad hoc month-to-month arrangements are recognized when usage occurs; under resident library arrangements, customers agree to use training courses for a period of time and revenue is recognized for the contracted course usage. Rental contracts generally range in term from one to five years and are billed to customers in annual installments. Custom contract revenues under time and materials contracts are recognized as costs are incurred, and revenues from fixed price contracts are recognized using the percentage-of-completion method. Industrial contract revenues are recognized when cash is received with appropriate recognition of estimated expenses relative to servicing such contracts.

Education Centers Revenues are recorded ratably over the terms of the courses which range from six to twenty-seven months. Course service costs are charged to expense as incurred. Advertising costs and salesmen's commissions are deferred and amortized into expense within nine months of incurrence.

Independent Study Contract Revenues are recognized when cash is received, but only to the extent such cash can be retained by the Company. Generally, the Company follows the guidelines of the National Home Study Council in determining retention rights. Advertising and promotional literature costs associated with independent study contracts are amortized over eighteen months.

Explain how the above-cited policies for revenues and costs accelerate revenue and defer expenses.

9. The earnings per share of Standard Register (SREG) decreased from $1.36 in 1987 to $1.28 in 1988. In analyzing this change in earnings per share, the following was reported in the April 12, 1989, issue of *Quality of Earnings Report*: (1) SREG's corporate tax rate declined to 37.8% in 1988 from 41.8% in 1987, with the lower tax rate equaling $0.08 per share; (2) SREG's selling and administrative expense declined in 1988 from its 1987 level, adding $0.23 per share to earnings after taxes; (3) SREG's repairs and maintenance expenditures declined in 1988 from their 1987 level which was estimated to improve earnings by $0.05 a share after taxes; and (4) SREG's depreciation expense declined in 1988 from its 1987 level, which was estimated to improve earnings by $0.06 per share after taxes. Based on the four items, comment on the quality of SREG's 1988 earnings.

10. a. For the first quarter of 1989, L.A. Gear reported earnings of $0.62 per share compared with $0.21 per share for the corresponding quarter in 1988. In L.A. Gear's 10-Q report for the first quarter for 1989, the following excerpt in reference to the company's accounting policy for expensing advertising costs appears:

For interim reporting purposes, the Company records advertising expense based on a percentage of net sales, which percentage is computed based upon the Company's total estimated advertising divided by the Company's estimated net sales for the year. This method of expense recognition may result in prepaid expenses or liabilities at any point in time if advertising expenditures do not correlate to recognition of net sales. During the three months ends February 28, 1989 and February 29, 1988, the Company expended approximately $3,293,000 and $2,148,000, respectively, for advertising costs, of which $3,900,000 and $149,000 have been deferred to be recognized in future quarters.

The warning that this policy to account for advertising "may result in prepaid expenses or liabilities at any point in time if advertising expenditures do not correlate to recognition of net sales" was not stated in previous published reports by L.A. Gear. Explain the implications of this policy for the increase in the first fiscal quarter's earnings per share and for L.A. Gear's ability to manipulate future earnings per share. (*Note*: It has been estimated that a deferral of expenses of $3.9 million increases earnings per share by $0.26.)

b. For L.A. Gear's first fiscal quarter of 1988, allowance for doubtful accounts was 4.6% compared with 10.1% for 1987. According to the May 15, 1989, issue of the *Quality of Earnings Report*, the decrease in the percentage for allowance for doubtful accounts changed earnings per share by $0.19. Explain whether this change in policy increased or decreased earnings per share.

c. Based on your answers to a and b, comment on the quality of L.A. Gear's earnings for the first fiscal quarter of 1988.

11. a. Explain two ways in which book value per share can be increased.

b. Explain why you agree or disagree with the following statement: "Earnings per share can be increased by increasing the book value per share."

12. a. Carefully explain the relationship between profit margins and rate of return on equity and on total capital for a given company.

b. Why would an increase in profit margin not necessarily increase the rate of return on total assets or the earnings per share?

13. Why should an investor carefully study unit sales data as well as dollar sales data?

14. In their book *The Investor's Equation* (Chicago: Probus Publishing, 1984), William M. Bowen and Frank P. Ganucheau suggest the following list of characteristics of a "good company" for investment (pages 122–130):

a. The ability to raise prices to cover rises in costs, even in poor economic times. This requires that the company face a relatively inelastic demand. Companies that offer unique high-quality goods or services or are in oligopolistic market situations with little threat of new entry are most likely to meet this condition. One must be careful, however, since pricing power may be more than built into the price of the company's stock. Careful valuation analysis is still necessary.

b. The company shows unit, as well as dollar, growth in sales. In other words, the growth in sales is real.

c. Leverage, both operating and financial, is favorable.

d. The company is able to retain a high or above-average return on total assets and owners' equity.

e. Labor cost are low in comparison to competitors'.

f. Pension plans are funded adequately, and cash flow seems able to support future needs without hurting the return to owners.

g. Research and development efforts have been successful historically. For most companies, research and development expenses are not voluntary. Failure to maintain this effort often will lead to failure of the company, since the innovations introduced by competitors will cause their product and/or service offerings to become obsolete. A healthy cash flow is needed to support the research and development effort.

h. A relatively low fixed-cost base, as indicated by a relatively high ratio of sales to each dollar of average gross plant value for the industry the company operates in.

i. A high earnings retention ratio that supports company growth and sustains capital during inflationary times.

j. A healthy cash flow over an extended period.

For each of the above, explain why the characteristics described by Bowen and Ganucheau for a "good company" are important.

15. **CFA** This question and the two to follow are adapted from the 1992 CFA Examination II.

You have recently joined the investment counseling firm of Cavalier Investment Management. The Investment Committee of the firm asked you to evaluate Monticello Corporation, a major holding in accounts managed by Cavalier. As part of your work on this project, you prepared a report containing the following information and data.

MONTICELLO CORPORATION

Monticello is a major American forest products company. Until 1990, it was entirely engaged in the manufacture and distribution of building materials, primarily wood products (lumber, plywood, etc.). The table below provides financial and operational results for selected years.

During 1990, Monticello acquired a major paper company, Great American Paper Corporation, a large producer of both pulp and newsprint. The transaction was for $3.5 billion and was financed entirely with debt.

The building material distribution operations are nationwide, but the manufacturing of building materials is concentrated in the southeastern United States (particularly Georgia), with five million acres of timberland owned to serve these facilities. The acquired paper operations are divided, with the pulp facilities in Georgia and the newsprint production in Maine.

The pulp mills (pulp is processed wood, used as the input for paper manufacturing) are low-cost pro-

MONTICELLO CORPORATION
YEARS ENDING DECEMBER 31
(In Millions Except Per Share Data)

	1980	1985	1987	1988	1989	1990	1991
Operational results:							
Net Sales	$4,554	$6,716	$8,603	$9,509	$10,171	$12,665	$11,000
Operating expenses	(4,242)	(6,294)	(7,747)	(8,534)	(8,824)	(11,340)	(10,290)
Interest expense	(79)	(132)	(124)	(197)	(260)	(606)	(700)
Pretax income	$ 233	$ 290	$ 732	$ 778	$ 1,087	$ 719	$ 10
Income taxes	(72)	(83)	(274)	(311)	(426)	$ (354)	(40)
Net income	$ 161	$ 207	$ 458	$ 467	$ 661	$ 365	$ (30)
Earnings per share	$ 1.48	$ 1.84	$ 4.23	$ 4.76	$ 7.42	$ 4.28	$ (0.35)
Dividends per share	$1.20	$ 0.80	$ 1.05	$ 1.25	$ 1.45	$ 1.60	$ 1.60
Average shares outstanding	108.8	112.5	108.3	98.1	89.1	85.3	86.0
Cash flow from operations	$ 350	$ 440	$ 781	$ 805	$ 1,075	$ 924	$ 630
Financial position at year-end:							
Current assets	$1,051	$1,291	$1,729	$1,892	$ 1,829	$ 1,766	$ 1,650
Other assets	3,266	3,575	4,141	5,223	5,227	10,294	10,465
Total assets	$4,317	$4,866	$5,870	$7,115	$ 7,056	$12,060	$12,115
Current liabilities	$ 710	$ 631	$ 996	$1,013	$ 924	$ 2,535	$ 2,000
Long-term debt	1,227	1,257	1,298	2,514	2,336	5,218	5,900
Other liabilities	311	675	896	953	1,079	1,332	1,400
Stockholders' equity	2,069	2,303	2,680	2,365	2,717	2,975	2,815
Total liabilities & equity	$4,317	$4,866	$5,870	$7,115	$ 7,056	$12,060	$12,115

ducers and are near an excellent deep-water port. As a result, much of the production is exported, particularly to Europe. There were no nearby timberlands owned by Great American, but the Monticello timberlands are now being utilized to supply these pulp operations.

The newsprint mills are not efficient and are in need of major capital expenditures. However, they are near two million acres of timberland which were owned by Great American and now by Monticello. An additional 50,000 acres of timberland were owned by Great American (now by Monticello) that are not used in any company operations.

The paper industry is capital-intensive, with large, modern mills necessary for a producer to be cost-competitive. The industry's products are mostly commodities in wide use. Wood is the primary raw material, so proximity to timberlands and an assured supply of timber through ownership or long-term contracts are important. Environmental concerns and a limitation on remaining potential sites for mills could restrict future industry expansion.

During your meeting with the Investment Committee, one member asked you to research Monticello's income tax situation because "in 1991 it reported an unusual tax rate, well over

100%." He wanted to know how this was possible and what the company's tax rate is likely to be in the future.

The following footnote appears in the *1991 Annual Report*:

The results for 1991 include net gains from asset sales of $60 million pretax ($40 million after tax). Also included is $100 million of goodwill amortization expense which is not tax deductible.

a. Calculate Monticello's marginal tax rate for 1991 after excluding the effects of asset sales and goodwill amortization expenses.

b. Calculate what the reported tax rate would be assuming pretax income of $1 billion after $100 million of goodwill amortization expense and the marginal tax rate calculated in part a. (*Note*: If you were unable to calculate the marginal tax rate in part a, assume 50%.)

c. In further analyzing Monticello's tax situation, you observe that a portion of federal taxes had been deferred and not paid.

d. Explain what causes some income taxes to be deferred, using one example to illustrate.

MONTICELLO CORPORATION
YEARS ENDING DECEMBER 31
(In Millions Except Per Share Data)

Income Statements			Balance Sheets		
	1992E	**1995E**		**1992E**	**1995E**
Net sales	$12,000	$16,000	Current assets	$1,800	$2,500
Operating expense	(10,920)	(14,150)	Other assets	10,400	8,500
interest expense	(680)	(300)	Total asssets	$12,200	$11,000
Pretax income	$400	$1,550			
Taxes	(200)	(660)	Current liabilities	$1,900	$1,700
Net income	$ 200	$ 890	Long-term debt	5,900	3,200
			Other liabilities	1,500	1,800
Shares outstanding	87	89	Stockholders' equity	2,900	4,300
Earnings per share	$2.30	$10.00	Total liabilities & equity	$12,200	$11,000

16. **CFA**   The Investment Committee at Cavalier Investment Management decided to retain its sizable position in the common stock of Monticello. You were asked by the Committee to be the primary person in the organization responsible for following the company. Over the past couple of weeks, you put together a brief update on Monticello containing the following projections for the current year and for 1995, which you assumed to be the peak of the next business cycle.

On Friday morning, the following press release appeared on the Dow Jones News Service:

Monticello Corporation and Charlottesville Paper Corporation have announced a preliminary agreement whereby Charlottesville will acquire certain assets from Monticello. The assets involved consist of the newsprint production facilities and the related two million acres of timberland acquired by Monticello in 1990. The companies indicated the purchase price will be approximately $1 billion.

The head of the Investment Committee called you soon after the appearance of this news. He indicated that trading in Monticello stock had been halted on the New York Stock Exchange prior to the announcement, and he felt it was unlikely to reopen until Monday morning. He asked you to meet with the Investment Committee before the market opens on Monday to discuss your assessment of the impact of this divestiture on Monticello and its stock.

Although the newsprint operations are not broken out in Monticello's financial reports, you have reviewed what has been said about them by Monticello and in previous Great American reports. Based on this work and your own knowl-

edge, you have arrived at the estimates below regarding the Monticello operations being sold.

NEWSPRINT OPERATIONS

	1992E	**1995E**
Net sales	$1,000	$1,500
Net income (loss)	(100)	100
Assets	$1,100	
Liabilities	200	
Net worth	$ 900	
Tax cost basis	$ 900	

Anticipating that the Investment Committee will have a strong interest in the financial impacts of the divestiture on Monticello, you decide to prepare the following information.

a. Recalculate your 1992 estimate of earnings per share from continuing operations of $2.30, allowing for the divestiture and based on the following assumptions:
   • The divestiture took place at the beginning of 1992.
   • The proceeds from the divestiture were used to retire debt with a 10% interest rate.
   • Monticello's marginal tax rate is 40%.

b. Recalculate your 1995 (peak of the next business cycle) estimate of earnings per share from continuing operations of $10, allowing for the divestiture and based on the following assumptions:
   • The divestiture takes place at the beginning of 1995.
   • The proceeds from the divestiture are used to retire debt with a 10% interest rate.
   • Monticello's marginal tax rate is 40%.

c. Recalculate your 1995 (peak of the next business cycle) estimate of earnings per share from continuing operations using the same assump-

tions as in part b except assume the proceeds from the divestiture are used to repurchase stock at $100 per share instead of retiring debt.
d. Prepare a pro forma balance sheet for Monticello at December 31, 1992, assuming:
   • The divestiture takes place at the end of 1992
   • The proceeds are used to retire debt.
   • Monticello's marginal tax rate is 40%.

17. **CFA** Anticipating possible questions from the Investment Committee regarding why Monticello acquired Great American in 1990, only to sell part of it, you prepare answers to the following questions.

a. Discuss four basic competitive forces that can influence an industry's profitability and how they probably were viewed by Monticello in analyzing the paper industry before making a major acquisition in it.
b. Discuss three basic company competitive strategies and how they may have influenced Monticello's decision to divest of the newsprint operations.

APPENDIX D
DEBT AND CASH FLOW ANALYSIS*

LEARNING OBJECTIVES

After reading this chapter you will be able to:

- explain the ratios used to analyze the ability of a firm to meet short-term debt obligations (current ratio, quick ratio, accounts receivable turnover, inventory turnover).

- describe the ratios used to measure a firm's financial leverage (long-term debt to equity ratio and total debt to equity ratio).

- discuss the ratios used to analyze the ability of a firm to meet long-term debt obligations: interest coverage ratio and fixed-charge coverage ratio.

- explain what is meant by the cash flow of a firm.

- explain why cash flow analysis is superior to ratio analysis for assessing the ability of a firm to satisfy its debt obligations.

- describe the statement of changes in financial position and its limitations.

- explain how financial data combined with market-related data can be used to predict the systematic risk of security.

Our focus in Appendix C was on net income and earnings per share. In this chapter, our focus is on the ability of a firm to meet its debt obligations. Traditionally, this has involved the calculation of various ratios that attempt to measure the company's short-term solvency, financial leverage, and debt burden. Because of limitations in these ratios, we also discuss cash flow analysis. Finally, we look at how the measures described in this and the previous appendix have been used to estimate a company's risk.

RATIO ANALYSIS

In the previous chapter we discussed several measures that can be used to assess the potential profitability of a firm. Three sets of ratios are used as indicators to assess the ability of a firm to satisfy its obligations: (1) short-term

---

*This chapter is coauthored with Professor John C. Ritchie, Jr., of Temple University. Part of the discussion on cash flow analysis draws from some material published by Thornton L. O'Glove in his *Quality of Earnings Reports.* Permission to use this material is granted by Thornton L. O'-Glove.

solvency ratios, which assess the ability of the firm to meet debts maturing over the coming year, (2) capitalization (or financial leverage) ratios, which assess the extent to which the firm relies on debt financing, and (3) coverage ratios, which assess the ability of the firm to meet the fixed obligations brought about by debt financing.

Short-Term Solvency Ratios

Short-term solvency ratios are used to judge the adequacy of liquid assets for meeting short-term obligations as they come due. Firms go bankrupt or get into financial difficulty because they cannot pay obligations as they come due, not because they are not profitable. Therefore, before buying a stock, an investor should assure himself or herself that liquidity problems are not likely to appear.

A complete analysis of the adequacy of working capital for meeting current liabilities as they come due and assessing management's efficiency in using working capital would require a thorough analysis of cash flows, sources and applications of funds, and forecasts of fund flows in future periods that will be discussed in the next section. Ratios, however, can in many instances provide a crude but useful assessment of working capital. The following four ratios should be calculated to assess the adequacy of working capital for a firm: (1) the current ratio, (2) the acid-test ratio, (3) the inventory turnover ratio, and (4) the receivable turnover ratio. We described the last two ratios in the previous appendix. These two ratios indicate the approximate time needed to translate accounts receivable and inventory into cash, and as such, they are important for purposes of judging the adequacy of working capital. Below we discuss the first two ratios.

Current Ratio   The **current ratio** is calculated by dividing current assets by current liabilities:

$$\text{Current ratio} = \frac{\text{current assets}}{\text{current liabilities}}$$

The current ratio indicates the company's coverage of current liabilities by current assets. For example, if the ratio were 2 to 1, the firm could realize only half the values stated in the balance sheet in liquidating current assets and still have adequate funds to pay all current liabilities. Table D-1 shows the calculation of the current ratio for The Home Depot, Inc., for 1991 and 1990. The balance sheet data are given in Table B-4 of Appendix B.

A general standard for this ratio (such as 2 to 1) is not useful. Such a standard fails to recognize that an appropriate current ratio is a function of the nature of a company's business and would vary with differing operating cycles of different businesses.

As explained in Appendix B, a current asset is one that is expected to be converted into cash in the ordinary operating cycle of a business. Inventory, therefore, is a current asset. In a tobacco or liquor company, inventory may be as much as 80% to 90% of current assets. However, for a liquor company, that inventory may have to age four years or more before it can be converted into a salable asset. Such a company typically would require a much higher current ratio than average to have adequate liquidity to meet current liabilities maturing in one year. For a public utility company where there is no

TABLE D-1		
CALCULATION OF FINANCIAL RATIOS FOR THE HOME DEPOT, INC.: 1991 AND 1990		
Financial Measure	**1991**	**1990**
Current ratio:		
$\dfrac{\text{Current assets}}{\text{Current liabilities}}$	$\dfrac{\$713{,}574{,}000}{\$412{,}707{,}000} = 1.73$	$\dfrac{\$566{,}240{,}000}{\$292{,}389{,}000} = 1.94$
Acid-test (quick) ratio:		
$\dfrac{\text{Current assets} - \text{inventories*}}{\text{Current liabilities}}$	$\dfrac{\$204{,}552{,}000}{\$412{,}707{,}000} = 0.50$	$\dfrac{\$184{,}788{,}000}{\$292{,}389{,}000} = 0.63$
Long-term debt to equity ratio:		
$\dfrac{\text{Long-term debt †}}{\text{Shareholders' equity}}$	$\dfrac{\$543{,}394{,}000}{\$683{,}402{,}000} = 0.80$	$\dfrac{\$313{,}016{,}000}{\$512{,}129{,}000} = 0.61$
Total debt to equity ratio:		
$\dfrac{\text{Current liabilities} + \text{long-term debt}}{\text{Shareholders' equity}}$	$\dfrac{\$956{,}101{,}000}{\$683{,}402{,}000} = 1.40$	$\dfrac{\$605{,}405{,}000}{\$512{,}129{,}000} = 1.18$
Interest coverage ratio:		
$\dfrac{\text{Earnings before taxes} + \text{Interest charges paid}}{\text{Interest charges paid}}$	$\dfrac{\$265{,}635{,}000}{\$5{,}807{,}000} = 45.7$	$\dfrac{\$184{,}649{,}000}{\$2{,}634{,}000} = 70.1$

* Items classified as other current assets are ignored.

† Lease obligations added to long-term debt.

inventory or receivables collection problem, a current ratio of 1.1 or 1.2 to 1 has proved satisfactory. We suggest looking at industry averages, such as those produced by organizations like Dun & Bradstreet or Robert Morris Associates, rather than considering an overall standard. Industry averages have their faults, but they are preferable to general standards that do not recognize operating differences among classes of companies.

The current ratio has a major weakness as an analytical tool. It ignores the composition of current assets, which may be as important as their relationship with current liabilities. Assume the components of the current ratio for XYZ Corporation are shown in Table D-2.

While this firm has a 2 to 1 current ratio, which would more than meet the average in many industries, one could question its liquidity. The inventory has not been sold yet and appears high relative to the total of current assets. Therefore, current ratio analysis must be supplemented by other working capital ratios.

Acid-Test (Quick) Ratio   Since the problem in meeting current liabilities may rest on slowness or even inability to convert inventories into cash to meet

TABLE D-2			
CURRENT RATIO COMPONENTS FOR XYZ CORPORATION			
Current Assets		**Current Liabilities**	
Cash	$ 1,000	Accounts payable	$ 5,000
Receivables	1,000	Bank loans	2,000
Inventory	12,000		
Total	$14,000		$ 7,000

current obligations, the **acid-test ratio** (also called the **quick ratio**) is recommended. This is the ratio of current assets minus inventories, accruals, and prepaid items to current liabilities; that is,

$$\text{Acid-test ratio} = \frac{\text{Current assets} - \text{inventories} - \text{accruals} - \text{prepaid items}}{\text{Current liabilities}}$$

This ratio does assume that receivables are of good quality and will be converted into cash over the next year. Table D-1 shows this calculation for The Home Depot, Inc. The strength of a firm's working capital position can also be usefully assessed by studying the inventory turnover and receivables ratios discussed in Appendix C. Turnover of a firm's current assets is expected to provide the funds to pay current liabilities.

Capitalization Ratios

Analysts also calculate **capitalization ratios** to determine both the extent to which the corporation is trading on its equity and the resulting financial leverage. These ratios, also called **financial leverage ratios**, can be interpreted only in the context of the stability of industry and company earnings and cash flow. The assumption is that the greater the stability of industry and company earnings and cash flow, the more the company is able to accept the risk associated with financial leverage, and the higher the allowable ratio of debt to total capitalization (the total dollar amount of all long-term sources of funds in the balance sheet).

Many variations are to be found within the industry to calculate capitalization ratios. Two such ratios are shown below:

$$\text{Long-term debt to equity ratio} = \frac{\text{long-term debt}}{\text{shareholders' equity}}$$

$$\text{Total debt to equity ratio} = \frac{\text{current liabilities} + \text{long-term debt}}{\text{shareholders' equity}}$$

For both ratios, the higher the ratio, the greater the financial leverage. The values used to measure debt in both ratios is the book value. It is useful to calculate shareholders' equity at market as well as at book value for the purpose of determining these ratios. A market calculation for common equity may indicate considerably more or less financial leverage than a book calculation.

Commercial rating companies (discussed earlier in this book) and most Wall Street analysts rely heavily upon the long-term debt to equity ratio, and this is often provided in research reports sent out to clients. While this ratio can be useful, it should be noted that in recent years, given the uncertain interest rate environment, many corporations have taken to financing a good deal of their business with short-term debt. Indeed, an imaginative treasurer with a keen insight into money market activities can earn as much for a company as a plant manager, simply by switching debt from long term to short, and vice versa, at the right time.

Other considerations in using the long-term debt to equity ratio involve leased assets. Many corporations rent buildings and equipment under long-term lease contracts. Required rental payments are contractual obligations similar to bond coupon and repayment obligations. However, assets acquired through leasing (i.e., those leases classified as operating leases) may not be capitalized and shown in the balance sheet. Two companies, therefore, might work with the same amount of fixed assets and produce the same profits before interest or rental payments, but the one leasing a high proportion of its productive equipment could show significantly lower financial leverage.

Table D-1 shows the two capitalization ratios for The Home Depot, Inc. In the calculation, capital leases are obligations that are added to long-term debt.

Coverage Tests

The earnings of a corporation are the basic source of cash flows. **Coverage ratios** are used to test the adequacy of cash flows generated through earnings for purposes of meeting debt and lease obligations.

Tests of the adequacy of earnings are applied to the past record of the company, although the future record is the one that will determine the soundness of the judgment exercised in buying a security. These ratios must, therefore, be interpreted using the assumption that the past financial record offers a reasonable indication of future performance.

Calculation of Earnings Available to Cover Interest and Fixed Charges   The calculation of an **interest coverage ratio** is simple: Earnings available for paying the interest for a given year are divided by the annual interest expense. Interest expense is tax-deductible, and, therefore, all earnings before taxes are available for paying such charges. Also, the interest should be added back to earnings before taxes to determine the amount available to meet annual interest expenses. The calculation is shown in equation form below:

$$\text{Interest coverage ratio} = \frac{\text{earnings before taxes} + \text{interest charges paid}}{\text{interest charges paid}}$$

The interest coverage ratio for The Home Depot, Inc., for 1991 and 1990 is shown in Table D-1.

Annual obligations other than interest payments may have to be satisfied by a firm, the most important of which are lease payments. A more comprehensive coverage ratio that takes into account lease payments is the **fixed-charge coverage ratio,** which in equation form is:

$$\text{Fixed-charge coverage ratio}$$
$$= \frac{\substack{\text{earnings before} \\ \text{taxes}} + \substack{\text{interest charges} \\ \text{paid}} + \substack{\text{rental payments under} \\ \text{long-term leases}}}{\text{interest charges paid} + \text{rental payment under long-term leases}}$$

Suggested standards for coverage ratios are based on experience and empirical studies relating the incidence of defaults over a number of years to such ratios. Different standards are needed for a highly cyclical company than for a stable company. Data suggest that average coverage over a business cycle should be 8 or better to be classed as higher grade for a cyclical company, while the coverage ratio should not fall below 4 in any one year. For stable companies, an average coverage ratio of 5 or better and a minimum ratio of 2.5 in any year suggests relatively high quality.

CASH FLOW ANALYSIS

Cash flow is typically used on Wall Street, in the financial press, and in company reports to designate net earnings after taxes with depreciation, depletion and other non-cash expense items of the period added back. It is important to realize, however, that depreciation and depletion (and other non-cash expenses) are real expenses, even though they did not require a cash outflow in the current period. Any attempt to downgrade the importance of depreciation or depletion as an expense can lead to an erroneous conception of true corporate earning power over time. Inability to generate adequate earnings after depreciation may lead to serious financial problems and inability to replace assets as they wear out or become obsolete. Keep in mind that management must replace the asset base that is wearing out if the firm is to continue to produce income.

Depreciation or depletion is often considered a source of funds (and listed as such in a cash flow or funds flow statement) in the sense that funds generated by sales are not siphoned off by depreciation or depletion since no expenditures are currently made. However, a situation where there is no profit before depreciation or where there is a loss before depreciation clearly emphasizes that depreciation by and of itself is not a source of funds. Sales revenues are the basic source of all funds derived from operations.

Statement of Changes in Financial Position

Fragmentary information on sources and uses of funds and cash can be obtained from comparative balance sheets and income statements. However, a much better picture of the cash flow of a business can only be gained from a **statement of changes in financial position**, which can be found in an annual report. This statement can help provide answers to important questions such as:

1. How were the funds that were provided by operations, and from other sources, used in the business?
2. Where did the funds come from to maintain dividends in the face of potential losses?
3. How did the business get the funds to accomplish the debt repayment that took place during the period?
4. What were the sources of increases in working capital during the period, or what uses were made of withdrawals from working capital?
5. How did the company finance a large investment project?

Moreover, analysts forecast future fund flows under varying assumptions to assess the ability of the firm to finance its growth plans, maintain its capital base, and reward owners.

A Cash Focus

Statements of changes in financial position often focus on explaining changes in working capital, but there are increasing demands that these statements focus on cash.[1] Analysts should concentrate on the nature of cash inflows and outflows to provide a better basis for assessing future cash flows. Net income and cash flow are two different things, since the determination of net income is based on accrual accounting techniques. For example, depreciation is listed as an expense in a given year, thereby reducing reported profits, when there has been no corresponding cash outflow. Net income becomes even less adequate for assessing cash flow during inflationary periods. The gap between reported earnings and cash flow widens during inflationary periods, since a growing investment in receivables and inventories is not offset by corresponding increases in trade credit.

---

[1]See FASB, Statement of Financial Accounting Concepts No. 1, "Objectives of Financial Reporting by Business Enterprises" (Stamford, CT, 1978).

To highlight the importance of cash flow, consider the study by Largay and Stickney, who analyzed the financial statements of W. T. Grant during the 1966–1974 period preceding its bankruptcy in 1975 and ultimate liquidation.[2] They noted that financial indicators such as profitability ratios, turnover ratios, and liquidity ratios showed some down trends but provided no definite clues to the company's impending bankruptcy. A study of cash flows from operations, however, revealed that company operations were causing an increasing drain on cash, rather than providing cash. This necessitated an increased use of external financing, the required interest payments on which exacerbated the cash flow drain. Cash flow analysis clearly was a valuable tool in this case.

A financially healthy firm will generate cash from operations on a consistent basis. Professor Bernstein has pointed out that "the unsuccessful firm will find its cash drained by slowdowns in receivables and inventory turnovers, by operating losses, or by a combination of these factors."[3] The investor should look for companies that report real earnings, not those that are the result of inflation, and that have healthy cash flows. The investor should also have sound reasons for assuming that these cash flows will continue in the future.

Inflation and Cash Flow

Profits reported to stockholders during inflationary periods are in part real earnings and in part illusion. If the need to replace worn-out plant and equipment and inventories that were used to generate the cash inflows is considered, there may be no real profits. A real profit means that the firm has more real assets at the end of the period than when it began the period.

Richard Greene illustrates this problem by contrasting Dow Chemical and Union Carbide, two giant chemical companies.

> Over the four years from 1976 to 1979, Dow showed earnings totaling about $2.5 billion. Over the same period, Union Carbide reported cumulative earnings of some $1.8 billion. It would appear that both firms were robust money-makers in the same league.
>
> But, take it a step further and look at cash. Kidder, Peabody & Co. did this and, although Kidder's methodology is a bit controversial, the question is a matter of degree—not direction. Kidder came up with a number called discretionary cash flow. That's the figure representing how much money a firm has left to grow with—after taking out the amount necessary to maintain its property, plant and equipment after dividends. Companies don't really set aside money to replace equipment but ultimately they have to put out the cash—and it's not going toward growth.
>
> Dow's discretionary cash flow is at a healthy level with $924 million over the four year period. But Union Carbide has a different story, negative discretionary cash flow of $663 million. That means, according to Kidder, Union Carbide was paying dividends for that whole period of time with borrowed money. It was, in effect, cannibalizing its capital structure to keep the stock price up. That's not a healthy habit. But it's common among the kind of huge firms you'd think would know better.[4]

---

[2]J. A. Largay III and C. P. Stickney, "Cash Flows, Ratio Analysis and the W. T. Grant Company Bankruptcy," *Financial Analysts Journal* (July–August 1980), pp. 51–54.

[3]Leopold A. Bernstein, *Financial Statement Analysis: Theory, Application, and Interpretation,* 3d ed. (Homewood, IL: Richard D. Irwin, Inc., 1983), p. 405.

[4]Richard Greene, "Are More Chryslers in the Offering?" *Forbes* (Feb. 2, 1981), pp. 69–73, as reported in William M. Bowen and Frank P. Ganucheau, *The Investor's Equation* (Chicago: Probus Publishing, 1984), p. 111.

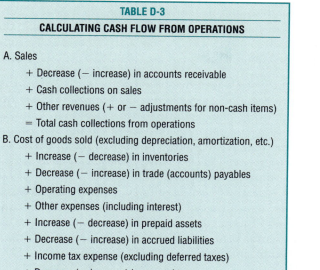

TABLE D-3

CALCULATING CASH FLOW FROM OPERATIONS

A. Sales
- \+ Decrease (− increase) in accounts receivable
- \+ Cash collections on sales
- \+ Other revenues (+ or − adjustments for non-cash items)
- = Total cash collections from operations

B. Cost of goods sold (excluding depreciation, amortization, etc.)
- \+ Increase (− decrease) in inventories
- \+ Decrease (− increase) in trade (accounts) payables
- \+ Operating expenses
- \+ Other expenses (including interest)
- \+ Increase (− decrease) in prepaid assets
- \+ Decrease (− increase) in accrued liabilities
- \+ Income tax expense (excluding deferred taxes)
- \+ Decrease (− increase) in accrued taxes
- = Total cash outflows from operations

C. Net cash flows from operations = $A - B$

Source: Leopold A. Bernstein, *Financial Statement Analysis: Theory, Application, and Interpretation*, 3d ed. (Homewood, IL: Richard D. Irwin, Inc., 1983), pp. 411–413.

Calculating Cash Flow from Operations

A knowledge of just how much cash a company takes in from its operating activities during any given time period is the kind of information that forms the bedrock of analysis. This is known as the *cash flow from operations (CFFO)*, to be distinguished from the term "cash flow," which refers to the sum of profits plus depreciation allowances. There are major problems in measuring CFFO because of the many and confusing methods of presentation of the data. Investors instinctively know this is an important matter. After wading through annual reports, they wonder if the companies emerged from the year in better shape than when they began. Leopold Bernstein and Mostafa Masky wrote:

> The best defense that can be used by credit and equity analysts against the misleading presentations of CFFO is to approach the analysis of financial statements armed with a clear understanding of what CFFO is and how it is computed. At present, an analyst who accepts a published figure designated as CFFO or by similar terminology runs the risk of working with inaccurate and misleading measures. A working knowledge of how CFFO is computed will enable the analyst to assess the validity of the figure disclosed and, if need be, to adjust it to the correct amount.[5]

Professor Bernstein suggests a more detailed approach to calculating cash flow from operations, as shown in Table D-3. This offers a more complete basis for analysis of cash flow, since it considers changes in working capital

[5]Leopold A. Bernstein and Mostafa M. Masky, "Again Now: How Do We Measure Cash Flow from Operations?" *Financial Analysts Journal* (July–August 1985), p. 77.

as well as dividends and capital expenditures and begins with sales rather than reported earnings.

FUNDAMENTAL RISK ESTIMATION

In Chapter 5, the measurement of risk was discussed. It was explained that systematic risk (beta) can be estimated using historical returns for a stock and some stock index. The resulting beta is called *historical beta*. Calculation of historical beta requires only the use of price data to obtain the returns. As explained in Chapter 5, adjustments are made to historical beta to account for the sampling error (uncertainty) for each common stock beta estimate. The result is called a Bayesian-adjusted historical beta.

Barr Rosenberg and Vinay Marathe have developed a much more extensive model to predict the fundamental risk of a security using not only price data but other market-related and financial data.[6] The product of their model is what they refer to as **fundamental beta**, and is the cornerstone of an important service, BARRA, now used by institutional investors. We discussed this in the appendix to Chapter 15.

The procedure for estimating fundamental beta begins by describing the company in terms of ratios reflecting the fundamental condition of the company. Each ratio is called a *descriptor*. The descriptors are then classified into the following six categories, called **risk indexes**: (1) market variability, (2) earnings variability, (3) low valuation and unsuccess, (4) immaturity and smallness, (5) growth orientation, and (6) financial risk. Each category represents a distinct source of risk. The description of each risk index is such that the higher the value, the greater the risk. For example, for the first risk index, market variability, the greater the index value, the greater the risk.

Table D-4 gives the six risk indexes and the components of each. The ratios in the first group, market variability, are called **technical descriptors** since they rely on market-related data. The other five groups of ratios are called **fundamental descriptors** because they use financial data other than price data, many of which we have described in this and the previous two appendixes.

Also included as a descriptor are the industries in which a company operates. As explained in Appendix C, information about the various industries in which a company operates is provided in the annual report. While these data were not available at the time of the original work by Barr and Marathe, they are included in the current model used by BARRA. The industry categories are fundamental descriptors.

The statistical methodology for calculating the model that is used to predict a fundamental beta is beyond the scope of this appendix.[7]

Rosenberg and Marathe empirically investigated their fundamental risk model.[8] They found that by using only technical descriptors, they were able to calculate a beta that could explain 57% more of the variance in the return of stocks than by using the Bayesian-adjusted historical beta. By using

[6]Barr Rosenberg and Vinay Marathe, "The Prediction of Investment Risk: Systematic and Residual Risk," *Proceedings of the Seminar on the Analysis of Security Prices*, University of Chicago (November 1975), pp. 85–225.

[7]For a detailed explanation, see Rosenberg and Marathe, op. cit., or Andrew Rudd and Henry K. Clasing, *Modern Portfolio Theory* (Berkeley, CA: Andrew Rudd, 1988), pp. 111–120.

[8]See Section 7 of Rosenberg and Marathe, op. cit.

TABLE D-4

COMPONENTS OF RISK INDEXES FOR PREDICTING FUNDAMENTAL BETA

1. Index of market variability
   Historical beta estimate
   Historical sigma estimate
   Share turnover, quarterly
   Share turnover, 12 months
   Share turnover, five years
   Trading volume/variance
   Common stock price (ln)
   Historical alpha estimate
   Cumulative range, one year

2. Index of earnings variability
   Variance of earnings
   Extraordinary items
   Variance of cash flow
   Earnings covariability
   Earnings-price covariability

3. Index of low valuation and unsuccess
   Growth in earnings per share
   Recent earnings change
   Relative strength
   Indicator of small earnings-price ratio
   Book-price ratio
   Tax/earnings, five years
   Dividend cuts, five years
   Return on equity, five years

4. Index of immaturity and smallness
   Total assets (log)

    Market capitalization (log)
    Market capitalization
    Net plant/gross plant
    Net plant/common equity
    Inflation-adjusted plant/equity
    Trading regency
    Indicator of earnings history

5. Index of growth orientation
   Payout, last five years
   Current yield
   Yield, last five years
   Indicator of zero yield
   Growth in total assets
   Capital structure change
   Earnings-price ratio
   Earning-price, normalized
   Typical earnings-price ratio, five years

6. Index of financial risk
   Leverage at book
   Leverage at market
   Debt/assets
   Uncovered fixed charges
   Cash flow/current liabilities
   Liquid assets/current liabilities
   Potential dilution
   Price-deflated earnings adjustment
   Tax adjusted monetary debt

Source: Barr Rosenberg and Vinay Marathe, "The Prediction of Investment Risk: Systematic and Residual Risk," *Proceedings of the Seminar on the Analysis of Security Prices*, University of Chicago (November 1975).

only the fundamental descriptors, they found that they could calculate a beta that could explain 45% more than by using the Bayesian-adjusted historical beta. Finally, using both technical and fundamental descriptors to calculate beta, they could explain 86% more than by using the Bayesian-adjusted historical beta. This evidence therefore suggests that the systematic risk of a security can best be described by combining both market-related and financial data.

■ SUMMARY

Debt and cash flow analysis are used to evaluate the ability of a firm to satisfy its debt obligations. Ratios that are used include short-term solvency ratios, capitalization (or financial leverage) ratios, and coverage tests. Short-term solvency ratios measure the ability of a firm to meet obligations coming due within one year. Capitalization ratios indicate the degree to which the firm is financed by creditors. Cover-

age tests measure the ability of a firm to meet long-term obligations.

While these ratios are useful for analyzing the debt-paying ability of an issuer, a better indication is an analysis of the firm's cash flow. The starting point for this analysis is the statement of financial condition.

Both financial data and market-related data can be used by an analyst to predict the systematic risk of a security. This risk measure is called the security's fundamental beta. Empirical evidence indicates that fundamental beta is a better measure of systematic risk than historical beta, which uses just price data.

■ KEY TERMS

acid-test ratio
capitalization ratios
coverage ratios
current ratio
financial leverage ratios
fixed-charge coverage ratio

fundamental beta
fundamental descriptors
interest coverage ratio
quick ratio
risk indexes
short-term solvency ratios

statement of changes in financial
    postion
technical descriptors
total debt to equity ratio

■ QUESTIONS

1. **a.** What is the major weakness of the current ratio as a measure of the short-run solvency of a firm?
   b. How does the acid-test ratio attempt to remedy this limitation of the current ratio?

2. "A current ratio less than 1 indicates that regardless of the industry that the company is in, it will have difficulty in meeting its short-term obligations." Explain why you agree or disagree with this statement.

3. Why may a substantial increase in the day's sales outstanding in accounts receivable be an indication that a company will find it difficult to meet its short-term obligations.

4. Explain the effect of using the FIFO versus the LIFO inventory valuation method in periods of rising prices on each of the following financial ratios:
   a. Current ratio
   b. Acid-test ratio
   c. Total debt to total equity ratio

5. **a.** Suppose that a company has a long-term debt to equity ratio of 0.75. Why do you think it is important for the analyst to know the annual interest payments on all the debt and whether the interest rate is a fixed or a floating rate in order to assess if the debt burden is excessive?

   b. What ratios can be used to determine if a company may be overburdened with debt?
   c. Why are long-term lease obligations treated as long-term debt?

6. "The cash flow of a company is the net income plus accrued expenses and is a good indicator of a company's ability to meet its financial obligations as they come due." Explain why you agree or disagree with this statement.

7. "Since the focus of the statement of changes in financial position is cash, a better approach to evaluate the ability of a firm to meet its obligations is to analyze this statement rather than look at short-term solvency ratios and capitalization ratios." Explain why you agree or disagree with this statement.

8. Why is the cash flow from operations calculated as suggested by Professor Leopold Bernstein superior to the cash flow defined by net income plus depreciation allowance?

9. **a.** What is meant by a fundamental risk beta?
   b. In developing a fundamental risk beta, risk indexes are constructed. These risk indexes can be classified as technical descriptors and fundamental descriptors. Describe both.

GLOSSARY*

A

abnormal returns See excess returns.

accounts receivable turnover The ratio of net credit sales to average accounts receivable, a measure of how quickly customers pay their bills.

accrued interest The accumulated coupon interest, paid to the seller of a bond by the buyer (unless the bond is in default).

accumulated benefit obligation (ABO) An approximate measure of the liability of the plan in the event of a termination at the date the calculation is performed. Compare **projected benefit obligation**.

acid-test ratio Also called the *quick ratio*, the ratio of current assets minus inventories, accruals, and prepaid items to current liabilities.

active portfolio strategy A strategy that uses available information and forecasting techniques to seek a better performance than a portfolio that is simply diversified broadly. Compare **passive portfolio strategy**.

after-tax profit margin The ratio of net income to net sales.

agency basis A means of compensating the broker of a program trade solely on the basis of commission established through bids submitted by various brokerage firms.

agency incentive arrangement A means of compensating the broker of a program trade using benchmark prices for issues to be traded in determining commissions or fees.

agency pass-throughs Mortgage pass-through securities whose principal and interest payments are guaranteed by government agencies, such as the Government National Mortgage Association ("Ginnie Mae"), Federal Home Loan Mortgage Corporation ("Freddie Mac"), and Federal National Mortgage Association ("Fannie Mae").

alpha In a Jensen Index, a factor to represent the portfolio's performance that diverges from its beta, representing a measure of the manager's performance.

American Depositary Receipt (ADR) The U.S. version of the International Depositary Receipt.

American option An option that may be exercised at any time up to and including the expiration date. Compare **European option**.

annual fund operating expenses For investment companies, the management fee and "other expenses," including the expenses for maintaining shareholder records, providing shareholders with financial statements, and providing custodial and accounting services. For 12b-1 funds, selling and marketing costs are included.

annuity A regular periodic payment made by an insurance company to a policyholder for a specified period of time.

arbitrage The simultaneous buying and selling of a security at two different prices in two different markets, resulting in profits without risk. Perfectly efficient markets present no arbitrage opportunities.

arbitrage-free option-pricing models See **yield curve option-pricing models**.

arbitrage pricing theory (APT) An alternative model to the capital asset pricing model developed by Stephen Ross and based purely on arbitrage arguments.

arithmetic mean return An average of the subperiod returns, calculated by summing the subperiod returns and dividing by the number of subperiods.

arithmetic average (mean) rate of return See **arithmetic mean return**.

---

*This glossary was prepared by Michael Buchman, development editor for this book.

ask price A dealer's price to sell a security. Compare **bid price**.

asset Any possession that has value in an exchange.

asset allocation decision The decision regarding how the institution's funds should be distributed among the major classes of assets in which it may invest.

asset-backed securities Securities backed by assets that are not mortgage loans. Examples include assets backed by automobile loans and credit card receivables.

asset classes Categories of assets, such as stocks, bonds, real estate, and foreign securities.

asset/equity ratio The ratio of total assets to stockholders' equity.

asset/liability management Also called *surplus management*, the task of managing funds of a financial institution to accomplish the two goals of a financial institution: (1) to earn an adequate return on funds invested and (2) to maintain a comfortable surplus of assets beyond liabilities.

asset swap An interest rate swap used to alter the cash flow characteristics of an institution's assets so as to provide a better match with its liabilities.

asset turnover The ratio of net sales to total assets.

attribute bias The tendency of stocks preferred by the dividend discount model to share certain equity attributes such as low price-earnings ratios, high dividend yield, high book-value ratio, or membership in a particular industry sector.

auditor's report A section of an annual report containing the auditor's opinion about the veracity of the financial statements.

average (across-day) measures An estimation of price that uses the average or representative price of a large number of trades.

B

back-end loan fund A mutual fund that charges investors a fee to sell (redeem) shares, often ranging from 4% to 6%. Some back-end load funds impose a full commission if the shares are redeemed within a designated time period after purchase, such as one year, reducing the commission the longer the investor holds the shares. The formal name for the back-end load is the contingent deferred sales charge, or CDSC.

balance sheet Also called the statement of financial condition, a summary of the assets, liabilities, and owners' equity.

balanced fund An investment company that invests in both stocks and bonds.

balloon maturity Any principal due at maturity for a bond with a sinking fund requirement.

bank discount basis A convention used for quoting bids and offers for Treasury bills in terms of annualized yield based on a 360-day year.

bankers acceptance A security representing a bank's promise to repay a loan created in a commercial transaction in case the debtor fails to perform. Commonly used in international transactions.

barbell strategy A strategy in which the maturities of the securities included in the portfolio are concentrated at two extremes.

BARRA's performance analysis (PERFAN) factor model A method developed by BARRA, a consulting firm in Berkeley, California, which is commonly used by institutional investors applying performance attribution analysis to evaluate their money managers' performances.

base interest rate See **benchmark interest rate**.

base probability of loss The probability of not achieving a portfolio expected return.

basis Regarding a futures contract, the difference between the cash price and the futures price observed in the market.

basis risk The uncertainty about the basis at the time a hedge may be lifted. Hedging substitutes basis risk for price risk.

basket trades See **program trades**.

before-tax profit margin The ratio of net income before taxes to net sales.

bellwether issues See **benchmark issues**.

benchmark The performance of a predetermined set of securities, for comparison purposes. Such sets may be based on published indexes or may be customized to suit an investment strategy.

benchmark interest rate Also called the *base interest rate*, the minimum interest rate that investors will demand for investing in a non-Treasury security. The yield to maturity offered on a comparable-maturity Treasury security that was most recently issued ("on-the-run").

benchmark issues Also called *on-the-run* or *current-coupon issues* or *bellwether issues*. In the secondary market, the most recently auctioned Treasury issues for each maturity.

beta The slope (β) of the market model for the asset, which measures the degree to which the historical returns on the asset change systematically with changes in the market portfolio's return. Hence, beta is referred to as an index of that systematic risk due to general market conditions that cannot be diversified away.

biased expectations theories Expectations theories, including the liquidity theory of the term structure and the preferred habitat theory, which assert that factors other than expected future short-term rates affect forward rates. Compare **pure expectations theory**.

bid price A dealer's price to buy a security. Compare **ask price**.

Black-Scholes option-pricing model A model for pricing call options based on arbitrage arguments that uses the stock price, the exercise price, the risk-free interest rate, the time to expiration, and the standard deviation of the stock return.

block trade A large trading order, defined on the New York Stock Exchange as an order that consists of 10,000 shares of a given stock or that has a total market value of $200,000 or more.

bond An instrument in which the issuer (debtor/borrower) promises to repay to the lender/investor the amount borrowed plus interest over some specified period of time.

bond-equivalent basis The method used for computing the bond-equivalent yield.

bond-equivalent yield The annualized yield to maturity computed by doubling the semiannual yield.

bond indenture The contract that sets forth the promises of a corporate bond issuer and the rights of investors.

bond indexing Designing a portfolio so that its performance will match the performance of some bond index.

BONDPAR A system that monitors and evaluates the performance of a fixed-income portfolio as well as the individual securities held in the portfolio. BONDPAR decomposes the return into those elements beyond the manager's control, such as the interest rate environment and client-imposed duration policy constraints, and those that the management process contributes to, such as interest rate management, sector/quality allocations, and individual bond selection.

book value The total owners' equity shown in the balance sheet.

book value per share The ratio of stockholders' equity to the average number of common shares. Book value per share should not be thought of as an indicator of economic worth, since it reflects accounting valuation (and not necessarily market valuation).

bootstrapping A process of creating a theoretical spot rate curve, using one yield projection as the basis for the yield of the next maturity.

bottom-up equity management style A management style that de-emphasizes the significance of economic and market cycles and focuses instead on the analysis of individual stocks.

break-even time See **premium payback period**.

broker An entity that acts as the agent of an investor who wishes to execute orders; no position is taken by the broker in the security that is the subject of the trade.

broker loan rate See **call money rate**.

bull spread A spread strategy in which an investor buys an out-of-the-money put option and finances this purchase by selling an out-of-the-money call option on the same underlying.

bulldog market The foreign market in the United Kingdom.

bullet contract A guaranteed investment contract purchased with a single (one-shot) premium. Compare **window contract**.

bullet strategy A strategy in which a portfolio is constructed so that the maturities of its securities are highly concentrated at one point on the yield curve.

business risk The risk that the cash flow of an issuer will be impaired because of adverse economic conditions, making it difficult for the issuer to meet its operating expenses.

busted convertible See **fixed-income equivalent**.

butterfly shift A non-parallel shift in the yield curve involving the humpedness of the curve.

buy-and-hold strategy A passive investment strategy with no active buying and selling of stocks once the portfolio is created until the end of the investment horizon.

buy hedge See **long hedge**.

buy limit order A conditional trading order that indicates that a security may be purchased only at the designated price or lower. Compare **sell limit order**.

buy-side analyst A financial analyst employed by a non-brokerage firm, typically one of the larger money management firms that purchase securities on their own accounts.

buying on margin A transaction in which an investor borrows to buy additional shares using the shares themselves as collateral.

C

calendar effect The tendency of stocks to perform differently at different times, including such anomalies as the January effect, month-of-the-year effect, day-of-the-week effect, and holiday effect.

call date A date before maturity, specified at issuance, when the issuer of a bond may retire part of the bond for a specified call price.

call money rate Also called the broker loan rate, the interest rate that banks charge brokers to finance margin loans to investors. The broker charges the investor the call money rate plus a service charge. Also see **buying on margin**.

call option Also called a *call*, an option that grants the buyer the right to purchase the underlying from the writer.

call price The price, specified at issuance, at which the issuer of a bond may retire part of the bond at a specified call date.

call protection A feature of some callable bonds that establishes an initial period when the bonds may not be called.

call provision An embedded option granting a bond issuer the right to buy back all or part of the issue prior to maturity.

call risk The combination of cash flow uncertainty and reinvestment risk introduced by a call provision.

call swaption A swaption in which the buyer has the right to enter into a swap as a fixed-rate payer. The writer therefore becomes the fixed-rate receiver/floating-rate payer.

capital asset pricing model (CAPM) An economic theory that describes the relationship between risk and expected return, and serves as a model for the pricing of risky securities. The CAPM asserts that the only risk that is priced by rational investors is systematic risk, because that risk cannot be eliminated by diversification. The CAPM says that the expected return of a security or a portfolio is equal to the rate on a risk-free security plus a risk premium.

capital market The market for trading long-term debt instruments (those that mature in more than one year).

capital market line (CML) The line defined by every combination of the risk-free asset and the market portfolio.

capitalization method A method of constructing a replicating portfolio in which the manager purchases a number of the largest-capitalized names in the index stock in proportion to their capitalization.

capitalization ratios Also called *financial leverage ratios*, ratios that compare debt to total capitalization and thus reflect the extent to which a corporation is trading on its equity. These ratios can be interpreted only in the context of the stability of industry and company earnings and cash flow.

capitalized Recorded in asset accounts and then depreciated or amortized, as is appropriate for expenditures for items with useful lives greater than one year.

carry See **net financing cost**.

cash-equivalent items Temporary investments of currently excess cash in short-term, high-quality investment media such as Treasury bills and bankers acceptances.

cash flow matching Also called *dedicating a portfolio*, an alternative to multiperiod immunization in which the manager matches the maturity of each element in the liability stream, working backward from the last liability to assure all required cash flows.

cash markets Also called spot markets, markets that involve the immediate delivery of a security or instrument. Compare **derivative markets**.

cash settlement contracts Futures contracts, such as stock index futures, which settle for cash, not involving the delivery of the underlying.

cash-surrender value An amount the insurance company will pay if the policyholder ends a whole life insurance policy.

certificate of deposit (CD) Also called a *time deposit*, a certificate issued by a bank or thrift that indicates a specified sum of money has been deposited at the issuing depository institution. A CD bears a maturity date and a specified interest rate, and can be issued in any denomination.

characteristic line The market model applied to a single security. The slope of the line is a security's beta.

chartists See **technical analysts**.

cheapest to deliver issue The acceptable Treasury security with the highest implied repo rate, the rate that a seller of a futures contract can earn by buying an issue and then delivering it at the settlement date.

clean opinion An auditor's opinion reflecting an unqualified acceptance of a company's financial statements.

closed-end fund An investment company that sells shares like any other corporation and usually does not redeem its shares. A publicly traded fund sold on stock exchanges or over the counter that may trade above or below its net asset value. Compare **open-end fund**.

cluster analysis A statistical technique that identifies clusters of stocks whose returns are highly correlated within each cluster and relatively uncorrelated between clusters. Cluster analysis has identified groupings such as growth, cyclical, stable, and energy stocks.

coefficient of determination A measure of the goodness of fit of the relationship between a dependent and independent variable in a regression analysis—for instance, the percentage of the

delta Also called the *hedge ratio*, the ratio of the change in price of a call option to the change in price of the underlying stock.

demand deposits Checking accounts that pay no interest and can be withdrawn upon demand. Compare **negotiable order of withdrawal accounts**.

derivative instruments Contracts such as options and futures whose price is derived from the price of the underlying financial asset.

derivative markets Markets for derivative instruments.

deterministic models Liability-matching models that assume that the liability payments and the asset cash flows are known with certainty. Compare **stochastic models**.

differential disclosure The practice of reporting conflicting or markedly different information in official corporate statements including annual and quarterly reports and the 10-Ks and 10-Qs.

diffusion process A conception of the way a stock's price changes that assumes that the price takes on all intermediate values.

dirty price See **full price**.

disclaimer of opinion An auditor's statement disclaiming any opinion regarding the company's financial condition.

discount Referring to the selling price of a bond, a price below its par value. Compare **premium**.

discount rate The interest rate that the Federal Reserve charges a bank to borrow funds when a bank is temporarily short of funds. Collateral is necessary to borrow, and such borrowing is quite limited because the Fed views it as a privilege to be used to meet short-term liquidity needs, and not a device to increase earnings.

diversifiable risk See **unsystematic risk**.

dividend discount model (DDM) A model for valuing the common stock of a company, based on the present value of the expected cash flows.

dividend rate The fixed or floating rate paid on preferred stock based on par value.

dividend yield The cash yield of a stock or stock index, used in determining the net financing cost for a stock index future contract.

dollar duration The product of modified duration and the initial price.

dollar return The return realized on a portfolio for any evaluation period, including (1) the change in market value of the portfolio and (2) any distributions made from the portfolio during that period.

dollar safety margin The dollar equivalent of the safety cushion for a portfolio in a contingent immunization strategy.

dollar value of an 01 See **price value of a basis point**.

dollar-weighted rate of return Also called the *internal rate of return*, the interest rate that will make the present value of the cash flows from all the subperiods in the evaluation period plus the terminal market value of the portfolio equal to the initial market value of the portfolio.

domestic market Part of a nation's internal market, representing the mechanisms for issuing and trading securities of entities domiciled within that nation. Compare **external market** and **foreign market**.

dual-currency issues Eurobonds that pay coupon interest in one currency but pay the principal in a different currency.

duration A common gauge of the price sensitivity of an asset or portfolio to a change in interest rates.

dynamic asset allocation An asset allocation strategy in which the asset mix is mechanistically shifted in response to changing market conditions, as in a portfolio insurance strategy, for example.

dynamic hedging A strategy that involves rebalancing hedge positions as market conditions change; a strategy that seeks to insure the value of a portfolio using a synthetic put option.

E

earnings per share Earnings calculated by dividing the earnings available to common stock holders by the weighted average number of common shares outstanding over the year for which the calculation takes place.

earnings surprises Positive or negative differences from the consensus forecast.

economic surplus For any entity, the difference between the market value of all its assets and the market value of its liabilities.

effective convexity The convexity of a bond calculated with cash flows that change with yields.

effective date In an interest rate swap, the date the swap begins accruing interest.

effective duration The duration calculated using the approximate duration formula for a bond with an embedded option, reflecting the expected change in the cash flow caused by the option.

efficient portfolio A portfolio that provides the greatest expected return for a given level of risk, or equivalently, the lowest risk for a given expected return.

embedded option An option that is part of the structure of a bond, as opposed to a bare option, which trades separately from any underlying security.

emerging markets The financial markets of developing economies.

endowment funds Investment funds established for the support of institutions such as colleges, private schools, museums, hospitals, and foundations. The investment income may be used for the operation of the institution and for capital expenditures.

enhanced indexing Also called indexing plus, an indexing strategy whose objective is to exceed the total return performance of the index.

equilibrium market price of risk The slope of the capital market line (CML). Since the CML represents the return offered to compensate for a perceived level of risk, each point on the line is a balanced market condition, or equilibrium. The slope of the line determines the additional return needed to compensate for a unit change in risk.

equity cap An agreement in which one party, for an upfront premium, agrees to compensate the other at specific time periods if a designated stock market benchmark is greater than a predetermined level.

equity claim Also called a *residual claim*, a claim to a share of earnings after debt obligations have been satisfied.

equity collar The simultaneous purchase of an equity floor and sale of an equity cap.

equity floor An agreement in which one party agrees to pay the other at specific time periods if a specific stock market benchmark is less than a predetermined level.

equity-linked policies See **variable life**.

equity market See **stock market**.

equity options Options in which the underlying is either a stock or a stock index.

equity swap A swap in which the cash flows that are exchanged are based on the total return on some stock market index and an interest rate (either a fixed rate or a floating rate). Compare **interest rate swap**.

equivalent taxable yield The yield that must be offered on a taxable bond issue to give the same after-tax yield as a tax-exempt issue.

Euro straight A fixed-rate coupon Eurobond.

Eurobond A bond that is (1) underwritten by an international syndicate, (2) offered at issuance simultaneously to investors in a number of countries, and (3) issued outside the jurisdiction of any single country.

Eurodollar bonds Eurobonds denominated in U.S. dollars.

Euroequity issues Securities sold in the Euromarket. That is, securities initially sold to investors simultaneously in several national markets by an international syndicate.

Euromarket See **external market**.

European option Option that may be exercised only at the expiration date. Compare **American option**.

Euroyen bonds Eurobonds denominated in Japanese yen.

evaluation period The time interval over which a money manager's performance is evaluated.

event risk The risk that the ability of an issuer to make interest and principal payments will change because of (1) a natural or industrial accident or some regulatory change or (2) a takeover or corporate restructuring.

ex ante return The expected return of a portfolio based on the expected returns of its component assets and their weights.

ex post return See **holding period return**.

except for opinion An auditor's opinion reflecting the fact that the auditor was unable to audit certain areas of the company's operations because of restrictions imposed by management or other conditions beyond the auditor's control.

excess reserves Any excess of actual reserves above required reserves.

excess returns Also called *abnormal returns*, returns in excess of those required by some asset pricing model.

exchange rate risk Also called *currency risk*, the risk of an investment's value changing because of currency exchange rates.

exchangeable security A security that grants the securityholder the right to exchange the security for the common stock of a firm *other* than the issuer of the security.

execution costs The difference between the execution price of a security and the price that would have existed in the absence of a trade, which can be further divided into market impact costs and market timing costs.

exercise price Also called the *strike price*, the price to be paid for a security if an option is exercised.

expectations theories Theories including the pure expectations theory, the liquidity theory of the term structure, and the preferred habitat theory, which share a hypothesis about the behavior of short-term forward rates and also assume that the forward rates in current long-term contracts are closely related to the market's expectations about future short-term rates. These three theories differ, however, on whether other factors also affect forward rates, and how.

expected return The return expected on a risky asset based on a probability distribution for the possible rates of return.

expected value The weighted average of a probability distribution.

expensed Charged to an expense account, fully reducing reported profit of that year, as is appropriate for expenditures for items with useful lives under one year.

expiration date The date when an option contract ends.

external efficiency See **pricing efficiency.**

external market Also referred to as the *international market*, the *offshore market*, or, more popularly, the *Euromarket*, the mechanism for trading securities that (1) at issuance are offered simultaneously to investors in a number of countries and (2) are issued outside the jurisdiction of any single country. Compare **internal market.**

extrapolative statistical models Models that apply a formula to historical data and project results for a future period. Such models include the simple linear trend model, the simple exponential model, and the simple autoregressive model.

F

face value See **par value.**

fair price The equilibrium price for futures contracts. Also called the *theoretical futures price.*

feasible portfolio A portfolio that an investor can construct given the assets available.

feasible set of portfolios The collection of all feasible portfolios.

federal funds Deposits held in reserve for depository institutions at their district Federal Reserve Bank.

federal funds market The market where banks can borrow or lend reserves, allowing banks temporarily short of their required reserves to borrow reserves from banks that have excess reserves.

federal funds rate The interest rate charged to borrow funds in the federal funds market.

federally related institutions Arms of the federal government that are exempt from SEC registration and whose securities are backed by the full faith and credit of the U.S. government (with the exception of the Tennessee Valley Authority).

fill or kill order A trading order that is canceled unless executed within a designated time period. Compare **open order.**

filter The percentage by which the price of a security must change in order to trigger its purchase or sale.

financial analysts Also called *securities analysts* and *investment analysts*, professionals who analyze financial statements, interview corporate executives, and attend trade shows, in order to write reports recommending either purchasing, selling, or holding various stocks.

financial leverage ratios See **capitalization ratios.**

financial market An organized institutional structure or mechanism for creating and exchanging financial assets.

financial risk The risk that the cash flow of an issuer will not be adequate to meet its financial obligations.

first-in-first-out (FIFO) A method of valuing the cost of goods sold that uses the cost of the oldest item in inventory first.

fixed-charge coverage ratio A measure of a firm's ability to meet its fixed-charge obligations: the ratio of (net earnings before taxes plus interest charges paid plus long-term lease payments) to (interest charges paid plus long-term lease payments).

fixed-income equivalent Also called a *busted convertible*, a convertible security that is trading like a straight security because the optioned common stock is trading low.

fixed-income instruments Assets that pay a fixed-dollar amount, such as bonds and preferred stock.

fixed-income market The market for trading bonds and preferred stock.

fixed-rate payer In an interest rate swap the counterparty who pays a fixed rate, usually in exchange for a floating-rate payment.

flattening of the yield curve A change in the yield curve where the spread between the yield on a long-term and short-term Treasury has decreased. Compare **steepening of the yield curve** and **butterfly shift.**

floating-rate contract A guaranteed investment contract where the crediting rate is tied to some variable ("floating") interest rate benchmark, such as a specific-maturity Treasury yield.

floating-rate payer In an interest rate swap, the counterparty who pays a rate based on a reference rate, usually in exchange for a fixed-rate payment.

flow-through method The practice of reporting to shareholders using straight-line depreciation and accelerated depreciation for tax purposes and "flowing through" the lower income taxes actually paid to the financial statement prepared for shareholders.

foreign market Part of a nation's internal market, representing the mechanisms for issuing and trading securities of entities domiciled outside that nation. Compare **external market** and **domestic market**.

forward contract An agreement for the future delivery of the underlying at a specified price at the end of a designated period of time. Unlike a futures contract, a forward contract is traded over the counter, and its terms are negotiated individually. There is no clearinghouse for forward contracts, and the secondary market may be non-existent or thin.

forward rate A projection of future interest rates calculated from either the spot rates or the yield curve.

full-faith-and-credit obligations The security pledges for larger municipal bond issuers, such as states and large cities which have diverse funding sources.

full price Also called *dirty price*, the price of a bond including accrued interest.

fully modified pass-throughs Agency pass-throughs that guarantee the timely payment of both interest and principal. Compare **modified pass-throughs**.

fund family Set of funds with different investment objectives offered by one management company. In many cases, investors may move their assets from one fund to another within the family at little or no cost.

fundamental beta The product of a statistical model to predict the fundamental risk of a security using not only price data but other market-related and financial data.

fundamental descriptors In the model for calculating fundamental beta, ratios in risk indexes other than market variability, which rely on financial data other than price data.

funding ratio The ratio of a pension plan's assets to its liabilities.

funding risk See **interest rate risk**.

futures contract A firm legal agreement whereby two parties agree to transact with respect to some financial asset at a predetermined price at a specified future date. One party agrees to buy the financial asset; the other agrees to sell the financial asset. Both parties are obligated to perform, and neither party charges a fee.

futures contract multiple A constant, set by an exchange, which when multiplied by the futures price gives the dollar value of a stock index futures contract.

futures option An option on a futures contract. Compare **options on physicals**.

futures price The price at which the parties to a futures contract agree to transact on the settlement date.

G

gamma The ratio of the change in a call option's delta to the change in price of underlying stock.

general obligation bond A debt instrument of a municipality which is secured by the issuer's unlimited taxing power.

generally accepted accounting principles (GAAP) Standard accounting procedures promulgated by the Financial Accounting Standards Board (FASB) and its predecessor.

geographic risk Risk that arises when an insurer has policies concentrated within certain geographic areas, such as the risk of damage from a hurricane or an earthquake.

geometric mean return Also called the *time-weighted rate of return*, a measure of the compounded rate of growth of the initial portfolio market value during the evaluation period, assuming that all cash distributions are reinvested in the portfolio. It is computed by taking the geometric average of the portfolio subperiod returns:

$$\text{Geometric mean return} = [(1 + \text{return}_1) \times (1 + \text{return}_2) \dots (1 + \text{return}_N]^{1/N} - 1$$

good till canceled order See **open order**.

Gordon-Shapiro model See **constant-growth model**.

government-sponsored enterprises Privately owned, publicly chartered entities (such as the Student Loan Marketing Association) created by Congress to reduce the cost of capital for certain borrowing sectors of the economy including farmers, homeowners, and students.

gross profit margin The ratio of gross profit to net sales.

group rotation manager A top-down manager who infers the phases of the business cycle and allocates assets accordingly.

growth manager A money manager who seeks to buy stocks that are typically selling at relatively high P/E ratios due to high earnings growth, with the expectation of continued high (or higher) earnings growth.

growth phase A phase of development in which a company experiences rapid earnings growth as it produces new products and expands market share. See **three-phase DDM**.

guaranteed investment contract (GIC) A pure investment product in which a life company agrees, for a single premium, to pay the principal amount and a predetermined annual crediting rate over the life of the investment, all of which is paid at the maturity date.

H

hedge fund A fund that may employ a variety of techniques to enhance returns, such as both buying and shorting stocks based on a valuation model.

hedge ratio The ratio of volatility of the portfolio to be hedged and the return of the volatility of the hedging instrument.

hedged portfolio A portfolio consisting of the long position in the stock and the short position in the call option, so as to be riskless and produce a return that equals the risk-free interest rate.

hedger An investor who seeks to put well-defined limits on the risk of a portfolio.

hedging The process of constructing a portfolio that limits risk by anticipating offsetting losses and gains from the assets selected, often employing derivative securities and short selling.

high-yield bond See **junk bond**.

holding period return Also called the *ex post return*, the return on a portfolio over a period of time.

homogeneous expectations assumption An assumption of Markowitz portfolio construction that investors have the same expectations with respect to the inputs that are used to derive efficient portfolios: asset returns, variances, and covariances.

horizon analysis An analysis of returns using total return to assess performance over some investment horizon.

horizon matching See **combination matching**.

horizon return Total return over a given horizon.

horizontal analysis The process of dividing each expense item of a given year by that same expense item in the base year. This allows for the exploration of changes in the relative importance of expense items over time and the behavior of expense items as sales change.

host security The security to which a warrant is attached.

hybrid security A convertible security whose optioned common stock is trading in a middle range, causing the convertible security to trade with the characteristics of both a fixed-income security and a common stock instrument.

I

immunization strategy A bond portfolio strategy whose goal is to immunize a portfolio against a general change in the rate of interest.

implied repo rate The rate that a seller of a futures contract can earn by buying an issue and then delivering it at the settlement date. See **cheapest to deliver issue**.

implied volatility The expected volatility in a stock's return derived from its option price, using an option-pricing model.

income statement A statement showing the revenues, expenses, and income (the difference between revenues and expenses) of a corporation over some period of time.

index warrant A stock index option issued by either a corporate or sovereign entity as part of a security offering, and guaranteed by an option clearing corporation. Compare **warrant**.

indexing A passive instrument strategy consisting of the construction of a portfolio of stocks designed to track the total return performance of an index of stocks.

indifference curve The graphical expression of a utility function, where the horizontal axis measures risk and the vertical axis measures expected return.

inflation risk Also called *purchasing-power risk*, the risk that changes in the real return the investor will realize after adjusting for inflation will be negative.

information coefficient (IC) The correlation between predicted and actual stock returns, sometimes used to measure the value of a financial analyst. An IC of 1.0 indicates a perfect linear relationship between predicted and actual returns, while an IC of 0.0 indicates no linear relationship.

information costs Transaction costs that include the assessment of the investment merits of a financial asset. Compare **search costs**.

information-motivated trades Trades in which an investor believes he or she possesses pertinent information not currently reflected in the stock's price.

informationless trades Trades that are the result of either a reallocation of wealth or an implementation of an investment strategy that only utilizes existing information.

initial margin requirement When buying securities on margin, the proportion of the total market value of the securities that the investor must pay for in cash. The Security Exchange Act of 1934 gives the board of governors of the Federal Reserve the responsibility to set initial margin requirements, but individual brokerage firms are free to set higher requirements. In futures contracts, initial margin requirements are set by the exchange.

input-output tables Tables that indicate how much each industry requires of the production of each other industry in order to produce each dollar of its own output.

institutional investors Organizations that invest, including insurance companies, depository institutions, pension funds, investment companies, and endowment funds.

institutionalization The gradual domination of financial markets by institutional investors, as opposed to individual investors. This process has occurred throughout the industrialized world.

insured bond A municipal bond backed both by the credit of the municipal issuer and by commercial insurance policies.

insured plans Defined benefit pension plans that are guaranteed by life insurance products. Compare **non-insured plans**.

intangible asset A legal claim to some future benefit, typically a claim to future cash. Financial assets, also called financial instruments or securities, are intangible assets.

interest coverage ratio The ratio of the earnings available for paying the interest for a given year to the annual interest expense.

interest rate agreement An agreement whereby one party, for an upfront premium, agrees to compensate the other at specific time periods if a designated interest rate (the reference rate) is different from a predetermined level (the strike rate).

interest rate cap Also called an *interest rate ceiling*, an interest rate agreement in which payments are made when the reference rate *exceeds* the strike rate.

interest rate ceiling See **interest rate cap**.

interest rate floor An interest rate agreement in which payments are made when the reference rate *falls below* the strike rate.

interest rate risk For a bond, the risk that a rise in interest rates will decrease the bond's price. For a depository institution, also called *funding risk*, the risk that spread income will suffer because of a change in interest rates.

interest rate swap A binding agreement between counterparties to exchange periodic interest payments on some predetermined dollar principal, which is called the notional principal amount.

intermarket sector spread The spread between the interest rate offered in two sectors of the bond market for issues of the same maturity.

intermarket spread swaps An exchange of one bond for another based on the manager's projection of a realignment of spreads between sectors of the bond market.

internal market The mechanisms for issuing and trading securities within a nation, including its domestic market and foreign market. Compare **external market**.

internally efficient market See **operationally efficient market**.

internal rate of return See **dollar-weighted rate of return**.

International Depositary Receipt (IDR) A receipt issued by a bank as evidence of ownership of one or more shares of the underlying stock of a foreign corporation that the bank holds in trust. The advantage of the IDR structure is that the corporation does not have to comply with all the regulatory issuing requirements of the foreign country where the stock is to be traded. The U.S. version of the IDR is the American Depositary Receipt (ADR).

international market See **external market**.

intramarket sector spread The spread between two issues of the same maturity within a market sector. For instance, the difference in interest rates offered for five-year industrial corporate bonds and five-year utility corporate bonds.

intrinsic value An option's economic value if it were exercised immediately.

inventory turnover The ratio of the cost of goods sold to the average inventory for a year.

investment analysts See **financial analysts**.

investment grade A bond that is assigned a rating in the top four categories by commercial credit rating companies. Compare **high-yield bond**.

investment income The revenue from a portfolio of invested assets.

investment management Also called *portfolio management* and *money management*, the process of managing money.

investment manager Also called a *portfolio manager* and *money manager*, the individual who manages a portfolio of investments.

investment value See **straight value**.

investor The owner of a financial asset.

investor's equity The balance of a margin account. See **buying on margin** and **initial margin requirement**.

invoice price The price that the buyer of a futures contract must pay the seller when a Treasury bond is delivered.

issue A particular financial asset.

issuer An entity that issues a financial asset.

J

Jensen Index An index that uses the capital asset pricing model to determine whether a money manager outperformed a market index.

junk bond Also called a *high-yield bond*, one with a quality rating below triple B.

K

kappa The ratio of the dollar price change in the price of an option to a 1% change in the expected price volatility.

L

ladder strategy A bond portfolio strategy in which the portfolio is constructed to have approximately equal amounts invested in every maturity within a given range.

last-in–first-out (LIFO) A method of valuing inventory that uses the cost of the most recent item in inventory first.

law of one price An economic rule stating that a given security must have the same price regardless of the means by which one goes about creating that security. This implies that if the payoff of a security can be synthetically created by a package of other securities, the price of the package and the price of the security whose payoff it replicates must be equal.

leveraged buy-out (LBO) A transaction used for taking a public corporation private, financed through the use of debt funds: bank loans and bonds. Because of the large amount of debt relative to equity in the new corporation, the bonds are typically rated below investment grade, properly referred to as high-yield bonds or junk bonds. Investors can participate in an LBO through either the purchase of the debt (i.e., purchase of the bonds or participation in the bank loan) or the purchase of equity through an LBO fund that specializes in such investments.

leveraged portfolio A portfolio that includes risky assets purchased with funds borrowed.

liability A financial obligation, or the cash outlay that must be made at a specific time to satisfy the contractual terms of such an obligation.

liability funding strategies Investment strategies that select assets so that cash flows will equal or exceed the client's obligations.

liability swap An interest rate swap used to alter the cash flow characteristics of an institution's liabilities so as to provide a better match with its assets.

limit order A conditional trading order designed to avoid the danger of adverse unexpected price changes, executed only if the limit price or a better price can be obtained. Also see **buy limit order**, **sell limit order**, and **stop-limit order**. Compare **market order**.

limit order book A record of unexecuted limit orders that is maintained by the specialist. These orders are treated equally with other orders in terms of priority of execution.

limited-tax general obligation bond A general obligation bond that is limited as to revenue sources.

liquidity The ease with which an asset may be converted into cash.

liquidity risk The risk that arises from the difficulty of selling an asset. It can be thought of as the difference between the "true value" of the asset and the likely price, less commissions.

liquidity theory of the term structure A biased expectations theory that asserts that the implied forward rates will not be a pure estimate of the market's expectations of future interest rates because they embody a liquidity premium.

listed stocks Stocks that are traded on an exchange.

load fund A mutual fund that tends to impose large commissions, typically ranging from 8.5% on small amounts invested down to 1% on amounts of $500,000 or over. Compare **no-load fund**.

loan value The amount a policyholder may borrow against a whole life insurance policy at the interest rate specified in the policy.

local expectations theory A form of the pure expectations theory which suggests that the returns on bonds of different maturities will be the same over a short-term investment horizon.

lognormal distribution A distribution where the logarithm of the variable follows a normal distribution. Lognormal distributions are used to describe returns calculated over periods of a year or more.

long futures See **long position**.

long hedge A hedge undertaken to protect against rising prices of future intended purchases; also called a *buy hedge* since the hedger buys a futures contract to implement this strategy.

long position In the cash market, the ownership of securities. In the futures market, the purchase of a futures contract with no offsetting short position. In the options market, the purchase of an option with no offsetting short position. Compare **short position**.

long straddle A straddle in which a long position is taken in both a put and call option.

long-term debt to equity ratio A capitalization ratio comparing long-term debt to shareholders' equity.

low price-earnings ratio effect The tendency of portfolios of stocks with a low price-earnings ratio to outperform portfolios consisting of stocks with a high price-earnings ratio.

M

Macaulay duration The weighted-average term to maturity of the cash flows from the bond, where the weights are the present value of the cash flow divided by the price.

magic of diversification The effective reduction of risk (variance) of a portfolio, achieved without reduction to expected returns through the combination of assets with low or negative correlations (covariances). See **Markowitz diversification**.

maintenance margin requirement The minimum balance needed in the investor's equity account compared with the total market value. Maintenance requirements are set by the exchange and are lower than initial margin requirements. See also **margin call** and **variation margin**.

management fee An investment advisory fee charged by the financial advisor to a fund based on the fund's average assets, but sometimes determined on a sliding scale that declines as the dollar amount of the fund increases.

margin call A broker's notification to an investor requiring additional funds when the investor's margin account falls below the minimum maintenance margin. If the investor fails to put up the additional cash, the position is liquidated.

margin income See **spread income**.

mark to market To price at market value as determined by the latest available information.

market conversion price Also called *conversion parity price*, the price that an investor effectively pays for common stock by purchasing a convertible security and then exercising the conversion option. This price is equal to the market price of the convertible security divided by the conversion ratio.

market-if-touched order A trading order to buy (or sell) that becomes a market order if the price of a security rises (or falls) to a designated level. Compare **stop order**.

market impact costs Also called *price impact costs*, the result of a bid/ask spread and a dealer's price concession.

market model This relationship is sometimes called the *single-index model*. The market model says that the return on a security depends on the return on the market portfolio and the extent of the security's responsiveness as measured by beta (β_i). In addition, the return will also depend on conditions that are unique to the firm. Graphically, the market model can be depicted as a line fitted to a plot of asset returns against returns on the market portfolio.

market order A trading order executed at the currently best price available in the market. Compare **limit order**.

market portfolio A portfolio consisting of all assets available to investors, with each asset held in proportion to its market value relative to the total market value of all assets.

market risk See **systematic risk**.

market sectors The classifications of bonds by issuer characteristics, such as state government, corporate, or utility.

market segmentation theory A biased expectations theory that asserts that the shape of the yield curve is determined by the supply of and demand for securities within each maturity sector.

market timer A money manager who assumes he or she can forecast when the stock market will go up and down.

market timing costs Costs that arise from price movement of the stock during the time of the transaction which is attributed to other activity in the stock.

marketplace price efficiency The degree to which the prices of assets reflect the available marketplace information. Marketplace price efficiency is sometimes estimated as the difficulty faced by active management of earning a greater return than passive management would, after adjusting for the risk associated with a strategy and the transactions costs associated with implementing a strategy.

Markowitz diversification A strategy that seeks to combine assets in a portfolio with returns that are less than perfectly positively correlated, in an effort to lower portfolio risk (variance) without sacrificing return. Compare **naive diversification**.

Markowitz efficient frontier The graphical depiction of the Markowitz efficient set of portfolios representing the boundary of the set of feasible portfolios that have the maximum return for a given level of risk. Any portfolios above the frontier cannot be achieved. Any below the frontier are dominated by Markowitz efficient portfolios.

Markowitz efficient portfolio. Also called a *mean-variance efficient portfolio*, a portfolio that has the highest expected return at a given level of risk.

Markowitz efficient set of portfolios The collection of all efficient portfolios, graphically referred to as the Markowitz efficient frontier.

matador market The foreign market in Spain.

matching concept The accounting principle that requires the recognition of all costs that are associated with the generation of the revenue reported in the income statement.

mathematical programming An operations research technique that solves problems in which an optimal value is sought subject to specified constraints. Mathematical programming models include linear programming, quadratic programming, and dynamic programming.

maturity date For a bond, the date on which the principal is required to be repaid. In an interest rate swap, the date that the swap stops accruing interest.

maturity phase A phase of company development in which earnings continue to grow at the rate of the general economy. See **three-phase DDM**.

maturity spread The spread between any two maturity sectors of the bond market.

maturity value See **par value**.

mean-variance efficient portfolio See **Markowitz efficient portfolio**.

medium-term note A corporate debt instrument that is continuously offered to investors over a period of time by an agent of the issuer. Investors can select from the following maturity bands: 9 months to 1 year, more than 1 year to 18 months, more than 18 months to 2 years, etc., up to 30 years.

minimum variance zero-beta portfolio The zero-beta portfolio with the least risk.

modified duration The ratio of Macaulay duration to $(1 + y)$, where y = the bond yield. Modified duration is inversely related to the approximate percentage change in price for a given change in yield.

modified pass-throughs Agency pass-throughs that guarantee (1) timely interest payments and (2) principal payments as collected, but no later than a specified time after they are due. Compare **fully modified pass-throughs**.

money center banks Banks that raise most of their funds from the domestic and international money markets, relying less on depositors for funds.

money management See **investment management**.

money manager See **investment manager**.

money market The market for trading short-term debt instruments (those that mature in less than one year). Compare **capital market**.

money market demand account An account that pays interest based on short-term interest rates.

mortgage A loan secured by the collateral of some specified real estate property which obliges the borrower to make a predetermined series of payments.

mortgage-backed securities Securities backed by a pool of mortgage loans.

mortgage bond A bond in which the issuer has granted the bondholders a lien against the pledged assets. Compare **collateral trust bonds**.

mortgage pass-through security Also called a *pass-through*, a security created when one or more mortgage holders form a collection (pool) of mortgages and sell shares or participation certificates in the pool.

mortgage rate The interest rate on a mortgage loan.

mortgagee The lender of a loan secured by property.

mortgager The borrower of a loan secured by property.

most distant futures contract When several futures contracts are considered, the contract settling last. Compare **nearby futures contract**.

multifactor CAPM A version of the capital asset pricing model derived by Merton that includes extra-market sources of risk referred to as factors.

multiperiod immunization A portfolio strategy in which a portfolio is created that will be capable of satisfying more than one predetermined future liability regardless if interest rates change.

multiple regression The estimated relationship between a dependent variable and more than one explanatory variable.

multirule system A technical trading strategy that combines mechanical rules, such as the CRISMA (*c*umulative volume, *r*elative *s*trength, *m*oving *a*verage) Trading System of Pruitt and White.

mutual fund See **open-end fund**.

N

naive diversification A strategy whereby an investor simply invests in a number of different assets and hopes that the variance of the expected return on the portfolio is lowered. Compare **Markowitz diversification**.

naked strategies An unhedged strategy making exclusive use of one of the following: long call strategy (buying call options), short call strategy (selling or writing call options), long put strategy (buying put options), and short put strategy (selling or writing put options). By themselves, these positions are called *naked* strategies because they do not involve an offsetting or risk-reducing position in another option or the underlying security. Compare **covered or hedge option strategies**.

National Association of Securities Dealers Automatic Quotation (NASDAQ) System An electronic quotation system that provides price quotations to market participants about the more actively traded common stock issues in the OTC market. About 4,000 common stock issues are included in the NASDAQ system.

national market See **internal market**.

nearby futures contract When several futures contracts are considered, the contract with the closest settlement date is called the nearby futures contract. The next futures contract is the one that settles just after the nearby futures contract. The contract farthest away in time from settlement is called the most distant futures contract.

negative carry See **net financing cost**.

negative convexity A bond characteristic such that the price appreciation will be less than the price depreciation for a large change in yield of a given number of basis points.

neglected firm effect The tendency of firms that are neglected by security analysts to outperform firms that are the subject of considerable attention.

negotiable order of withdrawal (NOW) account Demand deposits that pay interest.

net asset value (NAV) per share The basis of a mutual fund's share price, which is found by subtracting from the market value of the portfolio the mutual fund's liabilities and then dividing by the number of mutual fund shares outstanding.

net financing cost Also called the *cost of carry* or, simply, *carry*, the difference between the cost of financing the purchase of an asset and the asset's cash yield. Positive carry means that the yield earned is greater than the financing cost; negative carry means that the financing cost exceeds the yield earned.

net operating margin The ratio of net operating income to net sales.

next futures contract The contract settling immediately after the nearby futures contract.

no-load fund A mutual fund that does not impose a sales commission. Compare **load fund**.

non-cumulative preferred stock Preferred stock whose holders must forgo dividend payments when the company misses a dividend payment. Compare **cumulative preferred stock**.

non-insured plans Defined benefit pension plans that are not guaranteed by life insurance products. Compare **insured plans**.

non-parallel shift in the yield curve A shift in the yield curve in which yields do not change by the same number of basis points for every maturity. Compare **parallel shift in the yield curve**.

non-reproducible assets A tangible asset with unique physical properties, like a parcel of land, a mine, or a work of art.

normal deviate See **standardized value**.

normal distribution A probability distribution forming a symmetrical bell-shaped curve.

normal portfolio A customized benchmark that includes all the securities from which a manager normally chooses, weighted as the manager would weight them in a portfolio.

normalizing method The practice of making a charge in the income account equivalent to the tax savings realized through the use of different depreciation methods for shareholder and income tax purposes, thus washing out the benefits of the tax savings reported as final net income to shareholders.

notes Debt instruments with maturities of less than 10 years.

notional principal amount In an interest rate swap, the predetermined dollar principal on which the exchanged interest payments are based.

O

odd lot A trading order for less than 100 shares of stock. Compare **round lot**.

offer price The price at which the mutual fund will sell the shares, equal to the net asset value per share plus any sales commission, or load.

official statement A statement published by an issuer of a new municipal security describing itself and the issue.

offshore market See **external market**.

on-the-run issues See **benchmark issues**.

open-end fund Also called a *mutual fund*, an investment company that stands ready to sell new shares to the public and to redeem its outstanding shares on demand at a price equal to an appropriate share of the value of its portfolio, which is computed daily at the close of the market.

open interest The number of identical derivative contracts that have been entered into but not yet liquidated, reported by an exchange as a useful statistic for measuring the liquidity of a contract.

open order Also called a *good till canceled order*, a trading order that is good until specifically canceled.

operating cycle The average time intervening between the acquisition of materials or services and the final cash realization from those acquisitions.

operationally efficient market Also called an *internally efficient market*, one in which investors can obtain transactions services that reflect the true costs associated with furnishing those services.

opinion shopping A practice prohibited by the SEC which involves attempts by a corporation to obtain reporting objectives by following questionable accounting principles with the help of a pliable auditor willing to go along with the desired treatment.

opportunity costs The difference in the performance of an actual investment and a desired investment adjusted for fixed costs and execution costs. The performance differential is a consequence of not being able to implement all desired trades.

optimal portfolio An efficient portfolio most preferred by an investor because its risk/reward characteristics approximate the investor's utility function. A portfolio that maximizes an investor's preferences with respect to return and risk.

optimization approach to indexing An approach to indexing which seeks to optimize some objective, such as to maximize the portfolio yield, to maximize convexity, or to maximize expected total returns.

option An options contract.

option-adjusted spread (OAS) The spread over an issuer's spot rate curve, developed as a measure of the yield spread that can be used to convert dollar differences between theoretical value and market price.

option premium The option price.

option price Also called the option premium, the price paid by the buyer of the options contract for the right to buy or sell a security at a specified price in the future.

option seller Also called the *option writer*, the party who grants a right to trade a security at a given price in the future.

option writer See **option seller**.

options contract A contract that, in exchange for the option price, gives the option buyer the right, but not the obligation, to buy (or sell) a financial asset at the exercise price from (or to) the option seller within a specified time period, or on a specified date (expiration date).

options contract multiple A constant, set at $100, which when multiplied by the cash index value gives the dollar value of the stock index underlying an option. That is, dollar value of the underlying stock index = cash index value × $100 (the options contract multiple).

options on physicals Interest rate options written on fixed-income securities, as opposed to those written on interest rate futures contracts.

out of the money A description of an option whose exercise would not be profitable.

over-the-counter market (OTC) A decentralized market (as opposed to an exchange market) where geographically dispersed dealers are linked together by telephones and computer screens.

overfunded pension plan A pension plan that has a positive surplus (i.e., assets exceed liabilities).

overlay strategy A strategy of using futures for asset allocation by pension sponsors to avoid disrupting the activities of money managers.

overnight repo A repurchase agreement with a term of one day.

overreaction hypothesis The supposition that investors overreact to unanticipated news, resulting in exaggerated movement in stock prices followed by corrections.

P

par value Also called the *maturity value* or *face value*, the amount that the issuer agrees to pay at the maturity date.

parallel shift in the yield curve A shift in the yield curve in which the change in the yield on all maturities is the same number of basis points. Compare **non-parallel shift in the yield curve**.

parity value See **conversion value**.

participating GIC A guaranteed investment contract where the policyholder is not guaranteed a crediting rate, but instead receives a return based on the actual experience of the portfolio managed by the life company.

pass-through See **mortgage pass-through security**.

pass-through coupon rate The interest rate paid on a securitized pool of assets, which is less than the rate paid on the underlying loans by an amount equal to the servicing and guaranteeing fees.

passive portfolio strategy A strategy that involves minimal expectational input, and instead relies on diversification to match the performance of some market index. A passive strategy assumes that the marketplace will reflect all available information in the price paid for securities. Compare **active portfolio strategy**.

payment-in-kind (PIK) bond A bond that gives the issuer an option (during an initial period) either to make coupon payments in cash or to give the bondholder a similar bond. Compare **deferred-interest bond** and **step-up bond**.

Pension Benefit Guaranty Corporation (PBGC) A federal agency that insures the vested benefits of pension plan participants (established in 1974 by the ERISA legislation).

pension plan A fund that is established for the payment of retirement benefits.

pension sponsors Organizations that have established a pension plan.

perfect hedge A hedge in which the profit and loss are equal.

performance attribution analysis The decomposition of a money manager's performance results to explain the reasons why those results were achieved. This analysis seeks to answer the following questions: (1) What were the major sources of added value? (2) Was short-term factor timing statistically significant? (3) Was market timing statistically significant? And (4) was security selection statistically significant?

performance evaluation The evaluation of a manager's performance which involves, first, determining whether the money manager added value by outperforming the established benchmark (performance measurement) and, second, determining how the money manager achieved the calculated return (performance attribution analysis).

performance measurement The calculation of the return realized by a money manager over some time interval.

perpetual warrants Warrants that have no expiration date.

pit committee A committee of the exchange that determines the daily settlement price of futures contracts.

plan sponsors The entities that establish pension plans, including private business entities acting for their employees; state and local entities operating on behalf of their employees; unions acting on behalf of their members; and individuals representing themselves.

plowback rate See **retention rate**.

policy asset allocation A long-term asset allocation method, in which the investor seeks to assess an appropriate long-term "normal" asset mix that represents an ideal blend of controlled risk and enhanced return.

portfolio A collection of investments.

portfolio insurance A strategy using a leveraged portfolio in the underlying stock to create a synthetic put option.

portfolio internal rate of return The rate of return computed by first determining the cash flows for all the bonds in the portfolio and then finding the interest rate that will make the present value of the cash flows equal to the market value of the portfolio.

portfolio management See **investment management**.

portfolio manager See **investment manager**.

portfolio turnover rate For an investment company, an annualized rate found by dividing the lesser of purchases and sales by the average of portfolio assets.

positive carry See **net financing cost**.

positive convexity A property of option-free bonds whereby the price appreciation for a large change in interest rates will be greater (in absolute terms) than the price depreciation for the same change in interest rates.

posttrade benchmarks Prices after the decision to trade.

preferred habitat theory A biased expectations theory which rejects the assertion that the risk premium must rise uniformly with maturity. Instead, the extent that the demand for and supply of funds in a given maturity range do not match will induce some participants to shift to maturities showing the opposite imbalances. However, such investors will need to be compensated by an appropriate risk premium whose magnitude will reflect the extent of aversion to either price or reinvestment risk.

preferred stock A class of stock that shares characteristics of both common stock and debt.

premium Referring to the selling price of a bond, a price above its par value. Compare **discount**.

premium payback period Also called *break-even time*, the time it takes to recover the premium per share of a convertible security.

prepayment speed Also called *speed*, the estimated rate at which mortgagers pay off their loans ahead of schedule, critical in assessing the value of mortgage pass-through securities.

prepayments Payments made in excess of scheduled mortgage principal repayments.

prerefunded bond See **refunded bond**.

pre-trade benchmarks Prices occurring before or at the decision to trade.

price compression The limitation of the price appreciation potential for a callable bond in a declining interest rate environment, based on the expectation that the bond will be redeemed at the call price.

price discovery process The process of determining the prices of the assets in the marketplace through the interactions of buyers and sellers.

price-earnings (P/E) ratio The current market price of the stock divided by some measure of earnings per share.

price impact costs See **market impact costs**.

price momentum See **relative strength**.

price persistence See **relative strength**.

price risk The risk that the value of a security (or a portfolio) will decline in the future.

price value of a basis point (PVBP) Also called the *dollar value of an 01*, a measure of the change in the price of the bond if the required yield changes by one basis point.

price-volume relationship A relationship espoused by some technical analysts that signals continuing rises and falls in security prices based on accompanying changes in volume traded.

pricing efficiency Also called *external efficiency*, a market characteristic where prices at all times fully reflect all available information that is relevant to the valuation of securities.

primary market The market for newly issued financial assets. Compare **secondary market**.

private-label pass-throughs See **conventional pass-throughs**.

probability distribution Also called a *probability function*, a function that describes all the values that the random variable can take and the probability associated with each.

probability function See **probability distribution**.

profit margin The ratio of earnings available to stockholders to net sales.

program trades Also called *basket trades*, orders requiring the execution of trades in a large number of different stocks at as near the same time as possible. Compare **block trade**.

projected benefit obligation (PBO) A measure of a pension plan's liability at the calculation date assuming that the plan is ongoing and will not terminate in the foreseeable future. Compare **accumulated benefit obligation**.

protective put buying strategy A strategy that involves buying a put option on the underlying security that is held in a portfolio. See **covered or hedge option strategies**.

provisional call feature A feature in a convertible issue that allows the issuer to call the issue during the non-call period if the price of the stock reaches a certain price.

purchasing-power risk See **inflation risk**.

pure expectations theory A theory that asserts that the forward rates exclusively represent the expected future rates. Compare **biased expectations theories**.

pure index fund A portfolio that is managed so as to perfectly replicate the performance of the market portfolio.

put See **put option**.

put-call parity relationship The relationship between the price of a put and the price of a call on the same underlying with the same expiration date, which prevents arbitrage opportunities.

put option Also called a *put*, an option that grants the buyer the right to sell the underlying to the writer.

put swaption A swaption in which the buyer has the right to enter into a swap as a floating-rate payer. The writer of the swaption therefore becomes the floating-rate receiver/fixed-rate payer.

Q

quality option Also called the *swap option*, the seller's choice of deliverables in Treasury bond and Treasury note futures contract. See also **cheapest to deliver issue**.

quality spread Also called *credit spread*, the spread between Treasury securities and non-Treasury securities that are identical in all respects except for quality rating. For instance, the difference between yields on Treasuries and those on single-A-rated industrial bonds.

quick ratio See **acid-test ratio**.

R

random variable A variable that can have more than one possible value.

rate anticipation swaps An exchange of bonds in a portfolio for new bonds that will achieve the target portfolio duration, based on the investor's assumptions about future changes in interest rates.

reference rate A benchmark interest rate (such as LIBOR), used to specify conditions of an interest rate swap or an interest rate agreement.

refunded bond Also called a *prerefunded bond*, one that originally may have been issued as a general obligation or revenue bond but that is now secured by an "escrow fund" consisting entirely of direct U.S. government obligations that are sufficient for paying the bondholders.

refunding The redemption of a bond with proceeds received from issuing lower-cost debt obligations ranking equal to or superior to the debt to be redeemed.

regression analysis A statistical technique that can be used to estimate relationships between variables.

regulatory pricing risk Risk that arises when regulators restrict the premium rates that insurance companies can charge.

regulatory surplus The surplus as measured using regulatory accounting principles (RAP) which may allow the non-market valuation of assets or liabilities and which may be materially different from economic surplus.

reinvestment risk The risk that proceeds received in the future will have to be reinvested at a lower potential interest rate.

relative strength Also called *price momentum* or *price persistence*, the ratio of the price of a stock to some price index. Changes in the ratio can be interpreted as uptrends or downtrends relative to the price index,

relative yield spread The ratio of the yield spread to the yield level.

Rembrandt market The foreign market in the Netherlands.

replicating portfolio A portfolio constructed to match an index or benchmark.

reproducible assets A tangible asset with physical properties that can be reproduced, such as a building or machinery.

repurchase agreement An agreement with a commitment by the seller to buy a security back from the purchaser at a specified price at a designated future date. Also called a repo, it represents a collateralized short-term loan, where the collateral may be a Treasury security, money market instrument, federal agency security, or mortgage-backed security.

required reserves The dollar amounts based on reserve ratios that banks are required to keep on deposit at a Federal Reserve Bank.

required yield Generally referring to bonds, the yield required by the marketplace to match available returns for financial instruments with comparable risk.

reserve An accounting entry that properly reflects the contingent liabilities of an insurance company.

reserve ratios Specified percentages of deposits, established by the Federal Reserve Board, that banks must keep in a non-interest-bearing account at one of the twelve Federal Reserve Banks.

reset frequency In an interest rate swap, the frequency with which the floating rate changes.

residual claim See **equity claim**.

residual risk See **unsystematic risk**.

retail investors Individual investors. Compare **institutional investors**.

retention rate The percentage of present earnings held back or retained by a corporation.

return The change in the value of a portfolio over an evaluation period, including any distributions made from the portfolio during that period.

return on stockholders' equity The ratio of earnings to stockholders' equity.

return on total assets The ratio of earnings available to common stock holders to total assets.

return-to-maturity expectations interpretation A variant of pure expectations theory which suggests that the return that an investor will realize by rolling over short-term bonds to some investment horizon will be the same as holding a zero-coupon bond with a maturity that is the same as that investment horizon.

revenue bond A bond issued by a municipality to finance either a project or an enterprise where the issuer pledges to the bondholders the revenues generated by the operating projects financed, for instance, hospital revenue bonds and sewer revenue bonds.

revenue fund A fund accounting for all revenues from an enterprise financed by a municipal revenue bond.

risk averse A risk-averse investor is one who when faced with two investments with the same expected return but two different risks will prefer the one with the lower risk.

risk-free or riskless asset An asset whose future return is known today with certainty. The risk-free asset is commonly defined as short-term obligations of the U.S. government.

risk indexes Categories of risk used to calculate fundamental beta, including (1) market variability, (2) earnings variability, (3) low valuation and unsuccess, (4) immaturity and smallness, (5) growth orientation, and (6) financial risk.

risk premium The reward for holding the risky market portfolio rather than the risk-free asset. The spread between Treasury and non-Treasury bonds of comparable maturity.

risk premium approach The most common approach for tactical asset allocation to determine the relative valuation of asset classes based on expected returns.

risky asset An asset whose future return is uncertain.

round lot A trading order typically of 100 shares of a stock or some multiple of 100. Compare **odd lot**.

round-trip transactions costs Costs of completing a transaction, including commissions, market impact costs, and taxes.

S

safety cushion In a contingent immunization strategy, the difference between the initially available immunization level and the safety-net return.

safety-net return The minimum available return that will trigger an immunization strategy in a contingent immunization strategy.

samurai market The foreign market in Japan.

savings deposits Accounts that pay interest, typically at below-market interest rates, that do not have a specific maturity; and that usually can be withdrawn upon demand.

scenario analysis The use of horizon analysis to project bond total returns under different reinvestment rates and future market yields.

search costs Costs associated with locating a counterparty to a trade, including explicit costs (such as advertising) and implicit costs (such as the value of time). Compare **information costs**.

secondary market The market where securities are traded after they are initially offered in the primary market.

securities analysts See **financial analysts**.

securitization The process of creating a pass-through, such as the mortgage pass-through security, by which the pooled assets become standard securities backed by those assets.

security market line (SML) A description of the risk-return relationship for individual securities, expressed in a form similar to the capital market line.

sell hedge See **short hedge**.

sell limit order A conditional trading order that indicates that a security may be sold at the designated price or higher. Compare **buy limit order**.

sell-side analyst Also called a *Wall Street analyst*, a financial analyst who works for a brokerage firm and whose recommendations are passed on to the brokerage firm's customers.

selling short A trade in which the investor (working through a broker) borrows a security, sells it, repurchases it at a later time, and then returns it to the party who initially loaned the security. If the price has fallen, the short seller profits. When the security is returned, the investor is said to have "covered the short position."

semistrong form efficiency A form of pricing efficiency where the price of the security fully reflects all public information (including, but not limited to, historical price and trading patterns). Compare **weak form efficiency** and **strong form efficiency**.

serial bonds Corporate bonds arranged so that specified principal amounts become due on specified dates. Compare **term bonds**.

settlement date Also called the *delivery date*, the designated date at which the parties to a futures contract must transact.

settlement price The value at the end of the day of a futures contract as determined by the pit committee of an exchange. The exchange uses the settlement price to mark to market the futures position so that brokers can adjust each investor's equity account.

settlement rate The rate suggested in Financial Accounting Standard Board (FASB) 87 for discounting the obligations of a pension plan. The rate at which the pension benefits could be effectively settled if the pension plan wished to terminate its pension obligation.

shareholders' letter A section of an annual report where one can find jargon-free discussions by management of successful and failed strategies which provides guidance for the probing of the rest of the report.

Sharpe benchmark A statistically created benchmark that adjusts for a managers' index-like tendencies.

Sharpe Index A measure of a portfolio's excess return relative to the total variability of the portfolio. Compare **Treynor Index**.

short futures See **short position**.

short hedge A hedge used to protect against a decline in the future cash price of the underlying; also called a *sell hedge* since the hedger sells a futures contract to implement this strategy.

short position In the cash market, a sale of securities not owned. The securities sold are borrowed. In the futures market, the sale of a futures contract with no offsetting long position. In the options market, the sale of an option with no offsetting long position.

short straddle A straddle in which one put and one call are sold.

short-term solvency ratios Ratios used to judge the adequacy of liquid assets for meeting short-term obligations as they come due, including (1) the current ratio, (2) the acid-test ratio, (3) the inventory turnover ratio, and (4) the accounts receivable turnover ratio,

shortfall risk The risk of falling short of any investment target.

simple linear regression A regression analysis between only two variables, one dependent and the other explanatory.

simple linear trend model An extrapolative statistical model that asserts that earnings have a base level and grow at a *constant amount* each period.

simple moving average The mean, calculated at any time over a past period of fixed length.

single-index model See **market model**.

single-premium deferred annuity An insurance policy bought by the sponsor of a pension plan for a single premium. In return, the insurance company agrees to make lifelong payments to the employee (the policyholder) when that employee retires.

sinking fund requirement A condition included in some corporate bond indentures that requires the issuer to retire a specified portion of debt each year. Any principal due at maturity is called the balloon maturity.

small-firm effect The tendency of small firms (in terms of total market capitalization) to outperform the stock market (consisting of both large and small firms).

specialist On an exchange, the member firm that is designated as the market maker (or dealer) for a listed common stock. Only one specialist can be designated for a given stock, but dealers may be specialists for several stocks. In contrast, there can be multiple market makers in the OTC market.

speed See **prepayment speed**.

spot markets See **cash markets**.

spot rate The theoretical yield on a zero-coupon Treasury security.

spot rate curve The graphical depiction of the relationship between the spot rates and maturity.

spread income Also called *margin income*, the difference between income and cost. For a depository institution, the difference between the assets it invests in (loans and securities) and the cost of its funds (deposits and other sources).

spread strategy A strategy that involves a position in one or more options so that the cost of buying an option is funded entirely or in part by selling another option in the same underlying.

standard deviation The square root of the variance. A measure of dispersion of a set of data from their mean.

standardized value Also called the *normal deviate*, the distance of one data point from the mean, divided by the standard deviation of the distribution.

stated conversion price At the time of issuance of a convertible security, the price the issuer effectively grants the securityholder to purchase the common stock, equal to the par value of the convertible security divided by the conversion ratio.

statutory surplus The surplus of an insurance company determined by the accounting treatment of both assets and liabilities as established by state statutes. Compare **regulatory surplus** and **economic surplus**.

steepening of the yield curve A change in the yield curve where the spread between the yield on a long-term and short-term Treasury has increased. Compare **flattening of the yield curve** and **butterfly shift**.

step-up bond A bond that pays a lower coupon rate for an initial period which then increases to a higher coupon rate. Compare **deferred-interest bond** and **payment-in-kind bond**.

stochastic models Liability-matching models that assume that the liability payments and the asset cash flows are uncertain. Compare **deterministic models**.

stock exchanges Formal organizations, approved and regulated by the Securities and Exchange Commission (SEC), that are made up of members that use the facilities to exchange certain common stocks. The two major national stock exchanges are the New York Stock Exchange (NYSE) and the American Stock Exchange (ASE or AMEX). Five regional stock exchanges include the Midwest, Pacific, Philadelphia, Boston, and Cincinnati. The Arizona Stock Exchange is an after-hours electronic marketplace where anonymous participants trade stocks via personal computers.

stock index option An option in which the underlying is a common stock index.

stock market Also called the *equity market*, the market for trading equities.

stock option An option in which the underlying is the common stock of a corporation.

stock replacement strategy A strategy for enhancing a portfolio's return, employed when the futures contract is expensive based on its theoretical price, involving a swap between the futures/Treasury bills portfolio and a stock portfolio.

stop-limit order A stop order that designates a price limit. In contrast to the stop order, which becomes a market order if the stop is reached, the stop-limit order becomes a limit order if the stop is reached.

stop order A trading order that specifies that the order is not to be executed until the market moves to a designated price, at which time it becomes a market order. Also see **stop order to buy**, **stop order to sell**, and **stop-limit order**.

stop order to buy A stop order that specifies that the order is not to be executed until the market rises to a designated price (i.e., trades at or above, or is bid at or above, the designated price).

stop order to sell A stop order that specifies that the order is not to be executed until the market price falls below a designated price (i.e., trades at or below, or is offered at or below, the designated price).

straddle A combination strategy in which the same position is taken in the same number of puts as calls

straight value Also called *investment value*, the value of a convertible security without the conversion option.

stratified equity indexing A method of constructing a replicating portfolio in which the stocks in the index are classified into stratum, and each stratum is represented in the portfolio.

stratified sampling approach to indexing An approach in which the index is divided into cells, each representing a different characteristic of the index, such as duration or maturity.

stratified sampling bond indexing A method of bond indexing that divides the index into cells, each cell representing a different characteristic, and that buys bonds to match those characteristics.

strike index For a stock index option, the index value at which the buyer of the option can buy or sell the underlying stock index. The strike index is converted to a dollar value by multiplying by the option's contract multiple. Compare **strike price**.

strike price See **exercise price**.

strong form efficiency Pricing efficiency, where the price of a security reflects all information, whether or not it is publicly available. Compare with **weak form efficiency** and **semistrong form efficiency**.

structured portfolio strategy A strategy in which a portfolio is designed to achieve the performance of some predetermined liabilities that must be paid out in the future.

structured settlement An agreement in settlement of a lawsuit involving specific payments made over a period of time. Property and casualty insurance companies often buy life insurance products to pay the costs of such settlements.

subject to opinion An auditor's opinion reflecting acceptance of a company's financial statements subject to pervasive uncertainty that cannot be adequately measured, such as information relating to the value of inventories, reserves for losses, or other matters subject to judgment.

subordinated debenture bond An unsecured bond that ranks after secured debt, after debenture bonds, and often after some general creditors in its claim on assets and earnings. Compare **debenture bond**, **mortgage bond**, and **collateral trust bonds**.

subperiod return The return of a portfolio over a shorter period of time than the evaluation period.

substitution swap A swap in which a money manager exchanges one bond for another bond that is similar in terms of coupon, maturity, and credit quality, but offers a higher yield.

surplus management See **asset/liability management**.

swap assignment See **swap sale**.

swap buy-back The sale of an interest rate swap by one counterparty to the other, effectively ending the swap.

swap option See **quality option**.

swap reversal An interest rate swap designed to end a counterparty's role in another interest rate swap, accomplished by counterbalancing the original swap in maturity, reference rate, and notional amount.

swap sale Also called a *swap assignment*, a transaction that ends one counterparty's role in an interest rate swap by substituting a new counterparty whose credit is acceptable to the other original counterparty.

swaptions Options on interest rate swaps. The buyer of a swaption has the right to enter into an interest rate swap agreement by some specified date in the future. The swaption agreement will specify whether the buyer of the swaption will be a fixed-rate receiver or a fixed-rate payer. The writer of the swaption becomes the counterparty to the swap if the buyer exercises.

symmetric cash matching An extension of cash flow matching that allows for the short-term borrowing of funds to satisfy a liability prior to the liability due date, resulting in a reduction in the cost of funding liabilities.

synchronous data Data available at the same time. In testing option-pricing models, the price of the option and of the underlying should be synchronous, representing the same moment in the market.

systematic risk Also called *undiversifiable risk* or *market risk*, the minimum level of risk that can be obtained for a portfolio by means of diversification across a large number of randomly chosen assets. Compare **unsystematic risk**.

T

tactical asset allocation (TAA) An asset allocation strategy that allows active departures from the normal asset mix based upon rigorous objective measures of value.

tangible asset An asset whose value depends on particular physical properties. These include reproducible assets such as buildings or machinery and non-reproducible assets such as land, a mine, or a work of art. Compare **intangible asset**.

tax-exempt sector The municipal bond market where state and local governments raise funds. Bonds issued in this sector are exempt from federal income taxes.

technical analysts Also called *chartists* or *technicians*, analysts who use mechanical rules to detect changes in the supply of and demand for a stock and capitalize on the expected change.

technical descriptors In the model for calculating fundamental beta, ratios in the market variability risk index which rely on market-related data.

technician See **technical analysts**.

term bonds Often referred to as bullet-maturity bonds or simply bullet bonds, bonds whose principal is payable at maturity. Compare **serial bonds**.

term life insurance A contract that provides a death benefit but no cash build-up or investment component. The premium remains constant only for a specified term of years, and the policy is usually renewable at the end of each term.

term repo A repurchase agreement with a term of more than one day.

term structure of interest rates The relationship between the yields on otherwise comparable securities with different maturities, often depicted as a yield curve.

term to maturity The time remaining on a bond's life, or the date on which the debt will cease to exist and the borrower will have completely paid off the amount borrowed.

term trust A closed-end fund that has a fixed termination or maturity date.

theoretical futures price Also called the *fair price*, the equilibrium futures price.

theoretical spot rate curve A curve derived from theoretical considerations as applied to the yields of actually traded Treasury debt securities because there are no zero-coupon Treasury debt issues with a maturity greater than one year. Like the yield curve, this is a graphical depiction of the term structure of interest rates.

theta Also called *time decay*, the ratio of the change in an option price to the decrease in time to expiration.

three-phase DDM A version of the dividend discount model which applies a different expected dividend rate depending on a company's lifecycle phase, growth phase, transition phase, or maturity phase.

tick-test rules SEC-imposed restrictions on when a short sale may be executed, intended to prevent investors from destabilizing the price of a stock when the market price is falling. A short sale can be made only when either (1) the sale price of the particular stock is higher than the last trade price (referred to as an uptick trade) or (2) if there is no change in the last trade price of the particular stock, the previous trade price must be higher than the trade price that preceded it (referred to as a zero uptick).

tilted portfolio An indexing strategy that is linked to active management through the emphasis of a particular industry sector, selected performance factors such as earnings momentum, dividend yield, price-earnings ratio, or selected economic factors such as interest rates and inflation.

time decay See **theta**.

time deposit See **certificate of deposit**.

time premium Also called *time value*, the amount by which the option price exceeds its intrinsic value.

time value of an option See **time premium**.

time-weighted rate of return See **geometric mean return**.

timing option For a Treasury bond or note futures contract, the seller's choice of when in the delivery month to deliver.

top-down equity management style A management style that begins with an assessment of the overall economic environment and makes a general asset allocation decision regarding various sectors of the financial markets and various industries. The top-down manager then selects a portfolio of individual securities within the favored sectors.

total asset turnover The ratio of net sales to total assets.

total debt to equity ratio A capitalization ratio comparing current liabilities plus long-term debt to shareholders' equity.

total return In performance measurement, the actual rate of return realized over some evaluation period. In fixed income analysis, the potential return that considers all three sources of return (coupon interest, interest on interest, and any capital gain/loss) over some investment horizon.

tracking error In an indexing strategy, the difference between the performance of the benchmark and the replicating portfolio.

tranche One of several related securities offered at the same time.

trade date In an interest rate swap, the date that the counterparties commit to the swap.

transactions costs See **round-trip transactions costs**, **information costs**, and **search costs**.

transition phase A phase of development in which the company's earnings begin to mature and decelerate to the rate of growth of the economy as a whole. See **three-phase DDM**.

Treasuries See **Treasury securities**.

Treasury bills Debt obligations of the U.S. Treasury that have maturities of one year or less.

Treasury bonds Debt obligations of the U.S. Treasury that have maturities of 10 years or more.

Treasury notes Debt obligations of the U.S. Treasury that have maturities of more than 2 years but less than 10 years.

Treasury securities Securities issued by the U.S. Department of the Treasury.

Treynor Index A measure of the excess return per unit of risk, where excess return is defined as the difference between the portfolio's return and the risk-free rate of return over the same evaluation period and where the unit of risk is the portfolio's beta. Compare **Sharpe Index**.

12b-1 funds Mutual funds that do not charge an upfront or back-end commission, but instead take out up to 1.25% of average daily fund assets each year to cover the costs of selling and marketing shares, an arrangement allowed by the SEC's Rule 12b-1 (passed in 1980).

two-factor model Black's zero-beta version of the capital asset pricing model.

two-fund separation theorem The theoretical result that all investors will hold a combination of the risk-free asset and the market portfolio.

U

underfunded pension plan A pension plan that has a negative surplus (i.e., liabilities exceed assets).

underlying The "something" that the parties agree to exchange in a derivative contract.

underwriting income For an insurance company, the difference between the premiums earned and the costs of settling claims.

undiversifiable risk See **systematic risk**.

universal life A whole life insurance product whose investment component pays a competitive interest rate rather than the below-market crediting rate.

unsystematic risk Also called the *diversifiable risk*, *residual risk*, or *company-specific risk*, the risk that is unique to a company such as a strike, the outcome of unfavorable litigation, or a natural catastrophe. Compare **systematic risk**.

upstairs market A network of trading desks for the major brokerage firms and institutional investors that communicate with each other by means of electronic display systems and telephones to facilitate block trades and program trades.

uptick trade See **tick-test rules**.

utility function A mathematical expression that assigns a value to all possible choices. In portfolio theory the utility function expresses the preferences of economic entities with respect to perceived risk and expected return.

V

value manager A manager who seeks to buy stocks that are at a discount to their "fair value" and sell them at or in excess of that value. Also called *contrarians* because they see value where many other market participants do not.

variable life A whole life insurance policy that provides a death benefit that depends on the market value of the insured's portfolio at the time of the death. Typically the company invests premiums in common stocks, and hence variable life policies are referred to as *equity-linked policies*.

variance A measure of dispersion of a set of data points around their mean value.

variance minimization approach to tracking An approach to bond indexing that uses historical data to estimate the variance of the tracking error.

variation margin An additional required deposit to bring an investor's equity account up to the initial margin level when the balance falls below the maintenance margin requirement.

venture capital An investment in a start-up business that is perceived to have excellent growth prospects but does not have access to capital markets.

vertical analysis The process of dividing each expense item in the income statement of a given year by net sales to identify expense items that rise faster or slower than a change in sales.

W

Wall Street analyst See **sell-side analyst**.

warrant An options contract often sold with another security. For instance, corporate bonds may be sold with warrants to buy common stock of that corporation. Warrants are generally detachable.

weak form efficiency A form of pricing efficiency where the price of the security reflects the past price and trading history of the security. Compare **semistrong form efficiency** and **strong form efficiency**.

weighted-average portfolio yield The weighted average of the yield of all the bonds in a portfolio.

whole life insurance A contract with both insurance and investment components: (1) It pays off a stated amount upon the death of the insured, and (2) it accumulates a cash value that the policyholder can borrow against or redeem.

wild card option The right of the seller of a Treasury bond futures contract to give notice of intent to deliver at or before 8:00 p.m. Chicago time after the closing of the exchange (3:15 p.m. Chicago time) when the futures settlement price has been fixed. Compare **timing option**.

window contract A guaranteed investment contract purchased with deposits over some future designated time period (the "window"), usually between 3 and 12 months. All deposits made are guaranteed the same credit rating. Compare **bullet contract**.

Y

Yankee market The foreign market in the United States.

yield curve The graphical depiction of the relationship between the yield on bonds of the same credit quality but different maturities. See also **term structure of interest rates**.

yield curve option-pricing models Also called *arbitrage-free option-pricing models*, models that can incorporate different volatility assumptions along the yield curve, such as the Black-Derman-Toy model.

yield curve strategies Positioning a portfolio to capitalize on expected changes in the shape of the Treasury yield curve.

yield ratio The quotient of two bond yields.

yield spread strategies Strategies that involve positioning a portfolio to capitalize on expected changes in yield spreads between sectors of the bond market.

yield to call For a bond that may be called prior to maturity, the yield to the first call date.

yield to maturity The interest rate that will make the present value of a bond's remaining cash flows (if held to maturity) equal to the price (plus accrued interest, if any).

yield to worst The bond yield computed by always using the lower of either the yield to maturity or the yield to call on every possible call date.

Z

zero-beta portfolio A portfolio constructed to represent the risk-free asset, that is, having a beta of zero.

zero-coupon bond A bond in which no periodic coupon is paid over the life of the contract. Instead, both the principal and the interest are paid at the maturity date.

zero uptick See **tick-test rules**.

NAME INDEX

SUBJECT INDEX